PUBLIC PAPERS OF THE PRESIDENTS
OF THE
UNITED STATES

PUBLIC PAPERS OF THE PRESIDENTS
OF THE
UNITED STATES

George W. Bush

2006

(IN TWO BOOKS)

BOOK II—JULY 1 TO DECEMBER 31, 2006

UNITED STATES GOVERNMENT PRINTING OFFICE
WASHINGTON : 2010

Published by the
Office of the Federal Register
National Archives and Records Administration

Foreword

This volume collects my speeches and papers from the second half of 2006.

This was a period when many important pieces of legislation came to my desk. In July, I signed the Voting Rights Reauthorization and Amendments Act, continuing America's commitment to ensure that every citizen's sacred right to vote is protected by law. The Congress also sent me a bill that would have overturned my Administration's balanced policy on embryonic stem cell research and compelled American taxpayers, for the first time in our history, to fund the deliberate destruction of human embryos. I vetoed that bill. On the same day, I signed a law prohibiting one of the most egregious abuses in biomedical research: trafficking in human fetuses created for the sole purpose of being aborted and harvested for parts.

This was also a time when Americans joined together to commemorate a terrible anniversary. On September 11, the Nation paused to remember the terrorist attacks perpetrated against us 5 years earlier.

On this anniversary, I addressed the Nation from the Oval Office. I said, "We look to the day when moms and dads throughout the Middle East see a future of hope and opportunity for their children. And when that good day comes, the clouds of war will part, the appeal of radicalism will decline, and we will leave our children with a better and safer world. On this solemn anniversary, we rededicate ourselves to this cause. Our nation has endured trials, and we face a difficult road ahead. Winning this war will require the determined efforts of a unified country, and we must put aside our differences and work together to meet the test that history has given us. We will defeat our enemies. We will protect our people. And we will lead the 21st century into a shining age of human liberty."

The following week, I addressed the United Nations General Assembly and spoke about the importance of freedom in the Middle East. I said, "Some have argued that the democratic changes we're seeing in the Middle East are destabilizing the region. This argument rests on a false assumption, that the Middle East was stable to begin with. The reality is that the stability we thought we saw in the Middle East was a mirage. For decades, millions of men and women in the region have been trapped in oppression and hopelessness. And these conditions left a generation disillusioned, and made this region a breeding ground for extremism."

My Administration acted forcefully against the extremist threat at home and abroad. In the fall, I signed the "SAFE Port Act of 2006," which enhanced our Nation's ability to help keep our major shipping centers secure without unduly burdening foreign trade. I signed the Military Commissions Act, which allowed our intelligence community to continue questioning suspected terrorists and created the ability to prosecute these extremists for war crimes through fair trials. I also hosted the presidents of Afghanistan and Pakistan at the White House to discuss our continuing efforts against radicalism in their countries.

These months also saw violence increase dramatically in Iraq. Terrorists waged a brutal effort to keep the people of Iraq's young democracy from succeeding. Our men and women in uniform performed valiantly against these challenges—but it became clear that a change in strategy was required. In November, I traveled to the Middle East, where I met with Iraqi Prime Minister Nouri Al-Maliki and American commanders on the ground to discuss a new way forward in Iraq. To help carry out our new strategy, I named a new Secretary of Defense—Robert Gates.

In the closing days of 2006, the Iraqi people made an important break with their past when Saddam Hussein was convicted and executed for crimes against his own people. In the early days of 2007, America would take a decisive new step toward stemming the violence in Iraq and helping the Iraqi people secure their democracy.

Preface

This book contains the papers and speeches of the 43d President of the United States that were issued by the Office of the Press Secretary during the period July 1–December 31, 2006. The material has been compiled and published by the Office of the Federal Register, National Archives and Records Administration.

The material is presented in chronological order, and the dates shown in the headings are the dates of the documents or events. In instances when the release date differs from the date of the document itself, that fact is shown in the textnote. Every effort has been made to ensure accuracy: Remarks are checked against a tape recording, and signed documents are checked against the original. Textnotes and cross references have been provided by the editors for purposes of identification or clarity. At the request of the Office of the Press Secretary, the Bush property known as Prairie Chapel Ranch in Crawford, Texas, is referred to simply as the Bush Ranch. Speeches were delivered in Washington, DC, unless indicated. The times noted are local times. All materials that are printed full-text in the book have been indexed in the subject and name indexes, and listed in the document categories list.

The Public Papers of the Presidents series was begun in 1957 in response to a recommendation of the National Historical Publications Commission. An extensive compilation of messages and papers of the Presidents covering the period 1789 to 1897 was assembled by James D. Richardson and published under congressional authority between 1896 and 1899. Since then, various private compilations have been issued, but there was no uniform publication comparable to the Congressional Record or the United States Supreme Court Reports. Many Presidential papers could be found only in the form of mimeographed White House releases or as reported in the press. The Commission therefore recommended the establishment of an official series in which Presidential writings, addresses, and remarks of a public nature could be made available.

The Commission's recommendation was incorporated in regulations of the Administrative Committee of the Federal Register, issued under section 6 of the Federal Register Act (44 U.S.C. 1506), which may be found in title 1, part 10, of the Code of Federal Regulations.

A companion publication to the Public Papers series, the Weekly Compilation of Presidential Documents, was begun in 1965 to provide a broader range of Presidential materials on a more timely basis to meet the needs of the contemporary reader. Beginning with the administration of Jimmy Carter, the Public Papers series expanded its coverage to include additional material as printed in the Weekly Compilation. That coverage provides a listing of the President's daily schedule and meetings, when announced, and other items of general interest issued by the Office of the Press Secretary. Also included are lists of the President's nominations submitted to the Senate, materials released by the Office of the Press Secretary that are not printed full-text in the book, and proclamations, Executive orders, and other Presidential documents released by the Office of the Press Secretary and published in the *Federal Register*. This information appears in the appendixes at the end of the book.

Volumes covering the administrations of Presidents Herbert Hoover, Harry S. Truman, Dwight D. Eisenhower, John F. Kennedy, Lyndon B. Johnson, Richard Nixon, Gerald R. Ford, Jimmy Carter, Ronald Reagan, George Bush, and William J. Clinton are also included in the Public Papers series.

The Public Papers of the Presidents publication program is under the direction of Michael L. White, Managing Editor, Office of the Federal Register. The series is produced by the Presidential and Legislative Publications Unit. The Chief Editor of this book was Stacey A. Mulligan, assisted by William K. Banks, Loretta F. Cochran, Lois Davis, Kathleen M. Fargey, Stephen J. Frattini, Michael J. Forcina, Allison M. Gavin, Gwendolyn J. Henderson, Diane Hiltabidle, Alfred Jones, Joshua H. Liberatore, Heather N. McDaniel, Ashley Merusi, Amelia E. Otovo, Jennifer M. Partridge, D. Gregory Perrin, Matthew R. Regan, and Michael J. Sullivan.

The frontispiece and photographs used in the portfolio were supplied by the White House Photo Office. The typography and design of the book were developed by the Government Printing Office under the direction of William J. Boarman, Public Printer.

Raymond A. Mosley
Director of the Federal Register

David S. Ferriero
Archivist of the United States

Contents

Cabinet

Secretary of State .... Condoleezza Rice

Secretary of the Treasury .... John W. Snow
(resigned 6/30)
Henry M. Paulson, Jr.
(confirmed 6/28)

Secretary of Defense .... Donald H. Rumsfeld

Attorney General .... Alberto R. Gonzales

Secretary of the Interior .... Gale A. Norton
(resigned 3/31)
Dirk Kempthorne
(confirmed 5/26)

Secretary of Agriculture .... Mike Johanns

Secretary of Commerce .... Carlos M. Gutierrez

Secretary of Labor .... Elaine L. Chao

Secretary of Health and Human
Services .... Michael O. Leavitt

Secretary of Housing and Urban
Development .... Alphonso R. Jackson

Secretary of Transportation .... Norman Y. Mineta
(resigned 7/7)
Mary E. Peters
(confirmed 9/30)

Secretary of Energy .... Samuel W. Bodman

Secretary of Education .... Margaret Spellings

Secretary of Veterans Affairs .... R. James Nicholson

Secretary of Homeland Security .... Michael Chertoff

Chief of Staff .... Andrew H. Card, Jr.
(resigned 4/14)
Joshua B. Bolten
(appointed 4/14)

Administrator of the Environmental
Protection Agency .... Stephen L. Johnson

United States Trade Representative .... Robert J. Portman
(resigned 5/30)
Susan C. Schwab
(confirmed 6/8)

Director of the Office of Management
and Budget .... Joshua B. Bolten
(resigned 4/14)
Robert J. Portman
(confirmed 5/26)

Director of National Drug Control
Policy .... John P. Walters

Administration of George W. Bush

2006

The President's Radio Address
July 1, 2006

Good morning. Laura and I wish all Americans a safe and happy Fourth of July weekend. I'm looking forward to spending Independence Day with members of our Armed Forces and their families at Fort Bragg, North Carolina. These brave men and women risk their lives to defend the ideals of our founding generation, and I will have the honor of thanking many of them personally for their service in freedom's cause.

In 1776, John Adams predicted to his wife, Abigail, that America's Independence Day would be celebrated by succeeding generations as the great anniversary festival. He wrote that "this anniversary should be commemorated with pomp and parade, with shows, games, sports, bells, bonfires, and illuminations from one end of this continent to the other, from this time forward, forever more."

Since then, generations of Americans have done just that. Each year, we look forward to the family gatherings and the grand celebrations that take place across the Nation on the Fourth of July. And amid the music and barbeques and fireworks, we give thanks for our freedom, and we honor the bravery and sacrifices of all those who have made that freedom possible.

On Independence Day, we recall the courage and high ideals of our Nation's Founders, who waged a desperate fight to overcome tyranny and live in freedom. Recent years have brought a renewed interest in the lives and achievements of our Founders, and we have learned once again that they possessed extraordinary talents as well as ordinary human failings, which only makes their accomplishments all the more remarkable.

For the brave men and women of our founding generation, victory was far from certain. They were certain only of the cause they served, the belief that freedom is the gift of God and the right of all mankind. The strength of their convictions made possible the birth of the free Nation in which we are blessed to live.

On the Fourth of July, we also honor the sacrifices made by each American generation to secure the promises of the Declaration of Independence. For more than two centuries, from the camps of Valley Forge to the mountains of Afghanistan, Americans have served and sacrificed for the principles of our founding.

Today, a new generation of American patriots is defending our freedom against determined and ruthless enemies. At this hour, the men and women of our Armed Forces are facing danger in distant places, carrying out their missions with all the skill and honor we expect of them. And their families are enduring long separations from their loved ones with great courage and dignity. Our troops and our military families deserve all our support and gratitude, and on this Fourth of July weekend, I ask every American to find a way to thank those who defend our freedom. To find out about efforts in your community, please visit the web site americasupportsyou.mil.

As we celebrate the Fourth, we also remember that the promises of liberty contained in our Declaration apply to all people. Because Americans believe that freedom is an unalienable right, we value the freedom of every person in every nation. And because we are committed to the God-given worth of every life, we strive to promote respect for human dignity. Today, all

1313

who live in tyranny and all who yearn for freedom can know that America stands with them.

As citizens of this good Nation, we should be proud of our heritage, grateful for our liberty, and confident in our future. Two hundred and thirty years after America declared its independence, the spirit of '76 lives on. And our Nation remains proud to carry freedom's torch. We still place our trust in the protections of divine providence. We still pledge our lives, our fortunes, and our sacred honor to freedom's defense. And we still believe in the promise of freedom for all.

Thank you for listening.

NOTE: The address was recorded at 7:45 a.m. on June 30 in the Cabinet Room at the White House for broadcast at 10:06 a.m. on July 1. The transcript was made available by the Office of the Press Secretary on June 30 but embargoed for release until broadcast. The Office of the Press Secretary also released a Spanish language transcript of these remarks.

Remarks at an Independence Day Celebration at Fort Bragg, North Carolina
July 4, 2006

Thank you all. Thanks for the warm welcome. It's a pleasure to be back here at Fort Bragg, home of our Airborne and Special Forces.

I flew down on Air Force One, and our pilot, Colonel Tillman, he said, "I can open the hatch and drop you out by parachute." [*Laughter*] I said he had the wrong President Bush. [*Laughter*] Old 41, I call him— who happens to be my dad—has jumped five times with the Golden Knights of Fort Bragg. Mother appreciates you helping him down safely. [*Laughter*] He's the only skydiving President, and that's a distinction I think he's going to keep. [*Laughter*]

Ever since I left the White House this morning, I've been looking forward to coming here and saying, Hooah!

Audience members. Hooah!

The President. It's a pleasure to get out of Washington, to spend some time in the real "center of the universe." It's good to be with the men and women of the 8th [18th] ° Airborne Corps and the quiet professionals of the Army Special Operations Command.

—————
° White House correction.

I can't think of a better way to spend the Fourth of July than with the "All-Americans" of the 82d Airborne. You're Airborne all the way, and I'm proud to be here with you. We also welcome the men and women of Pope Air Force base, who put the "air" in Airborne. I'm privileged to be in the presence of so many courageous military families who have borne the hardships of war with dignity and devotion. By supporting a loved one in uniform, you are serving our country, and America is grateful for your service and your sacrifice.

Today we mark the 230th anniversary of American independence. And on this day, when we give thanks for our freedom, we also give thanks for the men and women who make our freedom possible. Each of you have stepped forward to serve, knowing the risks and dangers that accompany freedom's defense.

I've come to thank you for your valor and to thank you for your patriotism. I've come to share with you and with the American people how your dedication and your sacrifice are helping us win the war on terror. You are serving our country at a time when our country needs you. And because of your courage, every day is Independence Day in America.

Laura sends her best and her love. I'm a lucky man that she said yes when I asked her to marry me. I appreciate Lieutenant General John Vines for his introduction. I want to thank all the commanding officers, all the sergeant majors, all who wear our uniform for welcoming me here today. It's a pleasure to be with you.

I'm honored to be here with Senator Richard Burr, United States Senator from the State of North Carolina. He strongly supports the men and women who wear the uniform. And I'm proud to serve with him in Washington, DC.

I want to thank all the local officials who are here. Thank you for supporting the good folks who live here and work here and train here. It means a lot to the families to know that the local communities extend the hand of friendship and support.

Two hundred and thirty years ago, 56 brave men signed their names to a document that set the course of our Nation. It changed the history of the world. Our Declaration of Independence was a bold statement of revolutionary principles. It laid down a creed of freedom and equality that has lifted the lives of hundreds of millions here in America and around the world. Yet without the courage of the soldiers of our Continental Army, the words of the Declaration would have been forgotten by history, dismissed as the radical musings of a failed revolution.

We celebrate Independence Day each year because that ragtag group of citizen soldiers challenged the world's most powerful military, secured our liberty, and planted a standard of freedom to which the entire world has aspired.

Since that first Fourth of July, some 43 million Americans have defended our freedom in times of war. These brave men and women crossed oceans and continents to defeat murderous ideologies and to secure the peace for generations that followed. We live in liberty because of the courage they displayed. From Bunker Hill to Baghdad, from Concord to Kabul, on this Independence Day, we honor their achievements and we thank them for their service in freedom's cause.

At this hour the men and women of Fort Bragg are carrying on this great legacy, facing danger in distant lands and carrying out their missions with all the skill and honor we expect of them. In a time when the terrorists have attacked our homeland and hope to strike again, Americans take comfort in knowing that the soldiers of Fort Bragg are on duty and standing watch for our freedom.

Fort Bragg is the home to some of our country's best and bravest, the men and women of the United States Army Special Operations Command. Army Special Forces define their mission in a motto: "To Liberate the Oppressed." And in the war on terror, you've done just that, overthrowing cruel regimes in Afghanistan and Iraq and bringing freedom to more than 50 million people.

Green Berets were the first U.S. forces on the ground in both Operation Enduring Freedom and our Operation Iraqi Freedom. And along with others, you remain on the offense against the terrorists today. A few weeks ago, I had a chance to visit Baghdad and visit with some of Fort Bragg's finest soldiers, the special operation forces who helped bring justice to the terrorist Zarqawi.

They were the first coalition forces to arrive on the scene after the bombing of Zarqawi's safe house. They administered compassionate medical care to a man who showed no compassion to his victims. And when this brutal terrorist took his final breath, one of the last things he saw was the face of an American soldier from Fort Bragg, North Carolina.

We're on the offense. In the weeks since Zarqawi's death, coalition and Iraqi forces have launched more than 190 raids on targets across the country. We've captured more than 700 enemy operatives and killed some 60 more. In these raids, we've uncovered caches of weapons and suicide vests and Iraqi Army uniforms to be used as disguises in brutal terrorist attacks. We've seized new intelligence information that is helping us keep the pressure on the terrorists and the insurgents. At this moment of vulnerability for the enemy, we will continue to strike their network, we will disrupt their operations, and we will bring their leaders to justice.

Last week, Iraqi security forces announced the capture of an Al Qaida terrorist from Tunisia named Abu Qadama. He's one of the men responsible for the bombing of the Golden Mosque in Samarra. The Golden Mosque is one of Shi'a Islam's holiest sites, and the terrorists blew it up in the hope that this vicious act would provoke sectarian reprisals and drag the nation into civil war and derail the formation of a unity government. Hundreds of Iraqis were killed in the violence that ensued.

But in the end, Iraqis stepped back from the abyss. They want to live in a free and peaceful society. Their mothers are no different from the mothers here in America who want their children to grow up and be able to realize dreams. They came together to form a new Government. Iraqi and coalition forces, by working together, have brought justice to a key player in the Samara attack. We're going to continue to strike blows against the terrorists. We'll continue working to support Iraq's new Government.

When I spoke here a year ago, Iraqis still had a transitional government that was operating under an administrative law issued before the restoration of sovereignty. Today, Iraqis have a permanent Government chosen in free elections under a democratic Constitution that they wrote and they approved. And the Iraqi people have a courageous leader in Prime Minister Maliki, who has formed a cabinet and laid out a clear agenda for the people of Iraq.

I met the Prime Minister. I met with his team. I was impressed by them. I was impressed by his strength. I was impressed by his character. I was impressed by his determination to succeed. He's laid out an ambitious plan to improve its economy and deliver essential services and to defeat the enemies of a free Iraq. And I told him this: That as he stands up for freedom, the United States of America will stand with him.

There's more work to be done in Iraq. The Iraqi people face deadly enemies who are determined to stop Iraq's new unity Government from succeeding. They can't stand the thought of liberty. Our strategy is clear. Our goals are easy to understand. We will help Iraq's new leaders; we will help the people of Iraq build a country that can govern itself and sustain itself and defend itself as a free nation. Our troops will help the Iraqi people succeed because it's in our national interests. A free Iraq in the heart of the Middle East will make America and the world more secure.

I'm going to make you this promise: I'm not going to allow the sacrifice of 2,527 troops who have died in Iraq to be in vain by pulling out before the job is done.

General Casey is working with the Iraqi Government on a path forward. But we're not going to set an artificial timetable for withdrawal. Setting an artificial timetable would be a terrible mistake. At a moment when the terrorists have suffered a series of significant blows, setting an artificial timetable would breathe new life into their cause. Setting an artificial timetable would undermine the new Iraqi Government and send a signal to Iraq's enemies that if they wait just a little bit longer, America will just give up. Setting an artificial timetable would undermine the morale of our troops by sending the message that the mission for which you've risked your lives is not worth completing. We're not going to set an artificial timetable to withdraw from Iraq. I will make decisions about troop levels in Iraq based on the advice that matters most: the measured judgment of our military commanders.

I'll make you another pledge: We're going to make sure you have the resources you need to defeat our enemies in Iraq and secure the peace for generations to come. I believe in you, and I believe in all the men and women who are serving in the cause of freedom with such courage and such determination. You're winning this war, and our enemies understand that too.

We get all kinds of evidence when we raid these safe houses about their concerns. They bemoan the fact that we're keeping the pressure on them. They see the successes we're having in training. They know we're damaging their cause. This moment when the terrorists are suffering from the weight of successive blows is not the time to call retreat. We will stay, we will fight, and we will prevail.

Prevailing in Iraq is going to require more tough fighting; it's going to require more sacrifice. And when the job in Iraq is done, it will be a major victory in the battle against the terrorists. By achieving victory in Iraq, we will deny the terrorists a safe haven from which to plot and plan new attacks on America and other free nations. By achieving victory in Iraq, we will send a signal to our enemies that America's resolve is firm and that our country will not run in the face of thugs and assassins.

By achieving victory in Iraq, we will help Iraqis build a free nation in the heart of a troubled region and inspire those who desire liberty, those democratic reformers from Damascus to Tehran. By achieving victory in Iraq, we will honor the sacrifice of the brave men and women who have risked their lives and given their lives for a just and noble cause.

Victory in Iraq will not, in itself, end the war on terror. We're engaged in a global struggle against the followers of a murderous ideology that despises freedom and crushes all dissent and has territorial ambitions and pursues totalitarian aims. This enemy attacked us in our homeland on September the 11th, 2001. They're pursuing weapons of mass destruction that would allow them to deliver even more catastrophic destruction to our country and our friends and allies across the world. They're dangerous. And against such enemy there is only one effective response: We will never back down, we will never give in, and we will never accept anything less than complete victory.

We will keep the pressure on them. We will stay on the offense. We'll fight the terrorists in Afghanistan and Iraq and every battlefront in this struggle. Yet in the long run, we will defeat the terrorists and their hateful ideology by spreading the hope of freedom across the world. Our strategy to protect America is based on a clear premise: The security of our Nation depends on the advance of liberty in other nations.

On September the 11th, 2001, we saw that problems originating in a failed and oppressive state 7,000 miles away could bring murder and destruction to our country. And we learned an important lesson: Decades of excusing and accommodating the lack of freedom in the Middle East did nothing to make it safe. So long as the Middle East remains a place where freedom does not flourish, it will remain a place where terrorists foment resentment and threaten American security.

And so we pursue a forward strategy of freedom in the Middle East. We ought to be confident in the pursuit of that strategy because liberty is universal. And by standing with those who desire liberty, we will help extend freedom to millions who have not known it and lay the foundations of peace for generations to come.

These are historic times, and I thank you for putting on the uniform and for volunteering to serve this country during these important times. I have confidence in our country, and I have faith in our cause, because I see—I know the character of the men and women who wear our Nation's uniform. And I know the character of the men and women here at Fort Bragg. We see that character in 24 servicemembers from Fort Bragg and Pope Air Force Base who have received the Silver Star for gallantry in combat. We see that character in men and women who have received serious wounds in battle but fought on, exposing themselves to enemy fire to save their comrades and complete their missions.

We see that character in special operations soldiers like Captain Chip Eldridge. In December 2004, Captain Eldridge was deployed at a coalition base near Shkin, Afghanistan, where he got a report that the terrorists were preparing to attack the base with a rocket. When his unit went out to look for them, his Humvee was hit by an antitank mine, and his unit came under a barrage of gunfire. He was pulled out of his vehicle, and he looked down, and he saw that part of his left leg had been blown off. Despite the intense pain, he refused pain killers offered by a field medic so he could stay alert to deal with the enemy. Soon, a team of A–10 Warthogs arrived and took care of the terrorists, and Chip and his men were evacuated.

Eventually, Chip was transported to Walter Reed Army Medical Center, where doctors told him that he would be in recovery for at least a year. He told his doctors he had a change of command in 6 months and that he'd be out of recovery by then. To speed his recovery, he tripled his daily physical therapy regime. He told his physical therapists, "I'm going to need to run, swim, jump out of planes, possibly ride horses; I'm not going to accept anything different." His therapist recalls how angry he was when someone told him he'd never run a sub-7 minute mile again. Chip proved him wrong.

Today, his commanding officer says, "I'd say he's fitter than 90 percent of the people in the unit he commands. In a room with four people, I bet he could beat three of us in a mile run." Chip is here at Fort Bragg. He's jumping out of planes, he's training with his men, and next April, he's heading back to Afghanistan, where he'll once again command a unit in the zone of combat. America is blessed to have brave soldiers like Chip Eldridge. With men like this leading our forces in the battle, the enemy doesn't have a chance.

Like Chip, some of our service men and women have returned from war with terrible injuries, wounds they will carry with them for the rest of their lives. Others left our shores to defend freedom and did not live to make the journey home. They left loved ones behind who mourn a loss that time can never fully heal. We hold the families of the fallen in our hearts, and we lift them up in our prayers, and America will always honor their sacrifice.

In the past 5 years, the men and women of Fort Bragg have met hardships together, and you have looked out for each other. Last year, more than 6,400 members of the Fort Bragg community served as volunteers, put in more than 725,000 hours of service to your friends and neighbors at this base. You've coached little league teams, you've comforted children who miss moms and dads deployed on missions far from home, and you helped returning soldiers make the adjustments from life in a combat zone to life at home.

As you stand with one another here at Fort Bragg, you need to know, America stands with you. We support you. Last week, at the White House, I met with leaders of military service organizations from across this country. These groups are sending letters to our troops and offering scholarships for the children of our fallen and severely wounded soldiers. And they're providing millions of dollars in assistance to families of service men and women in need.

I met some remarkable people at that meeting. I met a lady named Emily Dieruf who lost her husband Nich in Iraq. Emily Dieruf has dedicated her life to helping our service men and women and their families in difficult times. She travels the country raising funds for a group called USA Cares. And together, they provided more than $1.4 million in assistance to our military families.

I met a wonderful lady named Mary Harper. Mary has got five children and a son-in-law in the United States Army, all of them in the Army, and all of them have served in Iraq. Mary was concerned about our troops not receiving mail from home, and so she started something called Operation Shoe Box. Today, she has 500 volunteers working with her, shipping between 500 and 700 care packages a week to our troops in Afghanistan and Iraq and other fronts in the war on terror. People like Mary and Emily represent the heart and soul of our Nation, and they make this country proud.

Across our country, Americans are coming together to help our deployed forces and their families. And we can do more. So on this Fourth of July, I ask all Americans to take a moment and consider what you might do to support the men and women who wear our Nation's uniform. If you're interested in helping, go to a Department of Defense web site called americasupportsyou.mil. That's where you can find a place to volunteer, an opportunity to help. I ask every citizen to consider making a contribution to the men and women who defend us, because every one

of us owes our freedom to these courageous Americans.

The men and women who serve here at Fort Bragg are making a difference for America, and you're part of a great history. From the Battle of Trenton to the Battle of Tall 'Afar, brave soldiers have stepped forward to risk their lives for liberty. Two hundred and thirty years after America declared her independence, the spirit of '76 lives on in the courage that you show each day.

You've given our citizens a priceless gift, the opportunity to live in freedom and to pursue their dreams and enjoy lives of purpose and dignity. You've kept America what our Founders meant her to be: a light to the nations, spreading the good news of human freedom to the darkest corners of Earth.

I want to thank you for all you do for our country and for the world. May God bless you all, and may God continue to bless the United States of America.

NOTE: The President spoke at 9:58 a.m. in Iron Mike Plaza. In his remarks, he referred to Col. Mark Tillman, USAF, commander, Presidential Airlift Group; Lt. Gen. John R. Vines, USA, commanding general, XVIII Airborne Corps and Fort Bragg; Prime Minister Nuri al-Maliki of Iraq; and Gen. George W. Casey, Jr., USA, commanding general, Multi-National Force—Iraq.

Remarks on Immigration Reform in Alexandria, Virginia
July 5, 2006

The President. I just had a really interesting conversation. First of all, this business is owned by two Iranian American brothers. They are small-business owners; they are entrepreneurs; they are employing people. And then I met with the district manager, who works with the two Iranian

American brothers, happens to be a Guatemalan American citizen. She is learning business; she is taking on additional responsibility. Then I talked to the store manager, who was a Salvadoran American.

These people remind me that one of the great features of our country is that people are able to come here and realize dreams. One of the problems we have, because our economy is strong, is that small-business owners have trouble finding workers. People come here to work.

And one of the things we've got to do is to make sure that they have a verification plan that will enable them to determine, as they hire new workers, whether or not those workers are here illegally. See, it's against the law to hire somebody who is here illegally. And we intend to enforce that law. Part of a comprehensive immigration plan is to give employers the tools necessary to determine whether or not the workers they're looking for are here illegally in America. And we've got such a plan, Basic Pilot, it's called. It's working.

One of the reasons I came is I asked the owner of the business, was the plan working. He said, "Yes, it is. It makes it easier for us to verify whether the documents a person gives us are true." I also want—so therefore, I want this plan to be expanded. When I first became President, it was only in six States. Now it's across the Nation. But it's a voluntary plan; it ought to be a mandatory plan.

I'm strongly for a comprehensive immigration policy. It's one that enforces the border. And we're doing that by expanding agents and putting new technologies on our border. But part of a comprehensive immigration plan is to make sure we have interior enforcement, that we uphold our laws, and say to employers, "It's against the law for you to hire somebody who's here illegally. We intend to fine you when we catch you doing it." But we've got to get the employers the tools to make sure that the people who are here, are here legally.

Thirdly, I think there needs to be—I know there needs to be a worker program that says you can come here on a temporary basis and work here legally for jobs Americans aren't doing. If you talk to employers such as these folks, they'll tell you they need workers. And people are willing to do the work that others aren't willing

to do, but we want to make sure there's a legal way to do it.

So I look forward to working with Congress for a temporary-worker plan that will have background checks to make sure that people that are coming aren't criminals, that say you can come here for a temporary basis, that you can do work others aren't doing. And that's one way to make sure that employers know they're hiring people who are here legally.

We need to make sure we help people assimilate. I met four people here who assimilated into our country. They speak English; they understand the history of our country; they love the American flag as much as I love the American flag. That's one of the great things about America: We help newcomers assimilate. Here's four folks that are living the American Dream, and I think it helps renew our soul and our spirit to help people assimilate.

And finally, we cannot kick people out who have been here for a while. And so I look forward to working with Congress on a rational plan as to how to make sure people who have been here, the 11 million or so people who have been here for a while, are treated with respect and dignity. I'm absolutely opposed to amnesty. Amnesty says, you're automatically a citizen. That would be a mistake to grant amnesty. Amnesty would say to somebody, all I've got to do is wait it out; all I've got to do is get here illegally myself and I'll become a citizen. That would be bad policy.

But I'm also realistic to tell you that we're not going to be able to deport people who have been here, working hard and raising their families. And so I want to work with Congress to come up with a rational way forward.

Again, I want to thank you all for having me. I love being—I cannot tell you how I love being with entrepreneurs and dreamers and doers and people who are running things and managers, and to be with my fellow citizens as we talk about a very important public policy, and that's rational, comprehensive immigration reform.

Thank you all very much. See you back at the White House.

Q. Mr. President, North Korea—do you believe there should be——

The President. See you at the White House. April [April Ryan, American Urban Radio Networks], would you like me to buy you a cup of coffee?

Ms. Ryan. I would love you to.

The President. What would you want in it?

Ms. Ryan. Anything you want to give me.

The President. What would you like in it, cream and sugar?

Ms. Ryan. Sure, sir. [*Laughter*]

The President. All right. One more coffee please. I'm coming your way. It's in the spirit of——

Ms. Ryan. Spirit of what?

The President. Spirit of reaching out.

Ms. Ryan. All right. And you got money in your pocket? Do you typically keep money in your pocket?

The President. No, this is—Jared let me have this money. [*Laughter*] And I'll repay him—I'll repay him. See, the man offered to give me the coffee for free. You can't run a business if you give your coffee away. I understand how commerce works. He offers a product I want; I then pay for that product—I'll handle that, sir, thank you. [*Laughter*]

Ms. Ryan. Mr. President, thank you so much.

The President. April, anything for you.

NOTE: The President spoke at 11:02 a.m. in a Dunkin' Donuts/Baskin Robbins store. In his remarks, he referred to Abolhossein Ejtemai and Ali Assayesh, owners, and Reynaldo Ramos, store manager; and Adriana Hernandez, district manager, Dunkin' Brands, Inc. The Office of the Press Secretary also released a Spanish language transcript of these remarks.

Remarks Following Discussions With President Mikheil Saakashvili of Georgia and an Exchange With Reporters
July 5, 2006

President Bush. We'll have opening statements and a couple of questions.

First, Mr. President, welcome. I was—reminded the President about what a fantastic visit I had to Georgia. Laura and I will never forget your hospitality; we will never forget the food, for which Georgia is quite famous; we will never forget the fantastic folk dancing we saw. And then I'll never forget our visits and the speech to the Georgian people. It was a fantastic trip.

It was made fantastic because my friend not only was a good host, but he is a man who shares the same values I share. He believes in the universality of freedom. He

believes that democracy is the best way to yield the peace. The Georgian Government and the people of Georgia have acted on those beliefs. I want to thank you for your contribution in Iraq, to help the Iraqi people realize the great benefits of democracy. It's hard work, but it's necessary work.

We had a very good discussion about a variety of topics. I assured the President that Georgia is our friend, and we care deeply about the people of Georgia. It's—a remarkable experience has taken place. I congratulate the President and his Government on creating an economic climate that fosters growth and opportunity. I love the stories about the entrepreneurial spirit that's beginning to flourish.

And one of the interesting stories that captured my imagination is when the President first came into office and he cleaned out the police forces in order to rid the country of corruption in the law enforcement, understanding full well that the people must trust security in order for a society to flourish.

And so, Mr. President, you've got hard work ahead of you. You've tackled problems with vigor and enthusiasm. But most importantly, you've stayed true to a philosophy that I admire. So welcome back to the Oval Office, and please give your good wife all my very best.

President Saakashvili. I will certainly tell Sandra. And I mean, Mr. President, it was an incredible honor for me to stand next to you in the Freedom Square in Tbilisi. And I felt like it was, you know, after— it was vindication for all those Georgians, including my family members, who perished in gulag, who died fighting for their freedom, their liberty, their independence. And, basically, this was an incredible occasion, because I'm also—I've studied diplomacy for many years, and I can tell you, it was brilliant exercise of self-diplomacy, the way you appreciated our culture, our openness, our warmth. And we will certainly never forget it.

Georgia is, indeed, performing. It is a very—I mean, it has strong economic growth. This is a very beautiful country that attracts lots of investment now. We have low tax rates, but we dramatically increased our tax collection, which means that low taxes and less government is a very good thing to have, as you well know.

So basically, we are getting there. And one thing, you know, we discussed with President Bush the upcoming G–8 summit. And, certainly, there are lots of issues that are at stake there, and we believe very strongly in the same values, in the same principles. And we are talking to the President—to the country, which is the—for

Georgians, I mean, for generations of Georgians, American freedom are synonymous— they have been synonymous for me all my life, when I lived under Soviets and after that. And it still stays very much that way because all freedom-loving people today, whenever they have something to share with somebody, come to America. And this is a very strong thing.

And one thing I can tell, Mr. President, your freedom agenda does indeed work. I mean, you can see it in Georgia. We are seeing it in Iraq. And please stay there; please fight there until the end. We will stay with you there, whatever it takes, because your success in Iraq is success for countries like Georgia. It's a success for every individual that loves freedom, every individual that wants security, to live in more secure world for himself, herself, or their children. And whatever it takes to help you. We are not a big country; we are beautiful, small country with lots of attractions. I invited you to come. I had mountain biking here yesterday, and I invited you to come over and have mountain biking in Georgia.

But one thing is important, that you know we really cherish the same things. And I'm so honored to be here on the Independence Day, and I watched yesterday fireworks—and around the time of your birthday. So happy birthday. I'm honored to be invited now. [*Laughter*] And God bless you, America, Georgia, and the whole world. Thank you very much.

President Bush. Mr. President, thank you. Deb [Deb Riechmann, Associated Press].

North Korea

Q. Mr. President, on North Korea, how is it possible to punish a country that is one of the poorest and most isolated in the world? And secondly, had you been hoping for a stronger response from China?

President Bush. The North Korean Government can join the community of nations and improve its lot by acting in concert with those who—with those of us who believe that she shouldn't possess nuclear weapons, and by those of us who believe that there's a positive way forward for the North Korean Government and her people. In other words, this is a choice they make. Yesterday, as you know, they fired off a series of rockets. The world had—particularly those of us in the six-party talks—had asked for that not to happen. It's a matter of good faith. The Government made a different decision.

And so it's their choice to make. What these firing of the rockets have done is they've isolated themselves further, and that's sad for the people of North Korea. I am deeply concerned about the plight of the people of North Korea. I would hope that the Government would agree to verifiably abandon its weapons programs. I would hope that there would be a better opportunity to—for that Government and its people to move forward. The Chinese will play—have played and will continue to play a very important role in the six-party talks. It's my view that the best way to solve this problem diplomatically is for there to be more than one nation speaking to North Korea, more than America voicing our opinions.

And therefore, the five of us—Russia, South Korea, Japan, China, and the United States—spoke with one voice about the rocket launches, and we will work together to continue to remind the leader of North Korea that there is a better way forward for his people.

Georgia.

President Saakashvili. You know, regarding the—I mean, I'm not intervening off the agenda, but one thing I have to tell you, in Georgia, that I just sent over to President Bush the letter that Georgian freedom fighters sent him 7 years ago, and it never made it to the White House. It was intercepted by KGB, and all the people who wrote it were shot.

I'm sure lots of people out there in Korea are writing similar letters today. And I'm sure that North Korean missiles will never reach the United States, but those letters will, eventually, very soon, because that's a part of freedom agenda that President Bush has and what we strongly believe in.

President Bush. Do you want to call on a Georgian?

President Saakashvili. Please. Whatever.

Georgia/North Atlantic Treaty Organization

Q. Mr President, Georgia is planning IPP to NATO. What do you think, how fast can Georgia finish this IPP process and get Membership Action Plan? And do you think that Georgia should and will be a NATO member during your Presidency? Thank you, sir.

President Bush. Listen, I believe that NATO would benefit with Georgia being a member of NATO, and I think Georgia would benefit. And there's a way forward through the Membership Action Plan. And we'll work with our partners in NATO to see if we can't make the path a little smoother for Georgia. Georgia has got work to do, and the President understands that. But I'm a believer in the expansion of NATO. I think it's in the world's interest that we expand NATO.

Kelly [Kelly O'Donnell, NBC News].

North Korea

Q. Thank you, sir. On the North Korean missiles, what have you learned about their intentions or their capabilities, and what threat level do you think they still possess given that their intercontinental missile failed?

President Bush. I spoke with Secretary Rumsfeld yesterday. He called me right after the launch, and he said they had preliminary information that they were going to analyze about the trajectory of the larger rocket. The other five rockets that were fired, the scuds, were—their performance was pretty predictable. It's kind of a routine weapon that some of these nations have.

I asked him this morning again, when I met with him, about the information. They're still analyzing, trying to figure out the intention of the North Korean leader as to why he would have fired the rocket and what they were trying to learn from it.

One thing we have learned is that the rocket didn't stay up very long and tumbled into the sea, which doesn't, frankly, diminish my desire to solve this problem. So the first part of your question is, we're still analyzing what the intentions were. We're trying to analyze the data to determine flight path, for example.

I view this as an opportunity to remind the international community that we must work together to continue to work hard to convince the North Korean leader to give up any weapons programs. They've agreed to do that in the past, and we will hold them to account. And I also strongly believe that it is much more effective to have more than one nation dealing with North Korea. It's more effective for them to hear from a group of nations rather than one nation.

And so today the Secretary of State—starting last night, the Secretary of State has been in touch with counterparts. I, of course, will be on the phone as well. We want to send—to continue to send a clear message that there is a better way forward for the leader of North Korea. It's hard to understand his intentions. It's hard to understand why he would not only fire one missile that failed but five others. And so we're talking with our friends and allies on the subject.

Spread of Democracy/Georgia-U.S. Relations

Q. Mr. President, as you mentioned, you've faced a lot of important challenges in many places like Iran and Iraq, Afghanistan, and North Korea. And at the same time, the whole world recognizes your personal role in promoting democracy and freedom all around. And how do you think—is there any chance that Georgia's aspiration to build free and democratic country may be left off of your agenda?

President Saakashvili. Tricky question.

President Bush. Freedom—I believe freedom is universal. And I believe the spread of liberty is important for peace. And therefore, the freedom agenda will be at the heart of everything I do. The freedom agenda is ingrained in my—it's not only ingrained in my policy, it's ingrained in my soul. I believe it strongly. And I believe the United States has an obligation to work with others to help them secure their liberty.

I understand that elections are only the beginning of the freedom agenda and that there's work needed to be done around the world, including our own country, to continue to build strong institutions and build the organizations necessary for a civil society to develop. Remember, ours was a country that wrote a great Constitution but enslaved people for 100 years. It takes time. And so I understand that, and I want to work with our friends that ask. Georgia is a sovereign government, and when governments say, "Will you help," America must always listen to requests for help, and specifically to Georgia.

One of the signature pieces of policy in my administration has been the Millennium Challenge Account. It's a foreign funding mechanism that recognizes countries that fight corruption, support rule of law, invest in the health and education of their people, and adopt open markets. And one of the most robust Millennium Challenge Account projects is with Georgia. It's a sign—should be a sign to the people of Georgia and people in the neighborhood that the United States respects the decisions this Government has made and wants to work closely with the people of Georgia to help Georgia succeed, to help create the conditions for success.

And so to answer your question, yes, I've got a lot that comes to my desk here, absolutely. I've got a lot to think about. But my friend, the President, wouldn't be sitting here if I didn't have Georgia on my mind. [*Laughter*]

Thank you all very much.

NOTE: The President spoke at 2:15 p.m. in the Oval Office at the White House. In his remarks, he referred to Sandra Roelofs, wife of President Saakashvili; and Chairman Kim Jong Il of North Korea.

The President's News Conference With Prime Minister Stephen Harper of Canada
July 6, 2006

President Bush. Thank you all. Welcome. It's been my honor to visit with Stephen Harper, the Prime Minister of Canada, in the Oval Office. After this exercise in democracy, I'll be buying him lunch, where we'll continue our discussions. I'm impressed by his leadership style. I appreciate the fact that he doesn't mince words. He tells me what's on his mind, and he does so in a real, clear fashion.

We talked about a lot of subjects. We talked about Iran and our joint desire to convince the Iranian regime to give up its nuclear weapons ambitions. We talked about North Korea, and I shared with him our strategy to work with five other—four other nations to convince the North Koreans to adhere to agreements they had already reached with the world.

We talked about the war on terror, and I told the Prime Minister how pleased Americans were that the Canadian Government did the hard work necessary to disrupt terrorist plots. It just goes to show how safe Canada is. When you've got a government that's active and a police force that's capable, people ought to be rest assured that Canada is on top of any plots.

I thanked the Prime Minister and the Canadian people for their involvement in Afghanistan. This is a serious foreign policy decision by the Government, and it's a necessary decision, in my judgment, to help make this world a more peaceful place. It just goes to show the important role Canada can play in foreign policy. Canada has

got a set of values that are extremely important for the world to see.

And I do want to thank the families of those soldiers who are in Afghanistan for supporting their loved ones. Their soldiers are doing fantastic work. I asked prior to your visit here from our military folks how they were doing; they said, great. And they're making the country proud.

I appreciate very much our discussion about Darfur. I believe that Canada and the United States can make a difference in Darfur and should. As you know, our Nation declared the situation in Darfur a genocide. We will work with the international community to bolster the AU forces that are there now. I believe they ought to be blue-helmeted, and I believe there ought to be NATO involvement with a blue-helmeted, AU-augmented force on the ground. The message has got to be clear to the Government of Sudan: We're not going to tolerate this kind of activity.

I speak frequently with my Secretary of State on this issue, Mr. Prime Minister, to make sure that we expedite the arrival of augmented troops to save lives. I talked to Kofi Annan the other night, by the way, about this very subject. And so I appreciate your understanding, and I really appreciate your working on this.

You know, we cooperate closely in our neighborhood. We just renewed the NORAD accord, and I want to thank you for that. I remember going out—one of the hurricanes was about to hit us here, and I can remember talking to and having dinner with a Canadian general there, and it was a—it just reminded me of how close that our relations need to be.

We talked about trade. We have a lot of trade with Canada. It's in this Nation's interest to trade with Canada. It's in, I think, the Canadian interest to trade with the United States. I'll let the Prime Minister speak to that. But it's important when you have trade to have goods and services and people flow as smoothly as possible between our two countries.

We've had some disputes in the past, trade disputes. That's what you expect when you have a lot of trade. And probably the most nettlesome trade dispute was softwood lumber. And I appreciate the Prime Minister's leadership in helping us resolve this issue. It's a tough issue. It was a tough issue for the Canadian Government; it's a tough issue for us. Nevertheless, the fact that we were able to reach an accord just goes to show how trading partners can be active in trade and be willing—and solve problems. I think this is a really important solution, and I want to thank you for that.

Needless to say, the Prime Minister expressed deep concerns about the Western Hemisphere Travel Initiative. The last time I was with him, he expressed concerns. He basically was a little impatient, if I might clarify your—it seemed like you were impatient, at least—[*laughter*]—and straightforward. "Look," he said, "I understand there's a law on the books. Show us what's going to happen." And I understand the concerns. If you have a relationship like we have, where there's a lot of activity and a lot of people moving across the border, it makes sense for the Prime Minister of Canada to say, "Look, we just want to know what the rules are to determine whether or not it is compatible with our relationship."

And so I assured him that my view is—simple and easy to understand is the operative words. And we will continue our dis-

cussions about this initiative, particularly since the Secretary of Homeland Security, Chertoff—who is sitting right over there, by the way—will be joining us for lunch. Unless you don't want me to invite him. [*Laughter*]

We talked about—well, we talked about a lot of subjects, and that's what you'd expect friends to do.

Mr. Prime Minister, the floor is yours. I'm proud you're here, and thanks for coming.

Prime Minister Harper. Well, thank you very much, Mr. President, for the invitation and for the kind words. And thank you for doing something I never thought I'd see, which is have the Canadian media stand when I entered the room. But we certainly enjoy that.

[*At this point, Prime Minister Harper spoke in French, and no translation was provided. He then continued in English, as follows.*]

Prime Minister Harper. ——your hospitality. The United States and Canada have a strong relationship, strong and firm relationship based on the largest commerce and social interaction in the history of any two countries of the world, and we were able to discuss a wide range of bilateral and international matters where we, more often than not, share common values and common objectives.

We discussed many topics of interest to our respective countries and citizens, in particular, as the President mentioned, the Western Hemisphere Travel Initiative. The President and I agreed that the implementation of the provisions of the WHTI must not unduly hinder cross-border travel or tourism or trade. And to that end, we've tasked our officials to agree on common standards for securing alternate documents and, preferably, as soon as possible.

We discussed the critical role Canada, in particular our oil sands, can play in providing energy security. The President and

I have agreed to task our officials to provide a more forward-looking approach focused on the environment, climate change, air quality, and energy issues in which our Governments can cooperate. We raised the issue of how regulatory cooperation could increase productivity, while helping to protect our health, safety, and environment.

We also expressed, as the President just did, our mutual satisfaction on the significant progress made on the longstanding softwood lumber dispute. Both countries have now initialed the legal text. That legal text faithfully reproduces and documents the agreements reached between our Governments and various premiers on April the 27th, and I now urge all relevant parties to move forward with its implementation.

The President and I also discussed a number of important international issues, in particular our role in Afghanistan. We have 2,300 men and women on the ground as part of the Canadian forces. They're playing an important role in security and development in order to protect our national interest, rebuild Afghanistan, and ensure it never becomes again a safe haven for terrorists.

We also discussed recent developments in Iran, and we expressed our mutual concern about North Korea's latest provocative acts. We also discussed the upcoming G–8 meeting in Russia, where issues like energy security, infectious diseases, education, and innovation will be on the agenda. And finally, we did touch briefly on the recent Mexican election. Canada has full confidence in Mexico's institutions and processes, and I look forward very much to working with the next President of Mexico.

President Bush. Thank you, sir.

Keil [Richard Keil, Bloomberg News].

North Korea

Q. Thank you, Mr. President. Do you want the United Nations to impose sanctions on North Korea? And how will you go about persuading the Russians and the Chinese to back those moves if you make

them? And in addition to that, sir, what kind of threat do you think North Korea poses to world peace right now?

President Bush. Nontransparent societies run by Governments that aren't selected by the people are—very difficult to tell what's going on. That's part of the problem. We're dealing with a person who was asked not to fire a rocket by the Chinese, the South Koreans, the United States, the Japanese, and the Russians. And he fired seven of them, which then caused the Secretary of State and myself to get on the phone with our partners and reminded them that—of the importance of speaking with one voice.

It's to—saying to Kim Jong Il, there is a better way forward for you than isolating yourself from the rest of the world; that there is a opportunity for you to stick to some of your agreements, and that is to verifiably disarm; and that there will be a better life than being isolated and, most importantly, a better life for your people than isolation will bring.

And so I was on the phone this morning with Hu Jintao and President Putin, and last night I talked to Prime Minister Koizumi and President Roh. And my message was that we want to solve this problem diplomatically, and the best way to solve the problem diplomatically is for all of us to be working in concert and to send one message, and that is—to Kim Jong Il—that we expect you to adhere to international norms, and we expect you to keep your word.

One way to send a message is through the United Nations. And the Japanese laid down a resolution which we support. But we're working with our partners to make sure we speak with one voice. Diplomacy takes a while, particularly when you're dealing with a variety of partners. And so we're spending time diplomatically making sure that voice is unified.

I was pleased from the responses I got from the leaders. They, like me, were—are concerned, concerned about a person who doesn't seem to really care about what others say. And so we're working it, working it hard. And it's—and by the way, an effective policy is one which is not just the United States trying to solve problems. So I spent time talking to the Canadian Prime Minister about it. I mean, Canada is a, should be, and must be an active participant in helping deal with problems.

He brought up Haiti, for example, in the Oval Office. Canada has made a significant contribution to stability in Haiti in the past. And it's an important—my only point is, is that we will continue to work with others to deal with problems that crop up.

Q. How much of a threat to the world——

President Bush. Well, you know, Dick, I think that—let's put it this way—he's going to pose less of a threat the more isolated he becomes and the more we work together. And as I mentioned to you, it's hard to tell. This is a society in which there's very little freedom, including freedom of the press. There's not a lot of light shining in there.

And so we take his statements very seriously. He's kind of declared himself to be a nuclear power. We obviously watch very carefully his testings. We're trying to make sure, by the way, that the missile that he fired wasn't headed for Canada. We don't know for a fact where it was headed. But, for example, one thing that Stephen and I talked about is he could be seemingly firing a missile at the United States, say, at—I don't know, this is all speculation— but could be headed toward the Northwest of our country. And it wouldn't take much for it to get off course and end somewhere where he may not have intended.

My only point is, is that we will work very closely on these matters together. It's in our interests that we send a clear message to the leader of North Korea.

Canada-U.S. Border

Q. Christian St. Pierre, Radio Canada. Happy birthday, sir.

President Bush. It's amazing, the first birthday greeting I got from the press came from the Canadian press. [*Laughter*] Thank you. I am grateful. You're not 60 years old, are you? [*Laughter*] Well, let me just say this—it's a lot younger than you think.

Q. President Bush——

President Bush. Sure.

Q. My question is about the security at the border. On the passport issue, you seem very open, but there is a deadline of 2008.

President Bush. Yes.

Q. Is there any chance of getting a— of dealing? And Mr. Harper, can you comment in French and English, please?

President Bush. Thank you. We are responding to congressional law. And I—let me reinterpret your—is your question, is there flexibility in the law, basically? Yes, I think that if Congress decides there needs to be flexibility, there will flexibility. Interestingly enough, the Senate passed—made its intention clear to extend deadlines. That hasn't happened in the House yet. And so we are operating in the executive branch under the idea that nothing will change, and therefore, we need to get to the Canadian Government as quickly as possible our definition of what a reasonable policy is. If Congress decides to be flexible, we obviously will be flexible.

But the reason we're dealing with this issue is because the legislative branch put this into law, put the need to have these kind of documents into law. And as I told Chertoff, who is responsible for implementing the law, that I would like this— to the extent the law allows, for there to be a lot of flexibility and simplicity.

As the Governor of Texas, I'm used to a border situation where hundreds of thousands of people crossed every day. See, we—on our southern border, there are a lot of Mexican citizens who come into the United States and work on a daily basis and then go back home. It happens a lot. And therefore, I fully understand the need for there to be simplicity in the documentation. It needs to be easy for somebody who is known and a person that is—makes a living on the other side of the border. There's—a lot of kids go to college in, like, El Paso, Texas, and they're living in Mexico, so they've got to go back and forth on a regular basis. So I'm familiar with this issue a lot, and I really do emphasize the need for us to be mindful of what a onerous program could mean to good relations as well as facilitation of trade.

I can remember Stephen's concerns about the effect of this initiative might have on conventions, for example, in Canada. He brought up today an interesting example of Little League teams playing baseball in Manitoba. And so, in other words, there's a lot of just daily commerce that we've got to be mindful about, not just trade, but the movement of people. And we are, we are.

And so to answer your question, if the Congress provides flexibility, of course we will work with the Canadian Government to extend deadlines. If the Congress says, "No, this is what our intent is," we will work with the Canadian Government to make the law work.

[Prime Minister Harper spoke in French, and no translation was provided.]

Prime Minister Harper. We're on two tracks here. We've indicated we want to cooperate. We understand this is a congressional law the administration has to put into place. We're prepared to cooperate to make it work as smoothly and effectively as possible. We need more information, and we've been pressing for that for some time, and we'll continue to do so.

At the same time, our other track is obviously to encourage some reexamination of the law. The Senate has recently passed an amendment that would delay this process by a year and a half. We have some indications from some quarters of the House of Representatives, some will there to consider the same thing.

As I say, we—and I just want to emphasize—we in Canada share the United States security concerns and objectives. I think, as you all know, recently with events in Toronto, it's been brought home to all of us that we face exactly the same kind of security threats and are defending exactly the same kinds of values. And I would hate to see a law go into place that has the effect of not just limiting and endangering trade or tourism but endangering all those thousands of social interactions that occur across our border every day and are the reason why Canada and the United States have the strongest relationship of any two countries, not just on the planet but in the history of mankind.

And I would just urge the Congress to think carefully, that if the fight for security ends up meaning that the United States becomes more closed to its friends, then the terrorists have won. And I don't think either of us want that. So we're prepared to cooperate, and also urge the Congress to apply some flexibility in reaching their objectives of security.

President Bush. Thank you.

Jim Axelrod [CBS News].

North Korea/Foreign Policy

Q. Thank you, Mr. President. Kim Jong Il has been described as quirky, as odd. A member of your administration yesterday compared him to an unloved child looking for attention. And I'm wondering if you agree with that assessment. Does he pose——

President Bush. Who was that person? *[Laughter]*

Q. Does he pose—come to the booth, sir, I'll tell you who it was. *[Laughter]* Does he pose any particular unique problems to deal with? And do you feel that he's looking, for instance, at what's been offered to the Iranians by the world community in terms of incentives and saying, "I'd like a little of that for myself"?

President Bush. It's hard for me to tell you what's on his mind. He lives in a very closed society. It's unlike our societies where we have press conferences and people are entitled to ask questions, and there's all kinds of discussions out of administrations and people saying this, saying that, and the other. This is a very closed society.

We do know there's a lot of concentration camps. We do know that people are starving. As a matter of fact, our Nation has tried to help feed the hungry. But what we don't know is his intentions, and so I think we've got to plan for the worst and hope for the best. And planning for the worst means to make sure that we continue to work with friends and allies, as well as those who've agreed to be a part of the six-party talks, to continue to send a unified message.

We've also got a very strong Proliferation Security Initiative, because one of the threats that can emanate from a closed society, particularly one that claims to have nuclear weapons, is proliferation. One of the real dangers we face is weapons of mass destruction in the hands of people who would like to continue to hurt us, hurt the United States or hurt Canada, hurt anybody who has the courage to stand up and embrace freedom, see. That's the big threat.

And so we don't know, Jim, about his intentions, but we take—we're planning. And so one of the things we've done—and I thank Canada's contribution—is for there to be a very strong initiative to prevent proliferation, through what we call the Proliferation Security Initiative. And it's an important initiative. It's a way to say, we're not going to allow you to threaten us; we're not going to allow you to—the rocket— as I say, I'm not exactly sure what the azimuth was of the rocket. We've got our people still analyzing that. But, for example, we didn't—we don't know what was on the rocket. We don't know where the rocket was headed. It would have been helpful, of course, had he said, "Here's what we're going to do. Here's our intentions. Here's what—we want to work with you; we want

to explain it." Who knows—maybe send a satellite—who knows what his intention was.

But that's not the way he decided to deal with it. He just decided to say—to start firing, and he fired seven of them. And we take this seriously. We take, and we all should take, threats seriously. That's one of the lessons of September the 11th, is that what takes place in other parts of the world can come home to hurt the American people. See, a failed government in Afghanistan enabled plotters and planners to train and then come and kill 3,000 of our citizens. And so it used to be that's it's okay if something were happening from afar, oceans could protect us. I presume that's how some in Canada used to feel. The lesson of September the 11th is, is that we're vulnerable, and therefore, we've got to deal with each threat.

I've assured the American people and assured our friends and allies, we want to deal with threats diplomatically. The best way to deal with threats diplomatically is to encourage others to be a part of the process. And that's what we're doing. That's why we've got the six-party talks.

And one of the keys in the six-party talks is for all the nations to send clear messages to Kim Jong Il. That's why I was on the phone this morning, saying as clearly as I could to our fellow partners, four other leaders, to say, let's send a common message that you won't be rewarded for ignoring the world and that you'll be isolated if you continue to do this, and yet there's a way forward.

See, I care deeply about the people in North Korea. I truly do. It breaks my heart to know that young children are literally starving to death. And I wish—I just wish at some point in time there was an openness in that society where we could help save lives. I'm also realistic enough to realize what weapons of mass destruction could mean in the world in which we live.

And so we're working this issue hard. We're working the Iranian issue hard. Steve and I talked about a strategy going into the G–8 session. I talked to President Putin this morning abut making sure that not only do we send messages to the North Koreans but that our strategy will work with Iran.

And it's just really important for the American President to see the world the way it is, not the way we would hope it would be, and to deal with threats, and to do so in a way that will achieve results. And it takes a while. I mean, these threats didn't arise overnight, and these problems won't be solved overnight. But we've got strategies in place to deal with them.

And one of the reasons why it's important to have Steve here is so we can talk about how we can work together to deal with it. And they're not just threats to our security that normal people think of. HIV/AIDS on the continent of Africa is a threat to our security in the long run. That's why I'm proud to report the United States took the lead on setting up the Global Fund, as well as bilateral programs to help save people's lives. I think it's in our interests. I also happen to believe in the admonition, "To whom much is given, much is required."

And so we've got a robust foreign policy on a lot of fronts, and I intend to keep it that way. And I'm confident that what we're doing is going to make this world a better place. And I'm proud to have allies like Steve who understand the stakes of the 21st century.

Birthday Present for the President

Q. Mr. President, Mr. Prime Minister, before I ask you a question, I'm just curious what you think of that belt buckle the Prime Minister gave you as a birthday gift, and are you wearing it?

President Bush. I hadn't seen it yet. [*Laughter*] Oh, Lee, you gave it away. [*Laughter*]

North Korea/Missile Defense System

Q. Mr. President, on a serious note, in light of the North Korean missile test and the fact that North Korea could launch another series of missiles at any minute, did you ask Canada to reconsider joining in the Ballistic Missile Defense Shield?

And, Prime Minister, do you still think it's wrong and not in Canada's interest to join the BMD? And if—when you're responding, could you do it in French and English, please?

President Bush. Anyway, thanks for the belt buckle in advance. [*Laughter*]

Prime Minister Harper. No problem at all.

President Bush. Looking forward to getting it.

Prime Minister Harper. Figure if you're going to be 60, you should get something.

President Bush. That's right. Just hope the belt fits. [*Laughter*]

No, I didn't bring it up, because I figured if he was interested, he would tell me. I did explain to him, however, that we will continue to build a robust system, because I think it's in—I know it's in our interest to make sure that we're never in a position where somebody can blackmail us.

So we'll continue to invest and spend. And since this issue first came up, we've made a lot of progress on how to—towards having an effective system. And it's in our interest that we continue to work along these lines.

But, no, my attitude was—this is a—this was a particularly difficult political issue inside Canada, and my relationship is such that if Stephen thought it was of importance, he would have told me what's on his mind. Now, maybe he's going to bring it up over lunch, but he didn't bring it up earlier.

Prime Minister Harper. Let me just begin by saying——

President Bush. Interesting question, though.

Prime Minister Harper. Let me just begin by saying that—first of all, the question was asked earlier, I think, is North Korea a threat. I don't think the issue is whether North Korea is a threat. North Korea clearly wants to be a threat. And I think—I just want to repeat what the President has said. Given that that's a society of the kind of nature it is, I think this should concern us immensely, and the fact that it is prepared to arm itself and prepared to threaten to use such armaments—I think it is something that we should be gravely concerned about, as was said earlier.

Missiles that are fired in the direction of the United States constitute a threat to Canada. That's one of the reasons why our Government renewed, on a permanent basis, the NORAD treaty. Through NORAD we have a special relationship on air defense and we share information on these kind of matters. I think as you know, to answer your specific question, the Government of Canada is not prepared to open a missile defense issue at this time, but I will say that I think it should be obvious, when we look at this kind of threat, why the United States and others would want to have a modern and flexible defense system against this kind of threat. So I think that's something, at least, our Government fully understands.

[*Prime Minister Harper spoke in French, and no translation was provided.*]

President Bush. Welcome. Thank you for your birthday greetings.

President's Birthday

Q. Mr. President, happy birthday.

President Bush. Thank you very much. Yes.

Q. It's also my birthday.

President Bush. Today's your birthday, too?

Q. Yes, sir.

President Bush. It is? Come on up. Let's have a birthday picture. Come up, come up, come up. [*Laughter*] Come on. Get up here. Anybody else have their birthday today? [*Laughter*] It's your birthday? Yes, sure. It is your birthday? Come on. [*Laughter*] It's amazing how everybody's birthday is today.

[*All present sang Happy Birthday to the President and others celebrating birthdays.*]

President Bush. Dear Richard—he just told me he's 30 years old. [*Laughter*] Happy birthday. Happy birthday.

NOTE: The President's news conference began at 11:55 a.m. in the East Room at the White House. In his remarks, he referred to Secretary-General Kofi Annan of the United Nations; Chairman Kim Jong Il of North Korea; President Hu Jintao of China; President Vladimir V. Putin of Russia; Prime Minister Junichiro Koizumi of Japan; and President Roh Moo-hyun of South Korea.

Remarks Following a Meeting With United States Ambassador to Iraq Zalmay Khalilzad
July 6, 2006

The President. It's been my pleasure to sit here and talk to our Ambassador from Iraq. I want—first, Zal, I thank you for your service. I really appreciate your family supporting you on this very important mission. I know the Secretary of State and the National Security Adviser join me in

saying it gives us great comfort to know that we've got a man of your caliber there. It's a hard job. And Zal has earned the confidence of the new Iraqi Government, and I was able to see that firsthand in how the Prime Minister and other members of his administration related to him.

He brought back a report that is realistic. On the one hand, he said they've got a good Government—goal-oriented people who are working to achieve certain objectives. And I know that you've been impressed by Prime Minister Maliki's determination to succeed and his willingness to lay out a commonsense agenda and then hold people to account.

Zal also said it's still a dangerous place because there are people there that will do anything to stop the progress of this new Government. And you have to ask yourself, who's afraid of democracy? I mean, why would people be afraid of a peaceful civil society? And the answer is, people who want to not only harm Iraqis but want to harm us.

And I've assured Zal that—to assure the Iraqi people that when we give our word, we'll keep our word. And we intend to work closely with the Government and to help defend the people until this Government is more capable of defending itself.

And he talked about police training. There's more work to be done in training the police. And we talked about the training of the army, and it's gone quite well. Zal is concerned about foreign influences in the country, as am I.

I do appreciate your briefing on the Prime Minister's recent trip in the neigh-borhood, which looked like a very successful trip. We, of course, are concerned that some in the neighborhood may want to derail the progress of a free Iraq. And that is troubling and something that we'll work on.

But, Mr. Ambassador, you represent our country with a lot of class and dignity. And so, thank you. You may want to say a few comments.

Ambassador Khalilzad. Thank you, Mr. President. I came today to also wish the President a happy birthday. Happy birthday, Mr. President. And it's an honor to serve the United States in Iraq. Under your leadership, we're working very hard to make sure Iraq succeeds because Iraq is the defining challenge of our time. And what happens in Iraq will shape the future of the Middle East, and the future of the Middle East will shape the future of the world.

So it's an honor to see you again. And happy birthday, Mr. President.

The President. Thank you, sir. Thank you all.

NOTE: The President spoke at 2:12 p.m. in the Oval Office at the White House. In his remarks, he referred to Prime Minister Nuri al-Maliki of Iraq.

Remarks Following a Dinner With Mayor Richard M. Daley of Chicago and Business Leaders in Chicago, Illinois
July 6, 2006

Laura said, "What do you want for your birthday?" I said, "I want to have dinner in Chicago with the mayor." [*Laughter*] Thank you all for joining us. We've had a wonderful discussion. Chicago is a fabulous town, Mayor. And you're awfully kind to host us here.

Somebody said, "Well, what's your birthday wish?" I've got a lot of birthday wishes. I hope our troops are safe. I hope Roger Ebert does well. That's a birthday wish. I know a lot of people here in Chicago are praying for him. It's been a heck of a birthday party tonight, and I appreciate you all joining me, and looking forward to having my cake.

Thanks for coming.

NOTE: The President spoke at 8:21 p.m. in the Chicago Firehouse Restaurant. In his remarks, he referred to Chicago Sun-Times film critic Roger Ebert, who had emergency surgery on July 2. A tape was not available for verification of the content of these remarks.

The President's News Conference in Chicago
July 7, 2006

The President. Please be seated. Thank you. It's nice to be here in Chicago. Mr. Mayor, I thought you might have had enough of me last night. [*Laughter*] Thanks for the birthday party. I really enjoyed our dinner and enjoyed our conversation. Jesse, thanks for being here as well. It's awfully kind of you to come.

I do want to thank the trustees of this beautiful museum for opening up your facility for a press conference. I hope it doesn't ruin the atmosphere of the museum. I will try to make sure it doesn't. I'm looking forward to a tour of this museum after the press conference.

I'm sure you're wondering why I would have a press conference in Chicago. It's a fabulous city, plus I'd like to see what it's like to have a major press conference outside of Washington. It might do me some good. The truth of the matter is, it might do the White House press corps some good as well. So I welcome the Chicago reporters here. Thank you for coming.

I had a fine dinner last night at the Chicago Firehouse and a good breakfast today at Lou Mitchell's. It's really interesting sites here in Chicago, and it's a lot of fun going to them. And I want to thank the gracious hospitality of the restauranteurs and the people of Chicago for—by welcoming me.

I had some conversations with some of the business leaders last night and for breakfast, and there's kind of an interesting sense of optimism here in this part of the world, and the statistics bear that out. In the Chicago area, businesses have added over more than 74,000 new jobs over the past 2 years. And that's positive; it's a good sign. The unemployment rate in this area is 4.3 percent; that's below the national average. People are working. People are able to find jobs. Illinois created more jobs than any other State in the month of April. So the entrepreneurial spirit is strong here.

One of the things I detected from the business leaders, that there's a sense of optimism which encourages people to invest. And when you invest, you create the conditions for job growth. Major companies have announced plans to add even more jobs.

This morning we got some good news: The Nation added 121,000 new jobs for the month of June. That's over 5.4 million jobs since August of 2003; that's 34 months of job increases. In the first quarter, our economy grew at 5.6 percent. Productivity is high. People are better off. Things are working. And so the fundamental question we face in Washington is, how do we keep economic vitality alive? What do we do? What are the policies necessary to keep this growth strong?

And one policy is to keep taxes low. If you raise taxes, you take money out of the pockets of small businesses and entrepreneurs, which makes it harder to increase employment. One of the reasons I'm here at this museum is because one way to make sure we continue to grow our economy is to have a workforce that's capable of filling the jobs of the 21st century.

One of the subjects the mayor and I talked about last night was the No Child Left Behind Act and what the city of Chicago is doing to hold people to account and have high standards and to offer different choices to parents here in Chicago, through charter schools, for example. The mayor said something interesting; he said, "Reading scores are up." That's a good sign. It means people are measuring, and teachers are teaching. And when you have the basics—the basic foundation for good education laid, then you can focus on math and science.

So the truth of the matter is, we have to make sure our kids have got the math and science skills to fill the jobs of the 21st century. We live in a global economy in an interconnected world, and if we can't provide the employees for the jobs of the 21st century, they're going to go somewhere else. So education is crucial to make sure we're a competitive and vibrant nation.

Job training is really important. The Labor Department, working with the local folks here, have set up one-stop centers in Chicago to help connect workers with employers. You've got a good community college system here. Community colleges are really important to make sure that workers are given the skills to fill the jobs which actually exist. And the Lake Land Community College system is a strong program. There's Federal help, and there's State help, and there's local involvement, all aimed at making sure people have got the capacity to have the—to fill the jobs. I mean, you have got a growing economy like this; there's concern by employers whether or not they're going to be able to find people to do the work. And education is the gateway to make sure that we remain a competitive economy.

I also believe strongly that we've got to open up markets to goods produced here in Illinois, goods and services. In other words, one way to make sure this economy of ours grows is to reject protectionism and be confident in our capacity to trade. I'm getting ready to go to the G–8, and one of the topics there is going to be the Doha round of the WTO, which basically—the commitment is that a world that trades freely is a world in which people are going to be able to find work here at home, and it means we have better capacity to be able to help lift nations out of poverty.

We talked last night about immigration. I found it interesting that the people that were there with the mayor and me, employers and chamber of commerce-type people, put immigration as one of the issues they want to talk about. I told them this, I said, "First of all, I'll always remember that immigrants have helped shape the character of this Nation." We are a land of immigrants. I also reminded them that the system we got today isn't working, and it needs to be changed and reformed.

We're a nation of law, and we can be a compassionate nation when it comes to immigration, and the two don't conflict. So I've talked about a comprehensive immigration plan. Look, people in this country expect us to secure the border, and we will. And the way you do that is you add more manpower and you put new technologies on the border to keep people from sneaking across.

But in order to enforce this border, we've got to have a rational way that recognizes there are people sneaking across to do work Americans aren't doing. They're doing jobs Americans are not filling. And my attitude is this: When you find a willing worker and a willing employer, there ought to be a legal way to let somebody come here to work on a temporary basis. It takes pressure off the border. When you got people sneaking across to do work, it puts pressure on the border. If somebody can come in on a legal way, it's going to make it easier for our Border Patrol agents to do their job.

Secondly, one of the serious issues we have, and one of the issues that the—some of the leaders brought up yesterday was— the guy said, "We really shouldn't be in a position to be document verifiers." And when you make something illegal that people want, it's amazing what happens, kind of a whole industry of smugglers and inn-keepers and document forgers that sprung up. And so people show up and say, "I want to work." The guy says, "Show me your document," and they don't know whether it's real or not. And we got a Basic Pilot program to help people verify whether documents are real.

But one way to do it is, if you have a temporary-worker program, say, here's a tamper-proof card that will enable our employers to be able to verify whether someone is here legally to do work on a temporary basis and enable the Government to hold people to account for hiring illegal workers. See, it's against the law to hire somebody who is here illegally, and the American people expect us to enforce the law, and we will. But the system needs to be reformed.

I told the workers last night that there are about 11 million people here, more or less, who have been here for a while, that are building families, and they're good workers. And they said, "What are you going to do about it?" And I said, well, there's two extremes on this issue. One extreme is, kick them out, deport everybody. That's not going to work. It may sound like a kind of an interesting sound bite, kind of a nice throwaway line, but it's not going to work. It's impractical.

The other option is to say, well, you're an automatic citizen. That's called amnesty. That won't work. And the reason that won't work is, if you grant 8 or 9 million people who are here illegally automatic citizenship, it means another 8 or 9 million coming.

The best way to deal with this problem, in my judgment, is to say, look, you're here illegally; there's got to be a consequence. The consequence could be a penalty, a fine. It could be proof that you're not a criminal. In other words, there's got to be ways to say—make restitution for society for breaking the law; but say to the person, you can get in the citizenship line, but at the back of the line, not at the beginning. See, there are people in line who want to be-

come a citizen of the United States. It doesn't make sense to penalize those who are here legally, playing by the rules, to let people who have been here illegally get ahead of them.

This is a comprehensive plan. Look, the House has passed a bill; the Senate has passed a bill. And we're working in Washington to reconcile the differences. It's hard work. It's not an easy assignment. But I'm confident if we all keep working on it, we can get a comprehensive bill done, which will be good for the country and send the message that we're a land of different folks from different religions and different backgrounds, all united under the great American ideal.

I spend a lot of time worrying about the war on terror. I think about it every single day. My biggest job, frankly, is to protect the American people. And this is a dangerous world, and there are people out there lurking who are trying to figure out ways to hurt us. I know some dismiss that as empty rhetoric; I'm just telling you, it's the truth. And therefore, we're doing a lot of stuff in Washington. We're reforming our intelligence services to be able to react better. The FBI is now focusing on counterterrorist activities. The CIA is developing more human intelligence, which will make it easier to be able to do our duty.

We're also on the offense against the terrorists. We'll keep the pressure on them. We'll bring them to justice before they hurt our people.

The central front in the war on terror is Iraq. And I know Iraq is on the minds of a lot of people here in Chicago. It's hard work. It's hard work because we face an enemy that will kill innocent people in order to achieve an objective, and their objective is to drive us out of Iraq so they can have safe haven from which to launch attacks against modern Muslim nations, so they can spread their ideology of hate. They want us to—they believe capitalist societies and democracies are inherently weak. They do not believe that we've got the capacity to do the hard work necessary to help the Iraqis succeed.

And they're mistaken; they're just wrong. Success in Iraq is vital for the security of the United States, and success in Iraq is vital for long-term peace. And so therefore, we'll complete the mission.

And we've got good partners. Zal Khalilzad came in the other day, who is our Ambassador to Iraq. And he, like me, has confidence in Prime Minister Maliki. He's a guy who can set goals and follow through on those goals. He understands what needs to be done in order to succeed. And he represents the will of 12 million people who went to the polls. That's a pretty interesting sign that the Iraqi people want to live in freedom.

There's been a lot of sacrifice in the war on terror. People have lost life. We've lost, obviously, a lot of lives here on the homeland, and we've lost lives overseas. I think of Corporal Ryan Cummings, from right here in the Chicago area. He was an honor student at Hoffman Estates High School. He volunteered for the United States Marine Corps. He served two tours of duty in Iraq, and then he volunteered for a third. Ryan understood the stakes. He understood that we must win. And so he said, "I'd like to go back." And he was killed in Anbar Province last month.

Our prayers go out to Ryan's family. I marvel at the strength of his mother, when she said, "He wanted to be doing something that made a difference. He was doing what he wanted to do."

I have confidence in the capacity of liberty to transform hostile regions to peaceful regions. And I have confidence in our capacity to win the war on terror because of—people like Ryan Cummings are willing to step up and serve this Nation.

There's a lot of issues that I'm sure we'll be talking about today: North Korea and Iran, hopefully, the Middle East, maybe some local issues here in Chicago. It's my honor to be here. Thank you for coming. And now I'll start answering some questions, starting with one of the senior members of the press corps—are you over 60?

North Korea/Missile Testing

Q. [*Inaudible*]

The President. You look like you're about 65. Anyway, go ahead. [*Laughter*]

Q. Harsh. Mr. President, Japan has dropped the threat of sanctions from its proposed Security Council resolution about North Korea. Why was that necessary? And how do you punish or penalize a country that's already among the poorest and most isolated in the world?

The President. I think that the purpose of the U.N. Security Council resolution is to send a clear message to the leader of North Korea that the world condemns that which he did. Part of our strategy, as you know, has been to have others at the table, is to say as clearly as possible to the North Korean, "Get rid of your weapons, and there's a better way forward." In other words, there's a choice for him to make. He can verifiably get rid of his weapons programs and stop testing rockets, and there's a way forward for him to help his people.

I believe it's best to make that choice clear to him with more than one voice, and that's why we have the six-party talks. And now that he has defied China and Japan and South Korea and Russia and the United States—all of us said, don't fire that rocket. He not only fired one; he fired seven. Now that he made that defiance, it's best for all of us to go to the U.N. Security Council and say loud and clear, here are some red lines. And that's what we're in the process of doing.

The problem with diplomacy, it takes a while to get something done. If you're acting alone, you can move quickly. When you're rallying world opinion and trying to come up with the right language at the United Nations to send a clear signal, it takes a while.

And so yesterday I was on the phone with—I think I mentioned this to the press conference yesterday—to Hu Jintao and Vladimir Putin; the day before to President Roh and Prime Minister Koizumi. And Condi, by the way, was making the same calls out there to her counterparts, all aiming at saying, "It's your choice, Kim Jong Il; you've got the choice to make."

So we'll see what happens at the U.N. Security Council. I talked to Condi this morning first thing, in anticipation of this question, and she feels good about the progress that can be made there.

North Korea/Six-Party Negotiations

Q. [*Inaudible*]

The President. Well, what matters most of all is for Kim Jong Il to see the world speak with one voice. That's the purpose, really.

Here's the problem, it seems like to me, that there have been agreements with North Korea in the past. There's the '94 agreement. I think you were around here then, Sanger [David Sanger, New York Times]. And then it turns out he didn't live up to the agreement. He said—in September of '05, there was a joint declaration that talked about lasting peace, and we all signed on to a document that said we'll denuclearize the Korean Peninsula. That's a noble and important goal. This was signed by the five of us plus North Korea. He had also talked about the rocket moratorium. He assured Koizumi in '04, Prime Minister Koizumi, that he would adhere to that. And you just got to wonder whether the man's word means anything. And one way to make sure it does mean something is for nations other than the United States to say the same thing, to speak loud and clear. And that's what you're seeing evolve. Steve [Steve Holland, Reuters].

Chairman Kim Jong Il of North Korea

Q. Thank you, sir. Some experts say North Korea may be launching missiles to attract more concessions. Are you prepared to offer any more concessions beyond that already offered in the six-party format? And

have you ruled out the possible military option in responding to them?

The President. As you know, we want to solve all problems diplomatically. That's our first choice.

What was the first part of your question? This is what happens when you're 60——

Q. ——are they trying to exchange—[*inaudible*].

The President. Look, I don't know what the man's intentions are. I don't know what they are. It's an interesting question: Is he trying to force us to do something by defying the world? If he wants a way forward, it's clear. If he wants to have good relations with the world, he's got to verifiably get rid of his weapons programs like he agreed to do in 1994, stop testing missiles, and there is a way forward. Part of the discussions in September were, here's a way forward. Here's a way for—he's worried about energy, and our partners at the table said, well, here's an energy proposal for you to consider. And so the choice is his to make.

And I made it very clear to our partners that it seems like to me that the message ought to be one that said, you shouldn't be rewarded for violating that which you've said you're going to do and kind of ignoring what the world has said. And it's just—whether it be the Iranian issue or the North Korean issue, there is a way forward for these leaders that will lead to a better life for their people and acceptance into the international community. And one of the things we've done in the United States is to work with the coalition to send that message. It's a clear message. He knows what his options are.

Kelly [Kelly O'Donnell, NBC News]. A couple—then we'll start working the local thing. Warm up.

Hamdan v. Rumsfeld

Q. Hello, Mr. President.

The President. Yes.

Q. I'd like to ask you to speak on the broad implications of that recent Supreme

Court case—not the specifics of the case. But the Justices said that you overreached your authority, and your critics have been saying that too. Given your support and respect for the Court, are you willing to rethink how you use your Presidential authority?

The President. I am willing to abide by the ruling of the Supreme Court. And the Supreme Court said that in this particular case, when it comes to dealing with illegal combatants who were picked up off a battlefield and put in Guantanamo for the sake of our security, that we should work with the United States Congress to develop a way forward. They didn't say we couldn't have done—made that decision, see. They were silent on whether or not Guantanamo—whether or not we should have used Guantanamo. In other words, they accepted the use of Guantanamo, the decision I made. What they did say was, in terms of going forward, what should the court system look like? How can we use a military commission or tribunal?

And we'll work with the United States Congress. They have said, work with the Congress. I have been waiting for this decision in order to figure out how to go forward. I want to move forward. First of all, I stand by the decision I made in removing these people from the battlefield. See, here's the problem: These are the types of combatants we have never faced before. They don't wear uniforms, and they don't represent a nation-state. They're bound by an ideology. They've sworn allegiance to individuals but not to a nation. The Geneva Conventions were set up to deal with armies of nation-states. You've got standard rules of war.

So this is new ground. This is different than any President has been through before, in terms of how to deal with these kind of people that you're picking up off a battlefield and trying to protect the American people from.

So we have about 600 or so there, and 200 have been sent back home. We'd like to send more back to their countries of origin. Some need to be tried, and the fundamental question is, how do we try them? And so in working with the Supreme—in listening to the Supreme Court, we'll work with Congress to achieve that objective.

And so your question is slightly loaded, which is okay; I'm used to it. But the idea of making the decision about creating Guantanamo in the first place was upheld by the courts. Or let's say, the courts were silent on it.

Let's see. Jessica [Jessica Yellin, ABC News]. Go ahead and yell it out.

Q. Yell it out. All right, sir.

The President. Or don't yell it out.

North Korea/Missile Defense System

Q. It's been three days since North Korea fired those missiles. Yesterday you said you did not know the trajectory of the long-range missile. Can you now tell us, where was it headed? And if it were headed—if it had been headed at the United States, how would our national ballistic missile system have taken it down?

The President. I still can't give you any better answer than yesterday. I can embellish yesterday's answer. It may sound better. No, I—really, I haven't talked to the Secretary of Defense about that.

Our missile systems are modest; our antiballistic missile systems are modest. They're new. It's new research. We've gotten—testing them. And so I can't—it's hard for me to give you a probability of success. But nevertheless, the fact that a nontransparent society would be willing to tee up a rocket and fire it without identifying where it's going or what was on it means we need a ballistic missile system.

So that's about all I can tell you on that. Yes. Obviously, it wasn't a satisfactory answer.

Q. [*Inaudible*]

The President. Yes, I think we had a reasonable chance of shooting it down. At least that's what the military commanders told me.

Rick [Rick Pearson, Chicago Tribune]. Let's get a little local here, Ricky. Do you consider yourself local or national? Hybrid? Are you a hybrid?

CIA Employee Identity Leak Investigation

Q. It seems trendy——

The President. Yes, very trendy. You're kind of a trendy guy. Got the gray shirt.

Q. Thank you very much. Mr. President, the work of U.S. Attorney Patrick Fitzgerald in prosecuting alleged corruption is well-known here in Chicago as well as nationally. It's my understanding that technically, he hasn't been reappointed to his position and serves at your pleasure. Do you have any plans to formally reappoint him to the post, or any other position at Department of Justice?

The President. As a special prosecutor?

Q. And would you give us your assessment of the job that he's doing?

The President. I don't have any plans to reappoint him because I haven't thought about it. I will now think about it, now that you brought it up.

The only—I can give you an assessment of how I thought he handled the case in Washington. I haven't been following the cases here. I thought in Washington, he handled the case with professionalism; he was very professional about it. You didn't see a lot of leaks; you didn't see a lot of speculation; you didn't see a lot of people, kind of, dropping a little crumb here for the press to chew on. And I really thought he handled himself well.

But as far as reappointing him as a special prosecutor, I don't know whether the Attorney General is going to do that or not. That's his choice to make.

Chris. Or, Paul [Paul Mieke, Channel 7 TV]. Paul.

Energy/Alternative Fuel Sources

Q. Mr. President, gas prices are high, as you know. Oil is at 75 a barrel. There is a poll that suggests that three in four Americans are not content with your leadership on the issue, and that the State of the Union pitch for alternative fuel technology has fallen flat and is not moving. Why not call for an emergency energy summit and lift the issue to a higher priority?

The President. Well, I thought addressing the issue at the State of the Union was pretty much lifting it to a high priority. When you include it in the State of the Union, it means it's a top priority, and it is.

It took us a while to get in a position where we're reliant upon sources of energy from outside our boundaries, and it's going to take us a while to become less dependent. It just takes a while; things just don't happen instantly. I told the people, if I could lower gasoline prices with a snap of the fingers, I'd do it. And I've been talking about energy independence since I first got elected. And we've made some progress. We made progress by encouraging the spread of ethanol. And I think if you were to look at the facts, that ethanol has gone from low market penetration to pretty significant market penetration in selected parts of the country, relatively speaking, particularly in the Midwest.

There is more work to be done. There is a lot of ethanol plants being built as we speak, and there's incentives in Government law to do that. We've effected CAFE standards when it comes to light trucks, which will help consumers make a rational decision. We put incentives for people to buy hybrid vehicles in law. If you go out and buy a hybrid vehicle, you get a tax credit.

I happen to believe it's essential for us to promote nuclear power as a way to make us less dependent on natural gas from overseas, for example. Also, this will help us be wise stewards of our environment. We're spending a lot of money on technologies, battery technologies, for example, that would enable Chicago residents to drive the first 40 miles on electricity before one would have to use gasoline.

And so we do have a full-blown strategy to make this country less dependent on foreign sources of oil, to help relieve pressure at the gas pump. When the demand for crude oil in China rises, it affects the global price of crude oil, which affects your price of gasoline. And therefore, the strategy has got to be to diversify away from crude oil.

One of the issues that we're trying to get done here is that if you—if people are genuinely concerned about the price of gasoline, they ought to be supporting my initiative to encourage the construction of additional refinery capacity. Certainly, it's not the long-term solution, but it's an important solution for the short run. If you have constrained gasoline supplies and demand remains high, you're going to have higher prices of gasoline. We haven't built a new refinery in this country since the early 1970s. And so the truth of the matter is, I would hope people would contact their Members of Congress to insist that they support a—the bill that we ran up to the Hill, which would have made it much easier to permit and construct refineries.

So we have a comprehensive plan. This is a serious issue. I understand people are paying high gasoline prices here—it's like a tax. I understand it's like a tax. And we got a strategy to deal with it.

Anna [Anna Kukec, Daily Herald]. We're going to work our way down the row here. The Daily Herald, is that one of Pearson's competitors? It is?

Free Trade

Q. Well, we compete with everyone. My question is focusing, too, also, on technology. There's been a lot of mergers with companies in the technology industry, and one of the more recent ones was Lucent Technologies with Alcatel, which is French-owned. How do you feel about a lot of the foreign-owned companies buying out U.S. tech companies, especially those that have military contracts?

The President. We have laws that prevent sensitive technologies from being trans-ferred as a result of sale and/or merger. And we watch that very carefully.

On the broader scale, I have no problem with foreign capital buying U.S. companies; nor do I have a problem with U.S. companies buying foreign companies. That's what free trade is all about. As a matter of fact, there are workers working here in Illinois because of foreign investment. A foreign company takes a look at Illinois, they like the tax structure, they like the governance, they like the workforce, and they invest. And when they invest, they create jobs.

A lot of the jobs in America exist as a result of foreign companies investing here in our country. So I believe in opening markets. I do believe in protecting secrets, but we've got laws on the books to prevent secrets from being transferred or vital technology from being transferred. But I believe in free flows of capital, and I believe in free trade. And that's not a given in the United States. There are people who say, "Well, we can't compete with China; let's throw up roadblocks; let's protect ourselves," or, "We don't want foreigners coming to invest in our country." I think that would be a mistake. I think that's the early signs of protectionist sentiments, which would mean our economy wouldn't grow.

In my State of the Union—the very same State of the Union that I addressed the energy problem—I talked about trends that are worrisome. One trend would be protectionism, and its corollary would be isolationism. An isolationist world basically says, "Don't worry about what happens overseas; we'll just worry about what happens here at home. Don't worry about HIV/AIDS on the continent of Africa, not our problem. Don't worry about Darfur, it's not our problem. Don't worry about the fact that there's tyrannies in the Middle East; that's not our problem."

The truth of the matter is, all of these issues are our problem, and if we became isolationist, we would not do our duty to protect the American people and, kind of, lay the foundations for a better world.

People say, well, you know, China is too tough to compete with; let's just throw up tariffs. I completely disagree. I think competition is good and healthy. I think it's important to have a competitive world. It means that people are constantly producing a better product and a better service at a better price, which is good for consumers.

Yes, sir.

2006 Midterm Elections

Q. An aide to Judy Topinka was quoted as saying that given your low approval ratings in the polls, they prefer you to come here in the middle of the night.

The President. Didn't work. I'm coming at lunch. [*Laughter*]

Q. I'm wondering if you're offended by those remarks, and whether or not you think your presence may actually harm Republican candidates when you come out to campaign for them.

The President. I'm not offended. First of all, I think—am I offended that you read the person's remarks to me? No, I'm not offended that you were reading that at all, nor am I offended at what the person said. The first I've heard it was just then. And I'm coming to lunch. I think it's going to be a pretty successful fundraiser. And I—we will hold the House and the Senate. And I've spent a lot of time on the road. I like campaigning, and I'm proud she invited me. And—yes.

Q. [*Inaudible*]—approval ratings, do you think that—[*inaudible*].

The President. That's up to the candidates to decide. I was invited; I gladly came. And I think we're going to have a pretty successful fundraiser for her.

Here's how you win elections. You win elections by believing something. You win elections by having a plan to protect the American people from terrorist attack. You win elections by having a philosophy that has actually produced results, with economic growth, for example, or kind of changing the school systems for the better or providing prescription drug coverage for elders. That's how you win elections. And I'm looking forward to these elections. I think you'll be surprised. Or maybe you won't be surprised. You're probably a sophisticated political analyst; you know what's going on.

Iraq/North Korea

Q. Mr. President, a lot of people here in Chicago tell us that they see an incongruity in your foreign policy. We're involved in a shooting war in Iraq; yet we have a leader in North Korea who has announced his affection for nuclear weapons and no hesitation to use them against the United States. Is your policy consistent between the way you have dealt with Iraq, the way you have dealt with North Korea? And if so, are we headed toward a military action in North Korea? And if so, can this Nation sustain military action on three fronts: Iraq, Afghanistan, and North Korea?

The President. I have always said that it's important for an American President to exhaust all diplomatic avenues before the use of force. Committing our troops into harm's way is a difficult decision. It's the toughest decision a President will ever make. And I fully understand the consequences of doing so.

All diplomatic options were exhausted, as far as I was concerned, with Saddam Hussein. Remember that the U.N. Security Council resolution that we passed when I was the President was 1 of 16, I think— 16, 17? Give me a hand here. More than 15. [*Laughter*] Resolution after resolution after resolution saying the same thing, and he ignored them. And we tried diplomacy. We went to the U.N. Security Council— 15-to-nothing vote that said, "Disarm, disclose, or face serious consequences."

I happen to believe that when you say something, you better mean it. And so when we signed on to that resolution that said, disclose, disarm, or face serious consequences, I meant what we said. That's one way you keep the peace: You speak clearly, and you mean what you say.

And so the choice was Saddam Hussein's choice. He could have not fooled the inspectors. He could have welcomed the world in. He could have told us what was going on. But he didn't, and so we moved.

And we're in the diplomatic process now with North Korea; that's what you're seeing happening. Remember—remember, we put a coalition together at the United Nations that said, "Disclose, disarm, or face serious consequences." It was 15 to nothing. It wasn't a U.S. 1 to 14. It was 15 to nothing; other nations stood up and said the same thing we said.

So we're now working the diplomacy, and you're watching the diplomacy work, not only in North Korea but in Iran. It's kind of painful, in a way, for some to watch because it takes a while to get people on the same page. Everybody—not everybody thinks the exact same way we think. There are different—words mean different things to different people, and the diplomatic processes can be slow and cumbersome. That's why this is probably the fourth day in a row I've been asked about North Korea. It's slow and cumbersome. Things just don't happen overnight.

But what you're watching is a diplomatic response to a person who, since 1994, has said they're—not going to have a weapon.

Q. Do you believe the United States— [*inaudible*].

The President. I don't accept that hypothetical question. You're asking me a hypothetical. What I believe is we can solve the problem diplomatically.

Let's see here—Bret [Bret Baier, FOX News].

Upcoming G–8 Summit/Iran

Q. Mr. President, if the EU does not receive a definitive answer from Iran on the incentives package by next week, do you foresee the G–8 summit as being a springboard to bring that issue to the U.N. Security Council? And what do you say to Americans who are frustrated by the familiar roadblocks, it seems, of China and Russia on harsh sanctions?

The President. I said I wasn't going to answer a hypothetical; now you're trying to get me to answer a hypothetical. The G–8 will be an opportunity for those of us involved with this issue to make it clear to the Iranians that they—we're firm in our resolve for them not to have a nuclear weapon.

I talked to President Putin about North Korea; I also talked to him about Iran. I believe he understands the dangers of the Iranians having a nuclear weapon.

Some nations are more comfortable with sanctions than other nations, and part of the issue we face in some of these countries is that they've got economic interests. And part of our objective is to make sure that national security interests, security of the world interests, trump economic interests. And sometimes that takes a while to get people focused in the right direction.

You know, the first step of a diplomatic solution is for there to be a common goal agreed upon by those of us participating in the process. The goal in North Korea is a nuclear weapons-free peninsula—not just in North Korea but North and South Korea. And that's an important goal. It's important for the neighborhood to have embraced that goal.

The goal for Iran is for them to have a—verifiably get rid of their weapons program. The first step, however, is to—for their verifiable suspension. And by the way, if they will verifiably do which they said they would do in Paris, we will come back to the table. That's what we've said we will do.

And whether or not they—what their posture is, we're finding out as a result of the conversations of Mr. Solana of the EU and Mr. Larijani. I do appreciate Javier Solana's work on this issue. I saw him when I was in Austria, and I thanked him for doing a good job.

Yes. I'm trying to kind of tamp the followups down a little bit here.

Q. [*Inaudible*]

The President. Do I have a sense of urgency? I have a—I'm realistic about how things move in the world. Sanger will tell you—he's been covering North Korea since the mid nineties—these problems don't arise in a nanosecond. It takes a while for a problem to fester and grow, and then it takes a while to solve them diplomatically. That's just the nature of diplomacy. I wish we could solve them overnight. But I'm a realistic—one thing I'm not going to let us do is get caught in the trap of sitting at the table alone with the North Korean, for example. In my judgment, if you want to solve a problem diplomatically, you need partners to do so.

And a good partner to have at the table with us is China. They're in the neighborhood, got some influence in the neighborhood. Another good partner to have at the table is South Korea. They've got a lot at stake of what happens in North Korea, so it's important to have them at the table as well. My concern—I've said this publicly a lot—my concern about being—handling this issue bilaterally is that you run out of options very quickly. And sometimes it's easier for the leader of the nontransparent society to turn the tables and make a country like the United States the problem, as opposed to themselves.

The problem in North Korea and the problem in Iran is their leaders have made choices. And what we're saying is, "There's a better avenue for you. Here's a different route; here's a different way forward for your people."

I said yesterday—and I truly mean this—I am deeply concerned about the plight of the folks who live in North Korea. I'm concerned about starvation and deprivation. I'm concerned that little children are being denied enough food so they can develop a mental capacity to be citizens of this world. I'm concerned about concentration camps. There is a better way for the people of North Korea, and their leader can make better choices if he truly cares about their plight. And we have made clear what that choice is.

Suzanne [Suzanne Malveaux, Cable News Network].

North Korea

Q. Mr. President, if I could follow up, you say diplomacy takes time——

The President. Yes, it does.

Q. ——but it was 4 years ago that you labeled North Korea a member of the "axis of evil." And since then, it's increased its nuclear arsenal; it's abandoned six-party talks; and now these missile launches——

The President. Let me ask you a question. It's increased its—that's an interesting statement: "North Korea has increased its nuclear arsenal." Can you verify that?

Q. Well, intelligence sources say—if you can—if you'd like to dispute that, that's fine.

The President. No, I'm not going to dispute; I'm just curious.

Q. Our intelligence sources say that it's increased the number—its nuclear capability——

The President. Let me put it this way: The guy is dangerous—dangerous. He's got potential danger.

Q. It's increased its nuclear capabilities. It's abandoned six-party talks, and it's launched these missiles.

The President. Yes.

Q. Why shouldn't Americans see the U.S. policy regarding North Korea as a failed one?

The President. Because it takes time to get things done.

Q. What objectives has the U.S. Government achieved when it comes to North Korea? And why does the administration continue to go back to the same platform process if it's not effective in changing North Korea's behavior? Thank you.

The President. Suzanne, these problems didn't arise overnight, and they don't get solved overnight. It takes a while. Again, I think if you look at the history of the North Korean weapons program, it started probably in the eighties. We don't know—maybe you know more than I do about increasing the number of nuclear weapons. My view is, we ought to treat North Korea as a danger, take them seriously. No question that he has signed agreements and didn't stick by them. But that was done during—when we had bilateral negotiations with him, and it's done during the six-party talks.

You've asked what we've done. We've created a framework that will be successful. I don't—my judgment is, you can't be successful if the United States is sitting at the table alone with North Korea. You run out of options very quickly if that's the case. In order to be successful diplomatically, it's best to have other partners at the table. You ask what we've done. We got the six-party talks started. And that's a positive development. It's a way to solve this problem diplomatically.

Bill [Bill Plante, CBS News].

Usama bin Laden

Q. Mr. President——

The President. I just thought for a minute you might have known more than I do about—when you say, definitively say, he's increased the number of weapons. I don't think we know that.

Q. Maybe you know, but you're not telling.

The President. That's an option. [*Laughter*]

Q. Mr. President, you said some time ago that——

The President. Maybe I don't know and don't want to tell you I don't know. Anyway—[*laughter*]——

Q. You said some time ago that you wanted Usama bin Laden dead or alive. You later regretted the formulation, but maybe not the thought.

The President. I regretted the formulation because my wife got on me for talking that way.

Q. We suspected as much, sir. [*Laughter*] But the question I have is, it appears

that the CIA has disbanded the unit that was hunting him down. Is it no longer important to track him down?

The President. It's just an incorrect story. I mean, we got a lot of assets looking for Usama bin Laden. So whatever you want to read in that story, it's just not true, period.

Q. You're still after him?

The President. Absolutely. No ands, ifs, or buts. And in my judgment, it's just a matter of time, unless we stop looking. And we're not going to stop looking so long as I'm the President, not only for Usama bin Laden but anybody else who plots and plans attacks against the United States of America. We're going to stay on the offense so long as I'm your President. And my judgment is, if we let up the pressure on them, the world is more dangerous. In the short run, we will bring these people to justice. We will use good intelligence. We will share information with our allies. We will work with friends. We'll bring people to justice. In the long run, the way you defeat this enemy is to spread liberty, and that's what you're seeing unfold.

Yes, sir. You are?

Mayor Daley of Chicago

Q. Carlos [Carlos Hernandez-Gomez, CLTV Chicago].

The President. Who are you working for, Carlos?

Q. CLTV, the Tribune TV station in town.

The President. CLTV.

Q. I work with Pearson, so——

The President. You do?

Q. Well, thank you, Mr. President. Last summer, when you were here to sign the transportation bill in Denny Hastert's district, you described Mayor Daley as "a great mayor." If you've read the morning papers, you'll find that Patrick Fitzgerald has secured the conviction of one of the mayor's top—former top officials for rigging city jobs to benefit the mayor's political workers. Does that change your assessment of Mayor Daley's tenure?

The President. I still think he's a great mayor. This is a well-run city, and he gets a lot of credit for it. He doesn't get sole credit, but he gets a lot of credit. He's a leader. The thing I like about Daley is he—when he tells you something, he means it. Like, he told me, he said, we're going to whomp you in the 2000 election. He meant it. [*Laughter*] He's a—yes, I'm proud to call him friend. I'm proud to have shared my 60th birthday with your mayor.

Yes, sir. Yes, Mark [Mark Suppelsa, WFLD Chicago].

Progress in Iraq/U.S. Armed Forces

Q. Yes, sir. Thank you. Mr. President, three Illinois National Guard units left this week for Iraq. At a time when there's discussion about withdraw or drawdown of troops, what are the families of these Illinois National Guardsmen to expect?

The President. They expect that their loved one will be participating in a noble and important cause. If I didn't think it was important, I wouldn't have put out the orders to have people go there. And if I didn't think we could win, I wouldn't be there. That's what they can expect. They can expect tough work, tough sledding, and they can expect a grateful Commander in Chief and a grateful nation for their sacrifices.

In terms of troop levels, those decisions will be made by General Casey. There's a debate in Washington as to whether or not we set an artificial timetable for withdrawal. That's what it's about in Washington, DC. And the answer is, absolutely not. You can't win a war if you have an artificial timetable for withdrawal. You can't have people making troop decisions based upon political considerations. It just won't work. It's unfair to those families that we're sending—of the kids we're sending over, and it's unfair to the troops.

Artificial timetable for withdrawal sends the wrong message to the Iraqis; they're

seeing it's not worth it. There's a lot of Iraqis over there determined—trying to make up their mind whether they want to be a part of democracy or whether or not they're going to take to the hills and see what happens. Artificial timetable for withdrawal, kind of early withdrawal before this finishes, sends the message to the enemy, we were right about America. That's what they say. Al Qaida has said it's just a matter of time before America withdraws. They're weak; they're corrupt; they can't stand it; and they'll withdraw. And all that would do is confirm what the enemy thinks.

And getting out before we finish the job would send a terrible message to the troops who've sacrificed. We'll win. We'll achieve our objective, which is a free country that can govern itself, defend itself, and sustain itself and will be an ally in the war on terror. And we're making progress toward that goal.

The problem is that the enemy gets to define success better than we do. See, they'll kill innocent people like that; they don't care. Life is not precious to them. And they're willing to kill women and children in order to achieve a tactical objective. And it gets on our TV screens. And people mourn the loss of life. This is a compassionate nation that cares about people, and when they see people die on their TV screens, it sends a signal: Well, maybe we're not winning.

We occasionally are able to pop in with great success, like Zarqawi or 12 million people voting. But increasing electricity in Baghdad is not the kind of thing that tends to get on the news, or small-business formation is not the kind of thing to get— or new schools or new hospitals, the infrastructure being rebuilt that had been torn apart. And I'm not being critical. I'm just giving you a fact of something I have to deal with in order to make it clear to the American people that the sacrifice of those families is worth it. We are winning. And a free Iraq is an essential part of changing the conditions which causes the terrorists to be able to recruit killers in the first place.

For a long period of time, our foreign policy was just, kind of, excuse tyranny and hope for the best. It didn't work. The world may have seemed placid, it may have seemed calm, but beneath the surface was resentment and hatred, out of which came an attack that killed 3,000 of our citizens.

And so I am committed to the spread of liberty. It's, after all, how we were founded. And there's a debate here in the United States that says, well, maybe it's too much for the United States to insist others live in a free world. Maybe that's just too unilateral. I view that as cultural elitism for people who say that. It's like saying, we're okay to be free, but you're not.

I believe freedom is universal, and I believe etched in the soul of every person on the face of the Earth is the desire to be free. And I know that freedom has got the capacity to change regions of the world for the better.

Our press corps is bored with this story, but I'm going to tell it anyway—the Koizumi story. [*Laughter*] That's what you get when you get familiar with people; they can anticipate your remarks.

I hope you thought it was interesting that Prime Minister Koizumi and I went to Graceland. It was really a lot of fun, wasn't it? It's an interesting part of the development of our relationship, from one in which Japan was the enemy of the United States and today, the son of a person who fought the Japanese and the son of a person who resented the United States are close friends. We talk about keeping the peace. We talk about working together to change the world for the better: What do we do? How do we feed people who are hungry? How do we build roads in Afghanistan? What do we do?

And so what happened? What happened was, is that Japan adopted a Japanese-style democracy after World War II, and the conditions of our relationship, the condition

of the country changed; the attitude changed, and our relationship changed.

The Far East was a pretty difficult place. I know we spend a lot of time talking about the Far East today because of North Korea, but if you really look at the development in the Far East, it's pretty remarkable, isn't it? South Korea has emerged into a vibrant capitalist society. Japan has still got a little hangover from their previous activities in the region but, nevertheless, is a thriving partner in peace. Taiwan is making progress. China has got opening markets. Their economy is growing. Their entrepreneurial class is strong. They need to—the political system needs to evolve. But nevertheless, the region is relatively peaceful except for one outpost, one system that's not open and transparent, one system that doesn't respond to the will of the people, one system that's dark, and that's North Korea.

It took a while for that peaceful evolution to occur. And that's what's going to happen in the Middle East. It is. And it's hard work. And I want those parents to know that. These are historic times. We will lose if we leave too early. The stakes of success are vital, but a free Iraq is going to help inspire others to demand what I believe is a universal right of men and women.

General Casey will make the decisions as to how many troops we have there. And that's important for the families to know. It's really important. General Casey is a wise and smart man who has spent a lot of time in Baghdad recently, obviously. And it's his judgment that I rely upon. He'll decide how best to achieve victory and the troop levels necessary to do so.

I spent a lot of time talking to him about troop levels, and I told him this, I said, you decide, General. I want your judgment, your advice. I don't want these decisions being made by the political noise, by the political moment. It's just unfair to our troops, and it's unfair to their families. It's the reasoned judgment of our military commanders that the President must count on in order to achieve a victory that is necessary to help make this country more secure. And that's exactly how I'm going to make my decision.

So if the people are listening, they need to know I'm proud of their families. The cause is noble and necessary. And the size of the troops that will be there will depend upon the sound judgment of our military commanders.

Thank you for this press conference. I've enjoyed it. Appreciate it.

NOTE: The President's news conference began at 10 a.m. in the Museum of Science and Industry. In his remarks, he referred to Mayor Richard M. Daley of Chicago, IL; Rep. Jesse L. Jackson, Jr., of Illinois; Prime Minister Nuri al-Maliki and former President Saddam Hussein of Iraq; President Hu Jintao of China; President Vladimir V. Putin of Russia; President Roh Moo-hyun of South Korea; Prime Minister Junichiro Koizumi of Japan; Patrick J. Fitzgerald, U.S. Attorney for the Northern District of Illinois and Department of Justice CIA employee identity disclosure investigation special prosecutor; Judy Baar Topinka, Illinois gubenatorial candidate; Secretary General Javier Solana of the Council of the European Union; Secretary of the Supreme National Secretary Council Ali Larijani and President Mahmud Ahmadinejad of Iran; and Gen. George W. Casey, Jr., USA, commanding general, Multi-National Force—Iraq.

Remarks at a Lunch for Gubernatorial Candidate Judy Baar Topinka in Chicago
July 7, 2006

Thank you all. Go ahead; please be seated. Thanks for coming. I am honored to be here. I proudly stand with Judy Baar Topinka as the next Governor of the State of Illinois.

Laura sends her best. Like Judy says, "Sorry Laura didn't come." I say, "Yes, most candidates say that." [*Laughter*] I'm really lucky that Laura said yes when I asked her to marry me. And I think the country is lucky to have her as the First Lady. And she sends her very best to Judy. She, like me, hopes that Judy will win. And she, like me, knows that when Judy does win, she's going to be a fabulous Governor for the people of Illinois.

I'm glad to be here with the Speaker. Mr. Speaker, I'm proud you're here. Thanks for coming. Somebody said, "What is it like dealing with Hastert?" I said, "Solid as a rock." [*Laughter*] He's predictable. You can count on him. He's doing a fine job as the Speaker of the House of Representatives. I love working with you. We're getting a lot done. And I want to thank you for being here.

Jim Edgar, what a good man. Thanks for coming, Governor. I appreciate you being here. We're members of the ex-Governors club. [*Laughter*] And we got to know Jim and Brenda well during his time as Governor of Illinois, and he was a dandy. All you got to do is aspire to be as good as Jim Edgar, and you'll do a great job, Governor Topinka. He is—he set the standard, didn't he, for Governors here in Illinois. And I'm proud you're here, and thanks for helping Judy Baar.

I want to thank all the candidates who are here. There's a lot here, so I'm not going to try to rip them all off, but I do want to thank you for running statewide—Lieutenant Governor candidate, attorney general candidate, treasurer candidate, comptroller candidate. Maybe I ought to say it just to see if I can get some ink for you: Joe Birkett, running for Lieutenant Governor. [*Applause*] Yes, let's do it that way—Christine Radogno, running for State treasurer. Senator, thanks for coming. Senator Dan Rutherford, running for secretary of state—there he is. Senator Bill Brady, he's not running for anything statewide, but he's here. Senator, thank you.

It's a good sign to see all the senators. When senators and members start to swarm around, it means they're smelling victory. [*Laughter*] They want to be close to the next Governor. Judy Baar, it's a good sign when you've got people like Tom Cross, the Illinois house minority leader. He's from your district, right, Speaker? Yes. Stu Umholtz is running for attorney general. Thanks for coming, Stu. Yes.

I want to thank Andy McKenna and all the grassroots activists who are here. This has been an incredibly successful fundraiser. And I thank you for your hard work in supporting Judy Baar. It's hard to do a big fundraiser like this, and it takes a lot of good organizers and people willing to go out and pick up the phone and call and ask. And you've done a fantastic job. It's a good sign. People don't want to back somebody who can't win. And you're here to back Judy Baar because, one, you like her; two, you trust her; and, three, you know she can win and become the Governor of the State.

So I thank you all for contributing mightily to her campaign, and I urge those of you who are involved in grassroots politics to kind of warm up and get ready to turn out the vote come November. She's going to need people putting up the signs and stuffing the letters and making the phone calls and urging the good people of this State—Republican, Democrat, and independent—to show up to the polls and do their duty and to vote for Judy Baar. She's going to do a fine job as your Governor. She's a good, fine, honest person who knows what she's doing. She's got a track record. She can get the job done.

Having been a Governor, I know what it means to be a Governor. You got to have somebody who can set an agenda; somebody that doesn't try to be all things to all people; somebody that says, "Here's what I'm running for, and here is what I intend to do," and then is going to do it. That's what the people of Illinois want. They don't want a bunch of fancy footwork and empty slogans. They want a practical person to say, let's make this State, for example, the best State in the country to be an entrepreneur. Let's make sure this is a progrowth economic policy in the State of Illinois.

We share a philosophy: The role of government is not to create wealth; the role of government is to create an environment in which the entrepreneurial spirit flourishes. And Judy Baar wants to make sure Illinois is entrepreneurial heaven for people here.

And so how do you do that? How do you do it? Well, the first thing you do is make sure you keep the people's taxes low. And it works. It works. We have been in Washington, the Speaker and I and others, working together, have proven that low taxes can increase economic vitality. We believe that when a person has more money in his or her own pocket to save, spend, and invest the way she or he feels fit, the economy grows.

Remember what's happened in the last 5 years. We have faced a recession, a stock market correction, corporate scandals, an attack on the United States of America, two major military operations to defend ourselves, national disasters, high energy prices. And yet this economy, first quarter of 2006, grew at 5.6 percent. Today we found out we added another 121,000 new jobs. The national unemployment rate is 4.6 percent. The unemployment rate in Chicago is 4.3 percent. Productivity is high. More people own a home than ever before. Small businesses are being created. This economy is strong, and the reason it's strong is because we cut the taxes on the American people.

And the fundamental question is, can we keep them low to make sure the economy grows? Here's the interesting debate in Washington, and I'm proud that Dave McSweeney is here, because he gets it. He's running for the United States Congress. He understands what I'm about to say. Here's the trap: In Washington, they say, "Oh, all we got to do is raise taxes to balance the budget." That's not the way Washington, DC, works. Yes, they'll raise your taxes, but they will figure out new ways to spend your money. The best way to balance the budget—and Judy Baar understands this—is to keep progrowth economic policies in place through low taxes and be wise about how we spend the people's money.

Our progrowth policies are working. Pretty soon we're going to announce the new deficit projections. I told the people that if we're wise about spending the money and keep progrowth policies in place, we'll be able to cut the deficit in half by 2009. What's really interesting is that when you cut the taxes and your economy grows, guess what happens. You yield more tax revenues. It's working. And, Speaker, I think we're going to have a pretty good projection here in a couple of weeks that will remind the American people that it's good policy to let you keep more of your own money, that we got to set priorities with your money in Washington, DC, and we can grow our way out of our deficits.

You know, the country has got some tough decisions to make. And that is, do we fear the future and try to wall ourselves off from the world, or do we welcome the competition the world provides and shape the future? And Judy Baar Topinka understands that we shouldn't fear the future. We ought to put good policies in place to keep us the most innovative, technologically advanced country in the world.

And you start with making sure you've got a good education system. When I was Governor of Texas, I used to say, education is to a State what national defense is to the Federal Government. In other words, it's got to be the number-one priority of your Governor. And you got to have a Governor that's willing to set high standards and willing to challenge the status quo if you find mediocrity and failure.

We've got too much stateism in public education, too much excuse-making, too much process. See, it's so simple to give up on an inner-city kid and say, "Well, you're this age; you're supposed to be here," or just kind of shuffling children through. It is inexcusable behavior. And therefore, we passed the No Child Left Behind Act, which says, we'll have high standards, and we expect people, in return for Federal money, to measure.

And the reason we want people to measure is because we want to know. We want to know if the curriculum may need to be corrected; we want to know if a school is failing to meet standards; we want to know if children are simply being shuffled through the school system without regard to their capacity to read and write and add and subtract.

And, Judy Baar, you're going to hear all the excuses for no measuring. You know, it's too much State interference; this—you're teaching to test. If we hold people to account, we will make sure children are not left behind.

You know what's happening here in the city of Chicago? You're reading scores are up. And the reason why is because you measure and you correct problems early, before it's too late. I look forward to working with Governor Judy Baar Topinka to make sure we institute the No Child Left Behind Act so the great State of Illinois is on the leading edge of education reform.

If you want to be a good State, in which people risk capital, and a competitive State, you got to make sure you use your community college system wisely. The community college system is a vital part of making sure America is able to compete in the global economy because the community colleges have the capacity to work with employers to help train people for the jobs which actually exist. And I know Judy Baar Topinka is going to be—wisely use the community college system here in Illinois to make sure this State remains competitive and a good place for the entrepreneurial spirit to flourish.

I look forward to working with her to get rid of our dependence on oil, foreign sources of oil. We got a problem. When the demand for oil goes up in China or in India, it causes the price of crude oil to go up, which causes the price of gasoline to go up in Illinois. And we need people who have got good commonsense policies in place, and one commonsense policy is to make sure that we have the opportunity to grow ourselves out of dependence on oil.

I love ethanol, and I intend to work with the Governor here to make sure that is widespread, not only throughout Illinois but throughout the United States of America. Thank you for your understanding that we need alternative sources of energy.

One of the toughest jobs she's going to have is fight off all the lawsuits. I don't know if the trial lawyers are that tough here in Illinois. I suspect they are. [*Laughter*] They're real tough in Washington, DC, too. You know, I met an ob-gyn coming through the line here. First of all, I can't think of a more noble profession than being an ob-gyn. But there's a problem in the United States of America. We got these junk lawsuits running good doctors out of practice. You know, there's over 1,500 counties in America that don't have an ob-gyn because of all these junk lawsuits. And that's not right, and it's not fair, and it's inexcusable. And you better have yourself a Governor who's willing to look those trial lawyers right in the face and say, "We need tort reform to make sure Illinois holds up the promise for all its citizens."

And by the way, I want to thank the Speaker. I think not one time but two times, he's passed medical liability reform out of the House of Representatives. When I first went to Washington, I thought it was a mistake for there to be a Federal medical liability bill. See, I thought the States can handle it. Then it was explained to me that all these lawsuits are costing the Federal Government and you an additional $28 billion a year.

So we got some pretty big health programs. We got Medicare and Medicaid and veterans' benefits. And so when you get all these junk lawsuits out there, it's not only causing premiums to rise, which you pay for, it's also causing doctors to practice defensive medicine, which you pay for.

And so they estimate the tab to the Federal Government is about $28 billion a year. So medical liability reform is not just a State issue, it's a national issue. And I appreciate the Speaker's leadership on getting a good bill out of the House. It's time for the Senate to stop playing politics and pass good medical liability reform for the sake of the patients in the United States of America, for the sake of good, quality health care.

These are historic times we're living in, and this country can make the decision to be confident about the future or to retreat from the future. And I believe we ought to be confident. Our entrepreneurial spirit is strong; this economy is good; and we can put good policies in place—good educational policies, good research and technology policies. The Speaker passed a good bill, by the way, that will double the amount of Federal research—Federal monies that go into research for basic science. It's a smart thing to do. It's a way to make sure America stays on the leading edge of change and technology.

In order to make sure that this country is competitive, you've got to have Governors who understand the proper role of Government and how to properly stimulate the entrepreneurial spirit. And I firmly believe Judy Baar Topinka is that right person, and I want to thank you for supporting her.

Before the Speaker and I get on the helicopter and go see one of the incredibly advanced plants, I do want to talk about the war on terror. Before I do so, I do want to say a really cool place—if you're wondering where a good place is to celebrate your 60th birthday—[*laughter*]—yes, you ought to try—yes, okay, thank you. Thank you. I'm saying, come to Chicago. It's a good place to celebrate your birthday. That's all I'm trying to say. Had a fabulous night last night with the mayor. They asked me at a press conference about the mayor. I said, the mayor is a man of his word. He said, "You're going to get clobbered in Chicago in 2000," and he kept is word. [*Laughter*]

By the way, if you go to the Science Museum, take your kids. It is a special place. I know there are some members of the board who are here—it is really great. And I'm looking forward to shedding my entourage one of these days and spending a little quality time there at the museum. [*Laughter*]

But at my press conference, they spent a lot of time talking about the world. And I told them today, like I'm going to tell you now, that my biggest job is to protect— is to work to protect the American people. And I think about it all the time. They ask, what's the job like, to be President. And the answer to that—job is, you make a lot of decisions. It's a decisionmaking experience. Governor, you'll find it to be a decisionmaking experience.

Rule one on decisionmaking is you make decisions based upon principle, not based upon polls and focus groups. You can't make good decisions if you're chasing a poll. You can't make the hard decision necessary to secure this country and to yield peace if you're worried about whether somebody thinks you're popular. You got to stand for what you believe and do what you think is right. And after September the 11th, I vowed that I would use our national assets to protect the American people. I think about it; I talk about it; I act on it every day of my Presidency.

The enemy we face are a bunch of totalitarians. They have a philosophy. They believe that if you don't adhere to their view, that you ought to be punished. They don't believe in freedom of worship; they don't believe in freedom of speech. They're willing to kill innocent people in order to achieve their objectives. They have clearly stated their objectives, which are to drive the United States out of parts of the world so they can develop safe haven from which to launch further attacks.

There are some people who want to see the world the way they'd like it to be, and I can understand that. My job is to see the world the way it really is. And therefore, so long as I'm the President, we will stay on the offense and bring these people to justice before they hurt the American people again.

We must keep the pressure on all the time. And one of the central fronts in the war on terror, one of the theaters of the war—not the sole theater but a theater in the war on terror—is Iraq. And I know it's on your minds. It's on my mind. We're facing a group of killers there that can't stand the advance of freedom. It should say something about the nature of the people we face when they see a young democracy beginning to grow and they're willing to kill innocent people in order to try to stop the march of freedom. That's one way to describe the enemy.

What is it about a free society that bothers these people? What's troubling about a society in which people are able to worship an Almighty freely if they choose to do so? How come you can't stand dissent in the public square? The reason why is because they have a vision that is opposite of that. And that's why they're doing—taking desperate measures to stop the advance of a democratic society.

And the enemy has got the capacity to kill on a daily basis, which clouds our TV screens. And therefore, some Americans are wondering whether or not we can win. And to those Americans, I say, not only can we win, we are winning. I want them to remember that 12 million people went to the polls in the face of incredible threat; 12 million people stood up and said, "We want to be free." There's now a unity Government. Victory will be achieved when Iraq, a free Iraq, can sustain itself and govern itself and defend itself. And the mission of the United States of America is to help that Government succeed. It's in our national interests there be a free Iraq.

People have often asked me, "Would I have made the same decision I made before, knowing what I know today?" And the answer is, I didn't have that luxury, but getting rid of Saddam Hussein has made America and the world a better and safer place.

And now the question is, does this country have the will and the patience to stand by a new democracy so they can realize the benefits of liberty? And when I flew over to Baghdad to see Prime Minister Maliki, one of my missions was to determine whether or not he had the capacity to lead and to make the tough decisions. I came to the conclusion he does. And my other part of the mission was to tell the Iraqi people, when America gives her word, America will keep her word.

You know, there's a lot of talk about troop levels. Let me just tell you this—and I spoke to a reporter today who asked about Illinois National Guard troops going overseas, and my answer to him was this—it was a long answer, but this is part of the answer: I'm going to make my mind up based upon the measured judgment of the commanders on the ground, and they will make their mind up about what is necessary to achieve victory in Iraq. We will not be set—determining troop levels based upon politics. I will be making the troop level decisions based upon what General

George Casey recommends. We owe that to our troops; we owe that to their families; we owe that to the Iraqi.

I do not want the enemy to think that we will withdraw because of politics. The enemy should not think that when they hear talk about artificial timetables for withdrawal, that's what the American people think, nor that's what the Congress will do. This United States Congress and this President will stand squarely behind our troops and stand squarely behind a strategy for victory.

So our short-term strategy is to defeat the enemy overseas so we don't have to face them here at home. And we're keeping the pressure on them. And I appreciate the Speaker's steadfast support. The long-term strategy, we will defeat the ideology of hatred with an ideology that's hopeful and light. And that's the ideology of freedom. And it's worked. It's worked in the past. Freedom has been able to convert enemies into allies.

I—one of my alltime favorite stories is to talk about my relationship with Koizumi. It was enriched, by the way—my relationship reached a new level of friendship when we went to Graceland. [*Laughter*] Isn't that interesting? It should be, when you really put that visit in the context of—in historical context.

After all, my dad and his dad were both old enough to be participants in—observers of World World II. They were enemies. And yet, here his son is getting on the airplane—the son of the Japanese fellow getting on the airplane with George H.W. Bush's son, on Air Force One, to fly down to go to Graceland. And we were talking about the peace. That's what we were talking about. We were talking about the issue of North Korea and the need for Japan and the United States, as well as South Korea and China and Russia, to send a clear message to the leader of North Korea: Your behavior is unacceptable.

I was thanking him for the thousand troops he had in Iraq. It's pretty remarkable, when you think about it, that the Japanese Self-Defense Forces were sent to Iraq to help secure liberty for a new democracy. We talked about how to help people in Afghanistan. We talked about HIV/AIDS on the continent of Africa. We're talking about how to make the world a better place, yet 60 years ago we were at war.

You've got to ask yourself what happened. How can that possibly be? Is it just circumstance? My answer is, no. One of my predecessors, Harry S. Truman, believed in the power of liberty to transform an enemy to an ally, and so he worked to see to it that the Japanese were able to adopt a Japanese-style democracy.

Liberty has got the capacity to change the world. We shouldn't be surprised when 12 million people vote in Iraq because I believe—and I hope you do too—that the concept of liberty is universal; that it's not just a concept for Americans or Methodists, it's a concept that rests in the soul of everybody. That's what we believe in America. That's the basis of our founding.

And so the idea of our enemy becoming a friend shouldn't be a surprise. The lessons of World War II and the aftermath should be lessons applied today in helping us chart our path to victory in the war against these terrorists. Someday, an elected leader of Iraq, a free Iraq in the heart of the Middle East, will be sitting down with an American President talking about keeping the peace. And generations of children will be better off for it.

Thanks for helping Judy Baar. God bless.

NOTE: The President spoke at 12:27 p.m. at the Drake Hotel. In his remarks, he referred to Andy McKenna, chairman, Illinois Republican Party; Mayor Richard M. Daley of Chicago, IL; former President Saddam Hussein and Prime Minister Nuri al-Maliki of Iraq; Gen. George W. Casey, Jr., USA, commanding general, Multi-National Force—Iraq; Prime Minister Junichiro Koizumi of Japan; and Chairman Kim Jong Il of North Korea.

Remarks at Cabot Microelectronics Corporation in Aurora, Illinois
July 7, 2006

The President. Listen, thank you. Thanks for the tour. The Speaker and I really enjoyed coming. Bill, appreciate you.

William P. Noglows. It's an honor.

The President. It is an honor to be here.

This is an innovative company that is a sign of the times that are coming. This is a company that strives upon our country's greatest asset, which happens to be the brainpower of our citizens. And what's amazing as you walk through the labs and meet the people working here, you say, "What's your degree in?" Let me just say, there wasn't a lot of history majors: physicists, chemists, Ph.D.s, people with advanced degrees. It is clear that in order for this country of ours to be competitive in the future, we've got to understand the nature of the jobs of the future, and these jobs are going to require people who have got math and science skills.

And so one way to make sure this country is competitive is to enhance math and science in early grades and encourage people to take math and science in the later years. And there's all kinds of ways to do that. One is to encourage Advanced Placement programs in our Nation's schools and help train 30,000 teachers in Advanced Placement. Another is to get people from institutions like this to go into our middle schools and high schools and say, "It's okay to be a scientist," you know, "Math and science will be important for your future." In other words, try to inspire people. We call that an adjunct professor program.

We've got a role at the Federal Government to make sure that we're research-oriented in a technology-driven economy, and that is to spend your money on basic research, so that, for example, nanotechnology is a really important part of the economy—an important growing part of the economy. And I believe and the Speaker believes—as a matter of fact, the House of Representatives believes that it makes sense to double the basic research budget of our Federal Government to help companies like this stay on the leading edge of change.

And so we're here because we want our fellow citizens to understand that we've got some really innovative people here in our country, and that in order for us to be competitive in the future, we've got to emphasize math and science and research and technology.

And so I want to congratulate you for running a good company.

Mr. Noglows. Thank you.

The President. I want to thank the people who work here for making you look good. And I thank—I want to thank the Speaker for getting a bill out of the House that funds the American Competitiveness Initiative that I sent up to Congress. The Speaker did good work on that. I call upon the Senate to get it done. This will be a commitment to our Nation's future, so that people won't have to fear the future because we intend to shape the future.

Anyway, thanks for letting us come by. Proud to be here. You're a great company. Thanks for the good work you do. God bless.

NOTE: The President spoke at 2:12 p.m. In his remarks, he referred to William P. Noglows, chairman and chief executive officer, Cabot Microelectronics Corp.

The President's Radio Address
July 8, 2006

Good morning. This week, I visited the city of Chicago. In that great city and across America, our strong and growing economy is creating jobs and delivering prosperity to more of our people.

In the Chicago area, businesses have added more than 74,000 new jobs over the past 2 years. And in Illinois, the unemployment rate has fallen to 4.6 percent, the lowest rate there in over 5½ years.

We have good news about our national economy as well. On Friday, we learned that the American economy created 121,000 new jobs in June, and it has created over 5.4 million jobs since August 2003. We now have added jobs for 34

straight months, and the unemployment rate is 4.6 percent.

In the first quarter of 2006, our economy grew at an impressive annual rate of 5.6 percent. This follows our economic growth of 3.5 percent in 2005, the fastest rate of any major industrialized nation. And because taxes are low, our workers are keeping more of the money they earn.

Behind each of these positive statistics are countless stories, stories of workers who start each day with hope because they have a job that will help them build a better life, stories of families with more money in the bank for college tuition or a downpayment on a home, stories of small-business owners who know they can hire more workers and grow with confidence.

Our economic expansion is lifting the lives of millions of Americans, and to keep this expansion going, we must maintain the progrowth, low-tax policies that helped to launch it in the first place. The tax relief we delivered has helped unleash the entrepreneurial spirit of America and kept our economy the envy of the world. So I will continue to work with Congress to make that tax relief permanent.

Our economy is also thriving because America remains the world's most innovative nation. During my trip to Illinois, I visited a company called Cabot Microelectronics, which makes products for manufacturing semiconductor chips and other high-tech components. Cutting-edge firms like Cabot are creating good jobs for our workers and helping to keep America competitive in the global economy.

· To help companies like Cabot maintain our Nation's competitive edge, I proposed my American Competitiveness Initiative. This initiative will double Federal funding for research in promising areas such as nanotechnology, supercomputing, and alternative energy sources. The initiative will

also encourage bolder private sector investment in technology and help ensure that every American child has the math and science skills needed for the jobs of tomorrow.

Last month, the House of Representatives approved full funding for the basic research component of this initiative. I urge the Senate to follow the House's lead, so America can remain an innovative nation that competes with confidence.

Americans are living in times of great hope and great opportunity. By keeping our taxes low, keeping our country competitive, and keeping this a welcoming nation, we will add to our prosperity, and we will create a better America for future generations.

Thank you for listening.

NOTE: The address was recorded at approximately 10:06 a.m. on July 7 at the InterContinental Hotel in Chicago, IL, for broadcast at 10:06 a.m. on July 8. The transcript was made available by the Office of the Press Secretary on July 7 but was embargoed for release until the broadcast. The Office of the Press Secretary also released a Spanish language transcript of this address.

Remarks Following Discussions With Prime Minister Janez Jansa of Slovenia
July 10, 2006

President Bush. Mr. Prime Minister, thank you for coming. It's been a really fascinating discussion we've had. First, I want to thank you for your friendship. I thank you for your leadership. I really appreciate the fact that you have made the courageous decision to help two young democracies, Afghanistan and Iraq, succeed. Your contributions in Afghanistan and Iraq will make a difference in achieving peace. And so thank you for that very much.

I really appreciate your briefing on your neighborhood. The Prime Minister is a man who has got clear vision. He understands how to explain problems in a way that will help yield results. And so the fact that you talked about the Balkans in such clear fashion will help us work with you to achieve certain objectives. I want to thank you for that.

I fondly remember my visit to your beautiful country. It was a spectacular visit. I came back to the States, and I told people that if you really want to see an interesting slice of heaven, go to Slovenia. It's got a country that's got a lot to it. But the most important thing, it's got wonderful people. And I look forward to working with you, Mr. Prime Minister. I'm confident that by working together, we can improve the lives of our respective peoples as well as improve the lives of those who are struggling against forms of government that won't allow them to have free expression, won't allow them to self-govern.

And so welcome to the White House, and thank you for our wonderful meeting.

Prime Minister Jansa. Esteemed Mr. President, thank you very much for inviting me and my delegation to the White House. We still remember your visit in Slovenia, and we hope to continue with good cooperation in the future.

I found very useful your information regarding the development of events in the region of Western Balkans. I'm glad we share the same views regarding the pro-spectus of—in Western Balkans regarding the security and also the NATO. In spite of the fact that Slovenia is a small country, it completed its allotment of troops in the NATO operations.

Based on the fact that we got a lot of help during our entering the NATO—and European Union, we got a lot of help—we feel that now it's our obligation that we help others to do the same. As I mentioned before, Slovenia will be presiding the European Union in 2008, during which time there will be a summit between the European Union countries and the United States. We would be very happy if we could welcome you then in Slovenia.

President Bush. Thanks for coming. Appreciate it very much. Thank you.

NOTE: The President spoke at 10:51 a.m. in the Oval Office at the White House. Prime Minister Jansa spoke in Slovenian, and his remarks were translated by an interpreter.

Remarks at a Swearing-In Ceremony for Henry M. Paulson, Jr., as Secretary of the Treasury
July 10, 2006

Thank you all. Please be seated. Thanks for coming. Good morning. Thank you for being here. I'm pleased to be here at the Department of the Treasury to stand in one of its most historic rooms. A hundred years ago, the vaults of the Cash Room were stacked from floor to ceiling with bank notes and coins and bullion—right here in this room. Today there is no longer any cash in this room; there's a lot of talent in this room. But this historic space reminds us of our responsibility to treat the people's money with respect. And in a few moments, Chief Justice John Roberts will swear in a man that every American can have faith in—Hank Paulson.

Hank comes to his position with a lifetime of experience in business and finance. He has an intimate knowledge of global markets. He will work to keep this economy of ours competitive and growing, and he will work to ensure fair treatment for America's goods and services across the world.

We welcome his family here—his wife, Wendy, and his mom, Marianna, his son, Merritt, and daughter, Amanda. And the other members of the Paulson family who have joined us, thanks for coming. We join them in congratulating Hank as he is sworn in as America's 74th Secretary of the Treasury.

I appreciate the Chief Justice joining us today. I appreciate the members of my Cabinet who are here to welcome your new colleague. I want to thank Deputy Secretary Bob Kimmitt and all the folks who work here at the Department of Treasury. You're getting a good boss. You're getting somebody you can work with and respect.

I appreciate the Chairman of the U.S. Federal Reserve; Chairman Bernanke is with us. Thanks for coming, Ben. All right if I still call you, Ben? [*Laughter*] I appreciate the House majority leader, John Boehner, joining us. Thanks for coming, John. I appreciate the ranking member of the House Budget Committee, Congressman John Spratt. Thanks for coming, John. I appreciate you all joining us here today. I want to thank my friend Don Evans, former Secretary of the Commerce, joining us. Welcome.

The Treasury Department is one of the oldest in the Federal Government, and every person who leads this Department walks in the footsteps of our first Treasury Secretary, Alexander Hamilton. In more— in the more than two centuries since he led this department, his role has expanded and his responsibilities have increased. Today, the Treasury Secretary is responsible for policies effecting global financial markets, international trade and investment, taxes and spending, and other issues of vital importance to America's ability to compete in a worldwide economy. The Treasury Secretary also oversees the minting of the U.S. currency, the management of public finances, and the enforcement of important laws, including our efforts to crack down on terrorist financing.

As Treasury Secretary, Hank Paulson will be my leading policy adviser on a broad range of domestic and international economic issues, and he will be the principal spokesman for my administration's economic policies. He is supremely qualified to take on these important responsibilities. He has served as chairman and chief executive officer of one of the world's leading financial firms, the Goldman Sachs Group. His decades of experience have given him a keen insight into the workings of our global economy. As he showed in his Senate confirmation hearings, he has the ability to explain complex economic issues in clear terms. People understand him when he talks. His nomination received strong bipartisan support. He was confirmed unanimously by the United States Senate.

Hank is being sworn in in an optimistic time for our country and for our workers. In the first quarter of 2006, our economy grew at an annual rate of 5.6 percent. That's the fastest growth in 2½ years. We've added more than 5.4 million new jobs since August of 2003. The national unemployment rate is down to 4.6 percent. Consumers and businesses are confident in the future. Productivity is high. That's leading to higher wages and a higher standard of living for our people. And I look forward to working with Hank Paulson to keep this economy growing and to keep creating jobs and enhance opportunity for our people.

We have a broad agenda to pursue. Our first challenge is to keep taxes low. Hank shares my philosophy that the economy prospers when we trust the American people to save, spend, and invest their money as they see fit. Hank understands that cutting taxes have helped launch the strong economic expansion that is lifting the lives of millions of Americans. And he will work with the United States Congress to maintain a progrowth, low-tax environment so we can keep our expansion growing.

Our second challenge is to bring Federal spending under control. We'll continue to cut wasteful and unnecessary spending in the annual budget. Hank Paulson understands we also need to rein in the growth of spending for entitlement programs like Social Security and Medicare and Medicaid. We have a problem with these programs. They're growing fast; they're growing at a rate faster than inflation, faster than the economy, and faster than we can afford.

If Congress does not act, these vital programs will be jeopardized and unfairly burden future generations. And so we'll continue to call on the Congress to work with us to preserve important programs, like Social Security and Medicare and Medicaid, for our children and our grandchildren.

The third challenge is to expand opportunities for American workers and businesses to compete in a global economy. Hank understands that the fastest growing markets for American goods and services are overseas, and that so long as the playing field is level, American workers and businesses can compete with anybody. So we will work to open up new markets to American products and to ensure that our trading partners play by the rules and respect intellectual property rights and maintain market-based exchange rates for their currencies.

Our fourth challenge is to prevent the Federal Government from burdening our economy with excessive regulations that will drive jobs and capital overseas. As one of the Nation's most accomplished investment bankers, Hank understands how important it is to maintain our openness to foreign investment and to keep America an attractive place to do business. So he's going to be a watchdog to prevent creeping overregulation that burdens our economy and costs America jobs.

Our fifth challenge is to keep America competitive by fostering a spirit that rewards innovation and risk-taking and enterprise. America is the most innovative nation in the world because our free enterprise system unleashes the talent and creativity of our people. Hank will be a champion for our country's small businesses and entrepreneurs. And he's going to work to ensure that the American Dream is within reach of every one of our citizens.

As he pursues this agenda, Hank will build on the firm foundation laid by Sec-

retary John Snow. John is a good fellow. He's a good man and a fine public servant. And he assumed leadership of this Department at a difficult time for our economy. During his tenure, John oversaw a strong economic resurgence that created millions of jobs for our families and made America's economy the fastest growing in the industrialized world.

John has also been an important leader in the war on terror. He directed the Treasury Department's efforts to crack down on terrorist financing, including a vital program to track terrorists' use of the international banking system. John Snow has helped make America safer and more prosperous, and I'm grateful for his distinguished service.

I'm also grateful that Hank Paulson has agreed to succeed John. He grew up on an Illinois farm. He rose to one of the highest positions on Wall Street, and now he's about to be sworn in as the Treasury Secretary of the United States of America. He's shown his talent and initiative as a leader in the private sector, and today he's showing his character and patriotism by leaving his career to serve our country. I'm grateful that Hank has answered the call to service.

The men and women of this Department will have an outstanding leader in Hank Paulson. I look forward to working with— welcome him to our Cabinet. I'm looking forward to working with him for the good of our country. And now I ask Chief Justice John Roberts to administer the oath.

NOTE: The President spoke at 11:15 a.m. at the Department of the Treasury. The transcript released by the Office of the Press Secretary also included the remarks of Secretary Paulson.

Statement on a Report of the Commission for Assistance to a Free Cuba
July 10, 2006

Today I approved the second report of the Commission for Assistance to a Free Cuba. I also approved a Compact with the People of Cuba, which outlines how the United States will support the Cuban people as they transition from the repressive control of the Castro regime to freedom and a genuine democracy. The report demonstrates that we are actively working for change in Cuba, not simply waiting for change. I call on all our democratic friends and allies around the world to join us in supporting freedom for the Cuban people. I applaud the work of the Commission, cochaired by Secretary Rice and Secretary Gutierrez.

NOTE: The statement referred to President Fidel Castro Ruz of Cuba. The Office of the Press Secretary also released a Spanish language transcript of this statement.

Message to the Senate Transmitting Amendments to the International Telecommunication Union Constitution and Convention
July 10, 2006

To the Senate of the United States:

With a view to receiving the advice and consent of the Senate to ratification, I transmit herewith the amendments to the Constitution and Convention of the International Telecommunication Union (Geneva, 1992), as amended by the Plenipotentiary Conference (Kyoto, 1994) and the Plenipotentiary Conference (Minneapolis, 1998), together with the declarations and reservations by the United States, all as contained in the Final Acts of the Plenipotentiary Conference (Marrakesh, 2002).

I transmit also, for the information of the Senate, the report of the Department of State concerning these amendments.

The Plenipotentiary Conference (Marrakesh, 2002) adopted amendments that would expand the field of individuals eligible for election to the Radio Regulations Board; provide for functional privileges and immunities for members of the Radio Regulations Board; strengthen the finances of the International Telecommunication Union by, among others, providing for sector member contributions to defray the expenses of regional conferences in which they participate and clarifying that operational plans prepared by the International Telecommunication Union Secretary-General and Directors of each of the International Telecommunication Union sectors must reflect the financial implications of the activities proposed; provide for sector members to be represented as observers at meetings of the Council; and recognize the authority of the Radiocommunication Assembly, the World Telecommunication Standardization Assembly, and the World Telecommunication Development Conference to adopt working methods and procedures for their respective sectors.

Consistent with long-standing practices, the United States, in signing the 2002 amendments, made certain declarations and reservations. Subject to those declarations and reservations, I believe the United States should ratify the 2002 amendments to the International Telecommunication Union Constitution and Convention. Those amendments will contribute to the International Telecommunication Union's ability to adapt to changes in the telecommunication environment and, in so doing, serve the needs of the United States Government and United States industry. It is my hope that the Senate will take early action on this matter and give its advice and consent to ratification.

GEORGE W. BUSH

The White House,
July 10, 2006.

Remarks at a Dinner Honoring the Special Olympics
July 10, 2006

Ladies and gentlemen, thank you for coming—Mrs. Shriver and Special Olympics athletes, friends and family. Mr. President—the President of Iceland has joined us—proud you're here, President Grimsson. And First Lady of Panama, First Lady Torrijos, is with us as well. We've got Members of the Congress and Members of the Senate. Laura and I are glad you all are here. Welcome to this special occasion.

We're here to celebrate the Special Olympics and to honor a woman who made them possible, Eunice Kennedy Shriver. And we're here to celebrate her birthday. [*Laughter*]

In a moment, we'll hear from this woman who has made it her life's work to create opportunities for people with intellectual disabilities. She founded the Special Olympics in 1968 to get people with intellectual disabilities the chance to develop physical fitness, to create friendships, and experience the joy of sports competition and achievement. Today, the Special Olympics includes more than 2.25 million athletes in 150 countries. The games have become a source of unity and excitement for its participants. They've helped raise awareness of the challenges facing those with intellectual disabilities.

America upholds the values of every person and the possibilities of every life. And the Special Olympics are an example of America at its best. We share with the entire world the spirit of joy and kindness that the Special Olympics brings.

If you ever had any doubt about how much good one person can do, look no further than this kind and gracious lady. On this special occasion, I ask you to join me in a toast to the Special Olympics and to Eunice Kennedy Shriver and to her contributions to our Nation, past, present, and future. God bless.

NOTE: The President spoke at 7:40 p.m. in the East Room at the White House. In his remarks, he referred to Eunice Kennedy Shriver, founder and honorary chairman, Special Olympics; President Olafur Grimsson of Iceland; and Vivian Fernandez de Torrijos, wife of President Martin Torrijos Espino of Panama.

Interview With Foreign Journalists
July 10, 2006

The President. I'm looking forward to it. I'm going to see Angela Merkel on her home turf. She kindly invited me to go to her part of the country. I always view that as a sign of generous hospitality, when somebody says, "Come by my home area." And I'm looking forward to going, and I'm looking forward to having a good discussion with her on a variety of subjects.

I've spoken frequently with the Chancellor since she's gotten in, and that's important, because Germany has got a very important role to play, not only in Europe but around the world. So I'm looking forward to that a lot.

And then, of course, I'll be going to Russia and have—Laura and I and the Putins will be having dinner, which is a good chance to continue our friendship. We've got a good friendship with the Putins. We're comfortable around them. And then, of course, the next day we'll have a bilateral meeting, which will be more business than pleasure. I also am looking forward to that. I've spoken to Vladimir Putin frequently over the last couple of weeks on a variety of subjects. And the world is complex. There are problems that are surfacing. I've always felt like it's best to work with friends and allies to solve the problems. And so we'll have a variety of topics on the agenda.

And then we've got the G–8. I think the topics there are relevant: energy security. I view energy security, from my perspective, as how do we diversify away from hydrocarbons. That's the definition of security from an American perspective. I will be—it just so happens, it's a really interesting moment where there's the need to be—protect our national security, and economic security comes at a time when there's great concern about global warming, and it turns out that you can achieve economic and national security and protect the environment at the same time. For example, civilian nuclear power, that's going to be an important subject, as far as I'm concerned.

If you truly are concerned about protecting the environment, then it seems like to me that civilian nuclear power is a good way to go. Technologies have changed; we'll discuss that. Some agree; some don't agree.

But nevertheless, it's going to be a part of the dialog. I look forward to talking to them about our research and development efforts into new types of batteries that will be able to power automobiles for the first 40 miles without using gasoline, or talk about use of ethanol or our experimentation and our work with hydrogen. In other words, there's a variety of things we can talk about to help with energy—on the energy security issue.

We'll talk about infectious diseases. I thank the Russian President for putting that on the agenda. That's going to be a very important topic, if there were to be a pandemic flu outbreak. It's important for us to have discussed our individual plans and how we intend to work collectively on the problem.

We'll talk about education matters. I intend to talk about trade. We've got—the Doha round is out there, kind of—people are wondering whether or not we'll be able to move it. I'm still upbeat about it, by the way. I think we can get something done. I just finished meeting with my trade minister and our team involved on the subject. But this will be a good forum to talk about it, not only at the first days of the G–8 but when the members of the G–20 come. There will be an important discussion with the leader of Brazil and others.

As well, one of the things we will talk about are common values that are important—transparency, anticorruption, free markets—values that tend to bind us and that can unite us in common purpose. So I'm looking forward to it.

Michael [Michael Backfisch, Handelsblatt].

Germany-U.S. Relations

Q. Mr. President, German-American relations have improved since Angela Merkel became Chancellor. With Silvio Berlusconi being out of office and Tony Blair's days being numbered, has Germany become America's most important pillar in Europe, and would you even use a formula such as partnership and leadership, as your father dubbed the relationship with Helmut Kohl?

The President. First, let me say, we had disagreements over Iraq, obviously. But apart from that, I always felt our relationship with Germany was vital and important. Much has been made about the differences between Chancellor Schroeder and myself, and no question, there were differences. But I will tell you that from my perspective, and I think he would say this, is we've tried to work beyond that. There were other issues we had to deal with besides Iraq. So the relationship has been good since I've been the President.

Angela Merkel comes into office now at a time where we've gotten that behind us, and we're moving forward. Remember, one of the first decisions I made after 9/11 was to go into Afghanistan, and the Germans supported us on that. So there's—we've worked together, and I do believe that, as I mentioned to you, Germany has got a very important role to play in Europe and in the world. And Angela Merkel is assuming the mantle of leadership, for which I'm grateful.

From my perspective, I think the American President and the country must maintain a lot of good relations with Europe, since Europe is a—it's vital. It's a vital center of trade, and it's a vital center of exchange, and it's a vital center, I hope, of working together to, kind of, spread common values. But we've got a good relationship.

Andrei [Andrei K. Sitov, ITAR–TASS].

President's Birthday

Q. Thank you, sir, for inviting us, for giving us this opportunity.

The President. Any time.

Q. May I congratulate you, sir, on your recent birthday. I was on the South Lawn there, watching.

The President. You were watching me turn 60? [*Laughter*]

Q. No, the Fourth of July, the celebration.

The President. Let me ask you something, does that seem old to you, 60?

Q. No, not at all, sir.

The President. Good, yes. [*Laughter*]

Q. Sir, you are——

The President. The American press corps seems to—makes it seems like it's a very old age—people—how old are you, Tom [Tom Raum, Associated Press]?

Q. Sixty-one.

The President. See.

Q. Everybody knows your medical stats, sir. You are in good condition.

The President. Thank you for wishing me a happy birthday. Finally ended. Go ahead.

Russia-U.S. Relations/World Trade Organization

Q. Thank you, sir, for indulging us.

I wanted to ask you about the continuing Russian integration. Will there be——

The President. Continuing Russian integration?

Q. Integration into the world bodies. Will there be a deal on the WTO negotiations with Russia in St. Petersburg? And also, when do you expect Russia to gain a permanent seat at the financial G–7?

The President. First of all, as far as the G–8 goes, from my perspective, Russia is an active participant. President Putin has been there; he speaks; he talks; he acts; he interfaces. Plus, he's hosting it—is hosting this G–8.

Secondly, we talked about the WTO negotiations with Russia, and there is—I've presented the letter to the President, which makes it very clear, our position, so that there's no ambiguity about what needs to happen in terms of market access from both—the perspective of both countries. And we will continue to work, see if we can't get this done.

President Putin has got his issues at home; we've got issues here. And that is, we've got to make sure any agreement we strike is a good one. And there's two issues that are very important for—a lot of issues are important, but I would say the two areas where a lot of people will be paying attention to it here in America is, one, on agriculture, we want to make sure that if somebody says they're going to take our products into their country, they'll do it. And secondly, the other is intellectual property rights. And that's what a lot of people will be looking at from this perspective. I'm sure Vladimir Putin has got pressures on his side too.

I do believe it's in our country's interest to have Russia as a member of the WTO. It's been a difficult negotiation, because there's more than one constituency. That's what President Putin has got to understand. One issue—not just satisfying what our trade negotiators think is fair; we've got to make sure we can get it through the Congress.

But others are watching as well; other nations are watching the set of negotiations. So hopefully, we can get it done. I'm optimistic about it.

Mario [Mario Platero, IlSole24Ore], congratulations to you.

2006 World Cup

Q. Thank you. Thank you, Mr. President. Did you watch the game?

The President. I watched some of it.

Italy-U.S. Relations/War on Terror

Q. Mr. President, the new Italian Government has stated that there are, and I quote the Italian Foreign Minister, Mr. D'Alema, "evident differences with the U.S., certainly with respect to policies from the previous years." And a decision about whether to stay in Afghanistan will be made in the next few days, and a decision has been made to withdraw completely from Iraq, contrary to what the commitment of the previous Government was. Are you disappointed by that?

The President. First of all, I want to thank the Italian people and the Government for their contributions in Iraq. They

were there during some of the most difficult times. And the previous Government made a commitment and met its commitment, and we're very grateful for that. The current Government campaigned on not staying in Iraq; that's what they said. So when you win elections, you're supposed to do what you say you do. So I'm not surprised. I would hope—and I appreciate the commitments. I would hope they would—toward, for example, training through NATO or reconstruction aid. This is an historic time.

And one of the messages I'll be sending people at the G–8 is, liberty is universal; the world is better off when there's free societies. We'll worry about our own selves, of course, but we've also got to need to worry about others living under the—that may live under the clutches of a tyrant or others who are trying to build a democracy. And we would hope that established democracies would help young democracies grow, and there's all kinds of ways you can do that. There's a difference of opinion, obviously, in certain corners as to whether or not we should have gone into Iraq in the first place. But now that we're there, the hope is that we can work with nations to help build the new democracy. And that's not my appeal; that's the appeal of Prime Minister Maliki and others. So I'm confident we can work with the Government, looking forward to it.

Q. On Afghanistan, you hope they will stay?

The President. Of course I do. It's a new democracy. We'll see. Every country gets to make its own mind what to do, but I would hope that those who are weighing whether or not it makes sense to stay or go look at the consequences of failure and realize the great benefits of liberty for the people of Afghanistan. An elected government there—society is changing. It takes hard work. I happen to believe the hard work it takes is necessary for peace.

Masaomi [Masaomi Terada, The Yomiuri Shimbun]. Did I say it right?

North Korea

Q. Masaomi.

The President. Yes, see, pretty close. [*Laughter*]

Q. Thank you very much. I have a question on North Korea. Security Council is about to adopt North Korea resolution. The U.S. had vowed to continue diplomatic efforts to resolve the issue. But what kind of measures will you take to get North Korea back to the six-party talks?

The President. First of all, I want to thank the Japanese contribution in the Security Council. Secondly, I think there's an interesting new development, that the Japanese have decided to delay tabling the resolution to give the Chinese a chance to go to Pyongyang to have a discussion with the leader in North Korea, with the desire of having them come back to the table. So that's where we are—them being the North Koreans—come back to the table.

And that's where we are. And so the Security Council option is always there. But to answer your question, the strategy at this point in time is for the Chinese to travel and to make the claim that it would be in North Korea's interests that they come back to the table and remind them they've already been at the table and they agreed to a Korean Peninsula that is nuclear-weapons free. That's what they've agreed to—they being the North Koreans, along with the United States, the Russians, the South Koreans, the Japanese, and the Chinese. So that's where we are.

Michael.

Energy

Q. Mr. President, energy security, 25 percent of Europe's natural gas consumption is satisfied by Russia. In the case of Germany, it's more than one-third. Is Europe, is Germany too energy dependent on Russia, and do you see the ensuing danger that Russia has the means to potentially blackmail Europe?

The President. I think each nation or each group of nations has to make their own national security calculations. I can just give you my perspective where the United States is, and you can draw whatever conclusions you want from that.

I think we are dependent on oil from, in some cases, unstable parts of the world. And while you may be able to manage your way through the short term, in the long term, eventually, I think that will be a problem for national security purposes here. And therefore, when you talk about energy security, it is part—people say, "Well, security is how you guarantee supply." That's one view of security. It's just that supplies can get disrupted sometimes. I view security as diversification away from a particular source of energy that may be the cause of the worry about insecurity in the first place.

And so the German Government is going to have to make its decision as to whether or not it makes sense to have a supply—one-third of its supply from a single source. I can tell you this, I've told the American people we will spend billions to put technology in place or achieve technological breakthroughs that will enable future Presidents to say, "I no longer have to worry about a single source of supply; I no longer have to worry about disruption; I no longer have to worry about politics." And I think the world needs to go there, in my own judgment. I think the whole world would be better off if we're less reliant upon forms of hydrocarbon.

Is it possible? Yes, it's possible. We're spending over a billion dollars on hydrogen technologies and research to determine whether or not you can actually drive your automobiles with hydrogen, a byproduct of which is nothing, water. The issue with hydrogen, however, is, one, obviously, the technologies. But it takes a fair amount of power to create the hydrogen. And therefore, the question is, will nations such as ours, and others, be willing to use nuclear power to be able to provide the power to create the hydrogen in the first place? It's a policy choice countries are going to have to make.

We are working with India and China, for example, on nuclear power. I think it's in everybody's interest that these new, growing economies have—that the appetite for hydrocarbons in these growing economies is lessened with the advent of nuclear power. I know it's in—it really is in everybody's interest because of the globalization of energy demand. In other words, India demands more; it causes your prices to go up.

And so our contribution to trying to deal with energy security is to not only spend money here at home but also to work with developing countries to reduce their appetite for hydrocarbons. And to this end, we're working with Japan and Russia, France, and Great Britain to spend money to come up with a fast breeder reactor program, so that we can reprocess, burn, and reduce the amount of waste, which will hopefully then make the idea of additional civilian nuclear power in other countries more palatable politically.

Q. And Russia's potential blackmailing power?

The President. That's going to be up to the Europeans to make that decision. That's not an issue we worry about here at home. That's an issue that the European leaders are going to have to work through, particularly at the EU, to make sure that they're not in a position where somebody can change the equation. Obviously, there was—some of my friends who were the leaders in Europe were somewhat concerned about the Ukrainian issue. We expressed our opinion on that very clearly. But the decisionmakers, your leaders, are going to have to make the decision as to whether or not they view the current status as something that they need to diversify away from. And I just laid out some ideas as to how, at least, we're trying to do that. Andrei.

Alternative Fuel Sources/Georgia

Q. You just gave me an opening there——

The President. Well, I'm trying to, Andrei. I'm Mr. Thoughtful, as you know. [*Laughter*]

Q. ——by referring to Ukraine, sir. Russia, for years, has been subsidizing its neighbors with energy supplies. President Putin recently suggested that it was to the tune of $3 billion to $5 billion a year. Basically he said, "If any new friends of those countries want them to have cheap energy, are they willing to pay?" So is this country willing to pay the same amount for cheap gas for Ukraine and Georgia?

The President. Well, look, there's a pretty good market. I mean, there's a marketplace. And the definition of price—you can judge whether or not it's fair, given kind of comparable situations elsewhere. Michael's point is, if you've got a sole source of supply or a significant sole source of supply, sometimes that source of supply can set the market. And I would think that what most consumers would want was fair, transparent pricing.

One way to make sure you've got fair pricing is to have alternative sources of energy so that you're able to make different choices, and that's very difficult, particularly when it comes to natural gas. Gas is a hard product to transport. Gas requires enormous capital investment. Oil can be transferred by cart, by trucks. Gas has to be transferred by pipeline, more or less. Now there's a whole new technology coming, which is liquefied natural gas, so it can be transported by fleet. And so all I would ask is that there be transparency, that there be—that people know fully what the rules are, and that the contracts be open, easy to understand, and honored.

Q. And if I may stay with the neighborhood for a second there. You recently hosted the President of Georgia. Why do you think it's in NATO's interest to admit a country with two internal conflicts on its territory?

The President. I think it's in the world's interest that there be peaceful resolution of those two internal issues. I also think it's in NATO's interest to welcome countries which adhere to rule of law and marketplace economics, a country that is a democracy, a country which allows for public dissent and free press. I think those are all wonderful values that ought to be incorporated—that NATO—that will benefit NATO, with the incorporation of a country like Georgia. It's not a given that Georgia enters. All I said was that Georgia ought to be—that the way forward into NATO for Georgia ought to be clear, and the road ought to be clearly delineated so that they can then do the things necessary to earn NATO membership.

There's some question as to whether or not the United States was committed to this Georgian ascension, at least to be a part of the MAP Program. I think I cleared that up. I think people pretty understand—pretty well understand my position on that now.

Q. That's good. Thanks.

The President. Mario.

Italy-U.S. Relations

Q. Yes, Mr. President.

The President. So let me ask you something, Mario. Was your face painted yesterday? [*Laughter*]

Q. Mine wasn't, but one of a friend of mine was. But my dog had an Italian flag.

The President. Very good. [*Laughter*]

Q. So that created quite an impression. Mr. President, two senior officials of SISMI, the Italian counterintelligence service, have been arrested just recently.

The President. Mario, I'm going to give you a chance to ask another question because I'm not going to talk about ongoing cases. If you'd like to come up with another question——

Q. It's an open case. It's open in the sense that today there has been a request

from the magistrate for the extradition of 26 CIA——

The President. Mario—Mario——

Q. In principle, you would——

The President. Mario, no, I'm not going to talk about the case. You can ask another question, since I cut you off before you were able to ask your full question.

Q. You confuse me with the soccer. [*Laughter*]

The President. This is just in fairness.

Q. Okay.

The President. Gone from Mr. Thoughtful to Mr. Openminded here. [*Laughter*]

Q. Well, Mr. President, you've known Mr. Prodi for a long time, and you've known Mr. Berlusconi; you've known both of them. And how would you assess the personal relationship that you had with Mr. Prodi and with Mr. Berlusconi? Is there a difference how comfortable would you feel with one or the other?

The President. I feel very comfortable with both. The first thing that's important is I feel comfortable with the people of Italy. We've got very close ties.

And let me just take a step back. What's interesting about our country is that we've got—we've had close ties with a lot of countries. My ranch was settled by Germans.

Q. Really?

The President. Yes. There's a huge number of Italian Americans, a lot of Russian Americans. You know, Norm Mineta in my Cabinet is a Japanese American. In other words, so when you talk about relations with an American President, you've got to understand that there's a—at least I have, I know my predecessors have connections, close connections with people who have fond—either fond memories and/or great pride in their motherland.

And the way I like to define relations is that we've got—that I've got good relations and great respect for the country of Italy. Obviously, people are so different that you've just got to gauge your relationship to meet certain objectives. And our objective with our European friends is to have a Europe that is whole, free, and at peace and is in close concert with the United States.

And so I think in this case, Prodi and Berlusconi share that objective, both share the same objective; same in Germany. And so I deal with them differently. They're just different types of people with different backgrounds. But I've known Romano Prodi, particularly since he was the head of the EU. I've worked with him quite a bit. Ask him about the time when I was riding my mountain bike on the beaches of Sea Island, Georgia. I came roaring by as fast as I could. There was Prodi with his head down. I made some kind of noise or something startled him out of his walking shoes, you know. [*Laughter*] My point is, there he was. He's a guy who I felt comfortable enough roaring by on a mountain bike, three Secret Service agents spewing up sand. [*Laughter*]

I know him. I feel comfortable talking to him. I may—he may not agree with me. But the fundamental question I think you're searching for is, can you still have a good relationship even though you disagree on issues? And the answer is, yes. That's part of life. There's a—look, I'm the kind of person, I make decisions; I deal with problems; I want to solve them. And sometimes—and, you know, I make it clear where I stand. And that creates—in the world, people say, "Wow, that creates tension." But privately, it doesn't. That's what you've got to know, that there's a—and I work hard to make sure that I've got good personal relationships with these leaders so we can solve problems. And I'm confident that——

Q. Will you see him in——

The President. Prodi?

Q. ——in St. Petersburg, in a bilateral——

The President. I don't even know. I'm not the scheduler, Mario. But I will see him.

Q. In a bilateral?

The President. Well, I'll take him aside, just the two of us, if that's—I'll take your recommendation for it. When I see him, I'll take him aside and congratulate him. I don't know whether or not we're having bilaterals or not. Are we?

National Security Adviser Stephen J. Hadley. We're still looking at it.

The President. Mario, you want me focused on the big picture. I don't know my schedule. [*Laughter*]

Q. Thank you.

The President. All right. Masaomi.

Japan-U.S. Relations

Q. Mr. President, U.S.-Japan relations are enjoying a golden age, a so-called golden age, which can be credited to close friendship that you and Prime Minister Koizumi share. On the other hand, Japanese relations with China and South Korea have chilled on Koizumi's watch. So how will you build the U.S.-Japan alliance with the next Prime Minister? And what do you hope to see in his approach to diplomacy towards Asia?

The President. First of all, our relations are good. I'm not sure any President and Prime Minister are going to be able to duplicate our trip to Graceland. [*Laughter*] It's an unbelievable experience, if you think about it. It's really one of the interesting lessons of history, isn't it? And what I—I'm told these guys are sick of hearing me say this, but I'm going to say it anyway—what the President referred to by "these guys" are the American people sitting behind—so my dad fought the Japanese. And that is startling to me that his son takes the Prime Minister to Graceland. Something happened. We fought the Germans; now we're very close friends.

And what happened was, there's a—liberty took hold, a Japanese-style democracy. That's what we're working on in Afghanistan and Iraq. Those are the stakes, as far as I'm concerned.

And so we've got a great relationship, and I intend to keep it that way. It's in

American interests that we work closely with Japan. It's also in our interests that Japan have got better relations with China and South Korea. And that's going to be up to the Japanese leaders to make the determination of how to do that. I, of course, have said that to Prime Minister Koizumi: "We would hope that you would be able to improve relations." It's in our Nation's interest that our friends have good relations with other friends and acquaintances.

And so that's going to be an interesting issue as to whether or not that's the case, whether that's a campaign issue in your democracy, whether or not it even matters to the people of Japan. But that's why you have elections. That's why you have decisionmaking in the democratic process, to determine whether that's an important issue.

And that's—you know what's interesting about the world in which we live, if the Chinese are able to get the North Koreans back to the table, think about a negotiating arrangement where you've actually got the Japanese and the Chinese and the South Koreans and the Americans and the Russians all sitting down, trying to convince Kim Jong Il to give up his nuclear weapons program. It's pretty remarkable, when you think about it.

And it's—and so I happen to believe— and the same thing is remarkable, in some ways, that we're still working very closely together on Iran. Germany has been great on Iran, by the way. Appreciate the Chancellor's strong position.

And the reason I bring this up, these are issues which we will solve, and we're more likely to solve them more quickly when we work together to solve them. And it's—to me, it's a very positive development. It's a new framework. It's kind of an interesting—it's an interesting data point in history to know that nations with different backgrounds and at times warring with each other are now working together to deal the common—with the common

threats. And it's a threat if the Iranians have a nuclear weapon. It's a threat to world peace. It's a threat to all of us. It's a threat for North Korea to develop a nuclear weapon. It's a very destabilizing event in the Far East. So we're working very closely with each other to get it done.

Japan-China Relations

Q. Do you have any worry about the relations between Japan and China?

The President. Do I worry about it?

Q. Yes.

The President. Well, I would hope it would improve, is the best way to put it— hope it would improve. I think it's an important relationship. And I can't make it improve. That's up to the parties to make it improve. I can say, I hope it improves, to both parties, which I'm more than willing to do.

Anyway, looking forward to going. Who's going? You're going, Steve [Steve Holland, Reuters]? Tom? Stretch [Richard Keil, Bloomberg News], you going? You're going to be there.

Q. Mr. President——

The President. No more questions.

Q. That's it?

Q. One more?

The President. Okay, yes.

Iran

Q. Great. [*Laughter*] Mr. President, you were mentioning Germany's role vis-a-vis Iran. Provided that there is no positive Iranian response before the G–8 summit——

The President. I'm not sure I accept that yet.

Q. Yes, well, let's just give it a try.

The President. Well, it's hypothetical, Michael.

Q. Okay, let's give it a try. What measures——

The President. You can try it. Give me a head's up. [*Laughter*]

Q. What measures—what kind of sanctions will the administration strive for? And how do you want to convince Russia and China to come aboard?

The President. We spent a lot of time talking about these—more than one issue now, obviously, Russia and China. But part of diplomacy is just constant work, constant dialog, and constant discussion, and remind people that we have declared common goals. The goal on the Korean Peninsula is a nuclear weapons-free peninsula. The goal of the Iranians is no nuclear program.

And everybody has got different interests. And so everybody has got different pressures. So diplomacy takes a while. And what you're watching—what the world watches now is diplomacy in action. And we will work very quietly with our friends to work toward a resolution of the issue with the goal of achieving this thing diplomatically, of achieving this issue—success diplomatically but also with the goal of saying, you know, with common voice to, in this case, the Iranians, no weapons program.

I'm not sure I necessarily accept your hypothesis that something positive isn't going to happen. I don't know. But what I'm going to tell you is we'll react to it if it doesn't, if something positive doesn't happen.

Q. So far, nothing has happened. On the Iranian side, it's been going on for a long time.

The President. Right, but there's a meeting here pretty soon. Wednesday.

Q. So you're trusting the Iranians?

The President. No, no, no. You're asking me to—you're asking me—you're predicting the outcome of the meeting, and I'm saying, I'm not predicting the outcome of the meeting. And either way, we'll be prepared to react.

Q. So there is——

The President. Good try, though, on the hypothetical question.

Q. Very briefly.

The President. Yes, Andrei.

War on Terror

Q. The Russians got their Usama bin Laden, Shamil Basayev, who was responsible for killing the children in Beslan. What do you have to say to the Russians about that?

And also, will you be discussing with President Putin his new idea about the new binding treaty to replace the old START I that expires?

The President. I'll be talking to him about a variety of subjects. Yes, looking forward to hearing from that. And I—I guess we're gathering the details on the death of the guy, to find out more about it, you know. But if he's, in fact, the person that ordered the killing of children in Beslan, he deserved it.

Q. Mr. President, on the U.N.—United Nations, after Kofi Annan——

The President. It's an interesting thing about terrorists, by the way, they'll kill children like that. They don't care.

United Nations Secretary-General

Q. The name surfaced recently of Prince Zeid, who is a member of the royal family of Jordan—was the representative of Jordan to the U.N. And he would be the first Muslim in case he would run for it.

The President. You're trying to rope me into the——

Q. No, I'm saying, would you be against a moderate Muslim?

The President. You're trying to get me to commit a name, actually talk about names.

Q. No, no, no. In general. [*Laughter*]

The President. As I understand it, the—traditionally, there's kind of a—regions rotate, and we're really looking in the Far East right now to be the Secretary-General—Secretary-General there. Holland.

Q. Oh, sorry. [*Laughter*]

The President. Well, that's kind of where the current—that's kind of where the current—he's over 60. No, he's not—53?

Q. Fifty-one.

The President. Fifty-one. That's kind of—his birthday was recently. That's kind of—so the discussions mainly, at least the ones I've heard about this, somebody from the eastern—Far East——

Q. Asia.

The President. Asia, yes. So this is the first I've heard of this suggestion. And you'll find that we will work closely with friends and allies to come up with the best candidate, but we won't be committing publicly, like you're trying to get me to do.

Q. But with general principle, will you be against a Muslim, in Indonesia, for example, who is up for the position?

The President. Not at all, would not be against a Muslim. The criterion I'm for is somebody who wants to spread liberty and enhance the peace, do difficult things like confront tyranny, worry about the human condition, blow the whistle on human rights violations.

Yes, sir. Final question now, for certain. Michael roped me into another round there. [*Laughter*]

North Korea

Q. Going back to North Korea, do you still think U.S. can deal with Kim Jong Il in resolving the crisis, or do you have sort of regime change in mind?

The President. What we want is for the North Korean leader to give up his weapons programs. And the United States tried to deal with him bilaterally in the past, and it didn't work. So I changed the policy. I said it's not going to be just the United States dealing with the North Korean leader. We're also going to have other partners like Japan and South Korea and Russia and China.

See, in the past, negotiators from the United States sat down and said this, that, and the other, and the North Koreans didn't honor the agreement. So I'm trying a different approach. My last approach didn't work, so hopefully, this approach will work. And I think it's more likely to work

because you've got more than just one person saying it—you know, "Get rid of your weapons programs." Now we've got neighbors saying the same thing. And so that's where we are right now.

What's interesting, I thought, was that, you know, the Chinese, the United States, Japan, and South Korea, Russia all said, "Don't fire your weapon; don't fire your rockets." And he fired his rockets.

And that ought to be an interesting lesson to all of us involved in this relationship, that we've got to stay very close together and speak with one voice, because it's very—he must hear clearly that that kind of behavior is unacceptable. People have asked me, what do I think he's trying to achieve? I don't know. It's a nontransparent society. It's hard to tell. Like, if I were to make a decision, you'd be reading about it. People, reporters all over the place trying to—"Why did he do this; why did he do that?" And that's good. That's what an open society does. I don't know what objective he was trying to achieve.

But from my perspective, it sent a signal that he really was not afraid of isolating himself even further. My attitude is, is that the people of North Korea can have a much better life than they've—than their leader has chosen for them. There's tremendous starvation in North Korea. There's huge concentration camps. It's unacceptable behavior, as far as I'm concerned.

And I would hope that the North Korean leader would choose a different path forward. And the way to do that is to get rid of your weapons programs in a verifiable fashion. There's a better way forward for the Iranian leadership than isolation, and that is to get rid of the weapons programs in a verifiable fashion. It's their choice to make. We've made our—the United States has made its choice; Germany has made its choice; Russia has made her choice; Japan has made its choice. We've made our choice; the choice is theirs. And I would hope that these leaders would recognize that there is—there's benefits for their people. They truly care about their people. There's benefits for their people.

You know, one of the most moving moments of my Presidency came when the young—when the mother of—young daughter was kidnaped by the North Koreans. Imagine. Anybody got children here? Imagine if some foreign nation ordered your child to be kidnaped, just removed. And never—they never heard from the girl again. They went—she was telling me, she was wondering whether she was murdered, and they searched everywhere. It's unbelievable, isn't it? It turns out that they believe that she was in North Korea, a regime that just felt like there was no accountability and no regard for human rights and just took this young child.

So the mother was sitting there in the Oval Office with me. It was incredibly emotional. After all these years, she still felt this pain in her heart. And my point is, is that there's a better way forward than that, to live in a society like that. And the choice is his to make, in North Korea's case. I hope he makes the right choice. It's important for all of us to continue to make that very clear. If he chooses the other way, he'll be isolated and his people won't benefit.

Okay. Thank you all. I enjoyed it.

NOTE: The interview was taped at 2:30 p.m. in the Roosevelt Room at the White House. In his remarks, he referred to Chancellor Angela Merkel and former Chancellor Gerhard Schroeder of Germany; President Vladimir V. Putin of Russia, and his wife, Lyudmila; President Luiz Inacio Lula da Silva of Brazil; Prime Minister Nuri al-Maliki of Iraq; Chairman Kim Jong Il of North Korea; Prime Minister Romano Prodi and former Prime Minister Silvio Berlusconi of Italy; Prime Minister Junichiro Koizumi of Japan; Shamil Basayev, a Chechen separatist leader, who was killed on July 10; and Sakie Yokota, mother of Megumi Yokota, who was abducted by North Korean authorities. Reporters referred to former Chancellor Helmut J.M. Kohl of Germany; Prime Minister Tony Blair of the United Kingdom; Usama bin Laden, leader of the Al Qaida terrorist organization; Secretary-General Kofi Annan of the United Nations; and Prince Zeid Ra'ad Zeid al-Hussein of Jordan. The transcript was released by the Office of the Press Secretary on July 11. A tape was not available for verification of the content of this interview.

Remarks on the Office of Management and Budget Mid-Session Review
July 11, 2006

The President. Thank you. Thanks for coming. The White House is the people's house, and I'm here to talk about the people's money. We're glad you're here. As you know, every year, my administration produces a budget that lays out our priorities and our goals. And every summer, the Office of Management and Budget releases a report called the Mid-Session Review that tells the American people how much progress we're making towards meeting our fiscal goals.

Today OMB Director Rob Portman released the latest review. I'm pleased to report that it's got some good news for the American taxpayer. This economy is growing; Federal taxes are rising; and we're cutting the Federal deficit faster than we expected.

This good news is no accident. It's the result of the hard work of the American people and sound policies in Washington, DC. This morning I'm going to discuss the way forward; I'll explain why our progrowth policies are vital to our efforts to reduce the Federal deficit, what my administration is doing to work with Congress to eliminate wasteful spending, and why we need to confront the unsustainable growth in entitlement spending.

I appreciate our new Secretary of the Treasury, Hank Paulson, joining us today. Mr. Secretary, you've been on the job one day, and you've got a pretty strong record. I'm proud that Rob Portman is here, and he brought his lad with him. [*Laughter*] I thank the Senate President pro tem, Senator Ted Stevens, for joining us. Senator, thanks for coming. I'm proud you're here. Thank you for your leadership. I also want to thank David Dreier, Conrad Burns— Senator Conrad Burns, excuse me——

Senator Conrad Burns. That's okay. [*Laughter*]

The President. ——Congressman Joe Knollenberg, Ander Crenshaw, Marilyn Musgrave, thank you all for coming. Pence is with us; thanks for coming. I'm proud you're here, Mike. Thank you all for taking time to be here to hear this good news. You're responsible, in many ways, for creating the conditions for the good news we're about to talk about.

When I came to Washington, taxes were too high and the economy was headed into a recession. Some said the answer was to centralize power in Washington and let the politicians make the decisions about what to do with the people's money. That was one point of view.

We had a different point of view. I believe that the economy prospers when we trust the American people to make their own decisions about how to save, spend, and invest. So starting in 2001, my administration worked with the United States Congress, and we delivered the largest tax relief since Ronald Reagan was in the White House. We cut rates for everyone who pays income taxes. We reduced the marriage penalty; we doubled the child tax credit; and we cut the death tax. We cut the tax paid by most small businesses, because we understand that most new jobs are created by small businesses. And we encouraged economic expansion by cutting taxes on dividends and capital gains.

Together, these tax cuts left nearly $1.1 trillion in the hands of American workers and families and small-business owners, and they used this money to help fuel an economic resurgence that's now in its 18th straight quarter of growth. The tax cuts we passed work.

Last year, our economy grew at 3.5 percent, and in the first quarter of this year, it grew at an annual rate of 5.6 percent. Over the past 3 years, our economy has grown by more than $1.3 trillion, an amount that is larger than the size of the entire Canadian or South Korean economy.

Since August 2003, the U.S. economy has added more than 5.4 million new jobs. Our unemployment rate is down to 4.6 percent. People are working. Behind these numbers, there are American workers who start each day with hope because they have a job to help them build a better life. Behind these numbers, there are more families with more money in the bank for college tuition or a downpayment on their homes. Behind these numbers are small-business owners who are hiring more workers, expanding their businesses, and realizing the great promise of our country.

Our job in Washington is to keep this expansion growing—going and to promote progrowth policies that let Americans keep more of their hard-earned paychecks and aid us in reducing our fiscal deficit.

In order to reduce the deficit, you got to set priorities. And in working with Congress, we've set clear priorities. And the number-one priority of this administration and this Congress is to make sure men and women who are defending the security of the United States and helping to spread peace through the spread of liberty get all the help they need from our Government. We will always fund the troops in harm's way.

In an age when terrorists have attacked our country and want to hurt us again, we will do everything in our power to protect the American homeland. Those are the clear priorities of this administration, and the clear priorities of the United States Congress.

Fighting a war on terror and defending the homeland imposes great costs, and those costs have helped create budget deficits. Our responsibility is to win this war on terror and to keep the economy growing. And those are the kind of policies we have in place. Some in Washington say we had to choose between cutting taxes and cutting the deficit. You might remember those debates. You endured that rhetoric hour after hour on the floor of the Senate and the House. Today's numbers show that that was a false choice. The economic growth fueled by tax relief has helped send our tax revenues soaring. That's what's happened.

When the economy grows, businesses grow, people earn more money, profits are higher, and they pay additional taxes on the new income. In 2005, tax revenues grew by $274 billion, or 14.5 percent; it's the largest increase in 24 years. Based on tax collections to date, the Treasury projects that tax revenues for this year will grow by $246 billion, or an 11 percent increase. The increase in tax revenues is much better than we had projected, and it's helping us cut the budget deficit.

One of the most important measures of our success in cutting the deficit is the size of the deficit in relation to the size of our economy. Think of it like a mortgage. When you take out a home loan, the most important measure is not how much you borrow; it is how much you borrow compared to how much you earn. If your income goes up, your mortgage takes up less of your family's budget. Same is true of our national economy. When the economy expands, our Nation's income goes up and the burden of the deficit shrinks. And that's what's happening today. Thanks to

economic growth and the rise in tax revenues, this year the deficit will shrink to 2.3 percent of GDP. That's about the same as the average over the past 40 years.

Here are some hard numbers: Our regional projection for this year's budget deficit was $423 billion. That was a projection. That's what we thought was going to happen. That's what we sent up to the Congress: "Here's what we think." Today's report from OMB tells us that this year's deficit will actually come in at about $296 billion.

That's what happens when you implement progrowth economic policies. We faced difficult economic times. We cut the taxes on the American people because we strongly believe that the American people should lead us out of recession. Our small businesses flourished, people invested, tax revenue is up, and we're way ahead of cutting the deficit—Federal deficit in half by 2009.

As a matter of fact, we're a year ahead of fulfilling a pledge that I told the Congress and the American people. I said to the American people, give this plan a chance to work. We worked with Congress to implement this plan. I said, we can cut the Federal deficit in half by 2008—or 2009. We're now a full year ahead of schedule. Our policies are working, and I thank the Members of Congress for standing with us.

See, we cannot depend on just a growing economy, though, to keep cutting the deficit. That's just one part of the equation. We also got to cut out wasteful spending. See, it's okay to create revenue growth; that's good. But if we spend all that revenue growth on wasteful programs, it's not going to help us meet our objectives. And so the second half of the equation is for this administration to continue working with the Congress to be wise about how we spend the people's money.

Every year, Congress votes to fund the day-to-day spending of the Federal Government. That's called discretionary spending.

In other words, the Congress decides how much to spend on these types of programs on an annual basis. Every year since I took office, we've reduced the growth of discretionary spending that's not related to the military or homeland security. I told you, our priorities are our military and protecting the homeland. But on other programs, we've reduced the growth of that discretionary spending. The last two budgets have actually cut this kind of spending.

The philosophy is clear: Every American family has to set priorities and live within its budget, and so does the Federal Government. And I thank the Members of Congress for making the tough votes, setting priorities, and doing the hard work on behalf of the taxpayers of this country.

We made good progress with the emergency spending bill that Congress approved in June. You might remember the debate leading up to that supplemental bill. And there was a good, constructive debate. And I weighed in. I said that we got to make sure that the emergency funding in the bill supported our troops and provided help to citizens that were hit by last year's hurricanes and to prepare for the dangers of an outbreak of pandemic flu.

The onset—I also set limits that I thought were acceptable. In other words, we came up with our view of what would be a rational spending limit for this important piece of legislation. And I made it clear to the Congress, they sent me a bill that went over the limit, I'd veto it. We got good relations with Congress. People took that threat seriously because I meant it. Congress responded by removing nearly $15 billion in spending that had been added to the bill. By meeting the limit I'd set, Congress ensured funding for vital programs and provided a good example of fiscal discipline.

The next test is whether or not we can get a line-item veto out of the United States Senate. A line-item veto is an important tool for controlling spending. See, it will allow the President to target unneces-sary spending that sometimes lawmakers put into large bills. Today, when a lawmaker loads up a good bill with wasteful spending, I don't have any choices. I either sign the bill with the bad spending or veto the whole bill that's got good spending in it. And I think it would be wise if we're seriously concerned about wasteful spending to enable the executive branch to interface effectively with the legislative branch to eliminate that kind of wasteful spending.

And so we've proposed a line-item veto that the House of Representatives passed. Under this proposal, the President can approve spending that's necessary; redline spending that's not; and send back the wasteful, unnecessary spending to the Congress for a prompt up-or-down vote. In other words, it's a collaborative effort between the two branches of Government, all aimed at making sure we can earn the trust of the taxpayers.

Listen, the line-item veto works. Forty-three Governors of both parties have this authority, and they use it effectively to help restrain spending in their State budgets. I've talked to some of these Governors—used to be a Governor. I know what I'm talking about when it comes to line-item veto being an effective tool. The line-item veto provides a lot of advantages, and one of them is, it acts as a deterrent. See, when legislators think they can slip their individual items in a spending bill without notice, they do it.

If they think that they're going to try to slip something in that gets noticed, it means they're less likely to try to do so. We want to make sure that the system we have here in Washington is transparent and above-board and fair to the people's—taxpayers' money.

And one way to do so is to make sure that the President can work with the Congress through the line-item veto proposal I submitted. I strongly urge the United States Senate to take this matter up and pass it into law.

We're dealing with the short-term deficit, but there's another challenge that we face. In the long run, the biggest challenge to our Nation's economic health is the unsustainable growth in spending for entitlement programs, mandatory programs such as Social Security, Medicare, and Medicaid. Millions of our fellow Americans rely on these programs for retirement and health care needs. They're important programs. But the spending for these programs is growing faster than inflation, faster than the economy, and faster than our ability to pay for them.

To solve the problem, we need to cut entitlement spending. We need to do something about it, is what we need to do. One reason Secretary Paulson agreed to join this administration is because he wants to get something done about these entitlement programs, and I want to work with him.

You know it's so much—easy just to shove these problems down the road. The easy fix is to say, "Let somebody else deal with it." This administration is going to continue trying to work with Congress to deal with these issues. That's why I ran for office in the first place, to confront big problems and to solve them. That's why Henry Paulson made the tough decision to leave the comfort of private life to come in and do something good for this country. And the United States Congress needs to feel that same sense of obligation. The time of playing politics with Social Security and Medicare and Medicaid is over. We need to fix this for younger generations of Americans to come.

I'm optimistic about the future of this country because I'm optimistic about the— because I understand the nature of the people we got here. I mean, we are an entrepreneurial people. We're a hard-working, decent group of citizens. And the role of Government is to foster the entrepreneurial spirit. It's to encourage people. And one way you do that is to keep people's taxes low, let them keep more of their own money.

We've got great faith in the people's ability to spend their money wiser than the Federal Government can do. And our faith in the people has been proven by the numbers we're talking about today.

We said we got an economic issue, and we're going to let you have more of your own money to help us recover from recession, the stock market correction, and terrorist attacks and war and natural disasters. And the people haven't let us down, have they? This economy is strong.

We also said, let's just be patient about solving this Federal deficit; we're not going to take money out of your pocket; let's grow our way out of it. Let's keep—let's set priorities when it comes to spending and keep the people's taxes low, and these revenues will catch up into our Treasury. And they have. And we're reducing that Federal deficit, through the people's hard work and the wise policies in Washington, DC.

Today is a good day for the American taxpayer. Tax relief is working; the economy is growing; revenues are up; the deficit is down; and all across this great land, Americans are realizing their dreams and building better futures for their families.

I want to thank you all for supporting our policies. Thank you for giving me a chance to come to visit with you. I thank the Members of Congress for doing good work. God bless you all.

NOTE: The President spoke at 9:45 a.m. in the East Room at the White House.

Remarks at Allen-Edmonds Shoe Corporation in Port Washington, Wisconsin
July 11, 2006

The President. John, thanks for the shoes, and thanks for——

John J. Stollenwerk. You're welcome.

The President. ——employing people.

Mr. Stollenwerk. You're welcome.

The President. We're at one of America's great companies. It's a privately held company that is making a good product. This is a company that has benefited because of the tax cuts. It's a subchapter S company. You've often heard me talk about cutting taxes on individuals benefits small businesses; this is a company that had benefited from the tax cuts. It's also a company that made additional investments because of the tax relief we passed.

And when you make investments, it makes your company more productive. And when you're more productive, it makes you more competitive. And so the tax cuts we passed have helped this company. It made a lot of sense. They've also helped our country. This economy of ours is growing. The unemployment rate is 4.6 percent nationally, and that's good news for workers. People are making more money, and that's good news for workers.

And as a result of a growing economy, we collected more money for the Treasury. I told the American people we would keep spending down and keep progrowth policies in place to help cut the deficit in half by 2009. As a result of the Mid-Session Review, the numbers that came out of the Mid-Session Review, I'm able to tell the American people, we'll cut the deficit in half by 2008. The projected budget deficit over—of over 420 billion is now assumed to be 296 billion. See, what happens is, when you grow the economy by cutting taxes, more tax revenues come into the Treasury, and that's what we're seeing here.

I'm looking forward to working with Congress to make sure that we continue to hold spending down, to set priorities, and to be wise about how we spend the money. And one of the problems we have in Congress is, sometimes Congressmen and Senators stick unnecessary spending into bills. And I believe the President needs a line-item veto to help make sure that there's fiscal responsibility in Washington, DC.

I'm traveling with Congressman Ryan. He is the sponsor of the House bill, and I appreciate his leadership on this issue. The United States Senate needs to get the line-item veto to the President's desk so that the American people can have confidence in our ability to be wise about how we spend the money. This practice about stuffing stuff into these bills that never gets a hearing or the light of day is just—it's just not right. And one way to bring fiscal sanity to Washington and fiscal discipline to Washington is to give the President the line-item veto.

I'm thrilled to be here at Allen-Edmonds. I'm thrilled with my new shoes. [*Laughter*] I wish I had them on the Fourth of July. [*Laughter*]

Mr. Stollenwerk. You're a little late.

The President. But these shoes last a long period of time. I intend to be wearing them for a lot of Fourth of Julys in coming. This is an American-based company making good American products. And I'm proud of what you're doing here, John.

I'll tell you something interesting. So we're working the floor out there, talking to the people who make this company go, and he knows everybody's name. That's a good sign. That's a caring chief executive officer who cares first and foremost about the people here on the floor. And guess what happens when you have somebody like that who takes care of his workers? They make good product. And so I'm proud to be an Allen-Edmonds customer, and I'm proud to be here at this factory, and thanks for having me.

Mr. Stollenwerk. Thank you.

The President. Yes, sir.

Mr. Stollenwerk. And a paying customer at that.

The President. Oh, yes. [*Laughter*] Part of the accountability system in Washington. [*Laughter*] Thank you all.

Q. Do you have a comment on India?

The President. No comments today. Thank you very much. Thank you. Good to see you.

NOTE: The President spoke at 4:24 p.m. In his remarks, he referred to John J. Stollenwerk, president and chief executive officer, Allen-Edmonds Shoe Corp.

Remarks at a Reception for Gubernatorial Candidate Mark Green in Milwaukee, Wisconsin
July 11, 2006

Thanks for coming. Thanks for the introduction. Thanks for supporting the next Governor of Wisconsin, Mark Green.

I know a little something about what it means to be a Governor and a chief executive officer of government. Here is what you need: You need somebody who knows how to set an agenda; you need somebody who knows how to achieve the agenda; you need somebody who can get results without worrying about public opinion polls; you need somebody who stands on principle; you need somebody who shoots straight with the people. And that person is Mark Green.

There is no doubt in my mind he will be a great Governor for Wisconsin. I got to know him; this isn't the first time I've been with him before. I've seen him in action in Washington, DC. He is a highly respected Member of the United States Congress. People trust his word. When he says something, he means it. He is a positive influence in Washington, DC. He can bring people together, which is what you need in this State. He is an honorable, decent man, and I am proud to stand with him as he runs for Governor. I want to thank you all for supporting him.

I know something about running; you cannot win unless your friends step up. And

tonight you have stepped up. And I know Mark is grateful, and so am I, for coming tonight. So, thanks for being here.

You can't run for Governor unless you have a wife who loves you and a family standing with you. And the Green family is a fine, fine family. I want to thank Sue for being here and Rachel and Anna and Alex.

I was also proud to have met Jeremy and Elizabeth Green, the mom and dad. The mom kind of reminded me of my mom—[*laughter*]—constantly reminding Mark, you know, what to do, how to say it. [*Laughter*] I said, "Are you listening to her?" He said, "Yes, all the time." I said, "Then you're going to win." Thank you all for being here.

And by the way, Laura sends her love to the Greens. If you really need help coming down the stretch, I suggest you invite Laura to come here to Wisconsin. She'll help you win. She's a great First Lady.

We're having the time of our lives, by the way, and it really helps to—well, I have a 45-second commute. [*Laughter*] And it helps to commute to a home where there's somebody you respect and love there. And she sends her best. She knows what I know, that you can't win in politics alone. And so for those who have given money, thanks. And for those of you who are kind of warming up for the campaign, thanks in advance for what you're going to do, which is to put up the signs, knock on the doors, get on the telephones; go to your churches, community centers, your synagogues, your houses of worship and say, you've got a good, decent man in Mark Green who can lead this State.

So thanks for being here. It means a lot to Mark, and it means a lot to me. I'm traveling over from Washington, by the way, with another fine public servant from Wisconsin, and that's Congressman Paul Ryan.

By the way, we're working on an important piece of legislation in Washington. That is to give the President the opportunity to kind of take some of these special interest spending out of these spending bills. We call it the line-item veto. It's one way to bring some fiscal sanity to Washington, DC. It's one way to make sure that people don't play politics with your money. Interestingly enough, the bill passed the United States House of Representatives, and the bill sponsor was this fine Member from Wisconsin, Paul Ryan. I want to thank you for your leadership.

Green's leaving the House, and he's going to be succeeded by speaker John Gard. And I want to thank you for running, and I wish you all the very best in your run for the United States Congress, Mr. Speaker. You'll make a fine Member of the House of Representatives.

I want to thank all the local officials who are here in the statehouse. By the way, if you're a member of the statehouse, a senator or representative, you're fixing to have a sea change when Mark wins the governorship. You're going to find somebody that's going to be a joy to work with, somebody who will make an agenda, a clear agenda, somebody who is making decisions based upon sound principles. So I look forward on your behalf to get yourself a new Governor for the State of Wisconsin.

I want to thank the grassroots leaders who are here. First of all, Margaret Farrow is here, former Lieutenant Governor. Margaret, thank you for coming. I appreciate you being here. Good to see you again. I've spent some quality time here in the State of Wisconsin. Some of my most fond memories campaigning in 2000 and 2004 were in this State. And I had the honor of getting to know Margaret. So it's great to see you. Thanks for coming. Thanks for helping the next Governor. He needs your help.

I want the thank Rick Graber, who is the chairman of the Republican Party of Wisconsin. He is a good friend of mine and a good man. I want to thank Mary Buestrin, and I want to thank Klauser, Jim Klauser and thank all the grassroots activists again for coming.

These are historic times in which we live. And I'm glad to have had Congressman Green in Washington, DC, during a time where the President has had to make some tough decisions and the country has been through some tough times. We are a nation at war. I wish I could report differently. But you need to have a President and you need to have leaders who see the world the way it is, not the way we would hope it would be. And my biggest job, and the biggest job of people in Washington, DC, is to protect the American people from further attack. And the way to do that is to stay on the offense, to give the enemy no quarter, and to bring them to justice before they hurt us again, and that's precisely what this administration will continue to do.

Iraq is a part of the war on terror. It's the central front in the war on terror, and the reason it's a central front is because the enemy that attacked us has made it clear they would like to have a safe haven from which to attack us again. I didn't make this up. I'm just telling you what the enemy has said. In order to make sure this country is secure, you better have a Commander in Chief who listens carefully to what the enemy says and takes them seriously, which I do.

By the way, just so you know, when you're the Chief Executive Officer, you make a lot of decisions. And 9/11 affected my decisionmaking a lot. I vowed that the country would do everything—we would do everything to protect the country. I meant what I said. Iraq is part of protecting the country—not to revisit a lot of history.

But one of the lessons of September the 11th is when this Nation sees a threat, it must take these threats seriously before they fully materialize. That's a lesson we must learn and we must not forget. And we saw a threat; Republicans and Democrats saw a threat in Saddam Hussein. After all, he had attacked his neighbors. He had used weapons of mass destruction. At the very least, he had the capacity to make weapons of mass destruction. He had terrorist connections. He was shooting at American pilots. The decision I made was the right decision. America is safer and the world is better off without Saddam Hussein in power.

The enemy believes we're weak. That's what they say. They believe we'll lose our nerve. They believe it's just a matter of time before we pull out of Iraq. The stakes in Iraq are incredibly high. But we've got some things going for us. We've got a fantastic United States military. And I want to thank Mark Green and Brian for supporting these men and women. Listen, any time you have a man or a woman in uniform in harm's way, they deserve the full support of the United States Government. And thanks to these good Congressmen and this administration, we've given them the full support of the United States Government.

We also have 12 million people in Iraq who say, "I want to live in freedom." I know it seems like an eternity since the elections last December. I guess it's because we've got too many TV channels that things seem to move real quick. But it wasn't all that long ago that the people,

when given the chance, went to the polls and said, "We want to be free. We want to live in a Iraqi-style democracy. Just give us a chance." That's what they said.

And there are a group of killers, cold-blooded killers, that are trying to stop the advance of this young democracy. That's what they're trying to do. You got to ask yourself, what kind of people fear democracy? Who wouldn't want people to worship freely? What is the mindset where you can't go to the public square and express yourself openly? It's the same mindset that wants to attack us for what we believe in.

We're not going to lose in Iraq. As a matter of fact, we will win in Iraq so long as we stay the course. Twelve million people have voted. They've now got a unity government.

I went over there and saw the man, Prime Minister Maliki. You know what I was looking for? I was looking for, do we have someone there who can set an agenda; somebody who can follow through; somebody who is dedicated to a government of, by, and for the people. And I found a courageous man there. And he's wondering, he's wondering when he hears all the rhetoric in Washington, DC, and around the country, he's wondering whether the United States can keep its word. And I told him this, I said, "So long as you're willing to make the tough decisions, so long as you're willing to represent the people, the United States of America will keep our word."

It's in our interest we succeed in Iraq. And we're going to succeed in Iraq. And when we succeed in Iraq, we'll be a powerful example of freedom in the heart of the Middle East.

You know, you might have noticed recently that I went to Graceland—that's Elvis's place—[*laughter*]—with Prime Minister Koizumi. I think that's really interesting. I think we need to put that visit in perspective about what we're talking about and the hard decisions we've made in Washington, DC.

You see, 60 years ago my dad, and I'm sure some of your relatives, fought the Japanese. They were the sworn enemy of the United States of America. A lot of people lost their lives in that war, a lot.

By the way, as you might recall, they attacked us at Pearl Harbor. We lost more people on 9/11 than we did in Pearl Harbor. And yet 60 years later, after fighting this bloody war, I go to Graceland with Prime Minister Koizumi. Something happened. And what happened in between that war and today was the Japanese adopted a Japanese-style democracy.

Democracies yield the peace we want. And guess what we talked about after we got past talking about Elvis? [*Laughter*] We talked about North Korea. I congratulated Prime Minister Koizumi for committing 1,000 troops into Iraq to help this young democracy. And he did so because he knows what I know: The best way to defeat the terrorists in the short run is to find them and bring them to justice and to prevent them from having safe haven. The best way to defeat them in the long run is the spread of liberty. Freedom yields the peace we want. Freedom is able to convert. Liberty has the capacity of converting an enemy into an ally, and someday an American president will be talking with a duly elected leader of Iraq and talking about the peace.

We're doing the hard work necessary to protect ourselves, and we're doing the hard work of supporting young democracies. So we're laying the foundation of peace for generations to come. And I appreciate the vision and strength and courage of Mark Green on this tough issue.

So today I had an interesting announcement to make, and that is that the projected deficit of 423 billion is now down to 296 billion in one year. It now means the deficit is 2.3 percent of GDP, which is about average over the last 40 years. What's interesting about that announcement is that we were able to achieve deficit reduction primarily because the revenues

increased in spite of the fact that we cut taxes.

You might remember the history of this administration and working with Mark—he understands that and so does Ryan—that we've been through a recession and corporate scandals, a stock market correction, an attack on the United States of America, two wars—two battles in theaters to defend ourselves—Afghanistan and Iraq, major natural disasters, high energy prices. And yet this economy of ours is strong, and we intend to keep it that way.

And one of the reasons it's strong and one of the reasons we recovered is because we cut the taxes. We cut the taxes on small-business people. We cut the taxes on workers. We cut the taxes on families raising children. We cut the taxes on dividends. We cut the taxes on capital gains.

I was at Allen-Edmonds today; we accelerated depreciation, which caused him to buy more equipment, which makes him an incredibly, productive, competitive company. Cutting the taxes works. It makes this economy strong.

You need a Governor who will cut the taxes in Wisconsin. Mark Green is that Governor.

You know, it's amazing, the rhetoric in Washington is beyond belief at times. They say in order to solve the deficit, you've got to raise taxes. We just proved them wrong. In order to solve the deficit, you cut taxes, you increase economic vitality, which yields more taxes. That's how it works. You need a tax cutter as your Governor here. It's just a philosophical difference, by the way, between people like myself and others, me and Mark and others. And it's this: We trust you with your money. Who best to spend your money? You? Or the government?

We believe that you can best spend your money. Do you realize the tax cuts we passed left $1.1 trillion in the hands of workers and small-business owners and entrepreneurs and farmers?

And I made the point today: You have clearly shown that you can spend your money better than the Federal Government can, and therefore, our economy is strong. It's the envy of the world. One thing we've got to do in Washington, DC, is to make sure that we continue to grow. And one good way to do that is to make the tax cuts permanent.

The other equation in reducing the deficit, by the way, is to make sure we're wise about how we spend your money. You need a Governor who knows how to set priorities. I appreciate working with the Speaker and the leader in the Senate; we've set priorities. I told you what the priorities are. It's defending this country and giving our troops what they need to win the war on terror. Beyond that, believe it or not, we've actually cut discretionary spending on non-homeland and defense spending.

We're doing a good job about watching your money. And it's hard work. Everybody's got a good idea. Every program sounds fantastic. You've got to make sure you've got a good fiscal hawk in your Governor's seat. You've got to have somebody who's willing to take on the sacred cow. Somebody's asking, "Do these programs produce results?" Somebody who is willing to look beyond the title of the program to determine whether or not they're delivering result for the people. Mark Green is that kind of guy. He's going to do you a fine job as the Governor when it comes to watching your money.

This is a little off subject here, but the biggest problem we got in the long term is dealing with these entitlement programs that we can't pay for; that's Medicare and Social Security and Medicaid. If you're an older person, you're in good shape. If you're a younger person who is just working, you're in lousy shape. And I can't wait to work with Congress to solve the Social Security and Medicare issue.

One reason I ran for office is to solve problems and not pass them on to other Presidents and other Members of Congress.

It's time for the United States Congress to stop playing politics with Social Security and Medicare so a young generation of Americans can look at these entitlement programs and say, "I'm not putting my money into a black hole." And it's hard work.

It's hard work, but I'm confident we can get it done. I'm going to keep working it. That's what the people expect us to do. And I appreciate Congressman Ryan. He's not afraid to take on the tough issues—that's the kind of person you want in Washington, DC—and neither is Mark Green. You see, you've got to have somebody in the Governor's chair who sees a tough issue and says, "I'm going to take it on; that's why I ran." You've got too many people in politics who say, "Well, it might affect my poll numbers and therefore, I'm going to duck it." I just can't imagine people running for office and saying I'm going the duck the tough issue.

You've got to have you a Governor who is willing to stand up and make the tough calls. And Mark Green is that man. He also understands this. I used to tell people when I was the Governor of Texas that education is to a State what national defense is to the Federal Government. I really believe that a Governor has got to make education the number-one priority of the State. And Mark Green is going to do that.

I worked with him on passing the No Child Left Behind Act, and this is a powerful piece of legislation and necessary reform. Here's the way it works: It says, first of all, that we believe everybody can learn to read and write and add and subtract, and we refuse to accept a system that doesn't hold people to account if they're not learning to read and write and add and subtract. We said in Washington, DC, if you're going to receive Federal money, which States do, that we expect you, the State, to measure to determine whether we are achieving certain objectives.

There was a huge howl, of course, when you lay that kind of initiative out there.

People said, "How dare you measure." And my answer is, how dare we not measure. How can you expect the school system to be good unless you're willing to test to see whether or not children are learning to read and write and add and subtract. And guess what happens, by the way, in a school system that has no accountability? Guess who loses? Generally inner-city kids or parents who don't speak English as a first language.

See, it's easy to quit on those kinds of children. It's easy just to shuffle them through the grades: say, "When you're 10, you're supposed to be here; if you're 11, you're supposed to be in this grade." We blew the whistle on that kind of soft bigotry of low expectations. We said we were going to measure to determine whether or not the schools are succeeding. And if they're not succeeding, we're going to make sure a child gets extra help early, before it gets too late.

I know there's a big debate here about school choice, and there should be a debate. And it's an important debate. And my attitude is, when you find a child trapped in a school that will not teach and will not change, you have got to give parents other options.

In Mark Green you'll have a Governor who's willing to challenge the status quo in education, a Governor who's willing to insist upon high standards and excellence in the classroom, a Governor who will not rest if he finds children trapped in mediocrity. He understands that the future of a State depends upon the State's capacity to provide an excellent education for every child regardless of what he or she looks like. And that's the Governor Mark Green's going to be.

I bet the doctors in this State can't wait to get yourself a Governor who's willing to support medical liability reform. You can't have good health care; you cannot have affordable and available health care if you have a liability system that has run amok. And I know how tough these trial lawyers are in some of these States. I took them on in the State of Texas. And you need to have a Governor, for the sake of good medicine, for the sake of affordable medicine, for the sake of patients, and for the sake of needed professionals, to stand up to the trial bar and pass medical liability reform. And Mark Green is going to do that.

I think you can tell I'm quite enthusiastic about him. [*Laughter*] I do want to conclude by saying this about Mark: He and I understand that government is limited in its capacity to love. I mean government—you can pass laws, and you can hold people to account. And government is justice, as it should be. Government is fairness. But government can't put hope in a person's heart or a sense of purpose in a person's life. That happens when a loving person puts their arm around a lost soul and says, "I love you, brother," or, "I love you, sister. What can I do to help?"

I think the State of Wisconsin will benefit mightly from having a person as Governor who is willing to rally the faith-based community and community center groups to do their duty to help change Wisconsin one heart and one soul and one conscience at a time.

Our society should not fear the involvement of faith in helping to cure some of the intractable social ills. We ought to have leaders who welcome those who've heard the universal call to love a neighbor just like you'd like to be loved yourself, to make your State as good as it can possibly be. And that Governor is going to be Governor Mark Green. Thank you all for coming tonight. God bless.

NOTE: The President spoke at 5:51 p.m. at the Hilton Milwaukee City Center. In his remarks, he referred to Mary Buestrin, national committeewoman, Republican Party of Wisconsin; James R. Klauser, former secretary of the Wisconsin Department of Administration; former President Saddam Hussein and

Prime Minister Nuri al-Maliki of Iraq; and Prime Minister Junichiro Koizumi of Japan.

Statement on the Terrorist Attacks in Mumbai, India
July 11, 2006

On behalf of the American people, Laura and I send our deepest condolences to the friends and families of the victims of today's brutal attacks on commuter rail passengers in Mumbai. The United States stands with the people and the Government of India and condemns in the strongest terms these atrocities, which were committed against innocent people as they went about their daily lives. Such acts only strengthen the resolve of the international community to stand united against terrorism and to declare unequivocally that there is no justification for the vicious murder of innocent people.

Statement on Signing the Coast Guard and Maritime Transportation Act of 2006
July 11, 2006

I have today signed into law H.R. 889, the "Coast Guard and Maritime Transportation Act of 2006." The Act authorizes funding for and strengthens the ability of the United States Coast Guard to perform its missions.

The executive branch shall construe the reference to the "National Intelligence Director" in section 309 of the Act, amending section 70105(c) of title 46, United States Code, to be a reference to the position of Director of National Intelligence established by law (50 U.S.C. 403(a)(1)).

The executive branch shall construe section 408(c) of the Act, which purports to make consultation with a legislative agent a precondition to execution of the law, to call for but not mandate such consultation, as is consistent with the Constitution's provisions concerning the separate powers of the Congress to legislate and the President to execute the laws.

Section 801 of the Act purports to require the Secretary of the department in which the Coast Guard is operating to work at the International Maritime Organization with foreign nations toward specified international objectives. The executive branch shall construe the provision to be advisory, as is consistent with the constitutional commitment to the President of responsibility for conducting the foreign relations of the United States, including the exclusive responsibility for formulating the position of the United States in international fora and conducting negotiations with foreign nations.

GEORGE W. BUSH

The White House,

July 11, 2006.

NOTE: H.R. 889, approved July 11, was assigned Public Law No. 109–241.

Remarks at a Welcoming Ceremony in Stralsund, Germany
July 13, 2006

Chancellor Angela Merkel of Germany. Mr. President, Mrs. Bush, Minister President, Lord Mayor, ladies and gentlemen, citizens of Stralsund, let me say that I am delighted to be able to welcome you on behalf of the representatives of the land and also of the city. I'm delighted to welcome most warmly the President of the United States of America. Mr. President, a very, very warm welcome to you.

Mr. President, I'm delighted to be able to welcome you here in this part of our country that I can truly call my political home, the Hanseatic City of Stralsund. Stralsund was part of the League of Hanseatic Cities; that is to say, it is imbued with a spirit of openness to the rest of the world. And in 1989, it was also one of the many cities where, on Monday, demonstrations took place, where people went out into the streets to demand freedom, to demonstrate for freedom. And we're happy to say in these days it is part of the land of Mecklenburg-Vorpommern and also part of the Federal Republic of Germany.

And I think that this is a very good opportunity, indeed, to say a word of thanks. Thank you for the contribution, for the support that we have enjoyed throughout from the people of the United States of America, from the American Government, to help us along the way towards German unification. I think we owe you a big debt of gratitude for being able to finally live within one country in peace and freedom, one country, Germany.

I think one can safely say that ever since we were able to achieve German unity, a lot has happened and, indeed, Stralsund is a case in point. If you look at the fact that when the GDR finally collapsed, you had about 600 monuments here of historic importance in the city itself that were slowly decaying, that were slowly in ruins, and

part of them have been restored over time. But there are still quite a lot of problems that remain to be solved. One of them, obviously, is the fairly high unemployment in this particular part of the country. They urgently need economic progress, an economic upturn. And this is why I am also delighted to have you here, to show you here in my constituency what it means when people try to take their own fate, their own future into their own hands and try to turn it to something positive; they are willing to work for the future of the city, for the future of this region.

And I think it also clearly illustrates what we can do together in order to confront the international dangers, the threats at the international level that are common to us all, and that we can do in order to, together, work for peace and freedom for our two countries.

Yet again, a very, very warm welcome to you, Mr. President.

President Bush. Thank you all. Thank you, Chancellor Merkel. Thank you all for coming. Laura and I feel welcome here in Stralsund. To the mayor and Minister President and the people of this beautiful town, we say, *guten morgen.*

For decades, the German people were separated by an ugly wall. Here in the East, millions of you lived in darkness and tyranny. Today, your nation is whole again. The German people are at the center of Europe that is united and free and peaceful.

You've given Germany a fine Chancellor in Angela Merkel, who I'm proud to call friend. The American people and the German people see the same qualities of character in your nation's leader. We see a bold vision and a humble heart. We see that she's willing to make hard decisions and eager to build strong partnerships. And like many others in the international community, I respect her judgment and I value her opinion.

It's such an honor to be in her constituency. When I met with her in the Oval Office, she said, "When you come to Germany, you need to come to one of the best parts of Germany." She didn't predict the weather. [*Laughter*] But I want to thank the mayor for delivering such a beautiful day. And she forgot to tell me I was going to get some herring, and I thank you for that gift.

I bring a message from the American people: We're honored to call the German people friends and allies. We share common values and common interests. We want to work together to keep the peace.

We want to work together to promote freedom. There's so much that we can do, working together, and that's part of my visit today, is to pledge to you and the Chancellor, America and Germany stand side by side.

Thank you for your warm welcome. May God bless you all. Thank you very much.

NOTE: The President spoke at approximately 9:55 a.m. in Stralsund Market Square. In his remarks, he referred to Mayor Harald Lastovka of Stralsund, Germany; and Minister President Harald Ringstorff of the Federal State of Mecklenburg-Vorpommern, Germany. Chancellor Merkel spoke in German, and her remarks were translated by an interpreter.

The President's News Conference With Chancellor Angela Merkel of Germany in Stralsund
July 13, 2006

Chancellor Merkel. Ladies and gentlemen, I am delighted to be able to welcome the President of the United States here to Stralsund yet again. We had a lengthy conversation just now in the office of the mayor. We felt very much at home here in this beautiful city hall. We talked about all of the different issues on the global agenda.

We shall later on see a little bit more of the countryside here, of the city itself. I am really pleased to be able to show to the President of the United States how matters have developed here, with some problems still existing but also what sort of problems we've coped with quite successfully. And it's such a great thing to have this lovely weather for our visits.

Just now in our talks, we talked at great length about international issues. Unfortunately, there are quite a lot of problems that we need to deal with and for whose solution we feel responsible. The first and

foremost on top of the agenda is certainly Iran. The international community actually submitted a very substantial, very fundamental offer to Iran, starting from the firm view that Iran should not be in possession of a nuclear weapon, but that, on the other hand, Iran should have—should know good development. So far we have not received any sort of reaction from the Iranian leadership as to how their position is on this offer.

And this is why it was only consistent that yesterday the foreign ministers decided yet again to show clearly, also through a resolution in the U.N. Security Council, that should Iran not in any way reply to this offer and accept this offer, we unfortunately have to embark on a new course. The door has not been closed, but Iran must know that those who have submitted this offer are willing—and this is the success of yesterday's meeting—Russia, China, the E–3, and the United States of America, all of them together are willing to act in concert and to show this clearly through their action in the Security Council.

We also addressed the very disturbing situation in the Middle East, and it fills us with concern. And we have also stated clearly that everything needs to be done in order to come back to a peaceful resolution. We need to remind all of us again how this escalation started, with the kidnaping of a soldier, through rockets—for the firing of missiles against Israeli territory. And we can only urge all parties, appeal to all parties to stop, to cease violence, and to also release the kidnaped soldier and to stop this firing of missiles at Israeli territory.

We would like to appeal to the powers in the region to see to it that further escalation is warded off and that, first and foremost, the root causes of this conflict are removed. And only in this way will a negotiating process become possible again. We have every interest in seeing the Lebanese Government be strengthened and this Government being able to pursue its policies in a sensible and secure environment.

We also addressed matters of trade, global trade. Here we—and I'm saying this from a German perspective—have a common interest in seeing this world round be a successful one, this world trade round. But that means there has to be movement on all sides. And we're expecting a reasonable, sensible offer by the G–20, because this is where movement is necessary. Europe and others have submitted far-reaching proposals, and we would like to explore every possibility of these negotiations, but that means, as I said, movement on all sides. And here I see that the G–20 has to deliver.

We also addressed those issues that will be on the agenda at the G–8 in St. Petersburg. Here, first and foremost, energy policy, secure energy supply, was at the top of the agenda. We addressed African issues, Darfur and the Congo mission. We as Germans, as you know, have taken out a commitment as regards Congo. We also, however, see the situation in Darfur as a threatening one.

We found that there is a lot that we agree on, as regards our common responsibilities, responsibilities that we see for the two of us the world over. And I, for one, think that as regards, for example, Iran, this responsibility ought to be shouldered by more and more countries—that goes for Russia; that goes for China. It will only be if we act in concert that we will be able to vanquish the tyrants, remove dictatorships, and contain those who sponsor terrorism. And Germany would like to give its contribution to that.

President Bush. Chancellor, thank you very much. Thanks for the invitation. This is a beautiful part of the world, and Laura and I are so honored to come to your constituency and meet some of the friendly people who live here. I remember you coming to the Oval Office, and you said, "If you are coming to Germany, this is the part of Germany I want you to see." And now I can see why you suggested it. I'm looking forward to the feast you're going to have tonight. I understand I may have the honor of slicing the pig.

We had a good discussion—it's more than a discussion; it's really a strategy session, is the way I'd like to describe it. We talked about a lot of subjects. We talked about the Middle East and Iran, and I briefed the Chancellor on North Korea. We talked about Iraq and Afghanistan as well.

But when we talked about the issues, it's important for you to understand, we're really trying to figure out how to work together to solve problems. And I appreciate—appreciate the Chancellor's judgment a lot. It's an interesting conversation, you know, when you toss out what may seem to be a problem that's insoluble, and all of a sudden, two people start thinking about how to solve it, solve the problem. And that's what we're doing.

You know, on the Iranian issue, for example, the last time that we were together, we talked—spent a lot of time on Iran, and the Chancellor was wondering whether or not the United States would ever come to the table to negotiate with the Iranians. You made that pretty clear to me that you thought it was something—an option we ought to consider, which I did. And I made it clear to the Iranians that if they were to do what they said they would do, which is to stop enrichment in a verifiable fashion, we're more than pleased to come back to the table.

There's no question that this issue can be solved diplomatically, and there's no question that it can be solved diplomatically with Germany and the United States strategizing as how to solve it. And I want to thank the Chancellor's leadership on this issue. It's really important for Europe to speak with one common voice. And it's important for Angela and myself to work with Vladimir Putin, which we will do at the G–8, to continue to encourage him to join us in saying to the Iranians loud and clear, "We're not kidding; it's a serious issue. The world is united in insisting that you not have a nuclear weapons program."

We talked about the Israeli-Palestinian and the Israeli issues with Hizballah and our common desire to work together to help bring peace to that troubled region. My attitude is this: There are a group of terrorists who want to stop the advance of peace. And those of us who are peace-loving must work together to help the agents of peace—Israel, President Abbas, and others—to achieve their objective. You got to understand, when peace advances, it's in the terrorists' interests in some cases to stop it. And that's what's happening.

We were headed toward the roadmap; things looked positive. And terrorists stepped up and kidnaped a soldier, fired rockets into Israel. Now we've got two more kidnapings up north. Hizballah doesn't want there to be peace. The militant arm of Hamas doesn't want there to be peace. And those of us who do want peace will continue to work together to encourage peace.

We talked about North Korea. I assured the Chancellor that I'm committed to the six-party talks and that the five of us in the six-party talks will work to convince North Korea to come back to the table. I'm hopeful that we can get some U.N. action on North Korea.

We did talk about Doha, the trade round, and it's—look, these trade rounds are difficult to negotiate with. We've all got our own interests, but the good news is, we do share a common desire to open up markets. Germany is a great exporter. It's in Germany's interest that tariffs be reduced around the world. It's in our interests that tariffs be reduced around the world. And I committed to what I told the world back last September: We will reduce agricultural subsidies. But all we want is fair treatment when it comes to market access.

I'm optimistic we can still get something done on the Doha round. It's going to take work, but G–8 is a good place for us to continue the dialog, and we will.

And I guess that's about all—we discussed a lot of things, in other words. And thank you for having me. I'm looking forward to that pig tonight. [*Laughter*]

I'll be glad to answer a couple of questions. Do you want to start her off?

Iran

Q. Chancellor, you spoke about charting a new course as regards a response to the Iranian conflict. What new course will that be? You talked about the results of the foreign ministers' meeting where they will appeal to the Security Council. What sort of action will there be? Again, just a resolution that only demands certain things, or is the objective a resolution that will then actually threaten sanctions of a specific nature? This question is also addressed to the President.

Chancellor Merkel. Well, essentially what we're talking about here is not a totally new process; it's just another phase. We have waited patiently whether Iran will examine this offer and in which way it will react. So far we have not had any sort of reliable reaction. And for us, the precondition for talks has always been suspension of the enrichment activities, and a precondition for talks has always been, well, we will then, under the circumstances, not react with sanctions. But through this common action, we are now making clear, because we are not receiving a reply, that there will be a concerted action and that there will be specific steps. And we're defining what steps these will be if Iran continues to let us wait with its response.

So we wanted to demonstrate yet again that the international community is willing to show resolve to pursue this strategy further in every direction. Iran has received a proposal that I think is a very substantive one, a very good one, one that is good for the development of its own country, of its own interests—is in its own interests. But if Iran should not reply, if they think they can prevaricate in the hope of the international community being split, then this proves them wrong. And this is why I am so happy about the conclusion of that meeting of the foreign ministers.

President Bush. This notion that the Iranians must understand that they can't wait us out and can't hope to split a coalition—and so the first step is to go to the United Nations and speak with as common a voice as possible.

Your question really is, how fast should the process move along? And my attitude is, the answer to that is, it should move as fast as necessary to make it effective, which is a nonanswer, admittedly. But the truth of the matter is, diplomacy takes a lot of work, and there are different interests involved here. We do share a common goal of no nuclear weapon and no program. And by the way, we've already sanctioned Iran, so we've got a different position than others. It's easy for me to espouse sanctions, since it's already a *fait accompli*. But we

understand other nations have got—there's a pace to this diplomacy. And I assured the Chancellor that the United States will continue to work to make sure the process is steady as it moves forward.

The key first step is—common goal, which is no nuclear weapon or program—and united message to the Iranians. I truly think they're trying to wait us out. They think it's a matter of time before people lose their nerve or a matter of time before different interests are able to influence the process. And I think they're going to be sorely mistaken. I think they're going to be disappointed that this coalition is a lot firmer than they think.

It is in our interests to make sure they don't have a weapon. It would be dangerous if the Iranians had a nuclear weapon. And that's a recognizable fact now. So I appreciate the Chancellor's position on this.

Yes, Terry.

Russia

Q. Madam Chancellor, Mr. President—Terry Hunt with the AP [Associated Press]. Looking ahead to St. Petersburg, I'd like to ask you, do you think that Russia is honoring human rights and democratic freedoms and has a responsible approach to energy security?

And, Mr. President, were you surprised by President Putin replying to Vice President Cheney's criticism, saying that it was an "unsuccessful hunting shot?"

President Bush. Did I think it was a clever response? It was pretty clever. Actually, quite humorous—not to dis my friend the Vice President. I don't know, do you want to start with this? I'd be glad to—[*laughter*]. No, I think our job is to continually remind Russia that if she wants to do—have good relations, that she ought to share common values with us. We share common values; free press is a common value we share. And I've expressed my opinion to President Putin. You might remember my visit with him in Slovakia where I was quite pointed in my concerns about whether or not there is a free and vibrant press in Russia. We share concerns about the ability for people to go to the town square and express their opinions and whether or not dissent is tolerated, whether or not there's active political opposition.

And so I will continue to carry that message. My own view of dealing with President Putin, though, is that nobody really likes to be lectured a lot, and if you want to be an effective person, what you don't go is scold the person publicly all the time; that you remind him where we may have a difference of opinion, but you do so in a respectful way, so you can then sit down and have a constructive dialog.

And that's exactly how I'm going to continue my relations with President Putin. I'll be firm about my belief in certain democratic institutions; I'll be firm in my belief about the need for there to be an active civil society, and NGOs should be allowed to function in Russia without intimidation. But I'm also going to be respectful of the leader of an important country. And I may not tell you exactly what I talked to him about in private, and I would hope that he wouldn't tell you what he talks to me about in private.

But, yes, we've got issues. Listen, we've got common problems that we need to work together to solve—North Korea and Iran are two. And we've also got—I hope he continues to understand that it's in his country's interest to implement the values that Germany and Russia—Germany and the United States share.

Chancellor Merkel. Well, first, as to the issue of energy security, I can safely say that, looking at Germany over the past few decades, Russia has always proved to be a reliable supplier of energy. They have always abided by the treaties that we signed. But we would wish—and I've addressed this with the Russian President—that they actually bring the energy charter to its completion, that is to say, commit themselves to it, because then we would

have a greater degree of certainty and security that we understand our common commitments on this.

As regards—a strategic link between Russia and Europe obviously is of tremendous importance. It's important because we need energy supplies from Russia. And this is why we shall work towards Russia accepting that charter, that energy charter, so that we get a legitimate charter that is also based on contracts. But again, it has to be said that Russia has always been a reliable supplier.

As to democracy and human rights, during my visit to Russia, I met with a number of representatives of nongovernmental organizations. We discussed what is desirable, what ought to be there as regards Russia's further development, and what needs to be addressed, time and again. And let me tell you that I talked to the President about these issues.

I think also we ought to have an open, confidential dialog. We should not, sort of, speak loudly and in public about certain issues; that we have different ideas about how a pluralist society, a democratic society ought to work; that there ought to be a strong opposition is certainly one of the realities of life. There are differences of opinion between Russia and the European Union. We would wish for Russia to embark on a path that leads to a lively and very pluralistic political landscape, that they enter into a dialog with their civil society, which is at yet not there, for many reasons.

But we would like to share with them, also, the experience that we've made with democracy, that pluralism in a democracy, last but not least, actually enhances stability in a country. And that is an experience that we have made, and that is a very strong force which drives reform processes forward. For example, we've seen that in German unity. It's sometimes complicated to bring those decisionmaking processes forward in a democracy, but then you receive the necessary legitimacy. And that is the experience that informs us in our talks.

Situation in the Middle East

Q. A question addressed to you both. You talked about the Middle East, and what is your assessment of the military action of Israel in Lebanon? The French Foreign Minister already said it is disproportionate. Does that give you cause for Europe or the United States to intervene?

And apart from the pig, Mr. President, what sort of insights have you been able to gain as regards East Germany? [*Inaudible*]

Chancellor Merkel. Neither have I, but apparently a camera team was there when it was shot. So apparently it is already there, physically. [*Laughter*] I hope it's actually already roasting; otherwise, we won't be able to eat it tonight.

Well, as to the violence in the Middle East, particularly as regards Lebanon, I think that one needs to be very careful to make a clear distinction between the root causes and the consequences of something. So we started here from a case of kidnaping of a soldier, and one of the other root causes, also, is the activity of Hizballah. And it's most important for the Israeli Government to be strengthened, but it is also clearly shown that these incursions, such as the kidnaping of soldiers, is not acceptable.

And the parties to that conflict obviously have to use proportionate means, but I am not at all for, sort of, blurring the lines between the root causes and the consequences of an action. There has to be a good reaction now, not from the Israeli Government but from those who started these attacks in the first place.

President Bush. ——to help calm the situation, we've got diplomats in the region. Secretary of State Rice, who is here, is on the phone talking to her counterparts. I'll be making calls.

I gave you my initial impression earlier, and that is that it's a sad situation where—when there is a very good chance for there to be a two-state solution enacted—that is,

two states living side by side in peace—it's really sad where people are willing to take innocent life in order to stop that progress. As a matter of fact, it's pathetic.

And having said that, Israel has a right to defend herself. Every nation must defend herself against terrorist attacks and the killing of innocent life. It's a necessary part of the 21st century.

Secondly, we—whatever Israel does, though, should not weaken the Siniora Government in Lebanon. We're concerned about the fragile democracy in Lebanon. We've been working very hard through the United Nations and with partners to strengthen the democracy in Lebanon. The Lebanese people have democratic aspirations, which is being undermined by the actions and activities of Hizballah.

Thirdly, Syria needs to be held to account. Syria is housing the militant wing of Hamas. Hizballah has got an active presence in Syria. The truth of the matter is, if we really want there to be—the situation to settle down, the soldiers need to be returned, and President Asad needs to show some leadership toward peace.

To answer your question about involvement, we will be involved diplomatically and are involved diplomatically.

Steve [Steve Holland, Reuters].

Iran

Q. Thank you, sir. Just to follow up——

President Bush. Follow up on?

Q. On both of these. Does it concern you that the Beirut Airport has been bombed? And do you see a risk of triggering a wider war?

And on Iran, they've so far refused to respond. Is it now past the deadline, or do they still have more time to respond?

President Bush. I thought you were going to ask me about the pig.

Q. I'm curious about that too. [*Laughter*]

President Bush. The pig? I'll tell you tomorrow after I eat it.

The Iranian issue is—will be taken to the U.N. Security Council. We said that we have—to the Iranians, we said, "Here's your chance to move forward, and we'd like a response in a reasonable period of time." And we meant what we said. One of the important things about moving toward the Security Council, it shows that when we say something, we mean it. In order for—to help solve these problems, you just can't say things and not mean it. And so when we spoke, we said, reasonable period of time—weeks, not months—that's what we explained to the Iranians. They evidently didn't believe us. And so now we're going to go to the Security Council, and we're united in doing that.

Q. Their deadline has passed——

President Bush. Their deadline passed, right. That's why we're going to the U.N. Security Council.

Q. ——have time?

President Bush. Oh, they've got plenty of time. I mean, the U.N. Security Council—they've got time to react. They've got time to make a decision. By the way, it's their choice. We've made our choice. It's the Iranian choice. And as Angela mentioned, there was an offer put on the table, a reasonable offer, for them to make the choice as to the way forward.

And our choice is, look, we want to have relations with you, but you're not going to have a weapon or the capacity to make a weapon. It would be incredibly dangerous if we—5 years from now, Iran shows up with a nuclear weapon and threatens people in the neighborhood, and they're going to say, "Where were you? What were you doing during that period of time?" And that's what we're working on.

And so time—when we said, weeks, not months, we meant it. And now we're heading to the U.N. Security Council. They can show up any time and say, "Wait a minute. Now we'd like to go back and negotiate, now—take a look at the interests." We're not precluding any further negotiations with the Iranians.

In order for us to come to the table, however, what they must do is verifiably show that they're not enriching, like they said they would do earlier. This is not a—this is not a new statement by them. They agreed to this in Paris. All we're asking them to do is to honor what they said they would do in the past in a verifiable fashion.

The rest of your four-part question?

Situation in the Middle East

Q. Sorry about that, sir.

President Bush. That's okay. It just—it's a bad habit.

Q. Does the Beirut—the attack on the Beirut Airport, does that concern you, and are you concerned about triggering a wider Middle East war?

President Bush. As I mentioned, my biggest concern is whether or not actions taken will weaken the Siniora Government. Democracy in Lebanon is an important part of laying a foundation for peace in that region. We have worked really hard to get Syria out of Lebanon—U.N. Resolution 1559 and its followup, Resolution 1680, were manifestations of the work of the international community to get Syria out of Lebanon. We've always felt that a democracy in Lebanon is important for the Lebanese people, and it's important for the region.

So the concern is that any activities by Israel to protect herself will weaken that Government. And we have made that—or topple that Government—and we've made it clear in our discussions.

Having said all that, people need to protect themselves. There are terrorists who will blow up innocent people in order to achieve tactical objectives. In this case, the objective is to stop the advance of peace—which is a remarkable statement, isn't it—willing to kill to stop peace.

We have a good chance to get a two-state solution, two democracies living side by side in peace. It is a clear and achievable vision. There is a way forward called the roadmap to achieve that vision. What will prevent that vision from being achieved is—are terrorist activities, and that's what you're seeing taking place.

Thank you all.

Chancellor Merkel. Thank you.

NOTE: The President's news conference began at 12:34 p.m. in the Town Hall. In his remarks, he referred to President Vladimir V. Putin of Russia; President Mahmoud Abbas of the Palestinian Authority; Gilad Shalit, an Israeli soldier captured and held captive by militants in Gaza since June 25; Prime Minister Fuad Siniora of Lebanon; Ehud Goldwasser and Eldad Regev, Israeli soldiers captured and held captive by militants in Lebanon since July 12; and President Bashar al-Asad of Syria. A reporter referred to Minister of Foreign Affairs Philippe Douste-Blazy of France. Chancellor Merkel spoke in German, and her remarks were translated by an interpreter.

Remarks in a Discussion With Civic Leaders in St. Petersburg, Russia
July 14, 2006

Ambassador, thank you for setting up this meeting. I've just had a really interesting meeting. I've been meeting with young, vibrant Russian activists who, first, love their country; secondly, care deeply about the form of government of the country; and third, care deeply about the human condition in their country.

These folks come from a variety of different NGOs and civic groups, representing a variety of issues, all bound together to be involved in their governments, in their countries, so that it's the best it can possibly be.

I spent a lot of time listening to their concerns. I assured them that the United States of America cares about the form of government in Russia, that we believe in the universal values embedded in democracy. We believe in rule of law; we believe in human rights; we believe everybody has a right to be treated equally.

I explained to them that our own Government and our country took a while to evolve, but nevertheless, it's important to be aiming toward a better tomorrow.

I hope my visit here was encouraging to them; it certainly was instructional for me. I explained to them my strategy of dealing with Vladimir Putin, who is my friend. Some asked me to deliver messages, which I'd be more than happy to do. I explained to them that it's in the U.S. interests to remain engaged with Russia—Russia is a great country with a fantastic future— and that the foreign policy of my administration will be to work with Russia to solve common problems and, at the same time, be in a position where we can have a frank exchange of ideas and philosophies and views.

I told the young leaders here that this has been a very enriching experience for me. I shared the thought—shared the idea that I'm the father of 24-year-old twin daughters. I'm looking at some folks here at the table who are their age; I'm impressed by their courage and their idealism and their desire to make their societies a better place.

So I want to thank you all for your visit. Thank you for your frank exchanges. I will you all the very best, and I ask for God's blessings on the people of Russia.

NOTE: The President spoke at 4:06 p.m. at the Counsel General's residence. In his remarks, he referred to U.S. Ambassador to Russia William J. Burns; and President Vladimir V. Putin of Russia. A tape was not available for verification of the content of these remarks.

Statement Honoring Former President Gerald Ford's Birthday
July 14, 2006

President Gerald Ford's story is a true American story. It is the tale of a son of the Midwest who achieved great things through hard work, dedication, courage, and humility. President Ford played football at Michigan, received a law degree from Yale, served in the Navy during World War II, and for decades he represented western Michigan as a Republican Congressman from Grand Rapids.

Then came his appointment with history. He assumed the Presidency at a perilous moment for our country. A President had resigned; the United States was involved in a cold war; the economy was sputtering; and America's confidence was deeply shaken.

Few leaders have ever faced such challenges upon taking office. Yet President Ford met them with steadfastness and courage. His leadership helped heal a wounded nation.

Since leaving office, President Ford has set a high standard for grace and character. He has never forgotten his roots or lost sight of the things that matter, including his deep love for his wife and partner, Betty.

Laura and I join all Americans in wishing President Ford a happy birthday.

The President's News Conference With President Vladimir V. Putin of Russia in Strelna, Russia
July 15, 2006

President Putin. Dear ladies and gentlemen, I have just completed my meeting with the President of the United States. The Russian party is satisfied with the results of this meeting. The meeting has reaffirmed that Russia and the United States remain reliable and mutually interested partners. We have been able to reach a whole range of agreements on key issues on the bilateral and international agenda.

We have adopted a joint statement, the basis of which are our parallel initiatives on the secure development of nuclear energy. Its main goal is to contribute to the sustainability and reliability of the supply of this type of energy resource and the parallel reduction of the threat of the spread of nuclear weapons. We believe that this will be possible in the case of the creation of a system of international enrichment centers integrated into a single network and, of course, under strict control on the part of the IAEA.

It is equally important to pay a close attention to the development of innovative technology in the creation of new-generation reactors. The most productive way to go is to carry out this work on the basis of broad international cooperation. Such an approach will have a positive and stabilizing effect on the progress of international political and economic processes.

We have also supported the United States proposal on the Global Nuclear Energy Partnership. The Russian initiative on the creation of multilateral centers for the provision of nuclear fuel cycle services and the idea of a global partnership in this area complement each other very well, and we'll jointly work towards integrating these two initiatives. In order to achieve this, we'll have to resolve problems that have to do with the terms of trade in nuclear materials between Russia and the United States.

In addition to that, we have come up with a joint statement on fighting acts of nuclear terrorism. It reaffirms the shared desire of Russia and the United States to counter this dangerous threat and opens new horizons for our joint efforts. Our countries are demonstrating their commitment to taking the most serious measures to counter the acquisition, transport, or use of nuclear and radioactive materials by terrorists, as well as improvised explosive devices based on such materials. It is equally important to rule out any hostile actions against nuclear facilities. We hope that this initiative will draw the due attention of other participants in the G–8 and will deliver concrete results.

We have had a productive discussion of the entire range of international issues. Those include Iran's nuclear program, the situation in the Middle East, on the Korean Peninsula, and in other regions of the world.

We also discussed the settlement of persistent conflicts in regions that are Russia's neighbors. Both sides have expressed and reaffirmed their commitment to resolving all these problems through peaceful political and diplomatic means. We intend to step up our efforts in the spirit of solidarity to counter new threats and challenges. A good example is our joint initiative to hold in spring 2007 in Vienna a political conference on the partnership of governments, civil society, and business in counterterrorism.

On the whole, we hope that our joint proposals and agreements will lay a good groundwork for a successful G–8 summit. They will set the right constructive tone for the proceedings of a credible international forum.

We have also discussed bilateral cooperation in the light of the parallel instructions to the government agencies and departments of the two countries to step up our interaction. We have registered success in the achievement of our goals in all areas: economy, security, science and outer space, people-to-people contacts. Some of the instructions have already been fulfilled; others are still being carried out. New goals have been agreed upon that will be addressed in nearest future. Those include the peaceful use of nuclear energy, fighting money laundering, fighting avian influenza, and cultural cooperation.

We have not limited ourselves to the discussion of the current problems; quite the contrary. We have tried to glance at the Russian-U.S. relationship from the perspective of the future and in the broad context of the development of the system of international relations as a whole.

I would like to thank our American partners for a friendly and constructive atmosphere in which our meeting has taken place. Thank you for your attention.

President Bush. We did have a very good discussion today. It was started—actually, our discussion started last night over a really good dinner. And I want to thank you and Mrs. Putina for being such wonderful hosts.

You've got to admit this is a fantastic setting. It's beautiful. The cottages are very comfortable. I think that our fellow G–8 leaders are going to really enjoy being here.

Anyway, we had a good discussion this morning. One thing is clear, is relations between America and Russia are good, and they're important that they be good. We've got a lot to—we've got a lot to work on. We discussed North Korea and Iran. Those are two difficult issues, made less difficult because Russia and the United States are willing to work together to send clear messages to both governments that their nuclear weapons ambitions are not acceptable.

We talked about the Middle East. I explained my position, which I'm confident I'll be asked about here in a minute. The President talked about his concerns. We share the same concerns. We are concerned about the violence, and we're troubled by the loss of innocent life. President

Putin, like me, wants there to be peaceful dialog. And so we had a good, frank discussion about the issue.

We talked about our bilateral relations. I think it's indicative of the strength of our relationship that we're able to agree on nonproliferation matters. Not only agree on it, we're taking the lead on this issue. And I want to thank the President for his leadership on this issue.

We're talking about nuclear cooperation, and we're about to begin dialogs about how we can cooperate better when it comes to peaceful uses of nuclear power. We're talking about counterterrorism. Nation-states face the threat of terrorism, and we want to work together to deal with this threat.

I, of course—we talked philosophy. One thing, what happens when you get relaxed and are friendly with each other, you're able to share philosophies and able to ask questions about decisionmaking. And I appreciated very much our discussion last night and this morning about why the President has made decisions he's made, what decisions he intends to make, and the decisions I made. We don't always agree with each other, but nevertheless, it's important for leaders to be able to share philosophy, whether it be the philosophy of government or the philosophy of governing.

And our relationship is good. And I want to thank the President for his hospitality. I thank you for your good food, thank you for the 60th birthday gift you gave me last night, and thanks for the meeting this morning.

President Putin. Ladies and gentlemen, please ask your questions. There will be three questions on each side. We'll start with the Russian journalists.

Russia-U.S. Relations

Q. Thank you. Good afternoon. My question is to both leaders. Question one is to President Bush. Russia, at the negotiations with its international partners, has demonstrated openness and transparency in its economy but does not always receive an adequate response. We can see this at the talks on the accession of Russia to the WTO. Since 2001, the United States has been supportive of Russia's accession to the WTO, but why are you the key impediment for the completion of this process? I'm sure that you've discussed this issue at the negotiations.

And my question to Mr. Putin: Given such difficulties, can we afford to give up a proactive position with respect to the accession to the WTO? Thank you.

President Bush. We're tough negotiators. But—and the reason why is because we want the agreement that we reach to be accepted by our United States Congress. In other words, when we negotiate an agreement, it has to be approved—any trade agreement has to be approved. But I believe we're fair negotiators, and our negotiators come to the table trying to achieve the objective that I've sent out, that we want Russian accession into WTO. That's what we want. And we will continue negotiating.

Evidently, there was a false report in the press that said a deal was reached. Well, it's almost reached. In other words, we— a lot of the areas, we found accommodation in a lot of the areas. But there's more work to be done. And we discussed this today, and I assured the President that we'll continue to negotiate. And he assured me that we'll continue to negotiate in good faith to try to reach an agreement that has been difficult to achieve. I understand that.

But you've just got to understand the intention to achieve an agreement is there.

President Putin. I and my guest, my friend, the President of the United States, George W. Bush, are often asked the question, "Does our personal relationship help in progressing—in addressing this question, in resolving various international issues?" I know that he believes so, that this informal personal relationship is helping us in our work. I have to tell you that, at the same time, it does not hamper us in standing up for our national interests in this or that area.

The WTO accession talks are very concrete, calculable in their nature, which can be expressed in terms of millions of dollars or rubles. This is a complicated process that has lasted for quite a while, for quite a few years. This difficulty is not a surprise to us. We will continue to work further, pursuing our interest, the interest of our developing economy.

Situation in the Middle East

Q. The violence in the Middle East is escalating despite calls for restraint. What can you, President Bush and President Putin, do to stop the violence, stop the fighting, given that there is divisions among allies here about whether Israel is using excessive force?

President Bush. I think you'll find all parties here want the violence to stop. In my judgment, the best way to stop the violence is to understand why the violence occurred in the first place. And that's because Hizballah has been launching rocket attacks out of Lebanon into Israel and because Hizballah captured two Israeli soldiers. That's why we have violence.

And the best way to stop the violence is for Hizballah to lay down its arms and to stop attacking. And therefore, I call upon Syria to exert influence over Hizballah.

Now, here's my concern, is that we were making good progress toward a two-state solution in the Middle East. The Israeli Prime Minister came to Washington and talked to me about his desire for there to be a democracy living side by side with another democracy, said this was part of his strategic vision for Israel and for peace.

And he was working toward that end. As you know, he made efforts to reach out to President Abbas, who we support. He made efforts to reach out to countries in the neighborhood to help achieve this vision. And as the vision was progressing, certain elements—certain terrorist elements began to act to stop the advance of democ-

racy. The militant wing of Hamas made decisions to attack and to capture. Hizballah has made decisions to stop the advance of a two-state solution.

The solution—short-term solution is for Hizballah to stop the attacks. The longer-term solution is for nations around the world and nations in the neighborhood to support those who support the advance of democracy.

President Putin. I agree with the premise that it is absolutely unacceptable to try and reach this or that goal, including political goals, through the use of force, through abductions, through carrying out strikes against an independent state from the territory of another state. This is all true. And in this context, we consider Israel's concerns to be justified.

At the same time, we work under the assumption that the use of force should be balanced. And in any case, bloodshed should stop as soon as possible. This should be the point of departure for the efforts to create an enabling environment for the resolution of the entire set of problems. Escalation of violence, in our opinion, will not yield positive results.

At any rate, we share the approach with President Bush. We will take every necessary effort on both sides, and I hope that our G–8 colleagues will support us. We will find common ground on this front in order to bring the situation, as soon as possible, to a position where concrete results could be achieved, not only in terms of the cessation of combat but also in terms of building an enabling environment for the development of Israel within secure borders, in the context of security, as well as in terms of the building of the independent Palestine state.

Russia-U.S. Relations/Nuclear Proliferation

Q. Mr. President, let me address my question to both of you. There has been a lot of concerns about proliferation of weapons of mass destruction and missile delivery. Have you discussed this issue? If yes, could you share the results of your talks? And also, if you could let me, we all can see that you enjoy good personal relationships, but do you notice any deterioration of ties on a state level between the two countries? Thank you.

President Bush. What was the first part of the question?

Q. Have you discussed proliferation of weapons of mass destruction and missile delivery, and what are the results of your talks?

President Bush. We sure have. We talked about our concerns about Iran developing a nuclear weapon or Iran having the capacity to make a nuclear weapon, and we talked about North Korea. And the results of our talks are that we agree that we've got to work together to send a common message to both that there is a better way forward for these leaders.

And so we're working with Russia and our partners to develop Security Council resolutions that will send a clear message. One thing is for certain, that if the Iranians see that the United States and Russia are working together on this issue, they'll understand the seriousness of our intent.

And so we spent time talking about the issue—sure did. We understand that a grave threat that faces countries like America and Russia would be—is the ability of a terrorist organization to end up with a weapon of mass destruction. Both nations have had to deal with terrorism; both nations know what it's like to see people blown up. Russia suffered through one of the most horrible terrorist incidents in modern mankind, which is Beslan, where terrorists are willing to kill young children to achieve political objectives. And the President and I understand that when you make that kind of attitude with a weapon of mass destruction, you could be talking about greater catastrophe. And so we spent a lot of time talking about it.

I think relations between the United States and Russia are very good. There's a lot of skeptics on both sides of the equa-

tion as to whether or not the relationship is good. We've got people in Russia questioning U.S. motives, people in America questioning Russian motives. But that's what happens when you have—when you're big nations that have got influence, where you've got leaders willing to make tough decisions. And I would characterize, from my perspective, that our relationship is strong and necessary. That's the point I want to make to you, that a strong relationship will make the world a better place, in my judgment, because we'll be better able to confront the current problems that face us all.

President Putin. I have already mentioned that we will not participate in any crusades, in any holy alliances. This is true. I reaffirm our position in this matter. But our common goal is to make the world a more secure place, and certainly we'll be working with all our partners, including the United States, in order to address this problem. It is for this reason that we are joining our efforts with other G–8 countries.

And I have to say that this is not some kind of plot against a particular country, where a certain problem emerges, be it missile or nuclear proliferation. We are seeking not only for the possibility of controlling this or that process; we are seeking opportunities for ensuring their legal access to nuclear technology. It is to this end that we have adopted our joint initiative on the creation of international centers for uranium enrichment and reprocessing of spent nuclear fuel. These are not unilateral actions aimed at trying to block somebody's access to something. This is a search for solutions that could ensure development in the world, at the same time would make the development secure in terms of nuclear nonproliferation and missile nonproliferation.

We're satisfied with the level of exchanges at the working level, which we have achieved in terms of bilateral cooperation. At the summit's end, in the context of the U.N. Security Council, we will continue our work tonight and tomorrow in the course of our discussion with our partners who are arriving in St. Petersburg.

Iran

Q. Mr. President, we know that you talked about Iran and North Korea. Let me ask you if you moved forward at all on these issues? Did you ask Russia to take specific steps, for example with Iran, to agree to U.N. sanctions? Did you discuss what you could move on—in North Korea to move it forward?

And, President Putin, is Russia now willing, if necessary, to vote for sanctions in the United Nations to stop Iran's nuclear preparations?

President Bush. We strategized on both issues. But this isn't the first time that we've talked together to—on how to solve problems. You might remember that Russia proposed a very interesting way forward for Iran. It was the Putin Government that said to the Iranians, "If you want a civilian nuclear power program, we will support you in that; however, we will provide the fuel, and we'll collect the spent fuel." I thought it was a very innovative approach to solving the problem. I strongly supported the initiatives.

So, Bill [Bill Plante, CBS News], to answer your question, this isn't the first time that we have strategized on how to solve this problem. And, yes, we talked about the U.N. Security Council resolution. And, no, I'm not going to tell you the particulars about the conversation. I will tell you, however, that there is common agreement that we need to get something done at the U.N., and I'm confident we will be able to do that. And there's agreement that we need to get something done on North Korea at the United Nations.

Here's the thing, though, just so that everybody understands: Diplomacy is not two countries just saying, this is the way it is. Diplomacy is two countries agreeing to work together with other countries, in this case, to come up with common language that we can live with that sends the same message, and that is, no nuclear weapons programs.

Our goal and objective is to have a nuclear-free—nuclear weapons-free Korean Peninsula. Russia shares that objective, China shares the objective, Japan shares the objective, and South Korea shares the objective. So we've got common ground to move forward, and now we're working on language. And it was a very constructive meeting.

President Putin. You know, I have spoken on this count for many times. I can repeat, it is not in Russia's national interest to see a proliferation of weapons of mass destruction, including nuclear weapons, especially in such an explosive region as the Middle East.

This is something that we tell our Iranian partners directly. We have always told them about it. There is nothing novel or new about our position in this respect. But we work on the assumption that we have to find efficient ways of ensuring security around the world. We need to take efficient diplomatic steps that would not disrupt the gentle fabric of the negotiations in the search for mutually acceptable decisions. And we're satisfied with the status of the U.S.-Russia relationship in this area.

Q. I apologize, but I would like to follow up on the question of my U.S. colleague. Could you speak at greater detail? You have discussed the Iranian nuclear issue in terms of what has happened before and what may happen in the future. There is now the situation with the Iranian nuclear issue. How do you see it as of now? And most importantly, what are we to expect in the future?

President Bush. ——progress, because Russia and the United States agree that Iran should not have a nuclear weapon. In other words, the Iranians need to understand that we're speaking with one voice that they shouldn't have a weapon, and that's progress.

You see, my judgment is they're testing the resolve of the parties to determine whether or not we really are resolved to work together to prevent them from having a weapon. And the clearer they hear a message, the better off—or the closer we'll be to them recognizing there's a better way forward. See, we've made our choice, and that's progress. We've agreed to work together to achieve a common goal. That's considerable progress.

And now the choice is theirs to make. I have said the United States will change our posture on this issue if the Iranian Government does what they've already said they would do, which is to verifiably suspend their enrichment program, at which point, if they do so, we will come to the negotiating table. We will sit side by side.

Right now we're negotiating together to send a common message. We will come to the table. It's their choice to make, however. There is a better way forward for the Iranian people than to be isolated because of their Government's actions. And so I would say that we've made good progress on the issue.

President Putin. I can see that members of the Russian and U.S. press have colluded and are tormenting us with the same kind of questions. [*Laughter*]

President Bush. An old colluder, but a colluder.

Q. [*Inaudible*]

President Bush. That's right. [*Laughter*]

President Putin. I would like to add to what has been said by George, that Russia has agreed to participate in the six-way format for the discussion of the Iranian issue. We assume that in the course of the elaboration of the position of the six countries, the opinion of Russia will be taken into account, and we can see that our partners are acting along these lines, precisely.

What does this imply for us? This implies that if we elaborate common approaches to this difficult problem, we will see to it that our joint decisions are fulfilled. This is what we said honestly and directly to

our Iranian partners. I said it at the meeting with the President of the Islamic Republic of Iran in China quite recently.

True, it is extremely important to adhere to an approach within which the countries that are involved in the negotiations would be able to elaborate a shared approach to the resolution of the problem, but the approach has to be balanced and has to take into account the interests of the Iranian people in their desire to develop state-of-the-art, high-tech industries, including nuclear ones. This has to be done under the obligatory requirement that nonproliferation is ensured and the overall security situation around the world is improved.

Democracy in Russia

Q. President Bush, you said that you planned to raise, in a respectful way, your concerns about Russian democracy with President Putin. How did that conversation go? And I know you've already talked a lot about the U.S.-Russian relationship, but I'm wondering if both of you could elaborate on that and how the differences of opinion over the democracy issue are affecting the relationship.

President Bush. I thought the discussion was a good discussion. It's not the first time that Vladimir and I discussed our governing philosophies. I have shared with him my desires for our country, and he shared with me his desires for his. And I talked about my desire to promote institutional change in parts of the world like Iraq where there's a free press and free religion, and I told him that a lot of people in our country would hope that Russia would do the same thing.

I fully understand, however, that there will be a Russian-style democracy. I don't expect Russia to look like the United States. As Vladimir pointedly reminded me last night, we have a different history, different traditions. And I will let him describe to you his way forward, but he shared with me some very interesting thoughts that I think would surprise some of our citizens.

Now that I've lured you into the deal here, you know—like, for example, how do you promote land reform? So we discussed land reform. You know, one of the interesting decisions a government has to make, particularly this Government would have to make, is how do you encourage private ownership of land further than that which has already happened?

Anyway, he shared some thoughts with me. Sorry to put—lay the trap out there for you—but it was a good discussion. He's a strong man. Look, he's willing to listen, but he also explains to me, he doesn't want anybody telling him how to run his Government. He was elected. And so it was a cordial relationship. But he can speak for himself.

President Putin. We certainly would not want to have the same kind of democracy as they have in Iraq, I will tell you quite honestly. [*Laughter*]

President Bush. Just wait.

President Putin. But it is true that we have discussed this issue at length, on the initiative of the President of the United States and on my own initiative as well. It is true that we assume that nobody knows better than us how we can strengthen our own nation. But we know for sure that we cannot strengthen our nation without developing democratic institutions, and this is the path that we will certainly take. But certainly, we will do this by ourselves.

At the same time, as far as the forum and context in which we discussed this last night and earlier today, we believe that this is not only acceptable to us to have such discussions with our partners, but I personally believe that this is quite useful as well, because when we do this in a nonbiased manner, in a friendly manner, in an objective manner, when we recognize that the existence of problems in this part of the world, when we recognize that problems with democracy are universal in their nature—these are not specifically Russian problems, the problems of building democracy are universal—and when we honestly and openly discuss this, as was the case last night, as was the case earlier today, this will always be useful.

Thank you for your attention. Have a nice day.

NOTE: The President's news conference began at 12:29 p.m. at the International Media Center. In his remarks, President Bush referred to Lyudmila Putina, wife of President Putin; Ehud Goldwasser and Eldad Regev, Israeli soldiers captured and held captive by militants in Lebanon since July 12; Prime Minister Ehud Olmert of Israel; and President Mahmoud Abbas of the Palestinian Authority. President Putin referred to President Mahmud Ahmadi-nejad of Iran. President Putin spoke in Russian, and his remarks were translated by an interpreter.

Joint Statement by President George W. Bush and President Vladimir V. Putin of Russia Announcing the Global Initiative To Combat Nuclear Terrorism
July 15, 2006

The United States of America and Russia are committed to combating the threat of nuclear terrorism, which is one of the most dangerous international security challenges we face.

Today we announce our decision to launch the Global Initiative to Combat Nuclear Terrorism. Building on our earlier work, the Global Initiative reflects our intention to pursue the necessary steps with all those who share our views to prevent the acquisition, transport, or use by terrorists of nuclear materials and radioactive substances or improvised explosive devices using such materials, as well as hostile actions against nuclear facilities. These objectives are reflected in the International Convention for the Suppression of Acts of Nuclear Terrorism, the Convention on the Physical Protection of Nuclear Material and Nuclear Facilities as amended in 2005, the Protocol to the Convention for the Suppression of Unlawful Acts Against the Safety of Maritime Navigation, and other international legal frameworks relevant to combating nuclear terrorism.

The United States and Russia call upon like-minded nations to expand and accelerate efforts that develop partnership capacity to combat nuclear terrorism on a determined and systematic basis. Together with other participating countries and interacting closely with the International Atomic Energy Agency (IAEA), we will take steps to improve participants' capabilities to: ensure accounting, control, and physical protection of nuclear material and radioactive substances, as well as security of nuclear facilities; detect and suppress illicit trafficking or other illicit activities involving such materials, especially measures to prevent their acquisition and use by terrorists; respond to and mitigate the consequences of acts of nuclear terrorism; ensure cooperation in the development of technical means to combat nuclear terrorism; ensure that law enforcement takes all possible measures to deny safe haven to terrorists seeking to acquire or use nuclear materials; and strengthen our respective national legal frameworks to ensure the effective prosecution of, and the certainty of punishment for, terrorists and those who facilitate such acts.

We stress that consolidated efforts and cooperation to combat the threat of nuclear terrorism will be carried out in accordance with international law and national legislation. This Global Initiative builds on the International Convention for the Suppression of Acts of Nuclear Terrorism, which Russia and the United States were the first to sign on September 14, 2005. This unique international treaty provides for broad areas of cooperation between states for the purpose of detecting, preventing, suppressing, and investigating acts of nuclear terrorism.

One of our priority objectives remains full implementation by all countries of the provisions of UNSCR 1540, which was adopted in 2004 as a result of joint efforts by the United States and Russia. This resolution is an important non-proliferation instrument aimed at preventing weapons of mass destruction (WMD) from entering "black market" networks and, above all, keeping WMD and related material from falling into the hands of terrorists. The full implementation by all countries of UNSCR 1373, including the sharing of information pertaining to the suppression of acts of nuclear terrorism and their facilitation, also remains a priority.

We note the importance of IAEA activities in implementing the Convention on the Physical Protection of Nuclear Material and Facilities, as amended and its Plan entitled "Physical Nuclear Security—Measures to Protect Against Nuclear Terrorism," and we reaffirm our willingness to continue supporting and working with the IAEA in this area to enhance the effectiveness of national systems for accounting, control, physical protection of nuclear materials and radioactive substances, and the security of civilian nuclear facilities, and, where necessary, to establish such systems.

We trust that, through their participation in this new Global Initiative to Combat Nuclear Terrorism, all countries that share our common goals of suppressing and mitigating the consequences of acts of nuclear terrorism will—on a voluntary basis and on the basis of independent responsibility of each country for the steps taken within its jurisdiction—reinforce the joint efforts to increase international cooperation in combating this threat.

The United States and the Russian Federation reaffirm that issues related to safeguarding nuclear weapons and other nuclear facilities, installations and materials used for military purposes remain strictly the national prerogative of the nuclear weapons state parties to the Non-Proliferation of Nuclear Weapons Treaty (NPT), for which they bear special responsibility. The Joint Statement on Nuclear Security, which we adopted in Bratislava, noted that while the security of nuclear facilities in the United States and Russian Federation meets current requirements, these requirements must be constantly enhanced to counter evolving terrorist threats. We trust that the other nuclear weapon state parties to the NPT will also ensure a proper level of protection for their nuclear facilities,

while taking into account the constantly changing nature of the terrorist threat.

As part of this initiative, we intend to work with countries possessing sensitive nuclear technologies to reaffirm their commitment to take all necessary measures to ensure proper protection and safeguarding of nuclear facilities and relevant materials in their territory.

We will be prepared to work with all those who share our views to strengthen mechanisms for multilateral and bilateral cooperation to suppress acts of nuclear terrorism, with a view to practical implementation of the measures provided for in the International Convention for the Suppression of Acts of Nuclear Terrorism as well as in other relevant international legal frameworks.

NOTE: An original was not available for verification of the content of this joint statement.

The President's Radio Address
July 15, 2006

Good morning. This weekend, I am in Russia meeting with other world leaders at the G–8 summit. This annual summit gives us a chance to talk about key issues facing all our nations, such as energy security and the threat of infectious diseases like avian flu.

At this year's summit, we will also discuss how to promote the spread of freedom and democracy and how our countries can work together to expand trade and prosperity for all our citizens.

As the world's economic powers gather for the G–8, the American economy remains the envy of the world. And this week, we received even more positive news about our economy. On Tuesday, my administration's Office of Management and

Budget released its annual update on the budget outlook. This year's report is very encouraging. Because our economy continues to enjoy strong growth, Federal tax revenues are growing, and we are cutting the Federal deficit faster than expected.

This good news is no accident. It is the result of the hard work of the American people and progrowth economic policies in Washington, DC. Since 2001, we have cut taxes for everyone who pays income taxes, reduced the marriage penalty, doubled the child tax credit, and put the death tax on the road to extinction. We cut tax rates paid by most small businesses and further encouraged expansion by cutting taxes on dividends and capital gains.

Together, these tax cuts have left nearly $1.1 trillion in the hands of American small-business owners, workers, and families. And you have used this money to help spur an economic resurgence that has produced 18 straight quarters of growth.

Some in Washington think the choice is between cutting taxes and cutting the deficit. This week's numbers show that this is a false choice. The economic growth fueled by tax relief has helped send tax revenues soaring. When the economy grows, businesses grow with it, people earn more money, and they pay taxes on this new income.

In 2005, tax revenues posted the largest increase in 24 years, and they're projected to rise again this year. The increase in tax revenues is much better than we had projected, and it is helping us cut the budget deficit.

Our original projection for this year's budget deficit was $423 billion. This week's report from OMB projects that this year's deficit will actually come in at $296 billion, a reduction of $127 billion. That is a tremendous difference, and 90 percent of it is because our growing economy has produced a lot more tax revenues.

Because of these new revenues, we now project that we'll meet our goal of cutting the Federal deficit in half by 2008, a full year ahead of schedule. This is real progress, yet we cannot depend on a growing economy alone to cut the deficit. We must also cut waste and restrain unnecessary Government spending. And my administration is doing its part.

Every year since I took office, we have reduced the growth of discretionary spending that is not related to national security.

My last two budgets have actually cut this kind of spending. I am also working with Congress to pass a line-item veto, which will help me and future Presidents target wasteful spending that lawmakers tack on to large bills. The House has already passed this measure with significant bipartisan support. Now the Senate needs to act and get a line-item veto to my desk to sign into law.

Finally, I will continue to work with Congress to address the unsustainable growth of entitlement spending so that we can save programs like Social Security, Medicare, and Medicaid for our children and grandchildren.

This week's good news confirms the wisdom of trusting the American people with their own money and being wise with the money they send to Washington. By pursuing progrowth policies and restraining Government spending, we will keep our economy the envy of the world. We will create more jobs and opportunities for all our citizens, and we will deliver results for the American taxpayer.

Thank you for listening.

NOTE: The address was recorded at 8:50 a.m. on July 14 at the Kempinski Grand Hotel in Heiligendamm, Germany, for broadcast at 10:06 a.m., e.d.t., on July 15. The transcript was made available by the Office of the Press Secretary on July 14 but was embargoed for release until the broadcast. Due to the 8-hour time difference, the radio address was broadcast after the President's news conference in Strelna, Russia, and the accompanying joint statement. The Office of the Press Secretary also released a Spanish language transcript of this address.

Remarks Following Discussions With Prime Minister Romano Prodi of Italy in Strelna
July 15, 2006

President Bush. I've enjoyed my visit with the Prime Minister, Romano. I've known him for a long time. This isn't the first time we have had discussions, and so therefore, the discussions today were very cordial. They reflect the important relationship that the United States shares with Italy.

Before I say anything beyond this, I do want to congratulate your great country for winning the World Cup.

Prime Minister Prodi. I am happy to——

President Bush. I bet you are happy for it. And we were very excited for the Italian people as they celebrated the magnificent victory.

Romano and I talked about a lot of issues that face the world. No question, when Italy and the United States works together, along with other countries, we're able to achieve important breakthroughs. We talked about Iran; we talked about the Middle East; we talked about a variety of issues. We talked about energy; we spent a lot of time talking about energy.

I want to thank you for your time, thank you for your frank discussions. It's good to see you again.

Prime Minister Prodi. I hope that we can meet sometime again.

President Bush. Yes, sir, thank you.

Prime Minister Prodi. I confirm what George told—we had a very frank conversation concerning all that—[*inaudible*]— issues. But now—[*inaudible*]—first of all, Middle East, of course, then Iran and Iraq and Afghanistan. Then we spent a lot of time on the future. I think we—[*inaudible*]—for Africa—[*inaudible*]. There's certainly a vision between U.S. and Italy— [*inaudible*]—and our friendship is stronger, Mr. President.

President Bush. Yes, sir. Thank you, Romano.

NOTE: The President spoke at 6:44 p.m. in Cottage Nine at the Konstantinovsky Palace Complex. A tape was not available for verification of the content of these remarks.

Remarks Following Discussions With Prime Minister Tony Blair of the United Kingdom and an Exchange With Reporters in Strelna
July 16, 2006

President Bush. It's good to be here with my friend and our close ally. We just had a wide-ranging discussion. We talked about the Middle East, we talked about Iraq, we talked about Iran. I was pleased to inform and thank Tony for the good work in the United Nations on a unanimous resolution regarding North Korea.

We talked about trade. We're both committed to a world that trades freely. All in all, it's a typical Blair-Bush conversation;

it was wide-ranging and conclusive. And I appreciate your insight and your thoughts.

Prime Minister Blair. Well, thank you very much, Mr. President. The President has indicated to you the subjects we discussed. And we went through basically all of the international agenda, as evidence of a very strong common agreement on the key questions.

President Bush. Steve [Steve Holland, Reuters].

Situation in the Middle East

Q. Israel's offensive in Lebanon appears to have no end in sight at this point. Are you willing to go along with Lebanon's call for a cease-fire?

President Bush. One of the interesting things about this recent flareup is that it helps clarify a root cause of instability in the Middle East, and that's Hizballah and Hizballah's relationship with Syria and Hizballah's relationship to Iran and Syria's relationship to Iran. Therefore, in order to solve this problem, it's really important for the world to address the root cause.

We, of course, are in continued discussions with Israel. All sovereign nations have the right to defend themselves against terrorist attacks. However, we hope that there is restraint as people respond. And one of our concerns, of course, is the fragile democracy in Lebanon. So in order to solve this problem, the international community must address the root causes, otherwise there may be apparent calm and then all of a sudden, there will be more conflict.

Remember, Hizballah started this by capturing two Israeli soldiers and firing rockets into Israel. And as we talk about Hizballah, we must always remember that there is an issue in Gaza as well. And we've discussed this issue, and we will continue to work with the parties involved to solve that issue as well.

Prime Minister Blair's Upcoming Meeting With President Vladimir V. Putin of Russia

Q. Last night President Putin said that if you asked him about Russian democracy, he had some questions to ask you about Lord Levy. Do you feel that your ability to play a role in international states is now being seriously undermined by Lord Levy's activities?

Prime Minister Blair. No, I don't. I think—I'm sure we will have a discussion not just about that but about the full range of international issues that we've been discussing including, obviously, the most pressing issue on the international agenda at the moment.

Q. Do you expect him to raise Lord Levy with you?

Prime Minister Blair. No, I'm not, frankly.

President Bush. Keil [Richard Keil, Bloomberg News].

Situation in the Middle East

Q. Mr. President, you've talked here about your concern about the fragility of the democracy in Lebanon and the Prime Minister there calling for a cease-fire. Do you think that's needed now to protect his Government? And, if not, why?

President Bush. My message to Israel is that as a sovereign nation, you have every right to defend yourself against terrorist activities. And again, I repeat, this started because Hizballah decided to capture two Israeli soldiers and fire hundreds of rockets into Israel from southern Lebanon. That's the cause of the crisis.

And so our message to Israel is, look, defend yourself, but as you do so, be mindful of the consequences. And so we've urged restraint.

Q. What about a cease-fire?

President Bush. Well, it's really important; this is a moment of clarification. It's becoming clear for everybody to see some of the root causes of instability. I say, "some of the root causes of instability," because there's still a militant wing of Hamas that wants to stop progress.

But let's step back for a minute. We were making progress toward a two-state solution, two democracies living side by side in peace. There's a Prime Minister from Israel, Olmert, who is dedicated to a two-state solution. He comes to the United States and holds a press conference and says, "I am dedicated. As a matter of fact, I am so dedicated, I'm campaigning on the platform that if need be, we will unilaterally make the decision that there's a Palestinian state." That's a remarkable statement. He also said that he is willing to reach out to President Abbas, which he has done. He's also reached out to other nations in the neighborhood in order to make sure there's a negotiated settlement.

As progress was being made, it obviously scared those who can't stand the thought of democracy. So you have the militant wing of Hamas act first, and then you had Hizballah act. And in order to solve this problem, Dick, the world must address the root causes of the problem.

And so we have said to Israel—and we're in touch with Israel a lot—remember, there's a fledgling democracy on your northern border, which will ultimately help you achieve the peace you want. And today here at the G–8, we'll discuss this issue. And it's a—one of the interesting things about this moment is it's now become clear to a lot of people why we don't have peace in the Middle East. It's a moment of clarification. And therefore, it's a moment that requires all of us to work together to send a clear message not only to Hizballah but to the Iranians who finance Hizballah and to the Syrians who house Hizballah.

G–8 Summit/Middle East

Q. Mr. Prime Minister and Mr. President, do you get a sense among the other leaders who are gathered here today that you are all on the same wavelength when it comes to the Middle East? Or do some leaders have very different views about what's happening there?

President Bush. I think most leaders are now beginning to recognize the root cause of the problem. Clearly, the Prime Minister does. And our respective political directors and foreign ministers and Secretary of States have been talking about this issue a lot. And there seems to be a consensus growing that in order for us to have the peace we want, that the world is going to have to recognize that there are terrorist elements who are dedicated to stopping the advance of democracy and peace. And therefore, we must deal with those. And I repeat, there are two nation-states that

are very much involved with stopping the advance of peace, and that would be Iran, and that would be Syria.

War on Terror/Situation in the Middle East

Q. Mr. Prime Minister, can I just ask you on this: The Russians have said they feel Israel's use of force is excessive. What do you think of that? And could you just spell out exactly what influence the Russians, you think, have or could have in this situation?

Prime Minister Blair. Well, I think everyone is going to work very hard to find a common and unified position. But the essential point is this: We all want the situation to calm down, and we want it to calm down because we're mindful of the need to protect Lebanese democracy, and we're also deeply mindful of the need to try to reengage people with the negotiated process towards a two-state solution, Israel and an independent, viable state in Palestine.

Now the question is, how do we calm it down from this position now? And as the President was just saying a moment or two ago, the absolute essence of this, the only way we are going to get this situation calm and we're going to get the cessation of hostilities is if we address the reasons why the situation has arisen. And the basic reasons are that there are extremists who want to interrupt the process that can lead to that two-state solution—Israel with its security protectors, a proper independent Palestinian state—and there are also extremists backed, I'm afraid, by Iran and by Syria who want to disrupt the positions in Lebanon and who want to create a situation of tension and hostility there.

So if we're going to make this work— and we've got the U.N. mission that is out there now, and that's obviously very important, and we support it—if we want to make this work, we have got to deal with those underlying conditions that have given rise both to the problem in the Gaza and the problems into Lebanon. And I hope very much that everybody here, because we have a common position in supporting Lebanon and its democracy and supporting the security of Israel, and supporting the two-state solution, since we're agreed on those basic fundamentals, we should be able to agree on a position here. And I think it would be a very good signal to send out to the world at this moment that we can agree to such a position.

I think that sometimes, for understandable reasons, there's been a hesitation in putting the real truth of this situation up to people, and the fact is, there are those out in that region, notably Iran and Syria, who do not want this process of democratization and peace and negotiations to succeed.

President Bush. Let me just say one thing. You've triggered a brilliant thought. [*Laughter*] A couple of points—Kofi Annan is going to be here, and the United States, as well, supports the mission in the region. Secondly, of course, all of us care deeply about the loss of innocent life. And in thinking about that, I remember a year ago what took place during the G–8 hosted by Tony. There were terrorist attacks in London, and there was a loss of innocent life. And there was outrage, as there should have been, and a determination to work together to protect life.

And that same determination must be applied to the Middle East as well. The terrorists will do anything to achieve objectives. They went into London subways. They'll fire rockets into Israel, all aiming to disrupt, to destroy, to prevent free societies from flourishing, because they don't agree with freedom. And the stakes are high, and the stakes have been clarified once again, during yet another G–8. And Tony and I will call upon our fellow leaders to come together and to make it clear that we reject this kind of violence and that we will be steadfast in our support of freedom.

Thank you.

NOTE: The President spoke at 8:50 a.m. in Cottage Nine at the Konstantinovsky Palace Complex. In his remarks, he referred to Ehud Goldwasser and Eldad Regev, Israeli soldiers captured and held captive by militants in Lebanon since July 12; Prime Minister Ehud Olmert of Israel; President Mahmoud Abbas of the Palestinian Authority; and Secretary-General Kofi Annan of the United Nations. A reporter referred to Baron Michael A. Levy, Prime Minister Blair's personal envoy to the Middle East, who was arrested on July 12 in connection with a police investigation into possible infringements of honours and elections laws. A tape was not available for verification of the content of these remarks.

Remarks Following Discussions With President Jacques Chirac of France in Strelna
July 16, 2006

President Bush. I want to thank Jacques Chirac for coming over. It's always a pleasure to visit with Jacques. He is a man who is able to crystalize his thoughts, who is able to discuss issues in a very clear way.

Obviously, we're going to spend time talking about the Middle East. The United States is proud to work with France on Resolution 1559 of the United Nations, which is a clear statement of principle and concern about Lebanese democracy. I'm confident that other leaders will look at the spirit of 1559 and recognize that one way to help heal in the Middle East is to address the root causes of the problems there, and the root cause of the problem is Hizballah and Syria and the Iranian connection.

The President has taken a strong lead on this issue in the past. We are in discussions with his administration, and I'm confident that we'll be able to come up with a clear position between France and the United States on this vital issue.

I look forward to discussing other issues with my friend Jacques Chirac. It's good to be with you, sir. Thank you for coming by.

President Chirac. First of all, I just like to say how delighted I am to have this opportunity to meet with the American President. And I note, albeit it, that this has been difficult circumstances, as we have been witnessing the sad events that have been unfolding in the Middle East. But I'm especially struck and delighted by the fact that we share the same views of the issues at stake here. We witness the tremendous sadness, the hardship of the civilian population in this region. You know what longstanding ties France has always had with Lebanon. And when I say "this region," I refer not only to Lebanon but, of course, to what's happening to the Palestinians. So we would call—[*inaudible*]—for a show of moderation on the part of all parties involved, so that we can establish the conditions of a long-lasting, lasting cease-fire in the region.

Now, I entirely agree with the American President in what he said about supporting the U.N. mission, which is designed, among other things, to ensure the release of the Israeli soldiers being detained right now both by Hizballah and by Hamas and put an end to the firing of Kassam rockets.

Now, with respect to Gaza, which is a separate issue from that of Lebanon, we feel that it is essential—it is of the essence—that we renew dialog with Mahmoud Abbas.

Now, as regards Lebanon, I couldn't agree more with President Bush in saying that what is at the heart of this is the to-the-letter implementation of Security Council Resolution 1559. That is what must be done forthwith. And we must stop all those who are at present engaging in jeopardizing the security, the stability, and authority of Lebanon.

President Bush. Thank you all. Thank you, sir.

NOTE: The President spoke at 9:14 a.m. in Cottage Nine at the Konstantinovsky Palace Complex. President Chirac referred to Ehud Goldwasser and Eldad Regev, Israeli soldiers captured and held captive by militants in Lebanon since July 12; President Mahmoud Abbas of the Palestinian Authority. President Chirac spoke in French, and his remarks were translated by an interpreter. A tape was not available for verification of the content of these remarks.

Remarks Following Discussions With President Hu Jintao of China in Strelna
July 16, 2006

President Bush. Mr. President, thank you for coming by to say hello. I remember fondly your visit to Washington, DC, a very successful trip to our Nation's Capital and other parts of our country. I want to thank you for the discussion we've had today.

The United Nations Security Council unanimously passed a resolution dealing with the North Korean issue, and I want to thank you for your leadership on that, Mr. President. We're working together on the Iranian issue. We talked about the Middle East. I want to thank you very much for our continued dialog on bilateral issues. We spent a lot of time on economics and trade.

All in all, it's a continuation of the very good dialog we had during your trip to Washington, and I want to thank you for coming.

President Hu. Ladies and gentlemen, I'm very happy to have the opportunity to meet you here. As President Bush said just now, we had a very friendly and candid discussion. To start with the discussion, I expressed my heartfelt thanks to the American side for the warm reception afforded to me during my visit to the United States in April this year by President Bush, the American Government, and the American people.

In addition, we also had an in-depth discussion on the China-U.S. relationship and major international issues of mutual interest. Both President Bush and I speak highly of the development of China-U.S. relationship as it is today. We also are happy to see that the agreement President Bush and I reached on comprehensively moving forward the constructive and cooperative China-U.S. relationship is being gradually implemented.

We both agreed to continue to view and handle the China-U.S. relationship from a strategic plane—I mean, a long-term perspective. In addition, we also agreed to work hard to expand the convergent interests between the two countries and step up our pragmatic cooperation in the economic, trade, energy, science, technology, counterterrorism, nonproliferation, and the military fields.

At the same time, we also believe that we need to respect and properly address each other's concerns and properly handle the sensitive issues in the bilateral relationship so that we can continue to move forward this relationship.

We both believe that against the current backdrop of a complex and volatile international situation, to enhance the consultation and the coordination between China and the United States on major regional as well as international issues, serves the interests of both countries. This is also crucial to international peace and stability.

Both sides expressed their commitment to maintain peace and stability on the Korean Peninsula and in Northeast Asia as a whole, and both sides agreed to continue their efforts to move forward the six-party talks so that at the end of the day, the entire Korean Peninsula could be denuclearized in a peaceful way through dialog and in negotiations.

Both sides indicated their willingness to work together to continue to seek a peaceful solution to the Iranian nuclear issue. We also discussed the situation in the Middle East.

In this afternoon's discussion, we also spent quite a lot of time in an in-depth manner on our economic ties and trade and on the Taiwan question.

I am satisfied with the discussion with President Bush. Thank you.

President Bush. Thank you, Mr. President.

NOTE: The President spoke at 3:53 p.m. in Cottage Nine at the Konstantinovsky Palace Complex. President Hu spoke in Chinese, and his remarks were translated by an interpreter.

G–8 Leaders' Statement on the Situation in the Middle East
July 16, 2006

Today, we the G–8 Leaders express our deepening concern about the situation in the Middle East, in particular the rising civilian casualties on all sides and the damage to infrastructure. We are united in our determination to pursue efforts to restore peace. We offer our full support for the UN Secretary General's mission presently in the region. The root cause of the problems in the region is the absence of a comprehensive Middle East peace.

The immediate crisis results from efforts by extremist forces to destabilize the region and to frustrate the aspirations of the Palestinian, Israeli and Lebanese people for democracy and peace. In Gaza, elements of Hamas launched rocket attacks against Israeli territory and abducted an Israeli soldier. In Lebanon, Hizbollah, in violation of the Blue Line, attacked Israel from Lebanese territory and killed and captured Israeli soldiers, reversing the positive trends that began with the Syrian withdrawal in 2005, and undermining the democratically elected government of Prime Minister Fuad Siniora.

These extremist elements and those that support them cannot be allowed to plunge the Middle East into chaos and provoke a wider conflict. The extremists must immediately halt their attacks.

It is also critical that Israel, while exercising the right to defend itself, be mindful of the strategic and humanitarian consequences of its actions. We call upon Israel to exercise utmost restraint, seeking to avoid casualties among innocent civilians and damage to civilian infrastructure and to refrain from acts that would destabilize the Lebanese government.

The most urgent priority is to create conditions for a cessation of violence that will be sustainable and lay the foundation for a more permanent solution. This, in our judgment, requires:

- The return of the Israeli soldiers in Gaza and Lebanon unharmed;
- An end to the shelling of Israeli territory;
- An end to Israeli military operations and the early withdrawal of Israeli forces from Gaza;
- The release of the arrested Palestinian ministers and parliamentarians. The framework for resolving these disputes is already established by international consensus.

In Lebanon, UN Security Council Resolutions 1559 and 1680 address the underlying conditions that gave rise to this crisis. We urge the UN Security Council to develop a plan for the full implementation of these resolutions.

We extend to the Government of Lebanon our full support in asserting its sovereign authority over all its territory in fulfillment of UNSCR 1559. This includes the deployment of Lebanese Armed Forces to all parts of the country, in particular the South, and the disarming of militias. We would welcome an examination by the UN Security Council of the possibility of an international security/monitoring presence.

We also support the initiation of a political dialogue between Lebanese and Israeli officials on all issues of concern to both parties. In addition, we will support the economic and humanitarian needs of the Lebanese people, including the convening at the right time of a donors conference.

In Gaza, the disengagement of Israel provided an opportunity to move a further step toward a two state solution under the Road Map. All Palestinian parties should accept the existence of Israel, reject violence, and accept all previous agreements and obligations, including the Roadmap. For its part, Israel needs to refrain from unilateral acts that could prejudice a final settlement and agree to negotiate in good faith.

Our goal is an immediate end to the current violence, a resumption of security cooperation and of a political engagement both among Palestinians and with Israel. This requires:

- An end to terrorist attacks against Israel;
- A resumption of the efforts of President Abbas to ensure that the Palestinian government complies with the Quartet principles;
- Immediate expansion of the temporary international mechanism for donors established under the direction of the Quartet;
- Israeli compliance with the Agreement on Movement and Access of November 2005 and action on other steps to ease the humanitarian plight of the people of Gaza and the West Bank;
- Resumption of security cooperation between Palestinians and Israelis;
- Action to ensure that the Palestinian security forces comply with Palestinian law and with the Roadmap, so that they are unified and effective in providing security for the Palestinian people;
- Resumption of dialogue between Palestinian and Israeli political officials.

These proposals are our contribution to the international effort underway to restore calm to the Middle East and provide a basis for progress towards a sustainable peace, in accordance with the relevant UN Security Council Resolutions. The Quartet will continue to play a central role. The G–8 welcomes the positive efforts of Egypt, Saudi Arabia and Jordan as well as other responsible regional actors to return the region to peace. We look forward to the report of the Secretary General's mission to the Security Council later this week which we believe could provide a framework for achieving our common objectives.

NOTE: The statement referred to Secretary-General Kofi Annan of the United Nations; and President Mahmoud Abbas of the Palestinian Authority. An original was not available for verification of the content of this joint statement.

Letter to Congressional Leaders on Review of Title III of the Cuban Liberty and Democratic Solidarity (LIBERTAD) Act of 1996
July 16, 2006

Dear _____ :

Consistent with section 306(c)(2) of the Cuban Liberty and Democratic Solidarity (LIBERTAD) Act of 1996 (Public Law 104–114) (the "Act"), I hereby determine and report to the Congress that suspension for 6 months beyond August 1, 2006, of the right to bring an action under title III of the Act is necessary to the national interests of the United States and will expedite a transition to democracy in Cuba.

Sincerely,

GEORGE W. BUSH

NOTE: Identical letters were sent to Richard G. Lugar, chairman, and Joseph R. Biden, Jr., ranking member, Senate Committee on Foreign Relations; Thad Cochran, chairman, and Robert C. Byrd, ranking member, Senate Committee on Appropriations; Henry J. Hyde, chairman, and Tom Lantos, ranking member, House Committee on International Relations; and Jerry Lewis, chairman, and David R. Obey, ranking member, House Committee on Appropriations. This letter was released by the Office of the Press Secretary on July 17.

Remarks Following Discussions With Prime Minister Manmohan Singh of India in Strelna
July 17, 2006

President Bush. Thanks for coming over this morning. It's always a pleasure to be in your company. You're one of the really true gentlemen in the international arena. And you've got a wonderful heart. I know you've been through difficult times, and America mourns the loss of innocent life as a result of the terrorist attacks.

One of the issues that we've been discussing here at the G–8 is the recent terrorist activities in the Middle East. Yesterday, in working with other members of the G–8, we cobbled together a very important statement. I'm most pleased that the leaders came together to say, "Look, we condemn violence; we honor innocent life."

However, for the first time, we've really begun to address with clarity the root causes of the conflict, the recent conflict in the Middle East, and that is terrorist activity, mainly Hizballah, that's housed and encouraged by Syria, financed by Iran, are making these moves to stop the progress of peace. We would hope that by addressing the conditions of this violence, we could get to a situation where there was calm. We're going to work hard as nations to address the root cause. Yesterday was an important statement. The reason I tell you that is that you'll find nations willing to work together for the common good here.

I also look forward to discussing with you our trade matters as well as the wonderful deal you and I negotiated. Our Congress is working on that important piece of legislation that will encourage and allow India and U.S. cooperation, and I'm optimistic that we will get that passed.

At any rate, welcome, and thank you, sir. I'd be glad for you to make some comments.

Prime Minister Singh. Mr. President, thank you very much for your words of sympathy and support in the wake of these terrible terrorist acts in Mumbai and in Srinagar. I've just been there—200 people, innocent men, women, and children, have perished, about 800 citizens injured, and when I—[*inaudible*]—various hospitals, it was such a moving sight, people without limbs and all this—and I'm grateful to you—you gave me help from Germany, and I deeply appreciate your generosity. Your kindness, your sympathy and support mean a great deal to me, President, personally and to our Government and to our people.

Sir, your visit to our country in March, and in the company of the First Lady, was a landmark. We have set new goalposts for working together between our two countries. And I'm glad to report to you that we are making progress in all directions. India was the idea of getting the business community of our two countries engaged. You suggested we set up a CEOs forum. That forum is very active. It has produced a number of good ideas. We'll follow it up by an investors' summit towards the end of the year.

Sir, India is still very largely an agricultural country; 65 percent of all people live on land. And the initiative that you took, and that was also your ideas and knowledge initiative to usher in a second green revolution in our country. We have now agreed on a roadmap. We have identified sectors like agricultural education, food processing, water management—[*inaudible*]—as the key areas which will be the focus of this agriculture initiative. It means a great deal to us, to build a new trust to agricultural innovation, agricultural productivity. And I thank you for active support.

In science and technology also, Mr. President, we have now agreed to work together and invite national—[*inaudible*]—in science and technology. The coordinators have been appointed. They have no outline, a roadmap. And I am very happy that both our administrations are working very hard to give concrete meaning and substance to our cooperation.

And I thank you, Mr. President, for your efforts and Secretary Rice's effort in getting the legislation with regard to nuclear cooperation moving through the Congress. We have followed very intensely what has been written into these bills. And I must confess to you that while we deeply appreciate your personal involvement, Secretary Rice's magnificent efforts when she appeared before the Congress—there are some concerns which worry us and, we believe, our Parliament. And like you, we are a democracy; we have a Parliament which is very jealous of what we do and what we don't do. And we have—these concerns are made, and I sincerely hope that we can find constructive solutions to all these problems. So this truly is landmark cooperation.

I recall it—I said to you that, Mr. President, that this is a—[*inaudible*]—conciliation of India and the U.S.—[*inaudible*].

NOTE: The President spoke at 8:11 a.m. in Cottage Nine at the Konstantinovsky Palace Complex.

Remarks Following Discussions With President Luiz Inacio Lula da Silva of Brazil in Strelna
July 17, 2006

President Bush. It's an honor for me to have a discussion with my friend the President of Brazil. He represents a great country, right in the heart of our neighborhood.

We've got a lot to discuss. I'm, of course, interested in his views about different nations in our neighborhood. He's a man who looks at the world and is able to give a good assessment.

I'm interested in continuing our dialog about alternative energy. Brazil has been a leader in development of biofuels. I'm interested, as well, in talking to the President about how we can move the Doha round of WTO forward. He's one of the leaders when it comes to trade discussions. A lot of the world looks to his—to him for judgment. And so I view this as a very important meeting. We're committed to a successful Doha round. In order for the round to be successful, the United States and Brazil must continue to strategize.

And so, Mr. President, welcome. You're looking good. You're looking good.

President Lula da Silva. This is because of the election campaign that's going on. [*Laughter*]

Mr. President, for Brazil, the fact that the G–8 had decided to create, open a special moment to discuss the Doha round at the G–8 meeting is extremely important. After our phone conversations, I am convinced that now is the time for us to make a political decision, whatever might it be. We cannot leave in the hands of our negotiators only. They already have done immense work, but now it seems to me that they don't have any hidden card in their pockets anymore. Now we're the ones that have to take our cards from the pockets. So that's why it is extremely important that the G–8 discusses this subject matter.

And another important thing is that we see that we will open up the possibility for us to build partnership with the United States of America on the issue of renewable sources of energy and fuel. And we are advancing this field. The biodiesel program is already a reality. And now we have another novelty that is the H-bio that is directly, finally, in the refineries—of the blend of oil seeds and vegetable oil with petroleum.

I'd like to take advantage of this moment and hand over to you—[*laughter*]—our program of renewable sources of fuel. We have ethanol, biodiesel, H-bio—it's almost an in-

vitation, Mr. President, for us to build a major partnership.

President Bush. Thank you, sir. [*Laughter*]

NOTE: The President spoke at 8:55 a.m. in Cottage Nine at the Konstantinovsky Palace Complex. President Lula da Silva spoke in Portuguese, and his remarks were translated by an interpreter.

Joint Statement by President George W. Bush and President Vladimir V. Putin
July 17, 2006

The United States and the Russian Federation believe that strengthening their cooperation in civil nuclear energy is in the strategic interests of both our countries. It will serve as an additional assurance of access for other nations to economical and environmentally safe peaceful nuclear energy.

The United States and the Russian Federation are working together to meet the challenges posed by the combination of proliferation of weapons of mass destruction and international terrorism. We recognize the devastation that could befall our peoples and the world community if nuclear weapons or materials or other weapons of mass destruction were to fall into the hands of terrorists. We are closely cooperating to lessen that unacceptable danger, including by strengthening the non-proliferation regime and ensuring the security of nuclear weapons and fissile materials.

Cooperation in the Peaceful Uses of Nuclear Energy

The United States and the Russian Federation are convinced that reliable and sufficient energy supplies are the cornerstone of sustainable economic development and prosperity for all nations, and a necessary

condition for maintaining international stability. Today nuclear energy is a proven technology for providing reliable electric power without emissions of greenhouse gases, and is an essential part of any solution to meet growing energy demand.

We share the view that nuclear energy has an essential role in the promotion of energy security, which is an issue of special concern for the leaders of the G–8. Advancing nuclear energy will require further development of innovative technologies that reduce the risk of proliferation, provide for safe management of waste, are economically viable, and are environmentally safe.

Being consistent in our approach to assure access to the benefits of nuclear energy for all nations complying with their non-proliferation obligations, we have each proposed initiatives on the development of a global nuclear energy infrastructure, specifically the Russian proposal to establish a system of international centers to provide nuclear fuel services, including uranium enrichment, under International Atomic Energy Agency (IAEA) safeguards, and the U.S. proposal for the Global Nuclear Energy Partnership to develop innovative nuclear reactor and fuel cycle technologies.

Following up on these initiatives, the United States and the Russian Federation intend to work together, actively involving the IAEA, to allow all nations to enjoy the benefits of nuclear energy without pursuing uranium enrichment and spent fuel reprocessing capabilities.

The United States and the Russian Federation together with four other nuclear fuel supplier states have also proposed a concept for reliable access to nuclear fuel for consideration and development at the IAEA.

We call upon other countries to join us to facilitate the safe and secure expansion of nuclear energy worldwide. Proceeding from our national interests and common goals, and recognizing the benefits of civil commercial nuclear trade, we express our intent to develop bilateral cooperation in the peaceful use of nuclear energy.

We have directed our Governments to begin negotiations with the purpose of concluding an agreement between the United States and the Russian Federation on cooperation in the peaceful use of nuclear energy.

Countering Nuclear Proliferation

We recognize the vital role of the Treaty on the Non-proliferation of Nuclear Weapons (NPT) in the prevention of nuclear proliferation and the importance of the IAEA in implementing safeguards required by the NPT. We are working with our G–8 partners to make the Additional Protocol an essential norm for verifying compliance with nuclear safeguards obligations. We welcome the establishment of the IAEA Committee on Safeguards and Verification. We are actively fulfilling our obligations under Article VI of the NPT by substantially reducing nuclear forces as we implement the Moscow Treaty of May 24, 2002.

We reiterate our support for effective measures to prevent transfers of sensitive nuclear equipment, materials and technologies to states that may seek to use them for weapons purposes, or allow them to fall into terrorists' hands, and will work together to this end.

We reiterate our commitments undertaken under the Bratislava Joint Statement on Nuclear Security Cooperation of February 24, 2005. We have made substantial progress in the implementation of those commitments and we reaffirm our goal of completing nuclear security upgrades by the end of 2008.

We welcome the continued cooperation and the recent extension of the Cooperative Threat Reduction Agreement to ensure full implementation of the ongoing projects launched earlier under this Agreement. In this context, we take note of the start of operations of the Mayak Fissile Materials Storage Facility. We continue discussions on how best to implement our commitments to the disposition by each side of 34 metric tons of weapons grade plutonium.

We applaud the extension of UN Security Council Resolution 1540, the adoption by the UN General Assembly of the International Convention for the Suppression of Acts of Nuclear Terrorism, and the decision by the States Parties to strengthen the Convention on Physical Protection of Nuclear Material.

We will continue to advance the objectives of the Proliferation Security Initiative, which makes an important contribution to countering the trafficking in WMD, their delivery means, and related materials. We welcome increasing international endorsement for the initiative, as was demonstrated at the High Level Political Meeting in Warsaw. We take note of the discussion at that meeting on how PSI states can work cooperatively to prevent and disrupt proliferation finance, in furtherance of UNSCR 1540.

We look forward to reinforcing our partnership with India. We welcome the important nonproliferation commitments India has made, and India's closer alignment with the nonproliferation regime mainstream. We look forward to working with India on civil nuclear cooperation to address its energy requirements, and on further enhancing the global nonproliferation regime. We will continue to work together to strengthen the global non-proliferation regime.

We are especially concerned by the failure of the Iranian government to engage seriously on the proposals made by the P–5 countries and Germany. In this context, we stand fully behind the decision by Foreign Ministers on July 12. We are seriously concerned by North Korea's ballistic missile tests and urge it to return to a moratorium on such launches, to the Six-Party Talks, and to full implementation of the September 19, 2005 agreement. The United States and the Russian Federation are actively working for unity among the UN Security Council members on these sensitive issues. We will continue consultations with our G–8 partners to strengthen the global non-proliferation regime.

Through our cooperation in the field of nuclear nonproliferation we seek to improve the security of our own peoples and of all others in the world community. In doing so, we are building on the unique historic roles and responsibilities of the United States and the Russian Federation in nuclear science and technology, both military and civilian. We are united in our determination to help make the benefits of nuclear energy securely available to all for peaceful purposes.

NOTE: An original was not available for verification of the content of this joint statement.

Statement on the Landing of the Space Shuttle *Discovery*
July 17, 2006

On behalf of all Americans, I welcome home the crew of the space shuttle *Discovery* from a safe and successful mission. Your courage and commitment to excellence have inspired us all, and a proud Nation sends its congratulations on a job well done. The men and women of NASA have dedicated themselves to putting our space program back on track and implementing our Nation's vision for human and robotic space exploration. America's space program is a source of great national pride, and this mission has been another important accomplishment in advancing space science, human space flight, and space exploration.

Remarks Following a Meeting With Congressional Leaders and an Exchange With Reporters
July 18, 2006

The President. I just had the pleasure of briefing the key Members of the House and the Senate on my trip to St. Petersburg and to Germany. Thank you all for coming.

You know, prior to my traveling to St. Petersburg, I thought the issue was going to be whether or not we could bring the world together to deal with North Korea and Iran. And by the way, during my stay there, we did get an unanimous United Nations Security Council agreement on North Korea. And it was my pleasure to be able to thank the Chinese and the Russians and the Japanese and our European friends for voting favorably for that resolution. But instead, a lot of the discussion was on the Hizballian attacks into Israel.

What was really interesting was that—and I briefed this to the Members—that we were able to reach a very strong consensus that the world must confront the root causes of the current instability. And the root cause of that current instability is terrorism and terrorist attacks on a democratic country. And part of those terrorist attacks are inspired by nation-states like Syria and Iran. And in order to be able to deal with this crisis, the world must deal with Hizballah, with Syria, and to continue to work to isolate Iran.

I strongly believe every nation ought to be able to defend herself from terrorist attacks. We're also mindful—and I talked to the Members—about the need to make sure the Government of Lebanon does not collapse. It's in our interest that Lebanon be free and the Siniora Government succeed.

We also talked about the evacuation of U.S. citizens in Lebanon. And Condi briefed the Members about the joint plan with the Defense Department to make sure there's enough transportation to expeditiously provide transportation for those who want to leave. And we're in the process of doing that.

All in all, it was a very positive visit there in the G–8. We dealt with significant problems. Sometimes it requires tragic situations to help bring clarity in the international community. And it is now clear for all to see that there are terrorist elements who want to destroy our democratic friends and allies, and the world must work to prevent them from doing so.

With that, I'll be glad to answer a couple of questions. Let's see, here. Yes.

Situation in the Middle East

Q. In trying to defuse the situation in the Middle East, is the United States trying to buy time and give Israel a chance to weaken Hizballah militarily?

The President. Well, we have made it very clear that Israel should be allowed to defend herself. We've asked that as she does so, that she be mindful of the Siniora Government. It's very important that this Government in Lebanon succeed and survive.

Everybody abhors the loss of innocent life. On the other hand, what we recognize is that the root cause of the problem is Hizballah. And that problem must be addressed, and it can be addressed through—internationally by making it clear to Syria that they've got to stop their support to Hizballah.

Listen, Syria is trying to get back into Lebanon—it looks like to me. We passed United Nations Resolution 1559, and finally this young democracy—or this democracy became whole—by getting Syria out. And there's suspicions that the instability created by the Hizballian attacks will cause some in Lebanon to invite Syria back in, and it's against the United Nations policy, and it's against the U.S. policy.

Q. There's a Deputy Army Chief of Israel who said that for this offensive to reach its goal will take weeks. Are you comfortable with that kind of timeframe? Are you comfortable with letting the offensive go on for weeks?

The President. I want the world to address the root causes of the problem, and the root cause of the problem is Hizballah. I also—and we've been, of course, in touch with Israel. Condi spoke to Prime Minister Olmert yesterday on the airplane flying back. And we're never going to tell a nation how to defend herself, but we are urging caution when it comes to the survival of the Siniora Government. It's essential that the Government of Lebanon survive this crisis.

We've worked hard to free—and "we" being the international community—worked hard to free Lebanon from Syrian influence. And there's a young government there. And it's in our interest that Syria stay out of Lebanon and this Government survive. And so in our consultations with countries in the neighborhood, we have urged all to address the problem—that would be Hizballah and its terrorist attacks on Israel.

Remember, this started—this crisis started when Hizballah captured two Israeli soldiers. They were unprovoked, Hizballah were unprovoked, and they then took hostages. Imagine how the United States would react if somebody provoked us with that kind of action, and secondly, started firing rockets. And it's this provocation of

Hizballah that has created this crisis, and that's the root cause of the problem.

All right, thank you all.

NOTE: The President spoke at 3:57 p.m. in the Cabinet Room at the White House. In his remarks, he referred to Prime Minister Fuad Siniora of Lebanon; and Prime Minister Ehud Olmert of Israel. A reporter referred to Maj. Gen. Moshe Kaplinsky, Deputy Chief of the General Staff, Israel Defense Forces.

Message to the Congress on Continuation of the National Emergency Blocking Property of Certain Persons and Prohibiting the Importation of Certain Goods From Liberia
July 18, 2006

To the Congress of the United States:

Section 202(d) of the National Emergencies Act (50 U.S.C. 1622(d)) provides for the automatic termination of a national emergency unless, prior to the anniversary date of its declaration, the President publishes in the *Federal Register* and transmits to the Congress a notice stating that the emergency is to continue in effect beyond the anniversary date. In accordance with this provision, I have sent the enclosed notice to the *Federal Register* for publication, stating that the national emergency and related measures blocking the property of certain persons and prohibiting the importation of certain goods from Liberia are to continue in effect beyond July 22, 2006. The most recent notice continuing this emergency was published in the *Federal Register* on July 21, 2005 (70 *FR* 41935).

The actions and policies of former Liberian President Charles Taylor and his close associates, in particular their unlawful depletion of Liberian resources and their removal from Liberia and secreting of Liberian funds and property, continue to undermine Liberia's transition to democracy and the orderly development of its political, administrative, and economic institutions and resources. These actions and policies pose a continuing unusual and extraordinary threat to the foreign policy of the United States. For these reasons, I have determined that it is necessary to continue the national emergency and related measures blocking the property of certain persons and prohibiting the importation of certain goods from Liberia.

GEORGE W. BUSH

The White House,
July 18, 2006.

NOTE: The notice is listed in Appendix D at the end of this volume.

Letter to the Speaker of the House of Representatives Transmitting Budget Amendments for the Department of Health and Human Services
July 18, 2006

Dear Mr. Speaker:

I ask the Congress to consider the enclosed FY 2007 Budget amendments for the Department of Health and Human Services to enhance the preparedness and response capabilities of the agency based primarily on the findings of the *Federal Response to Hurricane Katrina: Lessons Learned* report of February 2006. The total discretionary budget authority in my FY 2007 Budget would not be increased by these requests.

The details of this proposal are set forth in the enclosed letter from the Director of the Office of Management and Budget.

Sincerely,

GEORGE W. BUSH

Letter to Congressional Leaders on Departure of American Citizens From Lebanon
July 18, 2006

Dear Mr. Speaker: *(Dear Mr. President:)*

Hostilities involving Israeli military forces and Hezbollah terrorists in Lebanon commenced on July 12, 2006, and have included military operations in the vicinity of the U.S. Embassy in Beirut.

Although there is no evidence that Americans are being directly targeted, the security situation has deteriorated and now presents a potential threat to American citizens and the U.S. Embassy. On July 14, the Department of State first requested Department of Defense assistance to support the departure of American citizens from Lebanon. On July 15, U.S. military helicopters temporarily deployed to Cyprus. On July 16, these combat-equipped helicopters delivered to U.S. Embassy, Beirut, a contingent of U.S. military personnel who will assist in planning and conducting the departure from Lebanon of U.S. Embassy personnel and citizens and designated third country personnel. The helicopters also transported U.S. citizens from Beirut to Cyprus. It is expected that these helicopters will continue to provide support to the Embassy, including for the departure of additional personnel from Lebanon. It is likely that additional combat-equipped U.S. military forces may be deployed to Lebanon and Cyprus and other locations, as necessary, in order to support further efforts to assist in the departure of persons from Lebanon and to provide security.

These actions are being undertaken solely for the purpose of protecting American citizens and property. United States forces will redeploy as soon as it is determined that the threat to U.S. citizens and property has ended and the departure of any persons, as necessary, is completed.

I have taken this action pursuant to my constitutional authority to conduct U.S. foreign relations and as Commander in Chief and Chief Executive. I am providing this report as part of my efforts to keep the Congress informed, consistent with the War Powers Resolution.

Sincerely,

GEORGE W. BUSH

NOTE: Identical letters were sent to J. Dennis Hastert, Speaker of the House of Representatives, and Ted Stevens, President pro

tempore of the Senate. This letter was released by the Office of the Press Secretary
on July 19.

Remarks on Signing the Fetus Farming Prohibition Act and Returning Without Approval to the House of Representatives the "Stem Cell Research Enhancement Act of 2005"
July 19, 2006

Good afternoon. Congress has just passed
and sent to my desk two bills concerning
the use of stem cells in biomedical research. These bills illustrate both the promise and perils we face in the age of bio-
technology. In this new era, our challenge
is to harness the power of science to ease
human suffering without sanctioning the
practices that violate the dignity of human
life.

In 2001, I spoke to the American people
and set forth a new policy on stem cell
research that struck a balance between the
needs of science and the demands of conscience. When I took office, there was no
Federal funding for human embryonic stem
cell research. Under the policy I announced
5 years ago, my administration became the
first to make Federal funds available for
this research, yet only on embryonic stem
cell lines derived from embryos that had
already been destroyed. My administration
has made available more than $90 million
for research on these lines. This policy has
allowed important research to go forward
without using taxpayer funds to encourage
the further deliberate destruction of human
embryos.

One of the bills Congress has passed
builds on the progress we have made over
the last 5 years, so I signed it into law.
Congress has also passed a second bill that
attempts to overturn the balanced policy
I set. This bill would support the taking
of innocent human life in the hope of finding medical benefits for others. It crosses

a moral boundary that our decent society
needs to respect, so I vetoed it.

Like all Americans, I believe our Nation
must vigorously pursue the tremendous
possibility that science offers to cure disease and improve the lives of millions. We
have opportunities to discover cures and
treatments that were unthinkable generations ago. Some scientists believe that one
source of these cures might be embryonic
stem cell research. Embryonic stem cells
have the ability to grow into specialized
adult tissues, and this may give them the
potential to replace damaged or defective
cells or body parts and treat a variety of
diseases.

Yet we must also remember that embryonic stem cells come from human embryos
that are destroyed for their cells. Each of
these human embryos is a unique human
life with inherent dignity and matchless
value. We see that value in the children
who are with us today. Each of these children began his or her life as a frozen embryo that was created for in vitro fertiliza-
tion but remained unused after the fertility
treatments were complete. Each of these
children was adopted while still an embryo
and has been blessed with the chance to
grow up in a loving family.

These boys and girls are not spare parts.
They remind us of what is lost when embryos are destroyed in the name of research. They remind us that we all begin
our lives as a small collection of cells. And
they remind us that in our zeal for new

treatments and cures, America must never abandon our fundamental morals.

Some people argue that finding new cures for disease requires the destruction of human embryos like the ones that these families adopted. I disagree. I believe that with the right techniques and the right policies, we can achieve scientific progress while living up to our ethical responsibilities. That's what I sought in 2001, when I set forth my administration's policy allowing Federal funding for research on embryonic stem cell lines where the life and death decision had already been made.

This balanced approach has worked. Under this policy, 21 human embryonic stem cell lines are currently in use in research that is eligible for Federal funding. Each of these lines can be replicated many times. And as a result, the National Institutes of Health have helped make more than 700 shipments to researchers since 2001. There is no ban on embryonic stem cell research. To the contrary, even critics of my policy concede that these federally funded lines are being used in research every day by scientists around the world. My policy has allowed us to explore the potential of embryonic stem cells, and it has allowed America to continue to lead the world in this area.

Since I announced my policy in 2001, advances in scientific research have also shown the great potential of stem cells that are derived without harming human embryos. My administration has expanded the funding of research into stem cells that can be drawn from children, adults, and the blood in umbilical cords, with no harm to the donor. And these stem cells are already being used in medical treatments. With us today are patients who have benefited from treatments with adult and umbilical-cord blood stem cells. And I want to thank you all for coming.

They are living proof that effective medical science can also be ethical. Researchers are now also investigating new techniques that could allow doctors and scientists to produce stem cells just as versatile as those derived from human embryos. One technique scientists are exploring would involve reprogramming an adult cell—for example, a skin cell—to function like an embryonic stem cell. Science offers the hope that we may one day enjoy the potential benefits of embryonic stem cells without destroying human life.

We must continue to explore these hopeful alternatives and advance the cause of scientific research while staying true to the ideals of a decent and humane society. The bill I sign today upholds these humane ideals and draws an important ethical line to guide our research. The Fetus Farming Prohibition Act was sponsored by Senators Santorum and Brownback—both who are here—and by Congressman Dave Weldon, along with Nathan Deal. Thank you, Congressmen. This good law prohibits one of the most egregious abuses in biomedical research, the trafficking in human fetuses that are created with the sole intent of aborting them to harvest their parts. Human beings are not a raw material to be exploited or a commodity to be bought or sold, and this bill will help ensure that we respect the fundamental ethical line.

I'm disappointed that Congress failed to pass another bill that would have promoted good research. This bill was sponsored by Senator Santorum and Senator Arlen Specter and Congressman Roscoe Bartlett. Thanks for coming, Roscoe. It would have authorized additional Federal funding for promising new research that could produce cells with the abilities of embryonic cells but without the destruction of human embryos. This is an important piece of legislation. This bill was unanimously approved by the Senate; it received 273 votes in the House of Representatives but was blocked by a minority in the House using procedural maneuvers. I'm disappointed that the House failed to authorize funding for this vital and ethical research.

It makes no sense to say that you're in favor of finding cures for terrible diseases as quickly as possible and then block a bill that would authorize funding for promising and ethical stem cell research. At a moment when ethical alternatives are becoming available, we cannot lose the opportunity to conduct research that would give hope to those suffering from terrible diseases and help move our Nation beyond the current controversies over embryonic stem cell research.

We must pursue this research. And so I direct the Secretary of Health and Human Services, Secretary Leavitt, and the Director of the National Institutes of Health to use all the tools at their disposal to aid the search for stem cell techniques that advance promising medical science in an ethical and morally responsible way.

Unfortunately, Congress has sent me a bill that fails to meet this ethical test. This legislation would overturn the balanced policy on embryonic stem cell research that my administration has followed for the past 5 years. This bill would also undermine the principle that Congress itself has followed for more than a decade, when it has prohibited Federal funding for research that destroys human embryos.

If this bill would have become law, American taxpayers would, for the first time in our history, be compelled to fund the deliberate destruction of human embryos. And I'm not going to allow it.

I made it clear to the Congress that I will not allow our Nation to cross this moral line. I felt like crossing this line would be a mistake, and once crossed, we would find it almost impossible to turn back. Crossing the line would needlessly encourage a conflict between science and ethics that can only do damage to both and to our Nation

as a whole. If we're to find the right ways to advance ethical medical research, we must also be willing, when necessary, to reject the wrong ways. So today I'm keeping the promise I made to the American people by returning this bill to Congress with my veto.

As science brings us ever closer to unlocking the secrets of human biology, it also offers temptations to manipulate human life and violate human dignity. Our conscience and history as a nation demand that we resist this temptation. America was founded on the principle that we are all created equal and endowed by our Creator with the right to life. We can advance the cause of science while upholding this founding promise. We can harness the promise of technology without becoming slaves to technology. And we can ensure that science serves the cause of humanity instead of the other way around.

America pursues medical advances in the name of life, and we will achieve the great breakthroughs we all seek with reverence for the gift of life. I believe America's scientists have the ingenuity and skill to meet this challenge. And I look forward to working with Congress and the scientific community to achieve these great and noble goals in the years ahead.

Thank you all for coming, and may God bless.

NOTE: The President spoke at 2:08 p.m. in the East Room at the White House. In his remarks, he referred to H.R. 810, the "Stem Cell Research Enhancement Act of 2005." S. 3504, approved July 19, was assigned Public Law No. 109–242.

Message to the House of Representatives Returning Without Approval the "Stem Cell Research Enhancement Act of 2005"
July 19, 2006

To the House of Representatives:

I am returning herewith without my approval H.R. 810, the "Stem Cell Research Enhancement Act of 2005."

Like all Americans, I believe our Nation must vigorously pursue the tremendous possibilities that science offers to cure disease and improve the lives of millions. Yet, as science brings us ever closer to unlocking the secrets of human biology, it also offers temptations to manipulate human life and violate human dignity. Our conscience and history as a Nation demand that we resist this temptation. With the right scientific techniques and the right policies, we can achieve scientific progress while living up to our ethical responsibilities.

In 2001, I set forth a new policy on stem cell research that struck a balance between the needs of science and the demands of conscience. When I took office, there was no Federal funding for human embryonic stem cell research. Under the policy I announced 5 years ago, my Administration became the first to make Federal funds available for this research, but only on embryonic stem cell lines derived from embryos that had already been destroyed. My Administration has made available more than $90 million for research of these lines. This policy has allowed important research to go forward and has allowed America to continue to lead the world in embryonic stem cell research without encouraging the further destruction of living human embryos.

H.R. 810 would overturn my Administration's balanced policy on embryonic stem cell research. If this bill were to become law, American taxpayers for the first time in our history would be compelled to fund the deliberate destruction of human embryos. Crossing this line would be a grave mistake and would needlessly encourage a conflict between science and ethics that can only do damage to both and harm our Nation as a whole.

Advances in research show that stem cell science can progress in an ethical way. Since I announced my policy in 2001, my Administration has expanded funding of research into stem cells that can be drawn from children, adults, and the blood in umbilical cords with no harm to the donor, and these stem cells are currently being used in medical treatments. Science also offers the hope that we may one day enjoy the potential benefits of embryonic stem cells without destroying human life. Researchers are investigating new techniques that might allow doctors and scientists to produce stem cells just as versatile as those derived from human embryos without harming life. We must continue to explore these hopeful alternatives, so we can advance the cause of scientific research while staying true to the ideals of a decent and humane society.

I hold to the principle that we can harness the promise of technology without becoming slaves to technology and ensure that science serves the cause of humanity. If we are to find the right ways to advance ethical medical research, we must also be willing when necessary to reject the wrong ways. For that reason, I must veto this bill.

GEORGE W. BUSH

The White House,

July 19, 2006.

NOTE: S. 3504, approved July 19, was assigned Public Law No. 109–242.

Remarks at the National Association for the Advancement of Colored People Annual Convention
July 20, 2006

The President. Thank you very much. Bruce, thanks for your introduction. Bruce is a polite guy—I thought what he was going to say, "It's about time you showed up." [*Laughter*] And I'm glad I did. See, I see this as a moment of opportunity. I have come to celebrate the heroism of the civil rights movement and the accomplishments of the NAACP.

I want to talk about ways to build what the NAACP has always sought: a nation united, committed to destroying discrimination and extending to every American the full blessings—the full blessings—of liberty and opportunity. It's important to me. It's important to our Nation. I come from a family committed to civil rights. My faith tells me that we're all children of God, equally loved, equally cherished, equally entitled to the rights He grants us all.

For nearly 200 years, our Nation failed the test of extending the blessings of liberty to African Americans. Slavery was legal for nearly 100 years and discrimination legal in many places for nearly 100 years more. Taken together, the record placed a stain on America's founding, a stain that we have not yet wiped clean.

When people talk about America's Founders, they mention the likes of Washington and Jefferson and Franklin and Adams. Too often they ignore another group of founders: men and women and children who did not come to America of their free will but in chains. These founders literally helped build our country. They chopped the wood; they built the homes; they tilled the fields; and they reaped the harvest. They raised the children of others even though their own children had been ripped away and sold to strangers. These founders were denied the most basic birthright, and that's freedom.

Yet through captivity and oppression, they kept the faith. They carved a great nation out of the wilderness, and later, their descendants led a people out of the wilderness of bigotry. Nearly 200 years into our history as a nation, America experienced a second founding, the civil rights movement. Some of those leaders are here. These second founders, led by the likes of Thurgood Marshall and Martin Luther King, Jr., believed in the constitutional guarantees of liberty and equality. They trusted fellow Americans to join them in doing the right thing. They were leaders. They toppled Jim Crow through simple deeds: boarding a bus; walking along the road; showing up peacefully at courthouses; or joining in prayer and song. Despite the sheriff's dogs and the jailer's scorn and the hangman's noose and the assassin's bullets, they prevailed.

I don't know if you remember, 3 weeks ago, I went to Memphis, Tennessee. A lot of people focused on the fact that my friend, the Prime Minister of Japan, was an Elvis fan, because we went to Graceland. But we also went to another stop, a stop Reverend Jesse Jackson knows all too well, a painful moment in his life and in the life of our Nation, reflected in the Lorraine Motel.

The Prime Minister and I went there, which is now the National Civil Rights Museum. By the way, if you haven't been there, you ought to go. Among the people greeting me there was Dr. Benjamin Hooks. It's good to see you again, sir. He led me out onto the balcony of Room 306. I remember, Dr. Hooks pointed to the window that was still half-cracked. You know what I'm talking about, Jesse. It's not very far away. It was a powerful reminder of the hardships this Nation has been through, the struggle for decency.

I was honored that Dr. Hooks took time to visit with me. He talked about the hardships of the movement. With the gentle wisdom that comes from experience, he made it clear: We must work as one. And that's why I've come today. We want a united America that is one Nation under God, where every man and child and woman is valued and treated with dignity. We want a hopeful America where the prosperity and opportunities of our great land reach into every block of every neighborhood. We want an America that is constantly renewing itself, where citizens rise above political differences to heal old wounds, to build the bonds of brotherhood, and to move us ever closer to the founding promise of liberty and justice for all.

Nearly 100 years after the NAACP's birth, America remains an unfolding story of freedom, and all of us have an obligation to play our part.

I want to thank your chairman, Julian Bond, for his introduction. And thanks for greeting me today, Mr. Chairman. I asked him for a few pointers on how to give a speech. [*Laughter*] It doesn't look like they're taking. [*Laughter*] I want to thank Roslyn Brock, the vice chairman of the board, as well. I thank all the board members, all the participants, all the Members of the United States Congress for joining us today as well.

I congratulate Bruce Gordon on his strong leadership. I've gotten to know him. See, shortly after he was elected, he came by the Oval Office. He doesn't mince words. [*Laughter*] It's clear what's on his mind. He's also a results-oriented person. I'm pleased to say that I have—I'm an admirer of Bruce Gordon, and we've got a good working relationship. I don't know if that helps you or hurts you. [*Laughter*] But it's the truth. I admire the man.

We've had frank discussions, starting with Katrina. We talked about the challenges facing the African American community after that storm. We talked about the response of the Federal Government. And most importantly, we talked about the way forward. We talked about what we can do, working together, to move forward. And as a result of that first meeting, we found areas where we share common purpose, and we have resolved to work together in practical ways. I don't expect Bruce to become a Republican—[*laughter*]—and neither do you. [*Laughter*] But I do want to work with him, and that's what I'm here to talk to you about.

And so we've been working together in helping the citizens along the gulf coast recover from one of the worst natural disasters in our Nation's history. You know, when we met, I told Bruce that I would work with the Congress to make sure we dedicated enough money to help the folks. He kind of looked at me like—sure he's heard these political promises before. It's not the first time that he had heard somebody say, "Well, we'll work together to see if we can't get enough money." And I suspect he might have thought, "Well, he's just trying to get me out of the Oval Office." [*Laughter*]

But I meant what I said, and I want to thank the United States Congress for joining with the administration. We've committed over $110 billion to help the people in the gulf coast. That's money to go to build new homes, good schools. Bruce and I talked a lot about how do we make sure the contracting that goes on down there in the gulf coast goes to minority-owned businesses.

The road to recovery is long and difficult, but we will continue to work together to implement the strategy that Bruce and I worked on, along with people—other people like Donna Brazile and other leaders. We've got a plan, and we've got a commitment. And the commitment is not only to work together, but it's a commitment to the people of the gulf coast of the United States to see to it that their lives are better and brighter than before the storm.

We also worked together to ensure that African Americans can take advantage of the new Medicare drug benefit. Look, I understand that we had a political disagreement on the bill. I know that. But I worked with the Congress to make sure that the days of seniors having to choose between food and medicine is over. And that's the case of this new Medicare benefit. The Federal Government pays over 95 percent of the cost for our Nation's poorest seniors to get this new drug benefit.

And I want to thank the NAACP for recognizing that it's important to help our seniors sign up for this benefit. We put politics aside. We said, the day is over of arguing about the bill; let's make sure people receive the benefits of this bill. Bruce Gordon has shown leadership on this important issue, and I want to thank you for that.

We'll work together, and as we do so, you must understand, I understand that racism still lingers in America. It's a lot easier to change a law than to change a human heart. And I understand that many African Americans distrust my political party.

Audience members. Yes!

The President. I consider it a tragedy that the party of Abraham Lincoln let go of its historic ties with the African American community. For too long, my party wrote off the African American vote, and many African Americans wrote off the Republican Party.

That history has prevented us from working together when we agree on great goals. That's not good for our country. That's what I've come to share with you. We've put the interests of the country above political party. I want to change the relationship. The America we seek should be bigger than politics. And today I'm going to talk about some areas where I believe we can work together to reduce the obstacles for opportunity for all our citizens. And that starts, by the way, with education.

Surely, we share the same goal: We want an excellent education for every child. Not just some children but every single child.

I can remember being the Governor of Texas—I don't know if there's any Texans here or not. [*Applause*] Tell them "hi" at home. [*Laughter*]

I remember going to a ninth grade class when I was the Governor. It was in a neighborhood that's—a low-income neighborhood there in Houston. And I asked the ninth grade teacher, I said, "How's it going?" The man looked me in the eye and said, "My students cannot read." That's wrong, to hear a ninth grade teacher say, "My students cannot read."

I decided to do something about it when I was the Governor, and I decided to do something about that when I became the President. See, we must challenge a system that simply shuffles children through grade to grade without determining whether they can read, write, and add and subtract. It's a system—see, I like to call it this: We need to challenge the soft bigotry of low expectations. If you have low expectations, you're going to get lousy results. We must not tolerate a system that gives up on people.

So I came to Washington and I worked with Democrats and Republicans to pass the No Child Left Behind Act. Let me tell you the strategy behind the act: It says that the Federal Government will spend more money on education in primary and secondary schools—and we have increased the budgets by 40 percent. It also says, and in return for additional help, you must measure. We didn't say, the Federal Government is going to measure; we said, we want the local—the States and the local districts to measure.

And so why do you ask that? Why do you say that in return for increased money, you need to measure? And the reason why is because in order to solve a problem, you've got to diagnose the problem. Measuring results can tell us whether or not teaching methodology is sound. Measuring results can enable us to figure out which children are falling behind early.

You know, one of the interesting things about the No Child Left Behind Act, it says that when we find a child falling behind early, there will be extra money for tutoring, extra money for help. The whole purpose is to make sure people are at the starting line. The whole purpose is to make sure that the teacher that told me that, "My children can't read," no longer happens in the ninth grade. Measuring helps us determine how we're doing.

There's an achievement gap in America that's wrong for America, an achievement gap that says we're not fulfilling the promise. One of the barriers to opportunity, one of the obstacles to success is the fact that too many of our children aren't reading at grade level. And we know that because we measure, and we're doing something about it. Actually, the achievement gap is beginning to close. There's more work to be done.

Measuring allows parents to see how the school that their child is going to is doing. It lets the parents determine whether or not they should be satisfied with the education their child is getting. I strongly believe that parental involvement is important for our school systems. And I believe— and I strongly believe a parent knows what's best for his or her child. That's what I believe. And therefore, when we find schools that are not teaching and will not change, our parents should have a different option. If you want quality education, you've got to trust the parents.

You know, an amazing thing about our society today is wealthier white families have got the capacity to defeat mediocrity by moving. That is not the case for lower-income families. And so therefore, I strongly believe in charter schools and public school choice. I believe in opportunity scholarships to be able to enable parents to move their child out of a school that's not teaching, for the benefit of the United States of America.

I also understand that we've got to do more for primary—more than just primary and secondary education. I'm proud to report that working with the United States Congress, the number of low-income Americans receiving Pell grants has increased by about a million Americans since I have become the President. Pell grants are an important part of educational excellence and opportunity.

We're expanding money for our community college system. I met my pledge to increase funding for Historically Black Universities by 30 percent. A decent education is the gateway to a life of opportunity. It is a fundamental civil right. And I look forward to working with the NAACP to enhance educational excellence all across the United States of America.

Second, I hope we can work together in an America where more people become owners, own something, something that they can call their own. From our Nation's earliest days, ownership has been at the heart of our country. Unfortunately, for most of our history, African Americans were excluded from the dream. That's the reality of our past. Most of your forefathers didn't come to this land seeking a better life; most came in chains as the property of other people. Today, their children and grandchildren now have an opportunity to own their own property, and good policies will encourage that. And that's what we ought to work together on.

For most Americans, ownership begins with owning your own home. Owning a home is a way to build wealth. Owning a home is to—give something they can leave behind to their children. See, one of the concerns I have is that because of the past, there hasn't been enough assets that a family can pass on from one generation to the next. And we've got to address that problem. And a good way to do so is through homeownership. Owning a home gives people a stake in their neighborhoods and a stake in the future.

Today, nearly half of African Americans own their own homes, and that's good for America. That's good for our country, but they've still got to do more. So we—working to do our part with helping people afford a downpayment and closing costs, helping families who are in rental assistance to become homeowners, helping people understand the fine print when it comes to mortgage documents.

One of the things I want to work with the NAACP on is to encourage more people to be able to open the front door of the place where they live and say, "Welcome to my home; welcome to my piece of property." I also want to work to home-ownership in other areas. We want to see more African Americans own their own businesses, and that's why we've increased loans to African American businesses by 40 percent. We're taking steps to make it easier for African American businesses to compete for Federal contracts. We're working to expand help to have African American workers own a piece of their own retirement.

You know, one of my friends is Bob Johnson, founder of BET. He's an interesting man. He believes strongly in ownership. He has been a successful owner. He believes strongly, for example, that the death tax will prevent future African American entrepreneurs from being able to pass their assets from one generation to the next. He and I also understand that the investor class shouldn't be just confined to the old definition of the investor class.

You know, an amazing experience—when I went to Canton, Mississippi, I asked the workers there, who were mainly African American workers, I said, "How many of you have your own 401(k)?" Nearly all the hands went up. That means they own their own assets. It's their money. They manage their own money. It's a system that says, we want you to have assets that you can leave from one generation to the next. Asset accumulation is an important part of removing the barriers for opportunity. I think it's really important, and I want to work with Bruce, if possible. The Federal Government should encourage ownership in the Government pension program, to give people a chance to own an asset, something they can call their own. Ownership is vital to making sure this country extends its hope to every neighborhood in the United States of America. And I look forward to working with the NAACP to encourage ownership in America.

I want to work with you to make sure America's communities are strong. I've got a friend named Tony Evans. Some of you may know Tony, from Dallas, Texas. He was one time giving a sermon, and I heard him speak, and I want to share with you what it was. He said—he told a story about the man who had a crack on one of the walls in his home. So he got the plasterer to come by, and the guy plastered the wall. And about four days later, the crack reappeared. Got another plasterer in; put the plaster on the wall; and it reappeared again. He's getting frustrated. He finally called a wise fellow over. The man explained what the problem was with the cracks on the wall. He said, look, in order to solve the cracks on the wall, you have to fix the foundation.

What I want to do is work with the NAACP to help fix the foundations of our society. We want strong families. We want to help people who need help. We want to help the addicted; we want to help the homeless; we want to help those who are trying to reenter society after having been incarcerated. That's what we want to do. We want to help lives be improved. Government can hand out money—and we do—but it cannot put hope in a person's heart or a sense of purpose in a person's life. That's why I strongly support institutions of faith and community service all around our country. I believe in the neighborhood helpers and healers.

And I put this policy in place: We've provided more than $5 billion to faith-based groups that are running the soup kitchens and sheltering the homeless and healing the addicted and helping people reenter our society, people who are providing compassionate care and love. Organizations of faith exist to love a neighbor like they'd like to be loved themselves. And I believe it's important for Government to not only welcome but to encourage faith-based programs to help solve the intractable problems of our society.

And this Faith-Based Initiative is being challenged in the courts. They claim that— they fight the initiative in the name of civil liberties, yet they do not seem to realize that the organizations they are trying to prevent from accessing Federal money are the same ones that helped win the struggle of civil rights. I believe if an organization gets good results and helps people turn their lives around, it deserves support of Government. We should not discriminate based upon religion. We ought to welcome religious institutions into helping solve and save America, one soul and one heart at a time.

Finally, you and I seek America that commits its wealth and expertise to helping those who suffer from terrible disease. We believe that every person in the world bears the image of our Maker and is an individual of matchless value. And when we see the scourge of HIV/AIDS ravaging communities at home and abroad, we must not avert our eyes.

Today, more than a million of our fellow Americans live with HIV, and more than half of all AIDS cases arise in the African American community. This disease is spreading fastest among African American women. And one of the reasons the disease is spreading so quickly is many don't realize they have the virus. And so we're going to lead a nationwide effort—and I want to work with the NAACP on this effort— to deliver rapid HIV/AIDS—HIV tests to millions of our fellow citizens. Congress needs to reform and reauthorize the Ryan White Act and provide funding to States so we can end the waiting lists for AIDS medications in this country.

To whom much is given, much is required. This Nation is a blessed nation, and

when we look at HIV/AIDS on the continent of Africa, we haven't turned away. We believe it's our Nation's responsibility to help those who suffer from this pandemic. We're leading the world when it comes to providing medications and help. Today, more than 40 million people around the world are living with HIV/AIDS; 26 million of those live in sub-Sahara Africa, including 2 million children under the age of 15. We're calling people together. We pledged $15 billion to provide medicine and help. We launched the Emergency Plan for AIDS Relief. Before this AIDS emergency plan was passed, only 50,000 people in sub-Sahara Africa were getting medicine. Today, that number has grown to more than 560,000 people, and more are getting help every day. By working together, we can turn the tide of this struggle against HIV/AIDS and bring new hope to millions of people.

These goals I've outlined are worthy of our Nation. In the century since the NAACP was founded, our Nation has grown more prosperous and more powerful. It's also grown more equal and just. Yet this work is not finished. That's what I'm here to say. The history of America is one of constant renewal, and each generation has a responsibility to write a new chapter in the unfinished story of freedom.

That story began with the founding promise of equality and justice and freedom for all men. And that promise has brought hope and inspiration to all peoples across the world. Yet our founding was also imperfect because the human beings that made our founding were imperfect. Many of the same Founders who signed their names to a parchment declaring that all men are created equal permitted whole categories of human beings to be excluded from these words. The future of our founding, to live up to its own words, opened a wound that has persisted to today.

In the 19th century, the wound resulted in a civil war. In the 20th century, it denied African Americans the vote in many parts of our country. And at the beginnings of the 21st century, the wound is not fully healed and whole communities—[*applause*]. To heal this wound for good, we must continue to work for a new founding that redeems the promise of our Declaration and guarantees the birthright of every citizen.

For many African Americans this new founding began with the civil rights movement and the Voting Rights Act of 1965. A generation of Americans that has grown up in the last few decades may not appreciate what this act has meant. Condi Rice understands what this act has meant. See, she tells me of her father's long struggle to register to vote, and the pride that came when he finally claimed his full rights as an American citizen to cast his first ballot. She shared that story with me. Yet that right was not fully guaranteed until President Lyndon Johnson signed the Voting Rights Act into law. President Johnson called the right to vote the lifeblood of our democracy. That was true then, and it remains true today.

I thank the Members of the House of Representatives for reauthorizing the Voting Rights Act. Soon the Senate will take up the legislation. I look forward to the Senate passing this bill promptly, without amendment, so I can sign it into law.

There's an old Methodist hymn that speaks of God guiding us with a hand of power and a heart of love. We cannot know God's plans, but we trust in his purposes, because we know that the Creator who wrote the desire for liberty in our hearts also gives us the strength and wisdom to fulfill it. And the God who has brought us thus far on the way will give us the strength to finish the journey.

Thank you for having me. May God bless.

NOTE: The President spoke at 10:35 a.m. at the Washington Convention Center. In his remarks, he referred to Bruce S. Gordon, president and chief executive officer, and Benjamin L. Hooks, former executive director, NAACP; Prime Minister Junichiro Koizumi of Japan; civil rights activist Rev. Jesse L. Jackson, Sr., founder and president Rainbow/PUSH Coalition; and Donna Brazile, chair, Democratic National Committee's Voting Rights Institute.

Statement on Legislation To Reauthorize the Voting Rights Act
July 20, 2006

Last week, the House of Representatives passed legislation to reauthorize the Voting Rights Act. This morning, in celebration of the heroism of the civil rights movement, I spoke to members of the National Association for the Advancement of Colored People at their 97th annual convention, here in Washington, DC. At the NAACP convention, I said that I looked forward to the Senate promptly passing the House bill without amendment. Today the Senate acted and voted to reauthorize this historic legislation.

The Voting Rights Act is one of the most important pieces of legislation in our Nation's history. It has been vital to guaranteeing the right to vote for generations of Americans and has helped millions of our citizens enjoy the full promise of freedom.

I will be pleased to sign the Voting Rights Act into law, and I will continue to work with Congress to ensure that our country lives up to our guiding principle that all men and women are created equal.

NOTE: The statement referred to H.R. 9.

Remarks Following Discussions With First Vice President of the Government of National Unity of Sudan and President of Southern Sudan Salva Kiir Mayardit
July 20, 2006

President Bush. It's been my honor to welcome a man who wears two hats to the Oval Office: Vice President of all Sudan, as well as the President of Southern Sudan. We've had a fascinating discussion. Welcome, Mr. Vice President, I'm glad you're here. Thank you for coming.

I assured our friend that the United States is committed to helping the Sudanese people; we're committed to making sure that the peace agreement that we helped you negotiate is implemented. We're also committed to helping the people in Darfur.

I want to thank you for spending time with me to strategize about what we can do to save lives in Darfur. Our strategy is that we want AU forces to be complemented and blue-helmeted; in other words, the United Nations should be invited in. We talked about how best to get that done in order to save lives. Obviously, there is still a lot of work to be done.

But I want to thank you for coming to our country and sharing with me some of your thoughts and your vision for the people you represent. So welcome to the Oval Office.

First Vice President Kiir. Thank you very much, Your Excellency, President. Well, we are delighted to be in this office at the invitation of His Excellency, the President of the United States of America. It is a very rare opportunity for the people of southern Sudan, in particular, to come to this office and to voice our—their concerns about whatever is happening in our country.

It is true we have been working together during the negotiations with the people of the United States and the Government of the United States of America to bring peace to Sudan. And that peace has taken a toll of our people. This dream has been achieved, and we are now together in the implementation.

There are so many other crises in Sudan—that is the problem of Darfur—that people have been talking about. And we are sure that we are going to solve the problem so that we don't hear about rapes and killings in Darfur—and all other parts of our country, like the eastern Sudan. We are now also negotiating in that province so that peace is also achieved all over the Sudan.

So we thank the President for all the efforts that he has been exerting and the concerns that he has about the people of Sudan.

President Bush. Thank you, sir, appreciate you.

NOTE: The President spoke at 12:15 p.m. in the Oval Office at the White House.

Statement on House of Representatives Passage of the United States-Oman Free Trade Agreement
July 20, 2006

I am pleased the House has approved our free trade agreement with Oman. This agreement will advance America's national security by strengthening our bilateral relations with a strategic friend and ally in the Middle East region. The agreement will also level the playing field for U.S. workers and businesses and will support Oman's leaders as they seek to create long-term opportunities for the Omani people. I look forward to signing this legislation and to continuing our efforts to build a Middle East free trade area.

Remarks Following a Meeting With Military Personnel and an Exchange With Reporters in Aurora, Colorado
July 21, 2006

[The President's remarks are joined in progress.]

The President. ——and this country supports you and admires you and appreciates your dedication. You're doing some hard work. It's hard work to defeat terrorists, killers that wanted to achieve their objective. But we'll succeed; we'll prevail.

I want our troops to understand that not only does the country support them, but we'll win. It's in our national interests that we win. And we will. We've got some powerful, powerful weapons on our side. We've got the men and women who wear the uniform, people who bring such dignity and honor and bring compassion to people who have been suffering under tyranny and are now wondering whether or not the future is bright for them. And we've got freedom on our side too, and freedom is a powerful weapon. People want to be free.

And again, I want to thank you all for your service. I want to thank your families. I wish they were here so I could thank them in person. But your sacrifice has meant a lot. Congratulations for stepping up and volunteering and being a part of history. Thanks for giving me a chance to visit and have a little lunch with you. God bless you all.

Secretary Rice's Upcoming Visit to the Middle East

Q. Mr. President, what do you hope Secretary Rice accomplishes on her trip to the Middle East, sir?

The President. I'm going to talk to her tomorrow when I—Sunday, when I get back to the White House. We're going to have a good visit.

Q. What do you hope she accomplishes, sir?

The President. I said I would talk to her tomorrow.

NOTE: The President spoke at 11:35 a.m. at Tamale Fiesta Kitchen. A tape was not available for verification of the content of these remarks.

Statement on Senate Passage of Child Protection and Safety Legislation
July 21, 2006

I applaud Members of the United States Senate for voting to strengthen our laws against convicted sex offenders.

The "Adam Walsh Child Protection and Safety Act of 2006" will ensure appropriate sentencing for sex offenders and will provide local law enforcement officials with thetools they need to track those who prey upon children. By supporting this legislation, the Senate has taken an important step towards providing our country with a strict, uniform system for monitoring sex offenders to ensure that they do not commit additional crimes against our Nation's children.

I urge the House of Representatives to pass this good legislation as quickly as possible, so that I can sign it into law.

NOTE: The statement referred to H.R. 4472.

The President's Radio Address
July 22, 2006

Good morning. This week, I returned from Russia, where I met with world leaders at the G–8 summit. The summit was an opportunity for important talks with these nations, and it brought progress on key issues. We had wide-ranging discussions on the global economy. We agreed on new steps to strengthen our collective security, including a United Nations Security Council resolution on North Korea. This resolution condemned North Korea's recent missile launches, and it urged the North Korean regime to abandon its nuclear programs and return to the six-party talks.

Much of our time at the summit was spent discussing the situation in the Middle East, especially the recent violence in Israel and Lebanon. The recent crisis in the region was triggered by the kidnaping of Israeli soldiers by the terrorist group Hizballah and the launch of rockets against Israeli cities. I believe sovereign nations have the right to defend their people from terrorist attack and to take the necessary action to prevent those attacks.

We're also mindful of the cost to innocent civilians in Lebanon and in Israel, and we have called on Israel to continue to exercise the greatest possible care to protect innocent lives. Throughout this crisis, I have spoken to leaders in the Middle East and around the world. Our efforts to resolve this dangerous situation are guided by an international framework that is already in place.

In 2004, the United Nations Security Council adopted Resolution 1559, which recognizes the sovereignty of Lebanon, calls for all foreign forces to withdraw from Lebanon, and calls for the disbanding and disarmament of all militias. Hizballah defied the world's just demands by maintaining armed units in the southern region of Lebanon and attacking Israel in defiance of the democratically elected Lebanese Government.

I've directed Secretary of State Rice to travel to the Middle East in the coming days to discuss the best ways to resolve this crisis with leaders in the region. Secretary Rice will make it clear that resolving the crisis demands confronting the terrorist group that launched the attacks and the nations that support it.

For many years, Syria has been a primary sponsor of Hizballah, and it has helped provide Hizballah with shipments of Iranian-made weapons. Iran's regime has also repeatedly defied the international community with its ambition for nuclear weapons and aid to terrorist groups. Their actions threaten the entire Middle East and stand in the way of resolving the current crisis and bringing lasting peace to this troubled region.

We're also concerned about the impact the current conflict is having on Lebanon's young democracy. This is a difficult and trying time for the people of Lebanon. Hizballah's practice of hiding rockets in civilian neighborhoods and its efforts to undermine the democratically elected Government have shown it to be no friend of Lebanon. By its actions, Hizballah has jeopardized Lebanon's tremendous advances and betrayed the Lebanese people.

Over the past week, nations like Saudi Arabia and Kuwait and the United Arab Emirates have stepped forward to offer humanitarian aid and assistance to the Lebanese Government. America and our allies will join these efforts. We're also working to help American citizens who wish to leave Lebanon. American military personnel and Embassy officials are working hard to ensure this operation proceeds smoothly and safely. We continue to pray for the safety of all people in Lebanon: Americans, Lebanese, and citizens of other countries.

America remains committed to lasting peace in the Middle East. The United States and our partners will continue to seek a return to the roadmap for peace

in the Middle East, which sets out the pathway to establishing a viable democratic Palestinian state that will live in peace with Israel. We will continue to support moderate leaders like Palestinian Authority President Abbas. We will continue to call on Hamas to end its acts of terror. And now, more than ever, the Palestinians need leaders who are not compromised by terror and who will help the Palestinian people provide a future for their children based on regional peace and security.

In the long term, this peace will come only by defeating the terrorist ideology of hatred and fear. The world's best hope for lasting security and stability across the Middle East is the establishment of free and just societies. America and our allies will act decisively because we know our security is at stake in this struggle and we know the cause of freedom will prevail.

Thank you for listening.

NOTE: The address was recorded at 7:50 a.m. on July 21 in the Cabinet Room at the White House for broadcast at 10:06 a.m. on July 22. The transcript was made available by the Office of the Press Secretary on July 21 but was embargoed for release until the broadcast. In his address, the President referred to Ehud Goldwasser and Eldad Regev, Israeli soldiers captured and held captive by militants in Lebanon since July 12; and President Mahmoud Abbas of the Palestinian Authority. The Office of the Press Secretary also released a Spanish language transcript of this address.

Remarks at a Naturalization Ceremony
July 24, 2006

Thank you all. Thanks for coming. Thanks for letting me come back, General, proud to be here. I'm really looking forward to witnessing what is going to be a very uplifting ceremony.

In a few moments, these men will swear the oath to become citizens of the United States of America. As part of the ceremony, they will promise to support and defend the Constitution and laws of the United

States of America against all enemies, foreign and domestic. This isn't going to be the first time these men have made such a promise. They took a similar oath when they became soldiers of the United States Army. And their presence here bears witness that they kept their word so that others might be free.

I appreciate General Farmer, and I want to thank all the folks who work here. I'm incredibly impressed by the health care and the decency and the compassion of the people who work here at Walter Reed. You bring great credit to our country. I can't tell you the number of times, when I travel around America, that I brag about Walter Reed and the health care you deliver.

I appreciate Dr. Emilio Gonzalez, who will be administering the oath of office. He's the Director of the U.S. Citizenship and Immigration Services. He's the head guy; he came over to deliver the oath. [*Laughter*]

I want to thank Colonel Deal and everybody else. I particularly want to say thanks to the families of these three men. Thank you for joining us today.

Through the generations, our Nation has remained strong and free because men and women put on our uniform and defend this country and defend our beliefs. The three men we honor today have brought honor to America. Like those who have come before, each of these men chose to protect our country because they love what America stands for.

Army Specialist Sergio Lopez had always wanted to join the Army, and in 2003, he volunteered. After basic training, he moved to Fort Hood, Texas, home of the 1st Cavalry Division and the 4th Infantry Division. Specialist Lopez then deployed to Iraq. He put his life on the line each day, driving between observation posts and his unit's forward operating base in the Baghdad area. In January, he was injured by an improvised explosive device. Specialist Lopez says that becoming a citizen, quote, "represents being acknowledged as having done

my duty, having done my part for the country, like the oath says, defending the United States."

Today we honor Army Private First Class Eduardo Leal-Cardenas. He was injured when an IED blew up his vehicle in Iraq. Private Leal-Cardenas is a man of few words, and he's a man of action. When some questioned whether he would ever walk again, he laughed, and he began his rehab while still in his bed. When Private Leal-Cardenas is asked what citizenship in America means to him, he just said one word: Freedom.

And finally, we honor Army Specialist Lito Santos-Dilone. He was injured while serving as part of the protection detail in Iraq. I first met Specialist Santos-Dilone at this year's National Hispanic Prayer Breakfast. I was working the rope line. He grabbed my hand, and he said, "I'm not a citizen of the United States, and I want to be one." Now, here's a man who knows how to take it directly to the top. [*Laughter*] I'm proud to be here when he gets sworn in.

We are stronger and more dynamic when we welcome new citizens like these. More than 33,000 non-U.S. citizens currently serve in our military. Isn't that interesting—33,000 people who weren't born here serve in our military. And just like everybody else who wears the uniform, they understand the stakes of what it means to serve in the United States military, particularly after September the 11th, 2001.

After that date, I signed an Executive order making foreign-born members of our military immediately eligible for U.S. citizenship when they serve on active duty. It made sense to me. If somebody is willing to risk their lives for our country, they ought to be full participants in our country.

As our Nation debates the future of our immigration policies, we must remember the contribution of these good men and all who dream of contributing to this country's future. It says something about our country that people around the world are willing to leave their homes and leave their families and risk everything to come to America. Their talent and hard work and love of freedom have helped make America the leader of the world. And our generation will ensure that America remains a beacon of liberty and the most hopeful society this world has ever known.

I believe this country can be a lawful society and a welcoming society at the same time. We're going to enforce our laws, but we'll also honor our proud immigrant heritage. I support a comprehensive immigration reform that will accomplish five clear objectives. First, we'll secure our borders. Second, we must create a temporary-worker program that provides foreign workers a legal and orderly way to come into the country and do jobs Americans aren't doing. We must hold employers to account for the workers they hire. In other words, it's against the law to hire an illegal immigrant, and we're going to hold employers to account. We must resolve the status of millions of illegal immigrants who are here already. We shouldn't be granting people automatic citizenship, nor is it possible to kick people out of the country. There's got to be a rational way, and I proposed a way forward. And finally, we've got to honor the great American tradition of the melting pot by helping newcomers assimilate into our society.

Congress is now considering legislation on immigration reform; that legislation must be comprehensive. All elements of the problem must be addressed together, or none of them will be solved at all.

This is a joyful day for these men, and it's a joyful day for me to be here with them, and it's a proud day for our Nation. We gain three new citizens today, men who knew the cost of freedom and are willing to pay that cost so others can live free. It's a privilege to be their Commander in Chief, and I look forward to calling them fellow citizens.

I want to congratulate you for your achievement. I want to thank you for your service. I ask for God's blessings on you and your family and for God's blessings on the United States of America.

And now we'll have the oath of citizenship administered.

NOTE: The President spoke at 10:12 a.m. at Walter Reed Army Medical Center. In his remarks, he referred to Maj. Gen. Kenneth L. Farmer, Jr., USA, commanding general, North Atlantic Regional Medical Command and Walter Reed Army Medical Center; and Col. Virgil T. Deal, USA, commander, Walter Reed Health Care System. The Office of the Press Secretary also released a Spanish language transcript of these remarks.

Statement on Signing the Freedom to Display the American Flag Act of 2005
July 24, 2006

Today I was pleased to sign into law the "Freedom to Display the American Flag Act of 2005." Americans have long flown our flag at their homes as an expression of their appreciation for our freedoms and their pride in our Nation. As our brave men and women continue to fight to protect our country overseas, Congress has passed an important measure to protect our citizens' right to express their patriotism here at home without burdensome restrictions.

NOTE: H.R. 42, approved July 24, was assigned Public Law No. 109–243.

The President's News Conference With Prime Minister Nuri al-Maliki of Iraq
July 25, 2006

President Bush. Thank you all. Please be seated.

Mr. Prime Minister, welcome to the White House. I just had a very constructive meeting with the leader of a Government that has been chosen by the Iraqi people in free and fair elections. I appreciate your vision for a free Iraq, and I appreciate you briefing me on a strategy to reduce violence and to rebuild your country.

You have a strong partner in the United States of America, and I'm honored to stand here with you, Mr. Prime Minister. It's a remarkable, historical moment, as far as I'm concerned, to welcome freely elected leader of Iraq to the White House.

We discussed a lot of issues. The Prime Minister has laid out a comprehensive plan. That's what leaders do. They see problems; they address problems; and they lay out a plan to solve the problems. The Prime Minister understands he's got challenges, and he's identified priorities.

Our priority is to help this Government succeed. It's in the national interest of the United States that a unity government, based upon a constitution that is advanced and modern, succeed. And that's what I told the Prime Minister. He comes wondering whether or not we're committed. He hears all kinds of stories here in the United States. And I assured him that this Government stands with the Iraqi people. We're impressed by your courage, Mr. Prime Minister, and we're impressed by the courage of the Iraqi people. And we want to help you.

We talked about security in Baghdad. No question, the terrorists and extremists are brutal. These are people that just kill innocent people to achieve an objective, which is to destabilize his Government. The Prime Minister tells me that he and his Government are not shaken by these actions. They're concerned about them; they're not shaken by them.

The Iraqi people want to succeed. They want to end this violence. Our strategy is to remain on the offense, including in Baghdad. Under the Prime Minister's leadership, coalition and Iraqi leaders are modifying their operational concept to bring greater security to the Iraqi capital. Coalition and Iraqi forces will secure individual neighborhoods, will ensure the existence of an Iraqi security presence in the neighborhoods, and gradually expand the security presence as Iraqi citizens help them root out those who instigate violence.

This plan will involve embedding more U.S. military police with Iraqi police units to make them more effective. The Prime Minister advised me that to support this plan, he and General Casey have agreed to deploy additional American troops and Iraqi security personnel in Baghdad in the coming weeks. These will come from other areas of the country. Our military commanders tell me that this deployment will better reflect the current conditions on the ground in Iraq.

We also agreed that Iraqi security forces need better tools to do their job. And so we'll work with them to equip them with greater mobility, firepower, and protection.

We still face challenges in Baghdad, yet we see progress elsewhere in Iraq. Iraqi security forces are growing in strength and capability, and recently, a key Province in southern Iraq was transferred to full Iraqi civilian control. In the midst of all the violence in Baghdad, sometimes a success is obscured. And this transfer of a key Province is the beginning of other Provinces to be transferred to full Iraqi control. It's a sign of progress. No question, it's tough in Baghdad, and no question, it's tough in other parts of Iraq. But there are also places where progress is being made, and the Prime Minister and I talked about that progress.

The Prime Minister and I agreed to establish a joint committee to achieve Iraqi self-reliance. This new partnership will seek to ensure the smoothest and most effective assumption of security responsibility by Iraqi forces. Prime Minister Maliki was very clear this morning: He said he does not want American troops to leave his country until his Government can protect the Iraqi people. And I assured him that America will not abandon the Iraqi people.

Tomorrow the Prime Minister and I will travel to Fort Belvoir in Virginia to visit with American troops and their families so we can thank them for their courage and their sacrifice. And we in the United States need to recognize the enormous sacrifice of the Iraqi people. The people are suffering hardships. These terrorists and killers are trying to shake the will of the Iraqi people. But despite large casualties, both civilian and military, the Iraqi people continue to stand for public office, enlist in their security forces, and, through their actions, demonstrate every day that they want to raise their families and live their lives like other free people around the world. And I'm impressed by the courage of the Iraqi citizens, Mr. Prime Minister.

Citizens continue to believe in the future of their country and to subscribe to the notion upon which America is also founded, that the freedom of their country is worth fighting for. America is proud to be allied with such people. And it's important the Iraqi people hear of our pride and our determination, Mr. Prime Minister.

We also discussed several new initiatives we're undertaking to create opportunity for the Iraqi people, and one of them is called the Iraqi Leaders Initiative. And starting next summer, 200 high school and university students from all regions of Iraq and all sectors of Iraqi society will come to America to study at local institutions and build personal friendships with the people of our country. This is going to be the largest program of its kind, and it will help build the next generation of leaders for a free and democratic Iraq.

Prime Minister and I spent time talking about Lebanon, and we had a frank exchange on—of views on this situation. I listened closely to the Prime Minister, and I valued a chance to hear his perspective. I heard him on the seriousness of the humanitarian crisis in Lebanon and the need to do more for the Lebanese people. I told him that Secretary Rice has announced greater humanitarian measures for Lebanon to include $30 million in aid. America is concerned about the women and children who suffer in that country, concerned about the loss of innocent life. I reminded him and told him that Condi is over there working to establish corridors to ensure the delivery of humanitarian aid and central relief supplies.

I told him I support a sustainable ceasefire that will bring about an end to violence. And I talked about the importance of strengthening the Lebanese Government and supporting the Lebanese people.

Prime Minister and I also discussed his proposal for an international compact for Iraq. The compact will outline Iraq's commitment to specific economic reforms and the international community's commitment to support those reforms. We expect the international compact will be signed later this year. And I told the Prime Minister that the United States will work to encourage other countries to support the compact and for other countries that have made pledges to Iraq to make good on their pledges.

In light of the recent violence in the Middle East, some are questioning whether democracy can take root in the region. I believe that the Iraqi people are showing us their answer. They're making enormous sacrifices to secure their freedom, and they've elected leaders who are making tough decisions.

And, Mr. Prime Minister, you're such a leader, and I welcome you here to the White House. Thanks for coming.

Prime Minister Maliki. Thank you very much. In the name of God, the most merciful and the passionate, I would like to thank President George Bush. Mr. President, I would like to thank you for your invitation to come here and visit the United States of America, and I would like to thank you for the warm welcome that myself and my delegation received. And I also—I appreciate very much your interest in the situation in Iraq and the responsible spirit that has dominated our discussions today.

We have discussed with President Bush, clearly and frankly, all the current challenges and the horizon and the future and ways of cooperation between our two countries in order to build a democratic, united, flourishing Iraq that enjoys its full national sovereignty. We have agreed that building the security and military institutions in Iraq, in terms of numbers, equipment, firearms, and as quickly as possible, represents the fundamental base in order to stabilize the country and to have security and defeat terrorism.

I reaffirmed to the President Iraq's need to—the cooperation from the international community and your cooperation. And I have seen a great deal of understanding for this very vital issue from the President. I also expressed my appreciation to the role that's been played by the multinational forces and the exerted efforts to support us and to help us in building our security organizations, to allow our organizations to

fully be in control of the security position and the security circumstances.

I agreed with the President to form a joint committee of experts and the connections in order to achieve the self-sufficiency for the Iraqi forces. This will allow these forces to bear the responsibility of protecting security and confronting terrorism in our country. And in this field, we have achieved our first and initial success when our forces assumed the responsibility in the Muthanna Governorate. This is a very important step—will be followed by similar steps in many other governorates in Iraq.

We are determined to defeat terrorism. And the security plan for Baghdad have entered the second phase, and it's achieving its objectives in hunting the terrorist networks and eliminating it.

I have informed the President about the national reconciliation plan, which I have launched in order to attract more Iraqi forces which have not engaged in the political process yet. This initiative represents, in addition to building the Iraqi Armed Forces, one of the initiatives that will contribute to choking terrorism and defeating terrorism in Iraq.

On the economic sphere and the reconstruction of Iraq, I have seen support from President Bush to ensure the success of the international impact, which we hope that, through it, we'll be able to have the support of the world community in reconstructing Iraq and improving the services that the Government is providing to its own Iraqi people. We hope that many other countries will participate and contribute in that conference that will be convened in the next few months in order to sign this international compact. I assured the President, Iraq's readiness to make this conference a success and accept the mutual commitments between Iraq and those who will sign the compact. The President reaffirmed his administration's commitment to encourage as many countries as possible to support this compact.

I also discussed with the President the issue of Lebanon in all seriousness, in a way that matches the importance of the size of destructions that happened to the Lebanese people as a result of the military air and ground attacks. And I also emphasized the importance of immediate cease-fire, and call on the international community to support the Lebanese Government and support the Lebanese people to overcome the damage and destruction that happened.

I also expressed to the President about Iraq's desire and Iraq's political leadership's desire to merge in the international community and its institutions and to participate effectively in the various issues on the basis of mutual interest and to be committed to the policy of not interfering or intervening in the domestic policies of other countries. I also reaffirmed the importance of approaching every issue through peaceful and diplomatic means to deal with the problems that exist in our region. These chronic problems requires a great deal of wisdom and patience and perseverance in order to find the just and successful and fair solution.

Mr. President, I thank you once again for your kind invitation and for your very warm hospitality and generosity.

President Bush. ——questions a side, starting with you, Tom [Tom Raum, Associated Press].

Security Situation in Baghdad

Q. Mr. President and Mr. Prime Minister, why should one expect this new security crackdown in Baghdad to succeed when all previous ones have failed?

And, Mr. President, you've said before that withdrawal of U.S. troops would depend on conditions on the ground. What do conditions on the ground now in Baghdad suggest in terms of whether there can be a significant withdrawal of American forces by the end of the year?

President Bush. I'll start—do you want to start? Go ahead.

Prime Minister Maliki. Actually, the circumstances that the Baghdad security plans, or other plans related to Basra and other places, are different in terms of circumstances from the previous plans. Today, Iraq has a national unity Government that—it is basically composed of—all elements of the Iraqi people are represented in this Government. Iraq has a parliament; it has a Constitution to face all these challenges. So what the Baghdad security plan gains, in terms of support, is support from all over the segments of the Iraqi population.

Secondly, by monitoring the reality on the ground, we will be able to ensure the success, especially what happens against the innocent people. The Baghdad security forces was able to eliminate many hotspots of crimes and troubles in Baghdad.

President Bush. One of the things that's important is for—and one of the reasons why you trust the commanders on the ground is because there needs to be flexibility. And I explained to the Prime Minister that I'll be making my decisions based upon the recommendations of General Casey. And obviously, the violence in Baghdad is still terrible, and therefore, there needs to be more troops. In other words, the commanders said, "What more can we do; how best to address the conditions on the ground?" And they have recommended, as a result of working with the Prime Minister, based upon his recommendation, that we increase the number of U.S. troops in Baghdad alongside of Iraqi troops. And we're going to do that.

The second request that the Prime Minister made was that he needs more equipment for his troops. And General Dempsey, along with General Casey, have reviewed his requests and his ideas. And I told the Prime Minister if this is what these generals recommend, it's what I support.

Conditions change inside a country, Tom. And the question is, are we going to be facile enough to change with—will we be nimble enough; will we be able to deal with the circumstances on the ground? And the answer is, yes, we will.

Mr. Prime Minister, would you like to call on somebody? There you go.

Iraq-U.S. Cooperation in the War on Terror

Q. I have two questions—one, President Bush. The first one: Is there an obvious change that could be made to the security status, you politically—particularly in Baghdad right now?

And the second question for you, Mr. Prime Minister. You said in a press conference in Baghdad that your visit to Washington, you will put—you will cross the t's and dot the i's, especially regarding the security needs. Did you cross the t's and dot the i's in your discussion with President Bush?

President Bush. ——a lot of time talking about security, and I can understand why. Because there's—there are people who are willing to destroy innocent life to achieve a political objective. And the Prime Minister is deeply concerned about the lives of his fellow citizens. And I appreciate that concern. I would be very worried if a Prime Minister came to talk about his country and did not mention, first and foremost, protecting people's lives. That's, after all, the most important responsibility of government.

And he believes, and I believe, that the—there needs to be more forces inside Baghdad who are willing to hold people to account. In other words, if you find somebody who's kidnaping and murdering, the murderer ought to be held to account. It ought to be clear in society that that kind of behavior is not tolerated.

And that's the attitude of the Prime Minister. My attitude is, we shouldn't try to gauge whether or not someone is justified or not; we ought to be saying that if you murder, you're responsible for your actions. And I think the Iraqi people appreciate that type of attitude.

And so we—so we're not only talking about adjusting a Baghdad plan at the Prime Minister's request to make it more effective—we're also talking about how to make the Iraqi Army more effective. But the truth of the matter is, the Iraqi Army is becoming a highly professional force that will help bring confidence to the people inside Iraq that the Government has got the capacity to protect them.

Prime Minister Maliki. Thank you, Mr. President. Actually, successful acts and large issues has to be based on a clear vision. And through the serious discussion and the clear and the frank conversation that I had with President George Bush, that we are truly crossing the t's and dotting the i's in terms of enhancing the security and supporting the reconstruction. Through the discussion, we were able to go through the details of the vision that will cover the future, because we are not talking here about a specific phase of the reconstruction, but we are facing the necessity of continuous work in order to make sure that the entire political experiment will succeed.

I believe with a great deal of confidence that I have reaffirmed through this, and I became convinced that—I have full confidence of victory, and we will be highly capable of defeating terrorism in Iraq.

Situation in the Middle East/Democracy in Iraq

Q. ——you had a frank exchange on the Middle East. How can you get Arab nations to apply pressure to stop the fighting in the Middle East if allies like the Prime Minister won't condemn Hizballah?

And, Mr. Prime Minister, what exactly is your position on Hizballah? Thank you.

President Bush. The terrorists are afraid of democracies. And what you've witnessed in Israel, in my judgment, is the act of a terrorist organization trying to stop the advance of democracy in the region.

I assured the Prime Minister that I care deeply about the suffering that takes place, that we understand the anguish of leaders in the region who see innocent people losing their life. I also assured him that Condi Rice's mission is to help get humanitarian aid to the Lebanese people. She's working on not only air corridors but sea corridors and land corridors to get aid to the people. And the United States will participate, as will other nations.

I also talked about making sure that we adhere to U.N. Resolution 1559, which basically—not basically—strongly urges political parties not to be armed. A key part of our strategy is to support democracy. And so not only do we support democracy in the Palestinian Territory, we also support the Lebanese democracy. I think the Prime Minister was pleased to hear my strong support for the Siniora Government.

And so Condi goes with the following messages: We support the Siniora Government; we care about the people; we will help to get aid to the people; and that we want a sustainable cease-fire. We don't want something that's short-term in duration. We want to address the root causes of the violence in the area, and therefore, our mission and our goal is to have a lasting peace, not a temporary peace but something that lasts.

And I believe that Iraq, in some ways, faces the same difficulty, and that is, a new democracy is emerging and there are people who are willing to use terrorist techniques to stop it. That's what the murder is all about. People fear democracy if your vision is based upon kind of a totalitarian view of the world. And that's the ultimate challenge facing Iraq and Lebanon and the Palestinian Territories, and that is, will the free world, and the neighborhood, work in concert to help develop sustainable democracy?

And Iraq took a long step along that— a big step on that path when they developed a Constitution that was ratified by the Iraqi people. And it's a modern Constitution, and it's a landmark moment in the history of freedom advancing in the Middle East.

I believe that deep in everybody's soul, Mr. Prime Minister, is a desire to be free. And when 12 million Iraqis went to the polls and said, "I want to be free," it was an amazing moment. I know it seems like a long, long time ago that that happened. But it was a powerful statement about what is possible in terms of achieving peace.

Prime Minister Maliki. Thank you. Here, actually, we're talking about the suffering of a people in a country. And we are not in the process of reviewing one issue or another, or any government position. The important thing here is what we are trying to do is to stop the killing and the destruction, and then we leave the room and the way for the international and diplomatic efforts and international organization to play the role to be there.

We are not here facing a situation only in Lebanon, but would be facing a variety of issues in different countries. I'm talking here about the approach that should be used in order to stop this process of promoting hatred; that has to be superior decisions coming from above in order to protect these experiments, particularly the democratic experiments that should be protected by those who are trying to oppose it.

Israel-U.S. Relations/Rule of Law in Iraq

Q. Thank you very much, Mr. Prime Minister. General Abizaid said that the danger that Iraq is facing is the religious danger. Do you agree with his assessment? And do you see that—is there any security plan that can really curb the religious violence?

[*Inaudible*]—humanitarian aid to Lebanon, yet there's also reports that your administration are speeding up delivery of laser-guided missiles to Israel and bunker-buster bombs. And do you see this—if this is true, do you see it as contradictory? On one hand, you allow Israel to kill people, and civilian, in particular, and on the other hand, you're trying to aid the very people that have been suffering and killed as a result?

President Bush. No, I don't see a contradiction in us honoring commitments we made prior to Hizballah attacks into Israeli territory. And I—like the Prime Minister, I'm concerned about loss of innocent life, and we will do everything we can to help move equipment—I mean, food and medicines to help the people who have been displaced and the people who suffer.

Prime Minister Maliki. Yes. I do not reduce the risk and the danger of the religious feelings, especially through some of the organizations that are trying to promote this hatred. And there are—some of the events are on the basis of religious divide, but I would like to assure the political, religious leaders, and civil societies that the Iraqi parties, politicians, religious leaders are rising to their responsibility and are condemning those who are cooperating with Al Qaida and those who are trying to start a civil war.

The one—the most important element in the security plan is to curb the religious violence, because we will not allow any Iraqis to use this background. This is one of the main objective of the security plan.

It is the policy of the Government: There is no killing or discrimination against anyone. Everything is by law and everything based on the Constitution and the law. The Government responsibility is to protect all Iraqis, regardless of their ethnic or religious background. It's important to say that we are shedding the light against those who are calling for sectarian religious, because we feel that this is a great danger to Iraq. And, God willing, there will be no civil war in Iraq.

Thank you very much.

President Bush. Thank you.

NOTE: The President's news conference began at 11:27 a.m. in the East Room at the White House. In his remarks, he referred to Gen. George W. Casey, Jr., USA, commanding general, Multi-National Force—Iraq; Lt. Gen. Martin E. Dempsey, USA, commander, Multi-National Security Transition Command—Iraq and NATO Training Mission—Iraq; and Prime Minister Fuad Siniora of Lebanon. A reporter referred to Gen. John P. Abizaid, USA, commander, U.S. Central Command. Prime Minister Maliki and some reporters spoke in Arabic, and their remarks were translated by an interpreter.

Statement on Senate Passage of Legislation Concerning the Transportation of Minors Across State Lines
July 25, 2006

Transporting minors across State lines to bypass parental consent laws regarding abortion undermines State law and jeopardizes the lives of young women. To combat this dangerous practice, the Senate today passed the "Child Custody Protection Act," which penalizes those who unlawfully attempt to circumvent parental notification requirements.

I appreciate the Senate's efforts to preserve the integrity of State law and protect our Nation's families. I look forward to the House and Senate resolving their differences in conference and sending this legislation for my signature.

NOTE: The statement referred to S. 403.

Remarks at a Lunch With Prime Minister Nuri al-Maliki of Iraq and Military Personnel at Fort Belvoir, Virginia
July 26, 2006

President Bush. Thank you all for such gracious hospitality. I thought I would drop by with the Prime Minister of Iraq. [*Laughter*] I wanted him to be with some of the finest citizens in the United States of America.

I appreciate our Ambassador to Iraq joining us today, Zal Khalilzad. Mr. Ambassador, thank you for coming. Ambassador Sumaydi, from Iraq to the United States, is with us. Ambassador, thank you for coming. I appreciate the Members of the United States Senate who have joined us, Senator Warner and Senator Allen. Thank you all for being here. I appreciate you joining us. I want to thank Congressman Jim Moran and Congressman Tom Davis for joining us.

Mr. Prime Minister, obviously, Members of the United States Congress are interested in you. [*Laughter*] They're also interested in the United States military. And they know what I know, that anytime we've got a man or woman in uniform in harm's way, they deserve all the possible support necessary to complete the mission.

I want to thank Colonel Lauritzen and all the folks who made this visit possible. It's an honor to be here, and it's an honor to be with the family members of our troops.

Mr. Prime Minister, when I speak to our troops, I also talk to their loved ones, because you can't have a strong United States military without the support of the military families. Our troops have sacrificed, and as they have done so, so have our military families. And so today we pay respect for the men and women who wear the uniform and their loved ones. We're proud of you.

There's no better place to come than Fort Belvoir, Mr. Prime Minister, because here there are some 120 military commands representing the Army, Navy, Air Force, Marine Corps, and Coast Guard, all branches of the United States military who have served with distinction in fighting the terrorists who would like to do us harm and prevent your good country from becoming a democracy.

I tell our folks that success in Iraq is necessary for the security of the United States, and it's necessary for the peace of the world. One of the things that—one of the lessons we can learn from history is that freedom and liberty and democracies have got the capacity to convert enemies into allies and to lay the foundation for peace.

Now, Mr. Prime Minister, we were deeply moved when 12 million of your citizens went to the polls last December. It was really a remarkable statement, wasn't it? Twelve million citizens, who at one time had lived under the thumb of a brutal tyrant, went to the polls and said, "We want to be free." And out of that election, Mr. Prime Minister, you and your Government have emerged.

We respect the fact that your Government represents the will of the Iraqi people. One thing the Prime Minister told me getting out of the limousine, after having flown on the helicopter—[*laughter*]—was that he longs for the day when the Iraqi children can live in a hopeful society. That's what he wants. He wants the Iraqi people to enjoy the benefits that most people in other countries enjoy. It is a simple concept in many ways, yet is profound, because my reaction upon hearing his words was, this man will succeed if he cares first and foremost about the people and the condition of the Iraqi people. If he's the kind of leader like I know he is, who cares about generations of Iraqis to come, he will be successful.

We've got hard work to do together, Mr. Prime Minister. We were talking here at the table, and I was commenting that it's amazing, isn't it, where some people decide to kill innocent lives to stop freedom. And frankly, that's a hard concept for some of us to understand. But I understand this: That in order for freedom to succeed, those folks have got to be brought to justice. They cannot be allowed to kill the innocent.

And that's why we've sent some of our finest citizens to help you, Mr. Prime Minister. We want you to succeed. It's in our Nation's interest that you succeed. And I'm confident we will succeed. The Prime Minister came, and he didn't say this directly to me, but I could tell by looking in my eyes, he wanted to make sure that this was a President who kept his word. I've told the Iraqi people, we stand with you, and that no matter how tough it gets, we will complete this mission. We owe it to those who have served in combat. We owe it to those who have lost a limb. We owe it to those who have lost a life.

Fort Belvoir lost a good man recently in Sergeant First Class Scott Smith. He was killed by an IED. He helped save lives. He helped lay that foundation for peace. And in honor of his memory and in the memory of others who have gone before him, in honor of the thousands of Iraqis who have died at the hands of terrorists, we will complete the mission. It's in our interest, Mr. Prime Minister, that we succeed together.

And so I've asked you to come, to be in the midst of those who have served our country. The amazing thing about our military is that people have had to say, "I want to serve." Every person you see here in uniform, Mr. Prime Minister, has volunteered to serve the United States of America. And in so doing, they have set a fantastic example for generations to come, and they have made the United States of America incredibly proud.

So I'd like to welcome you to the podium, Mr. Prime Minister. And as you come up here and look at the folks here in uniform, you've got to know how proud their Commander in Chief is to be able to serve alongside of them as we do our duty with honor for our country.

Mr. Prime Minister.

Prime Minister Maliki. I would like to thank the President for his invitation. And I would also like to thank the Members of Congress who are with us today here— and to the sons and families of the Armed Forces who are here with us in this celebration. When I stand here in front of you and I salute you, I would like to appreciate what you have done and what you have achieved.

I appreciate your colleagues who offered their lives on the land of Iraq, and I tell you that Iraqis will never forget these sacrifices because they have really participated in ridding Iraq of dictatorship, one of the ugliest regimes that the region has known. And we are happy to be partners in this holy task of fighting terrorism and establishing democracy.

Iraq, because of what you have offered, because of what your sons have offered, your families have offered, has now moved from dictatorship to democracy; from oppression, torture chambers, chemical weapons, and now into a space of freedom, liberty, and partnership; from depravation and absolute poverty into the condition where we now are looking forward to economic prosperity, because Iraq is a rich country, and the previous regime has wasted all the wealth of Iraq in his adventures.

I sympathize with those who made sacrifices, and I sympathize with the families who have lost some loved ones. And I appreciate this sacrifice and this suffering, because I am one of the people who sacrificed and suffered in Iraq. The previous regime had sentenced me to death and actually has executed 67 members of my family and relatives. And I can feel the bitterness of the loss when someone loses a dear member of his family, a son or a spouse.

When blood mixes together in the field, aiming to achieve one goal, this blood will help in establishing long-lasting relationship between us. Our relationship will stay forever.

Terrorists still carry out, on daily basis, these crazy actions against innocent civilians: their suicide bombs, their car bombs against the innocent civilians who have nothing to do with the conflict in Iraq. They want to kill democracy as they kill humans. But they will definitely fail, because we are committed to success, and we are committed to democracy. And the daily killing does not prevent Iraqis from carrying out and going along with their daily lives. And we are confident that we will succeed, because you and people like you are helping us to confront terrorism— terrorism that is spreading in our land— with foreign support.

Lastly, on behalf of myself and on behalf of the Iraqi people, I would like to thank you and thank your families. I would like to appreciate your losses, your sacrifices, appreciate the bitterness of those who have lost loved ones. I hope that you can go past your losses, and I hope that you can compensate it with—compensate it about what's happened.

And we feel pain and sorrow for every drop of blood that falls in Iraq. But once again, we give you all the salute—we salute you, and we thank you very much for all that you've offered to Iraq.

NOTE: The President spoke at 1:17 p.m. at the Fort Belvoir Community Club. In his remarks, he referred to Iraq's Ambassador to the U.S. Samir Shakir al-Sumaydi; Col. Brian W. Lauritzen, USA, garrison commander, Ft. Belvoir; and former President Saddam Hussein of Iraq. Prime Minister Maliki spoke in Arabic, and his remarks were translated by an interpreter.

Statement on House of Representatives Passage of Legislation Expanding American Homeownership
July 26, 2006

I am pleased the House passed the "Expanding American Homeownership Act of 2006."

The Federal Housing Administration has helped millions of Americans become homeowners in communities throughout our country. I appreciate the House's efforts to modernize this important program to ensure that it reflects the demands of today's marketplace and addresses the current needs of potential home buyers. By providing the FHA with increased flexibility for mortgage downpayment requirements and the authority to tailor financing to suit a family's unique situation, this bill will improve FHA's ability to help lower and moderate-income families achieve the American Dream.

I encourage the Senate to join the House and pass this critical legislation.

NOTE: The statement referred to H.R. 5121.

Remarks on Signing the Fannie Lou Hamer, Rosa Parks, and Coretta Scott King Voting Rights Act Reauthorization and Amendments Act of 2006
July 27, 2006

Thank you. Good morning. Welcome. Thanks for being here on this special day. Please be seated. America began with a declaration that all men are created equal. This declaration marked a tremendous advance in the story of freedom, yet it also contained a contradiction: Some of the same men who signed their names to this self-evident truth owned other men as property. By reauthorizing this act, Congress has reaffirmed its belief that all men are created equal, its belief that the new founding started by the signing of the bill by President Johnson is worthy of our great Nation to continue.

I'm proud to be here with our Attorney General, members of my Cabinet, leaders of the United States Senate and House of Representatives. I thank the bill sponsors. I thank the members of the Judiciary Committee. I appreciate so very much representatives of the Hamer family who have joined us, representatives of the Rosa and Raymond Parks Institute who have joined us, and members of the King family, in particular Reverend Bernice King and Martin Luther King. Thank you all for coming.

I'm honored to be here with civil rights leaders like Dr. Dorothy Height, Julian Bond, the chairman of the NAACP. Bruce Gordon—thank you, Bruce. Reverend Lowery—it's good to see you again, sir—fortunately, I got the mike this time. [*Laughter*] I'm proud to be here with Marc Morial. Thanks for coming, Marc. Juanita Abernathy is with us today. Jesse Jackson—good to see you, Jesse. Al Sharpton, Dr. Benjamin Hooks and Frances are with us. A lot of other folks who care deeply about this issue, we welcome you here.

It's good to welcome the mayor. Mr. Mayor, good to see you. Thanks for coming—Tony Williams. Everything is fine in the neighborhood; I appreciate it. [*Laugh-*

ter] And the mayor of Selma, Alabama, James Perkins, is with us. Mr. Mayor, proud you're here. Welcome, sir.

The right of ordinary men and women to determine their own political future lies at the heart of the American experiment, and it is a right that has been won by the sacrifice of patriots. The Declaration of Independence was born on the stand for liberty taken at Lexington and Concord. The amendments to our Constitution that outlawed slavery and guaranteed the right to vote came at the price of a terrible civil war.

The Voting Rights Act that broke the segregationist lock on the ballot box rose from the courage shown on a Selma bridge one Sunday afternoon in March of 1965. On that day, African Americans, including a Member of the United States Congress, John Lewis, marched across the Edmund Pettus Bridge in a protest intended to highlight the unfair practices that kept them off the voter rolls.

The brutal response showed America why a march was necessary. When the marchers reached the far side of the bridge, they were met by State troopers and civilian posse bearing billy clubs and whips, weapons they did not hesitate to use. The images of policemen using night sticks on peaceful protesters were carried on television screens across the country, and they stung the conscience of a slumbering America.

One week after Selma, President Lyndon Johnson took to the airwaves to announce that he planned to submit legislation that would bring African Americans into the civic life of our Nation. Five months after Selma, he signed the Voting Rights Act into law in the rotunda of our Nation's Capitol. In a little more than a year after Selma, a newly enfranchised black community used their power at the ballot box to help defeat the sheriff who had sent men with whips and clubs to the Edmund Pettus Bridge on that bloody Sunday.

For some parts of our country, the Voting Rights Act marked the first appearance of African Americans on the voting rolls since Reconstruction. And in the primaries and elections that followed the signing of this act, many African Americans pulled the voting lever for the first time in their lives.

Eighty-one-year-old Willie Bolden was the grandson of slaves, and in the spring of 1966, he cast his first ballot in Alabama's Democratic primary. He told a reporter, "It felt good to me. It made me think I was sort of somebody." In the America promised by our Founders, every citizen is a somebody, and every generation has a responsibility to add its own chapter to the unfolding story of freedom.

In four decades since the Voting Rights Act was first passed, we've made progress toward equality, yet the work for a more perfect union is never ending. We'll continue to build on the legal equality won by the civil rights movement to help ensure that every person enjoys the opportunity that this great land of liberty offers. And that means a decent education and a good school for every child, a chance to own their own home or business, and the hope that comes from knowing that you can rise in our society by hard work and God-given talents.

Today we renew a bill that helped bring a community on the margins into the life of American democracy. My administration will vigorously enforce the provisions of this law, and we will defend it in court. This legislation is named in honor of three heroes of American history who devoted their lives to the struggle of civil rights: Fannie Lou Hamer, Rosa Parks, and Coretta Scott King. And in honor of their memory and their contributions to the cause of freedom, I am proud to sign the Voting Rights Act Reauthorization and Amendments Act of 2006.

NOTE: The President spoke at 9:34 a.m. on the South Lawn at the White House. In his remarks, he referred to Bruce S. Gordon, president and chief executive officer, National Association for the Advancement of Colored People (NAACP); civil rights leader Rev. Joseph E. Lowery; Marc H. Morial, president and chief executive officer, National Urban League; Juanita Abernathy, wife of deceased civil rights leader Rev. Ralph D. Abernathy; civil rights leader Rev. Jesse L. Jackson, Sr., founder and president, Rainbow/PUSH Coalition; 2004 Democratic Presidential candidate Rev. Alfred C. Sharpton, Jr.; Dr. Benjamin L. Hooks, National Civil Rights Museum board chairman, and his wife, Frances; and Mayor Anthony A. Williams of Washington, DC. H.R. 9, approved July 27, was assigned Public Law No. 109–246.

Remarks Following Discussions With President Traian Basescu of Romania and an Exchange With Reporters
July 27 2006

President Bush. The Prime Minister and I will take a couple of questions a side after opening statements—Mr. President, excuse me. Welcome.

President Basescu. Thank you.

President Bush. The President and I are friends. Romania and the United States are friends, and we're allies. And as such, we've had an in-depth discussion about a variety of subjects. We talked about the international scene and how we can work together to promote democracy and peace. We talked about the neighborhood, and I assured him that the United States position on Moldova is that we support the territorial integrity of Moldova.

We talked about bilateral relations. One of the—of course, the issues that's on the President's mind is visa policy. He was very articulate and strong in his position that the United States must be forward-leaning when it comes to granting visas to the citizens of Romania. I listened very carefully. I assured him that there is a way forward; there's a roadmap that we'd like to work with our friends and allies on, and we will pay very careful attention to what the President said.

We've got a lot on our agenda because we're friends. And I do want to thank the people of Romania for their strong support for the young democracies in Iraq and Afghanistan. And your contribution, Mr. President, has been worthwhile and meaningful, and I know the Iraqi people are grateful, and so am I.

So welcome back to the Oval Office.

President Basescu. Thank you very much, Mr. President. In fact, we meet each other after one year; compare it with what we discussed last year. We conclude that both parties fulfilled assumed obligations. Romania will continue to remain an ally of the United States in supporting the democracy in Iraq and Afghanistan, in supporting democratic regimes in these countries like a key of freedom on the area.

In same time, we analyze together the bilateral relations and the problems which are around Black Sea, around of the region where Romania exists. We analyzed the Western Balkans situation; we analyzed the situation of Moldova and the necessity having Republic of Moldova in his territory unaffected by anybody.

In same time, we conclude that we have to continue our cooperation in economical area, in political area, and in security area.

And in same time, Romania will contribute with peace possibilities in spreading the democracy around of Romania, mainly on the Black Sea region.

That's all in a few words. I thank you very much, Mr. President, for our discussion.

President Bush. Thank you, sir.

Jennifer [Jennifer Loven, Associated Press].

Situation in the Middle East

Q. Thank you, sir. Israel's Justice Minister said that the lack of a call from the international community for an immediate cease-fire essentially gives Israel a green light to push harder. And the top general there says there will be several more weeks of fighting. Is your administration okay with these things?

President Bush. I believe this: I believe that, as Condi said yesterday, the Middle East is littered with agreements that just didn't work. And now is the time to address the root cause of the problem. And the root cause of the problem is terrorist groups trying to stop the advance of democracies.

Hizballah attacked Israel. I believe Hizballah—I know Hizballah is connected to Iran. And now is the time for the world to confront this danger. Look, we care deeply about the loss of life. And I'm troubled by the destruction that has taken place in Lebanon. You know, we grieve when Lebanese families lose innocent life. I've urged that there be caution when it comes to dealing with Hizballah. On the other hand, I fully understand that whatever is done diplomatically must address the root cause. And the root cause is terrorist activities. One of the things I said initially when these incidents first started happening was that it's important for the Lebanese democracy to survive and to become strong.

And so what you're watching is American policy aiming to address the root cause and aiming to strengthen Lebanese democracy so that we can have peace. I view this as a clash of forms of government. I see people who can't stand the thought of democracy taking hold in parts of—in the Middle East. And as democracy begins to advance, they use terrorist tactics to stop it.

And so I appreciate my Secretary of State's hard work. There's a lot of diplomacy being done. There's a lot of discussions about how to go forward. Yesterday's meetings were successful in this way: It showed a diplomatic way forward. And so you're seeing a lot of diplomacy take place.

But our objective is to make sure those who use terrorist tactics are not rewarded, and at the same time, help those who have suffered as a result of the responses.

Q. So several more weeks of fighting is okay to achieve those goals?

President Bush. My goal is exactly what I said it was, and that is to hopefully end this as quickly as possible and, at the same time, making sure there's a lasting peace—not a fake peace, not a fake, you know, kind of circumstances that make us all feel better, and then, sure enough, the problem arises again. And that's the goal of the United States. And we're working toward that end, and we're working hard diplomatically. Look, as soon as we can get this resolved the better, obviously, but it must be real. And it can't be fake. And so there's a serious diplomatic effort going forward, led ably by my Secretary of State.

You want to ask somebody from the Romanian press?

Romania's Participation in International Affairs

Q. Is there any role for the Romanian—for Romania in the American foreign policy strategies besides its participation within the American-led coalitions in Iraq and Afghanistan?

President Bush. Absolutely. I spent a lot of time listening to my friend's advice on the Black Sea region. We're going to spend time over lunch talking about specific issues related to the Balkans. And Romania's role

in this area and in her neighborhood is a vital role, one that I listen very carefully to his advice on, because this area of the world is one where there's emerging democracies. And it's an area of the world that is—where there has been historical conflict, and it's an area of the world where we've got to pay attention to it. And so the Romanian role is a vital role.

And so, as I say, we're going to spend time strategizing about the role over lunch.

Holland [Steve Holland, Reuters].

War on Terror

Q. Sir, thank you. Dr. Zawahiri has surfaced again with a new videotape urging Muslims to fight and become martyrs because of the conflict in Lebanon. What's your reaction to that?

President Bush. My answer is, I'm not surprised people who use terrorist tactics would start speaking out. It doesn't surprise me. I am—Zawahiri's attitude about life is that there shouldn't be free societies, and he believes that people ought to use terrorist tactics, the killing of innocent people, to achieve his objective. And so I'm not surprised he feels like he needs to lend his voice to terrorist activities that are trying to prevent democracies from moving forward.

Al Qaida has made it clear about their vision for the future, and it's one that is exactly opposite to what the American people believe and this Romanian President believes, and that is, people ought to be free: free to worship, free to speak their minds, free to participate in the process.

And so, you know, here's a fellow who is in a remote region of the world putting out statements basically encouraging people to use terrorist tactics to kill innocent people to achieve political objectives. And the United States of America stands strong against Mr. Zawahiri and his types.

U.S. Visa Policy

Q. Mr. President, sir, about a visa waiver, how soon can Romanians expect to travel to U.S. without a visa? And when taking this decision that Romanians are expecting, are you going to take under consideration, for instance, that Romanians will probably want to come and work in the United States in huge numbers? Is that the problem for the United States?

President Bush. No, no. It's an interesting question you bring up, however. I told the President we're dealing with an immigration debate here in the United States and that I'm hopeful that we'll get a comprehensive immigration bill that will accommodate people who want to work here, but we want them to work here on a temporary basis and in a legal way.

No, the issue with the visa policy first started because of what was an overstay problem based upon a history of people traveling to the United States during a different era. In other words, a lot of people during the previous era that era would be one defined by a nonfree society versus a free society—would come to the United States on a temporary visa and then would overstay their visa. And we have laws on the books that say countries who had people come and overstay their visas, therefore, must be viewed differently than others.

Now, one of the first changes we have made is that we have said, "Okay, that's a bygone era. Now let's look toward the future." Secondly, we've said to countries, "We want to work together on a roadmap to make sure the visa policy will work." And that's where we are with Romania as well as other countries. And so each country has to develop its own roadmap based upon its own particular circumstances.

And that's what we're doing, Mr. President. The answer is, as quickly as we can get these issues resolved, the better. But we've still got work to do.

President Basescu. If you allow me, Mr. President, mainly for the American journalists. Romanians don't look at the United States like immigration area. In fact, as a member of European Union, the Romanians have a lot of places to work around Romania.

The problem which we have now—and for this reason, I raised the subject of visas in discussions with the President—is in connection with our students, which are more and more present in American universities, with our intelligent peoples, which are working in IBM or in Oracle, with our business peoples—and if you look at the volume of the business in the last 3 years, was three times increased. And now a businessperson from Romania, in order to obtain a visa coming in United States, discussing about developing the business, need minimum 3 months.

And, in fact, the Romanians don't look at the United States like a place to immigrate illegally or to find a working place. This problem was settled for Romanians in Europe. We already have the people spread around of Europe, like Romania have people from Europe, from other countries which work in Romania. Romania will not be illegal immigration problem, or a problem from the point of view of jobs which exist in the United States.

Thank you, Mr. President.

President Bush. Good job. Thank you.

NOTE: The President spoke at 11:58 a.m. in the Oval Office at the White House. In his remarks, he referred to Ayman Al-Zawahiri, founder of the Egyptian Islamic Jihad and senior Al Qaida associate. A reporter referred to Minister of Justice Haim Ramon of Israel.

Remarks on Signing the Adam Walsh Child Protection and Safety Act of 2006
July 27, 2006

The President. Thank you all for coming. Please be seated. Welcome and good afternoon. In a few moments, I will sign the Adam Walsh Child Protection and Safety Act of 2006. Twenty-five years ago today, Adam Walsh was abducted from a department store, and he was later found murdered. In the years since, his parents, John and Reve Walsh, have become advocates for missing children. They've helped combat child abduction and exploitation across this country. And the bill I sign today will strengthen Federal laws to protect our children from sexual and other violent crimes, will help prevent child pornography, and will make the Internet safer for our sons and daughters. I want to thank you all for joining us today, and thank you for your tireless crusade.

I'm pleased to be up here with the Attorney General, Al Gonzales. I want to thank all the Members of the House and the Senate who have joined us. John, as you can see, you've attracted quite a crowd here.

John Walsh. S.W.A.T. team for kids.

The President. Yes, it is, S.W.A.T. team for kids.

I appreciate very much the bill sponsors who have joined us and the committee chairmen and the leadership that has made this bill possible. This is a good piece of bipartisan legislation, and I'm really going to be proud to sign it.

I want to thank all the family members of victims who have joined us today. I particularly want to say hello to Elizabeth Smart and Amie Zyla. Thank you all for coming.

You know, having someone harm your child is one of the worst nightmares a parent could face. And the families who have joined us today have felt that pain first-hand. In your suffering and loss, many of you have found the courage to become ad-vocates for the safety of other children. Because of your efforts, this important measure is going to become the law of the land, and the children of parents you may never meet will be spared the anguish your families have known. So thank you for your contribution.

Protecting our children is our solemn responsibility. It's what we must do. When a child's life or innocence is taken, it is a terrible loss; it's an act of unforgivable cruelty. Our society has a duty to protect our children from exploitation and danger. By enacting this law, we're sending a clear message across the country: Those who prey on our children will be caught, prosecuted, and punished to the fullest extent of the law.

I appreciate working with Congress in the past to give law enforcement the tools they need to go after criminals who kidnap and exploit children. In 2003, I signed the PROTECT Act, that expanded the use of Amber Alerts, that makes grants to all 50 States so law enforcement can quickly alert the public about missing children and their abductors. We also launched Operation Predator to help law enforcement track down and arrest foreign pedophiles and human traffickers and sex tourists and Internet pornographers who prey on our children.

Earlier this year, the Department of Justice, led by Al Gonzales, launched Project Safe Childhood to help Federal, State, and local enforcement officials investigate and prosecute crimes against children that are facilitated by the Internet and other electronic communications.

This new law I sign today builds on the progress in four important ways. First, the bill I sign today will greatly expand the

National Sex Offender Registry by integrating the information in State sex offender registry systems and ensuring that law enforcement has access to the same information across the United States. It seems to make sense, doesn't it? See, these improvements will help prevent sex offenders from evading detection by moving from one State to the next. Data drawn from this comprehensive registry will also be made available to the public so parents have the information they need to protect their children from sex offenders that might be in their neighborhoods.

Second, the bill I sign today will increase Federal penalties for crimes against children. This bill imposes tough mandatory minimum penalties for the most serious crimes against our children. It increases penalties for crimes such as sex trafficking of children and child prostitution, provides grants to States to help them institutionalize sex offenders who've shown they cannot change their behavior and are about to be released from prison.

Third, the bill I sign today will make it harder for sex predators to reach our children on the Internet. Some sex predators use this technology to make contact with potential victims, so the bill authorizes additional new regional Internet Crimes Against Children Task Forces. These task forces provide funding and training to help State and local law enforcement combat crimes involving the sexual exploitation of minors on the Internet.

Fourth, the bill I sign today will help prevent child abuse by creating a National Child Abuse Registry and requiring investigators to do background checks on adoptive and foster parents before they approve to take custody of a child. By giving child protective service professionals in all 50 States access to this critical information, we will improve their ability to investigate child abuse cases and help ensure that the vulnerable children are not put into situations of abuse or neglect.

This is a comprehensive piece of legislation, and it's an important bill. Our Nation grieves with every family that's suffered the unbearable pain of a child who's been abducted or abused. This law makes an important step forward in this country's efforts to protect those who cannot protect themselves.

I thank you for coming for witness to this. It's now my high honor to sign the Adam Walsh Child Protection and Safety Act of 2006.

NOTE: The President spoke at 1:11 p.m. in the Rose Garden at the White House. In his remarks, he referred to Elizabeth A. Smart and Amie Zyla, child protection advocates. H.R. 4472, approved July 27, was assigned Public Law No. 109–248.

Remarks to the National Association of Manufacturers
July 27, 2006

The President. John, thanks. Thanks for the good, short introduction. [*Laughter*] Thanks for having me here. I want to thank you all for doing what you do for the country. I appreciate your leadership. I appreciate the entrepreneurial spirit which is represented in this room. Our manufacturers make products that enrich our life, that drive and sustain our economy, that create jobs and opportunity. When America's manufacturing sector is healthy, this country is healthy. And that's what I want to come to talk about, how to make sure that this Nation has a healthy economy and how to make sure the manufacturing sector remains one of the most important parts of our economic vitality.

I want to thank John Luke for his chairmanship of the National Association of Manufacturers. I appreciate you hiring my buddy, the former Governor of Michigan, John Engler—[*laughter*]—who is doing a fine job, I might add. I'm proud to be joined today by a member of my Cabinet, Ambassador Susan Schwab, who is the U.S. Trade Representative. Thanks for coming. I'm going to talk a little bit about—[*applause*]—and I appreciate the members of the National Association of Manufacturers. Thanks for coming to Washington; thanks for giving me a chance to visit with you.

I understand the importance of manufacturing to our Nation's economic leadership and prosperity. Our economic growth is powered by manufacturing. Catch this fact: By itself, U.S. manufacturing output is greater in size than the eighth largest economy in the world. Our manufacturers pioneer the innovations, technology, and methods that maintain this Nation's economic leadership. And it's important that we remain the economic leader in the world, for the good of our people. Manufacturers are responsible for nearly three-fifths of all private sector research and development. In other words, if you want to be the economic leader, you must have research and development to constantly stay ahead of the competition. And the manufacturing sector of the United States spends a lot of money making sure this country is innovative.

Our Nation's standard of living depends on our manufacturers. America's manufacturers provide our people with rewarding careers and high-paying jobs. Manufacturing jobs pay over 20 percent more than the national average. If you're working for a manufacturing company, you're likely to be getting paid more than your neighbor. Your standard of living is higher.

For decades, our manufacturers have faced the pressures of increased competition and globalization, but you've handled that competition well. Not only have you handled it well, you've excelled.

Manufacturing today represents roughly the same share of the real economy as it did 20 years ago. Every day, American manufacturers confront the competitive challenges of the global marketplace. I know that. You especially know that. But every day you stay innovative and creative and work on productivity, you continue to lead this Nation. And so I'm here to thank you, to thank you and your workers.

You know, we've overcome a lot together. Sometimes it's easy to forget short-term history. I'm sure you still remember the days of recession; stock market adjustment; corporate scandals; the terrorist attack of September the 11th, 2001, that still drives my foreign policy; the response of our Government to defend ourselves; natural disaster; high energy prices. We've faced a lot. But as John mentioned, I'm the kind of fellow that sees a problem and likes to address it head on.

And working with the Congress, we cut the taxes on you to get this economy back. I believe that when you have more of your own money in your pocket to save, spend, or invest, this economy is going to grow. I would rather have the American people spending their own money to drive this economy forward than Government trying to drive the economy forward. And so we cut the taxes. We didn't cut the taxes on a few; we cut the taxes on everybody who pays taxes. We doubled the child tax credit. We reduced the marriage penalty. We created new incentives for small businesses to invest.

We cut the taxes on dividends and capital gains, and we did so because we thought it was important to lower the cost of capital. If you're counting on the private sector to help recover from the tough situations we've been through, what you want to do is make capital less expensive so you can borrow easier or raise money faster, to invest. Investment means jobs and expansion.

We put the death tax to the road—on the road to extinction. I believe it's unfair to say to somebody who's built up some assets—a farmer or businessowner—that the Government is going to tax you twice, once when you make your money and then once when you move on and try to pass it on to your relatives. That's called "taxation without respiration." [*Laughter*]

This Congress passed—repealed the death tax, and the Senate is working on it. I strongly urge the United States Senate to come together with the House and put an end to the death tax for the sake of economic expansion.

Our policies have worked. Let me rephrase that: Our policies to enable you to work better have worked. After all, the economy grew at an annual rate of 5.6 percent in the first quarter of 2006. In 2005, the American economy turned in a performance that's the envy of the industrialized world. Our economy grew at 3.5 percent. That's faster than any other major industrialized nation.

Since August 2003, this economy of ours has created 5.4 million new jobs. That's more than Japan and the 25 nations of the European Union combined. For 34 straight months, the American economy has added jobs. Our unemployment rate is 4.6 percent. That's below the average of each of the past four decades. Manufacturing employment has increased by 18,000 over the past year—it's the largest 12-month gain since the period ending September of 1998.

Across the United States, real after-tax income is up more than 7 percent per American. Since January 2001, productivity is on the rise. Our productivity has been growing at 3.5 percent for the past 5 years. That's the fastest rate in nearly four decades. American workers are more than 18 percent more productive than they were in early 2001.

Let me talk about productivity for a minute; it's kind of a concept that some may not relate to. From 1973 until 1995, productivity grew at 1.4 percent per year.

At that rate, it would take 50 years to double the standard of living for Americans. Our economists now project that productivity will grow by 2.7 percent over the long term, and at that rate, we can double the standard of living of Americans nearly twice as fast. In other words, the more productive a society it is, the better lifestyle our citizens will have.

Manufacturing activity is growing. For 37 straight months, the Institute of Supply Management's manufacturing index has indicated that the manufacturing sector is expanding. Over the past 12 months, industrial production has increased 4.5 percent. And this morning the Commerce Department reported that new orders for durable manufacturing goods were up 3.1 percent in the month of June. What I'm telling you is, the economic policies we have pursued are working.

And the fundamental question facing this country is, what do we need to do to ensure the economy remains strong? What is it that Congress and the administration can do to help the manufacturing sector continue to grow? What is it we must do to make sure the entrepreneurial spirit remains strong? What actions must we take to make sure America is the economic leader in the world?

Well, here are some ideas. One is, we've got to be wise about how we spend your money. We've got to be wise when we appropriate money here in Washington. Deficits can hurt economic vitality. And I understand that. So the first thing you've got to do here in Washington is set priorities when it comes to spending the people's money.

And I'll tell you my priority. My priority is this: So long as we have a man or woman wearing our uniform who is in harm's way they will get all they need to secure the victory. And we'll spend resources to protect this homeland. September the 11th reminded us that we're no longer an island, that we can't assume problems overseas won't come home to hurt us. Our most solemn duty in Washington, DC, is to protect the American people, and we take that duty seriously.

And that priority is reflected in the budgets. And so we've got to show spending restraint elsewhere in the budget if we're going to be wise about how we spend your money. We've reduced the rate of growth of nonsecurity discretionary spending since 2001, and my last two budgets have cut this kind of spending. We said to Congress, "Here's our priorities; you need to make tough choices." And they've come along with us. And I hope the appropriations bills coming out this fall match this same fiscal responsibility that we've shown in the past.

I also addressed mandatory spending earlier this year when I signed the Deficit Reduction Act, which saves taxpayers nearly $40 billion over the next 5 years. In other words, we're working with Congress to be wise about spending your money.

I set a goal for this country that we cut the deficit in half by 2009—just had an interesting statistic come out in the Mid-Session Review recently. That's the time we take a look and see how things are going. When Rob Portman, who is the Director of OMB, analyzed revenues and spending, he projected that tax revenues will grow by $246 billion during this year. In other words, when you cut the taxes and you grow your economy, more revenues come into the Treasury. And it looks like we're on track to balance our budget by 2008 [cut the deficit in half by 2008]. * The current deficit is now—projected to be 2.3 percent of GDP. We're fulfilling our responsibilities. We're meeting the goal of reducing this deficit. The best way to reduce the deficit is to keep progrowth economic policies in place by keeping this Tax Code—making these tax cuts permanent and being wise about how we spend your money.

If Congress really does want to work with the administration to make sure that there's

---

* White House correction.

fiscal sanity in Washington, they need to give me the line-item veto. And I appreciate your hard work on this issue. Thank you for supporting our attempt to work with Congress to make it easier for both parts of Government, both branches of Government, to be smart about how we spend the people's money.

Forty-three Governors have got the line-item veto. It's a useful tool. It works. It's time to bring the important tool to Washington. The line-item veto will allow a President to target unnecessary spending. See, sometimes they get these big spending bills and put a little something in there for their district. [*Laughter*] Sometimes they're able to do it without a hearing. Just kind of ends up in there, in the bill, without much scrutiny. They're able to put earmarks on large bills.

What the line-item veto would enable a President to do is take a look at the big bills and kind of call out some of the programs that might not fit into the national priorities, and then send it back up to the Hill for an up-or-down vote. That's one way to make sure there's fiscal sanity in the budget. But the line-item veto would do something else. It would make lawmakers hesitant to try to tack something into the bills in the first place if they knew that their programs would see the light of day. In other words, sometimes sunshine is the best way to heal a problem.

I want to thank you for helping get the bill out of the House of Representatives. A bipartisan majority supported this concept of a line-item veto, a concept where the executive branch and the legislative branch would work closely together. And the United States Senate needs to take up this important legislation.

I was pleased the other day when my opponent in the 2004 campaign, John Kerry, came down to visit with me in the Cabinet Room to endorse the line-item veto. He's one of the bill sponsors of the line-item veto. The Senate needs to get the bill passed and to my desk.

I understand what you understand, that one of the biggest drags on our economic growth is going to be Social Security and Medicare, unless we do something about it. See, we've got a lot of guys like me who are fixing to retire. [*Laughter*] I'll be 62 in 2008—which is a convenient time to turn 62. [*Laughter*] And there's a lot of baby boomers that are living longer and that are getting ready for the benefits that we have been promised—by the way, benefits that are larger than the previous generation's benefits.

And there are fewer people paying into the system to make sure that the promises that have been made to my generation are kept, which means these big programs are becoming insolvent very quickly. There's an overhang. There's unfunded liabilities that we've got to address. One of the reasons why Hank Paulson came to Washington is because he wants to address big problems—he's the new Secretary of the Treasury. He's a can-do kind of person, John; he can get things done. And I'm looking forward to working with Hank and working with the United States Congress to once and for all put Social Security and Medicare on the road to solvency. We owe it to a new generation of Americans coming up, and we owe it to our entrepreneurs and risk takers to solve this problem now.

It's so easy in Washington to say, "Well, it's not necessarily a crisis; let's just shove it down the road." That's not why I ran for office. I believe a President and a Congress must confront problems now and not pass them on to future generations, which is what I intend to do.

Here's some other ideas to make sure we're an economic leader. We've got to remain competitive. We've got to make the R&D tax credit permanent. I talked about—if you're somebody trying to figure out how much to spend on R&D and you're not sure whether or not the tax credit will be around in the out years, you're less likely to take risk, less likely to spend the money, less likely to invest in the fu-

ture, so the R&D tax credit—the permanency of the R&D tax credit makes sense if you want to remain a competitive nation.

And here at the Federal level, I have proposed doubling the Federal commitment to the most basic critical—the most critical basic research in physical sciences over the next 10 years. I'll tell you why I have. I think that the Federal Government can help leverage ideas. I know it's in our national interest to spend taxpayers' money on research. The research that we conduct today will enable future generations to remain competitive tomorrow. I don't know if you know this or not, but the iPod came about because of a lot of Federal research—or probably the most known one is the Internet. In other words, it makes sense to invest taxpayers' money because there's a greater good to be gained when it comes to investing in basic research.

You know what I know, that we better have an educated workforce if we're going to be able to compete in the 21st century. We've made great strides in early grade education. I don't know if you followed the debate on No Child Left Behind, but it's a really important piece of legislation. I'll tell you why it's important, is because for too long we had a system that just shuffled kids through the schools. You know, I spoke to the NAACP the other day, and I recounted a story of when I was a Governor. I remember going to a high school in a pretty tough neighborhood in Texas. I'll never forget the ninth grade teacher looking me in the eye and saying, "I'm having trouble teaching." And I said, "Why is that?" He said, "Because my kids can't read." In other words, they'd just been moved through.

We can't compete in the 21st century if we have a system that does not hold people accountable. And so we said, "In return for additional Federal money from Washington, DC, we expect you, the State, to measure." Why do you measure? Because you want to know early in a child's career whether they can read or write and add and subtract. And if a child is falling behind, there's extra money in No Child Left Behind. The whole purpose is to have an accountability system that is able to detect problems early, before it's too late. And guess what? Because we measure, we can now see that an achievement gap is closing.

But there's more to be done, particularly in math and science. We need to apply the same rigor of No Child Left Behind that we use in reading—in No Child Left Behind—in math in the middle grade. We're doing fine early in math. The problem is, is that the measurement shows us that we're falling behind in math in the middle grades. We need to measure and solve problems earlier for our children than high school when it comes to math and science.

I'm a big believer in Advanced Placement. These are programs that believe in high standards and high accountability. And so we're going to train 70,000 high school teachers over the next 5 years to head AP courses in math and science.

I'll never forget going into Dallas recently to see an AP class there. And presumably, this little school graduates more AP students than any school in the country, at least that's what the Texas teacher told me. But you know how we Texans are, we tend to—yes, we—[*laughter*]. Let's just say this: They graduate a lot. [*Laughter*] And there were Latinos and African Americans. These bright young kids will become—will be the scientists and engineers. But they need that rigor; they need to be challenged; they need to have high standards; and they need a teacher group that is capable of teaching Advanced Placement.

We need to have an adjunct teacher corps to bring 30,000 math and science professionals into the classroom. Sometimes science isn't viewed as cool. But we need to make sure that students understand that it is good to take science and engineering and math. As a matter of fact, we need

to be able to connect the fact that the jobs of the 21st century, the high-paying, high-quality jobs will depend on a person's ability to be able to be an engineer or a mathematician or a scientist.

And I want to thank John and your crowd for helping us with this American Competitiveness Initiative. It's vital for our country that we take action now to make sure that we remain the leader in the world when it comes to the economy.

We've got to do something about health care to make sure we're competitive. One thing we will do is we'll take care of the poor and the elderly. This Medicare bill I signed is a really good piece of legislation that now says to poor seniors, you no longer have to choose between your medicine and food and electricity. They've been talking about modernizing Medicare for a long period of time, and my administration, working with the United States Congress, finally got it done.

I'm a big believer in health savings accounts, because it puts customers in charge of the health decisions. I would hope that as you analyze your health care plans, look at health savings accounts as ways to save money, but equally importantly, ways to empower your employees to make rational choices about their health care.

In order to make sure customers have got more choice in their health care, you've got to have transparency. You know, health care is one of the few industries where you really don't know pricing. How many of you ever actually asked a doctor, "What are you going to charge me, doc?" Generally, you don't ask that because a third party pays the bill. If you're worried about rising health care costs, it seems like it makes sense to have transparency in pricing and quality and to give consumers more choices to make in the marketplace, to empower people to ask the questions necessary to make sure there is some rational pricing in health care.

And along those lines, we're strongly supporting health IT. Many of you are very productive because you've been able to employ information technology. In the health care field, you can find places of medicine where people are walking around with handwritten files, and sometimes it's hard to read a doctor's handwriting. And sometimes the files get misplaced, and a lot of times there are medical errors as a result of that and cost inefficiencies in the system. And so health information technology will help modernize our health care system.

And if you're truly interested in making sure that you have health care that's available and affordable for your employees, you need to join us in making sure we end these frivolous and junk lawsuits that are running good doctors out of practice.

A couple more ideas to make sure that we're strong economically. And I repeat: A strong economy is good for our people. That's why I want the—America to be the leader, economic leader in the world. It's because I want the American people to benefit. I want people's lifestyles to go up. I want people to be able to realize their dreams.

We got to make sure that our energy policy is diverse and balanced and sound if we expect to be competitive. This is an interesting moment where we're able to advance new technologies that will make us less dependent on foreign sources of oil and enable us to be good stewards of the environment. And we're investing a lot of money to be able to achieve energy—economic independence, national security independence, and being good environmental stewards when it comes to energy.

Here's some ideas. One, we must—we must expand our nuclear power industry if we want to be competitive in the 21st century. We have got to be wise—[applause]. We have got to push hard to build new plants. And the energy bill I signed last year is—it's a good step forward. This Government is going to spend a lot of money on fast breeder reactor technology. We're going to join with other countries to work on fast breeder reactor technology

so that we can burn reprocessed fuel which will reduce the waste on civilian nuclear energy. In other words, there's technological gains to be made that will enable us to even advance nuclear power even faster.

And by the way, it's not only in our interest to develop nuclear power, it's in the interest of our country that India and China develop nuclear power. In the global energy market, when demand for hydrocarbons goes up in energy in China, it affects your gasoline prices. And therefore, the more we can help these countries develop technology, the more we can help them develop a civilian nuclear industry that is safe, the better off it is for American consumers.

And yesterday—I want to applaud the House of Representatives for passing an important piece of legislation when it comes to America's relationship with India. We're spending a lot of money to make sure that we can have coal-fired electricity plants that reduce the amount of pollution they put out. We're spending money to make sure that liquefied natural gas terminals are more quickly permitted. We need to get more gas into the United States. The House of Representatives has passed a bill to open up more areas for offshore exploration in the Gulf of Mexico. I strongly pass that—support that piece of legislation. I urge the Senate to do so as well.

We're also working hard to promote alternative forms of energy. I mean, we want—look, I like the idea of people using ethanol to power their automobiles. So do our farmers. [*Laughter*] It makes sense, doesn't it, if you can grow a product that you can power your cars with, to do so. Every bushel of corn grown in the Midwest makes us less dependent on oil from overseas.

We're working on battery technologies. They say we're pretty close to a breakthrough in a battery—where you can drive the first 40 miles on a battery, and your car doesn't look like a golf cart. [*Laughter*]

One of these days our children will be driving cars powered by hydrogen. In other words, in order to make sure this country is competitive, we've got to be spending money on technology now, on research and development now, to change our habits and to make sure we're good stewards of our environment.

I'm excited about the energy future for this country, I really am. I think there's going to be some fantastic opportunities for people. And I'm going to look back on this period, and I know you will, that we made the right decisions for a new generation of Americans.

I'm also a big believer in trade. That's why Susan's here; so is she. But I'm—what I'm for is trade that opens up people's markets just like we open up ours; that's what I'm for. I believe good trade policy—[applause]. Here's my definition of good trade policy: It's fair. That's all we ask. See, we open up our markets; you open up yours. You treat us the way we treat you.

There's a lot of talk about the WTO and the Doha development round. We're very much in favor of it moving forward. We think it makes a lot of sense. We think it makes a lot of sense for American workers that we open up markets. We think it makes sense for people who are locked in impoverished nations that we open up markets. We think trade helps lift people out of poverty, that's what we believe. So we're strongly supportive of the WTO round.

I told Susan that she needed to be flexible; she needed to go in the meetings with flexibility, particularly when it comes to our agricultural subsidies. Look, I said to the world last September, we'll reduce them, just so long as our folks have got access to markets; that's all we ask. Just give us a chance to compete fairly.

And so we'll continue to work on this agreement. Susan is committed to getting a deal done, if we can. Secretary of Agriculture Mike Johanns, as well, will continue to reach out to other nations to achieve our objectives. I want to thank you for your support on this. My attitude is, we want to be treated fairly, and the American people and the American manufacturer and the American farmer can compete with anybody, anytime, anywhere, so long as the rules are fair.

So there are some ideas for Congress to consider and the administrative branch to promote, ways to make sure this country is competitive. One of my big fears is that we lose our nerve, is that we kind of say, "Well, there's some new emerging economies, and therefore, we can't compete; let's just retreat. Why don't we become protective. Why don't we throw up walls and barriers around the United States of America. Why don't we just try to isolate ourselves from competition."

That's not the America I know. The America I know is a country that is confident, confident in our capacity to compete, entrepreneurial by nature. There are some smart things we can do, and will do, to make sure we remain competitive. But one thing we must never do is to not be willing to do the right policies so we can remain the economic leader of the world. We owe it to our people to put good policies in place. We owe it to future generations of Americans to keep the entrepreneurial spirit strong, and here are some ideas as part of a strategy to do just that.

I want to appreciate what you're doing for the country. I thank you for the risks you take. I thank you for the folks you employ. Government is not going to stand in your way. We want to stand side by side with you to make sure the entrepreneurial spirit remains strong here in the country.

God bless.

NOTE: The President spoke at 1:47 p.m. at the Grand Hyatt Washington. In his remarks, he referred to John Engler, president and chief executive officer, National Association of Manufacturers.

The President's News Conference With Prime Minister Tony Blair of the United Kingdom
July 28, 2006

President Bush. Thank you all. Prime Minister Tony Blair, welcome back to the White House. As you know, we've got a close relationship. You tell me what you think. You share with me your perspective, and you let me know when the microphone is on. [*Laughter*]

Today the Prime Minister and I talked about the ways we're working to advance freedom and human dignity across the world. Prime Minister Blair and I discussed the crisis in the Middle East. In Lebanon, Hizballah and its Iranian and Syrian sponsors are willing to kill and to use violence to stop the spread of peace and democracy, and they're not going to succeed.

The Prime Minister and I have committed our Governments to a plan to make every effort to achieve a lasting peace out of this crisis. Our top priorities in Lebanon are providing immediate humanitarian relief, achieving an end to the violence, ensuring the return of displaced persons, and assisting with reconstruction. We recognize that many Lebanese people have lost their homes, so we'll help rebuild the civilian infrastructure that will allow them to return home safely.

Our goal is to achieve a lasting peace, which requires that a free, democratic, and independent Lebanese Government be empowered to exercise full authority over its territory. We want a Lebanon free of militias and foreign interference and a Lebanon that governs its own destiny, as is called for by U.N. Security Council Resolutions 1559 and 1680.

We agree that a multinational force must be dispatched to Lebanon quickly to augment a Lebanese Army as it moves to the south of that country. An effective multinational force will help speed delivery of humanitarian relief, facilitate the return of displaced persons, and support the Lebanese Government as it asserts full sovereignty over its territory and guards its borders.

We're working quickly to achieve these goals. Tomorrow Secretary Rice will return to the region. She will work with the leaders of Israel and Lebanon to seize this opportunity to achieve lasting peace and stability for both of their countries. Next week, the U.N. Security Council will meet as well. Our goal is a Chapter VII resolution setting out a clear framework for cessation of hostilities on an urgent basis and mandating the multinational force.

Also at the United Nations, senior officials from many countries will meet to discuss the design and deployment of the multinational force. Prime Minister Blair and I agree that this approach gives the best hope to end the violence and create lasting peace and stability in Lebanon. This approach will demonstrate the international community's determination to support the Government of Lebanon and defeat the threat from Hizballah and its foreign sponsors.

This approach will make possible what so many around the world want to see: the end of Hizballah's attacks on Israel, the return of Israeli soldiers taken hostage by the terrorists, the suspension of Israel's operations in Lebanon, and the withdrawal of Israeli forces.

This is a moment of intense conflict in the Middle East. Yet our aim is to turn it into a moment of opportunity and a chance for a broader change in the region. Prime Minister Blair and I remain committed to the vision of two democratic states, Israel and Palestine, living side by side in peace and security. This vision has been embraced by Israel, the Palestinians, and many others throughout the region and the world, and we will make every effort to make this vision a reality. The United States is committed to using all of its influence to seize this moment to build a stable and democratic Middle East.

We also talked about other regions and other challenges and other conflicts. The Prime Minister and I each met with the Prime Minister of Iraq this week. The U.S. and U.K. are working together to support the Prime Minister and his unity Government, and we will continue to support that Government. Afghanistan's people and their freely-elected Government can also count on our support.

Our two nations urge Iran to accept the EU–3 offer, which also has the backing of Russia, China, and the United States. We agree that the Iranian regime will not be allowed to develop or acquire nuclear weapons.

The suffering in Darfur deserves the name of genocide. Our two nations support a United Nations peacekeeping mission in Darfur, which is the best hope for the people in that region.

I want to thank you for coming. It's good to discuss these urgent matters with you. We will continue to consult with each other as events unfold in the Middle East and beyond. The alliance between Britain and America is stronger than ever because we share the same values, we share the same goals, and we share the same determination to advance freedom and to defeat terror across the world.

Mr. Prime Minister.

Prime Minister Blair. Thank you, Mr. President. Thank you for your welcome to the White House once again. And first of all, I'd like to say some words about the present Middle East crisis, and then we'll talk about some of the other issues that we discussed.

What is happening in the Middle East at the moment is a complete tragedy for Lebanon, for Israel, and for the wider region. And the scale of destruction is very clear. There are innocent lives that have been lost, both Lebanese and Israeli. There

are hundreds of thousands of people that have been displaced from their homes, again, both in Lebanon and in Israel. And it's been a tremendous and terrible setback for Lebanon's democracy.

We shouldn't forget how this began, how it started. In defiance of the U.N. Resolution 1559, Hizballah, for almost 2 years, has been fortifying and arming militia down in the south of Lebanon, when it is the proper and democratically elected Government of Lebanon and its armed forces who should have control of that area, as they should of the whole of Lebanon. They then, in defiance of that U.N. resolution, crossed the U.N. Blue Line. As you know, they kidnaped two Israeli soldiers; they killed eight more. Then, of course, there was the retaliation by Israel, and there are rockets being fired from the south of Lebanon into the north of Israel the entire time.

So we know how this situation came about and how it started, and the question is, now, how to get it stopped and get it stopped with the urgency that the situation demands.

Since our meeting in St. Petersburg for the G–8, we have been working hard on a plan to ensure that this happens. And as well as, obviously, the consultations that I've had with President Bush, I've spoken to President Chirac, Chancellor Merkel, Prime Minister Erdogan of Turkey, the President of the European Union, the Prime Minister of Finland, and many, many others.

And as the President has just outlined to you, I think there are three essential steps that we can take in order to ensure that there is the cessation of hostilities we all want to see.

The first is, I welcome very much the fact that Secretary Rice will go back to the region tomorrow. She will have with her the package of proposals in order to get agreement both from the Government of Israel and the Government of Lebanon on what is necessary to happen in order for this crisis to stop.

Secondly, we are bringing forward to Monday the meeting in the United Nations about the international stabilization force. And again, this is something we've been discussing with various different countries over the past few days. The absolute vital importance of that force is that it is able to ensure that the agreement the international community comes to, in respect of Lebanon, is enforced and that we have the Government of Lebanon able to make its writ run fully with its own armed forces in the south of Lebanon.

And then thirdly, as the President has just said to you, we want to see, tabled and agreed, a U.N. resolution as early as possible that will allow the cessation of hostilities. Provided that resolution is agreed and acted upon, we can, indeed, bring an end to this crisis. But nothing will work unless—as well as an end to the immediate crisis—we put in place the measures necessary to prevent it occurring again.

That is why I return at every opportunity to the basis of the United Nations Resolution 1559—almost 2 years ago now—that said precisely what should happen in order to make sure that the southern part of Lebanon was not used as a base for armed militia. The purpose of what we are doing, therefore, is to bring about, yes, the cessation of hostilities, which we want to see as quickly and as urgently as possible, but also to put in place a framework that allows us to stabilize the situation for the medium and longer term.

In addition to that, we, both of us, believe it is important that we take the opportunity to ensure that the Middle East peace process, which has been in such difficulty over the past few months, is given fresh impetus towards the two-state solution that we in the international community want to see. In the end, that is of fundamental importance, also, to the stability and peace of the region.

Now, in addition to all of these things— and obviously, we discussed Iraq, as the President has just said, and the work that our troops are doing in Iraq and, indeed, in Afghanistan. And if I might, let me once again pay tribute to the quite extraordinary professionalism, dedication, bravery, and commitment of the Armed Forces of both the United States and the United Kingdom and the many other countries that are working there with us.

In addition to that, as the President indicated to you, we discussed the situation in the Sudan. We will have an opportunity to discuss other issues later, notably, obviously the world trade talks and other such things. But I want to emphasize, just in concluding my opening remarks, by referring once again to the absolutely essential importance of ensuring that not merely do we get the cessation of hostilities now in Lebanon and in respect of Israel but that we take this opportunity—since we know why this has occurred; we know what started it; we know what the underlying forces are behind what has happened in the past few weeks—we take this opportunity to set out and achieve a different strategic direction for the whole of that region, which will allow the Government of Lebanon to be in control of its country, Lebanon to be the democracy its people want, and also allow us to get the solution in respect of Palestine that we have wanted so long to see.

If we are able, out of what has been a tragedy, a catastrophe for many of the people in the region, to achieve such a thing, then we will have turned what has been a situation of tragedy into one of opportunity. And we intend to do that.

President Bush. Good job.

Three questions a side. Tom [Tom Raum, Associated Press].

Situation in the Middle East/War on Terror

Q. Mr. President, Mr. Prime Minister, with support apparently growing among the Arab population, both Shi'a and Sunni, for

Hizballah by bounds, is there a risk that every day that goes by without a cease-fire will tip this conflict into a wider war?

And, Mr. President, when Secretary Rice goes back to the region, will she have any new instructions, such as meeting with Syrians?

President Bush. Her instructions are to work with Israel and Lebanon to get a—to come up with an acceptable U.N. Security Council resolution that we can table next week. And secondly, it's really important for people to understand that terrorists are trying to stop the advance of freedom, and therefore, it's essential that we do what's right and not necessarily what appears to be immediately popular.

There's a lot of suffering in Lebanon because Hizballah attacked Israel. There's a lot of suffering in the Palestinian Territory because militant Hamas is trying to stop the advance of democracy. There is suffering in Iraq because terrorists are trying to spread sectarian violence and stop the spread of democracy. And now is the time for the free world to work to create the conditions so that people everywhere can have hope.

And those are the stakes; that's what we face right now. We've got a plan to deal with this immediate crisis. It's one of the reasons the Prime Minister came, to talk about that plan. But the stakes are larger than just Lebanon.

Isn't it interesting, that when Prime Minister Olmert starts to reach out to President Abbas to develop a Palestinian state, militant Hamas creates the conditions so that there's crisis, and then Hizballah follows up? Isn't it interesting, as a democracy takes hold in Iraq, that Al Qaida steps up its efforts to murder and bomb in order to stop the democracy?

And so one of the things that the people in the Middle East must understand is that we're working to create the conditions of hope and opportunity for all of them. And we'll continue to do that, Tom. That's—this is the challenge of the 21st century.

Prime Minister Blair. It's very obvious what the strategy of terrorism is, and of the actions that Hizballah took. Their strategy is to commit an outrage that provokes a reaction and then on the back of the reaction, to mobilize extreme elements and then try and create a situation which even moderate people feel drawn to their cause. That's the strategy.

And you, quite rightly, say, "Well, isn't there a danger that the Arab street and people in Arab Muslim countries become more sympathetic to Hizballah as a result of what's happened?" That is their strategy. How do we counter it? We counter it, one, by having our own strategy to bring the immediate crisis to an end, which we do. That is what is important about the Secretary of State visiting the region, getting an agreement, tabling it to the United Nations, getting the endorsement of the United Nations, having an international stabilization force to move into the situation. We've got to deal with the immediate situation.

But then, as the President was saying a moment or two ago, we've then got to realize what has happened in the past few weeks is not an isolated incident. It is part of a bigger picture. Now, I'm going to say some more things about this in the days to come, but we really will never understand how we deal with this situation unless we understand that there is a big picture out in the Middle East which is about reactionary and terrorist groups trying to stop what the vast majority of people in the Middle East want, which is progress towards democracy, liberty, human rights, the same as the rest of us.

Now, that's the battle that's going on. And, yes, it is always very difficult when something like this happens, as it has happened over the past few weeks. So we've got to resolve the immediate situation, but we shouldn't be in any doubt at all, that will be a temporary respite unless we put in place the longer-term framework.

Lebanon/United Nations Security Council Resolution 1559

Q. Mr. President, you spoke of having a plan to rebuild houses in Lebanon. Wouldn't the people of Lebanon rather know when you're going to tell the Israelis to stop destroying houses?

And, Prime Minister, you've talked of having a plan today, but isn't the truth that you and the President believe that Israel is on the right side in the war on terror and you want them to win this war, not to stop it?

President Bush. Look, we care deeply about the people whose lives have been affected in Lebanon, just like we care deeply about the people whose lives have been affected in Israel. There's over a million people in Israel that are threatened by this consistent rocket attack coming out of Lebanon. And, yes, we want to help people rebuild their lives, absolutely. But we also want to address the root causes of the problem, and the root cause of the problem is you've got Hizballah that is armed and willing to fire rockets into Israel—a Hizballah, by the way, that I firmly believe is backed by Iran and encouraged by Iran.

And so for the sake of long-term stability, we've got to deal with this issue now. Listen, the temptation is to say, "It's too tough. Let's just try to solve it quickly with something that won't last; let's just get it off the TV screens." But that won't solve the problem. And it's certainly not going to help the Lebanese citizens have a life that is normal and peaceful.

What is necessary is to help the Siniora Government, and one way to help the Siniora Government is to make aid available to help rebuild the houses that were destroyed. Another way to help the Siniora Government is to implement 1559, which is the disarmament of armed militia inside his country.

And I—look, we care deeply about the lives that have been affected on both sides

of this issue, just like I care deeply about the innocent people who are being killed in Iraq and people being denied a state in the Palestinian Territory. But make no mistake about it, it is the goal and aims of the terrorist organizations to stop that type of advance. That's what they're trying to do. They're trying to evoke sympathy for themselves. They're not sympathetic people. They're violent, coldblooded killers who are trying to stop the advance of freedom.

And this is the calling of the 21st century, it seems like to me, and now is the time to confront the problem. And of course, we're going to help the people in Lebanon rebuild their lives. But as Tony said, this conflict started, out of the blue, with two Israeli soldiers kidnaped and rockets being fired across the border.

Now, we have urged restraint. We made it clear that we care about wanton destruction. On the other hand, in my judgment, it would be a big mistake not to solve the underlying problems. Otherwise, everything will seem fine, and then you'll be back at a press conference saying, "How come you didn't solve the underlying problems?"

Prime Minister Blair. We feel deeply for people in Lebanon and people in Israel who are the innocent casualties of this conflict. Of course we do. And we want it to stop, and we want it to stop now. And what we're putting forward today is actually a practical plan that would lead to a U.N. resolution—could be early next week—that would allow it, put in place the conditions for it to stop.

But what we've also got to do is to make sure that we recognize that this action wasn't simply aimed against Israel, and then Israel retaliated. It was also aimed against the proper Government of Lebanon being able to control its own country. And the very reason why, 2 years ago, the international community passed this resolution was because people could see that what was going to happen in southern Lebanon was that these Hizballah militias, that are armed and financed by Iran and by Syria, were going to move into the south of the country in order to be a focus of terrorism and discontent.

Now, that is the fact. And of course, all of us are appalled at the destruction and loss of life; of course, we are. And that's why we've actually come together today with a viable plan—if people can agree it, as I believe they can—to get it stopped. But once you stop this violence happening now—which, of course, we should do—once you do, it doesn't alter the underlying reality unless we've got a framework that allows us to put the Government of Lebanon properly back in charge of its own country; unless we've got the commitment to take forward the Israel-Palestine two-state deal, which is there and which everyone wants to see; and then if we can—unless we mobilize the international community, to deal with the threat that Iran poses.

And there's no other way out of this. We're not—we can, all of us, make whatever statements we want to do, use whatever words we want to do, but the brutal reality of the situation is that we're only going to get violence stopped and stability introduced on the basis of clear principles.

Now, as I say, we've set out a way to do this. But it requires the long term, as well as the short term.

Multinational Peacekeeping Force in Lebanon

Q. Thank you, Mr. President. On the issue of the multinational force, what shape should it take; who should lead it; who should be part of it? And also, should Hizballah agreeing to it be a precondition for setting up the force?

And, Mr. Prime Minister, you talked about a resolution leading to a cessation of hostilities, and I'm just wondering, should it include a call for an immediate cease-fire?

President Bush. In terms of the troops, that's what the meeting Monday is going to be about. And this is one of these issues that requires international consensus. People will put forth ideas, and we'll participate, in terms of trying to help develop a consensus about what the force ought to look like.

In a general sense, though, the force needs to serve as a complement to a Lebanese force. See, that's the whole purpose of the force, is to strengthen the Lebanese Government by helping the Lebanese force move into the area. The whole cornerstone of the policy for Lebanon is for Lebanon to be free and able to govern herself and defend herself with a viable force.

And so one of the things you'll see in discussions there is, how do we help the Lebanese Army succeed? What does it— what's required? What's the manpower need to be in order to help this force move into the south so the government can take control of the country. What it looks like— if I hold a press conference on Tuesday, I'll be able to answer that better. But since I probably won't be, read your newspaper.

Q. What about Hizballah——

President Bush. That's a part of the conditions that they'll be discussing. That's what they'll be talking about. The key is to have Lebanon agree with it. And the key is to have Israel agree with it. Those are the two parties. Hizballah is not a state. They're a supposed political party that happens to be armed. Now, what kind of state is it that has got a political party that has got a militia? It's a state that needs to be helped, is what that is. And we need to help the Siniora Government deal with a political party that is armed, that gets its arms and help from other parts of the world—in order for Lebanon's democracy to succeed.

A lot has changed in Lebanon. It wasn't all that long ago that Lebanon was occupied by Syria. And we came together and worked in the U.N. Security Council, and Syria is now out of Lebanon. But part of the resolution that enabled Syria to get out was that Hizballah would disarm. And if we truly want peace in the region, we've got to follow through on that 1559, and that's what the whole strategy is. And part of the peacekeepers will be to—or the multinational force, whatever you call them, will be in there trying to help the Government.

Prime Minister Blair. Just on the international force, the thing that's very important to realize is that the purpose of it, obviously, is to help stabilize the situation. But it's also to allow the Government of Lebanon's true armed forces to come down from the north and occupy the south themselves. In other words, the purpose of the force is almost as a bridge between the north and the south, in order to allow the forces of the Government of Lebanon to come down and do what Resolution 1559 always anticipated would happen.

And as for your second question, yes, of course, the U.N. resolution, the passing of it, the agreeing of it can be the occasion for the end of hostilities if it's acted upon and agreed upon. And that requires not just the Government of Israel and the Government of Lebanon, obviously, to abide by it but also for the whole of the international community to exert the necessary pressure so that there is the cessation of hostilities on both sides. Now, that will be important also in making it very clear to Hizballah and those that back Hizballah that they have to allow the stabilization force to enter.

But, yes, of course, look, anybody with any human feeling for what is going on there wants this to stop as quickly as possible. And we have a process that allows us to do this, but it's got to be acted on. It's not just going to be agreed in theory; it's got to be acted on too.

Iran/Syria

Q. Thank you. Mr. President and Prime Minister Blair, can I ask you both tonight what your messages are for the Governments of Iran and Syria, given that you say this is the crisis of the 21st century?

President Bush. Want me to start? My message is, give up your nuclear weapon and your nuclear weapon ambitions. That's my message to Syria—I mean, to Iran. And my message to Syria is, become an active participant in the neighborhood for peace.

Prime Minister Blair. The message is very, very simple to them. It is that you have a choice. Iran and Syria have a choice. And they may think that they can avoid this choice; in fact, they can't. And when things are set in train, like what has happened in Lebanon over the past few weeks, it only, in my view, underscores the fact they have this choice. They can either come in and participate as proper and responsible members of the international community, or they will face the risk of increasing confrontation.

And coming in and being proper members of the international community does not mean—though I would love to see both Syria and Iran proper democracies—does not mean to say that we insist that they change their government or even their system of government, although, of course, we want to see change in those countries. But it does mean Iran abides by its obligations under the nuclear weapons treaty. It does mean that Iran and Syria stop supporting terrorism. It does mean that instead of trying to prevent the democratically elected government of Iraq fulfill its mandate, they allow it to fulfill its mandate.

Now, that's their choice. It's a perfectly simple one. They can either decide they are going to abide by the rules of the international community or continue to transgress them. And look, in the end, that's the choice that they will have to make. But where I think they make a strategic miscalculation is if they think that because of all the other issues that we have to resolve and so on, that we are indifferent to what they are doing. There will be no sidetracking of our determination, for example, to make sure that Iran is fully compliant with the call that's been made on them from the whole of the international community in respect of nuclear weapons capability. And I hope they realize there is a different relationship that is possible with the international community, but only on the basis that has been set out.

President Bush. David Gregory [NBC News].

Iraq/U.S. Influence Abroad/War on Terror

Q. Thank you. Mr. President, both of you, I'd like to ask you about the big picture that you're discussing. Mr. President, 3 years ago, you argued that an invasion of Iraq would create a new stage of Arab-Israeli peace. And yet today, there is an Iraqi Prime Minister who has been sharply critical of Israel. Arab governments, despite your arguments, who first criticized Hizballah, have now changed their tune; now they're sharply critical of Israel. And despite, from both of you, warnings to Syria and Iran to back off support from Hizballah, effectively, Mr. President, your words are being ignored. So what has happened to America's clout in this region that you've committed yourself to transform?

President Bush. David, it's an interesting period because instead of having foreign policies based upon trying to create a sense of stability, we have a foreign policy that addresses the root causes of violence and instability.

For a while, American foreign policy was just, let's hope everything is calm, kind of managed calm. But beneath the surface brewed a lot of resentment and anger that was manifested in its—on September the 11th. And so we've taken a foreign policy that says, on the one hand, we will protect ourselves from further attack in the short run by being aggressive and chasing down the killers and bringing them to justice— and make no mistake, they're still out there, and they would like to harm our respective peoples because of what we stand for— in the long term, to defeat this ideology, and they're bound by an ideology. You de-

feat it with a more hopeful ideology called freedom.

And, look, I fully understand some people don't believe it's possible for freedom and democracy to overcome this ideology of hatred. I understand that. I just happen to believe it is possible, and I believe it will happen. And so what you're seeing is a clash of governing styles. For example, the notion of democracy beginning to emerge scares the ideologues, the totalitarians, those who want to impose their vision. It just frightens them, and so they respond. They've always been violent.

I hear this amazing, kind of, editorial thought that says, all of a sudden, Hizballah has become violent because we're promoting democracy. They have been violent for a long period of time. Or Hamas— one reason why the Palestinians still suffer is because there are militants who refuse to accept a Palestinian state based upon democratic principles.

And so what the world is seeing is a desire by this country and our allies to defeat the ideology of hate with an ideology that has worked and that brings hope. And one of the challenges, of course, is to convince people that Muslims would like to be free, that there's other people other than people in Britain and America that would like to be free in the world. There's this kind of almost—kind of—weird kind of elitism that says, well, maybe certain people in certain parts of the world shouldn't be free; maybe it's best just to let them sit in these tyrannical societies. And our foreign policy rejects that concept. We don't accept it.

And so we're working. And this is—as I said the other day, when these attacks took place, I said this should be a moment of clarity for people to see the stakes in the 21st century. I mean, there's an unprovoked attack on a democracy. Why? I happen to believe because progress is being made toward democracies. And I believe that—I also believe that Iran would like to exert additional influence in the region. A theocracy would like to spread its influence using surrogates.

And so I'm as determined as ever to continue fostering a foreign policy based upon liberty. And I think it's going to work unless we lose our nerve and quit. And this government isn't going to quit.

Q. I asked you about the loss of American influence, and are you worried about that.

President Bush. Well, David, we went to the G–8 and worked with our allies and got a remarkable statement on what took place. We're working to get a United Nations resolution on Iran. We're working to have a Palestinian state. But the reason why—you asked the question—is because terrorists are trying to stop that progress. And we'll ultimately prevail, because they have—their ideology is so dark and so dismal that when people really think about it, it will be rejected. They just got a different tool to use than we do: They kill innocent lives to achieve objectives. That's what they do. And they're good. They get on the TV screens, and they get people to ask questions about, well, this, that, or the other. I mean, they're able to kind of say to people, "Don't come and bother us because we will kill you."

And my attitude is, is that now is the time to be firm. And we've got a great weapon on our side, and that is freedom and liberty. And it's got—those two concepts have got the capacity to defeat ideologies of hate.

Prime Minister Blair. I don't think, actually, it's anything to do with a loss of American influence at all. I think we've got to go back and ask what changed policy, because policy has changed in the past few years. And what changed policy was September the 11th. That changed policy, but actually, before September the 11th, this global movement with a global ideology was already in being. September the 11th was the culmination of what they wanted to do. But actually—and this is probably where

the policymakers, such as myself, were truly in error—is that even before September the 11th, this was happening in all sorts of different ways in different countries.

I mean, in Algeria, for example, tens and tens of thousands of people lost their lives. This movement has grown; it is there; it will latch on to any cause that it possibly can and give it a dimension of terrorism and hatred. You can see this. You can see it in Kashmir, for example. You can see it in Chechnya. You can see it in Palestine.

Now, what is its purpose? Its purpose is to promote its ideology based upon the perversion of Islam and to use any methods at all, but particularly terrorism, to do that, because they know that the value of terrorism to them is—as I was saying a moment or two ago, it's not simply the act of terror; it's the chain reaction that terror brings with it. Terrorism brings the reprisal; the reprisal brings the additional hatred; the additional hatred breeds the additional terrorism, and so on. Look, in a small way, we lived through that in Northern Ireland over many, many decades.

Now, what happened after September the 11th—and this explains, I think, the President's policy, but also the reason why I have taken the view and still take the view that Britain and America should remain strong allies, shoulder to shoulder in fighting this battle, is that we are never going to succeed unless we understand they are going to fight hard. The reason why they are doing what they're doing in Iraq at the moment—and, yes, it's really tough as a result of it—is because they know that if, right in the center of the Middle East in an Arab, Muslim country, you've got a nonsectarian democracy—in other words, people weren't governed either by religious fanatics or secular dictators; you've got a genuine democracy of the people—how does their ideology flourish in such circumstances?

So they have imported the terrorism into that country, preyed on whatever reactionary elements there are to boost it. And that's why we have the issue there; that's why the Taliban are trying to come back in Afghanistan. That is why the moment it looked as if you could get progress in Israel and Palestine it had to be stopped. That's the moment when, as they saw there was a problem in Gaza, so they realized, well, there's a possibility now we can set Lebanon against Israel.

Now, it's a global movement; it's a global ideology. And if there's any mistake that's ever made in these circumstances, it's if people are surprised that it's tough to fight, because you're up against an ideology that's prepared to use any means at all, including killing any number of wholly innocent people.

And I don't dispute part of the implication of your question at all, in the sense that you look at what is happening in the Middle East and what is happening in Iraq and Lebanon and Palestine, and, of course, there's a sense of shock and frustration and anger at what is happening and grief at the loss of innocent lives. But it is not a reason for walking away. It's a reason for staying the course and staying it no matter how tough it is, because the alternative is actually letting this ideology grip larger and larger numbers of people.

And it is going to be difficult. Look, we've got a problem even in our own Muslim communities in Europe, who will half-buy into some of the propaganda that's pushed at it—the purpose of America is to suppress Islam, Britain has joined with America in the suppression of Islam. And one of the things we've got to stop doing is stop apologizing for our own positions. Muslims in America, as far as I'm aware of, are free to worship; Muslims in Britain are free to worship. We are plural societies.

It's nonsense; the propaganda is nonsense. And we're not going to defeat this ideology until we in the West go out with sufficient confidence in our own position and say this is wrong. It's not just wrong in its methods; it's wrong in its ideas; it's wrong in its ideology; it's wrong in every single wretched reactionary thing about it. And it will be a long struggle, I'm afraid. But there's no alternative but to stay the course with it. And we will.

Situation in the Middle East

Q. Can I ask you both how soon realistically you think there could be an end to the violence, given there's no signs at the moment of 1559 being met? I mean, do you think we're looking at more weeks, months, or can it be achieved sooner than that? And also, will the multinational force potentially be used to affect a cease-fire or simply to police an agreement once we eventually get to that?

Prime Minister Blair. Well, the answer to the first point is, as soon as possible. And if we can get the U.N. resolution agreed next week and acted upon, then it can happen, and it can happen then. We want to see it happen as quickly as possible, but the conditions have got to be in place to allow it to happen.

And in relation to the multinational force, what will be—it's not going to be the opportunity to fight their way in. But the very way that you posed that question underlines this basic point, which is, this can only work if Hizballah are prepared to allow it to work. And we've got to make sure, therefore, that we have the force go in as part of an agreement that the Government of Lebanon have bound itself to, the Government of Israel has bound itself to, the international community has bound itself to. And Hizballah have got to appreciate that if they stand out against that, then it's not really that they will be doing a huge disservice to the people of Lebanon, but they will also, again, face the fact that action will have to be taken against them.

President Bush. We share the same urgency of trying to stop the violence. It's why Condi Rice went out there very quickly. Her job is to—first and foremost, was to make it clear to the Lebanese people that we wanted to send aid and help work on the corridors necessary to get the aid to the Lebanese people. And she's coming back to the region tonight, will be there tomorrow. I could have called her back here and could have sat around, visited, and talked. But I thought it was important for her to go back to the region to work on a United Nations Security Council resolution.

So, like the Prime Minister, I would like to end this as quickly as possible as well. Having said that, I want to make sure that we address the root cause of the problem. And I believe the plan that Tony and I discussed will yield exactly what we want, and that is addressing the root cause of the problem.

Thank you all for coming.

NOTE: The President's news conference began at 12:36 p.m. in the East Room at the White House. In his remarks, President Bush referred to Prime Minister Nuri al-Maliki of Iraq; Prime Minister Ehud Olmert of Israel; President Mahmoud Abbas of the Palestinian Authority; Prime Minister Fuad Siniora of Lebanon; and Ehud Goldwasser and Eldad Regev, Israeli soldiers captured and held captive by militants in Lebanon since July 12. Prime Minister Blair referred to President Jacques Chirac of France; Chancellor Angela Merkel of Germany; Prime Minister Recep Tayyip Erdogan of Turkey; and Prime Minister Matti Taneli Vanhanen and Foreign Minister Erkki Tuomioja of Finland, whose country held the Council of the European Union Presidency.

The President's Radio Address
July 29, 2006

Good morning. This week, the international community continued to build a political and security framework to confront the crisis in the Middle East, a crisis that began with Hizballah's unprovoked terrorist attacks on Israel. Secretary of State Rice traveled to Lebanon, Israel, and Europe, and met with key leaders to discuss a way forward. In Rome, she met with representatives of more than a dozen nations and international organizations. Our Governments agreed to provide relief to the people of Lebanon, using corridors for humanitarian aid that Israel is opening. We pledged to support Lebanon's revival and reconstruction. And we agreed to continue to work for a sustainable cease-fire that will stop the current violence, end the suffering of people in Lebanon and Israel, and move us toward a lasting peace.

Yesterday I met with Prime Minister Tony Blair to discuss our strategy to achieve these shared goals. We agreed that Lebanon's democratic Government must be empowered to exercise full authority over its territory. Militias in Lebanon must be disarmed; the flow of illegal arms must be halted; and the Lebanese security services should deploy throughout the country. We also agreed that a robust multinational force must be dispatched to Lebanon quickly. An effective multinational force will help speed delivery of humanitarian relief, facilitate the return of displaced persons, and support the Lebanese Government as it asserts full sovereignty over its territory and guards its borders. In addition, Iran must end its financial support and supply of weapons to terrorist groups such as Hizballah, and Syria must end its support for terrorism and respect Lebanon's sovereignty.

Secretary Rice will return to the region this weekend, and she will work with the leaders of Israel and Lebanon to seize this opportunity to achieve lasting peace and stability for both countries. Next week, the United Nations Security Council will also meet. We will work with our allies to adopt a resolution that establishes a framework to end the violence quickly and mandates the multinational force. This approach will demonstrate the international community's determination to support the Government of Lebanon and defeat the threat from Hizballah and its foreign sponsors. And this approach will make possible what so many around the world want to see: the end of Hizballah's attacks on Israel; the return of Israeli soldiers taken hostage by terrorists; the suspension of Israel's operations in Lebanon; and the withdrawal of Israeli forces.

As we work to resolve this current crisis, we must recognize that Lebanon is the latest flashpoint in a broader struggle between freedom and terror that is unfolding across the region. For decades, American policy sought to achieve peace in the Middle East by promoting stability in the Middle East, yet these policies gave us neither. The lack of freedom in that region created conditions where anger and resentment grew, radicalism thrived, and terrorists found willing recruits. We saw the consequences on September the 11th, 2001, when terrorists brought death and destruction to our country, killing nearly 3,000 innocent Americans.

The experience of September the 11th made it clear that we could no longer tolerate the status quo in the Middle East. We saw that when an entire region simmers in violence, that violence will eventually reach our shores and spread across the entire world. The only way to secure our Nation is to change the course of the Middle East by fighting the ideology of terror and spreading the hope of freedom.

So we have launched a forward strategy for freedom in the broader Middle East, and that strategy has set in motion a transformation that is changing millions of lives for the better. From Kabul to Baghdad to Beirut and beyond, we've seen the birth of democratic governments that are striving to serve their people, reject terror, and work for peace. We're also seeing those

who oppose democracy fighting its progress with all the destructive power they can muster. We see this in Hizballah's attacks on Israel, in the suicide bombings that kill innocent Iraqis, and in Al Qaida's campaign of terror across the world.

The enemies of freedom have shown their ability to set back our efforts with deadly attacks, but ultimately, they will fail. They will fail because courageous leaders in the region have stepped forward to defend freedom and set the Middle East on a better course. And they will fail because millions of people who have suffered decades of oppression and violence will choose to live in peace with their neighbors.

In Iraq, we will help Prime Minister Maliki's unity Government defeat the terrorists, insurgents, and illegal militias and establish a democracy in the heart of the Middle East. In Lebanon, we will stand with the democratic Government in its efforts to rid the country of terrorists and foreign influence and bring about a better life for the Lebanese people. In the Palestinian Territories, we will work with President Abbas to support the forces of moderation and achieve our shared vision of two democratic states, Israel and Palestine, living side by side in peace and security.

This moment of conflict in the Middle East is painful and tragic, yet it is also a moment of opportunity for broader change in the region. Transforming countries that have suffered decades of tyranny and violence is difficult, and it will take time to achieve. But the consequences will be profound, for our country and the world. When the Middle East grows in liberty and democracy, it will also grow in peace, and that will make America and all free nations more secure.

Thank you for listening.

NOTE: The address was recorded at 2 p.m. in the Cabinet Room at the White House for broadcast at 10:06 a.m. on July 29. The transcript was made available by the Office of the Press Secretary on July 28 but was embargoed for release until the broadcast. In his address, the President referred to Prime Minister Tony Blair of the United Kingdom; Prime Minister Ehud Olmert of Israel; Prime Minister Fuad Siniora of Lebanon; Gilad Shalit, an Israeli soldier captured and held captive by militants in Gaza since June 25; Ehud Goldwasser and Eldad Regev, Israeli soldiers captured and held captive by militants in Lebanon since July 12; Prime Minister Nuri al-Maliki of Iraq; and President Mahmoud Abbas of the Palestinian Authority. The Office of the Press Secretary also released a Spanish language transcript of this address.

Remarks on the Situation in the Middle East
July 30, 2006

The current situation in the Middle East is a reminder that all of us must work together to achieve a sustainable peace. America mourns the loss of innocent life. It's a tragic occasion when innocent people are killed. And so our sympathies go out to those who've lost their lives today and lost their lives throughout this crisis.

I've been in touch with Secretary of State Rice twice today. She'll be returning tomorrow, where she'll brief me on her discussions with leaders in the Middle East. I also talked to Tony Blair. The United States is resolved to work with members of the United Nations Security Council to develop a resolution that will enable the region to have a sustainable peace, a peace that lasts, a peace that will enable mothers and fathers to raise their children in a hopeful world.

May God bless those who lost their lives. Thank you.

NOTE: The President spoke at 4:12 p.m. on the South Lawn at the White House. In his remarks, he referred to Prime Minister Tony Blair of the United Kingdom.

Letter to Congressional Leaders Certifying Exports to the People's Republic of China
July 28, 2006

Dear Mr. Speaker: (Dear Mr. President:)

In accordance with the provisions of section 1512 of the Strom Thurmond National Defense Authorization Act for Fiscal Year 1999 (Public Law 105–261), I hereby certify that the export to the People's Republic of China of the following items is not detrimental to the United States space launch industry, and that the material and equipment, including any indirect technical benefit that could be derived from such exports, will not measurably improve the missile or space launch capabilities of the People's Republic of China.

1. Two million pounds of bulk graphite for use by Smarteem Precision Manufacturing Company, Qingdao Dezong Trading Company, Qingdao Haier Moulds Company, Hi-P Shanghai Precision Mold and Die, Shanghai Sharp Mold and Manufacturing, Shanghai Koito Automotive Lamp

Company, Ningbo Yongyao Graphite Product, Heibei Ningjin Matsimiya Semiconductor, Heibei Ningjin Yangguang Electrodes, Jiaxiang Zhengda Xingxin Electrodes, Shanghai Shenhe Thermo-Magnetics and Genic (Shanghai) Company to manufacture electrodes, dies and molds for the production and handling of plastic, rubber, copper, tin, aluminum, and iron components.

2. One 36-inch micronizer to be used by Jiangsu Sopo Chemical of Zhenjiang, China, for processing azodicarbonomide for use in manufacturing plastics.

3. One 42-inch micronizer to be used by Cabot Performance Products Company, LTD. of Tianjin, China, for manufacturing carbon black to be used in rubber and plastics manufacturing.

Sincerely,

GEORGE W. BUSH

NOTE: Identical letters were sent to J. Dennis Hastert, Speaker of the House of Representatives, and Richard B. Cheney, President of the Senate. The letter was released by the Office of the Press Secretary on July 31.

Remarks at a White House Tee-Ball Game
July 30, 2006

Thank you very much. You know, as we listen to our national anthem, it reminds us how blessed we are to live in a land where our boys and girls can grow up in a peaceful world. And on today our hopes for peace for boys and girls everywhere extends across the world, especially in the Middle East. Today's actions in the Middle East remind us that the United States and friends and allies must work for a sustainable peace, particularly for the sake of children.

And so I want to welcome you here to the White House. What an honor to be with the commissioner, Willie Mays. See, when I was growing up, I wanted to be the Willie Mays of my generation, but I couldn't hit a curve ball. So instead, I ended up being President.

Laura and I welcome you here, along with the commissioner. It's a proud day for us to welcome—a little hot for baseball, but I know these teams are up for it. First, I want to welcome the Civitan Club of Frederick Challengers from Thurmont, Maryland. We're glad you all are here. We also want to welcome the mayor, Mayor Marty Burns of Thurmont. Welcome, Mr.

Mayor. Thanks for coming. There he is. Marty used to work at Camp David, by the way.

I also want to welcome the Challenger Braves from Shady Spring, West Virginia.

We welcome both teams, the coaches, the helpers, and the families. We're glad you're here. We're lucky today to have not only one Major Leaguer but three Major Leaguers with us—coaching first base, the lefty, Al Leiter; welcome, Al—at third base, Dan Wilson. Glad you're here, Dan. Thanks for coming. Proud you're here.

We welcome Steve Keener, who is the president and CEO of Little League International. We want to thank the Girl Scout Council of the Nation's Capital who carried the colors. I want to thank Nichola Kouzes, who sang the national anthem. Nichola, you did a fabulous job here on the South Lawn. Thank you. She did a good job, didn't she? Not only a good job but a great job.

We're lucky today to have an old hand at calling this game, the former announcer of the Washington Senators, Charlie Brotman. Welcome, Charlie. Glad you're here. Thanks for coming. Glad you're here.

And finally, we have a tradition here, and that is, we actually don't throw out the first ball; we actually put the first ball on the tee. And joining me today is Kevin Turley. He's a Special Olympics gold medalist. Kevin, thanks for coming. Thank you for being a part of this.

You ready? Everybody ready? And right before we play ball, we'll give the Little League Pledge. Ready for the pledge?

[*At this point, the pledge was recited.*]

Play ball.

NOTE: The President spoke at 2:45 p.m. on the South Lawn at the White House. In his remarks, he referred to White House Tee-Ball Commissioner Willie Mays. The transcript was released by the Office of the Press Secretary on July 31.

Remarks to Reporters in Miami, Florida
July 31, 2006

It's an honor to be here at one of Miami's most famous restaurants. Brother Jeb suggested we come here and have some coffee with some of south Florida's leading entrepreneurs. We've got people who have started their own business, people who are carrying on family traditions, all of whom share with me their optimism but also share with me some of the problems they face.

One of the key problems that many of the businesses face here is labor. The unemployment rate is unbelievably low right now, and therefore, businesses who are planning for the future are wondering whether or not they're going to be able to find people to help their businesses expand. I assured them that the administration is still working toward a comprehensive immigration policy that will be rational, that will be able to, one, enforce rule of law and, on the other hand, be compassionate about how this country treats people.

I assured them, as well, that we will continue to work to keep taxes low. It's very interesting, you know; when an entrepreneur gets their business started, they want to keep more of their own money so they can expand. And one way to do that is to make sure that taxes stay low, and that's what we will do.

We talked about health care; we talked about energy; we talked about Cuba. So I want to thank you all very much for being here. Thanks for giving me a chance to come.

And by the way, we also talked about the situation in the Middle East. And I assured the people here that we will work toward a plan in the United Nations Security Council that addresses the root causes of the problem so that whatever comes out of the Security Council will be able to last and that the people in both Lebanon and Israel will be able to grow—be able to remain in peace. That's what we want. We want there to be a long-lasting peace, one that's sustainable. And I'll speak to Condi Rice when she gets back tonight, to talk about what she saw and what she heard in the Middle East. And of course, there will be a way forward in the Security Council later on this week.

Thank you.

NOTE: The President spoke at 8:47 a.m. at the Versailles Restaurant and Bakery. In his remarks, he referred to Gov. Jeb Bush of Florida.

Remarks at the Port of Miami in Miami
July 31, 2006

Thanks for the warm welcome on a warm day. [*Laughter*] I'm proud to be here in this really dynamic city. You know it's an amazing part of our country when you walk off and a Member of the United States Congress says, "*Bienvenido a Miami.*"

This trip is a little different from the last time I spent the night here in Miami. Last night Jeb and I had some crabs with members of the 1972 Miami Dolphins; Dan Marino and his really dynamic wife; TV stars—Andy Garcia, a movie star. We had a fantastic experience. It's a lot better, by the way, than preparing for a presidential debate. [*Laughter*]

I'm glad to be here. I'm glad to be with brother Jeb. We're really proud of him in our family. He's a guy who does what he said he's going to do. He's a good man, *mi hermanito.*

Miami is a strong and vibrant city, and because your economy is strong and vibrant, you've helped this State's economy grow and you've helped the country grow. I want to spend some time talking about the economy and how we can keep our economy strong; no better place to do that than here in the Port of Miami. I'm proud to be with those who work in the port. I'm particularly proud to be with those who wear the uniform of the United States of America. Thanks for serving.

The Commandant of the United States Coast Guard has joined us today, Admiral Thad Allen. Thanks for coming. Rear Admiral David Kunkel is with us. I appreciate you being here, Admiral. I particularly want to thank all those who are on our ships, work in our ports. And I thank your families. You tell your wife or your husband how much this country appreciates the support of our families for our Coast Guard men and women.

I want to thank Bill Johnson, who is acting seaport director. I'm proud to be here

with the Federal Emergency Management Agency head, Dave Paulison—south Floridian by the way. Members of the United States congressional delegation are with us, starting with the Congresswoman from this district, Ileana Ros-Lehtinen. *Los hermanos* Diaz-Balart are with us today, Lincoln *y tambien* Mario. It's good to see you guys. Thanks for coming. Clay Shaw, Congressman Shaw is with us. I'm proud you're here.

The new speaker of the house, Marco Rubio, is with us today. Mr. Speaker, thank you. Mayor Carlos Alvarez is with us, *el alcalde.* Thank you. Mayor Manny Diaz is with us. Thank you, Manny. I want to thank all the local folks for coming, all the people who are concerned about south Florida— the local officials. I'm proud to be here.

Let me start by telling you I'm monitoring the situation in the Middle East very closely. Secretary Rice was in the region over the weekend, and she is working urgently to get a sustainable cease-fire, a cease-fire which will last. We're going to work with our allies to bring before the United Nations Security Council a resolution that will end the violence and lay the groundwork for lasting peace in the Middle East.

As we work with friends and allies, it is important to remember, this crisis began with Hizballah's unprovoked terrorist attacks against Israel. Israel is exercising its right to defend itself. And we mourn the loss of innocent life, both in Lebanon and in Israel. We're determined to deliver relief to those who suffer; we're determined to work to resolve this crisis.

To achieve the peace that we want, we must achieve certain clear objectives. Lebanon's democratic Government must be empowered to exercise sole authority over its territory. A multinational force must be dispatched to Lebanon quickly so we can help speed the delivery of humanitarian aid to the Lebanese people. Iran must end its financial support and supply of weapons to terrorist groups like Hizballah. Syria must end its support for terror and respect the sovereignty of Lebanon.

This approach will make it possible what so many around the world want to see: the end of Hizballah's attacks on Israel; the return of the Israeli soldiers taken hostage by the terrorists; the suspension of Israel's operations in Lebanon; and the eventual withdrawal of Israeli forces.

The current crisis is part of a larger struggle between the forces of freedom and the forces of terror in the Middle East. For decades, the status quo in the Middle East permitted tyranny and terror to thrive. And as we saw on September the 11th, the status quo in the Middle East led to death and destruction in the United States, and it had to change. So America is opposing the forces of terror and promoting the cause of democracy across the broader Middle East.

This task is long. It is difficult work, but it is necessary work. When democracy spreads in the Middle East, the people of that troubled region will have a better future. The terrorists will lose their safe havens and their recruits, and the United States of America will be more secure. The hard work of helping people realize the benefits of liberty is laying the foundation of peace for generations to come.

It's an honor to be here at the largest container port in Florida and one of the most important ports in our Nation. From these docks, ships loaded with cargo deliver products all around the world carrying that label, "Made in the USA." See, the Port of Miami is shipping what the world wants to buy. The Port of Miami is also the largest cruise port in the whole world. All you got to do is drive down the highway and look at the size of those ships. This is known as the "Cruise Capital of the World." And that's important. It's impor-

tant for the people who want to find a job here.

See, the Port of Miami not only enables us to ship products all over the world, which encourages job creation—people working here, getting those products moving around the world—but it's also a place where tourists come to travel the world on some great cruise ships, which means that chefs and grocers need to be hired to prepare food for the people on the ships or accountants and travel agents to handle the bookings or hotel workers to house the passengers before the ships depart.

One reason south Florida's economy is doing well is because of the importance of this port. But it's just not the port that is helping the people in south Florida. Do you realize that over the past 3 years, the Miami-Fort Lauderdale metropolitan area has created more than 200,000 new jobs? The unemployment rate in this area is down to 3.2 percent. It's amazing economic vitality in this part of the world, and I congratulate the entrepreneurs.

Today I met with some entrepreneurs. I met a guy named Nelson Gonzalez. Are you here, Nelson? Yes, there he is. And he's got a partner who's not here. But think about this; I want to tell you about Nelson's story. It is an American story. It's a story about two people who had a dream, and 10 years ago they sat in Nelson's garage talking about how to create a business. And they had $10,000 in capital to start their business. And so they decided to build high-performance, custom-designed personal computers. That was their dream. First year, the revenues were $87,000, like they started getting moving. Last year, the revenue was $192 million. They went from 2 people sitting in a garage to employing 750 people.

So here's the spirit behind Nelson's dream. He said, "Losing was not just in our vocabulary. We overcame a lot of things. We really didn't sit on our laurels, and we always look at what we can improve." See, one of the jobs of Government is to put policy in place that encourages the entrepreneurial spirit to flourish. We want more people owning their businesses. We want more dreamers working hard to accomplish their dreams. And when they do, more people find work.

One of the reasons why the national unemployment rate is at 4.6 percent is because the entrepreneurial spirit is strong in America. And we intend to keep it that way. And one of the ways to make sure entrepreneurs like Nelson and others are able to realize dreams is to keep the taxes low.

There's a great temptation in Washington to say, "We can spend your money better than you can," see. But when you start talking about raising taxes, you're talking about taking money away from entrepreneurs and small-business owners. Good policy is policy that says, we want to strengthen the small-business sector in America. We want the entrepreneurial spirit to flourish. And one of the ways to do so is to make the tax cuts we pass a permanent part of the Tax Code.

And here's another way that we can help the entrepreneurial spirit flourish and help make sure south Florida remains a vibrant part of our national economy, and that is to open up markets for trade. I'm worried about protectionist tendencies in the United States, people saying, "Well, we don't want to—really want to compete. Let's just kind of throw up some walls and barriers so people can't sell products into the United States." Such policies will damage the Port of Miami; such policies are short-sighted, as far as I'm concerned.

America is home to 5 percent of the world's population. That means 95 percent of the world's population are potential customers. The port is known as "The Gateway of the Americas" for a reason, because international trade is one of the key reasons why Miami prospers. I don't know if the folks realize that because of trade—in other words, the ability to move products over-

seas—120,000 jobs here in this part of the world are supported by trade.

I believe trade leads to opportunity, trade leads to jobs; trade means this port will remain vibrant. And so good policy from our Government perspective must be to continue to working up—working to open up markets for U.S. products, and say to people around the world, "You treat us the way we treat you." In other words, trade must be a two-way street. We must work to open up markets, but at the same time, we must say to foreign nations, "As we open our markets to your goods, you open your markets to our goods." The United States can compete with anybody, anywhere so long as the rules are fair.

Congress passed NAFTA, and as a result, Florida's exports to Mexico tripled. Two years ago, we passed a free trade agreement with Chile. Florida exports to that country have jumped by 40 percent. Now when you hear me say, "Florida's exports," that means exports of products made in the United States leaving ports like Miami, which creates jobs. Exports means work. Exports means vitality at our ports.

Last year, we passed CAFTA. I want to thank the Members of Congress who supported me on that important agreement. This port handles nearly one-half of all American exports to Central America. And as CAFTA takes hold, we can envision more products passing from the United States to Central America through the Port of Miami.

Now, one of the most promising ways to open up new markets for our workers and businesses is the Doha round of negotiations at the World Trade Organization. See, these talks are important talks. They have a chance to break down trade barriers around the world. They have a chance to expand the flow of commerce, which is what we want. They have a chance to create new jobs and economic growth not only here but elsewhere. And they have a chance to help lift millions of people out of poverty around the world. These are important negotiations taking place. And our Government is strongly committed to a successful outcome of the Doha round.

The problem is, is that some others aren't committed. Recent discussions broke down. In order to make sure that they don't break down permanently, I asked Trade Representative Susan Schwab to continue to work with her counterparts, to continue to discuss ways for the United States to be flexible, particularly on agricultural subsidies, and for our counterparts to be flexible when it comes to achieving fairness when it comes to trade.

We'll do everything we can to get Doha back on track. That's what the people in this port who rely upon the export of goods must understand. We understand how important exportation is to the Port of Miami. We understand how important trade is for the economy of the United States. And so Susan Schwab now has been in Brazil recently and will continue talking with other trade ministers. Completing the Doha round is going to demand tough choices. We're willing to make those choices, and others nations should as well. This is a once-in-a-lifetime opportunity to jump-start global trade and create opportunities around the world.

In order to make sure this country continues to remain strong, we must also ensure that America welcomes new immigrants, people who add to our prosperity. See, we can be a nation of law and a welcoming nation at the same time, and we don't have to choose.

Of all the places in our country, Miami understands the importance of the contribution that the newly arrived can make to a society. Jeb and I just went and had a little coffee at Versailles, which reminded me of the important influence that those who have fled oppression at home can make to our society. It's so hopeful when people who escape repression come to the land of the free and embrace that freedom. We welcome the Cuban influence in the

United States of America. We understand that people flee oppression and poverty and seek a better life. We understand the Haitians who have come here to seek freedom. We understand that this is the land of opportunity, and for millions, Miami is the first stop toward realizing their dreams.

To keep the dream alive, we must have comprehensive immigration reform. We must be logical about the approach we take to immigration. Of course, we want to enforce our borders. The Coast Guard works hard to enforce our borders. We got hard-working people on the Mexican border working hard to enforce our borders. And we'll provide more Border Patrol agents. And we'll provide new technologies to help those working hard. But in order to enforce the border, we have got to recognize that people are sneaking in here to work. The best way to enforce the border is to have a rational way for people who are doing jobs Americans aren't doing to come to this country on a temporary basis so they can realize their dreams. We need a guest-worker program as part of a comprehensive reform.

There's a lot of document forging going on. See, we got people being snuck across in 18-wheelers; we got people walking miles across the desert because of *coyotes*, or smugglers. There's also a lot of people who forge documents. It's hard for an employer to know whether someone's here legally or not. That's why we need to have a document that can't be forged and faked. So people say, "I'm here for a temporary basis to work. I'm here legally to do a job Americans aren't doing"—and that way we'll be able to have better worksite enforcement. It's against the law for somebody to hire somebody who is here illegally. In order to make sure that those laws work, we need to have tamper-proof documents in the hands of people applying for work.

Fourthly, it is unrealistic to think that we should give automatic citizenship to people who've been here illegally. That's not going to work. It basically says, fine;

then the next wave of people will come to try to become—get automatic citizenship. Amnesty is not the right approach. But neither is trying to remove the 10 or 11 million people who've been here illegally. Deportation is not going to work. What must work is a rational middle ground that says, you can pay a fine; you can learn English; you can prove you've been a lawful citizen; and then you can get in the citizenship line—but at the back of the line, not the front of the line.

And finally, we'll continue to work to help people assimilate into the United States. We want people learning English. We want people learning our history and our traditions. We're going to work hard to make sure we're one Nation under God. Rational immigration policy is possible, and it's important for Members of the United States Congress to work toward a comprehensive immigration plan.

Finally, I want to talk a little bit about what we're doing to secure this country. You got to understand, we're still a nation at war. I fully understand why the American citizens would hope there is no such thing as war. I know that. I know that people don't like to be reminded about the fact that there's still an enemy that lurks and plots and plans. But it's my job, a job that I really understood clearly on September the 11th. My job is to rally the Federal Government and to work with State and local government to protect you. It's the most important job of our Government, is to protect the American people. And so we work hard to—I work hard to remind people that there's still a war going on. But I also assure them that we're doing everything we can to bring the enemy to justice and to secure the homeland at the same time.

And one of the most important parts of securing our country is securing our ports. Port security is one of the top priorities of our Government. Since September the 11th, we've provided $700 million in grants to enhance physical security at our ports,

and the Port of Miami received about $25 million of those grants. We understand the important the Coast Guard plays to port security, and so we've increased funding for the Coast Guard by almost $2.9 billion.

We're using technologies to protect this country of ours, such as state-of-the-art x-ray and gamma-ray scanners to screen cargo and containers. We launched what we called the Container Security Initiative, which is to identify and inspect suspicious cargo at foreign ports before they depart for America. In other words, doesn't it makes sense for us to inspect product and cargo overseas, before they're shipped here? That's what we're doing. We've got a smart policy about how to protect our ports. And we'll continue to work with port authorities and custom officers and immigration agents and the Coast Guard and Jeb's office and local folks to do our duty, to do the duty the American people expect, which is, to the best of our ability, protect the United States against further attack.

I want you to know that I am optimistic about the future of this country. I'm confident that we're going to win the war on terror, because I understand that our vision of freedom, our belief in liberty, is more powerful than the ideology of hatred that the terrorists espouse.

I believe this economy will remain strong if we leave hands in the—if we leave people's money in their own hands so they can save, invest, and spend. I believe in the entrepreneurial spirit in America. I believe in our workers. I believe in our small-business owners. I believe that when people can dream and do and accomplish, our society is better off. I'm confident that the values of the United States will remain strong, because I understand the character of Americans by birth and by choice.

And so I understand we face a lot of challenges, but I believe this country can overcome those challenges. And I want to thank you for letting me come to the Port of Miami to discuss some of the challenges we face.

Thanks for your hard work. May God bless you all.

NOTE: The President spoke at 10:17 a.m. at the U.S. Coast Guard Integrated Support Command. In his remarks, he referred to Gov. Jeb Bush of Florida; former professional football player Daniel C. Marino, Jr., and his wife, Claire; Rear Adm. David W. Kunkel, USCG, district commander, Seventh Coast Guard District; Bill Johnson, acting director, Port of Miami; Marco Rubio, speaker-designate, Florida State House of Representatives; Mayor Carlos Alvarez of Miami-Dade County, FL; Mayor Manuel A. Diaz of Miami, FL; Gilad Shalit, an Israeli soldier captured and held captive by militants in Gaza since June 25; Ehud Goldwasser and Eldad Regev, Israeli soldiers captured and held captive by militants in Lebanon since July 12; and Nelson Gonzalez and Alex Aguila, founders, Alienware Corp.

Remarks Following a Tour of the Port of Miami in Miami
July 31, 2006

I want to thank Admiral Allen and the members of the Coast Guard for what has been a really interesting tour of the Port of Miami.

A couple of things: One, it's clear that the money we've been spending to help secure our ports is working. In other words, new technologies—there's new ways to investigate cargo that gets here. Obviously, there's more work to be done, but one of the most innovative projects we've done, by the way, is to have a—is to use ports of—the disembarkation to inspect cargo so that the cargo has been inspected before it arrives here.

So I want to thank you all for the tour. I'm real proud of our Coast Guard. The Coast Guard is really, really good. And part of our efforts is to work with the Coast Guard leadership to make sure the Coast Guard is modernized, that they've got the latest choppers, the good boats to be able to do their job.

We talked about a lot of issues besides port security. One of the big issues that people face here is the migration issue, a lot of people trying to sneak into Florida. And the Coast Guard is doing their job to enforce our policy, and I appreciate them for their hard work.

At the United Nations today, the Security Council passed a resolution regarding Iran's attempt to have nuclear weapons. It's a strong resolution. I want to thank our partners. This resolution follows up on North Korea resolution, and it goes to show that when America takes the lead and works with our friends, we're able to accomplish diplomatic objectives.

And now Condi Rice comes back from the Middle East and will be working with our friends and allies on a resolution regarding Lebanon. But the Iranians must hear loud and clear with this resolution: The world is intent upon working together to make sure that they do not end up with a nuclear weapon or the know-how to build a nuclear weapon.

Again, I want to thank our allies on this very important resolution and remind the American people that we've had a strategy in place to send a common message, a unified message to the Iranian leadership.

I want to thank you all. Appreciate it.

NOTE: The President spoke at 11:24 a.m. at the U.S. Coast Guard Integrated Support Command.

Remarks to Reporters at the National Naval Medical Center in Bethesda, Maryland
August 1, 2006

The President. I'm just amazed at the health care here at Bethesda. The Admiral runs an amazing operation. And it's really important for our citizens to know that if one of our men and women get hurt on the battlefield, they're going to get incredibly good health care.

And, Admiral, I can't thank you and your staff enough for serving the country with great dignity and class.

Rear Adm. Robinson. Thank you very much.

The President. Appreciate being here. God bless. Thank you.

I'm doing fine; my health is fine. I probably ate too many birthday cakes.

NOTE: The President spoke at 1:40 p.m. In his remarks, he referred to Rear Adm. Adam M. Robinson, Jr., USN, commander, National Naval Medical Center, and chief, Navy Medical Corps.

Remarks on the Renovation of the James S. Brady Press Briefing Room and an Exchange With Reporters
August 2, 2006

White House Press Secretary Tony Snow. All right, well, never mind. See, every once in a while, hideous threats have a clarifying effect. And sometimes they make people make important choices, and apparently the threat of my singing has persuaded the President of the United States to intervene on yet another mission of peace.

Mr. President.

The President. Dee Dee, how are you doing?

Margaret J. "Dee Dee" Myers. Mr. President.

The President. Marlin, you're looking as pretty as ever.

M. Marlin Fitzwater. Thank you, Mr. President. Really good to see you.

The President. Sarah, good to see you.

Sarah Brady. How are you?

The President. Jim, really good to see you, sir. Thank you.

James S. Brady. Nice seeing you too.

Q. Speech, speech.

Q. Press conference.

Q. Welcome, Mr. President.

Q. We have a few questions, if you don't mind.

Q. Just a couple of questions.

The President. I know you've been complaining about the digs for a while. [*Laughter*] So this is like the end of an old era. And let me just say, we felt your pain. And so we decided, you know, to help you renovate and come up with a new Brady center.

And so I want to thank the former spinmeisters for joining me up here. Tell my people how to do it, will you? I mean, it's a—[*laughter*].

But anyway, Laura and I wanted to come by and wish you all the best as you get to move headquarters for a while. I look forward to welcome you back here in, I guess, 6 or 7 months. Is that right?

Q. Nine months. We hope.

Q. We're setting no timetables, Mr. President. [*Laughter*]

The President. That's what you get when you bring your crackpot up from Texas. [*Laughter*]

Q. No comment, sir. [*Laughter*]

The President. So, like, suede chairs? [*Laughter*] Is that what you're looking—kind of velvet armchairs? Armchairs. Everybody wants to be able to lean back.

It looks a little crowded in here. And so you want to double the size?

Q. Yes.

The President. Forget it. [*Laughter*] You get to work like the rest of us. We may have some air conditioning if we decide to. [*Laughter*]

Anyway, good luck in the new building. Looking forward to seeing you over there.

Q. Can we come see you?

The President. I don't know. Does the air conditioner work better there than here? [*Laughter*]

Q. Yes.

The President. The last time I had a press conference in here, it felt like it was outside. As a matter of fact, some of your makeup was running. [*Laughter*]

Q. Mr. President, should Mel Gibson be forgiven? [*Laughter*]

The President. Is that you and Gregory [David Gregory, NBC News] standing back there?

Q. I was there first. [*Laughter*]

The President. You know——

Q. ——complaining that the Jews start all the wars——

The President. Is that Sam Donaldson? [*Laughter*] Forget it. You're a has-been. We don't have to answer has-been's questions.

Q. Ooh!

Q. Mr. President, do you want to say a little about the White House press corps, please?

The President. Say something about the White House press corps?

Q. Yes, sir.

The President. It's a beautiful bunch of people. [*Laughter*]

Q. How about your best moment in here, sir? Can you remember your——

The President. My best moment in here is when my press conference ended. [*Laughter*]

Q. [*Inaudible*]—about Mel Gibson——

The President. I can't hear you; I'm over 60, just like you. [*Laughter*]

Q. ——Ronald Reagan could get away with that, sir.

The President. He was over 60 as well. At any rate, as you can tell, I'm thrilled to be here. [*Laughter*] But we do wish you all the best. Looking forward to being here when you kick off the new room. You deserve better than this. I appreciate the relationship with the press. I know these folks enjoyed the—enjoyed dealing with you—well, another crowd of you, been dealing with you as well. It's an important relationship.

Joe Lockhart. Some of the same crowd.

The President. Well, you're the head of the whole thing. Like, have you got a thing—a role to play?

Q. No, no, no.

The President. Okay, good. But anyway, good luck.

Q. What about Crawford?

The President. For those of you going to Crawford, saddle up. All right, good to see you.

Press Secretary Snow. Thank you, everybody.

NOTE: The President spoke at 1:57 p.m. in the James S. Brady Press Briefing Room at the White House. Participating in the visit were former White House Press Secretaries Margaret J. "Dee Dee" Myers, M. Marlin Fitzwater, Joe Lockhart, Ron Nessen, and James S. Brady, and his wife, Sarah. In his remarks, he referred to ABC News national correspondent Sam Donaldson. A reporter referred to actor Mel Gibson.

Remarks Following a Tour of the Lake County Emergency Management Agency in Mentor, Ohio
August 2, 2006

I have just been briefed by the emergency management teams of Lake County and the other counties affected by the recent flooding. Law enforcement was there; firefighters were there; and our FEMA representative was there at the briefing.

A couple of impressions: One, the local response was really good. The interoperability between various jurisdictions was superb. And as a result, a lot of people's lives were saved. And I want to congratulate you, Sheriff, and congratulate Larry for your good work in helping people.

Secondly, FEMA has been on the ground here, and I signed a major disaster declaration for this part of the country, which means this: That individuals will be helped. Individuals will be helped with rental assistance; individuals will be helped with temporary housing; individuals will be helped with grants to help rebuild their homes; and small businesses will be helped with low-interest loans. In other words, the first wave of help from the Federal Government as a result of these disasters is now available for people whose lives were affected by the flooding.

There are still assessments going on for further Federal help and Federal assistance, and when those assessments are made, the proper help will be granted. For those people who are wondering about the Federal help, there's toll-free numbers. You can call the emergency center, they'll give you the toll-free numbers if you've been a citizen affected by these recent floods.

Again, I want to congratulate you all for a job well done. I had the honor of talking to dispatchers, hard-working people that are on the phone all the time helping people. And now, once the lives have been saved, with the exception of one soul, that it's now time to help the people rebuild their lives. There's a lot of people concerned and a lot of people working here, and the Federal Government will do its part with the local authorities.

Thank you all very much. Appreciate you.

NOTE: The President spoke at 5:47 p.m. at the Lake County Emergency Operations and Communications Center. In his remarks, he referred to Jesse Munoz, Federal Coordinating Officer, Federal Emergency Management Agency; Sheriff Daniel A. Dunlap of Lake County, OH; and Larry D. Greene, director, Lake County Emergency Management Agency.

Remarks on Immigration Reform in McAllen, Texas
August 3, 2006

Thank you all very much. It's good to be home. Thank you for coming. Please be seated. You know, when I left the Governor's office, I knew I would leave it in capable hands with Rick Perry. And I'm proud of the job he's done as Governor of the State of Texas, and I'm proud to have been introduced by the Governor of my State.

I want to thank you all for the warm welcome. It's nice to get out of Washington. [*Laughter*] It's even better to come down to Texas. And I'm proud to be with my fellow Texans.

I learned a lot growing up here; I learned a lot as your Governor. And as Rick said, I understand this border, and I want to talk to you today about border policy. We have an obligation to secure our border, and we have an obligation to treat people with decency and respect. And we're going to do both in the United States of America.

I just traveled and met some of the fine men and women of the National Guard and Border Patrol who are working long hours to do the—to keep this border secure. And I first—I want to say thanks to all the Border Patrol agents and the Guard men and women who are here. You've got a tough job, and the role of the Federal Government is to give you the tools necessary to do your job.

So we landed, and we saw choppers with all kinds of new equipment on it, airplanes that can interdict people flying in drugs, fast boats to stop the people trying to bring drugs or people up and down the coast of Texas. One of the things that you'll hear me talk about is the need to modernize the technology along this border. And that's what we're going to do.

I also recognized we needed more people to help the Guard and to help the Border Patrol do its job. And so last May, I said, we'll deploy up to 6,000 National Guard members to assist the Border Patrol. And I said we'd get it done by August 1st. Well, we got it done by August 1st. And I want to thank those in the National Guard who have joined us.

It's good to look out in the crowd and see a lot of folks that I got to know over the years. And most of the folks that I got to know over the years realize that I married well. And so Laura sends her deep affection to the people of south Texas and our friends here in the audience. She's doing just fine, by the way. She's a great First Lady.

I'm proud to be here with Congressman Ralph Hall, right out of the Dallas area. Thanks for coming, Congressman. He's a fine Texan who cares deeply about the people along the border here. I'm traveling today with the Commissioner of the U.S. Customs and Border Protection, Ralph Basham. Ralph, thank you for joining us.

So, what happens when the President sets policy in Washington, like on the Guard policy—I said, "We need to get 6,000 members of the Guard down to help the Border Patrol." And then that order goes down the chain of command, and the first person whose desk it landed on in the chain of command after Secretary Rumsfeld was Lieutenant General Steve Blum of the Guard Bureau. General Blum said, "Mr. President, we're going to get the job done." I said, "That's good, General Blum, because come August 1st, I'm going to come down to the area and take a look-see." And he did. Thank you, General Blum, for a job well done.

David Aguilar is the Chief of the U.S. Border Patrol. I don't know if you know this or not, but David's mother lives here in the area. And he made sure the first person I met when I got off the airplane, as far as he is concerned, was his mother. [*Laughter*] One reason he's advanced so highly in the Border Patrol, like the head of the whole thing, is because he has listened to his mother—[*laughter*]—just like I have listened to mine. So thank you for being here, David. Thanks for serving.

Major General Chuck Rodriguez, Adjutant General of the Texas National Guard, very instrumental in making sure we've got the troops here to help the Border Patrol. General, thank you very much. General Allen Dehnert, who's the Adjutant General for the Texas Air National Guard—General Dehnert, thank you very much as well. General Mike Kostelnik who's the Assistant Commissioner, Office of CBP Air and Marine, U.S. Customs and Border Patrol— look, he's the guy in charge of airplanes and boats. [*Laughter*]

We're here as well, with Lieutenant Colonel Jose Carrillo. He is the Rio Grande Valley Texas National Guard Task Force commander. See, in other words, when you got to bring people down from other States to help the Border Patrol do their job, you have to have an organization. You just can't send people down here. And one thing the Guard has done well is they've organized this effort. I'm also proud to be here with Chief Lynne Underdown. She is the Rio Grande Valley Border Patrol Sector chairman. Chief, thank you for being here. Thanks for serving.

I want to thank Mayor Salinas of Mission who's with us today. Mayor, thank you for joining us. Proud you're here. Mayor Cortez of McAllen is with us. Mayor, good to see you. Thank you very much. [*Applause*] Yes, that's a good sign, Mayor; it's a good sign.

Finally, one of my dear friends, I've known him for a long time, and that's Mayor John David Franz of Hidalgo. Mayor, it's good to see you. John David told me just as I got off the airplane—I said, "How is your family?" He said, "My son has just enrolled in West Point." And you tell him thank you, John David, on behalf of a grateful nation.

And for those of you who have got a loved one in the United States military, you tell them the Commander in Chief is incredibly proud of the job they're doing to help secure this Nation and bring peace to this world. We've got a fantastic military, and it's a military that will have the full support—[*applause*].

I'm going to talk today about comprehensive immigration reform. I say "comprehensive" because unless you have all five pieces working together, it's not going to work at all. This is an important debate facing our Nation, and the debate is, can we secure this border and, at the same time, honor our history of being a land of immigrants? And the answer is, absolutely, we can do both. And we will do both.

First, we've got to secure the border. We will keep it open to lawful trade and commerce, and we will work to secure the border to prevent people and goods and

weapons from being brought illegally here. That's our job. It's the job of the Federal Government—it's the job of the—working with the State government to get the job done. That's what the American people expect.

All this strategy has got to start with more money, and so we've increased funding for border security from $4.6 billion in 2001 to more than 7.6 billion in 2006. In other words, you can't say the American people are going to make a commitment to secure the border unless you spend money to secure the border, and we're doing just that. And I recently signed an emergency supplemental spending bill that provides an additional $1.9 billion in immediate funding for border security. And what does that mean? Well, it means we're going to give the Border Patrol, the people on the frontlines of securing this border, better technology, and we're going to expand the number of Border Patrol agents that will be able to use that technology. That's the strategy.

We put new resources in people's hands. And as a result of the hard work of Border Patrol since 2001, Federal agents have apprehended and sent home more than 6 million people entering America illegally.

I mean, people are working hard. There's people doing their job, but we could do more. There's more work to be done. And so we've called for increases in manpower and technology. We're going to train 6,000 additional agents so that you've got more people to help you do the job. And in the meantime, the reason we brought the Guard down here was because we knew we had an immediate need to enforce the border. And so until those 6,000 are trained, we're going to be using National Guard units from over 30 States here. And the plan is working. It makes sense. If we need more manpower and the need for manpower is immediate, it makes sense to call upon our Guard troops to come and help the Border Patrol do the job.

We're going to help build a virtual border by using infrared and motion sensors. We'll deploy unmanned aerial vehicles. In other words, we're going to leverage the manpower we have. It's amazing, the new technologies that are arriving. People are—these Border Patrol agents will tell you that they're seeing more and better equipment. You got heat sensors on guard stations that will enable people to detect movement. We got choppers that are able to send real-time video streams back to Border Patrol command centers that will then enable a dispatcher to help an agent catch somebody who's smuggling people or drugs in a near real-time basis.

This border is changing, and it needs to change so the Border Patrol can do its job. We call this, by the way, this operation when we moved the Guard down here, Operation Jump Start. So when you hear about Operation Jump Start, that means Guard.

And the Guard has helped a lot. You know, it's interesting that—and by the way, the Guard is not just in Texas. It's in New Mexico, Arizona, and California as well. In other words, Border Patrol agents all up and down this southern border are getting help from our Guard men and women. And the Guards are doing—look, they're not arresting people. We're not going to militarize this border. The job of arresting people is up to the Border Patrol. That's your job. That's what you're trained to do. That's what your skill level is. Their job is to help the Border Patrol by, you know, surveillance and construction, logistics. I mean, if you've got a Guard person dispatching, it means there's more—one more Border Patrol agent out on the frontline. And so we're going to use this Guard until we get 6,000 more people trained.

For the people who wonder whether the Guard could be effective down here, when we deployed Operation Jump Start—since we've deployed it, our agents have seen 17,000 pounds of illegal drugs and apprehended 2,500 illegal immigrants. In other

words, the Guard is leveraging—giving the Border Patrol more opportunity.

Last month, Border Patrol agents in this sector confiscated more than 4,200 pounds of marijuana that was hidden in a tractor-trailer. And the support of the Guard was important in making this seizure happen. So for those of you in the Guard, I want to thank you for coming down here and helping these good folks in the Border Patrol, and your presence is making a difference.

In order to make sure the Border Patrol is effective, we've got to stop what's called catch-and-release. For the veterans down here, they know what catch-and-release means. And it had to have been discouraging for you—risk your life, or you're spending long hours, and all of a sudden, you apprehend people who are sneaking here illegally. But we didn't have enough detention space to hold people. And so the people were given a court date, and they said, you check back in when your court date comes up. But a lot of folks didn't want to check in when their court date came up, so they just didn't show up. And one of the things I learned early on was how discouraging that can be for the people on the frontline of securing this border.

You can imagine what it must feel like to work hard and chase somebody down, treat them humanely, send them in for their court date, and then they don't show up. It seemed like wasted effort, didn't it? So this Government is committed to ending this unacceptable practice. Step one is to add detention beds. If you didn't have enough detention space in the first place, the way you solve the problem is, you add beds. And here in the Rio Grande Valley, we're going to add 1,500 beds in short order.

We're also accelerating the deportation process, particularly for people who are not from Mexico that we catch coming across the border. Last year, for example, we put together what was called Operation Texas Hold 'Em. We cut through redtape so we could quickly return Brazilians who we caught illegally crossing this border. And we sent a clear message: When we catch you, there will be immediate deportation. And guess what happened? As a result of that clear message, the number of illegal immigrants from Brazil has dropped significantly across the whole region.

That's the message we must continually send over and over again to people who feel like they can come from Central America, for example, and if caught, be let back into society, and if not caught, they're able to escape the Border Patrol. We want to send a clear message: We will enforce our border.

But in order to make sure these Border Patrol agents can do their job, we must have a temporary-worker program. You got to understand here, and I know you do, there are people doing jobs Americans aren't doing. There are people who have come across this border to do work Americans are not doing. And it makes sense to let them come on a temporary basis in a legal way.

Wouldn't you rather have people who are doing work Americans are not doing, not trying to sneak across the border? I know the Border Patrol agents would rather not have people try to sneak across the border. It makes sense to me to say to somebody, if you're going to do a job Americans aren't doing, you can come for a period of time—say, 3 years—and do that work and support your family back home, and then you go home after your time is up. That's the way to treat people humanely.

I don't like a system that's not working and a system that forces people who want to work, in the back of 18-wheelers. I don't like a system that encourages smuggling. I don't like a system that encourages people to walk across the desert to risk their life. I think we need to have a system that is orderly and fair and transparent.

We've got to enforce our immigration laws at the worksite. But as a result of illegal activities in trying to get people into

this country, there's a lot of document forgery. Our employers cannot be document verifiers. They don't know whether they've got a real document to look at or a fake document to look at. One of the temporary—parts of a temporary-worker program would be to give people a tamper-proof temporary-worker card, that they could say, I'm legal, see; I'm here to do the job; I'm going to work for a period of time, and then I'm going to go home after I work a period of time; I can be here legally. That will make it easier for us to have worksite enforcement.

Listen, we will hold people to account. It's against the law in the United States to employ somebody who is here illegally. And a nation of laws is a nation that upholds its laws. But we've got to be wise about the policy that we enforce. We've got to give people something that document forgers can't tamper with so our employers know whether or not they're hiring somebody who's here illegally or not.

Fourthly, we've got to make sure that we resolve the status of illegal immigrants who are already in this country. It's an interesting debate taking place in America. I'll give you my position. One, I do not think we ought to grant amnesty to people who are here illegally. And the reason I don't is I think that will encourage a whole other bunch of people to come. But I know you cannot deport 10 million people who have been here working. It's unrealistic. It may sound good in certain circles and political circles. It's not going to work.

The best plan is to say to somebody who has been here illegally, if you've been paying your taxes and you've got a good criminal record, that you can pay a fine for being here illegally, and you can learn English, like the rest of us have done, and you can get in a citizenship line to apply for citizenship. You don't get to get in the front; you get to get in the back of the line.

But this idea of deporting people is just not—it doesn't make any sense to me, and it doesn't make any sense to a lot of people who understand this issue. So here's a reasonable way to treat people with respect and accomplish what we want to accomplish, which is to be a country of law and a country of decency and respect.

And finally, in order to make a comprehensive immigration plan work, we've got to help folks assimilate into our society. And what does that mean? It means, help people learn English, to help people understand the traditions and history of the United States of America.

One of the fabulous things about our country is that our soul has constantly been renewed by people seeking the American Dream, people coming here to work to realize their dream, people wanting to raise a family in the United States of America. And we come from different backgrounds, but we're all united by the great ideal of being an American citizen. That's why we say, we're one Nation under God. And to help people assimilate will help us keep that in place.

And so it's good to be down here on our border. It's an exciting part of the United States of America. It's amazing how this country has grown and how vital the valley is of the State of Texas. It's got to be exciting for people to grow up in this part of the world and see the new prosperity. Gosh, it wasn't all that long ago that—I know these mayors can remember—the economy was tough down here. It was, kind of, farming, and that was all.

And now there's economic vitality. People are making a living, and the schools are improving. It's a great place to raise a family.

It's a great place to also come and honor those who wear the uniform of the United States of America, whether it be local law enforcement or the sheriff's departments or the Border Patrol or the United States military. We're a blessed country. We're a great country because we've got people who stand up and say, I want to serve. And it's the service of the men and women in uniform that are doing the job down here that the American people expect.

I can't tell you how proud I am to be the Commander in Chief of the military and to be the President of the United States, full of such decent and honorable people. I'm honored to be back in this part of the world. I want to thank you for coming out and giving me a chance to talk about a comprehensive immigration plan. I expect the United States Congress to do its duty and pass comprehensive immigration reform.

God bless.

NOTE: The President spoke at 2:40 p.m. at Anzalduas Park. In his remarks, he referred to Gov. J. Richard "Rick" Perry of Texas; Mayor Norberto "Beto" Salinas of Mission, TX; Mayor Richard F. Cortez of McAllen, TX; and John David Franz, Jr., son of Mayor John David Franz, Sr., of Hidalgo, TX.

Statement on the Situation in Cuba
August 3, 2006

The United States is actively monitoring the situation in Cuba following the announcement of a transfer of power. At this time of uncertainty in Cuba, one thing is clear: The United States is absolutely committed to supporting the Cuban people's aspirations for democracy and freedom.

We have repeatedly said that the Cuban people deserve to live in freedom. I encourage all democratic nations to unite in support of the right of the Cuban people to define a democratic future for their country. I urge the Cuban people to work for democratic change on the island. We will support you in your effort to build a transitional government in Cuba committed to democracy, and we will take note of those in the current Cuban regime who obstruct your desire for a free Cuba.

In the event of a transition in the Cuban Government, we stand ready to provide humanitarian assistance as needed to help the Cuban people. It has long been the hope of the United States to have a free, independent, and democratic Cuba as a close friend and neighbor. In achieving this, the Cuban people can count on the full and unconditional support of the United States.

NOTE: The Office of the Press Secretary also released a Spanish language version of this statement.

Letter to Congressional Leaders on Continuation of the National Emergency Regarding Export Control Regulations
August 3, 2006

Dear Mr. Speaker: (Dear Mr. President:)

Section 202(d) of the National Emergencies Act (50 U.S.C. 1622(d)), provides for the automatic termination of a national emergency unless, prior to the anniversary date of its declaration, the President publishes in the *Federal Register* and transmits to the Congress a notice stating that the emergency is to continue in effect beyond the anniversary date. In accordance with this provision, I have sent the enclosed notice, stating that the emergency caused by the lapse of the Export Administration Act of 1979, as amended, is to continue in effect for 1 year beyond August 17, 2006, to the *Federal Register* for publication.

Sincerely,

GEORGE W. BUSH

NOTE: Identical letters were sent to J. Dennis Hastert, Speaker of the House of Representatives, and Richard B. Cheney, President of the Senate. The notice is listed in Appendix D at the end of this volume.

Statement on Pension Reform Legislation
August 4, 2006

After a lifetime of work, American workers have earned the opportunity to enjoy a secure retirement. Last year, I asked Congress to strengthen protections for workers' pensions. Congress has now delivered the most comprehensive reforms to America's pension system in over 30 years.

This legislation sets the right target for pension plan soundness: 100 percent funding of all promises. It would allow employers to put more money into their pension plans during good times, building a cushion that can survive lean times. Congress has also acted to make it harder in the future for employers with underfunded pension plans to promise additional benefits to their workers without funding those new promises.

These measures will provide workers with better information about their pension plans, eliminate loopholes that interfere with strong pension funding, and increase the accuracy of pension plan measurements. The bill would reform the rules governing employer funding and premium contributions to strengthen the pension insurance system.

The legislation also contains provisions to help workers who save for retirement through defined contribution plans. The legislation will make it easier for workers to participate in such savings plans by removing regulatory barriers to automatic enrollment. It also gives workers more information about how their accounts are performing and greater control over how their accounts are invested. Workers will be allowed greater access to advice about how to safely invest for retirement. And finally, the bill will enable more workers to build larger retirement nest eggs by making permanent higher allowed contribution amounts in IRA and 401(k) plans.

I look forward to signing this important legislation into law soon.

NOTE: The statement referred to H.R. 4.

The President's Radio Address
August 5, 2006

Good morning. This week, my administration met a key objective in our efforts to better secure our Nation's border.

In May, I pledged to deploy up to 6,000 National Guard members to support the Border Patrol, and we fulfilled that pledge by August 1st. Through Operation Jump Start, National Guard members are now on duty supporting the Border Patrol in Texas, California, Arizona, and New Mexico.

On Thursday, I visited the Rio Grande Valley Border Patrol Sector in Texas. I saw firsthand how the National Guard is working with our Border Patrol agents to improve border security. National Guard troops are helping with surveillance, construction, and logistics. They're building and repairing fences, maintaining vehicles, and manning detection equipment on the border and in command centers.

The arrival of National Guard units has allowed the Border Patrol to move more agents into frontline positions, and this additional manpower is delivering results. With the support of the National Guard, Border Patrol agents have seized over 17,000 pounds of illegal drugs and caught more than 2,500 illegal immigrants since June 15th. Just last month, Border Patrol agents in the Rio Grande Valley Sector confiscated more than 4,200 pounds of marijuana hidden in a tractor trailer. And the support of the National Guard was important in making this seizure happen.

Rational and comprehensive immigration reform must begin with border security, and we have more to do. So I've asked Congress to fund dramatic increases in manpower and technology for the Border Patrol. We will add 6,000 new Border Patrol agents. We will build high-tech fences in urban corridors and new patrol roads and barriers in rural areas. And we will employ motion sensors, infrared cameras, and unmanned aerial vehicles to prevent illegal crossings. By deploying 21st century technologies, we will make our Border Patrol agents even more effective and our border more secure.

Yet to be successful, comprehensive immigration reform must also accomplish four other critical goals. We need a temporary-worker program that will create a legal and orderly path for foreign workers to enter our country to work on a temporary basis. This program will add to our security by helping us know who is in our country and why they are here. And by reducing pressure on our border, it will free up our Border Patrol to focus on making sure we stop terrorists, violent criminals, and drug smugglers from entering our country.

We need to enforce our immigration laws at our Nation's worksites. To enforce the law, we have launched raids on businesses that knowingly hire illegal immigrants. We are filing criminal charges against these employers, and we are prosecuting them to the fullest extent of the law.

To help honest businesses follow the law, I propose more effective tools to verify the legal status of workers. These tools should include a tamper-proof identification card for legal foreign workers. By taking these steps, we will make it easier for businesses to obey the law and leave them no excuse for violating it.

We need to resolve the status of illegal immigrants who are already here. They should not be given an automatic path to citizenship. This is amnesty, and I oppose it. Amnesty would be unfair to those who are here lawfully, and it would invite further waves of illegal immigration. We will find a rational middle ground between automatic citizenship for illegal immigrants and mass deportations of people who've

been living here for many years with jobs, families, and deep roots in our country.

Finally, we need comprehensive immigration reform that honors the American tradition of the melting pot by helping newcomers assimilate. Americans are bound together by our shared ideals, our history, and the ability to speak and write the English language. When immigrants assimilate, they advance in our society, realize their dreams, and add to the unity of America. We can fix the problem of illegal immigration and deliver an immigration system that is rational and compassionate.

By passing comprehensive immigration reform, we will uphold our laws, meet the needs of our economy, and keep America what she has always been—an open door to the future, a blessed and promised land, one Nation under God.

Thank you for listening.

NOTE: The address was recorded at 8:05 a.m. on August 4 at the Bush Ranch in Crawford, TX, for broadcast at 10:06 a.m. on August 5. The transcript was made available by the Office of the Press Secretary on August 4 but was embargoed for release until the broadcast. The Office of the Press Secretary also released a Spanish language transcript of this address.

The President's News Conference With Secretary of State Condoleezza Rice in Crawford, Texas
August 7, 2006

The President. Good morning. Since the crisis in Lebanon began more than 3 weeks ago, the United States and other key nations have been working for a comprehensive solution that would return control of Lebanon to its Government and to provide a sustainable peace that protects the lives of both the Lebanese and the Israeli people.

Secretary Rice and diplomats from other countries are developing United Nations resolutions to bring about a cessation of hostilities and establish a foundation for lasting peace.

The first resolution, which the Security Council is now considering, calls for a stop of all hostilities. Under its terms, Hizballah will be required to immediately stop all attacks. Israel will be required to immediately stop all offensive military operations. In addition, the resolution calls for an embargo on the shipment of any arms into Lebanon, except as authorized by the Lebanese Government.

A second resolution, which the Security Council will begin working on as soon as possible, will help establish a sustainable and enduring cease-fire and provide a mandate for a robust international force that will help the legitimate Government of Lebanon extend its authority over all of Lebanon's territory.

Under this second resolution, the Lebanese Armed Forces, supported by the international force, will deploy to southern Lebanon. This international force will help Lebanon patrol its border with Syria and prevent illegal arm shipments to Hizballah. As these Lebanese and international forces deploy, the Israeli Defense Forces will withdraw. And both Israel and Lebanon will respect the Blue Line that divides them.

These two resolutions are designed to bring an immediate end to the fighting, to help restore sovereignty over Lebanese soil to Lebanese democratic government—to Lebanon's democratic Government, excuse me—to strike a blow against the terrorists and their supporters, and to help bring lasting peace to the region. By taking these steps, it will prevent armed militias like Hizballah and its Iranian and Syrian sponsors from sparking another crisis. It will protect innocent Lebanese and Israelis. And it will help the international community deliver humanitarian relief and support Lebanon's revival and reconstruction.

The loss of life on both sides of the Lebanese-Israeli border has been a great tragedy. Millions of Lebanese civilians have been caught in the crossfire of military operations because of the unprovoked attack and kidnapings by Hizballah. The humanitarian crisis in Lebanon is of deep concern to all Americans, and alleviating it will remain a priority of my Government.

I also believe that innocent civilians in Israel should not have to live in bunkers in fear of missile attacks. To establish a lasting peace that protects innocent civilians on both sides of the border, we must address the underlying conditions that are the root cause of this crisis.

I believe that the two resolutions I have discussed and that Secretary Rice is working on will put us on that path.

And now I'll be glad to answer some questions. Nedra [Nedra Pickler, Associated Press].

United Nations Security Council Resolution on the Situation in the Middle East

Q. Thank you, Mr. President. Lebanon has rejected the draft proposal, and Israel is not speaking out in support of it. How do you get a resolution that both sides will support?

The President. Everyone wants the violence to stop. People understand that there needs to be a cessation of hostilities in order for us to address the root causes of the problem. That was the spirit that came out of the G–8 conference; it came out of the Rome conference that Secretary Rice attended. We all recognize that the violence must stop. And so that's what Secretary Rice is working toward with our friends and allies.

Look, everybody is—I understand both parties aren't going to agree with all aspects of the resolution. But the intent of the resolutions is to strengthen the Lebanese Government so Israel has got a partner in peace. The intent of the resolution is to make sure that we address the root cause— the resolution is to address the root cause, which was a state operating within the state. Hizballah was—or is an armed movement that provoked the crisis.

And so whatever comes out of the resolutions must address that root cause. And so the task today for the Secretary and her counterparts is to develop a resolution that can get passed. It is essential that we create the conditions for the Lebanese Government to move their own forces, with international help, into the south of Lebanon to prevent Hizballah and its sponsors from creating this—creating another crisis. And so that's where we're headed.

Steve [Steve Holland, Reuters].

Level of Violence in the Middle East/United Nations Security Council Resolution

Q. The Lebanese Prime Minister is demanding a quick and decisive cease-fire after an Israeli air raid today killed 40 people. When will we see this resolution? And if it's approved, when will we see a cessation of violence?

The President. I'll let Condi talk about the details of what she's going to do today, if you care to hear from her. But we will work with our partners to get the resolution laid down as quickly as possible. And the resolution will call for a cessation of violence. And the concern, by the way, from the parties in the region is whether or not the resolution will create a vacuum into which Hizballah and its sponsors will be able to promote more instability.

We all agree that we ought to strengthen this Government, the Lebanese Government—that's the purpose of the resolutions, as well as to stop the violence.

I don't know if you want to comment upon——

Secretary Rice. First of all, we are working from what we believe to be a strong basis for a cessation of hostilities, that is the U.S.-French draft, a strong basis for the cessation of hostilities, and then as the President said, to have a process then that can address the root causes. And we also believe that it's going to be very important that this first resolution lay a very quick foundation for passage of a second resolution. So these have to be worked, in a sense, together.

I spoke last night and yesterday with Prime Minister Olmert, with Prime Minister Siniora, with Secretary General Kofi Annan, with a number of others, and I think we believe that there is a way forward.

Now, we understand that this has been a very emotional and, indeed, devastating and tragic set of circumstances for Lebanon and for Israel. And obviously, the parties have views on how to stop this. Their views are not going to necessarily be consonant about how to stop it. The international community has a view, but, of course, we're going to take a little time and listen to the concerns of the parties and see how they can be addressed.

But I want to just note, we believe that the extant draft resolution is a firm foundation, is the right basis, but, of course, we're going to listen to the concerns of the parties and see how they might be addressed. And that's really what's going to be going on today, particularly after the Arab League meets and Prime Minister Siniora emerges from that.

The President. Yes, Peter [Peter Wallsten, Los Angeles Times].

U.S. Armed Forces

Q. Thanks. Mr. President, officials have been quoted saying that the international force would not include U.S. troops. And I wonder if you can explain why that is? Is it because the military is already overtasked? Is it because you're afraid that the U.S. doesn't have credibility in the region?

The President. No, I think, first of all, there has been a history in Lebanon with U.S. troops. Secondly, I have said that if the international force would like some help with logistics and command and control, we'd be willing to offer logistics and command and control. There are some places where—it's like Darfur; people say to me, "Why don't you commit U.S. troops to Darfur as part of an international peacekeeping?" And the answer there is that those troops would be—would create a sensation around the world that may not enable us to achieve our objective. And so when we commit troops, we commit troops for a specific reason, with the intent of achieving an objective. And I think command and control and logistical support is probably the best—is the best use of U.S. forces.

Mike Fletcher [Washington Post].

Syria/Iran

Q. Many strategists say that we'll never get to the bottom of this crisis unless the U.S. engages directly with Syria and Iran. Why not talk to them directly about this and have a back-and-forth conversation?

The President. Yes, that's an interesting question. I've been reading about that, that people have been posing that question. We have been in touch with Syria. Colin Powell sent a message to Syria in person. Dick Armitage traveled to Syria. Bill Burns traveled to Syria. We've got a consulate office in Syria. Syria knows what we think. The problem isn't us telling Syria what's on our mind, which is to stop harboring terror and to help the Iraqi democracy evolve. They know exactly what our position is. The problem is, is that their response hasn't been very positive. As a matter of fact, it hasn't been positive at all.

And in terms of Iran, we made it clear to the Iranians that if they would honor previous obligations and verifiably stop enrichment of nuclear materials, we would sit at a table. And so there's a way forward for both countries. The choice is theirs. Now, I appreciate people focusing on Syria and Iran, and we should, because Syria and Iran sponsor and promote Hizballah activities—all aimed at creating chaos, all aimed at using terror to stop the advance of democracies.

Our objective, our policy is to give voice to people through democratic reform, and that's why we strongly support the Siniora Government. That's why I've articulated a two-state solution between Israel and the Palestinians, two democracies living side by side in peace. That's why Condi went to see President Abbas, the President of the Palestinian Territories, to assure him that

we're committed to a democracy. That's why we're making sacrifices in Iraq—to build democracy.

In other words, we believe democracy yields peace. And the actions of Hizballah, through its sponsors of Iran and Syria, are trying to stop that advance of democracy. Hizballah launched this attack. Hizballah is trying to create the chaos necessary to stop the advance of peace. And the world community must come together to address this problem.

Let's see here. Jim [Jim Axelrod, CBS News].

United Nations Security Council Resolution 1559

Q. Mr. President, in the last couple of weeks, every time the question was asked, why not get an immediate cessation and then build a sustainable—terms for a sustainable cease-fire after you get the hostilities stopped, it was categorically rejected. Yet a few weeks later, here we are. Can you explain why this wasn't done a couple weeks ago?

The President. Sure. Because, first of all, the international community hadn't come together on a concept of how to address the root cause of the problem, Jim.

Part of the problem in the past in the Middle East is people would paper over the root cause of the problem, and therefore, the situation would seemingly be quiet, and then lo and behold, there'd be another crisis. And innocent people would suffer. And so our strategy all along has been, of course we want to have a cessation of hostilities, but what we want to do in the same time is to make sure that there is a way forward for the Lebanese Government to secure its own country so that there's peace in the region.

And that deals with an international peacekeeping force to complement a Lebanese army moving into the south to make sure that Resolution 1559, passed 2 years ago by the U.N., was fully upheld. Had the parties involved fully implemented

1559, which called for the disarmament of Hizballah, we would not be in the situation we're in today.

Let's see here. Yes, Richard [Richard Benedetto, USA Today].

Diplomatic Efforts in the Middle East

Q. Mr. President, what are the specific stumbling blocks that are preventing this first resolution from being passed quickly? What are the people—what are the parties objecting to in the language that needs to be altered?

Secretary Rice. I think that first of all, I don't—I'm not going to get into specifics about the views of the parties. I think that we have to do that privately and talk with the parties privately. But obviously, this particular resolution is important because it sets an agenda for the basis for a sustainable peace. And so it will not surprise you that the Lebanese have views of what should be on that agenda. The Israelis have views of what should be on that agenda. They aren't always the same views, and so working together to get to what that agenda should be is part of what's going on here.

But I will say something that's very interesting. There is more agreement than you might think about how to prevent, again, a situation in which you have a state within a state able to launch an attack across the Blue Line.

For instance, there is agreement that the Lebanese Government needs to extend its authority throughout the country, that it needs to have the Lebanese Armed Forces move to take care of this vacuum that has been existing in the south, that there should not be any armed groups able just to operate in the south in the way that Hizballah has been able to operate in the south, that there ought to be respect for the Blue Line. These are all agreements between the two parties.

And so there is going to be some pressure from both sides to get things onto the agenda because they want to get them onto the agenda. But I think we have a

reasonable basis here that both sides can accept. I think there are some issues of timing and sequence that need to be worked out. There are some concerns about when an international force would actually be available. And so we're going to continue to work to address those concerns of the two parties.

But as the President said, this last 3 weeks has been extremely important. Had we done this 3 weeks ago, we were talking about what people—an unconditional cease-fire that I can guarantee you would not have addressed any of these items that both sides know are going to have to be addressed if we're going to have a sustainable cease-fire in the future. So this has been time that's been well spent over the last couple of weeks, that everybody agrees it's time to have a cessation. We're going to work a little bit more with the parties, and I think this resolution will be the right basis, both to cease the hostilities and to move forward.

The President. Sheryl [Sheryl Gay Stolberg, New York Times].

Diplomatic Negotiations/Situation in the Middle East

Q. Mr. President, you've spoken with Prime Minister Blair and Chancellor Merkel about this. Have you spoken directly with Prime Ministers Olmert and Siniora? And if not, why not?

The President. Because Condi is handling those conversations, and she's doing a fine job of doing so.

Yes.

Hizballah/War on Terror

Q. Mr. President, you've been quite specific in Hizballah's role as the creator of this conflict. But what is the magnet, what is the pressure point, what is the hook to get this group to accept a cease-fire, to stop shooting, and to stop kidnaping soldiers from across the border of another country?

The President. Yes, I would hope it would be international pressure on not only Hizballah, the group of Hizballah within Lebanon, but also its sponsors. And that's the whole purpose of the United States working with allies and friends, is to send a clear message that sponsoring terror is unacceptable. It's the great challenge of the 21st century, really.

Q. Do you——

The President. Let me finish for a minute.

Q. I'm sorry.

The President. It is the great challenge of this century, and it's this: As young democracies flourish, terrorists try to stop their progress. And it's the great challenge of the United States and others who are blessed with living in free countries. Not only do terrorists try to stop the advance of democracy through killing innocent people within those countries, they also try to shape the will of the Western World by killing innocent westerners. They try to spread their jihadist message, a message I call—it's totalitarian in nature, Islamic radicalism, Islamic fascism. They try to spread it as well by taking the attack to those of us who love freedom.

And as far as this administration is concerned, we clearly see the problem, and we're going to continue to work to advance stable, free countries. We don't expect every country to look like the United States, but we do want countries to accept some basic conditions for a vibrant society—human rights, human decency, the power of the people to determine the fate of their governments. And, admittedly, this is hard work because it flies in the face of previous policy, which basically says stability is more important than form of government. And as a result of that policy, anger and resentment bubbled forth with an attack, with a series of attacks, the most dramatic of which was on September the 11th.

You know, your question is, can we get people to—a terrorist group to change their attitude? What we can do is we can get state sponsors of terror to understand this behavior is unacceptable and that we can convince some people in terrorist groups that there is a better way forward for them and their families.

Remember, Hizballah is a political party within Lebanon. They actually ran people for office. The problem is, is that they're a political party with a militia that is armed by foreign nations, and obviously, this political party with militia was willing to try to influence the Middle East through unprovoked attacks.

And what Condi is working on and I work on is to remind people about the stakes in the Middle East. And those stakes include not only helping the Lebanese Government firm up its democracy—remember, we worked with the French 2 years ago to boot out Syria. Syria was inside Lebanon, and we felt that in order for a democracy to flourish, Syria needed to remove not only her troops but her agents, her intelligence agents, for example.

And obviously, there are some in the region that don't want the Lebanese Government to succeed. I also happen to believe that as Prime Minister Olmert was making progress in reaching out to President Abbas and others in the region to develop a Palestinian state, that that caused a terrorist reaction. Remember, this all started with the kidnaping of an Israeli soldier by militant Hamas, followed shortly thereafter by the kidnaping of two Israeli soldiers by Hizballah.

And finally, the third most notable battleground in the advance of liberty is Iraq. It's interesting; if you go back to the work of Mr. Zarqawi, he talked about fomenting sectarian violence in order to stop the advance of democracy. The challenge of the 21st century is for free nations to help those who aspire to liberty. And, you know, the first question is, do people aspire to liberty? And the answer is, absolutely—look at the 12 million people who voted in Iraq. Or look at the people who went to the polls in Lebanon. It's just clear to me that there will be terrorist activities that will try to stop people from living a decent, hopeful life.

And what you're watching now is diplomatic efforts to address the problem. I know there's—I sense a certain impatience in your voice about diplomacy coming to a conclusion. What Secretary Rice is doing, as well as me, is we are dealing with a lot of different interests. Remember, each nation at the Security Council has got its own domestic issues to deal with, as well, and so it is—I wish things happened quicker in the diplomatic realm—sometimes it takes a while to get things done. But what the American people need to know is, we've got a strategy—a strategy for freedom in the Middle East which protects the American people in the long run. And we've got a strategy to deal with the situations that arise in the Middle East— first Lebanon; of course, the Iranian nuclear weapon issue.

And, as you remember, right before the G–8, the question on your mind was, would we ever get a resolution out of the U.N. on the Iranians' desire to have a nuclear weapon, as well as whether or not we'd ever get a resolution out of the U.N. to deal with North Korea? As a matter of fact, there was great skepticism, I felt, in some circles as to whether or not we'd be able to put a diplomacy in place that would deal with these two very difficult problems.

And, in fact, during the G–8, two resolutions were passed—by the way, those resolutions overshadowed by the situation in Lebanon. And I'm confident that working with our friends, if we stay on principle and remind people of the stakes, that we'll be able to accomplish the diplomatic objectives that we have set out, which is dealing with this problem and addressing the long-term issues.

A couple more questions, and we'll get out—Suzanne [Suzanne Malveaux, Cable News Network].

Spread of Democracy/Situation in the Middle East

Q. If I could follow Nedra's question. She had asked, Lebanon——

The President. I can't remember that far back. [*Laughter*]

Q. Lebanon's Parliament Speaker, Nabih Berri, who has been negotiating for Hizballah, has rejected the first resolution, saying it's unacceptable. They want the Israeli troops to pull out immediately. Is that a negotiable point? And also, Secretary Rice, will you be reaching out to Berri, as you had spoken with him before?

The President. Whatever happens in the U.N., we must not create a vacuum into which Hizballah and its sponsors are able to move more weapons. Sometimes the world likes to take the easy route in order to solve a problem. Our view is, it's time to address root causes of problems. And to create a vacuum, Suzanne, is unacceptable. It would mean that we haven't addressed the root cause.

The idea is to have the Lebanese Government move into the south so that the Government of Lebanon can protect its own territory and that there be an international force to provide the help necessary for the Lebanese Government to secure its country. Remember, in Germany, the first thing I said was—or one of the first things I said—I think I said this—help me out here, if I didn't——

Secretary Rice. I think you did.

The President. ——was we want the Siniora Government to survive and to be strengthened. The linchpin of the policy is to support democracies. And so the strategy at the U.N., the diplomatic strategy is to support that notion because a democracy in Lebanon will not only help that nation address its long-term issues—such as rebuilding and providing a hopeful life—but a democracy on Israel's northern border will stabilize—help stabilize the region. We are committed to a democracy in the Palestinian Territory.

President Abbas, in his conversations with Condi, talked about moving forward with democracy. There are people who can't stand the thought of a society based upon universal liberty from emerging. And that in itself ought to be a warning signal to those of us who care deeply for peace, that people would be willing to kill innocent citizens in order to stop the advance of liberty.

Now, I've talked a lot about the universal appeal of liberty, and I readily concede some people aren't willing to—some say, well, you know, liberty may not be universal in this sense—America imposes its will. We don't impose liberty; liberty is universal.

It's one of the interesting debates of the 21st century, I think, that some would be willing to say it's okay for people not to live in a free society. It's not okay for us. If you love peace, in order to achieve peace, you must help people realize that which is universal, and that is freedom.

She asked you a question.

Secretary Rice. Our point of contact for the Lebanese Government is obviously Prime Minister Siniora. As you know, I've also spoken to Speaker Berri on a couple of occasions.

I understand how emotional this is for the Lebanese. They've been through a very difficult war. It's emotional for Israel as well. They're in the midst of a difficult war.

Let me just say that in terms of what the end state will look like here, I don't think there is any disagreement that the right solution is the one that the President referred to. It's the Lebanese and the Lebanese Armed Forces able to secure their territory. And the international help is so that Lebanon can secure its territory. And I don't believe anybody anticipates that there should be foreign forces on Lebanese soil as a result of what has happened here.

And so I think there is room on this issue to work on this issue, because everybody has the same vision—that it's the Leb-

anese Army, with support from an international force, that can actually prevent that vacuum from obtaining again in the south, so that we're not right back here 3 or 4 or 5 months from now, in the same situation.

President Fidel Castro Ruz of Cuba

Q. Mr. President, I don't think we've heard from you since Fidel Castro has fallen ill. Can you give us what you know of his current condition, what your administration's contingency plans are for his death, and how they address the desire of Cuban exiles in this country to eventually go home and reclaim their property?

The President. First of all, Cuba is not a very transparent society, so the only thing I know is what has been speculated. And that is that, on the one hand, he's very ill, and on the other hand, he's going to be coming out of a hospital. I don't know. I really don't know.

And secondly, that our desire is for the Cuban people to be able to choose their own form of government, and we would hope that—and we'll make this very clear—that as Cuba has the possibility of transforming itself from a tyrannical situation to a different type of society, the Cuban people ought to decide. The people on the island of Cuba ought to decide. And once the people of Cuba decide their form of government, then Cuban Americans can take an interest in that country and redress the issues of property confiscation. But first things first, and that is, the Cuban people need to decide the future of their country.

Progress in Iraq

Q. Mr. President, if I could turn to Iraq for a moment.

The President. Sure.

Q. When you and Prime Minister Blair met at the White House a few months ago, you were asked about mistakes and missteps. And he said the one mistake he made was miscalculating in thinking that a young democracy, as you put it, would be born very quickly after the fall of Saddam. Are you prepared today to agree with him and acknowledge that you've had the same expectations, which were wrong?

The President. Actually, I think—I can't remember his answer; I'm sure you've characterized it perfectly. My attitude is that a young democracy has been born quite quickly. And I think the Iraqi Government has shown remarkable progress on the political front, and that is, is that they developed a modern constitution that was ratified by the people, and then 12 million people voted for a government—which gives me confidence about the future in Iraq, by the way.

You know, I hear people say, "Well, civil war this, civil war that." The Iraqi people decided against civil war when they went to the ballot box, and a unity government is working to respond to the will of the people. And frankly, it's quite a remarkable achievement on the political front, and the security front is where there have been troubles. And it's going to be up to the Maliki Government, with U.S. help, to use the trained forces and eventually a trained police force to take care of those who are trying to foment sectarian violence.

We've made some progress against some of those folks, particularly when Mr. Zarqawi met his demise. Remember, Al Qaida is in the country, all attempting to stop the advance of democracy. And the blowing up of the mosque created an opportunity for those who were trying to foment sectarian violence to achieve their objective. But the Iraqi people rejected that kind of sectarian violence; the army stood strong.

No question, it's still difficult. On the other hand, the political process is part of helping to achieve our objective, which is a free country, an ally in the war on terror that can sustain itself and govern itself and defend itself.

Okay, who else? I don't want to hurt any feelings. Yes, sir.

United Nations Security Council Resolution 1559/War on Terror

Q. Thank you very much.

The President. Identify yourself.

Q. Kevin Corke, NBC News, sir.

The President. Right. I knew that.

Q. Yes, sir.

The President. Just wanted to make sure you did.

Q. Yes, indeed. In reading the 1559 resolution and the draft as it's currently constructed, there are a lot of similarities, quite frankly. And I'm wondering if you could speak to, maybe, the frustration some Americans might be feeling that you've said we want sustainable peace; we don't want to come back here in a few months or a few years, and yet it seems like there will be another resolution, maybe another resolution, maybe another this, that, and the other. People get frustrated. Can you understand that and respond to that, sir?

The President. Well, the people who should get really frustrated are the Israelis and the Lebanese. They ought to be the ones who are frustrated, because 1559 clearly laid a way forward for there to be a strong democracy in Lebanon, which will more likely yield the peace. And there is a level of frustration around the world with organizations that will take innocent life to achieve political objectives. And our job is to remind people that this isn't a moment; this is a movement, and that we must deal with this movement. We must deal with this movement with strong security measures; we must bring justice to those who would attack us, and at the same time, defeat their ideology by the spread of liberty.

And it takes a lot of work. This is the beginning of a long struggle against an ideology that is real and profound. It's Islamofascism. It comes in different forms. They share the same tactics, which is to destroy people and things in order to create chaos in the hopes that their vision of the world become predominant in the Middle East.

And Condi and I will work hard—by the way, the United States can't win this war alone. We can do damage to the enemy. We can take the philosophical high ground and remind people of the importance of how freedom can change societies. But we will work with allies and friends to achieve this objective. And part of the challenge in the 21st century is to remind people about the stakes and remind people that in moments of quiet, there's still an Islamic fascist group plotting, planning, and trying to spread their ideology. And one of the things that—one of the things that came out of this unfortunate incident in the Middle East is, it is a stark reminder that there are those who want to stop the advance of liberty and destabilize young democracies. And they're willing to kill people to do so.

I repeat, this whole incident started because Hizballah kidnaped two soldiers and launched rocket attacks. And it's been unfortunate that people on both sides of the border have lost life. And we're committed to helping the Lebanese Government rebuild.

On the other hand, what we won't do is allow for a false hope. We believe that it's important to challenge the root cause now. We thought we had done so with 1559, but 1559 wasn't implemented. In other words, there was a way forward to deal with the problem. And now there's another chance to deal with the problem, and that's the role of the United States,

working with others to not only remind people about the problem but to come up with solutions in dealing with the problem. And the solutions that we are working with our friends are—in our judgment, is the best hope for achieving stability and peace.

But it takes a lot of work. And it takes commitment and focus. And that's what this administration will continue to do. We'll stay focused on the problem and stay focused on coming up with solutions that, when implemented, will leave behind a better world.

Thank you all very much for your interest.

NOTE: The President's news conference began at 8:59 a.m. at the Bush Ranch. In his remarks, he referred to former Secretary of State Colin L. Powell; former Deputy Secretary of State Richard L. Armitage; President Mahmoud Abbas of the Palestinian Authority; Prime Minister Ehud Olmert of Israel; Gilad Shalit, an Israeli soldier captured and held captive by militants in Gaza since June 25; Ehud Goldwasser and Eldad Regev, Israeli soldiers captured and held captive by militants in Lebanon since July 12; Prime Minister Tony Blair of the United Kingdom; and Prime Minister Nuri al-Maliki of Iraq. Secretary Rice referred to Prime Minister Fuad Siniora and Speaker of Parliament Nabih Berri of Lebanon; and Secretary-General Kofi Annan of the United Nations. A reporter referred to Chancellor Angela Merkel of Germany.

Remarks on Arrival in Green Bay, Wisconsin
August 10, 2006

Counterterrorism Efforts in the United Kingdom

The recent arrests that our fellow citizens are now learning about are a stark reminder that this Nation is at war with Islamic fascists who will use any means to destroy

those of us who love freedom, to hurt our Nation.

I want to thank the Government of Tony Blair and officials in the United Kingdom for their good work in busting this plot. I thank the officials in Washington, DC, and around our country who gather intelligence and who work to protect the American people. The cooperation on this venture was excellent—cooperation between U.K. and U.S. authorities and officials was solid. And the cooperation amongst agencies within our Government was excellent.

This country is safer than it was prior to 9/11. We've taken a lot of measures to protect the American people. But obviously, we're still not completely safe because there are people that still plot and people who want to harm us for what we believe in. It is a mistake to believe there is no threat to the United States of America, and that is why we have given our officials the tools they need to protect our people.

Travelers are going to be inconvenienced as a result of the steps we've taken. I urge their patience and ask them to be vigilant. The inconvenience is—occurs because we will take the steps necessary to protect the American people.

Again, I appreciate the close cooperation between our Government and the Government of the United Kingdom. The American people need to know, we live in a dangerous world, but our Government will do everything we can to protect our people from those dangers.

Thank you.

NOTE: The President spoke at 10:54 a.m. at Austin Straubel International Airport. In his remarks, he referred to Prime Minister Tony Blair of the United Kingdom.

Remarks on the National Economy in Green Bay
August 10, 2006

John, thank you very much for your hospitality.

I understand that the small-business sector of our economy is vital for economic growth. And that's why we cut taxes on people like—on businesses like John's business. See, when you reduce the income taxes, you affect many small businesses. And when he's got more money in his treasury to invest, the workers become more productive.

The reason why this company is successful is, one, they've got a good product; but, more importantly, they've got a workforce that is skilled and capable and treated well.

The bonus appreciation—accelerated depreciation schedules we passed for small businesses helped John buy new equipment. And when you buy new equipment, it helps the folks behind me become more productive; and the more productive you are, the better wages you make.

And so I'm here to herald small businesses in America and to remind the American people that by cutting taxes on small businesses, it encourages small businesses to grow. John was telling me they hired five new people over the past 3 weeks, and he's looking for more workers, workers that can do the job necessary to put out a good product.

I also want to make it clear that Congress needs to keep the taxes low on the working people. I'd much rather have these people spend their own money than the Government. We've got ample money in Washington to do what we need to do. And therefore, in my judgment, it's better that the folks behind me who are working hard have more money so they can save and invest and spend as they see fit. So I'm here to herald the tax cuts as they affected the small businesses of America but also as they affect the families of Wisconsin and America.

John, I want to thank you. I'm impressed by your operations. I particularly want to thank your workers for giving me a chance to come by and meet you. America is blessed by having a highly skilled workforce like we have, and that enables us to compete. This is a competitive company. It's a company that can't fill every order it gets because they're constrained by being able to find enough workers. It's one of the issues that faces America: Can we com- pete? And one way we compete is to make sure our education system educates people who've got the skills necessary to fill the jobs of the 21st century, just like they're being filled here at this company.

Thank you all very much.

NOTE: The President spoke at 11:29 a.m. at Fox Valley Metal-Tech, Inc. Participating in the event was John E. West, president, Fox Valley Metal-Tech, Inc.

Statement on Kleptocracy
August 10, 2006

For too long, the culture of corruption has undercut development and good governance and bred criminality and mistrust around the world. High-level corruption by senior government officials, or kleptocracy, is a grave and corrosive abuse of power and represents the most invidious type of public corruption. It threatens our national interest and violates our values. It impedes our efforts to promote freedom and democracy, end poverty, and combat international crime and terrorism. Kleptocracy is an obstacle to democratic progress, undermines faith in government institutions, and steals prosperity from the people. Promoting transparent, accountable governance is a critical component of our freedom agenda.

At this year's G–8 meeting in St. Petersburg, my colleagues joined me in calling for strengthened international efforts to deny kleptocrats access to our financial systems and safe haven in our countries; stronger efforts to combat fraud, corruption, and misuse of public resources; and increased capacity internationally to prevent opportunities for high-level public corrup- tion. Today I am announcing a new element in my administration's plan to fight kleptocracy, the National Strategy to Internationalize Efforts Against Kleptocracy, which sets forth a framework to deter, prevent, and address high-level public corruption. It identifies critical tools to detect and prosecute corrupt officials around the world, so that the promise of economic assistance and growth reaches the people.

Our objective is to defeat high-level public corruption in all its forms and to deny corrupt officials access to the international financial system as a means of defrauding their people and hiding their ill-gotten gains. Given the nature of our open, accessible international financial system, our success in fighting kleptocracy will depend upon the participation and accountability of our partner nations, the international financial community, and regional and multilateral development institutions. Together we can confront kleptocracy and help create the conditions necessary for people everywhere to enjoy the full benefits of honest, just, and accountable governance.

Statement on Terrorist Attacks in Najaf, Iraq
August 11, 2006

The terrorists in Iraq have again proven that they are enemies of all humanity. Yesterday they targeted innocent civilians in Najaf near a holy Muslim shrine and a symbol of peace throughout the world.

According to Iraqi officials, the terrorist who committed this atrocity was stopped by Iraqi police before he could enter the holy shrine. These police officers were killed in the attack. They died for their country and for the cause of freedom, and we honor their dedication and bravery. We also mourn the loss of every innocent life in this atrocity and other atrocities perpetrated in Iraq in recent months.

On behalf of the American people, I join Iraqi leaders of all communities who have condemned this barbarous action in the strongest possible terms. To the Iraqi people, I pledge the commitment of the United States to helping your new Government bring peace and security to all areas of your country.

The President's Radio Address
August 12, 2006

Good morning. This week, America received a stark reminder that terrorists are still plotting attacks to kill our people. Beginning on Wednesday night, authorities in Great Britain arrested more than 20 individuals who we believe were plotting to detonate liquid explosives aboard flights from the United Kingdom to the United States. If these terrorists had succeeded, they could have caused death on a massive scale. The plot appears to have been carefully planned and well-advanced. They planned to bring the components of their explosives on board in their carry-on luggage, disguised as bottled drinks and electronic devices.

We believe that this week's arrests have significantly disrupted the threat. Yet we cannot be sure that the threat has been eliminated. So as a precaution, on Thursday, the Federal Government took several steps to increase security at our airports and aboard our planes.

First, the Department of Homeland Security has raised our Nation's threat warning to Code Red—the highest level—for flights from Great Britain to America, in coordination with British authorities. Second, we've raised the threat warning for all domestic and international flights landing in the United States to Code Orange, the second highest level. We also have sent additional Federal air marshals to Great Britain to provide extra protection aboard flights from the United Kingdom to the United States.

This plot is further evidence that the terrorists we face are sophisticated and constantly changing their tactics. On September the 11th, 2001, they used box cutters to hijack airplanes and kill thousands of innocent people. This time, we believe they planned to use liquid explosives to blow up planes in mid-air. In response, we've adjusted our security precautions by temporarily banning most liquids as carry-on items on planes. I know many of you will be traveling during this busy summer vacation season, and I ask for your patience, cooperation, and vigilance in the coming days. The inconveniences you will face are for your protection, and they will give us time to adjust our screening procedures to meet the current threat.

I'm grateful for the outstanding work of intelligence and law enforcement officers in the United Kingdom and in our country. This week's arrests were the culmination of hard work, cooperation, and information sharing across different agencies and different governments. We're dealing with a new enemy that uses new means of attack and new methods to communicate. This week's events demonstrate the vital importance of ensuring that our intelligence and law enforcement personnel have all the tools they need to track down the terrorists and prevent attacks on our country.

Because of the measures we've taken to protect the American people, our Nation is safer than it was prior to September the 11th. Still, we must never make the mistake of thinking the danger of terrorism has passed. This week's experience reminds us of a hard fact: The terrorists have to succeed only once to achieve their goal of mass murder, while we have to succeed every time to stop them. Unfortunately, some have suggested recently that the terrorist threat is being used for partisan political advantage. We can have legitimate disagreements about the best way to fight the terrorists, yet there should be no disagreement about the dangers we face.

America is fighting a tough war against an enemy whose ruthlessness is clear for all to see. The terrorists attempt to bring down airplanes full of innocent men, women, and children. They kill civilians and American servicemen in Iraq and Afghanistan, and they deliberately hide behind civilians in Lebanon. They are seeking to spread their totalitarian ideology. They're seeking to take over countries like Afghanistan and Iraq so they can establish safe havens from which to attack free nations. These killers need to know that America, Great Britain, and our allies are determined to defend ourselves and advance the cause of liberty. With patience, courage, and untiring resolve, we will defend our freedom, and we will win the war on terror.

Thank you for listening.

NOTE: The address was recorded at 8:05 a.m. on August 11 at the Bush Ranch in Crawford, TX, for broadcast at 10:06 a.m. on August 12. The transcript was made available by the Office of the Press Secretary on August 11 but was embargoed for release until the broadcast. The Office of the Press Secretary also released a Spanish language transcript of this address.

Statement on the United Nations Security Council Resolution on the Situation in the Middle East
August 12, 2006

I welcome the resolution adopted yesterday by the United Nations Security Council, which is designed to bring an immediate end to the fighting sparked last month by an unprovoked terrorist attack on Israel by Hizballah, a terrorist group supported by Iran and Syria. The United States and its allies have been working hard since the beginning of this conflict to create the conditions for an enduring cease-fire and prevent armed militias and foreign-sponsored terrorist groups like Hizballah from sparking another crisis.

Yesterday's resolution aims to end Hizballah's attacks on Israel and bring a halt to Israel's offensive military operations. It also calls for an embargo on the supply of arms to militias in Lebanon, for a robust international force to deploy to southern

Lebanon in conjunction with Lebanon's legitimate armed forces, and for the disarming of Hizballah and all other militia groups operating in Lebanon. These steps are designed to stop Hizballah from acting as a state within a state, and put an end to Iran and Syria's efforts to hold the Lebanese people hostage to their own extremist agenda. This in turn will help to restore the sovereignty of Lebanon's democratic Government and help ensure security for the people of Lebanon and Israel.

The loss of innocent life in both Lebanon and Israel has been a great tragedy. Hizballah and its Iranian and Syrian sponsors have brought an unwanted war to the people of Lebanon and Israel, and millions have suffered as a result. I now urge the international community to turn words into action and make every effort to bring lasting peace to the region.

NOTE: The statement referred to United Nations Security Council Resolution 1701.

Remarks Prior to a Meeting With Secretary of Defense Donald H. Rumsfeld and the Defense Policy and Programs Team in Arlington, Virginia
August 14, 2006

Mr. Secretary, thanks for having me. The national security team from the White House is anxious to come over and get a briefing from you. We've got a lot to discuss. It's very important for the American people to know that we're constantly thinking about how to secure the homeland, protect our interests, and use all assets available to do our jobs.

I appreciate very much you and your team providing the very important briefing. We live in troubled times, but I'm confident in our capacity to not only protect the homeland, but I'm confident in our capacity to leave behind a better world. And one reason I feel so confident is because we've got a fantastic military. It's been an honor to travel the country to meet those who wear the uniform. We're a blessed nation to have men and women who are willing to volunteer during these difficult times.

And so, Mr. Secretary, thanks for the briefing; I'm looking forward to it. And thank you all for giving us your insights and inputs.

NOTE: The President spoke at 9:27 a.m. at the Pentagon. The Office of the Press Secretary also released a Spanish language transcript of these remarks.

Remarks Following a Meeting With Secretary of State Condoleezza Rice and the Foreign Policy Team and an Exchange With Reporters
August 14, 2006

The President. Good afternoon. Today I met with members of my national security team, both here at the State Department and at the Pentagon. I want to, first of all, thank the leadership of Secretary Condi Rice and Secretary Don Rumsfeld.

During those discussions, we talked about the need to transform our military to meet the threats of the 21st century. We discussed the global war on terror. We discussed the situation on the ground in three fronts of the global war on terror, in Lebanon and Iraq and Afghanistan.

Friday's U.N. Security Council resolution on Lebanon is an important step forward that will help bring an end to the violence. The resolution calls for a robust international force to deploy to the southern part of the country to help Lebanon's legitimate armed forces restore the sovereignty of its democratic Government over all Lebanese territory. As well, the resolution is intended to stop Hizballah from acting as a state within the state.

We're now working with our international partners to turn the words of this resolution into action. We must help people in both Lebanon and Israel return to their homes and begin rebuilding their lives without fear of renewed violence and terror.

America recognizes that civilians in Lebanon and Israel have suffered from the current violence, and we recognize that responsibility for this suffering lies with Hizballah. It was an unprovoked attack by Hizballah on Israel that started this conflict. Hizballah terrorists targeted Israeli civilians with daily rocket attacks. Hizballah terrorists used Lebanese civilians as human shields, sacrificing the innocent in an effort to protect themselves from Israeli response.

Responsibility for the suffering of the Lebanese people also lies with Hizballah's state sponsors, Iran and Syria. The regime in Iran provides Hizballah with financial support, weapons, and training. Iran has made clear that it seeks the destruction of Israel. We can only imagine how much more dangerous this conflict would be if Iran had the nuclear weapon it seeks.

Syria is another state sponsor of Hizballah. Syria allows Iranian weapons to pass through its territory into Lebanon. Syria permits Hizballah's leaders to operate out of Damascus and gives political support to Hizballah's cause. Syria supports

Hizballah because it wants to undermine Lebanon's democratic Government and regain its position of dominance in the country. That would be a great tragedy for the Lebanese people and for the cause of peace in the Middle East.

Hizballah and its foreign sponsors also seek to undermine the prospects for peace in the Middle East. Hizballah terrorists kidnaped two Israeli soldiers, Hamas kidnaped another Israeli soldier for a reason—Hizballah and Hamas reject the vision of two democratic states, Israel and Palestine, living side by side in peace and security. Both groups want to disrupt the progress being made toward that vision by Prime Minister Olmert and President Abbas and others in the region. We must not allow terrorists to prevent elected leaders from working together toward a comprehensive peace agreement in the Middle East.

The conflict in Lebanon is part of a broader struggle between freedom and terror that is unfolding across the region. For decades, American policy sought to achieve peace in the Middle East by promoting stability in the Middle East. Yet the lack of freedom in the region meant anger and resentment grew, radicalism thrived, and terrorists found willing recruits. We saw the consequences on September the 11th, 2001, when terrorists brought death and destruction to our country, killing nearly 3,000 of our citizens.

So we've launched a forward strategy of freedom in the broader Middle East. And that strategy has helped bring hope to millions and fostered the birth of young democracies from Baghdad to Beirut. Forces of terror see the changes that are taking place in their midst. They understand that the advance of liberty, the freedom to worship, the freedom to dissent, and the protection of human rights would be a defeat for their hateful ideology. But they also know that young democracies are fragile and that this may be their last and best opportunity to stop freedom's advance and steer newly free nations to the path of radical extremism. So the terrorists are striking back with all of the destructive power that they can muster. It's no coincidence that two nations that are building free societies in the heart of the Middle East, Lebanon and Iraq, are also the scenes of the most violent terrorist activity.

Some say that America caused the current instability in the Middle East by pursuing a forward strategy of freedom, yet history shows otherwise. We didn't talk much about freedom or the freedom agenda in the Middle East before September the 11th, 2001; or before Al Qaida first attacked the World Trade Center and blew up our Embassies in Kenya and Tanzania in the 1990s; or before Hizballah killed hundreds of Americans in Beirut and Islamic radicals held American hostages in Iran in the 1980s. History is clear: The freedom agenda did not create the terrorists or their ideology. But the freedom agenda will help defeat them both.

Some say that the violence and instability we see today means that the people of this troubled region are not ready for democracy. I disagree. Over the past 5 years, people across the Middle East have bravely defied the car bombers and assassins to show the world that they want to live in liberty. We see the universal desire for liberty in the 12 million Iraqis who faced down the terrorists to cast their ballots and elected a free government under a democratic Constitution. We see the universal desire for liberty in 8 million Afghans who lined up to vote for the first democratic Government in the long history of their country. We see the universal desire for liberty in the Lebanese people who took to the streets to demand their freedom and helped drive Syrian forces out of their country.

The problem in the Middle East today is not that people lack the desire for freedom. The problem is that young democracies that they have established are still vulnerable to terrorists and their sponsors.

One vulnerability is that many of the new democratic governments in the region have not yet established effective control over all their territory.

In both Lebanon and Iraq, elected governments are contending with rogue armed groups that are seeking to undermine and destabilize them. In Lebanon, Hizballah declared war on Lebanon's neighbor, Israel, without the knowledge of the elected Government in Beirut. In Iraq, Al Qaida and death squads engage in brutal violence to undermine the unity Government. And in both these countries, Iran is backing armed groups in the hope of stopping democracy from taking hold.

The message of this administration is clear: America will stay on the offense against Al Qaida; Iran must stop its support for terror. And the leaders of these armed groups must make a choice: If they want to participate in the political life of their countries, they must disarm. Elected leaders cannot have one foot in the camp of democracy and one foot in the camp of terror.

The Middle East is at a pivotal moment in its history. The death and destruction we see shows how determined the extremists are to stop just and modern societies from emerging in the region. Yet millions of people in Lebanon, Iraq, and Afghanistan and elsewhere are equally determined to live in peace and freedom. They have tired of the false promises and grand illusions of radical extremists. They reject the hateful vision of the terrorists, and they dream of a better future for their children and their grandchildren. We're determined to help them achieve that dream.

America's actions have never been guided by territorial ambition. We seek to advance the cause of freedom in the Middle East because we know the security of the region and our own security depend on it. We know that free nations are America's best partners for peace and the only true anchors for stability. So we'll continue to support reformers, inside and outside governments, who are working to build the institutions of liberty. We'll continue to confront terrorist organizations and their sponsors who destroy innocent lives. We'll continue to work for the day when a democratic Israel and a democratic Palestine are neighbors in a peaceful and secure Middle East.

The way forward is going to be difficult. It will require more sacrifice. But we can be confident of the outcome because we know and understand the unstoppable power of freedom. In a Middle East that grows in freedom and democracy, people will have a chance to raise their families and live in peace and build a better future. In a Middle East that grows in freedom and democracy, the terrorists will lose their recruits and lose their sponsors and lose safe havens from which to launch new attacks. In a Middle East that grows in freedom and democracy, there will be no room for tyranny and terror, and that will make America and other free nations more secure.

Now I'll be glad to answer a couple of questions. Deb [Deb Riechmann, Associated Press].

Situation in the Middle East/Israel

Q. Mr. President, both sides are claiming victory in a conflict that's killed more than 900 people. Who won, and do you think the cease-fire will hold?

The President. We certainly hope the cease-fire holds, because it is step one of making sure that Lebanon's democracy is strengthened. Lebanon can't be a strong democracy when there's a state within a state, and that's Hizballah.

As I mentioned in my remarks, Hizballah attacked Israel without any knowledge of the Siniora Government. You can't run a government, you can't have a democracy if you've got a armed faction within your country. Hizballah attacked Israel. Hizballah started the crisis, and Hizballah suffered a defeat in this crisis. And the

reason why is, is that first, there is a new—there's going to be a new power in the south of Lebanon, and that's going to be a Lebanese force with a robust international force to help them seize control of the country, that part of the country.

Secondly, when people take a look-see, take a step back and realize how this started, they'll understand this was Hizballah's activities. This was Hizballah's choice to make.

I believe that Israel is serious about upholding the cessation of hostilities. The reason I believe that is I talked to the Prime Minister of Israel about it. And I know the Siniora Government is anxious that the hostilities stop and the country begin to rebuild.

I can't speak for Hizballah. They're a terrorist organization. They're not a state. They act independently of, evidently, the Lebanese Government, and they do receive help from the outside.

Andrea [Andrea Mitchell, NBC News].

Hizballah/War on Terror

Q. Thank you, Mr. President——

The President. It's good to see you. Thanks for breaking in with us—kind of a rough crowd here, hanging out with you.

Q. Thank you. Despite what you've just said, there is a perception, a global perception, certainly in the Arab media and in many Western media as well, that Hizballah is really a winner here because they have proven that they could, as a guerrilla force, withstand the Israeli Army. They have been the sole source of humanitarian aid to many of the Lebanese people in the south. So they've improved their position politically, within Lebanon, and militarily and globally. They've gotten an aura of being able to stand up for so long against Israel. How do you combat that and the perception that we settled for less than we originally wanted in the U.N. resolution, a less robust force? And what actions can the United States or this international force take if Iran, for instance, tries to rearm Hizballah?

The President. Yes. First of all, if I were Hizballah, I'd be claiming victory too. But the people around the region and the world need to take a step back and recognize that Hizballah's action created a very strong reaction that, unfortunately, caused some people to lose their life, innocent people to lose their life. But on the other hand, it was Hizballah that caused the destruction.

People have got to understand—and it will take time, Andrea; it will take time for people to see the truth that Hizballah hides behind innocent civilians as they attack. What's really interesting is a mindset—is the mindsets of this crisis. Israel, when they aimed at a target and killed innocent citizens, were upset. Its society was aggrieved. When Hizballah's rockets killed innocent Israelis, they celebrated. I think when people really take a look at the type of mentality that celebrates the loss of innocent life, they'll reject that type of mentality.

And so Hizballah, of course, has got a fantastic propaganda machine, and they're claiming victories and—but how can you claim victory when at one time you were a state within a state, safe within southern Lebanon, and now you're going to be replaced by a Lebanese army and an international force? And that's what we're now working on, is to get the international force in southern Lebanon.

None of this would have happened, by the way, had we—had 1559, U.N. Resolution 1559 been fully implemented. Now is the time to get it implemented. And it's going to take a lot of work, no question about it. And no question that it's a different kind of war than people are used to seeing. We're fighting the same kind of war. We don't fight the armies of nation-states; we fight terrorists who kill innocent people to achieve political objectives. And it's a hard fight. It requires different tactics, and it requires solid will from those of us who understand the stakes.

The world got to see what it means to confront terrorism. I mean, it's the challenge of the 21st century. The fight against terror—a group of ideologues, by the way, who use terror to achieve an objective—this is the challenge. And that's why, in my remarks, I spoke about the need for those of us who understand the blessings of liberty to help liberty prevail in the Middle East. And the fundamental question is, can it? And my answer is, absolutely, it can.

I believe that universal—that freedom is a universal value. And by that I mean, I believe people want to be free. One way to put it is, I believe mothers around the world want to raise their children in a peaceful world. That's what I believe. And I believe that people want to be free to express themselves and free to worship the way they want to. And if you believe that, then you've got to have hope that, ultimately, freedom will prevail. But it's incredibly hard work, because there are terrorists who kill innocent people to stop the advance of liberty. And that's the challenge of the 21st century.

And the fundamental question for this country is, do we understand the stakes and the challenge, and are we willing to support reformers and young democracies, and are we willing to confront terror and those who sponsor them? And this administration is willing to do so. And that's what we're doing.

And you asked about Iran? What did you say about them? My answer was too long to remember the third part of your multipart question.

Syria and Iran/Sponsorship of Hizballah

Q. I'm sorry. How can the international force or the United States, if necessary, prevent Iran from resupplying Hizballah?

The President. The first step is—and part of the mandate in the U.N. resolution was to secure Syria's borders. Iran is able to ship weapons to Hizballah through Syria. Secondly is to deal—is to help seal off the ports around Lebanon. In other words, there's—part of the mandate and part of the mission of the troops, the UNIFIL troops will be to seal off the Syrian border.

But, as well, there's a diplomatic mission that needs to be accomplished. In other words, the world must now recognize that it's Iranian sponsorship of Hizballah that exacerbated the situation in the Middle East. People are greatly concerned about the loss of innocent life, as are the Americans—American people. We care deeply about that, the fact that innocents lost their life. But it's very important to remember how this all happened. And Hizballah has been emboldened because of its state sponsors. I know they claim they didn't have anything to do with it, but sophisticated weaponry ended up in the hands of Hizballah fighters, and many assume and many believe that that weaponry came from Iran through Syria.

And so the task is more than just helping the Siniora Government; the task is also—and the task is not just America's alone; the task is the world's—and that is to continually remind the Iranians of their obligations, their obligations not to develop a nuclear weapons program, their obligations not to foster terrorism and promote terrorism.

And we'll continue working with our partners to do that, just that.

Yes, Michael [Michael Allen, *Time*].

Counterterrorism Efforts in the United Kingdom/Security Measures

Q. Thank you, Mr. President. Until the other day, few Americans thought about liquid explosives when they got on a plane. What are the other emerging or evolving threats to the homeland that are most on your mind? That is, what else needs to be hardened as convincingly as cockpits have been hardened?

The President. Michael, we will take the actions that are necessary based upon the intelligence we gather. And obviously, if we find out that terrorist groups are planning and plotting against our citizens—or any other citizens, for that matter—we will notify the proper authorities and the people themselves of actions that we're taking.

Uncovering this terrorist plot was accomplished through the hard and good work of British authorities as well as our folks. And the coordination was very strong, and the cooperation, interagency and with the Brits, was really good. And I congratulate the Blair Government and the hard-working folks in Great Britain. And, by the way, they're still analyzing; they're still dealing with potential threats. And I want to thank our folks too. It was a really good effort.

But my point to you is that if we find out or if we believe that the terrorists will strike using a certain type of weapon or tactic, we will take the necessary precautions, just like we did when it came to liquids on airplanes.

Okay. Yes.

Israel

Q. The U.N. resolution says that Israel must stop all offensive action. What do you view as defensive action? If Hizballah——

The President. Somebody shoots at an Israeli soldier.

Q. They can respond in what way?

The President. Absolutely.

Q. Any way Israel responds to that, if they start another ground offensive, that is all defensive?

The President. I'm not going to—I keep getting asked a lot about Israel's military decisions, and we don't advise Israel on its military options. But as far as I'm concerned, if somebody shoots at an Israeli soldier, tries to kill a soldier from Israel, then Israel has the right to defend herself, has a right to try to suppress that kind of fire. And that's how I read the resolution. And that's how Ms. Rice reads the resolution.

Yes, Bill [Bill Plante, CBS News].

United Nations Security Council Resolution 1701

Q. Mr. President, to much of the rest of the world, the United States appeared to tolerate the bloodshed and ongoing fighting for a long time before assertively stepping in, and in the process, perhaps earned the further enmity of a lot of people in the rest of the world, particularly the Arab and Muslim world. What is your thought about that?

The President. My thought is that, first of all, we, from the beginning, urged caution on both sides so that innocent life would be protected. And secondly, I think most leaders around the world would give Condoleezza Rice and her team great credit for finally getting a U.N. resolution passed. We were working hard on a U.N. resolution pretty quickly, and it can be a painful process; diplomacy can be a painful process. And it took a while to get the resolution done. But most objective observers would give the United States credit for helping to lead the effort to get a resolution that addressed the root cause of the problem. Of course, we could have got a resolution right off the bat that didn't address the root cause. Everybody would have felt better for a quick period of time, and then the violence would have erupted again.

And our hope is that this series of resolutions that gets passed gets after the root cause. We want peace, Bill. We're not interested in process; what we want is results. And so—look, America gets accused of all kinds of things. I understand that. But if people analyze the facts, they were to find two things: One, we urged caution; and two, secondly, that we worked on a diplomatic process that we believe has got the best chance of achieving a long-term objective, which is peace.

Final question, then I got to go.

Homeland Security/Counterterrorism Efforts in the United Kingdom

Q. Mr. President, 4 days later, now do you believe that the U.K. terror plot was developed by Al Qaida leaders? Do you believe that there are terror cells operating within the U.S.? And along with Michael's question, what do you say to critics who say there are giant loopholes in homeland security?

The President. Well, first I would say that—I don't know the loophole question. Maybe you can give me some specific loopholes. But it sounded like to me Homeland Security did a good job, along with intelligence services and FBI, in working with the British to shut down a major plot that could have killed Americans.

First part of the question? That's what happens when you get 60.

Q. Do you believe the terror plot was developed by Al Qaida leaders?

The President. We certainly—I stand by the statements that initially came out of Chertoff, which was, it sure looks like it. It looks like something Al Qaida would do. But before we actually claim Al Qaida, we want to make sure that we have—we could prove it to you. Of course, the minute I say it's Al Qaida, then you're going to step up and say, prove it. So therefore, I'm not going to say it until we have absolute proof. But it looks like the kind of thing Al Qaida would do, and——

Q. As far as terrorist cells inside the U.S.?

The President. Any time we get a hint that there might be a terrorist cell in the United States, we move on it. And we're listening; we're looking. And one thing that's important is for us to make sure that those people who are trying to disrupt terrorist cells in the United States have the tools necessary to do so within the Constitution of the United States, see.

One of the things we better make sure is, we better not call upon the Federal Government and people on the frontlines of fighting terror to do their job and disrupt cells without giving people the necessary tools to disrupt terrorist plots before they strike. And that's what we're doing here in this Government.

And that's why the terrorist surveillance program exists, a program that some in Washington would like to dismantle. That's why we passed the PATRIOT Act, to give our folks the tools necessary to be able to defend America. The lessons of the past week is that there's still a war on terror going on, and there's still individuals that would like to kill innocent Americans to achieve political objectives. That's the lesson. And the lesson for those of us in Washington, DC, is to set aside politics and give our people the tools necessary to protect the American people.

Thank you.

NOTE: The President spoke at 3:40 p.m. at the State Department. In his remarks, he referred to Ehud Goldwasser and Eldad Regev, Israeli soldiers captured and held captive by militants in Lebanon since July 12, 2006; Prime Minister Ehud Olmert of Israel; President Mahmoud Abbas of the Palestinian Authority; Prime Minister Fuad Siniora of Lebanon; and Prime Minister Tony Blair of the United Kingdom.

Remarks Following a Meeting With the Counterterrorism Team in McLean, Virginia
August 15, 2006

It's been my honor to be here at the NCTC. A couple of observations: One, that because of the work being done here by some really fine Americans from different agencies in our Government, America is safer than it has been. But it's not yet safe. The enemy has got an advantage when it comes to attacking our homeland. They've got to be right one time, and we've got to be right 100 percent of the time to protect the American people.

I'm proud to report that there's a lot of good folks that are working hard to see to it that we're right 100 percent of the time. And I want to thank all the people in this building and around our Government who spend an incredible amount of time and energy and effort to do a very difficult job, and that's to protect the American people.

Recently we saw the fruits of their labor in conjunction with their counterparts in Great Britain. Because of the good work in Great Britain, and because of the help of the people there at NCTC, we disrupted a terror plot, a plot where people were willing to kill innocent life to achieve political objectives. And that plot is—and this building and the work going on here really is indicative of the challenge we face, not only this week but this year and the years to come, because the United States of America is engaged in a war against a extremist group of folks bound together by an ideology, willing to use terror to achieve their objectives.

Our most solemn duty in the Federal Government is to protect the American people, and I will assure the American people that we're doing everything in our power to protect you. And we've got some good assets, and the best asset we have is the people, people represented right here in this building.

So I've come to listen and learn and to look at reforms that have been put in place. And I've also come to thank the good people who work here and elsewhere in our Government for doing what they are doing.

Thank you very much.

NOTE: The President spoke at 12 p.m. at the National Counterterrorism Center.

Remarks at Harley-Davidson Vehicle Operations in York, Pennsylvania
August 16, 2006

I want to thank the folks here at the Harley plant for their wonderful hospitality. I've been impressed by Harley-Davidsons. It's one of America's finest products. And today I add to my impressions about the product with the impressions of the workforce. I was—really enjoyed walking the floor and shaking hands with the people who work here. I'm impressed by the esprit de corps; I'm impressed by the fact that these people really enjoy what they're doing; I'm impressed by the fact that they're impressed by the product they make.

One of the things we talked about with some of the employees here and some of the management was the need for Government to do a couple of things to help them here. One is to open up markets around the world for products like Harley-Davidsons. Harleys get shut out of certain markets, like other American products. And it makes sense that if you're making something people want around the world, that we ought to work hard to open up those markets. There's a direct correlation between exports and jobs. In other words, the more Harleys that are sold in a place like Vietnam or China or India, the more

likely it is somebody is going to be able to find work.

And so we talked about that. We also talked about the fact that one reason this company is successful is that they invest a lot in technologies and that there is a part of our Tax Code that encourages investment, called the research and development tax credit. And I assured them that when I said I'm for it being permanent, I meant I was for it being permanent. We hope Congress makes the research and development tax credit a permanent part of the Tax Code. That encourages folks here at Harley to make new investments; it means that the workforce becomes more productive; it means that the product is more likely to be able to compete.

And so I come away from this plant with a lot of very positive impressions, and it is a joy to be here. And again I want to thank you all for opening up your facility, and thank the good folks there on the line for being—for greeting me in such a warm fashion.

Thank you all.

NOTE: The President spoke at 3:55 p.m.

Remarks at a Reception for Gubernatorial Candidate Lynn C. Swann in Lancaster, Pennsylvania
August 16, 2006

Thank you all for coming. Thanks for being here. The people of Pennsylvania know that when you draft Lynn Swann—[*laughter*]—you get a man who performs. I am proud to be here with the next Governor of the great State of Pennsylvania, Lynn Swann. I know something about being a Governor. Here's what you need.

You need somebody who tells the truth, somebody who sets the people's agenda above political parties, somebody who makes decisions based upon principle, not based upon polls or focus groups, somebody who doesn't go around the State trying to become everybody's friend, but somebody who goes around the State to try to improve the lives of the people of the State. And there's no doubt in my mind that Lynn Swann has got the characteristics necessary to be a great Governor of this important State.

And I'm proud to be here with Lynn and Jim Matthews. You know, one of the interesting things I'll never forget, one time I was campaigning for my dad in the sixties in Texas. And I went to a county courthouse on his behalf, and it was empty. It turns out he was a Republican, and they were all Democrats. [*Laughter*] It was my first lesson of how important it is to stay in touch with the people who run the counties. You see, really good politicians and smart people understand that county politics is where you find the pulse of the people and where you're able to do your best work. And so it's a smart thing that Lynn Swann asked Jim Matthews, a man who understands the county structure in Pennsylvania, to run on his ticket. You've got vision and you've got experience side by side, which makes a powerful ticket for the people of Pennsylvania.

I just had my picture taken with some of you, and about every fourth person said, "Where's Laura?" [*Laughter*] What they're really saying, "How come you didn't send Laura and you stay at home?" [*Laughter*] Laura sends her love to the Swanns. She is very fond of Lynn and Charena. She respects them like I respect them. These are noble, decent people. They don't have to be running for politics, see. They can be sitting, doing a lot of other things— watching a football game, talking on TV— [*laughter*]—helping people help themselves. They're great, charitable people. They've got big hearts. But instead, they've decided to serve a State they love and a people they love. So Laura stands with me in saying to the people of Pennsylvania, you've got two really fine people in Lynn and Charena. Put them in office, and you'll be proud of the job they'll do for you.

It's good to meet Lynn's sons and Jim's sons. There's nothing better than having

a family by your side when you're running for office. This is a big State you got here, and it takes a lot of work. And these candidates are going to do the work necessary to get elected. I know they'll work hard. There's nothing better to—coming home to somebody you care for after a hard day's work. And so when you're voting for a candidate, you're really voting for a family as well.

And I like people who put their families ahead of all else in life. I like people who prioritize. I think it's going to be good for this State to have a Governor who sets the right priorities. It starts with faith and family, and then you can get into politics.

I'm proud to be here with Congressman Joe Pitts. Joe, thank you for serving the district with distinction. I'm glad you're here. I appreciate you being here.

I just came from the district next door, where they put me on a Harley-Davidson. [*Laughter*] It was a static display—[*laughter*]—fortunately. [*Laughter*] But that district is also represented by a person of dignity and character, and that's Todd Platts. Congressman, thanks for coming.

The attorney general—you're going to need to have a good attorney general by your side, Governor, and you got one in Tom Corbett. Thanks for coming, General.

I want to thank Rob Gleason and Bob Asher and all who else are involved with party politics. I want to thank those of you who have given of your hard-earned money to help these folks. You can't run unless the people are willing to contribute. That's just the way it is. And the fact that Lynn and Jim have raised so much money tonight is a good sign. I want to thank you for those of you who have helped organize this event, and thank you for giving of your money. It really means a lot to them. I know. I speak with firsthand experience how much it means to have people willing to contribute.

And now you need to contribute your time. You need to go to your coffee shops and your community centers and your houses of worship, and you need to talk to your friends and neighbors and let them know the quality of the people that are seeking their vote. You need to let them know that these two good men will do a fine job for the people of Pennsylvania. Getting ready, coming down the stretch here pretty soon, going to need you to put up the signs and lick the envelopes and make the phone calls and knock on the doors. They need your help. They'll work hard, but they can't win alone. And so it's one thing to give of your money, and now I hope you give of your time when they're coming down the stretch, because they can win this race. And when they do, Pennsylvania will be better for it.

Not only do you have to have the character to serve in office, but you have to run for a reason. There's got to be a compelling reason why you seek the vote, and Lynn Swann has got compelling reasons why he'll be a good Governor for the State of Pennsylvania. It starts with his philosophy about the role of government in the economy. He understands that governments don't create wealth, that governments create an environment in which the entrepreneur can flourish or which the small-business owner can grow bigger or which a person can realize their dreams by creating their own company. That's the kind of Governor you want. You want a Governor who understands entrepreneurship; a Governor, when the small-business person looks out and says, "That person understands my needs, and he understands my concerns." And that means you have to have a Governor who is willing to cut the taxes on the people, creating the jobs and doing the work.

He said, "I know how to prioritize a budget." If you don't prioritize in State government or Federal Government, they'll figure out how to spend every single dime that they raise from you. But if you can get somebody to prioritize, that leaves money for you to stay in your pocket. See, that's how you end up cutting the taxes.

You say, "Here's my priorities; here's what I think is essential," and then with the money left over—since I recognize it's your money, you get to keep it. It's amazing what happens to the economy when you cut the taxes on the people who work. I know him well enough to say to the people of Pennsylvania, when he says he's going to cut the taxes by a billion dollars, you can take it to the bank.

You know, one of the issues that hurts people a lot is property taxes. People struggle to own their own home. One of the things we stand for is ownership. We love it when somebody opens the door to the place they live and says, "Welcome to my home; this is my piece of property." We stand strong for the ownership society. It's harder to own a home when your property taxes are going up too high. It's good to have somebody running for Governor who says, "I hear the problems you have when it comes to owning your home, and I'll do everything I can to cut your property taxes as well."

I used to tell people this: Education is to a State what national defense is to the Federal Government. Education must be the number-one priority of your Governor. And it is the number-one priority for Lynn Swann. See, one of the reasons he's decided to run is because he's concerned about an education system that's not educating every child. Sure, it educates some children, but we want an education system to educate every child, and here's our vision of how it's done.

First, you must have leadership that sets high standards. It's amazing what happens when you have low standards. Guess what happens? You get low results. It's what I call the soft bigotry of low expectations. If you don't have high standards, you get lousy results, particularly in some neighborhoods. And that's unacceptable to a person like Lynn Swann and me.

Secondly, you measure. You say to somebody, "Are you achieving the results I expect?" There's a justified role for that, as far as I'm concerned, in government. The Federal Government spends a lot of money, about 7 percent of the education budget, around the country. I've said, since we're spending 7 percent, we'd like to see the results for the money we spent. Lynn Swann says the same thing. He understands the primary driver of education in Pennsylvania is the State. Therefore, he has got a legitimate right to say to the educators, "We like what you do; we stand squarely with you, but please show us whether or not a child can read or write and add and subtract early, before it's too late."

There's a pitiful practice in some schools that say, "You're too hard to educate; we're just going to shuffle you through." It may be the color of somebody's skin or somebody's demographics that says to somebody, "We're just going to quit on you." That's not right. It's not good for Pennsylvania. It's not good for the United States. You need to have a Governor who'll set high standards and hold people to account. And when you find people learning to read, write, and add and subtract, you say, thank you for what you're doing. But when you don't, you challenge the status quo so no child is left behind in America.

I like his education plan. It's well-thought-out. It makes a lot of sense. But most importantly, it's going to deliver the results for the families of Pennsylvania. And it doesn't matter whether you're Republican or Democrat or independent; these are results that affect all children. And that's the kind of Governor you need.

One of the things I learned when I campaigned here was that you had a problem with your doctors, like, a real problem. As a matter of fact, I was deeply concerned when I sat down at these roundtables with ob-gyns to find out what it's like to try to practice medicine in the State of Pennsylvania. You can't have good quality of life if you can't find good docs. And the truth of the matter is, many of your doctors are leaving the State or quitting practice because of the junk and frivolous lawsuits.

Now, I understand something, that these trial lawyers are strong politically. They're tough, and that's why you need a tough Governor to stare them down and say, for the sake of good medical care, for the sake of availability and affordability of medicine, we've got to end these frivolous and junk lawsuits that are hurting the people of Pennsylvania.

Now, he's got the right platform. He's running on the right issues, and he's running for the right reason. He's a fellow that doesn't need to say, "I try to make myself feel better by being Governor." He's had plenty of accolades—[*laughter*]—just ask the Dallas Cowboy fans. [*Laughter*] See, he's not running for his ego. He's running because he wants to serve the people of this State, and he's got a platform that makes a lot of sense. And I'm proud to help him. I'm proud to help him. And I know you are as well.

You know, we're living in historic times. These are difficult times for the American people because we're in a war. We're in a war we did not ask for but in a war that we must wage and win for the sake of our future generation of children. Much of my thinking about the world changed on September the 11th. I recognized on that day that we face a threat and that the responsibility of the Federal Government, working with State government, is to do everything we can to secure the homeland to protect the people. That's my most important job now, and it's the most important job of a lot of other people too.

I learned that we face an enemy that knows no bounds of cruelty. I understand the nature of this enemy. This is an enemy that has an ideology. Some people say, well, this may be a law enforcement matter. No, these are people that are politically driven. They've got motives. They do not believe in freedom. They don't believe in freedom of religion; they don't believe in freedom of dissent; they don't believe in women's rights. They have a backward view of the world. And yet they want to impose their vision on other people. That's what they're trying to do. And the United States of America must never retreat and let them have their way.

This is a different kind of war. Veterans of World War II and Korea would tell you, we were able to measure progress based upon miles gained or based upon tanks destroyed, or however people measured war in those days. This is different. We're facing people with an ideology but without a nation-state. Sometimes they have people sponsor them and help them, but this is not a nation-state. It's a different kind of conflict. And it's hard on the American people, and I understand that. But we shouldn't let the difficulties of facing this war force us to retreat from the world. If your most important responsibility is to protect the American people, the best way to do so is to stay on the offense and bring these people to justice before they hurt us again.

A different kind of war requires a different kind of approach. It means we better have good intelligence in order to be able to figure out the designs of the enemy before they strike. Just last week, we had good intelligence in working with our partners in Great Britain to disrupt a plot. I know it's hard for Americans to believe this, but the enemy that attacked us before has got people that want to act like them, are maybe taking instruction from—I can't tell you whether this plot we disrupted was Al Qaida. I'm not going to say that unless I'm certain it was. But it's the kind of activities that Al Qaida has done in the past, and that is to place suiciders on airplanes to destroy innocent life, trying to shake the will of the United States, trying to send a political message.

And so we've got to use new tactics, new efforts, new assets to protect ourselves against an enemy that will strike us at any moment. This war on terror is more than just chasing down people hiding in caves or preventing people from getting on airplanes to blow them up; the war on terror

is fought in many theaters, and the central front in the war on terror now is Iraq. I say it's the central front because that's what the enemy themselves have said, that they want to drive us from the region, that they view it as the central front as well. They've got objectives in Iraq. They want the United States to suffer a defeat in Iraq. They want us to retreat from Iraq. They want to create such havoc on our TV screens by killing innocent people that the American people finally say, we've had enough, leaving Iraq before the mission is complete.

And the mission is to have a country, a free country that can sustain itself and govern itself and defend itself and serve as an ally in the war on terror in the heart of the Middle East. That's the mission. And they want us to leave; they want us to cut and run. And there's some good people in our country who believe we should cut and run. They're not bad people when they say that; they're decent people. I just happen to believe they're wrong, and they're wrong for this reason: This would be a defeat for the United States in a key battleground in the global war on terror. It would create a—leaving before we complete our mission would create a terrorist state in the heart of the Middle East, a country with huge oil reserves that the terrorist network would be willing to use to extract economic pain from those of us who believe in freedom.

If we were to leave before the mission is complete, it would hurt U.S. credibility. Who would want to stand with the United States of America if we didn't complete the mission, and a mission that can be completed and will be completed? If we cut and run, if we don't complete the mission, what would that say to those brave men and women who have volunteered to wear the uniform of the United States of America? If we leave before the mission is complete, if we withdraw, the enemy will follow us home.

By defeating the enemy in Iraq, jihadists who try to spread sectarian violence through brutal suicide bombings, jihadists who have declared openly that their mission is to convert that country into a safe haven for them to launch attacks, when we defeat them, there will be a major defeat for the terrorists. It will strengthen the spread of democracy in the Middle East.

Look, our strategy is this: We will stay on the offense. And we are. Any time we get a hint that somebody is going to hurt us, we respond. And we're keeping the pressure on the enemy. By the way, anybody who follows me should always understand, you must keep the pressure on the enemy; otherwise, they will put the pressure on us. They still exist. It's important to understand this is a global war on terror, not an isolated moment of law enforcement. This is the first war of the 21st century, and the United States of America must lead that war. And we must be firm, and we must be resolved.

We will stay on the offense so we don't have to face them here in the United States of America. The way to defeat this enemy in the long term is to defeat their hateful ideology with a hopeful ideology; is for the United States of America to understand the power of liberty to help transform people's lives to the better and the power of liberty to help spread the peace that we want for our children and our grandchildren.

You know, when you have resentment and anger, that breeds hatred; that breeds recruiting grounds for people to become a suicider. Imagine the mentality of somebody willing to kill for an ideology that just doesn't—is not hopeful, and yet I believe a lot of that has to do with the fact that parts of the world breed resentment. And I believe that is due in part to the nature of the governments. I believe a system of government that encourages people to participate and a government that says, "We respond to your will," is the kind of government that ends up creating a hopeful alternative to resentment and hatred.

Our foreign policy in the past in the Middle East has been, let's just work for stability; let us not care what the form of government is; let's just make sure everything appears stable. The problem was, that foreign policy came home on September the 11th, 2001. It didn't work. What looked placid, what looked serene, what looked calm was not. Beneath the surface was this deep resentment brewing that caused people to come and kill 3,000 of our fellow citizens. The best way to defeat this enemy in the long run is to spread liberty, is to give people the hope of freedom.

Isn't it interesting today that the most violent parts of the world are where young democracies are trying to take root? Isn't it interesting that Hizballah would attack Israel, a democracy in the heart of the Middle East, try to destabilize the Middle East so that Lebanon doesn't get to be a strong democracy, and starts to try to turn the world against Israel? Isn't it interesting that the young democracy of Iraq is the place where the enemy is trying to stop the progress? That should tell the American people the following things: One, we face an enemy that has an ideology that can't stand freedom; and secondly, as freedom progresses, it changes the world for the better. Otherwise, the enemy wouldn't be trying to stop it.

And so in the long term, the United States of America must take the lead in spreading liberty. And we've got to have great confidence that it will work. I believe there's an Almighty, and I believe in the heart and soul of everybody is the gift of freedom from that Almighty. I believe Muslim women, Hindu women, Christian women, Jewish women want their children to grow up in peace and hope. I believe there is the universality of freedom, and I know it works.

You might remember, I recently went down to Graceland—that's Elvis's place—with the Prime Minister of Japan. Wasn't that interesting? [*Laughter*] I thought it was. [*Laughter*] More importantly, my guest thought it was. He was an Elvis fan. I bet you, in 1949, 1950, if somebody had stood up and said, "You know, I bet one of these days an American President is going to take the Japanese Prime Minister to visit the heartland," they'd have said, "Man, you are nuts." [*Laughter*]

It's interesting, isn't it, that the Prime Minister of a country with which we had a mighty war, thousands lost their lives— as a matter of fact, it took us, I don't know how long, a decade or so to even get racial slurs out of our vocabulary because of the enmity that arose as a result of fighting the Japanese. We couldn't stand them, and they couldn't stand us. And yet 60 years after the end of World War II, George W. Bush flies on the airplane with Junichiro Koizumi to go to Elvis's place. [*Laughter*] And we didn't spend much time talking about Elvis's place on the way down; we talked about the peace. Isn't that interesting? A former enemy, the sworn enemy of the United States, the leader of that country now sat down with the President of the United States doing something that our forefathers could not have possibly imagined—that we talked about the peace.

Something happened between World War II and today, and what happened was, Japan adopted a Japanese-style democracy. Something nobody would have thought as possible after World War II, except for

Harry S. Truman and some other people that had great faith in the desire for people to live in freedom and in the capacity to change—for freedom to change an enemy into an ally.

Someday, an American President will be sitting down talking to a duly elected leader of Iraq, talking about how to keep the peace. And our children will be better off.

The stakes are high. But I clearly see where we need to go. And the stakes are high in Pennsylvania, and Lynn Swann clearly sees where the State needs to go. You can't lead unless you see the end result. You've got a man who has got the vision. He's got the skills necessary to lead toward that vision. He's the right man for the job. I'm honored to be with him.

I want to thank you all for supporting Lynn Swann and Jim Matthews. God bless you all, and God bless America.

NOTE: The President spoke at 5:18 p.m. at the Lancaster Host Resort and Conference Center. In his remarks, he referred to James R. Matthews, candidate for Lieutenant Governor of Pennsylvania; Robert A. Gleason, Jr., chairman, Republican State Committee of Pennsylvania; Robert Asher, Pennsylvania national committeeman, Republican National Committee; and Prime Minister Junichiro Koizumi of Japan.

Remarks on Signing the Pension Protection Act of 2006
August 17, 2006

Thank you. Please be seated. Thanks. Welcome to the White House. We're glad you're here. In a few moments, I will have the honor of signing the most sweeping reform of America's pension laws in over 30 years, the Pension Protection Act of 2006. And we welcome you here to witness the signing.

Americans who spend a lifetime working hard should be confident that their pensions will be there when they retire. Last year, I asked Congress to strengthen protections for the pensions of our workers. Members of both parties came together to pass a good bill that will improve our pension system, while expanding opportunities for Americans to build their own nest eggs for retirement. And I'm really pleased to sign this bill into law.

I want to thank two members of my— three members of my Cabinet who have joined us today: Secretary of Treasury Hank Paulson, Secretary of Labor Elaine Chao, and the Director of the OMB Rob Portman. As an aside, while Portman served in Congress, he was the principal author of some of the important provisions of this bill.

I also want to welcome Members of the United States Senate and the House of Representatives here. I welcome Senator Mike Enzi, who is the chairman of the Health, Education, Labor, and Pensions Committee. I welcome Senator Blanche Lincoln from Arkansas. I welcome Congressman John Boehner, House majority leader, who was instrumental in getting this bill passed; along with Buck McKeon, who's the chairman of the Education and Workforce Committee, Congressman Bill Thomas, chairman of the Ways and Means Committee, Congressman John Kline of Minnesota. Thank you all for coming. Thanks for coming back from your vacations.

Many Americans work for private companies that offer traditional pensions, and most of those companies are meeting their obligations to their employees and their retirees. Yet, some businesses are not putting away the cash they need to fund the pensions they promised to their workers. These companies get into financial trouble and go bankrupt; their underfunded pension plans can leave some retirees with checks much smaller than the ones they were promised.

The Federal Government has created an insurance system for businesses offering private pensions, and that insurance is funded by premiums collected from these employers. When some businesses fail to fund their pension plans and are unable to meet their obligations to their employees, it puts a strain on the entire system.

And if there's not enough money in the system to cover all the extra costs, American taxpayers could be called on to make up the shortfall. Every American has an interest in seeing this system fixed, whether you're a worker at a company with an underfunded pension or a taxpayer who might get stuck with the bill.

The Pension Protection Act of 2006 will help shore up our pension insurance system in several key ways. It requires companies who underfund their pension plans to pay additional premiums. It extends the requirement that companies that terminate their pensions must provide extra funding for the system. This legislation insists that companies measure their obligations of their pension plans more accurately. It closes loopholes that allow underfunded plans to skip pension payments. It raises caps on the amount that employers can put into their pension plans so they can add more money during good times and build up a cushion that can keep pensions solvent in lean times.

Finally, this legislation prevents companies with underfunded pension plans from digging the hole deeper by promising extra benefits to their workers without paying for those promises up front. The problem of underfunded pensions will not be eliminated overnight. This bill establishes sound standards for pension funding, yet in the end, the primary responsibility rests with employers to fund the pension promises as soon as they can.

The message from this administration, from those of us up here today, is this: You should keep the promises you make to your workers. If you offer a private pension plan to your employees, you have a duty to set aside enough money now so your workers will get what they've been promised when they retire.

In addition to reforming the laws governing traditional private pensions, the bill I signed today also contains provisions to help workers who save for retirement through defined contribution plans like IRAs and 401(k)s. These savings plans are helping Americans build a society of ownership and financial independence.

And this legislation will make it easier for workers to participate in these plans. It will remove barriers that prevent companies from automatically enrolling their employees in these savings plans, ensure that workers have more information about the performance of their accounts, provide greater access to professional advice about investing safely for retirement, and give workers greater control over how their accounts are invested.

Finally, this bill makes permanent the higher contribution limits for IRAs and 401(k)s that we passed in 2001, and that will enable more workers to build larger nest eggs for retirement.

To ensure more secure retirement for all Americans, we've got more work to do. We must also prepare for the impact of the baby boomer generation's retirement, and what that impact will have on Federal entitlement programs like Social Security and Medicare. As more baby boomers stop contributing payroll taxes and start collecting benefits—people like me—it will create an enormous strain on our programs. Entitlement programs are projected to grow faster than the economy, faster than the population, and faster than the rate of inflation. If we fail to act, spending on Social Security and Medicare and Medicaid will be almost 60 percent of the entire Federal budget in the year 2030. And that's going to leave future generations with impossible choices: staggering tax increases, immense deficits, or deep cuts in benefits.

We have an obligation to confront this problem now. The Secretary of Treasury understands what I'm telling the Congress: Now is the time to move; now is the time to do our duty. I'm going to continue to work with the Congress and call on the Congress to work with the administration to reform these programs so we can ensure a secure retirement for all Americans.

Today we've taken an important step toward ensuring greater retirement security for millions of American workers. I want to thank the House and the Senate for their good work on this vital legislation. It's been hard work. It took a lot of pages to write that bill, as you can see. [*Laughter*] But the Members did good work, and now I'd ask them to join me as I sign into law the Pension Protection Act of 2006.

NOTE: The President spoke at 1:13 p.m. in Room 450 of the Dwight D. Eisenhower Executive Office Building. H.R. 4, approved August 17, was assigned Public Law No. 109–280.

Statement on Signing the Pension Protection Act of 2006
August 17, 2006

Today I have signed into law H.R. 4, the "Pension Protection Act of 2006." This legislation strengthens the pension insurance system and ensures that workers will receive better information about their pension plans. The legislation makes permanent the deductible limits for contributions to Individual Retirement Accounts and 401(k) plans, encourages employers to automatically enroll workers in 401(k) plans, and expands workers' access to investment advice.

The executive branch shall construe sections 221(a) and 1632(b)(1) of the Act, which call for the submission of legislative recommendations to the Congress, in a manner consistent with the constitutional authority of the President to supervise the unitary executive branch and to recommend for the consideration of the Congress such measures as the President shall judge necessary and expedient.

Section 1634(e) purports to require the United States Trade Representative to submit to congressional committees the contents of the negotiating positions of the United States and foreign countries in certain international trade negotiations. The executive branch shall construe section 1634(e) in a manner consistent with the President's constitutional authority to conduct the Nation's foreign affairs including negotiations with foreign countries, super-

vise the unitary executive branch, and to withhold information the disclosure of which could impair foreign relations, national security, the deliberative processes of the Executive, or the performance of the Executive's constitutional duties.

GEORGE W. BUSH

The White House,
August 17, 2006.

NOTE: H.R. 4, approved August 17, was assigned Public Law No. 109–280.

Remarks Following a Meeting With Economic Advisers and an Exchange With Reporters at Camp David, Maryland
August 18, 2006

The President. Thank you all for coming. We've just finished a really informative meeting with my economic team. I want to thank them for their service to the country. I'm really proud to be serving the American people alongside them. I've put together a really good team of people; smart, capable, decent, honorable people who are serving America with great distinction.

We discussed the state of the economy. We discussed where our economy is headed, and we discussed the steps that we're going to take to ensure that our economy continues to lead the world. The foundation of our economy is solid, and it's strong. Because of the tax cuts we passed, American workers and families and small businesses are keeping more of the money they earn. And they're using that money to drive this economy of ours forward.

The economy grew at 4 percent annual rate during the first half of 2006, and this means that our economy is maintaining solid growth and performing in line with expectations. Our solid economic growth is creating real benefits for American workers and families and entrepreneurs. Since Au-

gust 2003, we've added more than 5.5 million new jobs. The unemployment rate is 4.8 percent. Productivity growth is strong. Behind the numbers are stories of hard-working Americans who are realizing their dreams. The entrepreneurial spirit in this country is strong, and that's good for America.

You know, in Miami a couple of weeks ago, and I met a fellow named Nelson Gonzalez. Ten years ago, he and a friend started a computer business in a garage with $10,000. Their revenues are $192 million today. They employ about 750 people around the world.

I visited a fellow in Wisconsin named John West. He runs a manufacturing company. Over the past 2 years, John's factory has expanded from 65 employees to 90 employees. He told me he's receiving more orders than he can fill, and he's looking for more workers.

The other day I went to York, Pennsylvania, to visit the Harley-Davidson plant. They're selling motorcycles all over the world. Harley has doubled its workforce in the past decade. In other words, things are good for American workers and good for the entrepreneurs, and that's good for the country.

The economic growth has had a positive impact on the budget, and that's good for the taxpayers. Last year, economic growth pushed up Federal tax revenues by 14.5 percent; it's the largest increase in 24 years. This year tax revenues are projected to increase by another 11.4 percent, and at the same time, we are working with Congress to restrain Federal spending. We're meeting our priorities, and we're restraining Federal spending.

We recently learned that this year's deficit is projected to be 30 percent lower than we initially thought, and that means we're on track to cut the deficit in half by 2008, a full year ahead of the original goal.

We've got to keep this economy growing through progrowth economic policies. Taxes need to be kept low. We're working with Congress to restrain spending. Congress needs to pass the line-item veto so we can work together to cut out wasteful and unnecessary spending. We're going to work to make sure health care is more affordable for our businesses and our families. We will continue to invest in new energy technologies so we can promote alternative sources of energy and be wise stewards with the environment. We'll continue to work to stop the spread of junk lawsuits, and we'll continue to open up markets for American products.

We also discussed ways to keep this economy of ours competitive, flexible, and dynamic into the future. We discussed ways to make sure we improve education and job training. It's really important for our workers to have the skills necessary so we can remain a competitive country. It's really important for Congress to fully fund the American Competitiveness Initiative to make sure this country remains the economic leader we want it to be.

And we also talked about the need for this administration to work with Congress to really deal with the biggest challenge facing our budget and a huge challenge for our economic growth in the future, and that is the unsustainable growth of spending on programs like Social Security, Medicare, and Medicaid. These programs need to be reformed so that they will be available for our children and our grandchildren. It's a difficult issue, I know, for Members of Congress. The people here with me clearly see the problem, and we look forward to working with both Republicans and Democrats to do our duty, and that's to solve the problem.

All of us here are confident about the future of this country. Over the past 5 years, our economy has faced unprecedented challenges, from recession to corporate scandal to terrorist attack to natural disasters. And through it all, our free enterprise system has proved to be the most resilient and responsive in the world.

With hard work and wise policies, we'll meet every challenge that comes. And in so doing, we'll help more Americans realize their dreams and continue to make this country a grand—a land of great opportunities.

And now I'll answer a couple of questions. Deb [Deb Riechmann, Associated Press], you got any?

Situation in the Middle East/United Nations Security Council Resolution 1701

Q. Mr. President, on Lebanon, how can you say that Hizballah has suffered such a bad defeat when it's rebuilding—helping rebuild in southern Lebanon and it remains intact? And secondly, are you disappointed at all about France's decision to scale back its support of the international force?

The President. I think when people take a sober look at what took place in Lebanon, they'll realize that the destruction was caused by Hizballah. Hizballah caused the crisis. It was Hizballah's kidnaping of Israeli soldiers as well as Hizballah's launching rockets that caused Israel to defend herself from an action that the Lebanese Government didn't support.

Hizballah acted as a government within a government, and the world came to that recognition very quickly. I remember—I don't know if you traveled to St. Petersburg with us, but one of the first things that happened in the G–8 after this crisis occurred was that we all sat around the table and came to the conclusion very quickly, this type of behavior from a state within a state is intolerable for peace.

The first reaction, of course, of Hizballah and its supporters is, declare victory. I guess I would have done the same thing if I were them. But sometimes it takes people a while to come to the sober realization of what forces create stability and which don't. Hizballah is a force of instability. I appreciate the Siniora's Government's efforts to make it clear to the Lebanese people that they are the legitimate Government of Lebanon and they will work to rebuild that country. Prime Minister Siniora gave a very, I thought, a very interesting speech the other night, and a powerful speech, about how it's now time for the duly elected Government of Lebanon to do its duty and help rebuild. And they're getting help from around the international community to do so.

Other part of your—oh, the peacekeepers. Diplomacy takes a while, as you know. You watched the unfolding of the U.N. resolution necessary to get a ceasefire in the first place—it took a while. And we will continue to work with friends and allies to make it clear to them, now is the time to address the root causes of the problem, and that's being Hizballah's state within a state, particularly in southern Lebanon. And we'll work with nations to step up to the plate and do what they voted to do at the United Nations, and that is to provide robust international forces to help the Lebanese Army retake the south.

Hizballah, they're pretty comfortable there in south Lebanon. They're now going to find themselves not only that which caused the destruction, but they'll find themselves with now a Lebanese army, with

U.N. help, making it clear they won't have the safe haven necessary—that they think is necessary to launch attacks.

The issue is broader than just Hizballah. The issue is also Syria and Iran, two nations that supported Hizballah in its attempts to create enough havoc so that, I guess, people feel like they could take political advantage of the situation; we just can't let them do it.

French Role in Lebanon

Q. But what about France, though?

The President. France has said they'd send some troops. We hope they send more. And there's been different signals coming out of France. Yesterday they had a statement. Today they had a statement. We're working with France. France is a friend. France is an ally. France has got a great stake in the future of Lebanon.

President Chirac has made it very clear that he believes that democracy in Lebanon is very important—been supportive of the Siniora Government like we have. France and the United States cosponsored 1559. That's the U.N. resolution that was the beginning of the end of Syria's involvement in—or Syria's occupation in Lebanon. So we have common interests with France, and they are a very important part of the international scene and will be a very important player in Lebanon.

Toby [Tabassum Zakaria, Reuters].

North Korea

Q. Mr. President, are there indications that North Korea is preparing to conduct its first nuclear bomb test? And if that were to occur, how would the United States respond?

The President. Well, it's a hypothetical question, and you're asking me to divulge any intelligence information I have, and I'm not going to do that, as you know. I'm not going to break tradition.

If North Korea were to conduct a test, it's just a constant reminder for people in the neighborhood, in particular, that North

Korea poses a threat. And we expect there to be—we expect our friends and those sitting around the table with us to act in such a manner as to help rid the world of the threat.

War on Terror/Terrorist Surveillance Program

Q. Mr. President, the Federal ruling yesterday that declared your terrorist surveillance program unconstitutional—the judge wrote that it was never the intent of the Framers to give the President such unfettered control. How do you respond, sir, to opponents who say that this ruling is really the first nail in the coffin of your administration's legal strategy in the war on terror?

The President. I would say that those who herald this decision simply do not understand the nature of the world in which we live. You might remember, last week, working with the—with people in Great Britain, we disrupted a plot. People were trying to come and kill people. This country of ours is at war, and we must give those whose responsibility it is to protect the United States the tools necessary to protect this country in a time of war.

The judge's decision was a—I strongly disagree with that decision, strongly disagree. That's why I instructed the Justice Department to appeal immediately, and I believe our appeals will be upheld.

I made my position clear about this war on terror. And by the way, the enemy made their position clear yet again when we were able to stop them. And I—the American people expect us to protect them, and therefore, I put this program in place. We believe—strongly believe it's constitutional.

And if Al Qaida is calling in to the United States, we want to know why they're calling. And so I made my position clear. It would be interesting to see what other policymakers—how other policymakers react.

Listen, thank you all very much.

NOTE: The President spoke at 11:33 a.m. In his remarks, he referred to Ehud Goldwasser and Eldad Regev, Israeli soldiers captured and held captive by militants in Lebanon since July 12, 2006; Prime Minister Fuad Siniora of Lebanon; President Jacques Chirac of France; and U.S. District Court Judge for the Eastern District of Michigan Anna Diggs Taylor.

The President's Radio Address
August 19, 2006

Good morning. This week, I met with my national security, counterterrorism, and economic teams. We've set clear goals: We will defeat the terrorists and expand freedom across the world; we'll protect the American homeland and work tirelessly to prevent attacks on our country; and we will continue to unleash the entrepreneurial spirit of America and build a more prosperous future for all our citizens.

On Monday, I visited the Pentagon and the State Department, where we discussed the war on terror, including the recent conflict in Lebanon, a conflict which began with an unprovoked attack by Hizballah on Israel. Thanks to the leadership of Secretary Rice and Ambassador Bolton at the United Nations, the U.N. Security Council passed a resolution that will help bring an end to the violence and create a foundation for a sustainable peace.

The resolution calls for a robust international force to deploy to the southern part of Lebanon. This force will help Lebanon's legitimate armed forces restore the sovereignty of its democratic Government over all Lebanese territory and stop Hizballah from acting as a state within a state. The resolution will help make it possible for civilians in both Lebanon and Israel to return home in safety and begin rebuilding their lives without fear of renewed violence and terror.

The United States is now working with our international partners to turn the words of this resolution into action. The conflict in Lebanon is part of a broader struggle between freedom and terror that is unfolding across the region. Terrorists and their sponsors recognize that the Middle East is at a pivotal moment in its history. Freedom has brought hope to millions, and it's helped foster the development of young democracies from Baghdad to Beirut.

Yet these young democracies are still fragile, and the forces of terror are seeking to stop liberty's advance and steer newly free nations to the path of radicalism. The terrorists fear the rise of democracy because they know what it means for the future of their hateful ideology.

It is no coincidence that two nations that are building free societies in the heart of the Middle East, Lebanon and Iraq, are also the scenes of the most violent terrorist activity. We will defeat the terrorists by strengthening young democracies across the broader Middle East.

The way forward will be difficult, and it will require sacrifice and resolve. But America's security depends on liberty's advance in this troubled region, and we can be confident of the outcome because we know the unstoppable power of freedom.

On Tuesday, I went to the National Counterterrorism Center, where I was briefed by the fine professionals who work day and night to protect our Nation from terrorist attacks. Their efforts are vital, as we saw with the recent terrorist plot to destroy airliners headed for America.

I thanked the men and women of the intelligence community for all they did to help the British Government uncover and disrupt this vicious plot. This attempted attack is a reminder to us all: The terrorists remain determined to destroy innocent life on a massive scale, and we must be equally determined to stop them.

On Friday, I met with my economic advisers at Camp David, where we discussed our efforts to keep our economy growing and creating jobs. Our economy has created more than 5.5 million new jobs since August of 2003, more jobs than Japan and the 25 nations of the European Union combined. The unemployment rate is 4.8 percent. The productivity of America's workers is rising, and our economy grew at a strong annual rate of 4 percent during the first half of 2006.

To keep this momentum going, we're pursuing a strategy to sustain our economic growth and keep our economy competitive for decades to come. We will keep taxes low, restrain Federal spending, open new markets for American products, invest in new energy technologies, and help American workers develop the skills they need to compete for high-wage jobs.

American workers also need affordable, high-quality health care, and more transparency in our health care system can help. Next week I will travel to Minnesota to discuss ways to ensure patients have access to more information about their health care. When patients know the facts about the price and quality of their health care options, they can make decisions that are right for them.

With all these steps, we're working to improve the health, security, and prosperity of the American people. Our Nation does not fear the future because we are determined to shape the future. We will build a more peaceful world and leave behind a stronger and better America for our children and grandchildren.

Thank you for listening.

NOTE: The address was recorded at 7:50 a.m. on August 18 at Camp David, MD, for broadcast at 10:06 a.m. on August 19. The transcript was made available by the Office of the Press Secretary on August 18 but was embargoed for release until the broadcast. In his address, the President referred to United Nations Security Council Resolution 1701. The Office of the Press Secretary also released a Spanish language transcript of this address.

The President's News Conference
August 21, 2006

The President. Thank you all. Please be seated. Fancy digs you got here. Thanks for your hospitality. It's good to visit with you. I look forward to taking some of your questions. I do want to talk to you about the latest developments in Lebanon and what we're doing to ensure U.N. Security Council 1701 is implemented and its words are quickly put into action.

Resolution 1701 authorizes an effective international force to deploy to Lebanon, which is essential to peace in the region, and it's essential to the freedom of Lebanon. An effective international force will help ensure the cessation of hostilities holds in southern Lebanon once the Israeli troops withdraw. An effective international force will help the Lebanese Army meet its responsibility to secure Lebanon's borders and stop them from acting as—and stop Hizballah from acting as a state within a state. An effective international force will help give displaced people in both Lebanon and Israel the confidence to return to their homes and begin rebuilding their lives without fear of renewed violence and terror.

An international force requires international commitment. Previous resolutions have failed in Lebanon because they were not implemented by the international community and, in this case, did not prevent Hizballah and their sponsors from instigating violence. The new resolution authorizes a force of up to 15,000 troops. It gives this force an expanded mandate. The need is urgent. The international community must now designate the leadership of this new international force, give it robust rules of engagement, and deploy it as quickly as possible to secure the peace.

America will do our part. We will assist the new international force with logistic support, command and control, communications, and intelligence. Lebanon, Israel, and our allies agreed that this would be the most effective contribution we can make at this time. We will also work with the leadership in the international force, once it's identified, to ensure that the United States is doing all we can to make this mission a success.

Deployment of this new international force will also help speed delivery of humanitarian assistance. Our Nation is wasting no time in helping the people of Lebanon. In other words, we're acting before the force gets in there. We've been on the ground in Beirut for weeks, and I've already distributed more than half of our $50 million pledge of disaster relief to the Lebanese people who have lost their homes in the current conflict. Secretary Rice has led the diplomatic efforts to establish humanitarian corridors so that relief convoys can get through, to reopen the Beirut airport to passenger and humanitarian aid flights, and to ensure a steady fuel supply for Lebanese powerplants and automobiles. I directed 25,000 tons of wheat be delivered in Lebanon in the coming weeks.

But we'll do even more. Today I'm announcing that America will send more aid to support humanitarian and reconstruction work in Lebanon, for a total of more than $230 million. These funds will help the

Lebanese people rebuild their homes and return to their towns and communities. The funds will help the Lebanese people restore key bridges and roads. The funds will help the Lebanese people rehabilitate schools so the children can start their school year on time this fall.

I've directed that an oil spill response team be sent to assist the Lebanese Government in cleaning up an oil slick that is endangering coastal communities; proposing a $42 million package to help train and equip Lebanon's armed forces. I will soon be sending a Presidential delegation of private sector leaders to Lebanon to identify ways that we can tap into the generosity of American businesses and nonprofits to continue to help the people of Lebanon.

We take these steps—and I'll also work closely with Congress to extend the availability of loan guarantees to help rebuild infrastructure in Israel, infrastructure damaged by Hizballah's rockets.

America is making a long-term commitment to help the people of Lebanon because we believe every person deserves to live in a free, open society that respects the rights of all. We reject the killing of innocents to achieve a radical and violent agenda.

The terrorists and their state sponsors, Iran and Syria, have a much darker vision. They're working to thwart the efforts of the Lebanese people to break free from foreign domination and build their own democratic future. The terrorists and their sponsors are not going to succeed. The Lebanese people have made it clear: They want to live in freedom. And now it's up to their friends and allies to help them do so.

I'll be glad to answer some questions, starting with you, Terry [Terence Hunt, Associated Press].

Progress in Iraq

Q. Thank you, Mr. President. More than 3,500 Iraqis were killed last month, the highest civilian monthly toll since the war began. Are you disappointed with the lack of progress by Iraq's unity Government in bringing together the sectarian and ethnic groups?

The President. No. I am aware that extremists and terrorists are doing everything they can to prevent Iraq's democracy from growing stronger. That's what I'm aware of. And therefore, we have a plan to help them—"them," the Iraqis—achieve their objectives. Part of the plan is political, and that is to help the Maliki Government work on reconciliation and to work on rehabilitating the community. The other part is, of course, security. And I have given our commanders all the flexibility they need to adjust tactics to be able to help the Iraqi Government defeat those who want to thwart the ambitions of the people. And that includes a very robust security plan for Baghdad.

We've, as you may or may not know, Terry, moved troops from Mosul, Stryker Brigade, into Baghdad, all aiming to help the Iraqi Government succeed.

You know, I hear a lot of talk about civil war. I'm concerned about that, of course, and I've talked to a lot of people about it. And what I've found from my talks are that the Iraqis want a unified country, and that the Iraqi leadership is determined to thwart the efforts of the extremists and the radicals and Al Qaida, and that the security forces remain united behind the Government. And one thing is clear: The Iraqi people are showing incredible courage.

The United States of America must understand, it's in our interests that we help this democracy succeed. As a matter of fact, it's in our interests that we help reformers across the Middle East achieve their objectives. This is the fundamental challenge of the 21st century. A failed Iraq would make America less secure. A failed Iraq in the heart of the Middle East will provide safe haven for terrorists and extremists. It will embolden those who are trying to thwart the ambitions of reformers. In this case, it would give the terrorists and extremists an additional tool besides safe haven, and that is revenues from oil sales.

You know, it's an interesting debate we're having in America, about how we ought to handle Iraq. There's a lot of people, good, decent people saying, "Withdraw now." They're absolutely wrong. It would be a huge mistake for this country. If you think problems are tough now, imagine what it would be like if the United States leaves before this Government has a chance to defend herself, govern herself, and listen to the—and answer to the will of the people.

Patsy [Patricia Wilson, Reuters]. We're working our way here everybody.

Iran/Democracy in the Middle East

Q. Thank you, Mr. President. Iran has indicated that it will defy the U.N. on nuclear enrichment. It's been holding military exercises, sending weapons and money to Hizballah. Isn't Tehran's influence in the region growing despite your efforts to curb it?

The President. The final history in the region has yet to be written. And what's very interesting about the violence in Lebanon and the violence in Iraq and the violence in Gaza is this: These are all groups of terrorists who are trying to stop the advance of democracy. They're trying to thwart the will of millions who simply want a normal, hopeful life. That's what we're seeing. And it's up to the international community to understand the threat.

I remember, right after Hizballah launched its rocket attacks on Israel, I said, this is a clarifying moment. It's a chance for the world to see the threats of the 21st century, the challenge we face.

And so to answer your question on Iran, Iran is obviously part of the problem. They sponsor Hizballah. They encourage a radical brand of Islam. Imagine how difficult this issue would be if Iran had a nuclear weapon. And so therefore, it's up to the international community, including the United States, to work in concert to—for effective diplomacy. And that begins at the United Nations Security Council.

We have passed one Security Council resolution, demanding that Iran cease its enrichment activities. We will see what their response is. We're beginning to get some indication, but we'll—let's wait until they have a formal response. The U.N. resolution calls for us to come back together on the 31st of August. The dates—dates are fine, but what really matters is will. And one of the things I will continue to remind our friends and allies is the danger of a nuclear-armed Iran.

But, no, you're right; this is a—they're a central part of creating instability, trying to stop reformers from realizing dreams. And the question facing this country is, will—do we, one, understand the threat to America? In other words, do we understand that a failed—failed states in the Middle East are a direct threat to our country's security? And secondly, will we continue to stay engaged in helping reformers, in working to advance liberty, to defeat an ideology that doesn't believe in freedom? And my answer is, so long as I'm the President, we will. I clearly see the challenge. I see the challenge to what these threats pose to our homeland, and I see the challenge—what these threats pose to the world.

Helen [Helen Thomas, Hearst Newspapers]. [*Laughter*] What's so funny about me saying "Helen"? [*Laughter*] It's the anticipation of your question, I guess.

Situation in the Middle East

Q. Israel broke its word twice on a truce. And you mentioned Hizballah rockets, but it's—Israeli bombs have destroyed Lebanon. Why do you always give them a pass? And what's your view on breaking of your oath for a truce?

The President. Yes, thank you. I like to remind people about how this started, how this whole—how the damage to innocent life, which bothers me—but again, what caused this?

Q. Why drop bombs on——

The President. Let me finish—let—ma'am, let me—ma'am, please let me finish the question. It's a great question, to begin with. The followup was a little difficult, but anyway. [*Laughter*] I know you're waiting for my answer, aren't you, with bated breath. There you go.

This never would have occurred had a terrorist organization, a state within a state, not launched attacks on a sovereign nation. From the beginning, Helen, I said that Israel, one, has a right to defend herself, but Israel ought to be cautious about how she defends herself. Israel is a democratically elected government. They make decisions on their own sovereignty. It's their decisionmaking that is—what leads to the tactics they chose.

But the world must understand that now is the time to come together to address the root cause of the problem. And the problem was, you have a state within a state. You had people launch attacks on a sovereign nation without the consent of the Government in the country in which they are lodged.

And that's why it's very important for all of us, those of us who are involved in this process, to get an international force into Lebanon to help the Lebanese Government achieve some objectives. One is their ability to exert control over the entire country; secondly is to make sure that the Hizballah forces don't rearm, don't get arms from Syria or Iran through Syria, to be able to continue to wreak havoc in the region.

Let's see, we'll finish the first line here. Everybody can be patient.

Q. Thank you.

The President. Yes. [*Laughter*] It's kind of like dancing together, isn't it? [*Laughter*]

Q. Yes, kind of. [*Laughter*]

Q. Very close quarters.

The President. If I ask for any comments from the peanut gallery, I'll call on you,

Herman [Ken Herman, Cox]. [*Laughter*] By the way, seersucker is coming back. I hope everybody gets—[*laughter*]—never mind.

Q. It's the summertime east Texas county commissioner look. [*Laughter*]

The President. Yes. Yes, Martha [Martha Raddatz, ABC News]. Sorry.

Iraq

Q. That's quite all right. Mr. President, I'd like to go back to Iraq. You've continually cited the elections, the new Government, its progress in Iraq, and yet the violence has gotten worse in certain areas. You've had to go to Baghdad again. Is it not time for a new strategy? And if not, why not?

The President. You know, Martha; you've covered the Pentagon. You know that the Pentagon is constantly adjusting tactics because they have the flexibility from the White House to do so.

Q. I'm talking about strategy——

The President. The strategy is to help the Iraqi people achieve their objectives and their dreams, which is a democratic society. That's the strategy. The tactics—now, either you say, yes, it's important we stay there and get it done, or we leave. We're not leaving, so long as I'm the President. That would be a huge mistake. It would send an unbelievably terrible signal to reformers across the region. It would say we've abandoned our desire to change the conditions that create terror. It would give the terrorists a safe haven from which to launch attacks. It would embolden Iran. It would embolden extremists.

No, we're not leaving. The strategic objective is to help this Government succeed. That's the strategic—and not only to help the Government—the reformers in Iraq succeed but to help the reformers across the region succeed, to fight off the elements of extremism. The tactics are—which change. Now, if you say, are you going to change your strategic objective, it means you're leaving before the mission is complete. And we're not going to leave before the mission is complete. I agree with General Abizaid: We leave before the mission is done, the terrorists will follow us here.

And so we have changed tactics. Our commanders have got the flexibility necessary to change tactics on the ground, starting with Plan Baghdad. And that's when we moved troops from Mosul into Baghdad and replaced them with the Stryker Brigade. So in essence, we increased troops during this time of instability.

Suzanne [Suzanne Malveaux, Cable News Network].

Q. Sir, that's not really the question. The strategy——

The President. Sounded like the question to me.

Q. You keep saying that you don't want to leave. But is your strategy to win working? Even if you don't want to leave— you've gone into Baghdad before; these things have happened before.

The President. If I didn't think it would work, I would change the—our commanders would recommend changing the strategy. They believe it will work. It takes time to defeat these people. The Maliki Government has been in power for less than 6 months. And yes, the people spoke. I've cited that as a part of—the reason I cite it is because it's what the Iraqi people want. And the fundamental question facing this Government is whether or not we will stand with reformers across the region. It's really the task. And we're going to stand with this Government.

Obviously, I wish the violence would go down, but not as much as the Iraqi citizens would wish the violence would go down. But, incredibly enough, they showed great courage, and they want our help. And any sign that says we're going to leave before the job is done simply emboldens terrorists and creates a certain amount of doubt for people so they won't take the risk necessary to help a civil society evolve in the country.

This is a campaign—I'm sure they're watching the campaign carefully. There are a lot of good, decent people saying, "Get out now; vote for me; I will do everything I can to"—I guess, cut off money is how— is what they'll try to do to get our troops out. It's a big mistake. It would be wrong, in my judgment, for us to leave before the mission is complete in Iraq.

Suzanne.

Situation in the Middle East/United Nations Security Council Resolution 1701

Q. Thank you, Mr. President. Back to Lebanon. The Lebanese Prime Minister, over the weekend, said that Israel flagrantly violated the cease-fire with its raid into Lebanon. And so far, the European allies who've committed forces, the U.N. security peacekeeping forces, have expressed reservations; those Muslim nations who've offered troops have been shunned by Israeli officials. Why shouldn't we see the cease-fire as one that essentially is falling apart? And what makes this more than a piece of paper if you don't have the will of the international community to back it up?

The President. Yes. No, listen—all the more reason why we need to help our friends and allies get the forces necessary to help the Lebanese forces keep the cessation of hostilities in place, intact. And that's why we're working with friends, with allies, with Security Council members, to make sure the force that is committed is robust and the rules of engagement are clear. And so it's an ongoing series of conversations and discussions, and hopefully, this will happen quite quickly.

Q. Will you pressure the French to contribute more troops?

The President. Well, we're pressing on all. I was asked about the French the other day at Camp David, and I—listen, France has had a very close relationship with Lebanon; there's historical ties with Lebanon. I would hope they would put more troops in. I mean, they understand the region as well as anybody. And so we're working with a lot of folks, trying to get this force up and running.

Look, like you—I mean, you sound somewhat frustrated by diplomacy. Diplomacy can be a frustrating thing. I think the strategy can work, so long as the force is robust and the rules of engagement are clear.

Iran/United Nations Security Council Resolution 1696

Q. Mr. President, as you mentioned, we're just 10 days from the U.N. Security Council deadline on Iran. Judging by the public comments from the Iranians, it appears, at least, highly unlikely that they're going to stop or suspend their enrichment program. Are you confident that the U.N. Security Council will move quickly on sanctions if Iran thumbs its nose at the world again?

The President. I certainly hope so. In order for the U.N. to be effective, there must be consequences if people thumb their nose at the United Nations Security Council. And we will work with people in the Security Council to achieve that objective, and the objective is that there's got to be a consequence for them basically ignoring what the Security Council has suggested through resolution.

Q. Understanding that diplomacy takes time, do you think that this could drag out for a while?

The President. You know, I don't know. I certainly want to solve this problem diplomatically, and I believe the best chance to do so is for there to be more than one voice speaking clearly to the Iranians. And I was pleased that we got a resolution, that there was a group of nations willing to come together to send a message to the Iranians—nations as diverse as China and Russia, plus the EU–3 and the United States.

Kelly [Kelly O'Donnell, NBC News].

Iraq/War on Terror

Q. Morning, Mr. President. When you talked today about the violence in Baghdad, first you mentioned extremists, radicals, and then Al Qaida. It seems that Al Qaida and foreign fighters are much less of a problem there, and that it really is Iraqi versus Iraqi. And when we heard about your meeting the other day with experts and so forth, some of the reporting out of that said you were frustrated; you were surprised. And your spokesman said, no, you're determined. But frustration seems like a very real emotion. Why wouldn't you be frustrated, sir, about what's happening?

The President. I'm not—I do remember the meeting; I don't remember being surprised. I'm not sure what they meant by that.

Q. About the lack of gratitude among the Iraqi people.

The President. Oh. No, I think—first of all, to the first part of your question, if you look back at the words of Zarqawi before he was brought to justice, he made it clear that the intent of their tactics in Iraq was to create civil strife. In other words, if you—look at what he said. He said, "Let's kill Shi'a to get Shi'a to seek revenge," and therefore, to create this kind of, hopefully, cycle of violence.

Secondly, it's pretty clear that—at least the evidence indicates that the bombing of the shrine was—it was an Al Qaida plot, all intending to create sectarian violence. No, Al Qaida is still very active in Iraq. As a matter of fact, some of the more— I would guess, I would surmise that some of the more spectacular bombings are done by Al Qaida suiciders.

No question there's sectarian violence as well. And the challenge is to provide a security plan such that a political process can go forward. And I know—I'm sure you all are tired of hearing me say 12 million Iraqis voted, but it's an indication about the desire for people to live in a free society. That's what that means, see.

And the only way to defeat this ideology in the long term is to defeat it through another ideology, a competing ideology, one that—where Government responds to the will of the people. And that's really—really the fundamental question we face here in the beginning of this 21st century is whether or not we believe as a nation, and others believe, it is possible to defeat this ideology.

Now, I recognize, some say that these folks are not ideologically bound. I strongly disagree. I think not only do they have an ideology; they have tactics necessary to spread their ideology. And it would be a huge mistake for the United States to leave the region, to concede territory to the terrorists, to not confront them. And the best way to confront them is to help those who want to live in free society.

Look, eventually Iraq will succeed because the Iraqis will see to it that they succeed. And our job is to help them succeed. That's our job. Our job is to help their forces be better equipped, to help their police be able to deal with these extremists, and to help their Government succeed.

Q. But are you frustrated, sir?

The President. Frustrated? Sometimes I'm frustrated—rarely surprised. Sometimes I'm happy. This is—but war is not a time of joy. These aren't joyous times. These are challenging times, and they're difficult times, and they're straining the psyche of our country. I understand that. You know, nobody likes to see innocent people die. Nobody wants to turn on their TV on a daily basis and see havoc wrought by terrorists. And our question is, do we have the capacity and the desire to spread peace by confronting these terrorists and supporting those who want to live in liberty? That's the question. And my answer to that question is, we must. We owe it to future generations to do so.

Bill [Bill Plante, CBS News].

Situation in the Middle East/United Nations Security Council Resolution 1559

Q. Mr. President, as you have reminded us a number of times, it was Hizballah that started the confrontation between Israel and Lebanon. But you were supportive of the holding off of any kind of cease-fire until Israel had a chance to clear out the Hizballah weapons. By all accounts, they did not exactly succeed in doing that. And by all accounts, the Lebanese Army, as it moved into southern Lebanon, had a-wink-and-a-nod arrangement with Hizballah not to disturb anything, to just leave things as they are, a situation not unknown in the Middle East. Do you demand that the peacekeeping force, if and when it gets up and running, disarm Hizballah?

The President. The truth of the matter is, if 1559, that's the United Nations Security Council resolution number, had been fully implemented, we wouldn't be in the situation we were in to begin with. There is—there will be another resolution coming out of the United Nations giving further instructions to the international force. First things first—is to get the rules of engagement clear so that the force will be robust, to help the Lebanese.

One thing is for certain—is that when this force goes in to help Lebanon, Hizballah won't have that safe haven or that kind of freedom to run on the—in Lebanon's southern border. In other words, there's an opportunity to create a cushion, a security cushion. Hopefully, over time, Hizballah will disarm. You can't have a democracy with a armed political party willing to bomb its neighbor without the consent of its Government, or just deciding, well, "Let's just create enough chaos and discord by lobbing rockets."

And so the reality is, in order for Lebanon to succeed—and we want Lebanon's democracy to succeed—the process is going to—the Lebanese Government is eventually going to have to deal with Hizballah.

Q. But it's the status quo if there's no disarming.

The President. Not really. I mean, yes, eventually, you're right. But in the meantime, there will be a—there's a security zone, something to—where the Lebanese Army and the UNIFIL force are more robust, UNIFIL force can create a security zone between Lebanon and Israel. That would be helpful.

But ultimately, you're right. Your question is, shouldn't Hizballah disarm, and ultimately, they should. And it's necessary for the Lebanese Government to succeed.

The cornerstone of our policy in that part of the world is to help democracies. Lebanon is a democracy; we want the Siniora Government to succeed. Part of our aid package is going to be, help strengthen the army of Lebanon so when the Government speaks, when the Government commits its troops, they do so in an effective way.

Knoller [Mark Knoller, CBS Radio].

Presidential Pardons

Q. Yes, sir.

The President. How are you feeling?

Q. I'm good, sir. It's good to be back.

The President. Good to see you. Yes, it's good to see you. Sorry we didn't spend more time in Crawford. I knew you were anxious to do so.

Q. Always am.

The President. That's good. [*Laughter*] That's why we love seeing you.

Q. Thanks. Let me ask you about Presidential pardons. Last week, you issued 17 of them. That brought the number of pardons you've issued in your Presidency to 97, and that's far fewer than most of your recent predecessors, except your dad. And I want to ask you, do you consider yourself to be stingy when it comes to pardons? What is your philosophy on granting Presidential pardons?

The President. You know, I don't have the criterion in front of me, Mark, but we have a strict criterion that we utilize—"we" being the Justice Department and the White House Counsel. And I, frankly, haven't compared the number of pardons I've given, to any other President. Perhaps I should. But I don't think a scorecard should, necessarily, be the guidepost for pardoning people.

McKinnon [John McKinnon, Wall Street Journal]. I'm going to go to you, Jackson [David Jackson, USA Today], and kind of work around.

Energy/Alternative Fuel Sources

Q. Thanks. Mr. President, what do you say to people who are losing patience with gas prices at $3 a gallon? And how much of a political price do you think you're paying for that right now?

The President. I've been talking about gas prices ever since they got high, starting with this—look, I understand gas prices are like a hidden tax—not a hidden tax, it's a tax; it's taking money out of people's pockets. I know that. All the more reason for us to diversify away from crude oil. That's not going to happen overnight. We passed law that encouraged consumption through different purchasing habits, like hybrid vehicles. You buy a hybrid, you get a tax credit. We've encouraged the spread of ethanol as an alternative to crude oil. We have asked for Congress to pass regulatory relief so we can build more refineries to increase the supply of gasoline, hopefully taking the pressure off of price.

And so the strategy is to recognize that dependency upon crude oil is—in a global market affects us economically here at home, and therefore, we need to diversify away as quickly as possible.

Jackson.

Hurricane Katrina Recovery Efforts

Q. Thank you, Mr. President. As you know, the one-year anniversary of Katrina is coming up. And there are a lot of retrospectives about what went wrong down there last year. Specifically, what has your administration done in the past year to help the folks down there, and what remains to be done?

The President. Yes, thanks. You know, I went to New Orleans, in Jackson Square, and made a commitment that we would help the people there recover. I also want the people down there to understand that it's going to take a while to recover. This was a huge storm.

First things—the first thing that's necessary to help the recovery is money. And our Government has committed over $110 billion to help. Of that, a lot of money went to—went out the door to help people adjust from having to be moved because of the storm. And then there's rental assistance, infrastructure repair, debris removal. Mississippi removed about 97 percent, 98 percent of its what they call dry debris. We're now in the process of getting debris from the waters removed. Louisiana is slower in terms of getting debris removed. The money is available to help remove that debris. People can get after it, and I would hope they would.

Q. What——

The President. Let me finish. Thank you.

We provided about $1.8 billion for education. That money has gone out the door. We want those schools up and running. As I understand, the schools are running now in New Orleans; a lot of schools are. Flood insurance—we're spending money on flood insurance. There is more work to be done, particularly when it comes to housing. We've spent about—or appropriated about 16 billion—$17 billion for direct housing grants to people in the gulf coast and in Louisiana.

I made the decision, along with the local authorities, that each State ought to develop a housing recovery plan. That's what they call the LRA in Louisiana. They're responsible for taking the Federal money and getting it to the people. Same in— Mississippi has developed its own plan.

I thought it would be best that there be a local plan developed and implemented by local folks. And so there's now, as I

mentioned, $16 billion of direct housing grants. Each State has developed its own plan, how much money goes to each homeowner to help these people rebuild their lives. And so I think the area where people will see the most effect in their lives is when they start getting this individualized CDBG grant money.

Q. Is there anything that's disappointed you about the recovery, the Federal response?

The President. I was concerned at first about how much Congress and the taxpayers would be willing to appropriate and spend. I think $110 billion is a strong commitment, and I'm pleased with that. Any time we—I named a man named Don Powell to go down there, and the thing that's most important is for the Government to eliminate any bureaucratic obstacles when we find something that's not moving quick enough.

I think, for example, about debris removal. There was the issue of whether or not the Government would pay for debris removal on private property, or not. So we worked out a plan with the local mayors and local county commissioners, local parish presidents to be able to designate certain property as a health hazard. And when they did so, then Government money could pay for it. In other words, we're trying to be flexible with the rules and regulations we have to deal with.

But the place where people, I'm sure, are going to be most frustrated is whether or not they're going to get the money to rebuild their homes. And my attitude is, we've appropriated the money, and now we'll work with the States to get the money.

April [April Ryan, American Urban Radio Networks], I suspect you have a followup on this.

State and Local Government Role in Hurricane Recovery

Q. Yes, I do, sir.

The President. Why don't you let her go?

Q. And another question, sir. The followup: Some have a concern that you've given all of this money, but the Federal Government has moved away to let the local government, particularly in New Orleans, handle everything, and things are not moving like they expected. And that's one of the concerns. And another question, if you——

The President. Well, let me address that, and I promise you can ask that other one.

As I mentioned to you, the strategy from the get-go was to work with the local folks in Mississippi and Louisiana, and they would then submit their plans to the Federal Government, particularly for housing. And that upon approval, we would then disburse the appropriated monies—in this case, about $17 billion for housing grants. And so each State came up with a grant formula, and I can't give you all the details. But it's—the whole purpose is intended to get money into people's pockets to help them rebuild. And once the strategy is developed at the State and local level, it makes sense for the monies to be appropriated at the State and local level. And if there's a level of frustration there, we will work with the LRA, in this case.

Second question.

Q. Well, I have one followup on that. Do you think——

The President. Well, how many—are you trying to dominate this thing? [*Laughter*]

Q. No, sir, but I don't get a chance to talk to you as much as the others.

The President. That's not—wait a minute. [*Laughter*]

Q. But a followup real quick. Do you think that more needs to be done? Does the Federal Government need to put its hands on what's going on? Because New Orleans is not moving——

The President. I think the best way to do this is for the Federal Government's representative, Don Powell, to continue to work with Mayor Nagin and Governor Blanco to get the money into the hands of the people. The money has been appropriated; the formula is in place; and now it's time to move forward.

Now, you have another question, I presume.

North Korea

Q. Yes, sir. And this is it, sir. Chinese officials are saying that you need to get involved in the six-party talks, and that, ultimately, you have to be a part of the six-party talks in dealing with North Korea. And also, they're saying that you need to stop dealing with the issue of money laundering and deal with the real issue of ballistic missiles. What are your thoughts?

The President. Well, counterfeiting U.S. dollars is an issue that every President ought to be concerned about. And when you catch people counterfeiting your money, you need to do something about it.

We are very much involved in the six-party talks. As a matter of fact, I talked to Hu Jintao this morning about the six-party talks and about the need for us to continue to work together to send a clear message to the North Korean leader that there is a better choice for him than to continue to develop a nuclear weapon. The six-party talks are—is an important part of our—the six-party talks are an important part of our strategy of dealing with Kim Jong Il. And the North Korean—the Chinese President recognized that in the phone call today. And so we talked about how we'll continue to collaborate and work together.

Jim [Jim Rutenberg, New York Times].

War on Terror/Public Debate

Q. Thank you, Mr. President. You mentioned the campaign earlier. Do you agree with those in your party, including the Vice President, who have said or implied that Democratic voters emboldened Al Qaida types by choosing Ned Lamont over Joe Lieberman, and then as a message that— how Americans vote will send messages to terrorists abroad? Thank you.

The President. You're welcome. What all of us in this administration have been saying is that leaving Iraq before the mission is complete will send the wrong message to the enemy and will create a more dangerous world. That's what we're saying. It's an honest debate, and it's an important debate for Americans to listen to and to be engaged in. In our judgment, the consequences for defeat in Iraq are unacceptable.

And I fully understand that some didn't think we ought to go in there in the first place. But defeat—if you think it's bad now, imagine what Iraq would look like if the United States leaves before this Government can defend itself and sustain itself. Chaos in Iraq would be very unsettling in the region. Leaving before the job would be done would send a message that America really is no longer engaged, nor cares about the form of governments in the Middle East. Leaving before the job was done would send a signal to our troops that the sacrifices they made were not worth it. Leaving before the job is done would be a disaster, and that's what we're saying.

I will never question the patriotism of somebody who disagrees with me. This has nothing to do with patriotism; it has everything to do with understanding the world in which we live. It's like the other day; I was critical of those who heralded the Federal judge's opinion about the terrorist surveillance program. I thought it was a terrible opinion, and that's why we're appealing it. And I have no—look, I understand how democracy works—quite a little bit of criticism in it, which is fine; that's fine; it's part of the process. But I have every right, as do my administration, to make it clear what the consequences would be of policy. And if we think somebody is wrong or doesn't see the world the way it is, we'll continue to point that out to people.

And therefore, those who heralded the decision not to give law enforcement the tools necessary to protect the American people simply don't see the world the way we do. They see, maybe these are kind of isolated incidents. These aren't isolated incidents; they're tied together. There is a global war going on. And somebody said, "Well, this is law enforcement." No, this isn't law enforcement, in my judgment. Law enforcement means kind of a simple, singular response to the problem. This is a global war on terror. We're facing extremists that believe something, and they want to achieve objectives. And therefore, the United States must use all our assets, and we must work with others to defeat this enemy. That's the call. And we—in the short run, we've got to stop them from attacking us. That's why I give the Tony Blair Government great credit, and their intelligence officers, and our own Government credit for working with the Brits to stop this attack.

But you know something—it's an amazing town, isn't it, where they say, on the one hand, "You can't have the tools necessary—we herald the fact that you won't have the tools necessary to defend the people," and sure enough, an attack would occur, and say, "How come you don't have the tools necessary to defend the people?" That's the way we think around this town.

And so, yes, we'll continue—Jim, we'll continue to speak out in a respectful way, never challenging somebody's love for America when you criticize their strategies or their point of view. And, you know, for those who say that, well, all they're trying to say is, we're not patriotic, simply don't listen to our words very carefully, do they?

What matters is that in this campaign that we clarify the different point of view. And there are a lot of people in the Democrat Party who believe that the best course of action is to leave Iraq before the job is done, period. And they're wrong. And the American people have got to understand the consequence of leaving Iraq before the job is done. We're not going to leave Iraq before the job is done, and we'll complete the mission in Iraq. I can't tell you exactly when it's going to be done, but I do know that it's important for us to support the Iraqi people, who have shown incredible courage in their desire to live in a free society. And if we ever give up the desire to help people who live in freedom, we will have lost our soul as a nation, as far as I'm concerned.

Ann [Ann Compton, ABC Radio].

2006 Midterm Elections/Iraq

Q. Is that a make-or-break issue for you, in terms of domestic politics? There's a Republican in Pennsylvania who says he doesn't think the troops should—would you campaign for Mike Fitzpatrick?

The President. I already have.

Q. And would you campaign against Senator Joe Lieberman, whose Republican candidate may support you, but he supports you too, on Iraq?

The President. I'm going to stay out of Connecticut. [*Laughter*]

Q. It's your native State, Mr. President. You were born there.

The President. Shhh. [*Laughter*] I may be the only person—the only Presidential candidate who never carried the State in which he was born. Do you think that's right, Herman? Of course, you would have researched that and dropped it out for everybody to see, particularly since I dissed that just ridiculous looking outfit. [*Laughter*]

Q. Your mother raised you better than that, Mr. President.

The President. That is—so I'm not going to say it——

Q. There is Al Gore.

The President. I don't want anybody to know that I think it's ridiculous. Look, I'm not through yet.

Q. ——make-or-break issue for you?

The President. And by the way, I'm staying out of Connecticut because that's what the party suggested, the Republican Party of Connecticut. And plus, there's a better place to spend our money, time, and resources——

Q. But you're the head of the party.

The President. Right. I've listened to them very carefully. I'm a thoughtful guy. I listen to people. [*Laughter*] I'm open-minded. I'm all the things that you know I am.

The other part of your question? Look, issues are won based upon whether or not you can keep this economy strong—elections are won based upon economic issues and national security issues. And there's a fundamental difference between many of the Democrats and my party, and that is, they want to leave before the job is completed in Iraq. And again, I repeat, these are decent people. They're just as American as I am. I just happen to strongly disagree with them. And it's very important for the American people to understand the consequences of leaving Iraq before the job is done.

This is a global war on terror. I repeat what our major general said—or leading general said, in the region. He said, "If we withdraw before the job is done, the enemy will follow us here." I strongly agree with that. And if you believe that the job of the Federal Government is to secure this country, it's really important for you to understand that success in Iraq is part of securing the country.

We're talking about a long-term issue here as well, Ann. In the short term, we've got to have the tools necessary to stop terrorist attack. That means good intel, good intelligence sharing, the capacity to know whether Al Qaida is calling into this country and why. We've got to have all those tools, the PATRIOT Act, the tearing down those walls between intel and law enforcement are a necessary part of protecting the country. But in the long term, the only way to defeat this terrorist bunch is through the spread of liberty and freedom.

And that's a big challenge. I understand it's a challenge. It requires commitment and patience and persistence. I believe it's the challenge of this—the challenge for this generation. I believe we owe it to our children and grandchildren to stay engaged and to help spread liberty and to help reformers.

Now, ultimately, success is going to be up to the reformers. Just like in Iraq, it's going to require Iraqis—the will of Iraqis to succeed. I understand that. And that's why our strategy is to give them the tools necessary to defend themselves and help them defend themselves, in this case, right now, mainly in Baghdad, but, as well, around the country.

At home, if I were a candidate, if I were running, I'd say, look at what the economy has done. It's strong. We created a lot of jobs—let me finish my question, please. These hands going up—I'm not—I'm kind of getting old and just getting into my peroration. [*Laughter*] Look it up. [*Laughter*] I'd be telling people that the Democrats will raise your taxes. That's what they said. I'd be reminding people that tax cuts have worked in terms of stimulating the economy. I'd be reminding people, there's a philosophical difference between those who want to raise taxes and have the Government spend the money, and those of us who say, you get to spend the money the way you want to—see fit; it's your money. I'd remind people that progrowth economic policies have helped us cut that deficit faster than we thought.

I'd also remind people, if I were running, that the long-term problem facing the budget is Social Security and Medicare. And they look—Republican or Democrat ought to say, "I look forward to working with the President to solve the problem." People expect us to come here to solve problems, and thus far, the attitude has been, let's just kind of ignore what the President has said and just hope somebody else comes and solves it for us.

And that's what I'd be running on. I'd be running on the economy, and I'd be running on national security. But since I'm not running, I can only serve as an adviser to those who are.

Yes, Herman.

Public Opinion Polls/Iraq

Q. Thank you, sir. Go ahead. [*Laughter*]

The President. I don't need to, now that you've stood up and everybody can clearly see for themselves. [*Laughter*]

Q. Mr. President, polls continue to show sagging support for the war in Iraq. I'm curious as to how you see this developing. Is it your belief that long-term results will vindicate your strategy and people will change their mind about it, or is this the kind of thing you're doing because you think it's right and you don't care if you ever gain public support for it? Thank you.

The President. Thank you. Look, I mean, Presidents care about whether people support their policies. I don't mean to say, I don't care; of course I care. But I understand why people are discouraged about Iraq—I can understand that. There is—we live in a world in which people, I guess, hope things happen quickly, and this is a situation where things don't happen quickly because there's a very tough group of people using tactics, mainly the killing of innocent people, to achieve their objective. And they're skillful about how they do this, and they also know the impact of what it means on the consciousness of those of us who live in the free world. They know that.

And so yes, I care; I really do. I wish— and so therefore, I'm going to spend a lot of time trying to explain as best as I can why it's important for us to succeed in Iraq.

Q. Can I follow——

The President. Let me finish. On the other hand, Ken, I don't think you've ever heard me say—and you've now been covering me for quite a while, 12 years—I don't think I've—12 years? Yes. Exactly. Yes. I don't think you've ever heard me say, "Gosh, I'd better change positions because the polls say this or that." I've been here long enough to understand, you cannot make good decisions if you're trying to chase a poll. And so the second part of your question is, look, I'm going to do what I think is right, and if people don't like me for it, that's just the way it is.

War on Terror/Spread of Democracy in the Middle East

Q. Quick followup: A lot of the consequences you mentioned for pulling out seem like maybe they never would have been there if we hadn't gone in. How do you square all of that?

The President. I square it because, imagine a world in which you had Saddam Hussein who had the capacity to make a weapon of mass destruction, who was paying suiciders to kill innocent life, who would—who had relations with Zarqawi. Imagine what the world would be like with him in power. The idea is to try to help change the Middle East.

Now, look, part of the reason we went into Iraq was—the main reason we went into Iraq at the time was we thought he had weapons of mass destruction. It turns out he didn't, but he had the capacity to make weapons of mass destruction. But I also talked about the human suffering in Iraq, and I also talked the need to advance a freedom agenda. And so my question—my answer to your question is, is that, imagine a world in which Saddam Hussein was there, stirring up even more trouble in a part of the world that had so much resentment and so much hatred that people came and killed 3,000 of our citizens.

You know, I've heard this theory about everything was just fine until we arrived, and then—kind of the "stir up the hornet's nest" theory. It just doesn't hold water, as far as I'm concerned. The terrorists attacked us and killed 3,000 of our citizens before we started the freedom agenda in the Middle East.

Q. What did Iraq have to do with that?

The President. What did Iraq have to do with what?

Q. The attack on the World Trade Center?

The President. Nothing, except for it's part of—and nobody has ever suggested in this administration that Saddam Hussein ordered the attack. Iraq was a—the lesson of September the 11th is, take threats before they fully materialize, Ken. Nobody has ever suggested that the attacks of September the 11th were ordered by Iraq. I have suggested, however, that resentment and the lack of hope create the breeding grounds for terrorists who are willing to use suiciders to kill to achieve an objective. I have made that case.

And one way to defeat that—defeat resentment is with hope. And the best way to do hope is through a form of government. Now, I said going into Iraq, we've got to take these threats seriously before they fully materialize. I saw a threat. I fully believe it was the right decision to remove Saddam Hussein, and I fully believe the world is better off without him. Now the question is, how do we succeed in Iraq? And you don't succeed by leaving before the mission is complete, like some in this political process are suggesting.

Last question. Stretch [Bill Sammon, Washington Examiner]. Who are you working for, Stretch?

Food and Drug Administration/Plan B Contraceptive Pill

Q. Washington Examiner.

The President. Oh, good. I'm glad you found work. [*Laughter*]

Q. Thank you very much. Mr. President, some pro-life groups are worried that your choice of FDA Commissioner will approve over the counter sales of Plan B, a pill that, they say, essentially can cause early-term abortions. Do you stand by this choice, and how do you feel about Plan B in general?

The President. I believe that Plan B ought to be—ought to require a prescription for minors; that's what I believe. And I support Andy's decision.

James S. Brady Press Briefing Room Renovation

The President. Thanks for letting me come by the new digs here.

Q. Do you like them?

The President. They may be a little too fancy for you.

Q. We'd be happy to go back.

Q. Are we coming back?

Q. Ever?

The President. Absolutely, you're coming back.

Q. Can we hold you to that?

The President. Coming back to the bosom of the White House. [*Laughter*] I'm looking forward to hugging you when you come back, everybody. When are you coming back?

Q. As soon as they can have us.

Q. You tell us.

Q. May.

The President. May, is that when it is scheduled?

Q. They've sealed off of our—they sealed off the door. We're wondering if we're really coming back or not.

Q. The decision will be made by commanders on the ground, sir. [*Laughter*]

Q. There's no timetable.

The President. What do you think this is, a correspondents dinner or something? [*Laughter*]

Thank you all.

Q. Thank you, sir.

Q. Want to come down and see our workspace?

The President. No. [*Laughter*]

NOTE: The President's news conference began at 10:02 a.m. at the White House Conference Center Briefing Room. In his remarks, he referred to Prime Minister Nuri al-Maliki and former President Saddam Hussein of Iraq; Gen. John P. Abizaid, USA, commander, U.S. Central Command; Prime Minister Fuad Siniora of Lebanon; Mayor C. Ray Nagin of New Orleans, LA; Gov. Kathleen Babineaux Blanco of Louisiana; President Hu Jintao of China; Chairman Kim Jong Il of North Korea; U.S. District Court Judge for the Eastern District of Michigan Anna Diggs Taylor; and Prime Minister Tony Blair of the United Kingdom. Reporters referred to senatorial candidates Ned Lamont and Alan Schlesinger of Connecticut; and former Vice President Al Gore.

Remarks in a Discussion on Health Care in Minneapolis, Minnesota
August 22, 2006

The President. Thank you very much. Thank you. Please be seated. Thank you for coming. Thanks for the warm welcome. We've got some work to do. [*Laughter*]

Thanks for being here today. And I want to thank our panelists for joining Secretary Leavitt and me to talk about health care. And before we do, I want to say a couple of words about some of the guests here. First, I'm real proud to be here with your Governor, Tim Pawlenty. Governor, thanks for being here. Senator Norman Coleman is with us. Senator, thanks for coming. Three Members of the Congress—Jim

Ramstad, whose district we're in; Mark Kennedy is with us; John Kline is with us. Thanks for coming.

We've got members of the statehouse here. We've got local officials—Mayor Jan Callison, the mayor of—Mayor, thanks for coming. This is the 50th anniversary of Minnetonka, right? Yes, good. Congratulations. Wait until you turn 60. [*Laughter*] It's not as old as it sounds. [*Laughter*]

We're going to have an interesting dialog today. I'm going to sign an Executive order after a while, but I want to explain why we're signing the Executive order to you.

We've got an interesting debate in health care in America. And I guess if I had to summarize how I view it, I would say there's a choice between having the government make decisions or consumers make decisions. I stand on the side of encouraging consumers. I think the most important relationship in health care is between the patient and their provider, the patient and the doc. [*Applause*] Thank you. And health care policy ought to be aimed at bolstering the consumer. Empowering individuals to be responsible for health care decisions is kind of the crux about what we're talking about.

Obviously, all of us are concerned about costs. You know, I hear it a lot. We talk about—we'll hear from Jane Brown here, who helps those who need help here in your community. She says health care costs oftentimes make it hard for people to buy food. You talk to small-business owners and one of the big concerns they have is the cost of health care, that many, in order to stay in business, you know, have to say to their employee, "You provide for yourself." And that's troubling. It's troubling. It doesn't matter what your political party is; it's an issue that needs to be addressed

And so the fundamental question is, how do you address cost, given the philosophy that I've just described to you? And so here are some ideas I'd like to share with you.

One way to help small businesses address the cost of rising insurance is to allow them to pool risk across jurisdictional boundaries. In other words, if you're a restaurant in Minnesota and you're a restaurant in Texas, you ought to be allowed to pool your employees into a employee risk pool so that the insurance is lower because of the spreading of risk. Those are called association health plans. One idea to—that says basically, the small-business owner will be in charge of the health care for his or her company—is to encourage association health plans.

Another idea is to make sure that—let me take a step back. There is a very important role for the Federal Government in health care. And that is to provide for the elderly and the poor. One of the things that Mike and I have worked on, and I hope some of you have helped with, is to encourage seniors to take a look at the new Medicare drug benefit. I was very concerned that Medicare had gone stale, and it needed to be reformed. Medicare is a vital program, and it's an important Federal program. And it worked.

The problem is, medicine had changed and Medicare hadn't. Medicare would pay, you know, $100,000 for an operation but not a dime for the prescription drugs that would prevent the operation from being needed in the first place. And it didn't make any sense. It didn't make any sense to the seniors, nor did it make any sense to the taxpayers. So we've changed Medicare. And if you're a poor senior in America, the Government is going to really help you with prescription drugs. And if you're not a poor senior, you'll save a half on your drug—prescription drugs. It's a good deal.

The Federal Government has also got a role in helping the poor through Medicaid. And one of the tasks that I've given to Michael Leavitt is to say to the Governors, "You should have the flexibility necessary to design a Medicaid program that meets the needs of your citizens."

Now, having said that, here's what we need to continue to do in the private sector. One of the problems to make sure health care is affordable and available is the legal system. And, look, it's out of kilter. We want everybody to have justice. But unfortunately, particularly in medicine, there are too many frivolous and junk lawsuits that are running good doctors out of practice and running up the cost of medicine. Do you realize that in order to avoid lawsuits, many doctors practice what's called defensive medicine? In other words, they prescribe medicines that may not be necessary or procedures that may not be necessary, just in case they get hauled into the court of law. As a matter of fact, it's estimated that the defensive practice of medicine costs your Federal Government, costs you, the taxpayer, $28 billion a year.

Now, when I first went to Washington, I said, "Well, this is an issue that ought to be solved at the State level," until I realized the budgetary impact that these lawsuits are having on you, the taxpayer. And so I went to Congress and worked with the House, and we got a good medical liability reform law out of the House. Unfortunately, it's stuck in the Senate. The trial lawyers are tough in Washington, by the way. They really don't want to see medical liability reform. But if you're interested in making sure the system works, if you want people to have access to affordable health care and have doctors that are around to practice to begin with, you need to have strong medical liability reform in order to make the health care system work.

Thirdly, have you ever watched how these files work in medicine? We're going to talk to Dr. Dean here in a minute. Her penmanship is probably pretty good—[*laughter*]—but most doctors don't write too well, and yet they write a lot in files. What I'm telling you is, medicine is really behind the times when it comes to information technology. And one of the things we'll talk about here is how to use information technology to wring the costs out of medicine and yet be able to deliver good quality care to our citizens.

It's estimated that between 25—that we can reduce costs by 25 to 30 percent with the advent of what we call medical—electric medical records, so each person has got their own electronic medical record that you've got data on. In other words, we'll be passing information from provider to provider via the Internet, via new technology as opposed to handwritten files that are carried from one office to the other. We're going to spend some time talking about that. It is a practical way to help control medical costs so people have got health care that's available and affordable.

Fourthly, we've got to make sure that we have plans that encourage consumer saving, in other words, insurance plans, products for people to be able to use in order to get health care that encourages savings. One idea is health savings accounts. These are plans where you buy a high-deductible catastrophic plan. You contribute money tax-free, but you're the consumer, you're the decisionmaker when it comes to health care. You decide. You decide what doctor you see.

Think about the system today as a third-party payer. How many of you have got insurance, and you never really cared about the cost because somebody else is paying the bill, right? You don't really care about the quality because some person in an office somewhere is paying the bill on your behalf. It's called a third-party payer system. It's the prevalent system today.

One of the things we're trying to encourage is the design of new opportunities for citizens to be able to get quality health care where they're in charge of the decisionmaking, that encourages people to make rational savings. If we have more consumer involvement in health care, then it makes sense—if that's the goal—then it makes sense to make sure that consumers have got rational data from which to make choices. And that's not the case today in medicine, really, when you think about it.

I don't know how many of you all have ever said, "Gosh, I wonder how much this procedure is going to cost me," or, "Before I go to see this person, I want to know how much it costs," or, "Maybe I need to know what this hospital charges." I doubt many of you have done that. I think the new trend in medicine is going to be to encourage transparency in pricing as well as transparency in quality. And that's the subject of today's discussion. How do we encourage consumerism. What do you do? Well, one thing you do is you make sure people understand their options, how much something costs. And if they decide to make a purchase, what do they expect;

what are the expectations from the consumer?

The Federal Government has got a lot to do with this because we spend a lot of money in health care, when you really think about Medicaid and Medicare, veterans' benefits, Department of Defense. And one of the initiatives Mike is now going to undertake is to say, "In order to do business with the Federal Government, you've got to show us your prices and you've got to help us develop a qualitative standard so the people that we're trying to help know what they're getting."

And so here are some practical ways to address the rising cost of medicine. These are ways that basically say, we want you, the consumer, in charge, that there is such thing as a market, and that markets function. You remember Lasik surgery, eye surgery? It's a place where—it was a procedure that cost a lot of money when it first came on, and yet there was quite a bit of competition. People said, "Look, I'm good at this. Why don't you come to my shop?" Or you noticed docs were advertising; all of a sudden, the cost of laser surgery has dropped precipitously. It's now affordable procedure. Markets work when consumers have got options to make in the marketplace.

And that's what this Executive order is going to do. I'm going to have Mike describe the Executive order to you here in a minute. But it's an order that basically commits the Federal Government to work with State and local and docs and hospitals to lead the way, to be a part of this new movement about transparency in pricing and quality.

Have I done it all right?

Secretary of Health and Human Services Michael O. Leavitt. You've done a good job, Mr. President. [*Laughter*]

The President. That's what he's supposed to say.

[*At this point, Secretary Leavitt made brief remarks.*]

The President. There's a lot of savings, by the way, when you're not writing things down on paper. Just ask some of the more modern businesses here in Minnesota, where your unemployment rate is, like, really low because of the productivity of your companies. One reason why is, they use information technology.

Sorry, Secretary.

[*Secretary Leavitt made further remarks.*]

The President. Yes. Why don't you talk to them about electronic medical records? I didn't do a very good job of describing it.

Secretary Leavitt. When——

The President. I'll give it a stab, and then you come back in.

Secretary Leavitt. All right. Got you. [*Laughter*]

The President. So one of these days, you're going to have all your medical records on a little key that you can then plug into a computer, and all of a sudden, information is at the provider's fingertips, which makes the system a lot more efficient, which means less costly, but also saves on medical errors. But the problem we face is that the—we've got to develop a standard language. Medicine is a fairly complicated—got a complicated dictionary, let's put it that way. So what's the procedure on that, Mike?

[*Secretary Leavitt made further remarks, concluding as follows.*]

Secretary Leavitt. My mother went to the doctor the other day. She told me that she filled out her name, address, insurance company name, birth date, telephone number—seven different times. Now, that's not necessary——

The President. My mother wouldn't have been so patient as your mother. [*Laughter*] I hope she's not watching. [*Laughter*] Good job, Michael.

Michael Howe is an interesting character here. He is an entrepreneur who's come up with a unique idea on how to help people have affordable and available health care.

Michael, did you start your deal—like, are you the classic entrepreneur, start in the garage?

Michael Howe. No, actually, I have to give credit; there were other groups. There were physicians and entrepreneurs that devised the mechanism, devised the innovation that MinuteClinic really represents.

The President. Okay, well, tell people what MinuteClinic is. If you haven't heard about it, it's worth listening.

[*Mr. Howe, chief executive officer, MinuteClinic, made brief remarks.*]

The President. What's process management? Tell people what that is.

Mr. Howe. Well, the interesting thing is, you can go through, and when you do something—strep test, a strep throat test—if you do thousands of strep throat tests, you can——

The President. You've got a problem, if there's thousands of strep tests. [*Laughter*]

Mr. Howe. You do. You have a problem. But you also have an opportunity.

The President. Yes, right. Okay. [*Laughter*] That's the spirit. [*Laughter*] Sorry. Go ahead.

Mr. Howe. No, no, it's all right. You have an opportunity to measure the effectiveness of one provider versus the next. You have an opportunity to measure treatment protocols.

[*Mr. Howe made further remarks.*]

The President. So do you have one in a shopping mall?

Mr. Howe. Absolutely. We have one in the Eden Prairie Mall right over here in Minnesota.

The President. Really? Isn't that interesting?

Mr. Howe. And the idea——

The President. A person walking down there looking, and says, "Here's the—if you need help, here are the costs."

Mr. Howe. That's right.

The President. Posted right there for them to see on——

Mr. Howe. Absolutely. And to compare it to where they go. It's also right-sized. And what I mean by that, it's a small facility. It's focused on a very specific scope of practice; common family ailments that some estimates are as high as 40 percent of the medical visits in today's society, are covered by these conditions.

So this is an opportunity to provide a higher quality care, transparent pricing, but also much more affordable. Our prices are 40 to 50 percent of what it would cost anywhere else.

The President. And are people going?

Mr. Howe. Well, in the last 6 years, we've completed 500,000 patient visits; we've had no malpractice claims; consumers tell us that their patient satisfaction runs between 97 and 98 percent; 99.6 percent of our patients tell us they'd use the service again, refer it to family and friend. Clearly, the providers we selected do a tremendous job making the emotional connection that delivers the end result that we're really looking for.

[*Mr. Howe made further remarks.*]

The President. Well, in order to have electronic medical records, there has to be a standardization in medicine to begin with.

You know, it's interesting, isn't it? It's an interesting idea he had, and it's meeting a consumer need. That stands in stark contrast to the government making the decisions for you, is to make different options available to patients. And you're providing health care at a 40 percent or 50 percent——

Mr. Howe. It's half the cost.

The President. Yes, it's great. Thanks for doing what you're doing. And you're in other States?

Mr. Howe. Yes, we have 86 clinics across 11 States at this point. We anticipate some very significant growth over the next few years.

The President. Yes, you ought to.

Mr. Howe. We're going to drive them very hard.

The President. Nothing better than being with an entrepreneur, isn't it? [*Laughter*] Thanks, Michael.

Marilyn, thanks for joining us.

Marilyn Carlson Nelson. Delighted to be here.

The President. We're thrilled you're here—chairman of the board, CEO of one of Minnesota's great companies, Carlson Companies. Thanks for joining us. What's on your mind?

Ms. Carlson Nelson. Well, first of all, I want to say thank you. I think we've been waiting at Carlson and in this community for about 20 years to hear what we've just heard, and that is inoperability, standards, quality standards, incentives.

At Carlson, we've worked with the Business Health Care Action Group for—I think we started almost 20 years ago now—to look at how to incentivize providers to have more transparency. We've worked on involving and engaging our employee base in preventative—various kinds of preventative activities. But recently we've put in several innovations—one, I have to say, a MinuteClinic in our headquarters.

The President. You saved 50 percent, I hope? [*Laughter*]

Ms. Carlson Nelson. Actually, we did the research. It looked as if a cost to us and our employees was about $40 to $50 through MinuteClinic for this certain set of services; it was, like, $100 in the doctor's office and dramatically more than that in the emergency room, where a lot of people end up going for that kind of care.

[*Ms. Carlson Nelson, chairman of the board, chief executive officer, and president, Carlson Companies, made brief remarks.*]

The President. This is an issue that we're focusing on the core problem, and that is, we're dealing with an industry that really is not modern, that needs help in the legal profession, and that needs more con-

sumerism. You know, you mentioned preventative health. Nothing that will cause somebody to take good care of their body than a—than having an insurance program that encourages savings. You make rational decisions and you exercise and you don't smoke and watch your drinking; it's amazing how your health improves. If you walk 2 miles every day, it really makes a big difference.

And if you have policies that say there's an incentive for you, you benefit from making that kind of rational decision, you monetarily benefit—like the health savings accounts, it helps with prevention. If people really watched what they ate, it's amazing how health care costs would also go down in America as well.

Yes, Michael.

Secretary Leavitt. Mr. President, there is—this is a good thing for our health, and it's a good thing for the system. It's also an economic imperative that we do it.

The President. Yes.

Secretary Leavitt. What Ms. Carlson suggested, I'm hearing from employers all over the country. Health care is now 16 percent of our gross domestic product, and it's headed for 20 percent. And there's really not a place on the economic leader board for a country that continues to spend more and more and more in one sector.

I was looking at the—and it's hitting consumers. I was looking in my home State at the teachers. They've got the largest increase——

The President. What is your home State?

Secretary Leavitt. That's Utah, by the way. [*Laughter*] And yet the teachers, many of them, end up having less take-home pay because of the cost of health care.

[*Secretary Leavitt made further remarks.*]

The President. Jim Chase. What do you do, Jim?

Jim Chase. Well, Mr. President, I work with an organization here in Minnesota that's been working on many of the things that you and Secretary Leavitt have talked about, and we're quite excited to have you here today.

[*Mr. Chase, executive director, MN Community Measurement made brief remarks.*]

The President. And so, like, what is your group—what's the name of your group?

Mr. Chase. We're called Minnesota——

The President. I know, but—[*laughter*].

Mr. Chase Minnesota Community Measurement. We're a non-profit that's been together for about 3 years.

The President. Really? And so the local folks came together and said, "Let's give old Jim some work and figure out how to do—[*laughter*]—have a health care system that works well."

Mr. Chase. My work came later. [*Laughter*] But I think what's exciting is that we're actually seeing some changes now. Being able to measure this, we're seeing the results change. And it's very encouraging, I think, for the providers out there who are—that's what they were in this for, was to find ways to treat their patients better.

[*Mr. Chase made further remarks.*]

The President. So, like, how many community measurement groups are there in the country, do you suspect? It sounds like it's pretty unique.

Mr. Chase. Yes. There are several that have started. In fact, we're pleased to be working with Secretary Leavitt in the Ambulatory Quality Alliance that has formed nationally, that are bringing together, to start with, six sites around the country that are in various stages of pulling together this kind of information.

[*Mr. Chase made further remarks.*]

The President. Good work. Thanks. It must be exciting to be, kind of, on the leading edge of substantial change.

Mr. Chase. It keeps us busy. [*Laughter*]

The President. That's good. I know the feeling. [*Laughter*]

We are joined by Dr. Laura Dean, ob-gyn. I will start off by telling you a startling statistic: There are 1,600 counties in the United States without an ob-gyn. I mean, we're talking about availability and affordability; obviously, 1,600 counties have got a serious problem.

Thanks for hanging in there.

Laura Dean. You're welcome.

The President. A lot of ob-gyns are leaving the practice because they're getting sued out of existence, pure and simple. I can't put it any more plainly than that. If you want to have ob-gyns in America, we need medical liability reform to protect these good people.

Step up, Doc. How long have you been practicing?

Dr. Dean. I've been practicing obstetrics and gynecology for 10 years in the community of Stillwater, and I've delivered more than 1,500 babies.

The President. Really?

Dr. Dean. Yes, sir.

The President. That's good. [*Laughter*] What's on your mind?

Dr. Dean. Well, I—certainly, as a physician, my goal is to help my patients make good decisions about their health care. And I'm excited about what you're here to talk about today, because I've been providing them with all kinds of medical information to help make decisions, but the financial piece has been missing. And people need that piece in order to make good and whole decisions.

The President. So, like, are you going to put on the window, you know, Dr. Laura Dean, 100 bucks? [*Laughter*] How does it—are you an individual practitioner?

Dr. Dean. I'm in a group practice with family practice doctors, other ob-gyns, internists, pediatricians.

[*Dr. Dean, ob-gyn, Stillwater Medical Group and Lakeview Hospital, made brief remarks.*]

The President. See, it's interesting, isn't it—kind of a mindset change. It used to be you'd go in and just take whatever they gave you, because somebody else is paying the bill. And if we can get a system down where people are able to have a good program, a good product, good insurance, but where the consumer has more to say with what's purchased or not, all of a sudden, the dynamic begins to change and costs begin to go down. You know, the good doc here volunteered to us all you don't need this procedure.

That cost—that saves money over time. The whole system benefits if we have a thousand providers making that same decision on an hourly basis. And so what Laura is saying is, if consumers have more information from which to make decisions, all of a sudden, costs begin to become less of a burden on the system, I think is what you're saying.

Dr. Dean. Absolutely.

The President. Lawsuits bothering you? Obviously, look, I led the witness. [*Laughter*] Not even a lawyer, and I led the witness. [*Laughter*]

Dr. Dean. Certainly it is something looming over the heads of physicians every day, the thought about lawsuits, really—maybe ordering tests to protect yourself and to make sure. I have many colleagues similar in age to me, which is not real old yet, in practice of medicine——

The President. Twenty-seven. [*Laughter*]

Dr. Dean. ——who have stopped delivering babies, who have stopped performing surgery.

The President. It's a problem; you've got a problem. It is a problem when society starts losing good souls that otherwise would be ob-gyns. It's a real problem, and we better do something about it. It's one thing to have good law; we want good law. But these frivolous lawsuits are a real problem for the people of Minnesota and all across the United States. It's serious business. These trial lawyers need to back off, and these politicians in the United States Senate, people like Coleman, need to step up. And he will. [*Laughter*] And he has.

No, he's been strong; he's been strong on medical liability reform. I'm not trying to turn this thing into a political deal. I'm just telling you, for the sake of this country, for the sake of good medicine, we better get some good medical liability reform out of the United States Senate.

Thanks, Dr. Dean.

Dr. Dean. Thank you.

The President. Thanks for practicing. One of the wonderful things about America is our health care providers are fantastic people. They really are decent, honorable people who've answered a higher calling. And we appreciate—[*inaudible*].

Dr. Dean. Thank you. Thank you, sir.

The President. Speaking about a higher calling, Jane Brown, executive director, Second Harvest Heartland. Has anybody ever heard of Second Harvest Heartland? Good. So you don't need to tell them what you do. Actually, you're feeding people who need help.

Rachel "Jane" Brown. That's correct, sir.

The President. Actually, if people need— I presume it's okay for me to say, you could use some contributions?

Ms. Brown. Oh, my, yes. That's a wonderful thing for you to say. [*Laughter*]

The President. Seriously. I know Marilyn will help you. [*Laughter*]

Ms. Brown. Thank you for that.

The President. She has.

Ms. Carlson Nelson. Yes. [*Laughter*]

The President. She has been helping, as has corporate Minnesota.

Ms. Brown. Yes, corporate Minnesota has been very good to us. And the Carlson Companies are wonderful.

Second Harvest Heartland is a food bank, and we have 800 agencies that get their food from us, so every little bit helps, so thank you for that.

The President. Yes. Well, we were talking—actually, the reason that this subject came up is I was asking her whether or not she had enough product to help people who need help, and the answer is, never enough.

Ms. Brown. Never enough, no, nowhere near enough yet.

The President. Yes. But you've done some interesting things through health care.

Ms. Brown. We have. We have—Marilyn and I were contrasting—she has a huge company; there are 76 employees at Second Harvest Heartland and 66 who receive their health insurance through our organization. And this last year, we offered an HSA for the first time as one of the options, and 15 percent—or 10 of those employees—opted to take it. And I'm one of those who opted to take it.

The President. Everybody understand what that is? It's, again, a high-deductible catastrophic plan, and that the person and/or company can put money in tax-free to cover up to the deductible.

Ms. Brown. That's great.

The President. Which actually saves money.

Ms. Brown. It saves money. It does so many things, and that's why we've chosen it.

[*Ms. Brown made brief remarks.*]

The President. And you contribute into the savings account?

Ms. Brown. Yes. As the employer, yes, we do.

The President. One hundred percent?

Ms. Brown. No. It's a shared responsibility, and that's very important, that there's a shared responsibility in that.

[*Ms. Brown made further remarks.*]

The President. Right, right. This is a—Jane has given her employees a very interesting option, and that is a consumer-driven plan where there is a incentive to save, to be a good shopper, and to make rational choices about how you live your life. And if you live a healthy lifestyle, you're going to spend less money out of the money she has contributed into their health account. But the money is yours. In other words, there's a catastrophic plan available; you may pay the first 3,000—the $3,000 is on the company, and anything above $3,000 goes to the insurance company.

So you can see, if you don't spend the $3,000, and you're able to roll it over, tax-free, and then there's another 3,000 contributed next year, and you roll over money you save, pretty soon you've got a good health savings account, because the Government doesn't tax any of it. It doesn't tax the money going in; it doesn't tax the earnings; and it doesn't tax the money coming out.

And if you change jobs—by the way, which is an interesting statistic in our society today. Somebody told me the other day that people change jobs about eight times before they're 32 years old. That wasn't the case when we were growing up.

Ms. Brown. No, it wasn't. [*Laughter*]

The President. Anyway, doesn't it make sense to have a plan that you can carry with you? That's called portability. And so what Jane has provided her employees is something that encourages consumerism but also helps meet their needs, and that's what medicine has got to do. It's got to meet the needs of the consumer, not the government. And that's what we're talking about, innovative ideas, innovative ways to help control costs in health care.

And I hope you've gained something from this conversation. At the very least, please leave with the notion that we're thinking differently, because you need to think differently. The system right now needs reform and needs to be fixed. And you're fortunate in the State of Minnesota that you've got leadership at the State and local and the corporate and individual level that is willing to think differently to help a new system evolve. And it's coming, and it's going to make a huge difference for people's lives.

And I want to thank all our panelists for joining us today. It's been a fascinating conversation. God bless you all.

Oh, wait a minute, now I'm going to sign an Executive order. And I think you'll find this interesting. It doesn't take very long, and we usually have people stand behind me when I do it. [*Laughter*]

You ready, Pawlenty?

[*The President signed the Executive order.*]

The President. Done.

NOTE: The President spoke at 2:41 p.m. at the Minneapolis Marriott Southwest. In his remarks, he referred to Mayor Jan Callison of Minnetonka, MN. The Executive order on promoting quality and efficient health care in Federal Government administered or sponsored health care programs is listed in Appendix D at the end of this volume.

Remarks Following a Meeting With Rockey Vaccarella
August 23, 2006

The President. I just had coffee with Rockey Vaccarella, St. Bernard Parish, Louisiana. He caught my attention because he decided to come up to Washington, DC, and make it clear to me and others here in the Government that there's people down there still hurting in south Louisiana and along the gulf coast.

And Roc is a plain-spoken guy. He's the kind of fellow I feel comfortable talking to. I told him that I understand that there's people down there that still need help. And I told him the Federal Government will work with the State and local authorities to get the help to them as quickly as possible.

Rockey Vaccarella. That's right.

The President. He met with my friend Don Powell. Don's job is to cut through bureaucracy. I told Rockey the first obligation of the Federal Government is to write a check big enough to help the people down there. And I want to thank the Members of Congress of both political parties that helped us pass over $110 billion of appropriations. And that's going to help the folks. And I told him that to the extent that there's still bureaucratic hurdles and the need for the Federal Government to help eradicate those hurdles, we want to do that.

Now, I know we're coming up on the first-year anniversary of Katrina, and it's a time to remember, a time to particularly remember the suffering that people went through. Rockey lost everything. He lost— he and his family had every possession they had wiped out. And it's a time to remember that people suffer, and it's a time to recommit ourselves to helping them. But I also want people to remember that a one-year anniversary is just that, because it's going to require a long time to help these people rebuild.

And thank you for your spirit.

Mr. Vaccarella. Thank you, Mr. President.

The President. It's an amazing country, isn't it, where——

Mr. Vaccarella. It is. You know, it's really amazing when a small man like me from St. Bernard Parish can meet the President of the United States. The President is a people person. I knew that from the beginning. I was confident that I could meet President Bush.

And my mission was very simple. I wanted to thank President Bush for the millions of FEMA trailers that were brought down there. They gave roofs over people's head. People had the chance to have baths—air condition. We have TV; we have toiletry; we have things that are necessities that we can live upon.

But now I wanted to remind the President that the job's not done, and he knows that. And I just don't want the Government and President Bush to forget about us. And I just wish the President could have another term in Washington.

The President. Wait a minute. [*Laughter*]

Mr. Vaccarella. You know, I wish you had another 4 years, man. If we had this President for another 4 years, I think we'd be great. But we're going to move on.

Mr. President, it's been my pleasure.

The President. You're a good man, Rockey. Thank you all.

Mr. Vaccarella. You are too. Thanks a bunch.

NOTE: The President spoke at 10:15 a.m. on the South Lawn at the White House. The Office of the Press Secretary also released a Spanish language transcript of these remarks.

Statement on France's Decision To Send Troops to Lebanon in Support of United Nations Security Council Resolution 1701
August 24, 2006

I welcome President Chirac's decision to send a total of 2,000 troops to Lebanon and to continue to exercise leadership on the ground in enforcing United Nations Security Council Resolution 1701. This is an important step towards finalizing preparations to deploy the United Nations Interim Force of Lebanon. I applaud the decision of France, as well as the significant pledges from Italy and our other important allies. I encourage other nations to make contributions as well. We are working with the United Nations and our partners to ensure the rapid deployment of this force to help Lebanon's legitimate armed forces restore the sovereignty of its democratic Government throughout the country and stop Hizballah from acting as a state within a state.

NOTE: The statement referred to President Jacques Chirac of France.

Letter to Congressional Leaders Transmitting a Notice of Intention To Enter Into a Free Trade Agreement With Colombia
August 24, 2006

Dear Mr. Speaker: (Dear Mr. President:)

Consistent with section 2105(a)(1)(A) of the Trade Act of 2002, (Public Law 107–210) (the "Trade Act"), I am pleased to notify the Congress of my intention to enter into a free trade agreement with the Republic of Colombia.

The United States-Colombia Trade Promotion Agreement will generate export opportunities for U.S. farmers, ranchers, and companies, help create jobs in the United States, and help American consumers save money while offering them more choices.

The Agreement will also benefit the people of Colombia by providing economic opportunity and by strengthening democracy.

Consistent with the Trade Act, I am sending this notification at least 90 days in advance of signing the Agreement. My Administration looks forward to working with the Congress in developing appropriate legislation to approve and implement this Agreement.

Sincerely,

GEORGE W. BUSH

NOTE: Identical letters were sent to J. Dennis Hastert, Speaker of the House of Representatives, and Richard B. Cheney, President of the Senate. The Office of the Press Secretary also released a Spanish language transcript of this letter. The notice is listed in Appendix D at the end of this volume.

Message on the 90th Anniversary of the National Park Service
August 24, 2006

I send greetings to those celebrating the 90th anniversary of the National Park Service.

Americans take great pride in our country's natural and historic treasures, and the National Park Service plays an important role in ensuring that our rich heritage is preserved and enjoyed for generations to come. Since its establishment in 1916, the National Park Service has grown to include almost 400 sites, with parks in nearly every state. These parks protect beautiful landscapes, tell important stories about our country's past, and encourage our citizens to conserve our natural environment and celebrate our national history.

Over the past five years, the National Park Service has made significant progress in conserving our natural resources and improving the condition of park facilities. I call on all Americans to help in these efforts and to enhance our parks as we get ready for the National Park Service's centennial celebration. Through continued cooperation and partnership, our national parks can endure for the next 100 years and beyond.

I appreciate the volunteers and employees of the National Park Service who dedicate their time and talents to maintaining and enhancing our national parks. Your efforts help advance environmental stewardship, promote outdoor recreation, and preserve our national memory.

Laura and I send our best wishes on this special occasion.

GEORGE W. BUSH

NOTE: This message was released by the Office of the Press Secretary on August 25. An original was not available for verification of the content of this message.

Memorandum on the Future of America's National Parks
August 24, 2006

Memorandum for the Secretary of the Interior

Subject: The Future of America's National Parks

In honoring its 90th anniversary, I have called on the National Park Service, and every American, to continue the cooperation necessary for our vibrant national parks to endure for the next 100 years and beyond.

Over the past 5 years, the National Park Service has built a strong foundation for the future, with 6,000 park improvements completed or underway. We should further enhance our national parks during the decade leading up to the 2016 centennial celebration.

Therefore, I direct you to establish specific performance goals for our national parks that, when achieved, will help prepare them for another century of conservation, preservation, and enjoyment. These goals should integrate the assessments of the past 5 years used in monitoring natural resources and improving the condition of park facilities. You are to identify signature projects and programs that are consistent with these goals and that continue the National Park Service legacy of leveraging philanthropic, partnership, and government investments for the benefit of national parks and their visitors.

You are directed to consult with the Director of the Office of Management and Budget and the Chairman of the Council on Environmental Quality as appropriate in implementing this memorandum. I encourage you to invite and receive suggestions from those who desire to preserve the scenic, cultural, historical, geological, and recreational values of our national parks.

You are to report the results of the implementation of this memorandum to me by May 31, 2007.

GEORGE W. BUSH

NOTE: This memorandum was released by the Office of the Press Secretary on August 25. An original was not available for verification of the content of this memorandum.

The President's Radio Address
August 26, 2006

Good morning. Earlier this week, I had coffee with Rockey Vaccarella in the White House. Rockey is from St. Bernard Parish in Louisiana, and he and his family lost everything they owned to Hurricane Katrina. Rockey drove to Washington to thank the Federal Government for its efforts to help people like him, and he brought a trailer along to help remind us that many good people along our gulf coast are still living in difficult conditions and that the hard work of rebuilding has only just begun.

This Tuesday marks the first anniversary of Katrina, one of the deadliest and most costly natural disasters in American history. In Mississippi, the storm wiped out virtually everything along an 80-mile stretch of the coast, flattening homes and destroying entire communities. In Louisiana, flooding left 80 percent of the city of New Orleans underwater. The human costs were even more terrible. More than a thousand people died, countless families lost their homes and livelihoods, and tens of thousands of men, women, and children were forced to flee the region and leave behind everything they knew.

During the storm and in the days that followed, Americans responded with heroism and compassion. Coast Guard and other personnel rescued people stranded in flooded neighborhoods and brought them to high ground. Doctors and nurses stayed behind to care for their patients, and some even went without food so their patients could eat. Many of the first-responders risking their lives to help others were victims themselves, wounded healers, with a sense of duty greater than their own suffering. And across our great land, the armies of compassion rallied to bring food and water and hope to fellow citizens who had lost everything. In these and countless other selfless acts, we saw the spirit of America at its best.

Unfortunately, Katrina also revealed that Federal, State, and local governments were unprepared to respond to such an extraor-dinary disaster. And the floodwaters ex-posed a deep-seated poverty that has cut people off from the opportunities of our country. So last year, I made a simple pledge: The Federal Government would learn the lessons of Katrina; we would do what it takes, and we would stay as long as it takes to help our brothers and sisters build a new gulf coast, where every citizen feels part of the great promise of America.

That was the same pledge I repeated to Rockey during his visit to the White House. This pledge meant stronger levees and rebuilt homes and new infrastructure. It also means safe streets and neighbor-hoods filled with locally-owned businesses and more opportunities for everyone.

Next week Laura and I will return to Mississippi and New Orleans to meet with local citizens and officials and review the progress we have made. The Federal Gov-ernment has conducted a thorough review of its response to natural disasters, and we're making reforms that will improve our response to future emergencies. With help from Congress, we have committed $110 billion to the recovery effort, and we are playing a vital role in helping people clear debris, repair and rebuild their homes, re-open their businesses and schools, and put their lives back together.

The Federal Government will continue to do its part. Yet a reborn gulf coast must reflect the needs, the vision, and the aspira-tions of the people of Mississippi and Lou-isiana. And their State and local officials have a responsibility to help set priorities and make tough decisions, so people can plan their futures with confidence.

One year after the storms, the gulf coast continues down the long road to recovery. In Mississippi and Louisiana, we can see many encouraging signs of recovery and re-newal, and many reminders that hard work still lies ahead. This work will require the sustained commitment of our Government, the generosity and compassion of the American people, and the talent and vision of people determined to restore their homes, neighborhoods, and cities. We will stay until the job is done, and by working together, we will help our fellow citizens along the gulf coast write a new future of hope, justice, and opportunity for all.

Thank you for listening.

NOTE: The address was recorded at 9:25 a.m. on August 24 in the Cabinet Room at the White House for broadcast at 10:06 a.m. on August 26. The transcript was made available by the Office of the Press Secretary on Au-gust 25 but was embargoed for release until the broadcast. The Office of the Press Sec-retary also released a Spanish language tran-script of this address.

Remarks Following a Lunch Meeting With Community Leaders in Biloxi, Mississippi
August 28, 2006

Listen, Laura and I are pleased to be down here again, and we want to thank a lot of the community leaders from the gulf coast region of Mississippi for sharing their thoughts and their concerns and their hopes and their aspirations.

I was just commenting upon how clean the beaches look, and that wasn't a given a year ago. Those beaches were cluttered with debris and garbage, the great, beau-tiful beaches here had been destroyed. And now they speak to the hope of this part of the world.

There's still a lot of problems left, Governor, but the people down here need to know the Federal Government is committed to working with you and the local people, and that, even though we've been through about one year together, one year doesn't mean that we'll forget. As a matter of fact, now is the time to renew our commitment and to let the people down here know that we will stay involved and helping the people of Mississippi rebuild their lives.

The truth of the matter is, the ultimate future for this region down here depends on the people of Mississippi. It requires the spirit and the courage of the people of this part of the world to rebuild, and I'm confident that's going to be the case.

We saw that spirit right after the storm hit, and we still see that spirit. And so I want to thank the good folks for letting us come by and say hello. We value our friends down here, and we really appreciate the good people of the gulf coast of Mississippi for what you stand for.

Governor, thank you; appreciate you.

NOTE: The President spoke at 12:39 p.m. in the Biloxi Schooner Restaurant. In his remarks, he referred to Gov. Haley R. Barbour of Mississippi.

Remarks on Hurricane Katrina Recovery Efforts in Biloxi
August 28, 2006

The President. Listen, thank you all for coming. I'm glad to be back here in Biloxi, and I'm glad Laura came with me. I've been in this neighborhood before. As a matter of fact, I was here a couple of days after Katrina hit. It's amazing, isn't it? It's amazing what the world looked like then and what it looks like now.

I remember meeting Patrick Wright. Remember, Patrick? I don't know if you all remember the picture of me seeing this fellow sitting in what used to be his home, a pile of rubble. Patrick, it's good to see you.

I also met Sandy and Lynn Patterson when I was walking down the street, your neighbor. They—well, just about everybody here, they'd lost everything they owned. People can't imagine what the world looked like then. I went by their home—just came out of their home. It's got air-conditioning—[*laughter*]—and electricity. You can see the reconstruction effort beginning here in this part of the world.

It's a sense of renewal here. It may be hard for those of you who have endured the last year to really have that sense of change, but for a fellow who was here and now a year later comes back, things are changing. And I congratulate you for your courage and your perseverance.

And there's still challenges. There's still more to be done. You can see it with the temporary trailers. I feel the quiet sense of determination that's going to shape the future of Mississippi. And so I've come back on this anniversary to thank you for your courage and to let you know, the Federal Government stands with you still. Laura and I really care for the people whose lives have been affected. We understand the trauma, and we thank you for your determination.

I want to thank Governor Haley Barbour and Marsha for joining us today. I appreciate the Federal Coordinator of Gulf Coast Rebuilding, Don Powell. He's my friend from Texas. We've got two of the military who helped after the storm. I think they made an enormous difference in people's lives: General Russ Honore and Admiral Thad Allen. Thank you for joining us. You've got two fine United States Senators from Mississippi, Thad Cochran and Trent

Lott. And I thank Tricia for joining us as well. I want to thank Congressman Chip Pickering who has joined us today. Congressman Pickering, like these two Senators, care a lot about the people of Mississippi.

I remember walking the block here with A.J. Holloway, your mayor. He—A.J. obviously was upset and concerned, but he also made it clear to me that with the proper amount of help, Biloxi can rebuild. And Biloxi is rebuilding. You got a fine mayor in A.J. Holloway.

I've had the pleasure of meeting some of the local officials up and down the coast—matter of fact, probably all of the local officials. One of the people that has intrigued me the most is Mayor Tommy Longo of Waveland. Mayor, good to see you, buddy. Thanks for coming. I'm always asking about you, Tommy.

Mayor J. Thomas Longo. I'm always asking about you.

The President. That's right. [*Laughter*] Check is in the mail. [*Laughter*]

You know, one of the interesting people I met was Malcolm Jones; he's a city attorney of Pass Christian. Malcolm, thanks for coming. He helped design the plan that enabled us to expedite the debris removal, and I appreciate your contribution. I want to thank Chipper McDermott, who is the mayor—with us—he's Pass Christian's mayor. Rusty Quave is with us today. Mr. Mayor, thanks for coming. Billy Skellie is with us as well. These are all mayors trying to help their communities recover, doing the hard work to helping the people improve their lives. I want to thank my friend Brent Warr. He's the mayor of Gulfport. Brent, good to see you. Thanks for coming. I want to thank the Biloxi firefighters who have joined us today. Thank you for your work. Thank you for staying the job.

When Katrina made landfall on August 29th at 6:10, it was one of the strongest hurricanes to ever hit America. The devastation and debris were unimaginable. You had to see it for yourself to fully under-stand the nature of this storm and the damage done. The terrible force of the storms tossed some of the giant casinos here onto the land. They twisted traffic lights. They ripped some of the beautiful trees from the ground. They stripped the cities of familiar landmarks and buildings.

In the days that followed, the people of Mississippi worked together to save lives. People reached out to those who were trapped by rising waters. Three people were pulled through a window in that house right there, to save their lives. People opened their homes to help the suffering. The people of Mississippi said, "We'll overcome this disaster," and worked together to do so.

Since the days of heroism and bravery, the gulf coast has begun one of the largest rebuilding efforts in our Nation's history. This is my 11th visit since the storm hit. You know, each visit you see progress. I was struck by the beauty of the beaches. The beaches were pretty rough after the storm, as you know. Today, they're pristine, and they're beautiful. They reflect a hopeful future, as far as I'm concerned.

I appreciate the fact that the people down here have embraced this amazing challenge with determination and grit. And your Governor is leading the way. He says this: He says, "With all its destruction, the storm gave birth to a renaissance in Mississippi that will surely result in building our State bigger and better than ever before." He believes that. A lot of the people in Mississippi believe that. And so do I.

A year ago, I committed our Federal Government to help you. I said, we have a duty to help the local people recover and rebuild. And I meant what I said. Working with Thad and Trent Lott and other Members of the United States Congress, we have appropriated $110 billion to help rebuild this area. It is a strong Federal commitment that we will keep.

We understand people are still anxious to get in their home. We understand people hear about help and wonder where it is. We know that. But the first thing is, is that this Federal Government has made a commitment to help, and it starts with a large check. It also means that in order for the rebuilding to be as strong as we want, there has to be a partnership with the Federal Government and the State and local governments.

Here's my attitude about the partnership: You know better than the people in Washington the needs of your communities. I'd rather listen to local mayors and county commissioners than folks sitting in Washington, DC, about what this part of Mississippi wants.

The first test of this partnership was to clear debris. You can't rebuild a community when the community is full of debris. We've now removed about 98 percent of the dry debris. I remember when we first came down here; the mayors weren't so happy with the debris removal. But we listened to them. We got the funding equations right. And we got after it, and the debris is basically gone, which is step one of making sure our partnership works, and step two about making sure we can rebuild this area bigger and better than before.

We're also working together to make sure we're better prepared to handle the hurricanes. Every Department of my administration participated in a comprehensive study that looked at our response to last year's hurricanes. Each Department came up with practical reforms, ways to do things better. And so we've been reviewing plans. We've been working with the State and local folks.

The people in Mississippi are prepared. And I want to thank Governor Barbour and the local folks for making impressive efforts to protect the people of Mississippi. The truth of the matter is, we can work together, and will, but when disaster strikes, the first people that you rely upon—the people that matter most—are your friends. It's friends helping friends that turns out to make an enormous difference in saving

lives and helping to get by the trauma of the first days.

We all have roles to play, but in every State hit by last year's storms, it was the bravery of the local citizens that meant the difference between life and death. It was the bravery of the first-responders on the scenes. I'm here to thank you all for showing the country how to respond to natural disaster.

See, there's a new Mississippi that's coming, and you're going to see it in the construction of homes and the return of local businesses. This requires a different kind of courage, but it's a courage, nevertheless, for people to take risk and to rebuild and to say, "I'm not going to let the storm disrupt my life forever."

See, you got people here leading the reconstruction. We'll help you. We've committed more than $3 billion in housing grants, and that money is beginning to flow to the homeowners. And I know there's some frustration, but I want to appreciate the State working hard to make sure that when that money is spent, it's spent well and it goes to people who deserve it. That's what you expect, and that's what's going to happen. The checks have begun to roll; they're beginning to move. And the Governor and his staff are on top of it. It's a huge undertaking that's going to require cooperation with government agencies, insurance companies, volunteers, and community leaders.

The folks right back here said they couldn't have rebuilt this house without the church, without volunteer organizations that have stepped up to help. Governor Barbour's Commission on Recovery, Rebuilding, and Renewal was an important step to bringing citizens together to develop a vision of how people can work together. It's a smart thing to have done.

See, I said, you develop the plan. We're not going to do it for you because you know better the local needs, and Mississippi stepped up. The Commission brought together more than 500 volunteers.

The Commission held more than 50 public forums in 33 counties. They heard from thousands of citizens on how to rebuild, and as a result, the recovery efforts began with concrete recommendations on how to improve the infrastructure, on how to revamp zoning laws and building codes, and how to increase local cooperation in planning for future storms.

It was a smart thing to do, Governor, and I appreciate you doing it. You have a strategy now to build smarter homes. You've got a strategy to have neighborhoods connected by parks and playgrounds. You've got a sound strategy.

And I understand that rebuilding neighborhoods begins one house at a time, and that's what's happening here. When somebody goes back to their home, it helps renew the community, and so part of our efforts and part of our focus is to make sure that people can get back in their homes as quickly as possible.

Sandy Patterson, she can tell you how important it is to feel reconnected. She says, "My house is my home again, and it's good to be home." And that's what we want; people to help people here in this part of the world.

Listen, the spirit is alive here in the small-business owners who are working hard to get their businesses open. One of the entrepreneurs, a fellow named Ernest Henley—he's here. He owns West End Cleaners. When Katrina hit, it blew out his windows, hurt his roof. Less than 2 weeks later, the windows were boarded up, but West End Cleaners was back in business. See, he wasn't going to let the storm stop him from realizing his dream, which is running his own business.

Bobby Mahoney is with us. He showed the same spirit when he opened Mary Mahoney's. That's a restaurant he named for his mother. That's a smart thing to do if you have a restaurant. [Laughter] Within 2 months of Hurricane Katrina, Mary Mahoney's was once again serving its world-famous gourmet seafood gumbo. Inside the restaurant you can see where Bobby painted the lines to mark how high the waters were for Camille and then Katrina. He says this: "The reason why Biloxi is going to get back real quick is because of businesses. You can come back and build a home with a job, but you can't come back and build a home without a job."

That's a smart man who understands that as this part of the world flourishes and businesses grow, people are going to find work and have the wherewithal to help rebuild the communities in their lives.

I appreciate the spirit of Pass Christian. After the hurricanes leveled many of its buildings, the city responded by permitting businesses and community organizations to set up trailers in War Memorial Park. The idea started when Hancock Bank set up a shop in an RV. Today, the park has two banks, an insurance agent, a real estate business, a convenience store, a construction company, a takeout restaurant, and a town library. Scott Naugle, he's with us today; he's the president of the chamber. He says, "We're going to do business even if we have to learn new ways to do it."

Optimism is the only option. We want to help. We want to help that optimism succeed. And so I signed legislation that creates what's called the Gulf Opportunity Zones. That means if you invest in this part of the world, you get tax breaks. In other words, they're using the Tax Code to say, come and invest your capital here. It's very important for the Congress to extend this legislation. It's important for planners and job creators to know that the incentive we created will still be there.

And also, we've put out small-business loans. In other words, what we're trying do is just help you. The spirit is here. The people want to succeed. And our job at the Federal level is to help you succeed. That's what I've come to tell you.

One of the remarkable things about this part of the world that was so affected by the storms was what happened to the schools. Laura has visited the gulf coast 13 times. She's carried the message that a lot of people in America feel, and that is, it's important to help children get back to school as quickly as possible. And you've done that.

For children who lost everything—their homes, their belongings, and their friends—going to school can be a place where they find stability and a familiar routine. The people of Mississippi understood that well. Teachers and community leaders worked hard to get the children back into school as quickly as possible.

Catch this: As a result of these efforts, in the past school year, every district closed after Katrina was reopened. It's a remarkable accomplishment by the good folks in this part of the world. Lizana Elementary School is a good example. In the days and weeks after Katrina, it first served as a Red Cross shelter. And to get school back on its feet, the citizens from Mississippi and all across the Nation helped it rebuild. They donated desks and file cabinets and even clothing and bookbags and pencils and paper. Vickie Williams is with us today. Here's what she said. She said, "None of the students had to purchase supplies. Through donation efforts across the country, everything got back to normal. It was a blessing from everywhere." Vickie, thanks for giving other people credit, but you and your staff deserve a lot of credit.

Charles B. Murphy and Gulfview elementary schools are another inspiring story. When the schools were destroyed, the teachers had to adapt, and they began to hold their classes in trailers. Teachers helped with maintenance duties, and parents pitched in, and volunteers came as far away as Vermont and Canada. And they assembled furniture and hauled boxes and set up computers and planted trees. There was an outdoor classroom that served as a meeting place for science and music and physical education.

Jan White is with us. She said this: "Last year was survival; this year is innovation."

The school system has not only survived, but they're going to be stronger and better than they were before.

One of the things that the Governor and the Senator said to the Federal Government, they said, "We need help. Our tax bases have been destroyed. We need operating cash to keep our schools running." And so we've spent almost $480 million to help the schools recover. But there's a lot more work to be done.

And one of the places where work can be done and is being done is in libraries. Laura Bush feels strongly about this. She's set up what's called the Laura Bush Foundation, and in working with the private sector, has awarded more than a million dollars in grants to 20 schools to purchase new books.

We see the new Mississippi because of the faith-based and community organizations that abound here. When the hurricane struck, men and women of faith stepped forward immediately. The following Sunday, Father Harold Roberts—he's with us today—and the congregation of Episcopal Church of the Redeemer gathered at the site where their church once stood. They carried lawn chairs, and they brought blankets to sit. Some of them had been through this before.

See, back in 1969, Hurricane Camille destroyed everything but the steeple and the old church bell. This time, nothing was left standing, and so the congregation had to ring the old bell from its new place in the rubble. On that first Sunday after Katrina, Father Harold Roberts read from the Book of Romans. Here's what he said: He said, "Rejoice in hope. Be patient in suffering. Persevere in prayer"—precisely what the people of this part of the world have done.

Father Roberts is working hard. His congregation began to rebuild their school, and now they're building—they're going to build a church on higher ground. In the meantime, they're gathering in the gymnasium. He said, "In spite of the challenges of the past year, we see the power of God working. The people have been incredibly patient. We will recover from this, and we will not rebuild until we can do it right."

Good citizens have risen up all over Mississippi to rebuild this State. Many volunteers traveled thousands of miles to be here. In other words, I hope you realized you weren't alone. One of the amazing groups was Hands On Gulf Coast.

Hands On Gulf Coast is a group of volunteers, total strangers to the people of this part of the world, in large part. They said, "What can I do to help?" They came en masse. They did all kinds of things. They cleaned up wreckage, and they removed mold, and they repaired roofs, and they provided clothing, and they tutored students. Somebody said, "We have a need." They said, "I want to help."

When the Coastal Family Health Center lost three buildings and more than 60 staff members, Hands On offered to help. They worked with nurses who came from the gulf coast. They got FedEx to supply funding for airfare. They provided food and housing. And as a result, the Coastal Family Health Center was able to provide critical help for good people in this part of the world.

Suzanne Stahl, who I happen to have met, is standing right over there. You've been down here for 12 months, see. Isn't that amazing? Somebody shows up and says, "I want to help," and is still here helping because she cares, as do a lot of other people. She said this: "It's been incredible to see the power and will of all the volunteers who have come to do something. If only I could have bottled the energy and enthusiasm of these volunteers. It's just about as unbelievable as the devastation."

So, I want to thank all those who have volunteered. I want to thank those who have given of their hard-earned money to help the good people down here recover. I want to remind those who are constantly looking for a way to serve your fellow man that there's still work to be done down here, that there's still hope. There's still a need for people to come and help.

The armies of compassion that conducted the millions of acts of kindness remind us that the true strength of the United States of America lies in the hearts and souls of our citizens, and we're thankful for that.

No doubt in my mind, Mississippi will have the renaissance that Governor Barbour talked about. You can't drive through this State without seeing signs of recovery and renewal. It's just impossible to miss the signs of hope. And you've done it the old-fashioned way, with vision and hard work and resolve.

Some of the hardest work is still ahead. We'll complete the clearing of the wet debris from the Mississippi Sound. We'll ensure Federal money reaches the individuals who need it to build their homes. We'll make sure the schools and libraries are rebuilt better than before, and we'll stand by you as long as it takes to get the job done. And when the job gets done, your children and your grandchildren will have a brighter and more hopeful future.

May God continue to bless the courageous people of Mississippi. Thank you for coming.

NOTE: The President spoke at 2:10 p.m. in an East Biloxi neighborhood. In his remarks, he referred to Gov. Haley R. Barbour of Mississippi and his wife, Marsha; Lt. Gen. Russel L. Honore, USA, commanding general, First United States Army; Patricia Thompson Lott, wife of Sen. C. Trent Lott; Mayor A.J. Holloway of Biloxi, MS; Mayor Rusty Quave of D'Iberville, MS; Mayor William Skellie, Jr., of Long Beach, MS; Vickie Williams, principal, Lizana Elementary School; and Jan White, principal, Gulfview-Charles B. Murphy Elementary School.

Remarks Following a Tour of United States Marine, Inc., and an Exchange With Reporters in Gulfport, Mississippi
August 28, 2006

The President. One of the interesting things I've learned here is that the good folks at United States Marine are looking for workers, and there's a shortage of workers here in the gulf coast. And the reason I bring that up is that if people are looking for work, they should come.

Obviously, part of the bottleneck is getting housing. And that's why we're working with Governor Barbour to make sure that the housing money starts moving. But people are going to have to—they're coming down to work; they're going to have to have a place to live. But what's fascinating about this part of the world is that in one year's time, it's gone from despair to hope and that if you're somebody who wants to find a job, you can find work in Mississippi, good-paying jobs. That's what the man just told me who runs the company. There is hope down here. There's still a lot of work to be done.

My message to the people down here is that we understand there's more work to be done, and just because a year has passed—the Federal Government will remember the people. This is an anniversary, but it doesn't mean it ends. Frankly, it's the beginning of what is going to be a long recovery. But I'm amazed by the opportunity, and I'm amazed by the hope that I feel down here. Anyway, thought you would be interested.

Federal Government Role in Hurricane Recovery Efforts

Q. Mr. President, in your remarks a few minutes ago, you talked about the role of faith-based organizations. Has the experience down here given you a new opinion about what the role of the Government can or should be in a situation like this?

The President. The role of Government here, first and foremost, is to provide enough money to say that the rebuilding effort will be robust. I felt it was very important for us to be generous, and the people of America responded. The people in the gulf coast region have got to understand that the American taxpayers have stepped forth with a lot of money. And you can't have hope unless there's a reason to be hopeful, and the $110 billion was a reason to be hopeful.

Now, obviously, there's a lot of work to be done, but the Federal Government had a very important role to play, and we're playing it, but so does the State and local government, whether it be here in Mississippi or in Louisiana. The citizens of our country and the citizens of this region have had an important role to play. In other words, this storm was so big it requires all aspects of American life to help the people here. It was a massive storm. It was the largest in the Nation's history or at least the most expensive.

Rebuilding Efforts on the Gulf Coast/Jobs

Q. How long do you imagine it will be before this area is fully rebuilt?

The President. Well, it's hard for me to say. I would say years, not months. On the other hand, the progress in one year's time has been remarkable. And I suspect that what you'll see, Toby [Tabassum Zakaria, Reuters], is there will be a momentum; momentum will be gathered. Houses will begat jobs; jobs will begat houses. And they're just beginning to get to that point where the infrastructures are being expanded, the houses are going to be—more houses will be added.

The Governor was talking to me today about an interesting modular concept to expedite the people getting out of trailers into something more permanent. But the storm was massive in its scope. You came down with me and saw it. Most Americans didn't get to see what it was like. It's hard to describe the devastation down here. It was massive in its destruction, and it spared nobody. United States Senator Trent Lott had a fantastic home overlooking the bay. I know because I sat in it with he and his wife. And now it's completely obliterated. There's nothing. And I remember coming down here—these giant piles of debris were here.

People say, "How can we rebuild with debris?" Now it's gone. Now, there's more work, but to answer your question, I can't predict, but I do know how massive the effort is going to be, and I know how massive it's been. There's just more work to be done. The people down here need to know the Federal Government is helping, and we understand that there are still issues, and people are still hurting, and people want to get into their homes.

Okay, final question before we all go.

Funding for Hurricane Recovery Efforts

Q. Sir, is $110 billion the end of it? And which promises from Jackson Square are you finding hardest to make a reality?

The President. One hundred and ten billion, hopefully, that will work. Hopefully, that's enough. It's certainly enough to get us through the next period of time. And the hardest part has been to get the State reconstruction effort up and running. Mississippi's is up and running. In other words, I said early on that the States and local governments have got to devise a plan to rebuild. And the reason I said that is because the people of Mississippi know best how to rebuild Mississippi, and the Governor stepped up, and he put this fantastic commission together, and they developed a plan. And now that plan has been funded. The money is beginning to go out the door, so people can rebuild their lives.

In Louisiana, it's been a little slower. And I look forward to talking to the folks there tomorrow and this evening about what we can do to work together to expedite these plans being implemented, because we funded the housing. And I think when people begin to see the checks that come—that say, "Okay, here's some money to help you rebuild," they'll have a lot better spirit. They'll feel a lot better about their future.

Anyway, thank you all. Good to see you.

NOTE: The President spoke at 3:19 p.m. In his remarks, he referred to Gov. Haley R. Barbour of Mississippi; John Dane III, cochairman, United States Marine, Inc.; and Patricia Thompson Lott, wife of Sen. C. Trent Lott.

Remarks in a Discussion on the Gulf Coast School Library Recovery Initiative in New Orleans, Louisiana
August 29, 2006

The President. Laura and I want to thank the educators and students who have taken time to come over and help us make the point that renewal requires good education, and that there are a lot of good folks up and down the gulf coast who understand that, and that part of good education means having good books and strong libraries.

And so I'm going to turn it over to the person who's the strong, good library person in our family.

The First Lady. Well, I'm so excited today to get to see each one of you. I had a foundation already for school libraries, and we were just getting ready to disband the fundraising arm of that, the advisory committee, last year, last October. And when we met for our last meeting, they said, "Let's keep going, and let's raise money now specifically for the gulf coast and try to raise enough money so that if every school comes up and is functional again and is staffed, that they can apply for a grant for—to stock their library."

And it's been a thrill to be associated with school people. I know how school people work. You're first-responders, just like firemen and policemen. You know you've got to get your schools up and going immediately. And I want to thank you for your determination and for your very hard work, because I know that many of the people on every school staff who rebuilt their schools are also having to rebuild their own lives. They lost their own houses, or they are living in FEMA trailers. And so they're doing double work, and I want to thank you very, very much for that.

This is the second round of grants that we're announcing today; we gave 10 schools, 7 in Louisiana and 3 in Mississippi, earlier this summer. And this is our second round of grants to 10 more schools, once again 7 in Louisiana and 3 in Mississippi.

These grants, for the press, might want to know that these are for materials to re-stock a school library. They come in the form of a check because we know that school librarians want to build their library the way that it will support their curriculum and be most appropriate and perfect for their schoolchildren. So this is not—this is not a book distribution; this is a check to

these schools so they can do what all pro-fessional librarians want to do, and that is restock their libraries with the best books possible, including, of course, books that are especially bound for libraries so they can get a lot of use.

So I'm so excited to be here with all of you. I especially want to thank four foun-dations which have been very, very gen-erous for the second round of grants. The AT&T Foundation, Conoco/Philips, Target, and Enterprise Corporation have been very generous so that we can continue to give grants across the gulf coast. And I want to thank them, their representatives of their corporations here. Thank you all very much for that.

And I also want to thank Marshall Payne out of Dallas, who's the chairman of the Gulf Coast Recovery Initiative. He's back here—and Pam Willeford, who's our direc-tor.

So, Pam, I believe we'll take it over to you next.

[*At this point, the public portion of the event concluded; the discussion continued, however, and no transcript was provided.*]

NOTE: The President spoke at 11:04 a.m. at Warren Easton Senior High School. The First Lady referred to Marshall B. Payne, chairman, Gulf Coast School Library Recov-ery Initiative; and Pamela P. Willeford, chair, advisory committee, Laura Bush Foundation for America's Libraries.

Remarks on Hurricane Katrina Recovery Efforts in New Orleans
August 29, 2006

Thank you all. Thank you. Good morn-ing. From our beginnings as a nation, the church steeple and the schoolhouse door have been enduring symbols of the Amer-ican community, and so it is today in New Orleans. Earlier this morning, we gathered

at St. Louis Cathedral in the presence of a just God who asks us to love our neigh-bors as ourselves. And now we stand inside Warren Easton Senior High School.

Warren Easton is the oldest public school in New Orleans. In a little more than a week, its classrooms will again be filled with young men and women who will write the future of this great American city. And that future draws from a rich past: the music of Fats Domino, the stories of Tennessee Williams, shotgun houses and iron-lattice balconies, seafood gumbo, red beans and rice on Mondays.

Over the course of nearly three centuries, a city that once was the center of slave trade has been transformed to a unique and great American city. This city is a story of hope and dignity and perseverance. And it's these qualities that have seen you through trials of war and prejudice and natural disaster.

One year ago today, your beloved New Orleans and surrounding parishes and counties and the great State of Mississippi were struck by a cruel hurricane. And here in this city, there was flooding on a biblical scale. Less than 3 weeks later, with many of the homes and churches and schools still under water, I came to Jackson Square. I said we could not imagine America without the Crescent City and pledged that our Government would do its part. And today Laura and I have come back to discuss that pledge and your future.

I want to thank Don Powell, the Federal Coordinator of the Gulf Coast Rebuilding, who is with us today. I appreciate Admiral Thad Allen, who's now the Commandant of the United States Coast Guard, who is with us today. And I want to thank Lieutenant General Russ Honore.

I appreciate the members of the congressional delegation who have joined us today: Senator Mary Landrieu as well as Senator David Vitter and his wife, Wendy. Thank you both for being here. I want to thank Congressman William Jefferson and Andrea; Congressman Bobby Jindal; and Congressman Charlie Melancon and his wife, Peachy. Thank you all for joining us. Proud to be working with you.

I noticed that Mary brought her brother, Mitch, the Lieutenant Governor of the great State of Louisiana. Mitch, thanks for coming.

I want to thank the attorney general of the State of Louisiana. General, thank you for joining us. He's an alumnus of Warren Easton Senior High School. I appreciate so very much the superintendent of schools; State Superintendent of Schools Cecil Picard is with us today. I thank all those State and local officials who have come. I appreciate Jean Case, who is the chair of the President's Council on Service and Civic Participation.

I want to thank one of the fine, fine citizens of your State, a man who brings great dignity in anything he does, and that's Dr. Norman Francis, who is the chairman of the Louisiana Recovery Authority.

I want to thank Lexi Medley, who is the principal of Warren Easton Senior High School. Happy birthday. Today is her birthday. We're not telling, are we? [*Laughter*] No, 25, okay.

I want to thank all those school administrators, teachers, librarians, and students who are here from not only—they're not only here from New Orleans, but they're from around the area, including Mississippi. Welcome. Thanks for coming.

When the waters broke through the levees a year ago, southern Louisiana was consumed by flood waters, and New Orleans faced the greatest disaster in its history. Eighty percent of your city was under water. Thousands of businesses were hurt. Tens of thousands of homes were damaged and destroyed, and hundreds of thousands of folks fled the region in perhaps the greatest dislocation of American citizens since the Dust Bowl of the 1930s.

Your fellow Americans offered you more than sympathy. They responded with action. Those of you who were stranded on rooftops looked to the sky for deliverance, and then you saw the Coast Guard choppers come. Members of Louisiana National Guard, who had just come back from Iraq, stepped forward to bring food and water and ice. On every street, in every parish, there were constant acts of selflessness.

Doctors and nurses stayed with patients; they went without food so that the sick and the infirm might be able to eat. Fishermen used their flat-bottom boats to form the "Cajun Navy" and pulled women and children and the elderly out of flooded homes and brought them to dry ground. Volunteers embraced frightened boys and girls with warm blankets and loving arms to reassure them somebody cared. In these and countless other acts of courage, we saw the very best of America.

Unfortunately, the hurricane also brought terrible scenes that we never thought we would see in America: citizens drowned in their attics, desperate mothers crying out on national TV for food and water, a breakdown of law and order, and a government at all levels that fell short of its responsibilities.

When the rain stopped and this wounded city was laid bare, our television screens showed faces worn down by poverty and despair. For most of you, the storms were only the beginning of your difficulties. Katrina exposed the big things that need repairing; yet its most devastating impact has been on the rhythms of everyday life.

Some of you still don't know whether you have a neighborhood to come back to. Others of you who made the decision to return are living in trailers. Many are separated from their loved ones and simply long just to go to church on a Sunday afternoon with somebody you care about. Many of you find yourself without jobs and struggling to make do without the convenience of a supermarket nearby. Many fear for your safety because of violent criminals. The challenge is not only to help rebuild, but the challenge is to help restore the soul.

I take full responsibility for the Federal Government's response, and a year ago I made a pledge that we will learn the lessons of Katrina and that we will do what it takes to help you recover. I've come back

to New Orleans to tell you the words that I spoke on Jackson Square are just as true today as they were then.

Since I spoke those words, Members of the United States Congress from both political parties came together and committed more than $110 billion to help the gulf coast recover. I felt it was important that our Government be generous to the people who suffered. I felt that step one of a process of recovery and renewal is money.

I also put a good man in charge of coordinating the Federal response for local rebuilding. I've already introduced him; his name is Don Powell. He's a good fellow. He's no nonsense. He's a good listener, and when he finds hurdles in the way between intentions and results, he works to remove them. He's on the job now, and he's going to stay on the job until we get the job done. And I appreciate you, Don, for your service.

To make sure that we keep our promises and to make sure this good area recovers, we have got to give assurance to the citizens that if there is another natural disaster, we'll respond in better fashion. Every Department of my administration has looked at its response to last year's hurricanes and has recommended practical reforms, things to do to make sure that the response is better.

Chertoff—Secretary Chertoff has increased manpower and training for FEMA, strengthened partnerships with the Red Cross and the Department of Defense, improved communications among local, State, and Federal emergency teams, and has expanded supplies so that FEMA can feed up to a million people for about a week. We looked at what went right, and we looked at what went wrong, and we're addressing that which went wrong.

In Louisiana, we have pre-positioned supplies in advance of this year's hurricane season. The people of the gulf coast can know that at the Federal level and at the State level and at the local level, we've all assessed, and we're now working together in better fashion. We're better prepared. And step one of rebuilding is to assure people, if another hurricane comes, there will be a better, more effective response.

Secondly, in order to make sure that people understand there's hope and renewal in this area, they've got to have confidence in a stronger levee system. It became clear to me in my first of my many visits down here—the people said, "It's fine—you can talk all you want, just get the levees stronger." I think that was your message, Senator. [*Laughter*]

The Army of Corps of Engineers has been working nonstop—and I mean nonstop—to repair the damage and make 350 miles of the system stronger. I say 350 miles. Most people in America don't understand the nature of your levee system. They're extensive and require a lot of work, including rebuilding I-walls with T-walls. In other words, that strengthens the foundations of levees. We're storm-proofing the pumping stations, and the pumping stations' capacities are being increased. We're elevating electrical systems so they can work during a flood.

Today, almost the entire flood protection system around New Orleans has been restored to pre-Katrina level. And in many places, the system is now better than it was before Katrina. We're working to make the levees stronger than ever by 2010, and we will study what we need to do to give New Orleans even greater protection.

One thing that the American people have got to understand is that in order to make sure the levee system works, there has to be a barrier system to protect the State of Louisiana. I strongly urge the United States Congress to pass energy legislation that will give the State of Louisiana more revenues from offshore leases so they can restore the wetlands.

The Army Corps of Engineers has been working with local citizens in difficult circumstances. I've been on the levees; I've seen these good folks working. One such fellow is Kevin Wagner. He's with us today. He's an engineer whose house had 12 feet of water after the storm. I think it's important for people to listen to what Kevin said. He said, "For me, it's personal. My whole family lived down there in St. Bernard Parish. Everyone who's working on this effort has the same motivation and the same sense of urgency."

There is a sense of urgency, and I want to thank those in the corps and those who are helping the corps send reassuring messages to the people who live here and the people who want to move back here.

A more hopeful New Orleans means we've got to get rid of the broken furniture and old refrigerators and get rid of the wreckage. You can't rebuild until you remove the rubble. The sheer tonnage of debris in Louisiana is many times greater than any previous disaster. And after many months and more than $1.8 billion from the Federal Government, from the taxpayers, more than three-quarters of the debris has now been cleared.

You know, it's amazing when you really think about the effort. Of course, government has a part, but the truth of the matter is, a lot of the effort, a lot of the success, and a lot of results were achieved because of faith-based and community groups. Groups like Katrina Krewe have mobilized thousands of volunteers, ranging from students on spring break to moms and retirees. Isn't it interesting to have a country where people are willing to show up to help clean out houses and remove debris for someone they didn't even know? It's a spectacular nation, isn't it, when compassion overflows to overwhelming?

The Krewe's founder, Becky Zaheri, is with us. She left; then she came back. And she said, "I went and visited other States and they were beautiful, but they were not home." That's the spirit that we're trying to capture. That's the spirit we want people who are watching from afar to understand; this "home" is beginning to be.

The debris is getting cleaned. As a matter of fact, in order to make sure that the Federal—that we continue to clean the remaining debris, the Federal Government has agreed to pay 100 percent of reimbursement costs through the end of the year on the five hardest hit parishes.

We need to get homes available for people. A renewed New Orleans is a New Orleans with new homes. Everybody understands that. The people here, and those who have left, they all tell me one thing—particularly those who—"I miss New Orleans," is what they say. But we got to make sure they have a place to move to. Trailers are only temporary. The goal is to make sure that communities are restored because there's new homes. That's the goal. And we will help.

I want to thank the Louisiana Recovery Authority. Dr. Francis and his team have done a really good job of developing a strategy, a plan, to help renew communities through homes. You know, when we first got going in this deal, we had choices to make, and a lot of people said, "Why don't you just take it over, Washington? Why don't you make all the decisions for the local folks?" That's not the way I think. I trust the people like Dr. Francis and the parish presidents and the mayors and the city councilmen to make the right decisions for the people of this community. And so the Federal Government is working with the Louisiana Recovery Authority to help people get back in their homes. And we've appropriated more than $10 billion to help people achieve that dream.

Under this program, eligible homeowners will receive up to $150,000 for damage not covered by insurance or other Federal assistance. All of us agree, at all levels of government, that we've got to get the money as quickly as possible in the hands of the people, so they can rebuild their lives and help this city recover.

A more hopeful New Orleans means replacing a school system that didn't work with one that will. And I congratulate the good people of New Orleans and the LRA for coming up with a novel plan to address failure that had caused—in many cases, was a root cause of poverty. I'm excited for you about the innovative charter school system you have put in place. I applaud you for thinking differently. I can't thank you enough for seizing the moment to say to the good folks and the families, we will do a better job with the school system here in New Orleans.

I know Margaret Spellings was down here recently; she's been down here a lot, and she should. We provided about a billion dollars to help the school system to get people back in school. The Federal Government has helped. It's very important, however, that people understand that the best way to make sure the school system delivers excellence is there be local control of schools, that people be charge of the future—local people be in charge of the future of the New Orleans schools.

Warren Easton Senior High School is a new charter school. One year ago, the classrooms and corridors were covered by about 10 feet of water. Like many other schools in New Orleans, Warren Easton is now reopened. When you say "charter school," it means the funding actually follows the students, which makes schools more accountable to parents. It means parents will be more involved in the schools.

By reopening as a charter school, Warren Easton is providing a new model. The motto of this school is, "We believe in success." A revitalized New Orleans needs a reformed public school system where everybody can say, "We not only believe in success; we see success for the good of the future of this State."

Laura mentioned that the First Lady's foundation established a Gulf Coast School Library Recovery Initiative, and they started granting—giving grants—more grants today to help libraries restock. Her view is the view of many, in that the center of a school is the library. Without a library, schools can't realize their full potential. And so she and her foundation and folks in the private sector have awarded more than a million dollars in grants to 20 schools, including $70,000 to the library here at this high school.

Nancy Hernandez is the librarian. She is a graduate from this high school. She puts it this way: "I think the library is the heart of the school. For a child, there is nothing that can replace the joy that comes from a book." And she is right. And I want to thank you, Laura, for helping people realize dreams with new books, in the midst of helping this public school system recover.

New Orleans's school system is enriched by the religious schools here. And the Cathedral Academy has been educating in New Orleans for nearly three decades. There's an interesting story I'm about to tell you. Last October, Cathedral Academy became the first school to reopen. That was last October. Sister Mary Rose is the principal, and she believes this: No child would be turned away from her school's front door.

For 10-year-old Aaliyah Carr, who is with us today here, the return to school was a day she will never forget. I love what she said. She said, "I was so happy, I could hear the choir singing in my head. It was a long time before I thought I'd see a school again, and I'm so glad to be walking these halls." Aaliyah says it better than I can. Education is the gateway to a brighter future. Education provides the light of hope for a young generation of children.

It's really important. I look forward to working with the Federal Government to provide opportunity scholarships for the poorest of our families so they have a choice as to whether they go to a religious school or a public school. It's good for New Orleans to have competing school systems. It's good for our country to have a vibrant parochial school system. And I applaud those who are very much involved with the Catholic school system here in the great city of New Orleans.

I predict, a year from now people are going to be wondering where they can find workers and wondering what they're going to do about the equipment shortages, supply shortages. I see an incredibly bright future for the entrepreneur. A lot of the revitalization of New Orleans and the area—surrounding area is going to come because there's more businesses opening and more shops reopening.

I believe that Government has a role to play in encouraging entrepreneurship, and so I worked with Members of the United States Congress, both political parties, to pass GO Zone legislation. GO Zone legislation gives entrepreneurs and small businesses tax incentives to invest in this area, to help jump-start this economy and provide jobs. The GO Zone legislation is set to expire. The United States Congress needs to extend this good piece of legislation.

There's a guy named Joe Peters—he's here with us. Where are you, Joe? Somewhere. Got a lousy seat. [*Laughter*] I want to tell you what he said. He's a Vietnam vet. He runs a tire store on St. Claude Avenue. Right after the flood, the waters went up to his desktop. He and his workers, though, reopened the shop. They had a job to do. They were fixing tires for police cruisers and family cars that were trying to get to safety. They were providing an important service. Here's what Joe says about this city's future. See, he's an entrepreneur. He's a can-do person. He believes in the future. He said, "This ain't nothing. This is New Orleans. We were here before there was a United States. You cannot kill a city like this."

I have returned to make it clear to people that I understand we're marking the first anniversary of the storm, but this anniversary is not an end. And so I come back to say that we will stand with the people of southern Louisiana and southern Mississippi until the job is done.

A lot of work has been accomplished, and I congratulate the people here. But there's more work to be done. The work ahead includes making sure that your streets are safe. And to make sure that people understand we at the Federal level understand we still have a continuing commitment, Attorney General Al Gonzales came down here. And he announced a new Justice Department initiative to send more Federal agents and prosecutors to New Orleans to help local law enforcement crack down on violent crime. If you want there to be renewal and recovery, like we all do, you've got to crack down on violent crime. You've got to send a message that the streets of New Orleans are safe. And we'll help you do so. The work ahead includes—[*applause*].

Last night I had dinner with your parish presidents and Mayor Nagin and Oliver Thomas and the good doctor and a lot of other good folks, and one message was clear to me: That for this city to recover, there needs to be help on infrastructure. There needs to be better sewers and better infrastructure around which a new New Orleans can emerge. I listened carefully, and to the extent there's bureaucracy standing in the way, me and Don Powell will—or Don Powell and I—excuse me, darlin'—Don Powell and I will work to get rid of them.

We can also—we'll work with your leaders to achieve a larger goal, and that is this: To rebuild a New Orleans where every child who grows up here feels a great part of the American promise. That's the challenge. And we've got a role to play, and we'll play it. That's what I'm here to say: We'll play it.

But I also want to remind you that the Federal Government cannot do this job alone, nor should it be expected to do the job alone. This is your home; you know what needs to be done. And a reborn Louisiana must reflect the views of the people down here and their vision and your priorities. State and parish authorities have a responsibility to set priorities, and they're doing so. We all have a responsibility to

clear obstacles that stand in the way of meeting goals. And we've got to make sure the money that has started to flow continues to flow.

At this critical moment, there are a lot of people making big decisions about where their future lies. I understand that, and so does the LRA and Governor Blanco and local authorities. We all understand that. We know there are people weighing a big decision. We want to make sure that when they do make the decision to rebuild, that the rules are clear and that the zoning decisions by local authorities make sense. That's a local decision to make. But we are going to make sure that we work closely together to clear up any ambiguity. See, we want people coming home. We want the rules clear, so when people come home, they know that they'll be coming to a safer, better place.

I appreciate the fact that State and local authorities are working together and making tough decisions. It hadn't been easy, but the storm was a big storm that created a lot of damage, and the good folks down here are working together. They're thinking smart. They've got a plan, a strategy to help rebuild, and the Federal Government will stand with you.

The private sector has a responsibility to help down here. You know, during the storm, American companies showed a lot of resourcefulness to get supplies and relief to the affected areas, and I know everybody down here thanks private—corporate America for doing that. But now that the immediate crisis has passed, the people of this region are looking to corporate America to see if they're here for the long haul. So I ask America's business leaders to show the people here the same commitment you showed during the flood. New Orleans is going to rise again, and by planting your corporate flag here now and contributing to this city's rebirth, you'll gain some loyal customers when times get better.

The people of this city have a responsibility as well. I know you love New Orleans, and New Orleans needs you. She needs people coming home. She needs people—she needs those saints to come marching back, is what she needs. New Orleans is calling her children home. I hear it from all of the local officials. They say they got a plan in place and money coming to make New Orleans a hospitable place.

One woman who's come back is a woman named Samantha George. She is with us today. A year ago, the future looked bleak for Samantha and her four young daughters. Their home in Mid-City had five feet of water in it. Everything they owned was gone. And so they left, and they went to Mississippi and Georgia, as this good mother searched for work. At one point, Samantha and her daughters were living in cars. She felt alone and abandoned. And that's when she walked into the office of Catholic Charities and met a lady named Peggy Matthews, who's also here.

Peggy wiped the tears off Samantha's face. She gave her love and encouragement. Samantha agreed to enroll in Peggy's job-training class and give it one more try. And within 2 weeks, she found work. And at the same time, Catholic Charities helped her with food and clothes and diapers and a gift card to Wal-Mart that allowed her to buy the uniform she would need for her new job. She found help and love.

Catholic Charities also helped Samantha find a house in the Carrollton neighborhood near Lafayette Academy. It's a new charter school that her daughters will be attending very soon. Recently she found a new job she loves; she's now a nurse. For the first time in her life, Samantha says she feels a sense of ownership and control over her future. Here's what she says: "I was just hoping for some motivation so I could keep going. I think God sent me to Catholic Charities, and I think of myself as blessed because now I'm able to help other people who cannot help themselves."

Samantha's story is a story of renewal. And it may sound like a familiar story to people who know the history of New Orleans; it's always been a city of second chance. When your first settlement was leveled by a storm, you rebuilt again. When fire struck, you replaced the wood buildings with brick. When you were ravaged by war and epidemics of malaria and smallpox and yellow fever, you picked yourself up and you prospered. And when the hurricanes hit in the past, you cleaned up, you salvaged what you could, and you rebuilt. Every time New Orleans came back louder, brasher, and better.

We see the same resolve today. In keeping with the tradition of this city, New Orleans again looks to music to express her feelings. And these feelings were captured on a benefit album called "Higher Ground." One of those songs is called "Come Sunday," written by Duke Ellington. In her rendition of this classic, Cassandra Williams implores a loving God to "please look down and see my people through."

Sunday has not yet come to New Orleans, but you can see it ahead. And as you approach that joyful day, you can move forward with confidence in your abilities, trust in the compassion of your fellow Americans, and faith in a loving God who makes the path through mighty waters. God bless.

NOTE: The President spoke at 11:35 a.m. at Warren Easton Senior High School. In his remarks, he referred to Lt. Gen. Russel L. Honore, USA, commanding general, First United States Army; Andrea Green-Jefferson, wife of Rep. William J. Jefferson; Louisiana State Attorney General Charles C. Foti, Jr.; Sister Mary Rose Bingham, principal, Cathedral Academy of New Orleans; Mayor C. Ray Nagin of New Orleans, LA; Oliver M. Thomas, Jr., president, New Orleans City Council; Gov. Kathleen Babineaux Blanco of Louisiana; and entertainer Cassandra Wilson. The transcript released by the Office of the Press Secretary also included the remarks of the First Lady, who introduced the President. The related Executive order improving assistance for disaster victims is listed in Appendix D at the end of the volume.

Remarks at Cotham's in the City and an Exchange With Reporters in Little Rock, Arkansas
August 30, 2006

The President. Asa recommended I come in and get some fried chocolate chip pie, so I did. I'm looking forward to eating it. It's a pleasure to be here with you. I've known Asa for a long time. He's the kind of fellow who can set an agenda and then achieve the results necessary to get the job done. I've seen him first hand in Washington. He's a fellow I called upon to help us get the Homeland Security Department up and running. And so I want to thank you for having me come here.

Asa Hutchinson. Thank you, Mr. President.

The President. I'm proud to call you friend, and thanks for the advice.

Mr. Hutchinson. You can't beat the fried pie here at Cotham's in Little Rock.

The President. Well, I'm looking forward to eating it. When you get to 60, you've got to be a little careful about what you eat. But nevertheless, I'm going to give it a shot, on the recommendation of my friends. Anyway, it's good to be back here in Little Rock. This is a good town. I've come here a lot, as candidate and as President. I appreciate my friends here; I appreciate the values of the people that live in this State. I hope to be back soon. Anyway——

Mr. Hutchinson. Mr. President, we're glad to have you. It's been a great visit. Thanks for helping us out. And we welcome you back anytime. And thank you for your leadership.

The President. Thank you, sir. We'll see you all in Tennessee.

President's Upcoming Speeches/War on Terror

Q. Sir, do you think your new series of speeches are going to have an impact on midterm elections?

The President. My series of speeches, they're not political speeches. They're speeches about the future of this country, and they're speeches to make it clear that if we retreat before the job is done, this Nation would become even more in jeopardy.

These are important times, and I seriously hope people wouldn't politicize these issues that I'm going to talk about. We have a duty in this country to defeat terrorists. That's why we'll stay on the offense and bring them to justice before they hurt us, and that's why we'll work to spread liberty in order to spread the peace.

Anyway, thank you all.

NOTE: The President spoke at 2 p.m. Participating in the event was gubernatorial candidate Asa Hutchinson of Arkansas. A tape was not available for verification of the content of these remarks.

Remarks at a Dinner for Senatorial Candidate Robert Corker and the Tennessee Republican Party in Nashville, Tennessee
August 30, 2006

Thanks for the warm welcome. Appreciate you treating this Texan with such a warm Tennessee welcome. What Corker didn't tell you was, is that the first choice was Laura for the dinner—[*laughter*]—who, by the way, sends her love to all our friends and agrees with me that Bob Corker is the right man for the United States Senate for Tennessee.

I think it makes sense to send somebody up to Washington who's not a lawyer. Nothing wrong with lawyers, but we got a lot of them up there. [*Laughter*] It makes sense to have somebody who understands how the economy works because he was a businessman. It makes sense to send somebody up there who understands how local communities work because he was the mayor of an important Tennessee city. It makes sense to send a man of integrity and decency to Washington, DC. And that man is Bob Corker.

I'm proud to call him friend, and you'll be proud to call him United States Senator. And I want to thank you for your help. I thank you for giving of your money, and I urge you to give of your time. I know there's a lot of grassroots activists who are here. And Bob and Elizabeth are going to be counting on your help coming down the stretch. He's got the message; he's got the courage; but he's going to need you to put up the signs and make the phone calls and go to community centers and remind the good people of this State—Republican, Democrat, and independent—that when you have somebody of his caliber, they need to go to the polls and put him in office.

So thanks for coming. Thanks for organizing this great dinner. And I'm proud to be here. And when Corker gets elected, he's going to be replacing one of the finest citizens your State has ever produced in Bill Frist. It's been my high honor to serve with him, and we're not through yet. He's going to get back up there in September and make sure we get legislation to help protect this country. It's been a joy working with a citizen like Bill. We're going to miss him in Washington, DC. But I take comfort in knowing that he'll be replaced by a fine citizen of this State in Bob Corker. Mr. Leader, thank you for your friendship, and thank you for your courage.

I'm proud also to be here with members of the Tennessee congressional delegation, Congressman Jimmy Duncan, Congressman Zach Wamp, and Congresswoman Marsha Blackburn.

Earlier, I had the privilege of meeting a man who is running hard for Governor of this important State, and I ask you to support Senator Jim Bryson in his quest to be the Governor of the State of Tennessee. And by the way, Senator, if you want some good advice, you ought to turn to Winfield Dunn or Don Sundquist, members who served—people who served well in this important State. I'm glad those two former Governors are here. Thank you for coming.

I'm also proud to be here with a man who served our country with such distinction as the Senate majority leader and under my administration as the Ambassador to Japan, and that would be Senator Howard Baker. I thank Senator Ron Ramsey for being here. He's the majority leader of the senate. I want to thank all the local folks and State folks who have come. Thanks for running; thanks for serving. I appreciate you working hard to make this State a fantastic place.

I bring a message of optimism to you. I believe, and I know, our party is a political party that trusts the wisdom of the American people. Ours is a party that is willing to confront challenges instead of passing them on to future generations. Ours is the party with a positive vision that makes a difference for every citizen of this country. I appreciate you supporting the Republican Party as you support Bob Corker.

We face historic times here in this country. These are tough times. They're difficult times because we face an enemy that longs to hurt America. Much of my thinking about the world in which we live, of course, was shaped on that fateful day of September the 11th, 2001. It's a day I'll never forget. It's a day—after that day, I vowed to the American people that we will do whatever it takes to defend this country from further attack. And I need people in the United States Senate standing by—side by side who understand our most important task is the security of the United States of America.

I need people in Washington, DC, who are willing to give those who are responsible for protecting America all the tools they need—tools such as the PATRIOT Act; tools such as programs that say if Al Qaida is calling into the United States, we want to know why, in order to protect the United States of America.

We face an enemy that has an ideology; they believe things. The best way to describe their ideology is to relate to you the fact that they think the opposite of the way we think. We treasure the freedom to worship. We value the freedom for people to express themselves in the public square. We honor the right for people to be able to raise their children in a peaceful society so they can realize their dreams. The enemy we face doesn't believe in dissent. They don't believe in the freedom to worship. They got a narrow view of freedom. But this enemy is particularly lethal because they're willing to use whatever tactic is necessary to achieve their objective.

You know, right after September the 11th, I knew that one of my challenges would be to remind the American people about the dangers of the world. I knew that the natural tendency for our country would be to hope that the lessons of September the 11th would be faded memory. Earlier this month, thanks to the good intelligence work of Great Britain, and with our help, we uncovered yet another plot, a plot in which these killers who do not share our belief of freedom were willing to take innocent lives in order to achieve their objective.

These are historic times, and we must have people in the United States Congress who understand the stakes. After September the 11th, I vowed to the American people we would use all assets at our disposal to protect you. And the best way to defend America is to stay on the offense against these killers and bring them to justice before they hurt this country again.

We got brave troops around the world who are on the hunt, who are doing their duty to protect the American people. I can't tell you how inspiring it is to be the Commander in Chief of a United States military full of men and women who understand the dangers and have volunteered to serve our country. And we need people in the United States Senate who will make sure that these troops have all the equipment, all the training, all the support they need to do their jobs and protect this country.

In the short run, we'll defend this country by staying on the offense; in the long run, we've got an equally effective weapon, and that is freedom and liberty. The way to defeat an ideology of hate, the way to defeat an ideology that exploits hopelessness and despair, is to spread liberty. It's the calling of our time. The United States of America must understand that freedom is universal, that there is an Almighty, and the great gift of that Almighty to each man and woman in this world is the desire to be free. I strongly believe, deep in the soul of people all across the globe is the desire to live in liberty. I strongly believe that mothers all across the world long to raise their children in a hopeful society. And it's up to us, working with our friends and allies, to defeat the ideology of hate with an ideology of hope. And that hope is based upon the universal principle of liberty and freedom.

One of the lessons of September the 11th is that this Nation must take threats seriously before they come to hurt us; that we just can't hope anymore that things calm down or that there's a rational way of thinking with an enemy; that we must be bold in our actions in defense of the American people. I saw a threat in Iraq, and so did Members of the United States Congress of both political parties. Saddam Hussein was a state sponsor of terror. Saddam Hussein had used weapons of mass destruction. Saddam Hussein had been shooting at our pilots. Saddam Hussein paid families of suicide bombers. Saddam Hussein was a threat, and the world is better off without Saddam Hussein in power.

And now the central front in the war on terror, the central front in this struggle to protect ourselves, is Iraq. You know, amazing things have happened in Iraq, when you think about it. Oh, I know the news is full with terrible suiciders, and it shakes our will. I know that. It's troubling for many of our citizens, no matter what their political party is. But that's what the enemy wants. They want to trouble us. They're willing to take innocent life to cause us to forget our mission and purpose and the calling of this in the 21st century.

But when you really think about it, amazing progress has been made. Twelve million people went to the polls. These are people who had just recently lived under the thumb of a brutal tyrant who killed hundreds of thousands of his own people. And yet, when given a chance, these Iraqis said, "We want to be free; we want to self-govern; we want a government of and by and for the people." And since then a government has been formed, a unity government headed by a good man named Prime Minister Maliki.

Our task is to stand with those who reject extremism and violence. Our task is to train the Iraqis so they can defend themselves. Our task is to achieve a goal of an ally in the war on terror that can defend itself, sustain itself. And we're on our way to achieving that mission.

Now I understand there's a serious—[*applause*]—there are Saddamists, Al Qaida, extremists, militia, all attempting to stop the advance of democracy. That should say something to the American people: What type of mentality is it that fears freedom? What kind of mentality is it that can't stand the thought of liberty? It's a mentality based upon an ideology that is foreign to our way of thinking. It's a mentality based upon an ideology of hate, and they have aspirations. Their goal—this is what they said, not me—is to drive us out of the Middle East because they want to spread their view, their vision.

If we leave Iraq before the job is done, as some have advocated, this will be a major defeat for the United States of America in the global war on terror. If we leave Iraq before the job is done, it will embolden an enemy that wants to harm the American people. If we leave Iraq before the job is done, it will create a terrorist state in the heart of the Middle East; a terrorist state much more dangerous than Afghanistan was before we removed the Taliban; a terrorist state with the capacity to fund its activities because of the oil reserves of Iraq. If we leave before the job is done, it will shred the credibility of the United States of America. If we leave before the job is done, it will have meant incredibly brave souls will have given their lives for nothing. And if we leave Iraq before the job is done, as General Abizaid has said, "They will follow us here."

The stakes in Iraq are high. It's very important for the American people to understand that the security of the United States of America, the capacity for our children to grow up in a peaceful world, in large part depends on our willingness to help this young Iraqi democracy succeed.

And we will succeed. And when we succeed, it will be a major defeat for the ideologues of hate. And when we succeed, it will serve—democracy will serve as a powerful example for others in a region that is desperate for free societies. And when we succeed, we'll create a valuable ally in the global war on terror.

Our mission must be to stay on the offense and defeat them overseas so we do not have to face them here at home. This country ought to have confidence in our capacity to succeed. We have faced these kind of challenges before. We have stared down and defeated the ideology of fascism. We won a cold war. The path to victory was never straight-lined, but the path to victory required perseverance, strength of character, and determination. It's important to have Members of the United States Senate like Bob Corker who share that sense of purpose and determination.

You know, recently I was just right down the road here with the Prime Minister of Japan, and he and I went to Graceland. [*Laughter*] It was an interesting moment. [*Laughter*] I chose to take my friend Prime Minister Koizumi there—one, I had never been there. [*Laughter*] So it was a little selfish. Secondly, he's an Elvis fan; he loved Elvis. And I thought it would be fun to take him there. Thirdly, I wanted to send a message to the American people. Imagine somebody in the late forties saying, one of these days an American President will be taking a Prime Minister from Japan to the home of a famous singer. You know, right after that war, you can imagine what the reaction would have been. They'd say, "Man, that guy is off his rocker." [*Laughter*]

We had fought the Japanese in a bloody, bloody conflict. And it was a brutal war. I find it ironic that my dad fought the Japanese, and yet some 60 years later, I was on Air Force One flying down to Memphis, Tennessee, with the Prime Minister

of a former enemy. And on that plane we weren't talking about Elvis's songs; we were talking about how to work together to keep the peace. We were talking about North Korea. I thanked this good man for sending 1,000 Japanese troops to help the young democracy in Iraq succeed. He understands what I know: Democracy yields the peace.

If we want peace for the long run for our children and grandchildren, we must work hard to spread liberty. Something happened between World War II and my trip to Graceland, and what happened was, Japan adopted a Japanese-style democracy. Democracy and liberty have the capacity to change an enemy into an ally. Someday, an American President will be sitting down with duly elected leaders from the Middle East talking about how to keep the peace, and our children and our grandchildren will be better off.

I appreciate Bob Corker's understanding of the role of government in our economy. He and I know the role of Government is not to create wealth; the role of Government is to create an environment in which the entrepreneurial spirit can flourish in the United States of America. And that means—[*applause*]—and that starts with letting the American taxpayer keep more of their own money.

Here's what we know: We know that when a soul has more of his or her own money to spend, save, or invest, the economy grows. There's a philosophical difference between what we think and what the other bunch thinks. They think they can spend your money better than you can. We believe the more of the money you have in your pocket, the stronger the economy grows and the more hopeful America is.

And our philosophy is working. Our economy is growing at 4.2 percent annual rate in the first 6 months of this year. That's faster than any other major industrialized nation in the world. For 35 straight months, our economy has added jobs. People are working in the United States of

America. The unemployment rate is 4.8 percent, and since August of 2003, we've added 5.5 million new jobs. The tax cuts we provided for the entrepreneurs and small businesses of America are making a difference for the working people of this country.

Now the question is, how do we keep the economy growing? Well, it starts with making sure the tax cuts we passed are permanent, so Congress can't undo them. We want there to be certainty in the Tax Code. We want people planning their future knowing that taxes will remain low, and I need a man like Bob Corker who understands that.

You know, you hear the talk in the campaign. They say, "Oh, well, we've got to balance the budget." We'll balance the budget, but we're not going to balance the budget and wreck the economy at the same time. You see people say, "The best way to balance the budget"—some in Washington say—"just give us more of your own money." But that's not the way Washington works. If you send more of your own money up there, they will figure out new ways as to how to spend your money. The best way to balance this budget is to keep progrowth economic policies in place and be fiscally sound with the people's money.

You know, something happened the other day that's interesting. This budget—I said, we'll try to—we'll cut the budget in half, the deficit in half by 2009. We're ahead of goal—ahead of that goal. It's amazing what happens when the economy grows. Guess what happens? More tax revenues come into the Treasury. Progrowth economic policies work. And I need people in Washington, DC, like Bob Corker who understand, one, you set priorities; two, you eliminate programs that might sound good but don't deliver the results; and three, you help people who can't help themselves. And my number-one priority is making sure we have enough money to defend the United States of America against attack again.

I think it's interesting what Bob Corker said. He said, "America must be the world leader in new technology." Our young people need an exceptional education in the sciences in order to compete for the jobs of the future. You see, the real challenge facing this country is, is to make sure we're the economic leader of the world. I'm not interested in being second place. I think it's—I know it's best for the future of this country that we remain the leader.

And how do you do that? Well, first and foremost, you make sure each child gets a good-quality education. And we're on our way. You know, the No Child Left Behind Act will be up for renewal, and we really need people in the United States Congress who understands the wisdom of that act. And here's the wisdom: It says that we must challenge the soft bigotry of low expectations. We cannot tolerate a system that just simply shuffles kids through school. We must set high expectations and measure to make sure our children are learning to read and write and add and subtract early. And if they're not, we'll provide extra money to make sure no child is left behind.

And I understand people say, "Well, we don't like that; we don't like to be measured; we don't want there to be accountability." There must be accountability in the public schools of the United States of America, to make sure the promise of this country is met.

Senator Frist and I have been working on policies to get us less dependent on foreign sources of oil. It's really the challenge of our time. We have got to use technologies to make us less dependent on energy from unstable parts of the world. It's in our economic interests, and it's in our national security interests. And there's some exciting technologies coming along. One of these days you'll be able to drive the first 40 miles in your car—and it won't look like a golf cart—using a new battery. We'll be using Tennessee crops to power our automobiles.

We must proceed with civilian nuclear power as a source of electricity. We must make sure we promote clean coal technologies. I look forward to having a United States Senator who understands that technology will help us become less dependent on foreign sources of oil.

I've got two other things I want to say; then you'll be liberated. [*Laughter*] One of my most important jobs is to put people on the bench who know the difference between a legislator and a judge. And I thank Senator Bill Frist for his strong leadership in getting two new Supreme Court judges through the United States Senate, Judge Roberts and Judge Alito. There will be more picks to be made. There will be picks throughout all the judiciary. And I need a United States Senator who understands that we need people on the bench who will strictly interpret the Constitution and not use the bench to legislate. And that man is Bob Corker.

And finally, one of the most important initiatives that my administration has pursued is what I call the Faith-based and Community-based Initiative. This initiative recognizes a couple of things: One, the true strength of this country lies in the hearts and souls of the American people. It recognizes there are social entrepreneurs all over America who feed the hungry, provide shelter for the homeless, love those who need love, without one single law emanating out of Washington, DC. I believe Government has an obligation to open its coffers for competitive bidding to faith-based and community-based groups in order to make sure America—America's souls are saved one person at a time.

You know, here is my great buddy, Michael W. Smith. He's an interesting man; he's a good musician, obviously, but he, too, is a social entrepreneur. I remember visiting with Michael's team who helped found what's called Rocket Town. It's an example of what I'm talking about. Rocket Town came into existence because there

was a need to provide a place where people could find love. You see, government is not a loving organization. [*Laughter*] Government is about law and justice. Love comes from the hearts and souls of individuals. And I need a soul like Bob Corker in the United States Senate who understands that many of the social problems we face require something greater than government, require the help of people who hear a higher calling to love their neighbor just like they would like to be loved themselves.

America can change one heart and one soul and one conscience at a time. Government should not fear faith; government ought to welcome the good works of faith-based and community-based organizations to help make this country as strong as it possibly can be.

And so I want to thank you for coming tonight. I'm proud to share the stage with a good man who is leaving the United States Senate. People of this State will be able to say, Bill Frist, job well done. And I'm proud to be serving—sharing this stage with a man who I look forward to serving with, to do what's right for this country. He doesn't need to take a poll; he doesn't need to run a focus group to determine what's right and what we need to do. He'll make you proud. He's the kind of United States Senator you want. It's my honor to endorse and strongly support Bob Corker for the United States Senate.

Thank you all for coming.

NOTE: The President spoke at 5:45 p.m. at the Loews Vanderbilt Hotel. In his remarks, he referred to Elizabeth Corker, wife of senatorial candidate Robert Corker; former President Saddam Hussein and Prime Minister Nuri al-Maliki of Iraq; Gen. John P. Abizaid, USA, commander, U.S. Central Command; and Prime Minister Junichiro Koizumi of Japan.

Remarks on Arrival in Salt Lake City, Utah
August 30, 2006

War on Terror

Thank you all for coming out. I can't thank you enough for this fantastic Utah welcome. I am delighted to be here in Salt Lake City. My only regret is that Laura is not here to see this great crowd. She sends her best; she sends her love.

I want to thank the Governor for being here today. Governor, thank you for coming. I want to thank your two fine United States Senators, Senator Hatch and Bennett for joining us. I thank Congressmen Matheson, Bishop, and Cannon for being here as well. I want to thank you all for coming.

Most of all, I want to thank you all for staying up a little past your bedtime, for some of you, to greet me.

I'm looking forward to talking tomorrow to our veterans. I'm going to tell the veterans how much America appreciates their service to the United States of America. And I want to thank our veterans for setting such a great example for incredibly fine men and women who wear the uniform of the United States military today.

These are challenging times. I wish I could report to you that all is well, but there's still an enemy that wants to harm the United States of America because of what we stand for. We learned that lesson earlier this month, when, because of the good work of our friends in Great Britain and some of our own help, we stopped a terrorist plot against the United States. This is the challenge of our time and my most important duty. And the most important duty of our Government is to protect the American people from further attack.

We will stay on the offense and defeat the terrorists abroad so we do not have to face them here at home. And as we do so, we'll remember the power of freedom and liberty to transform regions of hate to regions of compassion. I believe there's an Almighty, and I believe the great gift of the Almighty to every man and woman on the Earth is the desire to live in freedom.

Iraq is the central front in this war on terror. If we leave the streets of Baghdad before the job is done, we will have to face the terrorists in our own cities. We will stay the course. We will help this young Iraqi democracy succeed, and victory in Iraq will be a major ideological triumph in the struggle of the 21st century.

I firmly believe we'll succeed. We'll succeed in spreading liberty. And as we do so, we can say that this generation did our duty and laid the foundation of peace for generations to come.

For those of you with loved ones in the United States military, I thank you from the bottom of my heart. I can't tell you how proud I am to be the Commander in Chief of such a fantastic group of young men and women. And I'll make this pledge to you: Our Government will make sure your loved ones have all the support, all the help, all the training necessary to do their job of defending freedom, defending America, and spreading liberty that will yield the peace we all want.

So I want to thank you all for coming. It warms my heart to see such a huge crowd. May God bless the great State of Utah, and may God bless America. Thank you all very much.

NOTE: The President spoke at 9:04 p.m. at the Utah Air National Guard base at the Salt Lake International Airport. In his remarks, he referred to Gov. Jon M. Huntsman, Jr., of Utah.

Remarks at the American Legion National Convention in Salt Lake City
August 31, 2006

Thank you all very much. Please be seated. Thanks for the warm welcome. It's great to join you here in one of America's most beautiful cities. I appreciate your hospitality. I'm proud to stand before some of our country's finest patriots: our veterans and their families. And I'm pleased to call you my fellow Legionnaires—I suspect I may be the only one here, though, from Post 77, Houston, Texas. That's what I thought. [*Laughter*] If you're from Post 77, behave yourself here in Salt Lake. [*Laughter*]

Laura did remind me the other night, though, that a few of my fellow members— at least I've joined a few of my fellow members in another illustrious organization, the "Over 60 Club." [*Laughter*]

For almost 90 years, Legionnaires have stood proudly "for God and country." From big cities to small towns, the American Legion name brings to mind the best of our Nation: decency, generosity, and character. I thank you for a lifetime of service. I thank you for the positive contributions you make to our Nation, and I'm proud to join you today.

First, I want to thank Tom Bock, the national commander, for his kind introduction and his strong leadership. I always am pleased to welcome the commander to the Oval Office to discuss common issues, and you've done a fine job leading this organization, Tom. I also want to thank your wife, Elaine, and I particularly want to pay respect to your son, Captain Bock of the United States Army, who's joined us today.

I appreciate being here with Carol Van Kirk, the national president of the American Legion Auxiliary. And I want to thank all the Auxiliary members who are with us here today as well.

I'm proud that the Governor of this great State, Jon Huntsman, and his wife, Mary Kaye, have joined us. Governor, thank you for your time. I'm also proud to be joined by two United States Senators who are strong supporters of the United States military, Senator Orrin Hatch and Senator Bob Bennett.

Members of the congressional delegation from the State of Utah have joined us, Congressman Rob Bishop and Congressman Chris Cannon. Thank you both for coming. Proud you're here. I thank the State Senator John Valentine, who is the president of the Utah State Senate. I appreciate Speaker Greg Curtis. I want to thank all the State and local officials who have joined us here today. Most particularly, I want to thank you all for giving me a chance to come and speak to you. I particularly want to thank all the Gold Star families who have joined us today. May God bless you. May God bless you.

As veterans, all of you stepped forward when America needed you most. From north Africa to Normandy, Iwo Jima to Inchon, from Khe Sanh to Kuwait, your courage and service have made it possible for generations to live in liberty. And we owe you more than just thanks; we owe you the support of the Federal Government. And so in my first 4 years as President, we increased funding for veterans more than the previous administration did in 8 years. Since then, we've increased it even more. My budget for this year provides more than $80 billion for veterans. That's a 75-percent increase since I took office. It's the highest level of support for veterans in American history.

For many veterans, health care is a top priority, and it's a top priority of my administration. When Congress passes my 2007 budget, we will have increased the VA health care budget by 69 percent since 2001. We've extended treatment to a million additional veterans, including more than 300,000 men and women returning from Afghanistan and Iraq. We're building new VA facilities in places where veterans are retiring so that more veterans can get top-quality health care closer to their homes.

I appreciate the Legion's strong history of care and compassion for your fellow veterans. Earlier this week, I traveled to Mississippi and Louisiana to mark the first anniversary of Hurricane Katrina. Veterans were hit hard by this storm, and American Legion posts all across the United States responded with vital relief. In an hour of suffering, you showed the good heart of our Nation, and you showed the world that America can always count on Legionnaires.

I also appreciate the Legion's long history of supporting wise legislation in the Nation's Capital. Earlier this year, the Senate voted on a constitutional amendment to ban flag desecration; we came within a single vote of passing it. The administration looks forward to continuing working with the American Legion to make sure we get this important protection in the Constitution of the United States of America.

Your organization supported another good piece of legislation called the Respect for America's Fallen Heroes Act. This bill ensures that families of fallen servicemembers will not have to endure protests during military funerals.

My administration will also continue to work to locate the men and women in uniform whose fate is still undetermined, our prisoners of war and personnel missing in action. We will not forget these brave Americans. We must not rest until we've accounted for every soldier, sailor, airman, coastguardsman, and marine. And we will always honor their courage.

At this hour, a new generation of Americans in uniform is showing great courage in defending our freedom in the first war of the 21st century. I know that Legionnaires are following this war closely, especially those of you with family and friends who wear our uniform. The images that

come back from the frontlines are striking and sometimes unsettling. When you see innocent civilians ripped apart by suicide bombs or families buried inside their homes, the world can seem engulfed in purposeless violence. The truth is, there is violence, but those who cause it have a clear purpose. When terrorists murder at the World Trade Center or car bombers strike in Baghdad or hijackers plot to blow up planes over the Atlantic or terrorist militias shoot rockets at Israeli towns, they are all pursuing the same objective: to turn back the advance of freedom and impose a dark vision of tyranny and terror across the world.

The enemies of liberty come from different parts of the world, and they take inspiration from different sources. Some are radicalized followers of the Sunni tradition who swear allegiance to terrorist organizations like Al Qaida. Others are radicalized followers of the Shi'a tradition who join groups like Hizballah and take guidance from state sponsors like Syria and Iran. Still others are "homegrown" terrorists, fanatics who live quietly in free societies they dream to destroy. Despite their differences, these groups from—form the outlines of a single movement, a worldwide network of radicals that use terror to kill those who stand in the way of their totalitarian ideology. And the unifying feature of this movement, the link that spans sectarian divisions and local grievances, is the rigid conviction that free societies are a threat to their twisted view of Islam.

The war we fight today is more than a military conflict; it is the decisive ideological struggle of the 21st century. On one side are those who believe in the values of freedom and moderation, the right of all people to speak and worship and live in liberty. And on the other side are those driven by the values of tyranny and extremism—the right of a self-appointed few to impose their fanatical views on all the rest. As veterans, you have seen this kind of enemy before. They're successors to Fascists, to Nazis, to Communists, and other totalitarians of the 20th century. And history shows what the outcome will be: This war will be difficult; this war will be long; and this war will end in the defeat of the terrorists and totalitarians and a victory for the cause of freedom and liberty.

We're now approaching the fifth anniversary of the day this war reached our shores. As the horror of that morning grows more distant, there is a tendency to believe that the threat is receding and this war is coming to a close. That feeling is natural and comforting—and wrong. As we recently saw, the enemy still wants to attack us. We're in a war we didn't ask for, but it's a war we must wage and a war we will win.

In the coming days, I'll deliver a series of speeches describing the nature of our enemy in the war on terror, the insights we've gained about their aims and ambitions, the successes and setbacks we've experienced, and our strategy to prevail in this long war. Today I'll discuss a critical aspect of this war: the struggle between freedom and terror in the Middle East, including the battle in Iraq, which is the central front in our fight against terrorism.

To understand the struggle unfolding in the Middle East, we need to look at the recent history of the region. For a half-century, America's primary goal in the Middle East was stability. This was understandable at the time. We were fighting the Soviet Union in the cold war, and it was important to support Middle Eastern governments that rejected communism. Yet over the decades, an undercurrent of danger was rising in the Middle East. Much of the region was mired in stagnation and despair. A generation of young people grew up with little hope to improve their lives, and many fell under the sway of radical extremism. The terrorist movement multiplied in strength, and resentment that had simmered for years boiled over into violence across the world.

Extremists in Iran seized American hostages. Hizballah terrorists murdered American troops at the Marine barracks in Beirut and Khobar Towers in Saudi Arabia. Terrorists set off a truck bomb at the World Trade Center. Al Qaida blew up two U.S. Embassies in east Africa and bombed the USS *Cole*. Then came the nightmare of September the 11th, 2001, when 19 hijackers killed nearly 3,000 men, women, and children.

In the space of a single morning, it became clear that the calm we saw in the Middle East was only a mirage. We realized that years of pursuing stability to promote peace had left us with neither. Instead, the lack of freedom in the Middle East made the region an incubator for terrorist movements.

The status quo in the Middle East before September the 11th was dangerous and unacceptable, so we're pursuing a new strategy. First, we're using every element of national power to confront Al Qaida, those who take inspiration from them, and other terrorists who use similar tactics. We have ended the days of treating terrorism simply as a law enforcement matter. We will stay on the offense. We will fight the terrorists overseas so we do not have to face them here at home.

Second, we have made it clear to all nations, if you harbor terrorists, you are just as guilty as the terrorists. You're an enemy of the United States, and you will be held to account.

And third, we've launched a bold new agenda to defeat the ideology of the enemy by supporting the forces of freedom in the Middle East and beyond. The freedom agenda is based upon our deepest ideals and our vital interests. Americans believe that every person of every religion on every continent has the right to determine his or her own destiny. We believe that freedom is a gift from an Almighty God, beyond any power on Earth to take away. And we also know, by history and by logic, that promoting democracy is the surest way to build security. Democracies don't attack each other or threaten the peace. Governments accountable to the voters focus on building roads and schools, not weapons of mass destruction. Young people who have a say in their future are less likely to search for meaning in extremism. Citizens who can join a peaceful political party are less likely to join a terrorist organization. Dissidents with the freedom to protest around the clock are less likely to blow themselves up during rush hour. And nations that commit to freedom for their people will not support terrorists; they will join us in defeating them.

So America has committed its influence in the world to advancing freedom and democracy as the great alternatives to repression and radicalism. We will take the side of democratic leaders and reformers across the Middle East. We will support the voices of tolerance and moderation in the Muslim world. We stand with the mothers and fathers in every culture who want to see their children grow up in a caring and peaceful world. And by supporting the cause of freedom in a vital region, we'll make our children and our grandchildren more secure.

Over the past 5 years, we've begun to see the results of our actions, and we have seen how our enemies respond to the advance of liberty. In Afghanistan, we saw a vicious tyranny that harbored the terrorists who planned the September the 11th attacks. Within weeks, American forces were in Afghanistan. Along with Afghan allies, we captured or killed hundreds of Al Qaida and Taliban fighters; we closed down their training camps; and we helped the people of Afghanistan replace the Taliban with a democratic government that answers to them.

Our enemies saw the transformation in Afghanistan, and they've responded by trying to roll back all the progress. Al Qaida and the Taliban lost a coveted base in Afghanistan, and they know they will never reclaim it when democracy succeeds. And

so they're trying to return to power by attacking Afghanistan's free institutions, and they will fail. Forces from 40 nations, including every member of NATO, are now serving alongside American troops to support the new Afghan Government. The days of the Taliban are over. The future of Afghanistan belongs to the people of Afghanistan, and the future of Afghanistan belongs to freedom.

In Lebanon, we saw a sovereign nation occupied by the Syrian dictatorship. We also saw the courageous people of Lebanon take to the streets to demand their independence. So we worked to enforce a United Nations resolution that required Syria to end its occupation of the country. The Syrians withdrew their armed forces, and the Lebanese people elected a democratic Government that began to reclaim their country.

Our enemies saw the transformation in Lebanon and set out to destabilize the young democracy. Hizballah launched an unprovoked attack on Israel that undermined the democrat Government in Beirut. Yet their brazen action caused the world to unite in support for Lebanon's democracy. Secretary Rice worked with the Security Council to pass Resolution 1701, which will strengthen Lebanese forces as they take control of southern Lebanon and stop Hizballah from acting as a state within a state.

I appreciate the troops pledged by France and Italy and other allies for this important international deployment. Together we're going to make it clear to the world that foreign forces and terrorists have no place in a free and democratic Lebanon.

This summer's crisis in Lebanon has made it clearer than ever that the world now faces a grave threat from the radical regime in Iran. The Iranian regime arms, funds, and advises Hizballah, which has killed more Americans than any terrorist network except Al Qaida. The Iranian regime interferes in Iraq by sponsoring terrorists and insurgents, empowering unlawful militias, and supplying components for improvised explosive devices. The Iranian regime denies basic human rights to millions of its people. And the Iranian regime is pursuing nuclear weapons in open defiance of its international obligations.

We know the death and suffering that Iran's sponsorship of terrorists has brought, and we can imagine how much worse it would be if Iran were allowed to acquire nuclear weapons. Many nations are working together to solve this problem. The United Nations passed a resolution demanding that Iran suspend its nuclear enrichment activities. Today is the deadline for Iran's leaders to reply to the reasonable proposal the international community has made. If Iran's leaders accept this offer and abandon their nuclear weapons ambitions, they can set their country on a better course. Yet so far the Iranian regime has responded with further defiance and delay. It is time for Iran to make a choice. We've made our choice: We will continue to work closely with our allies to find a diplomatic solution, but there must be consequences for Iran's defiance, and we must not allow Iran to develop a nuclear weapon.

In Iraq, we saw a dictator who harbored terrorists, fired at military planes, paid the families of Palestinian suicide bombers, invaded a neighbor, and pursued and used weapons of mass destruction. The United Nations passed more than a dozen resolutions demanding that Saddam Hussein fully and openly abandon his weapons of mass destruction. We gave him a last chance to comply, and when he refused, we enforced the just demands of the world. And now Saddam Hussein is in prison and on trial. Soon he will have the justice he denied to so many for so long. And with this tyrant gone from power, the United States, Iraq, the Middle East, and the world are better off.

In 3 years since Saddam's fall, the Iraqi people have reclaimed the sovereignty of their country. They cast their ballots in free elections. They drafted and approved a democratic constitution and elected a constitutional democracy at the heart of the Middle East.

Over the same period, Iraq has seen a rise of terrorist and insurgent movements that use brutal and indiscriminate violence to frustrate the desire of the Iraqi people for freedom and peace. Al Qaida terrorists, former elements of Saddam's regime, illegal militias, and unlawful armed groups are all working to undermine Iraq's new democracy. These groups have different long-term ambitions but the same immediate goals. They want to drive America and our coalition out of Iraq and the Middle East so they can stop the advance of freedom and impose their dark vision on the people of the Middle East.

Our enemies in Iraq have employed ruthless tactics to achieve those goals. They've targeted American and coalition troops with ambushes and roadside bombs. They've taken hostage and beheaded civilians on camera. They've blown up Iraqi Army posts and assassinated government leaders. We've adapted to the tactics. And thanks to the skill and professionalism of Iraqi and American forces, many of these enemies have met their end. At every stop along the way, our enemies have failed to break the courage of the Iraqi people, they have failed to stop the rise of Iraqi democracy, and they will fail in breaking the will of the American people.

Now these enemies have launched a new effort. They have embarked on a bloody campaign of sectarian violence which they hope will plunge Iraq into a civil war. The outbreak of sectarian violence was encouraged by the terrorist Zarqawi, Al Qaida's man in Iraq who called for an "all-out war" on Iraqi Shi'a. The Shi'a community resisted the impulse to seek revenge for a while. But after this February bombing of the Shi'a Golden Dome Mosque in

Samarra, extremist groups mobilized and sectarian death squads formed on the streets of Baghdad and other areas. Our Ambassador reports that thousands of Iraqis were murdered in Baghdad last month, and large numbers of them were victims of sectarian violence.

This cruelty and carnage has led some to question whether Iraq has descended into civil war. Our commanders and our diplomats on the ground in Iraq believe that's not the case. They report that only a small number of Iraqis are engaged in sectarian violence, while the overwhelming majority want peace and a normal life in a unified country. Iraqi leaders from all backgrounds remember the elections that brought them to power, in which 12 million Iraqis defied the car bombers and killers to proclaim, "We want to be free."

Iraq's Government is working tirelessly to hold the nation together and to heal Iraq's divisions, not to exploit them. The Iraqi people have come a long way. They are not going to let their country fall apart or relapse into tyranny. As Prime Minister Maliki told the United States Congress, "Iraqis have tasted freedom, and we will defend it absolutely."

America has a clear strategy to help the Iraqi people protect their new freedom and build a democracy that can govern itself and sustain itself and defend itself. On the political side, we're working closely with Prime Minister Maliki to strengthen Iraq's unity Government and develop—and to deliver better services to the Iraqi people. This is a crucial moment for the new Iraqi Government; its leaders understand the challenge. They believe that now is the time to hammer out compromises on Iraq's most contentious issues.

I've been clear with each Iraqi leader I meet: America is a patient nation, and Iraq can count on our partnership as long as the new Government continues to make the hard decisions necessary to advance a unified, democratic, and peaceful Iraq. Prime Minister Maliki has shown courage in laying out an agenda to do just that, and he can count on an ally, the United States of America, to help him promote this agenda.

On the security side, we're refining our tactics to meet the threats on the ground. I've given our commanders in Iraq all the flexibility they need to make adjustments necessary to stay on the offense and defeat the enemies of freedom. We've deployed Special Operation forces to kill or capture terrorists operating in Iraq. Zarqawi found out what they can do. We continue to train Iraqi police forces to defend their own nation. We've handed over security responsibility for a southern Province to Iraqi forces. Five of Iraq's 10 army divisions are now taking the lead in their areas of operation. The Iraqi security forces are determined. They're becoming more capable, and together we will defeat the enemies of a free Iraq.

Recently we also launched a major new campaign to end the security crisis in Baghdad. Side by side, Iraqi and American forces are conducting operations in the city's most violent areas to disrupt Al Qaida, to capture enemy fighters, crack down on IED makers, and break up the death squads. These forces are helping Iraq's national police force undergo retraining to better enforce law in Baghdad. And these forces are supporting the Iraqi Government as it provides reconstruction assistance.

The Baghdad Security Plan is still in its early stages. We cannot expect immediate success. Yet the initial results are encouraging. According to one military report, a Sunni man in a diverse Baghdad neighborhood said this about the Shi'a soldiers on patrol: "Their image has changed. Now you feel they're there to protect you." Over the coming weeks and months, the operation will expand throughout Baghdad until Iraq's democratic Government is in full control of its capital. The work is difficult and dangerous, but the Iraqi Government and their forces are determined to reclaim their country. And the United States is determined to help them succeed.

Here at home, we have a choice to make about Iraq. Some politicians look at our efforts in Iraq and see a diversion from the war on terror. That would come as news to Usama bin Laden, who proclaimed that the "third world war is raging" in Iraq. It would come as news to the number-two man of Al Qaida, Zawahiri, who has called the struggle in Iraq, quote, "the place for the greatest battle." It would come as news to the terrorists from Syria, Saudi Arabia, Egypt, Sudan, Libya, and Yemen and other countries, who have come to Iraq to fight the rise of democracy.

It's hard to believe that these terrorists would make long journeys across dangerous borders, endure heavy fighting, or blow themselves up in the streets of Baghdad for a so-called diversion. Some Americans didn't support my decision to remove Saddam Hussein; many are frustrated with the level of violence. But we should all agree that the battle for Iraq is now central to the ideological struggle of the 21st century. We will not allow the terrorists to dictate the future of this century, so we will defeat them in Iraq.

Still, there are some in our country who insist that the best option in Iraq is to pull out, regardless of the situation on the ground. Many of these folks are sincere, and they're patriotic, but they could be— they could not be more wrong. If America were to pull out before Iraq can defend itself, the consequences would be absolutely predictable and absolutely disastrous. We would be handing Iraq over to our worst enemies: Saddam's former henchmen, armed groups with ties to Iran, and Al Qaida terrorists from all over the world who would suddenly have a base of operations far more valuable than Afghanistan under the Taliban. They would have a new sanctuary to recruit and train terrorists at the heart of the Middle East, with huge oil riches to fund their ambitions. And we know exactly where those ambitions lead.

If we give up the fight in the streets of Baghdad, we will face the terrorists in the streets of our own cities.

We can decide to stop fighting the terrorists in Iraq and other parts of the world, but they will not decide to stop fighting us. General John Abizaid, our top commander in the Middle East region, recently put it this way: "If we leave, they will follow us." And he is right. The security of the civilized world depends on victory in the war on terror, and that depends on victory in Iraq. So the United States of America will not leave until victory is achieved.

Victory in Iraq will be difficult, and it will require more sacrifice. The fighting there can be as fierce as it was at Omaha Beach or Guadalcanal. And victory is as important as it was in those earlier battles. Victory in Iraq will result in a democracy that is a friend of America and an ally in the war on terror. Victory in Iraq will be a crushing defeat to our enemies who have staked so much on the battle there. Victory in Iraq will honor the sacrifice of the brave Americans who have given their lives. And victory in Iraq would be a powerful triumph in the ideological struggle of the 21st century. From Damascus to Tehran, people will look to a democratic Iraq as inspiration that freedom can succeed in the Middle East and as evidence that the side of freedom is the winning side. This is a pivotal moment for the Middle East. The world is watching. And in Iraq and beyond, the forces of freedom will prevail.

For all the debate, American policy in the Middle East comes down to a straightforward choice. We can allow the Middle East to continue on its course—on the course it was headed before September the 11th, and a generation from now, our children will face a region dominated by terrorist states and radical dictators armed with nuclear weapons. Or we can stop that from happening by rallying the world to confront the ideology of hate, and give the people of the Middle East a future of hope. And that is the choice America has made.

We see a day when people across the Middle East have governments that honor their dignity, unleash their creativity, and count their votes. We see a day when leaders across the Middle East reject terror and protect freedom. We see a day when the nations of the Middle East are allies in the cause of peace. The path to that day will be uphill and uneven, but we can be confident of the outcome because we know that the direction of history leads toward freedom.

In the early years of our Republic, Thomas Jefferson said that we cannot expect to move "from despotism to liberty in a featherbed." That's been true in every time and place. No one understands that like you, our veterans, understand that. With the distance of history, it can be easy to look back at the wars of the 20th century and see a straight path to victory. You know better than that. You waged the hard battles; you suffered the wounds; you lost friends and brothers. You were there for dark times and the moments of uncertainty, and you know that freedom is always worth the sacrifice.

You also know what it takes to win. For all that is new about this war, one thing has not changed: Victory still depends on the courage and the patience and the resolve of the American people. Above all, it depends on patriots who are willing to fight for freedom. Our Nation is blessed to have these men and women in abundance. Our military forces make this Nation strong; they make this Nation safe; and they make this Nation proud.

We thank them and their families for their sacrifice. We will remember all those who have given their lives in this struggle. And I vow that we will give our men and women in uniform all the resources they need to accomplish their missions.

One brave American we remember is Marine Corporal Adam Galvez from here in Salt Lake City. Yesterday Adam's mom and dad laid their son to rest. We're honored by their presence with us today. About a month ago, Adam was wounded by a suicide bomb in Iraq's Anbar Province. When he regained consciousness, he found he was buried alive, so he dug himself out of the rubble. And then he ran through gunfire to get a shovel to dig out his fellow marines. As soon as he recovered from his injuries, Adam volunteered to go back to the frontlines. And 11 days ago, he was killed when a roadside bomb hit his convoy.

Here is what Adam's mom and dad said about the cause for which their son gave his life: "Though many are debating the justification of this war, Adam believed in his country; Adam's belief in his country did not waver, even to the point of the ultimate sacrifice. It's our hope and our prayer that people share the same conviction and dedication to our troops and fellow Americans."

Our Nation will always remember the selflessness and sacrifice of Americans like Adam Galvez. We will honor their lives by completing the good and noble work they have started. And we can be confident that one day, veterans of the war on terror will gather at American Legion halls across the country and say the same things you say: "We made our Nation safer; we made a region more peaceful; and we left behind a better world for our children and our grandchildren."

Thanks for having me. May God bless our veterans. May God bless our troops. And may God continue to bless the United States of America.

NOTE: The President spoke at 9:08 a.m. at the Salt Palace Convention Center. In his remarks, he referred to U.S. Ambassador to Iraq Zalmay Khalilzad; Prime Minister Nuri al-Maliki of Iraq; Usama bin Laden, leader of the Al Qaida terrorist organization; Ayman Al-Zawahiri, founder of the Egyptian Islamic Jihad and senior Al Qaida associate; and Gen. John P. Abizaid, USA, commander, U.S. Central Command.

Remarks at a Reception for Senatorial Candidate Orrin G. Hatch in Salt Lake City
August 31, 2006

Thank you all very much. Thank you all. Please be seated. Thanks for the warm welcome. It's great to be here in Utah. Gosh, I landed at the airport last night—a couple of thousand people out there to say hello. I just had the honor of speaking to the American Legion; then come to a hall filled with great citizens concerned about the reelection of Orrin Hatch. I'm telling—here to tell you, this guy is doing a great job and you need to send him back to the United States Senate.

I'm proud to call him friend. And he's an effective person in Washington. I don't know if you can tell it this far away from Washington, but he's effective. He gets things done. People like to hear him; they listen to him; they trust him; they trust his judgment. And so do I. And every time I'm around Orrin Hatch, after he gets through talking about Utah, he finally gets to the country. [*Laughter*] In other words, he loves Utah, and he loves the citizens of Utah.

And he married well. We're proud to be here with Elaine and the Hatch family. Laura said to me, she said, "You get over to Utah, and you help our friends come back to Washington, DC." She sends her love. I married well, just like Orrin married well. It helps to have somebody you love stand by your side when you're in politics. There's nothing better than having a person that you care deeply about and—to share the experience. And that's the way the Hatchs have been, and they've served a great example for a lot of younger political families. And thank you for having the right priorities, faith and your family and your friends.

And so I've come to say as best as I can and in as plain English as I can possibly speak—which sometimes gets a little distorted—[*laughter*]—please send Orrin Hatch back to the United States Senate.

I want to thank the Governor and Mary Kaye for joining us. I appreciate you all taking time to come to support the senior Senator from the State of Utah. It's smart politics. [*Laughter*] You're doing a fine job, and the people of Utah are proud of you.

I want to thank the other Senator, Senator Bob Bennett, for his courageous leadership and friendship. I want to thank Congressman Rob Bishop and Congressman Chris Cannon for joining us today and for serving the country. Glad you all are here. Cannon's brother is the chairman of the Republican Party. I like to remind the chairman that he's the cuter Cannon. [*Laughter*] Is that okay? No. [*Laughter*]

I want to thank all the statehouse folks who've joined us today too. I appreciate John Valentine who is the senate president—leader, and Greg Curtis, the speaker. I want to thank all of you who are senators and representatives. I appreciate you serving your communities. I had—some of the greatest experiences I've ever had in politics—was working with our State senate and our house of representatives in the State of Texas. And I hope, Governor, you're having as much fun working with them as I had. And if not, just keep telling them what to do, and eventually they'll get the message. [*Laughter*] But thank you all for serving.

I appreciate all the local folks here. I particularly want to say thanks to former Senator Jake Garn, who is with us. Senator, good to see you. I appreciate you coming. And I see my friend Jim Hansen is with us today. Congressman, good to see you, thanks for being here. And I wish LaVar Christensen all the best in his run for the congressional seat here in Utah. Good luck to you. Appreciate you.

And most of all, thanks for helping Orrin. It takes a lot of work to get this many people in the room. And for those of you who organized this event, thank you. I know how hard you worked, and so does he. This is an incredibly successful fundraiser, and he deserves it.

And for those of you involved in grassroots politics, thanks a lot for your hard work. Thanks for making sure that Utah was solid in 2004, and thank you for making sure that Utah remains solid in 2006. I appreciate you putting up the signs. I appreciate you making the phone calls. I appreciate you knocking on the doors.

A lot of times, people kind of forget the efforts you make, but I don't, and I know Orrin doesn't. I know the Governor appreciates all the grassroots activists. So thanks for the good work you're doing here in the great State of Utah.

These are historic times in which we're living. This generation of ours is being challenged, and it's a tough challenge because we're facing an enemy that knows no bounds of decency, an enemy that uses tactics that are beyond our imagination to achieve certain objectives. The President has to make a lot of decisions. Mine is a decisionmaking experience. And I just want you to know that a lot of the decisions I have made were based upon the experiences of the attacks on September the 11th. See, I vowed that day that I would never forget our most important duty in Washington, DC, is to protect the American people.

And Orrin Hatch understands that. He is a strong supporter of our strategy to defend the country. That strategy starts with understanding this doctrine: One, you can't rationalize with these people; you cannot negotiate with these extremists, these terrorists, these people who are bound together by an ideology that is hateful. The only way to protect the American people is to stay on the offense and defeat them overseas so we do not have to face them here at home.

But it's important to understand the nature of this war. This is more than just a military conflict. This is the decisive ideological struggle of the 21st century. Some would like to assign this war to something as simple as law enforcement. That shows a lack of understanding of the nature of the enemy. Law enforcement means we wouldn't use all assets at our disposal to protect the American people. This is an ideological struggle, and it's the struggle of the century. And it's the struggle in which we must prevail for the sake of our children and our grandchildren.

On the one side of this struggle are those who believe in freedom and moderation, the right of people to speak, the right of people to worship freely—one of the great privileges in America, isn't it? I'm proud as the President to be able to say you're equally American if you're Jew, Muslim, Christian, agnostic, atheist; we're all equally American. And one of the great treasured rights of our society is for people to be able to worship freely.

On this struggle are those who believe in the universality of liberty. I personally believe there's an Almighty, and I believe that one of the great gifts of that Almighty to every man, woman, and child on the face of the Earth is the desire to live in freedom.

And on the other side of this ideological struggle are those who are driven by tyranny and extremism, the right of a self-appointed few to impose their fanatical views over the rest of us. And that's the struggle. And it's important that our fellow citizens understand that struggle.

We didn't ask for this war, but we will answer history's call with confidence. And it's important to have Members of the United States Senate who understand the call of history and are willing to stand strong in the face of an enemy who is relenting. That's the challenge of the 21st century.

As I told you, we'll stay on the offense. As well, I made it clear that if you harbor a terrorist, you're just as guilty as the terrorists, and you're an enemy of the United States, and you will be held to account. In other words, this is a war in which nation-states aren't necessarily in the league, as previous wars, in, but they provide safe haven for. It's important when the President speaks, he means what he says. I spoke clearly to the world that if you harbor a terrorist, you're equally as guilty as the terrorists. The Taliban didn't take our word seriously. And thanks to a fantastic United States military, along with allies, we removed the Taliban. We upheld doctrine, we freed 25 million Afghan citizens, and the world is better off.

A lesson of September the 11th is that when this Nation sees a threat, we must take it seriously, before it fully materializes. If there is a threat, we must recognize that threat and deal with it before it comes home to hurt us. You know, the tendency in any difficult situation is for some to want to forget the lessons, put the past behind and think about a more comforting future. And I can understand that. As a matter of fact, part of my job is to assure the American people that we understand the threat and that people should go on about their lives. Let us worry about it. That's why I've asked to make sure we have all the tools necessary to protect the American people, tools like the PATRIOT Act, which Orrin helped get passed, tools like the capacity to listen to an Al Qaida phone call. If they're calling into the United States, we want to know why so we can protect the American people.

I saw a threat in Iraq. As a matter of fact, members of both political parties in the United States Congress saw the same threat. Nations around the world saw the threat. And the threat was a tyrant who brutally murdered thousands of his own citizens; a tyrant who had invaded his neighbors; a tyrant who had used weapons of mass destruction on his people; a tyrant who previous administrations had declared a state sponsor of terror; a tyrant who,

when the world spoke through the United Nations, ignored the world. I think when the world speaks, it must mean what it says. And so we gave the tyrant one last chance to disclose and disarm, or face serious consequences. It was his choice to make. The world is safer, the Iraqi people are better, the cause for liberty is more advanced because Saddam Hussein is no longer in power.

Iraq is the central front in the war on terror. Usama bin Laden has made that clear. Zawahiri has made that clear; he's the number-two man in Al Qaida. Their mission is to drive us out of Iraq in order to achieve safe haven, safe haven from which to launch further attacks against moderate elements in the Middle East, safe haven from which to plan and plot attacks against the United States of America. They're not going to succeed.

There are powerful forces inside Iraq that to me—causes me to be optimistic, starting with the Iraqi people themselves. You know, last December seems like an eternity, particularly to those of us in political office. But that's not too long in the march of history, is it? Last December, 12 million Iraqis, in defiance of terrorists and killers and suicide bombers, said loud and clear, "We want to be free. We want a government of, by, and for the people."

And since then, under a constitution that is one of the most modern constitutions ever in the Middle East, a unity government has formed, a government desirous of responding to the people, a government working hard to reject the extremists who want to stop the advance of democracy and freedom. This is a tough war. It's a tough war because the enemy will use any tactic to cause the Iraqis to split apart or any tactic trying to drive the United States out of the Middle East. We must persevere. We must continue to work with this democratically elected Government of Iraq. We must continue to give their army the skills necessary to fight. And we must stay on the hunt for terrorist elements, which we are doing. We'll succeed in Iraq, and when we do, this country will be more secure.

I understand there's a debate, and, of course, there should be a debate. I mean, I welcome debates in our society. One of the great things about America is, people can go into the public square and express themselves openly without fear of the state. That's what we welcome. In these 2006 campaigns, there will be a lot of debate. There will be people—good people, decent people, patriotic people—who say, "Now is the time to leave Iraq," and they are wrong.

If we leave before Iraq can defend itself and govern itself and sustain itself, this will be a key defeat for the United States of America in this ideological struggle of the 21st century. If we leave before this young democracy has its roots firmly in place, so that an example of liberty flourishes in a region that's so desperate for something other than a society that's caused resentment and hopelessness, if we leave, it will embolden the enemy. The enemy has said this is the front in the war on terror. That's what they have proclaimed. They'll become even more bold. If we leave before the job is done, we'll help create a terrorist state in the heart of the Middle East that will have control of huge oil reserves. If we leave before the job is done, this country will have no credibility. People will look at our words as empty words. People will not trust the judgment and the leadership of the United States. Reformers will shrink from their deep desire to live in a free society. Moderates will wonder if their voice will ever be heard again. If we leave before the job will be done, those who sacrificed, those brave volunteers who sacrificed in our United States military will have died in vain. And as General Abizaid has said, if we leave before the job is done, if we leave the streets of Baghdad, the enemy will follow us to our own streets in America.

The stakes are high. I believe the only way we can lose is if we leave before the job is done. That's what I believe. I'm making my decisions based upon the recommendations of commanders on the ground. I want to assure you, polls and focus groups will not decide the Iraq policy in the global war on terror. And when we win and when we achieve our stated objective, it will be a major defeat for the terrorists in this global war on terror. It will strengthen the spread of democracy in the Middle East. Imagine what the example of a democratic Iraq, a country that has adopted a democracy based upon its history and its traditions, imagine the signal it will send to those reformers in Iran or those hopeful Palestinians that say, "Someday, we want a state to live in peace with our neighbor Israel." When we succeed in Iraq, we'll have created a valuable ally in the global war on terror.

I don't know if you remember this, but recently I had the honor of and privilege of taking my friend the Prime Minister of Japan to Graceland, Elvis's place. [*Laughter*] I've never been to Graceland. I thought it would be fun to go, but more importantly, he wanted to go. See, he was an Elvis buff. [*Laughter*] I also thought it would send an interesting message that I hope helps explain the stakes of this ideological struggle we're in. Can you imagine somebody after World War II saying, "I predict one day an American President will be going to a singer's home with the Prime Minister of Japan?" They'd have thought the guy was off his rocker. Isn't it interesting that a son of a Navy torpedo fighter who fought the Japanese with all his soul and all his might, like many of your relatives did, flew down on Air Force One with the Prime Minister of the former enemy? I think it is. And I think it's an historical lesson that we all can learn something about.

And by the way, when we were on the plane, guess what we talked about—how we can work together to keep the peace. We talked about North Korea. We talked about what it meant for Japan to send

1,000 troops into Iraq to help this young democracy fight off the ideologues of hate. We talked about our HIV/AIDS initiative in Africa. We talked about building roads in Afghanistan. I found it incredibly interesting that I was able to sit down with the Prime Minister of a former enemy and talk about the peace. Something happened between 41's time in the U.S. Navy and 43's time talking with the Prime Minister of Japan. Japan adopted a Japanese-style democracy.

Liberty has the capacity to transform enemies into allies. One of these days, American Presidents will be sitting down with duly elected leaders of the Middle East, and they will be talking about keeping the peace. And this generation will be able to say, the world was safer for our children and grandchildren.

And this Senator understands the stakes, and I'm proud to serve with him. Both of us are honored to be able to say, we're laying the foundation of peace for generations to come.

He also understands this, that the more money you have in your pocket, the more you're going to save, invest, and spend, and the better our economy does. The classic debate in Washington, DC, really centers around this: Who best to spend your money, you or the Government? Senator Hatch and I believe you can spend it better than the Government, and therefore, we strongly believe—[*applause*]. And that's why, when things got tough, economically tough, we cut the taxes on everybody who paid taxes. And it worked. This economy of ours is strong. Progrowth economic policies work. And the way to make sure this economy remains strong is to make the tax relief we passed a permanent part of the Tax Code.

The unemployment rate is 4.8 percent. Since August of 2005, we've created more than 5.5 million new jobs. Productivity is high. The economy has grown now for 35 straight months. It has added jobs for 35 straight—your unemployment rate, Gov-

ernor, congratulations, is 3.4 percent. People are working. Productivity is high. That's good; we're a productive society. We're constantly trying to improve. Entrepreneurship is strong. Minorities are owning businesses. Homeownership has been high. I mean, this is a productive period of time for the American people. It's because our philosophy works; cutting taxes, trusting people with their own money makes sense.

And you know what else happens? It increases revenues for the Treasury. You know, there's been a lot of talk about the deficits, and there should be. We're concerned about the deficit. As a matter of fact, I said to the Congress, join us in being fiscally responsible about how we spend the people's money, and we can cut that deficit. The deficit is going to be cut in half, not by 2009 but by 2008, because progrowth economic policies work. The best way—and by the way, in Washington, you'll hear them say, "Well, in order to balance the budget, we need to raise more revenues." But that's not the way it works in Washington. Yeah, they'll raise revenues; they'll increase your taxes; but they will figure out new ways to spend your money. The best way to balance the budget is to keep taxes low and be fiscally responsible with the taxpayers' money. And that's what we're doing.

Orrin said, "Keep it short." I obviously didn't listen very carefully. I want to work with him to make sure this country becomes less dependent on foreign sources of oil. It's in our economic interests that we become less dependent on foreign sources of oil, and it is in our national security interests. And so therefore, we will continue to spend money wisely on new technologies.

We're big believers in the nuclear power industry's capacity to make sure that we protect the environment with renewable sources of energy. I see automobiles being driven by batteries that can drive the first 40 miles on electricity. I know we got clean coal technologies that will eventually work. It's the calling of our time to make sure that we do smart things with your money to enable us to diversify away from oil from countries, particularly those countries that don't like us. I look forward to working with Orrin to make sure that we remain competitive by spending money, wisely spending money on research and development both at the Federal level and at the private level, which is why we need to make permanent the research and development tax credit.

I look forward to working with Orrin and other Members of the United States Senate to once and for all do something about junk lawsuits, particularly those that are running good doctors out of practice. People worry about the cost of health care. One way to deal with the cost of health care is to get rid of these junk lawsuits.

It's one thing, if you got a problem, to have your day in court. But these junk lawsuits—you see, when I first got to Washington, I said, "Well, the States can figure it out." Governor, you know, you all write your own laws. And then I realized the defensive practice of medicine costs you, the taxpayers, about $28 billion a year. Docs and providers providing unnecessary services in order to defend themselves against junk lawsuits cost the Federal Government—because of Medicaid, Medicare, and veterans health benefits—about 28 billion. I came to the conclusion, therefore, this is a Federal problem that requires a Federal solution.

Congress passed—the House passed a good piece of legislation. I'm going to continue to work with Senators Hatch and Bennett to get good legislation out of the United States Senate to make sure health care is available and affordable for folks all across the United States of America.

And speaking about health care, you did a fine job of training my Secretary for Health and Human Services, Leavitt. He's doing a great job. He really is. And he said he's down there—somebody said he was fishing with him recently. So when you see him again, tell him to get back to work. [*Laughter*]

Finally, I want to say something about the judiciary. I've had no stronger ally than Orrin Hatch in making sure that we appoint judges who know the difference between being a judge and a legislator. One of my most important responsibilities is to make sure we have people on the Federal bench who strictly interpret the Constitution and not use the bench from which to legislate. And I had the honor of naming two members of the Supreme Court—and I took my time, and I looked at a lot of good folks, and I came up with some fine names. And thanks to the support and leadership of Senator Orrin Hatch, Chief Justice John Roberts and Justice Sam Alito now sit on the bench, and the United States is better off for it.

He just told me, if I didn't end, he's going to make me listen to one of his songs. [*Laughter*] Actually, the man has got some talent. [*Laughter*] And he's a great songwriter but not as good a Senator—as he is a Senator. And that's saying a lot. You've got a fine man in the United States Senate in Orrin Hatch. He's decent; he's honorable; he gets the job done. I thank you for supporting him. Send him back to Washington, and Utah and America will benefit—continue to benefit from his service.

I thank you for the warm welcome here. It's been such a joy to come back to your beautiful State. May God bless you all.

NOTE: The President spoke at 11 a.m. at the Grand America Hotel. In his remarks, he referred to Gov. Jon M. Huntsman, Jr., of Utah, and his wife, Mary Kaye; Joseph A. Cannon, chairman, Utah Republican Party; LaVar Christensen, candidate for Congress in Utah's Second Congressional District; former President Saddam Hussein of Iraq; Usama bin Laden, leader of the Al Qaida terrorist organization; Ayman Al-Zawahiri, founder of the Egyptian Islamic Jihad and senior Al Qaida associate; Gen. John P.

Abizaid, USA, commander, U.S. Central Command; and Prime Minister Junichiro Koizumi of Japan.

Message on the Observance of Labor Day
September 1, 2006

I send greetings to those celebrating Labor Day 2006.

America is the most innovative Nation in the world because our free enterprise system unleashes the talent and creativity of our people. American workers are vital to our Nation's economic prosperity, and they help us confront the competitive challenges of the global marketplace.

My Administration remains committed to fostering an environment where innovation succeeds and opportunity thrives. Since August 2003, our economy has created more than 5.7 million jobs, and manufacturing production has risen 5.6 percent in the last year. Our economic expansion is lifting the lives of millions of our citizens, and we will continue to work toward developing sound economic polices that keep our economy moving forward and create more jobs for American workers.

Each year on Labor Day, we recognize the dedicated men and women of our Nation's workforce. By working hard each day, these highly-skilled individuals build better lives for themselves and their families and make America stronger.

Laura and I send our best wishes on this special occasion.

GEORGE W. BUSH

NOTE: An original was not available for verification of the content of this message.

The President's Radio Address
September 2, 2006

Good morning. This week, I spoke to the American Legion in Salt Lake City. I thanked the military veterans for their lifetime of service to our country. And I gave them an update on the war that America is now fighting in defense of freedom in our time.

We're approaching the fifth anniversary of the September the 11th attacks, and since that day, we have taken the fight to the enemy. Yet this war is more than a military conflict; it is the decisive ideological struggle of the 21st century. On one side are those who believe in freedom and moderation, the right of all people to speak, worship, and live in liberty. On the other side are those driven by tyranny and extremism—the right of a self-appointed few to impose their fanatical views on all the rest. We did not ask for this war, but we're answering history's call with confidence, and we will prevail.

We are using every element of national power to defeat the terrorists. First, we're staying on the offense against the terrorists, fighting them overseas so we do not have to face them here at home. Second, we made it clear to all nations, if you harbor terrorists, you're as guilty as the terrorists; you're an enemy of the United States, and you will be held to account. And third, we have launched a bold new agenda to defeat the ideology of the enemy by supporting the forces of freedom and moderation in the Middle East and beyond.

A vital part of our strategy to defeat the terrorists is to help establish a democratic Iraq, which will be a beacon of liberty in the region and an ally in the global war on terror. The terrorists understand the threat a democratic Iraq poses to their cause, so they've been fighting a bloody campaign of sectarian violence which they hope will plunge that country into a civil war. Our commanders and diplomats on the ground believe that Iraq has not descended into a civil war. They report that only a small number of Iraqis are engaged in sectarian violence, while the overwhelming majority want peace and a normal life in a unified country. America will stand with the Iraqi people as they protect their new freedom and build a democracy that can govern itself, sustain itself, and defend itself.

Working side by side with Iraqi forces, we recently launched a major new campaign to end the security crisis in Baghdad. This operation is still in its early stages, yet the initial results are encouraging. The people of Baghdad are seeing their security forces in the streets, dealing a blow to criminals and terrorists. According to one military report, a Sunni man in a diverse Baghdad neighborhood said this about the Shi'a soldiers on patrol: "Their image has changed. Now you feel they are there to protect you." Over the coming weeks and months, the operation will expand throughout Baghdad until Iraq's democratic Government is in full control of the capital. This work is difficult and dangerous, but Iraqi forces are determined to succeed, and America is determined to help them.

Here at home, some politicians say that our best option is to pull out of Iraq, regardless of the situation on the ground. Many of these people are sincere and patriotic, but they could not be more wrong. If America were to pull out before Iraq can defend itself, the consequences would be disastrous. We would be handing Iraq over to the terrorists, giving them a base of operations and huge oil riches to fund their ambitions. And we know exactly where those ambitions lead. If we give up the fight in the streets of Baghdad, we will face the terrorists in the streets of our own cities. The security of the civilized world depends on victory in the war on terror, and that depends on victory in Iraq, so America will not leave until victory is achieved.

For all the debate, American policy in the Middle East comes down to a straightforward choice: We can allow the Middle East to continue on the course that led to September the 11th, and a generation from now, our children will face a region dominated by terrorist states and radical dictators armed with nuclear weapons. Or we can stop that from happening by rallying the world to confront the ideology of hate, by supporting the forces of liberty and moderation in the region, and by helping give the people of the Middle East a future of hope. And that is the choice America has made.

The path to victory will be uphill and uneven, and it will require more patience and sacrifice from our Nation. Yet we can be confident of the outcome, because America will not waver and because the direction of history leads toward freedom.

Thank you for listening.

NOTE: The address was recorded at 9:55 a.m. on August 31 at the Grand America Hotel in Salt Lake City, UT, for broadcast at 10:06 a.m. on September 2. The transcript was made available by the Office of the Press Secretary on September 1 but was embargoed for release until the broadcast. The Office of the Press Secretary also released a Spanish language transcript of this address.

Remarks on Labor Day in Piney Point, Maryland
September 4, 2006

The President. Thank you all. Please be seated. Happy Labor Day.

Audience members. Happy Labor Day.

The President. Yes, thanks. Listen, I'm thrilled that Michael invited me to come and visit with you this Labor Day. But this isn't the first time he invited me. [*Laughter*] He invited me for last year, and I committed. And then we had a terrible storm hit, and I hope you understood— understand why I needed to be there than up here last year.

Now he invited me again. And I couldn't wait to say yes and couldn't wait to come here. I must confess, Michael, I didn't realize how strong your facility—facilities are here. I wasn't sure what to expect, but this is a fantastic facility. It speaks to your leadership and the leadership and the importance of your union. And so here on Labor Day, I say to the union members who are here, happy Labor Day, and thanks for supporting leadership that is progressive, smart, capable, and has your best interests at heart.

I'm proud to be here with the family members. Michael, thanks for inviting family members. As you know, I think family is an important part of life, and that—invite the family here—families here today was a smart thing to do. And I look forward to shaking as many hands as I can this morning.

Today on Labor Day, we honor those who work. And we honor those who work because, in so doing, we recognize that one of the reasons why we're the economic leader in the world is because of our workforce. And the fundamental question facing the country is, how do we continue to be the economic leader in the world? What do we do to make sure that when people look around the world next year and 10 years from now, they say, "The United States is still the most powerful economy in the world"? I think that's an important goal to have, because when we're the most powerful economy in the world, it means our people benefit. It means there's job opportunities. That's what we want. We want people working. We want people to realize their dreams.

And so the best thing to do is to keep progrowth economic policies in place as the first step to making sure we're the most powerful economy in the world. And I think that means keeping those taxes low, letting you keep more of your own money. See, when you have more money in your pocket, you get to spend the money. You get to make the decisions. And the fundamental question facing government is, who best to spend your money, you or the government? I believe you ought to do it.

So we ought to make the tax relief permanent. I like it when people are working for a living, having more after-tax money in their pocket. That's what I like. And I think that ought to be a policy of the United States Government. So to make sure that we're the economic leader of the world, we got to keep taxes low.

But we also got to do some other things that's smart, and it starts with making sure our workers have the skills necessary to compete in the 21st century. And that's one of the primary reasons I came to this facility.

Now, I just happened to be over here at the training building, and they put me behind the wheel of a Coast Guard cutter in Baltimore Harbor, and they made the boat rock a little bit. [*Laughter*] And I got slightly discombobulated. [*Laughter*] It's one of the most amazing training tools I have ever seen. But it shows this union's commitment, along with industry's commitment, to making sure that those who pilot the boats, those who are engineers on the boats, have the absolute best training possible. See, as we constantly—as the world constantly changes, we better make sure that our workforce has the skills necessary to compete if we want to be the world's leading economy.

And so I applaud the Seafarers Union, and I applaud the employers working together to make sure that those who work for a living have what it takes to be competitive. And we got to make sure that's the case throughout all the workforce. And we got to make sure that our community colleges are accessible to people who need to gain new skills of the 21st century. See, as the workforce stays productive—in other words, if you keep getting a good education, it increases your standard of living, but also helps this country remain strong economically.

A couple of other things we need to do as well. We got to do something about energy in order to make sure that we're competitive, that this economy will remain strong, that people are able to find work. By the way, the unemployment rate is 4.7 percent. That's a good sign if you're somebody looking for a job. It means people are working here in the United States.

But one thing is clear, is that dependence on foreign oil jeopardizes our capacity to grow. I mean, the problem is, we get oil from some parts of the world and they simply don't like us. And so the more dependent we are on that type of energy, the less likely it will be that we are able to compete and—so people have good, high-paying jobs.

And so I've got a plan to work with—to spend money on technologies. See, the technological development here at this school has been dramatic. Well, we can achieve the same technological breakthroughs when it comes to energy. And that starts with how we drive our automobiles. You know, one of these days, you're going to have a—batteries in your automobile that will enable you to drive the first 40 miles without gasoline, and your car doesn't have to look like a golf cart. [*Laughter*] I mean, I bet the people down in this part of the world like to drive pickups, Mike. [*Laughter*] But we're going to have a battery that makes those pickups go.

And the reason why is, is that we're spending money to develop new technologies to enable us to become less dependent on oil. And that makes sense. And so in order to think about how we remain competitive as a nation, we've got to be aggressive in promoting new technologies, particularly on the energy front.

You know, in the Midwest, a lot of people are beginning to fuel their cars with more and more ethanol. Ethanol is derived from corn. So you've got to get out there growing corn. The corn goes into an ethanol plant, and out comes fuel to drive the car. That seems to make a lot of sense to me, to say, in order to become less dependent on foreign oil, why don't we become more reliant upon America's farmers to produce energy for our automobiles. And that's the kinds of things we're doing.

You know, we flew over—coming here, we flew over a nuclear powerplant, and it's a modern, safe plant. In my judgment, this country ought to continue to expand nuclear power if we want to become less dependent on foreign sources of energy. Nuclear power is safe; nuclear power is clean; and nuclear power is renewable. And so what I'm telling you is, and what I want the country to understand is, is that technologies has enabled this workforce, this union to become—have a more productive workforce; technology is going to enable us to become less dependent on oil. And we've got to continue to pursue technologies.

And finally, one of the ways to make sure that we're a competitive nation is to continue opening up markets for U.S. products. If I was somebody who was driving a ship or an engineer on a ship, I'd want to hear a President say, "We want you to be selling U.S. products—transporting U.S.

products around the world." See, we've got 5 percent of the world's people here in the United States, which means 95 percent are potential customers. And therefore, it's important for us to be aggressive about opening up markets.

And my message to the world is this: Just treat us the way we treat you. That's all we expect. We just want the rules to be fair—because I believe this country can compete with anybody, anytime, anywhere, so long as the rules are fair.

So Mike asked me to come and talk about ways to make sure we're competitive. He said, "What are you going to do, Mr. President? There you are; things are going okay now, but what about 5 years from now; what will the world look like?" And I hope here are some good ideas for you to think about, about how to make sure that the United States is competitive.

In the meantime, it's important for Presidents to embrace the Jones Act. Sacco's constantly talking to me about that. I have, so far, 5½ years as the President, supported the Jones Act and will continue to do so as the President.

I can't help but look at a man over there in uniform and think about our military right now on Labor Day. First, thank you for serving. And our soldiers and sailors and Coast Guard men and marines and Air Force have got to understand this— that this country supports them in the mission; that they may hear all the political discourse going on, but the people of this country, the people of the United States of America stand squarely behind the men and women who wear our uniform. And on Labor Day, we think about those who are sacrificing for our freedom and peace, and we think about their families too.

And so I want to thank you for greeting me. I look forward to coming to say hello to you. I appreciate you taking time out of your day to say hi. I know you're a little disappointed that Laura didn't come. [*Laughter*] You probably wish she'd have come and I stayed at home. [*Laughter*] But she sends her greetings. God bless you all, and may God continue to bless the United States of America.

NOTE: The President spoke at 11:38 a.m. at the Paul Haul Center for Maritime Training and Education. In his remarks, he referred to Michael Sacco, president, Seafarers International Union of North America, AFL–CIO.

Remarks Following Discussions With Amir Sabah al-Ahmad al-Jabir al-Sabah of Kuwait
September 5, 2006

President Bush. Your Highness, thank you for coming. It's been my honor to welcome you and your delegation here to the Oval Office. I congratulate you for taking on the very important responsibilities of our close friend and ally, Kuwait.

We've had a important strategic dialog about how to work together to promote peace and stability in the Middle East. I thank you for your leadership. I congratulate you for your steady reforms in your country. They have served as a notable ex-

ample for others in the region. I thank you very much for your steadfast support of our United States military. It means a lot, Your Highness, to know that we can count on your friendship.

I appreciated your advice on a variety of matters. His Highness has got a clear vision about how we can work together strategically as well as commercially. And I want to thank you for that vision. I assured His Highness that I fully understand that the United States has an obligation to work to promote the peace. And we will work to promote the peace with our friends.

And so I welcome you here, sir. It's great to see you again. And I'm honored that you would take time to visit me.

Amir Sabah. Thank you very much, Mr. President. I would like really to express my gratitude on my own behalf and the behalf of the delegation that accompanying me for this kind invitation. We have conducted a very fruitful talk. We have covered several issues, bilateral issues, economic issues related to strengthening the bilateral relation between our two countries. And also, we have discussed some regional matters related with the aim of both of us to achieve stability in the region.

Yes, I do agree that there are differences between points of view from the United States and some of our region. But, nevertheless, I would like also to say that there are differences between ourselves, the region. But the goal is to achieve peace and security, and we have seen in a lot of our positions that we are seeing our—the positions eye to eye. Therefore, I am very grateful for the outcome of this visit.

President Bush. Thank you, sir. Thank you.

NOTE: The President spoke at 11:54 a.m. in the Oval Office at the White House. Amir Sabah spoke in Arabic, and his remarks were translated by an interpreter.

Remarks to the Military Officers Association of America
September 5, 2006

Thank you all. Please be seated. General Hendrix, thank you for the invitation to be here. Thanks for the kind introduction. I'm honored to stand with the men and women of the Military Officers Association of America. I appreciate the board of directors who are here and the leaders who have given me this platform from which to speak. I'm proud to be here with active members of the United States military. Thank you for your service. I'm proud to be your Commander in Chief.

I want to—pleased also to stand with members of the diplomatic corps, including many representing nations that have been attacked by Al Qaida and its terrorist allies since September the 11th, 2001. Your presence here reminds us that we're engaged in a global war against an enemy that threatens all civilized nations. And today, the civilized world stands together to defend our freedom; we stand together to defeat the terrorists; and we're working to secure the peace for generations to come.

I appreciate my Attorney General joining us today, Al Gonzales. Thank you for being here. The Secretary of Homeland Security, Michael Chertoff, is with us. Three Members of the United States Senate—I might say, three important Members of the United States Senate—Senate President pro tem Ted Stevens of Alaska. Thank you for joining us, Senator—chairman of the Appropriations Committee, Senator Thad Cochran of Mississippi; the chairman of the Armed Services Committee, John WarnerNM of Virginia.

I thank Norb Ryan, as well, for his leadership. I do appreciate all the folks that are at Walter Reed who have joined us today. I'm going to tell the parents of our troops, we provide great health care to those who wear the uniform. I'm proud of those folks at Bethesda and Walter Reed—are providing you the best possible care to help you recover from your injuries. Thank you for your courage. Thank you for joining us here today. May God bless you in your recovery.

Next week, America will mark the fifth anniversary of September the 11th, 2001, terrorist attacks. As this day approaches, it brings with it a flood of painful memories. We remember the horror of watching planes fly into the World Trade Center and seeing the towers collapse before our eyes. We remember the sight of the Pentagon broken and in flames. We remember the rescue workers who rushed into burning buildings to save lives, knowing they might never emerge again. We remember the brave passengers who charged the cockpit of their hijacked plane and stopped the terrorists from reaching their target and killing more innocent civilians. We remember the cold brutality of the enemy who inflicted this harm on our country—an enemy whose leader, Usama bin Laden, declared the massacre of nearly 3,000 people that day, I quote, "an unparalleled and magnificent feat of valor, unmatched by any in humankind before them."

In 5 years since our Nation was attacked, Al Qaida and terrorists it has inspired have continued to attack across the world. They've killed the innocent in Europe and Africa and the Middle East, in central Asia and the Far East and beyond. Most recently they attempted to strike again in the most ambitious plot since the attacks of September the 11th, a plan to blow up passenger planes headed for America, over the Atlantic Ocean.

Five years after our Nation was attacked, the terrorist danger remains. We're a nation at war, and America and her allies are fighting this war with relentless determination across the world. Together with our coalition partners, we've removed terrorist sanctuaries, disrupted their finances, killed and captured key operatives, broken up terrorist cells in America and other nations, and stopped new attacks before they're carried out. We're on the offense against the terrorists on every battlefront, and we'll accept nothing less than complete victory.

In the 5 years since our Nation was attacked, we've also learned a great deal about the enemy we face in this war. We've learned about them through videos and audio recordings and letters and statements they've posted on web sites. We've learned about them from captured enemy documents that the terrorists have never meant for us to see. Together, these documents and statements have given us clear insight into the mind of our enemies: their ideology, their ambitions, and their strategy to defeat us.

We know what the terrorists intend to do because they've told us. And we need to take their words seriously. So today I'm going to describe, in the terrorists' own words, what they believe, what they hope to accomplish, and how they intend to accomplish it. I'll discuss how the enemy has adapted in the wake of our sustained offensive against them and the threat posed by different strains of violent Islamic radicalism. I'll explain the strategy we're pursuing to protect America by defeating the terrorists on the battlefield and defeating their hateful ideology in the battle of ideas.

The terrorists who attacked us on September the 11th, 2001, are men without conscience, but they're not madmen. They kill in the name of a clear and focused ideology, a set of beliefs that are evil but not insane. These Al Qaida terrorists, and those who share their ideology, are violent Sunni extremists. They're driven by a radical and perverted vision of Islam that rejects tolerance, crushes all dissent, and justifies the murder of innocent men, women, and children in the pursuit of political power. They hope to establish a violent political utopia across the Middle East, which they call a caliphate, where all would be ruled according to their hateful ideology. Usama bin Laden has called the 9/11 attacks, in his words, "a great step towards the unity of Muslims and establishing the righteous caliphate."

This caliphate would be a totalitarian Islamic empire encompassing all current and former Muslim lands, stretching from Europe to north Africa, the Middle East, and Southeast Asia. We know this because Al Qaida has told us. About 2 months ago, the terrorist Zawahiri—he's Al Qaida's second in command—declared that Al Qaida intends to impose its rule in "every land that was a home for Islam, from Spain to Iraq." He went on to say, "The whole world is an open field for us."

We know what this radical empire would look like in practice, because we saw how the radicals imposed their ideology on the people of Afghanistan. Under the rule of the Taliban and Al Qaida, Afghanistan was a totalitarian nightmare, a land where women were imprisoned in their homes; men were beaten for missing prayer meetings; girls could not go to school; and children were forbidden the smallest pleasures, like flying kites. Religious police roamed the streets, beating and detaining civilians for perceived offenses. Women were publicly whipped. Summary executions were held in Kabul's soccer stadium in front of cheering mobs. And Afghanistan was turned into a launching pad for horrific attacks against America and other parts of the civilized world, including many Muslim nations.

The goal of these Sunni extremists is to remake the entire Muslim world in their radical image. In pursuit of their imperial aims, these extremists say there can be no compromise or dialog with those they call infidels, a category that includes America, the world's free nations, Jews, and all Muslims who reject their extreme vision of Islam. They reject the possibility of peaceful coexistence with the free world. Again, hear the words of Usama bin Laden earlier this year: "Death is better than living on this Earth with the unbelievers among us."

These radicals have declared their uncompromising hostility to freedom. It is foolish to think that you can negotiate with them. We see the uncompromising nature of the enemy in many captured terrorist documents. Here are just two examples.

After the liberation of Afghanistan, coalition forces searching through a terrorist safe house in that country found a copy of the Al Qaida charter. This charter states that "There will be continuing enmity until everyone believes in Allah. We will not meet the enemy halfway. There will be no room for dialog with them." Another document was found in 2000 by British police during an antiterrorist raid in London, a grisly Al Qaida manual that includes chapters with titles such as "Guidelines for Beating and Killing Hostages." This manual declares that their vision of Islam "does not make a truce with unbelief, but rather confronts it." The confrontation calls for "the dialog of bullets; the ideals of assassination, bombing, and destruction; and the diplomacy of the cannon and machine gun," end quote.

Still other captured documents show Al Qaida's strategy for infiltrating Muslim nations, establishing terrorist enclaves, overthrowing governments, and building their totalitarian empire. We see this strategy laid out in a captured Al Qaida document found during a recent raid in Iraq, which describes their plans to infiltrate and to take over Iraq's western Anbar Province. The document lays out an elaborate Al Qaida governing structure for the region that includes an education department, a social services department, a justice department, and an execution unit responsible for "sorting out, arrest, murder, and destruction."

According to their public statements, countries that have—they have targeted stretch from the Middle East to Africa to Southeast Asia. Through this strategy, Al Qaida and its allies intend to create numerous, decentralized operating bases across the world, from which they can plan new attacks and advance their vision of a unified, totalitarian Islamic state that can confront and, eventually, destroy the free world.

These violent extremists know that to realize this vision, they must first drive out the main obstacle that stands in their way— the United States of America. According to Al Qaida, their strategy to defeat America has two parts. First, they're waging a campaign of terror across the world. They're targeting our forces abroad, hoping that the American people will grow tired of casualties and give up the fight. And they're targeting America's financial centers and economic infrastructure at home, hoping to terrorize us and cause our economy to collapse.

Bin Laden calls this his "bleed-until-bankruptcy plan," end quote. And he cited the attacks of 9/11 as evidence that such a plan can succeed. With the 9/11 attacks, Usama bin Laden says, "Al Qaida spent $500,000 on the event, while America lost—according to the lowest estimate—$500 billion," meaning that every dollar of Al Qaida defeated a million dollars of America. Bin Laden concludes from this experience that "America is definitely a great power, with unbelievable military strength and a vibrant economy, but all these have been built on a very weak and hollow foundation." He went on to say, "Therefore, it is very easy to target the flimsy base and concentrate on their weak points, and even if we're able to target one-tenth of these weak points, we will be able to crush and destroy them."

Secondly, along with this campaign of terror, the enemy has a propaganda strategy. Usama bin Laden laid out this strategy in a letter to the Taliban leader, Mullah Omar, that coalition forces uncovered in Afghanistan in 2002. In it bin Laden says that Al Qaida intends to launch, in his words, "a media campaign to create a wedge between the American people and their Government." This media campaign, bin Laden says, will send the American people a number of messages, including "that their Government will bring them more losses, in finances and casualties." And he goes on to say that "They are being sacrificed to serve the big investors, especially the Jews." Bin Laden says that by delivering these messages, Al Qaida "aims at creating pressure from the American people on the American Government to stop their campaign against Afghanistan."

Bin Laden and his allies are absolutely convinced they can succeed in forcing America to retreat and causing our economic collapse. They believe our Nation is weak and decadent and lacking in patience and resolve. And they're wrong. Usama bin Laden has written that the "defeat of American forces in Beirut in 1983 is proof America does not have the stomach to stay in the fight." He's declared that "In Somalia, the United States pulled out, trailing disappointment, defeat, and failure behind it." And last year, the terrorist Zawahiri declared that Americans "know better than others that there is no hope in victory. The Vietnam specter is closing every outlet."

These terrorists hope to drive America and our coalition out of Afghanistan so they can restore the safe haven they lost when coalition forces drove them out 5 years ago. But they've made clear that the most important front in their struggle against America is Iraq, the nation bin Laden has declared the "capital of the caliphate." Hear the words of bin Laden: "I now address the whole Islamic nation: Listen and understand. The most serious issue today for the whole world is this third world war that is raging in Iraq." He calls it "a war of destiny between infidelity and Islam." He says, "The whole world is watching this war," and that it will end in "victory and glory or misery and humiliation." For Al Qaida, Iraq is not a distraction from their war on America; it is the central battlefield where the outcome of this struggle will be decided.

Here is what Al Qaida says they will do if they succeed in driving us out of Iraq. The terrorist Zawahiri has said that Al Qaida will proceed with "several incremental goals. The first stage: Expel the Americans from Iraq. The second stage: Establish an Islamic authority or emirate, then develop it and support it until it achieves the level of caliphate. The third stage: Extend the jihad wave to the secular countries neighboring Iraq. And the fourth stage: The clash with Israel."

These evil men know that a fundamental threat to their aspirations is a democratic Iraq that can govern itself, sustain itself, and defend itself. They know that given a choice, the Iraqi people will never choose to live in the totalitarian state the extremists hope to establish. And that is why we must not and we will not give the enemy victory in Iraq by deserting the Iraqi people.

Last year, the terrorist Zarqawi declared in a message posted on the Internet that democracy "is the essence of infidelity and deviation from the right path." The Iraqi people disagree. Last December, nearly 12 million Iraqis from every ethnic and religious community turned out to vote in their country's third free election in less than a year. Iraq now has a unity government that represents Iraq's diverse population, and Al Qaida's top commander in Iraq breathed his last breath.

Despite these strategic setbacks, the enemy will continue to fight freedom's advance in Iraq, because they understand the stakes in this war. Again, hear the words of bin Laden in a message to the American people earlier this year. He says, "The war is for you or for us to win. If we win it, it means your defeat and disgrace forever."

Now, I know some of our country hear the terrorists' words and hope that they will not or cannot do what they say. History teaches that underestimating the words of evil and ambitious men is a terrible mistake. In the early 1900s, an exiled lawyer in Europe published a pamphlet called "What Is To Be Done?"—in which he laid out his plan to launch a Communist revolution in Russia. The world did not heed Lenin's words and paid a terrible price. The Soviet Empire he established killed tens of millions and brought the world to the brink of thermonuclear war. In the 1920s, a failed Austrian painter published

a book in which he explained his intention to build an Aryan super-state in Germany and take revenge on Europe and eradicate the Jews. The world ignored Hitler's words and paid a terrible price. His Nazi regime killed millions in the gas chambers and set the world aflame in war before it was finally defeated at a terrible cost in lives.

Bin Laden and his terrorist allies have made their intentions as clear as Lenin and Hitler before them. The question is, will we listen? Will we pay attention to what these evil men say? America and our coalition partners have made our choice. We're taking the words of the enemy seriously. We're on the offensive; we will not rest; we will not retreat; and we will not withdraw from the fight until this threat to civilization has been removed.

Five years into this struggle, it's important to take stock of what's been accomplished and the difficult work that remains. Al Qaida has been weakened by our sustained offensive against them. And today, it is harder for Al Qaida's leaders to operate freely, to move money, or to communicate with their operatives and facilitators. Yet Al Qaida remains dangerous and determined. Bin Laden and Zawahiri remain in hiding in remote regions of this world. Al Qaida continues to adapt in the face of our global campaign against them. Increasingly, Al Qaida is taking advantage of the Internet to disseminate propaganda and to conduct virtual recruitment and virtual training of new terrorists. Al Qaida's leaders no longer need to meet face to face with their operatives. They can find new suicide bombers and facilitate new terrorist attacks without ever laying eyes on those they're training, financing, or sending to strike us.

As Al Qaida changes, the broader terrorist movement is also changing, becoming more dispersed and self-directed. More and more, we're facing threats from locally established terrorist cells that are inspired by Al Qaida's ideology and goals but do not necessarily have direct links to Al Qaida, such as training and funding. Some of these groups are made up of homegrown terrorists, militant extremists who were born and educated in Western nations, were indoctrinated by radical Islamists or attracted to their ideology, and joined the violent extremist cause. These locally established cells appear to be responsible for a number of attacks and plots, including those in Madrid and Canada and other countries across the world.

As we continue to fight Al Qaida and these Sunni extremists inspired by their radical ideology, we also face the threat posed by Shi'a extremists who are learning from Al Qaida, increasing their assertiveness, and stepping up their threats. Like the vast majority of Sunnis, the vast majority of Shi'a across the world reject the vision of extremists. And in Iraq, millions of Shi'a have defied terrorist threats to vote in free elections and have shown their desire to live in freedom. The Shi'a extremists want to deny them this right. This Shi'a strain of Islamic radicalism is just as dangerous and just as hostile to America and just as determined to establish its brand of hegemony across the broader Middle East. The Shi'a extremists have achieved something that Al Qaida has so far failed to do. In 1979, they took control of a major power, the nation of Iran, subjugating its proud people to a regime of tyranny and using that nation's resources to fund the spread of terror and pursue their radical agenda.

Like Al Qaida and the Sunni extremists, the Iranian regime has clear aims. They want to drive America out of the region, to destroy Israel, and to dominate the broader Middle East. To achieve these aims, they are funding and arming terrorist groups like Hizballah, which allow them to attack Israel and America by proxy. Hizballah, the source of the current instability in Lebanon, has killed more Americans than any terrorist organization except Al Qaida. Unlike Al Qaida, they've not yet attacked the American homeland. Yet they're directly responsible for the murder

of hundreds of Americans abroad. It was Hizballah that was behind the 1983 bombing of the U.S. Marine barracks in Beirut that killed 241 Americans. And Saudi Hizballah was behind the 1996 bombing of Khobar Towers in Saudi Arabia that killed 19 Americans, an attack conducted by terrorists who we believe were working with Iranian officials.

Just as we take the words of the Sunni extremists seriously, we must take the words of the Shi'a extremists seriously. Listen to the words of Hizballah's leader, the terrorist Nasrallah, who has declared his hatred of America. He says, "Let the entire world hear me. Our hostility to the Great Satan, America, is absolute. Regardless of how the world has changed after 11 September, death to America will remain our reverberating and powerful slogan. Death to America."

Iran's leaders, who back Hizballah, have also declared their absolute hostility to America. Last October, Iran's President declared in a speech that some people ask— in his words—"whether a world without the United States and Zionism can be achieved. I say that this goal is achievable." Less than 3 months ago, Iran's President declared to America and other Western powers: "Open your eyes and see the fate of pharaoh. If you do not abandon the path of falsehood, your doomed destiny will be annihilation." Less than 2 months ago, he warned, "The anger of Muslims may reach an explosion point soon. If such a day comes, America and the West should know that the waves of the blast will not remain within the boundaries of our region." He also delivered this message to the American people: "If you would like to have good relations with the Iranian nation in the future, bow down before the greatness of the Iranian nation and surrender. If you don't accept to do this, the Iranian nation will force you to surrender and bow down." America will not bow down to tyrants.

The Iranian regime and its terrorist proxies have demonstrated their willingness to kill Americans, and now the Iranian regime is pursuing nuclear weapons. The world is working together to prevent Iran's regime from acquiring the tools of mass murder. The international community has made a reasonable proposal to Iran's leaders and given them the opportunity to set their nation on a better course. So far, Iran's leaders have rejected this offer. Their choice is increasingly isolating the great Iranian nation from the international community and denying the Iranian people an opportunity for greater economic prosperity. It's time for Iran's leader to make a different choice. And we've made our choice. We'll continue to work closely with our allies to find a diplomatic solution. The world's free nations will not allow Iran to develop a nuclear weapon.

The Shi'a and Sunni extremists represent different faces of the same threat. They draw inspiration from different sources, but both seek to impose a dark vision of violent Islamic radicalism across the Middle East. They oppose the advance of freedom, and they want to gain control of weapons of mass destruction. If they succeed in undermining fragile democracies like Iraq and drive the forces of freedom out of the region, they will have an open field to pursue their dangerous goals. Each strain of violent Islamic radicalism would be emboldened in their efforts to topple moderate governments and establish terrorist safe havens.

Imagine a world in which they were able to control governments, a world awash with oil, and they would use oil resources to punish industrialized nations. And they would use those resources to fuel their radical agenda and pursue and purchase weapons of mass murder. And armed with nuclear weapons, they would blackmail the free world and spread their ideologies of hate and raise a mortal threat to the American people. If we allow them to do this, if we retreat from Iraq, if we don't uphold our duty to support those who are desirous to live in liberty, 50 years from now, history will look back on our time with unforgiving

clarity and demand to know why we did not act.

I'm not going to allow this to happen, and no future American President can allow it either. America did not seek this global struggle, but we're answering history's call with confidence and a clear strategy. Today we're releasing a document called the National Strategy for Combating Terrorism. This is an unclassified version of the strategy we've been pursuing since September the 11th, 2001. This strategy was first released in February 2003; it's been updated to take into account the changing nature of this enemy. This strategy document is posted on the White House web site, whitehouse.gov, and I urge all Americans to read it.

Our strategy for combating terrorism has five basic elements. First, we're determined to prevent terrorist attacks before they occur, so we're taking the fight to the enemy. The best way to protect America is to stay on the offense. Since 9/11, our coalition has captured or killed Al Qaida managers and operatives and scores of other terrorists across the world. The enemy is living under constant pressure, and we intend to keep it that way. And this adds to our security. When terrorists spend their days working to avoid death or capture, it's harder for them to plan and execute new attacks.

We're also fighting the enemy here at home. We've given our law enforcement and intelligence professionals the tools they need to stop the terrorists in our midst. We passed the PATRIOT Act to break down the wall that prevented law enforcement and intelligence from sharing vital information. We created the terrorist surveillance program to monitor the communications between Al Qaida commanders abroad and terrorist operatives within our borders. If Al Qaida is calling somebody in America, we need to know why in order to stop attacks.

I want to thank these three Senators for working with us to give our law enforcement and intelligence officers the tools necessary to do their jobs. And over the last 5 years, Federal, State, and local law enforcement have used those tools to break up terrorist cells and to prosecute terrorist operatives and supporters in New York and Oregon and Virginia and Texas and New Jersey and Illinois, Ohio, and other States. By taking the battle to the terrorists and their supporters on our own soil and across the world, we've stopped a number of Al Qaida plots.

Second, we're determined to deny weapons of mass destruction to outlaw regimes and terrorists who would use them without hesitation. Working with Great Britain and Pakistan and other nations, the United States shut down the world's most dangerous nuclear trading cartel, the A.Q. Khan network. This network had supplied Iran and Libya and North Korea with equipment and know-how that advanced their efforts to obtain nuclear weapons. And we launched the Proliferation Security Initiative, a coalition of more than 70 nations that is working together to stop shipments related to weapons of mass destruction on land, at sea, and in the air. The greatest threat this world faces is the danger of extremists and terrorists armed with weapons of mass destruction, and this is a threat America cannot defeat on her own. We applaud the determined efforts of many nations around the world to stop the spread of these dangerous weapons. Together, we pledge we'll continue to work together to stop the world's most dangerous men from getting their hands on the world's most dangerous weapons.

Third, we're determined to deny terrorists the support of outlaw regimes. After September the 11th, I laid out a clear doctrine: America makes no distinction between those who commit acts of terror and those that harbor and support them, because they're equally guilty of murder. Thanks to our efforts, there are now three

fewer state sponsors of terror in the world than there were on September the 11th, 2001. Afghanistan and Iraq have been transformed from terrorist states into allies in the war on terror. And the nation of Libya has renounced terrorism and given up its weapons of mass destruction programs and its nuclear materials and equipment. Over the past 5 years, we've acted to disrupt the flow of weapons and support from terrorist states to terrorist networks. And we have made clear that any government that chooses to be an ally of terror has also chosen to be an enemy of civilization.

Fourth, we're determined to deny terrorist networks control of any nation or territory within a nation. So, along with our coalition and the Iraqi Government, we'll stop the terrorists from taking control of Iraq and establishing a new safe haven from which to attack America and the free world. And we're working with friends and allies to deny the terrorists the enclaves they seek to establish in ungoverned areas across the world. By helping governments reclaim full sovereign control over their territory, we make ourselves more secure.

Fifth, we're working to deny terrorists new recruits by defeating their hateful ideology and spreading the hope of freedom— by spreading the hope of freedom across the Middle East. For decades, American policy sought to achieve peace in the Middle East by pursuing stability at the expense of liberty. The lack of freedom in that region helped create conditions where anger and resentment grew and radicalism thrived and terrorists found willing recruits. And we saw the consequences on September the 11th, when the terrorists brought death and destruction to our country. The policy wasn't working.

The experience of September the 11th made clear, in the long run, the only way to secure our Nation is to change the course of the Middle East. And so America has committed its influence in the world to advancing freedom and liberty and democracy as the great alternatives to repression and radicalism. We're taking the side of democratic leaders and moderates and reformers across the Middle East. We strongly support the voices of tolerance and moderation in the Muslim world. We're standing with Afghanistan's elected Government against Al Qaida and the Taliban remnants that are trying to restore tyranny in that country. We're standing with Lebanon's young democracy against the foreign forces that are seeking to undermine the country's sovereignty and independence. And we're standing with the leaders of Iraq's unity Government as they work to defeat the enemies of freedom and chart a more hopeful course for their people. This is why victory is so important in Iraq. By helping freedom succeed in Iraq, we will help America and the Middle East and the world become more secure.

During the last 5 years, we've learned a lot about this enemy. We've learned that they're cunning and sophisticated. We've witnessed their ability to change their methods and their tactics with deadly speed, even as their murderous obsessions remain unchanging. We've seen that it's the terrorists who have declared war on Muslims, slaughtering huge numbers of innocent Muslim men and women around the world.

We know what the terrorists believe. We know what they have done, and we know what they intend to do. And now the world's free nations must summon the will to meet this great challenge. The road ahead is going to be difficult, and it will require more sacrifice. Yet we can have confidence in the outcome, because we've seen freedom conquer tyranny and terror before. In the 20th century, free nations confronted and defeated Nazi Germany. During the cold war, we confronted Soviet communism, and today, Europe is whole, free, and at peace.

And now freedom is once again contending with the forces of darkness and tyranny. This time the battle is unfolding in a new region, the broader Middle East. This time we're not waiting for our enemies to gather in strength. This time we're confronting them before they gain the capacity to inflict unspeakable damage on the world, and we're confronting their hateful ideology before it fully takes root.

We see a day when people across the Middle East have governments that honor their dignity and unleash their creativity and count their votes. We see a day when, across this region, citizens are allowed to express themselves freely, women have full rights, and children are educated and given the tools necessary to succeed in life. And we see a day when all the nations of the Middle East are allies in the cause of peace.

We fight for this day, because the security of our own citizens depends on it. This is the great ideological struggle of the 21st century, and it is the calling of our generation. All civilized nations are bound together in this struggle between moderation and extremism. By coming together, we will roll back this grave threat to our way of life. We will help the people of the Middle East claim their freedom, and we will leave a safer and more hopeful world for our children and our grandchildren.

God bless.

NOTE: The President spoke at 1:15 p.m. at the Capital Hilton Hotel. In his remarks, he referred to Gen. John W. Hendrix, USA (Ret.), chairman of the board, and Vice Adm. Norbert R. Ryan, Jr., USN (Ret.), president, Military Officers Association of America; President Mahmud Ahmadi-nejad of Iran; and A.Q. Khan, former head of Pakistan's nuclear weapons program.

Remarks on the Nomination of Mary E. Peters To Be Secretary of Transportation
September 5, 2006

The President. Good afternoon, and welcome to the White House. I'm pleased to announce that I intend to nominate Mary Peters to be the next Secretary of Transportation.

Our Nation's transportation infrastructure is vital to our prosperity and competitiveness; it's critical to the everyday lives of our citizens. The Secretary of Transportation is responsible for maintaining a safe, reliable, and efficient transportation system. In addition, the Secretary of Transportation plays an important role in our Nation's coordinated efforts to guard against terrorist threats to our aircraft, our seaports, and our infrastructure. It is the job that requires vision and strong leadership.

Mary Peters is the right person for this job. She brings a lifetime of experience on transportation issues, from both the private and public sectors. She now serves as a senior executive for transportation policy at a major engineering firm. Before that, Mary served in my administration as the head of the Federal Highway Administration. As Administrator, Mary led efforts to improve safety and security, reduce traffic congestion, and modernize America's roads and bridges.

And before coming to Washington, Mary served in the Arizona Department of Transportation for more than 15 years, rising through the ranks to become the director in 1998. Mary has a reputation for character and common sense. She's an innovative thinker. She knows how to set priorities and to solve problems. And as a member of my Cabinet, Mary will work closely with State and local leaders to ensure that America has a state-of-the-art transportation system that meets the needs of our growing economy.

When confirmed by the Senate, Mary will succeed one of our Nation's finest Secretaries of Transportation in Norm Mineta. When I came to Washington, I asked Norm to continue his service by joining my Cabinet. And he shows that when we put politics aside, people from different political parties can work together to achieve results for the American people.

He was the Secretary of Transportation on September the 11th, 2001, and he led the unprecedented effort to bring tens of thousands of passengers aboard commercial aircraft to safe landings. And since then, he's worked to strengthen the security at America's airports and seaports. He's played a critical role in keeping America safe from terrorist attacks. Norm also worked hard to modernize the aviation market. And after Hurricane Katrina, Norm and his team swung into action to repair and reopen major highways and seaports and airports and pipelines along America's gulf coast.

Norm Mineta has served America with integrity and dedication and distinction. He leaves office as the longest serving Secretary of Transportation in our Nation's history. I appreciate Norm's lifetime of service to our country. I wish him and Deni and all his family all the best. I also want to thank Maria Cino for her outstanding leadership of the Department since Norm stepped down in July.

Mary Peters knows the legacy she has to live up to at the Department of Transportation. She will take this new post during a time of historic challenges for our economy and our transportation system. I want to thank Mary for her willingness to serve yet again. She's going to make an outstanding Secretary of Transportation, and I call upon the United States Senate to confirm her promptly. Congratulations.

[*At this point, Secretary-designate Peters made brief remarks.*]

The President. Good job, thank you. Thank you all.

NOTE: The President spoke at 2:36 p.m. in the Roosevelt Room at the White House. In his remarks, he referred to Danealia "Deni" Mineta, wife of former Secretary of Transportation Norman Y. Mineta; and Maria Cino, Acting Secretary of Transportation. The transcript released by the Office of the Press Secretary also included the remarks of Secretary-designate Peters.

Statement on the Resignation of Mark B. McClellan as Administrator of the Centers for Medicare & Medicaid Services
September 5, 2006

Mark McClellan has served my administration in a number of pivotal positions and in doing so has bettered the lives of millions of Americans. He played an instrumental role in transforming the Nation's health care system, and his efforts will continue to make a difference for generations.

Mark first served as a member of my Council of Economic Advisers, focusing on health care and related economic issues. He then became head of the Food and Drug Administration, where he provided steady leadership to empower consumers and to ensure rapid access to products that are safe and effective. For the last 2½ years, Mark has run the Center for Medicare and Medicaid Services in the Department of Health and Human Services. As CMS Administrator, Mark was critical in the successful implementation of the Medicare prescription drug benefit, the most important health care reform in 40 years. He has also worked to ensure that price and quality information are available to consumers and led reforms that brought principles of private sector competition to Government programs, thereby moving the country toward a system in which Americans will receive better care at lower overall prices.

Mark has been a trusted adviser, and he leaves behind a strong record of accomplishment. I wish all the best to Mark, his wife, Stephanie, and their children.

Letter to Congressional Leaders on Continuation of the National Emergency With Respect to Certain Terrorist Attacks
September 5, 2006

Dear Mr. Speaker: (*Dear Mr. President:*)

Section 202(d) of the National Emergencies Act, 50 U.S.C. 1622(d), provides for the automatic termination of a national emergency unless, prior to the anniversary date of its declaration, the President publishes in the *Federal Register* and transmits to the Congress a notice stating that the emergency is to continue in effect beyond the anniversary date. Consistent with this provision, I have sent to the *Federal Register* the enclosed notice, stating that the emergency declared with respect to the terrorist attacks on the United States of September 11, 2001, is to continue in effect for an additional year.

The terrorist threat that led to the declaration on September 14, 2001, of a national emergency continues. For this reason, I have determined that it is necessary to continue in effect after September 14, 2006, the national emergency with respect to the terrorist threat.

Sincerely,

GEORGE W. BUSH

NOTE: Identical letters were sent to J. Dennis Hastert, Speaker of the House of Representatives, and Richard B. Cheney, President of the Senate. The notice is listed in Appendix D at the end of this volume.

Message to the Senate Transmitting the Patent Law Treaty and Regulations Under the Patent Law Treaty
September 5, 2006

To the Senate of the United States:

With a view to receiving the advice and consent of the Senate to ratification, subject to the reservation outlined below, I transmit herewith the Patent Law Treaty and Regulations Under the Patent Law Treaty (the "Treaty"), done at Geneva on June 1, 2000, between the Governments of 53 countries including the United States of America. I also transmit, for the information of the Senate, the Key Provisions of the Patent Law Treaty report prepared by the Department of State.

Strong intellectual property protection is a cornerstone of free trade and global market access. This Treaty promotes patent protection by codifying, harmonizing, and reducing the costs of taking the steps necessary for obtaining and maintaining patents throughout the world. The provisions set forth in the Treaty will safeguard U.S. commercial interests by making it easier for U.S. patent applicants and owners to protect their intellectual property worldwide.

The Treaty generally sets forth the maximum procedural requirements that can be imposed on patent applicants, and in addition, provides standardized requirements for obtaining a filing date from which no party may deviate. Additionally, the Treaty provides that applicants cannot be required to hire representation for, among other things, the purpose of filing an application

and that patents may not be revoked or invalidated because of noncompliance with certain application requirements, unless the noncompliance is a result of fraud. The Treaty does not limit the United States from providing patent requirements that are more favorable to the patent applicant or patent owner than those set forth in the Treaty or from prescribing requirements that are provided for in our substantive law relating to patents. Additionally, the Treaty is not intended to limit the United States from taking actions that it deems necessary for the preservation of its essential security interests.

This Treaty is in harmony with current U.S. patent laws and regulations, with minor exceptions to be addressed in proposed legislation. Because U.S. law does not require that each patent application apply to only one invention or inventive concept, and because the U.S. Patent and Trademark Office assesses that implementing a provision of the Treaty requiring "unity of invention" for all national applications would require a substantive and impractical change to our Patent Law, I recommend that the following reservation be included in the U.S. instrument of ratification, as allowed by the Treaty:

Pursuant to Article 23, the United States declares that Article 6(1) shall not apply to any requirement relating to unity of invention applicable under the Patent Cooperation Treaty to an international application.

I recommend that the Senate give early and favorable consideration to this Treaty and give its advice and consent to its ratification, subject to the reservation described above.

GEORGE W. BUSH

The White House,
September 5, 2006.

Remarks Following a Cabinet Meeting
September 6, 2006

I want to thank my Cabinet for what has been a very fruitful discussion. I thank you for your continued service to our country. Congress is coming back into town, and we welcome them back, and we look forward to working with them on a variety of matters.

One of the most important tasks is for Congress to recognize that we need the tools necessary to win this war on terror, and we'll continue to discuss with Congress ways to make sure that this Nation is capable of defending herself.

Secondly, I recognize this is a political season. There's elections coming down the road, but I made sure the Cabinet understands that we'll continue to address the concerns of the American people. That's what the people expect us to do. And those concerns include being fiscally wise with the people's money. So when Congress starts appropriating money, we will continue to urge them to be wise with the people's money.

We talked about the economy; we talked about energy; we talked about health care and a variety of other matters. I'm looking forward to working with Congress, Members of both political parties, to do the job that the American people expect us to do.

Thank you.

NOTE: The President spoke at 10:17 a.m. in the Cabinet Room at the White House.

Remarks on the War on Terror
September 6, 2006

Thank you. Thanks for the warm welcome. Welcome to the White House. Mr. Vice President, Secretary Rice, Attorney General Gonzales, Ambassador Negroponte, General Hayden, Members of the United States Congress, families who lost loved ones in the terrorist attacks on our Nation, and my fellow citizens: Thanks for coming.

On the morning of September the 11th, 2001, our Nation awoke to a nightmare attack. Nineteen men armed with box cutters took control of airplanes and turned them into missiles. They used them to kill nearly 3,000 innocent people. We watched the Twin Towers collapse before our eyes, and it became instantly clear that we'd entered a new world and a dangerous new war.

The attacks of September the 11th horrified our Nation. And amid the grief came new fears and urgent questions. Who had attacked us? What did they want? And what else were they planning? Americans saw the destruction the terrorists had caused in

New York and Washington and Pennsylvania, and they wondered if there were other terrorist cells in our midst poised to strike; they wondered if there was a second wave of attacks still to come.

With the Twin Towers and the Pentagon still smoldering, our country on edge, and a stream of intelligence coming in about potential new attacks, my administration faced immediate challenges. We had to respond to the attack on our country. We had to wage an unprecedented war against an enemy unlike any we had fought before. We had to find the terrorists hiding in America and across the world, before they were able to strike our country again. So in the early days and weeks after 9/11, I directed our Government's senior national security officials to do everything in their power, within our laws, to prevent another attack.

Nearly 5 years have passed since these—those initial days of shock and sadness, and we are thankful that the terrorists have not succeeded in launching another attack on our soil. This is not for the lack of desire or determination on the part of the enemy. As the recently foiled plot in London shows, the terrorists are still active, and they're still trying to strike America, and they're still trying to kill our people. One reason the terrorists have not succeeded is because of the hard work of thousands of dedicated men and women in our Government, who have toiled day and night, along with our allies, to stop the enemy from carrying out their plans. And we are grateful for these hard-working citizens of ours. Another reason the terrorists have not succeeded is because our Government has changed its policies and given our military, intelligence, and law enforcement personnel the tools they need to fight this enemy and protect our people and preserve our freedoms.

The terrorists who declared war on America represent no nation, they defend no territory, and they wear no uniform. They do not mass armies on borders or flotillas of warships on the high seas. They operate in the shadows of society. They send small teams of operatives to infiltrate free nations; they live quietly among their victims; they conspire in secret, and then they strike without warning. In this new war, the most important source of information on where the terrorists are hiding and what they are planning is the terrorists themselves.

Captured terrorists have unique knowledge about how terrorist networks operate. They have knowledge of where their operatives are deployed and knowledge about what plots are underway. This intelligence—this is intelligence that cannot be found any other place, and our security depends on getting this kind of information. To win the war on terror, we must be able to detain, question, and, when appropriate, prosecute terrorists captured here in America and on the battlefields around the world.

After the 9/11 attacks, our coalition launched operations across the world to remove terrorist safe havens and capture or kill terrorist operatives and leaders. Working with our allies, we've captured and detained thousands of terrorists and enemy fighters in Afghanistan, in Iraq, and other fronts of this war on terror. These enemy—these are enemy combatants who were waging war on our Nation. We have a right under the laws of war, and we have an obligation to the American people, to detain these enemies and stop them from rejoining the battle.

Most of the enemy combatants we capture are held in Afghanistan or in Iraq, where they're questioned by our military personnel. Many are released after questioning or turned over to local authorities, if we determine that they do not pose a continuing threat and no longer have significant intelligence value. Others remain in American custody near the battlefield to ensure that they don't return to the fight.

In some cases, we determine that individuals we have captured pose a significant threat or may have intelligence that we and our allies need to have to prevent new attacks. Many are Al Qaida operatives or Taliban fighters trying to conceal their identities, and they withhold information that could save American lives. In these cases, it has been necessary to move these individuals to an environment where they can be held secretly, questioned by experts, and, when appropriate, prosecuted for terrorist acts.

Some of these individuals are taken to the United States Naval Base at Guantanamo Bay, Cuba. It's important for Americans and others across the world to understand the kind of people held at Guantanamo. These aren't common criminals or bystanders accidentally swept up on the battlefield. We have in place a rigorous process to ensure those held at Guantanamo Bay belong at Guantanamo. Those held at Guantanamo include suspected bombmakers, terrorist trainers, recruiters and facilitators, and potential suicide bombers. They are in our custody so they cannot murder our people. One detainee held at Guantanamo told a questioner questioning him—he said this: "I'll never forget your face. I will kill you, your brothers, your mother, and your sisters."

In addition to the terrorists held at Guantanamo, a small number of suspected terrorist leaders and operatives captured during the war have been held and questioned outside the United States, in a separate program operated by the Central Intelligence Agency. This group includes individuals believed to be the key architects of the September the 11th attacks and attacks on the USS *Cole*, an operative involved in the bombings of our Embassies in Kenya and Tanzania, and individuals involved in other attacks that have taken the lives of innocent civilians across the world. These are dangerous men with unparalleled knowledge about terrorist networks and their plans of new attacks. The security of

our Nation and the lives of our citizens depend on our ability to learn what these terrorists know.

Many specifics of this program, including where these detainees have been held and the details of their confinement, cannot be divulged. Doing so would provide our enemies with information they could use to take retribution against our allies and harm our country. I can say that questioning the detainees in this program has given us information that has saved innocent lives by helping us stop new attacks, here in the United States and across the world.

Today I'm going to share with you some of the examples provided by our intelligence community of how this program has saved lives, why it remains vital to the security of the United States and our friends and allies, and why it deserves the support of the United States Congress and the American people.

Within months of September the 11th, 2001, we captured a man named Abu Zubaydah. We believe that Zubaydah was a senior terrorist leader and a trusted associate of Usama bin Laden. Our intelligence community believes he had run a terrorist camp in Afghanistan, where some of the 9/11 hijackers trained, and that he helped smuggle Al Qaida leaders out of Afghanistan after coalition forces arrived to liberate that country. Zubaydah was severely wounded during the firefight that brought him into custody, and he survived only because of the medical care arranged by the CIA.

After he recovered, Zubaydah was defiant and evasive. He declared his hatred of America. During questioning, he at first disclosed what he thought was nominal information, and then stopped all cooperation. Well, in fact, the "nominal" information he gave us turned out to be quite important. For example, Zubaydah disclosed Khalid Sheikh Mohammed, or KSM, was the mastermind behind the 9/11 attacks and used the alias Muktar. This was a vital piece of the puzzle that helped our intelligence community pursue KSM. Zubaydah also provided information that helped stop a terrorist attack being planned for inside the United States, an attack about which we had no previous information. Zubaydah told us that Al Qaida operatives were planning to launch an attack in the U.S. and provided physical descriptions of the operatives and information on their general location. Based on the information he provided, the operatives were detained, one while traveling to the United States.

We knew that Zubaydah had more information that could save innocent lives, but he stopped talking. As his questioning proceeded, it became clear that he had received training on how to resist interrogation. And so the CIA used an alternative set of procedures. These procedures were designed to be safe, to comply with our laws, our Constitution, and our treaty obligations. The Department of Justice reviewed the authorized methods extensively and determined them to be lawful. I cannot describe the specific methods used. I think you understand why; if I did, it would help the terrorists learn how to resist questioning and to keep information from us that we need to prevent new attacks on our country. But I can say the procedures were tough, and they were safe and lawful and necessary.

Zubaydah was questioned using these procedures, and soon he began to provide information on key Al Qaida operatives, including information that helped us find and capture more of those responsible for the attacks on September the 11th. For example, Zubaydah identified one of KSM's accomplices in the 9/11 attacks, a terrorist named Ramzi bin al-Shibh. The information Zubaydah provided helped lead to the capture of bin al-Shibh. And together these two terrorists provided information that helped in the planning and execution of the operation that captured Khalid Sheikh Mohammed.

Once in our custody, KSM was questioned by the CIA using these procedures, and he soon provided information that helped us stop another planned attack on the United States. During questioning, KSM told us about another Al Qaida operative he knew was in CIA custody, a terrorist named Majid Khan. KSM revealed that Khan had been told to deliver $50,000 to individuals working for a suspected terrorist leader named Hambali, the leader of Al Qaida's Southeast Asian affiliate known as JI. CIA officers confronted Khan with this information. Khan confirmed that the money had been delivered to an operative named Zubair and provided both a physical description and contact number for this operative.

Based on that information, Zubair was captured in June of 2003, and he soon provided information that helped lead to the capture of Hambali. After Hambali's arrest, KSM was questioned again. He identified Hambali's brother as the leader of a JI cell and Hambali's conduit for communications with Al Qaida. Hambali's brother was soon captured in Pakistan and in turn led us to a cell of 17 Southeast Asian JI operatives. When confronted with the news that his terror cell had been broken up, Hambali admitted that the operatives were being groomed at KSM's request for attacks inside the United States, probably using airplanes.

During questioning, KSM also provided many details of other plots to kill innocent Americans. For example, he described the design of planned attacks on buildings inside the United States and how operatives were directed to carry them out. He told us the operatives had been instructed to ensure that the explosives went off at a point that was high enough to prevent the people trapped above from escaping out the windows.

KSM also provided vital information on Al Qaida's efforts to obtain biological weapons. During questioning, KSM admitted that he had met three individuals involved in Al Qaida's efforts to produce anthrax, a deadly biological agent, and he identified one of the individuals as a terrorist named Yazid. KSM apparently believed we already had this information, because Yazid had been captured and taken into foreign custody before KSM's arrest. In fact, we did not know about Yazid's role in Al Qaida's anthrax program. Information from Yazid then helped lead to the capture of his two principal assistants in the anthrax program. Without the information provided by KSM and Yazid, we might not have uncovered this Al Qaida biological weapons program or stopped this Al Qaida cell from developing anthrax for attacks against the United States.

These are some of the plots that have been stopped because of the information of this vital program. Terrorists held in CIA custody have also provided information that helped stop a planned strike on U.S. marines at Camp Lemonier in Djibouti—they were going to use an explosive laden water tanker. They helped stop a planned attack on the U.S. consulate in Karachi using car bombs and motorcycle bombs, and they helped stop a plot to hijack passenger planes and fly them into Heathrow or the Canary Wharf in London.

We're getting vital information necessary to do our jobs, and that's to protect the American people and our allies. Information from the terrorists in this program has helped us to identify individuals that Al Qaida deemed suitable for Western operations, many of whom we had never heard about before. They include terrorists who were set to case targets inside the United States, including financial buildings in major cities on the east coast. Information from terrorists in CIA custody has played a role in the capture or questioning of nearly every senior Al Qaida member or associate detained by the U.S. and its allies since this program began. By providing everything from initial leads to photo identifications to precise locations of where terrorists were hiding, this program has helped

us to take potential mass murderers off the streets before they were able to kill.

This program has also played a critical role in helping us understand the enemy we face in this war. Terrorists in this program have painted a picture of Al Qaida's structure and financing and communications and logistics. They identified Al Qaida's travel routes and safe havens and explained how Al Qaida's senior leadership communicates with its operatives in places like Iraq. They provided information that allows us—that has allowed us to make sense of documents and computer records that we have seized in terrorist raids. They've identified voices in recordings of intercepted calls and helped us understand the meaning of potentially critical terrorist communications.

The information we get from these detainees is corroborated by intelligence, and we've received—that we've received from other sources, and together this intelligence has helped us connect the dots and stop attacks before they occur. Information from the terrorists questioned in this program helped unravel plots and terrorist cells in Europe and in other places. It's helped our allies protect their people from deadly enemies. This program has been and remains one of the most vital tools in our war against the terrorists. It is invaluable to America and to our allies. Were it not for this program, our intelligence community believes that Al Qaida and its allies would have succeeded in launching another attack against the American homeland. By giving us information about terrorist plans we could not get anywhere else, this program has saved innocent lives.

This program has been subject to multiple legal reviews by the Department of Justice and CIA lawyers; they've determined it complied with our laws. This program has received strict oversight by the CIA's Inspector General. A small number of key leaders from both political parties on Capitol Hill were briefed about this program. All those involved in the questioning of the terrorists are carefully chosen, and they're screened from a pool of experienced CIA officers. Those selected to conduct the most sensitive questioning had to complete more than 250 additional hours of specialized training before they are allowed to have contact with a captured terrorist.

I want to be absolutely clear with our people and the world: The United States does not torture. It's against our laws, and it's against our values. I have not authorized it, and I will not authorize it. Last year, my administration worked with Senator John McCain, and I signed into law the Detainee Treatment Act, which established the legal standard for treatment of detainees wherever they are held. I support this act. And as we implement this law, our Government will continue to use every lawful method to obtain intelligence that can protect innocent people and stop another attack like the one we experienced on September the 11th, 2001.

The CIA program has detained only a limited number of terrorists at any given time, and once we've determined that the terrorists held by the CIA have little or no additional intelligence value, many of them have been returned to their home countries for prosecution or detention by their governments. Others have been accused of terrible crimes against the American people, and we have a duty to bring those responsible for these crimes to justice. So we intend to prosecute these men, as appropriate, for their crimes.

Soon after the war on terror began, I authorized a system of military commissions to try foreign terrorists accused of war crimes. Military commissions have been used by Presidents from George Washington to Franklin Roosevelt to prosecute war criminals, because the rules for trying enemy combatants in a time of conflict must be different from those for trying common criminals or members of our own military.

One of the first suspected terrorists to be put on trial by military commission was one of Usama bin Laden's bodyguards, a man named Hamdan. His lawyers challenged the legality of the military commission system. It took more than 2 years for this case to make its way through the courts. The Court of Appeals for the District of Columbia Circuit upheld the military commissions we had designed, but this past June, the Supreme Court overturned that decision. The Supreme Court determined that military commissions are an appropriate venue for trying terrorists but ruled that military commissions needed to be explicitly authorized by the United States Congress.

So today I'm sending Congress legislation to specifically authorize the creation of military commissions to try terrorists for war crimes. My administration has been working with members of both parties in the House and Senate on this legislation. We put forward a bill that ensures these commissions are established in a way that protects our national security and ensures a full and fair trial for those accused. The procedures in the bill I am sending to Congress today reflect the reality that we are a nation at war and that it's essential for us to use all reliable evidence to bring these people to justice.

We're now approaching the 5-year anniversary of the 9/11 attacks, and the families of those murdered that day have waited patiently for justice. Some of the families are with us today. They should have to wait no longer.

So I'm announcing today that Khalid Sheikh Mohammed, Abu Zubaydah, Ramzi bin al-Shibh, and 11 other terrorists in CIA custody have been transferred to the United States Naval Base at Guantanamo Bay. They are being held in the custody of the Department of Defense. As soon as Congress acts to authorize the military commissions I have proposed, the men our intelligence officials believe orchestrated the deaths of nearly 3,000 Americans on September the 11th, 2001, can face justice. We'll also seek to prosecute those believed to be responsible for the attack on the USS *Cole* and an operative believed to be involved in the bombings of the American Embassies in Kenya and Tanzania. With these prosecutions, we will send a clear message to those who kill Americans: No longer—how long it takes, we will find you, and we will bring you to justice.

These men will be held in a high-security facility at Guantanamo. The International Committee of the Red Cross is being advised of their detention and will have the opportunity to meet with them. Those charged with crimes will be given access to attorneys who will help them prepare their defense, and they will be presumed innocent. While at Guantanamo, they will have access to the same food, clothing, medical care, and opportunities for worship as other detainees. They will be questioned subject to the new U.S. Army Field Manual, which the Department of Defense is issuing today. And they will continue to be treated with the humanity that they denied others.

As we move forward with the prosecutions, we will continue to urge nations across the world to take back their nationals at Guantanamo who will not be prosecuted by our military commissions. America has no interest in being the world's jailer. But one of the reasons we have not been able to close Guantanamo is that many countries have refused to take back their nationals held at the facility. Other countries have not provided adequate assurances that their nationals will not be mistreated or they will not return to the battlefield, as more than a dozen people released from Guantanamo already have. We will continue working to transfer individuals held at Guantanamo and ask other countries to work with us in this process. And we will move toward the day when we can eventually close the detention facility at Guantanamo Bay.

I know Americans have heard conflicting information about Guantanamo. Let me give you some facts. Of the thousands of terrorists captured across the world, only about 770 have ever been sent to Guantanamo. Of these, about 315 have been returned to other countries so far, and about 455 remain in our custody. They are provided the same quality of medical care as the American servicemembers who guard them. The International Committee of the Red Cross has the opportunity to meet privately with all who are held there. The facility has been visited by government officials from more than 30 countries and delegations from international organizations as well. After the Organization for Security and Cooperation in Europe came to visit, one of its delegation members called Guantanamo "a model prison," where people are treated better than in prisons in his own country. Our troops can take great pride in the work they do at Guantanamo Bay, and so can the American people.

As we prosecute suspected terrorist leaders and operatives who have now been transferred to Guantanamo, we'll continue searching for those who have stepped forward to take their places. This Nation is going to stay on the offense to protect the American people. We will continue to bring the world's most dangerous terrorists to justice, and we will continue working to collect the vital intelligence we need to protect our country. The current transfers mean that there are now no terrorists in the CIA program. But as more high-ranking terrorists are captured, the need to obtain intelligence from them will remain critical. And having a CIA program for questioning terrorists will continue to be crucial to getting lifesaving information.

Some may ask: Why are you acknowledging this program now? There are two reasons why I'm making these limited disclosures today. First, we have largely completed our questioning of the men, and to start the process for bringing them to trial, we must bring them into the open. Second, the Supreme Court's recent decision has impaired our ability to prosecute terrorists through military commissions and has put in question the future of the CIA program.

In its ruling on military commissions, the Court determined that a provision of the Geneva Conventions known as Common Article Three applies to our war with Al Qaida. This article includes provisions that prohibit "outrages upon personal dignity" and "humiliating and degrading treatment." The problem is that these and other provisions of Common Article Three are vague and undefined, and each could be interpreted in different ways by American or foreign judges. And some believe our military and intelligence personnel involved in capturing and questioning terrorists could now be at risk of prosecution under the War Crimes Act, simply for doing their jobs in a thorough and professional way.

This is unacceptable. Our military and intelligence personnel go face to face with the world's most dangerous men every day. They have risked their lives to capture some of the most brutal terrorists on Earth. And they have worked day and night to find out what the terrorists know so we can stop new attacks. America owes our brave men and women some things in return. We owe them their thanks for saving lives and keeping America safe. And we owe them clear rules, so they can continue to do their jobs and protect our people.

So today I'm asking Congress to pass legislation that will clarify the rules for our personnel fighting the war on terror. First, I'm asking Congress to list the specific, recognizable offenses that would be considered crimes under the War Crimes Act so our personnel can know clearly what is prohibited in the handling of terrorist enemies. Second, I'm asking that Congress make explicit that by following the standards of the Detainee Treatment Act, our personnel are fulfilling America's obligations under Common Article Three of the Geneva Conventions. Third, I'm asking that Congress make it clear that captured terrorists cannot use the Geneva Conventions as a basis to sue our personnel in courts—in U.S. courts. The men and women who protect us should not have to fear lawsuits filed by terrorists because they're doing their jobs.

The need for this legislation is urgent. We need to ensure that those questioning terrorists can continue to do everything within the limits of the law to get information that can save American lives. My administration will continue to work with the Congress to get this legislation enacted, but time is of the essence. Congress is in session just for a few more weeks, and passing this legislation ought to be the top priority.

As we work with Congress to pass a good bill, we will also consult with congressional leaders on how to ensure that the CIA program goes forward in a way that follows the law, that meets the national security needs of our country, and protects the brave men and women we ask to obtain information that will save innocent lives. For the sake of our security, Congress needs to act and update our laws to meet the threats of this new era. And I know they will.

We're engaged in a global struggle, and the entire civilized world has a stake in its outcome. America is a nation of law. And as I work with Congress to strengthen and clarify our laws here at home, I will continue to work with members of the international community who have been our partners in this struggle. I've spoken with leaders of foreign governments and worked with them to address their concerns about Guantanamo and our detention policies. I'll continue to work with the international community to construct a common foundation to defend our nations and protect our freedoms.

Free nations have faced new enemies and adjusted to new threats before, and we have prevailed. Like the struggles of the last century, today's war on terror is, above all, a struggle for freedom and liberty. The adversaries are different, but the stakes in this war are the same. We're fighting for our way of life and our ability to live in freedom. We're fighting for the cause of humanity against those who seek to impose the darkness of tyranny and terror upon the entire world. And we're fighting for a peaceful future for our children and our grandchildren.

May God bless you all.

NOTE: The President spoke at 1:45 p.m. in the East Room at the White House. In his remarks, he referred to Usama bin Laden, leader of the Al Qaida terrorist organization; Khalid Sheikh Mohammed, senior Al Qaida leader responsible for planning the September 11, 2001, terrorist attacks, who was captured in Pakistan on March 1, 2003; Ramzi bin al-Shibh, an Al Qaida operative suspected of helping to plan the September 11, 2001, terrorist attacks, who was captured in Karachi, Pakistan, on September 11, 2002; and Nurjaman Riduan Isamuddin (also known as Hambali), Al Qaida's chief operational planner in Southeast Asia, who was captured in Thailand on August 11, 2003.

Message to the Congress Transmitting Draft Legislation on Military Commissions
September 6, 2006

To the Congress of the United States:

I transmit for the consideration of the Congress draft legislation entitled the "Military Commissions Act of 2006." This draft legislation responds to the Supreme Court of the United States decision in *Hamdan v. Rumsfeld*, 126 S. Ct. 2749 (2006), by establishing for the first time in our Nation's history a comprehensive statutory structure for military commissions that would allow for the fair and effective prosecution of captured members of al Qaeda and other unlawful enemy combatants. The Act also addresses the Supreme Court's holding that Common Article 3 of the Geneva Conventions applies to the conflict with al Qaeda by providing definitions rooted in United States law for the standards of conduct prescribed by Common Article 3.

The military commission procedures contained in this draft legislation reflect the result of an extended deliberation both within the executive branch and between representatives of my Administration and Members of Congress. The draft legislation would establish a Code of Military Commissions that tracks the courts-martial procedures of the Uniform Code of Military Justice, but that departs from those procedures where they would be impracticable or inappropriate for the trial of unlawful enemy combatants captured in the midst of an ongoing armed conflict, under circumstances far different from those typically encountered by military prosecutors.

Five years after the mass murders of 9/11, it is time for the United States to begin to prosecute captured al Qaeda members for the serious crimes that many of them have committed against United States citizens and our allies abroad. As we provide terrorists the justice and due process that they denied their victims, we demonstrate that our Nation remains committed to the rule of law.

I ask that the Congress carefully consider this legislation and respectfully urge its speedy passage for enactment into law.

GEORGE W. BUSH

The White House,
September 6, 2006.

Remarks to the Georgia Public Policy Foundation in Atlanta, Georgia
September 7, 2006

Thank you all very much. Please be seated. Thank you. Sonny, thanks for the introduction. Thanks for your leadership. It's always a pleasure to be in Georgia. I appreciate you coming, and I appreciate this chance to speak here before the Georgia Public Policy Foundation. And I thank you for what you do. For 15 years, you've been researching and writing on issues that matter. You take on tough questions; you apply innovative thinking; you push for action; and you do it all without regard to politics. Come on up to Washington. [*Laughter*]

I have come here to Atlanta to continue a series of speeches marking the fifth anniversary of the September the 11th, 2001, attacks. Last week at the American Legion Convention in Salt Lake City, Utah, I outlined the ideological struggle between the forces of moderation and liberty and the forces of extremism across the Middle East. On Tuesday in Washington, I described our enemies in their own words and set forward a strategy to defeat them. Yesterday I announced that the men we believe orchestrated the 9/11 attacks have been transferred to Guantanamo Bay, and I called on the United States Congress to pass legislation creating military commissions to bring these people to justice.

Today I'll deliver a progress report on the steps we have taken since 9/11 to protect the American people, steps we've taken to go on the offense against the enemy, and steps we are taking to win this war on terror.

Today I traveled with two United States Senators who clearly see the issues before us, and I appreciate and I'm proud to be associated and friends with Senator Saxby Chambliss and Senator Johnny Isakson.

I do thank Brenda Fitzgerald for encouraging the board of governors to invite me and for taking the lead for the Georgia Public Policy Foundation. And I want to thank the board of governors for your kind invitation. I appreciate very much being with Major General Terry Nesbitt. He's the director of the Georgia office of Homeland Security.

Joining us today is a man I got to know quite well under trying circumstances, and that would be Lieutenant General Russ Honore of the United States Army— Honore. He issued one of the great lines I've ever heard, and you're welcome to use it: "Don't get stuck on stupid." It's good advice for people in Washington, DC. [*Laughter*]

I welcome the other State and local officials here. Thank you all for letting me come by.

In Atlanta, you know the pain of terrorism firsthand. This summer, you marked the 10th anniversary of the bombing in Centennial Olympic Park. That was the act of one madman. Next Monday is the fifth anniversary of an attack on our Nation, and on that day, we awoke to a new kind of terrorism. Instead of a localized strike, we faced multiple attacks by a network of sophisticated and suicidal extremists. In the years since, we've come to learn more about our enemies. We've learned more about their dark and distorted vision of Islam. We've learned about their plan to build a radical Islamic empire stretching from Spain to Indonesia. We learned about their dreams to kill more Americans on an even more devastating scale. That's what they have told us. As President, I took an oath to protect this country, and I will continue using every element of national power to pursue our enemies and to prevent attacks on the United States of America.

Over the past 5 years, we have waged an unprecedented campaign against terror at home and abroad, and that campaign has succeeded in protecting the homeland. At the same time, we've seen our enemies strike in Britain, Spain, India, Turkey, Russia, Indonesia, Jordan, Israel, Afghanistan, Iraq, and other countries. We've seen that the extremists have not given up on their dreams to strike our Nation. Just last month, police and intelligence officers from Great Britain, with the help of the United States and other allies, helped break up a terror cell in London. Working together, we foiled a suicide plot to blow up passenger planes on their way to the United States.

Many Americans look at these events and ask the same question: Five years after 9/11, are we safer? The answer is, yes, America is safer. We are safer because we've taken action to protect the homeland. We are safer because we are on the offense against our enemies overseas. We're safer because of the skill and sacrifice of the brave Americans who defend our people. Yet 5 years after 9/11, America still faces determined enemies, and we will not be safe until those enemies are finally defeated.

One way to assess whether we're safer is to look at what we have done to fix the problems that the 9/11 attacks revealed. And so today I'll deliver a progress report. The information about the attacks in this report is largely drawn from the work of the 9/11 Commission and other investigations of the terrorist attacks. I'll begin by looking back at four key stages of the 9/11 plot, the gaps in our defenses that each stage exposed, and the ways we've addressed those gaps to make this country safer.

In the first key stage of the 9/11 plot, Al Qaida conceived and planned the attacks from abroad. In the summer of 1996, Usama bin Laden issued a fatwa from Afghanistan that said this: "By the grace of Allah, a safe base here is now available." And he declared war on the United States. A month later, the Taliban seized control of Kabul and formed an alliance with Al Qaida. The Taliban permitted bin Laden to operate a system of training camps in

the country which ultimately instructed more than 10,000 in terrorist tactics. Bin Laden was also free to cultivate a global financing network that provided money for terrorist operations. With his fellow Al Qaida leaders, Usama bin Laden used his safe haven to prepare a series of attacks on America and on the civilized world.

In August 1998, they carried out their first big strike, the bombing of two U.S. Embassies in east Africa, which killed more than 200 people and wounded thousands. Shortly after the Embassy bombings, bin Laden approved another attack. This one was called the "planes operation." Our intelligence agencies believe it was suggested by a fellow terrorist named Khalid Sheikh Mohammed, or KSM. KSM's plan was to hijack commercial airliners and to crash them into buildings in the United States. He and bin Laden selected four preliminary targets—the World Trade Center, the Pentagon, the Capitol Building, and the White House. The "planes operation" would become the 9/11 plot, and by the middle of 1999, KSM was at work recruiting suicide operatives to hijack the airplanes.

The first stage of the 9/11 plot exposed serious flaws in America's approach to terrorism. Most important, it showed that by allowing states to give safe haven to terrorist networks that we made a grave mistake. So after 9/11, I set forth a new doctrine: Nations that harbor or support terrorists are equally guilty as the terrorists and will be held to account. And the Taliban found out what we meant. With Afghan allies, we removed the Taliban from power, and we closed down the Al Qaida training camps. Five years later, Taliban and Al Qaida remnants are desperately trying to retake control of that country. They will fail. They will fail because the Afghan people have tasted freedom. They will fail because their vision is no match for a democracy accountable to its citizens. They will fail because they are no match for the military forces of a free Afghanistan, a NATO alliance, and the United States of America.

Our offensive against the terrorists includes far more than military might. We use financial tools to make it harder for them to raise money. We're using diplomatic pressure, and our intelligence operations are used to disrupt the day-to-day functions of Al Qaida. Because we're on the offense, it is more difficult for Al Qaida to transfer money through the international banking system. Because we're on the offense, Al Qaida can no longer communicate openly without fear of destruction. And because we're on the offense, Al Qaida can no longer move widely without fearing for their lives.

I learned a lot of lessons on 9/11, and one lesson is this: In order to protect this country, we will keep steady pressure, unrelenting pressure on Al Qaida and its associates. We will deny them safe haven. We will find them, and we will bring them to justice.

Key advantages that Al Qaida enjoyed while plotting the 9/11 attack in Afghanistan have been taken away, and so have many of their most important leaders, including Khalid Sheikh Mohammed. For the past 3 years, KSM has been in the custody of the Central Intelligence Agency. He's provided valuable intelligence that has helped us kill or capture Al Qaida terrorists and stop attacks on our Nation. I authorized his transfer to Guantanamo Bay, and the sooner the Congress authorizes the military commissions I have called for, the sooner Khalid Sheikh Mohammed will receive the justice he deserves.

In the second key stage of the 9/11 plot, KSM and bin Laden identified, trained, and deployed operatives to the United States. According to the 9/11 Commission, two of the first suicide hijackers to join the plot were men named Hazmi and Mihdhar. KSM's plan was to send these two men to infiltrate the United States and train as pilots so they could fly the hijacked planes

into buildings. Both operatives attended a special training camp in Afghanistan, and then traveled to Malaysia and Thailand to prepare for their trip to America. KSM doctored Hazmi's passport to help him enter the United States. And from Thailand, the two men flew to Los Angeles in January of 2000. There they began carrying out the plot from inside our Nation. They made phone calls to planners of the attack, overseas, and they awaited the arrival of the other killers.

Our intelligence community picked up some of this information. CIA analysts saw links between Mihdhar and Al Qaida, and officers tracked Mihdhar to Malaysia. Weeks later, they discovered that he had been accompanied by Hazmi and that Hazmi had flown to Los Angeles. This gave the CIA reason to be suspicious of both these men. Yet at the time, there was no consolidated terrorist watch list available to all Federal agencies and State and local governments. So even though intelligence officers suspected that both men were dangerous, the information was not readily accessible to American law enforcement, and the operatives slipped into our country.

Since 9/11, we've addressed the gaps in our defenses that these operatives exploited. We've upgraded technology. We've added layers of security to correct weaknesses in our immigration and visa systems. Today, visa applicants like Hazmi or Mihdhar would have to appear face to face for interviews. They would be fingerprinted and screened against an extensive database of known or suspected terrorists. And when they arrived on American soil, they would be checked again to make sure their fingerprints matched the fingerprints on their visas. Those procedures did not exist before 9/11. With these steps, we made it harder for these—people like these guys to infiltrate our country.

Nine-Eleven also revealed the need for a coordinated approach to terrorist watch lists. So we established common criteria for posting terrorists on a consolidated terrorist watch list that is now widely available across Federal, State, and local jurisdictions. Today, intelligence community officials would immediately place terrorist suspects like Hazmi and Mihdhar on a consolidated watch list. And the information from this list is now accessible at airports, consulates, border crossings, and for State and local law enforcement. By putting terrorists' names on a consolidated watch list, we've improved our ability to monitor and to track and detain operatives before they can strike.

Another top priority after 9/11 was improving our ability to monitor terrorist communications. Remember, I told you the two had made phone calls outside the country. At my direction, the National Security Agency created the terrorist surveillance program. Before 9/11, our intelligence professionals found it difficult to monitor international communications such as those between the Al Qaida operatives secretly in the United States and planners of the 9/11 attacks. The terrorist surveillance program helps protect Americans by allowing us to track terrorist communications so we can learn about threats like the 9/11 plot before it is too late.

Last year, details of the terrorist surveillance program were leaked to the news media, and the program was then challenged in court. That challenge was recently upheld by a Federal district judge in Michigan. My administration strongly disagrees with the ruling. We are appealing it, and we believe our appeal will be successful. Yet a series of protracted legal challenges would put a heavy burden on this critical and vital program. The surest way to keep the program is to get explicit approval from the United States Congress. So today I'm calling on the Congress to promptly pass legislation providing additional authority for the terrorist surveillance program, along with broader reforms in the Foreign Intelligence Surveillance Act.

When the FISA was passed in 1978, there was no widely accessible Internet,

and almost all calls were made on fixed landlines. Since then, the nature of communications has changed quite dramatically. The terrorists who want to harm America can now buy disposable cell phones and open anonymous e-mail addresses. Our laws need to change to take these changes into account. If Al Qaida commander or associate is calling into the United States, we need to know why they're calling. And Congress needs to pass legislation supporting this program.

In the third key stage of the 9/11 plot, the rest of the 19 Al Qaida operatives arrived in the United States. The first two hijackers in America, Hazmi and Mihdhar, had given up flight training, so Khalid Sheikh Mohammed selected operatives from a cell in Germany to become the new pilots. These men, led by Mohammed Atta, obtained visas, and they traveled to the United States, and then they enrolled in flight training schools. Atta and his team visited airports and flight training centers along the east coast, including here in Georgia. Atta was pulled over by police. On his way, one of his coconspirators, the terrorist who would go on to pilot Flight 93, was also stopped. Yet there was no information that the men were dangerous, so the officers treated the encounters as routine traffic stops. By September the 10th, the hijackers had moved to their final destinations near major airports and were ready to execute their attacks.

As these terrorists finalized their plans, Al Qaida dispatched another operative named Moussaoui to the United States. Moussaoui took flight lessons in Oklahoma and Minnesota. He communicated with an Al Qaida leader abroad. But he remained isolated from the other operatives and was not a suicide hijacker on the day of the attacks, didn't participate in the 9/11 attacks.

During this stage, law enforcement and intelligence authorities failed to share the insights they were learning about the 9/11 plot. For example, the FBI intelligence analyst working at the CIA came across information that raised her suspicions about Hazmi and Mihdhar. But she did not relay her concerns to FBI criminal investigators because of a wall—or "the wall" that had developed over the years between law enforcement and intelligence. You see, throughout the Government, there was an assumption that law enforcement and intelligence were legally prohibited from sharing vital information. At one point, key officials from the CIA, the intelligence branch of the FBI, the criminal branch of the FBI were all sitting around the same table in New York, but they believed that "the wall" prohibited them from telling each other what they knew about Hazmi and Mihdhar, and so they never put the pieces together.

By the summer of 2001, intelligence about a possible terrorist attack was increasing. In July, an FBI agent in Phoenix noted that a large number of suspicious men were attending flight schools in Arizona. He speculated that this activity might be part of a bin Laden plan to attack inside the United States. The following month, the FBI field office in Minneapolis began an investigation into Moussaoui. He was soon arrested on immigration charges, and Minneapolis agents sought a FISA warrant to search his computer. FBI Headquarters turned them down, saying the case did not justify a FISA request because there was not enough intelligence tying Moussaoui to a foreign power. The FBI later learned that Moussaoui had attended an Al Qaida training camp in Afghanistan, but the information didn't arrive until September the 13th.

It is clear, after 9/11, that something needed to be done to the system; something needed to be changed to protect the American people. And it is clear to me that this started with transforming the FBI to ensure that it effectively and quickly respond to potential terrorist attacks. And so now the top priority of the FBI, since 9/11—the culture of that important Agency, full of decent people, has changed. The top priority is to protect the American peo-

ple from terrorist attack. The Bureau has hired large numbers of counterterrorism agents and analysts. They're focusing resources on what they need to do to protect America. They created a unified National Security Branch to coordinate terrorist investigations. They expanded the number of Joint Terrorism Task Forces. And the Bureau is submitting more FISA requests in terrorist cases. In other words, they understand the challenge, and the FBI is changing to meet those challenges. The FBI is responding to terrorist threats like Moussaoui more quickly, more effectively, and with more resources. At every level, America's law enforcement officers now have a clear goal: to identify, locate, and stop terrorists before they can kill again.

Since the attacks, we've also worked with Congress to do something about that wall that prevented intelligence and criminal investigators from talking to each other. The wall made no sense. It reflected an old way of thinking. And so I called upon Congress to pass a piece of legislation that would tear down the wall, and that was called the PATRIOT Act. The PATRIOT Act has increased the flow of information within our Government, and it has helped break up terrorist cells in the United States of America. And the United States Congress was right to renew the terrorist act— the PATRIOT Act, the terrorist prevention act called the PATRIOT Act.

We created the National Counterterrorism Center, where law enforcement and intelligence personnel work side by side in the same headquarters. This center hosts secure video teleconferences every day that allow for seamless communication among the FBI, the CIA, and other agencies. Now officials with critical threat information are sitting at the same table and sharing information. We created the position of the Director of National Intelligence to operate the intelligence community as a single unified enterprise. We set up the Terrorist Screening Center, which maintains the

Government's master list of suspected terrorists and helps get this information in the hands of State and local law enforcement. Today, a police officer who stops a driver for a routine traffic violation can access terrorist watch lists and be automatically directed to the Terrorist Screening Center if there's a match.

We've learned the lessons of September the 11th. We're changing how people can work together. We're modernizing the system. We're working to connect the dots to stop the terrorists from hurting America again.

The fourth and final stage of the 9/11 plot came on the morning of the attack. Starting around 6:45, the 19 hijackers, including Hazmi and Mihdhar, checked in, cleared security, and boarded commercial jets bound for the west coast. Some of the hijackers were flagged by the passenger prescreening system. But because the security rules at the time focused on preventing bombs on airplanes, the only precaution required was to hold the operatives' checked baggage until they boarded the airplane. Several hijackers were also carrying small knives or box cutters, and when they reached the security checkpoints, they set off metal detectors. The screeners wanded them but let them board their planes without verifying what had set off the alarms. When the flights took off, the men hijacked each plane in a similar way: They stabbed or subdued the pilots and crew, they seized control of the cockpit, and they started flying the airplane. By 9:03 a.m., the hijackers had driven two of the flights in the World Trade Center. By 9:37, they had struck the Pentagon. And shortly after 10 a.m., the fourth plane crashed into a field in Pennsylvania. The passengers realized what was happening, and they rose up against their captors. These brave passengers saved countless lives on the ground; they likely spared the Capitol or the White House from destruction; and they delivered America its first victory in the war on terror.

We have taken many steps to address the security gaps that the hijackers exploited that morning. We created the Transportation Security Administration to ensure that every passenger and every bag is screened. We increased the number of Federal air marshals on domestic and international flights. We trained and authorized thousands of pilots to carry firearms. We hardened cockpit doors to prevent terrorists from gaining access to the controls. We merged 22 Government agencies into a single Department of Homeland Security and tripled spending for homeland security on our airlines, on our ports, and our borders and other critical areas. We will continue to provide the resources necessary to secure this homeland.

Even if all the steps I've outlined this morning had been taken before 9/11, no one can say for sure that we would have prevented the attack. We can say that if America had these reforms in place in 2001, the terrorists would have found it harder to plan and finance their operations, harder to slip into the country undetected, and harder to board the airplanes and take control of the cockpits and succeed in striking their targets.

We are grateful to all those who have worked to implement these important reforms. We're grateful to our Federal and State and local law enforcement officers who are working tirelessly to protect our country. We're grateful to all the intelligence and homeland security and military personnel. Together these dedicated men and women are keeping their fellow Americans safe, and Americans are proud of their important service to our country.

On the morning of 9/11, we saw that the terrorists have to be right only once to kill our people, while we have to be right every time to stop them. So we had to make a larger choice about how to respond to the threats to our country. Some suggested that our effort should be purely defensive, hunkering down behind extreme homeland security and law enforcement measures. Others argue that we should respond overseas, but that our action should be limited to direct retaliation for 9/11. I strongly disagree with both approaches. Nine-Eleven lifted the veil on a threat that is far broader and more dangerous than we saw that morning, an enemy that was not sated by the destruction inflicted that day and is determined to strike again. To answer this threat and to protect our people, we need more than retaliation; we need more than a reaction to the last attack; we need to do everything in our power to stop the next attack.

And so America has gone on the offense across the world. And here are some of the results. We've captured or killed many of the most significant Al Qaida members and associates. We've killed Al Qaida's most visible and aggressive leader to emerge after 9/11, the terrorist Zarqawi in Iraq. We've kept the terrorists from achieving their key goal, to overthrow governments across the broader Middle East and to seize control. Instead, the governments they targeted, such as Pakistan and Saudi Arabia, have become some of the most valuable allies in the war on terror. These countries are joined by the largest coalition in the history of warfare, more than 90 nations determined to find the terrorists, to dry up their funds, to stop their plots, and to bring them to justice.

This coalition includes two nations that used to sponsor terror but now help us fight it, the democratic nations of Afghanistan and Iraq. In Afghanistan, President Karzai's elected Government is fighting our common enemies. In showing the courage he's showing, he's inspired millions across the region. In Iraq, Prime Minister Maliki's unity Government is fighting Al Qaida and the enemies of Iraq's democracy. They're taking increasing responsibility for the security of their free country.

The fighting in Iraq has been difficult, and it has been bloody, and some say that Iraq is a diversion from the war on terror. The terrorists disagree. Usama bin Laden

has proclaimed that the "third world war is raging" in Iraq. Al Qaida leaders have declared that Baghdad will be the capital of the new caliphate that they wish to establish across the broader Middle East. It's hard to believe that extremists would make large journeys across dangerous borders to endure heavy fighting and to blow themselves up on the streets of Baghdad for a so-called "diversion." The terrorists know that the outcome in the war on terror will depend on the outcome in Iraq. And so to protect our citizens, the free world must succeed in Iraq.

As we fight the enemies of a free Iraq, we must also ensure that Al Qaida, its allies, and the extremists never get their hands on the tools of mass murder. When we saw the damage the terrorists inflicted on 9/11, our thoughts quickly turned to the devastation that could have been caused with weapons of mass destruction. So we launched the Proliferation Security Initiative, a coalition of more than 70 countries that are cooperating to stop shipments related to deadly weapons. Together with Russia, we're working on a new Global Initiative to Combat Nuclear Terrorism. We worked with Great Britain to persuade Libya to give up its nuclear weapons program, and now the components of that program are secured right here in the United States. We uncovered the black market nuclear network of A.Q. Khan, who was shipping equipment to Iran and North Korea; that network is now out of business. And now the world is uniting to send a clear message to the regime in Tehran: Iran must end its support of terror; it must stop defying its international obligations; and it must not obtain a nuclear weapon.

Our enemies have fought relentlessly these past 5 years, and they have a record of their own. Bin Laden and his deputy Zawahiri are still in hiding. Al Qaida has continued its campaign of terror with deadly attacks that have targeted the innocent, including large numbers of fellow Muslims. The terrorists and insurgents in Iraq have killed American troops and thousands of Iraqis. Syria and Iran have continued their support for terror and extremism. Hizballah has taken innocent life in Israel and succeeded briefly in undermining Lebanon's democratic Government. Hamas is standing in the way of peace with Israel. And the extremists have led an aggressive propaganda campaign to spread lies about America and incite Muslim radicalism. The enemies of freedom are skilled, and they are sophisticated, and they are waging a long and determined war. The free world must understand the stakes of this struggle. The free world must support young democracies. The free world must confront the evil of these extremists. The free world must draw full measure of our strength and resources to prevail.

We see that full measure and the strength of this Nation in the men and women in uniform who fight this war and we have—and who have given their lives in the cause of liberty and freedom. One of these soldiers was a young lieutenant named Noah Harris, who was killed last summer in Iraq when his Humvee was hit by a roadside bomb. Noah grew up here in Georgia. He graduated from the University of Georgia. He volunteered for the Army after September the 11th, 2001. He told his dad that people had an obligation to serve a cause higher than themselves. In Iraq, Lieutenant Harris was an officer known for his toughness and his skill in battle and for the Beanie Babies that he carried with him to hand out to the Iraqi children. He was also known for the photo of his parents' home in Ellijay that he used as a screensaver on his computer. When his troops asked why he chose that picture, he explained, "That is why I'm here."

Lieutenant Harris understood the stakes in Iraq. He knew that to protect his loved ones at home, America must defeat our enemies overseas. If America pulls out of Iraq before the Iraqis can defend themselves, the terrorists will follow us here, home. The best way to honor the memory of brave Americans like Lieutenant Harris is to complete the mission they began. So we will stay, we will fight, and we will win in Iraq.

The war on terror is more than a military conflict, it is the decisive ideological struggle of the 21st century. And we're only in its opening stages. To win this struggle, we have to defeat the ideology of the terrorists with a more hopeful vision. So a central element in our strategy is the freedom agenda. We know from history that free nations are peaceful nations. We know that democracies do not attack each other and that young people growing up in a free and hopeful society are less likely to fall under the sway of radicalism. And so we're taking the side of democratic leaders and reformers across the Middle East. We're supporting the voices of tolerance and moderation in the Muslim world. We're standing with mothers and fathers in every culture who want to see their children grow up in a caring and peaceful world. And by leading the cause of freedom in the vital region, we will change the conditions that give rise to radicalism and hatred and terror. We will replace violent dictatorships with peaceful democracies. We'll make America, the Middle East, and the world more secure.

In the early days after 9/11, I told the American people that this would be a long war, a war that would look different from others we have fought, with difficulties and setbacks along the way. The past 5 years have proven that to be true. The past 5 years have also shown what we can achieve when our Nation acts with confidence and resolve and clear purpose. We've learned the lessons of 9/11, and we have addressed the gaps in our defenses exposed by that attack. We've gone on the offense against our enemies and transformed former adversaries into allies. We have put in place the institutions needed to win this war. Five years after September the 11th, 2001, America is safer, and America is winning the war on terror. With vigilance, determination, courage, we will defeat the enemies of freedom, and we will leave behind a more peaceful world for our children and our grandchildren.

God bless.

NOTE: The President spoke at 10:24 a.m. at the Cobb Galleria Center. In his remarks, he referred to Gov. George E. "Sonny" Perdue of Georgia; Brenda Fitzgerald, chairman, board of governors, Georgia Public Policy Foundation; Lt. Gen. Russel L. Honore, USA, commanding general, First United States Army; Usama bin Laden, leader of the Al Qaida terrorist organization; Khalid Sheikh Mohammed, senior Al Qaida leader responsible for planning the September 11, 2001, terrorist attacks, who was captured in Pakistan on March 1, 2003; U.S. District Court Judge for the Eastern District of Michigan Anna Diggs Taylor; Zacarias Moussaoui, an Al Qaida operative who was sentenced on May 4 for helping to plan the September 11, 2001, terrorist attacks; President Hamid Karzai of Afghanistan; Prime Minister Nuri al-Maliki of Iraq; and Ayman Al-Zawahiri, founder of the Egyptian Islamic Jihad and senior Al Qaida associate. He also referred to the National Commission on Terrorist Attacks Upon the United States (9/11 Commission).

Remarks at a Reception for Congressional Candidate Max Burns in Pooler, Georgia
September 7, 2006

Thanks for coming. I want to thank you all for coming and joining me in supporting my friend Max Burns to be the next Congressman from this district.

Max, this is a good sign that so many people would show up. [*Laughter*] And I thank you for supporting him. I know him quite well. See, as he mentioned, we have worked together before. He's not an unknown quantity. You don't have to guess about his political philosophy. You don't have to worry about whether he will do the right thing. Max Burns is a man who is the right man to represent the 12th Congressional District for the State of Georgia. And I want to thank you for giving him this strong support.

Max not—I not only think Max is the right guy, but so does Laura. [*Laughter*] She sends her love to the Burns family, to Lora and Max. She sends her thanks to all of you. And she reminded me to remind—to thank you for the fantastic experience we had down here in 2004. If you ever want to host an international conference, I strongly suggest this part of the country. The G–8 was a great success, primarily because of the beauty of the coastline and, more importantly, the warmth of the people here on the coastline. And so we're proud to be back in Savannah. This is good country with good people. And I'm proud to be back, and I'm real proud to be supporting Max.

Today I'm traveling from Atlanta, where I gave a speech, the third of three speeches on what we're doing to secure this country, and I traveled over on Air Force One with a man who is doing a fabulous job as the Governor of an important State, and that's Governor Sonny Perdue. Sonny, thanks for coming. He's a straightforward fellow. He's the kind of guy, frankly, that the Texas voters would be comfortable with. [*Laughter*] He's no-nonsense. He's down-to-earth. What you see is what you get. And even though he didn't ask, I do want to remind you to support him for his reelection. He deserves it.

Max is going to be working with a really important and a very fine senatorial group of folks from Georgia. I know firsthand because I work with them all the time. This State has done a very smart thing in sending Saxby Chambliss and Johnny Isakson to the United States Senate. I'm proud they're here, and I thank them for coming.

I'm looking forward to getting my instructions on Air Force One flying back to Washington. [*Laughter*] They're not shy about telling me what's on their mind, and it usually starts with, "Here's what's best for Georgia."

I'm proud to be here with Eric Johnson, president pro tem of the Georgia State Senate. Thanks for coming, senator. Tommie Williams, who is the majority leader of the Georgia State Senate, is with us. Senator, thank you for coming as well.

I know Max appreciates the statehouse people supporting him. I know he is proud to have the support of those who run for office themselves. It's a good sign. When people have been out there knocking on doors saying, "I'm for this man for Congress," they know what the grassroots are thinking; they know what the people want. The people want Max Burns to return to the United States Congress, and so do I.

Swainsboro mayor, Mayor Charles Schwabe is with us today. Mayor, thank you for coming. I appreciate Karen Handel, who's the candidate for secretary of state, joining us today. Perry McGuire, the candidate for the attorney general for the State of Georgia, is with us as well. Brent Brown and Gary Black—they're colorful characters—[*laughter*]—running for the labor commissioner and agriculture commissioner.

I appreciate—let me just say this—I appreciate all of you running statewide. It's hard work. I know you want me to say this—these folks need your help too. It's not easy to be a candidate; it just isn't. And when you find somebody as honest as Max, who's willing to step up there and run, I believe you owe him more than just writing a check; I believe you owe him putting up those signs. That's what I believe. I believe you owe him time, if you don't mind me saying so. He's counting on it, and so am I. It's important to have good, strong, decent, honorable people like Max Burns representing you in the United States Congress.

I want to thank Mike Wiggins, the candidate for the Georgia Supreme Court. I appreciate you being here, Mike.

And finally, I can't—I want to thank the original members of the Mighty Eighth Air Force. I want to thank the museum director. This is a spectacular facility, and we're grateful that we could use it.

These are historic times in which we live. These are—and that's why it's important to have people in the Congress who clearly see the challenges this Nation faces. We are a nation at war. I can't tell you how much I wish I could come to Savannah, Georgia, and say we weren't at war. I wish I could report that to you, but I can't.

It should have been clear to the American people that we're still under threat when a couple of weeks ago, working with Great Britain, we uncovered yet another plot. People were going to get on airplanes bound for the United States and destroy them because they can't stand what we believe. We're facing ideologues.

In other words, these are people that have a belief system. The best way to understand the belief system they have is to think opposite of what we believe. We believe in the freedom of people to worship. See, you're equally American if you're Christian, Jew, Muslim, Hindu, agnostic, whatever. You're equally American. You have the right to choose. The people that face us, the radicals and extremists who attack us, believe you ought to worship one way, the way they believe, or else you're condemned. We believe in people being able to express themselves in the public square. We believe in dissent. We believe in the freedom of the press. We believe in freedom, and they don't.

I will be in New York City and in Pennsylvania and at the Pentagon next Monday with Laura. It is a day for us to remember the sorrow and the horror of that day. It's a day for us to remember the incredible bravery of first-responders who were willing to rush into danger to save life. It's a day to remember those on the airplane that drove that airplane into the ground, which was the first victory in the war on terror.

And it's also a day to remember the lessons learned. And the first lesson learned from that day is that the most important duty that those of us in the executive branch and the legislative branch have is to protect the American people from harm. And the best way to do so is to stay on the offense, is to defeat the enemy overseas so we do not have to face them here at home.

So I need Members of Congress who understand that we must give our troops and intelligence and those responsible for protecting America all the support they need. See, in order to stay on the offense, we have got to support those on the frontline of protecting the American people. We will use all assets to defend this Nation.

I learned another lesson, and that is, in order to protect the country, we must deny the enemy safe haven. See, the people were plotting and planning to attack us from Afghanistan, and so I laid out a doctrine that said, if you harbor a terrorist, you're equally as guilty as the terrorist. You'll be an enemy of the United States, and we will hold you to account.

The Taliban found out what I meant, and so over the last 5 years, we liberated 25 million people in Afghanistan but, equally important, denied the radicals, the extremists, a safe haven from which to plot and plan. I need Members of Congress who understand—Members like Max Burns—that when the President says something, he better mean what he says, in order to make sure the world is a more peaceful place.

A lesson of September the 11th, an important lesson for the President and Members of Congress and people of the United States is that when we see a threat, we must take the threat seriously before they come to the United States and hurt us. I saw a threat in Iraq. I not only saw the threat; nations around the world saw the threat. Republicans and Democrats in the United States Congress saw the same threat. We went to the United Nations and said to Saddam Hussein, "Disclose, disarm, or face serious consequences." I believe that when the President and the world speaks, they better mean what they say, in order to keep the peace. I meant what it said. Saddam Hussein didn't. He ignored the demands of the free world. Our coalition removed Saddam Hussein from power, and the world is better off.

And now the question is, will the United States of America keep its word and help this young democracy survive? It's really the challenge. And it's hard work. I fully understand why Americans are troubled by the death and destruction they see on their television screens. I know that. You see, it's easy to understand because I understand the compassion of the United States of America. Isn't it a wonderful country when people suffer when they see a child maimed by an extremist's car bomb. It's the nature of our country. We care deeply. We suffer when one of our youngsters lose their life in combat.

The stakes in Iraq are incredibly high, however. It's really important that we succeed. It's important for a lot of reasons. If we were to leave before the job is done, and the job is this: to help this young democracy govern itself, sustain itself, and defend itself; to help this young democracy that has formed because 12 million people went to the polls and said, "We're tired of tyranny; we're tired of subjugation; we want to be free."

That's the challenge. If we leave before the job is done, if we leave before this country's forces are able to defend themselves from the enemies of freedom who want to destroy this young democracy, if we forget the words of Usama bin Laden, who has declared that Iraq is the central part of this war on terror, if we ignore the words of Zawahiri, the number-two man in Al Qaida, who has said that what we're going to do is drive America out of Iraq; we'll be able to use Iraq then as a launching pad to destroy moderate governments in the Middle East; we'll be able to launch attacks against our enemy, America. If we ignore those words, if we ignore the hopes and aspirations of the Iraqi people, we will have failed when history looks back.

We will have created a situation that is more dangerous than today. We will have said to our enemies that we will give you a key victory in the war on terror. We will have said to our friends, "You can't count on us." We will have said to the reformers and moderates in the Middle East who are so desperate to live in a society that is hopeful that "You don't matter." We will say to the troops and their families who have sacrificed, "Your sacrifice wasn't worth it."

Make no mistake about it, if the United States leaves before the mission is complete, the enemy will follow us here to America. The stakes are high. We will help this Government succeed, and we will achieve victory in Iraq.

I have defined the struggle we're in as the ideological struggle of the 21st century. You see, we face the task not only of protecting ourselves in the short run by staying on the offense and improving our intelligence and finding people before they come here; we also have a weapon for the long term. And that is, in order to win an ideological struggle, you have to be able to have an ideology of hope that defeats an ideology of hate.

And we have such an ideology; we live it. It's an ideology based upon liberty. It's this notion that we strongly believe here in America that democracies don't war, that a free society is the best way to prevent radicalism and extremism from convincing people to become suiciders. Free societies equal hopeful societies.

You know, one of the challenges I face as your President is to make it absolutely clear the stakes in this war on terror. And what I'm saying is, the stakes are more than just protecting you from attack. The stakes really are protecting future generations from attack. If we were to leave early and concede the Middle East to the enemies of freedom, imagine a world in which moderate governments get toppled. Imagine a world in which extremists and radicals have control of oil that they'll be able to use to inflict incredible economic damage on those of us who love liberty. Imagine a world in which state sponsors of terror have a nuclear weapon to be able to blackmail the world. Imagine such a world. I can see it coming if America does not do our duty and support moderation over extremism.

The other day in a speech, I said, "Fifty years from now, if the United States does not rise to the challenge, a generation of our citizens will look back and say, 'What happened? What happened to America?' " No President is going to allow this to happen, and I'm not going to allow this to happen. We will—[*applause*].

And I got great confidence in the outcome. You know, I guess the best way for me to describe why I'm confident is to tell you about my experience with Prime Minister Koizumi of Japan. You might remember, recently I had the pleasurable experience of going to Elvis's place—[*laughter*]—Graceland, right there in Memphis, Tennessee. Isn't that interesting? I thought it was. [*Laughter*] I invited him to go down to Graceland, and I'd never been to Graceland. I thought it would be kind of fun to go down there, and Laura wanted to go. [*Laughter*] More importantly, he wanted to go. See, he's an Elvis fan. [*Laughter*] I also wanted to send a message to our fellow citizens that is relevant today, and here it is. One way to put it is—and can you imagine somebody in 1948, after World War II, after the bloody battles and fighting the Japanese—the sworn enemy of the United States—saying, "You know, I'll make a prediction for you; someday, an American President is going to be taking a Japanese Prime Minister to the home of a famous American singer." [*Laughter*] I don't think that person would have had much credibility. [*Laughter*]

Something happened between when my dad and many of your relatives fought the Japanese in a bloody war, and the 43d President is on Air Force One flying down to see Elvis Presley. Something happened: Japan adopted a Japanese-style democracy. Liberty has got the capacity to convert enemies into allies. That's what history tells us. You know, when the Prime Minister and I flew down on Air Force One to Elvis's place, we didn't talk about Elvis. We talked about keeping the peace. We talked about North Korea. We talked about the fact that he had 1,000 troops helping this young democracy in Iraq, because he understands what I know: Liberty can transform areas of hate into areas of hope. Someday, an American President is going to be sitting down with duly elected leaders in the Middle East talking about keeping the peace, and a generation of Americans will be better off.

Max Burns understands the stakes. He's going to be the right guy to represent you in Washington. He also understands this: He, like me, understands that if you're worried about whether your economy is going to grow, that the best way to encourage growth is to just let you keep more of your own money. See, we have a theory that says, if you have more money in your pocket to save, invest, or spend, the economy will grow.

And you know what? We tested our theory in the face of recession, corporate scandal, war, Katrina, high energy prices, and it works. Today, the national unemployment rate is 4.7 percent. We've added over 5½ million jobs since August of 2003. Our economy is the strongest of any major industrialized nation in the world. Lowering your taxes has worked.

I want to work with Max to make sure the tax cuts we passed are permanent. You know, it's interesting in Washington; you'll hear people say, "Well, we just need to raise your taxes to balance the budget." That's the language of a lot of folks up there. That's not the way Washington works. Max understands this, as do I. Here's the way it works: They'll say, "Okay, we'll raise your taxes, but we will figure out new ways to spend your money." [*Laughter*] The best way to balance this budget—and we're on the way to doing so. I said we'll cut the deficit in half by 2009; we're cutting it in half by 2008. The best way to balance the budget is to keep progrowth economic policies in place—that means low taxes and be wise about how we spend your money—is to set priorities about how we spend your money.

And here are my priorities. Here are my priorities. The first priority is to spend enough money to make sure we can protect the homeland. The Port of Savannah, I understand, is an important part of securing the homeland. You need a Congressman who can pick up the phone and say, "Mr. President, you came and talked about the Port of Savannah when you campaigned for me." That Congressman is going to be Max Burns.

And the other priority is to make sure our troops, our brave men and women who wear the uniform of the United States of America, have all it takes to defend the United States of America. Max understands that. He understands when you put a kid in harm's way, they deserve the full support of the United States Government.

A couple other things I want to talk about right quick is, you know, the country shouldn't fear the future. We really shouldn't. As a matter of fact, we ought to welcome the future and shape the future. And the best way to remain the world's leading economy, which I strongly think we ought to do, is not only keep taxes low and keep lawsuits reasonable, make sure the entrepreneurial spirit is strong—is to do some things on energy. I am concerned about the fact that we are addicted to foreign oil. I know that might sound odd for somebody from Texas to say, but I am a realistic fellow. See, I get to see the consequences of needing energy from parts of the world that don't like us. That creates a national security issue.

The world is connected today so that when demand for crude oil goes up in China and India, it affects the price of gasoline in Savannah, Georgia. There are economic consequences, and there are national security consequences for being dependent on foreign sources of oil, and we have started a very strong initiative to diversify away from oil. And I'm going to work with Max to make sure that the ethanol initiative that we promoted—an initiative that says we want Georgia farmers growing energy on behalf of the American people.

Old Max said this—I thought this was an interesting quote—so for all the farmers who might be listening to what your Congressman thinks, he said, "I already know Georgia farmers are the best providers of food and fiber in the world, and if we can grow it, eat it, drink it, and wear it, then certainly we can burn it." And we need to be selling that which Georgia grows.

Now, I know the trade is important for the Port of Savannah. I just want to tell you my view on trade. I believe it's in the interest of Georgia farmers—I know it's in the interest of Savannah, people who depend upon the Port of Savannah—to have more markets for U.S. goods.

We're 5 percent of the people in the world, in the United States. That means 95 percent of the world is potential customers. But trade means this to me—it just says—let me put it to you this way: I want the other people to treat us the way we

treat them. That's all I ask. Treat us fairly. America can compete with anybody, anytime, anywhere, so long as the playing field is level, and that's what we'll be working for in Washington, DC.

In order for America to be a great nation, we got to make sure that we have got an education system that is giving the kids the skills necessary to be able to compete in a global economy. And that starts with the early grades. It means we got to make sure a child can read, write, and add and subtract early, before it's too late.

I'm a strong believer in the No Child Left Behind Act. It believes in local control of schools. It says the Governor sets the policy. But it also says that, in return for Federal money, you measure, so we can know. There's nothing worse than a system that guesses on whether a child has got the skills necessary to compete. We need to know early. And if we find a child that needs extra help, we'll provide extra help so no child is left behind.

Max is an educator. He knows what he's talking about when it comes to education. And 2007 is going to be an important year when it comes to reauthorizing No Child Left Behind. This district would be wise to send a good man, who knows what he's talking about when it comes to educating children, to Washington, DC.

Laura said, "Don't talk too long when you get up there." I'm running out of oxygen, and so are you. [*Laughter*]

I do want to share one other thought about our country. I mean there's a lot of issues, and Max will be talking about them. One of the most important initiatives that I have started in Washington is called the Faith-Based and Community-Based Initiative.

The reason it's an important initiative is because it taps into the strength, the true strength of the American people, and that is the hearts of the American people. We are a compassionate neighbor. It's just an amazing country, isn't it, where there are millions of acts of kindness that take place on a daily basis without one government edict. People are listening to a—many times, to a higher calling, a calling much higher than government.

De Tocqueville, a Frenchman, came to America in the 1830s and saw the spirit of America. He saw the fact that America is a unique place because there were voluntary associations where people bound together to help solve community problems.

I strongly believe that many of the most intractable problems in society require something more than government, and therefore, our society must welcome the healers and helpers and people full of love as a part of solving and improving the human condition. And one practical thing—the way to do this is to open up Federal money for competitive grants to houses of worship.

See, I firmly believe that there are some neighborhoods in which the church or the synagogue or the mosque can be much more effective than the government program. After all, people who go to the houses of worship go because they want to love a neighbor just like they'd like to be loved themselves.

Ours is a fantastic country, full of the armies of compassion that feed the hungry and find shelter to the homeless and put their arm around somebody and says, "I love you, brother; what can I do to help?" Government is of law and justice; love comes from a higher calling. And I need Members of the United States Congress who are willing to stand strong to make sure the Faith-Based Initiative in Washington, DC, is strong, active, and alive, so we can help change America one heart, one soul, one conscience at a time.

And so I've come back to Savannah with a simple message: Please send a good man—a good, smart man—a good, honest, smart man, who loves his family and loves the people of this district, to the United States Congress. And that man is Max Burns.

Thanks for coming. May God bless.

NOTE: The President spoke at 1:46 p.m. at the Mighty Eighth Air Force Museum. In his remarks, he referred to Walter E. Brown, president and chief executive officer, Mighty Eighth Air Force Museum; former President Saddam Hussein of Iraq; Usama bin Laden, leader of the Al Qaida terrorist organization; Ayman Al-Zawahiri, founder of Egyptian Islamic Jihad and senior Al Qaida associate; and Prime Minister Junichiro Koizumi of Japan.

The President's Radio Address
September 9, 2006

Good morning. This Monday our Nation will mark the fifth anniversary of the attacks of September the 11th, 2001. On this solemn occasion, Americans will observe a day of prayer and remembrance, and Laura and I will travel to New York City, Pennsylvania, and the Pentagon to take part in memorial ceremonies. Our Nation honors the memory of every person we lost on that day of terror, and we pray that the Almighty will continue to comfort the families who had so much taken away from them.

On this anniversary, we also remember the brutality of the enemy who struck our country and renew our resolve to defeat this enemy and secure a future of peace and freedom.

So this week, I've given a series of speeches about the nature of our enemy, the stakes of the struggle, and the progress we have made during the past 5 years. On

Tuesday in Washington, I described in the terrorists' own words what they believe, what they hope to accomplish, and how they intend to accomplish it. We know what the terrorists intend because they have told us. They hope to establish a totalitarian Islamic empire across the Middle East, which they call a caliphate, where all would be ruled according to their hateful ideology.

Usama bin Laden has called the 9/11 attacks "a great step towards the unity of Muslims and establishing the righteous caliphate." Al Qaida and its allies reject any possibility of coexistence with those they call "infidels." Hear the words of Usama bin Laden: "Death is better than living on this Earth with the unbelievers amongst us." We must take the words of these extremists seriously, and we must act decisively to stop them from achieving their evil aims.

On Wednesday at the White House, I described for the first time a CIA program we established after 9/11 to detain and question key terrorist leaders and operatives, so we can prevent new terrorist attacks. This program has been invaluable to the security of America and its allies and helped us identify and capture men who our intelligence community believes were key architects of the September the 11th attacks.

Information from terrorists held by the CIA also helped us uncover an Al Qaida cell's efforts to obtain biological weapons, identify individuals sent by Al Qaida to case targets for attacks in the United States, stop the planned strike on a U.S. Marine base in Djibouti, prevent an attack on the U.S. consulate in Karachi, and help break up a plot to hijack passenger planes and fly them into Heathrow Airport or the Canary Wharf in London.

Information from the terrorists in CIA custody has also played a role in the capture or questioning of nearly every senior Al Qaida member or associate detained by the U.S. and its allies since this program

began. Were it not for this program, our intelligence community believes that Al Qaida and its allies would have succeeded in launching another attack against the American homeland. We have largely completed our questioning of these men, and now it is time that they are tried for their crimes.

So this week, I announced that the men we believe orchestrated the 9/11 attacks had been transferred to Guantanamo Bay. And I called on Congress to pass legislation creating military commissions to try suspected terrorists for war crimes. As soon as Congress acts to authorize these military commissions, we will prosecute these men and send a clear message to those who kill Americans: No matter how long it takes, we will find you and bring you to justice.

As we bring terrorists to justice, we're acting to secure the homeland. On Thursday in Atlanta, I delivered a progress report on the steps we have taken since 9/11 to protect the American people and win the war on terror. We are safer today because we've acted to address the gaps in security, intelligence, and information sharing that the terrorists exploited in the 9/11 attacks. No one can say for sure that we would have prevented the attacks had these reforms been in place in 2001, yet we can say that terrorists would have found it harder to plan and finance their operations, harder to slip into our country undetected, and harder to board the planes, take control of the cockpits, and succeed in striking their targets.

America still faces determined enemies. And in the long run, defeating these enemies requires more than improved security at home and military action abroad. We must also offer a hopeful alternative to the terrorists' hateful ideology. So America is taking the side of democratic leaders and reformers and supporting the voices of tolerance and moderation across the Middle East. By advancing freedom and democracy as the great alternative to repression and radicalism and by supporting young democracies like Iraq, we are helping to bring a brighter future to this region, and that will make America and the world more secure.

The war on terror will be long and difficult, and more tough days lie ahead. Yet we can have confidence in the final outcome because we know what America can achieve when our Nation acts with resolve and clear purpose. With vigilance, determination, and courage, we will defeat the enemies of freedom, and we will leave behind a more peaceful world for our children and our grandchildren.

Thank you for listening.

NOTE: The address was recorded at 7:50 a.m. on September 8 in the Cabinet Room at the White House for broadcast at 10:06 a.m. on September 9. The transcript was made available by the Office of the Press Secretary on September 8 but was embargoed for release until the broadcast. In his address, the President referred to Usama bin Laden, leader of the Al Qaida terrorist organization. The Office of the Press Secretary also released a Spanish language transcript of this address.

Statement on the Visit of Prime Minister Tony Blair of the United Kingdom to the Middle East
September 9, 2006

I am pleased that Prime Minister Blair will be visiting Lebanon, Israel, and the Palestinian Territories. The deployment of increasing numbers of international forces in an enhanced United Nations Interim Force in Lebanon (UNIFIL), which enabled the lifting of the air and sea blockade of Lebanon, makes this a timely visit. The Prime Minister will be discussing ways to facilitate the full implementation of United Nations Security Council Resolution (UNSCR) 1701, including enforcing the ban on unauthorized arms shipments to Hizballah from Iran and Syria. I understand the Prime Minister will also be exploring ways to advance the dialog between Israelis and Palestinians and the two-state solution, a democratic Israel and democratic Palestine living side by side in peace and security. I wish him well in his efforts to promote peace and stability in the region.

Remarks Following a Tour of the Tribute WTC Visitor Center in New York City
September 10, 2006

Laura and I approach tomorrow with a heavy heart. It's hard not to think about the people who lost their lives on September the 11th, 2001. You know, you see the relatives of those who still grieve—I just wish there were some way we could make them whole. So tomorrow is going to be a day of sadness for a lot of people.

It's also a day of remembrance. And I vowed that I'm never going to forget the lessons of that day. And we spent time in there looking at some of the horrific scenes—inside this fantastic place of healing—and it just reminded me that there's still an enemy out there that would like to inflict the same kind of damage again.

So tomorrow is also a day of renewing resolve. I asked—today at the church service I asked for God's blessings on—of those who continue to hurt.

Thank you.

NOTE: The President spoke at 7:04 p.m. A tape was not available for verification of the content of these remarks.

Address to the Nation on the War on Terror
September 11, 2006

Good evening. Five years ago, this date—September the 11th—was seared into America's memory. Nineteen men attacked us with a barbarity unequaled in our history. They murdered people of all colors, creeds, and nationalities and made war upon the entire free world. Since that day, America and her allies have taken the offensive in a war unlike any we have fought before. Today, we are safer, but we are not yet safe. On this solemn night, I've asked for some of your time to discuss the nature of the threat still before us, what we are doing to protect our Nation, and the building of a more hopeful Middle East that holds the key to peace for America and the world.

On 9/11, our Nation saw the face of evil. Yet on that awful day, we also witnessed something distinctly American: ordinary citizens rising to the occasion and responding with extraordinary acts of courage. We saw courage in office workers who were trapped on the high floors of burning skyscrapers and called home so that their last words to their families would be of comfort and love. We saw courage in passengers aboard Flight 93, who recited the 23d Psalm and then charged the cockpit. And we saw courage in the Pentagon staff who made it out of the flames and smoke and ran back in to answer cries for help. On this day, we remember the innocent who lost their lives, and we pay tribute to those who gave their lives so that others might live.

For many of our citizens, the wounds of that morning are still fresh. I've met firefighters and police officers who choke up at the memory of fallen comrades. I've stood with families gathered on a grassy field in Pennsylvania who take bittersweet pride in loved ones who refused to be victims and gave America our first victory in the war on terror. I've sat beside young mothers with children who are now 5 years old and still long for the daddies who will never cradle them in their arms. Out of this suffering, we resolve to honor every man and woman lost, and we seek their lasting memorial in a safer and more hopeful world.

Since the horror of 9/11, we've learned a great deal about the enemy. We have learned that they are evil and kill without mercy but not without purpose. We have learned that they form a global network of extremists who are driven by a perverted vision of Islam, a totalitarian ideology that hates freedom, rejects tolerance, and despises all dissent. And we have learned that their goal is to build a radical Islamic empire where women are prisoners in their homes, men are beaten for missing prayer meetings, and terrorists have a safe haven to plan and launch attacks on America and other civilized nations. The war against this enemy is more than a military conflict. It is the decisive ideological struggle of the

21st century and the calling of our generation.

Our Nation is being tested in a way that we have not been since the start of the cold war. We saw what a handful of our enemies can do with box cutters and plane tickets. We hear their threats to launch even more terrible attacks on our people. And we know that if they were able to get their hands on weapons of mass destruction, they would use them against us. We face an enemy determined to bring death and suffering into our homes. America did not ask for this war, and every American wishes it were over. So do I. But the war is not over, and it will not be over until either we or the extremists emerge victorious. If we do not defeat these enemies now, we will leave our children to face a Middle East overrun by terrorist states and radical dictators armed with nuclear weapons. We are in a war that will set the course for this new century and determine the destiny of millions across the world.

For America, 9/11 was more than a tragedy. It changed the way we look at the world. On September the 11th, we resolved that we would go on the offense against our enemies, and we would not distinguish between the terrorists and those who harbor or support them. So we helped drive the Taliban from power in Afghanistan. We put Al Qaida on the run and killed or captured most of those who planned the 9/11 attacks, including the man believed to be the mastermind, Khalid Sheikh Mohammed. He and other suspected terrorists have been questioned by the Central Intelligence Agency, and they provided valuable information that has helped stop attacks in America and across the world. Now these men have been transferred to Guantanamo Bay so they can be held to account for their actions. Usama bin Laden and other terrorists are still in hiding. Our message to them is clear: No matter how long it takes, America will find you, and we will bring you to justice.

On September the 11th, we learned that America must confront threats before they reach our shores, whether those threats come from terrorist networks or terrorist states. I'm often asked why we're in Iraq when Saddam Hussein was not responsible for the 9/11 attacks. The answer is that the regime of Saddam Hussein was a clear threat. My administration, the Congress, and the United Nations saw the threat. And after 9/11, Saddam's regime posed a risk that the world could not afford to take. The world is safer because Saddam Hussein is no longer in power. And now the challenge is to help the Iraqi people build a democracy that fulfills the dreams of the nearly 12 million Iraqis who came out to vote in free elections last December.

Al Qaida and other extremists from across the world have come to Iraq to stop the rise of a free society in the heart of the Middle East. They have joined the remnants of Saddam's regime and other armed groups to foment sectarian violence and drive us out. Our enemies in Iraq are tough, and they are committed, but so are Iraqi and coalition forces. We're adapting to stay ahead of the enemy, and we are carrying out a clear plan to ensure that a democratic Iraq succeeds.

We're training Iraqi troops so they can defend their nation. We're helping Iraq's unity Government grow in strength and serve its people. We will not leave until this work is done. Whatever mistakes have been made in Iraq, the worst mistake would be to think that if we pulled out, the terrorists would leave us alone. They will not leave us alone. They will follow us. The safety of America depends on the outcome of the battle in the streets of Baghdad. Usama bin Laden calls this fight "the third world war," and he says that victory for the terrorists in Iraq will mean America's "defeat and disgrace forever." If we yield Iraq to men like bin Laden, our enemies will be emboldened; they will gain a new safe haven; they will use Iraq's resources to fuel their extremist movement.

We will not allow this to happen. America will stay in the fight. Iraq will be a free nation and a strong ally in the war on terror.

We can be confident that our coalition will succeed because the Iraqi people have been steadfast in the face of unspeakable violence. And we can be confident in victory because of the skill and resolve of America's Armed Forces. Every one of our troops is a volunteer, and since the attacks of September the 11th, more than 1.6 million Americans have stepped forward to put on our Nation's uniform. In Iraq, Afghanistan, and other fronts in the war on terror, the men and women of our military are making great sacrifices to keep us safe. Some have suffered terrible injuries, and nearly 3,000 have given their lives. America cherishes their memory. We pray for their families. And we will never back down from the work they have begun.

We also honor those who toil day and night to keep our homeland safe, and we are giving them the tools they need to protect our people. We've created the Department of Homeland Security. We have torn down the wall that kept law enforcement and intelligence from sharing information. We've tightened security at our airports and seaports and borders, and we've created new programs to monitor enemy bank records and phone calls. Thanks to the hard work of our law enforcement and intelligence professionals, we have broken up terrorist cells in our midst and saved American lives.

Five years after 9/11, our enemies have not succeeded in launching another attack on our soil, but they've not been idle. Al Qaida and those inspired by its hateful ideology have carried out terrorist attacks in more than two dozen nations. And just last month, they were foiled in a plot to blow up passenger planes headed for the United States. They remain determined to attack America and kill our citizens, and we are determined to stop them. We will continue to give the men and women who protect us every resource and legal authority they need to do their jobs.

In the first days after the 9/11 attacks, I promised to use every element of national power to fight the terrorists, wherever we find them. One of the strongest weapons in our arsenal is the power of freedom. The terrorists fear freedom as much as they do our firepower. They are thrown into panic at the sight of an old man pulling the election lever, girls enrolling in schools, or families worshiping God in their own traditions. They know that given a choice, people will choose freedom over their extremist ideology. So their answer is to deny people this choice by raging against the forces of freedom and moderation. This struggle has been called a clash of civilizations. In truth, it is a struggle for civilization. We are fighting to maintain the way of life enjoyed by free nations. And we're fighting for the possibility that good and decent people across the Middle East can raise up societies based on freedom and tolerance and personal dignity.

We are now in the early hours of this struggle between tyranny and freedom. Amid the violence, some question whether the people of the Middle East want their freedom and whether the forces of moderation can prevail. For 60 years, these doubts guided our policies in the Middle East. And then on a bright September morning, it became clear that the calm we saw in the Middle East was only a mirage. Years of pursuing stability to promote peace had left us with neither. So we changed our policies and committed America's influence in the world to advancing freedom and democracy as the great alternatives to repression and radicalism.

With our help, the people of the Middle East are now stepping forward to claim their freedom. From Kabul to Baghdad to Beirut, there are brave men and women risking their lives each day for the same freedoms that we enjoy. And they have one question for us: Do we have the confidence to do in the Middle East what our fathers and grandfathers accomplished in Europe and Asia? By standing with democratic leaders and reformers, by giving voice to the hopes of decent men and women, we're offering a path away from radicalism. And we are enlisting the most powerful force for peace and moderation in the Middle East, the desire of millions to be free.

Across the broader Middle East, the extremists are fighting to prevent such a future. Yet America has confronted evil before, and we have defeated it, sometimes at the cost of thousands of good men in a single battle. When Franklin Roosevelt vowed to defeat two enemies across two oceans, he could not have foreseen D-Day and Iwo Jima, but he would not have been surprised at the outcome. When Harry Truman promised American support for free peoples resisting Soviet aggression, he could not have foreseen the rise of the Berlin Wall, but he would not have been surprised to see it brought down. Throughout our history, America has seen liberty challenged, and every time, we have seen liberty triumph with sacrifice and determination.

At the start of this young century, America looks to the day when the people of the Middle East leave the desert of despotism for the fertile gardens of liberty and resume their rightful place in a world of peace and prosperity. We look to the day when the nations of that region recognize their greatest resource is not the oil in the ground but the talent and creativity of their people. We look to the day when moms and dads throughout the Middle East see a future of hope and opportunity for their children. And when that good day comes, the clouds of war will part, the appeal of radicalism will decline, and we will leave our children with a better and safer world.

On this solemn anniversary, we rededicate ourselves to this cause. Our Nation has endured trials, and we face a difficult road ahead. Winning this war will require the determined efforts of a unified country, and we must put aside our differences and work together to meet the test that history has given us. We will defeat our enemies. We will protect our people. And we will lead the 21st century into a shining age of human liberty.

Earlier this year, I traveled to the United States Military Academy. I was there to deliver the commencement address to the first class to arrive at West Point after the attacks of September the 11th. That day I met a proud mom named RoseEllen Dowdell. She was there to watch her son, Patrick, accept his commission in the finest Army the world has ever known. A few weeks earlier, RoseEllen had watched her other son, James, graduate from the Fire Academy in New York City. On both these days, her thoughts turned to someone who was not there to share the moment, her husband, Kevin Dowdell. Kevin was one of the 343 firefighters who rushed to the burning towers of the World Trade Center on September the 11th and never came home. His sons lost their father that day but not the passion for service he instilled in them. Here is what RoseEllen says about her boys: "As a mother, I cross my fingers and pray all the time for their safety. But as worried as I am, I'm also proud, and I know their dad would be too."

Our Nation is blessed to have young Americans like these, and we will need them. Dangerous enemies have declared their intention to destroy our way of life. They're not the first to try, and their fate will be the same as those who tried before. Nine-Eleven showed us why. The attacks were meant to bring us to our knees, and they did, but not in the way the terrorists intended. Americans united in prayer, came to the aid of neighbors in need, and resolved that our enemies would not have the last word. The spirit of our people is the source of America's strength. And we go forward with trust in that spirit, confidence in our purpose, and faith in a loving God who made us to be free.

Thank you, and may God bless you.

NOTE: The President spoke at 9:01 p.m. in the Oval Office at the White House. In his remarks, he referred to Khalid Sheikh Mohammed, senior Al Qaida leader responsible for planning the September 11, 2001, terrorist attacks, who was captured in Pakistan on March 1, 2003; Usama bin Laden, leader of the Al Qaida terrorist organization; and former President Saddam Hussein of Iraq. The Office of the Press Secretary also released a Spanish language transcript of this address.

Statement on House of Representatives Passage of Federal Funding Accountability and Transparency Legislation
September 13, 2006

I applaud the House for today's passage of S. 2590, the "Federal Funding Accountability and Transparency Act of 2006," and look forward to final passage by the Senate soon. This legislation demonstrates Congress's commitment to giving the American people access to timely and accurate information about how their tax dollars are spent.

This bill builds on existing administration initiatives to help ensure Federal agencies clearly reflect how they spend the tax-payers' money. Expectmore.gov is one such resource, allowing Americans to see which Federal programs are successful and which ones fall short.

In addition to these reforms, I urge the Senate to follow the House in passing the line item veto, a critical tool that will help rein in wasteful spending and bring greater transparency to the budget process. I call on the Senate to pass this important legislation this month.

Memorandum on the 2006 Combined Federal Campaign
September 13, 2006

Memorandum for the Heads of Executive Departments and Agencies

Subject: 2006 Combined Federal Campaign

Admiral Thad W. Allen, Commandant of the United States Coast Guard, has agreed to serve as the Chair of the 2006 Combined Federal Campaign of the National Capital Area. I ask you to enthusiastically support the CFC by personally chairing the campaign in your agency and by encouraging top agency officials around the country to do the same.

The Combined Federal Campaign is an important way for Federal employees to support thousands of worthy charities. Public servants not only contribute to the campaign but also assume leadership roles to ensure its success.

Your personal support and enthusiasm will help positively influence thousands of employees and will guarantee another successful campaign.

GEORGE W. BUSH

NOTE: An original was not available for verification of the content of this memorandum.

Remarks to Reporters Following a Meeting With the House Republican Conference
September 14, 2006

Thank you very much. It's an honor to meet with the Capitol press corps, and a few White House—a few White House folks scattered in. Just had a great visit with House Members—House Republican Members. I talked about a lot of issues and answered questions. I thanked them for the House Armed Services Committee passing a very important piece of legislation in a bipartisan fashion that will give us the tools and wherewithal to protect this country. I reminded them that the most important job of Government is to protect the homeland, and yesterday they advanced an important piece of legislation to do just that. I'll continue to work with Members of the Congress to get good legislation so we can do our duty.

It's nice seeing you all. Thank you very much.

NOTE: The President spoke at 10:44 a.m. at the U.S. Capitol. In his remarks, he referred to H.R. 6054, the "Military Commissions Act of 2006." A tape was not available for verification of the content of these remarks.

Remarks Following Discussions With President Roh Moo-hyun of South Korea and an Exchange With Reporters
September 14, 2006

President Bush. Welcome to the White House. I will give an opening statement; the President will give an opening statement; we will answer two questions a side.

Mr. President, thank you for coming. The relationship between the United States and South Korea is a strong and vital relationship. Today we talked about how to strengthen our commitment to peace and security on the Korean Peninsula. All our discussions began with the notion that our alliance is important to security and peace in the Far East. I thank the President, the South Korean Government, and the people of South Korea for sending troops into Iraq to help that young democracy realize the benefits of liberty.

We reaffirmed our commitment to the six-party talks so that we can peacefully deal with the North Korean issue. We talked about our economic relations and the importance of a free trade agreement to benefit our respective peoples.

And finally, the President talked to me about a visa waiver policy. He strongly advocated the need for there to be a visa waiver for the people of South Korea. I assured him we will work together to see if we can't get this issue resolved as quickly as possible.

We've had a very friendly and very meaningful dialog, and I'm glad you came, Mr. President. Please.

President Roh. First of all, I would like to offer my sincere condolences and sympathies, and those of the Korean people, for the tragedy of 9/11, which struck 5 years ago.

President Bush. Thank you, sir.

President Roh. I would like to also reiterate our support for the war against terror and of President Bush, the people of the United States. And we stand with you, President Bush, and the people of America in your fight against terror.

President Bush. Thank you, sir.

President Roh. Prior to our summit meeting, we have closely coordinated the agenda and issues of interest. And on this basis, we had very sufficient and very satisfactory talks.

And President Bush spoke about the three issues that we discussed. If I may add to one of them, of the wartime operational control, I was very happy that the President reassured me of the continued commitment of the United States for the defense of the Korean Peninsula.

As for the remaining issue of timing of the transfer of OPCON, we agreed that this is not a political issue; this is an issue that will be discussed through the working-level talks. And we will continue to work together on this issue.

And also, the President and I agreed to work together for the restart of the six-party talks. And as for specific steps that we can take before the resumption of the six-party process, our ministers and staff will be consulting closely.

And, Mr. President, I would like to thank you again for the open and understanding that you have shown in these difficult issues.

President Bush. Thank you, sir. Caren [Caren Bohan, Reuters]—I mean, Nedra [Nedra Pickler, Associated Press].

"Military Commissions Act of 2006"

Q. Thank you, Mr. President. Your former Secretary of State endorsed the plan to block the terror suspect interrogation legislation that you have proposed. He says it would raise doubts about the moral basis for the U.S. fight against terrorists and would put U.S. troops at risk. Does this hurt your efforts?

President Bush. We have proposed legislation that will enable the Central Intelligence Agency to be able to conduct a program to get information from high-value detainees in a lawful way. And that idea was approved yesterday by a House committee in an overwhelmingly bipartisan fashion. It is very important for the Amer-

ican people to understand that in order to protect this country, we must be able to interrogate people who have information about future attacks.

So the question I ask about any piece of legislation is, will the program provide legal clarity so that our professionals will feel comfortable about going forward with the program? That's what I'm going to ask. And I will resist any bill that does not enable this program to go forward with legal clarity. And there's all kinds of letters coming out, and today, by the way, active duty personnel in the Pentagon, the JAG, supported the concept that I have just outlined to you. This is an important program for the security of this country. And we want to work with Congress to make sure that the program can go forward. If there's not clarity, if there's ambiguity, if there's any doubt in our professionals' minds that they can conduct their operations in a legal way, with support of the Congress, the program won't go forward and the American people will be in danger.

President Bush. Mr. President.

U.S. Armed Forces in South Korea/North Korea

[At this point, a question was asked in Korean, and no translation was provided.]

President Bush. Okay, I'll interpret the question for you. *[Laughter]* "How come you look so beautiful in your blue tie, Mr. President?" *[Laughter]*

No, he asked about operational control and the date—the appropriate date of operational control. My message to the Korean people is that the United States is committed to the security of the Korean Peninsula. Decisions about the placement of our troops and the size of our troops will be made in consultation with the South Korean Government. We will work in a consultative way at the appropriate level of government to come up with an appropriate date.

I agree with the President that the issue should not become a political issue. I have talked to our Secretary of Defense about making sure that the issue is done in a consultative way and at the appropriate level of government, and that's how we will end up deciding the appropriate transfer of operational authority.

Did he ask you a question?

President Roh. Yes, that was a very good answer. Thank you, Mr. President. [*Laughter*]

President Bush. Hope everybody else agrees with it.

President Roh. As for the question about the common and broad approach being talked about between our two countries for the restart of the six-party talks, I must tell you that we are at the working level of consulting very closely on this issue, but we have not yet reached a conclusion. And this issue is very complex, so I would be hesitant—and it would be difficult for me to answer the question at the moment.

The important thing to remember, that South Korea now faces the issue of North Korean nuclear issue. And this, I would say, is one important issue that we're facing. On the other hand, the United States has a host of other issues to deal with: the Iran/Lebanon crisis; the war in Iraq. So what is important to remember is that— the fact that we are consulting closely on the North Korean nuclear issue, and we are consulting on ways to restart the six-party process. And I believe this is the important point, that this is, in fact, very meaningful that the United States is devoting much of its efforts to resolving the North Korean issue. This is very significant for the Korean Government.

President Bush. Thank you. Caren.

North Korea's Participation in the Six-Party Talks

Q. Mr. President, North Korea has refused to engage in the six-party talks for nearly a year. What's the incentive to get them back to the table?

President Bush. No, I appreciate that. First and foremost, the incentive is for Kim Jong Il to understand there is a better way to improve the lives of his people than being isolated; that stability in the region is in his interest, the ultimate interests for the people of North Korea to be able to benefit and for families to be able to have food on the table.

His refusal to come back to the six-party talks has really strengthened an alliance of five nations that—who are determined to solve this issue peacefully, but recognize a threat posed by a country in the region armed with a nuclear weapon. If he were to verifiably get rid of his weapons programs, there is clearly a better way forward. And that is the message we've been sending to the North Korean Government through the six-party talks.

Final question. Do you want to call on somebody?

South Korea-North Korea Relations

[*A question was asked in Korean, and no translation was provided.*]

President Roh. As for your question, that there is a concern in Korea that the United States will take further sanctions against North Korea and whether this will jeopardize the chance of a successful six-party process, my answer is that we are working very hard on restarting the six-party talks. That is what the President and I have discussed this morning, and this is not the appropriate time to think about the possibility of a failure of the six-party process. So this is my answer.

And my Government has taken certain measures. And although—because we do not want to hurt the inter-Korean relations, we do not label this—these measures as sanctions; we are, in fact, taking measures tantamount to sanctions after the North Korean missile launches. This is—we have suspended rice and fertilizer aid to North Korea, and this is, in fact, similar to sanctions in its effect.

And we are, in fact—this measure of suspension of aid to North Korea, I believe, is in line with the implementation of the U.N. security resolution on North Korea. And as for other sanctions you have mentioned by the United States, these are being done in line with the U.S. law enforcement. And so we would be—we would not delve into this at this time.

President Bush. Thank you, sir. Thank you.

NOTE: The President spoke at 11:53 a.m. in the Oval Office at the White House. In his remarks, he referred to Chairman Kim Jong Il of North Korea. A reporter referred to former Secretary of State Colin L. Powell.

Statement on the Death of Ann Richards
September 14, 2006

Laura and I are deeply saddened by the passing of Governor Ann Richards of Texas. Ann loved Texas, and Texans loved her. As a public servant, she earned respect and admiration. Ann became a national role model, and her charm, wit, and candor brought a refreshing vitality to public life. We extend our sympathies to Ann's family and friends. Texas has lost one of its great daughters.

Statement on House of Representatives Action on Earkmark Reform
September 14, 2006

I applaud the House of Representatives for voting again this week in support of greater transparency and accountability in Government. H.R. 1000 [H. Res. 1000] ° would shine a brighter light on earmarks by requiring disclosure of the sponsors of each provision. This reform would help improve the legislative process by making sure both lawmakers and the public are better informed before Congress votes to spend the taxpayers' money.

Statement on Senate Passage of Port Security Improvement Legislation
September 14, 2006

Today the Senate passed legislation to strengthen my administration's efforts to secure our ports and detect dangers before they reach America's shores.

By furthering our coordination with responsible countries throughout the world, the "Port Security Improvement Act of 2006" will help secure the global supply chain and help ensure the smooth flow of commerce into and out of the United States. I am pleased this bill codifies several administration efforts that have already substantially improved security at our ports, including the Container Security Initiative,

---

° White House correction.

which identifies and inspects cargo at foreign ports before they are placed on vessels destined for the United States, and the Customs-Trade Partnership Against Terrorism, which helps our international trading partners secure their supply chains before shipping goods into our country.

I look forward to the House and Senate resolving their differences in conference and sending this legislation to me for my signature.

NOTE: The statement referred to H.R. 4954.

The President's News Conference
September 15, 2006

The President. It's always a pleasure to be introduced into the Rose Garden. Thank you, Wendell [Wendell Goler, FOX News Channel]. Thank you for coming. I'm looking forward to answering some of your questions.

This week, our Nation paused to mark the fifth anniversary of the 9/11 attacks. It was a tough day for a lot of our citizens. I was so honored to meet with family members and first-responders, workers at the Pentagon, all who still had heaviness in their heart. But they asked me a question—you know, they kept asking me, "What do you think the level of determination for this country is in order to protect ourselves?" That's what they want to know.

You know, for me, it was a reminder about how I felt right after 9/11. I felt a sense of determination and conviction about doing everything that is necessary to protect the people. I'm going to go back to New York to address the United Nations General Assembly. I'm going to talk to world leaders gathered there about our obligation to defend civilization and liberty, to support the forces of freedom and moderation throughout the Middle East. As we work with the international community to defeat the terrorists and extremists, to provide an alternative to their hateful ideology, we must also provide our military and intelligence professionals with the tools they need to protect our country from another attack. And the reason they need those

tools is because the enemy wants to attack us again.

Right here in the Oval Office, I get briefed nearly every morning about the nature of this world, and I get briefed about the desire of an enemy to hurt America. And it's a sobering experience, as I'm sure you can imagine. I wish that weren't the case, you know. But it is the case. And therefore, I believe it is vital that our folks on the frontline have the tools necessary to protect the American people.

There are two vital pieces of legislation in Congress now that I think are necessary to help us win the war on terror. We will work with members of both parties to get legislation that works out of the Congress. The first bill will allow us to use military commissions to try suspected terrorists for war crimes. We need the legislation because the Supreme Court recently ruled that military commissions must be explicitly authorized by Congress. So we're working with Congress. The Supreme Court said, "You must work with Congress." We are working with Congress to get a good piece of legislation out.

The bill I have proposed will ensure that suspected terrorists will receive full and fair trials without revealing to them our Nation's sensitive intelligence secrets. As soon as Congress acts on this bill, the man our intelligence agencies believe helped orchestrate the 9/11 attacks can face justice.

The bill would also provide clear rules for our personnel involved in detaining and questioning captured terrorists. The information that the Central Intelligence Agency has obtained by questioning men like Khalid Sheikh Mohammed has provided valuable information and has helped disrupt terrorist plots, including strikes within the United States.

For example, Khalid Sheikh Mohammed described the design of planned attacks of buildings inside the U.S. and how operatives were directed to carry them out. That is valuable information for those of us who have the responsibility to protect the American people. He told us the operatives had been instructed to ensure that the explosives went off at a high— a point that was high enough to prevent people trapped above from escaping. He gave us information that helped uncover Al Qaida cells' efforts to obtain biological weapons.

We've also learned information from the CIA program that has helped stop other plots, including attacks on the U.S. Marine base in East Africa or American consulate in Pakistan or Britain's Heathrow Airport. This program has been one of the most vital tools in our efforts to protect this country. It's been invaluable to our country, and it's invaluable to our allies.

Were it not for this program, our intelligence community believes that Al Qaida and its allies would have succeeded in launching another attack against the American homeland. Making us—giving us information about terrorist plans we couldn't get anywhere else, this program has saved innocent lives. In other words, it's vital. That's why I asked Congress to pass legislation so that our professionals can go forward, doing the duty we expect them to do. Unfortunately, the recent Supreme Court decision put the future of this program in question. That's another reason I went to Congress. We need this legislation to save it.

I am asking Congress to pass a clear law with clear guidelines based on the Detainee Treatment Act that was strongly supported by Senator John McCain. There is a debate about the specific provisions in my bill, and we'll work with Congress to continue to try to find common ground. I have one test for this legislation; I'm going to answer one question as this legislation proceeds, and it's this: The intelligence community must be able to tell me that the bill Congress sends to my desk will allow this vital program to continue. That's what I'm going to ask.

The second bill before Congress would modernize our electronic surveillance laws and provide additional authority for the terrorist surveillance program. I authorized the National Security Agency to operate this vital program in response to the 9/11 attacks. It allows us to quickly monitor terrorist communications between someone overseas and someone in the United States, and it's helped detect and prevent attacks on our country. The principle behind this program is clear: When an Al Qaida operative is calling into the United States or out of the country, we need to know who they're calling, why they're calling, and what they're planning.

Both these bills are essential to winning the war on terror. We will work with Congress to get good bills out. We have a duty, we have a duty to work together to give our folks on the frontline the tools necessary to protect America. Time is running out. Congress is set to adjourn in just a few weeks. Congress needs to act wisely and promptly so I can sign good legislation.

And now I'll be glad to answer some questions. Terry [Terence Hunt, Associated Press].

War on Terror/Counterterrorism Efforts

Q. Thank you, Mr. President. Mr. President, former Secretary of State Colin Powell says the world is beginning to doubt the moral basis of our fight against terrorism. If a former Chairman of the Joint

Chiefs of Staff and former Secretary of State feels this way, don't you think that Americans and the rest of the world are beginning to wonder whether you're following a flawed strategy?

The President. If there's any comparison between the compassion and decency of the American people and the terrorist tactics of extremists, it's flawed logic. I simply can't accept that. It's unacceptable to think that there's any kind of comparison between the behavior of the United States of America and the action of Islamic extremists who kill innocent women and children to achieve an objective, Terry.

My job, and the job of people here in Washington, DC, is to protect this country. We didn't ask for this war. You might remember the 2000 campaign. I don't remember spending much time talking about what it might be like to be a Commander in Chief in a different kind of war. But this enemy has struck us, and they want to strike us again. And we will give our folks the tools necessary to protect the country; that's our job.

It's a dangerous world. I wish it wasn't that way. I wish I could tell the American people, "Don't worry about it; they're not coming again." But they are coming again. And that's why I've sent this legislation up to Congress, and that's why we'll continue to work with allies in building a vast coalition to protect not only ourselves but them. The facts are—is that after 9/11, this enemy continued to attack and kill innocent people.

I happen to believe that they're bound by a common ideology. Matter of fact, I don't believe that, I know they are. And they want to impose that ideology throughout the broader Middle East. That's what they have said. It makes sense for the Commander in Chief and all of us involved in protecting this country to listen to the words of the enemy. And I take their words seriously. And that's what's going to be necessary to protect this country, is to listen

carefully to what they say and stay ahead of them as they try to attack us.

Steve [Steve Holland, Reuters].

Q. Can I just follow up?

The President. No, you can't. Steve. If we follow up, we're not going to get—I want Hillman [G. Robert Hillman, Dallas Morning News] to be able to ask a question. It's his last press conference—not yet, Hillman. [*Laughter*] Soon. You and Wendell seem——

"Military Commissions Act of 2006"

Q. Thank you very much, sir. What do you say to the argument that your proposal is basically seeking support for torture, coerced evidence, and secret hearings? And Senator McCain says your plan will put U.S. troops at risk. What do you think about that?

The President. This debate is occurring because of the Supreme Court's ruling that said that we must conduct ourselves under the Common Article 3 of the Geneva Convention. And that Common Article Three says that there will be no outrages upon human dignity. It's very vague. What does that mean, "outrages upon human dignity"? That's a statement that is wide open to interpretation. And what I'm proposing is that there be clarity in the law so that our professionals will have no doubt that that which they are doing is legal. You know, it's—and so the piece of legislation I sent up there provides our professionals that which is needed to go forward.

The first question that we've got to ask is, do we need the program? I believe we do need the program. And I detailed in a speech in the East Room what the program has yield—in other words, the kind of information we get when we interrogate people within the law. You see, sometimes you can pick up information on the battlefield; sometimes you can pick it up through letters; but sometimes you actually have to question the people who know the strategy and plans of the enemy. And in this case, we questioned people like Khalid Sheikh

Mohammed, who we believe ordered the attacks on 9/11, or Ramzi bin al-Shibh or Abu Zubaydah, coldblooded killers who were part of planning the attack that killed 3,000 people. And we need to be able to question them, because it helps yield information, information necessary for us to be able to do our job.

Now, the Court said that you've got to live under Article 3 of the Geneva Convention, and the standards are so vague that our professionals won't be able to carry forward the program, because they don't want to be tried as war criminals. They don't want to break the law. These are decent, honorable citizens who are on the frontline of protecting the American people, and they expect our Government to give them clarity about what is right and what is wrong in the law. And that's what we have asked to do.

And we believe a good way to go is to use the amendment that we worked with John McCain on, called the Detainee Treatment Act, as the basis for clarity for people we would ask to question the enemy. In other words, it is a way to bring U.S. law into play. It provides more clarity for our professionals, and that's what these people expect. These are decent citizens who don't want to break the law.

Now, this idea that somehow we've got to live under international treaties, you know—and that's fine; we do; but oftentimes the United States Government passes law to clarify obligations under international treaty. And what I'm concerned about is if we don't do that, then it's very conceivable our professionals could be held to account based upon court decisions in other countries. And I don't believe Americans want that. I believe Americans want us to protect the country, to have clear standards for our law enforcement, intelligence officers, and give them the tools necessary to protect us within the law.

It's an important debate, Steve. It really is. It's a debate that really is going to define whether or not we can protect ourselves.

I will tell you this: I've spent a lot of time on this issue, as you can imagine, and I've talked to professionals, people I count on for advice; these are people that are going to represent those on the frontline of protecting this country. They're not going forward with the program. They're not going—the professionals will not step up unless there's clarity in the law. So Congress has got a decision to make: Do you want the program to go forward or not?

I strongly recommend that this program go forward in order for us to be able to protect America.

Hillman. This is Hillman's last press conference, so—sorry, sorry, about that.

Immigration Reform

Q. Thank you, Mr. President. On another of your top priorities, immigration, leaders of both parties have indicated that any chance of comprehensive immigration reform is dead before the election. Is this an issue you would like to revisit in a lame-duck session after the election? Or would it be put off until the new Congress?

The President. Bob, I strongly believe that in order to protect this border, Congress has got to pass a comprehensive plan that on the one hand provides additional money to secure the border and on the other hand recognizes that people are sneaking in here to do jobs Americans aren't doing. It would be better that they not sneak in, that they would come on a temporary basis, in an orderly way, to do work Americans aren't doing and then go home. And I will continue to urge Congress to think comprehensively about this vital piece of legislation.

I went up to the Hill yesterday, and of course this topic came up. It's exactly what I told the Members of Congress. They wanted to know whether or not we were implementing border security measures that they had funded last January, and the answer is, we are. One of the key things I told them was we had ended what's called catch-and-release. That was a—you know,

a Border Patrol agent would find somebody, particularly from—not from Mexico,
and would say, "Well, we don't have
enough detention space, so why don't you
come back and check in with the local person you're supposed to check in with," and
then they'd never show back up. And that,
of course, frustrated the Border Patrol
agents; it frustrates American citizens; it
frustrates me. And we ended it because
Congress appropriated money that increased the number of beds available to
detain people when we get them sneaking
into our country illegally.

The border has become modernized.
And Secretary Chertoff here, later on this
month, will be announcing further mod-
ernizations, as he has led a contract that
will use all kinds of different technologies
to make the border more secure. But in
the long run, to secure this border, we've
got to have a rational work plan.

And finally, we're going to have to treat
people with dignity in this country. Ours
is a nation of immigrants, and when Congress gets down to a comprehensive bill,
I would just remind them, it's virtually impossible to try to find 11 million folks—
who have been here, working hard and,
in some cases, raising families—and kick
them out. It's just not going to work. But
granting automatic citizenship won't work
either. To me, that would just provide an
additional incentive for people to try to
sneak in, and so therefore, there is a rational way forward. I'll continue working—I
don't know the timetable. My answer is,
as soon as possible; that's what I'd like to
see done.

Thank you. Let's see, Wendell. Coming
your way. Everybody is going to get one.

United Nations/Iran

Q. My apologies, Mr. President, for talking too long at the start.

The President. Don't worry. I'm not
going to apologize for talking too long to
your answer. [*Laughter*]

Q. Talk as long as you'd like, sir. [*Laughter*]

When you go to New York next week,
it's our thinking that one of the things
you'll be trying to do is to get more international support for taking a tough stance
against Iran. I wonder how much that is
frustrated by two things: one, the war in
Iraq and world criticism of that; and the
other, the Iraqi Prime Minister going to
Iran and basically challenging your administration's claim that Iran is meddling in Iraqi
affairs.

The President. First, Wendell, my decision, along with other countries, to remove
Saddam Hussein has obviously created
some concern amongst allies, but it certainly hasn't diminished the coalitions we
put together to deal with radicalism. For
example, there's 70 nations involved with
the Proliferation Security Initiative, and
that's an initiative to help prevent weapons
of mass destruction and/or component parts
from being delivered to countries that
could use them to hurt us; or the broad
war on terror, the intelligence sharing or
financial—sharing of financial information;
or Afghanistan, where NATO troops are
there now, along with ours.

In other words, there's a broad coalition.
Most nations recognize the threat of Iran
having a nuclear weapon in the middle of
the Middle East. And there's common consensus that we need to work together to
prevent the Iranian regime from developing
that nuclear weapons program.

I am pleased that there is strong consensus. And now the objective is to continue reminding the Iranian regime that
there is unanimity in the world and that
we will move forward together. And we
expect them to come to the table and negotiate with the EU in good faith. And should
they choose to verifiably suspend their program, their enrichment program, we'll
come to the table. That's what we have
said; offer still stands.

During the Hizballah attacks on Israel,
the United Nations did pass a resolution

with our European friends and ourselves and, of course, Russia and China voting for the resolution. I think it passed 14 to 1; one nation voted against the resolution toward Iran. So there is common consensus. And you've heard me lament oftentimes, it takes a while to get diplomacy working. There's one nation of Iran and a bunch of nations like us trying to kind of head in the same direction. And my concern is that they'll stall; they'll try to wait us out.

So part of my objective in New York is to remind people that stalling shouldn't be allowed. In other words, we need to move the process. And they need to understand we're firm in our commitment, and if they try to drag their feet or get us to look the other way, that we won't do that, that we're firmly committed in our desire to send a common signal to the Iranian regime.

It is important for the Iranian people to also understand we respect them; we respect their history; we respect their traditions; we respect the right for people to worship freely; we would hope that people would be able to express themselves in the public square; and that our intention is to make the world safer. And we'll continue to do so.

Suzanne [Suzanne Malveaux, Cable News Network] and then Martha [Martha Raddatz, ABC News].

Iran's Nuclear Enrichment Program

Q. Thank you, Mr. President. If I could follow up on that question.

The President. Yes.

Q. Mahmud Ahmadi-nejad, the Iranian President, will actually be in the same building as you next week, in Manhattan for the United Nations General Assembly. You say that you want to give the message to the Iranian people that you respect them. Is this not an opportunity, perhaps, to show that you also respect their leader? Would you be willing to, perhaps, meet face to face with Ahmadi-nejad, and would

this possibly be a breakthrough, some sort of opportunity for a breakthrough on a personal level?

The President. No, I'm not going to meet with him. I have made it clear to the Iranian regime that we will sit down with the Iranians once they verifiably suspend their enrichment program. And I meant what I said.

Martha.

Saddam Hussein

Q. Mr. President, you have said throughout the war in Iraq and building up to the war in Iraq that there was a relationship between Saddam Hussein and Zarqawi and Al Qaida. A Senate Intelligence Committee report a few weeks ago said there was no link, no relationship, and that the CIA knew this and issued a report last fall. And yet a month ago, you were still saying there was a relationship. Why did you keep saying that? Why do you continue to say that? And do you still believe that?

The President. The point I was making to Ken Herman's [Austin American-Statesman] question was that Saddam Hussein was a state sponsor of terror and that Mr. Zarqawi was in Iraq. He had been wounded in Afghanistan, had come to Iraq for treatment. He had ordered the killing of a U.S. citizen in Jordan. I never said there was an operational relationship. I was making the point that Saddam Hussein had been declared a state sponsor of terror for a reason, and therefore, he was dangerous.

The broader point I was saying, I was reminding people was why we removed Saddam Hussein from power. He was dangerous. I would hope people aren't trying to rewrite the history of Saddam Hussein; all of a sudden, he becomes kind of a benevolent fellow. He's a dangerous man. And one of the reasons he was declared a state sponsor of terror was because that's what he was. He harbored terrorists; he paid for families of suicide bombers. Never have I said that Saddam Hussein gave orders to attack 9/11. What I did say was, after 9/11, when you see a threat, you've got to take it seriously. And I saw a threat in Saddam Hussein, as did Congress, as did the United Nations. I firmly believe the world is better off without Saddam in power, Martha.

Dave [David Gregory, NBC News]. He's back.

"Military Commissions Act of 2006"

Q. Sorry, I've got to get disentangled——

The President. Would you like me to go to somebody else here, until you—[*laughter*].

Q. Sorry.

The President. But take your time, please. [*Laughter*]

Q. I really apologize for that. Anyway——

The President. I must say, having gone through those gyrations, you're looking beautiful today, Dave. [*Laughter*]

Q. Mr. President, critics of your proposed bill on interrogation rules say there's another important test—these critics include John McCain, who you've mentioned several times this morning—and that test is this: If a CIA officer, paramilitary or special operations soldier from the United States were captured in Iran or North Korea, and they were roughed up, and those governments said, "Well, they were interrogated in accordance with our interpretation of the Geneva Conventions," and then they were put on trial and they were convicted based on secret evidence that they were not able to see, how would you react to that, as Commander in Chief?

The President. David, my reaction is, is that if the nations such as those you named, adopted the standards within the detainee detention act, the world would be better. That's my reaction. We're trying to clarify law. We're trying to set high standards, not ambiguous standards.

And let me just repeat, Dave, we can debate this issue all we want, but the practical matter is, if our professionals don't

have clear standards in the law, the program is not going to go forward. You cannot ask a young intelligence officer to violate the law. And they're not going to. They—let me finish, please—they will not violate the law. You can ask this question all you want, but the bottom line is—and the American people have got to understand this—that this program won't go forward, if there is vague standards applied, like those in Common Article 3 from the Geneva Convention; it's just not going to go forward. You can't ask a young professional on the frontline of protecting this country to violate law.

Now, I know they said they're not going to prosecute them. Think about that: Go ahead and violate it; we won't prosecute you. These people aren't going to do that, Dave. Now, we can justify anything you want and bring up this example or that example; I'm just telling you the bottom line, and that's why this debate is important, and it's a vital debate.

Now, perhaps some in Congress don't think the program is important. That's fine. I don't know if they do or don't. I think it's vital, and I have the obligation to make sure that our professionals who I would ask to go conduct interrogations to find out what might be happening or who might be coming to this country—I got to give them the tools they need. And that is clear law.

Q. But sir, this is an important point, and I think it depends——

The President. The point I just made is the most important point.

Q. Okay.

The President. And that is, the program is not going forward. David, you can give a hypothetical about North Korea or any other country; the point is that the program is not going to go forward if our professionals do not have clarity in the law. And the best way to provide clarity in the law is to make sure the Detainee Treatment Act is the crux of the law. That's how we define Common Article 3, and it sets a good standard for the countries that you just talked about.

Next man.

Q. No, but wait a second, I think this is an important point——

The President. I know you think it's an important point.

Q. Sir, with respect, if other countries interpret the Geneva Conventions as they see fit—as they see fit—you're saying that you'd be okay with that?

The President. I am saying that I would hope that they would adopt the same standards we adopt, and that by clarifying Article 3, we make it stronger; we make it clearer; we make it definite.

And I will tell you again, David, you can ask every hypothetical you want, but the American people have got to know the facts. And the bottom line is simple: If Congress passes a law that does not clarify the rules—if they do not do that, the program is not going forward.

Q. This will not endanger U.S. troops, in your——

The President. Next man.

Q. This will not endanger U.S. troops——

The President. David, next man, please. Thank you. It took you a long time to unravel, and it took you a long time to ask your question.

Democracy Efforts in Iraq/Insurgency and Terrorist Attacks

Q. Morning, sir. I'd like to ask you another question about Iraq. It's been another bloody day there. The last several weeks have been 40, 50, 60 bodies a day. We've been talking for the last several months about Iraq being on the brink of a civil war. I'd like to ask you if it's not time to start talking about Iraq as being in a civil war, and if it's not, what's the threshold?

The President. Well, it seems like it's pretty easy to speculate from over here about the conditions on the ground. And so what I do is I talk to people like our

Ambassador and General Casey, which I just did this morning. And they and the Iraqi Government just don't agree with the hypothesis it is a civil war. They believe that there's, no question, violence; they believe that Al Qaida is still creating havoc; they know there's people taking reprisal; they're confident there are still Saddamists who are threatening people and carrying out attacks.

But they also believe that the Baghdad security plan is making progress. There was a lot of discussion about Al Anbar Province recently, and I spent some time talking with our commanders. No question, it's a dangerous place. It's a place where Al Qaida is really trying to root themselves; it's a place from which they'd like to operate. You know, this business about Al Qaida, Al Anbar's loss is just not the case; it's not what our commanders think.

So to answer your question, there's no question, it's tough. What I look for is whether or not the unity Government is moving forward, whether or not they have a political plan to resolve issues such as oil and federalism, whether or not they're willing to reconcile, and whether or not Iraqi troops and Iraqi police are doing their jobs.

Q. But how do you measure progress with a body count like that?

The President. Well, one way you do it is you measure progress based upon the resilience of the Iraqi people: Do they want there to be a unity government, or are they splitting up into factions of people warring with the head leaders, with different alternatives of governing styles and different philosophies? The unity Government is intact. It's working forward. They're making tough decisions, and we'll stay with them. We'll stay with them because success in Iraq is important for this country. We're constantly changing our tactics. We're constantly adapting to the enemy. We're constantly saying, "Here's the way forward; we want to work with you." But this is really the big challenge of the 21st century, whether or not this country and allies are willing to stand with moderate people in order to fight off extremists. It is the challenge.

I said the other night in a speech, this is like the ideological war of the 21st century, and I believe it. And I believe that if we leave that region, if we don't help democracy prevail, then our children and grandchildren will be faced with an unbelievable chaotic and dangerous situation in the Middle East. Imagine an enemy that can't stand what we believe in getting a hold of oil resources and taking a bunch of oil off the market in order to have an economic punishment. In other words, they say, "You go ahead and do this, and if you don't, we'll punish you economically." Or imagine a Middle East with an Iran with a nuclear weapon threatening free nations and trying to promote their vision of extremism through Hizballah.

I find it interesting that young democracies are being challenged by extremists. I also take great hope in the fact that, by far, the vast majority of people want normalcy and want peace, including in Iraq; that there is a deep desire for people to raise their children in a peaceful world; the desire for mothers to have the best for their child. And it's not—this isn't—you know, Americans—you've got to understand, this is universal. And the idea of just saying, well, that's not important for us—to me—or the future of the country, it's just not acceptable.

And I know it's tough in Iraq. Of course it's tough in Iraq, because an enemy is trying to stop this new democracy, just like people are trying to stop the development of a Palestinian state, which I strongly support, or people trying to undermine the Lebanese democracy. And the reason why is because the ideologues understand that liberty will trump their dark vision of the world every time. And that's why I call it an ideological struggle. And it's a necessary struggle, and it's a vital struggle.

Richard [Richard Benedetto, USA Today].

United Nations

Q. Mr. President, as you prepare to go up to the United Nations next week to address the General Assembly, Secretary Kofi Annan has been critical of some of U.S. policies, particularly in Afghanistan, lately. How would you characterize the relationship between the United States and the United Nations at this point?

The President. Yes. First of all, my personal relationship with Kofi Annan is good. I like him. And we've got a good relationship, personal relationship. I think a lot of Americans are frustrated with the United Nations, to be frank with you. Take, for example, Darfur—I'm frustrated with the United Nations in regards to Darfur. I have said and this Government has said, there's genocide taking place in the Sudan. And it breaks our collective hearts to know that.

We believe that the best way to solve the problem is there be a political track as well as a security track. And part of the security track was for there initially to be African Union forces supported by the international community, hopefully to protect innocent lives from militia. And the AU force is there, but it needs—it's not robust enough. It needs to be bigger. It needs to be more viable.

And so the strategy was then to go to the United Nations and pass a resolution enabling the AU force to become blue-helmeted—that means, become a United Nations peacekeeping force—with additional support from around the world. And I suggested that there also be help from NATO nations in logistics and support in order to make the security effective enough so that a political process could go forward to save lives.

The problem is, is that the United Nations hasn't acted. And so I can understand why those who are concerned about Darfur are frustrated; I am. I'd like to see more robust United Nations action. What you'll hear is, "Well, the Government of Sudan must invite the United Nations in for us to act." Well, there are other alternatives, like passing a resolution saying, we're coming in with a U.N. force in order to save lives.

I'm proud of our country's support for those who suffer. We've provided, by far, the vast majority of food and aid. I'm troubled by reports I hear about escalating violence. I can understand the desperation people feel for women being pulled out of these refugee centers and raped. And now is the time for the U.N. to act.

So you asked if there are levels of frustration; there's a particular level of frustration. I also believe that the United Nations can do a better job spending the taxpayer—our taxpayers' money. I think there needs to be better management structures in place, better accountability in the organization. I hope the United Nations still strongly stands for liberty. I hope they would support my call to end tyranny in the 21st century.

So I'm looking forward to going up there to—it's always an interesting experience, Richard, for a west Texas fellow to speak to the United Nations. And I'm going to have a strong message, one that's hope—based upon hope and my belief that the civilized world must stand with moderate reformist-minded people and help them realize their dreams. I believe that's the call of the 21st century.

Let's see, who else? The front row people have all asked. Hutch [Ron Hutcheson, Knight Ridder].

Terrorist Surveillance Program

Q. Good morning.

The President. Good morning. Thank you.

Q. On both the eavesdropping program and the detainee issues——

The President. We call it the terrorist surveillance program, Hutch.

Q. That's the one.

The President. Yes.

Q. You're working with Congress sort of after the fact, after you established these programs on your own authority. And Federal courts have ruled in both cases, you overstepped your authority. Is your willingness to work with Congress now an acknowledgment that that is a fact?

The President. First of all, I strongly believe that the district court ruling on the terrorist surveillance program was flawed. And there's a court process to determine whether or not my belief is true. That's why it's on appeal. We're working with Congress to add certainty to the program.

In terms of the Hamdan decision, I obviously believed that I could move forward with military commissions. Other Presidents had. The Supreme Court didn't agree, and they said, "Work with Congress." And that's why we're working with Congress.

McKinnon [John McKinnon, Wall Street Journal].

National Economy/2006 Midterm Elections

Q. Thank you, sir. Polls show that many people are still more focused on domestic issues like the economy than on the international issues in deciding how to vote in November. And I'd just like to ask you if you could contrast what you think will happen on the economy if Republicans retain control of Congress versus what happens on the economy if Democrats take over?

The President. If I weren't here—first of all, I don't believe the Democrats are going to take over, because our record on the economy is strong. If the American people would take a step back and realize how effective our policies have been, given the circumstances, they will continue to embrace our philosophy of government. We've overcome recession, attacks, hurricanes, scandals, and the economy is growing, 4.7 percent unemployment rate. It's been a strong economy. And I've strongly believed the reason it is because we cut taxes and, at the same time, showed fiscal responsibility here in Washington, with the people's money. That's why the deficit could be cut in half by 2009 or before.

And so I shouldn't answer your hypothetical, but I will. I believe if the Democrats had the capacity to, they would raise taxes on the working people. That's what I believe. They'll call it tax on the rich, but that's not the way it works in Washington, see. For example, running up the top income tax bracket would tax small businesses. A lot of small businesses are subchapter S corporations or limited partnerships that pay tax at the individual level. And if you raise income taxes on them, you hurt job creation. Our answer to economic growth is to make the tax cuts permanent so there's certainty in the Tax Code and people have got money to spend in their pockets.

And so yes, I've always felt the economy is a determinate issue, if not the determinate issue in campaigns. We've had a little history of that in our family and— [*laughter*]—you might remember. But it's a—I certainly hope this election is based upon economic performance.

Let's see here, kind of working my way— yes, Mark [Mark Silva, Chicago Tribune].

USA PATRIOT Act

Q. Thank you, Mr. President. I'd also like to ask an election-related question. The Republican leader in the House this week said that Democrats—he wonders if they are more interested in protecting the terrorists than protecting the American people. Do you agree with him, sir? And do you think that's the right tone to set for this upcoming campaign, or do you think he owes somebody an apology?

The President. I wouldn't have exactly put it that way. But I do believe there's a difference of attitude. I mean, take the PATRIOT Act, for example—an interesting debate that took place, not once, but twice, and the second time around there was a lot of concern about whether or not the PATRIOT Act was necessary to protect the

country. There's no doubt in my mind we needed to make sure the PATRIOT Act was renewed to tear down walls that exist so that intelligence people could serve— could share information with criminal people. It wasn't the case, Mark, before 9/11.

In other words, if somebody had some intelligence that they thought was necessary to protect the people, they couldn't share that with somebody who's job it was to rout people out of society to prevent them from attacking. It just made no sense. And so there was a healthy debate, and we finally got the PATRIOT Act extended after it was passed right after 9/11. To me, it was an indication of just a difference of approach.

No one should ever question the patriotism of somebody who—let me just start over. I don't question the patriotism of somebody who doesn't agree with me; I just don't. And I think it's unwise to do that. I don't think that's what leaders do. I do think that—I think that there is a difference of opinion here in Washington about tools necessary to protect the country—the terrorist surveillance program—or what did you call it, Hutcheson? Yes, the illegal eavesdropping program is what you wanted to call it—[*laughter*]—IEP as opposed to TSP. [*Laughter*] There's just a difference of opinion about what we need to do to protect our country, Mark. I'm confident the leader, you know, meant nothing personal. I know that he shares my concern that we pass good legislation to get something done.

Ken.

Former Governor Ann Richards of Texas

Q. Thank you, sir. I'd be interested in your thoughts and remembrances about Ann Richards, and particularly what you learned in running against her 12 years ago.

The President. Yes. Obviously, Laura and I pray for her family. I know this is a tough time for her children. She loved her children, and they loved her a lot.

Running against Ann Richards taught me a lot. She was a really, really good candidate. She was a hard worker. She had the capacity to be humorous and yet make a profound point. I think she made a positive impact on the State of Texas. One thing is for certain: She empowered a lot of people to be—to want to participate in the political process that might not have felt that they were welcome in the process.

I'll miss her. She was a—she really kind of helped define Texas politics in its best way. And one of the things we have done is we've—in our history, we've had characters, people larger than life, people that could fill the stage; when the spotlight was on them, wouldn't shirk from the spotlight but would talk Texan and explain our State. And she was really good at that.

And so I'm sad she passed away, and I wish her family all the best—and all her friends. She had a lot of friends in Texas. A lot of people loved Ann Richards.

And anyway, as I understand, they're working on the deal and how to honor her, and she'll be lying in state in the capitol, and——

Q. Will you be sending anybody to——

The President. Yes, I will send somebody to represent me. I don't know who it is going to be yet. Well, we're trying to get the details. Before I ask somebody, I've got to find out the full details.

Thanks for asking the question. Let's see, New York Times, Sheryl [Sheryl Gay Stolberg].

"Military Commissions Act of 2006"

Q. Hi, Mr. President.

The President. Fine. How are you doing?

Q. I'm well today. Thank you. [*Laughter*]

The President. Did you start with, "Hi, Mr. President"?

Q. Hello, Mr. President.

The President. Okay, that's fine. Either way, that's always a friendly greeting. Thank you.

Q. We're a friendly newspaper.

The President. Yes. [*Laughter*] Let me just say, I'd hate to see unfriendly. [*Laughter*]

Q. Mr. President——

The President. Want me to go on to somebody else and you collect your— [*laughter*]. Sorry, go ahead, Sheryl.

Q. Mr. President, your administration had all summer to negotiate with lawmakers on the detainee legislation. How is it that you now find yourself in a situation where you have essentially an open rebellion on Capitol Hill led by some of the leading members of your own party, very respected voices in military affairs? And secondly, would you veto the bill if it passes in the form that the Armed Services Committee approved yesterday?

The President. First, we have been working throughout the summer, talking to key players about getting a bill that will enable the program to go forward, and was pleased that the House of Representatives passed a good bill with an overwhelming bipartisan majority out of their committee, the Armed Services Committee. And I felt that was good progress. And obviously, we've got a little work to do in the Senate, and we'll continue making our case. But, no, we've been involved—ever since the Supreme Court decision came down, Sheryl, we've been talking about both the military tribunals and this Article 3 of the Geneva Convention.

The Article 3 of the Geneva Convention is hard for a lot of citizens to understand. But let's see if I can put it this way for people to understand. There is a very vague standard that the Court said must kind of be the guide for our conduct in the war on terror and the detainee policy. It's so vague that it's impossible to ask anybody to participate in the program for fear— for that person having the fear of breaking the law. That's the problem.

And so we worked with members of both bodies and both parties to try to help bring some definition to Common Article 3. I really don't think most Americans want international courts being able to determine how we protect ourselves. And my assurance to people is that we can pass law here in the United States that helps define our treaty—international treaty obligations. We have done that in the past. It is not the first time that we have done this. And I believe it's necessary to do it this time in order for the program to go forward.

Peter [Peter Baker, *Washington Post*].

Q. Thank you, Mr. President. Sheryl's second question was whether you would veto the bill as it passed yesterday.

The President. Oh, I don't—that's like saying, can you work with a Democrat Congress, when I don't think the Democrat Congress is going to get elected. I believe we can get a good bill. And there is—as you know, there's several steps in this process. The House will be working on a bill next week—the Senate will be. Hopefully, we can reconcile differences. Hopefully, we can come together and find a way forward without ruining the program.

So your question was Sheryl's question?

Q. No, sir.

The President. Oh, you were following up on Sheryl's question?

Q. Yes, sir.

The President. That's a first. [*Laughter*]

Iraqi Military and Security Forces/U.S. Armed Forces

Q. We're a friendly paper too. [*Laughter*] Mr. President, you've often used the phrase "stand up/stand down," to describe your policy when it comes to troop withdrawals from Iraq—as Iraqi troops are trained and take over the fight, American troops will come home. The Pentagon now says they've trained 294,000 Iraqi troops and expect to complete their program of training 325,000 by the end of the year. But American troops aren't coming home, and there are more there now than there were previously. Is the goalpost moving, sir?

The President. No, no. The enemy is changing tactics, and we're adapting. That's

what's happening. And I asked General Casey today, "Have you got what you need?" He said, "Yes, I've got what I need."

We all want the troops to come home as quickly as possible. But they'll be coming home when our commanders say the Iraqi Government is capable of defending itself and sustaining itself and is governing itself. And you know, I was hoping we would have—be able to—hopefully, Casey would come and say, you know, "Mr. President, there's a chance to have fewer troops there." It looked like that might be the case, until the violence started rising in Baghdad, and it spiked in June and July, as you know—or increased in June and July.

And so they've got a plan now. They've adapted. The enemy moved; we'll help the Iraqis move. And so they're building a berm around the city to make it harder for people to come in with explosive devices, for example. They're working different neighborhoods inside of Baghdad to collect guns and bring people to detention. They've got a "clear, build, and hold" strategy.

The reason why there are not fewer troops there, but are more—you're right; it's gone from 135,000 to about 147,000, I think, or 140-something thousand troops—is because George Casey felt he needed them to help the Iraqis achieve their objective.

And that's the way I will continue to conduct the war. I'll listen to generals. Maybe it's not the politically expedient thing to do, is to increase troops coming into an election, but we just can't—you can't make decisions based upon politics about how to win a war. And the fundamental question you have to ask—and Martha knows what I'm about to say—is, can the President trust his commanders on the ground to tell him what is necessary? That's really one of the questions.

In other words, if you say, "I'm going to rely upon their judgment," the next question is, how good is their judgment, or is my judgment good enough to figure out whether or not they know what they're doing? And I'm going to tell you, I've got great confidence in General John Abizaid and General George Casey. These are extraordinary men who understand the difficulties of the task and understand there is a delicate relationship between self-sufficiency on the Iraqis' part and U.S. presence.

And this is not a science but an art form in a way, to try to make sure that a unity government is able to defend itself and, at the same time, not be totally reliant upon coalition forces to do the job for them. And the issue is complicated by the fact that there are still Al Qaida or Saddam remnants or militias that are still violent. And so to answer your question, the policy still holds. The "stand up/stand down" still holds, and so does the policy of me listening to our commanders to give me the judgment necessary for troop levels.

Richard [Richard Wolffe, Newsweek] and then Allen [Mike Allen, Time].

Usama bin Laden/Pakistan's Role in the War on Terror

Q. Thank you, Mr. President. Earlier this week, you told a group of journalists that you thought the idea of sending Special Forces to Pakistan to hunt down bin Laden was a strategy that would not work.

The President. Yes.

Q. Now recently you've also——

The President. It's because, first of all, Pakistan is a sovereign nation.

Q. Well, recently you've also described bin Laden as a sort of modern day Hitler or Mussolini. And I'm wondering why—if you can explain why you think it's a bad idea to send more resources to hunt down bin Laden, wherever he is?

The President. We are, Richard. Thank you. Thanks for asking the question. They were asking me about somebody's report, well, Special Forces here—Pakistan—if he is in Pakistan, which this person thought

he might be, who is asking the question—Pakistan is a sovereign nation. In order for us to send thousands of troops into a sovereign nation, we've got to be invited by the Government of Pakistan.

Secondly, the best way to find somebody who is hiding is to enhance your intelligence and to spend the resources necessary to do that. Then when you find him, you bring him to justice. And there is a kind of an urban myth here in Washington about how this administration hasn't stayed focused on Usama bin Laden. Forget it. It's convenient throw-away lines when people say that. We have been on the hunt, and we'll stay on the hunt until we bring him to justice. And we're doing it in a smart fashion, Richard, we are.

And I look forward to talking to President Musharraf. Look, he doesn't like Al Qaida. They tried to kill him. And we've had a good record of bringing people to justice inside of Pakistan, because the Paks are in the lead. They know the stakes about dealing with a violent form of ideological extremists.

And so we will continue on the hunt. And we've been effective about bringing to justice most of those who planned and plotted the 9/11 attacks, and we've still got a lot of pressure on them. The best way to protect the homeland is to stay on the offense and keep pressure on them.

Last question. Allen.

American Culture

Q. Thank you, Mr. President. It was reported earlier this week that in a meeting with conservative journalists, you said you'd seen changes in the culture. You referred to it as a "Third Awakening." I wonder if you could tell us about—what you meant by that, what led you to that conclusion? And do you see any contradictory evidence in the culture?

The President. No, I said—Mike, thanks. I was just speculating that the culture might be changing, and I was talking about when you're involved with making decisions of historic nature, you won't be around to see the effects of your decisions. And I said that when I work the ropelines, a lot of people come and say, "Mr. President, I'm praying for you"—a lot. As a matter of fact, it seems like a lot more now than when I was working ropelines in 1994. And I asked them—I was asking their opinion about whether or not there was a "Third Awakening," I called it.

I'd just read a book on Abraham Lincoln, and his Presidency was right around the time of what they called the Second Awakening, and I was curious to know whether or not these smart people felt like there was any historical parallels. I also said that I had run for office the first time to change a culture—Herman and Hutch remember me saying, you know, the culture that said, "If it feels good, do it, and if you've got a problem, blame somebody else"—to helping to work change a culture in which each of us are responsible for the decisions we make in life. In other words, ushering in a responsibility era. And I reminded people that responsibility means, if you're a father, love your child; or if you're corporate America, be honest with the taxpayers; if you're a citizen of this country, love your neighbor.

And so I was wondering out loud with them. It seems like to me that something is happening in the religious life of America. But I'm not a very good focus group either. I'm encapsulated here. I'm able to see a lot of people, and from my perspective, people are coming to say, "I'm praying for you." And it's an uplifting part of being the President; it inspires me. And I'm grateful that a fellow citizen would say a prayer for me and Laura.

Anyway, thank you all very much.

NOTE: The President's news conference began at 11:15 a.m. in the Rose Garden at the White House. In his remarks, he referred to Khalid Sheikh Mohammed, senior Al Qaida leader responsible for planning the September 11, 2001, terrorist attacks, who was captured in Pakistan on March 1, 2003; Ramzi bin al-Shibh, an Al Qaida operative suspected of helping to plan the September 11, 2001, terrorist attacks, who was captured in Karachi, Pakistan, on September 11, 2002; Abu Zubaydah, a leader of the Al Qaida terrorist organization, who was captured in Faisalabad, Pakistan, on March 28, 2002; U.S. Ambassador to Iraq Zalmay Khalilzad; Gen. George W. Casey, Jr., USA, commanding general, Multi-National Force—Iraq; Gen. John P. Abizaid, USA, commander, U.S. Central Command; Usama bin Laden, leader of the Al Qaida terrorist organization; and President Pervez Musharraf of Pakistan. The President also referred to H.R. 6054, the "Military Commissions Act of 2006," and S. 2455 and S. 3874, both concerning the terrorist surveillance program. A reporter referred to Prime Minister Nuri al-Maliki of Iraq.

The President's Radio Address
September 16, 2006

Good morning. On Monday I visited New York, Pennsylvania, and the Pentagon to attend memorials marking the fifth anniversary of the 9/11 attacks. It was an emotional day for me and for our country. On that day, we remembered those who lost their lives, and we paid tribute to those who gave their lives so that others might live. We rededicated ourselves to protecting the American people from another attack.

Next week I will return to New York, where I will address the United Nations General Assembly. I look forward to talking to the world leaders gathered there about our obligation to defend civilization and how we must work together to support the forces of freedom and moderation throughout the Middle East.

As we work with the international community to defeat the terrorists and extremists, we must also provide our military and intelligence professionals the tools they need to keep our country safe. Congress is considering two vital pieces of legislation to help us do just that. My administration is working closely with members of both parties to pass these bills.

The first bill would allow us to use military commissions to try suspected terrorists for war crimes. We need this legislation because the Supreme Court has ruled that military commissions must be explicitly authorized by Congress.

Recently I announced that 14 suspected terrorists, including Khalid Sheikh Mohammed, the man believed to be the mastermind of the 9/11 attacks, had been transferred to Guantanamo Bay. As soon as Congress acts to authorize the military commissions I have proposed, the men our intelligence agencies believed helped orchestrate the deaths of nearly 3,000 Americans on September the 11th, 2001, can face justice.

This bill will also provide clear rules for our personnel involved in detaining and questioning captured terrorists. The information the Central Intelligence Agency has obtained by questioning men like Khalid Sheikh Mohammed has helped disrupt terrorist plots, including planned strikes inside the United States and on a U.S. Marine base in east Africa, an American consulate in Pakistan, and Britain's Heathrow Airport. This CIA program has saved American lives and the lives of people in other countries.

Unfortunately, the recent Supreme Court decision put the future of this program in question, and we need this legislation to save it. There is debate about the specific proposals in this bill, and my administration will work with Congress to find common ground. I have one test for this legislation:

The intelligence community must be able to tell me that the bill Congress sends to my desk will allow this vital program to continue.

The second bill before Congress would modernize our electronic surveillance laws and provide additional authority for the terrorist surveillance program. I authorized the National Security Agency to operate this vital program in response to the 9/11 attacks. It allows us to quickly monitor terrorist communications between someone overseas and someone in America. It has helped detect and prevent terrorist attacks on our own country. The principle behind this program is clear: When Al Qaida operatives are calling into or out of our country, we need to know who they are calling, why they are calling, and what they are planning.

Both these bills are essential to winning the war on terror, so we will work with legislators from both sides of the aisle to get them passed. By passing these critical bills, we will bring terrorists to justice, continue collecting vital intelligence from captured terrorists in a lawful way, and monitor terrorist communications, so we can stop new attacks on our Nation.

Thank you for listening.

NOTE: The address was recorded at 7:50 a.m. on September 15 in the Cabinet Room at the White House for broadcast at 10:06 a.m. on September 16. The transcript was made available by the Office of the Press Secretary on September 15 but was embargoed for release until the broadcast. In his address, the President referred to Khalid Sheikh Mohammed, senior Al Qaida leader responsible for planning the September 11, 2001, terrorist attacks, who was captured in Pakistan on March 1, 2003. He also referred to H.R. 6054, the "Military Commissions Act of 2006," and S. 2455 and S. 3874, both concerning the terrorist surveillance program. The Office of the Press Secretary also released a Spanish language transcript of this address.

Remarks at the White House Conference on Global Literacy in New York City
September 18, 2006

Thank you all. Thank you for attending this important conference. I look around the room and see some familiar faces— my mother. [*Laughter*] How are you doing? It's good to see you; my mother-in-law. [*Laughter*] Both of these ladies have instilled a great passion for literacy not only in Laura and me but for others around our country. Thank you all for coming. Laura, thank you for your leadership.

Laura believes strongly in the power of literacy to change societies, and that's really what we're here to talk about. The capacity of—the simple act of teaching a child to read or an adult to read has the capacity to transform nations and yield the peace we all want.

So I want to thank you for being here. I particularly want to thank the First Ladies who are here and the ministers from different Governments around the world. We're really proud you've taken time to join us here today.

As you probably can tell, our Government takes this initiative seriously. After all, we've got the Secretary of State, Condoleezza Rice, and the Secretary of Education, Margaret Spellings, both here. It should say to people loud and clear that when you combine the resources of the Department of Education and the State Department, that we're serious about helping global literacy. And then we've added Randy Tobias, who's the head of USAID. He's the fellow who's got the responsibility of handing out some money—[*laughter*]— which is what we're doing because we believe strongly in this initiative. So I want to thank you all for taking time out of your busy schedules to send a clear message to folks.

I want to thank Mr. Matsuura of UNESCO. Thank you very much for serving. Thanks for leading this vital organiza-tion. We want to work with you. And I see you're sitting next to one of my great friends—the Ambassador, Karen Hughes, is here as well.

I want to thank Paul LeClerc of the— of this fantastic library. Isn't this a wonderful place to meet? Obviously, it makes sense to meet in a library if you're going to talk about literacy. It's really one of the most special spots here in New York. And I also want to thank Catie Marron for allowing us to use this facility. She's the chairman of the board, and Paul, of course, is the president and CEO of the New York Public Library.

I want to thank those who have participated in panels. I had the honor of meeting some of the panelists and the panel leaders. I met Gerri Elliott, who is a corporate vice president of Microsoft. The reason I bring up Gerri Elliott is because in America, we believe that there is a combined responsibility to help. We believe government has got a vital role, but we also believe corporate America and our citizens have got a vital role to play in helping others benefit from learning how to read. And so I want to thank Gerri for setting such a good example.

I call upon others in our country to understand the importance of this initiative and to step forth. After all, a literacy initiative will help spread prosperity and peace. And that's really why we're here at the UNGA. I've been looking forward to coming here. As you know, it's an annual event. Every year, I get to come. It gives me a chance to meet with fellow leaders, and it gives me a chance to clearly explain, the goals of this country are to help those who feel hopeless; the goals of this country are to spread liberty; the goals of this country is to enhance prosperity and peace.

You can't have prosperity unless people can read. It's just as simple as that. You know, one of the things that we have committed ourselves to in America is to help eradicate persistent poverty. But there is a direct link between illiteracy and persistent poverty. Oftentimes when we're talking about prosperity and helping this world become a more prosperous place, we tend to focus only on trade. And no question, good trade agreements and tearing down the barriers that prevent the free flow of goods will help enhance prosperity. But you can't be a prosperous nation if you don't have people who can read.

I mean, think about it. It's pretty clear, in order to be an informed consumer, you have to read. In order to be able to take advantages of jobs that may come to your country as a result of expanding economic opportunity, you've got to read. In order to be a productive worker, you have to be able to read the manual. And so part of this initiative, part of the practical application of this initiative is to encourage prosperity by enhancing people's capacity to read. And I want to thank you for your focus on that important issue.

I also strongly believe that those of us who have the benefits of living in free society must help others realize the benefits of liberty. I believe that. I believe that's part of America's responsibility in the world. I realize we can't impose our vision of government, nor should we try. But we believe here in America in the universality of freedom. We don't believe freedom belongs only to the United States of America; we believe that liberty is universal in its applications. We also believe strongly that as the world becomes more free, we'll see peace. That's what we believe. And we're going to act on those beliefs.

But one thing that's for certain: It is very hard to have free societies if the citizens cannot read. Think about that. It's much harder for a society to realize the universal blessings of liberty if your citizens can't read the newspaper in order to be able to make informed choices and decisions about what may be taking place in a country. You can't realize the blessings of liberty if you can't read a ballot or if you can't read what others are saying about the future of your country.

I am deeply concerned about the spread of radicalism, and I know you are as well. We long for the days when people don't feel comfortable or empowered to take innocent life to achieve an objective. One reason radicals are able to recruit young men, for example, to become suicide bombers is because of hopelessness. One way to defeat hopelessness is through literacy, is to giving people the fantastic hope that comes by being able to read and realize dreams.

So this literacy initiative is vital as far as the United States of America is concerned, and we want to help. That's what I'm here to say. I want to thank you for being here, and let you know that we want to lend our help.

I know Laura talked about our initiative on the continent of Africa. It is a firm, real, dedicated commitment to helping folks become literate. We share—we have that same sense of commitment in more places than Africa. I mean, for example, in our own neighborhood, we are deeply concerned about illiteracy, and we believe it's in our national interest to help folks become literate in Central and South America.

One of the most, I guess, heartwarming literacy initiatives that I have witnessed as President was the Women's Teacher Training Institute in Kabul. I know there's some people from Afghanistan here, and I want to thank you for your courage and your bravery. I don't know if you know what the institute has been doing, but think back to the days prior to liberation when women really weren't let out of the house; young girls couldn't go to school. There was an underground teacher movement because of the great passion teachers feel for their students. And so after the liberation of the country, we have worked with that institute to teach trainers—teach teachers how to teach, in the knowledge that when they leave the institute, they'll then go to their village.

It's kind of this cascading movement of skill so that people can fulfill their compassion, fulfill their dreams about a more literate Afghanistan. This young democracy will survive. And one of the reasons it will survive is because of the committed effort by a lot of folks, not just the United States but by people around the world, to help the brave educational entrepreneurs that recognize hope and peace come about as a result of education.

We—a lot of times you hear a lot of words—people are pretty good talkers in this society of ours. People step up and make promises and, kind of, flowery statements. I want it to be said that our Government is doing more than just talking, that our Government is willing to act. We've doubled the development assistance since I've been the President. We have set forth what's called the Millennium Challenge Account. We said we were going to help people, particularly those who fight corruption, those who believe in markets, but equally important, those who invest in the education and health of their citizens.

We believe strongly that this world must confront the pandemic of HIV/AIDS and believe that to whom much is given, much is required in order to solve disease and poverty—a lot of it brought about because—a lot of that poverty brought about because of illiteracy.

And so one thing I'd like for you to take away from today is, one, we're committed. We believe that the United States of America must not isolate ourselves from the problems of the world. We believe we have an opportunity to help you solve problems of the world.

There is nothing more hopeful, there's no greater gift than to teach a person to read. When I was the Governor of Texas, I remember an African American woman walking up to me, and we were talking about the importance of teaching every child to read—not just a few, but every child to read. We believe in America that reading shouldn't be the right of just a few people; it ought to be—it's universal as well. And the woman walked up to me, and she said, "Mr. Governor," she said, "I want you to understand how people in my community feel." She said, "Reading is the new civil right." I feel the same way about global literacy. Reading will yield the peace we want.

So thanks for coming. God bless.

NOTE: The President spoke at 12:10 p.m. at the New York Public Library. In his remarks, he referred to Koichiro Matsuura, director-general, United Nations Educational, Scientific and Cultural Organization. The transcript released by the Office of the Press Secretary also included the remarks of the First Lady, who introduced the President. The Office of the Press Secretary also released a Spanish language transcript of these remarks.

Remarks Following Discussions With Prime Minister Abdullah bin Ahmad Badawi of Malaysia in New York City
September 18, 2006

President Bush. It's been my honor, Mr. Prime Minister, to be with you. You're one of the outstanding leaders in a very important part of the world. I want to thank you for strategizing our discussions. We talked about a lot of things. The main thing we talked about is how we can work together to keep the peace. And I want to thank you for your time.

Prime Minister Abdullah. Thank you, Mr. President. You shared me—with me Americans nation's, and your views on many issues is very, very impressive. And I am certainly most likely to see that you are very concerned for peace and U.N. peace-keeping in the Middle East.

President Bush. Yes, sir. Thank you, sir. Thank you.

NOTE: The President spoke at 2:58 p.m. at the Waldorf-Astoria Hotel. A tape was not available for verification of the content of these remarks.

Remarks Following Discussions With President Jacques Chirac of France and an Exchange With Reporters in New York City
September 19, 2006

President Bush. It's been a pleasure to have a meaningful, strategic dialog with Jacques Chirac. We talked about a lot of subjects. It's important that France and the United States work closely to keep the peace. We talked about Iran; we talked about Syria; we talked about the Palestinian-Israeli issue; we talked about Darfur; we talked about common problems and how to solve those problems. It was a very constructive and important dialog.

Mr. President, welcome back to America, and thank you for your time.

President Chirac. We're always welcome in the United States. Relations between the United States and France are longstanding and deeply rooted.

Well, indeed, today we have discussed and evidenced the fact that we have common approaches and a common sense of the main issues that we discussed, relating as they do to peace and to development throughout the world. In fact, this coincides with the 61st U.N. General Assembly, which is going to meet today.

So we discussed peace and development. And particularly on the subject of peace-related issues, we addressed the issue of Iran, of the Israeli-Palestinian conflict; we addressed Lebanon and, of course, Africa, in particular—in Africa. And with respect to Africa, we addressed the issue of what's going on in Darfur.

And we, as a result of this, have once again confirmed that we are entirely on the same wavelength. We have the same approach to the different issues, which are of deep and grave concern to us, as they challenge and jeopardize peace in different parts of the world.

I repeat what I've already said, namely that we concur, our views concur on these matters, particularly on the issue of a possible agreement with the Iranians. And therefore, France—I'm convinced the United States, the American administration and the French Government see eye to eye on these matters and on how to address them.

President Bush. One question a side. Nedra [Nedra Pickler, Associated Press].

Iran/Nuclear Weapons Development

Q. Yes, thank you, Mr. President. President Chirac has proposed suspending the threat of sanctions against Iran as an incentive to get them to the negotiating table. What do you think of that idea?

President Bush. First of all, France and the United States share the same goal, and that is for the Iranians not to have a nuclear weapon.

Secondly, we share the same goal. We'd like to solve this problem diplomatically, and we understand working together is important. And the Iranians have got to understand, we share the same objective, and we're going to continue to strategize together.

The EU–3 will continue to dialog with the Iranians to get them to the table so that they will suspend, verifiably suspend, their enrichment activities, in which case, the United States will come to the table. And we believe time is of the essence. Should they continue to stall, we will then discuss the consequences of their stalling. And one of those consequences, of course, would be some kind of sanction program.

But now is the time for the Iranians to come to the table. And that's what we discussed.

President Chirac. For the past 2 days, I've had the opportunity to speak very clearly on the subject—at least I hope I've been very clear—and let me take this opportunity once again to say that the present views of the United States and I again see eye to eye on this one. I totally agree with President Bush. We are both determined to push forward on this one, to move ahead in a constructive manner. And the first thing we need to do is to find a solution so that, indeed—and end be put to the uranium enrichment activity being engaged in, and then we can move on to finding solutions to the other problems that arise and stem from this issue.

President Bush. Final question. Do you want to call on somebody?

[At this point, a question was asked in French, and no translation was provided.]

President Chirac. There never has been any ambiguity as to the positions adopted respectively by the Europeans, by the six, by the United States, and in particular, by France. We have always said very clearly that any negotiations—and let's face it, this is the normal course of events; this negotiation is the normal way in which one expects to address and, indeed, settle, solve such a thorny issue as this one—that negotiations are the way we are heading.

Nonetheless, we have equally said that we cannot have negotiations if we do not have prior suspension, on the one hand, of uranium enrichment activity on the part of Iran, and on the other, on the part of the six, the agreement not to approach the Security Council on this matter—in particular, this will include the possibility of examining a sanction program.

I think this has been said abundantly clearly time and again, and I do not really understand what kind of controversy has arisen or misunderstanding could have crept in, insofar as this, as I said, has been repeatedly said. Maybe it's due to a lack of understanding of the situation, but there's no ambiguity on our side.

President Bush. Thank you, Jacques.

NOTE: The President spoke at 10:10 a.m. at the Waldorf-Astoria Hotel. President Chirac spoke in French, and his remarks were translated by an interpreter.

Remarks to the United Nations General Assembly in New York City
September 19, 2006

Mr. Secretary-General, Madam President, distinguished delegates, and ladies and gentlemen, I want to thank you for the privilege of speaking to this General Assembly.

Last week, America and the world marked the fifth anniversary of the attacks that filled another September morning with death and suffering. On that terrible day, extremists killed nearly 3,000 innocent people, including citizens of dozens of nations represented right here in this chamber. Since then, the enemies of humanity have continued their campaign of murder. Al Qaida and those inspired by its extremist ideology have attacked more than two dozen nations. And recently a different group of extremists deliberately provoked a terrible conflict in Lebanon. At the start of the 21st century, it is clear that the world is engaged in a great ideological struggle between extremists who use terror as a weapon to create fear and moderate people who work for peace.

Five years ago, I stood at this podium and called on the community of nations to defend civilization and build a more hopeful future. This is still the great challenge of our time; it is the calling of our generation. This morning I want to speak about the more hopeful world that is within our reach, a world beyond terror, where ordinary men and women are free to determine their own destiny, where the voices of moderation are empowered, and where the extremists are marginalized by the peaceful majority. This world can be ours if we seek it and if we work together.

The principles of this world beyond terror can be found in the very first sentence of the Universal Declaration of Human Rights. This document declares that the "equal and inalienable rights of all members of the human family is the foundation of freedom and justice and peace in the world." One of the authors of this document was a Lebanese diplomat named Charles Malik, who would go on to become President of this Assembly. Mr. Malik insisted that these principles apply equally to all people of all regions, of all religions, including the men and women of the Arab world that was his home.

In the nearly six decades since that document was approved, we have seen the forces of freedom and moderation trans-

form entire continents. Sixty years after a terrible war, Europe is now whole, free, and at peace, and Asia has seen freedom progress and hundreds of millions of people lifted out of desperate poverty. The words of the Universal Declaration are as true today as they were when they were written. As liberty flourishes, nations grow in tolerance and hope and peace. And we're seeing that bright future begin to take root in the broader Middle East.

Some of the changes in the Middle East have been dramatic, and we see the results in this chamber. Five years ago, Afghanistan was ruled by the brutal Taliban regime, and its seat in this body was contested. Now this seat is held by the freely elected Government of Afghanistan, which is represented today by President Karzai. Five years ago, Iraq's seat in this body was held by a dictator who killed his citizens, invaded his neighbors, and showed his contempt for the world by defying more than a dozen U.N. Security Council resolutions. Now Iraq's seat is held by a democratic Government that embodies the aspirations of the Iraq people, represented today by President Talabani. With these changes, more than 50 million people have been given a voice in this chamber for the first time in decades.

Some of the changes in the Middle East are happening gradually, but they are real. Algeria has held its first competitive Presidential election, and the military remained neutral. The United Arab Emirates recently announced that half of its seats in the Federal National Council will be chosen by elections. Kuwait held elections in which women were allowed to vote and run for office for the first time. Citizens have voted in municipal elections in Saudi Arabia, in parliamentary elections in Jordan and Bahrain, and in multiparty Presidential elections in Yemen and Egypt. These are important steps, and the governments should continue to move forward with other reforms that show they trust their people.

Every nation that travels the road to freedom moves at a different pace, and the democracies they build will reflect their own culture and traditions. But the destination is the same, a free society where people live at peace with each other and at peace with the world.

Some have argued that the democratic changes we're seeing in the Middle East are destabilizing the region. This argument rests on a false assumption that the Middle East was stable to begin with. The reality is that the stability we thought we saw in the Middle East was a mirage. For decades, millions of men and women in the region have been trapped in oppression and hopelessness. And these conditions left a generation disillusioned and made this region a breeding ground for extremism.

Imagine what it's like to be a young person living in a country that is not moving toward reform. You're 21 years old, and while your peers in other parts of the world are casting their ballots for the first time, you are powerless to change the course of your government. While your peers in other parts of the world have received educations that prepare them for the opportunities of a global economy, you have been fed propaganda and conspiracy theories that blame others for your country's shortcomings. And everywhere you turn, you hear extremists who tell you that you can escape your misery and regain your dignity through violence and terror and martyrdom. For many across the broader Middle East, this is the dismal choice presented every day.

Every civilized nation, including those in the Muslim world, must support those in the region who are offering a more hopeful alternative. We know that when people have a voice in their future, they are less likely to blow themselves up in suicide attacks. We know that when leaders are accountable to their people, they are more likely to seek national greatness in the achievements of their citizens, rather than in terror and conquest. So we must stand

with democratic leaders and moderate reformers across the broader Middle East. We must give them—voice to the hopes of decent men and women who want for their children the same things we want for ours. We must seek stability through a free and just Middle East where the extremists are marginalized by millions of citizens in control of their own destinies.

Today I'd like to speak directly to the people across the broader Middle East. My country desires peace. Extremists in your midst spread propaganda claiming that the West is engaged in a war against Islam. This propaganda is false, and its purpose is to confuse you and justify acts of terror. We respect Islam, but we will protect our people from those who pervert Islam to sow death and destruction. Our goal is to help you build a more tolerant and hopeful society that honors people of all faiths and promotes the peace.

To the people of Iraq: Nearly 12 million of you braved the car bombers and assassins last December to vote in free elections. The world saw you hold up purple ink-stained fingers, and your courage filled us with admiration. You've stood firm in the face of horrendous acts of terror and sectarian violence, and we will not abandon you in your struggle to build a free nation. America and our coalition partners will continue to stand with the democratic Government you elected. We will continue to help you secure the international assistance and investment you need to create jobs and opportunity, working with the United Nations and through the International Compact with Iraq endorsed here in New York yesterday. We will continue to train those of you who stepped forward to fight the enemies of freedom. We will not yield the future of your country to terrorists and extremists. In return, your leaders must rise to the challenges your country is facing and make difficult choices to bring security and prosperity. Working together, we will help your democracy succeed, so it can become a beacon of hope for millions in the Muslim world.

To the people of Afghanistan: Together we overthrew the Taliban regime that brought misery into your lives and harbored terrorists who brought death to the citizens of many nations. Since then, we have watched you choose your leaders in free elections and build a democratic government. You can be proud of these achievements. We respect your courage and your determination to live in peace and freedom, and we will continue to stand with you to defend your democratic gains. Today, forces from more than 40 countries, including members of the NATO alliance, are bravely serving side by side with you against the extremists who want to bring down the free Government you've established. We'll help you defeat these enemies and build a free Afghanistan that will never again oppress you or be a safe haven for terrorists.

To the people of Lebanon: Last year, you inspired the world when you came out into the streets to demand your independence from Syrian dominance. You drove Syrian forces from your country, and you reestablished democracy. Since then, you have been tested by the fighting that began with Hizballah's unprovoked attacks on Israel. Many of you have seen your homes and your communities caught in crossfire. We see your suffering, and the world is helping you to rebuild your country and helping you deal with the armed extremists who are undermining your democracy by acting as a state within a state. The United Nations has passed a good resolution that has authorized an international force, led by France and Italy, to help you restore Lebanese sovereignty over Lebanese soil. For many years, Lebanon was a model of democracy and pluralism and openness in the region. And it will be again.

To the people of Iran: The United States respects you; we respect your country. We admire your rich history, your vibrant culture, and your many contributions to civilization. You deserve an opportunity to determine your own future, an economy that rewards your intelligence and your talents, and a society that allows you to fulfill your tremendous potential. The greatest obstacle to this future is that your rulers have chosen to deny you liberty and to use your nation's resources to fund terrorism and fuel extremism and pursue nuclear weapons. The United Nations has passed a clear resolution requiring that the regime in Tehran meet its international obligations. Iran must abandon its nuclear weapons ambitions. Despite what the regime tells you, we have no objection to Iran's pursuit of a truly peaceful nuclear power program. We're working toward a diplomatic solution to this crisis. And as we do, we look to the day when you can live in freedom and America and Iran can be good friends and close partners in the cause of peace.

To the people of Syria: Your land is home to a great people with a proud tradition of learning and commerce. Today, your rulers have allowed your country to become a crossroad for terrorism. In your midst, Hamas and Hizballah are working to destabilize the region, and your Government is turning your country into a tool of Iran. This is increasing your country's isolation from the world. Your Government must choose a better way forward by ending its support for terror and living in peace with your neighbors and opening the way to a better life for you and your families.

To the people of Darfur: You have suffered unspeakable violence, and my nation has called these atrocities what they are, genocide. For the last 2 years, America joined with the international community to provide emergency food aid and support for an African Union peacekeeping force. Yet your suffering continues. The world must step forward to provide additional humanitarian aid, and we must strengthen the African Union force that has done good work but is not strong enough to protect you. The Security Council has approved a resolution that would transform the African

Union force into a blue-helmeted force that is larger and more robust. To increase its strength and effectiveness, NATO nations should provide logistics and other support. The regime in Khartoum is stopping the deployment of this force. If the Sudanese Government does not approve this peace-keeping force quickly, the United Nations must act. Your lives and the credibility of the United Nations is at stake. So today I'm announcing that I'm naming a Presidential special envoy, former USAID Administrator Andrew Natsios, to lead America's efforts to resolve the outstanding disputes and help bring peace to your land.

The world must also stand up for peace in the Holy Land. I'm committed to two democratic states, Israel and Palestine, living side by side in peace and security. I'm committed to a Palestinian state that has territorial integrity and will live peacefully with the Jewish State of Israel. This is the vision set forth in the roadmap, and helping the parties reach this goal is one of the great objectives of my Presidency. The Palestinian people have suffered from decades of corruption and violence and the daily humiliation of occupation. Israeli citizens have endured brutal acts of terrorism and constant fear of attack since the birth of their nation. Many brave men and women have made the commitment to peace. Yet extremists in the region are stirring up hatred and trying to prevent these moderate voices from prevailing.

This struggle is unfolding in the Palestinian Territories. Earlier this year, the Palestinian people voted in a free election. The leaders of Hamas campaigned on a platform of ending corruption and improving the lives of the Palestinian people, and they prevailed. The world is waiting to see whether the Hamas Government will follow through on its promises or pursue an extremist agenda. The world has sent a clear message to the leaders of Hamas: Serve the interests of the Palestinian people; abandon terror; recognize Israel's right to

exist, honor agreements, and work for peace.

President Abbas is committed to peace and to his people's aspirations for a state of their own. Prime Minister Olmert is committed to peace and has said he intends to meet with President Abbas to make real progress on the outstanding issues between them. I believe peace can be achieved and that a democratic Palestinian state is possible. I hear from leaders in the region who want to help. I've directed Secretary of State Rice to lead a diplomatic effort to engage moderate leaders across the region, to help the Palestinians reform their security services and support Israeli and Palestinian leaders in their efforts to come together to resolve their differences. Prime Minister Blair has indicated that his country will work with partners in Europe to help strengthen the governing institutions of the Palestinian administration. We welcome his initiative. Countries like Saudi Arabia and Jordan and Egypt have made clear they're willing to contribute the diplomatic and financial assistance necessary to help these efforts succeed. I'm optimistic that by supporting the forces of democracy and moderation, we can help Israelis and Palestinians build a more hopeful future and achieve the peace in a Holy Land we all want.

Freedom, by its nature, cannot be imposed; it must be chosen. From Beirut to Baghdad, people are making the choice for freedom. And the nations gathered in this chamber must make a choice as well: Will we support the moderates and reformers who are working for change across the Middle East, or will we yield the future to the terrorists and extremists? America has made its choice: We will stand with the moderates and reformers.

Recently a courageous group of Arab and Muslim intellectuals wrote me a letter. In it, they said this: "The shore of reform is the only one on which any lights appear, even though the journey demands courage and patience and perseverance." The

United Nations was created to make that journey possible. Together we must support the dreams of good and decent people who are working to transform a troubled region, and by doing so, we will advance the high ideals on which this institution was founded.

Thank you for your time. God bless.

NOTE: The President spoke at 12:15 p.m. in the General Assembly Hall. In his remarks, he referred to Secretary-General Kofi Annan of the United Nations; Sheikha Haya Rashed Al Khalifa, President, 61st Session of the U.N. General Assembly; President Hamid Karzai of Afghanistan; former President Saddam Hussein and President Jalal Talabani of Iraq; President Mahmoud Abbas of the Palestinian Authority; Prime Minister Ehud Olmert of Israel; and Prime Minister Tony Blair of the United Kingdom. The Office of the Press Secretary also released a Spanish language transcript of these remarks.

Remarks at a Luncheon Hosted by Secretary-General Kofi Annan of the United Nations in New York City
September 19, 2006

Mr. Secretary-General, distinguished members of the United Nations community, Your Excellencies, ladies and gentlemen, we're proud to welcome you here to our country.

I'm pleased to be with you at the 61st session of the United Nations General Assembly, this year under the President—under the leadership of President Sheikha Khalifa from Bahrain, the first woman from the Middle East to serve in this position. We welcome her presence on the podium.

Mr. Secretary-General, it is appropriate that we offer you a toast today, a toast based upon our gratitude for your 10 years of service to this important body. We need to toast your compassion, when the world saw the United Nations respond to natural disasters. We need to toast your desire for peace. We need to toast the fact that you're a hard worker. For those of you who have had the honor of taking phone calls from Kofi Annan, you know that he's not always calling from the same address. I've talked to him a lot of times during my time as President, and a lot of times my discussions with him came from when he was in far-away places, because he cares deeply about the world.

We need to toast the fact that he loves his wife, and his wife loves him. We need to toast the fact that he is a decent, honorable man. We need to raise our glasses to 10 years of extraordinary service and be thankful that a man such as Kofi Annan was willing to stand up and serve the cause of justice and peace.

And so now if you'll join me in a toast to a good man and a good friend, and we ask for God's blessings on you.

NOTE: The President spoke at 2:14 p.m. at the United Nations Headquarters. In his remarks, he referred to Sheikha Haya Rashed Al Khalifa, President, 61st Session of the U.N. General Assembly; and Nane Maria Annan, wife of Secretary-General Annan. The transcript released by the Office of the Press Secretary also included the remarks of Secretary-General Annan. A tape was not available for verification of the content of these remarks.

Remarks Following Discussions With President Jalal Talabani of Iraq in New York City
September 19, 2006

President Bush. I want to thank the President of Iraq for joining us. President Talabani, you and your colleagues here have given us time so we can strategize together to help you succeed, help you become a democracy, a country that can sustain itself and govern itself and defend itself, in the heart of the Middle East.

I want to congratulate the Iraqi people on your courage. These are tough times. There is still violence in your midst because extremists want to stop the advance of a free society. We spent time strategizing on how we can continue to help the Iraqi Government provide security for her people. It's not only security that comes from troops but security that comes from economic vitality.

We had a very good meeting yesterday on the compact for Iraq. The international community came and listened very carefully to the Iraqi Government's proposals and pledged support for this new democracy, and that ought to hearten the Iraqi people. I made it very clear to the President that it's important for the Government of Iraq to continue to make very difficult decisions so that the people of Iraq see progress, to see different political parties capable of working together for the good of the country and for the good of the people. I'm optimistic that this Government will succeed. And I've told the President of Iraq that America has given her word to help you, and we will keep our word. The people of Iraq must know that.

I spoke today at the United Nations, and in my speech, I spoke directly to the people of Iraq. I wanted them to know that we're thinking about them during this difficult period of time. I want them to know we appreciate their courage. And I want them to know that the United States of America stands with them, so long as the Government continues to make the tough choices necessary for peace to prevail.

So, Mr. President, thank you for coming again. I appreciate your time. I appreciate your longstanding courage and support for freedom and liberty. History will judge you kindly, Mr. President, when they look back and realize that under your leadership, a new democracy began to flourish in the heart of the Middle East, called Iraq.

Welcome.

President Talabani. Thank you. Today we were honored to meet President Bush, who we consider him as the hero of liberation of Iraq and who we are—very much appreciate the sacrifice of brave American Army, those who gave their life to liberate our country from the worst kind of dictatorship, which left behind mass graves with hundreds of thousands of innocent Iraqis in it. And the liberation of Iraq from this kind of dictatorship opened the door for Iraqi people to enjoy democracy, human rights, and all kinds of liberties, and to have free election, the National Assembly then elects the Presidency and Speaker and Prime Minister, and to have national unity, a Government headed by Dr. Maliki.

This Government is representing main portions of Iraqi people, of course Arabs, Sunnis, Shi'as, Turkomans, Christians, Muslims, everyone represented in this Government, and is working well for national reconciliation. I briefed his Excellency, President, about the steps we have taken towards implementing—implementation of national reconciliation program. And also, I told him that we are trying to do our best to remove all obstacles in the way of national reconciliation, to try to review some of those like de-Ba'athification and look to the amendment of a Constitution and also try to have some kind of discussion, free discussion about federation and some other issues. We have also our roadmap in Iraq, which was decided by a political council of national security for solving other problems of Iraqi people.

We, again, expressed our gratitude to his Excellency, our dear friend, President George Bush, and to American people. We hope that America also understand that we are grateful to them, to the America, and we will never forget those friends who helped us in the difficult days of Iraq, and Iraq will be always in the future in very good relation and be the friend of the United States and partner of United States in fighting against tyranny, dictatorship, and terrorism. You can count on the Iraqi people, Mr. President, in fighting against terrorism and for democratization of whole Middle East.

President Bush. Thank you, sir.

NOTE: The President spoke at 4:16 p.m. at the Waldorf-Astoria Hotel. President Talabani referred to Prime Minister Nuri al-Maliki of Iraq. A tape was not available for verification of the content of these remarks.

Statement on Senate Passage of the United States-Oman Free Trade Agreement
September 19, 2006

I commend the Senate for passing the U.S.-Oman free trade agreement, which will deliver benefits to both America and Oman. This agreement will level the playing field for U.S. workers and businesses, provide additional market access for U.S. goods, help Oman's leaders develop long-term opportunities for their people, and advance our shared goal of building a Middle East free trade area.

By strengthening our relations with a strategic friend and ally in the Middle East, this important agreement will also help protect America's national security interests.

I look forward to signing this legislation into law.

Statement on Senate Confirmation of Alice S. Fisher as Assistant Attorney General for the Criminal Division at the Department of Justice
September 19, 2006

I am pleased that the Senate acted today to confirm Alice S. Fisher as Assistant Attorney General for the Criminal Division at the Department of Justice.

Alice is a talented and effective public servant. As Acting Assistant Attorney General, she has led hundreds of DOJ attorneys and other staff in their efforts to combat terrorism, gang violence, drug trafficking, corruption, fraud, and crimes against children. I am confident she will continue to dedicate herself to keeping Americans safe from crime and bringing those who violate our laws to justice.

I continue to encourage the Senate to provide all of my nominees a prompt up-or-down vote.

Remarks Following Discussions With President Mahmoud Abbas of the Palestinian Authority in New York City
September 20, 2006

President Bush. Mr. President, thank you for coming. Yesterday in my speech to the United Nations, I said that you're a man of peace who believes in a two-state solution. And after our conversation today, once again you confirmed that.

I, too, believe that the best way to bring peace to the Holy Land is for two democratic states living side by side in peace. I said in my speech yesterday that the Palestinian state must have territorial integrity. I firmly believe that. I also said in my speech that the—one of the great objectives of my administration is to achieve this vision. I fully understand that in order to achieve this vision, there must be leaders willing to speak out and act on behalf of people who yearn for peace, and you are such a leader, Mr. President.

I can't thank you enough for the courage you have shown. I assure you that our Government wants to work with you in order— so that you're able—capable of delivering the vision that so many Palestinians long for, and that is a society in which they can raise their children in peace and hope. And I know that society is possible. And I appreciate your vision along those lines.

So, welcome to Washington, DC [the United States]°; I think this is our fifth visit. Every time, I've left our visits inspired by your vision.

President Abbas. Mr. President, thank you very much. I'm honored to meet with you, as you said, for the fifth time during these past years.

First of all, I would like to thank you greatly for the wonderful speech that you have delivered yesterday before the United Nations, and talk about the Palestinian issues and your vision of two states, and you adopt this vision. Mr. President, you are the first American President to adopt the vision of two states living side by side.

Of course, I've talked with the President about the situation in the Palestinian Territories and the difficulties that the Palestinian people are facing, as well as the possible solution that can get us out of these difficulties. And I mentioned to the President that more than 70 percent of the Palestinian population, they believe in the two-state solution, a state of Palestine and a state of Israel living in peace and security next to each other. That means that the Palestinian people desire peace, and there is no power on Earth that can prevent the Palestinian people from moving toward the peaceful solution and living and coexisting in peace.

Of course, we look forward to activate the various plans and various resolutions and the roadmap in order to be in a position to reach, with our neighbors, the desired objectives.

We always, Mr. President—we look forward to your support and your help and your aid, because we are in dire need for your help and support. Mr. President, we will always be faithful and truthful to peace, and we will not disappoint you.

President Bush. Thank you, sir. Thank you very much.

° White House correction.

NOTE: The President spoke at 10:33 a.m. at the Waldorf-Astoria Hotel. President Abbas spoke in Arabic, and his remarks were translated by an interpreter.

Statement on the Creation of the United States-China Strategic Economic Dialogue
September 20, 2006

I am pleased to welcome the creation of the Strategic Economic Dialogue between the United States and China. My leading economic adviser, Secretary of the Treasury Henry Paulson, will chair the U.S. side of the dialog, with support from Allan Hubbard, the Director of my National Economic Council. Deborah Lehr will serve as Secretary Paulson's special envoy to the dialog. President Hu and I agree on the importance of maintaining strong and mutually beneficial U.S.-China economic relations and on the need to establish an overarching bilateral economic framework between our two countries. The Strategic Economic Dialogue will help us achieve those objectives.

The economies of the United States and China have been engines of global growth. We must ensure that citizens of both countries benefit equitably from our growing economic relationship and that we work together to address economic challenges and opportunities.

Letter to the Speaker of the House of Representatives Transmitting Budget Amendments for the Federal Coordinator for Gulf Coast Rebuilding Office
September 20, 2006

Dear Mr. Speaker:

I ask the Congress to consider the enclosed FY 2007 Budget amendments for the Federal Coordinator for Gulf Coast Rebuilding Office in the Department of Homeland Security. The total discretionary budget authority in my FY 2007 Budget would not be increased by this request.

The details of this proposal are set forth in the enclosed letter from the Director of the Office of Management and Budget.

Sincerely,

GEORGE W. BUSH

Remarks at a Reception for Congressional Candidate Gus Bilirakis in Tampa, Florida
September 21, 2006

Gus, thanks. There's nothing wrong with a son following in his father's footsteps, particularly when you've got such a good son as Gus Bilirakis. [*Laughter*] He's the right man for the United States Congress, and I appreciate you all coming to support him.

I've been looking for Brother. [*Laughter*] He claims he's working. [*Laughter*] But I know he sends his best. He, like me, recognizes that Gus is the right man to serve you in the United States Congress. He really is. He's a good, decent, honorable, family-oriented man who will represent the interests of the folks down here. So Jeb sends his best.

But more importantly, so does Laura. [*Laughter*] Like me, Gus married well—

[*laughter*]—and it was my privilege to meet Eva and the four boys who are here. It's good to see you guys. Thanks for coming. Thanks for helping Dad get elected. He's going to need your help putting up those signs. And he's going to need the help of a family standing with him. And that's why it's important to have people who go to Washington, DC, who have prioritized their families. And the Bilirakis is a family-oriented group of folks. They understand that families are important for a stable society, and I'm proud to be here with Gus and all his friends.

Thank you all for coming. It's not easy to have a fundraiser this successful, it really isn't. And I know how much work it took, Gus, to convince this many people for coming. It's a good sign when you're running for Congress, Gus, and you get this many people to stand up and say, "We're willing to help you." And for those of you who have given, thanks. And for those of you who wonder if there's still more to do, there is. And so I urge you to think about putting up signs and getting on the telephone and turning out the votes. Go to your churches and places of worship, community centers, and remind people, when you've got somebody who is honest and decent and who shares the values of the people in Tampa, vote for him and send him to Washington, DC.

We not only married well, we share something else in common: We've got strong-willed mothers. [*Laughter*] And I'm glad to be here with Evelyn. The only difference between Ms. Bilirakis and my mother is, my mother's hair is white. [*Laughter*] Both of them speak their mind. As a matter of fact, when I ran into Miss Bilirakis earlier, she said to me—this is in Washington—she says, "My boy is running, and you get down there and help him as quickly as you can." [*Laughter*] Isn't that right? [*Laughter*] I'm proud to be with you. And thanks for serving. You married a good man. He served this district well, as will his son.

I'm proud to be here with Congresswoman Katherine Harris, running for the United States Senate. I want to thank Bing Kearney, who is the event chairman, and all the organizers. Appreciate you coming. Thanks for your help.

I'm looking forward to the campaign. I'm looking forward to reminding the American people there are significant differences in between what our party believes and what the other party believes. If there's a—it's easy to tell us apart. And the first place you can start is looking at taxes. There's a fundamental difference in this campaign and campaigns all across the country about who best to spend your money. We believe that the best people to spend your money is you. We believe that once you set priorities, it's important to have money in their pocket, because we know that when you save, invest, and spend, it helps this economy grow.

And so working with Members of the United States Congress, we passed the largest tax relief since Ronald Reagan was the President. We cut the taxes on everybody who pays income taxes. We doubled the child credit. We reduced the marriage penalty. We didn't think it made sense, by the way, to penalize marriage. We think in society, you ought to encourage marriage.

We cut the taxes on capital and—capital gains and dividends to encourage investment. We understand the role of Government is not to create wealth but to create an environment in which the entrepreneurial spirit flourishes. We put the death tax on the road to extinction, because we want to help our small businesses and farmers. There should be no doubt in anybody's mind where we stand on cutting taxes.

And the Democrats in Washington have got a record of their own, and there should be no doubt in anybody's mind where they stand. When we first cut taxes back in 2001 to get this economy going, when we cut taxes to recover from a recession, when we cut taxes to make sure we recovered from a corporate scandal, almost 85 percent of the House Democrats voted against it. When we cut taxes in 2003, nearly 95 percent of the House Democrats voted against you having more money in your pocket. And when we extended the key tax cuts earlier this year, more than 92 percent of the House Democrats voted against it. I think you're beginning to get a drift of their philosophy about your money.

One leading Democrat predicted this: He said the tax cuts would do nothing to create jobs. That's what they were saying when we said we were going to cut the taxes on the small-business owners and the working people to make sure you had more money in your pocket, which would stimulate job growth. And one of the leaders said, "No, that's not going to do anything to create jobs." Well, since those words were uttered in May of 2003, our economy has added nearly 5.7 million new jobs. That's more jobs than Canada, France, Germany, Great Britain, Italy, Japan, all put together. This economy is strong because of progrowth economic policies.

You see, what our opponents don't understand is that the economy grows when you control more of your own money. The tax cuts we passed put more than a trillion dollars in the hands of American workers and families and businesses. And you used that money to help us become a strong economy, the world leader.

And now we've got a choice to make, and that's what elections are all about, giving the people clear choices. Do you want to keep your taxes low so we can keep the economy growing, or do we raise taxes and let the politicians in Washington try to grow the economy?

Gus has made his position clear, and so have I. We're going to let you keep more of your own money. But the Democrats have made their position clear too. I want you to remember, the last time they had control of the United States Congress back in 1993, they passed a massive tax increase. In the 13 years since then, they've worked

hard to sustain their record as the party of high taxes.

A majority of House Democrats have voted against reducing the marriage penalty not once, not twice, but 26 times. It's a clear record. A majority of House Democrats have voted against a higher child tax credit 19 times. It's a clear record. If they get control of the House of Representatives, they'll raise your taxes, and it will hurt our economy, and that's why we're not going to let them get control of the House of Representatives—and elect people like Gus Bilirakis.

Just this week, the top Democrat on the House tax-writing committee said this—it's important for the American people to know there's a difference in point of view; they just think differently, got different philosophies about to do—what to do with your money. Here's what the top Democrat said on the committee that's going to write—determine what happens to your taxes. He said, "I can't think of one of our tax cuts that should be extended."

That's one way of saying, they're going to raise your taxes, because, you see, if you don't extend the tax cuts, your taxes go up. They may not call it a tax increase; they may want you to think something different. But if they don't extend the tax cuts that are set to expire, the working people, the small-business owners, those who are struggling to put food on the table for their families, the taxes are going to go up.

Now, they're going to say—they may not tell you they're going to raise your taxes. They're just going to say they're just going to let the tax relief expire. That's like a boss who came in and said, "You know something, I'm going to let your last pay raise expire." [*Laughter*] We're not going to let it happen. We're going to make it clear the differences between our desire to keep your taxes low and their desire to run your taxes up. Good economic policy says, we got plenty of taxes in Washington, DC; let's make sure the entrepreneurs and small businesses have enough money in their pocket to expand this job base so people can find work.

And I'm looking forward to talking about this until election day. I think it's a big issue. I think there are plenty of people across the country—Republicans, discerning Democrats, and wise independents—who understand they're paying plenty of taxes to Washington, DC. Oh, you'll hear this; they're going to say—and Gus, I'm sure you'll have to deal with this—they're going to say, "Look, we've got to raise your taxes to balance the budget." That's not the way Washington, DC, works. They will raise your taxes and figure out new ways to spend your money. The best way to balance the budget is to keep progrowth economic policies in place that are generating additional tax revenues into the Treasury and be wise about how we spend your money.

We've got to set clear priorities in Washington, DC, and the top priority is to make sure our troops will have what it takes to defend the United States of America.

There's a lot of issues. A lot of issues will be—I'll be working with Gus on. One issue, of course, is to make sure we diversify our energy supplies. We've got to make sure we get off of hydrocarbons as quickly as possible. But in the meantime, we'll be exploring for hydrocarbons, and we'll do so in an environmentally friendly way that protects the coast of the State of Florida. I told you that I would support reasonable limits, extended limits, about offshore drilling, and I've kept my word to the Governor. I've kept my word to the people of Florida, and I'm going to continue working with this Congressman to make sure that we have good, sane energy policy.

I'm going to continue to work with this Congressman-to-be on making sure seniors have got prescription drugs that they can afford. You might remember, before I came into Washington, DC, Medicare was an important policy, but it was growing tired and old. Medicine was changing—there's a lot of doctors out here who know what I'm talking about—Medicare wasn't changing with it. It was a system that just simply wasn't meeting the needs of our seniors. So I said to Congress, "Why don't we modernize Medicare; why don't we make sure that our seniors have got prescription drug coverage as a part of a modern Medicare system."

We worked hard; we got the legislation out. And now I'm going to make sure we work with the United States Congress, the new Congress after this election, to make sure the Medicare reforms we put in place that are benefiting seniors of all political parties all across the Nation don't get watered down by people who think the best way to run medicine is to have the Federal Government make every single decision.

I'm looking forward to working with Gus Bilirakis to make sure the good reforms we put in place to make sure every child gets a good education stays there. The No Child Left Behind Act is making a significant difference for the United States of America, and Congressman, I look forward to working with you on its reauthorization.

And I'm looking forward to working with this good man to keep the peace. This is a nation at war. And we've got to have people in the United States Congress who see the world the way it is, not the way we would like it to be. We can't afford to not be realistic about the world in which we live. The stakes are too high. There's an enemy that still wants to attack us. I wish I could report otherwise, but that is not the reality of the world in which we live. And therefore, the most important job the Congressman will have—will—to join with other Members of Congress and the administration to protect the United States of America.

If somebody is—associated with Al Qaida is making a phone call into the United States of America, we want to know why, so we can protect the United States against further attack. If somebody associated with terrorism is moving money around, we need to know why, so we can protect the

United States of America from attack. If there are walls that make it hard for intelligence gatherers and those charged with protecting this country, make it hard for them to communicate, we want to tear down those walls so we can protect the United States of America from attack. Our most important job in Washington is to protect you, and we'll do everything we can.

I remind people that the enemy has got to be right once, and we got to be right 100 percent of the time in order to protect us. So the best way to protect the United States of America is to stay on the offense and bring the enemy to justice before they come here and hurt us in America.

And that's exactly what we're doing. Every day, you just need to know, some of America's finest folks are on the offense. We're running down every lead possible. It's hard to plot and plan attacks against the United States when you're on the run. I need Members of Congress who understand that you can't negotiate with these folks; you can't hope that they change their mind; that the best way to protect the American people is to defeat them overseas so we do not have to face them here at home.

And the central front on this war on terror is Iraq. Now, I know some Americans say, "Well, it's not associated with the war on terror." Well, all I ask them to do is listen to what Usama bin Laden says when he calls Iraq the third—world war III. All I ask is that our fellow citizens be realistic about the world and listen to the words of senior Al Qaida when they say our objective is to—their objective is to run us out of the Middle East so they can topple moderate governments, so they could have energy resources at their disposal to inflict economic damage on those of us who refuse to kowtow to their demands, run us out of the Middle East so that they could achieve one of their objectives, which is the destruction of our close ally Israel.

Iraq is a central front in this war on terror, and we've got a plan to defeat the enemy. And it starts with answering to the will of 12 million brave Iraqis who said, when given a chance to vote, "We want to be free."

There's big debate about Saddam Hussein. My view is today as it was then; he was a threat. You see, after 9/11, we had to take threats seriously before they came home to hurt us. In order to protect this country—if you think the most important obligation of the Federal Government is to protect the country, then you must recognize that we do two things. One, if we find somebody harboring terrorists, we hold them to account, and we've got to take threats seriously before they come home to hurt us. Saddam Hussein was a threat.

And don't let people rewrite the history of the way the world was. He was a state sponsor of terror. He paid family of suiciders. He had attacked his neighbors. He had used weapons of mass destruction. He was a sworn enemy of the United States of America. And he had been given ample time to disclose, disarm, or face serious consequences by over a dozen United Nations Security Council resolutions. Getting rid of Saddam Hussein was the right thing to do, and the world is peaceful because of it. The world is more peaceful because of it.

And the world will be more peaceful when democracy takes hold in Iraq. And it's hard work. It's hard work because Al Qaida understands that democracies in the Middle East defeat their ideological vision of an extremist caliphate. It's hard because Saddamists are upset that they're no longer in power. It's hard because people are taking revenge for past history. But it's necessary work. It's necessary for our security.

If we were to leave before the mission was done, what kind of signal would that send to the extremists and radicals who want to harm either the United States or our close allies? What kind of signal would it send to the reformers and dreamers of a better life, that the United States has lost its will? What kind of signal would it send to those who count on the United States for its leadership? Our credibility would be damaged. Our enemies would be emboldened.

We're constantly changing tactics, but our strategy has not changed. We will help the Iraqis build a military where they can defend their freedom. We will help them build the institutions necessary for a free society to work. We will do our job and stand by the people of Iraq, and the world will be better for it when democracy takes hold.

You know, people ask me all the time—people ask me all the time, you know—they say, "What do you mean, when democracy takes hold? Do you think—really think people in the Middle East want to be free?" And the answer is, absolutely. We believe in the United States and the universality of freedom. I personally believe there's an Almighty, and I think a great gift from that Almighty is the desire in everybody's soul to be free. I'm not talking about just American Methodists. I believe in everybody's soul is the desire to be free. And I know that when you look at history, liberty has got the capacity to defeat resentment and ideologies of hate.

You know, one of the stories I like to share with people is my experience with the Prime Minister of Japan, Prime Minister Koizumi. You might remember, I had an interesting trip. [*Laughter*] He and I went down to Elvis's place. [*Laughter*] Went down there for a couple of reasons: One, I had never been to Elvis's place, and I'd like to go, you know. I thought it would be kind of fun. [*Laughter*] More importantly, he wanted to go. [*Laughter*] He loves Elvis. [*Laughter*] He can sing all the songs, you know—[*laughter*]—collects the memorabilia.

But I also wanted to send a signal to the American people about what's possible when liberty takes hold. A fellow came through the line recently here, and he said,

"My grandfather served on the USS *San Jacinto* with your dad." They were in the Pacific Ocean, young guys who had been called into action because the Japanese had attacked us, and we were in a brutal war with Japan—a really tough war.

The hatred for—of America for Japan was intense, and so intense, you can imagine how people would react if somebody had stood up and said, "I predict, someday, an American President and the Japanese Prime Minister would be going to, you know, a singer's house." [*Laughter*] They would have run him out of town, probably, you know. [*Laughter*]

But that's, in fact, what happened. And when we were on the airplane going down from Washington to Memphis, we were talking about keeping the peace. The Prime Minister of a country with which we were at war, a brutal war—young kids went off and never came home, unbelievable devastation and destruction in that war, a war ended by massive bombing—the Prime Minister of that country and the President of the United States were talking about peace. We were talking about North Korea, what we could do together to keep the peace. We were talking about the need to help this young democracy in the heart of the Middle East succeed so it could defeat an ideology of hatred. We were talking about how democracy has got the capacity to defeat the conditions that create resentment and hopelessness that cause young men to decide to become suicide bombers.

It's an amazing lesson of history, isn't it? It strikes me as so ironic, in a way, that my dad fought the Japanese, and his son sits down with the Prime Minister of the same country to keep the peace. What happened was, Japan adopted a Japanese-style democracy. Liberty has got the unbelievable capacity to convert enemies into allies, to change nations from hopelessness to hope. Someday, an American President will be sitting down talking to duly elected leaders of the Middle East about how to keep the peace, and a generation of American children will be better off for it.

And those are the stakes. We're in the great ideological struggle of the 21st century. It's a struggle playing out now in the Middle East between decent, honorable people who want something better for their children than war and turbulence versus extremists and radicals who use terrorism and murder to create fear. And the United States must lead in this ideological struggle to achieve the peace we all want.

And so I'm proud to stand with a man who sees the world the way it is; a person who understands that this great country has got responsibilities not only to protect our-selves but responsibilities to lay the foundation for peace for generations to come.

It's an exciting time to be representing the greatest nation on the face of the Earth. You'll like it up there, Gus. [*Laughter*] And I hope you all work hard to make sure he gets there. Thanks for coming. May God bless you.

NOTE: The President spoke at 1:36 p.m. at Raymond James Stadium. In his remarks, he referred to Gov. Jeb Bush of Florida; Usama bin Laden, leader of the Al Qaida terrorist organization; and former President Saddam Hussein of Iraq.

Remarks on Senate Action on Military Commissions Legislation in Orlando, Florida
September 21, 2006

I want to thank the Members of the United States Senate for working with my administration to meet our top legislative priority, and that is a law that will help us crack the terror network and to save American lives.

I had a single test for the pending legislation, and that's this: Would the CIA operators tell me whether they could go forward with the program, that is a program to question detainees to be able to get information to protect the American people? I'm pleased to say that this agreement preserves the most single—most potent tool we have in protecting America and foiling terrorist attacks, and that is the CIA program to question the world's most dangerous terrorists and to get their secrets.

The measure also creates military commissions that will bring these ruthless killers to justice. In short, the agreement clears the way to do what the American people expect us to do: to capture terrorists, to detain terrorists, to question terrorists, and then to try them. I hope the Congress will send me legislation before it wraps up their business next week.

Thank you.

NOTE: The President spoke at 5:04 p.m. at the Ritz-Carlton Orlando. In his remarks, he referred to S. 3930. The Office of the Press Secretary also released a Spanish language transcript of these remarks.

Remarks at a Reception for Gubernatorial Candidate Charles J. Crist, Jr., and the Republican Party of Florida in Orlando
September 21, 2006

The President. Thank you all. Thanks for coming. I appreciate you all being here. Thanks for your time. From "Chalkboard Charlie" to "Governor Charlie." Thanks for helping this good man. He's a good, decent man. He's had plenty of experience. He knows what he needs to do. He's been the commissioner of education; he's been your attorney general; he's been a State senator. He's the right guy for the job, and I want to thank you very much for standing strong when you find somebody who is decent and honorable, willing to serve the State of Florida, and that's Charlie Crist.

And you're right, Charlie, you're following a good man. He's made our family proud. But more importantly, he's done a fine job for the people of Florida. He's the kind of guy—[*applause*]—and, Charlie, I know you'll follow this example about you—he doesn't need a poll or a focus group to tell him what to think.

And that's what is necessary to make the hard decisions when you're the chief executive officer of a State, or in my case, the United States. I'm proud to be here with Charlie. I know something about being a Governor; I was one once. It requires a man with vision and a person who knows how to set the right priorities for a State. There's no doubt in my mind Charlie Crist will make a great Governor for the State of Florida, and I want to thank you for helping him.

And my wife feels the same way. If you were smart, Charlie, you'd get Laura down here to campaign for you. She sends her love; she sends her love to Jeb; and she sends her love to our friends here in Florida. And we've got a lot of friends. We've been blessed in this great State to have made a lot of friends. And I want to thank all my buddies who were there when nobody thought we could win in 2000, and

then came back through in 2004. Now you're back in 2006, and I'm grateful. It's for a good cause.

I want to thank Jeff Kottkamp, the next Lieutenant Governor of the State of Florida, who is with us today. I, too, encourage you to vote for Katherine Harris for the United States Senate. Welcome, Katherine.

One of my long-time friends here in Orange County is a guy whose son made him famous—[*laughter*]—a while ago. You might remember the incident. I was up there giving one of my best speeches. [*Laughter*] I was putting 100 percent into it. I thought I had the crowd on their feet, until I looked behind me. And Crotty's son was sound asleep. [*Laughter*] So, Crotty, you tell him, stay awake the next time he comes to one of these things. It kind of hurts an old guy's feelings. But I'm glad to be here with Rich Crotty. He's doing a fine job in Orange County.

I want to thank all the other State and local officials who are here. I want to thank the party activists who are here, starting with Carole Jean Jordan, who is the chairman of the Republican Party of Florida, and my friend Al Austin, who is the finance chairman of the Republican Party of Florida.

And raising money is one thing, and tonight is an extraordinarily successful event, and I thank you. I know it takes a lot to organize one of these events, and you've done a marvelous job. But I also want to remind you, in order for Charlie to win, he's going to need people to put up the signs and make the phone calls and stuff the envelopes—those quiet heroes of grassroots politics. So for those of you who have been involved with grassroots politics here in Florida, thank you for what you have done and thank you for what you're going to do to help this good man get elected Governor of the State of Florida.

You know, it's—one of the big issues that faces our country and your State is the issue of taxes. I think you're taxed too much; so does Charlie. And I think there's going to be a clear difference in this race, and there's certainly a clear difference nationally. You know, the—we share a philosophy, and that is, the role of Government is not to try to create wealth, but the role of Government is to create an environment in which the entrepreneurial spirit flourishes and which small businesses can grow to be big businesses. It's an environment in which people get to keep their own money. And the fundamental question facing this Nation and this State is, who best to spend your money? We believe the best people to spend your money is you.

The Democrats believe they can spend it better than you can.

Audience members. Noo!

The President. And it's a fundamental, philosophical difference. I aim to make taxes a key issue across this country, and we've got a good record on taxes, and so does Brother Jeb, and so will Governor Crist.

I was proud to sign the largest tax relief since Ronald Reagan was President of the United States. I did so because I felt we had enough money to spend on your behalf in Washington, DC, and I knew that if you had more money in your pocket to save, invest, or spend, this economy would grow.

There's a fundamental difference in Washington. When we cut the taxes on child care, most Democrats voted against— on the child credit, most Democrats voted against it. We tried to get rid of the marriage penalty. It's a simple concept, by the way. You shouldn't penalize marriage in the Tax Code; you ought to encourage—most Democrats voted against it. When we tried to get the death tax on the road to extinction, most Democrats voted against it. We've got a record of cutting taxes, and

they've got a record of opposing tax cuts. It's night and day. It is a clear example of the philosophical difference that divides Republicans and Democrats.

I remember in 2003 when we cut the taxes, one of the leading Democrats stood up and said, "Cutting taxes will do nothing to create jobs." Well, since that person uttered those famous words, our economy has added 5.7 million new jobs. This economy is strong.

This economy is strong because we let you have more of your own money, and we intend to keep it that way. Just the other day, a top Democrat—the top Democrat on the House tax writing committee—that's called the Ways and Means Committee; they'll be the people who decide whether or not your taxes go up or down—said this, "I can't think of one of our tax cuts that should be extended."

Now let me try to boil down Washington-speak for you. If the tax cuts are not extended, your taxes go up. It's kind of like an employer saying, you know, "I'm not going to extend your pay raise," see. And so if they're going to say, "Well, we're just not going to extend the tax cuts," that means they're going to run up your taxes. Running up your taxes would be wrong for our economy, and it would be wrong for the working families of the United States.

So I asked Charlie, I said, what's he making a priority? He said, "I'm making property taxes a priority in the State of Florida." You put him in office, he's going to cut your property taxes, and you can take that to the bank.

You know, we enacted some good legislation when it came to making sure our seniors have got good health care. You might remember, the Medicare program had gone a little stale. We would pay for surgeries but not for the prescription drugs that would prevent the surgery from being needed in the first place. And that didn't make any sense. My attitude is, if you're going to provide a service for our seniors, let's provide a good service.

And so we modernized Medicare, and today, the bills that seniors pay for prescription drugs is way down, and the days of seniors—poor seniors having to choose between food and medicine, those days are over. And I'm going to need a Governor, just like Jeb did, to make sure the modernization of this Medicare program is available for all of Florida's seniors.

When I was the Governor of Texas, I used to say, education is to the State what national defense is to the Federal Government. I think it's the most important priority of a State, is to make sure the public school system insists upon excellence for every single child. And that's what Charlie thinks too. That's why I called him "Chalkboard." [*Laughter*] He understands that a Governor, just like your Governor has done, needs to lead when it comes to challenging mediocrity when we find it in the public schools.

It's essential that our public schools work. It's essential that we set high standards and measure to make sure children are learning how to read and write and add and subtract. And if we find it early, we'll correct problems early so no child is left behind in America or in the State of Florida.

These are the issues that the people of Florida are going to have to decide upon, you know: taxes, fiscal sanity, making sure the health care system works, and making sure every single child gets educated. And I think if Floridians of all parties—or even if they're not of a party—pay attention to the debate, they'll find that Charlie Crist stands with them. He'll be a people's Governor. He likes to shake hands; he likes people. That's the kind of Governor you want. You want somebody who feels comfortable with the people of a State, somebody who can make decisions, and somebody who can set a clear vision on behalf of this vital State. And that's Charlie Crist.

I want to talk a little bit about the stakes of the world in which we live. We're at war. We're at war with a group of ideologues that use murder as a weapon to intimidate and create fear. I wish I could report otherwise.

I vowed after September the 11th, 2001, that I would use every one of our national assets in order to protect you. The most important job of any government in this day and age is to protect the American people from further attack. That starts with making sure our homeland is secure and making sure those on the frontline of protecting you have the tools necessary to be able to protect you. We have to find out what the enemy is thinking in order to stop attacks. If an Al Qaida or an Al Qaida associate is making a phone call into the United States, we need to know why in order to be able to protect you from further attacks.

If somebody is moving money around to finance a terrorist operation, we want to know why they're moving money around, to protect you. If the CIA and the FBI need to be able to share information to protect you, we need to make sure those walls are permanently torn down. In order to protect the United States of America, we must give those on the frontline that are protecting this Nation the tools necessary to do so within the Constitution of the United States, and that is precisely what this administration is doing.

But the facts are these: The enemy only has to be right one time to protect you— to hurt us, and we've got to be right 100 percent of the time to protect you, which means that the best way to protect the American people is to stay on the offense against these killers, defeat them overseas so we do not have to face them here at home, and bring them to justice before they hurt us again.

And that's exactly what the United States of America is doing, with a lot of other nations. We're keeping the pressure on them. It's hard to plot and plan when you're on the run. And that's what we have been doing for 5½ years, and that's what we will continue to do so long as I'm your

President. The most important job we have is to protect the American people.

You know, there's an enemy that still wants to strike. I mean, it should be clear to the American people, particularly after we recently, working with the Brits, foiled suicide attacks, bombing these airplanes when they're flying into the United States. These are ruthless people. You cannot negotiate with them; you can't hope that their ambitions go away; you can't try to—you know, therapy won't work. [*Laughter*] The only thing that matters is to bring them to justice. And make no mistake about it— [*applause*].

And so our strategy is twofold. On the one hand, we'll protect you by staying on the offense. But we've got another weapon beside a fantastic military and great intelligence people, and another weapon is liberty and freedom.

First, let me talk about the first part of our strategy. One is that when the President says something, he better mean it. And when I said, "If you harbor a terrorist, if you feed a terrorist or house a terrorist, you're equally as guilty as the terrorist, and you will be held to account." That's why we removed the Taliban that was providing safe haven for Al Qaida, from Afghanistan. Twenty-five million people now are free.

The second part of the strategy is, when you see a threat, you must take threats seriously before they come and hurt us in the United States. It's a different doctrine than we had in the past, but these threats are different than the threats we've had in the past.

I want to remind you that—what the world was like in 2001. In Iraq, there was a state sponsor of terror. There was a tyrant who brutalized his own people. This man was the sworn enemy of the United States of America. He paid suicide—families of suicide bombers to attack young democracies, for example. He had used weapons of mass destruction. He was a threat.

Now, before the President commits troops, he must try diplomacy. I want you to walk back in that period of time and remember resolution after resolution after resolution that came through the United Nations, and yet the tyrant didn't change his mind. Saddam Hussein chose war, and war he got, and the world is better off without Saddam Hussein in power.

And now Iraq is the central front on the war on terror. I hear people in the United States, "Well, that's not true." My advice to them is to listen carefully to the words of the enemy. Usama bin Laden has called Iraq world war III. He and Mr. Zawahiri, the number-two man in Al Qaida, have made it clear that their intention is to drive us out of Iraq. They want the death and suffering we see on our TV screens to cause us to abandon the 12 million people who said, "We want to be free."

And they want us to leave because they want to topple moderate governments in the region. They want to get a hold of oil resources. Imagine these radical jihadists, these extremists who've subverted a great religion, controlling oil. They would—they would love to create economic havoc on the United States of America. They have clearly stated their ambitions. The Commander in Chief must always take the words of the enemy seriously. And like them, I see Iraq as the central front in the war on terror, and unlike them, however, I refuse to yield to their barbarism. And we're going to stand strong with the 12 million Iraqis and help that young democracy survive for the sake of peace for our children and our grandchildren.

And it is hard work, but America has done this kind of work before. I believe we're in a great ideological struggle. It's the ideological struggle of the 21st century. On the one hand, you have reasonable people—moms who want their children to grow up in a peaceful world; decent people who can't stand terror and violence and who long to be free—versus ideologues, people bound together by a common philosophy who use murder as a weapon. These are the stakes of the 21st century.

And I'm confident we will prevail, because I believe that liberty, liberty and freedom have got the capacity to overcome the dark vision of these ideologues.

We've seen it happen in our history before. We have seen liberty triumph over hopelessness and despair. See, in the short run, we will stay on the offense, and we will help those brave souls who want to fight the enemy overseas so we don't have to face them here. In the long run, we will lay the foundation of peace for our children by spreading liberty.

Now, one way to make this point to you and to the American citizens is to remind people about an interesting experience that I just had, when I flew to Memphis, Tennessee, with the Prime Minister of Japan. Prime Minister Koizumi and I went to Elvis's place. [*Laughter*] It was an interesting experience. I chose to go for three reasons: One, I had never been to Elvis's place—[*laughter*]—and I thought that would be fun to do; plus, Laura wanted to go to Elvis's place. [*Laughter*] Secondly—and secondly, the Prime Minister wanted to go to Elvis's place—[*laughter*]—because he's a big Elvis fan. He loved Elvis Presley. Isn't that interesting? The Prime Minister of Japan thought Elvis was "It."

But I also wanted to make a point to the American citizens, and it's this: My dad, and many of your relatives, fought the Japanese. They were the sworn enemy of the United States of America. And yet his son had invited the Prime Minister of the former sworn enemy to travel to Elvis Presley's place. And on that plane going down there, we talked about peace. We talked about what we could do, working together, to deal with Kim Jong Il in North Korea. We talked about the fact that Japan had 1,000 of her troops alongside our brave troops in Iraq to help this young democracy defeat the forces of hatred. We talked about HIV/AIDS on the continent of Africa and how the United States and Japan can work together to save lives. We talked about feeding the hungry. We talked about

helping the fledgling democracy in Afghanistan survive against the Taliban's attempts to overthrow them.

Isn't it interesting? My dad fought the Japanese—or our dad fought the Japanese, and his son is now talking about the peace with the sworn enemy. Can you imagine somebody in 1948, after this terrible war, with all the hatred and bloodshed, standing up in front of the country and saying, "I predict an American President someday will be taking a leader of the sworn enemy to the singer's house." [*Laughter*] They would have run him out of town. [*Laughter*]

But it happened; it happened because Japan adopted a Japanese-style democracy. And the lesson of history is that liberty has got the capacity to change enemies into allies. Liberty has got the capacity to lay the foundation of peace. Someday, an American President will be sitting down with duly elected leaders in the Middle East talking about the peace, and a generation of Americans will be better off.

These are trying times for our country. We've got a lot of stuff going for us, though, you know. We've got a fantastic military. And I will assure you this, that our military will have whatever it takes to do their job and defend this country.

But we also have a lot of people who understand that liberty is not just an American concept. Liberty is universal. I personally believe there is an Almighty, and I believe that that Almighty's gift to each man and woman on the whole face of the Earth is the desire to be free. And I know that when people are able to realize that ambition, no matter what their religion, no matter where they live, the world will become a more peaceful place.

It's an honor to be the President of a country that has got such good values, determined country, a country that knows that history can repeat itself with perseverance and strength of character. No, these are challenging times, but out of these times will come a more secure America and a more peaceful world.

Thanks for helping Charlie. May God bless you all.

NOTE: The President spoke at 5:55 p.m. at the Ritz-Carlton Orlando. In his remarks, he referred to Gov. Jeb Bush of Florida; Mayor Richard T. Crotty of Orange County, FL, and his son, Tyler; former President Saddam Hussein of Iraq; Usama bin Laden, leader of the Al Qaida terrorist organization; and Chairman Kim Jong Il of North Korea.

Message on the Observance of Rosh Hashanah, 5767
September 21, 2006

I send greetings to those around the world celebrating Rosh Hashanah.

During these holy days, Jewish people begin the new year by answering the call of the Shofar and gathering in synagogues. It is a time to reflect on the past, celebrate the beginning of life, and welcome the promise of the future with a spirit of renewal and hope.

On this sacred holiday, I appreciate the Jewish people for your efforts to ensure that your values and traditions are passed on to future generations. As you begin the Days of Awe, your faith in the Almighty reminds us of the gift of religious freedom in our country and helps make the world a more hopeful place.

Laura and I send our best wishes for a peaceful Rosh Hashanah.

GEORGE W. BUSH

NOTE: An original was not available for verification of the content of this message.

Message to the Congress on Continuation of the National Emergency With Respect to Persons Who Commit, Threaten To Commit, or Support Terrorism
September 21, 2006

To the Congress of the United States:

Section 202(d) of the National Emergencies Act (50 U.S.C. 1622(d)) provides for the automatic termination of a national emergency unless, prior to the anniversary date of its declaration, the President publishes in the *Federal Register* and transmits to the Congress a notice stating that the emergency is to continue in effect beyond the anniversary date. In accordance with this provision, I have sent the enclosed notice to the *Federal Register* for publication, stating that the national emergency with respect to persons who commit, threaten to commit, or support terrorism is to continue in effect beyond September 23, 2006. The most recent notice continuing this emergency was published in the *Federal Register* on September 22, 2005 (70 *FR* 55703).

The crisis constituted by the grave acts of terrorism and threats of terrorism committed by foreign terrorists, including the terrorist attacks in New York, in Pennsylvania, and against the Pentagon of September 11, 2001, and the continuing and immediate threat of further attacks on United States nationals or the United States that led to the declaration of a national emergency on September 23, 2001, has not been resolved. These actions pose a continuing unusual and extraordinary threat to the national security, foreign policy, and economy of the United States. For these reasons, I have determined that it is necessary to continue the national emergency declared with respect to persons who commit, threaten to commit, or support terrorism, and maintain in force the comprehensive sanctions to respond to this threat.

GEORGE W. BUSH

The White House,
September 21, 2006.

NOTE: The notice is listed in Appendix D at the end of this volume.

Message on the Observance of Ramadan
September 21, 2006

I send greetings to the many Muslims observing Ramadan in America and around the world.

Ramadan is the holiest time of the Muslim year and an important holiday when Muslims take time for prayer, fasting, and personal sacrifice. According to Islamic teachings, this month represents when God delivered His word to the prophet Muhammad in the form of the Qur'an. Ramadan is also an opportunity to gather with friends and family and show thanks for God's blessings through works of charity.

Ramadan and the upcoming holiday seasons are a good time to remember the common values that bind us together. Our society is enriched by our Muslim citizens whose commitment to faith reminds us of the gift of religious freedom in our country.

Laura and I send our best wishes for a blessed Ramadan. Ramadan Mubarak.

GEORGE W. BUSH

NOTE: The transcript was released by the Office of the Press Secretary on September 22. An original was not available for verification of the content of this message.

The President's News Conference With President Pervez Musharraf of Pakistan
September 22, 2006

President Bush. Thank you very much. Please be seated. Laura and I appreciate the opportunity to welcome President and Mrs. Musharraf here to Washington. We remember fondly, Mr. President, your great hospitality in Pakistan, and we remember the importance of that visit. It reconfirmed our friendship, gave you and me a chance to discuss important issues. And there's no more important issue than defending our peoples.

This President is a strong defender of freedom and the people of Pakistan, and I appreciate your leadership.

President Musharraf. Thank you very much.

President Bush. He understands that we are in a struggle against extremists who will use terror as a weapon. He understands it just about as good as anybody in the world; after all, they've tried to take his life. These extremists, who can't stand the thought of a moderate leader leading an important country like Pakistan, want to kill the President. That should say things to the people of Pakistan and the people of America, that because he has been a strong, forceful leader, he has become a target of those who can't stand the thought of moderation prevailing.

I admire your leadership. I admire your courage. And I thank you very much for working on common strategies to protect our respective peoples.

We had a good discussion here today. We talked about how our intelligence cooperation can continue. I want to remind the people of Pakistan and the people of America that because of the good work of our intelligence forces and Pakistani intelligence forces, as we helped people in the United Kingdom, we prevented the loss of innocent life. That kind of cooperation is necessary in a world in which extremists and radicals are willing to kill to try to achieve political objectives.

We talked about the earthquake recovery, and our Nation was proud to support you, Mr. President, because we care when we see people suffering. And I was briefed by you and your administration when I was there, and I was impressed by the great organization and compassion shown for the Pakistani people by your Government. I hope all is going well, particularly for those who suffered mightily.

We talked about economic development and the need to move forward on a reconstruction opportunity zones as well as a bilateral investment treaty. In other words, our relationship is more than just helping to secure our respective homelands. Ours is a relationship that recognizes that through economic prosperity, people can embetter themselves.

We had a very interesting briefing on the federally administered tribal areas. The governor of the areas are with us here, and he briefed me and members of my national security team on the strategy to strengthen governance and to promote economic development.

We talked about education. The first time I ever met President Musharraf, he talked about the need to make sure that school systems in Pakistan worked well. I was impressed then and I'm impressed now by your commitment to an education system that prepares students for the—and gives students the skills necessary to compete in a global economy.

We talked about democracy. The last time I was with the President, he assured me and assured the people that were listening to the news conference that there would be free and fair elections in Pakistan in 2007. He renewed that commitment because he understands that the best way to defeat radicalism and extremism is to give people a chance to participate in the political process of a nation.

We talked about India in relations—and the President's relations with India. I was pleased to see that in Havana Prime Minister Singh and President Musharraf had another discussion. I think it's very important that the issue of Kashmir move forward and be resolved peacefully. And I appreciate your efforts, Mr. President.

We talked, of course, about Afghanistan. And President Musharraf and President Karzai and I will have dinner right here in the White House next week. And it's going to be an important discussion. It's going to be an important discussion because one of the most important avenues for peace is for Afghanistan to succeed. And it's in our mutual interests that we work together to help that country that's been devastated by war succeed. And so I'm looking forward to our trilateral discussion, Mr. President. It's going to be a good one, and it's going to be an interesting one. And it's an important discussion.

All in all, we've had yet another good meeting between people who are able to speak frankly with each other and people who share the common desire for our people to live in security and peace.

Welcome.

President Musharraf. Thank you very much. I would like to, first of all, express my gratitude, and also on behalf of my entire delegation, for the warmth and hospitality that we have received and many courtesies that are being extended to us since our arrival in the United States.

I had an excellent meeting with President Bush. We, first of all, reinforced our trust and confidence in each other. I trust President Bush, and I have total confidence in him that he desires well for Pakistan and for our region. And I trust him also that he's trying to do his best for bringing peace to the world. And I trust him also that he's trying to resolve the core issue of the Palestinian dispute.

We discussed the entire gambit of relations bilaterally between the United States and Pakistan and also in our region and on international issues. Bilaterally, we reinforced our desire to have this relationship on a long-term basis, broad-based, and a strategic relationship. When we are talking of broad-based, whatever the President has said, it involves all aspects which we discussed. It has its political and diplomatic aspects, which we reinforced, and then our desire to fight terrorism and succeed against terrorism.

Other than that issue, in the social sector, on the economy, how whatever assistance is being given to us, whatever assistance we require, our requests on that—especially in the field of trade and investment, which are the main areas which we require assistance in—otherwise, on a broad-based level, assistance in the education and health sector, on the defense side, the F–16 deals, all this was discussed.

On the regional issues, on the international plain, we did discuss the core issue of the Palestinian dispute, which needs to be resolved, and being at the core. And I am extremely glad that the President has a desire and a will to resolve this Palestinian dispute. I wish him very well because

that lies at the heart of all problems, even at the heart of terrorism and extremism.

On the regional side, in our region, we also discussed the rapprochement going on between Pakistan and India. And I proudly told the President that we had—I had an excellent meeting with Prime Minister Manmohan Singh in Havana. And it was a step forward towards resolution of disputes between India and Pakistan. I did tell him on the way forward that we are moving on the Kashmir dispute especially.

Coming on the other side, we had an in-depth discussion on what is happening in Afghanistan and our tribal agency. They are—I explained to him whatever we are doing in the form of the peace treaty that we have just signed through a grand jirga, which is an assembly of elders.

This treaty is not to deal with the Taliban; it is actually to fight the Taliban. The misperception in the media, I did clarify to the President. And may I very briefly say—and what I explained to the President—that this is a holistic approach that we are taking to fighting terrorism in Pakistan, in the tribal agencies of Pakistan. This is a political site of the holistic strategy—the holistic strategy being the military arm being used, a political element, an administrative element, and a reconstruction element.

So we want to move on all these aspects forward, confining myself to this deal. This deal is not at all with the Taliban; as I said, this is against the Taliban, actually. This deal is with the tribal elders of North Waziristan Agency. And the deal has three bottom lines which we fixed for ourselves. And this is very important, which I explained to the President.

Number one: There will be no Al Qaida activity in our tribal agency or across the border in Afghanistan. There will be no Taliban activity in our tribal agency or across in Afghanistan. There will be no Talibanization, which is an obscurantic thoughts or way of life—no Talibanization. So all these three have been agreed by the tribal elders who signed that deal. And when they signed the deal, they are honorbound—and they have a very strict honor code—to not only abide by it but also that whoever violates it, they'll move against them.

So this is, in brief, the deal which I explained to the President. And I know that he's satisfied with that deal. And maybe this shows the light or the way forward for bringing peace to the region.

So this is what we discussed holistically. I would like to conclude by saying we had a total understanding of views between President Bush and myself. And as I said, we reinforced our trust and confidence in each other. Thank you very much.

President Bush. Good job.

Two questions apiece. Deb [Deb Riechmann, Associated Press].

Pakistan's Role in the War on Terror

Q. Mr. President, after 9/11, would the United States have actually attacked Pakistan if President Musharraf had not agreed to cooperate with the war on terrorism? He says that the United States was threatening to bomb his country back into the Stone Age.

And, President Musharraf, would Pakistan have given up its backing of the Taliban if this threat had not come from Armitage?

President Bush. First, let me—she's asking about the Armitage thing. The first I've heard of this was when I read it in the newspaper today. You know, I was—I guess I was taken aback by the harshness of the words.

All I can tell you is, is that shortly after 9/11, Secretary Colin Powell came in and said, "President Musharraf understands the stakes, and he wants to join and help rout out an enemy that has come and killed 3,000 of our citizens." As a matter of fact, my recollection was that one of the first leaders to step up and say that the stakes have changed, that attack on America that killed 3,000 of the citizens needs to be

dealt with firmly, was the President. And if I'm not mistaken, Colin told us that, if not the night of September the 11th, shortly thereafter. Now, I need to make sure I get my facts straight, but it was soon.

I don't know of any conversation that was reported in the newspaper like that. I just don't know about it.

President Musharraf. I would like to— I am launching my book on the 25th, and I am honorbound to Simon and Schuster not to comment on the book before that day. [*Laughter*]

President Bush. In other words, buy the book, is what he's saying. [*Laughter*]

Islam/Religious Freedom

Q. My question is for the U.S. President. Your Excellency, President Musharraf has issued a call for building bridges and promoting interfaith harmony between the West and the Islamic world, which is in upheaval and in complete turmoil. So your comments of Islamic fascists and then the comments of the Pope have inflamed the Islamic world. And my question is that— would you take the leading role, along with President Musharraf, to build these bridges and promote interfaith harmony to avert any wrong notion of class of civilizations, sir?

President Bush. I appreciate the President's leadership in promoting harmony. There is unbelievable propaganda in the Middle East these days that try to inflame passion. The propagandists are attempting to create conditions where terror is justified. And so at my speech at the United Nations, I stood up and said loud and clear, America respects Islam. And we do. We don't respect people who kill in the name of Islam to achieve political objectives, like the terrorists do.

As a matter of fact, these extremists exploit propaganda in order to justify their behavior. All of us need to step up and talk about a world in which we respect each other's religions. As a matter of fact, it's very important for Muslims around the world to know, there's a lot of Muslims living at peace here in the United States. They are proud Americans, and they're equal to me as a citizen. We respect their religions.

I repeat to you, however, that the free world and the moderate world must stand up to these extremists and not let them spread their hateful propaganda, not let them try to incite people to acts of violence, because these extremists are not only against Western people, they're also against moderate people. And the President is reaching out to help understand—the world to understand that the Muslim religion is a peaceful religion—is very important. And we can help, and we will help.

One way we can help is to work with the Palestinians and the Israelis to achieve peace. I'm the first President ever to have articulated a two-state solution. I believe a Palestinian state, as a democracy living side by side with Israel, will yield the peace. What's important is for people to understand that in order to have that peace and that Palestinian state, people have got to recognize Israel's right to exist in order for this to happen. You can't ask people to negotiate with people who say you shouldn't exist.

We will continue to give aid to people who suffer. We didn't ask the question whether—you know, what was the nature of the religion of the people who suffered in Pakistan when we spent a half a billion dollars to help this President. We said, they're suffering, and we want to help. And so we will continue to outreach.

It's important, however, for people in the Middle East to reject the extremist propaganda that is spreading, in many cases, absolute lies about the intentions of the United States. They love to say this is a war against Islam; I can't think of anything more false. These are moderate, reasonable people who reject extremism in order for there to be peace. And so I'll work hard to do my part. Thank you for that question.

Steve [Steve Holland, Reuters].

Usama bin Laden/Pakistan-U.S. Cooperation in the War on Terror

Q. Thank you, sir. There's been a back-and-forth this week over whether the U.S. needs permission to strike inside Pakistan if Usama bin Laden is located. Could each of you give your position on that? And did you—are you satisfied with his assurances on the tribal deal?

President Bush. Well, first of all, I appreciate the briefing on the tribal deal. When the President looks me in the eye and says, "The tribal deal is intended to reject the Talibanization of the people and that there won't be a Taliban and won't be Al Qaida," I believe him, you know. This is a person with whom I've now had close working relationships for 5½ years. And when he says, "If we find—when we find Usama bin Laden, he will be brought to justice," I believe him. And we'll let the tactics speak for themselves after it happens.

We're on the hunt together. It's in the President's interest that Al Qaida be brought to justice, and it's in our interest. And we collaborate and we strategize and we talk a lot about how best to do this.

Q. So you do have permission to go inside Pakistan?

President Bush. All I can tell you is, is that when Usama bin Laden is found, he will be brought to justice. And that's what we've continually discussed.

President Musharraf. May I add?

President Bush. Yes, please.

President Musharraf. I think, as the President said, we are on the hunt together against these people. Now why are we bothering—or how to—the semantics of the tactics of how to deal with the situation? We will deal with it. We are on the hunt together. You want the person—if at all we confront him, if at all we find out his location, we are quite clear what to do.

But let's not get involved in how it ought to be done, by whom it ought to be done. There's total coordination at the intelligence level between the two forces.

There's coordination at the operational level, at the strategic level, even at the tactical level. So therefore, we are working together, and when the situation arises, we need to pick the right decision to strike. That's how I——

President Bush. You probably don't want to let them know what we're thinking about anyway, do we?

President Musharraf. And may I also say that we need to have—ladies and gentlemen here, we have the pieces of—a relationship is trust and confidence. Now, if we don't have that trust and confidence in each other, and we think that we are bluffing each other—I don't think that's a good way of moving forward, anyway.

Kashmir/Situation in the Middle East

Q. Mr. President, I have two-part question. And first, I must—[*inaudible*]—the remarks which you gave at the outset about President Musharraf. And second is, Mr. President, in Pakistan, we cherish the idea of having strategic and long partnership with United States of America. But we found that there is—a discriminate reality is being followed by your great country pertaining to the—[*inaudible*]—of the nuclear technology for the peaceful purpose. Pakistan needs energy, and we have been denied of that. Could you ensure us that this discrimination will come to an end after this great meeting with President Musharraf?

And the second part of my question, Mr. President, is that President Musharraf has been asking resolution of the problem of Palestine and Kashmir for the sustainable peace in the world, especially in this part of the world. Aren't you going to contemplate—are you contemplating some step to take, some initiative to resolve these two problems?

And question for Mr. President is, is how far did——

President Musharraf. Three in one. [*Laughter*]

President Bush. If I ask him—then I'll remember yours.

Q. ——talk about these discussions with President Bush and the agenda, the item for which you are going to take up with the President of the United States, how far have you been successful? Thank you, sirs.

President Bush. Man, you represented the entire press corps there; that's good. [*Laughter*] We talked about energy, and we talked about our need to work through the recent history that we've had together on dealing with proliferation matters.

Secondly, in terms of Kashmir and Palestine, Kashmir issue will be solved when two leaders decide to solve it. And we want to help. The United States can't force nations to reach an agreement just because we want there to be an agreement. Lasting agreements occur when leaders of nations say, "Let's get the past behind us, and let's move forward."

I am encouraged by the meetings that the President and the Prime Minister of India have had. It is an indication that there is desire at the leadership level to solve this long-standing problem.

Leadership is also going to be required between Israel and Palestine. We, of course, can help and will help. But it's important for you to understand that we cannot impose peace. We can help create the conditions for peace to occur. We can lay out vision. We can talk to world leaders, and we do. We can provide aid to help institutional building so that a democracy can flourish.

But ultimately, peace, longstanding peace, depends upon the will of leaders. I'm impressed by this President's will to get something done in Kashmir. He and I have talked about this issue in the past. He has said he was going to reach out to the Prime Minister of India, and he has. And our hope is that this process continues forward.

I asked the President, just like I would ask the Prime Minister of India, what can we do to help? What would you like the United States to do to facilitate an agreement? Would you like us to get out of the way? Would you like us not to show up? Would you like us to be actively involved? How can we help you, if you so desire, achieve peace? And that's the role of the United States, as far as I'm concerned.

President Musharraf. Thank you. I think I've already answered. We've had far-reaching discussion encompassing bilateral issues, regional, and international. I think we have general consensus on all issues.

President Bush. Thank you, Mr. President. Good job.

President Musharraf. Thank you.

President Bush. Buy the book. [*Laughter*]

NOTE: The President's news conference began at 10:21 a.m. in the East Room at the White House. In his remarks, he referred to Sehba Musharraf, wife of President Musharraf; Prime Minister Manmohan Singh of India; President Hamid Karzai of Afghanistan; and former Deputy Secretary of State Richard L. Armitage.

Statement on Senate Confirmation of Kenneth L. Wainstein as Assistant Attorney General for National Security at the Department of Justice
September 22, 2006

I am pleased the Senate has confirmed Kenneth Wainstein as the first Assistant Attorney General for National Security at the Department of Justice. As head of this new division, Ken will bring together our national security, counterterrorism, counterespionage, and foreign intelligence surveillance litigation under one Assistant Attorney General. Ken is an effective leader, who will play an important role in our efforts to combat terrorism.

Ken's confirmation fulfills one of the critical recommendations of the WMD Commission and further strengthens our ability to protect all Americans.

I urge the Senate to give all my nominees a prompt up-or-down vote.

The President's Radio Address
September 23, 2006

Good morning. This week, I traveled to New York City to address the United Nations General Assembly. In my speech to the leaders gathered there, I spoke about a more hopeful world that is within our reach, a world beyond terror, where ordinary men and women are free to determine their own destiny, where the voices of moderation are empowered, and where the extremists are marginalized by the peaceful majority.

I said that every nation must make a choice: We can support the moderates and reformers working for change across the broader Middle East, or we can yield the future to the terrorists and extremists. America has made its choice: We're standing with the moderates and reformers.

In New York, I met with two such leaders, President Talabani of Iraq and President Abbas of the Palestinian Authority. In my meeting with President Talabani, I told him that America will continue to support Iraq's democratic Government as it makes the tough decisions necessary to bring security and prosperity to the Iraqi people. I assured President Talabani that America will not abandon the Iraqi people in their struggle to defeat the terrorists and build a free society in the heart of the Middle East.

In my meeting with President Abbas, I told him that America remains committed to the vision of two democratic states, Israel and Palestine, living side by side in peace and security. President Abbas shares this goal. He's working hard to oppose violent extremists and build a society in which the Palestinian people can raise their children in peace and hope. By supporting moderate leaders such as President Abbas, the United States can help Israelis and Palestinians build a more hopeful future and achieve the peace we all want in the Holy Land.

Next week I will host a meeting at the White House with two courageous leaders, President Karzai of Afghanistan and President Musharraf of Pakistan. These two leaders are working to defeat the forces of terrorism and extremism. Under President Musharraf, Pakistan is siding with the forces of freedom and moderation and helping to defend the civilized world. Many Pakistani forces have given their lives in the fight against terrorists. President Musharraf understands the stakes in the war on terror because the extremists have tried more than once to assassinate him. They know he's a threat to their aspirations because he's working to build modern democratic institutions that could provide an alternative to radicalism. And it is in America's interest to help him succeed.

In Afghanistan, President Karzai continues the work of building a safer and brighter future for his nation. Today, forces from more than 40 countries, including members of the NATO alliance, are bravely serving side by side with Afghan forces. These forces are fighting the extremists who want to bring down the free Government that the people of Afghanistan have established. America and its allies will continue to stand with the people of Afghanistan as they defend their democratic gains. Working with President Karzai's Government, we will defeat the enemies of a free Afghanistan and help the Afghan people build a nation that will never again oppress them or be a safe haven for terrorists.

In the broader Middle East, the world faces a straightforward choice: We can allow that region to continue on the course it was headed before September the 11th, and a generation from now, our children will face a region dominated by terrorist states and radical dictators armed with nuclear weapons; or we can stop that from happening by confronting the ideology of hate and helping the people of the Middle East build a future of hope. All civilized nations, especially those in the Muslim world, are bound together in this struggle between moderation and extremism. By working together, we will roll back this grave threat to our way of life, we will help the people of the Middle East claim their freedom, and we will leave a safer and more hopeful world for our children and grandchildren.

Thank you for listening.

NOTE: The address was recorded at 7:50 a.m. on September 22 in the Cabinet Room at the White House for broadcast at 10:06 a.m. on September 23. The transcript was made available by the Office of the Press Secretary on September 22 but was embargoed for release until the broadcast. The Office of the Press Secretary also released a Spanish language transcript of this address.

Remarks Following a Meeting With Business Leaders on the U.S.-Lebanon Partnership Fund
September 25, 2006

I've just had a fascinating discussion with four business leaders and members of my administration, all of whom are strategizing on how to help the good people of Lebanon recover from the recent crisis.

Our goal and our mission is to help Lebanese citizens and Lebanese businesses not only recover but to flourish, because we believe strongly in the concept of a democracy in Lebanon. Right from the beginning of the crisis, I had stated that our objective is to help the Siniora Government—the Siniora Government, which is a democratically elected government. And now we've got generous citizens of the United States, people who are very busy in their own right, who are willing to step forward and to strategize and raise monies to help people in Lebanon.

And this is a very important mission for our country. It's a public/private partnership. Our Federal Government has committed $250 million; OPEC [OPIC],* under Chairman Mosbacher's lead, has arranged financing. And now private sector individuals and businesses will work together to send a clear message to the Lebanese people: We care about you; we want you to live in a free society; we've got great hopes for you; we believe in your Prime Minister, Prime Minister Siniora; and we will back up our words with actions.

So I appreciate John Chambers, who has taken the lead for this group, and I appreciate you all taking time to go over to Lebanon and show the face of America. We're a compassionate people; we care when people suffer; and we care about the type of governments that people live under. And we strongly support the young democracies in the Middle East; we support the democracy of Lebanon; we support the democracy of Iraq. And our dream is one day for there to be a Palestinian democracy living side by side in peace with Israel.

Thank you all very much for your commitment. May God bless the good people of Lebanon. Thank you.

NOTE: The President spoke at 9:38 a.m. in the Oval Office at the White House. In his remarks, he referred to John T. Chambers, president and chief executive officer, Cisco Systems, Inc.

Remarks Following a Tour of Meyer Tool, Inc., in Cincinnati, Ohio
September 25, 2006

I've come to this company because, first of all, I like to honor the entrepreneurial spirit. We've got a father and a son who are running this company and making sure of two things: One, they're on the leading edge of technological change, and two, they got a workforce that is trained and prepared to be able to provide product.

This is a company that has benefited from the tax cuts. They've increased their employment by about 125 over the past 12 months. They've expanded because of the bonus depreciation schedule; in other words, the tax cuts encouraged them to buy equipment, and when you buy equipment, you expand your business. Plus, this

---

* White House correction.

is a company that benefited from the cut in the individual income tax rates; this is a subchapter S.

This economy of ours is strong. And one of the main reasons it's strong is because of the tax cuts that we passed. And the fundamental question facing the country is, will we keep taxes low? Some have advocated that we ought to raise taxes on individuals, which would take money out of the pockets of this company. And if you take money out of the treasury of this company, it means it's less likely somebody is going to find work. So I think we ought to keep taxes low so companies like this can continue to expand and grow.

This is an important debate facing the United States of America. I believe that small businesses are the backbone to economic vitality. I know that most new jobs are created by small businesses just like this one, and I know the tax cuts we passed have helped this small business expand. Congress needs to make the tax cuts we passed permanent so these entrepreneurs can plan. You hear people say, "Well, we're not going to extend the tax cuts," that means they're going to raise taxes on the small business just like this one. And it's bad economic policy, and it will be bad for our country.

Anyway, I want to thank you all for letting us join you. I'm impressed by your company. I know your workforce is vibrant, growing, well trained. I know you know that you couldn't be doing what you're doing without a good workforce. So I want to thank you for taking care of them as well. Thank you.

NOTE: The President spoke at 4:22 p.m. In his remarks, he referred to Arlyn Easton, president and principal owner, and Beau Easton, director of continuous improvement, Meyer Tool, Inc. The Office of the Press Secretary also released a Spanish language transcript of these remarks.

Remarks on Signing the Federal Funding Accountability and Transparency Act of 2006
September 26, 2006

The President. Thank you, and sit down. Please be seated, except for you all. [*Laughter*] Welcome. Every April, Americans sit down and fill out their tax returns, and they find out how much of their hard-earned money is coming here to Washington. Once the tax dollars arrive here, most Americans have little idea of where the money goes, and today our Government is taking steps to change that. We believed that the more we inform our American citizens, the better our Government will be.

And so in a few moments, I'll sign the Federal Funding Accountability and Transparency Act of 2006. This bill is going to create a web site that will list the Federal Government's grants and contracts. It's going to be a web site that the average citizen can access and use. It will allow Americans to log onto the Internet just to see how your money is being spent. This bill will increase accountability and reduce incentives for wasteful spending. I am proud to sign it into law, and I am proud to be with members of both political parties who worked hard to get this bill to my desk.

This has been a good effort by concerned Members of the House and the Senate to say to the American people, "We want to earn your trust; when we spend your money, we want you to be able to watch us."

I want to thank Rob Portman, who is in my Cabinet—he's the Director of the OMB—and my good friend Clay Johnson— is the Deputy Director—for insisting on accountability when it comes to taxpayers' money. I know this has been a particular project—a fond project of Clay, and I'm glad that Members of Congress got it here.

I want to thank Susan Collins, who is the chairman of the Homeland Security and Governmental Affairs Committee. I want to thank the bill sponsors, Tom Coburn from Oklahoma, Tom Carper from Delaware, and Barack Obama from Illinois.

I appreciate Roy Blunt, who is the majority whip. He's a sponsor of the House companion bill. I also want to thank Tom Davis, who is the chairman of the Government Reform Committee, as well as cosponsors of the bill, Jeb Hensarling and Randy Kuhl.

You know, we spend a lot of time and a lot of effort collecting your money, and we should show the same amount of effort in reporting how we spend it. Every year, the Federal Government issues more than $400 billion in grants and more than $300 billion in contracts to corporations, associations, and State and local governments. Taxpayers have a right to know where that money is going, and you have a right to know whether or not you're getting value for your money.

Under Clay's leadership, we launched a new system for measuring how Federal programs are doing. In other words, Federal programs say, "We want to achieve this result," we're trying to figure out whether or not they're meeting the results. In other words, it makes sense for all of us in Washington, DC, to say, "We're a results-oriented Government." I know Henry Waxman believes that. [*Laughter*] Thank you for coming. Proud you're here, sir. I was just praising the bipartisan support that this bill has received, and you're confirmation of that bipartisan support. [*Laughter*] Thank you, appreciate you coming.

And so we've got—we're measuring, and we put a web site out called expectmore.gov. In other words, people can go onto that web site and determine whether or not the results are being met for programs.

And now Congress has come forth with an additional sense of accountability here in Washington, additional way for taxpayers to figure out whether or not we're being wise with your money. And the Federal Funding Accountability Act—Accountability and Transparency Act will create a new web site that will list Government grants and contracts greater than $25,000. We'll list all grants except for those above 25,000—except for those that must remain classified for national security reasons.

The web site will allow our citizens to go online, type in the name of any company, association, or State or locality, and find out exactly what grants and contracts they've been awarded. It will allow citizens to call up the name and location of entities receiving Federal funds and will provide them with the purpose of the funding, the amount of money provided, the agency providing the funding, and other relevant information.

By allowing Americans to Google their tax dollars, this new law will help taxpayers demand greater fiscal discipline. In other words, we're arming our fellow citizens with information that will enable them to demand we do a better job—a better job in the executive branch and better job in the legislative branch.

Information on earmarks will no longer be hidden deep in the pages of a Federal budget bill—will be but just a few clicks away. This legislation will give the American people a new tool to hold their Government accountable for spending decisions. When those decisions are made in broad daylight, they will be wiser and they will be more restrained. This is a good piece of legislation, and I congratulate the Members here.

Recently, the House made an important rule change that will also improve transparency in the legislative process. Under the rule change, the sponsor of each project will now be disclosed before the bills come to a vote. This is a wise change. It will shine the light on earmarks. It's going to help the American taxpayers know whether or not they're getting their money's worth here in Washington.

Rule change, along with the bill I'll sign today, are important steps, but there's more to be done. This President needs a line-item veto. Here's the problem: I get a big bill, an important bill to my desk, and in that bill, there may be some bad spending items, some kind of last minute cram-ins, or items that may not have seen the full light of day during the legislative process. I then either have to accept those or veto a good bill. And there's a better way forward, at least the House thought there was a better way forward in the legislative process, and that's the line-item veto.

Under the proposal, the President can approve spending that is necessary, redline spending that is not, and send the wasteful and unnecessary spending back to the Congress for an up-or-down vote. I think this is an important part of making sure we have accountability here in Washington, DC.

I want to thank the House for passing the bill. I would hope the Senate would take it up. We can work together to inspire confidence in the appropriations process here in Washington. And it's in the interest of both political parties to do so, and it's in the interest of both branches of Government to do so.

Right now, however, I have the honor of signing this new bill. It's a bill that empowers the American taxpayer, the American citizen. And we believe that the more transparency there is in the system, the better the system functions on behalf of the American people.

Again, I thank the Members. It's my honor now to sign the Federal Funding Accountability and Transparency Act of 2006.

[At this point, the President signed the bill.]

The President. All right, dismissed.

NOTE: The President spoke at 9:47 a.m. in Room 350 of the Dwight D. Eisenhower Executive Office Building. S. 2590, approved September 26, was assigned Public Law No. 109–282.

The President's News Conference With President Hamid Karzai of Afghanistan
September 26, 2006

President Bush. Thank you. Please be seated. It's my honor to welcome President Karzai back to the White House. Mr. President, Laura and I fondly remember your gracious hospitality when we met you in your capital. We had a chance today to reconfirm our strong commitment to work together for peace and freedom. And I'm proud of your leadership.

You've got a tough job——

President Karzai. Yes, sometimes it is.

President Bush. ——and you're showing a lot of strength and character. And we're proud to call you ally and friend. I really am.

We discussed how the Government is building institutions necessary for Afghans to have a secure future. We talked about how America and our international partners can continue to help.

Our allies are working on initiatives to help the Afghan people in building a free

Afghanistan. And we discussed those initiatives. We discussed whether or not they could be effective, and we discussed how to make them effective. We discussed our cooperation in defeating those who kill innocent life to achieve objectives, political objectives.

The Afghan people know firsthand the nature of the enemy that we face in the war on terror. After all, just yesterday, Taliban gunmen assassinated Safia Ama Jan—coldblooded kill—she got killed in cold blood. She was a leader who wanted to give young girls an education in Afghanistan. She was a person who served her Government. She was a person who cared deeply about the future of the country. And, Mr. President, Laura and I and the American people join you in mourning her loss.

And her loss shows the nature of this enemy we face. They have no conscience. Their objective is to create fear and create enough violence so we withdraw and let them have their way. And that's unacceptable. It's unacceptable behavior for the free world and the civilized world to accept, Mr. President.

I know that Taliban and Al Qaida remnants and others are trying to bring down your Government, because they know that as democratic institutions take root in your country, the terrorists will not be able to control your country or be able to use it to launch attacks on other nations. They see the threat of democratic progress.

In recent months, the Taliban and other extremists have tried to regain control, mostly in the south of Afghanistan. And so we've adjusted tactics, and we're on the offense to meet the threat and to defeat the threat. Forces from dozens of nations, including every member of NATO, are supporting the democratic Government of Afghanistan. The American people are providing money to help send our troops to your country, Mr. President, and so are a lot of other nations around the world.

This is a multinational effort to help you succeed.

Your people have rejected extremism. Afghan forces are fighting bravely for the future of Afghanistan, and many of your forces have given their lives, and we send our deepest condolences to their families and their friends and their neighbors.

The fighting in Afghanistan is part of a global struggle. Recently British forces killed a long-time terrorist affiliated with Al Qaida named Omar Farouq. Farouq was active in Bosnia and Southeast Asia. He was captured in Indonesia; he escaped from prison in Afghanistan; he was killed hiding in Iraq. Every victory in the war on terror enhances the security of free peoples everywhere.

Mr. President, as I told you in the Oval Office, our country will stand with the free people of Afghanistan. I know there's some in your country who wonder or not—whether or not America has got the will to do the hard work necessary to help you succeed. We have got that will, and we're proud of you as a partner.

President Karzai. Wonderful. Great.

President Bush. We discussed our efforts to help the Government deliver a better life. President Karzai said this about his aspirations—he said he "wants to make Afghanistan a great success and an enduring example of a prosperous and democratic society."

We're helping you build effective and accountable Government agencies. We discussed different agencies in your Government and how best to make them accountable to the people. We're going to help you build roads. We understand that it's important for people to have access to markets. I thought our general had a pretty interesting statement; he said, "Where the road ends, the Taliban tries to begin." The President understands that.

We're helping you with a national literacy program.

President Karzai. Yes.

President Bush. We understand that a free society is one that counts upon a educated citizenry. The more educated a populace is, the more likely it is they'll be active participants in democratic forms of government. We're helping you build schools and medical centers.

We talked about the illegal drug trade. The President gave me a very direct assessment of successes in eradicating poppies and failures in eradicating poppies. It was a realistic assessment of the conditions on the ground. And he talked about his strategy, particularly in dealing in Helmand Province. And, Mr. President, we will support you on this strategy. We understand what you understand, and that is, we've got to eradicate drug trade for the good of the people of Afghanistan.

Tomorrow President Karzai and President Musharraf and I will have dinner. I'm looking forward to it. It's going to be an interesting discussion amongst three allies, three people who are concerned about the future of Pakistan and Afghanistan. It will be a chance for us to work on how to secure the border, how we can continue to work together and share information so we can defeat extremists, how we can work together to build a future of peace and democracy in your region, Mr. President.

I thank you for coming today. I'm looking forward to our discussion tomorrow evening. Welcome back to the White House. The podium is yours.

President Karzai. Thank you very much, Mr. President. It's a great honor to be in your very beautiful country once again, especially during fall with all the lovely leaves around. And thank you very much for the great hospitality that you and the First Lady are always giving to your guests, especially to me. And thanks also for your visit to Afghanistan and for seeing us in our country, for seeing from close as to who we are and how we may get to a better future.

I'm very grateful, Mr. President, to you and the American people for all that you have done for Afghanistan for the last 4½ years, from roads to education to democracy to parliament to good governance effort to health and to all other good things that are happening in Afghanistan.

Mr. President, I was, the day before yesterday, in the Walter Reed Hospital. There I met wounded in Iraq and Afghanistan. And there also I met a woman soldier with six boys, from 7 to 21, that she had left behind in America in order to build us a road in a mountainous part of the country in Afghanistan. There's nothing more that any nation can do for another country, to send a woman with children to Afghanistan to help. We are very grateful. I'm glad I came to know that story, and I'll be repeating it to the Afghan people once I go back to Afghanistan.

We discussed today all matters that concern the two countries: the question of the reconstruction of Afghanistan, improvement for the reconstruction of Afghanistan, the equipping of the Afghan Army, the training of the Afghan Army, the police in Afghanistan, and all other aspects of reconstruction.

We also discussed the region around us, discussed our relations with Pakistan and the question of the joint fight that we have together against terrorism. And I am glad, Mr. President, that you are, tomorrow, hosting a dinner for me and President Musharraf. And I'm sure we'll come out of that meeting with a lot more to talk about to our nations in a very positive way for a better future.

Mr. President, we, the Afghan people, are grateful to you and the American people for all that you have done. I have things in mind to speak about, and you did that, so I'll stop short and let the questions come to us.

President Bush. Thanks. We'll have two questions a side. We'll start with Jennifer Loven [Associated Press].

National Intelligence Estimate/Situation in Afghanistan

Q. Thank you, sir. Even after hearing that one of the major conclusions of the National Intelligence Estimate in April was that the Iraq war has fueled terror growth around the world, why have you continued to say that the Iraq war has made this country safer?

And to President Karzai, if I might, what do you think of President Musharraf's comments that you need to get to know your own country better when you're talking about where terror threats and the Taliban threat is coming from?

President Bush. Do you want to start?

President Karzai. Go ahead, please. [*Laughter*]

President Bush. I, of course, read the key judgments on the NIE. I agree with their conclusion that because of our successes against the leadership of Al Qaida, the enemy is becoming more diffuse and independent. I'm not surprised the enemy is exploiting the situation in Iraq and using it as a propaganda tool to try to recruit more people to their murderous ways.

Some people have guessed what's in the report and have concluded that going into Iraq was a mistake. I strongly disagree. I think it's naive. I think it's a mistake for people to believe that going on the offense against people that want to do harm to the American people makes us less safe. The terrorists fight us in Iraq for a reason: They want to try to stop a young democracy from developing, just like they're trying to fight this young democracy in Afghanistan. And they use it as a recruitment tool, because they understand the stakes. They understand what will happen to them when we defeat them in Iraq.

You know, to suggest that if we weren't in Iraq, we would see a rosier scenario with fewer extremists joining the radical movement requires us to ignore 20 years of experience. We weren't in Iraq when we got attacked on September the 11th.

We weren't in Iraq, and thousands of fighters were trained in terror camps inside your country, Mr. President. We weren't in Iraq when they first attacked the World Trade Center in 1993. We weren't in Iraq when they bombed the *Cole*. We weren't in Iraq when they blew up our Embassies in Kenya and Tanzania. My judgment is, if we weren't in Iraq, they'd find some other excuse, because they have ambitions. They kill in order to achieve their objectives.

You know, in the past, Usama bin Laden used Somalia as an excuse for people to join his jihadist movement. In the past, they used the Israeli-Palestinian conflict. It was a convenient way to try to recruit people to their jihadist movement. They've used all kinds of excuses.

This Government is going to do whatever it takes to protect this homeland. We're not going to let their excuses stop us from staying on the offense. The best way to protect America is defeat these killers overseas so we do not have to face them here at home. We're not going to let lies and propaganda by the enemy dictate how we win this war.

Now, you know what's interesting about the NIE? It was a intelligence report done last April. As I understand, the conclusions—the evidence on the conclusions reached was stopped being gathered on February—at the end of February. And here we are, coming down the stretch in an election campaign, and it's on the front page of your newspapers. Isn't that interesting? Somebody has taken it upon themselves to leak classified information for political purposes.

I talked to John Negroponte today, the DNI. You know, I think it's a bad habit for our Government to declassify every time there's a leak, because it means that it's going to be hard to get good product out of our analysts. Those of you who have been around here long enough know what I'm talking about. But once again, there's a leak out of our Government, coming right down the stretch in this campaign, to create confusion in the minds of the American people, in my judgment, is why they leaked it.

And so we're going to—I told the DNI to declassify this document. You can read it for yourself. We'll stop all the speculation, all the politics about somebody saying something about Iraq, somebody trying to confuse the American people about the nature of this enemy. And so John Negroponte, the DNI, is going to declassify the document as quickly as possible. He'll declassify the key judgments for you to read yourself. And he'll do so in such a way that we'll be able to protect sources and methods that our intelligence community uses. And then everybody can draw their own conclusions about what the report says.

Thank you.

Q. My question——

President Bush. What was that question?

Q. Why is that declassification not——

President Bush. Because I want you to read the documents, so you don't speculate about what it says. You asked me a question based upon what you thought was in the document, or at least somebody told you was in the document. And so I think, Jennifer, you'll be able to ask a more profound question when you get to look at it yourself—*[laughter]*—as opposed to relying upon gossip and somebody who may or may not have seen the document trying to classify the war in Iraq one way or the other.

I guess it's just Washington, isn't it, where, you know, we kind of—there's no such thing as classification anymore, hardly. But, anyway, you ought to take a look at it, and then you'll get to see.

Why don't you ask somebody. Yes, you've got the two-part question.

President Karzai. Ma'am, before I go to the remarks by my brother, President Musharraf, terrorism was hurting us way before Iraq or September 11th. The President mentioned some examples of it. These extremist forces were killing people in Af-ghanistan and around for years, closing schools, burning mosques, killing children, uprooting vineyards with vine trees, grapes hanging on them, forcing populations to poverty and misery.

They came to America on September 11th, but they were attacking you before September 11th in other parts of the world. We are a witness in Afghanistan to what they are and how they can hurt. You are a witness in New York. Do you forget people jumping off the 80th floor or 70th floor when the planes hit them? Can you imagine what it will be for a man or a woman to jump off that high? Who did that? And where are they now? And how do we fight them; how do we get rid of them, other than going after them? Should we wait for them to come and kill us again? That's why we need more action around the world, in Afghanistan and elsewhere, to get them defeated: extremism, their allies, terrorists and the like.

On the remarks of my brother, President Musharraf, Afghanistan is a country that is emerging out of so many years of war and destruction and occupation by terrorism and misery that they've brought to us. We lost almost two generations to the lack of education. And those who were educated before that are now older. We know our problems. We have difficulties. But Afghanistan also knows where the problem is—in extremism, in madrassas preaching hatred, preachers in the name of madrassas preaching hatred. That's what we should do together to stop.

The United States, as our ally, is helping both countries. And I think it is very important that we have more dedication and more intense work with sincerity, all of us, to get rid of the problems that we have around the world.

An Afghan press? You?

War on Terror/Progress in Afghanistan

Q. ——from Voice of America. Mr. President, what is your strategy—your new strategy to fight against terrorism and also to deal with narcotics in Afghanistan? Thank you.

President Karzai. All right. This was to me or to President Bush? Okay. Ma'am, there is no new strategy on the fight against terrorism. We are continuing the strategy that we have. We are implementing the strategy. We are moving further in that strategy. We are getting more of them. We are trying to clean the country of these elements and the region of these elements by doing more reconstruction, by doing more search for the terrorist elements hiding around there. So the fight against terrorism will continue the way we started it.

Q. Mr. President, sorry, do you think it's working now the way it's going?

President Karzai. It is absolutely working. We come across difficulties as we are moving forward, and that's bound to happen. And we get over those difficulties, we resolve them, and we go to the next stage of this fight against terrorism for all the allies.

At one stage 4 years ago, we had a war against them to dislodge them from Afghanistan, to remove them from being the Government of Afghanistan. And then there were major operations against them to arrest or to chase them out. And then we began to rebuild the country, to have roads, to have schools, to have health clinics, to have education, to have all other things that people need all over the world. And now we are at a stage of bringing more stability and trying to get rid of them forever. The desire is to do that sooner, but a desire is not always what you get. So it will take time, and we must have the patience to have the time spent on getting rid of them for good.

On narcotics, it is a problem. It is an embarrassment to Afghanistan. And I told President Bush earlier in my conversation with him that we feel very much embarrassed for having narcotics growing in our country. But again, it has come to Afghanistan because of years of our desperation

and lack of hope for tomorrow. I know Afghan families, ma'am, who destroyed their pomegranate orchards or vineyards to replace them with poppies because they did not know if they were going to have their children the next day, if they were going to be in their own country the next day, if they were going to be having their home standing the next day. It has become a reality because of jobs and years of misery.

We have worked on the problem. In some areas of the country, we have succeeded; in other areas of the country, we have failed because of the circumstances and because of our own failures. We have discussed that, and we will continue to be very steadfast. It is Afghanistan's problem, so Afghanistan is responsible for it, and Afghanistan should act on it with the help of our friends in the United States and the rest of the world.

President Bush. Caren [Caren Bohan, Reuters].

Former President William J. Clinton/War on Terror

Q. Thank you, Mr. President. Former President Clinton says that your administration had no meetings on bin Laden for 9 months after he left office. Is that factually accurate, and how do you respond to his charges?

President Bush. You know, look, Caren, I've watched all this finger-pointing and naming of names and all that stuff. Our objective is to secure the country. And we've had investigations; we had the 9/11 Commission; we had the look back this; we've had the look back that. The American people need to know that we spend all our time doing everything that we can to protect them. So I'm not going to comment on other comments.

But I will comment on this—that we're on the offense against an enemy who wants to do us harm. And we must have the tools necessary to protect our country. On the one hand, if Al Qaida or Al Qaida affiliates are calling somebody in the country, we need to know why. And so Congress needs to pass that piece of legislation. If somebody has got information about a potential attack, we need to be able to ask that person some questions. And so Congress has got to pass that piece of legislation.

You can't protect America unless we give those people on the frontlines of protecting this country the tools necessary to do so within the Constitution. And that's where the debate is here in the United States. There are some decent people who don't believe—evidently don't believe we're at war and therefore shouldn't give the administration what is necessary to protect us.

And that goes back to Jennifer's question, you know. Does being on the offense mean we create terrorists? My judgment is, the only way to defend the country is to stay on the offense. It is preposterous to think if we were to withdraw and hope for the best, things would turn out fine against this enemy. That was my point about, before we were in Iraq, there were thousands being trained in Afghanistan to strike America and other places. The only way to protect this country is to stay on the offense, is to deal with threats before they fully materialize and, in the long term, help democracy succeed, like Afghanistan and Iraq and Lebanon and a Palestinian state.

But there's a difference of opinion. It will come clear during this campaign, where people will say, "Get out, leave before the job is done." And those are good, decent, patriotic people who believe that way; I just happen to believe they're absolutely wrong. So I'm going to continue to work to protect this country. And we'll let history judge—all the different finger-pointing and all that business. I don't have enough time to finger-point. I've got to stay—I've got to do my job, which comes home every day in the Oval Office, and that is to protect the American people from further attack.

Now, there are some who say, "Well, maybe it's not going to happen." Well, they don't see what I see. All I ask is that they look at that terror plot that, along with the Brits, we helped stop—people who were going to get on an airplane and blow up innocent lives in order to achieve political objectives. They're out there; they're mean; and they need to be brought to justice.

International Support for the War on Terror/Afghanistan-Pakistan Relations

Q. Thank you, sir. Mr. President, are you convinced, like President Bush, that the deal General Musharraf signed with the tribal leaders in Waziristan actually meant to fight the Taliban? And why are you convinced that Usama bin Laden is not in Afghanistan?

If I may, Mr. President, do you agree with the analysis from the counter chief European—counterterrorism chief European spokesman who said today that the international support for terrorism has receded? Do you agree with that? And do you see the tension between two important allies of yours, Pakistan and Afghanistan, undermining your effort to get Usama bin Laden? Thank you.

President Bush. It's a four-part question. First of all, I didn't—what was this person a spokesman for?

Q. Counterterrorism chief in Europe.

President Bush. Some obscure spokesman?

Q. No, actually, he has a name.

President Bush. Okay, he's a got a name. [*Laughter*] Well, no, I don't agree with the spokesman for the obscure organization that said that the international commitment to fighting terror is declining. It's quite the contrary, starting with the evidence that NATO has committed troops in Afghanistan. These are troops who are on the ground who are serving incredibly bravely to protect this country.

Secondly, when the Brits, along with our help, intercepted the plot to attack us, everybody started saying, "They're still there." They began to realize that their hopes that the terrorist threats were going away weren't true. Since September the 11th, it's important for the American people to remember, there have been a lot of attacks on a lot of nations by these jihadists. And some of them are Al Qaida and some of them are Al Qaida inspired. The NIE talked about how this group of folks are becoming more dispersed. That's what I've been saying as well. After all, look inside of Great Britain. These are people inspired by, perhaps trained by Al Qaida, but nevertheless plotted and planned attacks and conducted attacks in the summer of 2005, and then plotted attacks in the summer of 2006. See, they're dangerous, and the world knows that.

And so from my perspective, intelligence sharing is good, cooperation on the financial fronts is good, and that more and more nations are committing troops to the fight, in Afghanistan in particular.

Now, the other question——

Q. The tension between two allies—does this undermine the efforts of getting bin Laden?

President Bush. No. No, it doesn't. It's in President Karzai's interest to see bin Laden brought to justice. It is in President Musharraf's interest to see bin Laden brought to justice. Our interests coincide. It will be interesting for me to watch the body language of these two leaders to determine how tense things are.

President Karzai. I'll be good. [*Laughter*]

President Bush. Yes. From my discussions with President Karzai and President Musharraf, there is an understanding that by working together, it is more likely that all of us can achieve a common objective, which are stable societies that are hopeful societies, that prevent extremists from stopping progress and denying people a hopeful world.

I know that's what President Karzai thinks, and I know that's how President Musharraf thinks. And so—I'm kind of teasing about the body language for the dinner tomorrow night, but it's going to

be a good dinner, and it's an important dinner.

So to answer your question, no. What you perceive as tension is stopping us from bringing high-value targets to justice, quite the contrary, we're working as hard as ever in doing that.

President Karzai. On the question of Waziristan, ma'am, President Musharraf, when he was in Kabul, explained what they had done there. My initial impression was that this was a deal signed by the Taliban, and then later I learned that they actually signed with the tribal chiefs. It will have a different meaning if it is that signed with the tribal chiefs—that for us, for the United States, for the allies against terror.

The most important element here is item number one in this agreement, that the terrorists will not be allowed to cross over into Afghanistan to attack the coalition against terror, that is, the international community and Afghanistan together. We will have to wait and see if that is going to be implemented exactly the way it is signed. So from our side, it's a wait-and-see attitude. But generally, we will back any move, any deal that will deny terrorism sanctuary in North Waziristan or in the tribal territories of Pakistan.

President Bush. Mr. President, thank you.

President Karzai. Thank you, sir.

President Bush. Well done.

NOTE: The President's news conference began at 11:37 a.m. in the East Room at the White House. In his remarks, he referred to senior Al Qaida associate Omar al-Farouq, who was killed in Iraq on September 26; Lt. Gen. Karl W. Eikenberry, USA, commander, Combined Forces Command—Afghanistan; President Pervez Musharraf of Pakistan; Usama bin Laden, leader of the Al Qaida terrorist organization; and Gijs de Vries, counterterrorism coordinator, European Union.

Statement on the Report of the Commission on the Future of Higher Education
September 26, 2006

Today Education Secretary Margaret Spellings released the report of a commission whose focus was to help make America's higher education system more affordable and more accessible and to provide parents and students with information that will help them make better-informed choices. I strongly support the thrust of this important report and look forward to working with Secretary Spellings, the higher education community, the Congress, and the States to ensure that our higher education system remains the finest in the world.

America's colleges and universities have always played an important role in advancing innovation, opportunity, and prosperity throughout our Nation and the world. We must all work to provide our students with the knowledge and skills they need to shape a hopeful future for our country.

NOTE: The Office of the Press Secretary also released a Spanish language transcript of this statement.

Statement on the Death of Byron Nelson
September 26, 2006

I was saddened to learn today of the passing of Byron Nelson. Byron Nelson was a legend in the game of golf, setting extraordinary standards for excellence on the course. More importantly, he was a true gentleman and role model for generations of golfers. Laura and I join fellow Texans and the sports world in extending our sympathies to his wife, Peggy, and his family and friends.

Statement on House of Representatives Passage of Military Commissions Legislation
September 27, 2006

Earlier this month, I discussed with the American people a CIA program that has proven to be one of our most effective tools in the war on terror. Under this program, suspected terrorists have been detained and questioned about threats against our country. Because a Supreme Court decision put the future of this program in question, I asked Congress to provide legislation to save this important tool.

Today the House passed legislation that would allow this vital program to continue and help keep our country safe. The "Military Commissions Act of 2006" addresses the Supreme Court's ruling regarding the application of Common Article 3 of the Geneva Conventions and clarifies the standards for U.S. personnel who detain and question unlawful enemy combatants. The act also creates a comprehensive statutory structure for military commissions so that we can prosecute suspected terrorists.

I appreciate the House's commitment to strengthening our national security. I urge the Senate to act quickly to get a bill to my desk before Congress adjourns.

NOTE: The statement referred to H.R. 6166.

Remarks Prior to Discussions With President Hamid Karzai of Afghanistan and President Pervez Musharraf of Pakistan
September 27, 2006

President Bush. Tonight it's my honor to host a dinner with President Musharraf of Pakistan and President Karzai of Afghanistan. These two men are personal friends of mine; they are strong leaders who have a understanding of the world in which we live; they understand that the forces of moderation are being challenged by extremists and radicals. And we're working closely together to help improve the lives of the people in Afghanistan and the people in Pakistan.

President Musharraf kindly greeted me to Pakistan. I had the great privilege of meeting many in his Government. I met people in the civil society there. I met those who were helping the Pakistan citizens who were—whose lives were turned upside down by the devastating earthquake. I saw the compassion of this Government, and I was very proud that the American people were helping them recover.

I also had the opportunity to visit President Karzai. He's leading a young democracy. It's a democracy that was formed as a result of the Afghan people voting, having shed itself, with American help, from the Taliban regime.

We've got a lot of challenges facing us. All of us must protect our countries, but at the same time, we all must work to make the world a more hopeful place. And so today's dinner is a chance for us to strategize together, to talk about the need to cooperate, to make sure that people have got a hopeful future.

It's very important for the people in Pakistan and Afghanistan to understand that America respects religion, and we respect the right for people to worship the way they see fit. We welcome Muslim leaders here in the White House. I look forward to having dinner with friends of mine who don't happen to share the same faith I do, but nevertheless share the same outlook for a hopeful world.

As we work for a more hopeful world, we will continue to make sure that extremists, such as Usama bin Laden, that wants to hurt my friend here as well as upset the democracy in Afghanistan is brought to justice. The main thing I was looking forward to talking about is how the United States Government and the people of the United States can help these two countries provide a foundation for hope. And so I want to thank you for coming. We're proud to have you here, Mr. President.

President Musharraf. My pleasure.

President Bush. Proud to have you here, Mr. President. Let's go eat dinner. Thank you, sir.

President Musharraf. Thank you very much.

President Karzai. Thanks very much.

NOTE: The President spoke at 7:35 p.m. in the Rose Garden at the White House. In his remarks, he referred to Usama bin Laden, leader of the Al Qaida terrorist organization.

Message to the Senate Transmitting the United States-European Union Agreement on Mutual Legal Assistance
September 27, 2006

To the Senate of the United States:

With a view to receiving the advice and consent of the Senate to ratification, I transmit herewith the Agreement on Mutual Legal Assistance between the United States of America and the European Union (EU), signed on June 25, 2003, at Washington, together with 25 bilateral instruments that subsequently were signed between the United States and each European Union Member State in order to implement the Agreement with the EU, and an explanatory note that is an integral part of the Agreement. I also transmit, for the information of the Senate, the report of the Department of State with respect to the Agreement and bilateral instruments.

A parallel agreement with the European Union on extradition, together with bilateral instruments, will be transmitted to the Senate separately. These two agreements are the first law enforcement agreements concluded between the United States and the European Union. Together they serve to modernize and expand in important respects the law enforcement relationships between the United States and the 25 EU Member States, as well as formalize and strengthen the institutional framework for law enforcement relations between the United States and the European Union itself.

The U.S.-EU Mutual Legal Assistance Agreement contains several innovations that should prove of value to U.S. prosecutors and investigators, including in counterterrorism cases. The Agreement creates an improved mechanism for obtaining bank information from an EU Member State, elaborates legal frameworks for the use of new techniques such as joint investigative teams, and establishes a comprehensive and uniform framework for limitations on the use of personal and other data. The Agreement includes a non-derogation provision making clear that it is without prejudice to the ability of the United States or an EU Member State to refuse assistance where doing so would prejudice its sovereignty, security, public, or other essential interests.

I recommend that the Senate give early and favorable consideration to the Agreement and bilateral instruments.

GEORGE W. BUSH

The White House,

September 27, 2006.

NOTE: This message was released by the Office of the Press Secretary on September 28. An original was not available for verification of the content of this message.

Message to the Senate Transmitting the United States-European Union Agreement on Extradition
September 27, 2006

To the Senate of the United States:

With a view to receiving the advice and consent of the Senate to ratification, I transmit herewith the Agreement on Extra-

dition between the United States of America and the European Union (EU), signed on June 25, 2003, at Washington, together with 22 bilateral instruments that subsequently were signed between the United States and European Union Member States in order to implement the Agreement with the EU, and an explanatory note that is an integral part of the Agreement. I also transmit, for the information of the Senate, the report of the Department of State with respect to the Agreement and bilateral instruments. The bilateral instruments with three EU Member States, Estonia, Latvia, and Malta, take the form of comprehensive new extradition treaties, and therefore will be submitted individually.

A parallel agreement with the European Union on mutual legal assistance, together with bilateral instruments, will be transmitted to the Senate separately. These two agreements are the first law enforcement agreements concluded between the United States and the European Union. Together they serve to modernize and expand in important respects the law enforcement relationships between the United States and the 25 EU Member States, as well as formalize and strengthen the institutional framework for law enforcement relations between the United States and the European Union itself.

The U.S.-EU Extradition Agreement contains several provisions that should improve the scope and operation of bilateral extradition treaties in force between the United States and each EU Member State. For example, it requires replacing outdated lists of extraditable offenses included in 10 older bilateral treaties with the modern "dual criminality" approach, thereby enabling coverage of such newer offenses as money laundering. Another important provision ensures that a U.S. extradition request is not disfavored by an EU Member State that receives a competing request for the person from another Member State pursuant to the newly created European Arrest Warrant. Finally, the Extradition Agreement simplifies procedural requirements for preparing and transmitting extradition documents, easing and speeding the current process.

I recommend that the Senate give early and favorable consideration to the Agreement and bilateral instruments.

GEORGE W. BUSH

The White House,
September 27, 2006.

NOTE: This message was released by the Office of the Press Secretary on September 28. An original was not available for verification of the content of this message.

Remarks Following a Meeting With the Republican Senate Conference
September 28, 2006

I just had a really constructive and interesting session with Republican Members of the United States Senate. I'm impressed by the leadership here in the Senate. I'm impressed by the caliber of people that serve our country.

I want to congratulate the House for passing a very vital piece of legislation that will give us the tools necessary to protect the American people, and that's the Hamdan legislation. That's the legislation that will give us the capacity to be able to interrogate high-valued detainees and, at the same time, give us the capacity to try people who—in our military tribunals.

In speaking to the Senate, I urged them to get this legislation to my desk as soon as possible. Senator Frist and Senator McConnell committed to that end. The American people need to know we're working together to win this war on terror. Our most important responsibility is to protect the American people from further attack, and we cannot be able to tell the American people we're doing our full job unless we have the tools necessary to do so. And this legislation passed in the House yesterday is a part of making sure that we do have the capacity to protect you.

Our most solemn job is the security of this country. People shouldn't forget there's still an enemy out there that wants to do harm to the United States. And therefore, a lot of my discussion with the Members of the Senate was to remind them of this solemn responsibility. And so I look forward to you passing good legislation, Senators. Thank you for having me. Appreciate your time.

NOTE: The President spoke at 9:16 a.m. at the U.S. Capitol. In his remarks, he referred to H.R. 6166.

Remarks on Energy in Hoover, Alabama
September 28, 2006

You know, the price of gasoline has been dropping, and that's good news for the American consumer, it's good news for the small-business owners, it's good news for the farmers. But it's very important for us to remember that we still have an issue when it comes to dependence on foreign oil. And one way to become less dependent on foreign oil is for us to develop new ways to power our automobiles right here in America.

And so I've come to Hoover, Alabama, to recognize this city for being innovative and progressive and for having a good football team. [*Laughter*] I want to thank Mayor Tony Petelos and the city council for serving and leading. See, what we have just witnessed is a police force that is filling up its vehicles with a fuel called E–85. When you hear somebody talk about fuel E–85, that means 85 percent of the fuel comes from ethanol. And ethanol is produced from corn, and corn is grown right here in the United States of America.

One way to become less dependent on foreign oil is to use American-grown products to power our automobiles. And that's what we just witnessed. So I asked Officer Parker of the Hoover Police Department, I said, "Do you like using E–85?" See, he has a choice, because there are what we call flex-fuel vehicles. He can either use ethanol-based fuel or regular gasoline. As a matter of fact, there's a lot of cars in the United States that are flex fuel, and some of you probably don't even know you've got a car that's flex fuel. It doesn't cost much money, by the way, to convert a regular automobile, an automobile that uses gasoline, to a flex-fuel car.

So anyway, so I said to Officer Parker, I said, first, I told him thanks for serving. And then I said, "You've got a choice, don't you, between gasoline and E–85?" He said, "I do." I said, "Which one do you pick?" He said, "E–85." I said, "Why?" He said, "Because it's got a little better get up to it." In other words, it works just fine.

And it works just fine for other reasons as well. It works just fine because it helps keep our air clean. It works just fine because it helps address a national security issue. So one of the important policies of governments ought to be to encourage the production and use of ethanol. And there's a Federal role for that. In other words, we provide tax credits. We think it's in our national interest that ethanol penetrate more market—in other words, more people use ethanol.

We're providing research dollars, and one reason you provide research dollars is because it's going to be important for us to use something beyond corn to make ethanol. In other words, corn is good, and so is sugar, but you can imagine, it's going to put a little strain on the corn market after a while if the only raw material we use for ethanol is corn. After all, you've got to feed the cows and feed the hogs and feed people as well as feed automobiles with fuel.

And so the Federal Government has committed to spending a fair amount of your money to research other ways to make ethanol. And one such place where good research is going on is right here in the State of Alabama at Auburn University.

And I just had the honor of meeting a professor who came here from South Africa and is now one of the eminent scholars there at Auburn, who spends his time developing new ways to make ethanol. See, what's happening here in America is, is that we have made it a focused effort of our Government to diversify our fuel, and we're spending your money to do it.

The doc was telling me that one of these days, we could be using switchgrass to be making ethanol. That's pretty good news for people. You know, if that ever becomes a reality, there's going to be a lot of switchgrass growers.

He was talking to me about how they're spending time and money figuring out whether or not we can use wood products to make ethanol. Imagine if we can achieve a technological breakthrough that enables us to use wood chips. You got a lot of wood here in Alabama. You'll become one of the leading ethanol producers if—when we achieve that breakthrough. And that's good news for America.

I like the idea of a President or a Governor saying, "You know something, there's a lot of corn, and we're less dependent on oil from overseas," or, "We've got some new breakthroughs, which makes us less dependent on oil." And the good news is, this technology also helps us be good stewards of the environment.

And so I want to thank the good folks from Hoover, Alabama, for thinking differently, for being on the leading edge of change. I appreciate the mayor and the city council for thinking about how best to represent your people, and you're making a fine contribution to our country as well.

It's an honor to be here. I'm thrilled to see this E–85 plant operating right here in the State of Alabama. I predict there are more coming, and when more come, this country is going to be better off.

Thanks for having me, and God bless.

NOTE: The President spoke at 12:06 p.m. at the Hoover Public Safety Center. In his remarks, he referred to Mayor Tony Petelos of Hoover, AL; Reggie Parker, officer, Hoover Police Department; and David Bransby, professor of agronomy and soil, Auburn University. The Office of the Press Secretary also released a Spanish language transcript of these remarks.

Remarks at a Luncheon for Gubernatorial Candidate Robert R. Riley in Birmingham, Alabama
September 28, 2006

Thanks for coming. It is a joy to be back in Alabama, and I appreciate your warm welcome. I am proud to stand with one of the Nation's finest Governors and ask for your help in reelecting Bob Riley as Governor of Alabama.

He deserves to be reelected because he's got a record he can run on. He has made you proud. He listens to the people. He shares your values for the good of Alabama and for the good of all citizens, regardless of their political party. Bob Riley needs to be reelected as your Governor.

I'm proud to be here with Patsy, first lady of the great State of Alabama. Riley and I married well, and we're both wise enough to listen to our wives. [*Laughter*] So Laura said, "When you get down to Alabama, say hello to our friends on her behalf," and so I do. I bring greetings from Laura Bush, a wonderful mother, a fantastic wife, and a great First Lady for the United States of America. And Patsy, thank you for being here. Thank you for serving your State with dignity, just like Riley is serving the State with dignity.

I'm also proud to recognize the candidate for the Lieutenant Governor, a man who will stand tall for the State of Alabama—[*laughter*]—my friend Luther Strange. I have gotten to know your State attorney general, Troy King. He is an accomplished attorney, who brings great credit to the office he holds. I can say without a doubt, he's the right candidate to serve as the State attorney for this great State of Alabama. Troy, thanks for serving; it was an honor to meet your wife, Paige. I want to thank the State auditor, Beth Chapman, who is with us here today. I thank Twinkle Cavanaugh, who is the chairman of the Alabama Republican Party, and I want to thank all the grass roots activists who have joined us here today.

This is a fantastic fundraiser. The next thing that needs to be done is a fantastic grass roots effort to turn out the vote. For those of you who are stuffing the envelopes and putting up the signs and getting on the telephones, and turning people out to vote, I want to thank you in advance for what you're going to do for this excellent Governor.

You win campaigns by having somebody who has got a vision and can carry the message, and you also win campaigns by finding your voters and turning them out.

For all the grass roots activists here today, thanks for coming, and thanks for what you do.

I want to thank the State and local officials who are here. Thanks for serving. I appreciate your willingness to be a public servant. I want to thank the Selma High School Choir. I appreciate you lending your beautiful voices to this important occasion.

One of the most important jobs of a Governor is to set a tone for a State. Bob Riley and I share a philosophy about the role of government when it comes to the economy. The role of government is not to create wealth; the role of government is to create an environment in which the entrepreneurial spirit can flourish, in which small business grow to be big businesses, an environment in which people are able to find work.

I was noticing that the unemployment rate in the great State of Alabama is 3.5 percent, which says Riley knows what he's doing when it comes time to this economy. When you have people working, it makes sense to put the man in charge of setting the tone for the State back in office.

You know, one of the things Bob and I understand is that one way to grow the economy is to let people keep more of their own taxes. You see, we believe that when you've got more of your own money in your pocket to save, spend, or invest, the economy grows.

He told me that he's running on cutting taxes, another reason to put him back in office as the Governor of Alabama. And I'm telling you, cutting taxes works.

You might remember what this economy of ours has been through. We've been through a recession and corporate scandals, a terrorist attack, a war, hurricanes, and high gasoline prices. Yet we're growing, and we intend to keep growing. And the best way to keep growing is to keep the people's taxes low.

The the tax cuts we passed are working, and it's a campaign issue as far as I'm concerned. There's no doubt in my mind that if the national Democrats had control of the House or the Senate, they'd raise your taxes. And there's no doubt in my mind raising your taxes will hurt this economy. The best way to keep the people in Alabama working and the best way to keep the people across this country working is to make the tax cuts we passed permanent.

When I was the Governor of Texas, I used to tell people education is to a State what national defense is to the Federal Government. The single most important priority of a State is to make sure the people get educated. And Bob Riley has made the school system of Alabama his top priority, but he's made the school system in Alabama a priority in a different kind of way. See, he refuses to accept the status quo when he finds mediocrity or failure.

You know, I was talking to Margaret Spellings. She's my buddy from the State of Texas who is now the Secretary of Education. And Margaret Spellings, if she were here, would tell you that Alabama has some of the most innovative programs in the United States of America when it comes to making sure every single child gets an education. You got a Governor who is an education Governor and needs to be returned to your State capitol.

He is spending money on schools, and that's important. But he also understands money alone won't bring excellence to the classrooms. And that's why he has set high standards, and that's why he insists upon strong accountability measures. The best way to achieve educational excellence for every child in your State is to measure, is to determine whether a child is learning how to read, write, and add and subtract, and if not, correct problems early before it's too late.

I'm proud of the standards your Governor has set. I'm proud to call my friend an educational innovator. I'm proud that he has made reading a top priority. I'm proud he's challenging the soft bigotry of low expectations. I'm proud he's working

hard to make sure no child is left behind in the State of Alabama.

Riley and I just went over to—excuse me—Governor Riley—[*laughter*]—and I went over to Hoover, Alabama, today, the home of the mighty Bucs, the number one high school football team in the United States. That's kind of hard for a Texan to say. [*Laughter*] But we went over for a different reason, because we both understand that in order for America to remain competitive in the 21st century, in order for Alabama to remain competitive in the 21st century, we must diversify away from foreign sources of oil.

And so we went to a E–85 ethanol distribution place. See, what happened is, is that the fine mayor of Hoover and its city council decided that they were going to use ethanol as the primary fuel for their police automobiles. That's called innovation. It's called thinking ahead.

I found it to be really interesting to talk to the officers who drive the vehicles that are run on fuel that is 85 percent ethanol, in other words, fuel made from corn. So I said to the guy, do you—see, he has a choice, he can either use gasoline or ethanol. I said, "Which one do you use?" He says, "I like the ethanol." I said, "Why?" He said, "It's got a lot of get up and go to it." In other words, it works well.

What we're beginning to see is a change in how we fuel our automobiles. We're spending a lot of money at the Federal level, your money, to try to advance new technologies to make us less dependent on oil. It's in the national interests that we become less dependent on oil from overseas. After all, a lot of the oil we get is from parts of the world that don't particularly care for us right now.

I look forward to the day when more and more of you have flex-fuel vehicles and you can go and make the decision as to whether or not you want to use ethanol as the primary source of energy in your automobile or gasoline. I look forward to the day when I can say to the American people, "Because we've got more corn growing, we're less dependent on foreign sources of oil." I look forward to the day when you can use wood chips from Alabama trees as the feedstock for ethanol. I look forward to the day when we have these great breakthroughs of research and technology done right here in Auburn University to say to the American people, the research we're doing today means your children are going to be less dependent on oil in the future.

And Bob Riley is a partner in encouraging diversification away from hydrocarbons that we import from overseas. And I appreciate his stance. I appreciate his vision. He's got a vision for the people of Alabama, and he's got the skill and capability of implementing that vision. He's done an excellent job for the people. And I want to thank you for supporting him to put him back in office. It's good for this State that Bob Riley is the Governor. I want to talk about—I want to spend a little time on what else occupies my mind, other than making sure our economy grows. And it's this: My most solemn responsibility and the most solemn duty of the Federal Government, as a matter of fact governments at all levels, is to protect the American people.

We are a nation at war. I wish I could report differently, but you need to have a President who sees the world the way it is, not the way somebody would hope it would be. In order to protect this people, we must understand the nature of the threats we face. We face an enemy that is brutal, an enemy that is determined, an enemy that has a set of beliefs that is the opposite of our beliefs.

I'll never forget the lessons of September the 11th, 2001, and I will continue to use, as I vowed then to the American people, every element of national power to defeat the terrorists and to defend the freedom of the United States of America.

And that starts with making sure those responsible for defending you have all the

tools necessary to do so. As the Commander in Chief of the finest group of men and women produced in this country, I'll make you this pledge: Our troops will have whatever it takes to do the job we have asked them to do.

And we have got to make sure that our intelligence officers have the tools they need to protect you and our law enforcement officers have the tools they need to protect you. So working with the Congress, we passed what was called the PATRIOT Act, an act that broke down barriers and walls that prevented the intelligence community from sharing information with the law enforcement community.

You see, we recognize that in order to protect you, all elements of national government must be able to communicate freely to defeat this enemy. If somebody that we think is Al Qaida or an Al Qaida affiliate gets on the telephone and is making a phone call into the United States, we want to know why, in order to protect the American people.

In order to make sure we get the information necessary to protect you—see, this is a different kind of war. We cannot measure the enemy's progress based upon the movement of tanks or airplanes. These people hide in remote regions of the world and then strike with lethality, as we learned firsthand in our country.

And therefore we must find kernels of information that then will enable us to track them down and bring them to justice before they hurt Americans. And that's why it's essential that I created a program with the professionals in the Central Intelligence Agency to detain and question key terrorist leaders and operatives that were captured on the battlefield. As a result of this program, we have—we've learned information that enabled us to save American lives.

I also believed it was important to set up military commissions that will enable us to bring to justice the people that ordered the attacks on the United States of America. The Supreme Court said, you must work with the legislature to achieve these objectives, and we're doing just that.

Last night—yesterday afternoon, the House of Representatives voted on the legislation we put forward to create military commissions and to continue that vital program of questioning detainees. The bill passed, but I want to remind you about the vote. The bill passed over the objections of 160 House Democrats, including the entire Democrat leadership.

We must give our professionals the tools necessary to protect the American people in this war on terror, and those in the House of Representatives were wrong to vote against this bill.

Ours is an important job to protect you. We have to be right 100 percent of the time, and the enemy only has to be right once. And that's why it's important that we do the—pass the laws that we've asked the Senate and the House to pass. And that's also why it's important that we must defeat the enemy overseas so we do not have to face them here at home.

And there's a lot of debate in Washington about this war on terror. And perhaps you heard something about what's called a National Intelligence Estimate. The National Intelligence Estimate is a classified document that, in this case, analyzed the threat we faced from terrorists and extremists.

As you know, parts of that classified document were recently leaked to the press, a sure sign that elections are right around the corner. Some in the other party have been quoting selectively from the document for partisan political gain, and so I felt that it was important for people to actually see what was in the document, and so I declassified it.

And I'd like to share some thoughts about what was in the NIE with you today. It offers a frank assessment of where we are in the war on terror. It confirms that we face a determined and capable enemy. It lists four underlying factors that are fueling the extremist movement: longstanding grievances such as corruption and injustice, or fear of Western domination; the second such factor was the jihad in the Iraq; the third was the slow pace of reform in Muslim nations; and the fourth factor that the leaders of this extremist movement were using to recruit was anti-Americanism.

It concludes that the terrorists are exploiting all these factors to enhance their movement. The debate over this document raises really an important question about the war on terror: Should we be on the offense or not? Some in Washington—some decent people, patriotic people—feel like we should not be on the offensive in this war on terror. Here's what a senior Democrat in Congress put it when she was discussing Iraq. She said, "The President says that fighting them there makes it less likely we'll have to fight them here. The opposite is true." She went on to say, "Because we are fighting them there, it may become more likely that we'll have to fight them here."

History tells us that logic is false. We didn't create terrorism by fighting terrorism. Iraq is not the reason why the terrorists are at war against us. Our troops were not in Iraq when the terrorists first attacked the World Trade Center. They were not in Iraq when they blew up our Embassies in Kenya and Tanzania. They were not in Iraq when they bombed the USS *Cole*. And we were not in Iraq when the extremists killed nearly 3,000 of our people on September the 11th, 2001.

Five years after the 9/11 attacks, some in Washington, DC, still don't understand the nature of the enemy. The only way to protect our citizens at home is to keep the pressure on the enemy across the world. When terrorists spend their days working to avoid capture, they are less able to plot and plan and execute new attacks. We will stay on the offense. We will fight them across the world, and we will stay in this fight until the fight is won.

In order to win this war, we need to understand that the terrorists and extremists are opportunists. They will grab onto any cause to incite hatred and to justify the killing of innocent men, women, and children. If we weren't in Iraq, they would be using our relationship and friendship with Israel as a reason to recruit, or the Crusades, or cartoons as a reason to commit murder. They recruit based upon lies and excuses, and they murder because of their raw desire for power. They hope to impose their dominion over the broader Middle East and establish a radical Islamic empire where millions are ruled according to their hateful ideology. We know this because Al Qaida has told us.

The terrorist Zawahiri, number two man in the Al Qaida team—Al Qaida network, he said, we'll proceed with several incremental goals. The first stage is to expel the Americans from Iraq; the second stage is to establish an Islamic authority, then develop it and support it until it achieves the level of caliphate; the third stage, extend the jihad wave to secular countries neighboring Iraq; and the fourth stage, the clash with Israel.

This is the words of the enemy. The President of the United States and the Congress must listen carefully to what the enemy says in order to be able to protect you. It makes sense for us to take their words seriously, if our most important job is the security of the United States. Mr. Zawahiri has laid out their plan. That's why they attacked us on September the 11th. That's why they fight us in Iraq today. And that is why they must be defeated.

Some Democrats in Congress say that we should not be fighting the terrorists in Iraq; it was a mistake to go into Iraq in the first place. I believe these Democrats need to answer a simple question: Do they really believe that we would be better off if Saddam Hussein were still in power? In a recent interview, the top Democrat on the Intelligence Committee was asked this very question. And his answer was, "Yes, yes, and, yes."

If this is what the Democrats think, they need to make this case to the American people; they need to make the case that the world would be better off it Saddam Hussein were still in power. If Saddam Hussein were still in power, he would still be sponsoring terror and paying families of suicide bombers. If he were still in power, he would still be pursuing weapons of mass destruction. He would still be killing his own people. He would still be firing at our pilots. He would still be defying the United Nations. He would still be bilking the Oil-for-Food Programme and using one of the largest oil reserves in the world to threaten Western economies and to fuel his ambitions.

After the attacks of September the 11th, it became clear that the United States of America must confront threats before they come and hurt us. Saddam Hussein's regime was a serious threat, a risk the world could not afford to take. America, Iraqis, and the world are safer because Saddam Hussein is not in power.

In a recent series of speeches, I made it clear that we're in the early hours of a long struggle for civilization. I have made it clear that we're in the ideological struggle of the 21st century. I've also made it clear that the safety of the American people depends on the outcome of the battle in the streets of Baghdad.

I strongly believe that Iraq is a central front in the war on terror. The Democrats may not think so, but Usama bin Laden does. Here are the words of bin Laden, "I now address the whole Islamic nation: Listen and understand. The most serious issue today for the whole world is this third world war is raging in Iraq." He calls it "a war of destiny between infidelity and Islam." He says, "The whole world is watching this war," and that it will end in "victory and glory or misery and humiliation."

For Al Qaida, Iraq is not a distraction from their war on America; it is a central battlefield where there's—outcome of the struggle will be decided.

The NIE I quoted earlier says this about Iraq. It said, "Perceived jihadist success there," in Iraq, "would inspire more fighters to continue the struggle elsewhere." It also says that "Should jihadists leaving Iraq perceive themselves, and be perceived, to have failed, we judge fewer fighters will be inspired to carry on the fight."

Democrats in Washington have been quoting the NIE a lot in recent days, but you don't hear them quoting that part of the document. The Democrats can't have it both ways. Either they believe that Iraq is a distraction from the war on terror or they agree with the intelligence community and the terrorists themselves that the outcome of Iraq is important in the war on terror. Truth is, the Democrats are using the NIE to mislead the American people and justify their policy of withdrawal from Iraq.

The American people need to know what withdrawal from Iraq would mean. By withdrawing from Iraq before the job is done, we would be doing exactly what the extremists and terrorists want. The terrorists' entire strategy is based on the belief that America is weak and does not have the stomach for the long fight. Bin Laden has called American withdrawals from places like Beirut and Somalia as proof that if the terrorists are patient, America will lose her nerve and withdraw in disgrace.

The greatest danger is not that America's presence in Iraq is drawing new recruits to the terrorist cause; the greatest danger is that an American withdrawal from Iraq would embolden the terrorists and help them find new recruits to carry out even more destructive attacks on the American homeland. And that is why the United States of America will stand with the brave Iraqis and defeat the terrorists in Iraq.

The stakes are high in this war. It's really important that the United States of Amer-ica understands the nature of this enemy and understands what it would mean to leave Iraq before the job is done. If we were to abandon this young democracy to the extremists, imagine what other reformers and people of moderation would think about the United States of America. If we were to abandon our mission in Iraq where many have sacrificed, imagine what the enemy would think about the United States of America and our will.

If we were to abandon Iraq and create a vacuum in that country and that country were then taken over by the extremists, make no mistake about it, they would have mighty assets to use in order to inflict economic pain on the United States of America. We're not going to let this happen. America is a nation that keeps its commitments to those who long for liberty and want to live in peace. America is a nation that will keep its commitment to make sure that you're secure. America is a nation that does not retreat in the face of thugs and assassins.

We're going to help the Iraqi people. Remember, 12 million of them voted in elections last December. That probably seems like a decade ago to you, but when the history is finally written, it will be just a comma. Twelve million people stood up in the face of assassins and car bombers and said, "We want to be free."

I'm not surprised. I was pleased. I'm not surprised because I believe in this principle, a principle which should be a guiding light of American foreign policy: There is an Almighty, and a gift of that Almighty to every man, woman, and child on the face of the Earth is freedom. I believe deep in the soul of every person is the desire to live in liberty, and I know that liberty will yield the peace we want for generations to come.

From the beginning of the struggle, I've made it clear that we will defend this country by giving people the tools needed, that we'll defend America by staying on the offense, that we will find the terrorists and bring them to justice so they can't hurt us here at home. But I've also made it clear that defeating the terrorists in the long run requires defeating their hateful ideology.

The NIE explicitly states, the National Intelligence Estimate, that I have been discussing and has been widely discussed in the newspapers states this, that the terrorists greatest vulnerability is that their ideology is "unpopular with the vast majority of Muslims." People want to be free. People want to be able to express themselves freely. Mothers in the Muslim world share the same thing as mothers here; they want their children to grow up in a peaceful world.

And that's why it's essential that the United States of America stand with moderates and reformers and peaceful people, millions of men and women in the Muslim world who want a normal life and a more hopeful future for their children and their grandchildren. And as this powerful majority gains control over the destiny—over their destiny through the democratic progress, they will marginalize the radicals and extremists and their hateful vision of the world.

The transition from tyranny to democracy is tough work, but it's necessary work. It's the calling of history. It's the challenge to our generation to defend America and to lay the foundation of peace for generations to come. The extremists and the radicals will exploit these difficulties in every way they can. They will try to shake our will. They will use the murder of innocent men and women and children in order to convince America that the fight isn't worth it. Yet in the long run, America, if we keep our faith in our principles, will prevail.

Encouraging the rise of free societies across the broader Middle East is the only way to overcome the threat of terrorism and to protect the American people in the long run. We owe it to a generation of children to come to do the hard work now.

Imagine a Middle East where there's competing factions of extremism. Imagine a Middle East where the radicals control oil. Imagine a Middle East where there's an armed theocracy with a nuclear weapon. Fifty years from now, people will say, "Couldn't they see it; why couldn't they see the threat?"

Now is the time for the United States of America to lay the foundation of peace, to confront the challenges we have square on, to protect our country, to do our duty so that generations will look back and say, "Thank God this generation of Americans was willing to serve and serve strong."

The stakes in this war are high, and so are the stakes this November. Americans face the choice between two parties with two different attitudes on this war on terror. Five years after 9/11, the worst attack on American homeland in our history, the Democrats offer nothing but criticism and obstruction and endless second-guessing. The party of FDR and the party of Harry Truman has become the party of cut-and-run.

Our party's record is clear. We see the stakes. We understand the nature of the enemy. We know that the enemy wants to attack us again. We will not wait to respond to the enemy. We're not going to wait for them to attack us in order to respond. We will fight them wherever they make a stand. We will settle for nothing less than victory.

Thanks for coming. God bless.

NOTE: The President spoke at 1:34 p.m. at the Birmingham Jefferson Convention Complex. In his remarks, he referred to Mayor Tony Petelos of Hoover, AL; former President Saddam Hussein of Iraq; and Usama bin Laden, leader of the Al Qaida terrorist organization.

Statement on Senate Passage of Military Commissions Legislation
September 28, 2006

Today the Senate sent a strong signal to the terrorists that we will continue using every element of national power to pursue our enemies and to prevent attacks on America. The "Military Commissions Act of 2006" will allow the continuation of a CIA program that has been one of America's most potent tools in fighting the war on terror. Under this program, suspected terrorists have been detained and questioned about threats against our country.

Information we have learned from the program has helped save lives at home and abroad. By authorizing the creation of military commissions, the act will also allow us to prosecute suspected terrorists for war crimes.

Our most solemn responsibility is protecting America's security, and I thank the Senate for passing this vital legislation.

NOTE: The statement referred to S. 3930.

Message on the Observance of Yom Kippur, 5767
September 28, 2006

Know therefore that the LORD your God is God, the faithful God who keeps covenant and steadfast love with those who love him and keep his commandments, to a thousand generations . . .

DEUTERONOMY 7:9

On this most holy day of the Jewish calendar, Jews celebrate God's goodness and reflect on their lives. Yom Kippur is a solemn time to express thanksgiving that the Almighty remembers the names of all His children. During this blessed Day of Atonement, Jewish people gather in synagogues, consider their deeds and actions, and celebrate as the sound of the Shofar proclaims the forgiveness and mercy shown by the Creator of life.

As the High Holy Days come to an end, the Jewish people in America and around the world remind us of the gift of religious freedom and the blessings of God's steadfast love. On Yom Kippur and throughout the year, your deep commitment to faith helps make the world a more hopeful and peaceful place.

Laura and I send our best wishes for a blessed Yom Kippur.

GEORGE W. BUSH

NOTE: An original was not available for verification of the content of this message.

Remarks to the Reserve Officers Association
September 29, 2006

Thanks, Captain Smith, for your kind introduction. Thank you all for being here, and thank you for the warm welcome. I am honored to stand with the men and women of the Reserve Officers Association. For more than 80 years, this organization has stood up for America and its citizen soldiers, and I appreciate your contribution to our country. We're safer because you stand ready to put on the uniform. I am grateful for your service, and I am proud to be your Commander in Chief.

I want to speak to you today about the struggle between moderation and extremism that is unfolding across the broader Middle East. At this moment, terrorists and extremists are fighting to overthrow moderate governments in the region so they can take control of countries and use them as bases from which to attack America and from which to impose their hateful ideology. This is the challenge of our time. This is the call of a generation, to stand against the extremists and support moderate leaders across the broader Middle East, to help us all secure a future of peace.

This week in Washington, I met with two courageous leaders who are working for peace, President Karzai of Afghanistan and President Musharraf of Pakistan. These leaders understand the stakes in the struggle, in the ideological struggle of the 21st century. They understand the stakes from a personal perspective as well, since the extremists have tried to assassinate them. They are courageous people. They have seen the destruction that terrorists have caused in their own country, and they know this: That the only way to stop them is to work together and to stay on the offense. By standing with brave leaders like these, we are defending civilization itself and we're building a more peaceful world for our children and grandchildren.

I appreciate very much the Ambassador from Afghanistan, Ambassador Jawad, and Ambassador Durrani from Pakistan for joining us here today. Thank you all for coming. I appreciate members of my administration who have joined us. I appreciate people wearing the uniform who have joined us. I appreciate those from Walter Reed who have joined us and from Bethesda. I thank you for your sacrifice.

I also want to thank those from Walter Reed who are—and Bethesda who are giving you the help you need to recover from your wounds. It gives me great comfort to be able to tell the loved ones of those who wear our uniform that if you get hurt, you will receive first-class, compassionate care from the United States military. And so to the healers who are here, thank you for doing your duty and providing these brave folks the help they need to recover.

Earlier this month, our Nation marked the fifth anniversary of the September the 11th, 2001, terrorist attacks. We paused on that day to remember the innocent people who were killed that day. We paused to remember the rescue workers who rushed into burning towers to save lives. After 9/11, I stood in the well of the House of Representatives and declared that every nation, in every region, had a decision to make: Either you were with us, or you stood with the terrorists. Two nations, Afghanistan and Pakistan, made very different decisions with very different results.

Five years ago, Afghanistan was ruled by the brutal Taliban regime. Under the Taliban and Al Qaida, Afghanistan was a land where women were imprisoned in their own homes, where men were beaten for missing prayer meetings, where girls couldn't even go to school. What a hopeless society that was, under the rule of these hateful men. Afghanistan was the home to terrorist training camps. Under Al Qaida and the Taliban, Afghanistan was a terrorist safe haven. It was a launching pad for the horrific attacks that killed innocent people in New York City on September the 11th, 2001.

After 9/11, America gave the leaders of the Taliban a choice. We told them that they must turn over all of the leaders of Al Qaida hiding in their land. We told them they must close every terrorist training camp and hand over every terrorist to appropriate authorities. We told them they must give the United States full access to the terrorist training camps so they could make sure they were no longer operating. We told them these demands were not up for negotiation, and that if they did not comply immediately and hand over the terrorists, they would share in the same fate as the terrorists.

I felt these were reasonable demands. The Taliban regime chose unwisely, so within weeks after the 9/11 attacks, our coalition launched Operation Enduring Freedom. By December 2001, the Taliban regime had been removed from power, hundreds of Taliban and Al Qaida fighters had been captured or killed, and the terrorist camps where the enemy had planned the 9/11 attacks were shut down. We did what we said we were going to do. We made our intentions clear. We gave the Taliban a chance to make the right decision. They made the wrong decision, and we liberated Afghanistan.

The liberation of Afghanistan was a great achievement, and for those of you who served in that effort, thank you. I thank you on behalf of America, and the Afghan people thank you. But we knew that it was only the beginning of our mission in Afghanistan. See, the liberation was only the start of an important mission to make this world a more peaceful place. We learned the lesson of the 1980s, when the United States had helped the Afghan people drive the Soviet Red army from Kabul and then decided our work was finished and left the Afghans to fend for themselves.

The Taliban came to power and provided a sanctuary for bin Laden and Al Qaida, and we paid the price when the terrorists struck our Nation and killed nearly 3,000 people in our midst. So after liberating Afghanistan, we began the difficult work of helping the Afghan people rebuild their country and establish a free nation on the rubble of the Taliban's tyranny.

With the help of the United Nations and coalition countries, Afghan leaders chose an interim Government. They wrote and approved a democratic Constitution. They held elections to choose a new President, and they elected leaders to represent them in a new parliament. In those parliamentary elections, more than 6 million Afghans defied terrorist threats and cast their ballots. They made it clear they wanted to live in a free society. As I travel around the country, I tell people that I'm not surprised when people say, "I want to live in liberty." I believe liberty is universal. I believe deep within the soul of every man, woman, and child on the face of the Earth is a desire to live in freedom. And when we free people, we not only do our duty to ourselves, but we help the rise of decent human beings.

As Afghans have braved the terrorists and claimed their freedom, we've helped them, and we will continue to help them. It's in our interests that we help this young democracy survive and grow strong. We helped them build security forces they need to defend their democratic gains. In the past 5 years, our coalition has trained and equipped more than 30,000 soldiers in the Afghan National Army, and at this moment, several thousand more are in training at a Kabul Military Training Center. These Afghan soldiers are on the frontlines with coalition troops. Some have suffered terrible wounds in battle; others have given their lives in the fight against the terrorists. Afghans in uniform are determined to protect their nation and fight our common enemies, and we're proud to fight alongside such brave allies.

Our coalition has also trained about 46,000 members of the Afghan National Police. The training of the Afghan police has not gone as smoothly as that of the army. The police have faced problems with corruption and substandard leadership, and we've made our concerns known to our friends in the Afghan Government. When we see a problem, we adjust; we change. And so this year President Karzai's Government announced a new team to lead the National Police. As the police become more capable and better led and more disciplined, they will gain legitimacy and they will earn the respect of the Afghan people.

Listen, the Afghan people want to live in a peaceful world. It's important for the American citizens to understand, an Afghan mother wants the same thing for her child that our mothers want for our children: the chance to grow up and realize dreams; the chance to live in peace. And it's important for the Afghan Government to provide the kind of security so the citizens have trust that their Government can enable the peace to evolve in that strife-ridden part of the world.

The army and police are good fighters. At this moment, more than 21,000 American troops and more than 20,000 personnel from 40 countries are deployed in Afghanistan. In the summer of 2003, NATO took over the International Security Assistance Force—it's called ISAF—in Afghanistan, NATO's first mission outside the Euro-Atlantic area. Other nations besides the United States understand the importance of helping this young democracy survive and thrive and grow.

Since then, NATO has expanded ISAF from a small force that was operating only in Kabul into a robust force that has taken responsibility for security in nearly 60 percent of the country. And this week, NATO announced that it would take over security operations in all of Afghanistan in the coming weeks. Under the plan, the U.S. will transfer 12,000 of our troops that are now serving in the country to the NATO force, while the rest will remain under coalition command and continue antiterrorist operations across the country.

We saw the effectiveness of NATO forces this summer when NATO took responsibility from the United States for security operations in southern Afghanistan. The Taliban saw the transfer of the region from the United States to NATO control as a window of opportunity. They saw it as an opportunity to test the will of nations other than the United States. See, they've been testing our will. And they understand it's strong, and they need to understand it will remain strong.

So the Taliban massed an estimated 800 to 900 fighters near Kandahar to face the NATO force head on, and that was a mistake. Earlier this month, NATO launched Operation Medusa. Together with the Afghan National Army, troops from Canada and Denmark and the Netherlands and Britain and the United States engaged the enemy, with operational support from Romanian and Portuguese and Estonian Forces. According to NATO Commanders, NATO forces killed hundreds of Taliban fighters. NATO's Supreme Allied Commander, General Jones, a United States Marine, says this about the NATO operation in southern Afghanistan: "The Taliban decided to make a test case of this region, and they paid a very heavy price for it. The operation sent a signal to the insurgents that NATO forces would not back down." The operation also sent a clear message to the Afghan people, that NATO is standing with you.

I appreciate the courage of the NATO forces. I appreciate the governments of our allies in NATO understanding the importance of helping the Afghan people achieve their dream, and that is a stable country. The people from NATO must understand that they're helping a young democracy defend itself and protect its people. And in so doing, they're helping to lay the foundation of peace in the ideological struggle of the 21st century.

The NATO deployment has begun to bring security and reconstruction to a region that had previously had little and has allowed the United States and Afghan forces to stay on the offense. And so we launched another major offensive in the east called Operation Mountain Fury. The operation is ongoing. It's aimed at clearing out enemy safe havens in five Afghan Provinces, including three Provinces bordering Pakistan. The operation is being led by about 4,000 Afghan forces and supported by about 3,000 of our finest. And Afghan and coalition forces clear out the enemy— then we will follow up with reconstruction assistance—so we can improve the quality of life for local Afghans and help extend the authority of the central Government to distant areas of the country.

See, the enemy understands what we're doing, and they don't like it. That's why they're reacting the way they're reacting. They understand that the arrival of Afghan and coalition forces in the region means that the Government is beginning to win the hearts of the people. In many of these regions, the Taliban and Al Qaida fighters and drug traffickers and criminal elements have had—enjoyed free reign. There hasn't been any countervailing force to their presence. And you can imagine how that makes innocent people feel, you know, when you've got these killers in your midst. It creates an atmosphere of fear. As a matter of fact, people like Al Qaida, whose ideology is hateful, have got one major tool at their disposal. They kill innocent life to create fear. And what a contrast it is to the United States of America and coalition partners and decent Afghans who believe in hope.

These haters of humanity know that when the Government in Kabul can reach out and improve the lives of local Afghans in distant parts of the country, the population will gain confidence in Afghanistan's democracy. That's part of the struggle, this ideological struggle we're engaged in. And so they are going to try to do everything they can to stop the progress. And they'll fight Afghan and coalition forces, and that's what you're seeing today.

But they do more than just fight our forces. They destroy schools, and they destroy clinics. They do everything in their power to intimidate local folks. The enemies of a free Afghanistan are brutal, and they're determined, and we're not going to let them succeed. NATO and coalition and Afghan forces will continue to fight the enemy. We will stay on the offense, and we're going to help this Government of President Karzai bring a better life to his people.

In order to bring a better life to the Afghan people, our coalition and NATO forces have deployed 23 Provincial Reconstruction Teams across Afghanistan. These teams are important because we're talking about a country that has been torn apart because of war over the years. The teams are led by Sweden and Norway and Germany and Hungary and Italy and Spain and Lithuania and Canada and Britain and the Netherlands and the United States. And these teams are bringing security and reconstruction assistance to distant regions of the country. And to link the distant regions to the capital, we've got a strategy—it's called building roads. This is a country that is in dire need for transportation. And since the liberation of Afghanistan, we've provided more than $4.5 billion for reconstruction throughout the country. We're helping with electricity and irrigation and water and sanitation and other necessities.

Our coalition is working with President Karzai to strengthen the institutions of Afghans—Afghanistan's young democracy. We understand that the institutions must be strengthened and reformed for democracy to survive. And one of the areas most in need of reform is the nation's legal system. Recently President Karzai took important steps to strengthen the rule of law when he appointed a new Attorney General and judges to serve on Afghanistan's Supreme Court. Our coalition is helping his Government institutionalize these changes. Italy, for example, is helping to train Afghan judges and prosecutors and public defenders and court administrators so all Afghans can receive equal justice under the law.

And from the beginning, our actions in Afghanistan have had a clear purpose—in other words, our goals are clear for people to understand—and that is to rid the country of the Taliban and the terrorists and build a lasting free society that will be an ally in the war on terror. And from the beginning, the American people have heard the critics say we're failing, but their reasons keep changing. In the first days of

Operation Enduring Freedom, the critics warned that we were headed toward a quagmire. And then when the Taliban fell and operations began in Iraq, the critics held up the multinational coalition in Afghanistan as a model and said it showed that everything we were doing in Iraq was wrong. And now some of the critics who praised the multinational coalition we built in Afghanistan claim that the country is in danger of failing because we don't have enough American troops there.

Look, in order to win war, in order to win the ideological struggle of the 21st century, it is important for this country to have a clear strategy and change tactics to meet the conditions on the ground, not try to constantly respond to the critics who change their positions. And so I listen to the advice of those who matter in Afghanistan, and that is President Karzai and our commanders. We will continue to help Afghanistan's Government defeat our common enemies.

I've constantly told the American people, we must defeat the enemy overseas so we do not have to face them here at home. I will continue to remind the American people that is—you deal with threats before they materialize. In this war that we're in, it is too late to respond to a threat after the—after we've been attacked. I'm not going to forget the lessons of September the 11th, 2001, and I know you won't either. We must take threats seriously now in order to protect the American people.

So we're going to help the people of Afghanistan, and we're going to help them build a free nation. We're going to help them be a successful part of defeating an ideology of hate with an ideology of hope. And think what that will mean for reformers and moderate people in a region that has been full of turmoil. Imagine the effect it will have when they see a thriving democracy in their midst.

No, this ideological struggle of the 21st century will require tough military action, good intelligence. It will require the United States to give our folks on the frontline of terror the tools necessary to protect us, including listening to phone calls from Al Qaida coming into the country—so we know what they're getting ready to attack—or questioning people we capture on the battlefield. That's what it's going to include.

But it also means helping the millions who want to live in liberty to do so. In the long term, we will help our children and grandchildren live in a peaceful world by encouraging the spread of liberty.

Five years ago, another country that faced a choice was Pakistan. At the time of 9/11, Pakistan was only one of three nations that recognized the Taliban regime in Afghanistan. Al Qaida had a large presence in Pakistan. There was a strong radical Islamic movement in that country. Some of the 9/11 hijackers were housed and trained in Pakistan. Pakistan's future was in doubt, and President Musharraf understood that he had to make a fundamental choice for his people. He could turn a blind eye and leave the people hostage to the extremists, or he could join the free world in fighting the extremists and the terrorists. President Musharraf made the choice to fight for freedom, and the United States of America is grateful for his leadership.

Within 2 days of the September the 11th attacks, the Pakistani Government committed itself to stop Al Qaida operatives at its border, to share intelligence on terrorist activities and movements, and to break off all ties with the Taliban government if it refused to hand over bin Laden and the Al Qaida. President Musharraf's decision to fight the terrorists was made at great personal risk. They have tried to kill him as a result of his decision because they know he has chosen to side with the forces of peace and moderation and that he stands in the way of their hateful vision for his country.

President Musharraf's courageous choice to join the struggle against extremism has saved American lives. His Government has helped capture or kill many senior terrorist leaders. For example, Pakistani forces helped capture Abu Zubaydah, a man we believe to be a trusted associate of Usama bin Laden. Pakistani forces helped capture another individual believed to be one of the key plotters of the 9/11 attacks, Ramzi bin al-Shibh. Pakistani forces helped capture the man our intelligence community believes masterminded the 9/11 attacks, Khalid Sheikh Mohammed.

Once captured, these men were taken into custody of the Central Intelligence Agency. The questioning of these and other suspected terrorists provided information that helped us protect the American people. They helped us break up a cell of Southeast Asian terrorist operatives that had been groomed for attacks inside the United States. They helped us disrupt an Al Qaida operation to develop anthrax for terrorist attacks. They helped us stop a planned strike on a U.S. Marine camp in Djibouti and to prevent a planned attack on the U.S. consulate in Karachi and to foil a plot to hijack passenger planes and to fly them into Heathrow Airport and London's Canary Wharf.

Were it not for the information gained from the terrorists captured with the help of Pakistan, our intelligence community believes that Al Qaida and its allies would have succeeded in launching another attack against the American homeland. Our close cooperation with the Government of Pakistan has saved American lives, and America is grateful to have a strong and steadfast ally in the war against these terrorists.

President Musharraf understands that the terrorists hide in remote regions and travel back and forth across the border between Afghanistan and Pakistan. And so we're helping his Government establish stronger control over these border areas. We are helping him to equip the nation's paramilitary Frontier Corps that is policing the border regions. The United States is funding the construction of more than 100 border outposts, which will provide Pakistani forces with better access to remote areas

of the country's western border. We're providing high-tech equipment to help Pakistani forces better locate terrorists attempting to cross the border. We are funding an air wing with helicopters and fixed-wing aircraft to give Pakistan better security and surveillance capabilities.

And as we work with President Musharraf to bring security to his own country, we're also supporting him as he takes steps to build a modern and moderate nation that will hold free and fair elections next year. In an address to his fellow citizens earlier this year, President Musharraf declared this: "We have to eliminate extremism in our society. It will eat us up from within. So it is my appeal to all of you to shun extremism. Adopt the path of moderation. We will eliminate this extremism in our society, and then Pakistan will be considered a moderate, developed country." President Musharraf has a clear vision for his country as a nation growing in freedom and prosperity and peace. And as he stands against the terrorists and for the free future of his country, the United States of America will stand with him.

In both Pakistan and Afghanistan, America has strong allies who are committed to rooting out the terrorists in their midst. And with their help, we've killed or captured hundreds of Al Qaida leaders and operatives, and we put the others on the run. Usama bin Laden and other terrorists are still in hiding. Our message to them is clear: No matter how long it takes, we will find you, and we're going to bring you to justice.

On Wednesday night, I had dinner with Presidents Musharraf and Karzai at the White House. We had a long—and we had a frank conversation about the challenges we face in defeating the extremists and the terrorists in their countries and providing the people of these two nations an alternative to the dark ideology of the enemy. We discussed the best ways to improve intelligence sharing so that we can target and eliminate the leaders of Al Qaida and the Taliban.

We resolved to strengthen the institutions of civil society in both countries. We agreed on the need to support tribal leaders on both sides of the border. By helping these local leaders build schools and roads and health clinics, we will help them build a better life for their communities and strengthen their hand against—the fight against the extremists. It was clear from our conversation that our three nations share the same goals: We will defeat the Taliban; we will defeat Al Qaida; and the only way to do it is by working together.

Our meeting took place at a time when there is a debate raging in Washington about how best to fight the war on terror. Recently parts of a classified document called the National Intelligence Estimate was leaked to the press. As I said yesterday in Alabama, it's an indication that we're getting close to an election. [*Laughter*] The NIE is a document that analyzes the threat we face from terrorists and extremists. And its unauthorized disclosure has set off a heated debate here in the United States, particularly in Washington.

Some have selectively quoted from this document to make the case that by fighting the terrorists—by fighting them in Iraq, we are making our people less secure here at home. This argument buys into the enemy's propaganda that the terrorists attack us because we're provoking them. I want to remind the American citizens that we were not in Iraq on September the 11th, 2001.

And this argument was powerfully answered this week by Prime Minister Tony Blair. Here is what he said. He said, "I believe passionately that we will not win until we shake ourselves free of the wretched capitulation to the propaganda of the enemy that somehow we are the ones responsible." He went on to say, "This terrorism is not our fault. We didn't cause it, and it is not the consequence of foreign policy." He's right. You do not create terrorism by fighting terrorism. If that ever

becomes the mindset of the policymakers in Washington, it means we'll go back to the old days of waiting to be attacked and then respond. Our most important duty is to protect the American people from a future attack, and the way to do so is to stay on the offense against the terrorists.

Iraq is not the reason the terrorists are at war against us. They are at war against us because they hate everything America stands for. And we stand for freedom. We stand for people to worship freely. One of the great things about America is you're equally American if you're a Jew, a Muslim, a Christian, an agnostic, or an atheist. What a powerful statement to the world about the compassion of the American people—that you're free to choose the religion you want in our country. They can't stand the thought that people can go into the public square in America and express their differences with government. They can't stand the thought that the people get to decide the future of our country by voting. Freedom bothers them because their ideology is the opposite of liberty; it is the opposite of freedom. And they don't like it because we know they know we stand in their way of their ambitions in the Middle East, their ambitions to spread their hateful ideology as a caliphate from Spain to Indonesia.

We'll defeat the terrorists in Iraq. We'll deny them the safe haven to replace the one they lost in Afghanistan. We're going to make it harder for them to recruit a new generation of terrorists. And we're going to help the Iraqis build a free society, a hopeful country that sends a powerful message across the broader Middle East and serves with those of us who believe in moderation and hope as an ally in the war against these extremists.

We can have confidence in the outcome of the war on terror because our Nation is determined. We've done this kind of hard work before, and we have succeeded. And we can be confident because we've got incredible men and women who wear our Nation's uniform. I am constantly amazed at the incredible courage that our fellow citizens who wear the uniform show on a regular basis.

I think of two Navy SEALs named Matthew Axelson and Danny Dietz. In June of 2005, they were part of a SEAL team operating deep in the mountains of Afghanistan on a mission to kill or capture a Taliban leader. They were discovered, and they were soon surrounded in a mountain ravine by 30 to 40 Taliban fighters. During the firefight that ensued, Axelson urged an injured teammate to escape, and he provided cover before suffering a mortal wound. Fighting nearby, his partner, Dietz, was also mortally wounded, but he stood his ground and kept firing until finally—he finally died.

Because of the courage of Petty Officers Axelson and Dietz, their wounded teammate made it out alive. For their heroism, these two petty officers were awarded the Navy Cross. But I want you to hear what Petty Officer Dietz's wife said about her husband and his comrades in arms. She said, "Danny and his brothers went toward evil and ran forward and gave their last breath."

We live in freedom because of the courage of men like Matthew and Danny, and we will honor their sacrifice by completing the mission. From Afghanistan and Iraq to Africa and Southeast Asia, we are engaged in a struggle against violent extremists, a struggle which will help determine the destiny of the civilized world. We've borne these responsibilities before, and we have seen our faith in freedom vindicated by history. In this young century, a new generation of Americans is being called to defend liberty, and once again, the cause of liberty and peace will prevail.

Thank you for coming. God bless.

NOTE: The President spoke at 9:36 a.m. at the Wardman Park Marriott Hotel. In his remarks, he referred to Capt. Michael P. Smith, USN (Ret.), national president, Reserve Officers Association; Usama bin Laden, leader of the Al Qaida terrorist organization; Attorney General Abdul Jabbar Sabbit of Afghanistan; and Prime Minister Tony Blair of the United Kingdom.

Remarks Following Discussions With President Nursultan Nazarbayev of Kazakhstan
September 29, 2006

President Bush. Mr. President, thank you for coming. It's been my honor to welcome the President of Kazakhstan back to the Oval Office. He informed me that the first time he was here was when my dad was the President. And I welcome you back.

We've just had a very important and interesting discussion. We discussed our desire to defeat extremism and our mutual desire to support the forces of moderation throughout the world. I thanked the President for his contribution to helping a new democracy in Iraq survive and thrive and grow.

I thank very much the President for his concerns about Afghanistan's democracy and his willingness to help in Afghanistan. We talked about our mutual—our bilateral relations and our mutual desire to—for Kazakhstan to join the WTO. We talked about our commitment to institutions that will enable liberty to flourish.

I have watched very carefully the development of this important country from one that was in the Soviet sphere to one that now is a free nation. And I appreciate your leadership, Mr. President. And I welcome you here to the White House, and I'm looking forward to buying you lunch. [*Laughter*]

President Nazarbayev. Thank you very much, Mr. President, for hospitality and for warm feelings that I feel in this country and for the invitation. This is the third time that I'm in the Oval room since the independence of our country and as I am the President of Kazakhstan. And Kazakh nation never had experienced statehood before, and I had this blessing of becoming the first President of Kazakhstan, and the United States was the country that supported our independence and recognized it from the very first days. Thus in economics, in energy partnership, in policy, in war on terrorism, we've truly become close partners.

And Kazakhstan today is very proud that we have the highest rate of economic growth in the world, and a lot of countries learn from the experience of Kazakhstan today. But that wouldn't be possible if Taliban would not be defeated in Afghanistan. And that war was led by United States. And nobody in central Asia will feel safe and peace if we'd be surrounded by countries populated with terrorist people,

and if we'd be surrounded by countries where some people crave to put their hands on the nuclear weapons, which Kazakhstan renounced in the past voluntarily, and thus contributed significantly to global security.

The United States is the major investor, foreign investor into Kazakhstan. One-third of all foreign investments in Kazakhstan are from United States. And after this meeting, we'll publish the joint declaration, and you will—in that declaration, you will read about the details and what we have discussed and what we have achieved during these negotiations.

And I'm here today to tell once again that Kazakhstan is a friend of the United States because the United States is the country that guaranteed stability and protection of Kazakhstan when Kazakhstan renounced nuclear weapons. And we will continue to work in all fields of our cooperation that exist today.

President Bush. Thank you.

NOTE: The President spoke at 11:51 a.m. in the Oval Office at the White House. President Nazarbayev spoke in Russian, and his remarks were translated by an interpreter.

Joint Statement by the United States of America and the Republic of Kazakhstan
September 29, 2006

We express satisfaction with the progress the United States and Kazakhstan have made in advancing our strategic partnership, and declare our commitment to a shared vision of stability, prosperity, and democratic reform in Central Asia and the broader region.

We affirm our commitment to advancing that vision through an increasingly dynamic and varied partnership that advances our global and regional objectives. We will deepen our cooperation in fighting international terrorism and the proliferation of

weapons of mass destruction. We will strengthen our cooperation to enhance regional security and economic integration and the reconstruction of Afghanistan and Iraq. We will expand our joint activities to ensure the development of energy resources, while supporting economic diversification and reform, market principles, and the development of small- and medium-size enterprises. We recognize that peaceful democratization invests citizens in the future of their nation. Developing democratic institutions is therefore the crucial condition of long-term stability.

The United States and Kazakhstan reaffirm the importance of democratic development, and are committed to accelerating Kazakhstan's efforts to strengthen representative institutions that further invest its citizens in the political process, such as an independent media, local self-government, and elections deemed free and fair by international standards. We note that our two governments are signatories to international human rights covenants and our common membership in organizations whose goal is to support democracy and human rights, including the Organization for Security and Cooperation in Europe. The United States supports efforts to promote democracy, strengthen religious freedoms, and bolster civil society in Kazakhstan. With the full participation of all political parties and non-governmental organizations, the United States supports the activity of the State Commission to develop a program of democratic reforms. Kazakhstan supports the assistance of American and other international non-governmental organizations promoting these objectives and will take the necessary steps to facilitate their legal functioning.

The United States commends Kazakhstan's traditions of religious tolerance and its efforts to promote inter-ethnic harmony and cooperation. We welcome the initiatives Kazakhstan has taken internationally to promote mutual understanding and strengthen religious freedoms, such as the Congress of Leaders of World and Traditional Religions, as well as initiatives to promote peace, such as the Conference on Interaction and Confidence-Building Measures in Asia. These initiatives bring important contributions to inter-religious and inter-ethnic tolerance, as well as international security and conflict resolution. We commit to deepening our cooperation to help ensure mutual understanding and security in the world.

The United States recognizes Kazakhstan's leadership and commends its efforts in preventing the proliferation of weapons of mass destruction, thus enhancing global security. Kazakhstan was the first country to voluntarily renounce its nuclear weapons after the break up of the former Soviet Union and also closed its nuclear test site. This example reflects our shared commitment to threat reduction and nonproliferation remains a cornerstone of our joint effort to ensure global and regional security. We welcome new agreements to blend down highly enriched uranium in Kazakhstan and Kazakhstan's strong policy of strengthening the regime of nuclear nonproliferation as concrete steps in support of the recently launched Global Initiative to Combat Nuclear Terrorism.

The United States and Kazakhstan are steadfast partners in the international war on terrorism. The United States is grateful to Kazakhstan for its unwavering commitment to strengthening stability in Afghanistan and Iraq. We commit to further strengthening the excellent cooperation already achieved by our two countries, and confirm the determination to strengthen our close cooperation in the fight against international terrorism and illegal trafficking in drugs, persons, and dangerous weapons.

We commit to further cooperation between our armed forces in counterterrorism and peacekeeping operations, both bilaterally and through NATO's Partnership for Peace Program.

We commend our energy partnership which has helped move Kazakhstan into the ranks of the world's leading reliable suppliers of hydrocarbon reserves. The United States welcomes Kazakhstan's recent accession to the Baku-Tbilisi-Ceyhan pipeline which has made a valuable contribution to this important multilateral project. Our energy partnership will promote the participation of U.S. companies in exploring the reserves of Kazakhstan, as well as in the development of nuclear energy. Our nations pledge to enhance common efforts to expand global energy supplies and will seek new means to deliver those resources to the international market.

We share a commitment to economic diversification across a range of industries and sectors. Recognizing Kazakhstan's macro-economic reforms and impressive economic successes, the United States will continue to assist in Kazakhstan's transformation into a strong, economically developed country. Both sides view liberalization and diversification of the economy as a key to sustained growth. The United States supports Kazakhstan's plan to join the world's fifty most competitive nations consistent with the strategy outlined by President Nursultan Nazarbayev. Strengthening the rule of law, taking steps to improve Kazakhstan's investment climate, and reducing business risk will contribute to that shared goal. We pledge our support for efforts under the Extractive Industries Transparency Initiative (EITI) to ensure that companies in the petroleum and mining industries observe international standards of transparency and accountability.

The United States supports Kazakhstan's membership in the World Trade Organization, and welcomes Kazakhstan's efforts to prepare for membership, recognizing that a market access agreement will enhance free trade and contribute to the continuing modernization of Kazakhstan's economy. The United States will send a team of experts to Kazakhstan in the coming months to continue this joint work. Both sides pledge to facilitate Kazakhstan's graduation under the Jackson-Vanik Amendment.

In order to strengthen friendship between our peoples, we intend to expand our cultural and humanitarian cooperation, including exchanges of students. We also intend to strengthen scientific and technical cooperation between researchers and students at universities, research institutes, and in the private sector.

The United States supports Kazakhstan's leadership in regional integration efforts including its significant investment throughout Eurasia and in Afghanistan. We declare our common commitment to strengthen the independence, sovereignty and security of, and to develop democratic institutions in, the countries of the region, ensuring their sustainable development and prosperity. We pledge to support legal trade by improving border crossings and customs procedures, the implementation of transportation and infrastructure projects, and the use of cross-border resources.

Confirming our commitment to this shared view to implementing the agreements achieved today, we declare our intention to further strengthen our strategic partnership through enhanced strategic dialogues on energy, military cooperation, trade and investment, and democratization. We express firm confidence that an enhanced strategic partnership between our countries will promote security and prosperity and foster democracy in the 21st Century.

NOTE: An original was not available for verification of the content of this joint statement.

Statement on Congressional Passage of Department of Defense Appropriations Legislation
September 29, 2006

I applaud Congress for passing legislation that will provide our men and women in uniform with the necessary resources to protect our country and win the war on terror. As our troops risk their lives to fight terrorism, this bill will ensure they are prepared to defeat today's enemies and ad-

dress tomorrow's threats. I look forward to signing this bill into law.

NOTE: The statement referred to H.R. 5631.

Statement on Signing the Department of Defense Appropriations Act, 2007
September 29, 2006

Today, I have signed into law H.R. 5631, the "Department of Defense Appropriations Act, 2007." The Act appropriates the funds needed to fight the war on terror, advance other United States interests around the world, and support our Armed Forces. The Act also continues funding for Government programs for which the Congress has not yet enacted regular appropriations acts.

Sections 8007, 8084, and 9005 of the Act prohibit the use of funds to initiate a special access program or a new start program, unless the congressional defense committees receive advance notice. The Supreme Court of the United States has stated that the President's authority to classify and control access to information bearing on the national security flows from the Constitution and does not depend upon a legislative grant of authority. Although the advance notice contemplated by sections 8007, 8084, and 9005 can be provided in most situations as a matter of comity, situations may arise, especially in wartime, in which the President must act promptly under his constitutional grants of executive power and authority as Commander in Chief of the Armed Forces while protecting certain extraordinarily sensitive national security information. The executive branch shall construe these sections in a manner consistent with the constitutional authority of the President.

Section 8050 of the Act provides that, notwithstanding any other provision of law, no funds available to the Department of Defense for fiscal year 2007 may be used

to transfer defense articles or services, other than intelligence services, to another nation or an international organization for international peacekeeping, peace enforcement, or humanitarian assistance operations, until 15 days after the executive branch notifies six committees of the Congress of the planned transfer. To the extent that protection of the U.S. Armed Forces deployed for international peacekeeping, peace enforcement, or humanitarian assistance operations might require action of a kind covered by section 8050 sooner than 15 days after notification, the executive branch shall construe the section in a manner consistent with the President's constitutional authority as Commander in Chief.

A proviso in the Act's appropriation for "Operation and Maintenance, Defense-Wide" purports to prohibit planning for consolidation of certain offices within the Department of Defense. Also, sections 8010(b), 8032(b), and 8089 purport to specify the content of portions of future budget requests to the Congress. The executive branch shall construe these provisions relating to planning and making of budget recommendations in a manner consistent with the President's constitutional authority to require the opinions of the heads of departments, to supervise the unitary executive branch, and to recommend for congressional consideration such measures as the President shall judge necessary and expedient.

Section 8005 of the Act, relating to requests to congressional committees for reprogramming of funds, shall be construed as calling solely for notification, as any other construction would be inconsistent with the constitutional principles enunciated by the Supreme Court of the United States in *INS v. Chadha*.

The executive branch shall construe section 8093, relating to integration of foreign intelligence information, in a manner consistent with the President's constitutional authority as Commander in Chief, including for the conduct of intelligence operations, and to supervise the unitary executive branch. Also, the executive branch shall construe sections 8095 and 8101 of the Act, which purport to prohibit the President from altering command and control relationships within the Armed Forces, as advisory, as any other construction would be inconsistent with the constitutional grant to the President of the authority of Commander in Chief.

The executive branch shall construe provisions of the Act relating to race, ethnicity, gender, and State residency, such as sec-

tions 8013, 8018 and 8048, in a manner consistent with the requirement to afford equal protection of the laws under the Due Process Clause of the Constitution's Fifth Amendment.

Sections 8039 and 8064 of the Act purport to allocate funds for specified purposes as set forth in the joint explanatory statement of managers that accompanied the Act and to direct compliance with a classified annex which was not incorporated into the Act and for which presentment was not made. The executive branch shall construe all these provisions in a manner consistent with the bicameral passage and presentment requirements of the Constitution for the making of a law.

GEORGE W. BUSH

The White House,
September 29, 2006.

NOTE: H.R. 5631, approved September 29, was assigned Public Law No. 109–289.

Memorandum on Extension of the Safety, Health, and Return-to-Employment (SHARE) Initiative
September 29, 2006

Memorandum for the Heads of Executive Departments and Agencies

Subject: Extension of the Safety, Health, and Return-to-Employment (SHARE) Initiative

On January 9, 2004, I established the 3-year Safety, Health, and Return-to-Employment (SHARE) Initiative, and directed all executive branch agencies to participate in this Government-wide effort to improve safety and health in Federal workplaces. SHARE's four goals focus attention in the most critical areas of a safety, health, and injury case management program: lower total injury and illness case rates, lower lost-time injury and illness case rates, im-

proved timely reporting of injuries and illnesses, and reduced rates of lost production days due to work-related injuries and illnesses.

During the first 2 years of SHARE, most departments and agencies reduced their injury and illness and lost production day rates, and significantly improved the timely reporting of incidents. From 2003 to 2005 the Government as a whole achieved a 5.5 percent reduction in an injury and illness case rate, a 2.6 percent reduction in its lost-time injury and illness case rate, and a 43 percent increase in timely reporting. According to the Department of Labor, which leads the SHARE Initiative and tracks and reports its performance results,

Fiscal Year 2006 results will be even more favorable.

Therefore, I am extending the SHARE Initiative through Fiscal Year 2009 to reaffirm my commitment to improving the safety of Federal workplaces and reducing the significant personal and financial costs of occupational injuries and illnesses.

The four goals of the SHARE Initiative will continue to use FY 2003 as the baseline. The goals for the timely filing of workers' compensation claims (Goal 3) and reduction of lost production days (Goal 4) have been modified to recognize consistent and superior agency performance and, at the same time, to hold low-end performers to more significant and challenging performance levels.

Each executive department and agency will collaborate with the Department of Labor to establish ambitious annual goals based on its current performance in each of the four areas. Agencies are encouraged to work with the Department of Labor's Occupational Safety and Health Administration and Employment Standards Administration's Office of Workers' Compensation Programs to develop and refine strategies for improving workplace safety and health. The Department of Labor will continue to lead the SHARE effort by measuring and tracking performance and reporting to me annually on performance, both Government-wide and by agency.

Safety and health and return-to-work are important employment values. To ensure that workers are protected from harm, Federal supervisory personnel must concentrate their attention and use all the management tools and resources at their disposal to prevent workplace injuries and illnesses. Managers and supervisors should encourage Federal employees to perform their jobs safely, effectively, and alertly to remain injury-free. A safe and healthy Federal workforce not only preserves the Government's valuable human resources, but also contributes to the effective and efficient delivery of Government services to the American people.

GEORGE W. BUSH

NOTE: An original was not available for verification of the content of this memorandum.

Message to the Congress Transmitting the District of Columbia's Fiscal Year 2007 Budget Request
September 29, 2006

To the Congress of the United States:

Pursuant to my constitutional authority and consistent with section 446 of The District of Columbia Self-Governmental Reorganization Act as amended in 1989, I am transmitting the District of Columbia's 2007 Budget Request Act.

The proposed 2007 Budget Request Act reflects the major programmatic objectives of the Mayor and the Council of the District of Columbia. For 2007, the District estimates total revenues and expenditures of $7.61 billion.

GEORGE W. BUSH

The White House,
September 29, 2006.

The President's Radio Address
September 30, 2006

Good morning. Today I want to talk to you about a matter of national security that has been in the news, the National Intelligence Estimate on terrorism. The NIE is a classified document that analyzes the threat we face from terrorists and extremists. Parts of this classified document were recently leaked to the press. That has created a heated debate in our Nation's Capital and a lot of misimpressions about the document's conclusions. I believe the American people should read the document themselves and come to their own conclusions, so I declassified its key judgments.

The National Intelligence Estimate confirms that we are up against a determined and capable enemy. The NIE lists four underlying factors that are fueling the extremist movement: first, longstanding grievances such as corruption, injustice, and a fear of Western domination; second, the jihad in Iraq; third, the slow pace of reform in Muslim nations; and fourth, pervasive anti-Americanism. It concludes that terrorists are exploiting all these factors to further their movement.

Some in Washington have selectively quoted from this document to make the case that by fighting the terrorists in Iraq, we are making our people less secure here at home. This argument buys into the enemy's propaganda that the terrorists attack us because we are provoking them. Here is what Prime Minister Tony Blair said this week about that argument: "This terrorism isn't our fault. We didn't cause it. It's not the consequence of foreign policy." Prime Minister Blair is right. We do not create terrorism by fighting terrorism. The terrorists are at war against us because they hate everything America stands for and because they know we stand in the way of their ambitions to take over the Middle East. We are fighting to stop them from taking over Iraq and turning that country into a

safe haven that would be even more valuable than the one they lost in Afghanistan.

Iraq is not the reason the terrorists are at war against us. Our troops were not in Iraq when terrorists first attacked the World Trade Center in 1993 or when terrorists blew up our Embassies in Kenya and Tanzania or when they bombed the USS *Cole* or when they killed nearly 3,000 people on September the 11th, 2001. Five years after the 9/11 attacks, some people in Washington still do not understand the nature of the enemy. The only way to protect our citizens at home is to go on the offense against the enemy across the world. When terrorists spend their days working to avoid capture, they are less able to plot, plan, and execute new attacks on our people. So we will remain on the offense until the terrorists are defeated and this fight is won.

In my recent speeches, I've said we are in the early hours of a long struggle for civilization and that our safety depends on the outcome of the battle in Iraq. The National Intelligence Estimate declares, quote, "Perceived jihadist success there would inspire more fighters to continue the struggle elsewhere." It also says that, quote, "Should jihadists leaving Iraq perceive themselves, and be perceived, to have failed, we judge fewer fighters will be inspired to carry on the fight."

Withdrawing from Iraq before the enemy is defeated would embolden the terrorists. It would help them find new recruits to carry out even more destructive attacks on our Nation, and it would give the terrorists a new sanctuary in the heart of the Middle East, with huge oil riches to fund their ambitions. America must not allow this to happen. We are a nation that keeps its commitments to those who long for liberty and want to live in peace. We will stand with the nearly 12 million Iraqis who voted for their freedom, and we will help them fight and defeat the terrorists there so we do not have to face them here at home.

Thank you for listening.

NOTE: The address was recorded at 7:55 a.m. on September 29 in the Cabinet Room at the White House for broadcast at 10:06 a.m. on September 30. The transcript was made available by the Office of the Press Secretary on September 29 but was embargoed for release until the broadcast. In his address, the President referred to Prime Minister Tony Blair of the United Kingdom. The Office of the Press Secretary also released a Spanish language transcript of this address.

Statement on Senate Confirmation of Mary E. Peters as Secretary of Transportation
September 30, 2006

I am pleased that the Senate swiftly confirmed Mary Peters as Secretary of Transportation.

Mary is an innovative thinker who will work with State and local leaders to confront challenges and solve problems. I look forward to working with her to reduce highway and aviation congestion, modernize our Nation's infrastructure, and increase the efficiency of travel in our country. Her leadership will enable the Department to maintain a safe, reliable, and efficient transportation system.

I congratulate Mary and her family on her confirmation and thank her for her service to our Nation.

Statement on Congressional Passage of Legislation Supporting Iran's Freedom
September 30, 2006

My administration is working on many fronts to address the challenges posed by the Iranian regime's pursuit of weapons of mass destruction, support for terrorism, efforts to destabilize the Middle East, and repression of the fundamental human rights of the citizens of Iran. We are engaged in intense diplomacy alongside our allies and have also undertaken financial measures to counter the actions of the Iranian regime.

I applaud Congress for demonstrating its bipartisan commitment to confronting the Iranian regime's repressive and destabilizing activities by passing the Iran Freedom Support Act. This legislation will codify U.S. sanctions on Iran while providing my administration with flexibility to tailor those sanctions in appropriate circumstances and impose sanctions upon entities that aid the Iranian regime's development of nuclear weapons.

I applaud the efforts of Chairman Richard Shelby, Ranking Member Paul Sarbanes, Rick Santorum, and Bill Nelson in the Senate and Chairman Henry Hyde, Ranking Member Tom Lantos, Ileana Ros-Lehtinen, and Gary Ackerman in the House. I look forward to signing this bill into law, which will facilitate America's support for the Iranian people in their efforts to build a just, free, and peaceful society.

NOTE: The statement referred to H.R. 6198.

Message to the Senate Transmitting the Protocol Amending the Denmark-United States Taxation Convention
September 29, 2006

To the Senate of the United States:

I transmit herewith, for Senate advice and consent to ratification, a Protocol Amending the Convention Between the Government of the United States of America and the Government of the Kingdom of Denmark for the Avoidance of Double Taxation and the Prevention of Fiscal Evasion with Respect to Taxes on Income signed at Copenhagen May 2, 2006 (the "Protocol"). A related exchange of notes is enclosed for the information of the Senate. Also transmitted for the information of the Senate is the report of the Department of State with respect to the Protocol.

The Protocol eliminates the withholding tax on certain cross-border dividend payments. Like a number of recent U.S. tax agreements, the proposed Protocol provides for the elimination of the withholding tax on dividends arising from certain direct investments and cross-border dividend payments to pension funds. In addition, the Protocol modernizes the Convention to bring it into closer conformity with current U.S. tax-treaty policy, including strengthening the treaty's provisions preventing so-called treaty shopping.

I recommend that the Senate give early and favorable consideration to the Protocol and give its advice and consent to ratification.

GEORGE W. BUSH

The White House,
September 29, 2006.

NOTE: This message was released by the Office of the Press Secretary on October 2.

Message to the Senate Transmitting the Protocol Amending the Finland-United States Taxation Convention
September 29, 2006

To the Senate of the United States:

I transmit herewith, for Senate advice and consent to ratification, a Protocol Amending the Convention Between the Government of the United States of America and the Government of the Republic of Finland for the Avoidance of Double Taxation and the Prevention of Fiscal Evasion with Respect to Taxes on Income and on Capital, signed at Helsinki May 31, 2006 (the "Protocol"). Also transmitted for the information of the Senate is the report of the Department of State with respect to the Protocol.

The Protocol eliminates the withholding tax on certain cross-border dividend payments. Like a number of recent U.S. tax agreements, the proposed Protocol provides for the elimination of the withholding tax on dividends arising from certain direct investments and cross-border dividend payments to pension funds. The Protocol also eliminates the withholding tax on cross-border royalty payments. In addition, the Protocol modernizes the Convention to bring it into closer conformity with current U.S. tax-treaty policy, including strengthening the treaty's provisions preventing so-called treaty shopping.

I recommend that the Senate give early and favorable consideration to the Protocol and give its advice and consent to ratification.

GEORGE W. BUSH

The White House,

September 29, 2006.

NOTE: This message was released by the Office of the Press Secretary on October 2.

Message to the Senate Transmitting the Protocol Amending the Germany-United States Taxation Convention
September 29, 2006

To the Senate of the United States:

I transmit herewith, for Senate advice and consent to ratification, a Protocol Amending the Convention Between the United States of America and the Federal Republic of Germany for the Avoidance of Double Taxation and the Prevention of Fiscal Evasion with Respect to Taxes on Income and Capital and to Certain Other Taxes, Signed on August 29, 1989, signed at Berlin June 1, 2006 (the "Protocol"), along with a related Joint Declaration. Also transmitted for the information of the Senate is the report of the Department of State with respect to the Protocol.

The Protocol eliminates the withholding tax on certain cross-border dividend payments. Like a number of recent U.S. tax agreements, the proposed Protocol provides for the elimination of the withholding tax on dividends arising from certain direct investments and cross-border dividend pay-ments to pension funds. The Protocol also provides for mandatory arbitration of certain cases before the competent authorities. This provision is the first of its kind in a U.S. tax treaty. In addition, the Protocol also modernizes the Convention to bring it into closer conformity with current U.S. tax-treaty policy, including strengthening the treaty's provisions preventing so-called treaty shopping.

I recommend that the Senate give early and favorable consideration to the Protocol, along with the Joint Declaration and give its advice and consent to ratification.

GEORGE W. BUSH

The White House,
September 29, 2006.

NOTE: This message was released by the Office of the Press Secretary on October 2.

Message to the Senate Transmitting the Estonia-United States Extradition Treaty
September 29, 2006

To the Senate of the United States:

With a view to receiving the advice and consent of the Senate to ratification, I transmit herewith the Extradition Treaty between the United States of America and the Government of the Republic of Estonia, signed on February 8, 2006, at Tallinn. I also transmit, for the information of the Senate, the report of the Department of State with respect to the treaty.

The new extradition treaty with Estonia would replace the outdated extradition treaty between the United States and Estonia, signed on November 8, 1923, at Tallinn, and the Supplementary Extradition Treaty, signed on October 10, 1934, at Washington. The treaty also fulfills the requirement for a bilateral instrument between the United States and each European Union (EU) Member State in order to implement the Extradition Agreement between the United States and the EU. Two other comprehensive new extradition treaties with EU Member States—Latvia and Malta—likewise also serve as the requisite bilateral instruments pursuant to the U.S.-EU Agreement, and therefore also are being submitted separately and individually.

The treaty follows generally the form and content of other extradition treaties recently concluded by the United States. It would replace an outmoded list of extraditable offenses with a modern "dual criminality" approach, which would enable extradition for such offenses as money laundering and other newer offenses not appearing on the list. The treaty also contains a modernized "political offense" clause. It further provides that extradition shall not be refused based on the nationality of the person sought; in the past, Estonia has declined to extradite its nationals to the United States. Finally, the new treaty incorporates a series of procedural improvements to streamline and speed the extradition process.

I recommend that the Senate give early and favorable consideration to the treaty.

GEORGE W. BUSH

The White House,
September 29, 2006.

NOTE: This message was released by the Office of the Press Secretary on October 2.

Message to the Senate Transmitting the Latvia-United States Extradition Treaty
September 29, 2006

To the Senate of the United States:

With a view to receiving the advice and consent of the Senate to ratification, I transmit herewith the Extradition Treaty between the United States of America and the Government of the Republic of Latvia, signed on December 7, 2005, at Riga. I also transmit, for the information of the Senate, the report of the Department of State with respect to the treaty.

The new extradition treaty with Latvia would replace the outdated extradition treaty between the United States and Latvia, signed on October 16, 1923, at Riga, and the Supplementary Extradition Treaty, signed on October 10, 1934, at Washington. The treaty also fulfills the requirement for a bilateral instrument between the United States and each European Union (EU) Member State in order to implement the Extradition Agreement between the United States and the EU. Two other comprehensive new extradition treaties with EU Member States—Estonia and Malta—likewise also serve as the requisite bilateral instruments pursuant to the U.S.-EU Agreement, and therefore also are being submitted separately and individually.

The treaty follows generally the form and content of other extradition treaties recently concluded by the United States. It would replace an outmoded list of extraditable offenses with a modern "dual criminality" approach, which would enable extradition for such offenses as money laundering and other newer offenses not appearing on the list. The treaty also contains a modernized "political offense" clause. It further provides that extradition shall not be refused based on the nationality of the person sought; in the past, Latvia has declined to extradite its nationals to the United States. A national who has been convicted in the courts of the other Party may request to be allowed to serve the resulting sentence in his state of nationality. Finally, the new treaty incorporates a series of procedural improvements to streamline and speed the extradition process.

I recommend that the Senate give early and favorable consideration to the treaty.

GEORGE W. BUSH

The White House,
September 29, 2006.

NOTE: This message was released by the Office of the Press Secretary on October 2.

Message to the Senate Transmitting the Malta-United States Extradition Treaty
September 29, 2006

To the Senate of the United States:

With a view to receiving the advice and consent of the Senate to ratification, I transmit herewith the Extradition Treaty between the United States of America and the Government of Malta, signed on May 18, 2006, at Valletta, that includes an exchange of letters that is an integral part of the treaty. I also transmit, for the information of the Senate, the report of the Department of State with respect to the treaty.

The new extradition treaty with Malta would replace the outdated extradition treaty between the United States and Great Britain, signed on December 22, 1931, at London, and made applicable to Malta on June 24, 1935. The treaty also fulfills the requirement for a bilateral instrument between the United States and each European Union (EU) Member State in order to implement the Extradition Agreement between the United States and the EU. Two other comprehensive new extradition treaties with EU Member States—Estonia and Latvia—likewise also serve as the requisite bilateral instruments pursuant to the U.S.-EU Agreement, and therefore also are being submitted separately and individually.

The treaty follows generally the form and content of other extradition treaties recently concluded by the United States. It would replace an outmoded list of extraditable offenses with a modern "dual criminality" approach, which would enable extradition for such offenses as money laundering and other newer offenses not appearing on the list. The treaty also contains a modernized "political offense" clause. It further provides that extradition shall not be refused based on the nationality of a person sought for any of a comprehensive list of serious offenses; in the past, Malta has declined to extradite its nationals to the United States. Finally, the new treaty incorporates a series of procedural improvements to streamline and speed the extradition process.

I recommend that the Senate give early and favorable consideration to the treaty.

GEORGE W. BUSH

The White House,

September 29, 2006.

NOTE: This message was released by the Office of the Press Secretary on October 2.

Remarks Following a Meeting With Special Envoy to Sudan Andrew S. Natsios
October 2, 2006

The President. Recently, I named my friend Andrew Natsios to be the Presidential Special Envoy to Sudan to help us deal with the issue in Darfur. The reason I named Andrew is, one, he knows the area well; he's been involved in this area for a long period of time. Secondly, he, like me, shares a deep concern about the suffering in Darfur.

We believe the world has a responsibility to respond to what this Government has called genocide. And Andrew Natsios is going to help rally the world to solve the problem. The United Nations can play an important role in helping us achieve our objective, which is to end human suffering and deprivation. In my view, the United Nations should not wait any longer to approve a blue-helmeted force, a U.N. force of peacekeepers to protect the innocent people.

And Andrew knows my opinion and knows my beliefs. And I appreciate him very much implementing the strategy that our Government will develop to save lives. And I thank you for your efforts again, and thank you for your commitment.

Special Envoy Natsios. Thank you. I've been going to Sudan now for 17 years. I know leaders in all regions of the country, and I'm going to use those contacts and that history to move this process along. I have a great affection, personally, for the Sudanese people, north and south. My first trip to Darfur was 17 years ago, during the first Darfur war—this is the third war in Darfur in 17 years.

And I think what our objective is, is not just to have a temporary fix for 2 months but to try to deal with the root causes of this so we don't have another fourth war in 5 years—should we end this one successfully.

So I'm going to work on that. I think with the President's strong support—both of us are committed to this, and we're going to see what we can do.

The President. Thank you, Andrew. Appreciate it.

Special Envoy Natsios. Thank you.

NOTE: The President spoke at 9:50 a.m. in the Oval Office at the White House.

Remarks Following Discussions With Prime Minister Recep Tayyip Erdogan of Turkey
October 2, 2006

President Bush. Mr. Prime Minister, welcome back to Washington. We just had a extensive and important dialog about how Turkey and the United States can and must work together to achieve peace. We talked about our determined efforts to fight terror and extremism. We talked about our common efforts to bring stability to the Middle East. We had an important discussion about

both Iraq and Iran. Our desire is for— to help people who care about a peaceful future to reject radicalism and extremism.

I made it very clear to the Prime Minister, I think it's in the United States interests that Turkey join the European Union. And I congratulate the Prime Minister and his Government for the economic reforms that have enabled the Turkish economy to be strong, for the good of the Turkish people.

And finally, we shared our deep desire to improve the lives of those who are suffering in Darfur. The Prime Minister shared with me a personal account of what he saw, the suffering he saw, the human— the pitiful human condition he personally saw in Darfur. He shared with me his Government's anxiousness to help the people there, and I assured him I shared the same concern. And it's important for the United Nations and the Government of Sudan to take forward steps to help the—end the suffering.

I consider the Prime Minister a friend and a man of peace, and I welcome him.

Prime Minister Erdogan. Thank you. Distinguished members of the press, it is a great honor and pleasure to be here upon the invitation of President Bush, an ally. The United States is a strategic partner, a very important strategic partner for Turkey and an ally for many years.

In our meeting, we had the opportunity to discuss many points, especially terrorism. And the joint steps that we have taken in order to pursue with determination our fight against terrorism continues to be very important in our relations. In fact, we do share the same opinion about forming a joint platform in order to combat terrorism on a global scale.

We also had opportunity to discuss Lebanon as well as Israel and Palestine.

It was important to hear the President say that their support for Turkey's membership to the European Union will continue. We have also had the opportunity to discuss Cyprus, and I have expressed our sensitivities with regard to the issues related to Cyprus. And we had an opportunity to extensively discuss what we can do in the Middle East, what Turkey specifically can do in the Middle East.

We have also discussed Turkey's progress and reforms with regards to the European Union—the Copenhagen political criteria as well as Maastricht criteria—and the recent work that is ongoing with the screening process at the EU for Turkey's accession.

All in all, I think we had a very positive meeting, and I would like to thank the President for that.

President Bush. Thank you, sir.

NOTE: The President spoke at 11:40 a.m. in the Oval Office at the White House. Prime Minister Erdogan spoke in Turkish, and his remarks were translated by an interpreter.

Remarks at a Reception for Congressional Candidate Dean Heller in Reno, Nevada
October 2, 2006

Thank you all for coming. It's good to be back in Reno. I appreciate the invitation. I'm here to say as clearly as I can, Dean Heller is the right person for the United States Congress. And I want to thank you for helping him.

I appreciate the fantastic fundraiser. It's a good sign, Dean, when your friends and neighbors are willing to put a little hard-earned cash into the hat in order to help you. [*Laughter*] But he's going to need more than your money; he's going to need your time. And so coming down the stretch, I call on the grassroots activists and those who have been participating in campaigns to put up the signs and go to your houses of worship or your community centers and say, "We've got a good man in Dean Heller; he loves his family; he loves his country; he loves the people of the Second Congressional District. Let's send him to Washington, DC."

All he's got to do is get his family to go to work for him. [*Laughter*] I met a bunch of them today. I'm really proud to be with—[*laughter*]—with Lynne and the four children. I like a man who knows his priorities. We need people in Washington who have got the right priorities. And the priorities—he and I share a priority: our faith, our family, and our country.

Now, I wasn't Dean's first choice. [*Laughter*] He wisely had put in a request for Laura—[*laughter*]—who sends her love and her best to all our friends out here in Reno, in Nevada. We're blessed with friends. I wouldn't be standing here without the people of this good State voting for me, not once but twice. And in selecting me, you selected a really fine person to be the First Lady. I can't tell you how proud I am of Laura. I am a lucky man that she said yes when I asked her to marry me, and some of her friends in Texas wondered whether it was a wise decision or not, but we're doing great.

And we're really proud—I'm proud to be here. She, like me, understands Dean Heller will make a great United States Congressman. I want to thank his predecessor, Jim Gibbons. I've been honored to work with Jim on behalf of the people. Another predecessor is here; Barbara Vucanovich is with us. Barbara, it's good to see you. I'm proud you're here. Mother and Dad send their best. [*Laughter*] This Barbara knows the other Barbara. [*Laughter*]

I want to thank Kenny Guinn and Dema for joining us today. Kenny Guinn has been a great Governor for the State of Nevada. We're proud to call him friend, and I'm proud to call Dema friend. You know, one of the interesting things that we get to do is to share the White House with our friends from around the country. We've had the Governor and his wife spend the night with us when the National Governors were in town. And I remember Kenny walking around the White House saying, "My good-ness, I can't believe I'm here." [*Laughter*] And then he looked at me. [*Laughter*]

I hope you all support Jim Gibbons to replace Governor Kenny Guinn. And now that I'm going down the election roster and—make sure you put Ensign back in too; he's a great United States Senator.

I want to thank Brian Krolicki; he's going to be the Lieutenant Governor of the State of Nevada. Thanks for coming, Brian. We've got the mayor here, Bob Cashell. Bob, good to see you again. Mr. Mayor, proud you're here. And all the local officials—it's a good sign when the local officials are coming. It's when they stay away from the rallies, is when you get nervous. [*Laughter*]

I want to thank you all. It really is important you're here. Obviously, this is a race that my administration considers to be an important race. That's why I got on the airplane after meeting with the Prime Minister of Turkey to come out here and help Dean.

I want to thank Troy Marston; he led the Pledge of Allegiance—Private 1st Class, 3d Brigade, 101st Airborne, recently returned from Iraq. It is an honor to be the Commander in Chief of the finest military in the world. And the reason we're the finest military in the world is because of the men and women who have volunteered to wear the uniform of the United States of America. And being—one of your jobs and one of my jobs is to make sure our troops have all that is necessary to do their job and protect the United States of America.

I've been looking forward to this campaign because it gives me a chance to travel around the country making it clear there are significant differences in what we believe and what the other bunch believes. You take taxes, for example. You know, Dean talked about the fact that when we came in, we had a recession and then there was a terrorist attack and then we went to war and there was corporate scandals; there was hurricanes and high gasoline prices. And yet this economy is growing. And the reason it's growing, and the primary reason in my mind it's growing is because we cut the taxes on the working people; we cut the taxes on the small-business owners; we cut taxes on families with children.

We put an end to the marriage penalty—or started to put an end to the marriage penalty. I really don't understand a tax code that penalizes marriage. [*Laughter*] We ought to be encouraging marriage in the United States. The tax cuts we passed have worked.

And this election campaign is one in which the people have got a stark choice. You listen to those Democrats in Washington talk. I don't know how they're talking in Nevada, but I can tell how they're talking in Washington. And they're saying, "Well, we're not going to—we're going to let these tax cuts expire," see, hoping the American people don't pay attention to those words.

See, if you let the tax cuts expire—in other words, if you don't make the tax cuts permanent—it means your taxes are going to go up. It's a tax increase. The way I like to put it is, if the Democrats take control of the United States Congress, they're going to have their hand in your pocket; they're going to be running up your taxes. Raising the taxes on the people who work for a living, raising the taxes on the farmers and ranchers, raising the taxes on the small-business owners is bad economic policy. And that's why we need Dean Heller in the United States Congress.

Oh, you'll hear them tell you up there, or over there, they'll say, "Well, we need to raise taxes just on some of you in order to balance the budget." That's not the way Washington, DC, works. They'll raise your taxes, and they'll figure out new ways to spend your money. The best way to balance the budget is to keep progrowth economic policies in place so this economy grows and to prioritize how we spend your money. And the priorities I've set for the United

States Congress is winning this war on terror and making sure we've got what it takes to defend the American people.

You know, it's amazing what happens when you grow the economy. See, cutting taxes is counterintuitive for some in Washington, but when you reduce taxes, it causes the economy to grow. And when the economy grows, there's more tax revenues coming in. And that's what's happened recently. And that's why we're cutting the deficit in half prior to the goal I set in 2009. We need fiscally responsible people in Washington, DC. And Dean Heller will be a fine Congressman when it comes to watching your money.

We need people in Washington, DC, who understand that we need to make sure health care is available and affordable. Now, there's an interesting debate up there in the Nation's Capital, and it's this: who best to decide how to make decisions for health care, who best to make that decision—the Federal Government, or the doctors and patients? We believe that the doctors and patients should be making the health care decisions in the United States of America. And one way to make sure health care is available and affordable is to do something about these junk lawsuits that are running good doctors out of practice.

Now, I'm looking forward to working with Dean on good domestic policy that keeps this economy growing and keeps the power—decisionmaking power in the hands of the people. And I'm looking forward to working with him to do our most solemn duty, and that's to protect you.

You know, when I ran in 2000—I remember campaigning here—you know, I didn't want to be a war President. As a matter of fact, anybody who says, "Vote for me; I want to be a war President"—don't vote for him. [*Laughter*] No one should ever wish that. But an enemy declared war on us, a war we didn't want, but it's a war we must engage. September the 11th made it abundantly clear that the most solemn responsibility of the Federal Government is to protect the American people.

We're fighting an enemy that knows no rules. They're inhumane. They are evil people who have taken the religion and kill in the name of that religion to achieve geopolitical objectives. They're bound by a common ideology. They want to establish a caliphate that ranges from Indonesia to Spain. I'm not making this up. I'm simply repeating that which we have learned about the enemy from their own words.

You can't negotiate with these people. Therapy is not going to work. [*Laughter*] The best way to deal with this enemy is to bring them to justice before they hurt the American people again.

You know, it's a difficult task to protect the homeland, because we've got to be right 100 percent of the time, and these killers have got to be right once. And therefore, I thought it was important to make sure that those on the frontline of fighting terror and the extremists had all the tools necessary to protect the American people.

And that's why I called upon Congress to eliminate the walls and barriers that had arisen over time between the intelligence services and the criminal justice people, so they can share intelligence that is necessary to protect you. And that's why I thought it was important to set up a program that said, if Al Qaida or an Al Qaida affiliate is making a phone call into the United States of America, we need to know why in order to protect the American people.

And I want our fellow citizens to look at who voted for those proposals and what political party voted against them. There's a clear difference of opinion about how to protect this homeland.

You know, recently, we just had an important debate in Washington, DC. It's a debate over whether or not the Central Intelligence Agency should have a program that enabled our professionals to question high-value detainees to determine if they had information that could help protect the homeland. Obviously, I thought that was an important program. I submitted the bill after a speech in the East Room of the White House. I submitted that bill to the Congress. See, I understand the nature of the information we received from people such as Khalid Sheikh Mohammed; he is the mastermind of the September the 11th attacks.

I'll be signing that bill pretty soon. The Congress passed the bill, but I want you all to remember, when you go to the polls here in Nevada, what political party supported the President to make sure we had the tools necessary to protect the American people, and which political party didn't.

I have made the decision that the best way to protect the American people is to get on the offense against this enemy and stay on the offense. There is a difference of opinion in Washington. If you listen closely to some of the leaders of the Democrat Party, it sounds like they think the best way to protect the American people is, wait until we're attacked again. That's not the way it's going to be under my administration. We will stay on the offense, we will defeat the enemy overseas so we do not have to face them here at home.

And it's hard work, but it's necessary work. It's the calling of the 21st century. It's the call of a generation to determine whether we have the will and the vision to protect the American people.

Now, the lesson I have learned from September the 11th was two—one—many, but two of the most notable ones were, if you find somebody harboring a terrorist, they're equally as guilty as the terrorists and must be held to account. And that's why we removed the Taliban from Afghanistan and freed 25 million people from the clutches of a barbaric regime.

And I saw a threat in Iraq, and so did Members of the United States Congress and people on the United Nations Security Council. Saddam Hussein was a state sponsor of terror. He had killed thousands of his own people. He had used weapons of mass destruction. He was a sworn enemy of the United States. He paid families of suicide bombers. He was a threat, and the United Nations said that loud and clear. It was his choice to make, of whether or not he wanted war. He chose war, and the world is better off without Saddam Hussein in power.

And I think it's a legitimate question to ask candidates running for Congress or United States Senators who have been critical of policy, whether or not they think the world would be better off with Saddam Hussein in power. You know, when this question was asked to a senior member of the Intelligence Committee, the Democrat member, he said, "Yes, the world would be better off, given the world today, with Saddam Hussein in power."

Well, I just see it differently. I think it's important we take threats before they come home to hurt us. America cannot wait to be attacked again. In order to protect the United States of America, we must stay on the offense, and we will do so.

The other thing you hear coming out of the Nation's Capital is whether Iraq is a distraction on the war on terror: You know, it's not part of the war on terror. I happen to think it's a central front in the war on terror. Success in Iraq will help make this country more secure. Failure in Iraq will mean that we will have left behind a treacherous world for children and our grandchildren.

But if you don't take my word, take the word of Usama bin Laden or Mr. Zawahiri about the importance of Iraq. The number one and two of Al Qaida have made it clear that Iraq is the central front in the war on terror, and their ambitions are to drive the United States out of Iraq and to abandon the 12 million people who went to the polls and to say it's not worth it. They believe it's worth it. Al Qaida thinks it's necessary in order to defeat America. They want us to leave so they can have a safe haven from which to plot and plan

new attacks against the United States of America.

Imagine a world where moderate governments have been toppled by extremists and extremists get ahold of oil. If you think it was tough at $70 a barrel, imagine what it will be like when these extremists get ahold of a valuable resource and say to the free world, "Do it our way, or we're going to have an unbelievable economic peril." And couple with that an Iran with a nuclear weapon, and 20 or 30 years from now, the world will look back and say, "What happened to America? How come they couldn't see the threat?"

The threat is real. We will help those 12 million people who demanded freedom in Iraq achieve a stable democracy that can govern itself, defend itself, and sustain itself, and America and generations of Americans will be more secure.

You know, people ask me all the time, do you really think people in the Middle East want to be free? It's a legitimate question, I guess. But it belies the fact that we believe in the universality of freedom. Freedom is not just an American possession. It's not our gift to the world. I happen to believe there is an Almighty, and I believe one of the great gifts of that Almighty is the desire to be free, to every man, woman, and child on the face of the Earth.

So in the short term, our strategy is clear: We will stay on the offense; we will bring people to justice before they can hurt us again. In the long term, we will defeat the ideology of hatred with an ideology of hope.

I have made it clear to the American people, I view the struggle we're in as the great ideological struggle of the 21st century. It's akin to the cold war in some ways. It is the difference between tyranny and freedom, between moderation and extremism. Make no mistake about it: Most moms in the Middle East yearn for the same things our mom's want, which is a peaceful world in which to raise their children. Most people in the Middle East long for peace. What we're dealing with are radicals and extremists who have a dark vision for the future. And the fundamental question facing this country is, will we have the nerve, will we have the willpower, will we have the perseverance to do the hard work today so a generation of younger Americans can grow up in a more peaceful world?

And I take great hope, and I'm optimistic about achieving our objectives. First, I know how good our military is. Point them in the right direction, give them a clear goal, and they'll achieve the objective. Second, I know how hard people are working to protect you. Our intelligence is getting better. See, it's a different kind of war. You used to—could measure progress based upon the number of airplanes in the air or number of ships on the sea. It's hard to measure progress in this kind of war. But I'm just telling you, we're dismantling Al Qaida one person at a time. We're on the hunt. And it's just a matter of time before Usama bin Laden gets the justice he deserves.

You know, let me conclude by sharing this story with you. You might remember, I had an interesting experience recently when I went down with the former Prime Minister of Japan, my buddy, Koizumi, who just left office recently. And we went down to Elvis's place—[*laughter*]—in Memphis. It was an interesting experience. [*Laughter*] I went there for a couple of reasons. One, I wanted to see Elvis's place; I'd never been—[*Laughter*]—60 years old and had never been to Graceland. Plus, Laura wanted to go. Secondly, Prime Minister Koizumi really wanted to go. [*Laughter*] He likes Elvis; he likes his songs; he likes everything about Elvis.

Thirdly, I wanted to tell a story about what's possible and what will happen if we keep faith in the values that led to our formation and has led to us doing hard work in order to keep the peace. You see, the story I tell is the one that started with 18-year-old George H.W. Bush, my dad,

when he joined the United States Navy to fight the sworn enemy, the Japanese. A lot of other people did too. It was a brutal war. A lot of folks died.

And I find it interesting—not only interesting, I find it ironic in many ways that some 60 years later, the son of the 18-year-old fighter pilot was on Air Force One, flying to Memphis, Tennessee, with the Prime Minister of the former enemy, talking about how to keep the peace. We talked about North Korea. We talked about the fact that the way you defeat extremists and radicals is by helping people realize the blessings of liberty. Isn't that interesting? The Prime Minister of the former enemy talking about the blessings of liberty and freedom.

Something happened between World War II and 2006, and that was, Japan adopted a Japanese-style democracy. Liberty has the capacity to transform enemies into allies. Liberty has the capacity to transform regions of hate into regions of hope. What you're seeing is the beginning of a victory against an ideology of extremists, by an ideology that yields the blessings of peace, an ideology that enables the sons of former enemies to sit down, crafting strategy to make the world a better place for generations to come.

And that's what's going to happen some day. Elected leaders in the Middle East will be sitting down with an American President, talking about how to keep the peace. And our children and our grandchildren will be better off for it.

And those are the stakes in this election. It's an important election. And we need people in the United States Congress who see the world the way it is, not the way we would hope it would be now. We have to have clear-eyed realists on the one hand but people who have got faith in the great values, the universal values that can enable us to look back when history passes by and say, we did our jobs. We were called to serve, and we served by leaving behind a better world—and Dean Heller is such a man.

Thanks for coming. God bless.

NOTE: The President spoke at 5:29 p.m. at the Mercury Air Center. In his remarks, he referred to Lynne Heller, wife of congressional candidate Dean Heller; Gov. Kenny C. Guinn of Nevada and his wife, Dema;

Mayor Bob Cashell of Reno, NV; Prime Minister Recep Tayyip Erdogan of Turkey; Khalid Sheikh Mohammed, senior Al Qaida leader responsible for planning the September 11, 2001, terrorist attacks, who was captured in Pakistan on March 1, 2003; and former President Saddam Hussein of Iraq. He also referred to S. 3930, the "Military Commissions Act of 2006."

Memorandum on Promoting Sustainable Fisheries and Ending Destructive Fishing Practices
October 2, 2006

Memorandum for the Secretary of State and the Secretary of Commerce

Subject: Promoting Sustainable Fisheries and Ending Destructive Fishing Practices

It shall be the policy of the United States, in advancing the interests of the American people, to support the maintenance and use of sustainable fisheries (1) as a source of nutritious food for the United States and the rest of the world, and (2) to meet the needs of commercial and recreational fishing. To implement the policy set forth above, the Secretary of State, after consultation with the Secretary of Commerce, shall:

(1) work with other countries and international organizations to eliminate fishing practices that (a) jeopardize fish stocks or the habitats that support them, or (b) provide a commercial advantage to those who engage in such practices that is unfair in comparison with their competitors;

(2) work within Regional Fishery Management Organizations (RFMOs), and through other cooperative arrangements, to establish rules based on sound science to enhance sustainable fishing practices and to phase out destructive fishing practices;

(3) work with other countries to establish new RFMOs, or other cooperative institutional arrangements, to protect ecosystems in high seas areas where no competent RFMO or other arrangement exists, including calling on all nations to protect vulnerable marine ecosystems by prohibiting their vessels from engaging in destructive fishing practices in areas of the high seas where there are no applicable conservation or management measures or in areas with no applicable international fishery management organization or agreement, until such time as conservation and management measures consistent with the goals of the Magnuson-Stevens Fishery Conservation and Management Act (Public Law 94–265, as amended), the United Nations Fish Stocks Agreement, and other relevant instruments are adopted and implemented to regulate such vessels and fisheries;

(4) work with other countries to develop and promulgate criteria to guide the determination of which marine ecosystems are or are not at risk of damage or loss because of destructive fishing practices; and

(5) work with other countries to combat through enhanced monitoring and surveillance, including through the use of Vessel Monitoring Systems and other technologies, fishing that is unlawful, unregulated, and unreported.

Further, to implement the policy set forth above, the Secretary of State, after consultation with the Secretary of Commerce, shall carry out diplomatic activities for the purposes of (a) ending destructive fishing practices, and (b) promoting rules based on sound science to support sustainable fisheries and to end destructive fishing practices.

As used in this memorandum, the term "destructive fishing practices" are practices that destroy the long-term natural productivity of fish stocks or habitats such as seamounts, corals, and sponge fields for short-term gain.

This memorandum shall be implemented consistent with applicable law and subject to the availability of appropriations. It is intended only to improve the internal management of the executive branch and is not intended to, and does not, create any right or benefit, substantive or procedural, enforceable at law or in equity by a party against the United States, its departments, agencies, entities, officers, employees, or agents, or any other person.

GEORGE W. BUSH

NOTE: This memorandum was released by the Office of the Press Secretary on October 3. An original was not available for verification of the content of this memorandum.

Remarks at a Breakfast for Congressional Candidate Richard W. Pombo in Stockton, California
October 3, 2006

Thank you all very much. Thanks a lot. Please be seated. I don't want your eggs to get cold. [*Laughter*] Mr. Chairman, thank you for welcoming me to your district. I'm proud to be here on behalf of Richard Pombo, and I'm proud to be able to tell the people of the State of California, he's doing a fine job for the people of this district.

I know firsthand; I watch him up close; I've seen him in action. I think it makes sense for people from the State of California to send somebody to Washington, DC, who trusts the people of California. And that's Richard Pombo. I think it makes sense to send somebody from the State of California to Washington, DC, who knows what it means to make a living off the land. And that's Richard Pombo.

In all due respect to those of you who are here who are attorneys of law—[*laughter*]—we've got enough of those kind of people in Washington. [*Laughter*] It makes sense to have a rancher and a farmer speak commonsense language. See, what we need is some common sense in Washington, DC. Chairman Richard Pombo brings common sense to the big debates of our time. He brings practical experience when it comes to promoting cooperative conservation.

He understands, like I understand, that being dependent on foreign oil endangers the United States of America. It's a national security risk and an economic security risk. Richard Pombo thinks strategically on behalf of the people of this district and the United States. I'm proud to support his efforts to pass comprehensive energy. See, he and I know that technology is going to help us become less dependent on foreign sources of energy in the longer term. We'll be using ethanol from a product grown right here in California to power our cars. We'll have plug-in hybrid batteries. We'll be using hydrogen to power our automobiles. But in the meantime, we need to be exploring in environmentally friendly ways for energy from the United States of America, to make us less dependent on foreign sources of energy.

I'm proud to support Richard Pombo, a commonsense leader in the House of Representatives, and urge you to send him back to the United States Congress.

I want to thank you all for coming. I told Richard when I walked up here, it's a good sign when the home folks show up in the numbers like you have. [*Laughter*] It's always a good indication that when the people who know you best support you the strongest. So I want to thank you for contributing of your hard-earned dollars and urge you to help this good man as we're coming down the stretch. And that means turning out the vote, finding those solid Republicans, discerning Democrats, and wise independents to go to the polls and send Richard Pombo back to the United States Congress.

Laura sends her best. She sends her best to Richard, she sends her best to Annette and the Pombo family, and she sends her best to our many friends here in California. I'm a lucky man, when Laura said yes when I asked her to marry me. She has got to be the most patient woman in America. I realize I'm not very objective, but I'll report from the homefront, America's got a fabulous First Lady in Laura Bush.

And old Richard, the chairman, married well himself; Annette, thank you for being here. Thank you for supporting Richard. And I'm proud to be here with Rena and Rachel. It's good to see you young women. Thanks for coming today. I know you'll be putting up the signs and making those phone calls for old dad coming down the stretch.

I'm proud to be with Ralph and Onita Pombo, Richard's mom and dad. I suspect that Mrs. Pombo has something in common with my mother, that they're both not afraid to tell us what to do. [*Laughter*] And my only advice, Richard, is you make sure you listen to her, because I'm listening to mine, you'll be happy to know.

I'm proud to be here with Mayor Ed Chavez, the mayor of Stockton, California. Mr. Mayor, thank you for coming. It gives me great joy to be able to look out in the audience and see one of the city's finest citizens and a family we call friend in my household, somebody who's been a friend with you during good times and somebody who's a friend with you during not-so-good times but somebody who's always a friend, and that's the Spanos family. Alex and Faye, thank you for coming.

I want to thank all the local and State officials who have joined us. I especially want to thank Specialist Gerry Lee, United States Army National Guard, who not only served in Iraq but went down and helped those souls recovering from Hurricane Katrina. It's an honor to be the Commander in Chief of such fine, fine men and women, people who put on the uniform to the protect this country. And I'll tell you one thing about Richard Pombo. You don't have to worry, and I don't worry about him making sure our troops have all that's needed to do their job to support the United States of America and its people.

There's a lot of issues I could talk about, because there's big differences of opinion in Washington, DC. I don't know how it gets translated back here at home. Sometimes they go up to Washington and say one thing, and then come back and talk differently when they—in front of the home people. You don't have to worry about Richard Pombo. He tells you exactly what he thinks. You don't have to try to read between the lines. You don't have to worry about him taking a poll to determine what he believes. He stands on principle, and that's what you need in Washington, DC.

And he and I share a principle, and that is what to do with your money, how do we deal with the hard-working people's money. And make no mistake about it, there is a philosophical divide in Washington, DC. You might remember what this Nation went through, what our economy went through over the last 5½ years. We had a recession. We had corporate scandals. There was, obviously, the devastating attack on September the 11th, 2001. We responded and protected this people by taking a war to the enemy. We've had hurricanes. We've had high energy prices. Yet our economy is the envy of the industrialized world.

The national unemployment rate is low. The entrepreneurial spirit is high. Small businesses are making a living. Our farmers and ranchers—they probably don't want to admit it, but our farmers and ranchers are doing fine. See, I'm used to farmers and ranchers; after all, I'm from Texas, you might remember. I also want to take a step back and tell you, though, that a strong farm economy and a strong ranching economy is really important to the national economy.

And so in spite of these obstacles, the economy has grown. And something happened, and what happened was, we cut the taxes on the working people. We understand the role of government is not to try to create wealth but to create an environment in which the entrepreneurial spirit flourishes. The tax relief we passed is working, and the American economy is strong. And the fundamental question is, how do we keep it strong? And Richard Pombo and I believe the best way to keep this economy growing is to make the tax relief we passed permanent.

And the Democrats don't agree. If the Democrats were to gain power, they will raise your taxes, because they believe they can spend your money better than you can. Oh, you'll hear all kinds of excuses: "Let

us raise your taxes to balance the budget." That's not how Washington works. They will raise your taxes and figure out new ways to spend your money. The best way to balance the budget is to keep the taxes low so we can grow our economy, which increases more tax revenues, and be wise about how we spend your money. We're on our way to cutting this deficit in half before the year 2009 because of the progrowth economic policies we put in place and because of fiscal conservatives like Richard Pombo.

The issue on the economy is a big issue in any campaign. And I want the people of this district to know, plain and simple, that if Richard's opponent wins, your taxes will go up. Make no mistake about it. The Democrat Party is anxious to get their hands on your money. If you want to keep taxes low, if you want to make sure this environment for small-business growth and farmers and ranchers remains strong, put Richard Pombo back in the United States Congress, and we'll work to make the tax cuts we passed permanent.

I also appreciate his strong support in this war on terror. I wish I could tell you that there wasn't a war, but that's not the truth. That is not the reality of the world in which we live. There's an enemy that still plots and plans, that wants to attack us again. They're a group of ideologues bound together by this evil vision of the world, that want to inflict harm on the United States because we stand in the way of their ambitions and because we strongly believe in liberty.

The most important job of the Federal Government in the beginning of the 21st century is to do everything in our power to protect you from further attack. The key issue in this campaign is the security of the United States of America. You got to understand, a lot of my thinking about the world changed on September the 11th, 2001. I make a lot of decisions on your behalf, and many of those decisions were affected by the fact that we lost nearly

3,000 of our citizens, 3,000 innocent lives on our soil on that fateful day. I vowed then, and I've vowed ever since, to use every national asset at my disposal to protect the American people. And the best way to do so is to defeat those people overseas so we do not have to face them here at home.

I thank Richard's support. I appreciate the fact we've got Members of Congress who clearly see the enemy for what they are. You can't negotiate with these people. You cannot hope that they will go away. I like to remind people, therapy isn't going to work. The best way to deal with these folks is to bring them to justice before they hurt America again.

You know, there's a debate in Washington, DC, about how to wage this war, and that's positive. Ours is a democracy; I welcome the debate. But I also have a responsibility to make it clear the consequences of some of the positions our opponents take. They say that Iraq is a distraction in the war on terror. I strongly disagree. I think Iraq is a central front in the war on terror, and we must defeat the enemy in Iraq if we want America to be secure.

But don't take my word for it about Iraq. Our fellow citizens ought to listen to the words of Usama bin Laden and Mr. Zawahiri, who is his number two in Al Qaida. They have clearly stated that Iraq is a central front in their war against us. They have made their ambitions clear, and that is to inflict harm and damage on innocent life to the point where America says it's not worth it and retreats and leaves before the job is done. They have made their ambitions clear: to topple moderate governments. Al Qaida's leadership has told us loud and clear in their own words, their ambitions are to develop new safe haven from which to launch attacks.

Imagine a world in which there are competing forms of religious extremists trying to achieve dominance, a world in which moderate governments feel no longer capable of defending themselves against these radicals and extremists, a world in which they control oil, and a world in which a theocracy may have a nuclear weapon. Those are the stakes as we begin the 21st century. We're in the midst of an ideological struggle. And the fundamental question is, will we have people in the United States Congress who see the world the way it is, who clearly see the threats?

I'm going to tell you this: 20 or 30 years from now it's not going to be said, during my administration or during Richard Pombo's time in Congress, that the United States of America didn't confront these threats now, in order to make our children live in a more peaceful world.

It's hard work, but it's necessary work. Iraq is a central part on the war on terror, and we have a plan for victory there. We have a security plan that will chase down those extremists and radicals who would like to do us harm, and enable the Iraqis to defend themselves. We have a political strategy, and that is to stand squarely with the 12 million people who said loud and clear, "We want to be free."

You know, it must seem like an eternity to you, when you think about those elections last December. It certainly does to me, in some ways. Ultimately, when this chapter of history will be written, however, it's going to be a comma; the Iraqis voted, comma, and the United States of America understood that Iraq was a central front in the war on terror and helped this young democracy flourish so that a generation of Americans wouldn't have to worry about the extremists emanating from that country to hurt the American people.

The stakes are high. The Democrats are the party of cut-and-run. Ours is a party that has got a clear vision and says we will give our commanders and troops the support necessary to achieve that victory in Iraq. We will stay in Iraq, we will fight in Iraq, and we will win in Iraq.

Our strategy is to stay on the offense, and we will do that. You just got to know there's some fine, fine, brave men and women in uniform—and some not in uniform—in the intelligence services, doing everything they can to find the enemy every single day. It's hard to plot and plan when you're hiding in a cave and are on the run. And that's our strategy, and that's the way we're going to keep it.

But we got to do a job here at home too. See, our job is one in which we got to be right 100 percent of the time to protect you, and the enemy has got to be right one time. And that's why, in the days after 9/11, I would—I vowed that we would give those responsible for defending you the tools they need to do so. We worked with Congress—my administration worked with Congress to pass what's called the PATRIOT Act. It's the first measure we took that would break down barriers that prevented intelligence and law enforcement personnel from sharing information with each other.

It's probably hard for you to understand, but law enforcement and intelligence officers couldn't talk, and so the PATRIOT Act addressed that issue. How can you protect the American people if you don't have all branches of government sharing information, is what we thought.

We also established the terrorist surveillance program to monitor terrorist communications in and out of our country. We created a program with the Central Intelligence Agency to detain and question key terrorist operatives that were captured on the battlefield. I told the American people we would give our folks on the frontline of fighting terror to protect you the tools necessary.

On each of these programs, the Democrats have said they share our goals. But when it comes time to vote, they consistently oppose giving our personnel the tools they need to protect us. Time and time again, the Democrats want to have it both ways. They talk tough on terror, but when the votes are counted, their softer side comes out.

Let's take the PATRIOT Act. In the weeks after 9/11, we passed this vital law, and I want to thank Richard Pombo for his support. You don't have to worry about him. He understands that those on the frontline of fighting terror need to have the tools necessary to protect you. And in the 5 years since that law was passed, it has proved invaluable to stopping new attacks on our country. Our law enforcement community has used the law to break up terror cells or prosecute terrorist operatives and supporters in California, in Texas and New Jersey and Illinois and North Carolina and Virginia, Ohio, New York, and Florida.

In 2001, the vote in the United States Senate to pass this law was 98 to 1. But when the bill came up for renewal in 2005, Senate Democrats filibustered it, that means, tried to talk it to death. That's what filibuster means up in Washington-speak. They didn't want it to pass. In fact, the Senate Democrat leader bragged, "We killed the PATRIOT Act." That's what he said. When he was asked later by a reporter whether killing the PATRIOT Act was really something to celebrate, he answered, "Of course it is." The Democrat attempt to filibuster the PATRIOT Act follows an approach that might sound familiar: They voted for it before they voted against it.

Eventually, common sense prevailed. The bill was passed, and I signed it into law, and I firmly believe the American people are safer because that bill was renewed.

After 9/11, we recognized the need for new tools to learn what the terrorists are planning and then to be able to move quickly to stop them. See, this is a different kind of war—that is, different kind of threats—and we've got to make sure the tools are given to those on the frontline of protecting you. If the biggest issue and the biggest job of the Federal Government is to protect you, we must have the tools necessary to do so.

So I directed the National Security Agency to establish the terrorist surveillance program to track terrorist communications between someone overseas and someone in the United States. The philosophy behind this program is pretty clear: If Al Qaida operatives are making calls in the United States, we need to know who they're calling, why they're calling, and what they're planning.

Apparently, this simple logic is not very clear to the Democrats in the United States Congress. Last week, when legislation providing additional authority for the terrorist surveillance program came before the House of Representatives, 177 Democrats voted against listening in on terrorists communications.

The stakes in this election couldn't be more clear. If you don't think we should be listening in on the terrorists, then you ought to vote for the Democrats. If you want your government to continue listening in when Al Qaida planners are making phone calls into the United States, then you vote Republican.

We got to make sure people have got the tools necessary to defeat this enemy in a new kind of war. After the 9/11 attacks, I established a CIA program to detain and question key terrorist operatives and leaders who were captured on the battlefield in this war on terror. Captured terrorists have unique knowledge about where their operatives are deployed and what plots may be underway. In other words, they know. And it seems like it makes sense for us to know what they know, in order to protect you.

See, I know the security of the United States depends on getting this kind of information. For the past 5 years, the good and decent professionals of the CIA have worked tirelessly to get information from captured terrorists that enabled us to stop new attacks on our homeland and to save American lives.

Every American must understand what this program has meant to the security of our country. Information from the terrorists questioned by the CIA helped break up a cell of Southeast Asian terrorist operatives that had been groomed for attacks inside the United States. The program helped us stop an Al Qaida cell from developing anthrax for attacks against the United States. This program helped us stop a planned strike on a U.S. Marine camp in Djibouti. It helped prevent a planned attack on the U.S. consulate in Karachi. It helped foil a plot to hijack planes and fly them into Heathrow Airport and London's Canary Wharf.

Were it not for the information gained from the terrorists questioned by the Central Intelligence Agency, our intelligence community believes that Al Qaida and its allies would have succeeded in launching another attack against the American homeland. The CIA program has saved lives, and it remains one of the most vital tools our Nation has in the war against these extremists and terrorists.

Last week, Congress held a vote on the future of this CIA program. The choice before every Member was clear: Should the CIA program continue or not? Congress voted to continue the program. I look forward to signing it into law.

The vote tells us a great deal about where the two parties stand when it comes to defending America in this war on terror. In the House of Representatives, 160 Democrats—including the entire Democrat leadership—voted against continuing this program. Think about that. Almost 80 percent of the House Democrats want to stop a program that has provided invaluable intelligence that's saved American lives. In the Senate, 32 Democrats, including every member of the Senate leadership save one, voted to kill this vital program. That means almost three-quarters of the Democrats in the Senate, including both of your Senators here in California, voted to stop the men and women of the CIA from continuing a program to get information from terrorists like Khalid Sheikh Mohammed about planned attacks on the United States.

During the debate on the Senate floor, one senior Democrat, their ranking member on the Judiciary Committee, compared the brave Americans who question these terrorists to the Taliban and Saddam Hussein. This exposes a dangerous mindset on the part of Democrats in Congress. You can't defend America if you cannot tell the difference between the CIA officers who protect their fellow citizens and brutal dictators who kill their fellow citizens.

Another Senate Democrat said that allowing the CIA to go forward with this program to question the most dangerous terrorists we have captured would diminish the security and safety of Americans everywhere. If they feel we are safer without this program, the Democrats in the United States Senate need to explain to the American people which of the attacks that the CIA program stopped would they have been willing to let go forward.

We got a clear record on this issue. We know this program is making Americans safer, and we're not going to allow the Democrats in Congress to take it away.

People of this district have got to understand, there's a different mindset. Look, people in Washington are patriotic people. The Democrats are good people; they've just got a different view of the world than I have. They don't see it the way I see it. The House Democrat leader summed up her party's approach to the midterm elections. She said this—and I quote—she said this election, quote, "should not be about national security." I strongly disagree. The security of this country comes first, as far as I'm concerned. And this Government, with supporters like Richard Pombo, will do everything we can to protect you. Of course, to give the leader some credit, given her party's record on national security, I can see why she feels that way. [Laughter] I wouldn't want to be talking about the record, either.

The difference between our parties comes down to this: Democrats take a law enforcement approach to terrorism. That means America will wait until we're attacked again before we respond. We believe we're at war, and we will prevent those attacks from happening in the first place.

Their record is clear. When people go to the polls here in this district and districts around the country, I want them to look at the record, to look at the facts. Democrats have voted time and again to deny our personnel the tools they need to protect you. Republicans are giving you the tools they need—giving our folks the tools they need to keep this country safe. If you want leaders in Washington that understand the enemy we face and who are not going to sit back and wait for them to attack us again, I urge you to send Richard Pombo back to the United States Congress.

Again, I want to thank you for coming. I believe the decisions that I have made have made this country safer. And I believe the decisions I have made to take the enemy on overseas and to promote liberty and freedom to people who are desperate to be free, I believe those decisions are laying the foundation of peace for a generation to come.

I'm proud to be on the stage with a fellow citizen who understands the power of liberty to bring the peace we want. I'm proud to be with you all as you help this good man get reelected. I thank you for your prayers. I thank you for being here, and may God bless you all.

NOTE: The President spoke at 9:22 a.m. at the Stockton Memorial Civic Auditorium. In his remarks, he referred to Annette Pombo, wife of Rep. Richard W. Pombo; Alex G. Spanos, owner, San Diego Chargers professional football team, and his wife, Faye; Usama bin Laden, leader of the Al Qaida terrorist organization; Khalid Sheikh Mohammed, senior Al Qaida leader responsible for planning the September 11, 2001, terrorist attacks, who was arrested in Pakistan on March 1, 2003; and former President Saddam Hussein of Iraq.

Remarks at George W. Bush Elementary School in Stockton
October 3, 2006

The President. I want to thank Sylvia Ulmer, the principal of George W. Bush Elementary School, for welcoming me. It's such an honor, Sylvia—and Jack, thank you, sir—it's such an honor to have a school named after me. When I pulled in the parking lot and I saw George W. Bush Elementary, I couldn't think of a higher tribute to a person, and I thank you all and the citizens of this community for this honor and tribute. Frankly, I was a little emotional when I pulled in——

Sylvia Ulmer. So am I. So am I.

The President. I want to thank the teachers and the faculty here. I can't wait to tell Laura that I went into the Laura Bush Library and saw teachers working hard to teach kids how to read. It's just a blessing to be there.

You know, being at this school reminds us, we have a special responsibility to protect our children. One of the most important jobs of those involved with schools and government is to make sure that children are safe. And Laura and I were saddened and deeply concerned, like a lot of other citizens around the country, about the school shootings that took place in Pennsylvania and Colorado and Wisconsin. We grieve with the parents, and we share the concerns of those who worry about safety in schools.

Yesterday I instructed Attorney General Gonzales and Secretary of Education Margaret Spellings to convene a meeting next Tuesday, a meeting of leading experts and stakeholders, to determine how best the Federal Government can help States and local governments improve school safety.

Our schoolchildren should never fear their safety when then enter to a classroom. And, of course, the superintendent and principal know that.

We also had a reminder of the need for people in positions of responsibility to uphold that responsibility when it comes to children, in the case of Congressman Mark Foley. I was dismayed and shocked to learn about Congressman Foley's unacceptable behavior. I was disgusted by the revelations and disappointed that he would violate the trust of the citizens who placed him in office.

Families have every right to expect that when they send their children to be a congressional page in Washington, that those children will be safe. We have every right as citizens to expect people who hold higher office behave responsibly in that office. I fully support Speaker Hastert's call for an investigation by law enforcement into this matter. This investigation should be thorough, and any violations of the law should be prosecuted.

Now, I know Denny Hastert; I meet with him a lot. He is a father, teacher, coach, who cares about the children of this country. I know that he wants all the facts to come out, and he wants to ensure that these children up there on Capitol Hill are protected. I'm confident he will provide whatever leadership he can to law enforcement in this investigation.

Again, I want to thank you for your hospitality. It's an honor to be here. Appreciate your time. God bless. Thank you.

NOTE: The President spoke at 10:28 a.m. In his remarks, he referred to Jack McLaughlin, superintendent, Stockton Unified School District.

Remarks at a Reception for Congressional Candidate John T. Doolittle in El Dorado Hills, California
October 3, 2006

Thank you for coming. Thanks for the warm welcome. It's good to be in El Dorado County. [*Laughter*] I can see why you live here. It's a beautiful part of the world. And I'm honored to be standing here with a man who has done a fine job as a Member of the United States Congress, John Doolittle.

He was telling me on the way in, you did a pretty good job filling the hat— [*laughter*]—and I want to thank you for doing that. He deserves your support. He's a straightforward, honest, decent man with a lot of common sense. That's what we need in Washington, DC, a lot of common sense. And I'm proud to be standing with John Doolittle, and I appreciate Julie, and I appreciate his family.

I'm also proud to be here with the Congressman from the next district, and that would be Dan Lungren. Dan, thank you for coming, and I'm glad you brought Bobbi with you. I also appreciate Doug Ose, a former Congressman. Doug is with us, a good friend of mine; I'm proud to be with him.

The truth of the matter is, old John, when he's thinking about who could come and speak, really didn't want me first. [*Laughter*] He had somebody else in mind for this event—not Barbara—[*laughter*]— Laura. That shows good judgment. [*Laughter*] Laura sends her best to the Doolittles. She, like me, strongly believes John deserves to be reelected to the United States Congress. And we want to thank you for doing that.

By the way, I know I'm not very objective, but I think Laura is a fabulous First Lady. I know she's a great wife and a fabulous mother, and she's got to be the most patient woman in America. [*Laughter*]

I believe strongly that our philosophy represents the philosophy that is the most hopeful for all Americans. I believe our philosophy is one that works, because we've seen it work. Take, for example, the economy. I want you all to remember that the past 5 years, this economy has been through a lot. It's been through a recession, corporate scandals; it's been through a terrorist attack on the United States. The economy had to endure the fact that I decided to protect this country by going on the offense against the terrorists, and so we had a war in Afghanistan and a war in Iraq, and natural disasters we had to deal with, high energy prices. And yet the economy of the United States is the envy of the industrialized world. People are working. The entrepreneurial spirit is strong. Our farmers and ranchers are doing well. Small businesses are growing. Productivity is up.

Something happened, and what happened was, we cut the taxes on the working people and the small-business owners. Our philosophy is that the more money you have in your pocket, the better off the economy is. We like it when you've got more money to save, spend, and invest. We know that when you save, spend, or invest, the economy grows.

That stands in stark contrast to our opponents, the Democrats. They believe they can spend your money better than you can. And make no mistake about it, one of the fundamental differences of this campaign is what will the tax rates look like. If you vote Republican, we're going to keep the taxes low. If the people vote Democrat, the Government is getting into your pocket and spend your money on your behalf.

Now, you might not—listen carefully to the rhetoric in this campaign. You see, we've got these tax cuts in place, and a lot of them are going to expire. So when you hear people say, "Well, we're not going to extend the tax cuts," that really means they're going to raise your taxes. It's like saying to somebody, just giving them a raise and say, "Well, I'm going to take the raise away from you." That's not a raise.

In order to make sure this economy continues to grow, in order to make sure the entrepreneurial spirit remains strong, in order to make sure our small-business sector continues to lead economic growth, we need to make the tax cuts permanent. And John Doolittle understands that. He knows it loud and clear. He stands on principle in Washington, DC. He trusts you with your own money.

You'll hear these—all kinds of excuses about why they want to raise your taxes. Perhaps the one you hear the most of is, well, we just need to raise your taxes to balance the budget. The problem is, that's not the way Washington, DC, works. I've been up there long enough to know how it works. They'll figure out new ways to spend your money when they raise your taxes. They'll have more money to spend on pet projects. The best way to balance the budget is to keep taxes low, grow the economy, which yields more tax revenues, set priorities with your money, and be fiscally sound. And that's what we're going to continue to do.

And the single biggest priority to spend with your money is to make sure our troops have all the equipment, training, and support they need to do their job. And Congressman John Doolittle understands that. And I'm proud to say that by working with people in the Congress like Congressman Doolittle, our military is well-funded and

the esprit de corps is high. I can't tell you how great it is to be the Commander in Chief of such wonderful people, men and women who, in the face of danger, said, "I volunteer to serve the United States of America to protect our freedoms." Our military is great, and we intend to keep it that way, for your sake.

I couldn't help but notice there's a lot of farmers and ranchers in this part of the world. I strongly suggest making sure you've got a Congressman in Washington, DC, who understands how important it is to have a strong agricultural sector. I personally believe that when the ag sector is strong, our economy is strong. And I know full well we've got to have a strong agricultural sector for national security reasons. John Doolittle understands farming, and he understands ranching, and he's representing you well in the United States Congress.

Speaking about national security, we got to make sure we become less dependent on foreign sources of oil. There's a complacency, I'm sure, that's going to start setting in here because gasoline prices are low. And I'm glad they're going down. I'm glad for the sake of the working people in the United States. I'm glad for the sake of the farmers and ranchers. I'm glad, for the sake of those who make a living on the highways, that the price of gasoline is going down. But that doesn't lessen the national security consequences of being dependent on foreign sources of oil.

And so I look forward to working with John Doolittle to fund research and development on technologies that will enable us to drive automobiles with ethanol or to be able to have new batteries that will enable you to drive the first 40 miles on electricity—and your car is not going to have to look like a golf cart—[*laughter*]—or eventually powering your automobiles by hydrogen. And this is coming. We're spending a lot of your money on research to enable this country to become less dependent on foreign sources of oil, and in the meantime, we need to be exploring for oil and gas in environmentally friendly ways right here in the United States of America.

There's a lot of issues I look forward to working with Congressman Doolittle on: making sure our education system continues to hold people to account; making sure the health care system empowers patients and providers—and not the Federal Government—when it comes to making decisions for you; making sure we get legal liability for our doctors. We got too many junk lawsuits that are running good doctors out of practice, which is running up the cost of your medicine.

And I look forward to working with John to make sure our faith-based and community-based initiative still has support in the United States Congress. Let me tell you something about this country. The great strength of America is not in our military or not in the size of our wallets but exists in the hearts and souls of our fellow citizens. I am proud of and complimentary of the fact that thousands of our citizens volunteer on a daily basis to feed the hungry, find shelter for the homeless, without one single law. People hear that call to love a neighbor just like you'd like to be loved yourself. And it's changing our country, and it's saving souls. And the Federal Government ought not to fear the influence of faith in our society, but we ought to welcome faith-based and community projects to help solve America's most intractable problems.

There's going to be a lot of domestic issues we will be working on. But by far the biggest issue of this campaign and the biggest issue confronting the Federal Government is this: the security of you, the security of the United States. Make no mistake about it, there's an enemy that still lurks, an enemy that still plans, an enemy that still plots, an enemy that still wants to hurt the United States of America. These are ideologues bound by a hateful ideology. They can't stand what America stands for.

We believe strongly in the right of people to worship any way they see fit. As a matter of fact, one of the great strengths of the United States of America is you're equally American if you're a Muslim or a Jew or a Christian or a Hindu or an agnostic or atheist. You have a right to choose in the United States of America, and that right is a sacred right. But that's not the case with these ideologues. If you don't worship the way they want you to worship, there's penalty, and harsh penalties at that. They don't believe in the public square. They don't believe in people being able to dissent. They're bound by this ideology, and they've got objectives. And their objective is to drive the United States from parts of the world so they can spread their ideology throughout the Middle East in the form of a caliphate.

I like to remind people that we're in the ideological struggle of the 21st century. It's a struggle between good and evil. It's a struggle between moderate people and extremists. It's a struggle between those who believe in democracy and those who support tyranny. And the decisions that we make today will affect the security of the United States and affect the type of world your children and grandchildren live in.

These are historic times, and they're tough times, and they require steady leadership from the United States of America. And I need steady support in the United States Congress to protect this country. After 9/11, I came to these conclusions: One, that in order to protect you, in order to defeat this enemy of hatred, that we must stay on the offense. We must defeat the enemy overseas so we do not have to face them here at home. I concluded that where we find people harboring these terrorists, they should be judged equally as guilty as the terrorists. And the Taliban found out what the United States meant when they refused to turn over Al Qaida. And today, because of the actions of our coalition in Afghanistan, terrorist training camps and safe havens have been eliminated, 25 million people now live in freedom, and the world is better off for it.

And of course, the great debate is Iraq. The debate you'll hear a lot of talk about is, what should the United States of America do in Iraq? The first thing I would ask the Democrats is, do they truly believe the world would be better off with Saddam Hussein still in power? And if so, they need to say it loud and clear, because I know full well that this state sponsor of terror, a person who had used weapons of mass destruction, a person who invaded his neighbors, the sworn enemy of the United States, someone who was shooting at U.S. pilots, someone who defied the United Nations resolution, removing him from power has made America safer and the world a better place.

The debate is active and alive, and that's good. You hear people in Washington, DC, say that Iraq is a distraction from the war on terror. I believe it is a central front in the war on terror, and I believe we must defeat the enemy and help that young democracy succeed in order to make sure this homeland is more secure. But don't believe me. Just listen to the words of Usama bin Laden or Zawahiri, the number two in Al Qaida. They have loudly proclaimed that Iraq is central to their ambitions. They have made it abundantly clear that they will continue their murderous ways to drive us out of Iraq so they can establish safe haven from which to launch further attacks.

They want a capacity to be able to topple moderate governments who do not subscribe to their view of the world. Imagine a world 20 or 30 years from now where moderate governments have been toppled, where extremists are battling for power in the Middle East, where these killers have got control of oil resources, which they would use to punish the free world economically if the free world didn't concede to their demands. Imagine that kind of world in the midst of which was a country with a nuclear weapon aiming to—and vowing to—destroy our close friend Israel. If that world were ever to exist because the

United States of America lost its nerve during this battle in Iraq, history would look back and say, what happened to them? How come they couldn't see the problem? How come they lost their nerve and left a generation of Americans to deal with a troubled world?

Now is the time to confront this group of killers and these extremists. Now is the time to defend the United States of America by defeating the enemy overseas. Now is the time to stand with the 12 million people who demanded their liberty. Now is the time to help young democracies and moderates around the world, so when history looks back, they can say they did their duty and they laid the foundation of peace for a generation to come.

The challenge of defending you here at home is immense because we've got to be right 100 percent of the time, and the enemy has only got to be right one time. And that's why, after 9/11, I called upon the Congress to make sure that those responsible for defending you have got all the tools necessary to do so. I worked with Congress to pass the PATRIOT Act to break down walls that prevented the intelligence services from talking to the criminal justice, the law enforcement personnel. I can't explain very well why that was the case. I'm sure you're wondering how come somebody who gathered intelligence in the United States couldn't share that same information with law enforcement, but nevertheless, that's the way it was.

You cannot defend this country unless all branches of government have the capacity to talk to each other, to share information. This is a different kind of war. This isn't a war measured by the number of platoons or size of a navy. This is a war in which we must find about the intentions of the enemy and take care of them before they come and hurt us.

And so therefore, our people need the tools necessary to protect you. And that's why I established the terrorist surveillance program to monitor terrorist communications coming into this country and out of this country. Listen, after 9/11, we created the program with the Central Intelligence Agency to detain and question key leaders that we picked up off the battlefield. When I said, we're going to give these people tools, those are the kind of tools I was talking about.

On each of these programs—the PATRIOT Act and the terrorist surveillance program and the legislation to authorize aggressive interrogation of terrorists—the Democrats say they share our goals, but when it comes time to vote, they have consistently opposed giving our personnel the tools they need to protect us. And this is an issue in this campaign.

The issue in this campaign is which party, which group of individuals have got the will and the foresight necessary to give our professionals the tools necessary so they can do the most important job facing our Government, and that is to protect you from further attack. Time and time again, the Democrats want to have it both ways. They talk tough on terror, but when it comes time—when their votes are counted, their softer side comes out. [Laughter]

You don't have to worry about Doolittle. [Laughter] He understands the stakes. He understands the cause.

If you've got a second, I'd like to review these three acts and the legislative history in the hopes of clarifying the differences between how we think and how the other people think. First, on the PATRIOT Act: In the weeks after 9/11, we passed this vital law, and in the 5 years since, it has proved invaluable to stopping further attacks. In other words, it's worked. The law enforcement community has used the law to break up terror cells or prosecute terrorist operatives and supporters in California and Texas, New Jersey, Illinois, North Carolina, Virginia, Ohio, New York, Oregon, and Florida.

In 2001, the vote in the United States Senate was 98 to 1. And then 5 years later,

when the bill came up for renewal, the Senate Democrats filibustered it. That's Washington-talk for trying to kill it. They didn't want it to go forward. As a matter of fact, the Senate Democrat leaders, when they were filibustering, said, "We killed the PATRIOT Act." And a reporter said whether that was something to celebrate—does that really make sense to celebrate that maneuver? And his answer was, "Of course it is."

See, there's a difference of opinion in Washington, DC. It's a difference of opinion in this campaign and campaigns around the country. As a matter of fact, saying they were for the PATRIOT Act and then working to kill the PATRIOT Act kind of reminds me of another campaign. [Laughter] We may be heading back to the old days. Finally, the filibuster died, and I signed the law, and the United States of America is safer because of it.

I know you're familiar with the program of the National Security Agency called the terrorism surveillance program that I installed. I did so to protect you. The philosophy behind the program is pretty clear, pretty simple to understand: If Al Qaida or an Al Qaida associate is calling into the United States, we want to know why. We want to know their intentions. We want to be able to prevent an attack.

People say, "Well, how do you know they're Al Qaida?" Well, a lot of times, we're picking up information on the battlefield—say, one of these people we pick up has got a phone number on their possession, and it happens to be a U.S. phone number. I think it makes sense—I don't care whether you're Republican or Democrat or independent—for the United States—[laughter]—wondering why somebody would be calling that phone number. [Laughter]

Last week, when the legislation providing additional authority for the terrorist surveillance program came before the House of Representatives, 177 Democrats voted against listening in on terrorist communications. See, it's a clear position. It's a clear signal of how they view the world in which we live. I'm not saying these people are not patriotic; they are. I'm not saying they don't love America; they do. They just see the world differently, and it's an important issue in this campaign, as to how we see the world.

I see the world as a dangerous place. I see the world with enemies coming to try to hurt us. I see our most important job is to protect you. And therefore, we will give our folks on the frontline of terror the tools necessary to do so.

I want to spend a little time on this CIA program. I set up the program to detain and question key terrorist operatives and leaders who were captured on the battlefield. You see, a captured leader may have some information that will help protect you. You know, they may know plans; they may understand what plots are underway. And I know that our security depends on getting this kind of information.

In the past 5 years, the good and decent professionals of the CIA have worked tirelessly to get information from captured terrorists that enabled us to stop new attacks on the homeland. In other words, we were able to get vital information that we can act on to protect you. Every American has got to understand the importance of this program. Information from the terrorists questioned by the CIA helped break up a cell of Southeast Asian terrorist operatives that had been groomed for an attack on the United States. The program helped us stop an Al Qaida cell from developing anthrax for attacks against the United States. It helped stop a planned strike on a U.S. Marine camp in Djibouti, prevent a planned attack on the U.S. Consulate in Karachi. It helped foil a plot to hijack airplanes and fly them into Heathrow or London's Canary Wharf.

In other words, from this program, we got vital information that enabled us to act to protect you. Were it not for this informa-

tion from the terrorists questioned by the CIA, our intelligence community believes that Al Qaida and its allies would have succeeded in launching another attack against the United States.

Last week, the Congress held a vote on the future of this program. The choice before every Member was clear: Should the CIA program continue or not? Congress voted to continue the program, thankfully, for the security of the country. I'm looking forward to signing this bill into law. And I thank John Doolittle for his strong support in helping getting that bill out of the United States House of Representatives.

In this campaign season, this vote tells us a great deal—the vote on this bill tells a great deal where the two parties stand. In other words, you can get rid of all the rhetoric and you can look where the parties stand. In the House of Representatives, 160 Democrats, including the entire Democrat leadership, voted against continuing this program. Eighty percent of House Democrats want to stop a program that has provided invaluable intelligence that has saved American lives.

In the Senate, 32 Democrats, including every member of their Senate leadership save one, voted to kill the program, which means that about three-quarters of the Democrats in the Senate, including both of the Senators from the State of California, voted to stop the men and women of the CIA from continuing a program to get information from terrorists like Khalid Sheikh Mohammed about planned attacks on the United States of America.

We just have a fundamental difference, and it's a key difference for all Americans to look at and listen to. During the debate on the Senate floor, one senior Democrat, their ranking member on the Judiciary Committee, compared the brave Americans who question the terrorists to the Taliban and Saddam Hussein. I believe this exposes a dangerous mindset on the part of Democrats in the United States Congress. You can't defend America if you can't tell the difference between brave CIA officers who protect their fellow citizens and brutal dictators who kill their citizens.

I'm not making any of this up. [*Laughter*] Another Senate Democrat said that allowing the CIA to go forward with its program to question the most dangerous terrorists we have captured would, in this person's words, "diminish the security and safety of Americans everywhere." We just have a different mindset, a different view of the world. If they feel safer without this program, the Democrats in the Senate need to explain to the American people which of the attacks that the CIA program stopped would they have been willing to let go forward.

Protecting your country is the number-one priority as far as I'm concerned, and it's the number-one priority as far as Congressman Doolittle is concerned. We must see the world the way it is and stay on the offense and bring these people to justice before they hurt any American citizen.

But there is a different point of view in Washington. The House Democratic leader, right here from the State of California, summed up her party's approach to the midterm elections this way: She said, "This election shouldn't be about national security." Well, I think it's about national security, and I think when the people take a good look about the dangers confronting the United States of America, they'll think it's about national security. Democrats take a law enforcement approach to terrorism that means America will wait until we're attacked again to respond. That's kind of a pre-9/11 mentality, and it's not going to make this country any safer.

We believe that we're in a war and that we must prevent attacks from happening in the first place by staying on the offense. If you want leaders in Washington who understand the enemy we face and will give our folks the tools necessary to protect you, if you want people in Washington who are not going to sit back and wait to be attacked again, you make sure you send people like John Doolittle back to the United States Congress.

I'm an optimistic fellow. I believe strongly in my heart of hearts that not only will we secure this country, but we will do the hard work necessary to help moderates and reasonable people and people who long for peace in the Middle East achieve their dreams. When we find young democracies attacked by extremists, we'll help them survive. When we find liberty challenged in dark corners of the world, we'll stand with those reformers and those reasonable people who are anxious to see the extremists defeated and marginalized. This is the call of the 21st century. This is the challenge for our generation. And I'm confident— I'm confident that our generation will rise to that challenge. And when history looks back, they will say, job well done.

Thanks for coming. God bless.

NOTE: The President spoke at 2:12 p.m. at the Serrano Country Club. In his remarks, he referred to Julia Harlow, wife of Rep. John T. Doolittle; Bobbi Lungren, wife of Rep. Daniel E. Lungren; former President Saddam Hussein of Iraq; Usama bin Laden, leader of the Al Qaida terrorist organization; and Khalid Sheikh Mohammed, senior Al Qaida leader responsible for planning the September 11, 2001, terrorist attacks, who was captured in Pakistan on March 1, 2003.

Remarks on the California Wildfires in Los Angeles, California
October 3, 2006

Thank you all very much for joining me on Air Force One. I had a briefing on the fires that have been ravaging country here in California. I was proud to be here with the members of the U.S. Forest Service—as you can see, one of the yellow shirts. These are the people on the frontline of fighting these fires.

And they brought me up to date, particularly on the Day Fire. And that fire has been contained, which is good news for the people of California. I congratulate the Forest Service for their planning and operational planning on fighting this fire.

I really want to thank the brave firefighters who risk their lives on a daily basis to contain the fires. I was briefed on the Healthy Forest Initiative, particularly in the urban interface, and was pleased to hear we're making progress on helping to contain fires once they start. We've got a lot more work to do. I believe Congress needs to pass further law that will enable us to restore forests once they've been burned.

But all in all, it's been a good lesson for us to watch these Forest Service people do their job, and I'm really proud of them. I want to thank you for joining me, and I congratulate you for your good work.

Thank you.

NOTE: The President spoke at 4:52 p.m. upon arrival at Los Angeles International Airport.

Remarks at a Breakfast for Congressional Candidate Richard G. Renzi in Scottsdale, Arizona
October 4, 2006

Thank you all. Thanks for coming. Please be seated. I'm honored to be here. Thanks for a warm Arizona welcome. You know, there's nothing like waking up in Arizona with a fantastic sunrise. What a great way to brighten the spirit. And thank you for coming. It brightens my spirits, as well, to know that there are a lot of good folks from northern Arizona and other parts of this State who are willing to stand up and support a good man, Rick Renzi, in his quest to be reelected to the United States Congress. So thank you for coming. Both of us are really glad you're here. I remember campaigning for Rick in Flagstaff in a rain storm. That didn't dampen our spirits, nor did it dampen my enthusiasm in saying as clearly as I could, I'm confident he will make a great Congressman. And he has proven me right. He deserves to be reelected to the United States Congress, and I thank you for helping him.

I say he deserves it because he's got a record. And I'm going to talk a little bit about what we have done together to make Arizona and the country a better place. But one thing about Renzi, he stands strong on principle. He's got his priorities straight. He prioritizes his faith. He loves his family, all of them. [*Laughter*] Three of his boys are here, Rob, Ron, and Rick. Listen, when you got 12 kids, it's good to have their names start with the same letter; that way you don't forget them. [*Laughter*] But I want to thank the Renzi boys for being here. Thanks for supporting your dad.

I'm sorry mama is not here; Roberta is taking care of the kids. I understand that. But one of the good things about Rick is his family stands squarely with him, and it's important when you're in public service, when you're serving the people, that your family is with you. And that ought to give people in northern Arizona comfort, to know that they got a Congressman who not only works hard on their behalf in Washington and when he's back in the district, but he's got good priorities. I'm proud to support Rick Renzi in his reelection effort, and I thank you for coming.

I've got somebody else here who is running for reelection, and he's a man who has brought a lot of dignity to the office of United States Senator. He's solid; he is strong; he is influential, and that is Senator Jon Kyl. And I appreciate you coming, Senator—he brought Caryll along.

I appreciate Congressman J.D. Hayworth, who's up for reelection, and I urge you to vote for J.D. Thanks for coming, J.D. J.D. has got him a race, and I hope the people of his district are wise enough to send him back to Washington, DC.

I'm proud to be here with another Congressman, and that would be U.S. Congressman Trent Franks, who brought his wife, Josie, with him. Trent, thanks for coming—and sweet Josie.

Last night when I got here at the airport, I was greeted by a young person running for Governor, an attractive man—[*laughter*]—a family man, an honest man, and that's Len Munsil. I appreciate you coming, Governor. I'm glad you're here, and I wish you all the very best.

I know Renzi well enough to know that he can be a plain-spoken fellow, and he said to me, "I want you to know, you weren't my first choice for this breakfast." [*Laughter*] I said, "Well, thanks for having me fly all the way out here," you know. [*Laughter*] I said, "Who might that have been?" He said, "Well, I really wanted Laura to come." [*Laughter*] Another reason to put him back in Congress is because he's got good judgment. [*Laughter*]

Laura sends her best. She's proud of your service. She says hello to all our friends here in the great State of Arizona. I'm a lucky man that Laura Bush said yes when I asked her to marry me.

We're getting ready for—we're coming down the stretch in these campaigns. I'm looking forward to traveling the country, making it clear, there are substantial differences in the philosophy we adhere to and the philosophy advocated by the Democrats. I like campaigns. It's a good opportunity to explain to the American people why we make the decisions we make. It's a good chance to explain the philosophy of the two different parties.

I'd like to start with talking about our economic philosophy. Rick and I believe that the way to grow an economy is to let you keep more of your own money so you can save, spend, or invest. We strongly believe that the more money you have in your pocket, the more likely it is somebody is going to be able to find work. That is not only our philosophy; that is a practice that we adhere to.

See, you might remember—and when you're out there campaigning—I know Rick says, look what we have been through. In other words, we're not just talkers; we're doers. We've been through a recession. We had corporate scandals. We had a significant stock market correction. We had to suffer a terrorist attack on the United States of America, which hurt our economy. I made the decision to defend this country, and we have been in two theaters in this war on terror with troops. We had hurricanes, high energy prices, and yet the American economy is the envy of the industrialized world.

It's one thing to go out and advocate a philosophy; it's another thing to put it into effect. Progrowth economic policies work. We cut the taxes on people who were paying taxes. Small businesses are growing. The entrepreneurial spirit is strong. Productivity is up. Our farmers and ranchers are doing well. The progrowth economic policies of the Republican Party have made a significant difference to the working people in the United States.

And if the other bunch gets elected, they're going to raise your taxes. Make no mistake about it, we have a different philosophy. See, they think they can spend your money better than you can. They want more of your money to enhance their vision of bigger government. Oh, I know that words get couched in different ways or—the reason we campaign is, we help clarify Washington-speak. You'll hear people say, "Well, all we're going to do is just let the tax cuts expire"—those would be tax cuts on people who have got children, small businesses, those who are married—"Oh, we'll just let them expire." What that means is, they're going to raise your taxes. See, if those tax cuts expire, your taxes are going up. It's like an employer saying to somebody, I'm going to give you a raise, and a couple of weeks later, I'm going to take it away, but I hope you still think you got the raise. [*Laughter*]

Rick and I strongly believe that the best way to keep this economy growing, the best way to keep America to be entrepreneurial heaven is to make the tax cuts we passed permanent. Oh, you'll hear them say in Washington, "Oh, we just need to raise some of the people's taxes in order to balance the budget." You know, I've been there long enough to tell you, that's not how it works. Yeah, they'll raise your taxes, all right, but they will figure out new ways to spend your money. The best way to balance the budget is to keep taxes low so we grow the economy and to prioritize how we spend your money. You know, I said we can cut the deficit in half by 2009; because of progrowth economic policies and strong fiscal policy out of the House of Representatives, because of votes like Rick Renzi, this deficit is going to be cut in half by 2008. The worst way to treat the budget is to run up your taxes, slow down economic growth, and expand Federal Government. And we're not going to let them do it. We're going to win the

election because we're progrowth and wise about the money.

It's really important that Congress prioritize, set priorities. If you try to be all things to all people, we're going to spend foolishly. And I've set some priorities. And I want the people of Arizona to understand that the number-one priority for this Government is to defend this country and to make sure our troops have all that is necessary to do their job for the sake of security. And I thank Congressman Renzi and the other Congressmen here in this audience and Senator Kyl for standing strong for those brave men and women who put on the uniform of the United States of America. What an honor it is to be the Commander in Chief of such a fine group of people.

I appreciate the fact that Rick joins me in what I call cooperative conservation. That means we're going to work with local folks, local stakeholders, and States to conserve our environment. You know, there is a mindset in Washington that says, we'll tell the folks in Arizona how to do it. That's not my view. See, I'm from Texas; I believe that Texans can manage the environment in Texas plenty fine. And I believe the same thing in Arizona.

I worked with Rick to pass what's called the Healthy Forest Initiative. See, his district has got a lot of important forests. It means that we can work together with local folks to thin out those forests so they're not full of combustionable fuel, to be able to help deal with the catastrophic fires that have plagued this State and other States. It is a wise use of government resources to plan and affect good environmental policy by working with the local folks. Rick understands that. People in northern Arizona must feel confident that their Representative, Rick Renzi, trusts their judgment and is willing to work on behalf of them in Washington, DC, in a cooperative way.

Rick and I firmly believe that it's really important that we diversify away from foreign sources of oil. Look, we're all applauding the fact that gasoline prices are going down. I'm sure it pleases you if you drive a car. I know it helps our small-business owners and our families who are concerned about whether or not they'll have enough money to save for their child's education, for example. Declining gasoline prices are good for the economy, but they should not cause us to forget that dependence upon foreign oil is a national security problem. It's a national security concern. And therefore, I look forward to continuing to work with the Arizona delegation and Congressman Renzi to provide research and development money to enable us to fuel our automobiles in different ways.

I can't wait for the day when we can continue to say, "Corn is up, and therefore, dependence upon oil is down." I can't wait that we develop new ways to develop ethanol, like from wood chips, so that people in northern Arizona become significant producers of energy that will enable this country to diversify away from reliance on foreign crude oil. One day we'll have hybrid vehicles with new batteries, plug-in hybrids, and you'll be able to drive the first 40 miles on electricity, and your car won't have to look like a golf cart. [*Laughter*] When these kids are learning to drive, they'll be having hydrogen-powered automobiles at their disposal. In other words, we're on a massive effort to diversify away from foreign sources of oil.

And in the meantime, we need to be exploring for natural gas and oil in our own hemisphere in environmentally friendly ways. We've got a comprehensive plan to help this Nation's national security and economic security by having a comprehensive energy bill, and I want to thank Congressman Renzi for working on that.

Oh, there's going to be a lot of domestic issues we'll work on, but there's no issue more important than protecting the American people. It's the calling of the 21st cen-

tury. The most important job for the Federal Government is to protect you. After 9/11, I vowed that we would do everything in our power to prevent a further attack. We're at war with an enemy that would like to hurt us again. I know some would hope that the President wouldn't say that, but that's the reality of the world in which live. I live it every day. I think about the importance of defending this country every single day of my Presidency.

It's important to have Members of Congress who see the world the way it is and who understand the nature of the enemy. These are evil people who have taken the tenets of a great religion and used it to their ends to achieve objectives. These are ideologues. These are people bound by an ideology of hate. Their ideology is opposite of what we believe. We believe that anybody can worship any way they want and be an equal citizen of the United States of America. We believe Jew, Muslim, Christian, atheist, agnostic are all equally American. We believe in the great right of an individual to choose how to worship as they see fit. The enemy says, "If you don't worship the way we worship, you're guilty."

We believe in dissent in the public square. Oh, sometimes it gets a little loud, but nevertheless, we welcome dissent. We welcome the fact that in our country, people can express themselves any way they want. If you express dissent with these ideologues, they will hold you to account. They have a dark vision of the world. It stands in stark contrast with those of us who believe in liberty, who love freedom. And they'll do anything they can to drive us out of parts of the world so they can achieve their ambitions. They will murder innocent lives in the hopes that the United States of America will lose its will to confront them.

After 9/11, I vowed that in order to protect the United States of America, we must stay on the offense. We must defeat the enemy overseas so we don't have to face them here. We must bring them to justice before they hurt Americans again. And that's what we're doing. We're on the offense every single day. It's hard to plot, plan, and kill when you're running or when you're hiding in a cave. We've got fantastic people working on your behalf, unbelievably brave men and women in our intelligence services or in the United States military who are pressing this enemy every single day.

And now we're involved in a great conflict in the war on terror in Iraq. And there's a debate in Washington, DC, and the debate is whether or not Iraq is a part of the war on terror. You'll hear the Democrats say, "Well, it's a distraction on the war on terror." I strongly disagree. I fully understand the nature of this enemy. I fully understand their intent is to drive us out of the Middle East so they can topple moderate governments and get a hold of oil resources, develop weapons of mass destruction and safe havens from which to attack the United States again.

If you don't believe me, listen to the words of Usama bin Laden and the number two of Al Qaida, Zawahiri. They have made their intentions clear. They have made it clear that Iraq is a central front in this war on terror. They have made their intentions known, out loud—well, they probably didn't want us to hear it, but nevertheless, we did—that they want to drive us out of Iraq. It's just a matter of time, in their mind. They believe that the lessons of Somalia will apply to Iraq. They think that with enough carnage and bloodshed and death and the murder of the innocent, the United States will let them have their way.

They're wrong. The United States understands that the security of the United States of America, for our children, depends upon victory in Iraq. We will stand with the 12 million brave citizens who demanded their freedom. We will help the new unity Government succeed. We will train Iraqis so they can take the fight to the enemy. In the meantime, we will stay in the battlefield

and achieve the victory for a generation of Americans to come.

Right after 9/11, I said to the American people, we'll make sure that those on the frontline of defending this country have the tools necessary to do so. The reason I said that is because I understand the nature of this war. See, it's a different kind of battle. The old World War II vets here—and I thank you for your service—will remember—or the Korean war vets—will remember the days that you could measure success against an enemy based upon the number of ships sunk or aircraft shot out of the air. This is a different kind of war. It's a war that depends upon our capacity to find individuals and bring them to justice before they strike again. And therefore, it requires intelligence and tools that we didn't need in other wars.

And so I vowed—and the reason I know this is because, you see, we've got to be right 100 percent of the time to protect you. And the enemy has got to be right one time. And therefore, I worked with people like Rick Renzi and other Members of Congress to make sure those on the frontline of terror had what it needed— had what they needed to defend you.

That's why I proposed and worked hard to pass the PATRIOT Act. See, the PATRIOT Act—prior to the PATRIOT Act, intelligence and law enforcement could not communicate. I know that's hard for you to believe, but matter—somebody whose job it is to collect intelligence on what might be happening in the United States, and because of walls that had grown up over the years, it was impossible for them to share that intelligence with law enforcement. You cannot protect the United States if our—those responsible for protecting you cannot communicate.

And so I said to Congress, "This is ridiculous. Let's tear down the walls that prevented good people from talking." And they agreed. The House passed a bill; right after 2001, the Senate did, 98 to 1. But I want you all to remember, when the bill came up again for renewal in 2005, Democrat Senators filibustered the bill. Evidently, their attitude changed. Filibuster is Washington-speak for, like, try to talk it to death. I promise I'm not going to filibuster you here today. [*Laughter*] As a matter of fact, during that period—I think it is illustrative for people to hear the words of the Senator minority leader. He bragged, "We killed the PATRIOT Act." That's what he said. And then when pressed by the press, he said—they said, "Are you sure this is the right thing to do, to celebrate killing the PATRIOT"—he said, "Of course it is."

See, we just have a different attitude about the war on terror. My attitude is, we've got to give people the tools necessary to protect you and not wait for another attack. You know, they filibustered the PATRIOT Act and then—after they had voted for it—kind of sounds familiar. [*Laughter*] That old refrain from 2004—[*laughter*]—appears to be coming back to—coming back into the political dialog.

The reason I bring this up is, in an election year, I want the American people and the people of Arizona to understand, there is a clear difference of opinion about how to protect this country. Oh, they can talk good talk. But when it came time to vote, the American people can see exactly where the Democrat Party stands in protecting this country.

You might remember that I instituted a program through the National Security Agency to establish what's called the terrorist surveillance program. I felt it was very important for those of us whose job it is to protect you to understand the nature of the enemy. And if somebody from Al Qaida is calling into the United States, in order to protect you, we need to know why and what they're planning and what they're thinking. See, this is a different kind of war, and we need to know the intention of the enemy now in order to protect you from attack.

This bill came up—the idea of providing additional authority for the terrorist surveil-

lance program came to the House floor recently. And there was a vote, and people got to, stand up and declare whether or not this program was important: 177 Democrats voted against listening in on terrorist communications; 177 of the opposition party said, "You know, we don't think we ought to be listening to the conversations of terrorists."

If the people of Arizona, if the people of the United States don't think we ought to be listening in on the conversations of people who could do harm to the United States, then go ahead and vote for the Democrats. If you want to make sure those on the frontline of protecting you have the tools necessary to do so, you vote Republican, for the safety of the United States of America.

After the 9/11 attacks, I established a CIA program to detain and question key terrorist operatives and leaders who we captured on the battlefield. I did so because I believed that those who were responsible—we think were responsible for planning attacks, such as the 9/11 attack, might be able to tell us some information about how the enemy operates, where they operate, and what they intend. I understand this is a different kind of war and our most solemn duty is to protect you. And I felt—I know it's vital to get this kind of information. For 5 years, really fine professional people at the CIA have worked tirelessly to get information from these captured terrorists.

It's important for people of Arizona and the Nation to understand what this program has meant to our security. Information from the terrorists questioned by the CIA helped break up a cell of Southeast Asian extremists and terrorist operatives who had been groomed for attacks inside the United States of America. The program helped stop an Al Qaida cell from developing anthrax for attacks against the United States. Information that we gained helped to stop a planned strike on a Marine base in Djibouti and helped prevent an attack on the U.S. consulate in Karachi and helped foil a plot to hijack passenger planes and fly them into Heathrow and London's Canary Wharf.

The reason I bring—I declassified this information because I wanted the American people to understand the stakes of the debate on the detainee program, and I wanted them to understand with clarity that this program is essential to help get information to protect you. Were it not for information gained from the terrorists questioned by the CIA, our intelligence community believes that Al Qaida and its allies would have succeeded in launching another attack against the United States of America. And these are the facts.

And the Congress held a vote on the future of this CIA program, and the choice between every Member of Congress was clear: Should this program continue or not? Congress, fortunately, continued the program. I'm going to sign it into law, and I thank them for their leadership.

But I want you to understand what happened during this vote. In the House of Representatives, 160 Democrats, including the entire Democrat leadership, voted against continuing the program. I want you to understand that I would never question a person's patriotism; I don't. They just have a different point of view about the war on terror, and it's a point of view that the American people must understand.

Think about that vote. Think about what it says between different philosophies. Think about the difference of how we view the world. Eighty percent of the House Democrats—nearly 80 percent want to stop the program that has provided invaluable intelligence that saved lives, that saved lives of the United States of America. In the Senate, 32 Democrats, including every member of their Senate leadership save one, voted to kill the vital program. This means that nearly three-quarters of the Democrats in the United States Senate voted to stop the men and women of the CIA from continuing a program to get in-

formation from extremists and terrorists like Khalid Sheikh Mohammed about planned attacks on the United States of America.

We just think differently. And it's important, during a campaign, for the American people to understand the facts. There is a difference between rhetoric and action in Washington, DC. And the votes of the Democrats to deny the tools necessary to protect you speak loud and clear about their vision of the world in which we live.

We've got a clear record. We believe strongly that we must take action to prevent attacks from happening in the first place. They view this election—they view the threats we face like law enforcement, and that is, we respond after we're attacked. And it's a fundamental difference, and I will travel this country for the next 5 weeks making it clear the difference of opinion.

You know, the House Democrat leader summed up her party's approach to the midterm elections this way. She said, "This election should not be about national security." I strongly disagree. There's an enemy that wants to hurt the American people. The most solemn responsibility of the President and those of us who have been honored to serve you is to do what is necessary to protect the American people, and we will continue to do so.

I'm optimistic we will prevail in the great ideological struggle of the 21st century. You are witnessing historic times, and this is an historic election. You're witnessing a struggle between moderation and extremists, tyranny and freedom. You're witnessing a struggle between those who would impose their dark vision on others and people who just want to live in peace. These are historic times, and it's going to require strong U.S. leadership to help win this ideological struggle.

But I have got great faith. I believe in the universality of freedom. I believe all souls want to be free, and if given a chance, they will help us yield the peace we want. I believe the hard work that we're doing to protect you is also laying the foundation of peace for generations to come. I want it to be said when people look back at this moment of history that the United States of America had confidence in the values that caused our founding to begin in the first place; that we believed strongly in an obligation to help others realize the blessings and benefits of liberty. We did our duty; we did what we were called to do. And that's going to happen.

I want to thank you for your interest. I thank you for supporting good, solid peo-

ple who share my vision of peace. May God bless you all, and may God continue to bless the United States.

NOTE: The President spoke at 8:32 a.m. at the Camelback Inn. In his remarks, he referred to Caryll Kyl, wife of Sen. Jon Kyl; Usama bin Laden, leader of the Al Qaida terrorist organization; and Khalid Sheikh Mohammed, senior Al Qaida leader responsible for planning the September 11, 2001, terrorist attacks, who was captured in Pakistan on March 1, 2003.

Remarks on Signing the Department of Homeland Security Appropriations Act, 2007, in Scottsdale
October 4, 2006

Thank you all for coming. Pretty soon, I'm going to sign an important piece of legislation that will highlight our Government's highest responsibility, and that's to protect the American people. The Department of Homeland Security plays a critical role in fulfilling this responsibility every day. Since its creation in 2003, the Department has strengthened security of our borders, airports, seaports, and other key infrastructure. It's helped give our partners in local and State law enforcement the tools they need to do their jobs.

The legislation I sign today provides about $33.8 billion in funding to help secure the homeland. This is a good bill. It will help us deploy nuclear detection equipment at our ports of entry, raise security standards at the Nation's chemical plants, safeguard American cities against weapons of mass destruction, and stop terrorists seeking to enter our country.

The bill will also help our Government better respond to emergencies and natural disasters by strengthening the capabilities of the Federal Emergency Management Agency. This legislation will give us better

tools to enforce our immigration laws and to secure our southern border.

This bill is going to make this country safer for all our citizens. And I appreciate the Members of the Congress who have joined me to witness this signing, Senator Jon Kyl, J.D. Hayworth, Trent Franks, and Rick Renzi. These Members supported this good bill, and I thank them for their support. I'm also pleased that Governor Janet Napolitano has joined us. Governor, thank you for being here. We're honored to have you up here with us.

The bill I sign helps us address one of the central issues facing all States but particularly a State like Arizona, and that's illegal immigration. I understand full well that illegal immigration puts pressure on the public schools and hospitals. It strains State and local budgets. In some communities, it increases crime. The administration and Congress have been taking decisive steps to address this issue.

Since I took office, we've increased funding for our border security from $4.6 billion in 2001 to $9.5 billion in 2006. We have increased the number of Border Patrol agents from about 9,000 to 12,000. We significantly decreased the time it takes to return illegal immigrants to their home countries. We've apprehended and sent home more than 6 million people entering this country illegally. We've stepped up worksite enforcement against companies who knowingly hire illegal workers. We're sending a clear signal that we're a nation of law, and laws will be enforced.

We've made progress in addressing illegal immigration, but there is a lot more work to be done. This May, I asked Congress to fund improvements in infrastructure, technology, and manpower at the border, and I appreciate Congress delivering upon my requests.

The bill I sign today includes nearly $1.2 billion in additional funding for strengthening the border, for new infrastructure and technology that will help us do our job. It provides funding for more border fencing, vehicle barriers, and lighting, for cutting-edge technology, including ground-base radar, infrared cameras, and advance sensors that will help prevent illegal crossings along our southern border. That's what the people of this country want. They want to know that we're modernizing the border so we can better secure the border.

The bill also supports our efforts to increase the number of Border Patrol agents to about 18,000 by the end of 2008. I recognized, Congress recognized that we needed more Border Patrol agents to do the job. So we were in Artesia, New Mexico, earlier and went to the Border Patrol Training Center; they were thanked firsthand, the men and women who are willing to go out and do hard work and help secure a really long border. And I appreciate the service of the Border Patrol.

It provides funding for about 1,500 additional Border Patrol agents. In other words, this is part of a doubling of the Border Patrol that I called for earlier in my administration. I fully understand it's going to take time to recruit and train these Border Patrol, and that's why, in coordination with

the Governors, we deployed 6,000 National Guard members to the southern border, and they're doing a fine job.

I remember the outcry when I thought it was a good—told the American people I thought it was a good idea to send them down there. But, thankfully, we did. And they're helping the Border Patrol. And when the Border Patrol agencies—number of agents double, then we're not going to need the National Guard. But in the meantime, America owes them a debt of gratitude and thanks.

The bill I sign today also includes a 25-percent increase for funding for immigration and customs enforcement. This funding will help Federal agents better enforce our immigration laws inside our country. It will allow us to add at least 6,700 new beds in detention centers. Part of the problem we face is that illegal immigrant was caught sneaking into the country, and, because there was no detention beds, the Border Patrol would say, "Why don't you check back in with us after a while. There's no place to hold you, so check back in with the judges." And of course, they didn't check back in. It created a lot of frustration with the Border Patrol.

So we're in the process of ending catch-and-release. This bill will help us end catch-and-release. You see, when people know that they'll be caught and sent home if they enter the country illegally, they're going to be less likely to try to enter illegally in the first place.

The funds that Congress has appropriated are critical for our efforts to secure this border and enforce our laws. Yet we must also recognize that enforcement alone is not going to work. We need comprehensive reform that provides a legal way for people to work here on a temporary basis. It's going to relieve pressure on the border. It will enable our Border Patrol agents to do a better job when we reduce the number of people trying to sneak into the country. It will free up our law enforcement officers to focus on criminals and drug dealers and terrorists and others who mean us harm.

We'll continue to work with Congress to pass comprehensive immigration reform that secures this border, upholds our laws, and honors our Nation's proud heritage as a land of immigrants.

I want to thank the Members of Congress who have joined me for this important bill signing. And now it's my honor to sign the Department of Homeland Security Appropriations Act for 2007.

NOTE: The President spoke at 9:37 a.m. at the Camelback Inn. H.R. 5441, approved October 4, was assigned Public Law No. 109–295. The Office of the Press Secretary also released a Spanish language transcript of these remarks.

Statement on Signing the Department of Homeland Security Appropriations Act, 2007
October 4, 2006

Today, I have signed into law H.R. 5441, the "Department of Homeland Security Appropriations Act, 2007" (the "Act"). The Act appropriates the funds needed to protect the United States against terrorism, secure the Nation's borders, assist States and localities in dealing with natural disasters, and perform the other important functions of the Department of Homeland Security. The Act also strengthens the capabilities of the Federal Emergency Management Agency to prepare for and respond to emergencies requiring action by the Federal Government.

The executive branch shall construe as calling solely for notification the provisions of the Act that purport to require congressional committee approval for the execution of a law. Any other construction would be inconsistent with the principles enunciated by the Supreme Court of the United States in *INS v. Chadha*. These provisions include those under the headings "United States Visitor and Immigrant Status Indicator Technology;" "Automation Modernization, Customs and Border Protection;" "Border Security Fencing, Infrastructure, and Technology, Customs and Border Protection;" "Air and Marine Interdiction, Operations, Maintenance, and Procurement, Customs and Border Protection;" "Automation Mod-

ernization, Immigration and Customs Enforcement;" "Protection, Administration, and Training, United States Secret Service;" "Preparedness, Management and Administration;" "United States Citizenship and Immigration Services;" "Management Administration, Science and Technology;" "Research, Development, Acquisition, and Operations, Science and Technology;" and sections 504, 505, 509, 511, and 552.

Section 513 of the Act purports to direct the conduct of security and suitability investigations. To the extent that section 513 relates to access to classified national security information, the executive branch shall construe this provision in a manner consistent with the President's exclusive constitutional authority, as head of the unitary executive branch and as Commander in Chief, to classify and control access to national security information and to determine whether an individual is suitable to occupy a position in the executive branch with access to such information.

To the extent that section 514 of the Act purports to allow an agent of the legislative branch to prevent implementation of the law unless the legislative agent reports to the Congress that the executive branch has met certain conditions, the executive branch shall construe such section as advisory, in accordance with the constitutional principles enumerated in the *Chadha* decision.

The executive branch shall construe section 522 of the Act, relating to privacy officer reports, in a manner consistent with the President's constitutional authority to supervise the unitary executive branch.

To the extent that provisions of the Act, such as section 558, purport to direct or burden the conduct of negotiations by the executive branch with foreign governments or other entities abroad, the executive branch shall construe them as advisory. Such provisions, if construed as mandatory rather than advisory, would impermissibly interfere with the President's constitutional authorities to conduct the Nation's foreign affairs, participate in international negotiations, and supervise the unitary executive branch.

Provisions of the Act, including under the heading "Office of the Secretary and Executive Management" and sections 521, 539, 540, and 559, refer to joint explanatory statements of managers accompanying conference reports on specified acts. Such statements do not satisfy the constitutional requirements of bicameral approval and presentment to the President needed to give them the force of law.

Section 503(c) of the Homeland Security Act of 2002, as amended by section 611 of the Act, provides for the appointment and certain duties of the Administrator of the Federal Emergency Management Agency. Section 503(c)(2) vests in the President authority to appoint the Administrator, by and with the advice and consent of the Senate, but purports to limit the qualifications of the pool of persons from whom the President may select the appointee in a manner that rules out a large portion of those persons best qualified by experience and knowledge to fill the office. The executive branch shall construe section 503(c)(2) in a manner consistent with the Appointments Clause of the Constitution.

Also, section 503(c)(4) purports to regulate the provision of advice within the executive branch and to limit supervision of an executive branch official in the provision of advice to the Congress. The executive branch shall construe section 503(c)(4) in a manner consistent with the constitutional authority of the President to require the opinions of heads of departments and to supervise the unitary executive branch. Accordingly, the affected department and agency shall ensure that any reports or recommendations submitted to the Congress are subjected to appropriate executive branch review and approval before submission.

Section 507(f)(6) of the Homeland Security Act of 2002, as amended by section 611 of the Act, and sections 689i(a)(4)(B)(iv) and 689j(b)(2)(E) of the Act, purport to require in certain circumstances that an executive branch official submit legislation for the consideration of the Congress. The executive branch shall construe such provisions in a manner consistent with the President's constitutional authority to supervise the unitary executive branch and to recommend for congressional consideration such measures as the President shall judge necessary and expedient.

Several provisions of the Act purport to direct the President to perform the President's duties "acting through" a particular officer. These provisions include section 303(b) of the Robert T. Stafford Disaster Relief and Emergency Assistance Act, as amended by section 633 of the Act, section 1802 of the Homeland Security Act of 2002, as amended by section 671 of the Act, and sections 643, 644, 689i, and 689j of the Act. The executive branch shall construe such provisions in a manner consistent with the constitutional authority of the President to supervise the unitary executive branch.

The executive branch shall construe provisions of the Act relating to race, ethnicity, and gender, such as sections 623 and 697 of the Act, in a manner consistent with the requirement of the Due Process Clause of the Fifth Amendment to the Constitution to afford equal protection of the laws.

Section 1802(a) of the Homeland Security Act of 2002, as amended by section 671 of the Act, calls for the Secretary of Homeland Security "in cooperation with the Department of National Communications System (as appropriate)" and others to develop and update a National Emergency Communications Plan. An examination of the text and structure of the Act reveals that the term "Department of National Communications System" in section 1802(a) is most reasonably construed as a reference to the National Communications System in the Preparedness Directorate of the Department of Homeland Security, to which section 611 of the Act refers in amending section 505 of the Homeland Security Act of 2002, and the executive branch shall so construe it.

GEORGE W. BUSH

The White House,
October 4, 2006.

NOTE: H.R. 5441, approved October 4, was assigned Public Law No. 109–295.

Remarks at a Reception for Gubernatorial Candidate Bob Beauprez and the Colorado Republican Party in Englewood, Colorado
October 4, 2006

Thanks for coming. I appreciate those kind words, Governor. I'm proud to be here with Bob Beauprez. I've gotten to know him quite well. See, we both served in Washington, DC, together. [*Laughter*] He is a straight thinker. He is a clear thinker. He's a person who understands that as the chief executive officer of a State, that you have to have a vision and the capacity to make decisions necessary to achieve that vision. There's no doubt in my mind he'll make a great Governor for the State of Colorado, and I thank you for supporting him.

And there's no doubt in my mind Claudia will make a fine first lady for the State of Colorado. I know something about first ladies. [*Laughter*] I'm a fortunate man that Laura said yes when I asked her to marry me. We're both west Texans. At the time, I can promise you, neither of us dreamt that I'd be President and she'd be First Lady. As a matter of fact, if she thought at that time—[*laughter*]. Thankfully, she is our First Lady, and I know I'm not objective, but I feel like she's doing a fabulous job on behalf of the American people.

It's important to have—to be able to follow somebody in office who's done a good job. See, Beauprez is going to be a fine Governor, and one of the reasons he's going to be a fine Governor is, he's following another fine Governor, and that's Bill Owens. I appreciate Bill's leadership; I appreciate his steadfast adherence to principles. I'm proud to be with Bill and my friend Frances today, and I want to thank you both for serving your State.

I appreciate Lieutenant Governor Jane Norton and Mike Norton for joining us. Thank you all for coming. I am proud to be here with a fine United States Senator in Wayne Allard, and his wife, Joan. Thank you all for serving, and thanks for joining us.

Colorado is going to lose a really fine Congressman in Joel Hefley. I'm proud to call Joel friend. He brought honor and dignity to the office of United States Congressman. He represents the folks of Colorado Springs and the area with a lot of class. I appreciate him coming today, and

I'm honored also to be here with Lynn. Thank you both for coming.

I want to thank the State attorney general, John Suthers, and Janet for joining us today. Thank you for serving. I thank State treasurer Mike Coffman and Cynthia for joining us today; proud you both are here. By the way, just in case you might forget, Mike is running for Colorado secretary of state. And in case the people of Colorado forget, he is a United States marine who, when this Nation called, served with distinction in this battle against these terrorists. Mike, I want to thank you very much. Proud to have been able to call you commander in chief—[*laughter*]—for me to call—as Commander in Chief, call you proud marine. [*Laughter*]

I want to thank Commissioner Janet Rowland—Mesa County—and Lance, candidate for Lieutenant Governor. Thanks for coming, Janet. Bill Armstrong is with us. Bob Martinez is with us. John Elway is with us. Bruce Benson is with us. I'm proud everybody is here. Thanks for contributing.

I do want to remind you, however, that campaigns are more than just raising money. It helps; don't get me wrong. [*Laughter*] But the next Governor is going to need your help turning out the vote. I know what it means to have a grassroots organization in Colorado working on one's behalf. Many in this room worked on my behalf to help me become the President. I want to thank you for what you've done and encourage you to support Bob Beauprez and turn out that vote come November. And while you're doing it, make sure we get these congressional candidates back in office too.

Before I talk about some of the issues, I do want to talk about an event that just recently occurred here in Colorado, in Bailey, Colorado. A lot of Americans, and I know a lot of folks in Colorado, express our deepest sympathy to the folks in that good community about the tragic loss of Emily Keyes. She died one week ago of an unspeakable act of violence. It wasn't necessary. We join her family in prayer. We extend our deepest sympathies to those good people.

This next week, I have asked Attorney General Al Gonzales and Secretary of Education Margaret Spellings to convene a meeting of leading experts and officials to determine how the Federal Government can help State and local folks deal with these shootings and the tragedies. Look, we wanted to make us certain around the country that the schoolhouse is a safe place for children to learn. And so I'm looking forward to the results of that meeting, how we can facilitate help, and how we can help these communities heal and recover from the tragic events like those that have taken place in three States over the past couple of weeks. May God bless Emily's family.

Speaking about education, when I was the Governor of Texas, I used to say this: I said, education is to a State what national defense is to the Federal Government. Education is by far the most important priority for State government, as far as I'm concerned. And I know the next Governor feels the same way. I appreciate Bill Owens's approach to education, and I'm looking forward to continuing to work with Bob Beauprez. And here's the approach: We're setting high standards. We believe every child can learn to read and write and add and subtract. And we're willing to measure to determine whether or not each school is educating each child. And we measure early so we can correct problems early, so that the people of Colorado will be able to say no child is being left behind in the State of Colorado when it comes to public education.

I know that a Governor can set the tone for a State. Your Governor has set the tone for the State, and your next Governor must set the tone. And the tone for a State is, one, it's a safe place to live; two, the schools are worthy of the dollars being spent; and three, this is a good place for people to invest so people can find work. A Governor has the capacity to say loud and clear to risk takers and people looking at your State, "Please come and invest in the State of Colorado. Please come to this State of entrepreneurial dreams." I know that Bob Beauprez will be able to do this because I worked with him to help overcome a recession and a corporate scandal and a terrorist attack on the United States, war, two hurricanes, and high energy prices. And yet our economy is the envy of the industrialized world.

Our people are working. The unemployment rate is low in the State of Colorado. Productivity is up, small businesses are on the rise. I've always felt it's important for the State and the Nation to be able to say, entrepreneurs welcome here. The role of government is not to create wealth but to create an environment in which the entrepreneurial spirit can flourish. And so when it came time to overcome the economic obstacles we faced, I went to the United States Congress, spoke directly to people like Bob Beauprez and said, "Why don't we cut the taxes on everybody who is paying taxes. Why don't we let the people have more of their own money in their pocket so they can save, invest, and spend."

Progrowth economic policies work. This economy is on the run—on the rise. And this is an issue in this national campaign. It really is. The issue is, the Democrats get control of the Congress, they're going to have their hands on your wallet. [*Laughter*] They'll be running up your taxes; make no mistake about it. The best way to keep this economy growing is to make the tax cuts we passed permanent and to make sure Republicans control the House and the Senate.

The most important job of government in this day and age is to protect you. It is a vital call for those of us who serve in Washington or in State government. The reason I say that is because we're at war with an enemy that still wants to inflict harm. I wish I could report differently to you, but that's not my job. See, my job isn't to paint a picture of the way we'd like it to be; my job, in order to protect you, is to travel this country and explain to people exactly what's at stake. And what is at stake is your security and our freedoms, because there's a group of cold-blooded killers bound together by a common ideology that wants to strike us again.

I think about this every day, as your President. I resolved after 9/11 that we would use all assets at our disposal to do the most important job for a Federal Government, and that's to protect the American people. And the best way to do that is to stay on the offense against these people and defeat them overseas so we do not have to face them here.

And that's exactly what we're doing. There's some incredibly brave people working on your behalf: great intelligence officers, people in diplomatic corps, and people who have volunteered to wear the uniform of the United States of America. And the job of us in Washington, DC—of those of us in Washington is to make sure that these brave men and women have all that is necessary to do the job we have asked them to do. And we will continue to do just that.

This offense against these terrorists is waged in different fronts and in different ways. And the current front, the most visible front against the killers who would do harm in the United States, is in Iraq. And there's a difference of opinion. I believe that we must achieve victory in Iraq to make sure America is secure. Democrats in Washington believe Iraq is a distraction from the war on terror. These are decent people, and they're patriotic people; they just happen to be wrong people. [*Laughter*]

If you don't believe me, if people in Colorado are doubtful about whether Iraq is important to the security of the United States, I would hope they would listen to the words of Usama bin Laden or the number-two man in Al Qaida, Zawahiri, both of whom have proclaimed loud and clear that Iraq is essential to their plans. See, they believe America is weak, and if they can kill enough innocent people, we'll retreat. That's precisely what they want. They want us to leave the Middle East so they can establish safe haven from which to plot, plan, and attack again. They want to get their hands on oil reserves so that when they demand the free world to capitulate and there is resistance, they can wreak economic havoc. And into this mix of hatred comes a country that wants to have a nuclear weapon that has made their ambitions clear.

This is the world we face today. If America were to retreat, if we were to cut and run, if we were to abandon our friends and allies, 30 years from now, historians will look back, the country will look back, and say, "What happened to them? What happened to the people in charge of providing security for the United States of America? How come they couldn't see the threat to future generations of Americans?" I want you to know I clearly see the threat we face today, and I clearly see the threat we face in years to come. The United States of America will stand with those who long to live in freedom. We will support those moderates who stand in opposition to the extremists. We will keep the pressure on the enemies of freedom. We will help Iraq become a democracy that can sustain itself, defend itself, and govern itself, which will be yet another blow to Al Qaida and the haters. The United States of America will not retreat. We will achieve victory in Iraq. We will have done our duty for a generation of Americans to come.

After 9/11, I recognized this fact that we must be right 100 percent of the time to protect you, and the enemy only has to be right one time. And that's the challenge we face. It really is. It's a daunting challenge. The challenge is made easier, by the way, by keeping these folks on the run. It's a lot harder to plot and plan if you're hiding in a cave or you're moving around the world. And that's why a chief part of our strategy is to keep the pressure on them. But I also recognized that I needed to call upon Congress to help us develop tools so that those on the frontline of protecting you could do so.

One of the tools was given to folks through the PATRIOT Act. There was an extensive debate on the PATRIOT Act, and it's an important debate. But it's important for you to know that prior to the PATRIOT Act, intelligence officials and law enforcement officials could not exchange information. Now, this is a different kind of war. In the old days, you could measure success based upon the number of aircraft that were flying or the number of ships that were sailing, but no longer. See, in this war, we have to find people—find their intentions and bring them to justice before they come and hurt us again. In other words, we're not isolated or immune from the attacks. That's the lesson we learned on September 11th.

And so I decided to work with Congress to tear down these barriers. And right after 9/11, everything went fine. As a matter of fact, in the United States Senate, the vote was 98 to 1. And then something happened, because when it came time to renew the act, Senate Democrats filibustered; that's Washington, DC-speak for talking until the bill dies. As a matter of fact, the Senate minority leader openly bragged in the press that "We killed the PATRIOT Act," as if that's some kind of noble gesture in the middle of a war against killers and terrorists. He was asked by a reporter whether killing the PATRIOT Act was really something to celebrate, and he answered loud and clear, "Of course it is."

Eventually we overcame the filibuster, and I signed the renewal of the PATRIOT Act. But the reason I bring this story up, as people are getting ready to go to the polls, people from both political parties and people not affiliated with a political party, they must understand there is a different attitude in Washington, a different mindset between the two political parties about the threats we face. I strongly believe that we've got to give our folks the tools necessary to protect you. In this case, Senate Democrats, key members of the Democrat Party, tried to kill a bill that would have given people the tools necessary to protect you.

I think it's important for us to understand the intentions of the enemy, understand what they're thinking and what they're saying. And that's why I instructed the National Security Agency to establish what is called the terrorist surveillance program to track communications between someone overseas making a phone call into the United States, someone we know is Al Qaida and/or Al Qaida affiliate. People say, "Well, how do you know?" Well, sometimes in the—pick people up on the battlefield that we know is Al Qaida or an Al Qaida affiliate, they might have some information in their possession. Take, for example, if they had a phone number in the United States; I think it makes sense for us to understand why somebody might be calling that phone number—if the most important job is to protect you, which it is. See, let me put it in plain talk: If Al Qaida is making a phone call into the United States, we want to know why they're making the call, where they're making the call, and what they intend to do.

People talk good in Washington, see. They say, we're going to do everything we can to protect you. Then, all of a sudden, the vote comes along which helps clarify the difference of opinion. And so when it came time for legislation to provide additional authority for the terrorist surveillance program, 177 Members of the—Democrat Members of the House of Representatives voted against listening in on terrorist communications. We just have a different point of view. And this is an issue in this campaign. It's an issue on how best to protect the United States. Our most important job is to get information so we can protect you before an attack comes. It is no longer acceptable to respond to an attack after

it happens. The lesson of 9/11 is we must take threats seriously now and deal with them, in order to protect the men and women of the United States.

I felt it was very important that we have the capacity to interrogate people once we have captured them on this battlefield in the war on terror. And we've captured a lot of key operatives, people that we think were intimately involved in the planning, people we suspect was involved in the planning of these attacks—a man named Khalid Sheikh Mohammed, Ramzi bin al-Shibh, Abu Zubaydah—these are people that we believe, we suspect were involved with planning the 9/11 attacks, and we captured them. And I thought it made sense to have a program that enabled our professionals in the CIA to see whether or not we could learn information about what they knew. If you're at war and you capture somebody—one of the key commanders—it's in the interests of the country that we find out what they're thinking.

And I'm going to tell you point-blank, this program worked. Let me give you some of the data that we learned, some of the information. As a result of the information from the interrogations, the CIA helped break up—we helped break up a cell of Southeast Asian terrorist operatives that had been groomed for attacks inside the United States. Information gained meant we were able to act to protect you. The program helped stop an Al Qaida cell from developing anthrax for attacks against the United States. The program helped stop a planned strike on a U.S. Marine camp in Djibouti. It helped prevent a planned attack on the U.S. consulate in Karachi. It helped foil a plot to hijack passenger planes and fly them into Heathrow and London's Canary Wharf. In other words, we gained information that enabled us to do the job you expect us to do.

Were it not for the information gained from the terrorists questioned by the CIA, our intelligence community believes that Al Qaida and its allies would have succeeded in launching another attack against the United States. That's the measured judgment of those professionals that we call upon to protect you.

The program is a vital program to protect the United States. And last week, Congress held a vote on the future of this program. Again, it was another clarifying moment. It was a chance for the American people to see which party would take the means necessary to protect the American people. In the House of Representatives, 160 Democrats, including the entire Democrat leadership, voted against continuing this program.

I want our fellow citizens in Colorado—of both political parties and those not affiliated with a political party—to think about that vote. Nearly 80 percent of the House Democrats want to stop a program that has provided invaluable intelligence that has saved American lives. There is a fundamental difference of opinion on how to best defeat the terrorists and to protect the American people. The good news is, for Colorado, you don't have to doubt where Bob Beauprez stands.

By the way, it just wasn't the House Democrats that voted against the bill, so did the Senate Democrats; 32 Democrats, including every member of their Senate leadership save one, voted to kill this vital program.

I'm going to continue to campaign as hard as I possibly can and remind people about the facts because I understand the threats we face. This isn't a political issue; this is an issue of national security, to make sure that we give those on the frontline of fighting the war on terror all the tools, all the support, all that is necessary to protect the American people.

You know, those votes and the comments that you hear out of Washington really reflect a different attitude and mindset about how to protect you. Democrats take a law enforcement approach to terrorism. That means America will wait until we're attacked before we respond. That is a pre-September the 11th, 2001, mindset. That won't work. It's just not going to work. The best way to do our duty is to stay on the offense, is to respond to intelligence and information, is to bring people to justice so they can't attack in the first place. And the best way to protect a generation of Americans that are counting on us, that are counting on this generation to do the hard work—like many generations before us were called to do—is to stay on the offense and, at the same time, spread liberty.

You know, recently I had an amazing experience. I went to Elvis's place with Prime Minister Koizumi. You should have been there. [*Laughter*] I went because I'd never been there. I went because Prime Minister Koizumi wanted to go there. [*Laughter*] And I went because I wanted to tell you a story. I find it ironic that I was traveling to Elvis's place, particularly since my dad and many of your relatives—my dad, as an 18-year-old Navy fighter pilot—fought the enemy, Japan. They were the sworn enemy, and it was a bloody war. A lot of people lost their lives. It was a war ended by a horrific bombing—one tough decision for a President to have to make. And yet here we were 60 years later, old George W. and Prime Minister Koizumi, flying down to Elvis's place. [*Laughter*]

But let me tell you what made the story even more amazing, was that on the way down, we were talking about keeping the peace. We were talking about North Korea. We were talking about the fact that Prime Minister Koizumi had committed 1,000 of his troops to help a young democracy in the heart of the Middle East succeed. He knows what I know: We're in the middle of an ideological struggle between good and evil, between moderation and extremism, between those who just want to live in peace and those who want to kill in the name of an ideology of hatred. He understands that.

We talked about how nations must respond to pandemic like HIV/AIDS, and I assured him the United States of America will continue to take the lead to help alleviate suffering. We talked about helping the young democracy in Afghanistan. I thought it was amazing, when I thought back about the same experience my dad, as a young man, had with the Japanese. Something happened between 41's time in the Navy and 43's time in the Presidency. And what happened was, Japan adopted a Japanese-style democracy, and the lesson is, liberty can convert enemies into allies. Someday an American President will be sitting down with duly elected leaders in the Middle East talking about how to keep the peace, and a young generation of Americans will be better off.

Those are the stakes. Thanks for helping. God bless.

NOTE: The President spoke at 1:27 p.m. at the Inverness Hotel and Conference Center. In his remarks, he referred to Frances W. Owens, wife of Gov. William F. Owens of Colorado; Lynn Hefley, wife of Rep. Joel Hefley; Janet Suthers, wife of Colorado State Attorney General John W. Suthers; Cynthia Coffman, wife of Colorado State Treasurer Mike Coffman; Lance Rowland, husband of Mesa County Commissioner and candidate for Colorado Lieutenant Governor Janet Rowland; former Sen. William L. Armstrong; Bob Martinez, State chair, Colorado Republican Party; pro football Hall of Famer John Elway; Bruce Benson, chair and president, Benson Mineral Group, Inc.; and former Prime Minister Junichiro Koizumi of Japan.

Remarks at the Department of Education
October 5, 2006

I want to thank Secretary Spellings and her fine team for welcoming me here to the Department of Education. I have just reassured the Secretary and the folks who work here that the reauthorization of the No Child Left Behind Act is a priority of this administration. And the reason I say it's a priority is because this act is working. We strongly believe in setting high standards for all students, and we strongly believe that in order to make sure those standards are met, we must measure to determine whether or not the schools are functioning the way we expect them to function and the way the parents expect them to function and the way the taxpayers expect them to function.

No Child Left Behind is working, and we've been strategizing here as to how to make sure we not only defend it during the reauthorization process but how we strengthen the law.

And so I want to thank you all for your work. I particularly want to thank the teachers and principals who have taken the No Child Left Behind Act and have implemented it and have seen the dramatic results that can be achieved by rigorous academics and strong curriculum and hard work in the classroom.

The most important function of Government at home is to make sure that a child receives an excellent education, and that's particularly important in a world that is becoming more globalized. I'm optimistic we can achieve our objectives. I know this law is working, and I look forward to working with Congress in the next legislative session to reauthorize and strengthen the No Child Left Behind Act.

Thank you.

NOTE: The President spoke at 10:03 a.m. The Office of the Press Secretary also re- leased a Spanish language transcript of these remarks.

Remarks at Woodridge Elementary and Middle Campus
October 5, 2006

Thank you all. Thank you for the warm welcome. Thank you for inviting Madam Secretary and me to your school. It's nice to be introduced by somebody with a Texas accent. [*Laughter*] She's a good buddy, and she is doing a fine job as the Secretary of Education. And so, Margaret, thank you very much for your service.

I'm glad to be at Woodridge as well. I'm here because this is one of America's fine public charter schools. I'm here to re- mind people that charter schools work, and they can make a difference in the lives of our children. So I want to thank you for letting me come. I want to thank the teachers and the administrators and the principals—and the principal for setting high expectations. I know that sounds sim- ple, but you know what happens when you set low expectations? You get low results. And so a center of excellence is always a place of learning where people believe the best. And I want to thank the folks here for setting high expectations. I want to thank you for achieving results.

I applaud the parents of the students who are here for being—and I applaud you for being involved in the life of your chil- dren, particularly when it comes to one of the most important aspects of their devel- opment, and that is school. And I want to thank the students for letting me come too.

I want to thank Mary, the principal. You know, one of the things I have found, and I've spent a lot of time in schoolhouses as a result of being the Governor and the President, is that a good school always has a good principal. And Mary Dunnock must be a good principal because this is a good school. And I applaud you for being an educational entrepreneur. An educational entrepreneur is somebody who is willing to challenge failure and mediocrity if she finds it because failure and mediocrity are unacceptable in any classroom anywhere in the United States.

I thank Donald Hense for joining us, founder and chairman of the board of trust- ees of the Friendship Public Charter School. Mr. Hense told me he had the opportunity of meeting my mother one time, and I said to him, "Well, you met the A-team then." [*Laughter*] "Now you met the B-team." [*Laughter*] But thank you for your leadership. I welcome the mem- bers of the Friendship Public Charter School Board. Thank you for coming.

Being on a school board is difficult work, I know. Being on a school board that chal- lenges the status quo is important work, and I thank you for that. It means a dif- ference—I was in Lyle Brown's class. Lyle is not here. He's still teaching. But one of the things I saw was a teacher who loves being a teacher. And I applaud the teachers in this school and teachers all around the country who are adding to the great future of our country.

I was in Max Brooks's class. He's not here either, but he is the facilitator in what's called a SmartLab. They didn't have SmartLabs when I was going to elementary or junior high school. They've got one here. And it's an innovative program that teaches people practical skills.

You know, one of the interesting ques- tions I like to ask to students when I go into the classroom is, how many of you are going to go to college? You'll be pleased—there you go—you'll be pleased to hear, the hands went up. See, that's a good sign, when the principal and students and parents have encouraged our children to set a goal. Going to college is an important goal for the future of the United States of America, and I'm pleased to report that when I asked that question in both classrooms I was invited to go to, there was unanimity.

The students have set a goal to go to college. And I reminded them that now is the time to work hard so you get to go: like, take advantage of the SmartLab, read more than you watch TV, practice your math and science. I want to applaud you, Madam Principal, for encouraging our students to aim high, and I thank the teachers for helping them achieve those dreams.

In recent days, we have seen some sad and shocking violence in our schools across America. Yesterday I was in Colorado, which is one of the States that had received this sad and shocking news firsthand.

Next week, Secretary Spellings and Attorney General Al Gonzales are going to host a conference here in Washington, DC, and it's an important conference. We're going to bring together teachers and parents and administrators and law enforcement officials and other experts to discuss ways to help our schools protect the children. See, it is paramount that the Federal Government work with the State government and local governments to make it clear that our schools are places of learning, not places where there will be violence. And so, Margaret, I want to thank you for that initiative, and I'm looking forward to hearing the results of the important discussions.

I'm here today to talk about the No Child Left Behind Act. It's a—this act is an important way to make sure America remains competitive in the 21st century. We're living in a global world. You see, the education system in America must compete with education systems in China and India. If we fail to give our students the skills necessary to compete in the world of the 21st century, the jobs will go elsewhere. That's just a fact of life. It's the reality of the world in which we live. And therefore, now is the time for the United States of America to give our children the skills so that the jobs will stay here.

Oh, there will be jobs, don't get me wrong. But I'm talking about the high-paying jobs, the quality jobs, the jobs that will be helping to lead the world in the 21st century. And there's no doubt in my mind we can achieve that objective. And the No Child Left Behind Act was all part of making sure that we get it right in the schools. So when I came here to Washington, I made a focused effort to work with Democrats and Republicans to pass this important law. And the theory behind the law is straightforward: We'll spend more money on education, but in return, we want to see results.

Oh, I know that may be too much to ask for some. It's not too much for this school. As a matter of fact, I get a little nervous when I hear people say, "Well, I don't want to be measured." My attitude is, what are you trying to hide? How can you solve a problem until you measure the problem? How can you make sure a child is achieving what we all want if you don't measure early to determine whether or not the skills are being imparted?

And so the No Child Left Behind says, look, we trust the local folks. I don't want Washington, DC, running the schools. That's up to the people in the States and the local community. I've been a strong believer in local control of schools. But I also believe it makes sense to ask the question whether or not a child can read, write, and add and subtract. I don't think it's too much to ask. I know it's an important question if we expect our children to have the schools necessary to compete in the 21st century. I know the kids don't like tests, and I didn't like it either, to be honest with you. You hear people say, "Well, we're testing too much." No, we're just trying to figure out whether or not people have got the skills necessary to succeed.

You know, I remember the debates when I was the Governor of Texas and Margaret and I were working on accountability systems. I remember somebody standing up and saying, "It is racist to test." I said, uh-uh, it is racist not to test because there are too many children being shuffled through our schools without understanding whether or not they can read and write and add and subtract. I think it's important to hold people to account now to make sure the education system functions for all. And that's the spirit of No Child Left Behind.

By measuring, it helps us determine whether or not a curricula works. Is the reading curriculum you're using working? That's a fundamental question a parent ought to ask or a principal ought to ask or a teacher ought to ask. The best way to find out is to measure to determine whether or not a child can read at grade level. And that helps you determine whether or not your curriculum are working.

One of the things that I think is most important about the No Child Left Behind Act is that when you measure, particularly in the early grades, it enables you to address an individual's problem today, rather than try to wait until tomorrow. My attitude is, is that measuring early enables a school to correct problems early.

See, let's be frank about it. We had a system that just shuffled kids through grade after grade. I know some say that wasn't the case, but it was—let me just say, my State, the place I was familiar with. It's so much easier, when you think about it, just to say, "Okay, if you're such and such a grade, you're supposed—age, you're supposed to be in this grade," and just shuffle them through. And guess who got shuffled through—inner-city kids, the hard to educate. It made it easy just to say, "Oh, gosh, let's just—you know, let's don't worry about whether or not you've got the skills. Let's

just put you here because that's where you belong." That's unfair to parents. That's unfair to the children. And the No Child Left Behind Act demands result for every child, for the good of the United States of America.

There's an achievement gap in America that's not good for the future of this country. Some kids can read at grade level and some can't, and that's unsatisfactory. I know it's unsatisfactory for the educators who are here. It's unsatisfactory if you're a parent, and it's unsatisfactory for the President.

You can't have a hopeful America if certain kids can read at grade level and others can't, and we don't address the problem. I'm proud to report the achievement gap between white kids and minority students is closing, for the good of the United States.

How do I know? Because we measure. In reading, 9-year-olds have made larger gains in the past 5 years than at any point in the previous 28 years. That's positive news. In math, 9-year-olds and 13-year-olds earned the highest scores in the history of the test. In reading and math, African American and Hispanic students are scoring higher, and the achievement gap is closing.

Oh, I know people say we test too much, but how can you solve a problem until you measure? And how can you hold people to account when there's an achievement gap that is not right for America, unless you measure? Measuring is the gateway to success.

Woodridge Elementary School gets measured. The accountability system helped your school identify struggling students and enabled them to get the help they need early. I appreciate the fact that you have intervention sessions with teacher assistance. In other words, we identify a particular child's problems, and then this school intervenes. You have specialized learning projects, extra tutoring.

Each child matters. Every child has potential. All hands went up and said, "I want to go to college." And this school recognizes that some students need a little extra help early to make sure they can realize those dreams. That's what measuring helps you to do.

Woodridge has met standards for 3 years in a row. You've put in a lot of hard work, and you have the results to show for it, and I thank you for your contribution to the future of this country.

If you don't make progress, you get extra help. One of the most important initiatives is the Supplemental Service Initiative. This initiative says that when we find a child that needs help, that child gets extra help, in other words, if a child is falling behind. Remember, I keep talking about individual children. It used to be when they measured, they just measured everybody, you know. And now we're forcing them to disaggregate results. That's a fancy word for saying, just split individuals out so we know.

And when we find a child that needs extra help, there's money to do so. And there are options for parents, which is an important part of making sure there's parental involvement and making sure—an important part of making sure the strategy works.

A parent can enroll their child in a free intensive tutoring program. There's money for that. If your child is not up to grade level early on, there's extra help available for each family to do so. Parents can transfer their child to a better public school if that school refuses to change. In other words, at some point in time, there's got to be some accountability. It's one thing to be talking the talk about educational excellence, but pretty soon, if nothing happens, a parent ought to be allowed to walk, and that means to another public school, just like Woodridge, see.

If you're in a neighborhood and one school won't teach and change and another school will, I think it makes sense for a parent to have the option, with space available, to be able to say, "I've had it; I'm tired of my child being trapped in a failed school. I'm owed better as a parent and a property taxpayer than failure; therefore, I'd like to move my child to another school."

And that's what's happened to some of the students right here. Asia Goode, where's Asia? Oh, thank you for coming, Asia. Can I quote you? Thank you. I was going to quote you anyway. [*Laughter*] Asia first came to Woodridge; she was reading well below grade level. How do we know? Because she measured. Her teachers stayed after school to tutor her, and she caught up. Somebody said, "It is my job to make sure this individual is not left behind and not just shuffled through." And I thank that teacher for doing that.

Even after Asia reached grade level—in other words, we measure to determine whether a child can read at grade level—the teacher said, "Wait a minute; grade level is not good enough for you, Asia." I started off my speech by saying we're setting high standards. That's how you help somebody achieve educational excellence. Asia is now an honors student. She loves reading, and she sings in the school choir. And I congratulate her parent and the teachers and Asia for setting high standards and working hard to achieve those standards.

Washington, DC, has a really innovative and interesting program that I strongly support, as did your mayor, Mayor Williams. Oh, I know it's controversial for some, but it rests on the premise that a parent ought to have different options if a child is trapped in a school that won't teach and won't change. I happen to think that is a good, solid principle on which to operate, that the parent is the primary teacher of a child and the parent ought to have different options for his or her child.

And so the D.C. Opportunity Scholarship Program was enacted. And it wasn't easy to enact it. There are some who are willing to defend the status quo at all costs. That's okay. That's generally what happens some-times in the political arena. But this is a program that enables a parent to transfer his or her child to a private or religious school if the parent feels like the current school isn't working. This program is aimed particularly at low-income students.

Let's be frank about it: Upper income families have got school choice. They can afford it. Low-income families don't. This program enables low-income families to say, "I'm sick and tired of my child not receiving a quality education." Eighteen hundred low-income students have used these scholarships. One of them is Carlos Battle. Carlos isn't here, but I thought his quote might interest—he was in a school, and he transferred to Assumption Catholic School 2 years ago. In other words, his parents—family qualified, received a schol-arship, and off he went.

After transferring, he made the honor roll. He became the class president. He led the basketball team to its first cham-pionship. He said this: "There is no limit to what I can do. And that not only makes me happier, but my mom can't seem to stop smiling." It is really important that as we think about how to make sure every child gets a good education, that we not only measure but we say that if things don't change, parents ought to have different op-tions.

The No Child Left Behind Act is good progress, but we've got a lot of work to do, and it starts with making sure that here in Washington, we don't soften our desire to hold schools accountable. As I'll tell you, look, there's a lot of pressure, and I'm sure the Congressmen and Senators feel that pressure. They feel the pressure because people say, "Look, we're tired of meas-uring." They feel the pressure because, you know, "We're just teaching the test." I mean, there's every excuse in the book.

But as we come time to reauthorize the No Child Left Behind Act, my attitude is, instead of softening No Child Left Behind, we need to strengthen it. The law is work-ing. It makes sense. We must hold schools account—to account if we expect our chil-dren to be able to realize dreams. And if we want America to remain competitive, we must have high standards.

You know, there's a—kind of a mindset at times, a culture that says, "Well, you know, maybe certain kids can't learn, and therefore, let's don't have high standards." I reject that notion. I strongly believe every child has got the capacity. And all of us must demand that the high standards be set and met. And so one of the top prior-ities next year for me will be the reauthor-ization and the strengthening of the No Child Left Behind Act.

Here are some ways to improve the law. In order for every child to get up to grade level, there must be a quality teacher in every classroom. And one way to help the law is to help our teachers in an innovative way. We created what's called the Teacher Incentive Fund. It allows States and local districts to reward teachers who dem-onstrate strong results for their students. It's an interesting concept, isn't it? In other words, if your measurement system shows that you're providing excellence for your children, it seems to make sense that there ought to be a little extra incentive to do so through the bonus program, not run by the Federal Government: funded by the Federal Government, administered by States and local governments.

I think it's very important to encourage our good teachers to teach in some of the toughest school districts. You know, when you find a good teacher, a good, high-qual-ity teacher in a—for example, an inner-city district needs help, or a rural district needs help, there ought to be a bonus sys-tem available, an incentive program to say to a teacher, "Thanks; thanks for heading into some of the—you know, an area that is—that needs help, and here's a little in-centive to do so." So there's some ideas that Congress can work on in order to pro-vide incentives for our teachers.

I believe we ought to encourage math and science professionals to bring their expertise into the classrooms. I remember going to a school here in Maryland recently. Margaret and I went over there, and I met a guy who worked at NASA. And do you know what he was doing? He was in the classrooms basically saying to seventh and eighth graders, "Science is cool; take it seriously."

You know, it's important that you learn the skills necessary to be good scientists because it's important for the United States of America that we've got young scientists. And by the way, every neighborhood in America can produce young scientists. And therefore, encouraging these professionals in the classrooms as adjunct teachers makes a lot of sense, and Congress ought to fund that program.

We've got to improve options. One of the problems we have in the Public School Choice program is, parents aren't getting information on a timely basis. So in other words, you got your kid going to a school. The school's accountability system says, "Wait a minute; you're not doing as well as you should." And the parent gets notified after the next school year begins. That doesn't help.

It kind of looks like people are afraid to put out results for some reason. And so we'll work with Congress to clarify the law and to strengthen the law to make sure our parents get timely information and useful information so that they can take advantage of the No Child Left Behind Act's—law that provides flexibility and transferability.

We're going to work with school districts to help more students take advantage of free, intensive tutoring. You'd be amazed at the number of districts that don't use this extra tutoring. They don't take advantage of the extra money to help an individual child. Oh, they'll figure out ways to spend it, don't get me wrong. But the money is aimed for helping an individual succeed, and it's the cumulative effect of bringing these students up to grade level that will enable us all to say, we're more competitive for the future.

I believe in opportunity scholarships. I believe that the program here in Washington, DC, ought to be replicated around the country. I call on Congress to create such a program for 28,000 low-income children as a beginning step to help parents challenge failure.

We've got to do something about our high schools, by the way. I think there needs to be strong accountability in America's high schools. You've got strong accountability right here at Woodridge. It seems like it makes sense, if it's working, to extend that concept to our high schools.

One out of every four ninth graders in America does not graduate from high school on time. That's unacceptable. If we want to be competitive, we better make sure that the skills that are now being imparted at elementary school and junior high carry on through high school. We don't want the good work here at Woodridge to be lost because there's—because some say, "Well, I don't need to get out of high school," or the accountability systems in high school don't measure up. And so what I want to do is I want to have the same sense of accountability in our high schools that we have in our junior high and elementary schools, not to increase the testing burden but to help us understand whether or not we are achieving our national objective, which is giving our kids the skills necessary to be competitive.

And so I think we need to fund testing early in the high school systems and to help students fix problems like we're doing in elementary school and high schools. I proposed a billion-and-a-half dollar initiative; Congress needs to fund it. I've also proposed a program to train 70,000 teachers over 5 years to lead Advanced Placement classes in our high schools. Advanced Placement works. It is an excellent program that helps our high schools set high standards. And it calls—it challenges our students to achieve great things by raising the standards.

Many of you know about AP. It needs to be spread all throughout America. And step one is to make sure our teachers have the skills necessary to teach it. And step two is to help States develop programs that will help parents pay for the AP test. What we don't want is a child taking an AP class and having mom or dad say, "It's too expensive to take the test." You pass an AP test; you're on your way. If you've got the skills necessary to pass an AP test, it means the education system has done its job, and our country is better off.

And so here are some ideas for the Congress and the administration to work on

as we think about how to reauthorize the No Child Left Behind Act. I strongly believe this piece of legislation is working. I know it is necessary to have this kind of rigor in our school systems to say we have done our job and given our kids the skills necessary to succeed. And I want to thank you all for serving as a great example. Thank you for inviting me. Again, I thank the teachers for teaching and the parents for loving and the students for reading.

God bless.

NOTE: The President spoke at 11:02 a.m. In his remarks, he referred to Mayor Anthony A. Williams of Washington, DC. The Office of the Press Secretary also released a Spanish language transcript of these remarks.

Remarks on the National Economy
October 6, 2006

Secretary Paulson and I want to thank FedEx for inviting us here today to have a discussion about our economy and about entrepreneurship. We just met with a handful of small-business owners, business creators, people who had an innovative idea, followed up on their idea, and have now built healthy little businesses that are growing and employing people.

I don't necessarily want to speak for the Secretary, but I will tell you that it does my spirits good to be able to talk to risk takers and dreamers and doers. And one of the jobs of government is to make sure the entrepreneurial spirit is strong by creating an environment that encourages entrepreneurship, which means low taxes, less regulation, rational spending at the Government level, opening markets overseas so that the entrepreneur can trade but is treated fairly, and making sure that foreign countries don't steal products; that's called intellectual property rights. It's to really say

to the good folks in America that Government will help you as opposed to impede your ability to expand your company. And the entrepreneurial spirit is strong in America. Our economy is strong.

I say that because today we got more good news. The national unemployment rate is down to 4.6 percent. We have added 6.6 million new jobs since August of 2003. The wages are going up; energy prices are falling, which means people are going to have more money in their pocket to save, invest, or spend. And the fundamental question is, how do we make sure we sustain the economic growth? And one way to do so is to make the tax cuts we passed permanent. One sure way to hurt this economy is to take money out of the pockets of consumers or small-business owners and send it to Washington, DC.

And so I'm pleased with the economic progress we're making. The Secretary of the Treasury and I will continue to work as hard as we can to encourage entrepre-neurial—entrepreneurship and small-busi-ness growth.

And so, again, I want to thank the people of FedEx. This is a great example of what is possible in America. A fellow I knew long years ago, named Fred Smith, had a dream about how to better distribute mail and product. And he and a lot of other good folks built this into a great American company.

So I want to thank the folks here for letting us come by to say hello.

NOTE: The President spoke at 11:27 a.m. at the FedEx Express DCA Facility. In his re-marks, he referred to Frederick W. Smith, chairman, president, and chief executive offi-cer, FedEx Corp.

Remarks at a Reception Celebrating Hispanic Heritage Month
October 6, 2006

The President. Thank you. *Hola.* Please be seated.

Audience member. Viva Bush!

The President. Shhh. [*Laughter*] *Bienvenidos.* We are glad you're here. Thanks for coming. Laura sends her best. She, like me, greets you to come—to wel-come you to the *Casa Blanca*—[*laughter*]— *la casa de todos.* We are glad you're here. I am glad that so many of you joined us for Hispanic Heritage Month. Today we honor the contributions of Hispanic Ameri-cans to our country, to our culture, and to our national character.

We celebrate the values *de la familia y fe.* After all, those values are at the heart of the Hispanic American community. We welcome the diversity that enriches our lives, a diversity that makes America a stronger and better country. Thanks for coming.

I am proud to welcome a friend of my family's, His Royal Highness Prince Felipe de Borbon, the Crown Prince of the King-dom of Spain. Thank you for coming. His Royal Highness is here to help celebrate Hispanic Heritage Month, which I think is a kind gesture and a noble gesture from a very important country. We're proud you're here, sir. Thank you for coming. Please give your best to His Majesty and your mom. And I will do the same on be-half of you to my father and her majesty, my mother. [*Laughter*]

I am proud to be here with the Attorney General of the United States, Alberto Gonzales. The U.S. Treasurer, Anna Cabral—Anna, thank you for coming; *y su esposo,* Victor. Welcome, Victor. Good to see you.

Today we've got a special guest, Ana Cristina, who will perform two songs after I finish speaking, which probably means you want me to finish speaking soon, so that Ana can come up here. We're proud you're here, Ana. I want to thank my friend Emilio Estefan for arranging for the enter-tainment today. He's a great buddy of ours from Miami. It's good to see you, sir.

I am proud to be here with Lieutenant Colonel Consuelo Kickbusch. She's the winner of the Hispanic Heritage Award 2006. Interesting name, Kickbusch. [*Laugh-ter*] It sounds like the political campaign. [*Laughter*] Congratulations.

I appreciate all the Ambassadors who are here. Thanks for coming. We've got Ambas-sadors from neighboring countries. I like to remind people that the best foreign pol-icy is to make sure that we've got good foreign policy in our own neighborhood. And so we're glad you're here. Thanks for coming.

We've got distinguished members from the IDB, USO, all kinds of organizations. And I'm proud you're here. Thanks for coming.

We are a blessed nation to have thousands of people who claim Hispanic heritage. I firmly believe that. I know that to be true. I think our citizens must recognize the great contribution of Hispanic Americans to our country. Hispanic Americans are hard-working people. They're entrepreneurial people who dream big dreams. They're people who love their God and especially love their families. But most of all, they love their country, America.

As we celebrate Hispanic Heritage Month, we've got to recognize we have responsibilities in Government to make sure that all in this country can realize the American Dream. In the 21st century, the best way to do that is to make sure every child gets a good education—not just a few children—but every single child must receive a quality education.

I believe strongly that every child can learn regardless of the color of their skin or whether their parents speak English as a first language. And I know that in order to make sure every child gets educated, we've got to set high standards. And we've got to measure to determine whether or not schools are achieving that which we expect. And when we find a child cannot read at grade level, then that child deserves extra help to make sure that we make— to make sure that we meet a national objective, and that is, no child should be left behind.

I'm pleased to report that Hispanic students, in reading and math, are scoring higher, and an achievement gap in our country is beginning to close. We're making progress, but I assure you we will not rest until every child receives a quality education in our country.

I believe that America should remain the land of the entrepreneur, and that ours is a country that benefits when people have a dream and work hard to achieve that dream. The small-business community is strong here in America. It's strong because we have entrepreneurs in our midst. And the role of government is to encourage the entrepreneurial spirit. Government doesn't create wealth, but government can create an environment in which people who dream dreams have a chance to realize those dreams.

I'm proud to report that the number of Hispanic-owned businesses is growing at three times the national rate. And that's positive, particularly if you're a fellow like me who worries about whether or not people can find work, because the truth of the matter is, 70 percent of new jobs in our country are created by small businesses. And so when the small-business sector is growing, the job base is growing. And equally importantly, when the small business is growing, it means ownership is growing, and the more owners we have in the United States of America, the more hopeful country we will have for all of us.

We take pride in the service of Hispanic Americans. When we celebrate Hispanic Heritage Month, it's time to thank our fellow citizens for serving the country. I thank our Attorney General for serving the country. I thank the Secretary of Commerce, Carlos Gutierrez, for serving the country. They're in my Cabinet. These are men who serve at the highest councils of Government and can walk in the Oval Office any time they feel like it and say, "Mr. President, here is what's on my mind." I appreciate their counsel in helping me make good decisions on behalf of our country.

We've got Hispanic Americans all across the country who serve our country by loving a neighbor like they'd like to be loved themselves. Thousands of our fellow citizens feed the hungry or find shelter for the homeless or put their arm around a child who needs love in order to help create a society that is welcoming to all. And for those of you who are involved in our faith-based communities and charitable communities, I thank you on behalf of a grateful nation.

The Hispanic community is also known for its willingness to serve in the United States military and protect our freedoms. Today, we have over 200,000 Hispanic Americans wearing the uniform of the finest military on the face of the Earth. Today, we've got members of the Hispanic community who wear our uniform with us, representing those 200,000, and I want to thank you for your service.

These fine Americans, like the other Americans in our military, are working hard to secure this country. They're answering the call to history. They have volunteered to serve in an historic time, a time when this United States will do what it takes to defend ourselves from people who spread evil by killing the innocent; at a time when the United States understands that in order to spread the peace, we will stand with those who long for liberty. I'm proud to be the Commander in Chief of such a fantastic group of men and women.

And as we renew our commitment to our Hispanic Americans, we also must renew our commitment to make sure we're a welcoming society. We are a land of immigrants, and as we debate immigration policy, we must always keep that important fact in mind. One of the important things about our country is that we provide hope, and that we recognize that we're a stronger nation when we're bound together under one God—when we bind together under one God, different cultures and different heritages.

We will conduct this debate on immigration in a way that is respectful to our heritage. We are a nation of law, and we will enforce our law. But at the same time, we must remember that in order to secure our borders, in order to make sure we fulfill our heritage, immigration reform must be comprehensive in nature. We must understand that you can't kick 12 million people out of your country; that we must figure out a way to say to those that if you're lawful and if you've contributed to the United States of America, there is a way for you to eventually earn a citizenship.

Nobody in our land wants to grant automatic amnesty. But everybody in our land understands these people must be treated with respect and dignity. There are citizenship lines for people from our neighborhood. People ought to be given a chance to get at the back of the citizenship line and have a chance. And so I assure my friends here that I will—we will enforce the border as people expect us to do. But as we do so, we'll do so in a humane way, in a way that honors that great tradition of the United States of America, one Nation under God.

And so on this day that we recognize the contributions of our Hispanic Americans, we renew the great—our faith in the greatness of our country. I welcome you to the White House. I'm honored, Royal Highness, that you have joined us today. I thank you for serving the United States of America. And I now welcome to the stage Ana Cristina.

NOTE: The President spoke at 2:29 p.m. in the East Room at the White House. In his remarks, he referred to King Juan Carlos I and Queen Sofia of Spain; Victor G. Cabral, husband of U.S. Treasurer Anna Escobedo Cabral; Cuban American singer Ana Cristina Alvarez; Emilio Estefan, Jr., president, Estefan Enterprises, Inc.; and Lt. Col. Consuelo Castillo Kickbusch, USA (Ret.). The Office of the Press Secretary also released a Spanish language transcript of these remarks. The National Hispanic Heritage Month proclamation of September 14 is listed in Appendix D at the end of this volume.

The President's Radio Address
October 7, 2006

Good morning. In recent days, we have seen shocking acts of violence in schools across our Nation. Laura and I are praying for the victims and their families, and we extend our sympathies to them and to the communities that have been devastated by these attacks.

I have asked Secretary of Education Spellings and Attorney General Gonzales to host a conference on school safety this Tuesday. We will bring together teachers, parents, students, administrators, law enforcement officials, and other experts to discuss the best ways to keep violence out of our schools. Our goal is clear: Children and teachers should never fear for their safety when they enter a classroom.

As we work to keep our classrooms safe, we must also ensure that the children studying there get a good education. I believe every child can learn. So when I came to Washington, I worked with Republicans and Democrats to pass the No Child Left Behind Act, and I was proud to sign it into law. The theory behind this law is straightforward: We expect every school in America to teach every student to read, write, add, and subtract.

We are measuring progress and giving parents the information they need to hold their schools accountable. Local schools remain under local control. The Federal Government is asking for demonstrated results in exchange for the money we send from Washington. Thanks to this good law, we are leaving behind the days when schools just shuffled children from grade to grade, whether they learned anything or not.

Earlier this week, I visited the Department of Education, where I was briefed on our progress under the No Child Left Behind Act. The most recent national tests show encouraging results. In reading, 9-year-olds have made larger gains in the past 5 years than at any point in the previous 28 years. In math, 9-year-olds and 13-year-olds earned the highest scores in the history of the test. In both reading and math, African American and Hispanic students are scoring higher, and they are beginning to close the achievement gap with their white peers.

The No Child Left Behind Act also gives parents more options. If your child's school consistently fails to show progress, you can get free, intensive tutoring for your child or transfer your child to a better public school. By shining a spotlight on schools that are not performing and offering parents and children a way out, the No Child Left Behind Act is ushering in a new era of accountability and choice. And this is putting America's children on the path to a better life.

The No Child Left Behind Act has brought good progress, yet we still have a lot of work to do. So I will be talking more about education in the coming months, especially as we discuss the reauthorization of this law next year. I will focus on three areas where we can improve. First, we must improve teacher quality, so that every child has an excellent teacher. Second, we must give more options to parents whose children are trapped in struggling schools. And third, we need to bring the same high standards and accountability of the No Child Left Behind Act to our high schools, so that every high school graduate has the tools he or she needs to go to college and to get a good-paying job.

When we set expectations high, America's children will rise to meet them. And by helping our children succeed, we're creating a brighter future for them and for our Nation.

Thank you for listening.

NOTE: The address was recorded at 7:50 a.m. on October 6 in the Cabinet Room at the

White House for broadcast at 10:06 a.m. on October 7. The transcript was made available by the Office of the Press Secretary on October 6 but was embargoed for release until the broadcast. The Office of the Press Secretary also released a Spanish language transcript of this address.

Remarks at a Christening Ceremony for the USS *George H.W. Bush* in Newport News, Virginia
October 7, 2006

Mr. Secretary, thank you very much. Laura and I are honored to be here to honor our dad. We appreciate you coming. Mother, it's good to see you. Members of the Bush family, all of you, distinguished Members of Congress, Governor, ex-Governors, the men and women of the United States Navy, military veterans, the workers who helped build this great ship: I join you—I know you join me in saying to our father, President Bush, your ship has come in. [*Laughter*]

In a few minutes, my sister Dorothy will christen the newest and most advanced aircraft carrier in the Navy, the *George H.W. Bush*. For the pilots of the World War II generation who are with us today, this carrier may seem a little more inviting than the ones you landed on. As you can see, our Navy has made a few upgrades. The *George H.W. Bush* is the latest in the Nimitz line of aircraft carriers. She is unrelenting; she is unshakable; she is unyielding; she is unstoppable. As a matter of fact, probably should have been named the "Barbara Bush." [*Laughter*]

In accord with a long and honored tradition, we gather to christen this fine ship. We recall the service and sacrifice of earlier generations. And we pay tribute to a new generation of sailors and marines who have stepped forward to serve in freedom's cause.

The *George H.W. Bush* is named for a man who exemplifies the great character of our country. On the day Pearl Harbor was attacked, George H.W. Bush was a teenager, he was a high school senior. Six months later, he was sworn into the Navy. A year later, he received his wings at a ceremony in Corpus Christi, Texas. Here is what he said: He said, "I had an ensign's stripe and an admiral's confidence." [*Laughter*] "I was a Navy pilot."

Our dad would become known as one of the Navy's youngest pilots, but that wasn't his only distinction. While training along the Chesapeake Bay, the pilots in our dad's flight class learned about a beach across the way where young ladies liked to sunbathe. It became popular for the pilots to fly low over the beach. So one day he came in low to take a look. It just so happened to be the same day that a traveling circus had set up its tents. Dad's flyover upset an elephant, causing him to break loose and make a run throughout the town. He was called in for a reprimand from his commander. He puts it this way: "I was grounded for causing an elephant stampede"—probably the only Navy pilot in American history who can make that claim.

After training, he was assigned to a light carrier. He took part in the Great Turkey Shoot of the Marianas. He knew the horror of kamikaze attacks. He would complete 58 combat missions. These were tough days, but he had something that kept him going. And if you look closely at the photographs of the planes he flew, you will find what kept him going in the name he had painted under his cockpit: Barbara.

One of Dad's most important missions was a strike on a radio tower on an island called Chichi Jima. The Japanese were using that tower to intercept U.S. military radio transmissions and alert the enemy about impending American air strikes. On September 2, 1944, his squadron was given a simple assignment: to take it out. The pilots knew they would face heavy enemy fire because the Japanese had fortified the island. But Dad and his fellow pilots did their duty without complaint or hesitation. During that raid, his plane was hit by anti-aircraft artillery, and it caught on fire. Yet he kept his plane on course. He released his four bombs and scored four direct hits on that tower; he headed out to sea; he ejected.

Japanese boats were sent out to capture him. And after more than 2 harrowing hours at sea alone in a rubber life raft, he was rescued by the crew of the USS *Finback*. For his action, he earned the Distinguished Flying Cross. Yet it is characteristic that from those moments aboard his life raft to this ceremony today, Dad's thoughts have always been of the two fine members of his crew who did not make it home: Radioman Second Class John Delaney and Lieutenant (J.G.) Ted White. On that day over Chichi Jima, a young American became a war hero and learned an old lesson: With the defense of freedom comes loss and sacrifice.

The *George H.W. Bush* honors a generation that valued service above self. Like so many who served in World War II, duty came naturally to our father. In the 4 years of that war, 16 million Americans would put on the uniform, and the human costs were appalling. From the beaches of Normandy to the jungles of Southeast Asia, more than 400,000 Americans would give their lives.

From the beginning of that war, there were those who argued that freedom had seen its day and that the future belonged to the hard men in Tokyo and Berlin. Yet the war machines of Imperial Japan and Nazi Germany would be brought down by American GIs who only months before had been students and farmers and bank clerks and factory hands. The generation of World War II taught the world's tyrants a telling lesson: There is no power like the power of freedom and no soldier as strong as a soldier who fights for a free future for his children.

The *George H.W. Bush* will serve—as a new generation of Americans every bit as brave and selfless as those who have come before them. The 21st century—in the 21st century, freedom is again under attack, and young Americans are volunteering to answer the call. In the years since September the 11th, 2001, more than 1.6 million Americans have volunteered to wear the uniform of the United States. Today, they serve in distant lands and on far seas—from the islands of Southeast Asia to the Horn of Africa to the mountains of Afghanistan and in Iraq. And once again, with perseverance and courage and confidence in the power of freedom, a new generation of Americans will leave a more hopeful and peaceful world for generations to come.

The men and women of the United States military represent the best of America, and they deserve the best America can give them. And the *George H.W. Bush* is the best America can give them.

During his time in the South Pacific, Ensign Bush served on a light carrier called the USS *San Jacinto*. That ship was named for the 1836 Battle of San Jacinto. And in that battle, the free Texas forces led by Sam Houston defeated a Mexican army that was much larger in size, and Sam Houston succeeded in capturing the Mexican general responsible for the slaughter of the Alamo just a few weeks before. Yet on the eve of the battle, the outcome was far from certain, and the Mexicans seemed to hold the advantage. So Sam Houston called his Texans together, and he reminded them what they were fighting for. He told them: "Be men, be free men, that your children may bless their father's name."

On this proud day, the children of George H.W. Bush bless their father's name, the United States Navy honors his name, and the ship that bears his name sails into this young century as a symbol of American strength and freedom. May God watch over all those who sail this ship, all those who fly from her deck, and all those at home who pray for their safe return.

It is my honor to bring to you the 41st President, a great dad, George H.W. Bush.

NOTE: The President spoke at 10:55 a.m. at the Northrop Grumman Newport News Shipyard. In his remarks, he referred to Gov. Timothy M. Kaine of Virginia.

Statement on the Death of John J. "Buck" O'Neil
October 7, 2006

Buck O'Neil represented the best of America's national pastime. He devoted his long and full life to baseball and refused to allow injustice and discrimination to diminish his love of the game and his joyous, generous spirit. Laura and I extend our sympathies to his family and friends, and on behalf of all Americans, we give thanks for the life of one of the great ambassadors in baseball history.

Remarks on the Situation in North Korea
October 9, 2006

Last night the Government of North Korea proclaimed to the world that it had conducted a nuclear test. We're working to confirm North Korea's claim. Nonetheless, such a claim itself constitutes a threat to international peace and security. The United States condemns this provocative act. Once again North Korea has defied the will of the international community, and the international community will respond.

This was confirmed this morning in conversations I had with leaders of China and South Korea, Russia, and Japan. We reaffirmed our commitment to a nuclear-free Korean Peninsula, and all of us agreed that the proclaimed actions taken by North Korea are unacceptable and deserve an immediate response by the United Nations Security Council.

The North Korean regime remains one of the world's leading proliferator of missile technology, including transfers to Iran and Syria. The transfer of nuclear weapons or material by North Korea to states or non-state entities would be considered a grave threat to the United States, and we would hold North Korea fully accountable of the consequences of such action.

The United States remains committed to diplomacy, and we will continue to protect ourselves and our interests. I reaffirmed to our allies in the region, including South Korea and Japan, that the United States will meet the full range of our deterrent and security commitments.

Threats will not lead to a brighter future for the North Korean people nor weaken the resolve of the United States and our allies to achieve the denuclearization of the Korean Peninsula. Today's claim by North

Korea serves only to raise tensions, while depriving the North Korean people of the increased prosperity and better relations with the world offered by the implementation of the joint statement of the six-party talks. The oppressed and impoverished people of North Korea deserve that brighter future.

Thank you.

NOTE: The President spoke at 9:58 a.m. in the Diplomatic Reception Room at the White House. In his remarks, he referred to President Hu Jintao of China; President Roh Moo-hyun of South Korea; President Vladimir V. Putin of Russia; and Prime Minister Shinzo Abe of Japan.

Remarks Following Discussions With President Alan Garcia Perez of Peru
October 10, 2006

President Bush. Bienvenidos, Mr. Presidente, a la Casa Blanca. I'm proud to welcome the President of Peru to the Oval Office. We've had a fascinating and important discussion. First of all, I appreciated his experience, and I appreciated his advice on some key issues. He comes to the Oval Office as a friend, somebody with whom I can have good working relations.

We talked about world issues, we talked about issues regarding South America and Central America, and we talked about our bilateral relations. The central issue facing us right now is the passage of a free trade agreement. I assured the President that I will work with Congress as soon as possible to get this agreement passed. We talked about the need for both countries to work closely to fight drugs, and I appreciated the President's attitude and understanding of this important issue.

And we talked about the need to work together to help promote social justice. The President has a big heart. He cares deeply about those who suffer. And I assured the President it's in our Nation's interest that we work with our friends in the—in South America to promote good education and good health care and good opportunities.

All in all, it was an excellent meeting. And, Mr. President, welcome.

President Garcia Perez. Thank you. I am very happy to be here for the first time in the Oval Office. President Bush and I have agreed on the general topics that we discussed, in terms of strengthening democracy and also strengthening relations between developed countries and developing countries. And one basic tool for that goal is free trade. And we are very satisfied to have heard President Bush's promise to work with the Congress to push forward the passage of a free trade agreement with Peru.

And we have explained today that in terms of free trade, we are looking for an agreement that does much as focus on the most modern or the most significant economic groups in the country. We are also looking to have a free trade agreement that is focused internally and that will benefit our entire population, all our productive sectors, including the less advantaged sectors, so that they may export to the world and to the United States in particular.

We see the free trade agreement as one of our tools in our fight against poverty and also a tool for us to strengthen equality. Also, however, it is a tool that will help us achieve security through democracy and to give our population a road, a goal, and an aspiration in terms of economic development in the country.

We see our role as a country in terms of helping strengthen democracy and achieving friendship without threat in our region. And in this regard, Peru will continue to work towards the democratization of Latin America. As I said, it's a comprehensive democratization that we are looking for. We are looking to strengthen the options that our populations have in participating in the benefits of modernization and democratic civilization everywhere in the continent.

And one issue that we need to work on is a full eradication of the threat of drugs. And this is a commitment that we share with the United States. It's a commitment that will be strengthened and revised. And at some point, we will propose a high-level meeting on this topic in order to relaunch the fight against drugs, in terms of offering other alternatives, such as alternative development, and the free trade agreement is one of these tools. And the goal is to allow the poorest sectors, the farmers in the Andes, to have access to the buying power of the U.S. market and other markets in the world.

In the relationship between the United States and Latin America, there have been several missed opportunities in the 20th century. There was an opportunity that was put forward by President Roosevelt in the forties, with his proposal. There was also the Alliance for Progress, proposed here by the United States, by President Kennedy. And now we have a third possibility involving—or increasing world trade and the use of free trade as a tool to fight poverty. And it is an opportunity that Latin American countries must take advantage of this time. What could have been done almost 50 years ago with the Alliance for Progress is something that we can do now, thanks to the technological and computer

revolution that we are experiencing. And this is a way also to reach the poor in our countries and give them access to the world market.

And finally, I want to say that I'm a leader who belongs to a party that is a popular party, that believes in social justice and fights for sovereignty in our country. However, I recognize the opportunities that this time offers us in terms of our economies, and I believe it is important for our peoples to have specific and concrete gains in terms of the economy, education, and health. And I believe that this free trade agreement that we have been referring to is a very important tool in its regard.

And we have told the President that even though we are coming from a more modest position, we believe that with our leadership, we can stand side by side with the U.S. and make contributions in order to strengthen democracy and peace in the world and social justice among nations and also within our societies.

And I want to thank the President for his hospitality. I look forward to continuing to work together, and I hope that we will see the President soon in Peru. And thanks again for your invitation. Thank you a lot, Mr. President. Thank you very much.

President Bush. Muchas gracias, senor. Thank you.

NOTE: The President spoke at 10:11 a.m. in the Oval Office at the White House. President Garcia Perez spoke in Spanish, and his remarks were translated by an interpreter. The Office of the Press Secretary also released a Spanish language transcript of these remarks.

Joint Statement by the United States of America and the Republic of Peru
October 10, 2006

Presidents George W. Bush and Alan Garcia underscored the strong relationship between the United States and Peru, and reaffirmed their commitment to strengthening democracy and expanding free trade in the region as a means of improving the well-being of all citizens by securing freedom and delivering the greatest possible economic benefits to the largest number of people. They pledged to continue working together toward these and other shared objectives.

The two leaders agreed that democracies must strive to improve basic services for all citizens, and emphasized the importance of expanding health and education as a means of empowering citizens with the tools to fully participate in society, providing opportunities for economic growth and social development. They further concurred that democracy and democratic governance are the right and responsibility of all, and that an educated, engaged citizenry is the foundation for strong democratic institutions. They also agreed that all citizens should have the ability to participate fully and fairly in a modern economy, under the protection of the rule of law.

Both stressed the central role of initiatives such as the mutually beneficial U.S.-Peru Trade Promotion Agreement (PTPA) in strengthening bilateral ties while leveling the trade playing field, spurring job creation, and reducing poverty and inequality. In this regard, President Bush reaffirmed his commitment to securing congressional approval of the PTPA as quickly as possible. Both Presidents noted that domestic capacity-building programs, such as President Bush's Center for Education Excellence in Teacher Training and the Poverty Reduction and Alleviation Program initiatives, and President Garcia's Sierra Exportadora and "Internal FTA" programs, ensure that the opportunities derived from free and open markets accrue to the broadest number of Peruvians.

Presidents Bush and Garcia reaffirmed their strong commitment to protect their people and the hemisphere from the depredations of transnational terrorist and criminal organizations, pledging to promote speedy extradition of drug cartels' members. Among the many ways our countries work together to combat the scourge of narcotrafficking, based on the principle of shared responsibility, are Peru's comprehensive efforts against drug trafficking and illegal coca cultivation and U.S. programs that provide infrastructure and training to develop a police presence east of the Andes and alternative development to people in former coca growing areas, giving them hope for a sustainable, legal livelihood to provide for their families.

The Presidents reaffirmed their commitment to a strong bilateral relationship and to promoting prosperity and social justice for all people of the Americas.

NOTE: The Office of the Press Secretary also released a Spanish language version of this joint statement. An original was not available for verification of the content of this joint statement.

Remarks in a Discussion on School Safety in Chevy Chase, Maryland
October 10, 2006

The President. Thank you very much. Thank you all for coming. In many ways, I'm sorry we're having this meeting. In other ways, I know how important it is that we're having this meeting. The violence that has been occurring in our schools is incredibly sad, and it troubles a lot of folks, and it troubled me and Laura. And so I asked Margaret and Al to host a gathering of concerned citizens, the purpose of which is to come up with best practices and just shared experiences so that others might know how to react— to prevent and react to inexplicable and— violence that is hard to imagine.

All of us in this country want our classrooms to be gentle places of learning, places where people not only learn the basics—basic skills necessary to become productive citizens but learn to relate to one another. And our parents, I know, want to be able to send their child or children to schools that are safe places. And the violence we've seen, this is upsetting to a lot of people, and I know it's upsetting to the professionals who are with us. But rather than be upset, it's best for all of us who are responsible for helping folks not only cope but to prevent action from taking place. It's best to be proactive. And that's what this meeting is. And so I want to thank you all for joining.

I got a firsthand report on one of the panels from Laura, who said that—I think if I could summarize your words, it was, like, really interesting and very important. And so I thought what I would do is ask Al and Margaret to begin this session and maybe hear from some of the folks here, and then, if time permitting, hear from you all out in the audience.

Again, I want to thank Margaret and Al for setting this up, and really thank you all for coming and taking an interest. I know we got people from all around the country, and it's—this is a nationwide effort to help people who are responsible protect our children.

Attorney General Alberto Gonzales. Thank you. Mr. President, thank you for asking Margaret and I to host this important conference. We've had some good panel discussions, as you've already heard already. You've met some of the panelists that we've invited back. And just for our audience, again, we've asked Dr. Marleen Wong, Craig Scott, Fred Ellis, and Sheriff Jeff Dawsy to help us speak with the President about this important issue.

[*At this point, Attorney General Gonzales continued his remarks.*]

The President. I like the Secret Service too, Art. [*Laughter*]

[*Art Kelly, former police chief, New Bedford, MA, made brief remarks.*]

The President. Let me ask you a question, Al—not you, Chief, but—well, I can ask you too. I presume out of this there will be a series of best practices that you will share with principals and schools districts that explain, for example, what people could look for to determine whether or not there's an early warning sign, and then how to respond.

Attorney General Gonzales. Exactly.

The President. Okay, good. Thanks, Chief.

[*Attorney General Gonzales made further remarks, and Jeff Dawsy, sheriff, Citrus County, FL, made brief remarks.*]

The President. Is there an opportunity to share, between sheriffs around the country, how they're dealing with this issue? Does it make sense to have the National Sheriffs' Association contact members, ask for stories, practices, and then condense them and send them back out so that people can—who probably aren't listening to this will be able to——

Sheriff Dawsy. I think it would be a wonderful initiative. One of the things I learned today was not more about questions but more of solutions. There was many different speakers that came up and told us about different resources to use.

The President. Yes, that's my point.

Attorney General Gonzales. Mr. President, I think that Sheriff Dawsy would say that this program helps him to do his job, which means that I'm sure all the sheriffs around the country would like that kind of program as well, to help them do their job.

The President. That's my point. Yes. So who is responsible for talking to the head of the Sheriffs' Association or the police chiefs to make sure that happens?

Audience member. I'm right here, sir, and it will be done.

The President. Thank you, sir. Very good.

[*The discussion continued.*]

The President. Did you say 81 percent of the students were aware of a violent act?

Fred Ellis. Some of the data that I had heard today from the Secret Service and some of their research, that much information was out there.

The President. It seems like a pretty good opportunity to prevent an attack if 81 percent of the—there's an 81-percent awareness of a potential attack, which then, I guess, would lead to making sure principals explain to students: "When you hear something, please tell me."

[*Mr. Ellis, director, Office of Safety & Security, Fairfax County Public Schools, Centreville, VA, made brief remarks, and the discussion continued.*]

The President. Is it typical of a student that expresses a wish to die, makes that clear to his or her peers and to—if people are attuned to what that means, to pay attention to somebody who exhibits the behavior that says, "I am depressed, and I want to die"? I mean, is it—it's a pretty strong statement.

Marleen Wong. It's a wonderful question, because there are behaviors and there are expressions of hopelessness that come before that. And so I think we have to do a lot of education with just folks who say, you know, "They've changed. They don't have joy in life," and that this is an early warning sign.

The President. But is it easy to define the behavior that would tip off an adult in a school, or some—a coach or an art teacher that this is the kind of behavior that ought to say to us, we better pay attention to this person, this child?

Ms. Wong. Yes. There's a short list, and actually, the student who sat on the previous panel did an excellent job of naming all of those things. I was so proud of her. I thought she ought to come and do some training with our——

The President. And how many educators do you think that can name—good job, by the way—how many adults do you think around the schools in America can name the traits that would say, we better pay attention to this person?

Ms. Wong. Not enough.

The President. And therefore, what can we do to make sure that people understand what to look for? It seems like to me that a lot of our focus ought to be on preventing. And no question, we ought to worry about recovering, but preventing is—makes the recovery not necessary.

Secretary of Education Margaret Spellings. Chiarasay, you did such a nice job this morning. Why don't you go to the microphone real quick and tell us the nine signs.

The President. Where are you from, Chiarasay?

Chiarasay Perkins. Mr. President, I'm from Walton County, Florida.

The President. Good. I know your Governor. [*Laughter*]

[*Ms. Perkins, student, Walton Senior High School, DeFuniak Springs, FL, made brief remarks.*]

The President. That's great. Thank you.

Ms. Wong. Thank you.

The President. Let me ask you a question. From your experience, Marleen, if a teacher were to notice those traits, is it typical that someone would act on them? In other words, I'm just trying to make sure I understand. If a student sees—I mean, a teacher sees a student begin to change clothes and begin to—does a principal and a teacher tend to say, "Well, that's really not my business; it's the parents' business?" In other words, awareness requires, by the way, some kind of response.

Ms. Wong. And I think that varies around the country.

The President. Yes, I'm sure it does.

Ms. Wong. I think that more and more people are beginning to pay attention just because we have paid such a dear price for ignoring some of the warning signs.

The President. So maybe an outcome for this is to encourage—for you to get in touch with the principals' organizations or the teachers' organizations and help——

Secretary Spellings. ——them be aware of the warning signs.

The President. And then—I guess there's a certain confidence that has to come with interfering—not interfering, but interceding in a child's life. My only question is, is there hesitancy when an adult says, "Well, maybe this is just the way it's supposed to be," or, "Maybe it's none of my business"? And the question is, if that's the case—if you can determine that's the case, how do you get people to respond differently?

Secretary Spellings. Cathy Paine from Oregon told us about—where they had an incident there, that there were dozens of signs of this particular shooter and that the full picture didn't become clear until after the incident.

The President. Can you—do you mind sharing that? Thanks, Cathy.

[*Cathy Paine, special programs administrator, Springfield School District, Springfield, OR, made brief remarks.*]

The President. The whole purpose of this exercise is to help educate and, if there needs to be cultural change inside schools, for teachers to become more aware and more active—or principals—is to try to stimulate these kinds of discussions, obviously, outside of Washington, at the local level or State levels, in the hopes of preventing these from happening in the first place.

Thank you for coming to share your experience and appreciate your sharing your expertise.

Secretary Spellings. One of the people who's been doing that in a very meaningful way is Craig Scott, who has talked all over the country to teenagers and teachers and educators and school leaders. And he has a very powerful story, as you know. His sister, Rachel, was murdered in Columbine.

So, Craig, why don't you share your thoughts.

[*Craig Scott, former student, Columbine High School, Aurora, CO, made brief remarks.*]

The President. Good job. Whew. Which one of us up here can now talk after that? Thank you. Yes, that's great. You are changing our society. You may not realize it, but thank you—powerful statement.

I'd be glad to hear from people in the audience. [*Laughter*] Yes, I probably won't be able to hear from all of you in the audience.

That was great, Craig. Thank you. Could I have that?

Mr. Scott. Oh, absolutely.

The President. Thank you. Yes, sir.

*Character Education/Community
Involvement in Schools*

Q. Mr. President, I haven't had this feeling since I was 17, and that's the last time that I asked you a question in Herbert, Texas. I've spoken to hundreds of thousands of people since. Last time I was nervous was when I was 17 in Herbert, Texas, and you were campaigning in Herbert, Texas.

The President. Don't tell them I came in second place in a two-man race. [*Laughter*]

Q. My name is Pete Vargas. I'm the national director for Rachel's Challenge, the program——

The President. Oh, fantastic, Pete.

Q. ——that Craig just talked about. And I want to echo something that's very dear to my heart and Darrel, his father, who is sitting right here.

The President. Your dad is there? Where is your dad? Excuse me. Okay, thank you. Raised a good man here.

Q. I talk to thousands of educators every month—our team does—thousands. And one of the things that disturbs me is there's hundreds that say, "Pete, you all have changed the culture of our school." But then there's thousands that say, "It's so hard for us to fit our—we want your program so bad, but we have testing and testing and testing and this and that," and it made me think about something, President. It made me think about growing up—I was going the wrong direction completely. I was stealing; I was doing everything possibly wrong—vandalism, beating up kids. And in seventh grade there was a teacher, Mrs. Muldanado, who touched my heart. In 10th grade, there was a lady that you know from Herbert, Texas, that touched my heart. And in ninth grade my tennis coach touched my heart, and those three people changed my life. And as we—why I believe in what I'm doing so much is Darrel's motto is that if we touch the heart of the kid, the head will follow. If we touch their heart, the

head will follow, and the hands will make the difference.

My question to you today is, I don't want us to look at the warning signs; I want us to eliminate the warning signs.

The President. Right, right.

Q. What can we do—what can we do— and this is echoing Darrel and what Craig just said—what can we do from the government's standpoint to go back to touching the heart of the kid, to teaching character education? Because we hear that all the time about the testing.

The President. I agree. Pete, let me say— first on the tests. Thanks for coming. It's good to see you again. I was probably more nervous than you were when you asked the question. [*Laughter*]

Q. You look the same. [*Laughter*]

The President. I like selected memory. [*Laughter*]

First, in terms of testing, I don't think it's zero sum. I think you can make sure a child learns, and I think you can instill character at the same time. I don't think you have to choose. As a matter of fact, I know we can't say that one doesn't beget the other. I happen to believe that self-esteem comes when a child realizes he or she can read early, at grade level. And I think one of the real problems—[*applause*]—I think one of the real problems we have, Pete, is a school system across the country that basically gives up on children because we don't measure to determine whether or not they have the skills necessary to read, for example.

And so I'm concerned about a system that socially promotes children, because I think that at some point in time, that begins to affect a child's vision of the future, and a grim vision of the future may be that which triggers a response that is negative.

Character education is—I know we funded quite a bit of it when I was the Governor of Texas. Let me put the funding issue right on the table. The Federal Government is a limited funder of education, and I happen to believe that's the way it should be. I don't think it's possible for the people to have expectations that the Government should fund public schools. This is a local responsibility. It's been that way throughout our history. I think it makes sense to do so because it tends to make control of our schools more localized, which I happen to think is the best way to achieve excellence.

And so therefore, not to try to pass responsibilities—although we do have character education grants out of Washington, and we've got school safety grants out of Washington. But the best place to facilitate that kind of initiative, to make sure that character is taught in schools, is at the State level.

Secondly, it's really important, Pete, that people not think government is a loving entity. Government is law and justice. Love comes from the hearts of people that are able to impart love. And therefore, what Craig is doing is—he doesn't realize it— he's a social entrepreneur. He is inspiring others to continue to reach out to say to somebody who is lonely, "I love you." And I'm afraid this requires a higher power than the Federal Government to cause somebody to love somebody. And therefore, it's a—[applause]—and therefore, one of the things we can do, though, is to call upon people—we've got the USA Freedom Corps Initiative, for example, that calls on volunteers to take active participation in their communities.

You know, Craig said something interesting. I believe societies change one heart at a time. I don't mean to mimic what you said, but I was actually praising what you said, because that's how it works. And the truth of the matter is, if we really think about it, the primary responsibility, the primary teacher of character is the parent. That is the frontline of enabling our society to be a compassionate, decent place. You wouldn't be sitting here if your mother and father hadn't instilled in you a—something inside your soul that caused you to sit here

in front of the President of the United States and give an unbelievably eloquent testimony about compassion.

And the second line of defense in schools is, obviously, teachers. And the hope is, is that out of this violence and terror comes this notion that teachers have got to be— and by the way, the teachers have got an unbelievably hard job—to not only teach but to show concern and compassion. They've got their own lives to live. They've got their own families to raise many times, and now they've got to deal with yet another family situation, Pete. But yet, nevertheless, that is where the compassion—you notice, you didn't say, "I went to a program." You named three individuals that were heroic in your lives. And that's the way it works.

Now, teaching character matters—no question about it—and there's some great curriculum to do it. But the truth of the matter is, all this need to say, "I love you," comes from your soul. And so hopefully, out of these tragedies will come the sense of communal obligation all throughout our country, for people to take an extra effort to comfort the lonely. That could be a student or a teacher—Pete, in your case, a tennis coach. Still got a backhand? Anyway, thank you, buddy. It's good to see you again.

Yes, ma'am. Oh, yes, sir.

Voluntarism

Q. My name is John Kavelin. Up until yesterday, I was a Walt Disney Imagineer for 16 years, but I have quit that activity to commit myself for the rest of my life to a character education program that my sister, her husband, and I created 15 years ago, on a little island in the Pacific Northwest, called The Virtues Project. And it is exactly what I think many people are looking for because it reaches the heart. It is a multifaith, multicultural effort to simply teach five strategies that help people practice virtues in everyday life.

What we've learned in 85 countries where this is applied is that values are culture specific; virtues are universal to every sacred tradition. So simply practicing virtues in the home, in the school, in the workplace makes a shift in the culture.

And I am offering my love and my admiration for so many good-willed people in this room for bringing this group of people together. It's so exciting. And we're simply here to support whatever is going on.

The President. Yes, thanks for doing what you're doing. See, this is a—our country is blessed by the fact that we have people who stand up and say, "I want to contribute," like you. Just retired yesterday? You don't look a day over 60. Anyway— [*laughter*].

But see, Craig, what you're doing and what this gentleman is doing will stimulate a lot of—as you said, you've talked to a million kids, or a million people—same with you, sir. I believe that there is no single answer, no single program. It's a mosaic of programs all stimulated because people have decided to do something about the problem. And it's really the uniqueness of the country.

I like to remind our fellow citizens that de Tocqueville recognized this in 1832, the fact that voluntary organizations came together to help solve local problems. And it is—in my judgment, it is this capacity of citizens to take action to solve problems that defines the true greatness of America.

And, Pete, to answer your question about government: Government's role, in many ways, is to stimulate and to encourage and to thank people who have taken it upon themselves to either start character education or go into classrooms and to change society one person at a time.

Yes, sir.

Parent and Community Involvement in Schools

Q. Mr. President, my name is Marvin Nash. I represent the Bullying Hurts Program and the NASH Foundation, which stands for "No Adolescent Should Hurt," from Cheyenne, Wyoming. I want to let you know that I will be traveling back to Nashville, Tennessee, where Storme Warren, with Great American Country, and Charlie Daniels will be helping me make PSAs to address this issue. Instead of talking about my program though, I want to give my time up to this lady right here. She spent seven—she spent her time with 17 students locked in a closet at Columbine, and she has a question for you. So we're not going to talk about me; we're going to talk about her.

The President. Thank you, buddy. Nice-looking hat.

Q. Mr. President, Madam Secretary of Education, Marleen, Craig, and everybody else, my name is—[*inaudible*]—and I'm just a regular person. I don't have a radio talk show. [*Laughter*] And I don't—I'm not in charge of a big, major organization. I am a flight attendant for Frontier Airlines, and I'm shaking right now because I didn't think I was going to get up here. And I'm also a proud, retired teacher from Columbine High School.

And I think everything I was going to say just kind of flew out of my mind. I'm also a professional volunteer, and I am not here to ask for money for any program. When I said "professional volunteer," I don't mean I make money volunteering, but there are a whole group of just regular people like me out there. Even though I retired from Columbine, I have a daughter at Columbine right now who is a junior. I volunteer in the postgrad center there. I volunteer with the cheer squad, the football team, and it doesn't always take a lot of money to get things done. It's little people like me—I don't mean in size. I mean, it's little people like me who get there, little people like us. Like Grand Daddy Wong used to say, "Okay, one stick—you break it one at a time," but if we stick together, we can get it done.

I'm just saying, unless us volunteers— I always have time to volunteer, and I know other people do too. And it's what Craig was saying, it comes from the heart. President Bush, it's what you were saying. It's what our parents taught us, and it's what we need to teach our kids. It's that—I hope I don't pronounce it wrong—generativity, where we help to make the next generation better. So I'm sorry I forgot what my question was. [*Laughter*]

The President. What matters is your testimony, not your question. Thank you.

Last question, and I've got to go. Gonzales is also reminding me; actually I'm on a schedule here. I apologize. I'd like to sit here all day listening, and I am inspired that so many came to talk about this subject.

Yes, ma'am.

Character Education in State Curricula

Q. Good afternoon, Mr. President, Madam Secretary. My name is—[*inaudible*]—and I'm a youth programs director in New York City for a nonprofit called Art of Living Foundation. And like a lot of these wonderful people here, we teach a program in human values and stress management for teenagers and how to handle their negative emotions—which they just don't learn, I'm finding, nowadays. And what I have students constantly asking me is, "Can't this be a class in our school? Can we learn human values and universal ethics that are found in every culture?" But they're not being taught—a lot of times not at home—they're not being taught. And they're definitely not always being taught in schools. There's some amazing public school teachers, but there's also some very stressed-out public school teachers.

The President. Absolutely.

Q. Can this be—is there a way to have a class in public school where students learn stress management, the ability to deal with their own anger, frustration, and violent tendencies, and also to learn human values and actually practice them? Can they receive credit for a class like this? This is what students are asking, and I have superintendents coming to me saying, "What can you do?"—in our suspension centers—"We'll give credit to students for doing this." Is there a way we can do that?

Secretary Spellings. Well, those are State curriculum issues, and lots of States have included character education or programs like that as part of their required curriculum and give credit for it. But I would commend all those superintendents to their State board of education and put them to work. We had some of that in Texas and gave a lot of credit for peer mentoring and those sorts of things that are so supportive of kids.

The President. I am sorry for those of you standing in line. I know; I apologize.

Q. Time for one more?

The President. Okay, one final guy—go ahead. [*Laughter*]

Voluntarism

Q. I wanted to explain why I had on a bright red jacket.

The President. Yes, that's why. [*Laughter*]

Q. I appreciate it.

The President. Thank you for coming.

Q. My name is Michael Wade Smith, and I'm the national president for Family, Career, and Community Leaders of America. We are an in-school, high school, and middle school organization focusing on the family. Our main mission is to promote family as the basic unit of society.

And I'm happy I got to follow up after your question because we are—family consumer sciences—its curriculum in high schools and middle schools is teaching character education, that is teaching youth violence prevention. We're teaching career exploration. Because of our title, Family and Consumer Sciences and Family, Career, and Community Leaders of America, we address every one of the issues that's been presented in the discussions and in this room. And we are willing and wanting to partner with every single person in here to help students get this message out to students. We're about peer-to-peer message sharing. We want each and every student in our organization, which reaches about a quarter of a million students, to be a lot broader than that. We want to touch every student in America through our programs and through our mission to promote family as the basic unit of society and the values thereof.

So I thank you, Mr. President, Mrs. Bush——

The President. Why the red coat? [*Laughter*] Just so you got called on? I mean, is there a—[*laughter*].

Q. I just wanted that. No, our colors in the organization are red and white.

The President. Fabulous.

Q. So all of the officers wear our red jackets.

The President. I, once again, apologize. I've got to get on an airplane. But I do want to thank you all for coming. I hope you have found this interesting. I am a results-oriented person, and I expect from Margaret and Al to make sure that out of all this effort comes some concrete ac-

tion to help people understand what is possible, what is doable, the programs that are working. And the head of the sheriff's department readily sprung to his feet to say, "You can count on me."

The purpose has got to be more than just hoping somebody is listening to TV. The purpose has got to be—out of this— that we share information so that we can save lives, encourage parents, and help people respond.

And I want to thank you all very much for coming. I'm proud you're here. God bless you all.

NOTE: The President spoke at 1:24 p.m. at the National 4–H Conference Center. In his remarks, he referred to Gov. Jeb Bush of Florida. Participating in the event was Marleen Wong, director, Crisis Counseling and Intervention Services, Los Angeles Unified School District, and director, Trauma Services Adaptation Center for Schools and Communities, Los Angeles, CA.

Remarks at a Reception for Congressional Candidate Michael A. "Mac" Collins in Macon, Georgia
October 10, 2006

Thanks for coming. It's good to be in Macon. Thanks for coming out. One thing about old Mac is, you know where he stands. That's the kind of Congressman you need from this part of the world, and that's the kind of Congressman we need in Washington, DC, straightforward thinker, bringing common sense to the Nation's Capital.

I'm proud to stand here with Mac Collins. I know him well. I've worked with him; I've listened carefully to his ideas. No doubt in my mind he's the best person to represent the Eighth Congressional District from the State of Georgia.

I'm also for him because he married well. Of course, that's why he invited me,

because I married well. [*Laughter*] And I want you to know, Julie and Mac, that Laura sends her very best to you both. I know she was your first choice for this fundraiser. [*Laughter*] She's got to be the most patient woman in America. I know we've got some Texans here, and they went to the same college as Laura did. And when she went there, she, frankly, wasn't interested in politics and, I think, didn't care for politicians. [*Laughter*] Now here she is as the Nation's First Lady, and I firmly believe this country is better off with Laura as the First Lady.

I'm not only proud to be here with Mac Collins—and I want to thank you for supporting him, by the way. I cannot thank you enough for helping this good man. He not only needs to fill the hat in order to run a good campaign, he's going to need your work coming down the stretch. He's going to need you to help make the phone calls and put up the signs and turn out the vote. He's going to need the grassroots activists to step up and say to their fellow citizens, you've got a good man in Mac Collins. He knows what happens in Washington, DC. He's not a novice up there. When he gets back up there, he knows what he needs to do. And he's going to represent the will of the people of this district, see. That's the thing I like about Mac. And so I want to thank you for giving of your money, and thank you for giving of your time when we come down the stretch.

I also want to thank you for supporting one of the Nation's fine Governors, Governor Sonny Perdue. You know what—all Sonny is doing is—in office is what he said he's going to do. He said he's going to do this, he's going to do it, and he does. And I'm proud to be with Sonny, and I want to thank you for helping him.

I'm also proud to be able to work with a really fine United States Senator in Senator Saxby Chambliss, and I see sweet Julianne is with you. Thanks for coming, Julianne. Now, let me say this about Saxby: If you're interested in agriculture, you don't have to worry about your interests being represented in the United States Senate. The man has got some stroke up there in Washington—[*laughter*]—and he knows what he's talking about. And those of us in the White House listen to him. Senator, we're proud you're here.

Georgia has got a fine congressional delegation, and one of the Congressmen is with us today, Lynn Westmoreland. Congressman, thanks for coming. Good to see you. Appreciate your time. We've spent some quality time together, and I know he's a good one, and I know he's looking forward

to getting Mac up there to work with him to do what's right for the country.

I want to thank Alec Poitevint—with us; he's the chairman of—the national committeeman. It seems like I've been saying his name for two decades, or three decades. [*Laughter*] Thanks for coming, Alec. Perry McGuire—Perry McGuire is with us; he's the candidate for the attorney general for the State of Georgia. Perry, thanks for coming. Good luck to you, Perry.

I want to thank all the local officials and State officials who are here. Appreciate you serving.

There are a lot of issues that I'll be talking about. I know Mac will be talking about them. We've got issues such as making sure we become less dependent on foreign oil. It's going to be helpful to have these Georgia farmers growing oil—growing the feedstock for oil—[*laughter*]—like soy diesel or ethanol. It's coming. I look forward to working with Mac to spend some money to help new technologies evolve. We can't be complacent just because the price of gasoline is going down. Being dependent on oil from overseas is still a national security concern. And I intend to push hard for technologies that will enable us to diversify.

I'm going to work with Mac to make sure health care costs are reasonable so people can have affordable insurance. There's a lot of issues we can talk about, but one of the most important issues is taxes. It's a big national issue. I want to spend a little time talking about it today because there's a fundamental difference between the Republican and Democrat Parties on this important issue. And I'm going to discuss this issue and these differences between now and election day. And I'm going to spend some time right here in Macon, Georgia, talking about it.

Mac and I share a philosophy about taxes. We believe that the people who best know how to spend your money are the people who earn the money in the first place. And that's you. So we worked to ensure that working families are able to keep more of their paycheck. And that— those weren't just empty campaign words. Those are actually deliverables; that's what we did. Mac stood squarely for cutting the taxes. My administration and the Congress have enacted the largest tax relief since Ronald Reagan was in the White House. We cut the taxes for every American who pays taxes.

If you paid income taxes, we cut your taxes, see. We doubled the child tax credit; we reduced the marriage penalty; we cut taxes on small businesses; we cut taxes on capital gains and dividends to promote investment and jobs. And to reward family businesses and farmers for a lifetime of hard work and savings, we put the death tax on the road to extinction.

The Republican record on taxes is clear, and the Democrats in Washington have a clear record of their own. The trouble is, they don't want you to know about it. Recently the top Democrat leader in the House made an interesting declaration. She said, "We love tax cuts." Given her record, she must be a secret admirer. [*Laughter*] It's not just the so-called tax cuts for the rich she opposes. When we cut taxes for everybody who pays income taxes, she voted against it. When we reduced the marriage penalty, she voted against it. When we cut taxes on small businesses, she voted against it. When we lowered the taxes for families with children, she voted against it. When we put the death tax on the road to extinction, she voted against it. Time and time again, she had an opportunity to show her love for tax cuts— [*laughter*]—and she voted no. [*Laughter*] If this is a Democrat's idea of love—[*laughter*]—I wouldn't want to see what hate looks like.

Now she and other Democrats are trotting out their old line about how they're only going to raise taxes on the rich. We've heard that before. Sounds like a nice idea until you start doing the math. Let me just give you one example. Earlier this year,

the Democrats put forward a budget alternative that called for $177 billion in additional spending authority over the next 5 years, a number that does not include all the other spending they proposed. The problem is, even if they raise taxes on everyone making over $200,000, they would bring in only $108 billion of new revenues. And that means the Democrats would have to come up with $69 billion for additional spending they proposed. And guess who's going to have to pay?

When the Democrats find themselves short of money to pay for all their spending promises, it's the middle class Americans who get stuck with the bill. Recently, the top Democrat on the House Ways and Means Committee—that's the committee that writes taxes—said he can't think of one of our tax cuts that should be extended. Think of that, not one—not the tax cuts for families with children, not the reduction in the marriage penalty, not the tax cuts on small businesses, not the tax cuts on dividend and capital gains, not the cut in the death tax. Even when asked to explain his remarks, he refused to commit to extending a single tax cut we passed. If he's not going to commit to extending these tax cuts now, think of what he would do if the Democrats gained control over the United States Congress and he became chairman of this important committee.

The difference between our parties could not be clearer, and so is your choice on election day. If you want to keep the tax cuts we passed, vote Republican on November the 7th.

What they don't seem to understand, what the national Democrats don't seem to understand, is that the economy grows when you control more of your own money. The tax cuts we passed put more than a trillion dollars in the hands of American workers and families and small businesses. And you've used that money to help fuel our strong and growing economy. The national unemployment rate is now 4.6 percent. People are working in the United

States of America. Since August of 2003, our economy has added more than 6.6 million new jobs. Our progrowth economic policies work. They're making a difference for the people of America.

And this strong and growing economy has helped us reduce the Federal deficit. When I set a goal of cutting the deficit in half by 2009, Democrats said we couldn't get it done. Last year the ranking Democrat on the House Budget Committee said that my budget brought us nowhere near the goal of cutting the deficit in half. Here's what actually happened: A growing economy has helped produce record tax revenues, and in July, I announced that we were a year ahead of schedule in our plans to cut the deficit in half.

The Democrats' approach to cutting the deficit is taking more of your money to pay for their spending. The Republican approach is to restrain spending and let you keep more of your own money so this economy grows. And there's a fundamental difference, and it's clear as night and day.

Next month, our Nation has got this choice to make: Do we keep taxes low so we can keep this economy growing, or do we let the Democrats in Washington raise taxes and hurt the economic vitality of this country? The decision is yours to make in the voting booth. This decision will have a huge impact on the working people all across the United States of America. Whether you're a worker worried about the size of your paycheck or a business owner who's thinking about hiring more workers or a family worried about gas prices or health care costs, the last thing you need is higher taxes. To keep this economy growing and delivering prosperity to more Americans, we need to make the tax relief we passed permanent. And the best man for the Eighth Congressional District from Georgia to do that is Mac Collins.

Now, there are a lot of issues we got to discuss on the campaign trail, lot of domestic issues. But there is no bigger issue facing the voters than who best to protect the United States of America. You know, when I was campaigning in Georgia in 2000, I didn't believe I'd be saying such a statement. I didn't want to be a war President. I don't remember a lot of discussion about war in the 2000 campaign. But war came to our shores, a war we didn't ask for and a war we must win for the sake of future generations.

People ask me, what's it like to be the President. I said, it's a decisionmaking experience. [*Laughter*] And I make a lot. And a lot of decisions I make are based upon the knowledge I learned from that attack on September the 11th, 2001. I learned we face an enemy that is ruthless, that will kill the innocent in order to achieve objectives. I learned we face an enemy that has got an ideology, an ideology that is hard for a lot of Americans to understand, an ideology that does not believe in the same freedoms we believe.

Let's talk about religion for a second. One of the great, great beliefs of America and the fundamental cornerstone of our liberty is the fact that in America, you can worship any way you so choose. If you're a Jew, Christian, Muslim, Hindu, atheist, agnostic, you're equally American, equally American. That's a sacred right for all of our citizens. It's a right that we must never abandon in America. And it stands in stark contrast to what the enemies of freedom believe. They say if you don't worship the way they tell you to worship, you'll be held to account. They say that if you don't view religion the way they view religion, you'll be punished.

We're in the ideological struggle of the 21st century. It's a struggle between rational, reasonable people who believe in basic freedoms versus extremists and radicals who murder the innocent in order to achieve their objectives. Right after 9/11, I made it clear that if one were to harvest—harbor one of these extremists or radicals, they will be judged as equally as guilty as those who commit murder.

And that's why we went into Afghanistan. I said, "You've been harboring Al Qaida"—remember, they were providing safe haven for Al Qaida to train. I gave them time to turn over Al Qaida to us; they chose otherwise. And as a result of defending ourselves, which is the most important job of government, we liberated 25 million people from the clutches of that ideology.

This Nation cannot wait for threats to fully materialize. If we're to do our most important job, which is to protect the American people, we must make sure we deal with threats before they hurt us. That's one of the fundamental changes of September the 11th. And it's important to have people in Congress who understand that. It's important to have a person like Mac Collins who knows that we must deal with the threat overseas so we do not have to face that threat here at home. I saw a threat, the Congress saw a threat, the United Nations saw a threat in Saddam Hussein, and the world is better off without him in power.

And now the challenge is to do the hard work of helping the Iraqis defend their freedom, the hard work of helping this young democracy survive the onslaught of murder from those who would prevent democracy from taking root. It's in our interests that we do so because, you see, we must defeat the enemy overseas so we don't have to face them here at home. And if we were to retreat before the job is done, they would follow us straight to America.

And I understand it's hard on the American people, because the enemy is able to take innocent lives, and it gets on our TV screens. And it's hard. I know it's hard, because Americans are compassionate people. We care about innocent life. We care about the human condition. But it's necessary work. We'll continue to make sure our commanders have that which they need to do the job. We will be flexible in our tactics in order to help this young democracy survive. We will deploy the assets necessary to bring people to justice overseas

so we don't have to face them here at home.

And I need people by my side in the United States Congress like Mac Collins, who will make sure our brave men and women who wear the uniform have all that's necessary to defend the United States of America. We will stay; we will fight; and we will win, for the security of the United States.

But we must do more than just stay on the offense against these killers. We pressure them every day. It's harder to plot and plan when you're on the run or you're hiding in a cave. But I recognized after 9/11, we must also deploy all assets to protect you. I think about my job of protecting you every day. It's the most fundamental of all requirements of government. And so after 9/11, I called upon Congress, and sometimes—and a week later called upon Congress to give our folks on the frontline of fighting terror the tools necessary to protect you.

There were walls set up between intelligence and criminal investigators that made it impossible for folks to share intelligence with those who are hired to protect you. It's hard for me to explain why that was the case—just take my word for it. [*Laughter*] It was there. You had somebody get some intelligence; they couldn't share it with the person charged with criminal justice matters. And it made us vulnerable to attack.

And so I asked Congress to pass the PATRIOT Act. Congressman Mac Collins didn't hesitate. He said it's the right thing to do, to give those on the frontline of fighting terror the tools necessary to protect you. As a matter of fact, right after 9/11, it wasn't hard to get the bill passed. Five years later, however—or 4 years later, I came back and said, "We need to renew the bill," and on the floor of the United States Senate, Democrats filibustered the bill. See, that's Democrat-talk—I mean, Washington-talk for killing it, trying to kill it. They must think differently about this war on terror. It's a fundamental issue in this campaign, the difference about how to defend America.

The Senate minority leader openly bragged about—"We killed the bill," he said, killed the PATRIOT Act. To me, it speaks volumes in this campaign about which party clearly sees the enemy as it is and which party is willing to do the hard work necessary to protect the American people. I do not question the patriotism of anybody. I just know there's a different mindset, when they fought the PATRIOT Act's renewal.

As you know, I put in place a plan that said if Al Qaida is calling into the United States, we want to know why. We want to know why. In this war on terror, we're capturing people. And sometimes, for example, we might find something in somebody's pocket, and, say, it had a phone number of—an American phone number, and that phone number gets called from overseas—not with a call within the United States but from outside in. We need to know. If the most important job is to protect the American people, we need to know why that person, that Al Qaida and/or Al Qaida affiliate, is making a phone call.

So the United States Congress had a vote on this recently; out of the House of Representatives, 166 Democrats voted against the bill, voted against giving our people the tools necessary to protect you. These are fine people; I know a lot of them. They're decent citizens of our country. They just have a different view about the world in which we live. Perhaps one way to summarize it is, okay, we'll get tough; we'll respond after we're attacked. My attitude is, we better give our folks the tools necessary to protect you before we get attacked, to protect the American people.

As you, I'm sure, read, we have been capturing people on the battlefield—I call it a battlefield because this is a war—and we have interrogated those people in order to find out whether or not they know about attacks on the United States. In my discussion to the American people about this issue, I talked about some of the examples. For example, we have captured and interrogated a fellow named Khalid Sheikh Mohammed, who our intelligence people believe was the mastermind of the September the 11th attacks.

This country is under threat. The enemy still wants to hurt us. And therefore, it seemed like it made sense to me that when we found the mastermind, or the presumed mastermind of the September the 11th attacks, that our professionals should find out what this fellow knows. If the most important job is to protect the American people, we must give our professionals the tools necessary to protect you.

This bill came up for a vote recently in the House and the Senate. The overwhelming majority of Democrats voted against giving our professionals the tools necessary to protect you. There's a fundamental difference in this campaign, and it's a clear difference. And the American people need to understand there's a difference in this campaign. Our most important job is to protect you from attack, and the Republican Party will make sure our professionals have the tools necessary to defend you.

And the people of this congressional district don't need to worry about where Mac Collins stands. I look forward to working with this good man to help protect you from the threats we face.

We're in an ideological struggle. It's the challenge of our time. It's the call of our generation. We've got a great military. We've got wonderful professionals working hard to protect you. We've got one other fantastic way to defend America, a great asset, and that's freedom. I believe in the universality of freedom. I believe there's an Almighty. I believe one of the great gifts of the Almighty is the desire for people to be free. And I believe that the United States of America, it's in our interest that we promote liberty. Oh, not every democracy is going to look like ours. Each democracy ought to represent their own history and traditions. But it's in our interest that liberty flourish because that's how you ultimately win the ideological struggle that pits reasonable people against extremists. That's how you win a struggle with those who want their children to grow up in a reasonable society, a hopeful society, against those who will create chaos so that they can't do so.

You know, I recently—you might remember, I just had an interesting experience recently when the Prime Minister of Japan and I went down to Elvis's place. [*Laughter*] Laura and I had never been there, and so—[*laughter*]—I thought that would be fun. [*Laughter*] Prime Minister Koizumi really wanted to go there—[*laughter*]—because he is a—he's an Elvis fan. He loves Elvis. But I also wanted to tell a story. I'm going to tell it right quick and then head back up and have dinner with Laura. Here it is: I find it is a really interesting kind of twist of history, I guess you could put it, that I'm going to Elvis's place with the Prime Minister of Japan, and my dad fought the Japanese. Eighteen-year-old George H.W. Bush—I'm sure you've got relatives, the same thing happened to them—responded to the violent attack on the United States and said, "I want to volunteer," like thousands of other kids.

And we fought the Japanese with all we had. And it was a bloody war—really bloody war. And yet 60 years later, I'm on Air Force One flying to Memphis—[*laughter*]—talking about the peace, working with Prime Minister Koizumi on issues like North Korea. And I will tell you, we're more likely to solve this issue peacefully when we've got people like Japan and China and South Korea and Russia saying the exact same thing as the United States is to the man in North Korea.

It helps to be able to sit down and talk ally to ally about the peace. We talked about the fact that the Japanese had 1,000 troops in Iraq helping this young democracy fight off the extremists that can't stand the thought of a free society in their midst. We talked about the strategic implications of abandoning those who long for liberty in the Middle East. He knows what I know, that there could be a world in which moderate governments get toppled, which is precisely what the enemy said they want to do, so that these extremists control energy resources in which they'd be able to blackmail the free world.

And combine that with a nuclear weapon in the hands of an Iran, and Koizumi and I understand that the world would look back and say, "What happened to them? How come they couldn't see the threat?" We're all flying on Air Force One with the former Prime Minister of Japan—he recently left office—talking about the peace. And I found that to be amazing. Something happened between when George H.W. Bush became a Navy pilot, and his son is talking about the peace. And what happened was, Japan adopted a Japanese-style democracy. Liberty has got the capacity to change an enemy into an ally. Liberty has got the capacity to bring hope where hope is needed and light where there's darkness.

I believe if this generation does its duty to protect future generations of Americans, someday an American President will be sitting down talking with the duly elected leaders of the Middle East and talking about the peace, and a generation of Americans will be better off.

Those are the stakes of the elections of 2006, the stakes of the world in which we live. And I'll be proud to work with Mac Collins to bring the peace we all want. God bless.

NOTE: The President spoke at 5:35 p.m. at the Macon Centreplex. In his remarks, he referred to former President Saddam Hussein of Iraq; former Prime Minister Junichiro Koizumi of Japan; and Chairman Kim Jong Il of North Korea.

The President's News Conference
October 11, 2006

The President. Thank you. Before I take your questions, I'd like to discuss a couple subjects. First, I want to briefly mention that today we've released the actual budget numbers for the fiscal year that ended on September the 30th. These numbers show that we have now achieved our goal of cutting the Federal budget deficit in half, and we've done it 3 years ahead of schedule. The budget numbers are proof that progrowth economic policies work. By restraining spending in Washington and allowing Americans to keep more of what they earn, the economy is creating jobs and reducing the deficit and making our Nation a more prosperous nation for all our citizens.

I'm going to talk about the progrowth economic policies that helped bring about the dramatic reduction in the deficit, this afternoon, and I'm going to remind our fellow citizens that good tax policy has a lot to do with keeping the economy strong, and therefore, we'll continue to urge the Congress to make the tax cuts permanent.

I also want to talk about the unfolding situation in North Korea. Earlier this week, the Government of North Korea proclaimed to the world that it had conducted a successful nuclear test. The United States is working to confirm North Korea's claim, but this claim itself constitutes a threat to international peace and stability.

In response to North Korea's actions, we're working with our partners in the region and the United Nations Security Council to ensure there are serious repercussions for the regime in Pyongyang. I've spoken with other world leaders, including Japan, China, South Korea, and Russia. We all agree that there must be a strong Security Council resolution that will require North Korea to abide by its international commitments to dismantle its nuclear programs. This resolution should also specify a series of measures to prevent North Korea from exporting nuclear or missile technologies and prevent financial transactions or asset transfers that would help North Korea develop its nuclear and missile capabilities.

Last year, North Korea agreed to a path to a better future for its people in the six-party talks, September of last year. We had an agreement with North Korea. It came about in the form of what we call the six-party joint statement. It offered the prospect for normalized relations with both Japan and the United States. It talked about economic cooperation in energy, trade, and investment. In that joint statement, North Korea committed to abandoning all nuclear weapons and existing nuclear programs and to adhering to the Treaty on Nonproliferation of Nuclear Weapons and to IAEA safeguards. They agreed.

The United States affirmed that we have no nuclear weapons on the Korean Peninsula. We affirmed that we have no intention of attacking North Korea. With its actions this week, North Korea has once again chosen to reject the prospect for a better future offered by the six-party joint statement. Instead, it has opted to raise tensions in the region.

I'm pleased that the nations in the region are making clear to North Korea what is at stake. I thank China, South Korea, Japan, and Russia for their strong statements of condemnation of North Korea's actions. Peace on the Korean Peninsula requires that these nations send a clear message to Pyongyang that its actions will not be tolerated, and I appreciate their leadership.

The United States remains committed to diplomacy. The United States also reserves all options to defend our friends and our interests in the region against the threats from North Korea. So, in response to North Korea's provocation, we'll increase defense cooperation with our allies, including cooperation on ballistic missile defense to protect against North Korean aggression and cooperation to prevent North Korea from exporting nuclear and missile technologies.

Our goals remain clear: peace and security in Northeast Asia and a nuclear-free Korean Peninsula. We will take the necessary actions to achieve these goals. We will work with the United Nations. We'll support our allies in the region. And together we will ensure that North Korea understands the consequences if it continues down its current path.

I'd like to discuss the latest developments in Iraq. This morning I just had a meeting with Secretary Rumsfeld and General George Casey, who is in town today. General Casey, as you know, is the top commander on the ground in Iraq. The brutality of Iraq's enemies has been on full display in recent days. Earlier this week, Deputy President Tariq al-Hashimi lost his brother, Major General Hashimi, when gunmen dressed in police uniforms broke into his house and shot him in the head. Only a few months ago, his sister and other brother were assassinated. On behalf of the United States, I express my heartfelt condolences to the al-Hashimi family. And we express our condolences to all those who've suffered at the hands of these brutal killers.

The situation is difficult in Iraq, no question about it. The violence is being caused by a combination of terrorists, elements of former regime criminals, and sectarian militias. Attacks and casualties have risen during the Ramadan period. A rise in violence has occurred every Ramadan period in the last 3 years.

Attacks and casualties have also increased recently because our forces are confronting the enemy in Baghdad and in other parts of Iraq. The past weekend, U.S. and Iraqi forces engaged militias—or members of an illegal militia—during a mission to capture a high-value target. The reason I bring this up is that we're on the move. We're taking action. We're helping this young democracy succeed. The reasons we went after the illegal militia was to capture a man responsible for killing many innocent Iraqis, and we accomplished that mission. Our troops have increased their presence on the streets of Baghdad, and together with Iraqi forces, they're working to ensure that terrorists and death squads cannot intimidate the local population and operate murder rings.

Amid the violence, important political developments are also taking place. The Iraqi legislature reached a compromise and set up a process for addressing the difficult issues of federalism and constitutional reform. In addition, the Government of Prime Minister Maliki has taken three important steps to build confidence in his Government and in the Iraqi security forces. First, Prime Minister Maliki announced a plan to bring together Sunni and Shi'a parties and stop sectarian violence. The Prime Minister's plan has received support from every major political group in Iraq, including some hard-line Sunni elements that chose not to join the unity Government. Among the steps the Prime Minister announced is a new system of local and neighborhood committees, made up of both Sunni and Shi'a members, that will work directly with Iraqi security forces to resolve tensions and stop sectarian strife.

Second, this past weekend Prime Minister Maliki met with tribal leaders from the Anbar Province. These tribal leaders told him they've had enough of the terrorists seeking to control the Sunni heartland, and they're ready to stand up and fight Al Qaida. The Prime Minister told them that he welcomed their support and would help them.

Third, Prime Minister Maliki's Government suspended the Eighth Brigade, Second Division of the National Police after learning that this unit was not intervening to stop sectarian violence in and around Baghdad. This police brigade has been decertified by the Iraqi Ministry of Interior;

it's been removed from service; it's now being reviewed and retrained. With this action, the Iraqi Government has made clear, it's not going to tolerate the infiltration of the Iraqi security forces by militias and sectarian interests.

The reason I bring this up, these examples up, is that there's a political process that's going forward. And it's the combination of security and a political process that will enable the United States to achieve our objective, which is an Iraq that can govern itself, sustain itself, defend itself, and be an ally in this war on terror.

Iraq's Government—Iraq's democratic Government is just 4 months old. Yet in the face of terrorist threats and sectarian violence, Iraq's new leaders are beginning to make tough choices. And as they make these tough decisions, we'll stand with them, we'll help them. It's in our interests that Iraq succeed.

Look, I fully understand the American people are seeing unspeakable violence on their TV screens. These are tough times in Iraq. The enemy is doing everything within its power to destroy the Government and to drive us out of the Middle East, starting with driving us out of Iraq before the mission is done. The stakes are high. As a matter of fact, they couldn't be higher. If we were to abandon that country before the Iraqis can defend their young democracy, the terrorists would take control of Iraq and establish a new safe haven from which to launch new attacks on America. How do I know that would happen? Because that's what the enemy has told us would happen; that's what they have said. And as Commander in Chief of the United States military and as a person working to secure this country, I take the words of the enemy very seriously, and so should the American people.

We can't tolerate a new terrorist state in the heart of the Middle East, with large oil reserves that could be used to fund its radical ambitions or used to inflict economic damage on the West. By helping the Iraqis build a democracy—an Iraqi-style democracy—we will deal a major blow to terrorists and extremists, we'll bring hope to a troubled region, and we'll make this country more secure.

With that, I'll take some questions, starting with Terry Hunt [Associated Press].

Diplomatic Efforts With North Korea

Q. Thank you, Mr. President. Democrats say that North Korea's reported test shows that your policy has been a failure, that you got bogged down in Iraq, where there were no weapons of mass destruction, while North Korea was moving ahead with a bomb. Is your administration to blame for letting North Korea get this far?

The President. North Korea has been trying to acquire bombs and weapons for a long period of time, long before I came into office. And it's a threat that we've got to take seriously, and we do, of course.

In 1994, the Government—our Government—entered into a bilateral arrangement with the North Koreans that worked to make sure that they don't have the capacity to develop a bomb, and North Korea agreed that there would be no program whatsoever toward the development of a weapon. And yet we came into office and discovered that they were developing a program, unbeknownst to the folks with whom they signed the agreement, the United States Government. And we confronted them with that evidence, and they admitted it was true and then left the agreement that they had signed with the U.S. Government.

And my point—and then I—as I mentioned in my opening statement, we, once again, had North Korea at the table—this time with other parties at the table—and they agreed once again, through this statement as a result of the six-party talks, to verifiably show that they weren't advancing a nuclear weapons program. And they chose again to leave. And my point to you is that it's the intransigence of the North Korean leader that speaks volumes about the process. It is his unwillingness to choose a way forward for his country, a better way forward for his country. It is his decisions. And what's changed since then is that we now have other parties at the table who have made it clear to North Korea that they share the same goals of the United States, which is a nuclear weapons-free peninsula.

Obviously, I'm listening very carefully to this debate. I can remember the time when it was said that the Bush administration goes it alone too often in the world, which I always thought was a bogus claim to begin with. And now all of a sudden, people are saying, the Bush administration ought to be going alone with North Korea. But it didn't work in the past, is my point. The strategy did not work. I learned a lesson from that and decided that the best way to convince Kim Jong Il to change his mind on a nuclear weapons program is to have others send the same message.

And so in my phone calls that I recently made right after the test, I lamented the fact that he had tested to Hu Jintao and also lamented the fact that Hu Jintao had publicly asked him not to test. I talked to the South Korean President, and I said, "It ought to be clear to us now that we must continue to work together to make it abundantly clear to the leader in North Korea that there's a better way forward." When he walks away from agreement, he's not just walking away from a table with the United States as the only participant, he's walking away from a table that others are sitting at.

And my point to you is, in order to solve this diplomatically, the United States and our partners must have a strong diplomatic hand, and you have a better diplomatic hand with others sending the message than you do when you're alone. And so obviously, I made the decision that the bilateral negotiations wouldn't work, and the reason I made that decision is because they didn't. And we'll continue to work to come up with a diplomatic solution in North Korea.

This is a serious issue. But I want to remind our fellow citizens that the North Korean issue was serious for years. And I also remind our citizens that we want to make sure that we solve this problem diplomatically. We've got to give every effort to do so. But in my discussions with our partners, I reassured them that the security agreements we have with them will be enforced if need be, and that's in particular to South Korea and Japan.

Terry. I mean—you're not Terry; you're Steve [Steve Holland, Reuters].

Iraq Study Group/Democracy Efforts in the Middle East

Q. Thank you very much, sir.

The President. It's a huge insult, I know.

Q. Senator Warner says Iraq appears to be drifting sideways, and James Baker says a change in strategy may be needed. Are you willing to acknowledge that a change may be needed?

The President. Steve, we're constantly changing tactics to achieve a strategic goal. Our strategic goal is a country which can defend itself, sustain itself, and govern itself. The strategic goal is to help this young democracy succeed in a world in which extremists are trying to intimidate rational people in order to topple moderate governments and to extend a caliphate.

The stakes couldn't be any higher, as I said earlier, in the world in which we live. There are extreme elements that use religion to achieve objectives. And they want us to leave, and they want us to—and they want to topple government. They want to extend an ideological caliphate that is—has no concept of liberty inherent in their beliefs. They want to control oil resources, and they want to plot and plan and attack us again. That's their objectives. And so—and our strategic objective is to prevent them from doing that. And we're constantly changing tactics to achieve that objective.

And I appreciate Senator Warner going over there and taking a look. I want you to notice, what he did say is, if the plan is now not working—the plan that's in place isn't working, America needs to adjust. I completely agree. That's what I talk to General Casey about. I said, General, the Baghdad security plan is in its early implementation. I support you strongly, but if you come into this office and say we need to do something differently, I support you. If you need more troops, I support you. If you're going to devise a new strategy, we're with you, because I trust General Casey to make the judgments necessary to put the tactics in place to help us achieve an objective.

And I appreciate Jimmy Baker—willingness to—he and Lee Hamilton are putting this—have got a group they put together that I think was Congressman Wolf's suggestion—or passing the law. We supported the idea. I think it's good to have some of our elder statesmen—I hate to call Baker an elder statesmen—but to go over there and take a look and to come back and make recommendations. Somebody said he said, "Well, you know, cut-and-run isn't working." That's not our policy. Our policy is to help this country succeed, because I understand the stakes. And I'm going to repeat them one more time. As a matter of fact, I'm going to spend a lot of time repeating the stakes about what life is like in the Middle East.

It is conceivable that there will be a world in which radical forms, extreme forms of religion fight each other for influence in the Middle East, in which they've got the capacity to use oil as an economic weapon. And when you throw in the mix a nuclear weapon in the hands of a sworn enemy of the United States, you begin to see an environment that would cause some later on in history to look back and say, "How come they couldn't see the problem? What happened to them in the year 2006? Why weren't they able to see the problems now and deal with them before it came too late?", Steve.

And so Iraq is an important part of dealing with this problem. And my vow to the American people is, I understand the stakes, and I understand what it would mean for us to leave before the job is done. And I look forward to listening how—what Jimmy Baker and Lee Hamilton say about how to get the job done. I appreciate them working on this issue because I think they understand what I know, and the stakes are high.

And the stakes are high when it comes to developing a Palestinian state so that Israel can live at peace. And the stakes are high when it comes to making sure the young democracy of Lebanon is able to fend off the extremists and radicals that want to crater that democracy.

This is the real challenge of the 21st century. I like to tell people we're in an ideological struggle. And it's a struggle between extremists and radicals and people of moderation who want to simply live a peaceful life. And the calling of this country and in this century is whether or not we will help the forces of moderation prevail. That's the fundamental question facing the United States of America—beyond my Presidency. And you can tell I made my choice. And I made my choice because the most solemn duty of the American President and government is to protect this country from harm.

Martha [Martha Raddatz, ABC News]. Yes. I'm sure it was a profound followup. Okay.

Situation in North Korea/Six-Party Talks

Q. Can we go back to North Korea, Mr. President?

The President. Please.

Q. You talk about failures of the past administration with the policy towards North Korea. Again, how can you say your policy is more successful, given that North Korea has apparently tested a nuclear weapon? And also, if you wouldn't mind, what is the redline for North Korea, given what has happened over the past few months?

Photographic Portfolio

Overleaf: Speaking to military personnel at an Independence Day celebration at Fort Bragg, NC, July 4.

Left: Calling Prime Minister Nuri al-Maliki of Iraq from the Oval Office, September 29.

Right: Speaking with Staff Sgt. Ronell Bradley, USA, and his wife, Cynthia, during a visit to Walter Reed Army Medical Center, July 24.

Below: Having lunch with Prime Minister Nuri al-Maliki and military personnel at Fort Belvoir, VA, July 26.

Below right: Greeting military personnel following an Independence Day celebration at Fort Bragg, NC, July 4.

The President. My point was, bilateral negotiations didn't work. I appreciate the efforts of previous administrations. It just didn't work. And therefore, I thought it was important to change how we approached the problem so that we could solve it diplomatically. And I firmly believe that with North Korea and with Iran that it is best to deal with these regimes with more than one voice, because I understand how it works. What ends up happening is, is that we say to a country such as North Korea, "Here's a reasonable way forward." They try to extract more at the negotiating table, or they've got a different objective, and then they go and say, "Wait a minute; the United States is being unreasonable." They make a threat. They could—they say the world is about to fall apart because of the United States problem. And all of a sudden, we become the issue.

But the United States message to North Korea and Iran and the people in both countries is that we have—we want to solve issues peacefully. We said there's a better way forward for you. Here's a chance, for example, to help your country economically. And all you got to do is verifiably show that you—in Iran's case, that you suspended your weapons program, and in North Korea's case, that you've got international safeguards on your program—which they agreed to, by the way.

And so my point is, is that—to the American people I say, "Look, we want to solve this diplomatically." It's important for the President to say to the American people, diplomacy was what—is our first choice and that I've now outlined a strategy. And I think it is a hopeful sign that China is now a integral partner in helping North Korea understand that it's just not the United States speaking to them.

And it's an important sign to North Korea that South Korea, a country which obviously is deeply concerned about North Korean activities—South Korea is a partner, and that if North Korea decides that they don't like what's being said, they're not just stiffing the United States—I don't know if that's a diplomatic word or not—but they're sending a message to countries in the neighborhood that they really don't care what other countries think, which leads to further isolation. And when we get a U.N. Security Council resolution, it will help us deal with issues like proliferation and his ability—"he" being Kim Jong Il's ability—to attract money to continue to develop his programs.

Q. What about the redline, sir?

The President. Well, the world has made it clear that these tests caused us to come together and work in the United Nations to send a clear message to the North Korean regime. We're bound up together with a common strategy to solve this issue peacefully through diplomatic means.

Kevin [Kevin Corke, NBC News].

International Cooperation on the Situation in North Korea

Q. Thank you, Mr. President.

The President. If I might say, that is a beautiful suit.

Q. Thank you, sir. My tailor appreciates that.

The President. And I can't see anybody else who even comes close. [*Laughter*]

Q. Thank you very much. I'll be happy to pass along my tailor's number if you'd like that, sir.

The President. I'll take that back. I will recognize that on this—please.

Q. On May 23, 2003, sir, you said—you effectively drew a line in the sand. You said, "We will not tolerate a nuclear North Korea." And yet now it appears that they have crossed that line. And I'm wondering what now, sir, do you say to both the American people and the international community vis-a-vis what has happened over the last 48 hours?

The President. No, I appreciate that, and I think it's very important for the American people and North Korea to understand that that statement still stands, and that one way to make sure that we're able to achieve

our objective is to have other people join us in making it clear to North Korea that they share that objective. And that's what's changed. That's what's changed over a relatively quick period of time. It used to be that the United States would say that, and that would be kind of a stand-alone statement. Now when that statement is said, there are other nations in the neighborhood saying it.

And so we'll give diplomacy a chance to work. It is very important for us to solve these problems diplomatically. And I thank the leaders of—listen, when I call them on the phone, we're strategizing. This isn't, "Oh, please stand up and say something." This is, "How can we continue to work together to solve this problem?" And that is a substantial change, Kevin, from the previous times.

Suzanne [Suzanne Malveaux, Cable News Network]. First best dressed person here. Sorry.

Report on Iraqi Civilian Casualties

Q. Kevin and I coordinated.

The President. Yes. No, he actually looks——

Q. Thank you, Mr. President. Back on Iraq, a group of American and Iraqi health officials today released a report saying that 655,000 Iraqis have died since the Iraq war. That figure is 20 times the figure that you cited in December, at 30,000. Do you care to amend or update your figure, and do you consider this a credible report?

The President. No, I don't consider it a credible report; neither does General Casey and neither do Iraqi officials. I do know that a lot of innocent people have died, and that troubles me, and it grieves me. And I applaud the Iraqis for their courage in the face of violence. I am amazed that this is a society which so wants to be free that they're willing to—that there's a level of violence that they tolerate. And it's now time for the Iraqi Government to work hard to bring security in neighborhoods so people can feel at peace.

No question, it's violent, but this report is one—they put it out before; it was pretty well—the methodology was pretty well discredited. But I talk to people like General Casey, and, of course, the Iraqi Government put out a statement talking about the report.

Q. ——the figure of 30,000, Mr. President? Do you stand by your figure, 30,000?

The President. You know, I stand by the figure. A lot of innocent people have lost their life—600,000, or whatever they guessed at, is just—it's not credible. Thank you.

Baier [Bret Baier, FOX News].

2006 Midterm Elections

Q. Thank you, Mr. President. Since you last held a news conference here in the Rose Garden, about a month ago, Republicans across the country have seen races that were once safe, tighten, with the tide turning, according to several polls, towards the Democrats. Understanding that you don't lead by looking at polls——

The President. Thank you, sir. Thank you. Finally.

Q. ——as you've said many times, are you still confident Republicans will hold the House and the Senate?

The President. Yes, I am.

Q. If so, why? And do you believe that the biggest drag on the Republican Party is the situation in Iraq?

The President. I believe that the situation in Iraq is, no question, tough on the American psyche, like I said, I think, at this very spot last time I faced the press corps. And it's serious business. Look, the American people want to know, can we win—that's what they want to know—and do we have a plan to win. There are some who say, "Get out. It's not worth it." And those are some of the voices, by the way, in the Democrat Party. Certainly not all Democrats, but some of the loud voices in the party say, "Get out."

And so no question this is an issue, but so is the economy. And I believe there'll

be—I still stand by my prediction, we'll have a Republican Speaker and a Republican leader of the Senate. And the reason I say that is because I believe the two biggest issues in this campaign are, one, the economy. And the economy is growing. The national unemployment rate is 4.6 percent. We've just discovered, as the result of analyzing new data, that we added 6.6 million new jobs since August of 2003. Gas prices are down. Tax cuts are working.

And there's a difference of opinion in the campaign about taxes, and we will keep them low. Matter of fact, I would like to keep the—make the tax cuts we pass permanent. And the Democrats will raise taxes. Now, I know they say only on rich people, but that's—in my judgment, having been around here long enough to know, it's just code word. They're going to raise them on whoever they can raise them on.

And then on security, the American people know that our biggest job is to protect this country from further attack, and—because they know there's an enemy that still plots and plans. And there is; there is. Recently we learned that, when British intelligence and U.S. intelligence—with our help—broke up a plot to get on airplanes and blow them up, the planes that were going to fly from Great Britain to here. And they want to know—"they," the people—want to know what are we doing to protect them.

There have been some votes on the floor of the Senate and the House that make it abundantly clear, we just have a different view of the world. The vast majority of Democrats voted against a program that would enable us to interrogate high-value detainees. That was the vote. It's wide open for everybody to see: Should a CIA program go forward or not go forward? The vast majority of Democrats in the House voted against a program that would have institutionalized the capacity for this Government to listen to Al Qaida phone calls or Al Qaida affiliate phone calls coming from outside the country to inside the country.

It's very important for our fellow citizens to recognize that I don't question anybody's patriotism, but I do question a strategy that says, we can't give those on the frontline of fighting terror the tools necessary to fight terror. I believe that in order to defend America, we must take a threat seriously and defeat an enemy overseas so we don't have to face them here. I don't believe we can wait to respond after attack has occurred.

And so I think these are the two biggest issues, Bret. And Iraq is a part of the war on terror. Now, I recognize Democrats say that's not the case, and what I say to the American people when I am out there is, all you've got to do is listen to what Usama bin Laden says. Don't believe me that it's a part of the war on terror; listen to the enemy, or listen to Mr. Zawahiri, the number two of Al Qaida, both of whom made it clear that Iraq is central in their plans. And I firmly believe that American people understand that this is different from other war because in this war, if we were to leave early before the job is done, the enemy will follow us here.

And so I believe, Bret, that we'll maintain control because we're on the right side of the economic issue and the security issue.

Let's see. Yes, sir, Mr. NPR [Don Gonyea, National Public Radio]. Welcome to the front row. Yes, it's good.

Democratic Party/2006 Midterm Elections

Q. Thank you. It's good to be here. Appreciate it. Following up on that answer, one of the things Democrats complain about is the way you portray their position——

The President. Oh, really?

Q. ——in wanting to fight the war on terror. They would say you portray it as either they support exactly what you want to do, or they want to do nothing. We hear it in some of your speeches. Is it fair

to portray it to the American people that way?

The President. Well, I think it's fair to use the words of the people in Congress or their votes. The vote was on the Hamdan legislation: Do you want to continue a program that enabled us to interrogate folks or not? And all I was doing was reciting the votes. I would cite my opponent in the 2004 campaign when he said there needs to be a date certain from which to withdraw from Iraq. I characterize that as cut-and-run because I believe it is cut-and-run. In other words, I've been using either their votes or their words to characterize their positions.

Q. But they don't say "cut-and-run."

The President. Well, they may not use "cut-and-run," but they say "date certain is when to get out," before the job is done. That is cut-and-run. Nobody has accused me of having a real sophisticated vocabulary; I understand that. And maybe their words are more sophisticated than mine. But when you pull out before the job is done, that's cut-and-run as far as I'm concerned, and that's cut-and-run as far as most Americans are concerned. And so, yes, I'm going to continue reminding them of their words and their votes.

Jim [Jim Axelrod, CBS News].

Iraq Study Group/U.S. Armed Forces in Iraq

Q. Thank you, Mr. President. My best suit is in the cleaners.

The President. That's not even a suit.

Q. I know. [*Laughter*] You got to give me more time in the morning with a news conference.

The President. I know. You like to wake up about 8:30. [*Laughter*]

Q. I want to ask you——

The President. High-priced news guys.

Q. Yes, sure.

The President. Yes. [*Laughter*]

Q. I want to ask you a little bit about— I want to follow on the criticism that you've received for the suggestions from Senator

Warner and from James Baker, now Olympia Snowe. This is not exactly the board of directors for moveon.org. Do you——

The President. That's true.

Q. Do you feel in some way that there is some shift going on in terms of the general support for the war in Iraq and your strategy specifically? And do you ever feel like the walls are closing in on you in terms of support for this?

The President. [*Laughter*] Jim, I understand how hard it is, and I also understand the stakes. And let me go back to Senator Warner. Senator Warner said, "If the plan isn't working, adjust." I agree completely. I haven't seen Baker's report yet, but one of the things I remind you of is that I don't hear those people saying, get out before the job is done. They're saying, be flexible. And we are.

I believe that you empower your generals to make the decisions, the recommendations on what we do to win. You can't fight a war from Washington. In other words, you can't make the tactical decisions necessary to win. It just won't work. And I trust General Casey. I find him to be one of the really competent, decent guys.

Q. But——

The President. Let me finish, please, for a second. Plus, I couldn't hear you, but I saw you talking. Anyway, I think it's— I value his judgment. I value his—I know he wants to succeed, and I value his objectivity. And he—what's important for the President is when I open up that door in there and General Casey walks in, he feels confident to tell me what's on his mind, Jim—"Here's what's going right, and here's what's going wrong, and here's what we're doing about it."

And so for those folks saying, make sure there's flexibility, I couldn't agree more with you. And I think the characterization of, "Let's stay the course," is about a quarter right. "Stay the course" means, keep doing what you're doing. My attitude is, don't do what you're doing if it's not working; change. "Stay the course" also means,

don't leave before the job is done. And that's—we're going to get the job done in Iraq. And it's important that we do get the job done in Iraq.

Defeat in Iraq will embolden an enemy. And I want to repeat to you the reality of the world in which we live. If we were to leave before the job is done, the enemy is coming after us. And most Americans—back to your question, Bret—understand we've got to defeat them there so we don't face them here. It's a different kind of war, but nevertheless, it is a war.

Go ahead.

Insurgency and Terrorist Attacks in Iraq

Q. I'm just wondering—2 months ago, Prime Minister Maliki was here, and you talked about how we had to be nimble and facile in our approach. And my question is, are we being nimble and facile in the right way? Is what General Casey telling you the most effective advice? Because it would seem in the 2 months since Prime Minister Maliki was here, things have only gotten more bloody in Iraq.

The President. No question Ramadan is here; no question we're engaging the enemy more than we were before. And by the way, when you engage the enemy, it causes there to be more action and more kinetic action. And the fundamental question is, do I get good advice from Casey? And the answer is, I believe I do; I believe I do.

Please. Sanger [David Sanger, New York Times].

Diplomatic Efforts With North Korea

Q. Thank you, Mr. President. You spoke very passionately before about acting before it was too late on major issues. You faced one of those moments in early 2003. This was when the North Koreans had thrown out the international inspectors, said they were going to go ahead and turn their fuel into weapons. And you had a moment to tell them that they would face serious consequences if they were going to do that.

You also had what may have been the last moment for any American President to destroy their fuel supplies while they were all in one place.

The President. You mean, bombing them?

Q. Whatever action you might have needed to take, including military action, against the site—the one site at the time where they were getting ready——

The President. I just wanted to clarify. Sorry to interrupt you.

Q. Yes. And you chose not to. And I was wondering whether in retrospect you regret that decision at all, whether or not you think that, because of the long history of deception that you pointed out before, you should have acted differently?

The President. I used the moment to continue my desire to convince others to become equity partners in the Korean issue—North Korean issue, because, David, I obviously look at all options all the time, and I felt like the best way to solve this problem would be through a diplomacy effort that was renewed and reinvigorated by having China and South Korea and Japan and Russia joining us in convincing Kim Jong Il there's a better way forward.

And frankly, I was quite optimistic that we had succeeded last September when we had this joint statement, which you adequately covered. And yet he walked away from it. He decided, well, maybe his word doesn't mean anything.

And so we will continue to work diplomatically to solve the problem. That's what I owe the American people, to come up with a diplomatic solution. I also made it clear, and I will repeat, that we have security obligations in the region that I reconfirmed to our partners.

Sir. Washington Post man [Michael Fletcher, Washington Post].

Situations in Iran and North Korea

Q. Good morning, Mr. President.
The President. That would be Mike.

Q. Right. I'd like to follow up on an earlier question about your rhetoric on Iran and North Korea.

The President. Okay.

Q. You said yesterday in your statement that the North Korean nuclear test was unacceptable. Your chief negotiator for the six-party talks said last week that North Korea has a choice of either having weapons or having a future. When you spoke a month or so ago to the American Legion, you talked about Iran and said, "There must be consequences for Iran's defiance, and we must not allow Iran to develop a nuclear weapon." I am wondering, sir— your administration has issued these kinds of warnings pretty regularly over the last 5 years, and yet these countries have pursued their nuclear programs. I'm wondering if you—what is different about the current set of warnings, and do you think the administration and our Government runs a risk of looking feckless to the world by issuing these kinds of warnings regularly without response from the countries?

The President. That's a fair question. First of all, I am making it clear our policy hasn't changed. It's important for the folks to understand that we don't continually shift our goals based upon polls or whatever. See, I think clarity of purpose is very important to rally a diplomatic effort to solve the problem. And so I try to speak as clearly as I can and make sure there's no ambiguity in our position. I also found that's a pretty good way to help rally a diplomatic effort that I believe will more likely work.

I know this sounds—I'm just saying it over and over again, but it's—rhetoric and actions are all aimed at convincing others that they have an equal stake in whether or not these nations have a nuclear weapon, because I firmly believe, Mike, that that is the best strategy to solve the problem. One has a stronger hand when there's more people playing your same cards. It is much easier for a nation to hear what I believe are legitimate demands if there's more than

one voice speaking. And that's why we're doing what we're doing.

And to answer your question as to whether or not the words will be empty, I would suggest that, quite the contrary, that we not only have spoken about the goals, but as a result of working together with our friends, Iran and North Korea are looking at a different diplomatic scenario.

I thought you were going to ask the question, following up on Sanger, how come you don't use military action now? You kind of hinted it; you didn't say it. And some wonder that. As a matter of fact, I'm asked questions around the country— just go ahead and use the military. And my answer is, is that I believe the Commander in Chief must try all diplomatic measures before we commit our military. And I believe the diplomacy is—we're making progress when we've got others at the table.

I'll ask myself a followup. If that's the case, why did you use military action in Iraq? And the reason why is because we tried the diplomacy. Matter of fact, we tried resolution after resolution after resolution. All these situations are—each of them different and require a different response, a different effort to try to solve this peacefully. And we'll continue to do so.

The inability to convince people to move forward speaks volumes about them. It ought to say to all the world that we're dealing with people that maybe don't want peace—which, in my judgment, in order for there to be peace, requires an international response. It says volumes about a person who signs an agreement with one administration and signs an agreement or speaks about an agreement with another administration and doesn't honor the agreement. It points up the fact that these are dangerous regimes and requires an international effort to work in concert.

Roger [Roger Runningen, Bloomberg News].

Six-Party Talks With North Korea

Q. Thank you. I'd like to turn back to North Korea for a bit. You've said that bilateral talks didn't work. Secretary Baker has said that maybe they should be considered, maybe at some point under certain conditions. Are you prepared now to just take the possibility of one-one-one talks with North Korea off the table?

The President. I'm saying as loud as I can and as clear as I can that there is a better way forward for North Korea, and that we will work within the context of the six-party talks.

People say, "You don't talk to North Korea." We had a representative, a United States representative at the table in the six-party talks. The North Korean leader knows our position. It's easy to understand our position: There is a better way forward for his Government. And people need to review the September '05 document, the joint statement that talked about economics, and we won't attack North Korea. We agreed that we shouldn't have nuclear weapons on the peninsula. I mean, there is a way forward for the leader in North Korea to choose. We've made our choice, and so has China, South Korea, Japan, and Russia. And that's what's changed.

I also am deeply concerned about the lives of the citizens in that country. I mean there's—and that's why I named a envoy, Jay Lefkowitz, to talk about the human condition inside of North Korea. And the reason we did that is we care about how people live. We care about people starving. We care about the fact that there are large concentration camps.

You know, one of the most meaningful moments of my Presidency came when a Japanese mother came to the Oval Office to talk about what it was like to have her daughter kidnaped by North Korea. You can imagine what that was like. It broke my heart, and it should break everybody's heart. But it speaks to the nature of the regime. And therefore, we—I am con-

vinced that to solve this diplomatically requires more than just America's voice.

Let's see here. Mark [Mark Silva, Chicago Tribune].

Former Representative Mark Foley/2006 Midterm Elections

Q. Thank you, Mr. President.

The President. Yes.

Q. Mr. President, with growing numbers of House Members and staffers saying that they knew of and told others about a problem with Mark Foley some years ago, has House Speaker Hastert lost touch within his own ranks, and has the scandal damaged Hastert's credibility and effectiveness in maintaining party control in the midterm elections?

The President. No, I think the Speaker's strong statements have made it clear to not only the party members but to the country that he wants to find out the facts. All of us want to find out the facts. I mean, this is disgusting behavior when a Member of Congress betrays the trust of the Congress and a family that sent a young page up to serve in the Congress. And I appreciated Speaker Hastert's strong declaration of his desire to get to the bottom of it. And we want to make sure we understand what Republicans knew and what Democrats knew, in order to find the facts. And I hope that happens sooner rather than later.

Q. And his credibility, sir——

The President. Oh, Denny is very credible, as far as I'm concerned. And he's done a fine job as Speaker, and when he stands up and says, "I want to know the truth"— I believe yesterday he said that if somebody on his staff didn't tell him the truth, they're gone; I respect that and appreciate that and believe him. And—no, I think the elections will be decided by security and the economy. I really do, Mark. I know this is—this Foley issue bothered a lot of people, including me. But I think when they get in that booth, they're going to be thinking about how best to secure the country

from attack and how best to keep the economy growing.

I think the last time I was out here with you, I reminded you that I understand that the economy is always a salient issue in campaigns. We've had some experience with that in my family, I think I said. I still believe the economy is an important issue, and I believe on this issue there is a huge difference of opinion.

The other day, by the way, Don, I did bring up the words of the leader of the House when she said, "I love tax cuts." And then I reminded everybody that if she loved them so much, how come she voted against a lot of tax cuts? In other words, again, back to your question about whether it's fair to use people's words—I think to say, I love tax cuts, and then vote against tax cuts it's just—it's worthy—it's just worthy of people's consideration in the political process—I believe taxes are a big issue in the campaign, Mark.

And I know how—I know that—how best to protect the country is a big issue, a really big issue. And there's a kind of law enforcement mentality that says, "Well, we'll respond after attack." It's not going to work. It's just not going to work. We've got to deal with these problems before they come to—before they come to our territory.

I understand that some are saying, "Well, he's just trying to scare us." My job is to look at the intelligence and to—and I'm going to tell you, there's an enemy out there that would like to do harm again to the United States, because we're in a war. And they have objectives. They want to drive us out of parts of the world to establish a caliphate. It's what they have told us, and it's essential that we listen to the words of the enemy if we want to protect the American people.

And in this debate about which party can handle it better, I will—it's very important that no one question the patriotism or the loyalty to the country. There is a different mindset, however, that is worth

discussing in the course of a campaign. And I'm going to continue to do it. And I believe those two issues will be the issues that drive the election.

April [April Ryan, American Urban Radio Networks].

Diplomatic Efforts With North Korea/ Nuclear Weapons Development

Q. Thank you, sir. Mr. President, some in the national security community are wondering if, indeed, you're ready to live with a nuclear North Korea?

The President. No.

Q. Well, they're saying that that is a possibility.

The President. Well, they're wrong.

Q. Well, can I give you——

The President. Well, it was a short question and a short answer. [*Laughter*]

Q. One, China is not ready to put teeth behind sanctions—enough teeth to really threaten the regime. And also, economic sanctions have limited effect on North Korea.

The President. We got to try it diplomatically first, April. And this is back to old Michael's question about, am I serious about saying what I mean? It's why I say what I say, because some people are beginning to wonder whether or not it's the goal. The goal is no nuclear weapon. And again, I think I've shared with you my views of diplomacy. Diplomacy is—it's a difficult process because everybody's interests aren't exactly the same. We share the same goal, but sometimes the internal issues are different from ours. And therefore, it takes a while to get people on the same page, and it takes a while for people to get used to consequences.

And so I wouldn't necessarily characterize these countries' positions as locked-in positions. We're constantly dialoging with them to make sure that there is a common effort to send a clear message.

And the other part of your question was?

Q. And the followup, yes. Military options, there are a menu of options the

White House is saying. Once diplomacy has run its course and you've run through your timetable, what about military options against North Korea?

The President. Well, diplomacy hasn't run its course. That's what I'm trying to explain to you a la the Sanger question. And we'll continue working to make sure that we give diplomacy a full opportunity to succeed.

Yes, David [David Gregory, NBC News].

Retrospective Analysis of Iraq

Q. Thank you, Mr. President. You spoke of the troubles in Iraq. And as you know, we have Woodward [Bob Woodward, Washington Post] and we have a shelf full of books about Iraq, and many of them claim that administration policies contributed to the difficulties there. So I'm wondering, is there anything you wish you would have done differently with regard to Iraq?

The President. Speaking about books, somebody ought to add up the number of pages that have been written about my administration. There's a lot of books out there. A lot. I don't know if I've set the record or not, but I guess it means that I've made some hard decisions and will continue to make hard decisions.

And, David, this is the—this is about the fifth time I've been asked this type of question. And as you know, there are some things that I wish had happened differently: Abu Ghraib. I believe that really hurt us. It hurt us internationally. It kind of eased us off the moral high ground. In other words, we weren't a country that was capable of, on the one hand, promoting democracy, and then treating people decently. Now the world has seen that we've held those to account who are—who did this.

You know, there's just a lot of look-backs. Presidents don't get to look back, but I will tell you, the decision to remove Saddam was the right decision. And I would look forward to the debate where

people debate whether or not Saddam should still be in power.

As you know, a leader in the Senate Intel Committee on, I think it was CBS News, Axelrod, I'm not sure—you follow your news closely; you can verify this—said that the world would be better if Saddam were in power. I strongly disagree. So when it comes to that decision, which is a decision to cause a lot of people to write books, it's the right decision.

And now the fundamental question is, will this country help this young democracy succeed? And the answer is, we will. We'll change tactics when we need to change tactics to help this young democracy succeed. But the stakes are high if we were to leave. It means that we would hand over a part of the region to extremists and radicals who would glorify a victory over the United States and use it to become—use it to recruit. It would give these people a chance to plot and plan and attack. It would give them resources from which to continue their efforts to spread their caliphate. The stakes are really high.

Joe [Joseph Curl, Washington Times].

Immigration Reform

Q. Thank you. On a different topic, you've said you will sign the border fence bill to build 700 miles of fence along the U.S. border, but DHS has said it prefers a virtual fence of sensors and cameras rather than an actual wall. Are you committed to building the 700 miles of fence, actual fencing?

The President. Yes, we're going to do both, Joe. We're just going to make sure that we build it in a spot where it works. I don't—DHS said they want a virtual wall. I don't believe that's the only thing they've said. I think you might have truncated their statement, because we're actually building fence, and we're building double fence, in particular, in areas where there is a high vulnerability for people being able to sneak in.

You can't fence the entire border, but what you can do is you can use a combination of fencing and technology to make it easier for the Border Patrol to enforce our border. I happen to believe, however, that in order to make sure the border is fully secure, we need a guest-worker program, so people aren't sneaking in in the first place.

And so I look forward to not only implementing that which Congress has funded, in a way that says to folks, the American people, "We'll enforce our border," but I'm going to continue to campaign and work for a comprehensive bill so that whatever we do in terms of equipment and manpower works better. If somebody is not trying to sneak in to work, in other words, coming through in a way where they're showing a temporary-worker pass, where they're not using *coyotes* to smuggle across, where they're not going through tunnels, it's going to make it much easier for us to do our job, Joe, and that's enforce the border.

And so my judgment is, if the people want this country secure, we've got to do—have a smart border, which we're in the process of developing now. It's a combination of fencing and technologies—UAVs, sensors. I don't know if you've ever been down there, but it's a pretty vast part of country down there. It's hard to enforce that border. You've got some rugged country; you've got stretches of territory where you don't even know where the border is. You've got urban areas like El Paso or southern California where people have been able to sneak in by use of urban corridors. And so therefore, fencing makes sense there.

I went down to Arizona, the Arizona sector, and saw a place where there's literally neighborhoods abutting the border, and people come—100 of them would rush across the border into a little subdivision, and the Border Patrol would catch 2 or 3, and 97 would get in. And they're asking, what are you going to provide to help us do our job? And in this case, those who are in charge of coming up with the proper strategy to enforce the border said, "We need double fencing with space," so that the Border Patrol can use that fencing as leverage against people rushing into the country.

And my only point to you is, is that the strategy to develop this border requires different assets based on the conditions—based upon what the terrain looks like. And that's what we're doing.

But I repeat to you: When you've got a situation where people are sneaking in to do jobs Americans aren't doing, it's also going to keep a strain on the border. And so therefore, a temporary-worker plan, to me, makes sense, and it's a much more humane program—approach, by the way. It will certainly help stamp out all these illegal characters that are exploiting human beings. You know, these *coyotes* that stuff people in the back of 18-wheelers for money is just—that's not in character with how this Nation works. And I think we ought to—I think a good program that helps us enforce our border also will see to it that people are treated more humanely.

Thank you for your interest.

NOTE: The President's news conference began at 11:01 a.m. in the Rose Garden at the White House. In his remarks, he referred to Gen. George W. Casey, Jr., USA, commanding general, Multi-National Force—Iraq; Chairman Kim Jong Il of North Korea; President Hu Jintao of China; President Roh Moo-hyun of South Korea; James A. Baker III and Lee H. Hamilton, cochairs, Iraq Study Group; Usama bin Laden, leader of the Al Qaida terrorist organization; and Sakie Yokota, mother of Megumi Yokota, who was kidnaped by North Korean authorities.

Remarks on the National Economy and the Federal Budget
October 11, 2006

Thank you all. Please be seated. Good afternoon. Thanks for coming to the White House.

In 2004, I made a promise to the American people: We would cut the Federal budget deficit in half over 5 years. Today I'm pleased to report that we have achieved this goal, and we've done it 3 years ahead of schedule.

This morning my administration released the budget numbers for fiscal 2006. These budget numbers are not just estimates; these are the actual results for the fiscal year that ended February the 30th [September 30th]. ° These numbers show that the budget deficit has been reduced to $248 billion and is down to just 1.9 percent of the economy. As a percentage of the economy, the deficit is now lower than it has been for 18 out of the last 25 years. These budget numbers are proof that progrowth economic policies work. By restraining spending in Washington and allowing Americans to keep more of what they earn, we're creating jobs, reducing the deficit, and making this Nation prosperous for all our citizens.

Today I'm going to talk about the progrowth economic policies that helped bring a dramatic reduction in the Federal deficit. I'm going to remind the American people that we cannot afford to be complacent. I'll discuss some of the issues that I intend to address over the next 2 years to help ensure that our dynamic economy continues to grow and provide jobs.

Before I do so, I do want to recognize members of my Cabinet who have joined us. I want to thank the Secretary of the Treasury, Hank Paulson, for being here today. Mr. Secretary, thank you for your service. And the Director of the Office of Management and Budget, affectionately

---
° White House correction.

known as OMB, Rob Portman—thanks for coming, Rob. I thank Steve Preston, who is the Administrator of the U.S. Small Business Administration. Thanks for being here, Steve.

I see members of my staff who are here, who probably should be working—[*laughter*]—instead of taking time off. But I thank you for coming.

The reduction of the deficit I've announced today is no accident. It is the result of the hard work of the American people and because of sound fiscal policies here in Washington. When I first came to office, I thought taxes were too high—and they were—and this economy of ours was headed into a recession. Some people said the answer was to centralize power in Washington and to let politicians decide what to do with the people's money. I had a different approach. I have a different view. And therefore, we chose a different course of action.

See, I believe that our economy prospers when we trust the people to make the decisions on how to save, spend, or invest. And so starting in 2001, we worked with Members of the United States Congress to pass the largest tax relief ever passed since Ronald Reagan was the President. We cut taxes on everybody who pays income taxes. I was concerned about this kind of selective tax cutting. I didn't think that was fair. Our attitude was if you pay income taxes, you ought to get relief.

We reduced the marriage penalty. We doubled the child tax credit, and we put the death tax on the road to extinction. We cut the tax rate paid by most small businesses. Most small businesses are a subchapter S corporation, for example, or a limited partnership, and therefore, pay tax at the individual income tax rate. And therefore, when you cut the rates on people

who pay income taxes, you're cutting tax on small businesses.

And by the way, it was really the cornerstone, in many ways, of our economic recovery policy, because we understand that 70 percent of new jobs in America are created by small businesses, and therefore, when small businesses have more capital to spend, it is more likely they'll create jobs.

We increased the amount small businesses can expense, on the knowledge that providing incentive for people to buy plant and equipment will cause somebody to have to make the plant and equipment that the person purchases. We encouraged economic expansion by cutting taxes on dividends and capital gains, understanding that by cutting those types of taxes, we're reducing the cost of capital, which makes it easier for people to borrow so we can expand our economy. In other words, we had a comprehensive plan that, when enacted, has left nearly $1.1 trillion in the hands of American workers, families, investors, and small-business owners. And they have used this money to help fuel economic expansion that's now in its 37th straight month of growth.

The theory was, was that if we can encourage entrepreneurship and investment and consumption by reducing taxes, it will cause the economy to recover from a recession and a terrorist attack, corporate scandals, war, hurricanes. And it has. The progrowth policies have worked. Since August of 2003, this economy of ours has added more than 6.6 million new jobs. And the national unemployment rate is down to 4.6 percent. People are working, and that's good for our country.

Behind these numbers are millions of individual workers who start each day with hope because they have a job that will enable them to do their duties to support their families, or to put food on the table. Behind these numbers are small-business owners that are being rewarded for taking risk. Government can't make anybody suc-

cessful; we can make the environment such that people are willing to take risk. And when small businesses take risk, the economy flourishes and grows.

You know, last week, I went to a FedEx facility here in DC. The Secretary and I went, and we met with a group of entrepreneurs who are helping to drive this economic growth. It was a fascinating meeting. It was really exciting, wasn't it, Hank? I mean, it was so wonderful to sit with dreamers and doers. We met a guy—I think he said he was an engineering graduate from Purdue—who on his way from upstate New York to Purdue to go to college, he and his brother would stop and dive for golf balls—[*laughter*]—and then they'd sell the golf balls to help pay for college. He has since—he and his brother have since started an Internet company that sells golf clubs. And he's successful, and he's employing people, and he's excited, and he appreciates the tax cuts. [*Laughter*]

We talked to the Under Armour man. I don't know if you ever heard of that product. I know I'm not supposed to advertise—[*laughter*]—so I won't. [*Laughter*] But here's a dreamer. The man had an idea. He didn't like the way the cotton shirts that he wore absorbed his bodily fluids when he exercised, so he came up with a better product. And it worked. And now he's built a huge business, and he's talking about how to continue to expand, and he's worried about our trade policy. Here's a small-business guy who came out of a garage, and he's talking to the Secretary of the Treasury and the President of the United States about making sure we have intellectual property rights protection in China.

My point to you is, is that America must remain entrepreneurial heaven if we want to be the leading economy in the world, and we will do so through good policy. And that's by keeping taxes low. As a matter of fact, the best policy would be for Congress to have certainty in the Tax Code

by making the tax cuts we passed permanent.

Back to the budget. When we announced—when I announced the plan to cut the deficit in half by 2009, a lot of folks said, it's just simply not going to be done. They said that we had to choose between cutting the deficit and keeping taxes low. Or another way to put it, that in order to solve the deficit, we had to raise taxes. I strongly disagree with those choices. Those are false choices. Tax relief fuels economic growth, and growth—when the economy grows, more tax revenues come to Washington. And that's what's happened. It makes sense, doesn't it? As businesses expand, people pay more taxes, and when you pay more taxes, there's more revenues that come to our Treasury.

Tax revenues grew by $253 billion in 2006. That's an increase of 11.8 percent. Over the last 2 years, we've seen the largest back-to-back increases in tax revenues ever, and the largest percentage increase in 25 years. In other words, when you put policies in place that cause the economy to grow, tax revenues increase.

I know that sounds counterintuitive for some here in Washington. People say, "Well, they're cutting taxes; that means less revenue." But that's not what happened over the past 2 years. As a matter of fact, I'm convinced that if we had raised taxes, it would cause there to be an economic decline, which would make it harder to balance the budget over the years.

In February this year, we projected the Federal budget deficit for 2006 would be $423 billion. That was the best guess. Today's report, as I mentioned to you, shows that the deficit came out at 248 billion, so $175 billion less than anticipated. The difference is because we have a growing economy, and the difference is because we've been wise about spending your money.

Congress votes every year on day-to-day spending, and it's called discretionary spending. There's two types of spending in

Washington: discretionary spending, over which Congress has got discretion—and we're involved; we submit a budget; and we've got the capacity to veto to help bring some discipline to the process—or mandatory spending. Mandatory spending helped—just happens. It's formula driven. It's—the Congress doesn't allocate money for it; it just comes to be, based upon the circumstances involved.

Every year since I took office, we have reduced the growth of discretionary spending that is not related to the military and the homeland. And the reason that's the case is, I believe it's important for the President to lead and to set budget priorities, and so long as we've got kids in combat, they're going to have what it takes to do their job. And so long as there's an enemy that wants to strike us, we'll spend money to protect the homeland. Those are the most important jobs we have.

The last two budgets have actually cut nondefense, nonhomeland discretionary spending. And I want to applaud the Congress for making hard choices. Every program sounds fantastic in Washington, until you actually determine whether or not they're working. And a lot of times, the nice-sounding programs are not delivering the results that the people expect. And so we worked with Congress to focus on those programs that work and do away with those that don't work. It's not easy, by the way, to get rid of somebody's pet project that's not working. But you've just got to know that Rob and his office are working hard to do just that.

I believe Congress can make the President's job more effective in dealing with bad spending habits if they gave me the line-item veto, and let me tell you why. The President is presented with a dilemma. On the one hand, we sit down and we negotiate the budget with the Congress. We say, "Here's the top line we can live with," and they'll pass appropriations that meet our top line. But the problem is, within the appropriations are oftentimes

programs that may not have been properly debated, in other words, stuck in—earmarked. They may not be meeting national priorities. And therefore, the President is confronted with either vetoing a good budget bill because he doesn't like parts of the bill, or accepting the overall bill and the bad parts exist in it.

And so one way to remedy that is to give the President the capacity to analyze the appropriations process, to remove—approve spending that is necessary, redline spending that is not, and send back the wasteful and unnecessary spending to Congress for an up-or-down vote. That's how we define line-item veto.

It makes sure that the President is directly involved with the process in deciding the size of the slices of the pie, once the size of the pie has been delivered. But it also makes sure that Congress is involved with the process of approving, up or down, whether or not the spending is needed or not needed.

Governors have got this power; 43 Governors have got the authority, and they use it effectively. One of the advantages is this: That they know—if the chief executive has got the line-item veto, then legislators will understand that a program they may try to sneak into a bill will see the light of day, and therefore, make it less likely somebody will try to sneak something into the bill. It's kind of preventative maintenance.

The House has passed the bill. The Senate really needs to get the line-item veto to my desk. If Senators from both political parties are truly interested in helping maintain fiscal discipline in Washington, DC, and they want to see budgetary reform, one way to do so is to work in concert with the executive branch and pass the line-item veto.

And for those of you who are here, who are helping us get that legislation out of the Senate, I want to thank you for your work. The reason I brought it up is, I am absolutely convinced it is necessary to make sure that we continue to maintain budget discipline here in Washington, DC.

We've made good progress, as I mentioned to you, in getting the fiscal house in order, but there's another problem with our budget, and that has to do with mandatory spending, particularly with Social Security, Medicare and Medicaid. These are really important programs. They're called entitlement programs because when each of us retire, we're entitled to a benefit, in Social Security for example.

And yet the health of these programs, the health is in serious jeopardy. Why? Because there's a lot of people like me and Paulson who are fixing to retire. [*Laughter*] As a matter of fact, both of us reach retirement age at the same time, which is in 2008. That's quite convenient in my case. [*Laughter*]

But unlike the previous generation, there's a lot more of us, and we've been promised greater benefits than the previous generation. In other words, the Government has made promises with a future generation's money that we can't keep. And so the fundamental question facing the Government in Washington, DC, is, will we have the will necessary to deal with these entitlement programs to leave behind a better budget picture, to deal with the unfunded liabilities and the mandatory programs for future generations?

One reason Secretary Paulson came to work in this administration is because he wanted to understand whether or not we were committed to continue trying to bring Social Security reform, to modernize the system. Look, you don't have to cut benefits. You've just got to slow the rate at which benefits are growing in order to make sure a future generation is not strapped with a budgetary system that is unaffordable.

And I assured Hank that I was deeply committed to working to solve Social Security, because I believe the call for those of us who are blessed to be in public service is to confront problems now. It's so

much easier to quit and just say, "Let's let another Congress deal with it." The problem is, is that the longer we wait, the more costly it becomes for future Congresses. And so now is the time. Now is the time. And Hank and I are going to—after these elections come and go, we're going to work with the leaders and—to say, "We're all responsible for getting something done." My hope is, in the last 2 years of this administration, we can set aside needless politics and focus on what's right for the United States of America and solve these entitlement programs once and for all.

I hope you're optimistic about this country's future because I sure am. I am optimistic because I have great faith in American ingenuity, and I know how hard our people work. I am optimistic because we're an innovative society, and there's a lot of really capable, smart people continuing to make sure we remain innovative. I'm optimistic because the public sector and private sector encourages important research and development to make sure America is on the leading edge of change. I'm optimistic that we have put good policy in place that will encourage the entrepreneurial spirit. And I firmly believe, so long as this is an entrepreneurial-oriented country, America will remain the economic leader we want her to be.

I want to thank you all for coming to hear this proclamation of good news. [*Laughter*] God bless.

NOTE: The President spoke at 2:10 p.m. in Room 450 of the Dwight D. Eisenhower Executive Office Building. In his remarks, he referred to H.R. 4890, the "Legislative Line Item Veto Act of 2006."

Remarks at the National Renewable Energy Conference in St. Louis, Missouri
October 12, 2006

The President. Thanks for the warm welcome. I appreciate the chance to come and speak to the Renewable Energy Conference. I hope you're excited about being here because I sure am. This is—it's exciting to be with—[*applause*]. I view this as kind of a meeting of pioneers, people who are on the leading edge of change, and people whose research, thought, and production will all help this country become stronger and better. And so I appreciate you giving me a chance to come by and visit with you.

This is a—energy is a subject dear to my heart—as it should be for any President—because you can't grow your economy without energy. And yet it is apparent, and should be for most Americans, we've got to change our habits if we want to remain the economic leader of the world.

Before I share some of my thoughts with you, I do want to recognize members of my Cabinet who have joined you: the Secretary of Agriculture, Mike Johanns; the Secretary of Energy, Sam Bodman; and the Administrator of the EPA, Steve Johnson.

I think it is interesting that when we got an energy conference going on here, that we have the Secretary of Energy—which makes sense—[*laughter*]—but the Secretary of Agriculture as well. And the man who runs the EPA, whose job it is to make sure our environment is clean, is with us. And the reason I find that interesting is because we've got an interesting confluence of national security concerns and environmental concerns that come together, probably unlike any other time in our history. And I want to share some thoughts with you about that in a minute.

I do want to thank the United States Senators from the State of Missouri—both men believe strongly in the future of renewable energy—and that would be Kit Bond and Jim Talent. Thank you for coming. I appreciate Congressman Todd Akin being here, and his wife, Lulli.

You know, I—gasoline prices are down, and that's good news. [*Applause*] Yes. I mean, everybody in America ought to be applauding. [*Laughter*] It's like—if you're driving a truck for a living, it helps you. If you're trying to put food on the table and you got to drive to work, it helps you. If you're a small-business owner, it means you've got more capital to invest when the price of gasoline goes down.

My worry is, however, that a low price of gasoline will make it complacent—make us complacent about our future when it comes to energy, because I fully understand that energy is going to help determine whether or not this Nation remains the economic leader in the world. We're doing fine now. We've got a really strong economy, and in order to make sure it's strong tomorrow, we need to make sure we work on how we use energy.

Energy is—look, let me just put it bluntly: We're too dependent on oil. And, see, low gasoline prices may mask that concern. So, first, I want to tell you that I welcome the low gasoline prices; however it's not going to dim my enthusiasm for making sure we diversify away from oil.

We need to diversify away from oil for economic reasons. We live in a global world. When the demand for oil goes up in China or in India, it causes the price of crude oil to rise, and since we import about 60 percent of the crude oil we use, it causes our price to go up as well, which means the economy becomes less competitive.

And then, of course, there's the national security concern for oil. Why? Well, we get oil from some countries who don't particularly care for us. They don't like what we stand for. They don't like it when we

say, "For the sake of peace, let us work in a way that we don't develop nuclear weapons," for example.

I spend a lot of time on national security issues, which you expect your President to do. And a lot of times those national security issues are involved with countries that have oil. They have something we want, and so there's a national security issue when it comes to the status quo.

And then, of course, we have a great debate about the environment in America, and that's good. It's an important debate. We all want to be good stewards of our environment. We want to be good conservationists. And reliance upon oil and hydrocarbons has created some challenges when it comes to the environment.

And so this is one of the reasons why I believe so strongly that this country has got to use its talent and its wealth to get us off oil. And I believe we will do so, and I believe—I know the best way to do so is through technological breakthroughs.

And the Government has got a role to play. First, I understand there are some entrepreneurs here, some people that are investors, venture capitalists, and I welcome you here. I think it's a good sign for those of us who understand the need to diversify away from oil that private money is beginning to make investments into some of the technologies I'm going to be describing.

And we can help you in Washington, and one way we can help you is to reward people for investing in research and development. There's a research and development tax credit that's on the books. The problem is, it expires every year, on a year-by-year basis, which means you've got to come back to Congress on a year-to-year basis; which also means there's unpredictability in the Tax Code, and that's not wise, if you're trying to encourage people to invest dollars in the long term. And so in order to encourage private initiative and private investment in new energies, we ought to make the research and development tax credit a permanent part of the Tax Code.

And we need to continue what we're doing at the Federal level, which is spend your money on research. I think it's a legitimate use of taxpayers' money, to spend on grants, to find new ways to power our economy, new ways to conserve, new ways to protect the environment through new technologies.

Since I've been President, we've spent about $10 billion on research. A lot of it goes through Sam's shop. He's the Energy man. [*Laughter*] We will vigorously pursue new ways to power our automobiles. If you want to get off oil, the surest and quickest way to do so is to change how we power our automobiles. We consume a lot of oil through gasoline. And the more inefficient our cars are, the more we drive old clunkers, the more gasoline we use, which means we're more dependent on oil.

And so we've got some interesting initiatives at the Federal level to help change habits. One of them is—and it's probably the fastest way we can begin to change the consumer habits—is to promote hybrid vehicles. You all know what hybrids are; it's a combination of gas and—gasoline and electric battery that gets the driver a lot more miles per gallon.

And so one way to do this, one way to encourage people to buy hybrids, one way to stimulate demand so that the production will follow is to provide tax credits. You can get up to, now, $3,400 tax credit when you buy your hybrid automobile. In other words, the Government is using the Tax Code to stimulate demand, which then should stimulate more automobile—more production on the auto lines of hybrids. And the more hybrids we get on the road, the less oil we're going to be using.

Secondly, we're spending money on new battery technologies. See, we envision a day in which light and powerful batteries will become available in the marketplace so that you can drive the first 40 miles on electricity, on batteries, and your car won't have to look like a golf cart. [*Laughter*] In other words, it will be a technology that will meet consumer demand and, at the same time, meet a national need, which is less consumption of gasoline. These are called plug-in hybrid vehicles.

And the battery technology is coming. In order to expedite it, Sam's shop, the Department of Energy, is putting out grants. In other words, we're using your money to expedite the arrival of a new technology that will enable folks to drive the first 40 miles on electricity.

That's not going to help rural Missouri or rural Texas, but it's certainly going to help those who live in the cities. Most folks in the cities don't drive more than 40 miles, so you can envision consumer habits beginning to change: You drive to work; you go home; you plug in your automobile. And you go—ride to work and go home the next day, and you're still on electricity. It's going to change the consumption patterns. This new technology will change the consumption patterns on gasoline, which in turn will make us less dependent on crude oil, which meets a national security concern, an economic security concern, and helps us deal with an environmental concern.

Now, there's another technology that will enable us to help change our driving habits, and that's ethanol. See, I like the idea of promoting a fuel that relies upon our farmers. I happen to believe a good farm economy is important to a good national economy, and I also know it makes sense to have our—[*applause*]. Sounds like we might have some farmers here. [*Laughter*]

But I also know it makes sense to have our farmers growing the feedstock for new energy. The way I like to tell our citizens is, Johanns is going to come in someday and say, "Mr. President, corn is up, which means we're less dependent on oil." And that's good news for the country and good news for our economy.

People are using ethanol. For those of you who are in the ethanol business, you're on the leading edge of change. It's coming, and Government can help. That's why we

enhanced and extended the 10-cent-per-gallon tax credit. We did that to stimulate production. We've extended a 51-cent-per-gallon tax credit for ethanol blenders. We provided a 30-percent tax credit for the installation of alternative fuel stations, up to $30,000 a year.

In other words, I believe and Congress agrees that the proper use of tax credits will help stimulate a new industry that will help our economy and help us when it comes to national security. You know, we're up to, now, 5 billion gallons of ethanol sold this year. That's up from 1.6 billion gallons in 2000. Ethanol—there are now 100 ethanol refineries which are operating. There—it's anticipated there are going to be 40 more next year. In other words, we're just at the beginning stages of a new industry that is evolving. It's one of the reasons I'm excited to be here. For those of you on the cutting edge, I want to thank you and just let you know we want you to succeed. It's in our interests that you do succeed.

Today, there are 900 stations selling E–85. For those of you who don't know what that means, that's 85 percent ethanol. Look, a lot of Americans wonder whether or not this is feasible, what I'm talking about. A lot of folks aren't exposed to ethanol yet. In the Midwest you are; you've got a lot of corn. And it makes a lot of sense to have these plants where the feedstocks are. But ethanol is coming, and it doesn't require much money to convert a regular gasoline-driven car to a flex-fuel automobile. See, the technology is available. It takes about a hundred and something dollars to change a gasoline-only automobile to one that can use E–85. And it works.

And in my judgment, the thing that's preventing ethanol from becoming more widespread across the country is the lack of other types of feedstocks that are required to make ethanol—sugar works; corn works. And it seems like it makes sense to spend money, your money, on researching cellulosic ethanol, so that we could use wood chips or switchgrass or other natural materials.

And we've got an aggressive effort to research new raw materials to be used in ethanol. When I was down in Alabama—I'm going to tell you an interesting story when I was down there the other day. But I talked to a fellow from Auburn; he's a Ph.D.—just reminded me the difference between a Ph.D. and a C student. The C student is the President, and the Ph.D. is the adviser. [*Laughter*]

But he's telling me how optimistic he is that someday we're going to be able to take wood chips from those southern pine forests and convert that raw material into ethanol. He said it's right around the corner as far as he's concerned. It makes a lot of sense for the Federal Government to continue to invest taxpayers' money, because the more different raw materials that are practical in use, the more ethanol production facilities will spread around the country. And the more spread around—the more production there is, the more likely it is that the entire industry will evolve quicker.

So you've got a lot of plants here in the Midwest. The vision has got to be for these plants to be able to spread throughout the entire country. And when it does, ethanol will become a primary source for the fuel people use, which will help us meet our national security and economic concerns and objectives.

The Department of Energy announced $250 million in funding to establish and operate two new bioenergy research center, all aimed at accelerating basic research into cellulosic ethanol and other biofuels. I suspect we've got some soybean growers here. I know you've got some in Missouri. I have been to a biodiesel plant in Virginia. And it doesn't take much capital investment to refine biodiesel from soy, soybeans; it just doesn't. Biodiesel is coming. It makes a lot of sense for us to continue to invest in biodiesel technologies to make the production process even more efficient. I have

seen biodiesel poured into a new truck and watched that truck crank right up and realize it emitted no emissions. I know, because I put a handkerchief over the stack. [*Laughter*]

These are exciting times, and people are beginning to take advantage of them. I told you I was down in Alabama. I went to the Hoover Police Department. They're using E–85. Their people on the beat are filling up their cars with E–85. I asked a guy, one of the policemen—I said, "Why do you use it?" He said, "First of all, I like the fact that it keeps the environment clean"—that's a good reason. He said, "By the way, when you fill it up with the 85, it gives you better get-up-and-go." [*Laughter*] In other words, it works. That's a good sign when police departments begin to use E–85.

I was over at a FedEx place, and they've got what they call the OptiFleet E700; it's a new vehicle, all aimed at reducing emissions by 96 percent. In other words, people are thinking differently now. There's a whole new industry beginning to evolve. Users are beginning to understand the benefits of using ethanol or biodiesel. And these are exciting times.

And the Federal Government's job is to continue to research so that we provide our consumers, the American people, with more options. And one of the great options that's coming down the road is hydrogen. That's a longer term project. If you notice, I kind of talk about hybrids that are on the road today and how we stimulate demand, hybrids that are coming with new batteries, ethanol which is now evolving into a significant industry. Ultimately, in my judgment, one of the ways to make sure that we become fully less dependent on oil is through hydrogen. And we're spending $1.2 billion to encourage hydrogen fuel cells. It's coming; it's coming. It's an interesting industry evolution, to think about your automobiles being powered by hydrogen, and the only emission is water vapor.

Oh, I'm sure there are some people out there saying, "Well, you know, he's just dreaming." Well, I'm just listening to the dreamers who happen to be good, smart, capable people who know what they're talking about——

Audience member. Out of Iraq now! Out of Iraq now! Soldiers are not renewables!

The President. Since 2003, my administration has made hydrogen and fuel-cell technology a priority——

[*At this point, there was a disruption in the audience.*]

The President. ——and we will continue to research to make sure America is less dependent on foreign sources of oil.

As you can tell, I'm excited about new technologies. But I think we've got to be realistic about the timing. And in order to become less dependent on foreign sources of oil, we've got to explore for oil and gas in our own hemisphere in environmentally friendly ways. And one of the interesting technological developments is the capacity to find oil in unique places. I don't know if you followed recently the exploration in the Gulf of Mexico, where there was a well that was drilled five miles in depth in thousands of feet of water.

In other words, these new technologies enable us to go to new places, and they enable us to be wise stewards of the environment. I understand there's a big debate about whether or not you can explore for oil and gas and protect the environment. I believe you can. And I understand that as we transition to the ethanol era, we must also—or the hydrogen era, we must also find oil and gas in our own hemisphere if the objective is to become less dependent on foreign oil.

They estimate that the new discovery in the deep Gulf of Mexico could increase our reserves from 10 to 50 percent. In other words, this is a big deal. And Congress is debating an energy bill. They passed a good energy bill, by the way, in the past, that encourages conservation and

encourages a lot of the research that I was talking about, understands we've got to diversify away from our current structure. But there's another bill out there, and they need to get the work done. They need to come together between the House and the Senate version to encourage exploration in the Gulf of Mexico in new areas to make sure that we transition to a new day when it comes to energy.

And I believe that States ought to share in the royalties, because I know in the State of Louisiana, for example, they have committed their share of new royalties in this new exploration to help protect their coastline. And I believe Congress needs to get the bill to my desk as quick as possible. So when you finish the elections, get back and let me sign this bill so the American people know that we're serious about getting off foreign oil.

And that's going to be important because we can find a lot of natural gas offshore, for example. And we need natural gas in order to make sure we meet our second objective, and that's how we protect the environment and power our society.

I don't know if you know this or not, but electricity is generated from natural gas, about 18 percent; coal, 50 percent; nuclear power, 20 percent; and then solar and wind. And the fundamental question is, can the Federal Government help make sure that we have energy so we can power our economy, protect the environment, and grow? And the answer is, we can, and we can spend money to help you.

One thing we don't need to spend money on but need to do is permit more liquefied natural gas terminals. LNG is a new technology that is—it's not that new, but it's evolving technology. It means you can get—buy natural gas from overseas in liquefied form and deliquefy it. There's a lot of natural gas in the world, and it makes sense for us to be in a position to receive that natural gas in order to make sure you've got energy in your home.

A shortage of natural gas causes your electricity bills to go up. Supply of natural gas, increased supply, makes it more likely that you're going to have rational bills, more likely the economy will continue to grow. And natural gas protects the environment.

Secondly, on coal, we got a lot of coal. We got 250 years of coal. That's a lot, and yet coal presents us with an environmental challenge. And so we're spending quite a bit of money here at the Federal level to come up with clean-coal technologies. If you want to be less dependent on foreign sources of energy, it seems like it makes sense to me that we use the energies we have here at home and do so in environmentally friendly ways.

We're spending $2 billion to promote technologies that will enable our coal-fired plants to protect the environment. As a matter of fact, we got what's called a FutureGen Initiative. By the year 2012, we'll build the first clean-coal powerplant that will remove virtually all pollutants and greenhouse gases from burning coal. In other words, there's a way coming that's going to enable us to use this plentiful resource.

A controversial subject is nuclear power. You might remember, we've had a time in our country where people liked nuclear power, thought it was a strong solution to energy independence, and then we just shut her down because of engineering concerns. I strongly believe that if we want to keep this country competitive, if we want to make sure we can compete globally, we must promote civilian nuclear power. We must have more energy coming from nuclear power.

Nuclear power is renewable, and there are no greenhouse gases associated with nuclear power. One of the problems we've had is that nobody wants to build any plants. They're afraid of the costs of regulation and the litigious nature that surrounds the construction of nuclear powerplants—

litigious problems surrounding the construction of the nuclear powerplants.

And so in the energy bill that I signed, the Congress wisely provided incentives and risk insurance for nuclear powerplant construction. Last year, only three companies were seeking to build powerplants, nuclear powerplants. Today, 14 have expressed new interest in construction. In other words, there's a new industry beginning to come back.

I think it's very important for us to spend dollars on how to best deal with the waste—in other words, research new ways to be able to assure the American people that we'll be able to deal with the nuclear waste in a smart way. And that's why we're teaming up with France and Japan and Russia to spend money—$250 million from the United States perspective, and they're matching it—on what's called the Global Nuclear Energy Partnership, all designed to research reprocessing and fast-burner reactors.

The idea is to take the nuclear industry, take the spent fuel, reprocess it, put it into a fast-burner reactor, which will yield about 90 percent less of the waste than under the current system. What I'm telling you is, is that the engineering is much safer today than it has been in the past, and we're spending money to make sure that we can deal with the waste in a sane way, so that we can, with confidence, say to the American people, now is the time to accelerate the expansion of nuclear power, for the sake of national and economic security.

I believe that with the proper amount of research, whether it be public or private, we will have solar roofs that will enable the American family to be able to generate their own electricity. And it's coming.

I believe wind power has got the opportunity to help. All we need is to put a couple of windmills right there in Washington, DC, and we'll be—[*laughter*]—less dependent on foreign sources of energy.

What I'm talking about is a comprehensive approach to solving a national issue, which is dependence on oil and how best to protect this environment. You know, it's time to get rid of the old, stale debates on the environment and recognize new technologies are going to enable us to achieve a lot of objectives at the same time.

Technology will enable us to be able to say we can grow our economy and protect our environment at the same time. It's not a zero-sum game anymore. These technological breakthroughs are going to say to our farmers, "You're energy producers." And that's good for America. It's going to say to those entrepreneurs that are risk takers, this is a good place to try to make a good return on capital.

There's a lot of smart money in the United States going into energy diversification and to research. And for those of you here, thanks. I hope you make a good return. I think you will. There is no question in my mind that we're on the verge of significant breakthroughs. And so what I wanted to come and tell you is, one, thanks for your interest; thanks for showing up at a conference like this. You're the beginning of what's going to be a new environmental debate, an economy based upon new technologies, a new way to power our automobiles, and a way that says by making good decisions now and researching now, we'll leave behind a better world for our children.

Someday, some—the 56th President will be standing up here saying, I appreciate the fact that there was some pioneers back in America in those days; I can't spend too much time because I've got to go get my limousine filled up by hydrogen—[*laughter*]—but I appreciate the fact that the solar panels are working so you can see me. [*Laughter*] In other words, it's coming, and I'm excited to be a part of it. And I hope you're excited as well.

Thanks for letting me come by. God bless.

NOTE: The President spoke at 12:29 p.m. at the St. Louis Convention Center. In his remarks, he referred to David Bransby, professor of agronomy and soil, Auburn University.

Remarks at a Reception for Congressional Candidates Peter Roskam and David McSweeney and the Illinois Congressional Victory Committee in Chicago, Illinois
October 12, 2006

The President. Thank you very much. Thanks for coming. I'm proud you're here. Before I liberate the Speaker, so he doesn't have to stand up here for this long speech—[*laughter*]—I want to say this to you: I am proud to be standing with the current Speaker of the House who is going to be the future Speaker of the House.

Speaker Denny Hastert has a long record of accomplishment. You know, he's not one of these Washington politicians who spews a lot of hot air. He just gets the job done. I have worked with him up close. I know what it's like to work with a Speaker who is determined to protect the United States of America, and a Speaker who wants to make sure that everybody who wants a job in America can find one. He has delivered results for the people. This country is better off with Denny Hastert as the Speaker, and it will be better off when he's the Speaker, the next legislative session.

The Speaker has heard me give a lot of talks, so he wants to make sure if there's a chair nearby—[*laughter*]—but I want to thank you all for coming. Your support means a lot.

Audience member. We will win.

The President. Yes, sir. I am also proud to be with two fine candidates, Peter Roskam, David McSweeney. And I want to thank you for helping them. I have a sense of what it's like to run for office. [*Laughter*] I've done it before, and I know how important it is for two candidates who are out, day in and day out, campaigning to be able to look at an audience this size and realize they're getting fine support. Your support means a lot not only to their campaigns, in the sense that you're helping to fill the hat, but it means a lot to their spirits to realize there's a lot of people pulling for them.

And there's nobody better to pull for a candidate than his family—in this case, Peter's family, Elizabeth and his children, and in David's case, his wife, Margaret. And it's been my honor to be able to see both those families, and I want to thank the families for supporting these good men for running for office as well.

Speaking about wives—[*laughter*]—I was—I happened to have my picture taken a while ago with a group of citizens that came through, and one fellow—I guess I would define him as blunt—said, "You know, I was hoping to have my picture taken with Laura." [*Laughter*] I said, "It's not hurting my feelings, man. You got good taste." [*Laughter*] She sends her best to the Speaker and to the candidates; she sends her best to you all. I am a lucky man to have Laura Bush as my wife. And our country—in my nonobjective opinion—is lucky to have her as the First Lady.

I wish Kevin White all the very best in his run for the Fifth Congressional Delegation. Thanks for coming, Kevin; give Geraldine a hug for me.

Audience member. Right in front of you; right here. [*Laughter*]

Audience member. I'll do it for you.

The President. Yes, thank you. [*Laughter*]

Audience member. Give her a hug for me. [*Laughter*]

Audience member. Okay.

The President. That's your responsibility. [*Laughter*]

I am proud to be here with Congressman Don Manzullo from the great State of Illinois. My thanks to State Representative Tom Cross, who is the minority leader of the Illinois House. I want to thank all the State and local officials who've joined us. But most of all, thank you all for being here.

I thank my friend Pat Ryan. It's not easy to raise this much money, and I know how much organization it takes, and therefore, it takes a strong leader up top, and that's exactly what Pat Ryan is. He's a strong leader and a great American, and I'm proud to be with you, Pat.

I want to thank my friend Andy McKenna, who is the chairman of the Illinois Republican Party. The reason I mention grassroots activists is that you win campaigns by having candidates who can carry a strong message, and we have those candidates. You win a campaign because people are generous with their hard-earned money, and you have been so tonight. And you win campaigns when people get out and put up the signs and make the phone calls, go to the community centers and houses of worship and say, "Support these candidates." So I want to thank you for what you have done, and I encourage you to continue to work to turn out the vote come this November.

We've got a lot to do to make sure this country is prosperous and safe. I'm looking forward to working with these two new Congressmen as we work to diversify our energy supply. I'm going to tell you why we need to. I'm a little concerned at the price—the drop in gasoline prices, which I welcome, and I know you do too. [*Laughter*] However, masks the fact that it is not in our national interest to be dependent on foreign sources of oil. And so I look forward to working with these Congress-

men to promote alternative energy sources, such as ethanol, and new research and development into new battery technologies that will enable you to drive the first 40 miles on electricity, and your car won't have to look like a golf cart. [*Laughter*]

We've got an aggressive agenda to diversify our energy sources so that we're not dependent on Middle Eastern oil. It's in our national security interests.

I'm looking forward to working with these Members to make sure health care is available and affordable. We don't need the Federal Government telling doctors how to practice and telling patients who they got to go see. But we do need the Federal Government to do something about these junk and frivolous lawsuits that are running good doctors out of practice.

A big issue always facing the Congress is how to make sure that the entrepreneurial spirit remains strong in the United States. And we got a strong record. This administration has got a strong record on the economy, and so does Speaker Denny Hastert.

You might remember the facts. This country has been through a recession, a stock market correction. We've been through a terrorist attack on our Nation. We've been at war to defend this country. We've had major hurricanes. For a while, we had high energy prices. And yet America is the envy of the industrialized world when it comes to economic growth.

Our national unemployment rate is 4.6 percent. People are working; we've added 6.6 million new jobs since August of 2003. Our farm economy is strong. Productivity is up. Small businesses are on the rise. This economy is in good shape, and we need to keep Denny Hastert and the Republicans in charge of the United States Congress to keep it that way.

And we're in good shape because we cut the taxes on everybody who paid income taxes. We have a philosophy of government that says, if you have more of your own money in your pocket to save, spend, or

invest, this economy will do well. That stands in stark contrast to our opponents, who believe that they can spend your money better than you can spend your money. And so we cut the taxes, not once, but twice. We cut the taxes on families with children; we cut the taxes on people who were married; we put the death tax on the road to extinction; we cut the taxes on small-business people. As a result of good fiscal policy in Washington, DC, this economy is strong. And the best way to keep it there is to make the tax cuts we passed permanent.

That's the opposite view of the Democrats. You might remember the debate about the deficit—they go around the country saying, "Well, we got to solve the deficit, and we need to raise taxes." That's not the way Washington works. If they were to get in charge of the House of Representatives, they would raise your taxes and figure out new ways to spend your money. The best way to balance this budget—by the way, a couple of years ago, I stood up and said, we can cut the deficit in half by 2009. It's amazing what happens when you cut taxes; the economy grows; you end up with more tax revenues. When you couple that with fiscal discipline in Washington, DC, which we have exhibited, the deficit gets cut. As a matter of fact, we cut the deficit in half not by 2009, but by 3 years prior to that.

The best way to keep this economy growing, the best way to make sure we've got a fiscal situation that makes sure the economic growth continues is to keep taxes low and prioritize how we spend your money. And the number-one priority has got to be to protect America and make sure those who wear the uniform have all the support they need to do their job.

Our record on taxes is clear. The Democrats in Washington have a clear record of their own. The trouble is, they don't want you to know about it. Recently the top Democrat leader in the House made an interesting declaration. Here's what she said: "We love tax cuts." Given her record, she must be a secret admirer. [*Laughter*]

It's not just the so-called tax cuts for the rich she opposes, when we cut taxes for everybody who pays income taxes, she voted against it. When we reduced the marriage penalty, she voted against it. When we cut taxes on small businesses, she voted against it. When we lowered the taxes for families with children, she voted against it. When we cut the taxes on dividends and capital gains to stimulate investment, she voted against it. When we put the death tax on the road to extinction, she voted against it. Time and again, when she had an opportunity to show her love for tax cuts, she voted, no. If this is the Democrats' idea of love—[*laughter*]—I don't want to see what hate looks like. [*Laughter*]

A big issue in this campaign across the United States and here in Illinois with these two Congressmen is, who is going to keep your taxes low? When we win, we will keep your taxes low. And make no mistake about it, the Democrats will raise your taxes. It's a fundamental difference in this campaign. And I'm looking forward to leading us to victory to make sure the taxes on the people of the United States remain low and reasonable.

No, there's a lot of big domestic issues—and I'm sure our candidates are out there telling people what's on their mind—but the biggest issue facing this country is, who best to protect you? We are a nation at war. You know, I wish I didn't have to say that. I wish I could say everything is fine, but that's not the reality of the world in which we live. The most fundamental job of those of us in government is to protect you and to do everything in our power to protect the American people.

There's an enemy that lurks and plots and plans because they cannot stand—they can't stand our values and what we believe. They don't believe in the freedoms that we believe in. They're bound by an ideology, and they're willing to use murder

as a tool to achieve that ideology. It's a different kind of war, but it's real, as we learned on that fateful day of September the 11th, 2001.

On that day, I vowed that I would use all of my powers and national assets to protect the American people, and so did the Speaker. These are folks you can't negotiate with. These are ideologues who have stated clearly, their objective is to drive the United States out of the Middle East so they can establish a caliphate based upon their ideology of hate. They have made their plans clear, and it's essential that the President and the United States Congress listen carefully to the words of the enemy.

My view is, is that the best way to defeat this enemy is to stay on the offense and defeat them overseas so we do not have to face them here at home. And so we're keeping steady pressure on a group of people who would want to do America harm. It's hard to plan and plot when you're on the run. It's hard to plan and plot when you're in a cave. You just got to know, there's some incredibly brave Americans, working with allies, that are keeping the pressure on this enemy to keep you safe.

One of the terrible lessons of September the 11th is that oceans can no longer protect us, and therefore, it is essential that the United States treat threats seriously before they come home to hurt us, before they fully materialize. I saw a threat. Members of both parties in the United States Congress saw a threat. The United Nations saw a threat in Iraq. Removing Saddam Hussein from power was the right decision, and the world is better off for it.

Iraq is a central front in this war on terror. Oh, I know the Democrats say it's a diversion from the war on terror; some of them say that. But I would ask them to listen to the words of Usama bin Laden or Zawahiri, who is the number two of Al Qaida, who have said clearly, their ambitions are to drive us out of Iraq so they can establish a safe haven from which to launch further attacks; to drive us out of

Iraq so they can have resources to use to fund their ambitions; to drive us out of Iraq so they can topple moderate governments.

Imagine a world in which there are violent forms of extremists who've crushed the hopes of moderate, decent people because they have this ideology that is so foreign to us. Imagine a world in which they could use oil to blackmail the free world. Imagine that world, as well, with a group of people that don't care for America, with a nuclear weapon. If that were to happen, a generation of Americans would look and say: "What happened? What happened to the leaders? How come they couldn't see the threat?"

I see the threat. The Speaker sees the threat. We've got a plan for victory in this war on terror, and that includes helping those 12 million people who are desperate for freedom to achieve their dreams of democracy. We've got a goal, a clear goal, which is an Iraq that can defend itself and sustain itself, an Iraq that will be an ally in the war on terror.

We're constantly changing our tactics to meet those of the enemy. We're constantly adjusting. But make no mistake about it, our plan is victory. We will stay in Iraq, we will fight in Iraq, and we will win in Iraq for the security of the United States.

We have to be right 100 percent of the time to protect the country. The enemy has to be right one time. And therefore, it is incumbent upon those of us in government to make sure the professionals on the frontlines of protecting America have all the tools necessary to protect you. The Speaker understands that. These candidates running for office understand that.

And that is why I worked with the Congress to pass what's called the PATRIOT Act. It was an act that tore down walls that prevented the intelligence community and the criminal justice community from talking. I know that probably sounds strange that that happened, but it's the reality. You can't defend America unless all

elements of government are capable of sharing information so that we can prevent the attack from happening in the first place. I also believed it was essential—and by the way, the Speaker led the charge in making sure the House passed the PATRIOT Act the first time and then reauthorized it.

Secondly, I believe strongly that if an Al Qaida or Al Qaida affiliate was making a phone call into the United States from outside the country, we need to know why. If the most important job of government is to protect you, we need to understand what the enemy is thinking and what they're planning. I thank the Congress for getting the House of Representatives to endorse the terrorist surveillance program. I thought it was very important that when we captured a leader of the enemy on the battlefield that we detain and question that enemy. I thought it was essential to protect you, that we gain information from the leadership of those who would do us harm.

One of the people we captured was Khalid Sheikh Mohammed, who our intelligence officers believe was the mastermind of the 9/11 attacks. I thought it was important for this country to gain information from this mastermind in order to be able to say we're doing everything we can to protect you. And we learned a lot of information from those who we have captured, information that our intelligence service believes strongly has prevented attacks on the homeland. And yet we've had a debate on this issue, and the Speaker of the House led the House of Representatives to endorse this vision.

In other words, we've been giving people the tools necessary to protect the homeland, and our Democrat colleagues back in Washington have taken a very different approach to the war on terror. There is a difference of opinion. I'm not questioning anybody's patriotism or love for America, but I am questioning their view of how best to protect you. And this is an issue in this campaign. If the security of the United States is the most important issue, then part of this issue is which party has been willing to step up and give those charged with protecting you the tools necessary to do so.

In each vote, a clear pattern has emerged on which party can best protect the American people. More than 75 percent of the House Democrats voted to block the renewal of the PATRIOT Act. Almost 80 percent of the House Democrats voted against allowing the CIA to continue the interrogation program. Almost 90 percent of the House Democrats voted against continuing to monitor terrorist communications through the terrorist surveillance program. Rarely has a single series of votes summed up the difference between the two political parties so clearly. If the Democrats' Congress had their way, we wouldn't have had the PATRIOT Act or the interrogation program or the terrorist surveillance program. They can run from this record, but we're not going to let them hide.

You know, I was—recently read where the Democrat leader said this. She said, "The midterm elections should not be about national security." I strongly disagree. I want those discerning Democrats and independents and Republicans to hear loud and clear that the person who wants to be Speaker of the House has said that the midterm elections shouldn't be about national security.

I know this election ought to be about national security. I'm briefed every day on the threats this country faces. The United States of America cannot afford to wait and respond to an attack. The United States of America must be on the offense to make sure the attacks don't happen in the first place.

We've got one great asset at our disposal as well, and it's called liberty. I believe in the universality of liberty. I believe there is an Almighty, and I believe one of the great gifts of that Almighty is the desire for people to be free. I believe that. I believe that Muslim moms want to be free.

I believe that people all across the globe have this great desire and yearning to live in freedom. And I believe that freedom will help us yield the peace we want for our children and grandchildren.

The way to defeat—the way I like to put it is, we're in an ideological struggle. It's a struggle between extremists, radicals, and reasonable people who simply want to have a better life. And I believe it's incumbent upon the United States of America to stand with those who are reasonable and moderate against the extremists and radicals.

I believe it's our call to do so, and I have great faith in the power of liberty to transform regions of hate to regions of hope and to transform enemies to allies. And the reason I say that to you, I've had some amazing experience as your President, and perhaps one of the most unusual is my relationship with the Prime Minister of Japan. I must have told this story hundreds of times because it is so ironic that my relationship is so close, and yet my dad, when he was a young man, volunteered to fight the Japanese as a sworn enemy.

You know, recently I invited my friend, the former Prime Minister—he just left office—to go to Elvis's place. [*Laughter*] I'd never been there. [*Laughter*] He wanted to go there. See, he's an Elvis fan. But I also wanted to tell a story to the American people about ideological struggles and the faith we should have in liberty—because on Air Force One, going down to Memphis, Tennessee, the Prime Minister and I talked about keeping the peace. Isn't that interesting? My dad fought the enemy, fought the Japanese as the enemy, and now his son is talking about the peace.

We're talking about North Korea and how it's important for there to be more than one voice at the table when it comes to convincing the leader of North Korea. By the way, it's much better to have China at the table with the United States. It's much better to have Japan and South Korea—[*applause*].

We talked about the fact that Japan had deployed 1,000 troops in Iraq, because he understands what I know, the advent of democracy is a huge defeat to the extremists. That's why they're fighting so hard. That's why this is such a brutal battle. And I understand it affects the American people, because the enemy has got a weapon, and they use it, and that's the murder of innocent people. And it gets on our TV screens, and we're a nation of compassionate, decent people who care about human life in all its forms. And yet Prime Minister Koizumi knows what I know, that we will succeed as liberty progresses, and we will succeed by helping people who yearn for a better life, and we will succeed by marginalizing those extremists and radicals and, if need be, bring them to justice before they hurt us again.

Something happened between World War II and when I became the President, talking with this Japanese Prime Minister. And what happened was, Japan adopted a Japanese-style democracy. Liberty has got the capacity to transform an enemy into an ally. And someday, an American President will be sitting down with elected leaders in the Middle East talking about how to keep the peace, and a generation of Americans will be better off for it.

God bless.

NOTE: The President spoke at 5:25 p.m. at the Hilton Chicago. In his remarks, he referred to Patrick G. Ryan, executive chairman and founder, Aon Corp.; former President Saddam Hussein of Iraq; Usama bin Laden, leader of the Al Qaida terrorist organization; former Prime Minister Junichiro Koizumi of Japan; and Chairman Kim Jong Il of North Korea.

Statement on the Sixth Anniversary of the Terrorist Attack on the USS *Cole*
October 12, 2006

Six years ago, on October 12, 2000, Al Qaida attacked the USS *Cole*, a U.S. Navy warship refueling in Aden harbor in Yemen. This terrorist attack killed 17 sailors and injured many others, leaving the victims' loved ones and our Nation to mourn our collective loss.

On the sixth anniversary of this attack, we pause to remember those brave service men and women whose lives were cut short by this act of terrorism and to give thanks to the brave crew whose heroic actions saved their ship and fellow shipmates.

With the men we believe to be the key architects of that attack now in custody, this anniversary should serve to renew America's dedication to bring terrorists to justice and our gratitude to those men and women of the U.S. Government serving abroad who take great risks in protecting America.

Six years ago, our Nation was tested by terrorism. Terrorists continue to be an active threat to our Nation, but we are responding resolutely and forcefully. On this solemn anniversary, we rededicate ourselves to the fight against the enemies of humanity, offer our prayers and condolences to the families of the *Cole* victims, and offer thanks to the men and women of our Navy who protect our country and promote peace and freedom around the world.

Statement on Signing the Rio Grande Natural Area Act
October 12, 2006

Today, I have signed into law S. 56, the "Rio Grande Natural Area Act." The Act establishes the Rio Grande Natural Area in Colorado to help protect natural resources on Federal and non-Federal lands.

The Act establishes a commission to perform specified functions relating to the Natural Area. The Commission consists of nine individuals appointed by the Secretary of the Interior, of whom one must represent the Colorado State Director of the Bureau of Land Management, one must be a specified Federal employee, three must be appointed on the recommendation of the Governor of Colorado to represent various Colorado governmental entities, and four must be knowledgeable, experienced local citizens to represent the general public. Thus, the Act limits the qualifications of the pool of persons from whom the Secretary may select appointees to the Com-

mission in a manner that rules out a large portion of those persons best qualified by experience and knowledge to fill the positions, which the Appointments Clause of the Constitution does not permit if the appointees exercise significant governmental authority. To faithfully execute the Act to the maximum extent consistent with the Appointments Clause, the executive branch shall construe the provisions of the Act specifying functions for the Commission as specifying functions that are advisory only.

GEORGE W. BUSH

The White House,
October 12, 2006.

NOTE: This statement was released by the Office of the Press Secretary on October 13. S. 56, approved October 12, was assigned Public Law No. 109–337.

Statement on Signing the National Heritage Areas Act of 2006
October 12, 2006

Today, I have signed into law S. 203, the "National Heritage Areas Act of 2006." The Act establishes national heritage areas and reduces the royalty rate on certain minerals.

A number of provisions of the Act purport to give to management entities or local coordinating entities, composed of individuals who are not officers of the United States appointed in accordance with the Appointments Clause of the Constitution, significant governmental authority, such as authority to make grants from Federal appropriated funds to implement management plans for heritage areas. As is consistent with the Appointments Clause and with requirements in the Act concerning approval by the Secretary of the Interior of the management plans, the executive branch shall construe the provisions to require exercise by the Secretary of the Interior of the significant governmental authority given by the provisions, specifically including the exercise by the Secretary of final authority over any disbursement of Federal appropriated funds by a management entity or local coordinating entity.

GEORGE W. BUSH

The White House,
October 12, 2006.

NOTE: This statement was released by the Office of the Press Secretary on October 13. S. 203, approved October 12, was assigned Public Law No. 109–338.

Remarks on Signing the Security and Accountability For Every Port Act of 2006
October 13, 2006

Thank you all. Please be seated. Thank you, and welcome. I'm pleased to have you here as I sign a bill that will help protect the American people and our ports. The SAFE Port Act will make this Nation more prepared, more prosperous, and more secure.

I want to thank the Congress for its good work. I'm pleased that key Members of the Senate and the House have joined me here today, and I want to thank you for being here. I first want to thank the Secretary of Homeland Security, Michael Chertoff, for his service to the country. I appreciate that Senate Majority Leader Bill Frist has joined us. I'm pleased that Senator Susan Collins, who is the chairman of the Senate Homeland Security and Governmental Affairs Committee, has joined us. She is one of the sponsors of the bill, as is Peter King, who's the chairman of the House Homeland Security Committee. These two Members are strong, strong chairmen, and they're doing a fine job to help us protect this country. I appreciate very much Senator Bob Bennett and Senator Patty Murray and Senator Norm Coleman for joining us, as well as Congressman Dan Lungren.

The most solemn responsibility of the Federal Government is to protect the American people. And since September the 11th, the administration and the Congress have worked together, and we've led an unprecedented effort to safeguard our homeland. In other words, we learned the lessons of that attack. We've more than tripled spending on homeland security. We've

created a Federal Department of Homeland Security with a single mission: to protect the American people. We've trained and equipped hundreds of thousands of State and local first-responders. We've worked with public agencies and private companies to improve security at airports and aboard commercial airliners. We've strengthened protections at bridges and tunnels and other critical infrastructure. We have a responsibility to protect the homeland, and we're meeting that responsibility.

Protecting our homeland requires protecting our borders. Since I took office, we more than doubled funding for border security, from $4.6 billion in 2001 to 9.5 billion in 2006. We've increased the number of Border Patrol agents from around 9,000 to a little more than 12,000. We've upgraded technology and infrastructure along the border. We've apprehended and sent home more than 6 million people entering America illegally. This is important progress, but we've got a lot of more work to do.

Last week in Arizona, I signed a bill that will allow us to hire 1,500 more Border Patrol agents, deploy advanced technology like ground-based radar and infrared cameras, add beds in our detention facilities so we can work to end catch-and-release. Congress also passed a bill that will authorize the construction of about 700 miles of double-layered fencing along our Southern border. I'm going to sign that bill into law. I'll continue to work with Congress to pass comprehensive immigration reform that protects our country, enforces our laws, and upholds our values.

Protecting our homeland also requires protecting our seaports. Our seaports are a gateway to commerce, a source of opportunity, and a provider of jobs. Our ports could also be a target of a terrorist attack, and we're determined to protect them.

Since September the 11th, we've launched a series of new efforts to improve port security. We worked with Congress to pass the Maritime Transportation Security Act, which required American ports and vessels to adopt strict new security measures. We made wider use of intelligence to screen cargo and target suspicious containers for inspection. We've worked with foreign partners to improve their security procedures. And with the bill I sign today, we renew a clear commitment: We will work tirelessly to keep our Nation safe and our ports open for business.

The SAFE Port Act will build on progress and help us protect our ports in three key ways. First, the SAFE Port Act will strengthen physical security measures at our ports by helping us harness the power of technology. The bill authorizes the development of 21st century inspection equipment, so that Customs agents can check inside cargo containers for dangerous materials without having to open them. The bill also requires radiation detection technology at our 22 busiest ports by the end of next year. America has the best technology in the world, and with this bill, we will apply that technology to make our ports the safest in the world.

Second, the SAFE Port Act provides legislative authority for key elements of our port security strategy. The bill codifies into law the Container Security Initiative, which we launched in 2002. Through this initiative, we have deployed American inspectors to dozens of foreign ports on five continents where they are screening cargo before it leaves for our country.

The bill also codifies into law the Customs Trade Partnership Against Terrorism, a joint effort between the public and private sectors to improve cargo security. Under this partnership, private shippers agree to improve their own security measures, and in return, they can receive benefits, including expedited clearance through our ports.

And the bill provides additional authority for the Domestic Nuclear Detection Office, which we established to guard against the threat of terrorists smuggling a nuclear device into our country.

All these efforts are smart. They're working. And with this bill, they're here to stay.

Finally, the SAFE Port Act requires the Department of Homeland Security to establish a plan to speed the resumption of trade in the event of a terrorist attack on our ports or waterways. This bill makes clear that the Federal Government has the authority to clear waterways, identify cleanup equipment, and reestablish the flow of commerce following a terrorist attack. We'll do everything we can to prevent an attack, but if the terrorists succeed in launching an attack, we'll be ready to respond.

We take these steps to improve our port security, and as we do so, we thank the hard-working Americans who protect our people day in and day out. We're grateful to the Coast Guard's men and women, the Customs and Border Protection officers, our port workers and managers, State and local law enforcement officers, and all those in the private sector who do their part to keep America safe. We're going to protect our ports. We're going to defend this homeland. And we're going to win the war on terror.

With that, I'm now pleased to sign the SAFE Port Act into law.

NOTE: The President spoke at 10 a.m. in Room 350 of the Dwight D. Eisenhower Executive Office Building. H.R. 4954, approved October 13, was assigned Public Law No. 109–347.

Statement on Signing the Security and Accountability For Every Port Act of 2006
October 13, 2006

Today, I have signed into law H.R. 4954, the "Security and Accountability For Every Port Act of 2006," or the "SAFE Port Act" (the "Act"). The Act strengthens the Government's ability to protect the Nation's seaports and maritime commerce from attack by terrorists.

The executive branch shall construe provisions of the Act that purport to require executive branch officials to submit recommendations for legislation to the Congress, including section 201, in a manner consistent with the President's constitutional authority to recommend for the consideration of the Congress such measures as the President judges necessary and expedient and to supervise the unitary executive branch.

The executive branch shall construe provisions of the Act, including subsection 401(c) and subsection 2(d) of the Act of March 3, 1927, as amended by section 402 of the Act, that purport to make consultation with congressional committees a precondition to execution of the law, to call for but not mandate such consultation, as is consistent with the Constitution's provisions concerning the separate powers of the Congress to legislate and the President to execute the laws.

The executive branch shall construe subsection 301(h)(2) of the Customs Procedural Reform and Simplification Act of 1978, as amended by section 403 of the Act, which purports to give a subordinate official within the executive branch authority to prevent an action by the superior official to whom the subordinate official reports, in a manner consistent with the President's constitutional authority to supervise the unitary executive branch.

The executive branch shall construe section 709 of the Act, which purports to direct the President to perform the President's duties "acting through" a particular officer, in a manner consistent with the

constitutional authority of the President to supervise the unitary executive branch.

The executive branch shall construe as advisory provisions of the Act that purport to direct or burden the conduct of negotiations by the executive branch with foreign governments, international organizations, or other entities abroad, that purport to direct executive branch officials to negotiate with foreign governments or in international organizations to achieve specified foreign policy objectives, or that purport to require the executive branch to disclose deliberations between the United States and foreign countries. Such provisions include subsections 205(d) and (i) and 803(b) of the Act; subsection 431(b) of the Homeland Se-

curity Act of 2002, as amended by section 301 of the Act; and subsection 629(h) of the Tariff Act of 1930, as amended by section 404 of the Act. Such provisions, if construed as mandatory rather than advisory, would impermissibly interfere with the President's constitutional authorities to conduct the Nation's foreign affairs, participate in international negotiations, and supervise the unitary executive branch.

GEORGE W. BUSH

The White House,
October 13, 2006.

NOTE: H.R. 4954, approved October 13, was assigned Public Law No. 109–347.

Remarks Following a Meeting With the President's Management Council
October 13, 2006

It's been my pleasure to meet with members of my administration on a very important topic, and that is, how do we make sure that the taxpayers' money we're spending is getting the results we want. And I appreciate Clay Johnson of the OMB staff. And I appreciate the Director for spearheading this project, which says to our agencies, it's important to set clear goals and to set priorities for the dollars we spend. And once a goal is set, a goal that everybody can understand, it's important to make sure we measure to determine whether or not we're achieving the results.

See, the people expect—when they send their money up there—expect us to achieve certain results. And so we've been through a rigorous process in this administration of judging agencies' ability to get results, and I will tell you our agencies are responding well. It's important to measure results so that we know we're doing our job. It's also important to measure results to determine

whether or not the taxpayers' money is being spent wisely.

We've all dedicated ourselves to rallying around this model. We are results-oriented people, and we work on behalf of the taxpayers. And when we find wasteful spending, we work to eliminate it. When we find a program that is making a significant difference, we work to enhance it. And we are getting results for the people. And I want to thank everybody around this table for being public servants, people who are willing to serve the public and bring dignity to the process.

I want you to go back to your agencies and thank those who are working hard on behalf of the American people as well. Thank you.

NOTE: The President spoke at 2 p.m. in Room 350 of the Dwight D. Eisenhower Executive Office Building.

Letter to Congressional Leaders on Blocking Property of and Prohibiting Transactions With the Government of Sudan
October 13, 2006

Dear Mr. Speaker: (Dear Mr. President:)

Consistent with subsection 204(b) of the International Emergency Economic Powers Act, 50 U.S.C. 1703(b)(IEEPA), and section 301 of the National Emergencies Act, 50 U.S.C. 1631 (NEA), I hereby report that I have issued an Executive Order (the "order") to take additional steps with respect to the national emergency declared in Executive Order 13067 of November 3, 1997.

On October 13, 2006, I signed into law the Darfur Peace and Accountability Act of 2006 (DPAA), which, among other things, calls for support of the regional government of Southern Sudan, assistance with the peace efforts in the Darfur region of Sudan, and provision of economic assistance in specified areas of Sudan. Section 7 of the DPAA maintains the sanctions currently imposed on the Government of Sudan. However, section 8(e) of the DPAA exempts from the prohibitions of Executive Order 13067 certain areas in Sudan, including Southern Sudan, Southern Kordofan/Nuba Mountains State, Blue Nile State, Abyei, Darfur, and marginalized areas in and around Khartoum.

Pursuant to IEEPA and the NEA, I determined that the Government of Sudan continues to implement policies and actions that violate human rights, in particular with respect to the conflict in Darfur, where the Government of Sudan exercises administrative and legal authority and pervasive practical influence, and that the Government of Sudan has a pervasive role in the petroleum and petrochemical industries in Sudan. In light of these determinations, and in order to reconcile sections 7 and 8 of the DPAA, I issued this order to continue the country-wide blocking of the Government of Sudan's property and to prohibit transactions relating to the petroleum and petrochemical industries in Sudan.

The order blocks the property and interests in property of the Government of Sudan that are in the United States, that hereafter come within the United States, or that are or hereafter come within the possession or control of United States persons, including their overseas branches. The order also prohibits all transactions by United States persons relating to the petroleum or petrochemical industries in Sudan, including, but not limited to, oilfield services and oil or gas pipelines.

The order specifies that Executive Order 13067 remains in force, but that the prohibitions in section 2 of that order shall not apply to activities and transactions with respect to Southern Sudan, Southern Kordofan/Nuba Mountains State, Blue Nile State, Abyei, Darfur, or marginalized areas in and around Khartoum, provided that the activities or transactions do not involve any property or interests in property of the Government of Sudan.

Sincerely,

GEORGE W. BUSH

NOTE: Identical letters were sent to J. Dennis Hastert, Speaker of the House of Representatives, and Richard B. Cheney, President of the Senate. The Executive order is listed in Appendix D at the end of this volume.

The President's Radio Address
October 14, 2006

Good morning. Earlier this week, the Government of North Korea proclaimed to the world that it had conducted a successful nuclear weapons test. In response to North Korea's provocative actions, America is working with our partners in the region and in the United Nations Security Council to ensure that there are serious repercussions for the North Korean regime.

North Korea has been pursuing nuclear weapons and defying its international commitments for years. In 1993, North Korea announced that it was withdrawing from the Nuclear Nonproliferation Treaty. The United States negotiated with North Korea and reached a bilateral agreement in 1994: North Korea committed to giving up its pursuit of nuclear weapons in exchange for help with peaceful nuclear power.

After I came to office, we discovered that North Korea had been violating this agreement for some time by continuing work on a covert nuclear weapons program. My administration confronted the North Korea regime with this evidence in 2002, and the North Koreans subsequently walked away from the 1994 agreement.

So my administration decided to take a new approach. We brought together other nations in the region in an effort to resolve the situation through multilateral diplomacy. The logic behind this approach is clear: North Korea's neighbors have the most at stake, and they are North Korea's principal sources of food, energy, and trade, so it makes sense to enlist them in the effort to get the North Korean regime to end its nuclear program.

This diplomatic effort was called the six-party talks, and these talks included North and South Korea, China, Japan, Russia, and the United States. In September of last year, these diplomatic efforts resulted in a wide-ranging joint statement that offered a resolution to the problem and a better

life for the North Korean people. In this joint statement, North Korea committed to abandoning all nuclear weapons and existing nuclear programs. North Korea was offered the prospect of normalized relations with Japan and the United States, as well as economic cooperation in energy, trade, and investment. And the United States affirmed that we have no nuclear weapons on the Korean Peninsula and no intention to attack or invade North Korea.

Unfortunately, North Korea failed to act on its commitment. And with its actions this week, the North Korean regime has once again broken its word, provoked an international crisis, and denied its people the opportunity for a better life. We are working for a resolution to this crisis. Nations around the world, including our partners in the six-party talks, agree on the need for a strong United Nations Security Council resolution that will require North Korea to dismantle its nuclear programs. This resolution should also specify measures to prevent North Korea from importing or exporting nuclear or missile technologies. And it should prevent financial transactions or asset transfers that would help North Korea develop its nuclear or missile capabilities.

By passing such a resolution, we will send a clear message to the North Korean regime that its actions will not be tolerated. And we will give the nations with the closest ties to North Korea—China and South Korea—a framework to use their leverage to pressure Pyongyang and persuade its regime to change course.

As we pursue a diplomatic solution, we are also reassuring our allies in the region that America remains committed to their security. We have strong defense alliances with Japan and South Korea, and the United States will meet these commitments. And in response to North Korea's

provocation, we will seek to increase our defense cooperation with our allies, including cooperation on ballistic missile defense to protect against North Korean aggression and cooperation to prevent North Korea from importing or exporting nuclear or missile technologies.

Our goals remain clear: peace and security in Northeast Asia and a nuclear-free Korean Peninsula. We will do what is necessary to achieve these goals. We will support our allies in the region; we will work with the United Nations; and together we will ensure that North Korea faces real consequences if it continues down its current path.

Thank you for listening.

NOTE: The address was recorded at 7:50 a.m. on October 13 in the Cabinet Room at the White House for broadcast at 10:06 a.m. on October 14. The transcript was made available by the Office of the Press Secretary on October 13 but was embargoed for release until the broadcast. The Office of the Press Secretary also released a Spanish language transcript of this address.

Remarks at the United States Air Force Memorial Dedication in Arlington, Virginia
October 14, 2006

Thank you all. Thank you very much. Mr. Secretary, thank you for your kind words. Secretary Nicholson, General Hayden, General Pace, Secretary Wynne, General Moseley, Chief Master Sergeant McKinley, Ross Perot, Jr., Major General Grillo, members of the Armed Forces, military veterans, and distinguished guests: Laura and I are honored to join you on this historic day.

With today's ceremony, the United States Air Force begins a year-long celebration of its 60th birthday. As someone who recently crossed that milestone—[*laughter*]— it's not all that bad. [*Laughter*] I can think of no better way to begin the celebrations than by dedicating this magnificent monument. So, General Grillo, here in the company of the brave men and women of the United States Air Force, I proudly accept the Air Force Memorial on behalf of the American people.

A soldier can walk the battlefields where he once fought; a marine can walk the beaches he once stormed; but an airman can never visit the patch of sky he raced across on a mission to defend freedom. And so it's fitting that from this day forward, the men and women of the Air Force will have this memorial, a place here on the ground that recognizes their achievements and sacrifices in the skies above.

Building this memorial took a lot of talent and creativity and determination. Like the aircraft whose flight it represents, this memorial is a incredible feat of engineering. Like the country whose freedom it represents, this memorial is hopeful and optimistic. By its design, this monument raises our eyes toward the vast and open skies and focuses our mind on the endless possibilities of human flight.

Having flown an F–102, I know the exhilaration of flight, and as a son of an aviator who was shot down in combat, I am keenly aware of its dangers. I have spent a lot of time with the aviators, and one thing about them that has always struck me, aviators, by their nature, are optimistic people. It takes an optimist to climb into a steel tube, race to the sky at 1,500 miles an hour heading toward danger, and expect to return home safely. Yet this is precisely

what the men and women of the Air Force do for our country every day.

America is grateful for your service, and I'm proud to be the Commander in Chief of such fine men and women.

Today, it's hard to imagine a world without the Air Force protecting us in the skies above. Yet by the standards of history, air power is still a relatively new phenomenon. Men have been fighting on land and sea for thousands of years, but there are still Americans alive today who were born before man had ever flown. Over the past century, manned flight has gone from the dream of two brothers working in an Ohio bicycle shop to an indispensable tool in our Nation's arsenal.

We saw the importance of air power 6 days ago—six decades ago, after our Nation was attacked at Pearl Harbor. Soon after the attack, General Hap Arnold called Lieutenant Colonel Jimmy Doolittle into his office and gave him an unprecedented mission: retaliate against Tokyo. Just over 4 months later, Doolittle's raiders had shocked the world by striking the enemy capital some 4,000 miles away from Pearl Harbor. To do it, they had to load B–52 [B–25]° bombers on the deck of an aircraft carrier, sail within a few hundred miles of enemy territory, take off and drop their payloads, knowing they had little chance to make it safely to China.

But the Doolittle raid sent a clear message to America's enemies: If you attack this country and you harm our people, there is no corner of the Earth remote enough to protect you from the reach of the aviators who wear our Nation's uniform.

Five years ago, our enemies learned this lesson anew after the attacks of September the 11th, 2001. Within weeks of the attack, pilots at Whiteman Air Force Base in Missouri boarded B–2 stealth bombers, flew halfway across the world, refueling in mid-air, took out the Taliban and Al Qaida targets in Afghanistan, dropped into Diego

---

° White House correction.

Garcia for engine-running crew changes, and then made the journey home. Jimmy Doolittle would have been proud.

Together with Navy and Marine aircrew, submariners, Special Ops forces from every service, and a vast coalition of nations, the United States Air Force helped deliver justice to a regime nearly 7,000 miles away from the World Trade Center and helped put the terrorists on the run. Five years have passed since the opening salvos in the war on terror, and every day in this war, we depend on the skill and determination of the men and women of the United States Air Force. In this war, battlefield airmen on the ground scout out enemy positions, locate targets for aviators circling above, and use advanced laser guidance systems to steer bombs, allowing us to strike the terrorists and spare innocent civilians.

In this war, Air Force aviators in Nevada step into a camouflage trailer on their base, sit down in front of computer consoles, and fly Predator unmanned aerial vehicles half a world away over the skies of Iraq, using them to find and remove terrorist nests in remote corners of the world.

In this world—in this war, our airmen operate advanced space satellites circling the Earth. They beam down real-time images of terrorist positions to our troops on the ground so they can strike the enemy before the enemy can strike our country. In this war, Air Force C–130 crews deliver supplies to our troops on the frontlines; Air Force teams disarm and remove roadside bombs; Air Force maintenance squadrons keep our planes in the air; Air Force A–10 Thunderbolts provide close air support for troops in contact with the enemy. And Air Force search and rescue teams evacuate soldiers and sailors, airmen, and marines injured in the war on terror.

Whether they are serving on the frontlines or bases overseas or here in the homefront, the men and women of the United States Air Force bring honor to the uniform, and they are bringing us victory in the war on terror.

And the stakes in this war could not be higher. Terrorists and extremists are fighting to overthrow moderate governments across the broader Middle East so they can take control of countries and use them as bases from which to attack America. If we do not defeat these enemies now, we will leave our children to face a Middle East overrun by terrorist states and radical dictators armed with nuclear weapons. We are in a war that will set the course for this new century and determine the destiny of millions across the world. Defeating the terrorists and extremists is the challenge of our time and the calling of this generation.

And like generations that came before, we will answer history's call with confidence. We will confront the threats to our way of life; we will fight for our liberty without wavering; and we will prevail.

Victory in this war depends on the one thing that has not changed since the founding of the Air Force six decades ago: the courage of the men and women who wear the Air Force blue. We see that courage in the men and women of the Air Force who return from battle with wounds they will carry with them for the rest of their lives. We see that courage in the airmen who left our shores to defend freedom and did not live to make the journey home. They gave their lives so that their fellow Americans could enjoy a bright horizon of freedom and peace. We mourn every loss. We pray for their families. And here at this memorial, we consecrate their memory for the ages.

This memorial lies in sight of Arlington National Cemetery, where so many of those fallen airmen are buried. This memorial also lies in sight of the Pentagon, where our Nation came under attack. It is a fitting location. Under these magnificent spires, we pay tribute to the men and women of the Air Force who stand ready to give all for their country. And looking from this promontory to a place once filled with smoke and flames, we remember why we need them.

Every man and woman who has worn the Air Force uniform is part of a great history. From the Berlin Airlift to the Korean war to Vietnam to the Gulf war to Kosovo and today's war on terror, a long blue line of heroes has defended freedom in the skies above. To all who have climbed sunward and chased the shouting wind, America stops to say: Your service and sacrifice will be remembered forever and honored in this place by the citizens of a free and grateful nation.

May God bless you all.

NOTE: The President spoke at 2:48 p.m. In his remarks, he referred to Secretary of Defense Donald H. Rumsfeld, who introduced the President; Chief Master Sergeant of the Air Force Rodney J. McKinley; and H. Ross Perot, Jr., chairman of the board, and Maj. Gen. Edward F. Grillo, Jr., USAF (Ret.), president, Air Force Memorial Foundation.

Remarks on the United Nations Security Council Resolution on North Korea
October 14, 2006

Today the United Nations Security Council passed a unanimous resolution, sending a clear message to the leader of North Korea regarding his weapons programs. This action by the United Nations, which was swift and tough, says that we are united in our determination to see to it that the Korean Peninsula is nuclear-weapons free.

I have said all along there is a better way forward for North Korea. There's a better way forward for the people of North Korea. If the leader of North Korea were to verifiably end his weapons programs, the United States and other nations would be willing to help the nation recover economically.

The message today, however, says to the leader of North Korea that the world is united in our opposition to his nuclear weapons plans.

Thank you.

NOTE: The President spoke at 3:30 p.m. on the South Grounds at the White House. In his remarks, he referred to Chairman Kim Jong Il of North Korea. He also referred to U.N. Security Council Resolution 1718.

Remarks at the Iftaar Dinner
October 16, 2006

Please be seated. Good evening, and *Ramadan Karim.* Welcome to the White House. Laura and I are really glad you're here. This is the sixth year that we have been pleased to host an Iftaar at the White House. We're honored to be with you, and once again, we're honored to pay tribute to the month of Ramadan.

Islam is a religion that brings hope and comfort to more than a billion people around the world. It has transcended racial and ethnic divisions. It has given birth to a rich culture of learning and literature and science. And tonight we honor the traditions of a great faith by hosting the Iftaar here at the White House.

I'm so pleased our Secretary of State, Condi Rice, has joined us. Thank you, Madam Secretary. I'm pleased that Dr. Elias Zerhouni, who is the Director of the NIH, is with us. Good to see you, Elias. I thank Imam Eid from the Islamic Institute of Boston, who's with us. I welcome all the ambassadors and other members of the diplomatic corps.

Ramadan is the holiest month in the Muslim calendar. For Muslims in America and around the world, Ramadan is a special time of prayer and fasting, contemplation of God's greatness, and charity and service to those in need. And for people of all faiths, it is a good time to reflect on the values we hold in common, including love of family, gratitude to God, the importance of community, and a commitment to tolerance and religious freedom.

America is a land of many faiths, and we welcome and honor the Muslim faith in our Nation. Our society is enriched by our Muslim citizens. Your commitment to your faith reminds us all of the precious gift of religious freedom in our country. America is a more hopeful nation because of the talents and generosity and compassion of our Muslim citizens.

Tonight we have with us a group of special guests, American Muslims who are serving our country. We have with us New York City police officers and a EMT worker who risked their lives to save their fellow citizens on 9/11, a military doctor, and a member of the Navy's Chaplain Corps, members of our Foreign Service, and military veterans who have served in Afghanistan and Iraq to protect our country and help those nations build free and democratic futures.

One of our guests is Farooq Muhammad. Farooq is the son of Pakistani immigrants and was born and raised in Brooklyn. He spent the past decade with the New York City Fire Department, first as an emergency medical technician and now as a paramedic. Farooq was at the World Trade

Center on 9/11, treating victims when the towers collapsed; he narrowly escaped death himself. He also recently volunteered in the mountains of Kashmir, where he helped treat the victims of last year's devastating South Asian earthquake. Farooq's courage and compassion represent the best of the American spirit.

Paramedic Muhammad is a proud Muslim; he is a patriotic American. And those are characteristics he shares with the other special American guests gathered in this room. All of you bring credit to your faith. You make America a better and stronger country, and we're honored by your presence tonight.

The United States also appreciates the many Muslim nations who stand with us in the war on terror, some of whom are represented here tonight. You know that the majority of the victims of the terrorists have been innocent Muslims, and many of you have seen terrorist violence in your own cities and your streets. We welcome you here. We are proud to work with you to defeat the terrorists and extremists and help bring a brighter future to millions of Muslim people throughout the world who yearn for moderation and peace.

On this special evening, we celebrate the millions of Muslims that we are proud to call American citizens. We honor the many Islamic nations that America is proud to call friends. And we renew the ties of friendship that should bind all who trace their faith back to God's call on Abraham.

Laura and I are grateful that you're here. Once again, I wish you a blessed Ramadan. And now Imam Eid will say the blessing.

NOTE: The President spoke at 6:52 p.m. in the State Dining Room at the White House. In his remarks, he referred to Imam Talal Y. Eid, founder and director of religious affairs, Islamic Institute of Boston.

Remarks on Signing the Military Commissions Act of 2006
October 17, 2006

Please be seated. Welcome to the White House on an historic day. It is a rare occasion when a President can sign a bill he knows will save American lives; I have that privilege this morning.

The Military Commissions Act of 2006 is one of the most important pieces of legislation in the war on terror. This bill will allow the Central Intelligence Agency to continue its program for questioning key terrorist leaders and operatives like Khalid Sheikh Mohammed, the man believed to be the mastermind of the September the 11th, 2001, attacks on our country. This program has been one of the most successful intelligence efforts in American history. It has helped prevent attacks on our country. And the bill I sign today will ensure that we can continue using this vital tool to protect the American people for years to come. The Military Commissions Act will also allow us to prosecute captured terrorists for war crimes through a full and fair trial.

Last month, on the fifth anniversary of 9/11, I stood with Americans who lost family members in New York and Washington and Pennsylvania. I listened to their stories of loved ones they still miss. I told them America would never forget their loss. Today I can tell them something else: With the bill I'm about to sign, the men our intelligence officials believe orchestrated the murder of nearly 3,000 innocent people will face justice.

I want to thank the Vice President for joining me today. Mr. Vice President, appreciate you. Secretary Don Rumsfeld, I

appreciate your service to our country. I want to thank Attorney General Al Gonzales; General Mike Hayden, Director of the Central Intelligence Agency; General Pete Pace, Chairman of the Joint Chiefs of Staff.

I appreciate very much Senator John Warner, chairman of the Senate Armed Services Committee, and Congressman Duncan Hunter, chairman of the House Armed Services Committee, for joining us today. I want to thank both of these men for their leadership. I appreciate Senator Lindsey Graham from South Carolina joining us. Congressman Jim Sensenbrenner, chairman of the House Judiciary Committee; Congressman Steve Buyer of Indiana; Congressman Chris Cannon of Utah—thank you all for coming.

The bill I sign today helps secure this country, and it sends a clear message: This Nation is patient and decent and fair, and we will never back down from the threats to our freedom.

One of the terrorists believed to have planned the 9/11 attacks said he hoped the attacks would be the beginning of the end of America. He didn't get his wish. We are as determined today as we were on the morning of September the 12th, 2001. We'll meet our obligation to protect our people, and no matter how long it takes, justice will be done.

When I proposed this legislation, I explained that I would have one test for the bill Congress produced: Will it allow the CIA program to continue? This bill meets that test. It allows for the clarity our intelligence professionals need to continue questioning terrorists and saving lives. This bill provides legal protections that ensure our military and intelligence personnel will not have to fear lawsuits filed by terrorists simply for doing their jobs.

This bill spells out specific, recognizable offenses that would be considered crimes in the handling of detainees so that our men and women who question captured terrorists can perform their duties to the fullest extent of the law. And this bill complies with both the spirit and the letter of our international obligations. As I've said before, the United States does not torture. It's against our laws, and it's against our values.

By allowing the CIA program to go forward, this bill is preserving a tool that has saved American lives. The CIA program helped us gain vital intelligence from Khalid Sheikh Mohammed and Ramzi bin al-Shibh, two of the men believed to have helped plan and facilitate the 9/11 attacks. The CIA program helped break up a cell of 17 southeastern Asian terrorist operatives who were being groomed for attacks inside the United States. The CIA program helped us uncover key operatives in Al Qaida's biological weapons program, including a cell developing anthrax to be used in terrorist attacks.

The CIA program helped us identify terrorists who were sent to case targets inside the United States, including financial buildings in major cities on the east coast. And the CIA program helped us stop the planned strike on U.S. marines in Djibouti, a planned attack on the U.S. consulate in Karachi, and a plot to hijack airplanes and fly them into Heathrow Airport and Canary Wharf in London.

Altogether, information from terrorists in CIA custody has played a role in the capture or questioning of nearly every senior Al Qaida member or associate detained by the United States and its allies since this program began. Put simply, this program has been one of the most vital tools in our war against the terrorists. It's been invaluable both to America and our allies. Were it not for this program, our intelligence community believes that Al Qaida and its allies would have succeeded in launching another attack against the American homeland. By allowing our intelligence professionals to continue this vital program, this bill will save American lives. And I look forward to signing it into law.

The bill I'm about to sign also provides a way to deliver justice to the terrorists we have captured. In the months after 9/11, I authorized a system of military commissions to try foreign terrorists accused of war crimes. These commissions were similar to those used for trying enemy combatants in the Revolutionary War and the Civil War and World War II. Yet the legality of the system I established was challenged in the court, and the Supreme Court ruled that the military commissions needed to be explicitly authorized by the United States Congress.

And so I asked Congress for that authority, and they have provided it. With the Military Commission Act, the legislative and executive branches have agreed on a system that meets our national security needs. These military commissions will provide a fair trial, in which the accused are presumed innocent, have access to an attorney, and can hear all the evidence against them. These military commissions are lawful, they are fair, and they are necessary.

When I sign this bill into law, we will use these commissions to bring justice to the men believed to have planned the attacks of September the 11th, 2001. We'll also seek to prosecute those believed responsible for the attack on the USS *Cole*, which killed 17 American sailors 6 years ago last week. We will seek to prosecute an operative believed to have been involved in the bombings of the American Embassies in Kenya and Tanzania, which killed more than 200 innocent people and wounded 5,000 more. With our actions, we will send a clear message to those who kill Americans: We will find you, and we will bring you to justice.

Over the past few months, the debate over this bill has been heated, and the questions raised can seem complex. Yet, with the distance of history, the questions will be narrowed and few: Did this generation of Americans take the threat seriously, and did we do what it takes to defeat that threat? Every Member of Congress who voted for this bill has helped our Nation rise to the task that history has given us. Some voted to support this bill even when the majority of their party voted the other way. I thank the legislators who brought this bill to my desk for their conviction, for their vision, and for their resolve.

There is nothing we can do to bring back the men and women lost on September the 11th, 2001. Yet we'll always honor their memory, and we will never forget the way they were taken from us. This Nation will call evil by its name. We will answer brutal murder with patient justice. Those who kill the innocent will be held to account.

With this bill, America reaffirms our determination to win the war on terror. The passage of time will not dull our memory or sap our nerve. We will fight this war with confidence and with clear purpose. We will protect our country and our people. We will work with our friends and allies across the world to defend our way of life. We will leave behind a freer, safer, and more peaceful world for those who follow us.

And now, in memory of the victims of September the 11th, it is my honor to sign the Military Commissions Act of 2006 into law.

NOTE: The President spoke at 9:35 a.m. in the East Room at the White House. S. 3930, approved October 17, was assigned Public Law No. 109–366. The Office of the Press Secretary also released a Spanish language transcript of these remarks.

Remarks at a Swearing-In Ceremony for Mary E. Peters as Secretary of Transportation
October 17, 2006

Thank you very much. Good afternoon. We are here to congratulate Mary Peters on becoming our Nation's 15th Secretary of Transportation.

Mary is a dedicated public servant, an experienced leader, and one of our Nation's most innovative thinker on transportation issues. Mary brings more than two decades of knowledge and skill to her new post. She also brings to her position the love and support of her friends and her family. I want to thank her family for being here, especially Mary's husband, Terry.

I appreciate my Chief of Staff, Josh Bolten, who is here to administer the oath. Presidents can't administer the oath— [*laughter*]—so I tapped my man, Josh. [*Laughter*]

I want to thank Maria Cino, who is the Deputy Secretary, Acting Secretary. I thank you for your service and your friendship.

I appreciate my friend Secretary Norm Mineta. I got some other stuff to say about you here in a minute. [*Laughter*] I do want to thank Rodney Slater for joining us, former Secretary of Transportation, as well as Jim Burnley. Thank you both for coming. I'm proud you're here, and I know Secretary Peters appreciates it as well.

The job of Secretary of Transportation is one of the most important in our Federal Government. The American people rely on the Department of Transportation to maintain a safe, reliable, and efficient transportation system. And the future of our growing economy and changing infrastructure depend on the decisions made by the Secretary that will be put into action by this Department.

The Secretary of Transportation also plays an important role in our Nation's coordinated efforts to guard against terrorist threats to our aircraft, seaports, and infrastructure. For the past 6 years, these responsibilities have been carried out by Norm Mineta, who served our country with distinction, integrity, and dedication. Norm is our Nation's longest serving Secretary of Transportation, and he served at a time of great consequence for our country.

I remember after the attacks of September the 11th, when Norm led the successful effort to bring tens of thousands of passengers aboard commercial aircraft to safe landings. He grounded quite a few planes, including the ones my mom and dad were on. They've always thanked you for that, Norm. [*Laughter*]

After Hurricane Katrina, Norm and his team helped quickly repair and reopen the major—area's major highways, airports, seaports, and pipelines. He offered incentive-based contracts and used other innovative ideas, and as a result, the Department of Transportation was to get critical infrastructure in place faster than usual. I want to thank you for your leadership, Norm, and I want to thank you for your lifetime of service to our country, and I wish you all the very best. And I want to remind you, Maria made you look pretty good while you were in office. [*Laughter*]

Mary Peters is the right person to succeed Norm as the Secretary of Transportation. She worked for several years with Secretary Mineta, and she understands the fine legacy she has to live up to. She also knows firsthand the skills and dedication of the men and women who work here at the Department of Transportation. She's going to be a fine boss. She understands that to maintain our Nation's competitiveness and to sustain our growing economy, we need a Secretary who can see the challenges and be willing to confront them.

Mary Peters will provide strong leadership. She has spent a lifetime working on transportation issues in both the private and

public sectors. Most recently, she has served as senior executive for transportation policy at a major engineering firm. For 4 years before that, she led the Federal Highway Administration. Before coming to Washington, she served in the Arizona Department of Transportation. For more than 15 years, she rose through the ranks to become director in 1998.

At both the State and Federal level, Mary Peters has worked to improve safety and security on roads and bridges. She's worked to reduce traffic congestion and modernize America's transportation infrastructure. As Secretary of Transportation, Mary will work closely with Federal, State, and local leaders to ensure that America has a state-of-the-art transportation system so that we can meet the needs of our growing economy.

In her new position, she will face important challenges. Next year, she will lead the Department's efforts to reauthorize our Nation's aviation programs. Our Nation is outgrowing our aviation capacity. More people are flying every year, and so we must modernize our airports and our air traffic control.

We also face the challenges of reducing congestion in our surface and maritime transportation systems. To accomplish these tasks, America needs creative thinking and innovative solutions, and I believe Mary Peters will provide them.

As Mary works to build a better transportation system, she will be a careful steward of the people's money. She brings to her new position a reputation for fiscal discipline and integrity. As head of the Federal Highway Administration, Mary introduced better fiscal oversight and accountability. She improved management for the largest transportation projects. She worked closely with her department's inspector general to eliminate waste, fraud, and abuse. She's going to carry this kind of diligence into her new job.

She understands the importance of a modern infrastructure and good management. And I'm pleased she has agreed to serve her country once again. As she takes on this important position, she has my full trust and my confidence. Mary, I look forward to working with you as the new Secretary of Transportation. Congratulations.

It's now my honor to witness the swearing-in of Mary Peters.

NOTE: The President spoke at 1:16 p.m. at the Department of Transportation. In his remarks, he referred to Terryl Peters, Sr., husband of Secretary of Transportation Peters; and former Secretary of Transportation James H. Burnley IV. The transcript released by the Office of the Press Secretary also included the remarks of Secretary Peters.

Remarks Following Discussions With Prime Minister Ivo Sanader of Croatia
October 17, 2006

President Bush. It's been my honor to welcome the Prime Minister of Croatia here. Mr. Prime Minister, welcome.

Prime Minister Sanader. Thank you very much.

President Bush. We just had a very lengthy and interesting discussion, which is

what you would expect friends to do. I consider the Prime Minister a friend; I consider Croatia a friend as well.

We talked about foreign policy issues, issues of peace. I thank the people of Croatia for their support in Afghanistan of the young democracy. I also believe it's in the

world's interest that Croatia join NATO as well as the European Union. And to that end, when I go to Riga, I will make the case that Croatia should be admitted. It seems like a reasonable date would be 2008.

We talked about bilateral relations. We talked about investments, investment opportunities in Croatia. We talked about the need to enhance trade and commerce. The Prime Minister has invited me to come. I've heard unbelievably great things about your country, Mr. Prime Minister. I hear it's one of the most beautiful places on the face of the Earth. I'd love to come sometime. I've got to clear it first with my wife. [*Laughter*]

But nevertheless, all in all, it's been a very good meeting. And I welcome you here, and thank you for coming.

Prime Minister Sanader. Thank you, Mr. President. I've been touched by the warmth of this reception during this visit and of the interest and understanding you have shown in Croatia and the challenges facing Europe today.

About the only question we disagreed was whether Croatia or the United States had the most beautiful coastline.

President Bush. That's right. [*Laughter*]

Prime Minister Sanader. I will let you and Mrs. Bush judge for yourselves when you visit Croatia, where you certainly will be most welcome, Mr. President.

The President and I, we discussed a range of issues of bilateral concerns, especially of the preparations of my country to join EU and NATO. And I expressed my gratitude to the President for his constant support for Croatia on its way.

I also—we discussed a range of issues of—regarding our region of southeastern Europe: final status of Kosovo; Georgia; Ukraine; Moldova. We are very active. Croatia is not forgetting that we are in the region where we still need a strong U.S. and European cooperation. We believe strongly in transatlantic partnership. There is no alternative to this. I think that President Bush and the United States of America, along with the EU, have still to be very, very closely cooperating in a couple of issues in Europe.

So thank you very much, Mr. President, for warm reception and very fruitful discussion.

President Bush. Thank you, sir. I appreciate it. Good job. Thank you.

NOTE: The President spoke at 3:16 p.m. in the Oval Office at the White House.

Statement on Signing the Northern California Coastal Wild Heritage Wilderness Act
October 17, 2006

Today, I have signed into law H.R. 233, the "Northern California Coastal Wild Heritage Wilderness Act." The Act strengthens protection of certain lands in California.

Section 4(i)(2) of the Act purports to give binding legal effect to guidelines in an appendix to a report issued by a congressional committee, which was not incorporated into the Act and for which presentment was not made. Consistent with the bicameral approval and presentment requirements of the Constitution for the making of a law, the executive branch shall, in carrying out the Act, take appropriate account of the guidelines as a matter of comity between the executive and legislative branches.

GEORGE W. BUSH

The White House,
October 17, 2006.

NOTE: H.R. 233, approved October 17, was assigned Public Law No. 109–362.

Statement on Signing the John Warner National Defense Authorization Act for Fiscal Year 2007
October 17, 2006

Today, I have signed into law H.R. 5122, the "John Warner National Defense Authorization Act for Fiscal Year 2007" (the "Act"). The Act authorizes funding for the defense of the United States and its interests abroad, for military construction, for national security-related energy programs, and for maritime security-related transportation programs.

Several provisions of the Act call for executive branch officials to submit to the Congress recommendations for legislation, or purport to regulate the manner in which the President formulates recommendations to the Congress for legislation. These provisions include sections 516(h), 575(g), 603(b), 705(d), 719(b), 721(e), 741(e), 813, 1008, 1016(d), 1035(b)(3), 1047(b), and 1102 of the Act, section 118(b)(4) of title 10, United States Code, as amended by section 1031 of the Act, section 2773b of title 10 as amended by section 1053 of the Act, and section 403 of the Ronald W. Reagan National Defense Authorization Act for Fiscal Year 2005 (Public Law 108–375) as amended by section 403 of the Act. The executive branch shall construe these provisions in a manner consistent with the President's constitutional authority to supervise the unitary executive branch and to recommend for the consideration of the Congress such measures as the President deems necessary and expedient.

The executive branch shall construe sections 914 and 1512 of the Act, which purport to make consultation with specified Members of Congress a precondition to the execution of the law, as calling for but not mandating such consultation, as is consistent with the Constitution's provisions concerning the separate powers of the Congress to legislate and the President to execute the laws.

A number of provisions in the Act call for the executive branch to furnish information to the Congress or other entities on various subjects. These provisions include sections 219, 313, 360, 1211, 1212, 1213, 1227, 1402, and 3116 of the Act, section 427 of title 10, United States Code, as amended by section 932 of the Act, and section 1093 of the Ronald W. Reagan National Defense Authorization Act for Fiscal Year 2005 (Public Law 108–375) as amended by section 1061 of the Act. The executive branch shall construe such provisions in a manner consistent with the President's constitutional authority to withhold information the disclosure of which could impair foreign relations, the national security, the deliberative processes of the Executive, or the performance of the Executive's constitutional duties.

The executive branch shall construe as advisory section 1011(b)(2) of the Act, which purports to prohibit the Secretary of the Navy from retiring a specified warship from operational status unless, among other things, a treaty organization established by the U.S. and foreign nations gives formal notice that it does not desire to maintain and operate that warship. If construed as mandatory rather than advisory, the provision would impermissibly interfere with the President's constitutional authority to conduct the Nation's foreign affairs and as Commander in Chief.

The executive branch shall construe section 1211, which purports to require the executive branch to undertake certain consultations with foreign governments and follow certain steps in formulating and executing U.S. foreign policy, in a manner consistent with the President's constitutional authorities to conduct the Nation's foreign affairs and to supervise the unitary executive branch.

As is consistent with the principle of statutory construction of giving effect to each of two statutes addressing the same subject whenever they can co-exist, the executive branch shall construe section 130d of title 10, as amended by section 1405 of the Act, which provides further protection against disclosure of certain homeland security information in certain circumstances, as in addition to, and not in derogation of, the broader protection against disclosure of information afforded by section 892 of the Homeland Security Act of 2002 and other law protecting broadly against disclosure of such information.

GEORGE W. BUSH

The White House,
October 17, 2006.

NOTE: H.R. 5122, approved October 17, was assigned Public Law No. 109–364.

Statement on the Population of the United States Reaching 300 Million
October 17, 2006

For more than two centuries, America has been a beacon of hope and opportunity for people around the world, millions of whom came here to live in freedom and make better lives for themselves and their families. Today we celebrate a significant milestone: The population of the United States has now reached 300 million. Our continued growth is a testament to our country's dynamism and a reminder that America's greatest asset is our people.

America is built on a shared love of freedom and a belief in the dignity and match-less value of every human being. Our confidence in our people has carried us to ever greater achievements in all areas of human endeavor and allowed us to remain the world's most vibrant and innovative country. And so long as we insist on high standards in education, place our trust in the talents and ingenuity of ordinary Americans, and protect our freedoms, we will remain the land of opportunity for generations to come. We welcome this milestone as further proof that the American Dream remains as bright and hopeful as ever.

Remarks at Waldo C. Falkener Elementary School in Greensboro, North Carolina
October 18, 2006

Thank you very much, Madam Secretary. I've known Margaret, as she said, a long time, and I'm very proud of the job she's doing. She knows what she's talking about when it comes to the schools in America, and she and I are going to work to make sure that every child gets an excellent education.

I want to thank the good folks here at Falkener for inviting the President to come.

As you can tell, it's not an easy thing— [*laughter*]—to host the President. It's like, the entourage is pretty big, a lot of security. And so for the school folks here, thank you very much for accommodating us. I've come because I appreciate the example you set.

One of the things I like to do is to herald excellence. So the first thing I want to say is, congratulations to the principal and the teachers and the parents for working hard to make this a fantastically interesting place for our children to go to school.

I want to thank—you know, they say to me, "What do you want from the schools?" I don't know if you recognize this, but we just had six Nobel Prize winners recently announced—America had six Nobel—all of whom went to public schools in America. And my hope as I travel through the halls of these schools—like this one—I'm meeting Nobel Prize winners of the future. It's a noble aspiration for all of us to aim for. And so I want to thank you for letting me come.

I'm going to talk about No Child Left Behind. I think you're about to find out I am a passionate advocate of this important law, because I know it can save children's lives and I know it can help us meet a national objective, and that is, every child getting a good education in every school throughout the country.

I bring greetings from Laura. Most people say, "I wish Laura had come and the old boy stayed home." [*Laughter*] She's actually in El Paso, Texas, today—I think she's in El Paso, Texas, today—I'm confident—I think that's what she told me— where a new school out there is opening up the Laura Bush Library. And well deserved, I want you to know, because she has a great passion for making sure that every child can read. So I bring, as best I can, her passion here to this important school.

I'm proud to be here with Senator Richard Burr from the great State of North Carolina. Thank you for working on us— with—on educational excellence. I appreciate Virginia Foxx, the Congresswoman, who joined us as well. Amy Holcombe is the principal.

You might remember, I was a Governor of a State. And I used to say, education is to a State what national defense is to the Federal Government. And so I took my role as Governor and being involved in public school—just like Guy Hunt did— we overlapped as Governors, and we prioritized public education. And so I spent a lot of time with schools in Texas, and I learned one thing, that these little centers of excellence always depended upon having an aggressive principal, a principal who is willing to set high standards and not allow for mediocrity to set in. So, Amy, I want to thank you for your leadership and thank you for your hospitality.

I met Josette Hamrick, who is the teacher of the year. I congratulate you, Josette, for setting a good example. I think Josette is here somewhere—there she is. Thanks for being here. I also have recently gone to Mary Helen Parson's third grade school—third grade class. And Tom "Ned"—Tom Niedziela—he is a—both of whom are dedicated teachers. And so I want to say something about teaching. It is a noble profession. It is a necessary profession for this country. And for those of you who are teachers, I congratulate you and thank you for serving our country.

I oftentimes say to people that are asking me about—do you have any recommendations for what I should be doing, and my answer is, teach. And to parents I say, remember, you're the child's first teacher. As a matter of fact, schools succeed when a parent understands that teaching begins at home, and it makes the job of the classroom teacher so much easier. But I want to thank the teachers who are here, and thank you for setting a good example.

I want to thank the school board members who are here. I told the head of the school board and the other man on the school board, I said, "It's a pretty tough

job to be on the school board." [*Laughter*] One fellow said, "Do you want to switch jobs?" I said, "You know, I don't think so." [*Laughter*] But thank you all for serving. Local control of schools is important in order to achieve educational excellence, and I'm going to talk a little about that in a minute.

I also landed today and met a lady named Michelle Gilmore. Michelle is—there you are. Thanks for coming. Michelle and her husband, Tiran, are here. Michelle volunteers as a mentor. If you are concerned about the future of North Carolina or concerned about the future of our country and you want to make a difference, become a mentor. It's amazing what happens when an adult takes time out of her life, in this case, to say to a child, "I care about you, and I want to help." The true strength of the United States of America lies in the hearts and souls of our citizens. And the amazing thing about our country is that there are millions of acts of kindness that take place on a daily basis, and it hasn't required one government law.

And the reason I mention Michelle and the reason I welcomed her to Air Force One is because I want to, one, thank you as an individual, and remind people that you can serve America by loving a neighbor just like you'd like to be loved yourself. And I appreciate you being here, Michelle. Thanks for coming.

I like the fact that this—we're at a school named for a civil rights pioneer. I happen to believe reading is a modern-day civil right, that if you cannot read, you cannot realize the great promise of the United States of America. That's what I believe. And so I've come to this school because I believe schools should set high standards and insist upon results, like teaching a child to read. I don't think it's too much to ask in schools around the United States of America. I know what happens when a child can't read at grade level. I know the despondency that can be caused if a child is just simply shuffled through a school.

Falkener is a magnet school. In other words, it's a school that—I equate that with educational entrepreneurship. It means people are willing to try things differently. This school is one that, interestingly enough, has got a international baccalaureate program inherent in its curriculum. And that's important because international baccalaureate programs are programs that set high standards for children in later years. So in other words, it's kind of a pre-international baccalaureate experience, all aimed at making sure that a child who goes from here has a chance to even have a greater skill level than anticipated. So it's interesting to be in a school that's a magnet school, that has got a pre-international baccalaureate program.

We support magnet schools at the Federal level. First, let me just tell you my theory. Most education needs to be funded at the State and local level. I believe that is the proper role between the Federal Government and the State government. And yet there are incentive programs that come out of Washington; Title I money, for example, is an incentive program. We also have put money in our budget for magnet schools. As a matter of fact, the budget next year I've asked for has got about $100 million for magnet schools. I think magnet schools are interesting concepts to—that the local folks ought to decide to use. And so there's a little incentive from the Federal Government to encourage you.

I'm a—also understand, and I hope you do—I know those of you involved with public schools understand that we're now living in a global economy. North Carolina understands that about as much as any State. What happens abroad affects the lives of our students in the near future. If a child in China gets a good engineering degree and a child in America doesn't, it means China is likely to be more competitive in the 21st century. In other words, we've got to get education right not only

because it's a national responsibility but because we're in a global world. Whether we
like it or not, there is competition for jobs
of the future that are going to—that will
take place. And therefore, it's important
that we make sure that our children get
a solid foundation early in order—so that
our country can be competitive, as well as
our children.

Now, let me talk about No Child Left
Behind, because I'm really here to make
clear to people in Congress, not only who
are here but around the country, that the
reauthorization of this important bill is
going to be a top priority of mine. And
it's not only just the reauthorization, it's
the strengthening of the bill, and not the
weakening of the bill.

There's been a lot of talk about No Child
Left Behind Act. First, you've got to understand, it was a bipartisan effort. I readily
concede that's a rare occurrence in Washington, DC, but nevertheless, Republicans
and Democrats came together to get this
important piece of legislation passed.

It said, "We'll spend more money at the
Federal level, but in return, we expect results." It seems like a simple concept, but
nevertheless, it was not inherent in the
education programs out of the Federal
Government. We just never really asked;
we just assumed everything was fine. As
a matter of fact, in many schools around
the country, that's the way it was. If people
said it was fine, it was fine.

You know, I remember, one time, going
to a school in Houston, Texas, and I said
to the teacher, "How's everything? Thanks
for teaching." She said, "My kids can't
read." I think it was ninth or tenth grade.
It was a shock to the Governor. It should
be a shock to everybody when you hear
a teacher say, my kids can't read by the
time they get to high school. Something
was wrong.

The point was made to me—and this
is when Margaret and I started working
on this concept of measurement—that if
you don't measure, you don't know. And

the only way to prevent kids from just getting shuffled through schools—until the
point where the high school teacher says
they can't read—is to measure early. And
so part of the No Child Left Behind Act
says, "We expect results, and you measure."

I believe in local control of schools. I
do not believe the Federal Government
should be telling the people in North Carolina how to run their schools. I think that
would be a mistake if that were the case.
I don't think the Federal Government
ought to design the test; the people of
North Carolina should design the accountability tests. I do think the Federal Government ought to ask, "Can a child read?"

Look, I understand kids—I understand
the debate; you know, "They're teaching
the test." No, you're teaching a child to
read so they can pass a comprehensive test.
And if they can't pass a comprehensive test,
something is fundamentally wrong. You
know, "All we do is test." No, what you
do is you teach so that the accountability
system—when you do test, a child is proficient. You know, if you don't test, you
don't know. And if you don't know, you
can't correct. Active schools, schools that
are meeting excellence are those that find
problems early and solve the problems
early, before it's too late. That's why I'm
at this school. This school sets high standards.

And by the way, if you set low standards,
guess what happens in schools? You get
bad results. If you walk into a classroom
full of the hard to educate and not have
high standards, the hard to educate remains
hard to educate. So the law says: Set high
standards; use curriculum that works; you
can determine what works by measuring
whether or not students are meeting certain
standards; and correct problems early, before it's too late. That's what No Child Left
Behind is all about.

And it's working. It's working. You know,
the first year this school was tested under
No Child Left Behind, it didn't meet standards; like, it just wasn't good enough. This

school decided to do something about it. See, they recognized they had a problem, and so they used Federal funding to pay for new laboratories, teacher collaboration, research on what was going right and what was going wrong. There's a new focus on results; there was frequent testing; they set up a Saturday Academy for children with low test scores that needed extra help. And the results have been impressive. Four years ago, about 46 percent of third graders at this school were reading at grade level. That's okay if you're a parent of one of the 46 percent. It's not okay if you're a parent of one of the 54 percent. And the principal and the teachers understood there was a problem, and they took steps to change the status quo. And today, 76 percent are reading at grade level.

That's what No Child Left Behind does. It can't do the teaching; it can't be the leader; but it can help people who care deeply about the lives of a child—the life of a child to succeed, to recognize problems, address the problem, correct the problem, and teach a child to read. And that's what's—that's why I'm at Falkener. This is a school that has gone from mediocre to excellent, because they've used the tools of the No Child Left Behind Act.

In the fifth grade, about 68 percent of the students were reading at grade level 4 years ago; today, 88 percent of the students are reading at grade level. I cannot thank you enough for taking advantage of a law that really was living up to its name—no child being left behind. Here's what your principal said: She said, "Falkener has greatly benefited from this legislation. Our test scores tell our story of success."

I met Tom Ned—you call him "Ned," right?—Niedziela. He focused on reading comprehension and vocabulary, and his class made the largest reading gains in the fourth grade. One girl whose first language is Spanish—see, if the child's first language is Spanish, that child generally is what we call hard to educate. And sometimes that label becomes a self-fulfilling prophesy.

Inner-city kids tend to be labeled hard to educate, so all that mattered in the past was, if you're 10, you're supposed to be here, and if you're 11, you're supposed to be there. It's unacceptable for this country, by the way. That type of attitude is unacceptable.

This child started the year reading at the second grade level. Thanks to Mr. Ned, she now reads at the sixth grade level. I met her. There's nothing more than helping a child's self-esteem than to—teaching a child to read, just giving that child the basic skills necessary to succeed in a hopeful society.

Here's what Mr. Ned said: He said, "I told them, if you want to be good at something, you've got to practice. If you want to play football, you have to go to football practice. If you want to be good at reading, you have to practice reading." And he said, "I've never had a class work so hard." I want to thank Mr. Ned; I want to thank the students. There's nothing more heartwarming than to know that standards are being met.

We see the results in No Child Left Behind across the State of North Carolina. I don't know if you know this or not, but your State has been an innovative State. Your State has been one that has not shied away from accountability. In other words, you didn't use excuses about testing. You said, "Look, we want to test because we want to know." Your State was the first in the Nation to establish an accountability system and one of the first to have the testing plans approved under No Child Left Behind. In other words, your State led. And I congratulate the State leaders and those involved with education for being bold on behalf of the children of your State.

Your test scores are encouraging. The percentage of fourth graders with basic math skills rose 10 points between 2000 and 2005. The percentage of eighth graders with basic math skills rose about six points between 2000 and 2005. African American

fourth and eighth graders in North Carolina achieved some of the highest math scores in the Nation. How do we know? Because we measure.

It's got to make you feel good to hear African American kids are scoring some of the highest tests in the Nation. Can you imagine if the President came and said, "By the way, your kids are scoring the lowest scores in the Nation"? I suspect you'd want to be doing something about that. At least I would hope you would.

There are good results of No Child Left Behind across the Nation. In other words, we're measuring—each State measures, and you're able to norm to determine how States do relative to each other. In reading, 9-year-olds have made the largest gains in the past 5 years than at any point in the previous 28 years. That's good. In math, 9-year-olds and 13-year-olds earned the highest scores in the history of the test.

We have an achievement gap in America that is—that I don't like and you shouldn't like. It's the difference between reading of African American students and Latino students and White students. The gap is closing, and that's incredibly important for the United States of America, to see that achievement gap close. How do we know? Because we're measuring.

Inherent in No Child Left Behind are some interesting reforms. First, if we find a child falling behind early, there is extra Federal money to help that child. Think about that. For the first time, the Federal Government has said, "Not only do we want you to measure, but when we find a child falling behind, there is extra money to be used in either the private or public sector."

See, measuring encourages parental involvement. If you measure and a parent finds out that his or her child is not succeeding, most parents are going to say, "Do something about it." And what the Federal Government has said, "Here's some extra money to help you, to get tutoring, to get you back up to grade level."

If a school continues to fail—in other words, a school doesn't make progress—I believe parents ought to be liberated from that school district if they so choose and go to another public school. In other words, there has to be a consequence at some point in time for a school that won't—is not teaching and won't change, if you expect there to be concrete results.

This school started off with low scores, set high standards, and has achieved the objective. I suspect not many parents, even if they could, would want to leave, because you're meeting—you're doing the job. There are schools around the country that are not doing the job, and that is unacceptable to society. It ought to be unacceptable to school boards and parents and teachers.

In DC, we started something interesting. We said that if the school fails, continue to—if there's persistent failure, that a child ought to be able to go to not only a public school but a private school. We provide what are called opportunity scholarships. We work with the mayor to enhance—it's an interesting opportunity—said, if you fail, and the school won't change, then the DC came up with a scholarship that said this scholarship could be redeemed at a public school or a Catholic school, for example.

There is a debate going on about whether we ought to reauthorize the No Child Left Behind Act. I think you can get a sense for where I'm coming from. Not only do I think we ought to reauthorize it, I think we ought to strengthen it. I think it would be a huge mistake for the United States Congress not to reauthorize this important piece of legislation. And the reason I say that is that it's working. In other words, there's just more than words there; we have achieved concrete results.

I'm not suggesting the law shouldn't be improved; it should be improved. For example, we ought to make sure that scores are tested early, particularly for big districts, so that people understand what the results are. Oftentimes in—I don't know how many big districts, Margaret—but I've

heard complaints from school districts where the test scores get posted for the parents after the school year begins, which is like—it doesn't work. So the bureaucracy, frankly, has got to be a little more facile in getting the results out, and Margaret understands that.

I think we ought to continue doing what we call the Teacher Incentive Fund. This is a further reform. It allows States and school districts to reward teachers who demonstrate results for their students. If this school board decides they want to provide incentives for teachers based upon results, the Federal Government will provide money to help you do that. I like the idea. You may not like it, and that's fine. You got elected a school board member; I didn't. But nevertheless, I do believe we ought to make sure that school boards and school districts have the option.

I also think there ought to be incentives for teachers who make the decision to teach in some of the needier school districts, tougher schools—to provide an incentive. We have got a program I'm going to work with Congress on to encourage math and science professionals to come into classrooms. And the reason why is, in order for us to be competitive in the future, our students have got to be proficient in math and the sciences, and we have to have more emphasis on math and science. And there's no better way to encourage a child to take math and science than to have a professional come in the class. We call them adjunct professors.

Margaret and I, one time, went over to a school in Maryland, and there were some people from NASA there, two science guys from NASA that could talk the language of science. And their message was, it's cool to be a scientist. Some pretty cool guys that were there, but they were saying to eighth grade kids, "Science is interesting for you." Sometimes it takes somebody in the field to be able to lend practical knowledge to convince children to continue to focus on science and math and engineering.

I talked to you about how to make sure parents get better information. I do believe we ought to fund a national opportunity scholarship program to make sure parents have choices—particularly poor parents have choices beyond just public school choice.

I'm worried about high school, and I think the new law ought to focus a lot on high school. Four out of every—one out of every four ninth graders in America does not graduate from high school on time. That's a problem. If we live in a global world that's highly competitive, our kids have got to get out of high school, and they got to head to community college or college, if we're going to be competitive. And so we need to bring the same standards to our high schools that we have brought thus far to elementary and junior high schools.

We need to test. If it's okay to test in the third grade, it ought to be okay to test in high school to determine whether or not curricula works, whether or not teaching methodology is working, and whether or not our children are learning.

Again, I told you about the international baccalaureate program. It feeds into another way for us to enhance the competitiveness of this country, and that is to encourage AP programs—Advanced Placement programs—throughout classrooms all across America. One of the bottlenecks is—a bottleneck is the number of teachers that are capable of teaching AP. I think it's a good use of your taxpayers' money to train teachers in Advanced Placement; 70,000 teachers—is our initial goal to train in Advanced Placement, so that teachers have the skills necessary to teach AP. But it works.

It's amazing what happens when you set high standards and give people the tools necessary to effect those standards. And so these are ideas and ways to strengthen No Child Left Behind. We'll continue to listen to good ideas. We, of course, will listen to Members of Congress from both parties.

This is a State that had a good idea. They were deeply concerned about how to make sure that the accountability system would measure progress without—in an accurate way. And so Margaret worked with the State leaders, worked with the Senator to provide flexibility for the accountability system, without undermining the whole concept of measurement. And so in other words, we'll be rational and reasonable, but what we will not do is allow schools to lower standards. And what we will not do is allow people to get rid of accountability systems, because I believe the accountability system is the first step in making sure no child is left behind.

I understand what it means for public schools to guess whether or not a child can read and write and add and subtract, and I understand fully the consequences of a system that guesses. I also understand the consequences of a system which meas-

ures, and a system which measures and corrects problems is a system which will help meet the great promise of this country.

I want to thank you for giving me a chance to come and talk about something I feel strong about, deeply passionate about. I'm looking forward to getting these elections behind us and start working on the reauthorization of the No Child Left Behind Act, for the good of every child in the United States of America. God bless.

NOTE: The President spoke at 2:07 p.m. In his remarks, he referred to former Gov. James B. Hunt, Jr., of North Carolina; Alan W. Duncan, chairman, Guilford County Schools Board of Education; and Mayor Anthony A. Williams of Washington, DC. The Office of the Press Secretary also released a Spanish language transcript of these remarks.

Remarks Following a Tour of Victory Junction Gang Camp, Inc., in Randleman, North Carolina
October 18, 2006

The President. You know, it's a remarkable place. I can't tell you how thrilled I am to be with the Pettys and the champion race car drivers who have heard a call to help people who need help. And I wish our fellow citizens could see the physical layout here. And if you were here, you'd also feel a great sense of compassion. And, you know, the Petty family has been well known for a long time in America. And they've been known as great athletes—now they will be known as great humanitarians as well.

And so we really thank you.

Kyle Petty. Thank you, sir.
The President. This is a place that's in honor of their son, Adam. They have made a conscious decision to turn a tragic event into a loving event, and that's what I feel here. And you guys did a good job. Thanks for having me.

NOTE: The President spoke at 3:56 p.m. in Adam's Race Shop. In his remarks, he referred to NASCAR driver Kyle Petty and his wife, Pattie, founders, Victory Junction Gang Camp, Inc.

Remarks at a Reception for Congressional Candidate Don Sherwood and the Pennsylvania Victory Committee in La Plume, Pennsylvania
October 19, 2006

Thank you all very much. Please be seated. I'm glad to be back again. Thanks for welcoming me. I am pleased to be here with Don Sherwood. He is the right man to represent the people of the Tenth Congressional District from the State of Pennsylvania.

He has got a record of accomplishment. He has been a strong supporter of those brave men and women who wear our Nation's uniform. He has been a supporter of the Tobyhanna Army Depot. He's a strong supporter of Pennsylvania's dairy farmers. When it came time to make sure highway money was available for Pennsylvania, he did his job that you expect him to do. He's a person who has been working hard to increase jobs here in this part of the world. He's worked to cut taxes on the working people. He understands it's important to keep the people of the district safe. I strongly believe the people in this part of Pennsylvania need to send Don Sherwood back to the United States Congress.

And I'm glad Carol is here with us today. I read Carol Sherwood's letter to the citizens of this congressional district. I was deeply moved by her words. Carol's letter shows what a caring and courageous woman she is. I'm delighted to be here with Carol and their daughter Maria. Thanks for coming.

I am not Sherwood's first choice to be here at the fundraiser. [*Laughter*] Both he and Carol wanted Laura to come. [*Laughter*] But she sends her very best to the Sherwoods, and she, like me, strongly believes Don Sherwood ought to be reelected to the United States Congress.

I want to thank Dr. Ned Boehm, the president of Keystone College—and Regina. Regina told me she broke her foot playing golf. [*Laughter*] In 2½ years, I'm going to try that out myself. [*Laughter*] But thank you very much for letting us use this facility on this beautiful campus, and thanks very much for being involved in higher education. I appreciate your leadership, and I know the people of this part of the world do as well.

I thank very much Rob Gleason, who's the chairman of the Republican State Committee for Pennsylvania, and Bob Asher, who is the national committeeman. The reason I bring up these folks is that a lot of politics depends upon the capacity of the grassroots to do their job. So first, I want to thank you very much for raising the money, filling the hat. It's important for Don Sherwood's campaign to be able to advertise, and he will continue to do so. But in order for him to win, we got to turn out the vote. And so for those of you who are involved with grassroots politics, I want to thank you in advance for what you're going to do to get people to the polls come November.

I also want to thank my friend Bill Scranton, who's with us today. Bill and Maryla are fine citizens of this part of the world, and I'm proud to call him friend. And I really want to thank you for being here. Thanks for coming.

It's a big campaign coming up, and I like being out on the campaign trail because I like sharing with the people what I believe. And I'm looking forward to working with Congressman Sherwood the next time Congress convenes in—not in a lame-duck session. We got a lot to do. One thing we got to do is make sure we become less dependent on foreign sources of oil. You know, I understand the price of gasoline is dropping, but that should not obscure the fact that we have a national security problem when it comes to relying upon

oil from parts of the world that don't like us.

And so I want to continue to work with Congressman Sherwood to make sure we promote new technologies, new ways to power our automobiles. I envision a day when ethanol becomes more widespread, where Pennsylvania farmers are actually providing the fuel necessary to run our cars. For the sake of economic security and for the sake of national security, we must continue to diversify away from foreign sources of crude oil.

No, we'll work together on issues like health care. I appreciate the fact that he was a strong supporter of Medicare modernization. For the seniors who are on prescription drugs here in this part of the district, they understand that this new Medicare bill is a good bill. No longer do poor seniors have to choose between medicine and food, thanks to people like Congressman Don Sherwood.

But as this campaign gets closer to the stretch, you will hear a lot of rhetoric and a lot of partisan charges coming from the other side. Their goal is to distract you from the two main issues in this campaign, and they are these: Which party will keep your taxes low, and which party will take the steps necessary to defend the United States of America?

My administration, our party, and Don Sherwood have clear records on both these issues. Let me first start with taxes. Republicans have a clear philosophy. We believe that the people who know best how to spend your money are the people that earn that money, and that is you. The Democrats believe that they can spend your money better than you can. So we worked hard to ensure that the working families in this district and all around the country kept more of their paychecks when we enacted the largest tax cuts since Ronald Reagan was President of the United States.

Our record is clear, and so is the record of the Democrats in Washington, DC. When we cut taxes for everybody who pays income taxes, the Democrats voted against it. When we reduced the marriage penalty, Democrats voted against it. When we cut taxes on small businesses, Democrats voted against it. When we lowered taxes for families with children, the Democrats voted against it. We put the death tax on the road to extinction; the Democrats voted against it time and time again. When the Democrats had a chance to deliver tax relief for the American people, they voted no. This is a party that is genetically hostile to tax relief. [*Laughter*]

With every vote they have cast, they make clear to the American people, higher taxes are part of the congressional Democrats' DNA. When we passed tax relief over the Democrat objections in 2003, the minority leader in the House called it a tragedy and predicted it would not create jobs or grow our economy.

And here are the actual facts: The tax cuts we passed put more than a trillion dollars in the hands of American workers and families and small businesses and farmers, and the American people have used that money to fuel a strong and growing economy. The United States economy is the envy of the industrialized world.

Since overcoming the recession, the terrorist attacks, war, hurricanes, corporate scandals, this economy has had 37 straight months of job growth, since August of 2003. And since that day, we've added 6.6 million new jobs. The national unemployment rate is low. The progrowth economic policies that Don Sherwood supported have made this economy strong, and we intend to keep it growing.

As well, because of growing our economy, which increases tax revenues into the Federal Treasury, and being wise about how we spend your money, we met our goal of reducing our Federal deficit in half 3 years ahead of schedule. Democrats may call this a tragedy; we call it success.

And now you're going to hear that same old, tired rhetoric, Washington Democrats talking about how they're going to raise

taxes only on the rich. You know, they say they're for fairness and they're for tax relief for the middle class. But we've heard this before, and the American people shouldn't be fooled by this kind of rhetoric.

You might remember, back in 1992, the Democrats campaigned on a tax cut for the middle class. They won, but when they took office, the middle class tax cut they promised turned out to be the largest tax increase in American history. The moral of the story is that when you hear Democrats talk about fairness, there's a pretty good chance they're going to try to get in your pocket and raise your taxes.

There is no doubt in my mind that the key issue in this campaign, as far as domestic politics is concerned, is: Who is going to keep your taxes low, and who will raise your taxes? The Republican Party and Don Sherwood will make sure the working people have more money in their pocket.

Our most important job is to protect America. The most important job of the Federal Government is to use all our assets to protect the American people from an attack. We are still under threat. I wish I could report otherwise. I wish I could tell you everything was fine in the world and the enemy wasn't around that would come and try to harm us again. But I wouldn't be doing my job if I reported that. An enemy still plots and plans to attack the American people. These people are nothing but coldblooded killers. They're not religious people. I don't believe religious people kill innocent men and women and children. I believe the President must call these people by what they are: They are evil. And our most important job is to protect the American people from further attack.

You can't negotiate with these people. You can't hope to have a treaty with these people. The best way to defend America from an attack is to defeat them overseas so we do not have to face them here at home.

There are major differences between the political parties on the issue of how best to protect the American people. You know, the enemy has got to be right once, and we've got to be right 100 percent of the time to protect you.

And that's why I thought it was very important to institute a program that would enable our professionals at the Central Intelligence Agency to question people that we captured on the battlefield in order to be able to gain information necessary to do our most important job, which is to protect the American people.

And recently we had a vote on a program in the House of Representatives. When it came time to stand up and be counted, Don Sherwood voted to support the professionals at the CIA. And that cannot be said for most of his Democrat colleagues in the House. The American people must understand that nearly 80 percent of the House Democrats voted to take away this vital tool, which is necessary to protect the American people from further attack.

The other clear example is the PATRIOT Act. This good bill tore down the wall that made it impossible for law enforcement and intelligence to share information. I know that's hard for you to believe, that when intelligence had information, they couldn't share it with those who were responsible for protecting you. But that's what happened. Over time, there was a wall. And so I called for the Congress to pass the PATRIOT Act that enabled us to share information so we could break up terrorist cells, which we have—in California, in Texas, in New Jersey and Illinois and North Carolina, Ohio, New York, Virginia, and Florida. The tools inherent in the PATRIOT Act have been vital and necessary to enable us to do our job, which is to protect the American people from further attack. When this important piece of legislation came up for reauthorization, Congressman Don Sherwood supported this vital law, but more than 75 percent of the House Democrats voted to block it.

There's a fundamental difference of opinion all across the Nation about which party understands the stakes in this war on terror. After 9/11, I decided it was essential that if Al Qaida or an Al Qaida affiliate was making a phone call into the United States of America, we needed to know why in order to be able to do our job and protect you. Recently this bill came up for a vote in the United States Congress. The United States Congressman from the Tenth Congressional District of Pennsylvania voted to support our professionals who are doing everything we can to protect you, but almost 90 percent of the House Democrats voted against it.

Rarely has a single series of votes summed up the difference between the two parties so clearly. If the House Democrats had their way, the PATRIOT Act would have expired; the CIA interrogation program would have been shut down; the terrorist surveillance program would have been discontinued. And that is the record the Democrats have to run on, and it is no record to be proud of in a time of war. We Republicans understand that we must give our professionals all the tools necessary to protect the American people.

Iraq is an important issue in this campaign. I strongly believe that Iraq is a central front in the war on terror. Oh, I know some of them in Washington are saying Iraq is a diversion from the war on terror. That's not what Usama bin Laden thinks. That's not what the number-two man in Al Qaida thinks, Mr. Zawahiri. It's important to listen to the words of the enemy. Both of those men have said that it's just a matter of time for America to lose her nerve and to leave Iraq. And that's what they want to do, so they can have a safe haven from which to plot and plan and to attack America again.

These extremists are bound by a common ideology of hate, and their objective is to establish that ideology throughout the Middle East. Their objective is to topple moderate government. Their objective is to use energy as a resource to bring the West to its knees. And Iraq is a central part of this war against them.

On this question, the Democrats have been all over the place. Most leading Democrats argue we should pull our troops out of Iraq, some, "Right away," others, "In just a few months," even if the terrorists have not yet been defeated. Others recommend moving our troops to an island some 5,000 miles away. Nineteen House Democrats introduced legislation that would cut off all funds for our troops in Iraq. All these proposals have one thing in common: They would have our country quit in Iraq before the job is done. For the sake of the security of the United States of America, we must defeat the enemy in Iraq. For the sake of world peace, for the sake of peace for our children, we must not let the extremists have their way in this vital front in the war on terror. So America will stay, we will fight, and we will win in Iraq. [*Applause*] Thank you.

This summer, we saw what happens when a Democrat rejects his party's doctrine of cut-and-run. Senator Joe Lieberman, a three-term Democrat from Connecticut, supports completing the mission in Iraq, supports victory in Iraq. And for taking this stand, he was purged from his party. Think about what that means. Six years ago, the Democrats thought Joe Lieberman was good enough to run for Vice President of the United States. Now, because he supports victory in Iraq, they don't think he's fit to be in their party. There's only one position in the Democrat Party that everybody seems to agree on: If you want to be a Democrat these days, you can be for almost anything, but victory in Iraq is not an option.

The stakes in this war couldn't be higher. The security of the United States is at stake, and we have no illusions—it's tough. The fighting is tough, because an enemy understands what a defeat in Iraq would mean for their ambitions. We are a nation

at war, and we must do everything in our power to win that war.

Our goal in Iraq is clear and unchanging: Our goal is victory. What is changing are the tactics we use to pursue that goal and defeat our enemies. In Iraq, we face adversaries who are brutal, and they are sophisticated. Our commanders on the ground are constantly adjusting to stay ahead of the enemy. We have a strategy that allows us to be flexible and to adapt to changing circumstances. We will continue to make the changes necessary to support our troops, and to support those 12 million people in Iraq who want to be free, and to support the new democracy in Iraq that represents the unity of that country. There is one thing we will not do: We will not pull out our troops from Iraq before the terrorists are defeated. We will not pull out before Iraq can govern itself, sustain itself, and defend itself.

I'm going to make it clear to the American people what a policy of retreat would mean. Retreating from Iraq would allow the terrorists to gain a new state—new safe haven to replace the one they lost in Afghanistan. Retreating from Iraq would dishonor the service of our brave men and women who have sacrificed in that country and have given their lives in that country, which would mean their sacrifice would be in vain. Retreating from Iraq would crush the hopes of the millions of people who just simply want to live in peace, if America were to retreat. Retreating from Iraq would embolden the terrorists and make our country more vulnerable to new attacks. If we were to leave Iraq before the job is done, the enemy would follow us here to America.

We know this because that's what the terrorists tell us. Usama bin Laden states that early American withdrawal from places like Beirut and Somalia are proof that the United States does not have the stomach to stay in this fight. The terrorists are trying to wait us out. They're hoping we will lose our nerve and retreat in disgrace. If we

were to follow the Democrat's prescriptions and withdraw from Iraq, we would be fulfilling Usama bin Laden's highest aspirations. There can be legitimate disagreements on the best way to win this war, and there are. But we should at least be able to agree that the path to victory is not to do precisely what the terrorists want.

The stakes in this war are high, and so are the stakes in this election. I want to tell you—I want you to imagine what the House of Representatives would look like if the Democrats get their way this November. The chairman of the House Ways and Means would be a Congressman who suggested cutting off funding for our troops in Iraq. The Speaker of the House, the official third in line for the Presidency, would be a Congresswoman who voted against renewing the PATRIOT Act, against creating the Department of Homeland Security, against removing Saddam Hussein from power, against continuing the terrorist surveillance program, and against questioning terrorists in the CIA program. The Speaker would be a Congresswoman who has called liberating 25 million Iraqis a grotesque mistake. The Speaker would be a Congresswoman who said catching Usama bin Laden would not make America any safer. No wonder she says this election should not be about national security. [Laughter]

Given the Democrats' record on national security, I understand why they want to change the subject. I don't want to change the subject. I'm going to keep talking about this subject until election day. The most important job of the government is to protect you.

We'll win. We will protect the American people by staying on the offense. There's just a different attitude in Washington, if you really listen carefully to the debate. Some believe that we should respond after attack. I understand the consequences of attack, and so do you. We must take threats seriously before they fully materialize.

We got a fantastic group of men and women who wear our uniform. They are motivated, they are skilled, and Don Sherwood and I will make sure they have all the tools necessary to protect the American people.

And we have one other asset at our disposal to protect the American people, and that is the power of liberty. You know, there's an interesting debate in the world about whether or not liberty is universal or not. I believe it is. I believe there's an Almighty, and I believe a gift of the Almighty to each man and woman and child in this world is the desire to be free. That's what I believe. I'm not surprised when 12 million people defied car bombers and said, "We want to live in a land of liberty."

You know, I was amazed that they defied the car bombers, but I'm not surprised, because I believe everybody wants to be free. I believe people have a deep desire to live in peace, and I know that liberty can help yield the peace we want for generations to come. We're in an ideological struggle between those of us who love liberty and extremists who can't stand the thought of liberty. And it's the call of our generation. It's the challenge of our time. But I have great confidence that our generation will rise and meet the challenge like previous generations of Americans.

You know, I was reminded of that, and one of my favorite stories to share with our fellow citizens is my trip down to Memphis, Tennessee, to Elvis's place, with former Prime Minister Koizumi. He was sitting Prime Minister at the time. People say, "Why did you go down there?" I say, "Well, I had never been to Elvis's place, and I thought it would be kind of fun to go down there." Koizumi wanted to go to Elvis's place because he's an Elvis fan. But I also wanted to tell an interesting story about the power of liberty to our fellow citizens.

See, I find it very interesting that an 18-year-old George H.W. Bush volunteered

to fight the Japanese. After all, they were the sworn enemy of the United States of America. And then his son is on an airplane, Air Force One, flying down to Memphis, Tennessee, talking about the peace; talking about how we can work together to convince the leader in North Korea to give up his nuclear weapons ambitions; talking about why it was important for Japan to have a thousand troops helping that young democracy in the heart of the Middle East.

See, Koizumi understands what I know, that democracy will be a defeat to an ideology of hatred in the long run. I found it interesting that my dad fought the Japanese and his son is talking about the peace with the Prime Minister of the former enemy. Something happened, and what happened was, Japan adopted a Japanese-style democracy. Democracies yield the peace we all want. Someday an American President will be sitting down talking about the peace with duly elected leaders in the Middle East, and generations of Americans will be better off. That's the stake in the election. These are the stakes in this election.

I want to thank you for supporting Don Sherwood. I want to thank you for being involved in the process. Now go out and turn out the vote, and he's going to win.

May God bless you, and may God bless our country.

NOTE: The President spoke at 2:04 p.m. at Keystone College. In his remarks, he referred to Regina Boehm, wife of Edward G. Boehm, Jr., president, Keystone College; Pennsylvania gubernatorial candidate Bill Scranton, and his wife, Maryla; Usama bin Laden, leader of the Al Qaida terrorist organization; former President Saddam Hussein of Iraq; former Prime Minister Junichiro Koizumi of Japan; and Chairman Kim Jong Il of North Korea.

Remarks at a Reception for Senatorial Candidate George Allen in Richmond, Virginia
October 19, 2006

Thank you all. Thank you for coming. Thanks for the warm welcome, and thank you for supporting George Allen to be re-elected United States Senator of the great State of Virginia.

I'm proud to be here with him. He's a man who has earned the confidence of the people of this State as a delegate, as the Governor—and a very successful Governor—as a United States Senator. He's the kind of fellow who says he's going to—what he tells you on the campaign trail, he does in office. He doesn't need a poll or a focus group to tell him what to think or what to say. George Allen is a man of strong principle; he is a leader; he is the right man to be the United States Senator from the State of Virginia.

And he married well, and so did I. See, we got something in common. We're both named George, and we both married smart, beautiful women. Laura is very fond of the Allens. She understands that they are honorable, decent people—honest, good folks. We're proud to call them friends, and I know the people of Virginia are proud to call George Allen United States Senator.

I appreciate the Lieutenant Governor—Lieutenant Governor Bill Bolling and his wife, Jean Ann, and the family are with us today. Governor, thanks for coming. Speaker Bill Howell is with us. Appreciate you being here, Mr. Speaker.

I had the honor of meeting an interesting fellow at the airport today—as a matter of fact, he was at the steps there when I got off of Air Force One, and we traveled throughout his senatorial district a little bit because we went and bought some pumpkins. [*Laughter*] His name is State Senator Benny Lambert. See, the Allen campaign understands that you reach across party line. He did that as the Governor of the State of Virginia; he has done that as the

United States Senator. There's no doubt in my mind this good man will win by getting the votes of Republicans, discerning Democrats, and wise independents.

I really want to thank you all for coming. I appreciate you contributing to his campaign, and I want to thank the grassroots activists who are here for what you're fixing to do. See, we're getting close to voting time. We're coming down the stretch. And for those of you who are going to be putting up the signs and making the phone calls and going to your houses of worship or community centers urging people to do their duty as an American citizen and voting for George Allen, I want to thank you. A lot of times the grassroots folks don't get the thanks that you deserve. I'm here giving you thanks; I know the Senator gives you thanks. Work hard. We need him in the United States Senate, for the good of the United States of America.

I'm looking forward to continue to working with Senator Allen to diversify our energy. I'm looking forward to promoting ethanol and new technologies so that we can change our habits and become less dependent on foreign sources of oil. For the economic security of the United States and for the national security of the United States, we need to get off oil.

I'm looking forward to continue to work with Senator Allen to make sure that patients and doctors make the decisions for health care, not for people in Washington, DC. Now, there's a lot of domestic issues that I look forward to working with Senator Allen on, but there's no bigger issue than what we do with the people's money—no bigger issue.

There's a lot of rhetoric in these campaigns, a lot of needless noise in a campaign. A lot of time it's to obscure the

fundamental issues facing the people of Virginia and the people all across our Nation. And the two biggest issues in this campaign, in any campaign across the country, is which party will take the steps necessary to protect the American people and win the war on terror, and which party is going to keep your taxes low to keep this economy growing.

George Allen and I have made our position very plain. Nobody has to guess where we stand. We got a clear record on taxes, and our philosophy is easy to understand. It says: We trust the people. See, we understand it's your money, not the government's money. We think the best people to spend the hard-earned dollars that you make is you. We understand the economy grows when you have more money in your pocket to save, spend, or invest.

And therefore, we worked together to deliver the greatest tax cuts since Ronald Reagan was the President of the United States. We said, if you're going to have tax relief, then everybody who pays taxes ought to get relief. So we reduced the marriage penalty as well. We doubled the child tax credit. We understand that an economy grows when the small-business owners are growing. And so we cut taxes on small businesses; we cut taxes on capital gains and dividends to promote investment and jobs. And to reward family businesses and farmers right here in the great State of Virginia for a lifetime of hard work and savings, we put the death tax on the road to extinction.

Our record on cutting taxes is clear, and the Democrats in Washington, DC, have a record of their own. The trouble is, they don't want you to know about it. [*Laughter*] It's interesting that recently the top Democrat leader in the House of Representatives made an interesting declaration. She said, "We love tax cuts." Given her record, she must be a secret admirer. [*Laughter*] It's just not the so-called "tax cuts for the rich" she opposes.

When we cut taxes for everybody who pays income taxes, she voted against it. When we reduced the marriage penalty, she voted against it. When we cut taxes on small businesses, she voted against it. When we put the death tax on the road to extinction, she voted against it. Time and time again, she and her party voted against tax cuts. Time and time again, when she had an opportunity to show her love for tax cuts, she voted no. If this is the Democrats' idea of love—[*laughter*]—I wouldn't want to see what hate looks like. [*Laughter*]

But, by the way, this view of taxes extends beyond the House of Representatives. Democrats in the United States Senate had the same point of view. I remember when we cut the taxes in 2003. See, we were coming out of a recession, and we were dealing with the effects of a terrorist attack, and we were dealing with the effects of corporate scandal. And we knew that in order to recover, we had to let the people have more of their own money.

And one Democrat in the Senate said these tax cuts would do nothing to create jobs. One of his colleagues called the tax cuts the wrong prescription for our economy. Those were the predictions, and here are the results: The tax cuts we passed have put more than a trillion dollars in the hands of American workers and families and small businesses, including millions of families living right here in Virginia. And the amazing thing is, the people did a much better job with your money than the Government did or could have done.

Since August 2003, our economy has had 37 straight months of job growth. Since August of 2003, we added 6.6 million new jobs. Small businesses are flourishing. Homeownership is up. This economy is strong, and we intend to keep it that way.

You know, I'm sure you've heard the line that the Democrats are just going to raise taxes on the rich. They say it every time. But I want the people here in Virginia who

are listening to the debate on taxes to remember what happened back in 1992, after the Democrats campaigned on cutting the taxes for the middle class. Well, they won, and they came to power, and the middle class tax cut they promised turned out to be one of the largest tax increases in American history.

We just have a different view of the world when it comes to taxes. We believe you can spend your money well. The Democrats want the Government to spend your money. No, the best way to make sure that this economy stays strong is to make the tax cuts we passed permanent. And the best thing the Virginia citizens can do to make sure taxes stay low is to send George Allen back to the United States Senate.

It's interesting, if you look at the history of tax cuts, the Democrat Party always—didn't always feel the way they feel today. Back in the sixties, the Democrats understood that our economy grows when Americans keep more of what they earn, when Americans make their own decisions about how to save, spend, or invest. You might remember, when President John F. Kennedy became President, he proposed across-the-board tax cuts for American families and small businesses, including tax cuts on capital gains.

In his message to the Congress in 1963, he explained that cutting taxes across the board, in his words, "would help strengthen every segment of the American economy and bring us closer to every basic objective of American economic policy." John F. Kennedy was right in 1963, and George Allen and I are right in 2006.

Next month, the people of this State and people all across the United States have a basic choice to make: Do we keep taxes low so we can keep the economy growing, or do we let the Democrats in Washington raise taxes, which will hurt our economic growth? And I'm convinced, when people sift through all the noise and listen carefully to the debate, the people of this State and

the people across the United States will choose low taxes and strong economy policy and growth, and that means reelecting George Allen to the United States Senate.

The biggest issue we face is protecting the American people. It's the most important job of government. I learned that lesson on September the 11th, 2001, and so did George Allen and a lot of other good folks. And we learned that fateful day that our most important responsibility is to protect you, and this is a fundamental issue in this campaign: What candidate or what party has got the right policies to protect the American people from further attack?

We face a brutal enemy, an enemy that uses murder to achieve political objectives. You can't negotiate with these people. There's no such thing as a peace treaty with these kind of killers. The best way to protect the American people is to stay on the offense and bring them to justice before they hurt America again.

And the best way to protect America is to give our professionals the tools they need to protect you from attack. We recently had a debate—a series of debates in the House and the Senate that clarified the two political parties' position on the war on terror on how best to protect the American people.

I believe strongly that our CIA professionals should have authorization to question people we pick up on the battlefield, to determine whether or not they have information that is necessary to protect you. We're at war with a group of killers. We pick people up off the battlefield, and I believe that it's necessary to learn what they know so that we can anticipate attacks before they occur.

This bill came up before the—in front of the United States Senate, and one of the strongest advocates for making sure our professionals had the tools necessary to protect you was Senator George Allen of the State of Virginia.

The same cannot be said for his Democratic Senate colleagues. More than 70 percent of the United States Senators from the Democrat Party voted to take away this vital tool in the war on terror. We just have a different point of view, a different look at the world.

You know, another clear example of the difference of opinion came when we voted for and reauthorized what we call the PATRIOT Act. There was a wall that existed between law enforcement and intelligence gathering in the United States. I know that's hard to conceive, but it's true. In other words, intelligence officers could not speak with law enforcement officers. In this new war on terror against these extremists, we have to have good intelligence. And that good intelligence must be shared with professionals all throughout government, in order to be able to protect you.

Right after September the 11th, when people were deeply concerned about attacks and future attacks, George Allen voted yes on the PATRIOT Act, as did 97 of his colleagues in the Senate. And yet the bill needed to be reauthorized years later. And so I called upon the Senate. I said, "There's still a threat; we still face a threat." And yet Senate Democrats filibustered the bill, the reauthorization of a bill that would tear down the walls between intelligence and law enforcement. Filibuster means they don't want it to pass, so they talk a lot. [*Laughter*] It happens quite a bit in Washington. [*Laughter*] The Senate Democratic leader bragged, "We have killed the PATRIOT Act." Think about that. The main Democrat in the United States Senate said, "We killed the PATRIOT Act." He was asked later by a reporter whether killing the PATRIOT Act was really something to celebrate, and he answered, "Of course it is."

There's a fundamental difference of opinion between Democrats and Republicans on this issue. They voted for it right after 9/11; they tried to kill it 5 years later. Kind of sounds familiar, doesn't it? [*Laugh-ter*] They voted for it right before they voted against it. [*Laughter*] You don't have to worry about George Allen being steadfast and making sure our folks have the tools necessary to protect you. A fundamental issue in this campaign is—who best to protect the United States of America. Our record is clear, and you need to send George Allen back to the United States Senate so we can do our duty, so we can assume the responsibilities of this era and protect you from further attack.

A big issue in this campaign, of course, is Iraq. Iraq is a central front in the war on terror. Iraq is a part of defeating an enemy that would like to hurt us again. Oh, I know, I've heard all the rhetoric; I'm sure you've heard it too, that people say Iraq is just a distraction from the war on terror. That's what a lot of Democrats believe. Well, if you're out there listening and you're worried about who to vote for and worried about which party has the clearest vision about how to protect the American people, don't take my word for whether Iraq is part of the war on terror, listen to Usama bin Laden—or Mr. Zawahiri, he's the number-two man in Al Qaida.

These two killers have made it clear that Iraq is an important part of their campaign to establish a totalitarian form of government across the Middle East. They have made it clear in their words that they believe America is weak, that it's just a matter of time; if they murder enough people, that we will withdraw.

And they want us to withdraw. They want us to withdraw so that they can establish safe haven from which to launch attacks. They want us to withdraw so they can topple moderate governments. They want us to withdraw because they got designs on energy. They would like nothing more than to blackmail the free world with the fear of running up the price of energy; blackmail the free world to abandon our alliance with Israel; blackmail the free world to continue to force the West to

cater to their needs and their dark vision of the world.

When you couple all that with the possibility of Iran having a nuclear weapon, you begin to understand the stakes in the war on terror. You begin to think about how important it is that when we confront the enemy, we defeat the enemy.

I fully understand—[applause]—we have a fundamental disagreement in Washington, DC, on this central front in the war on terror. Most Democrats—most leading Democrats argue we should pull our troops out of Iraq—some, "right away"; others, "in just a few months," even if the terrorists have not been defeated. Others recommend moving our troops to an island 5,000 miles away. Nineteen House Democrats introduced legislation that would cut off funds for our troops in Iraq. All these programs have one thing in common: They would have our country quit in Iraq before the job is done. That's why they are the party of cut-and-run.

The United States of America will support our allies in Iraq. We will stand with the 12 million people who demanded freedom at the ballot box. Our goal of Iraq that can defend itself and govern itself and sustain itself and an ally in the war on terror is an important goal. We will give our commanders the flexibility they need to continue to change the tactics to achieve that goal. We will fight, we will stay, and we will win in Iraq.

And I want to thank Senator Allen's stand. This is tough; this is a tough fight. It's a tough fight when we see carnage on our television screens. It's a tough fight when somebody you know has volunteered to serve the United States and doesn't come home. It's tough, but it's tough for a reason: Because the enemy understands the stakes in Iraq. They have ambitions. And it's up to this generation to stand with our troops, to put forth a strategy for victory, to not abandon those voices in the Middle East, the millions of people who simply want to live in peace. This is the calling of our time.

You know, the Democrat Party made a clear statement about the nature of their party when it came to how they dealt with Senator Joe Lieberman. He's a three-term Democrat from Connecticut who supports completing the mission in Iraq. He took a strong, principled stand, and he was purged from the Democrat Party. Think about what it means. Six years ago, the Democrats thought that Joe Lieberman was a good enough man and a good enough politician to run as the Vice Presidential candidate. Now, because he supports victory in Iraq for the sake of security in the United States, they don't think he's fit to be in their party. There's only one position in the Democratic Party that everybody seems to agree on: If you want to be a Democrat these days, you can be for almost anything, but victory in Iraq is not an option.

These are serious times. It requires steadfast leadership, strong determination. People like George Allen need to be reelected, to stand strongly with our troops, the voices that desire peace. We'll stay on the offense; we will keep the enemy on the run. We will do the hard fight now so a generation of Americans can grow up in peace. We've got fantastic assets on our side. We've got a military that will get all the support and training they need to defend the American people.

We also have the power of liberty. Freedom is a powerful force. You know, I like to tell people about an interesting experience I had. That's when I went to Elvis's place—[laughter]—with the then sitting Prime Minister of Japan. I went down there. I'd never been to Elvis's place. I thought it would be interesting to go there. [Laughter] Prime Minister Koizumi wanted to go to Elvis's place because he loves Elvis. [Laughter]

But I wanted to tell a story, and I'm going to tell it to you right quick, the reason I went. You might remember, my dad,

and I know some of your relatives, fought the Japanese as a sworn enemy. There was a lot of kids in the early forties that signed up to fight the Japanese. They had attacked us, and this country was going to defend ourselves.

I find it amazing, and I hope you do too, that the son of Navy pilot George H.W. Bush, the sitting President of the United States, is on Air Force One, flying down with the Prime Minister of the former enemy talking about the peace. We're talking about North Korea and how we can work together to convince the leader in North Korea to give up his nuclear weapons ambitions. We're talking about the fact that Japan had 1,000 troops in Iraq because Prime Minister Koizumi and I know that freedom is how you defeat an ideology of hatred; that we understand that when you encourage liberty to flourish where it hadn't flourished, it provides hope; it helps defeat those who prey on hopelessness.

It's an amazing conversation—I've had several with him. But every time I have sat down with him, I find it interesting fact of history that my dad fought the Japanese, and today, his son is working to keep the peace. Something happened. Japan adopted a Japanese-style democracy. It's— the example is, liberty has the capacity to change an enemy into an ally. Liberty has the capacity to turn a region of hate into a region of compassion. Someday, an American President will be sitting down talking about the peace with duly elected leaders from the Middle East, and a generation of Americans will be better off.

God bless.

NOTE: The President spoke at 5:33 p.m. at the Science Museum of Virginia. In his remarks, he referred to Susan Allen, wife of Sen. George Allen; Usama bin Laden, leader of the Al Qaida terrorist organization; former Prime Minister Junichiro Koizumi of Japan; and Chairman Kim Jong Il of North Korea.

Letter to Congressional Leaders on Continuation of the National Emergency With Respect to Significant Narcotics Traffickers Centered in Colombia
October 19, 2006

Dear Mr. Speaker: (*Dear Mr. President:*)

Section 202(d) of the National Emergencies Act, 50 U.S.C. 1622(d), provides for the automatic termination of a national emergency unless, prior to the anniversary date of its declaration, the President publishes in the *Federal Register* and transmits to the Congress a notice stating that the emergency is to continue in effect beyond the anniversary date. In accordance with this provision, I have sent the enclosed notice to the *Federal Register* for publication, stating that the emergency declared with respect to significant narcotics traffickers centered in Colombia is to continue in effect beyond October 21, 2006.

The circumstances that led to the declaration on October 21, 1995, of a national emergency have not been resolved. The actions of significant narcotics traffickers centered in Colombia continue to pose an unusual and extraordinary threat to the national security, foreign policy, and economy of the United States and to cause unparalleled violence, corruption, and harm in the United States and abroad. For these reasons, I have determined that it is necessary to maintain economic pressure on significant narcotics traffickers centered in Colombia by blocking their property and interests in property that are in the United States or within the possession or control

of United States persons and by depriving them of access to the U.S. market and financial system.

Sincerely,

GEORGE W. BUSH

NOTE: Identical letters were sent to J. Dennis Hastert, Speaker of the House of Representatives, and Richard B. Cheney, President of the Senate. The notice is listed in Appendix D at the end of this volume.

Remarks on Medicare Reform
October 20, 2006

Medicare Reform

The President. Secretary Leavitt and I are pleased to be here at this counter where seniors come to buy prescription drugs. And one of the interesting things that happens at this counter is that these decent folks are constantly reminding seniors that there is a cost-saving benefit, Plan D in Medicare, available for them. It's a new plan; it just started last year. The Health and Human Services helped implement the plan, and millions of seniors are benefiting. Our seniors are saving money. They're getting better coverage. It's a plan that I'm real proud of.

We will continue to work to make it as good as it possibly can be. I really do want to thank these kind-hearted souls who say to a senior that you no longer—poor seniors, particularly—you no longer have to choose between food and medicine because there's a new way forward. Our compassionate approach to health care is working for America's seniors. And I want to thank you.

You want to say anything about the enrollment process?

Secretary of Health and Human Services Michael O. Leavitt. On November 15th, people can go through an open enrollment period. Eighty percent of seniors who are on this plan are satisfied with their plan, and if they're satisfied, they don't need to do anything. But over 80 percent will be able to find a plan that's cheaper, if they want to, or that may, in fact, fit their particular situation.

We'll have people available at 1–800–MEDICARE. There will be people at pharmacies and at senior centers—and others that can help them around the country. This has been a big success, and we're going to get better at it. We're getting better at it every year. It'll be better this year than it was last, and it will be better the year after that, just like Medicare was in 1965. This is a very important American success story that we'll now build upon.

The President. Thank you all very much. Appreciate it.

NOTE: The President spoke to reporters at 11:04 a.m. at a CVS Pharmacy.

Remarks at a National Republican Senatorial Committee Reception
October 20, 2006

Thanks for coming. Please be seated. I appreciate you being here. On the way down, Mr. McConnell said, "Keep it short; they haven't had their food yet." [*Laughter*]

But I want to thank you all for coming. As you well know, we're heading down the stretch here in this important political season. I want to thank you for helping our Senate candidates. It means a lot. I don't know about you, but I am absolutely confident that Mitch McConnell will be the leader of the United States Senate in 2007.

I appreciate Mitch's leadership, and I appreciate the leadership of Elizabeth Dole as well. These are two of the finest United States Senators we have.

Laura sends her best. She is a patient woman. [*Laughter*] She is doing just fine. I'm real proud of her. She is a fabulous First Lady.

Oh, there's going to be a lot of noise here at the end of the campaign. There always is. And sometimes it's all meant to obscure the main issues. Sometimes folks don't really want to talk about the core issues that will affect the future of this country. I think there are two big issues that we need to stay focused on and I know our candidates are talking about, and they're issues in which there are big differences of opinion. And the first issue is taxes.

There is a difference of opinion between—what we ought to be doing with your money, see. There are people in the Democrat Party who think they can spend your money far better than you can. And we believe that you're plenty capable of spending your own money. As a matter of fact, we believe that when you have more of your own money in your pocket to save, invest, or spend, all of us benefit; that the economy grows; that hope expands; that the entrepreneurial spirit is invigorated.

And so in times of economic difficulty, I worked with Members of the United States Senate and the United States House to pass the largest tax relief since Ronald Reagan was President of the United States. We didn't think the Tax Code ought to penalize marriage, so we reduced the marriage penalty. We cut taxes for small businesses. There's a reason why we cut taxes

for small businesses: Because we understand that 70 percent of new jobs in America are created by small-business owners.

We cut the taxes on capital gains and dividends, because we wanted to encourage investment. We understand that when people invest, it means that someone is more likely to be able to find a job. We cut the taxes on—we doubled the child tax credit. In other words, we cut the taxes on families with children. We put the death tax on the road to extinction. We don't think it's fair to tax you twice, once while you're living and once after you're dead. As a matter of fact, we cut taxes on everybody who pays taxes. [*Laughter*] We don't believe in this selective tax cutting. We said, if you're going to pay income taxes, you ought to get relief.

And we had a spirited debate about whether or not the tax cuts made sense. A lot of the Democrats in the United States Senate said, "These tax cuts are going to make the economy worse." They went around the United States saying tax cuts don't make any sense, but they did make sense.

We've created 6.6 million new jobs since August of 2003. This week, a new report showed that real wages grew 2.2 percent over the past 12 months. That's faster than the average for the 1990s. Because of our progrowth economic policies, this economy is strong. People are working. The entrepreneurial spirit is up. People are buying homes. Our plan works, and our candidates have something to run on coming this November.

There's a difference of opinion here in Washington, and I'm going to continue reminding people of the clear difference of opinion in this campaign. Let me tell you what the recent—the top leader, the Democrat leader in the House of Representatives said recently. This is a person who aspires to be the Speaker of the House. She said, "We love tax cuts." She actually said that. Given her record, she must be a secret admirer. [*Laughter*] Over

the past 5 years, she and her Democrat colleagues voted against every major tax cut that we passed. Time and time again, when she had her opportunity to show her love for tax cuts, she voted no. If this is the Democrats' idea of love, I wouldn't want to see what hate looks like. [*Laughter*]

Now they're trotting out their old lines. I'm sure Elizabeth and Mitch will tell you what they're hearing out there. They're saying, "Listen, we're just going to tax the rich." It is the same old, tired excuse for raising taxes. It sounds good, but that's not what they believe. Look at the record. In 1992, when they took over the White House and they campaigned on middle class tax cuts, when they got the capacity to deliver on their promises, they passed one of the largest tax increases in American history.

Raising taxes is what the Democrats want to do; make no mistake about it. If they take over the Senate, they will run up your taxes. Raising your taxes would hurt our economy. Raising our taxes would diminish the entrepreneurial spirit. Raising taxes would be bad for small-business owners. Raising taxes is a Democrat idea of growing the economy, and it won't work. The best way to keep this economy strong is to make the tax cuts we passed permanent.

The other issue in this campaign is which party, which group of leaders can keep America safe. We are at war, and it's a tough war, but it's a war that is necessary to protect you. Our most important job, the solemn responsibility of those of us who are honored to serve you in Washington, DC, is to do everything in our power to protect the American people from further attack.

There is an enemy which—[*applause*]—we face a coldblooded enemy. You can't negotiate with these people. You cannot hope for the best, because they are ideologues bound by the desire to inflict damage on nations which love freedom. They will murder the innocent. They have no conscience. And they murder to achieve

an objective, and that's what's important for our fellow citizens to understand. It may sound farfetched to some Americans out there, but this group of ideologues wants to establish a caliphate, a governing body, a—they want to spread their ideology of hate from Indonesia to Spain. That's what they have so declared. And they recognize in order to do that, they must inflict serious damage on America, to the point where we're willing to retreat from the Middle East, so they can topple moderate governments.

Imagine a world in which radical extremists not only topple moderate governments so they can have territory from which to plan, plot, and attack America and our allies, but they have the capacity to control oil resources, which they would be more than willing to use in order to blackmail America and our allies into further retreat. You can imagine a circumstance in which these radicals say, "We'll run up the price of oil by denying oil on the markets unless you abandon your allies such as Israel, or unless you further withdraw from the world." And compound that with a nuclear Iran, and the world 20 or 30 years from now is going to say, "What happened to them in 2006? How come they couldn't see the threat? What blinded these people in order that they did not do their job?"

One of the key issues in this election is who best sees the future and who best has the plan to deal with it? I firmly see the threats we face, and the best way for America to protect ourselves is to go on the offense and to stay on the offense. [*Applause*] Thank you all.

However, going on the offense is not going to be enough to protect you. It's a part of a comprehensive strategy. You know, we've got to be right 100 percent of the time in protecting this homeland from those who still want to attack, and the enemy has got to be right one time. And therefore, I felt it was vital that our professionals who are in charge of protecting you have all the tools necessary to

do so. And so right after September the 11th, we worked with Congress, in some cases—and in some cases, we felt like we didn't need to—to put tools in the hands of professionals.

One such tool was to tear down a wall that prevented law enforcement from talking to intelligence. I know that's hard to believe, but that's the reality of what had happened in our country; that's what grew up to be the case. How can you protect our country when you've got people gathering intelligence and they can't tell the law enforcement who are in charge of protecting you what they know?

And so after September the 11th, I went to the United States Congress and said, "Let's pass what we call the PATRIOT Act." It was a chance to make sure that we gave our folks on the frontlines of protecting you all the tools necessary to do so. Right after September the 11th, both the House and the Senate overwhelmingly passed the bill, but the bill needed to be reauthorized some years later. And when it came up for reauthorization, Democrat Members of the United States Senate tried to kill the bill—they, what we call here in Washington, filibustered. They didn't want to give that tool necessary to those who protect you.

There's just a difference of opinion. We believe we're at war and we should give all the folks protecting you the tools necessary to do so. Evidently, Democrats don't. As a matter of fact, the Democrat leader, the person who aspires to be the majority leader in the United States Senate, when asked about his filibuster, he said—he proudly proclaimed he killed the bill. And a reporter gave him a chance to recant; he said, "No, I'm proud of that."

I don't think that's the kind of attitude that is necessary—we can afford if the biggest job we have in Washington, DC, is to protect you. Fortunately, cooler heads prevailed, and I was able to sign the reauthorization of the PATRIOT Act, thanks to

people like Mitch McConnell and Elizabeth Dole.

I felt it was important that our professionals at the Central Intelligence Agency questioned people we picked up on the battlefield, in order to find out what they know, see. If you're at war, you need to make sure that you get as much information as possible, in order to protect you. It's a different kind of war. We can't measure the size of an infantry against these people. We don't go out and count the number of airplanes they have. This is a war that requires precise intelligence, good information, if the task is to protect you before an attack comes.

And so yes, sir, I set up a program that gave our CIA professionals the opportunity to question people like Khalid Sheikh Mohammed, the person our intelligence officials think is responsible for the killings on September the 11th—the mastermind. You could imagine my thought processes—they tell me they captured Khalid Sheikh Mohammed; my first question was, "What does he know? Does he know anything else that we need to know?"

And so as a result of a Supreme Court ruling, I took this bill to the United States Senate. The Court said, work with the Senate to set up a military tribunal. I felt it was important for us to give these killers the justice that they had denied others. But as a result of that bill, we also worked with the Senate to put legislation in place that would make it clear to our professionals that they could interrogate.

I view this as a clarifying moment for the country, a chance for Republicans, Democrats, and independents to learn firsthand the differences of opinion we have in Washington, DC, because 70 percent of the people in the United States Senate who call themselves Democrat voted against giving our professionals the tools necessary to question people so we can prevent attacks. These are fine people; they're patriotic people; but they're wrong. They don't understand the stakes in the war on terror. In

order to protect America, we must stay on the offense against the enemy and give our professionals the tools necessary to protect you.

It is interesting what's happened to the Democrat Party. I'm reading a lot of history these days, and I read about Franklin Roosevelt, who was strong in his confrontation of Nazi Germany and Imperial Japan. His strength of character, his vision helped set the course for victory in World War II—strong wartime leader. It was a Democrat, President Harry Truman, who confronted the rise of Soviet communism, and he set the course for victory in the cold war. John F. Kennedy declared America's commitment to, in his words, "pay any price and bear any burden" in the defense of freedom. These Presidents understood the challenges of their time and were willing to confront those challenges with strong leadership. And at the same time, they had great faith in the power of liberty and freedom.

And then something began to change. In 1972, the Democrats nominated a Presidential candidate who declared, "I don't like communism, but I don't think we have any great obligation to save the world from it." It was a—it began a slow shift of philosophy in the Democrat Party. A few years later, at the height of the cold war, a Democrat President told the country that America had gotten over, quote, "inordinate fear of communism." In the mid-1980s, a Senator from Massachusetts, whom Democrats would later choose as their Presidential nominee, declared that Americans should, quote, "abandon the kind of thinking that suggests we can gain a meaningful advantage over the Soviet Union in the nuclear arms race."

In other words, this is a different attitude. The philosophy of that party began to shift. Fortunately, in the 1980s, America had a Republican President who saw things differently. Ronald Reagan declared, "My theory of the cold war is that we win and they lose."

By this time, the Democrat Party did not share his optimism or his strategy for victory. See, they'd gotten to the point where they didn't think that we could win. Many of their leaders fought the Reagan defense buildup; they fought his strategic defense initiative; they opposed the liberation of Grenada; they didn't like America's support for freedom fighters resisting Soviet puppet regimes; they heaped scorn on him; they mocked him when he called the Soviet Union an "evil empire." Despite all the opposition that the President faced from the Democrats, he didn't waver. He stood for what he believed, and history will remember Ronald Reagan as the man who brought down the Soviet Union and won the cold war.

And now we're involved in what I have called the great ideological struggle of the 21st century. It's a struggle between the forces of liberty and the forces of a tyrannical vision that does not believe in freedom. It's a struggle between moderates who want to live in peace in the Middle East and extremists and radicals who will use murder to achieve their objective.

This is going to be a long struggle, but in order to prevail, it requires perseverance and determination and a strong belief in the power of liberty to conquer the ideology of hate. The Democrat Party that has evolved from one that was confident in its capacity to help deal with the problems of the world to one that is doubting today still has an approach of doubt and defeat. They believe that the war in Iraq is a diversion from the war on terror. I believe the war in Iraq is a central part in defeating the terrorists, in order that we protect ourselves.

If you don't believe me and if the citizens of our country don't believe me, then they ought to at least listen to Usama bin Laden—[*laughter*]—and the number-two man in Al Qaida, Mr. Zawahiri, both of whom have made it perfectly clear that Iraq is a central part of their strategy to establish their caliphate. They believe America

is weak, and it's just a matter of time before we will lose our nerve and abandon that young democracy in the heart of the Middle East. That's what they firmly believe, and they have said so and stated it clearly.

The same Democrats that doubt and don't believe this is a part of the war on terror also argue that we should pull out our troops before the job is done. The person I ran against for President said there ought to be a date certain for withdrawal. That means it doesn't matter what's happening on the ground; it just means, get out. You've had a leader in the House say, "Well, the best way to deal with this is to put our troops on an island some 5,000 miles away from Iraq." There's all kinds of difference of opinions, but none of them are, "Let's do the hard work necessary to secure America."

We have a difference of opinion. And that's why I have said that the Democrat Party, the party that—where some leaders have said we shouldn't spend another dime on Iraq; others have said, get out now; others said, get out in a couple of months. That's why they are the party of cut-and-run.

It's a difference of opinion, but it's a fundamental issue in this campaign. The voters out there need to ask the question, which political party will support the brave men and women who wear our uniform when they do their job of protecting America? Which political party is willing to give our professionals the tools necessary to protect the American people? Which political party has a strategy for victory in this war on terror?

Listen, I fully understand it's a tough fight in Iraq. I know it, you know it, and our troops know it. Last week—or earlier this week, I spoke with the Prime Minister of Iraq, Prime Minister Maliki, and we discussed the violence in his country. I told him I was amazed at how tough the Iraqis are when it comes to violence. Think about that. They haven't abandoned their hopes

for a government of, by, and for the people; 12 million people voted; they still long to live in a free society. Yet they're putting up with unspeakable violence.

There's a reason why the violence is increasing. One reason is that our forces, coalition and Iraqi forces, are focused on operations to bring security in Baghdad. In other words, we're on the move. We're confronting those who would like to sow sectarian violence. We're confronting the criminals who are taking advantage of the situation. We're confronting the militias who are harming innocent people. We're operating in some of the city's most violent neighborhoods to disrupt and bring to justice Al Qaida and IED makers and death squad leaders. We're engaging the enemies, and they're putting up a tough fight.

Another reason why is the terrorists are trying to influence public opinion around the world and right here in the United States. They carry video cameras, film their atrocities, e-mail images and video clips to Middle Eastern cable networks like Al Jazeera and opinion leaders throughout the West. They operate web sites where they say their goal is to, quote, "carry out a media war that is parallel to the military war."

Our goal in Iraq is clear, and it's unchanging: a country that can sustain itself, a country that can govern itself, a country that can defend itself, and a country which will be an ally in the war against these extremists. Our strategy is threefold: to help rebuild that country, to help the political process move forward, and to help the Iraqis stand up security forces that are capable of defeating the enemy themselves.

Our tactics are constantly changing. I talk to our generals who are in charge of these operations, and my message to them is, whatever you need, we'll give you; and whatever tactics you think work on the ground, you put in place. Our goal hasn't changed, but the tactics are constantly adjusting to an enemy which is brutal and violent.

My message to the United States of America is, victory in Iraq is vital for the security of a generation of Americans who are coming up. And so we will stay in Iraq, we will fight in Iraq, and we will win in Iraq. [*Applause*]

All right. Thank you. Sit down now. Thank you. I'm not through yet. [*Laughter*] I'm almost through. [*Laughter*] The waiter is signaling to me, you know, giving me one of these things. [*Laughter*]

I want to tell you one other thing we believe in, and I believe it's a difference between the philosophies of our parties— is that I believe in the power of liberty to transform regions and countries and yield the peace we want. That's what I believe. I believe this is an ideological struggle, and the way you defeat an ideology of hate is with an ideology of hope. I believe in the universality of freedom. I believe there's an Almighty, and I believe a great gift of that Almighty to every man, woman, and child on the Earth is freedom.

I believe people—I believe America should never condemn anybody to a society that does not embrace freedom. I believe in freedom so much that I wasn't surprised when 12 million people defied car bombers and said, "I want to be free." And I believe free societies yield the peace we want.

A story that I share all the time with people is the story about my relationship with the Prime Minister of Japan—former Prime Minister now, Prime Minister Koizumi. You might remember, the Prime Minister and I went down to Elvis's place—[*laughter*]—in Memphis, Tennessee. I went down there because I'd never been. [*Laughter*] He went down there—and asked me to take him down there because he liked Elvis. [*Laughter*]

But I wanted to tell a story to the American people. You see, my dad fought the Japanese. They were the sworn enemy of the United States. And many of your relatives did the same thing. They attacked us; we responded with the full force and might of the United States. Kids signed up; many didn't come home. They volunteered to fight for our freedom, just like the kids are doing today, volunteering to fight for our freedom.

One of them was an 18-year-old Navy fighter pilot. I find it really interesting that his son was on Air Force One with the Prime Minister of the former enemy talking about the peace. See, going down to Memphis from Washington, we didn't spend a lot of time analyzing Elvis's songs. [*Laughter*] We talked about North Korea and how Japan and the United States could work together to convince the leader of North Korea to give up his nuclear weapons ambitions. We talked about the fact that Japan had 1,000 troops in Iraq.

See, Prime Minister Koizumi knows what I know, that when you find a young democracy that's battling against extremists, it's in our interests to help that young democracy succeed. It's in the interests of not only this generation, who has got the charge of protecting ourselves from terrorists, but from future generations, to help democracies flourish. He understands what I know, that the reason we're talking about the peace is because something happened between World War II, when Japan was the sworn enemy of the United States, and 2006, when they're flying from Washington to Memphis on Air Force One. And what happened was, Japan adopted a Japanese-style democracy.

The lesson is, liberty has the capacity to change an enemy into an ally. And someday American Presidents will be sitting down with duly elected leaders from the Middle East talking about keeping the peace, and a generation of Americans will be better off for it.

Thank you for your help. God bless.

NOTE: The President spoke at 11:53 a.m. at the Mayflower Hotel. In his remarks, he referred to Usama bin Laden, leader of the Al Qaida terrorist organization; and Chairman Kim Jong Il of North Korea.

Remarks Following a Meeting With Organizations That Support the United States Military in Iraq and Afghanistan
October 20, 2006

I've had an uplifting and heartwarming conversation with fellow citizens of all ages from across our country who are supporting our troops. These folks don't really care about politics. What they care about is how best to send a strong message to the men and women who wear our uniform that America supports them.

And so we've had examples of people who started web pages to get different supplies to send to troops who are—who need a care package; to a woman who started a group of people to sew garments to help the wounded recover faster; to a guy who helped start video conferencing capabilities so that loved ones can share big moments in their lives together, even though one is in combat; to a child who started treasure hunts to raise money to help kids go to school. It's a remarkable country when we have people who decide to step up and help men and women who are serving their country in a time of need.

And I want to thank you all for coming, and I appreciate what you're doing. Americasupportsyou.mil is a web site where our fellow citizens can volunteer to help. You can become a part of a group and find out ways that you can support our men and women in uniform. These are brave, courageous people who deserve the full support of the American citizenry.

So I want to thank you all for coming. I appreciate you being here. Thanks very much.

NOTE: The President spoke at 2:35 p.m. in the Roosevelt Room at the White House.

Remarks at a National Italian American Foundation Dinner
October 20, 2006

Ian [Ken],° thank you for that kind introduction. But what you forgot to tell the people was that my mother said, "Listen, son, I know you're going to be going over there this evening. Remember your father has already spoken, so keep your remarks short." [*Laughter*]

I thank you for your kind words about my mother and father. I am real proud they're with you today. He is a remarkable guy and—[*applause*]. The only mistake you made was not to insist that Laura spoke instead of me. [*Laughter*] She's doing great. She said, "Look, you keep it short too, because the food is on the table." [*Laughter*]

But thanks for letting me come by to say hello. I'm honored to be with you. I love to pay homage to the Italian Americans that have made our country so great. And that's precisely what you do. The National Italian American Foundation is an important organization because it reminds people of the great Italian heritage of many of our citizens. It also heralds the great diversity of our country. So thanks for what you're doing. Thanks for letting me come by to say hello.

I'm honored to be here with the Ambassador from the great country of Italy. Mr. Ambassador, it's good to see you, sir. I am proud to say that Italy is a strong ally of the United States of America.

° White House correction.

I see we've got some of the third branch of Government with us, Justice Scalia and Justice Alito. Thank you all for being here. I know that you are paying Alito an honor, and I tell you, he paid this country an honor by agreeing to serve on the Supreme Court of the United States. I make a lot of decisions as your President, and one of the finest decisions I made was to ask this man to serve.

And I understand you're honoring Frankie Valli. Sorry I'm not going to be around to hear you, but rest assured, I've heard plenty of you when I was growing up. [*Laughter*] Congratulations to both you men. You picked fine winners here. Thanks for letting me come and pay homage to them as well.

I'm proud to be with Secchia—Peter Secchia. See, he picks up the phone, calls the Oval Office, and says, "Man, you're the only sitting President who's never come to this organization." He said, "You better get over here tonight." [*Laughter*] I said, "All right, Secchia." But I'm proud to call you friend.

You know, the story of this country is a story of immigrants, and we've always got to remember that. And some of the greatest stories of our country are the result of your ancestors who came to America and realized the big dream of our country. And what this country must always do is be a land of dreamers and doers, is to reward hard work and honor faith and family. And the Italian Americans inspire that greatness of America every day through your acts of kindness and generosity and through your contributions to the country.

You know, the list of Italian Americans that have made a significant contribution to our country is long. I mean, Tommy Lasorda, Yogi Berra, and for you Colt 45 fans—that's the old Houston baseball team—"Hollywood" Kenny Aspromonte. Where are you, Aspro? Yes, sir.

I'm sorry tonight that one outstanding Italian American can't join you, but he'll be joining me tomorrow at a meeting in the White House, and that's Peter Pace. Peter "Pac"—[*laughter*]—four-star general in the United States Marine Corps, Chairman of the Joint Chiefs. The reason I bring him up and the reason I'm meeting with him—first, there's no finer American than Peter Pace. He's an outstanding American, an outstanding Italian American.

I bring it up because we are in a titanic struggle between extremists and radicals who cannot stand the way of life of America. They don't like the thought that people from different backgrounds are able to live under a nation and work together and achieve greatness. They can't stand the thought of free societies flourishing in their midst.

And generations of Italian Americans before this generation have served with such valor to make sure freedom still stands, and now another generation of Americans is challenged. There are many Italian Americans who wear our uniform today, brave men and women who have volunteered in the great challenge of the 21st century, which is to protect our country from terrorist attack and, at the same time, spread the great blessings of liberty so that a generation of Americans can grow up in peace.

Taking the inspiration of those who have come before us, there's no doubt in my mind that this generation of Americans will succeed. We won't falter in the face of danger. We'll be steadfast in our resolve to protect you. We will be confident in the power of liberty to transform hostile regions into hopeful regions. And when we persevere, someday somebody will step up here to this mike, years from now, and say, "Thank goodness a generation of Americans did their duty for the sake of the security of the United States and the peace of the world."

So I come before you with a lot on my mind. But one of the things that's on my mind is how grateful I am to be the President of such a fabulous country, a country full of spirited, entrepreneurial, decent, compassionate people.

I hope you enjoy your evening tonight. Thanks for letting me come by. God bless you. God bless America.

NOTE: The President spoke at 7:43 p.m. at the Washington Hilton. In his remarks, he referred to A. Kenneth Ciongoli, chairman, and Ken Aspromonte, member of the board of directors, National Italian American Foundation; Italy's Ambassador to the U.S. Giovanni Castellaneta; entertainer Frankie Valli; former U.S. Ambassador to Italy Peter F. Secchia; and baseball Hall of Famers Tommy Lasorda and Yogi Berra. A tape was not available for verification of the content of these remarks.

The President's Radio Address
October 21, 2006

Good morning. Earlier this week, I spoke with Prime Minister Maliki of Iraq. We discussed the recent increase in violence in his country. Attacks have grown significantly during the first weeks of the Muslim holy month of Ramadan.

There are a number of reasons for this increase in violence. One reason is that coalition and Iraqi forces have been conducting focused operations to bring security to Baghdad. Side by side, Iraqi and American forces are operating in the city's most violent areas to disrupt Al Qaida, capture enemy fighters, crack down on IED makers, and break up death squads. As we engage our enemies in their stronghold, these enemies are putting up a tough fight. In a briefing in Iraq on Thursday, General William Caldwell said the operation to secure Baghdad has "not met our overall expectations." He also explained, "It's no coincidence that the surge in attacks against coalition forces coincides with our increased presence in the streets in Baghdad."

Our goal in Iraq is clear and unchanging: Our goal is victory. What is changing are the tactics we use to achieve that goal. Our commanders on the ground are constantly adjusting their approach to stay ahead of the enemy, particularly in Baghdad. General Pete Pace, the Chairman of the Joint Chiefs, recently put it this way: "From a military standpoint, every day is a reassessment day." We have a strategy that allows us to be flexible and to adapt to changing circumstances. We've changed the way we train the Iraqi security forces. We have changed the way we deliver reconstruction assistance in areas that have been cleared of terrorist influence. And we will continue to be flexible and make every necessary change to prevail in this struggle.

Iraq's new leaders are beginning to take the difficult steps necessary to defeat the terrorists and unite their country. The Prime Minister recently met with tribal leaders from Anbar Province, who told him they are ready to stand up and fight the terrorists. He's also taken action to clean up the Iraqi National Police. His government suspended a National Police unit after allegations that some of its members were linked to militias and death squads. A battalion commander was arrested for possible complicity in sectarian deaths. And earlier this week, two of Iraq's most senior police commanders were reassigned as part of a major restructuring of the national police force.

Another reason for the recent increase in attacks is that the terrorists are trying to influence public opinion here in the United States. They have a sophisticated propaganda strategy. They know they cannot defeat us in the battle, so they conduct high-profile attacks, hoping that the images of violence will demoralize our country and

force us to retreat. They carry video cameras and film their atrocities and broadcast them on the Internet. They e-mail images and video clips to Middle Eastern cable networks like Al Jazeera and instruct their followers to send the same material to American journalists, authors, and opinion leaders. They operate web sites where they post messages for their followers and readers across the world.

In one recent message, the Global Islamic Media Front, a group that often posts Al Qaida propaganda on web sites, said their goal is to "carry out a media war that is parallel to the military war." This is the same strategy the terrorists launched in Afghanistan following 9/11. In a letter to the Taliban leader Mullah Omar, Usama bin Laden wrote that Al Qaida intended to wage "a media campaign to create a wedge between the American people and their Government."

The terrorists are trying to divide America and break our will, and we must not allow them to succeed. So America will stand with the democratic Government of Iraq. We will help Prime Minister Maliki build a free nation that can govern itself, sustain itself, and defend itself. And we will help Iraq become a strong democracy that is a strong ally in the war on terror.

There is one thing we will not do: We will not pull our troops off the battlefield before the mission is complete. There are some in Washington who argue that retreating from Iraq would make us safer. I disagree. Retreating from Iraq would allow the terrorists to gain a new safe haven from which to launch new attacks on America. Retreating from Iraq would dishonor the men and women who have given their lives in that country and mean their sacrifice has been in vain. And retreating from Iraq would embolden the terrorists and make our country, our friends, and our allies more vulnerable to new attacks.

The last few weeks have been rough for our troops in Iraq and for the Iraqi people. The fighting is difficult, but our Nation has seen difficult fights before. In World War II and the cold war, earlier generations of Americans sacrificed so that we can live in freedom. This generation will do its duty as well. We will defeat the terrorists everywhere they make their stand, and we will leave a more hopeful world for our children and our grandchildren.

Thank you for listening.

NOTE: The address was recorded at 1:30 p.m. on October 20 in the Cabinet Room at the White House for broadcast at 10:06 a.m. on October 21. The transcript was made available by the Office of the Press Secretary on October 20 but was embargoed for release until the broadcast. In his address, the President referred to Prime Minister Nuri al-Maliki of Iraq; Maj. Gen. William B. Caldwell IV, USA, spokesman, Multi-National Force—Iraq; and Usama bin Laden, leader of the Al Qaida terrorist organization. The Office of the Press Secretary also released a Spanish language transcript of this address.

Message on the Observance of Eid al-Fitr
October 20, 2006

I send greetings to Muslims in the United States and around the world celebrating Eid al-Fitr.

Islam is a great faith that has transcended racial and ethnic divisions and brought hope and comfort to many people. Throughout Ramadan, Muslims have fasted to focus their minds on faith and to direct their hearts to charity. Eid al-Fitr marks the completion of this holy month with the

Festival of Breaking the Fast. During this joyous celebration, Muslims thank God for his guidance and blessings by gathering with family and friends, sharing traditional foods, and showing compassion to those in need.

America is strengthened by the countless contributions of our Muslim citizens, and we value our ties with Muslim nations throughout the world. For people of all faiths, Eid al-Fitr is an opportunity to reflect on the values we share and the friendships that bind all who trace their faith back to God's call to Abraham.

Laura and I send our best wishes for a joyous Eid and for health, happiness, and prosperity in the year ahead. Eid Mubarak.

GEORGE W. BUSH

NOTE: This message was released by the Office of the Press Secretary on October 23. An original was not available for verification of the content of this message.

Remarks at Urban Trust Bank
October 23, 2006

The President. I want to thank Bob Johnson and Dwight Bush for hosting this meeting here at the Urban Trust Bank. I also want to thank Tim and Tony and Kathy for joining us. These are local entrepreneurs who are living the American Dream, which is, they've started their own businesses; they're growing their own businesses; they are hoping to expand and hire more people.

One of the great things about America is that somebody can start with nothing and end up with something when it comes to business. People can have a dream, and they can work hard to achieve that dream. And the role of government, it seems to me, is to make sure that the dreamers are rewarded for their hard work and their ingenuity and success. And the best way to do that is to reduce taxes on people. The more money a entrepreneur has in his or her pocket, the more likely it is he or she will be able to expand that business, which will create jobs.

Government has got to be careful about the regulations it passes. We've got to be careful about the number of lawsuits that threaten these young companies. Government can do well at helping to team up with private corporations to enhance capital flows. But the strength of this economy depends upon the strength of the small-business sector.

We've added a lot of jobs since August of 2003, 6.6 million new jobs. And that's a result of small businesses growing and expanding. I was just talking to Tim. He's got 30 employees. That's up from zero 5 years ago. It's really enlightening and encouraging for me to talk to these hard-working people.

One of the interesting things about our economy that's also important is that as the economy has grown, the real wages for American workers has increased. Last year, it increased by 2.2 percent. That's the largest increase in recent years. And that's important, because not only does it mean the small businesses are doing well, it means our working families are doing as well.

And so I want to thank you, Bob, for letting me come by. Congratulations on the example you've set.

Robert L. Johnson. My pleasure, sir.

The President. Appreciate you very much.

Mr. Johnson. Thank you, Mr. President.

The President. Thank you.

NOTE: The President spoke at 2:01 p.m. In his remarks, he referred to Robert L. Johnson, founder and chairman, The RLJ Companies; Dwight L. Bush, president and chief executive officer, Urban Trust Bank; Timothy Sullivan, founder and chief executive officer, Fidelis Security Systems, Inc.; Tony Rome, president and chief executive officer, Maven Strategies; and Kathy Boden, president and chief executive officer, Bluehouse Water Solutions.

Remarks at a Reception for Congressional Candidate Vern Buchanan in Sarasota, Florida
October 24, 2006

Thank you all. I'm proud to be here. I appreciate you turning out to give me a chance to say that Vern Buchanan is the right man to be the United States Congressman from the 13th Congressional District. He is smart; he is capable; he is successful; he shares your values; he loves his family; he practices his faith with sincerity. He's a decent, honorable man who deserves to be elected to the United States Congress.

And I want to thank you for helping him. I appreciate you coming out. It makes me feel good. I know it makes the Congressman-to-be feel good. But it gives us a chance to remind you that we're in the final stretches of this campaign. And he's been working hard, and his family has been working hard. And he's going to count on you to turn out the vote.

So I want to thank you in advance for what you're going to do, which is to find our fellow Republicans, to remind our fellow citizens we have an obligation to vote, and when you get them headed toward the polls, tell them if they want a country that's strong and an economy that's strong, send Vern Buchanan to Washington, DC.

I was pleased to meet Sandy and James and Matt—Sandy would be the wife—[laughter]—James and Matt, the sons. I told them how much I appreciated them supporting Vern for his run. I know what it's like to run for office, and it's important to have a wife and family stand with you.

It can kind of get lonely out there on the campaign trail sometimes. And to have that strong family standing with him means a lot for this candidate.

I know what I'm talking about because I married well, just like Vern married well. And Laura sends her love to our good friends down here in Florida. And we've got a lot of friends down here. As a matter of fact, I don't have a lot of friends down here—I've got some relatives down here. You know, Jeb and I share the same campaign consultant—[laughter]—our mother. [Laughter] And so for you little ones here, my advice is, listen to your mother. At 60 years old, I'm still listening to mine. But Laura sends her love, Mother sends her love, and I know Jeb Bush is strongly for Vern Buchanan to be the next Congressman from this district.

I, too, want to thank my buddy, the Senator from the great State of Florida, Mel Martinez. Thank you for coming.

There's a lot of issues that we can talk about. I want to talk about two today. And the first issue I want to talk about is the taxes you pay. It's an important issue. We have made our position clear. We believe in lower taxes, and we intend to keep them that way. The Democrats consistently oppose cutting your taxes. It should tell you how they feel. See, we just have a fundamental disagreement. They think they can spend your money better than you can. We

believe you can spend your money far better than the Government can.

When you go to the voting booth in 2 weeks, the lever you pull will determine the taxes you pay for years to come. Americans will cast their ballots on November the 7th, but you will feel the results every April 15th. We share a philosophy that when you have more money in your pocket to save, spend, or invest, the economy benefits.

He knows what he's talking about. It's important for people from this part of the great State of Florida to have somebody who has been a successful entrepreneur represent you. This is an entrepreneurial State; this is an entrepreneurial area; this is a man who has taken risks. He's built businesses, but more importantly, he's employed people. He is successful; he understands how the economy works. He has lived the American Dream.

The Republican Party is dedicated to making sure the American Dream is viable for every single American. We understand that if you have more money in your pocket, it's easier to save for a child's education. We understand if you have more money in your pocket, a young Floridian can afford a downpayment on a new home. We understand that when small businesses have more money in their treasury, it makes it more likely that small business will grow and expand and hire new people. Our economy grows and the American Dream expands when you keep taxes low, and therefore I was able to lead the United States Congress to pass the largest tax relief since Ronald Reagan was the President of the United States.

And now the results of the tax relief are in. Tax cuts we passed have left more than a trillion dollars in the hands of American workers and families, farmers, and small-business owners. And the American people have used that money to help fuel strong economic expansion.

The Democrats said the tax cuts were not the solution to solving an economy that was slipping into recession, you might remember, back in 2001. The truth is, the tax cuts have helped make the American economy grow faster than any major industrialized nation. This economy is the envy of the world.

The Democrats said that the tax cuts would lead to a jobless recovery. The truth is that our economy has added jobs for 37 months in a row, and since August of 2003, our economy has created 6.6 million new jobs.

The Democrats said tax cuts would not help increase wages. Well the truth is, real wages have grown 2.2 percent over the last 12 months.

The Democrats said tax cuts would cause the deficit to explode. Well the truth is that tax cuts led to economic growth, and that growth has helped send tax revenues soaring. And as a result, the deficit has been cut in half 3 years ahead of schedule.

The Democrats have made a lot of predictions. Matter of fact, I think they may be measuring the drapes. [*Laughter*] If their electoral predictions are as reliable as their economic predictions, November 7th is going to be a good day for the Republicans.

And here's the truth. One of the reasons that the Democrats will lose on election day: Because they want to raise your taxes. No, I know they don't want to tell it that plainly, but that's what they're going to do. You know, the top Democrat leader in the House made an interesting statement recently. She said, "We love tax cuts." Given her record, she must be a secret admirer. [*Laughter*]

When we cut taxes on everybody that paid income taxes, she and her colleagues—most of her colleagues—voted against it. When we reduced the marriage penalty, she and most of her colleagues voted against it. When we cut the taxes on small businesses, she voted against it. When we lowered taxes for families with children, she voted against it. When we

reduced the taxes on capital gains and dividends, she voted against it. When we put the death tax on the road to extinction, she voted against it. Time and time again, she had an opportunity to show her love for taxes. [*Laughter*] If this is the Democrats' idea of love, I wouldn't want to see what hate looks like.

You know, you listen to the debate, and they're trotting out the same old stuff. They're saying they're only going to raise taxes on the rich. It's important for people in this district not to be fooled by that language. It's important for people all across the United States who are making up their mind who to vote for in these elections not to be fooled by the language, "Oh, we'll only tax the rich."

Some of you are old enough to remember 1992. [*Laughter*] They campaigned on saying they will—for a middle class tax cut. You might remember that rhetoric. But when they took office, the middle class tax cut they promised turned out to be one of the largest tax increases in history. See, here's what happens. You get up to Washington, DC, and you start spending the people's money if you're a Democrat, and you start making all these promises on the campaign trail. Then you get up and you say, "Well, I think I'm going to spend money here or there."

Earlier this year, the Democrats in the House, for example, put a budget alternative to call for 177 billion additional dollars than that which we're going to spend. The problem is, if they only raise taxes on the rich—raise taxes on people making $200,000 or more—they would fall far short of meeting their spending promises. So guess who gets to pay the bill? All of a sudden, the tax cut on the rich means you have to pay. It means the middle class in America have to pay. America should not be fooled by the empty rhetoric of the Democrats running for Congress. The best way to make sure that the Democrats don't raise your taxes is to put Congressman Vern Buchanan in Washington, DC.

It's important for you to understand this fact as you're rounding up people to go to the polls, as you're getting ready to get on the telephone, dial people and remind them to vote—and if somebody says, "Well, tell me about this election"—when it comes to taxes, here's the way it works in Washington. Under the current law, the tax cuts we passed, many of them, are set to expire. In other words, if Congress doesn't be proactive, the tax cuts will go away. And if the tax cuts go away, you're paying higher taxes. In other words, if Congress fails to act, your taxes go up.

And so they asked the ranking member of the Ways and Means Committee—that's the tax-writing committee; he would be the one who would take the lead in taxes— and his response to a question was, he couldn't think of one of our tax cuts he would extend. See, this is the attitude of those who want to run the House of Representatives on the Democrat side. He said, he couldn't think of one of the tax cuts— he couldn't even think of one that he would extend. Asked if he meant that would consider—asked if that meant he would consider tax hikes across the income spectrum, he said, "Of course it would." See, they're genetically—[*laughter*]—disposed to raise your taxes.

If there is no legislation renewing or extending the tax cuts, every tax rate will go back up to the old level. The marriage penalty will return. The death tax will spring back to life. The child credit will be cut in half, from $1,000 per child to just $500 per child. So I want people who are listening to the debate in this election to think about what that would mean, if the Democrats take control.

If you're sitting around the dinner table and there's two children, your taxes just went up $1,000, if they take control. If you're got three children at the dinner table, your taxes went up by $1,500. If you're a family of four and you're working hard to make ends meet and the Democrats take control of the House, your taxes

just went up $2,000. The best way to make sure you have more of your own money in your pocket to spend on your family is to vote for Vern Buchanan, and we'll work to make the tax cuts we passed permanent.

I want to talk about another issue, if you've got some time. The most important issue facing this Nation is to protect you. The most important job in Washington, DC, is to do everything we can to protect you from another attack. We face an enemy that is brutal; they have no conscience. They have an ideology which is the opposite of our ideology. They can't stand freedom. They have desires, and that is to spread a kind of caliphate, a governing organization, throughout the Middle East from which to launch attacks and spread their dark vision of the world. They use murder as a weapon to achieve their objectives. There is no negotiation possible with these kind of people. You can't reason with them. The best way to protect the American people is to stay on the offense and bring them to justice so they don't hurt us again.

We had a series of interesting votes in Washington, DC, recently that should explain the fundamental differences between how we view the war on terror and how the Democrats view the war on terror. I felt that the President should do everything in his power, within the Constitution, to protect you.

And therefore, after 9/11, I made a couple of decisions that recently were brought to a vote on the floor of the House of Representatives, which should give you an indication about the differences of opinion. I believe that we must work to prevent attacks from happening in the first place, but here in the homeland—by staying on the offense. But here in the homeland, I understand that the enemy has to be right one time, and we have to be right 100 percent of the time, in order to protect you. And therefore, I feel it's important

to make sure our professionals have the tools necessary to protect you.

I felt like that if Al Qaida or an Al Qaida affiliate was making a phone call into the United States of America from outside our country, our intelligence professionals need to know why. This is a different kind of war. Past wars—in past wars, you could watch flotillas of ships or count airplanes to determine the intent or the strength of the enemy; you could watch manpower being moved. This is a different kind of war. It's a war that requires intelligence so that we can make sure our professionals are able to protect you.

The idea of people—professionals being able to listen to Al Qaida and its affiliates came to a vote on the floor of the United States Congress. The American people must fully understand that the vast majority of Democrats opposed the right of this administration to have a tool necessary to protect you. We just have a different view. They must not think we're at war. They must think that the best way to protect you is to respond after the attack. I understand this is a war, and the United States of America will do everything we can to protect you before the enemy hits again.

This is a different kind of war, and we pick up people off the battlefield, and we want to know what they know. I'm sure you've been reading recently about some of the people that we have picked up since that fateful attack on us on September the 11th, 2001. We captured a man named Khalid Sheikh Mohammed, who our intelligence officers believe was the mastermind of the September the 11th attacks. I felt it was important that our professionals find out what he knew, in order to make sure I could say to you, standing right here, that we're doing everything we can to protect you.

I felt it was important for these brave souls who work for the intelligence service to have the tools necessary to inquire to these killers what they know, in order to be able to stop a further attack. This vote

came up on the floor of the United States House of Representatives. The vast majority of Democrats voted against giving our professionals the right to interrogate to protect America. These are patriotic souls, but their vision of the world is wrong, and we need to make sure that we continue to control the House of Representatives to provide the protection necessary for—[*applause*].

This is a global war. There are many fronts in the war on terror. We've got some fantastic men and women who wear our uniform. The best way to protect the American people is to keep the enemy on the run. It is hard to plot and plan when you're hiding in a cave. It's hard to plot and plan when you know the mighty United States military and/or our intelligence services are breathing down your neck. And therefore, it is important to have Members of the United States Congress who understand the stakes of the world in which we live and will join me in making sure our troops have all the equipment, all the support, all the pay that is necessary for them to do their job.

A central front in this war, a central part of protecting America from an enemy that would like to strike us again, is Iraq. It's tough fighting in Iraq. It is tough fighting because the enemy understands the stakes of success in Iraq. A lot of people in Washington, a lot of Democrats, say that Iraq is a diversion on the war on terror. As you know, I have a difference of opinion. I believe it is a central front in the war on terror.

And that's an honest debate to have, but if you haven't made up your mind yet, listen to the words of Usama bin Laden or his number-two person in Al Qaida, Mr. Zawahiri, both of whom made it clear that their objective is to inflict as much pain as possible so America will withdraw from Iraq, so they can have safe haven from which to plot and plan attacks, so they can have more resources to develop the weapons they would like to use against us, so they can topple moderate governments.

It is conceivable 20 years from now, people would look back on this period of time in the midst of a world in which radicalism and extremism was prevalent, in which allies such as Israel were surrounded by incredibly hostile forces, in which Iran had a nuclear weapon, in which governments were in control of these radicals who then cut off oil supplies to the West. That's the scenario that will happen if we withdraw before we achieve our objectives. People will look back and say, "What happened to them in the year 2006? How come they couldn't see the threat?" I see the threat. That is why we have got a strategy for victory in Iraq.

The stakes are high, and the enemy understands that. Our goal is to have a country that can defend itself, sustain itself, govern itself, and be an ally in the war on terror. Our goal was to remove a threat. I made the right decision in taking Saddam Hussein out of power. And now our goal is to help this young democracy succeed, is to help these brave souls defeat the thugs and the sectarians and the Al Qaida, from toppling their dreams.

Twelve million Iraqis went to the polls. They said, "We want to be free." You shouldn't be surprised. Freedom is universal. We don't own freedom in America. I believe there is an Almighty, and I believe one of the great gifts of the Almighty is the deep desire to be free.

For those of you who understand military, I'm running the war this way: I set the goal, and I count on our commanders on the ground and our Ambassador in Baghdad to set the tactics in order to achieve the goal. We're constantly changing. The enemy changes, and we change. The enemy adapts to our strategies and tactics, and we adapt to theirs. We're constantly changing to defeat this enemy.

But if the Democrats were to take control, their policy is pretty clear to me: It's cut-and-run. Oh, they try to claim it's not.

They try to claim it's not, but if you listen to their leaders, the man I ran against for President in 2004 said we need a date certain from which to withdraw. My attitude is, look, I want to bring our troops home as much as anybody, but I want to make sure they come home with victory, not with defeat.

For the sake of these little kids here, we will fight in Iraq, and we will win in Iraq. And when we achieve our goal, we will have dealt the enemy an incredible blow. You know, we've got great assets on our side. We've got a fantastic country, people that are strong. We've got a military that is bold and courageous. We got one other thing going for us, too, and that is the great power of liberty.

Liberty is a powerful, powerful tool. You see, liberty will yield the peace we want. Free societies will yield the peace. We're in an ideological struggle between extremists and radicals who hate and between moderate people who simply want to live in peace. It's a struggle between good and decent people and evil killers. It's a struggle that is going to take a while to achieve. But it is an ideological struggle, and you can defeat an ideology of hate with an ideology of hope, and freedom is that ideology of hope.

You know I—recently, I had an interesting experience. I share this with people all around our country because I want to bring to life that which we are now accomplishing. I went to Elvis's place—[laughter]—with the former Prime Minister of Japan. He was the sitting Prime Minister of Japan then. I went. I had never been there. [Laughter] The Prime Minister wanted to go there. [Laughter] See, he was an Elvis fan. [Laughter]

But I wanted to tell an interesting story. It's the story about a family—my family—and a story about liberty. My dad fought the Japanese. You've had relatives—I know people here whose families fought the Japanese. They were the sworn enemy of the United States. It was a bloody conflict.

Thousands of people lost their lives. Young kids volunteered to defend their country, just like people are volunteering today to defend our country, and a lot didn't come home.

As a matter of fact, it took us a while to get Japanese—slurs of Japanese people out of our vocabulary, the hate was so bad. I find it interesting that I'm on the airplane flying down to Elvis's place with the Prime Minister of a former enemy talking about the peace, talking about bringing peace to the world. For some of you young ones out there, 60 may seem like a long time. For those of us who are 60, it just seemed like a snap of the fingers. [Laughter]

Something happened between 18-year-old Navy fighter pilot George H.W. Bush and his President—and his son, the President, talking about keeping the peace with the Prime Minister of a former enemy. And what happened was, Japan adopted a Japanese-style democracy. Liberty has got the capacity to change hate into hope. Liberty has got the capacity to help change an enemy into an ally. Someday, someday an American President will be sitting down with duly elected leaders from the Middle East talking about the peace, and a generation of Americans will be better off.

The stakes in this election are high. I ask you to vote for Vern Buchanan. He'll be an ally in making sure your taxes stay low so the economy grows and an ally in making sure the United States Government does everything in our power to protect the American people and to make sure that a generation of Americans can grow up in peace.

God bless, and thanks for coming.

NOTE: The President spoke at 1:35 p.m. at the Sarasota Bradenton International Convention Center. In his remarks, he referred to Gov. Jeb Bush of Florida; Usama bin Laden, leader of the Al Qaida terrorist organization; U.S. Ambassador to Iraq Zalmay Khalilzad; and former Prime Minister Junichiro Koizumi of Japan.

Remarks Following a Tour of Gyrocam Systems, LLC, in Sarasota
October 24, 2006

I wanted to stop by here at Gyrocam for a couple of reasons. One, low taxes encourage small-business growth. One of the reasons why we're adding jobs in this country of ours is because our small-business sector is flourishing. And in order to make sure that companies such as this little company continue to expand, you got to keep taxes low. If we run up taxes, it's going to make it harder for the small businesses to expand.

There's a big—there's a significant issue in this campaign. Make no mistake about it, if the Democrats take control of the Congress, they'll raise taxes by letting the tax cuts expire. And we intend to keep taxes low.

The other thing that's interesting about this little company is one of the products they make is an IED detector. And I've been saying to the American people that our goal in Iraq has not changed, which is a country that can sustain itself, defend itself, govern itself. Our tactics are adjusting. And one of the adjustments we had to make in order to protect lives and achieve our mission was to better detect IEDs. And this little company right here makes an IED detector that enables our troops to be able to ferret out an IED before they come across it.

And one of the interesting things I was able to do was talk to a couple of Iraq vets who now work for this company. They're bringing their expertise off the battlefield to help this company design a product which will work. Interestingly enough, they then send people back to maintain the detectors.

At any rate, I want to thank you all for giving me a chance to come by. I'm proud to be with you. The entrepreneurial spirit must remain strong in this country. It is strong inside this company, and we intend to keep it strong by keeping taxes low, less regulation, hopefully less lawsuits, and our economy will remain strong. If we run up taxes, it will falter.

Thank you. Appreciate it.

NOTE: The President spoke at 2:40 p.m.

Statement on the Retirement of Chief Usher Gary Walters
October 24, 2006

Chief Usher Gary Walters has been a valued public servant to seven First Families for more than three decades at the White House. We have known Gary for many years and are especially grateful for making our family feel at home and for managing and overseeing the operations of the White House, a museum of American history. While we are sad to see him leave, we wish Gary all the best in his future endeavors.

NOTE: This statement was released by the Office of the Press Secretary as a statement by the President and the First Lady.

The President's News Conference
October 25, 2006

The President. Thank you all very much. I'm going to spend a little more time on my opening comments than I usually do, but I'll save plenty of time for questions.

Over the past 3 years, I have often addressed the American people to explain developments in Iraq. Some of these developments were encouraging, such as the capture of Saddam Hussein, the elections in which 12 million Iraqis defied the terrorists and voted for a free future, and the demise of the brutal terrorist Zarqawi. Other developments were not encouraging, such as the bombing of the U.N. headquarters in Baghdad, the fact that we did not find stockpiles of weapons of mass destruction, and the continued loss of some of America's finest sons and daughters.

Recently American and Iraqi forces have launched some of the most aggressive operations on enemy forces in Baghdad since the war began. They've cleared neighborhoods of terrorists and death squads and uncovered large caches of weapons, including sniper scopes and mortars and powerful bombs. There has been heavy fighting. Many enemy fighters have been killed or captured, and we've suffered casualties of our own. This month we've lost 93 American servicemembers in Iraq, the most since October of 2005. During roughly the same period, more than 300 Iraqi security personnel have given their lives in battle. Iraqi civilians have suffered unspeakable violence at the hands of the terrorists, insurgents, illegal militias, armed groups, and criminals.

The events of the past month have been a serious concern to me and a serious concern to the American people. Today I will explain how we're adapting our tactics to help the Iraqi Government gain control of the security situation. I'll also explain why, despite the difficulties and bloodshed, it remains critical that America defeat the enemy in Iraq by helping the Iraqis build a free nation that can sustain itself and defend itself.

Our security at home depends on ensuring that Iraq is an ally in the war on terror and does not become a terrorist haven like Afghanistan under the Taliban. The enemy we face in Iraq has evolved over the past 3 years. After the fall of Saddam Hussein, a sophisticated and a violent insurgency took root. Early on, this insurgency was made up of remnants of Saddam Hussein's Ba'ath Party as well as criminals released by the regime. The insurgency was fueled by Al Qaida and other foreign terrorists, who focused most of their attention on high-profile attacks against coalition forces and international institutions.

We learned some key lessons from that early phase in the war. We saw how quickly Al Qaida and other extremist groups would come to Iraq to fight and try to drive us out. We overestimated the capability of the civil service in Iraq to continue to provide essential services to the Iraqi people. We did not expect the Iraqi Army, including the Republican Guard, to melt away in the way that it did in the face of advancing coalition forces.

Despite these early setbacks, some very important progress was made in the midst of an incredibly violent period. Iraqis formed an interim government that assumed sovereignty. The Iraqi people elected a transitional government, drafted and adopted the most progressive democratic Constitution in the Arab world, braved the car bombs and assassins to choose a permanent government under that Constitution, and slowly began to build a capable national army.

Al Qaida and insurgents were unable to stop this progress. They tried to stand up to our forces in places like Fallujah, and they were routed. So they changed their tactics. In an intercepted letter to Usama

bin Laden, the terrorist Zarqawi laid out his strategy to drag Iraq's Shi'a population into a sectarian war. To the credit of the Shi'a population, they resisted responding to the horrific violence against them for a long time.

Yet the persistent attacks, particularly last February's bombing of the Golden Mosque in Samarra, one of Shi'a Islam's most holy shrines, eventually resulted in sectarian reprisals. The cycle of violence, in which Al Qaida insurgents attacked Shi'a civilians and Shi'a death squads retaliated against Sunnis, has sharply increased in recent months, particularly in Baghdad.

As the enemy shifts tactics, we are shifting our tactics as well. Americans have no intention of taking sides in a sectarian struggle or standing in the crossfire between rival factions. Our mission is to help the elected Government in Iraq defeat common enemies, to bring peace and stability to Iraq, and make our Nation more secure. Our goals are unchanging. We are flexible in our methods to achieving those goals.

On the military side, our commanders on the ground are constantly adjusting our tactics to stay ahead of our enemies. We are refining our training strategy for the Iraqi security forces, so we can help more of those forces take the lead in the fight and provide them better equipment and firepower to be successful. We've increased the number of coalition advisers in the Iraqi Ministries of Defense and Interior so they can better plan and execute security operations against the enemy.

We have changed our force structure so we can better respond to the conditions on the ground. For example, during the Iraqi elections, we increased our force levels to more than 150,000 troops to ensure people could vote. Most recently, we have moved additional coalition and Iraqi forces into Baghdad so they can help secure the city and reduce sectarian violence.

After some initial successes, our operations to secure Baghdad have encountered greater resistance. Some of the Iraqi security forces have performed below expectations. Many have performed well and are fighting bravely in some of Baghdad's toughest neighborhoods. Once again, American troops are performing superbly under very difficult conditions. Together with the Iraqis, they've conducted hundreds of missions throughout Baghdad. They've rounded up or killed key insurgents and death squad leaders.

As we fight this enemy, we're working with the Iraqi Government to perform the performance—to improve the performance of their security forces, so they can regain control of the nation's capital and eventually assume primary responsibility for their country's security.

A military solution alone will not stop violence. In the end, the Iraqi people and their Government will have to make the difficult decisions necessary to solve these problems. So in addition to refining our military tactics to defeat the enemy, we're also working to help the Iraqi Government achieve a political solution that brings together Shi'a and Sunnis and Kurds and other ethnic and religious groups.

Yesterday our Ambassador to Iraq, Zal Khalilzad, laid out a three-step approach. First, we're working with political and religious leaders across Iraq, urging them to take steps to restrain their followers and stop sectarian violence.

Second, we're helping Iraqi leaders to complete work on a national compact to resolve the most difficult issues dividing their country. The new Iraqi Government has condemned violence from all quarters and agreed to a schedule for resolving issues, such as disarming illegal militias and death squads, sharing oil revenues, amending the Iraqi Constitution, and reforming the de-Ba'athification process.

Third, we're reaching out to Arab States such as Saudi Arabia, the UAE, and Jordan and asking them to support the Iraqi Government's efforts to persuade Sunni insurgents to lay down their arms and accept

national reconciliation. The international community is also supporting the international compact that outlines the support that will be provided to Iraq as it moves forward with its own program of reform.

These are difficult tasks for any government. It is important for Americans to recognize that Prime Minister Maliki's unity Government has been in office for just over 5 months. Think about that. This young Government has to solve a host of problems created by decades of tyrannical rule. And they have to do it in the midst of raging conflict, against extremists from outside and inside the country who are doing everything they can to stop this Government from succeeding.

We're pressing Iraq's leaders to take bold measures to save their country. We're making it clear that America's patient is not unlimited. Yet we also understand the difficult challenges Iraq's leaders face, and we will not put more pressure on the Iraqi Government than it can bear. The way to succeed in Iraq is to help Iraq's Government grow in strength and assume more control over its country as quickly as possible.

I know the American people understand the stakes in Iraq. They want to win. They will support the war as long as they see a path to victory. Americans can have confidence that we will prevail because thousands of smart, dedicated military and civilian personnel are risking their lives and are working around the clock to ensure our success. A distinguished independent panel of Republicans and Democrats, led by former Secretary of State Jim Baker and former Congressman Lee Hamilton, is taking a fresh look at the situation in Iraq and will make recommendations to help achieve our goals. I welcome all these efforts. My administration will carefully consider any proposal that will help us achieve victory.

It's my responsibility to provide the American people with a candid assessment on the way forward. There is tough fighting ahead. The road to victory will not be easy. We should not expect a simple solution. The fact that the fighting is tough does not mean our efforts in Iraq are not worth it. To the contrary, the consequences in Iraq will have a decisive impact on the security of our country, because defeating the terrorists in Iraq is essential to turning back the cause of extremism in the Middle East. If we do not defeat the terrorists or extremists in Iraq, they will gain access to vast oil reserves and use Iraq as a base to overthrow moderate governments across the broader Middle East. They will launch new attacks on America from this new safe haven. They will pursue their goal of a radical Islamic empire that stretches from Spain to Indonesia.

I know many Americans are not satisfied with the situation in Iraq. I'm not satisfied either. And that is why we're taking new steps to help secure Baghdad and constantly adjusting our tactics across the country to meet the changing threat. But we cannot allow our dissatisfaction to turn into disillusionment about our purpose in this war. We must not look at every success of the enemy as a mistake on our part, cause for an investigation, or a reason to call for our troops to come home. We must not fall prey to the sophisticated propaganda by the enemy, who is trying to undermine our confidence and make us believe that our presence in Iraq is the cause of all its problems.

If I did not think our mission in Iraq was vital to America's security, I'd bring our troops home tomorrow. I met too many wives and husbands who have lost their partners in life, too many children who won't ever see their mom and dad again. I owe it to them and to the families who still have loved ones in harm's way to ensure that their sacrifices are not in vain.

Our country has faced adversity before during times of war. In past wars, we've lost young Americans who gave everything to protect our freedom and way of life. In this war, we've lost good men and

women who've given their lives for a cause that is necessary and it is just. We mourn every loss, and we must gird ourselves for the sacrifices that are yet to come. America's men and women in uniform are the finest in the world. I'm awed by their strength and their character. As General Casey reported yesterday in Iraq, "The men and women of the Armed Forces have never lost a battle in over 3 years in the war." Every American can take pride in our troops and the vital work they are doing to protect us.

Our troops are fighting a war that will set the course for this new century. The outcome will determine the destiny of millions across the world. Defeating the terrorists and extremists is the challenge of our time and the calling of this generation. I'm confident this generation will answer that call and defeat an ideology that is bent on destroying America and all that we stand for.

And now I'll be glad to answer some of your questions. Terry [Terence Hunt, Associated Press].

War on Terror/Democracy Efforts in Iraq

Q. Mr. President, the war in Iraq has lasted almost as long as World War II for the United States. And as you mentioned, October was the deadliest month for American forces this year—in a year. Do you think we're winning, and why?

The President. First of all, this is a different kind of war than a war against the fascists in World War II. We were facing a nation-state—two nation-states—three nation-states in World War II. We were able to find an enemy by locating its ships or aircraft or soldiers on the ground. This is a war against extremists and radicals who kill innocent people to achieve political objectives. It has a multiple of fronts.

Afghanistan was a front in this war against the terrorists. Iraq is now the central front in the war against the terrorists. This war is more than just finding people and bringing them to justice. This war is

an ideological conflict between a radical ideology that can't stand freedom and moderate, reasonable people that hope to live in a peaceful society.

And so it's going to take a long time, Terry. I am confident we will succeed. I am confident we'll succeed in Iraq, and the reason I'm confident we'll succeed in Iraq is because the Iraqis want to succeed in Iraq. The ultimate victory in Iraq, which is a government that can sustain itself, govern itself, and defend itself, depends upon the Iraqi citizens and the Iraqi Government doing the hard work necessary to protect their country. And our job is to help them achieve that objective. As a matter of fact, my view is, the only way we lose in Iraq is if we leave before the job is done.

And I'm confident we can succeed in the broader war on terror, this ideological conflict. I'm confident because I believe the power of liberty will defeat the ideology of hate every time, if given a chance. I believe that the radicals represent the few in the Middle East. I believe the majority of people want to live in a peaceful world. That's what I believe.

And I know it's incumbent upon our Government and others who enjoy the blessings of liberty to help those moderates succeed, because otherwise, we're looking at the potential of this kind of world: a world in which radical forms of Islam compete for power; a world in which moderate governments get toppled by people willing to murder the innocent; a world in which oil reserves are controlled by radicals in order to extract blackmail from the West; a world in which Iran has a nuclear weapon. And if that were to occur, people would look back at this day and age and say, "What happened to those people in 2006? How come they couldn't see the threat to a future generation of people?"

Defeat will only come if the United States becomes isolationist and refuses to, one, protect ourselves, and two, help those

who desire to become—to live in a moderate, peaceful world. And it's a hard struggle, no question about it. And it's a different struggle.

Q. Are we winning?

The President. Absolutely, we're winning. Al Qaida is on the run. As a matter of fact, the mastermind, or the people who they think is the mastermind, of the September the 11th attacks is in our custody. We've now got a procedure for this person to go on trial, to be held for his account. Most of Al Qaida that planned the attacks on September the 11th have been brought to justice.

Extremists have now played their hand; the world can clearly see their ambitions. You know, when a Palestinian state began to show progress, extremists attacked Israel to stop the advance of a Palestinian state. They can't stand democracies. Extremists and radicals want to undermine fragile democracy because it's a defeat for their way of life, their ideology.

People now understand the stakes. We're winning, and we will win, unless we leave before the job is done. And the crucial battle right now is Iraq. And as I said in my statement, I understand how tough it is, really tough. It's tough for a reason: Because people understand the stakes of success in Iraq. And my point to the American people is, is that we're constantly adjusting our tactics to achieve victory.

Steve [Steve Holland, Reuters].

Iraqi Military and Security Forces

Q. Thank you, Mr. President. Are you considering sending more U.S. troops to Iraq? What would be the justification for it? And how reliable is this new timetable of 12 to 18 months?

The President. I will send more troops to Iraq if General Casey says, "I need more troops in Iraq to achieve victory." And that's the way I've been running this war. I have great faith in General Casey. I have great faith in Ambassador Khalilzad. I trust our commanders on the ground to give the best advice about how to achieve victory. I want to remind you, victory is a government that can sustain itself, govern itself—a country that can govern itself, sustain itself, and defend itself and serves as an ally in the war on terror—which stands in stark contrast to a government that would be chaotic, that would be a safe haven for the enemy to launch attacks on us.

One way for the American people to understand what Iraq could look like is what Afghanistan looked like under the Taliban, a place where there was no freedom; a place where women were taken to the public square and beaten if they did not adhere to the strict, intolerant guidelines of the Taliban; a place where thousands trained to attack America and our allies. Afghanistan doesn't have nearly the resources that Iraq has. Imagine a safe haven for an enemy that ended up with the resources that it had.

It is—and so this is a war where I say to our generals, "Do you have what it takes to win?" Now, General Casey talked about part of our strategy, and part of the strategy is to give the Iraq Government the tools necessary to protect itself, to defend itself. If you're able to defend yourself, you're more likely to be able to govern yourself as well. But politics—the political way forward and the military way forward must go hand in hand.

And what the General was saying yesterday is that there is a three-step process to enable the Iraqi forces to be able to help this Government bring security. One was to train and equip. The goal is 325,000 troops, 137,000 military and the balance, police.

Second was to put the Iraqi security forces in the lead. Six of ten divisions now are in the lead in helping this Government defend itself. The strategy has been to embed U.S. personnel, officers and noncom officers, into these forces to help them gain the confidence and the capacity to be effective when they're in the lead.

And the third step is for the Iraqi security forces to be able to operate independently. And this, perhaps, is going to be one of the most difficult aspects of having the Iraqis ready to go, because that means they have to be able to drive themselves, maintain their vehicles, provide logistics, have combat service support. And that's what General Casey was describing.

The key is that our commanders feel that there—they have got enough flexibility to design the program to meet the conditions on the ground. You know, last spring, I thought for a period of time we'd be able to reduce our troop presence early next year. That's what I felt. But because we didn't have a fixed timetable and because General Casey and General Abizaid and the other generals there understand that the way we're running this war is to give them flexibility, have the confidence necessary to come and make the right recommendations here in Washington, DC, they decided that that wasn't going to happen. And so what he was describing to you was the way forward to make sure that the Iraqis are fully prepared to defend themselves.

Q. What about the 12 to 18 month estimate?

The President. It's a condition, a base estimate. And that's important for the American people to know. This notion about, you know, fixed timetable of withdrawal, in my judgment, is a—means defeat. You can't leave until the job is done. Our mission is to get the job done as quickly as possible.

Let's see here, Dave [David Gregory, NBC News].

Progress in Iraq

Q. Mr. President, for several years you have been saying that America will stay the course in Iraq; you were committed to the policy. And now you say that, no, you're not saying, stay the course, that you're adapting to win, that you're showing flexibility. And as you mentioned, out of Baghdad, we're now hearing about benchmarks and timetables from the Iraqi Government, as relayed by American officials, to stop the sectarian violence.

In the past, Democrats and other critics of the war who talked about benchmarks and timetables were labeled as defeatists, "defeatocrats," or people who wanted to cut and run. So why shouldn't the American people conclude that this is nothing from you other than semantic, rhetorical games and all politics 2 weeks before an election?

The President. David, there is a significant difference between benchmarks for a government to achieve and a timetable for withdrawal. You're talking about—when you're talking about the benchmarks, he's talking about the fact that we're working with the Iraqi Government to have certain benchmarks to meet as a way to determine whether or not they're making the hard decisions necessary to achieve peace. I believe that's what you're referring to. And we're working with the Iraqi Government to come up with benchmarks.

Listen, this is a sovereign government. It was elected by the people of Iraq. What we're asking them to do is to say, when do you think you're going to get this done, when can you get this done, so the people themselves in Iraq can see that the Government is moving forward with a reconciliation plan and plans necessary to unify this Government.

That is substantially different, David, from people saying, "We want a time certain to get out of Iraq." As a matter of fact, the benchmarks will make it more likely we win. Withdrawing on an artificial timetable means we lose.

Now, I'm giving the speech—you're asking me why I'm giving this speech today— because there's—I think I owe an explanation to the American people—and will continue to make explanations. The people need to know that we have a plan for victory. Like I said in my opening comments, I fully understand, if the people think we don't have a plan for victory, they're not

going to support the effort. And so I'll continue to speak out about our way forward.

Jessica [Jessica Yellin, ABC News].

Iran and Syria

Q. Sir, you've called Iran part of the axis of evil and Syria a state sponsor of terrorism. You said earlier today that your administration will consider any proposal that will help us achieve victory. So, I'm wondering, if it's determined that Iran and Syria could help you achieve victory in Iraq, would you be willing to work with them?

The President. Iran and Syria understand full well that the world expects them to help Iraq. We've made that very clear to them.

Let me talk about the Iranian issue. We've got a lot of issues with Iran. First is whether or not they will help this young democracy succeed. The second issue, of course, is whether or not they will help the Lebanese democracy succeed—the Siniora Government, which is—a priority of this Government is to help that Siniora Government. The big issue right now is whether or not Iran will end up with a nuclear weapon. And so our issues with Iran are many. And our position is very clear to the Iranians: There is a better way forward for the Government and the people than to be isolated.

And we will continue to work to make it clear to the Iranian Government that all three accounts and the sponsor of terrorists will cause more isolation. We've got a very active diplomatic effort taking place. The Iranians know our position on Iraq, and they know it clearly. More importantly, they know the Iraqis' position relative to Iran. We're helping a sovereign government succeed. And the Iraqis have sent messages to the Iranians: To help us succeed, don't interfere in the internal affairs.

As to Syria, our message to Syria is consistent: Do not undermine the Siniora Government in Lebanon; help us get back the—help Israel get back the prisoner that was captured by Hamas; don't allow Hamas

and Hizballah to plot attacks against democracies in the Middle East; help inside of Iraq. They know our position as well, Jessica.

Q. May I just follow? James Baker has himself said that he believes the U.S. should work with Iran. So would you be willing to work with Iran in a way that allows some sort of negotiations in Iraq, even if they don't come to the table in the P–3 and P–5 negotiations?

The President. Jessica, Iran has a chance to come to the table with the United States to discuss a variety of issues. And the way forward is one that I had made clear at previous press conferences, and that is, if they would verifiably stop their enrichment, the United States will be at the table with them. In the meantime, they understand our position, and they understand, more importantly, the Iraqi position about their interference inside their country.

Progress in Iraq

Q. Thank you, Mr. President. Prime Minister Maliki apparently gave his own news conference this morning, where he seemed to be referring to Ambassador Khalilzad and General Casey yesterday, when he said, nobody has the right to set any timetables in Iraq—and also seemed to be upset about the raid in Sadr City, saying he wasn't consulted. And I believe the quote was, "It will not be repeated." Do you still have full, complete, and total confidence in Prime Minister Maliki as a partner in Iraq? And what can you tell the American people about his ability to rein in the militias, since he seems to derive much of his power from them?

The President. Yes. First, this is back to the question that David asked about benchmarks. You called it "timetables."

Q. He did, sir.

The President. Okay, he called it "timetables;" excuse me. I think he was referring to the benchmarks that we're developing

that show a way forward to the Iraqi people, and the American people for that matter, about how this unity Government is going to solve problems and bring the people together. And if his point is, is that those benchmarks, or the way forward, can't be imposed upon Iraq by an outside force, he's right. This is a sovereign government. But we're working closely with the Government to be able to say, "Here's what's going to happen then; here's what we expect to happen now; here's what should be expected in the future."

Second part of your question?

Q. I was wondering—first of all, he seemed to be pushing back with——

The President. Oh, on the sectarian—on the militias. I heard that, and I asked to see his complete transcript of this press conference, where he made it very clear that militias harm the stability of his country. Militias—people out—who operate outside the law will be dealt with. That's what the Prime Minister said in his press conference. The idea that we need to coordinate with him is a—makes sense to me. And there's a lot of operations taking place, which means that sometimes communications may not be as good as they should be. And we'll continue to work very closely with the Government to make sure that the communications are solid.

I do believe Prime Minister Maliki is the right man to achieve the goal in Iraq. He's got a hard job. He's been there for 5 months, a little over 5 months, and there's a lot of pressure on him, pressure from inside his country. He's got to deal with sectarian violence; he's got to deal with criminals; he's got to deal with Al Qaida—all of whom are lethal. These are people that will kill. And he wants to achieve the same objective I want to achieve, and he's making tough decisions.

I'm impressed, for example, by the way, that he has got religious leaders, both Sunni and Shi'a, to start working together. I appreciate the fact that he has made a very clear statement on militias. And, by the way, death squad members are being brought to justice in this—during these operations in Baghdad.

I speak to him quite frequently, and I remind him we're with him, so long as he continues to make tough decisions. That's what we expect. We expect that the Iraqi Government will make the hard decisions necessary to unite the country and listen to the will of the 12 million people.

Let's see here. Yes, sir, Bret [Bret Baier, FOX News].

Situation in North Korea

Q. Thank you, Mr. President. North Korean leaders apparently today warned South Korea against joining international sanctions, saying South Korea would pay a high price if they did so. Are you still confident that South Korea and China will implement the full force of the U.N.-passed sanctions? And what happens if North Korea continues to thumb its nose at the world?

The President. I believe that—first of all, I've been briefed on this subject recently by the Secretary of State, who just came back from the Far East. She met with the Japanese, the South Koreans, the Chinese, and the Russians. Her report is that all countries understand we must work closely together to solve this problem peacefully. And that means adhering to the latest United Nations Security Council resolution that was passed.

The leader of North Korea likes to threaten. In my judgment, what he's doing is just testing the will of the five countries that are working together to convince him there is a better way forward for his people. I don't know the exact words he used, but he is—this is not the first time that he's issued threats. And our goal is to continue to remind our partners that when we work together, we're more likely to be able to achieve the objective, which is to solve this problem diplomatically. And so I would report to you the coalition remains firm, and we will continue to work to see to it that it does remain firm.

Baker [Peter Baker, Washington Post].

Secretary of Defense Rumsfeld

Q. Thank you, Mr. President. Thank you for taking questions today.

The President. What was that?

Q. Thank you for taking questions today.

The President. Baker, I'm just happy to be able to do so, brother. [*Laughter*] I can't tell you how joyful it is. [*Laughter*]

Q. When you first ran for President, sir, you talked about the importance of accountability. We learned from Bob Woodward's recent book that Secretary Card, on two occasions, suggested that you replace Secretary Rumsfeld, and both times you said no. Given that the war in Iraq is not going as well as you want, and given that you're not satisfied as you just told us today, why hasn't anybody been held accountable? Should somebody be held accountable?

The President. Peter, you're asking me why I believe Secretary Rumsfeld is doing a good job, I think, if I might decipher through the Washington code.

Q. Or someone else.

The President. Well, let's start with Rumsfeld, Secretary Rumsfeld. I've asked him to do some difficult tasks as the Secretary of Defense, one, wage war in two different theaters of this war on terror, Afghanistan and Iraq, and at the same time, asked him to transform our military posture around the world and our military readiness here at home. In other words, the transformation effort into itself is a big project for any Secretary to handle. But to compound the job he has, he's got to do that and, at the same time, wage war. And I'm satisfied of how he's done all his jobs.

He is a smart, tough, capable administrator. As importantly, he understands that the best way to fight this war, whether it be in Iraq or anywhere else around the world, is to make sure our troops are ready, that morale is high, that we transform the nature of our military to meet the threats, and that we give our commanders on the ground the flexibility necessary to make the tactical changes to achieve victory.

This is a tough war in Iraq. I mean, it's a hard fight, no question about it. All you've got to do is turn on your TV. But I believe that the military strategy we have is going to work. That's what I believe, Peter. And so we've made changes throughout the war; we'll continue to make changes throughout the war. But the important thing is whether or not we have the right strategy and the tactics necessary to achieve that goal. And I believe we do.

Dick [Richard Keil, Bloomberg News].

Q. And from the——

The President. Wait a minute, let me say—the ultimate accountability, Peter, rests with me. That's the ultimate—you're asking about accountability, that's—rests right here. It's what the 2004 campaign was about. If people want to—if people are unhappy about it, look right to the President. I believe our generals are doing the job I asked them to do. They're competent, smart, capable men and women. And this country owes them a lot of gratitude and support.

Yes, now Dick, sorry.

War on Terror

Q. Mr. President——

The President. It was a clever little followup you slipped in there. Sorry, Gregory. I mean, look—Gregory is still mad he didn't get the followup, but it's okay.

Q. You've said, Mr. President, several times here this morning that the definition of failure in Iraq would be to leave before the job was done. But you also said that you have no intention of seeing our troops standing in the crossfire of a sectarian war within that country. With many observers on the ground saying that civil war in Iraq is as close as it's ever been, how do you reconcile those two statements? And what happens if a full-fledged civil war breaks out?

The President. Dick, our job is to prevent the full-scale civil war from happening in

the first place. It's one of the missions, is to work with the Maliki Government to make sure that there is a political way forward that says to the people of Iraq, it's not worth it. Civil war is not worth the effort—by them. That's the whole objective, is to help this Government be able to defend itself and sustain itself so that the 12 million people that voted—they didn't vote for civil war; they voted to live under a Constitution that was passed. And so we will work to prevent that from happening. I——

Q. What about——

The President. Let me finish. I view that this is a struggle between radicals and extremists who are trying to prevent there to be a democracy, for a variety of reasons. And it's in our interest that the forces of moderation prevail in Iraq and elsewhere in the Middle East. A defeat there—in other words, if we were to withdraw before the job is done, it would embolden extremists. They would say, you know, we were right about America in the first place, that America did not have the will necessary to do the hard work. That's precisely what Usama bin Laden has said, for example. A defeat there would make it easier for people to be able to recruit extremists and kids, to be able to use their tactics to destroy innocent life. A defeat there would dispirit people throughout the Middle East who wonder whether America is genuine in our commitment to moderation and democracy.

And I told you what the scenario, Dick, could look like, 20 or 30 years from now, if we leave before the job is done. It's a serious business. And that's why I say it's the call of this generation. And I understand how tough it is, see, but I also said in my remarks, just because the enemy has been able to make some progress doesn't mean we should leave. Quite the contrary, we ought to do everything we can to help prevent them from making progress. And that is what our strategy is.

Elaine [Elaine Quijano, Cable News Network].

Q. What if there is a civil war?

Iraqi Government

The President. You're asking me hypotheticals. Our job is to make sure there's not one, see. You been around here 5½ years; you know I won't answer hypotheticals. Occasionally slip up, but——

Q. Thank you, Mr. President. You talk about the U.S. Government and the Iraqi Government working closely together on benchmarks. I'm wondering, sir, why was Prime Minister Maliki not at the news conference yesterday with General Casey and Ambassador Khalilzad? Would that not have sent a strong message about there being a very close level of cooperation between the two Governments?

The President. Elaine, I have no idea why he wasn't there.

Q. Was he invited, sir?

The President. I have no idea. I'm not the scheduler of news conferences. I do know they work very closely together, and they've got a very close working relationship, and that's important.

Iraqi Prime Minister al-Maliki

Q. May I ask you, sir, following up, when you say that you're not satisfied with the way things are going in Iraq, why should that not be interpreted by some to mean that you are dissatisfied with Prime Minister Maliki's performance?

The President. Because I know Prime Minister Maliki; I know how hard his job is; and I understand that he is working to make the decisions necessary to bring this country together. And he's—look, we'll push him, but we're not going to push him to the point where he can't achieve the objective. And we'll continue to work with him. He represents a government formed by the people of Iraq. It's a—and he's got a tough job. I mean, think about what his job is like. He's got to deal with political factions. He's got to deal with the hatred

that is left over from the tyranny of Saddam Hussein.

There's a lot of people still furious about what happened to them during Saddam Hussein's period. You can imagine that. What happens if your brother or sister had been assassinated by Saddam Hussein and his political party? You'd be—you wouldn't be happy about it. Reconciliation is difficult in a society that had been divided and tortured by a tyrant.

And Prime Minister Maliki has got the difficult job of reconciling these grievances and different political parties on top of that, plus dealing with violence. I've talked to him a lot. I like his spirit. I like his attitude. He's confident we can achieve the mission. He's not—he's realistic about how difficult it is in Iraq.

It's in our Government's interest that we help him succeed, because he wants a unified country. And I believe we will succeed. I know we're not going to succeed, however, if we set artificial timetables for withdrawal or we get out of there or we say to the enemy, "Just keep fighting; we'll leave soon." That's not going to work. What will work is a strategy that's constantly—tactics that constantly change to meet the enemy. And that's what I was describing in my speech; we're constantly adjusting. As the enemy changes, we change. War is not a—this war and other wars, they're not static. They're dynamic events. And we must adjust to meet those events, and we are.

Jim [Jim Rutenberg, New York Times].

Progress in Iraq

Q. Thank you, Mr. President. Does the United States want to maintain permanent bases in Iraq? And I would follow that by asking, are you willing to renounce a claim on permanent bases in Iraq?

The President. Jim, any decisions about permanency in Iraq will be made by the Iraqi Government. And frankly, it's not in much of a position to be thinking about what the world is going to look like 5 or

10 years from now. They are working to make sure that we succeed in the short term. And they need our help, and that's where our focus is.

But remember, when you're talking about bases and troops, we're dealing with a sovereign government. Now, we entered into an agreement with the Karzai Government. They weren't called permanent bases, but they were called arrangements that will help this Government understand that there will be a U.S. presence so long as they want them there. And at the appropriate time, I'm confident we'll be willing to sit down and discuss the long-term security of Iraq. But right now we're discussing how to bring security to Baghdad and what do we do in Al Anbar Province, where Al Qaida still uses violent methods to achieve political objectives.

You know, it's interesting, if you—I'm sure people who watch your TV screens think the entire country is embroiled in sectarian conflict and that there's constant killing everywhere in Iraq. Well, if you listened to General Casey yesterday, 90 percent of the action takes place in 5 of the 18 Provinces. And around Baghdad, it's within a 30-mile area. And the reason I bring that up is that while it seems to our American citizens that nothing normal is taking place—and I can understand why; it's a brutal environment there, particularly that which is on our TV screens—that there is farmers farming; there are small businesses growing; there's a currency that's relatively stable; there's an entrepreneurial class; there's commerce. General Abizaid was describing to me what it was like to go to Baghdad markets.

There's a lot of work to be done, don't get me wrong, but it is—there are people living relatively normal lives who, I believe—strongly believe that they want to continue that normalcy. And it's up to Prime Minister Maliki to do everything he can to make the situation as secure as possible.

Ann [Ann Compton, ABC News]. Sorry, Rutenberg, you're through.

2006 Midterm Elections

Q. Thank you, sir. Is the coming election a referendum on Iraq? Should it be?

The President. I think the coming election is a referendum on these two things: Which party has got the plan that will enable our economy continue—to continue to grow, and which party has a plan to protect the American people. And Iraq is part of the security of the United States. If we succeed—and when we succeed in Iraq, our country will be more secure. If we don't succeed in Iraq, the country is less secure.

The security of this country—and look, I understand here in Washington, some people say we're not at war. I know that. They're just wrong, in my opinion.

The enemy still wants to strike us. The enemy still wants to achieve safe haven from which to plot and plan. The enemy would like to have weapons of mass destruction in order to attack us. These are lethal, coldblooded killers. And we must do everything we can to protect the American people, including questioning detainees or listening to their phone calls from outside the country to inside the country. And there was—as you know, there was some recent votes on that issue. And the Democrats voted against giving our professionals the skill—the tools necessary to protect the American people.

I will repeat, like I've said to you often: I do not question their patriotism; I question whether or not they understand how dangerous this world is. And this is a big issue in the campaign. Security of the country is an issue, just like taxes are an issue. If you raise taxes, it will hurt the economy. If you don't extend the tax cuts, if you don't make them—in other words, if you let the tax cuts expire, it will be a tax increase on the American people.

Take the child tax credit. If it is not made permanent—in other words, if it ex-pires—and you got a family of four sitting around the breakfast table, the taxpayers can be sure that their taxes will go up by $2,000: 500 for that child, 500 for the one right there, 500 for this one, and 500 for that one. That is a tax increase. And taking $2,000 out of the pockets of the working people will make it harder to sustain economic growth.

So the two issues I see in the campaign can be boiled down to, who best to protect this country and who best to keep taxes low. That's what the referendum is about.

Let's see here, David [David Greene, Baltimore Sun]. Hold on for a minute. David.

Iraqi Prime Minister al-Maliki

Q. Thank you, sir. You've long talked about the importance when the Federal Government is involved in an effort, spending money and resources, of measuring success, accountability, as Peter said. Now you've set some benchmarks on the Maliki Government. You've said that you're expecting him to make tough decisions. Can you tell the American people how you plan to measure his success in reaching those benchmarks, and what happens if he doesn't hit those benchmarks?

The President. David, the first objective is to develop benchmarks that the Government agrees with and that we think are important. You can't—it's really important for the American people to understand that to say, "Okay, these are the benchmarks you must live with," is not going to work nearly as effectively as if we have—when we have buy-in from the Government itself, the sovereign Government of Iraq.

And so the step is to say to the Maliki Government—which we're doing—let us work in concert to develop a series of benchmarks to achieve different objectives. And the purpose of that is to assure the Iraqi people that this unity Government is going to work to—for the improvement of the Iraqi people. In other words, it will be beneficial for the Government to say

to the Iraqi people, "Here is what we intend to do, and here's when we intend to do it."

It will also be beneficial for the American people to be able to see that this Iraqi Government is going to make the difficult decisions necessary to move forward, to achieve the goal. And that's what we're talking about when it comes to benchmarks. It's—again, I repeat: One should not expect our Government to impose these benchmarks on a sovereign government. You'd expect us to work closely with that Government to come up with a way forward that the Government feels comfortable with. And there's probably going to be some bones of contention during these discussions, but nevertheless, we'll respect the fact that the Iraq Government is sovereign, and they must respect the fact that we've got patience but not unlimited patience.

Q. What happens if that patience runs out?

The President. See, that's that hypothetical Keil is trying to get me to answer. Why don't we work to see to it that it doesn't work out—run out? That's the whole objective. That's what positive people do. They say, "We're going to put something in place, and we'll work to achieve it."

Let's see here, Stephen [Stephen Dinan, Washington Times].

2006 Midterm Elections

Q. Thank you, Mr. President. With a Republican Congress, you failed to achieve three major goals of your second term: Social Security reform, a Tax Code overhaul, and a comprehensive immigration bill. Why shouldn't Americans give Democrats a chance to work with you on those issues, especially when divided government seemed to work in the late 1990s, on the budget?

The President. That's a tricky little question there. [*Laughter*] First, I haven't given up on any of those issues. I've got 2 years left to achieve them. And I firmly believe

it is more likely to achieve those three objectives with a Republican-controlled Congress and a Republican-controlled Senate. And I believe I'll be working with a Republican-controlled Congress and a Republican-controlled Senate.

I understand here in Washington, people have already determined the outcome of the election, like it's over even before the people actually start heading—voting. But that's not what I see when I'm on the campaign trail. You know, we've got some people dancing in the end zone here in Washington, DC. They've got them measuring their drapes; they're going over to the Capitol and saying, "My new office looks beautiful. I think I'm going to have this size drape there, or this color." But the American people are going to decide, and they're going to decide this race based upon who best to protect the American people and who best to keep the taxes low.

Secondly, I'll tell you what I see—you didn't ask, but I'm going to tell you anyway. I see there's a lot of enthusiasm amongst the grassroots activists. Our people are going out there to man the phones and to put up the yard signs. You know, they're showing up when it comes time to—these absentee votes. We're organized. We've got a fantastic grassroots organization to turn out the vote. This campaign has obviously got national implications to it, no question about it: the Iraq war, the security of the country, economic vitality and growth. But each of these elections turn out to be local in their scope and in their character.

And we've got good candidates running hard, and we're going to win. Now, I know that defies conventional wisdom here. I'm not suggesting anybody in this august crowd has determined the outcome of the election already, but they're running profiles on who this person is going to be running this office, or this one that's going to be—magazines have got all kinds of new stars emerging when they haven't won the votes yet.

And anyway, thanks for asking about the campaign. I'm enjoying it out there. I like

campaigning. It's what guys like me do in order to get here. We campaign. We shake the hands, you know, and give the speeches. And Laura is campaigning too. From my perspective, our people are ready to go out there and vote for—vote our candidates back into power.

Let me see here, Michael Allen [Time].

U.S. Armed Forces in Iraq

Q. Thank you, Mr. President. Your comment earlier that last spring, you believed that troops would be able to come home early next year——

The President. Yes.

Q. ——I wonder if you could talk to us about how you came to believe that and over what period of time or whether it was a single development because you realized that wasn't feasible.

The President. No, no, no, look, Mike, here's the way it works. I meet with our—or talk to our generals all the time. And the security situation looked like, at that point in time, that beginning next year, we could reduce our troop presence. That's what we felt—until the conditions on the ground changed. And when they changed, our generals changed their attitude. And when their attitude changed, my attitude changed.

Look, I want to get our troops home as fast as we can. But I do not want to leave before we achieve victory. And the best way to do that is to make sure we have a strategy that works, tactics that adjust to the enemy, and commanders that feel confident making recommendations to the Secretary and to the Commander in Chief. And that's how that happened. In other words, they're saying it looks like things are positive, things are stepping up. The security situation is—looks like it could be this way. And then when it changed, we changed. And that's important for the American people to know, that we're constantly changing tactics to meet the situation on the ground.

Knoller [Mark Knoller, CBS Radio].

Q. Excuse me——

The President. No.

Q. May I follow up?

The President. Well, you're taking Wolffe's time. Is this your question, Wolffe [Richard Wolffe, Newsweek]?

Q. No, sir, it's not.

The President. Okay, okay.

Q. But I yield.

The President. Then it's your question.

Q. Only for a moment.

The President. Okay.

Q. I just wanted to ask you quickly, sir, if you believe that Iraq will be able to defend, sustain, and govern itself by the time you leave office?

The President. Mike, I believe Iraq will be able to defend, govern, and sustain itself; otherwise, I'd pull our troops out. See, you all got to understand that, and the parents of our troops must understand, that if I didn't believe we could succeed and didn't believe it was necessary for the security of this country to succeed, I wouldn't have your loved ones there. That's what I want these parents to hear.

And that's a backhanded way of getting me to put a timetable. My answer is, we'll work as fast as we can get the job done.

Mark and then Richard.

Q. Thank you, sir.

The President. That way it will give you time to——

2006 Midterm Elections

Q. I understand why you would claim or assert that the Republicans will win the midterm elections. But if in your heart of hearts you really didn't think that, would you tell us so? [*Laughter*] And are you resentful that some Republican candidates seem to be distancing themselves from you?

The President. You know, no, I'm not resentful, nor am I resentful that a lot of Democrats are using my picture. All I ask is that they pick out a good one. [*Laughter*] Make me look good, at least, on the picture.

Mark, the first part of your question, the serious part, if I thought we were going to lose, would I tell you—we're not going to lose, in my heart of hearts. [*Laughter*] No, again, I understand how—look, I read the—look at the newspapers around here. I can see why you would think that I'm concealing something in my heart of hearts. The race is over as far as a lot of the punditry goes. They've got it all figured out. And they just—as I said, they're dancing in the end zone. They just haven't scored the touchdown, Mark, you know; there's a lot of time left. And these candidates are working hard out there. And my message to them is, keep talking about the security of the United States and keeping taxes low, and you'll come back here.

Last question. Richard.

Ethics in Government

Q. Thank you, Mr. President. Back in 2000, you campaigned around the country saying you wanted to usher in the responsibility era, to end the days when people said, "If it feels good, do it, and if you've got a problem, blame somebody else."

The President. Right.

Q. Yet over the last several months, we've seen many members of your own party in Congress embroiled in one scandal or another and all too ready to blame somebody else, whether prosecutors or Democrats or even the media. So I'm wondering, why do you think it is so many people in your own party have failed to live up to the standards of the responsibility era?

The President. If any person in any party fails to live up to high standards, they ought to be held to account, Richard. It's important for there to be trust in the Halls of Congress and in the White House and throughout government. People got to trust elected leaders in order for democracy to work to its fullest extent. And I fully expect people to be held to account if there's wrongdoing, just like I expect corporate executives to be held to account for wrongdoing, just like I expect people throughout our society to be held to account for wrongdoing.

People do have to take responsibility for the decisions they make in life. I take responsibility for the decisions I make. I also understand that those of us in positions of responsibility have the duty to bring honor to the offices we hold. People don't have to agree with somebody's opinion—there's all kinds of opinions here—but in order to make this country work and to make democracy succeed, there's got to be high standards, and people must be held to account to achieve those standards.

I thank you for your time. See you on the campaign trail.

NOTE: The President's news conference began at 10:31 a.m. in the East Room at the White House. In his remarks, he referred to former President Saddam Hussein and Prime Minister Nuri al-Maliki or Iraq; Usama bin Laden, leader of the Al Qaida terrorist organization; Gen. George W. Casey, Jr., USA, commanding general, Multi-National Force—Iraq; Khalid Sheikh Mohammed, senior Al Qaida leader responsible for planning the September 11, 2001, terrorist attacks, who was captured in Pakistan on March 1, 2003; Gen. John P. Abizaid, USA, commander, U.S. Central Command; Prime Minister Fuad Siniora of Lebanon; Gilad Shalit, an Israeli soldier captured and held captive by militants in Gaza since June 25; Chairman Kim Jong Il of North Korea; and President Hamid Karzai of Afghanistan. The Office of the Press Secretary also released a Spanish language transcript of this press conference.

Remarks Following Discussions With President Leonel Fernandez Reyna of the Dominican Republic
October 25, 2006

President Bush. Bienvenidos a mi amigo the President of the Dominican Republic. I'm proud to be with a strong leader who is focused on reform and rule of law and prosperity.

The President informed me that the economy of the Dominican Republic grew by 9 percent last year. And I want to congratulate you, Mr. President.

We talked about how to continue economic growth and vitality. It's in the interests of the United States that the Dominican Republic have a strong economy. We talked about the need for us to help with the multilateral institutions, to work with— for them to work with this Government to help with cash flows and cash demands so that this economy can continue its growth and strength.

We talked about DR–CAFTA and how important this piece of legislation is to the people of the Dominican Republic and to the people of the United States. And I assured the President that we will implement DR–CAFTA as quickly as possible, as soon as possible. And to that end, I had my trade minister, Ambassador Susan Schwab, here to make sure that we both heard the message of the President, that this was a very important piece of legislation and that we have committed—our Government has committed to working with you, Mr. President, to get this done as quickly as possible.

Y por fin, we talked about the need for us to work closely on drug trafficking. The United States of America must continue to work to diminish the demand for drugs, and we are. As well, we want to work with our partners in the hemisphere, particularly the Dominican Republic, to interdict the drugs and to help these countries be able to avoid and fight off the scourge of drugs, because there is a direct correlation between drugs and crime. And the more we can cut down on drug use and drug trafficking and drug supplies, the easier it will be for respective countries to protect their people.

Mr. President, I appreciate very much your presence here. I thank you for your leadership in the hemisphere. I appreciate the advice you have given me on how we can work together to make sure our own neighborhood is secure and peaceful and hopeful. Welcome.

President Fernandez Reyna. I thank you very much, Mr. President. It's a pleasure to be here. And I want to thank President Bush for the warm welcome that he has given me, along with my delegation, here to the Oval Office of the White House.

As the President indicated, we have touched on a number of issues of mutual interest to our two countries. First of all, DR–CAFTA, its implementation, hopefully, will take place very soon. We are now in the final phase. This is a bill now before our own Congress in the Dominican Republic. We are dealing with some minor legal amendments, and our two teams have been working very hard to obtain a speedy implementation of DR–CAFTA. President Bush and we have agreed to the need to accelerate this process to benefit both our countries.

Second, as President Bush indicated, we have also touched on the issues of disbursements by multilateral institutions. These are extremely important in order to help the progress of countries like the Dominican Republic to establish confidence, to maintain the confidence in our countries, and also to help us sustain ability of our economies.

The Dominican Republic has agreements with these multilateral institutions, and we hope that they will be honored soon, with

regard to these disbursements. The sooner that they are complied with, the better it will be for us.

And third, of course, we have touched on a number of issues such as the issue of drug trafficking, as President Bush mentioned, the issue of crime, the issue of the good relations that we have had for so many years between the United States and the Dominican Republic, the issue of good governance, the issue of respect for human rights, and a number of other things.

It has been a very good meeting. Thank you so much.

President Bush. Gracias por su tiempo.

NOTE: The President spoke at 2:20 p.m. in the Oval Office at the White House. President Fernandez Reyna spoke in Spanish, and his remarks were translated by an interpreter. The Office of the Press Secretary also released a Spanish language transcript of these remarks.

Remarks on Signing the Secure Fence Act of 2006
October 26, 2006

Thank you all. Thank you. Please be seated. I'm pleased that you all are here to witness the signature of the Secure Fence Act of 2006. This bill will help protect the American people. This bill will make our borders more secure. It is an important step toward immigration reform.

I want to thank the Members of Congress for their work on this important piece of legislation. I welcome you here to the White House. I'm looking forward to signing this bill.

I appreciate the Vice President joining us today. I thank the Deputy Secretary, Michael Jackson, of the Department of Homeland Security. Rob Portman—he happens to be the Director of the OMB. I want to thank Ralph Basham, who is the Commissioner of the U.S. Customs and Border Protection; David Aguilar is the Chief of the U.S. Border Patrol.

I appreciate the fact that Senate Majority Leader Bill Frist has joined us, as well as House Majority Leader John Boehner. I appreciate them coming in from their respective States as I sign this piece of legislation. I want to thank Congressman Peter King, who's the chairman of the Homeland Security Committee in the House of Rep-

resentatives. I appreciate you being here, Peter.

Ours is a nation of immigrants. We're also a nation of law. Unfortunately, the United States has not been in complete control of its borders for decades, and therefore, illegal immigration has been on the rise. We have a responsibility to address these challenges. We have a responsibility to enforce our laws. We have a responsibility to secure our borders. We take this responsibility seriously.

Earlier this year, I addressed the Nation from the Oval Office. I laid out our strategy for immigration reform. Part of that strategy begins with securing the border. Since I took office, we have more than doubled funding for border security—from $4.6 billion in 2001 to $10.4 billion this year. We've increased the number of Border Patrol agents from about 9,000 to more than 12,000, and by the end of 2008, we will have doubled the number of Border Patrol agents during my Presidency.

We've deployed thousands of National Guard members to assist the Border Patrol. We've upgraded technology at our borders. We've added infrastructure, including new fencing and vehicle barriers. We're adding thousands of new beds in our detention

facilities so we can continue working to end catch-and-release at our southern border. During the course of my administration, we have apprehended and sent home more than 6 million people entering our country illegally. And I thank the Border Patrol for their hard work.

The Secure Fence Act builds on this progress. The bill authorizes the construction of hundreds of miles of additional fencing along our southern border. The bill authorizes more vehicle barriers, checkpoints, and lighting to help prevent people from entering our country illegally. The bill authorizes the Department of Homeland Security to increase the use of advanced technology like cameras and satellites and unmanned aerial vehicles to reinforce our infrastructure at the border. We're modernizing the southern border of the United States so we can assure the American people we're doing our job of securing the border. By making wise use of physical barriers and deploying 21st century technology, we're helping our Border Patrol agents do their job.

The Secure Fence Act is part of our efforts to reform our immigration system. We have more to do. Meaningful immigration reform means that we must enforce our immigration laws in the United States. It is against the law to hire someone who is here illegally. We fully understand that most businesses want to obey that law, but they cannot verify the legal status of their employees because of widespread document fraud. So we're creating a better system for verifying documents and work eligibility and, in the meantime, holding people to account for breaking the law.

We must reduce pressure on our border by creating a temporary-worker plan. Willing workers ought to be matched with willing employers to do jobs Americans are not doing for a temporary—on a temporary basis.

We must face the reality that millions of illegal immigrants are already here. They should not be given an automatic path to citizenship; that is amnesty. I oppose amnesty. There is a rational middle ground between granting an automatic pass to citizenship for every illegal immigrant and a program of mass deportation. And I look forward to working with Congress to find that middle ground.

The bill I'm about to sign is an important step in our Nation's efforts to secure our border and reform our immigration system. I want to thank the Members of Congress for joining me as I sign the Secure Fence Act of 2006.

NOTE: The President spoke at 9:34 a.m. in the Roosevelt Room at the White House. H.R. 6061, approved October 26, was assigned Public Law No. 109–367. The Office of the Press Secretary also released a Spanish language transcript of these remarks.

Remarks at a Luncheon for Congressional Candidate Jeffery Lamberti and Iowa Victory 2006 in Des Moines, Iowa
October 26, 2006

Thanks for coming. Please be seated. Thank you for the warm Iowa welcome. It's kind of like old home week here when I look around. [*Laughter*] It's good to be in the midst of a lot of friends who made possible for me to stand here and address you as the President of the United States.

I'm proud to be here with Jeff Lamberti. No doubt in my mind he is going to be the next Congressman from this congressional district. He is smart, he is capable,

he is accomplished, he listens, and he cares. The right man to represent the Third Congressional District in Iowa is Jeff Lamberti.

I not only feel that way, but Laura feels that way. [*Laughter*] She sends her best to Jeff and Shannon and their family. She sends her best to you all. She has got to be the most patient woman in America. [*Laughter*] I also happen to believe, in all due respect to my mother, she's the greatest First Lady our country has ever had.

I am proud to be here with one of the finest United States Senators any State has ever produced in Chuck Grassley. Jeffrey, if you want to learn how to win, hire Grassley. [*Laughter*] Jeff and I were talking about what we can do together when he wins. And I said, well, why don't we work with Senator Grassley and Congressman Tom Latham, who is with us, and Congressman Steven King, who is with us, to make sure that this renewable fuels initiative we started continues to remain an important part of not only the Iowa economy but an important part of making sure we become less dependent on foreign sources of oil.

I can remember when this guy from Texas came here in 2000 and said, "I support ethanol." I think old Grassley didn't really believe me. [*Laughter*] I think he kind of thought, well, maybe that's just typical political talk. I meant what I said, and I mean what I say today. I'm looking forward to working with this new Congressman to make sure that we use Iowa farm crops to power the U.S. economy.

I do appreciate Congressman Latham coming down to say hello to the man you'll be serving with. And I appreciate Congressman Steve King coming over to be here with Jeff. These are two fine, fine Members of the United States Congress. I'm proud to call them friends. I'm proud to serve with you on behalf of the United States.

I ran into State Auditor Dave Vaudt. I said, "How's your campaign going?" [*Laughter*] He said, "Pretty good." [*Laughter*] What's it like to run unopposed?

[*Laughter*] But I'm proud of you, Dave, and I'm glad you're here with your wife, Jeanie. Thanks for coming. Now that you've got a little spare time on your hands, why don't you help our man get elected here in the Third Congressional District?

The next secretary of state of Iowa is somebody I know quite well. I used to see her all the time in the Oval Office; Mary Ann Hanusa is with us today. Thanks for running. Vote for her. She'll do a fine job.

I'm proud that members of the ex-Governors club are with us. [*Laughter*] I'm a member. [*Laughter*] Two of the better members are here: Governor Ray and Governor Branstad, two of the finest public servants the State has had. Thank you for coming. I particularly look forward to telling Mother and Dad that you're looking just fine, Bob. [*Laughter*] And so are they.

I want to thank all the grassroots activists who are here. I appreciate the chairman of the Iowa party, Ray Hoffmann. Thank you for coming. I want to thank all of you who are involved with helping this good man. I appreciate you giving—helping fill the hat. But I also want to encourage you to make sure you do more than contribute just of your money. I ask you to contribute of your time and your efforts. There's nothing better for a candidate coming down the stretch in a campaign to know that he's got a lot of folks standing side by side with him. I ask you to make the phone calls and put up the signs and turn out the vote.

I know the other side is already dancing in the end zone, except they haven't made the end zone yet. [*Laughter*] They're up there in Washington already kind of picking out their offices and measuring the drapes. [*Laughter*] This campaign only ends after the voters have had a chance to speak. No doubt in my mind, with your help, Dave [Jeff]° Lamberti will be the next United States Congressman.

° White House correction.

Dave [Jeff]° and I believe a lot of things. We believe that you ought to keep more of your own money. We believe in family values. We believe values are important. And we believe marriage is a fundamental institution of civilization.

Yesterday in New Jersey, we had another activist court issue a ruling that raises doubts about the institution of marriage. I believe that marriage is a union between a man and a woman, and I believe it's a sacred institution that is critical to the health of our society and the well-being of families, and it must be defended. And I'm looking forward to working with Jeff Lamberti to do just that.

I think one of the biggest issues in this campaign is, is what's going to happen to the money in your pocket. A big issue in this campaign is whether you're going to have more money to spend as you see fit. This election is going to have a direct impact on your family budget. When you go to the voting booth less than 2 weeks from today, the lever you pull will determine the taxes you pay. Americans will cast their ballots on November the 7th, but you're going to feel the results every April 15th. And make no mistake about it, there is a big difference in philosophy when it comes to taxes.

We believe—the Congressman-to-be and I believe—the Senator, Congressman-to-be, and two Congressmen and I believe that we think you can spend your money far better than the Federal Government can spend your money. We believe that when you have more of your own money in your pocket to save, spend, or invest, the economy benefits. We believe that the more money there is in the hands of private citizens, the more likely it is people from all walks of life will be able to realize the American Dream. That's what we believe.

Not only do we believe that; that's what we acted on. I was proud to sign the largest tax relief since Ronald Reagan was the President of the United States. And I thank Chairman—yes, Chairman Grassley—see,

he's the chairman of the Finance Committee—for taking the lead. These tax cuts would not have happened without the leadership of Chuck Grassley nor without the support of Latham and King.

And now the results of the tax cuts are in. What matters in this business is results—that's what matter. And the results are strong. Because of the tax cuts we passed, small businesses flourish, the farm economy is strong, American families have got more money in their pocket. The United States economy is the envy of the industrialized world.

The Democrats said the tax cuts were not a solution for the economy that was slipping into a recession. The truth is that the tax cuts have helped make the American economy the fastest growing of any major industrialized nation. The Democrats said the tax cuts would lead to a jobless recovery. The truth is that our economy has added jobs for 37 months in a row, and since August of 2003, our economy has created 6.6 million new jobs.

The Democrats have said the tax cuts would not help increase wages. The truth is that real wages have grown 2.2 percent over the past year. The Democrats said tax cuts would cause the deficit to explode. Well, the truth is the tax cuts led to economic growth, and that economic growth helped send our tax revenues soaring. As a matter of fact, we cut the deficit in half 3 years ahead of schedule.

And now the Democrats have another prediction—they're predicting they're going to win this November 7th. The truth is, if their electoral—election predictions are as good as their economic predictions—[laughter]—Lamberti is going to win.

One big reason we're going to win is because the truth is, the Democrats will raise your taxes. You know, you're not going to hear much about it; they're not going to go bragging about that fact. But they've got a record they're going to have to run on. They're going to have to answer to the

voters why, time and time again, they voted against the tax cuts we passed.

They don't want you to know the truth. As a matter of fact, recently, the top Democrat leader in the House made an interesting declaration. She said, "We love tax cuts." Given her record, she must be a secret admirer. [*Laughter*] It's just not—just the so-called tax cuts for the rich she opposes. When we cut taxes for everyone who pays income taxes, she and her colleagues voted against them. When we reduced the marriage penalty, she and her colleagues voted against them. When we cut the taxes on small businesses, she and her colleagues voted against them. When we lowered the taxes for families with children, she and her colleagues voted against them. When we put the death tax on the road to extinction, she and her colleagues voted against it. Time and time again, when she had the opportunity to show her love for taxes, she voted no. If this is the Democrats' idea of love—[*laughter*]—I wouldn't want to see what hate looks like. [*Laughter*]

Now they're throwing out the same old line. I don't know if it's happening in this campaign, but in district after district, you can hear them saying, "Oh, we're just going to tax the rich." But that's not the way it works when you've got a spending appetite as big as their appetite. You might remember what happened in 1992. They said, "We're going to run on middle-class tax cuts. Elect us, we're going to cut the taxes on the middle class." Sure enough, they got elected, and we had the largest—one of the largest tax increases in American history.

Now, the way it works is this: If the tax cuts we pass are not made permanent and they are left to expire, your taxes are going up. See, these tax cuts we passed are set to expire. And if they were to expire—something I'm against and something Jeff Lamberti is against and something Senator Grassley is against and these two Congressmen are against—your taxes go up.

And make no mistake about it, the Democrats want these tax cuts to expire.

Why do I say that? Recently the ranking Democrat on the House Ways and Means Committee—that's the committee that decides the level of your taxes—said he can't think of one of the tax cuts that he would extend. Those are his words, not mine. Asked if that meant he would consider tax hikes across the income spectrum, he answered, "No question about it."

I want you to think about that, what happens if the tax cuts aren't made permanent. Say you're just sitting around the breakfast table, and you have three children. If those tax cuts are not made permanent, you could look at that child and say, $500 more on my taxes going to go up. Or you can look at that other child sitting there with you, that's another 500. If you got three children, your taxes are going up $1,500. Now, that may not seem like a lot to these Washington, DC, Democrats, but it's a lot to the working people here in Iowa. The best way to make sure your taxes stay low, the best way to make sure we keep economic vitality alive, is to elect Jeff Lamberti to the United States Congress.

The biggest issue facing this country, as far as I'm concerned, is the security of the United States of America. I think about it every day. Every day I am briefed about the fact that there's still an enemy that lurks, plans, and plots and wants to kill Americans. I wish I did not have to report that. You know, when I campaigned here in 2000, I said [didn't say],* "I want to be a war President." No President wants to be a war President, but I am one. Not because the United States chose war, but because an enemy chose to attack us. And these folks are lethal, and they are brutal. And the best way to deal with them is to bring them to justice before they can hurt the American people again.

We face an enemy that has an ideology that is the opposite of what we believe.

---

* White House correction.

We believe in freedoms. We believe in the universality of freedom. We believe in the right for people to choose how they worship. We believe in freedom of the press. We believe in freedom of dissent. They don't believe in any of those freedoms. And what makes this war a tough war is that they're willing to kill innocent women and children to achieve their objectives. And they have objectives. They want to establish a governing authority from Spain to Indonesia in which they can impose their dark vision of the world. These are their words. The Commander in Chief must take the words of the enemy very seriously, particularly since the most important job that we have in Washington, DC, is to protect the American people from further attack.

Here at the homeland, we must be right 100 percent of the time in order to protect you, and the enemy only has to be right one time. And so therefore, after 9/11, after September the 11th, 2001, I vowed to give our professionals all the tools necessary to protect the American people from further attack. For example, if Al Qaida or an Al Qaida affiliate was making a phone call into the United States of America, in order to make sure that we're doing our job to protect you, we've got to understand what that person is saying. If the enemy is making a phone call, in this different kind of war that requires instant information to protect you, we better understand what the enemy is thinking and what they're planning.

Recently the terrorist surveillance program came up for a vote in the Halls of the United States Congress. Our Members stood strong in understanding that the number-one responsibility is to protect the American people and that we must give our professionals the tools necessary to protect you. Over 80 percent of the Democrats voted no, in giving the professionals the tools they need. There's just a different mindset in Washington, DC, in what we believe. They must not fear the enemy. You cannot wait to respond to the enemy after we have been attacked. To protect the

American people, we have got to make sure.

This is a different kind of war. I see we've got vets here, and I want to thank you for serving. But this is a war unlike any we have fought before. In past wars, you could determine success based upon the number of ships sunk or airplanes down or territory taken. This is a war that is global in nature, fought on a myriad of fronts, that requires precise knowledge as how to interface and react with this enemy. We pick people up off the battlefield. We pick people off the battlefield like Khalid Sheikh Mohammed, who our intelligence services believe was the mastermind of the attacks that killed over 3,000 of our citizens on September the 11th.

I felt that it was important to understand and find out what Khalid Sheikh Mohammed knew, in order to protect you. I authorized the professionals of the Central Intelligence Agency to set up a program to inquire to Mr. Khalid Sheikh Mohammed about what he knew. This bill came in front of the United States Congress to authorize the Government to be able to do so. Over 80 percent of the Democrats in the House of Representatives voted against giving our professionals the tools necessary to gain information so that we can protect you.

There is a difference of opinion, and our voters in Iowa and across the country must understand that the Democrats have a different view about this war on terror, a view that I think makes America less secure and makes it harder for us to do our job to protect the American people.

This front—this war on terror is on many fronts. And the central front right now is in Iraq. The lessons of September the 11th are many. One, we've got to stay on the offense and keep the enemy on the run. It's hard to plan, plot, and attack if you're on the run. It's hard to plan, plot, and attack if you're in a cave. And we got great professionals who are constantly keeping the pressure on this enemy. But there's

another lesson of September the 11th, and I just mentioned it—we cannot afford to wait when we see a threat. If this is a different kind of war, this country of ours must take threats seriously before they fully materialize. Saddam Hussein was a threat; the world is better off without Saddam Hussein in power.

And now the fundamental question is, does this country have the wherewithal and the perseverance to help this young democracy flourish in the heart of the Middle East? I will tell you, it's important to defeat the enemy overseas so we do not have to face them here at home.

It's tough fighting in Iraq. It's tough fighting because there are folks there who understand the stakes in this important battle in the war on terror. They understand that if we lose our nerve and leave before the job is done that they will be able to gain safe haven from which to launch further attacks. They understand that if the United States were to withdraw, it would be a significant victory for them in the war on terror. It would embolden them to recruit. It would enable them to more likely topple moderate governments.

I want you to envision a world 20 to 30 years from now in which there are violent forms of radicals—violent radicals fighting for power in the Middle East, in which moderate governments have been toppled, in which oil resources will have been used in order to blackmail Western countries into retreat. And couple all that with an Iran with a nuclear weapon, and a generation of Americans will look at our generation and say, "What happened to them? Couldn't they see the threats? Weren't they able to see the dangers?" Well, I want you to know I understand the dangers. I see—clearly see the threats. We will help this young democracy in Iraq succeed.

We will help the Iraqis defend their democracy. We will help this country become a nation that can govern itself and sustain itself and defend itself and serve as an ally in the war on terror. We will stand with the 12 million folks who went to the polls and said they want to live in freedom. We'll help train the Iraqis so they can take the fight to the enemy, and then our boys and girls will come home with the honor they have earned.

There's a mighty debate in the United States of America on this important subject. I will tell you, if we leave before the job is done, we will have let down a generation of Americans. If we leave before the job is done, we will have not honored the sacrifice of incredibly brave men and women who wear our uniform. If we leave before the job is done, we will embolden a dangerous enemy that still wants to strike the United States of America. No question, the fighting is tough, but the United States of America has done this kind of tough fighting before. We will adjust our tactics. We will support our troops. We will fight, and we will win in Iraq.

There is a difference of opinion in Washington on this important issue. The Democrat leadership and many of the Democrats have a more limited view of the war on terror. Recently the top Democrat in the House, who wants to become the Speaker, said this on a nationally televised interview: She said, quote, "It's not right to say that Iraq is part of the war on terror." She said, instead, "The war on terror is the war in Afghanistan."

Her position must come as news to Usama bin Laden, who has proclaimed that the "third world war is raging in Iraq." Her position would come as news to the number-two man of Al Qaida, who has called the struggle in Iraq "the place for the greatest battle." Her position would come as news to the terrorists from Syria, Saudi Arabia, Egypt, Sudan, Libya, Yemen, and other countries who come to Iraq to fight the rise of democracy and the United States. Her position must come as news to the people of Iraq who have lost loved ones to terrorist car bombings and assassinations and attacks in markets and

mosques. Her position would come as news to the American troops in Iraq who are risking their lives every day to fight the terrorists and prevent them from regaining the safe haven like they had in Afghanistan.

Her position on the war on terror, that it's contained only to Afghanistan, would come as news to the people in London and Madrid and Oman and Bali and Beslan and Riyadh and Istanbul and Casablanca and other cities where the terrorists have massacred and murdered innocent men, women, and children.

Her position in the war on terror is wrong. You cannot win a war if you do not believe we are in a war. It's very important for the citizens of this important State to understand that if we leave Iraq before the job is done, the enemy will follow us here. The best way to secure the peace for the United States, the best way to do— the most important job of the Federal Government is to support the troops, to support the young democracy, and defeat the enemy in Iraq and—what we'll do. And I'm proud to be standing here with Jeff Lamberti, who understands the stakes in this war.

We've got one other asset at our disposal I want to share with you, and that is the power of liberty. One of my favorite stories to share is the story that happened here a couple of weeks ago—or weeks ago— when I went to Elvis's place in Memphis with then-sitting Prime Minister Koizumi of Japan. The reason I like to share that story is because it's got a good lesson for our citizens, particularly younger citizens who may not have really studied that period of history too much, the history of Japan-U.S. relations.

People say, "Why did you go down there?" Well, I'd never been. [*Laughter*] And the Prime Minister, he wanted to go. [*Laughter*] He was an Elvis fan. [*Laughter*] But here's the story I want to tell. My dad fought the Japanese. He was an 18-year-old kid who volunteered, just like a lot of our troops are doing today—they're

all volunteers. By the way, these men and women understand the stakes. They understand the consequences of early retreat. They know what it's like to give up the ground to an enemy. They have volunteered during dangerous times. I want to thank you for your service, brother. Thanks for joining us.

That's what happened, too, after the Japanese attacked us, see. By the way, we lost more people on September the 11th than we did at Pearl Harbor. But a lot of the young folks signed up. One of them was George H.W. Bush. And he and a lot of other brave Americans fought tooth and nail to defeat the Japanese. They were the sworn enemy of the United States. And it was a bloody conflict, a tough fight. And yet, some 60 years later, the Navy pilot's son is on Air Force One flying down to Elvis's place talking about the peace.

You see, on the flight down, the Prime Minister of Japan, our former enemy, and I talked about what we could do to work together to make the world a more peaceful place. We talked about the fact that Japan had 1,000 troops in Iraq to help that young democracy fight off the extremists and moderates—to help the moderates fight off the extremists. See, Prime Minister Koizumi and I understand we're in an ideological struggle between moderate people and people who just want to live in peace and extremists and radicals who want to impose their view. He understands that. And he knows that as a free nation, we need to help struggling democracies survive if we want there to be peace for our children and our grandchildren.

And we talked about North Korea. We talked about helping HIV/AIDS victims in Africa. We talked about making this world a better place. Isn't it interesting that the son of a man who fought the Japanese is able to talk the peace with the Prime Minister of a former enemy? What happened was, Japan adopted a Japanese-style democracy. The power of the—of that lesson is this: Liberty has got the capacity

to transform an enemy into an ally, just like liberty has got the capacity to transform a region of hate into a region of hope. Someday an American President will be talking with elected leaders from the Middle East about the peace, and a generation of Americans, a generation to come, will be better off for it.

These are the stakes in this election. I'm proud you're here. Thank you for standing with Jeff. Take it to the final day, and he'll win. God bless.

NOTE: The President spoke at 12:42 p.m. at the Iowa State Fairgrounds. In his remarks, he referred to Robert Ray and Terry Branstad, former Governors of Iowa; former President Saddam Hussein of Iraq; Usama bin Laden, leader of the Al Qaida terrorist organization; and Ayman Al-Zawahiri, founder of the Egyptian Islamic Jihad and senior Al Qaida associate.

Remarks to Reporters in Clinton Township, Michigan
October 26, 2006

Purchase at Morley Candy Makers

The President. They asked me why I came here, and I said, one, I like small businesses, and two, I like sweets. [*Laughter*]

The entrepreneurial spirit is strong in this store. And the job of those of us in Washington who are lucky enough to serve the American people is to keep the taxes low on the small-business people, as well as the people who work for the small-business people.

And so we want to wish you all the best. Thanks for thinking the big dream.

Ronald W. Rapson. Thank you very much, Mr. President, for coming. Enjoy Sanders hot fudge, one of the best products in the State of Michigan.

The President. Looking forward to it. [*Laughter*]

Mr. Rapson. A couple of Michigan State and Michigan candy bars for you there.

The President. There you go. Now, the other thing is, is that the big money here is, of course, with the press corps. And I would fully suspect you all to shop. [*Laughter*] Fletcher [Michael Fletcher, Washington Post], how about it?

Q. Yes, sir.

The President. All right. Thank you. Good to be with you.

NOTE: The President spoke at 5:05 p.m. at Morley Candy Makers. Participating in the event was Ronald W. Rapson, president, Morley Brands LLC.

Remarks at a Reception for Senatorial Candidate Michael Bouchard in Warren, Michigan
October 26, 2006

Thank you all. Thanks for coming. The way to go from worst to first is elect Mike Bouchard to the United States Senate. I am impressed by Mike Bouchard's char-

acter, his decency, his compassion for the people of Michigan. And there's no doubt in my mind, with your hard work, he'll be elected to the United States Senate.

I thank you for coming. You know, it's an interesting year. The other side is dancing in the end zone, except they're on the 15-yard line. We got the issues on our side. We got the right candidates running. Mike Bouchard is going to win. And I appreciate you coming to support him.

And I'm proud to be here with Pam and his family. I thank—you know, there's nothing better than having a candidate who has got a strong family. I appreciate the fact that he puts family first in his life. And I know what it's like to have a loving wife and kids that love you because I've got a loving wife. And she understands what I know: Michael Bouchard is the right man for this job.

I appreciate Congressman Joe Knollenberg joining us. Congressman, I appreciate you coming. We got the State attorney general, Michael Cox. Michael, where are you? Thanks for coming, buddy. [Applause] There you go. He's a good man to be running with. He's a good, strong leader. I appreciate you coming, Mike.

I'm proud to be here with the grassroots activists for the State of Michigan, the party chairman, the national committeewoman; the cochair of the Michigan Republican Party happens to Jane Abraham. I know her husband quite well. [Laughter] The reason I bring up the grassroots activists is, I want to remind you that giving money is one thing; turning out the vote is the other. And coming down the stretch, this good man is going to give it his all, but he needs you by his side. He needs people getting on the telephones and putting up the signs and knocking on doors and reminding people of Michigan, if they want good government and good results, Mike Bouchard is the—should be the United States Senator.

And when he wins, we've got a lot to do together—got a lot to do together. One thing we're going to do together is to make sure we continue to develop alternative fuel for our automobiles. See, we've got a problem here in America. We are too dependent on foreign sources of oil. And the best way to diversify away from foreign sources of oil is to encourage renewable fuels like ethanol. We want Michigan farmers growing the fuel that runs our automobiles, for the sake of economic security and national security.

I'm looking forward to having this good Senator vote to confirm the judges I nominate to the Federal bench. Make no mistake about it, one of the key issues in this campaign is the type of judiciary we end up having in America. My job is to appoint judges who will strictly interpret the Constitution and not use the bench from which to legislate. And it would be—if you believe in that philosophy, it's important that you have at least one United States Senator from Michigan who will support a conservative judiciary, and that's Senator Mike Bouchard.

I mentioned his love for family. He understands what I know, that marriage is a fundamental institution of our civilization. Yesterday in New Jersey, we had another activist court issue a ruling that raises doubts about the institution of marriage. I believe that marriage is a union between a man and a woman. Mike and I believe that marriage is a sacred institution, that it is critical to the health of our society and the well-being of families, and marriage must be defended.

Another big issue in this campaign, and one I'm looking forward to working with Senator Bouchard on, is taxes. You know, we believe that we ought to keep your taxes low because we believe you can spend your money better than the Government can. The Democrats believe that they can spend your money better than you can and, therefore, will raise your taxes.

Make no mistake about it, this is a key issue in this campaign. When we were confronted with recession and corporate scandal and an attack on the United States and the war—needed to defend ourselves—and hurricanes and high energy prices, this

economy was able to withstand those challenges because we cut the taxes. See, if you have more money in your pocket to save, invest, or spend, this economy grows.

Oh, you heard all the rhetoric during those tax debates. For those people who are undecided in this campaign, you might want to look up the words of the respective candidates when it came to cutting taxes. You might want to make sure you understand the record of people who are running in this race for the United States Senate when it comes to taxes. You might remember, the Democrats said that tax cuts were not the solution for an economy that was slipping into recession. Truth is, the tax cuts have helped make America's economy the fastest growing of any major industrialized nation.

The Democrats said the tax cuts would lead to a jobless recovery. You might remember that rhetoric. The truth is that our economy has added jobs for 37 months in a row, and since August of 2003, our economy has created more than 6.6 million new jobs. Oh, the Democrats said the tax cuts would cause the deficit to explode. Well, the truth is that the tax cuts led to economic growth, and that growth has helped send tax revenues soaring. As a result, we cut the deficit in half 3 years ahead of schedule.

And now the Democrats are telling you they're going to win on election day. But the truth is, if their electoral predictions are as reliable as their economic predictions—[*laughter*]—November 7th is going to be a good day for Michigan because Mike Bouchard is going to win the United States Senate.

One of the reasons why we're going to hold the Senate and hold the House on election day is because the Democrats are determined to raise the taxes on the people that work in this country. Oh, I know, they're not going to admit it out loud, but I want to remind you of what the top Democrat leader in the House said recently. She said, "We love tax cuts." Given her record, she must be a secret admirer. [*Laughter*]

It's just not the so-called tax cuts for the rich that she opposes. When we cut taxes for everyone who pays income taxes, she and her House colleagues, as well as Members of the United States Senate, voted against that tax cut. When we reduced the marriage penalty, she and her colleagues in Washington, DC, voted against it. When we cut the taxes on small business, she and her colleagues voted against it. When we lowered taxes for families with children, she and her colleagues voted against it. When we reduced the taxes on capital gains and dividends, she and her colleagues in Washington, DC, voted against it. When we put the death tax on the road to extinction, she and her colleagues in Washington, DC, voted against it. Time and time again, when she had an opportunity to show her love for tax cuts—[*laughter*]—she voted no. If this is the Democrats' idea of love—[*laughter*]—I wouldn't want to see what hate looks like. [*Laughter*]

No, taxes are a big issue—big issue. Oh, you'll hear them try to obscure the deal by saying, "We're just—only going to tax the rich people." I want you to tell your fellow citizens who have yet to make up their mind that in 1992, they campaigned on, "We're going to give you a middle class tax cut." And when they had the power and the capacity to make the decisions about taxes in the White House and in the Congress, we had the largest—one of the largest tax increases—increases—in American history. Their record is clear. They can run, but they can't hide. If the people of Michigan want low taxes, you vote for Mike Bouchard as United States Senator.

I want to talk about taxes just a little bit more. [*Laughter*] See, I know how important they are for this economy of ours. I know how important they are for small businesses. I know how important it is for our farmers and ranchers to get tax cuts.

I know how important it is for people who are working for a living to be able to have more money in your pocket so you can make the decisions for your family. I know how important it is to keep taxes low. I've seen it work. We've got a record that we can run on.

You know, the way it works is, is that these tax cuts we passed are set to expire, so, therefore, they have to be renewed by Congress or made permanent. So recently they asked the head man on the Ways and Means Committee in the House of Representatives—he would be the head man, see, he's the ranking member on the Ways and Means Committee—they asked him about which tax cuts he would extend— the ones that maybe help the family with children, or the ones that get rid of the marriage penalty. He asked that—he couldn't think of one of those tax cuts that he would extend. In other words, by not extending, he's raising your taxes. See, they try to hide behind the language.

I don't know if your opponent is trying to hide behind the language, but I doubt that she's going to be there to make sure these tax cuts we passed stay intact. I want to tell you what that means. It means that if the child tax credit were cut in half, if these tax cuts aren't extended, if you're having breakfast with your family and you got one kid, your taxes go up $500, if they get control. Imagine having lunch with four children and the tax cuts don't get extended. That mother and father can rest assured that the Democrats will have caused their taxes to go up by 500 times four. That would be $2,000. That may not seem like a lot to the big spenders in Washington, DC, but it's a lot to the people who work for a living. If you want to keep your taxes low, you vote for Mike Bouchard for the United States Senate.

Mike mentioned an issue that's on my mind a lot. As a matter of fact, every day I think about how best to protect the American people, because that is the most important responsibility of your Govern-

ment. I wish I didn't have to say that, but as your Commander in Chief and as the person responsible for rallying the Federal Government to use all assets to protect you, I've got to speak plainly to the American people. An enemy still lurks; a dangerous enemy still exists, which will use any means they can to attack us again. And therefore, we must use every means we have at our disposal to protect you. The most important job I have, and the most important job this United States Senator will have, is to make sure that we do everything in our power to protect the American people.

See, we face an enemy that knows no bounds of decency. They're ideologues, but they're ideologues of hate. They have taken a great religion and have twisted it to their evil intentions. They want to establish a caliphate, a governing structure, from Spain to Indonesia, in which they're able to impose their dark vision on decent men and women. They want safe haven from which to launch attack against America again. They would like the wealth so they can develop weapons of mass destruction to use against us.

You cannot negotiate with these people. You cannot reason with these people. The best way to attack—the best way to defend America is to go on the attack, stay on the attack, and bring the people to justice before they hurt us again.

And Michigan needs a United States Senator who understands the stakes of the world in which we live, and that Senator will be Mike Bouchard. We need a Senator up there who understands this is a global war fought on a variety of fronts. One of the lessons of September the 11th is we must stay on the offense. Look, it's hard to plan, plot, and attack if you're running or hiding in a cave. And you got to know, we got immense pressure on those who would do harm to the United States.

The other lesson—another lesson is, is that when we see a threat overseas, we must take that threat seriously. America cannot wait to respond after we've been

attacked. One of the lessons of that fateful day is we must do everything in our power to protect you before there's an attack. I saw a threat in Iraq. Getting rid of Saddam Hussein has made the United States safer and the world better off.

And now our job is to complete the mission, and that is to help Iraq become a government—a country that can govern itself, sustain itself, defend itself, a country that will be an ally in the war against these extremists that want to harm us. And the stakes are high. It's important that we succeed. It's important that we understand there's an enemy that will kill innocent life so they can get their images on our TV screens, because they believe it's just a matter of time before we leave before the job is done.

If we were to listen to the Democrats in Washington, DC, who say, "Let's have a fixed date of withdrawal"—by the way, that's code word for saying, leave before the job is done—we would turn over this important country to radicals and extremists who would plot and plan and attack.

I want you to think about a world in which violent forms of extremists battle for power, a Middle East in which moderate governments have been toppled, a Middle East in which these extremists get ahold of oil and energy and enable—to enable them to blackmail the United States. Imagine the message: "If you don't abandon your relationship with Israel," for example, "we'll run the price of oil up to—if you don't retreat to allow us to continue to expand our caliphate or governing structure, we'll run the oil up." Imagine Iran with a nuclear weapon 20 or 30 years from now. People would look back at this period of time and say, "What happened to them? How come they couldn't see the threats to a generation of Americans who are growing up? Why weren't they able to see the dangers that persisted?"

I see the dangers. I understand the stakes. Victory in Iraq is essential for the security of the United States of America.

We will change our plans; we will adjust our tactics; but we will support our military. We will support this young democracy, and we will win in Iraq.

And there's a fundamental difference of opinion. You listen to the rhetoric of the leaders of the Democrat Party. They have a different view than I do about whether or not this is a global war on terror. They have a different view about how aggressive the United States should be in pursuing enemies overseas so we do not have to face them here at home.

I want you to listen to what the—one of the leaders in Washington, DC, said this past Sunday. She said—a Democrat leader in a nationally televised interview—she said, "It is not right to say that, quote, 'Iraq is part of the war on terror.'" In other words, they don't believe Iraq is a part of the war on terror. They believe it is a separate theater of some kind. I'm not sure what they believe. This is a global war we're—fight. You can't win a war if you don't believe we're in a war. And therefore, we need leaders in Washington, DC, who understand the stakes.

And her position on Iraq would come as news to Usama bin Laden, who has proclaimed that the "third world war is raging in Iraq." Her position would come as news to the number-two man of Al Qaida, Mr. Zawahiri, who has called the struggle in Iraq "the place for the greatest battle." Her position on Iraq would come as news to the terrorists from Syria, Saudi Arabia, Egypt, Sudan, Lybia, Yemen, and other countries who have come to Iraq to fight America and the coalition forces. Her position would come as news to the people of Iraq who have lost loved ones as a result of terrorist bombings and beheadings and brutal acts of terror. Her position would come as news to those brave men and women who wear the uniform of the United States of America who are risking their lives every day to protect the American people.

And her position that the war on terror—see, she went on to say it's only in Afghanistan—her position that the war on terror should be fought only in Afghanistan would come as news to the citizens of London and Madrid and Amman and Bali and Beslan and Riyadh and Istanbul and Casablanca and other cities where the terrorists have murdered innocent men, women, and children.

We need people in Washington, DC, who understand the stakes of the world in which we live. Our most important duty is to protect you. And the best way to protect the American people is to confront the enemy overseas so we do not have to face them here at home. And the best way to confront the enemy is to be clear-eyed and understand that if we were to leave Iraq before the job is done, the enemy would follow us right here to the United States of America. We will fight; we will win in Iraq.

We got a lot of assets at our disposal. We got the finest military that has ever existed, and we need a United States Senator who will support them. And when I say support them, I mean give them all the tools necessary so they can do their job. This Government owes these young men and women and their families all the support necessary, and I'm confident that Senator Mike Bouchard will help me provide that support.

But we've got another asset, and that's the power of liberty. I like to tell the story—as a matter of fact, I'm going to tell it as many times as people will listen—[*laughter*]—about my trip to Elvis's place. [*Laughter*] I went down there, as you might recall, with the then sitting Prime Minister of Japan, who no longer holds the office, Prime Minister Koizumi. He's a friend of mine. We went down there. I'd never been, thought it would be fun to go. He wanted to go a lot. [*Laughter*] He was an Elvis fan.

But I also wanted to tell a story. And here's the story. My dad, like many of your—who got relatives here, many of you whose relatives did the same thing, who are—you're here; the relatives probably aren't—[*laughter*]—joined the Navy to fight the Japanese. You know the kind of people I'm talking about. He's an 18-year-old kid; the Japanese had attacked America. They killed more people on 9/11 than were killed at Pearl Harbor. And yet he went, just like the kids who are signing up today. We've got unbelievable men and women who are saying, "I understand the stakes, and I want to go defend my country"—as volunteers. That's what happened in World War II. And it was a bloody war, and a lot of people lost their lives. It was a tough, tough fight.

I find it to be really interesting that the son of this Navy pilot is on Air Force One flying down to Memphis, Tennessee, with the Prime Minister of the former enemy, talking about peace, talking about the fact that this country of Japan has sent 1,000 troops into Iraq, because the—Prime Minister Koizumi and I understand that we're involved in an ideological struggle between decent people who want to live in peace and radicals and extremists who will battle democracy in order to be able to impose their will.

We talked about North Korea and the fact that not only the North Korea—man trying to get him a nuclear weapon and how destabilizing that would be, but we mourned the fact that thousands starve inside that country. We talked about HIV/AIDS on the continent of Africa and our understanding that to whom much is given, much is required, and that this great country, I assured him, would continue to take the lead in providing antiretroviral drugs to help save lives. And we talked about helping Afghanistan build up its democracy.

Isn't it amazing? My dad fought the Japanese, and I'm talking about keeping the peace. Something happened between World War II and today, and what happened was, Japan adopted a Japanese-style democracy. Democracies yield the peace.

Liberty has got the capacity to transform an enemy into an ally. Liberty has got the capacity to transform regions of hopelessness to regions of light and hope.

Someday an American President will be sitting down with duly elected leaders from the Middle East talking about keeping the peace, and our children and grandchildren will be better off for it.

God bless.

NOTE: The President spoke at 6:03 p.m. at the Mabry Banquet and Convention Center. In his remarks, he referred to Saulius Anuzis, chairman, and Holly Hughes, national committeewoman, Michigan Republican Party; former Secretary of Energy Spencer Abraham; former President Saddam Hussein of Iraq; Usama bin Laden, leader of the Al Qaida terrorist organization; and Chairman Kim Jong Il of North Korea.

Remarks Following Discussions With Secretary General Jakob Gijsbert "Jaap" de Hoop Scheffer of the North Atlantic Treaty Organization and an Exchange With Reporters
October 27, 2006

President Bush. I'm proud to welcome the Secretary General of NATO here to the Oval Office. We've just had a fascinating discussion.

First, Mr. Secretary General, you've been a very strong leader. As a matter of fact, you've made NATO a values-based organization that is capable of dealing with the true threats of the 21st century. I appreciate your leadership. I particularly appreciate the fact that you have led the 26 nations of NATO into Afghanistan to help this young democracy. You know what I know, that the real challenge for the future is to help people of moderation and young democracies succeed in the face of threats and attacks by radicals and extremists who do not share our ideology, have kind of a dark vision of the world.

I appreciate the fact that you're reaching out to global partners, nations which share our value but have not been considered a—necessarily considered a part of NATO. I want to thank your view of making sure NATO continues to provide the opportunity for other nations to join NATO.

I'm looking forward to Riga. The Riga summit is a time for us to celebrate the great successes of this partnership. Mr. Secretary General and I will be there reminding our partners that we have a lot of work to be done in the noble cause of peace.

So welcome.

Secretary General de Hoop Scheffer. Mr. President, thank you very much, and thank you for giving me your time. I can echo your words. NATO is delivering security in the 21st century. And that means defending values, and that means defending values not only in Europe but far away from NATO's traditional area. And the case in point, of course, is Afghanistan, where there was a regime which was grossly violating human rights, no women's rights, public executions. There we are trying to assist the Afghan Government to establish democracy, to establish human rights, to establish those values.

And let me say that when, in those actions of NATO, of those brave NATO soldiers, civilians are killed, as happened 2 days ago, that's always a tragedy. That's a tragedy.

But let me convince you to look at the broader picture. They are against democracy. Girls did not go to school when the Taliban was running Afghanistan. Now they go to school. Now there is a precedence. Now there is a government. Civilian victims are a tragedy, but we are there in favor

of democracy. They are there to destroy democracy, and they are there to destroy our values.

Mr. President, I'm looking forward to the Riga summit, where we'll see a 21st century NATO delivering security in many, many places of the world with 50,000 soldiers, including many Americans, on three continents. That is the challenge, but I can tell you that NATO is up to the challenge. NATO is delivering security, and NATO will continue to do this, indeed, with its presence, but also with global partners, because terrorism, proliferation, failed states, and failing states are global threats we have to face and to counter on a global scale.

Mr. President, once again, thank you very much for being here.

President Bush. Yes, sir.

I'll answer a couple of questions this morning. Jennifer [Jennifer Loven, Associated Press].

Iran

Q. Thank you, sir. What does it say to you that Iran is doubling its enrichment capacity?

President Bush. It says to me that we must double our effort to work with the international community to persuade the Iranians that there is only isolation from the world if they continue working forward on such a program. And I've read the speculation about that that's what they may be doing, but whether they've doubled it or not, the idea of Iran having a nuclear weapon is unacceptable. And it's unacceptable to the United States, and it's unacceptable to nations we're working with in the United Nations to send a common message.

Caren [Caren Bohan, Reuters].

Interrogation of Terrorists

Q. Sir, do you agree with the Vice President that a dunk in the water is a "no brainer" when it comes to interrogating a terror suspect?

President Bush. This country doesn't torture. We're not going to torture. We will interrogate people we pick up off the battlefield to determine whether or not they've got information that will be helpful to protect the country.

Keil [Richard Keil, Bloomberg News].

2006 Midterm Elections

Q. Mr. President, with the elections just about 10 days away, polls show that voters are more disenchanted with the Republican-led Congress than at any time since 1994, when the Democrats lost power. What explanation or answer do you have for people who feel that way?

President Bush. Keil, I understand people here in Washington have already determined the outcome of the elections. As I said in my press conference the other day, I've seen it before, where people start measuring the drapes in their new offices before the vote has been counted—in other words, they're taking the people's vote for granted.

This election is going to be determined by how our candidates run locally. And I believe if they continue to emphasize the big issues—keeping taxes low and protecting the American people—we'll win. And so we'll see how the outcome comes. I know there's a lot of speculation here in Washington, DC, and there's a lot of fascination about listening to these pundits and people who are giving their opinions.

All I can tell you is what I see: I see enthusiasm amongst Republicans; I see candidates who are saying, "Vote for me. I will work to make sure America doesn't get attacked again." And I'm seeing candidates saying, "I understand that if we run up your taxes like the Democrats do, it's going to hurt this economy, and so we'll keep your taxes low."

Thank you all very much.

NOTE: The President spoke at 10:53 a.m. in the Oval Office at the White House.

The President's Radio Address
October 28, 2006

Good morning. Election day is around the corner, and one of the biggest issues at stake in this campaign is your taxes. Here is my philosophy: I believe that our economy grows and the American Dream reaches more citizens when you keep more of what you earn. With more money in your pocket, it is easier for families to afford a good education, it is easier for young people to afford the downpayment on a home of their own, and it's easier for small-business owners to go out and invest and create jobs.

So my administration and the Republican Congress enacted the largest tax relief since Ronald Reagan was in the White House. We cut taxes for every American who pays income taxes. We doubled the child tax credit. We reduced the marriage penalty. We cut taxes on small business. We cut taxes on capital gains and dividends to promote investment and jobs. And to reward family businesses and farmers for a lifetime of hard work and savings, we put the death tax on the path to extinction.

Now the results of these tax cuts are in. The tax cuts we passed have left more than a trillion dollars in the hands of American workers, families, and small businesses, and you have used that money to fuel a strong and growing economy. Last year, our economy grew faster than any other major industrialized nation. This week, we learned that our economy grew by 1.6 percent during the third quarter of this year. As we expected, this rate is slower than in previous quarters. Yet the evidence still points to a vibrant economy that is providing more jobs and better wages for our workers and helping reduce the Federal deficit.

Since August 2003, the American economy has created more than 6.6 million new jobs, including over 1.7 million jobs in the past 12 months alone. Real take-home wages are up by 2.2 percent over the past year, which means an extra $1,300 for the typical family of four with two wage earners. And the economic growth spurred by tax cuts has helped reduce the deficit. Tax revenues have soared as the economy has grown, allowing us to meet our goal of cutting the Federal deficit in half, 3 years ahead of schedule.

All these signs point to one conclusion: Cutting your taxes worked. Unfortunately, the Democrats are still determined to raise your taxes, and if they gain control of the Congress, they can do so without lifting a finger. Under current law, many of the tax cuts we passed have to be renewed by Congress, or they will expire. In other words, if Congress fails to act, your taxes will automatically go up. If Democrats take control of the House, the committee in charge of all tax legislation would be chaired by a Democrat who recently said he cannot think of one of our tax cuts that he would extend. And if there's no legislation to renew and extend the tax cuts, every tax rate will go back up to its old, higher level.

Take just one example: If Democrats have their way, the child tax credit will be cut in half, from $1,000 per child to just $500 per child. And think of what that means for your family. Next time you're having dinner at home, look around the table and multiply the number of children you have by $500. That's how much more you will be sending to Washington in taxes if Democrats take control of the Congress. If you have two children, that is an extra $1,000 the Democrats will add to your tax bill every year. If you have three children, that's an extra $1,500. If you have four children, that's an extra $2,000. That may not seem like a lot to Democrats in Washington, but for working families across America, that is real money.

The decision you make on election day will have a direct impact on America's economy and on your family budget. So this coming week, I'll be traveling across America, and I'll be carrying this message: Whether you're a worker earning a paycheck, or a small-business owner who's thinking about hiring more workers, or a family worried about gas prices or health care costs, the last thing you need now is a higher tax bill. To keep this economy growing and delivering prosperity to more Americans, we need leaders in Washington who understand the importance of letting you keep more of your money and making the tax relief we delivered permanent.

Thank you for listening.

NOTE: The address was recorded at 7:50 a.m. on October 27 in the Cabinet Room at the White House for broadcast at 10:06 a.m. on October 28. The transcript was made available by the Office of the Press Secretary on October 27 but was embargoed for release until the broadcast. The Office of the Press Secretary also released a Spanish language transcript of this address.

Remarks at an Indiana Victory 2006 Rally in Sellersburg, Indiana
October 28, 2006

The President. Thank you all. Thank you for your warm welcome. I appreciate being here. You know, recently the First Lady was here. She told me there's no finer day to spend a Saturday than in southern Indiana. She also told me there's no finer Congressman for the people of this district than Mike Sodrel. As usual, Laura is right. Mike Sodrel needs to be sent back to the United States Congress.

As a member of the Indiana National Guard, he has served our country in uniform, and as a Congressman, he is a strong supporter of the United States military. Mike Sodrel supports the veterans.

I think it's good to have a man representing you who knows what it means to build a company from the bottom up, somebody who knows what it means to meet a payroll, somebody who brings fiscal discipline to the Nation's Capital. As a father and a grandfather, Mike Sodrel understands Indiana values, and he's standing up for those values in Washington, DC.

The stakes are high in this election. Your vote will have an impact not only on your lives here but a impact that will help determine the course of this Nation. I want to thank you for supporting this good man. The election of Mike Sodrel is important for the United States of America.

Laura sends her love. Sodrel told me coming over, he said, "The event with Laura was so great, we felt like asking you to stay at home and bring her back." [*Laughter*] I appreciate being with Keta—Keta Sodrel. I appreciate being with all the Sodrel children and the grandchildren. These are people who put family first, and that's important.

I want to thank all the statewide elected officials who are here today. Thank you for coming.

Audience members. U.S.A.! U.S.A.! U.S.A.!

The President. I want to thank all the grassroots activists who are here today. I thank you for putting up the signs. I thank you for making the phone calls. I thank you do the work—I thank you for, in advance, what you're going to do in the next week, and that's send this good man back to the United States Congress.

Election day is 10 days away, and we're going to sprint to the finish line. I understand you've probably been paying attention

to the pundits in Washington, DC. They think the election is already over. As a matter of fact, some of them in Washington are already measuring the drapes for their new offices.

Audience members. Boo!

The President. In other words, they're taking your vote for granted.

Audience members. Boo!

The President. This isn't the first time that's happened. You might remember, back in 2004, they were picking out new offices in the West Wing. [*Laughter*] Things turned out a little differently on election day. The movers never got the phone call. This November 7th, voters are going to defy all the pundits in Washington, DC, and send this good man back to the United States Congress. We will control the House of Representatives, and we will control the United States Senate. We will win this election because we've got good, strong candidates like Mike Sodrel, and we will win this election because we got a record to run on.

For decades, our public schools failed too many students. We passed the No Child Left Behind Act. We demanded high standards and strong accountability, and we are bringing America closer to the day when every single child in this country gets a good education.

For decades, we've been growing dependent on foreign oil. So we took the lead. We passed an energy bill that supports conservation and expands domestic production. But we're also spending money to make sure that Indiana farmers produce the fuel for our cars in the future. Mike and I understand this: When the agricultural economy is strong, that's good for the United States of America.

For decades, Medicare was outdated. It wasn't serving our seniors as well as it could. So we passed landmark legislation to modernize the Medicare system. Now 33 million seniors have more choices and access to affordable goods, and the days of our poor seniors having to choose between food and medicine are over.

For decades, we have not had complete control over our southern border, and illegal immigration has been on the rise. So we have acted. I sent National Guard troops down there to help our Border Patrol. We're adding thousands of new Border Patrol. We will reform our immigration system, and we will uphold the immigration laws of the United States.

Activist judges try to define America by court order. Just this week in New Jersey——

Audience members. Boo!

The President. ——another activist court issued a ruling that raises doubt about the institution of marriage. We believe that marriage is the union between a man and a woman, and should be defended. I will continue to appoint judges who strictly interpret the law and not legislate from the bench. America is better off because John Roberts and Sam Alito are serving on the Supreme Court of the United States.

We have a record to run on. And I appreciate Mike Sodrel's support on these important issues. There are big differences in Washington, DC, between Republicans and Democrats, and when it comes—and perhaps the biggest differences can be seen in two issues: Which party will keep your taxes low and keep this economy growing, and which party will take the necessary steps to protect you from the terrorists?

Let me start with taxes. We have a clear philosophy. We believe that you know how to spend your money far better than the Federal Government does. We believe that when you have more money in your pocket to save, invest, or spend, the economy benefits. The Democrats believe they should raise your taxes so they can spend your money.

Audience members. Boo!

The President. We not only have a philosophy, we acted on that philosophy. We passed the largest tax relief since Ronald Reagan was the President of the United

States. We cut the taxes on everyone who pays income taxes. We doubled the child tax credit. We reduced the marriage penalty. We cut taxes on small businesses. We cut taxes on capital gains and dividends to encourage investment. And to reward hard work and small-business owners and farmers for a lifetime of work, we put the death tax on the road to extinction.

You might remember the debate. The Democrats in Washington predicted the tax cuts wouldn't create jobs, would not create wages, and would cause the Federal deficit to explode. Truth is, the facts are in. The tax cuts have led to a growing economy that has added 6.6 million new jobs since August of 2003. Real wages have risen 2.2 percent over the past 12 months. We have cut the deficit in half 3 years ahead of schedule.

And now the Democrats in Washington have another prediction—they're telling you they're going win on election day. If their electoral predictions are as reliable as their economic predictions, November 7th is going to be a great day for the Republican Party.

They don't really want you to know their position when it comes to taxes. They really don't want you to know that they're going to raise up your taxes. As a matter of fact, the Member from California, the ranking leader, the minority leader in the House, who wants to be the Speaker——

Audience members. Boo!

The President. Here's what she said the other day. She said, "We love tax cuts." That's what she said. Given her record, she must be a secret admirer. [*Laughter*] She and her party voted against reducing the marriage penalty, voted against cutting taxes on small businesses, voting against lowering taxes on families with children, voted against getting rid of the death tax. Time and time again, when she and the Democrat Party had an opportunity to show their love for tax cuts, they voted no. If this is the Democrats' idea of love, I

wouldn't want to see what hate looks like. [*Laughter*]

See, here's the way it's going to work. If we don't make permanent the tax cuts or if the tax cuts are not extended, you're going to get a tax increase. And so they asked the man who would be head of the Ways and Means Committee if we don't win—we will win—he said he can't think of one of the tax cuts he would extend. See, in other words, he's going to let them all expire. Now, think about what that means if you are a small-business owner—and we've got a lot of small-business owners here in southern Indiana. If you're a small-business owner who pays taxes at the individual rate, the Democrats are going to raise your taxes. If you're a small-business owner who wants to expand and invest in new equipment, the Democrats are going to raise your taxes.

Audience members. Boo!

The President. If you're a small-business owner who wants to pass on your life's work to your children and grandchildren, the Democrats want to raise your taxes. If you're a small-business owner, you better vote for Mike Sodrel to make sure your taxes stay low.

When a Democrat can't—say they can't think of one of the tax cuts they would extend, I want you to think about what it means for our families. The child tax credit would be cut in half from $1,000 to $500. So when you're sitting around the dinner table this evening, and if you've got one child sitting there, you can rest assured that your taxes, if the Democrats take over, will go up by 500. If you happen to have two children, that's $1,000 tax increase. If you have four children, that's a $2,000 tax increase. That may not seem like a lot to the Democrats in Washington, DC, but we understand it's a lot for you, and we're going to keep your taxes low.

They want to get in your pocketbook, and we're not going to let them. A big

issue in this campaign is taxes. The Democrats will raise your taxes, and the Republicans will keep your taxes low.

This election is taking place in an historic time for our country. When people look back at this period of time, the question will be, did we do everything in our power to protect the American people and win the war on terror? And we are in a war. It came to our shores on September the 11th, 2001. And on that day, I vowed to use every element of national power to defend the American people and to defeat the terrorists.

Audience members. U.S.A.! U.S.A.! U.S.A.!

The President. We face an enemy that— which is brutal. There is no negotiation with these people. These are ideologues who have a backward and hateful vision of the world. They do not believe in freedom. They hate America because we do believe in freedom. For those who say, "Bring them at the table to discuss our differences," they do not understand the nature of these people. The best way to protect the American people is to bring them to justice before they hurt us again.

We have been implementing a strategy to protect you. You know, the enemy can be right one time, and we must be right 100 percent of the time to protect the American people. And that is why I said that we must break down walls that prevent the intelligence community and enforcement community from sharing information. And so, working with Members in Congress like Mike Sodrel, we passed the PATRIOT Act.

I understand this is a different kind of war. For you World War II vets here, this is not a war that can be determined by how many airplanes we shoot down or what kind of territory we take. It's a different kind of war. And it means good intelligence. In order to be able to protect you, we must know what the enemy is thinking and getting ready to do. That's why when Al Qaida or an Al Qaida affiliate is making a phone call from outside the United States to inside the United States, we want to know why.

In this new kind of war, we must be willing to question the enemy when we pick them up on the battlefield. We have captured people like Khalid Sheikh Mohammed, who our intelligence community thinks was the mastermind of the September the 11th attacks. When we captured him, I said to the Central Intelligence Agency, "Why don't we find out what he knows in order to be able to protect America from another attack."

In the past year, Congress has voted on each of these critical tools in the fight against terror, and these votes have revealed a clear pattern and a clear difference of opinion. When it came time to renew the PATRIOT Act, more than 75 percent of the House Democrats voted against it.

Audience members. Boo!

The President. When it came time on whether to allow the Central Intelligence Agency to continue to detain and question terrorists, almost 80 percent of the House Democrats voted against it.

Audience members. Boo!

The President. When it came time to vote on whether the NSA should continue to monitor terrorist communications through the terrorist surveillance program, almost 90 percent of House Democrats voted against it.

Audience members. Boo!

The President. In all these vital measures for fighting the war on terror, the Democrats in Washington follow a simple philosophy: Just say no. When it comes to listening in on the terrorists, what's the Democratic answer? Just say no. When it comes to detaining terrorists, what's the Democrat answer?

Audience members. Just say no!

The President. When it comes to questioning terrorists, what's the Democrat answer?

Audience members. Just say no!

The President. When it comes to trying terrorists, what's the Democrats' answer?

Audience members. Just say no!

The President. So when the Democrats ask for your vote on November the 7th, what are you going to say?

Audience members. Just say no!

The President. Here are some questions we're asking all around the country: Do you want your Government to listen in on the terrorists?

Audience members. Yes!

The President. Do you want your Government to detain the terrorists?

Audience members. Yes!

The President. Do you want your Government to question the terrorists?

Audience members. Yes!

The President. Do you want your Government to do whatever it takes to bring justice to the terrorists?

Audience members. Yes!

The President. And so when Republicans ask for your vote on November 7, what's your answer?

Audience members. Yes!

The President. We will continue to make sure our professionals have the tools necessary to protect you. And I want to thank Mike Sodrel for his strong support for our professionals on the frontline of protecting the American people. But the best way to protect you is to go on the offense and defeat the enemy overseas so we do not have to face them here.

One of the lessons of September the 11th is that when we see a threat, we must take it seriously before that threat comes home to hurt us. I saw a threat in Saddam Hussein; members of both political parties in Congress saw a threat in Saddam Hussein; the United Nations saw the threat in Saddam Hussein. Getting rid of Saddam Hussein was the right policy; the world is better off for it.

And now Iraq is a central front in this war against the terrorists. You know, in Washington, DC——

Audience member. You're the man, George!

The President. I want you to listen to the words of a senior Democrat in the House of Representatives. The person went on to say, "The President says that fighting them there makes it less likely we will have to fight them here. The opposite is true"— the person went on to say—"Because we're fighting them there, it may become more likely we will have to fight them here."

Here's what that person does not understand: You do not create terrorism by fighting the terrorists, and Iraq is not the reason the terrorists are at war against us. I would remind that Democrat that our troops were not in Iraq when the terrorists first attacked the World Trade Center in 1993. We were not in Iraq when they blew up our Embassies in Kenya and Tanzania. We were not in Iraq when they blew up the USS *Cole.* And we were not in Iraq when they killed nearly 3,000 of our citizens on September the 11th.

Five years after September the 11th, too many Democrats still do not get it. The best way to protect this homeland is to find the enemy and defeat them overseas. Oh, I know you've heard all the discussion about Iraq. They say—in Washington, the Democrats say, it's not a part of the war against the terrorists; it's a distraction. Well, don't take my word for it, listen to Usama bin Laden. He has made it clear that Iraq is a central part of this war on terror. He and his number-two man, Zawahiri, have made it abundantly clear that their goal is to inflict enough damage on innocent life and damage on our own troops so that we leave before the job is done. And why do they want to do that? They want to establish safe haven, like the safe haven they had in Afghanistan, from which to launch further attacks on the United States of America. They want to have a base from which to topple moderate governments.

Imagine a world in which violent radicals have seized power in the Middle East and they've toppled moderate governments and

they use oil to extract blackmail from the West. And couple that with an armed, nuclear Iran, and 30 years from now people are going to look back and say, "What happened to them in 2006? How come they couldn't see the danger?" And that is why we will defeat the enemy in Iraq.

We have a plan for victory. Our goal is a country that can sustain itself, govern itself, and defend itself and will be an ally in the war on terror. The enemy's goal is to get us to retreat before the job is done. I'm in close contact with our commanders. I tell them, "Whatever it takes to achieve victory, I support." They tell me that they're constantly adjusting their tactics to meet an enemy which is changing its tactics. Oh, the fighting is tough; I understand that. And it is brutal. The enemy has an advantage because they're willing to kill innocent people, and that gets on our TV screens. It's hard to measure the progress of a new hospital or new schools or people willing to be brave and tough. The enemy understands that it's a matter of time, in their mind, before we retreat. But they don't understand the American people, and they don't understand this administration. We will put a plan in place.

I can't tell you how proud I am to be the Commander in Chief of such incredibly brave men and women who have volunteered to wear the uniform of the United States.

Audience members. U.S.A.! U.S.A.! U.S.A.!

The President. And when it comes time—and when they send those bills up there to support our men and women in uniform, I don't have any doubt where Mike Sodrel is going to land. He is a strong supporter of the military. He knows what I know: Any time you have an American in harm's way, he or she deserves the full support of the American Government.

We've got a strong asset in our military. We've got something else going for us in Iraq, brave Iraqis. They have suffered unbelievable violence. But they remember the 12 million people that voted. They want to succeed. We've got a security track so that these Iraqis can defend themselves. We've got a political track so that the Government is of and by and for the people. We've got an economic track to help them realize the vast potential of that country. We'll succeed. The only way we will not succeed is if we leave before the job is done.

And all the people listening here, I want you to think about the Democrat plan for success: There isn't one. [*Laughter*] Iraq is the central front in this war, and yet leading Democrats argue we should pull out right now.

Audience members. Boo!

The President. Others suggest we should draw—withdraw on a specific date, even if we have not accomplished the mission.

Audience members. Noo!

The President. Others recommend moving our troops to an island some 5,000 miles away.

Audience members. Boo!

The President. Nineteen House Democrats introduced legislation that would cut off funds for our troops in Iraq.

Audience members. Boo!

The President. This week, one Democrat Senator explained her party's position this way: "We haven't coalesced around a single plan, but we're in general agreement on the basic principles." She's right. They are in agreement on one thing: They will leave before the job is done. And we will not let them.

I'm not saying these people are unpatriotic; I'm saying they're wrong. You cannot win a war if you're unwilling to fight the war. Retreat before the job was done would embolden the enemy. It would provide new safe haven. It would enable the enemy to recruit. It would dash the hope of millions who want to simply live in peace. It would dishonor the sacrifice of the men and women who have worn the uniform of the United States of America.

This is a different kind of war, and it's important for Republicans and Democrats and independents to understand this fact: If we were to leave before the job was done, the enemy would follow us to the United States. And that is why victory is our goal, and that is why we will achieve victory. A victory will be a blow to the terrorists. A victory will say to those in the Middle East—"Do you believe in freedom?"—that we do. A victory will make Iraq an ally on the war on terror. A victory in Iraq will make generations of young Americans more secure. And that is why we will stay, we will fight, and we will win.

I want to share a story with you. I want to share—if you can stand it, I want to share a story with you. I want to talk about something really powerful that we've got at our disposal. It's called liberty. I don't know if you remember, but recently I flew down to Elvis's place with the then-sitting Prime Minister of Japan. People said, "Why did you go down there?" And I said, "Well, one, I've never been there." [*Laughter*] Secondly, he wanted to go there. [*Laughter*]

But I also want to tell a story about the power of liberty, and here it is. In the late 1940s, we got attacked. And by the way, more people died on September the 11th than died at Pearl Harbor. And a lot of young Americans—many of them probably your relatives—volunteered to fight the sworn enemy, the Japanese. One of them was Navy fighter pilot George H.W. Bush, who at the age—[*applause*]. And he fought them with all he had, just like a lot of other brave Americans. Thousands and thousands didn't come home from that war.

And yet on Air Force One was the Prime Minister of the former enemy and this Navy fighter pilot's son talking about peace. We were talking about the fact that 1,000 Japanese troops were in Iraq helping this young democracy. See, the Prime Minister knows what I know: that the radicals and extremists want to overturn democracy; they want to spread their vision across what's called a caliphate, a vision opposite of what we believe. That's their ambitions. That's their goals. And yet when we find young democracies, those of us who live in freedom have a duty to support that democracy because democracies yield the peace.

We talked about North Korea, how we could work together to convince the leader of North Korea to give up his nuclear weapons ambitions. We talked about HIV/AIDS on the continent of Africa, and how "to whom much is given, much is required" ought to apply to the United States and Japan, and how we must end the suffering of those poor people on the continent of Africa. We talked about a lot of big issues.

But I find it interesting that my dad fought the Japanese, and his son is talking about the peace with the Japanese. Something happened, and what happened is, Japan adopted a Japanese-style democracy. And the lesson for our fellow citizens is, liberty has got the capacity to transform enemies into allies. Liberty has got the capacity to transform regions of hate to regions of hope. I firmly believe that someday an American President will be sitting down with duly elected leaders in the Middle East talking about the peace, and a generation of Americans will be better off.

These are historic times. These are challenging times. It is such an honor to represent the United States of America during these historic times. I ask you to go from here and to call up your friends and neighbors, find our fellow Republicans, discerning Democrats—[*laughter*]—intelligence independents—[*laughter*]—and remind them of the stakes, remind them that the outcome of this election will determine how much money you have in your pocket. And remind them the outcome of this election will determine whether this Government does its most fundamental job, and that is to protect the American people.

No doubt in my mind, with your help, we will win. Thanks for coming. God bless.

NOTE: The President spoke at 1 p.m. at Silver Creek High School. In his remarks, he referred to Keta Sodrel, wife of Rep. Michael E. Sodrel; former President Saddam Hussein of Iraq; Usama bin Laden, leader of the Al Qaida terrorist organization; Ayman Al-Zawahiri, founder of the Egyptian Islamic Jihad and senior Al Qaida associate; former Prime Minister Junichiro Koizumi of Japan; and Chairman Kim Jong Il of North Korea.

Remarks at Charleston Air Force Base, South Carolina
October 28, 2006

Thank you all very much. You know, I was in the neighborhood and thought I'd stop by to say hello here at Team Charleston. I am proud to be here with the men and women of the 437th and the 315th Air Wings. Yes, I'm proud to be with members of the United States Air Force and the United States Navy—proud to be with the rest of you too. [*Laughter*]

Laura sends her love, and she sends all her respect to those who support our military. I'm proud to be here with the Governor of the great State of South Carolina, Governor Mark Sanford, and his wife, Jenny, and their children. I thank Congressman Henry Brown for taking time out of a Saturday afternoon to come and say hello to his buddy, the President of the United States. I thank Colonel Glen Joerger for his hospitality. I thank Colonel Tim Wrighton. I thank you all for giving me a chance to come and share some thoughts with you.

The first thought I want to say is, I am proud to be the Commander in Chief of such a fine group of young men and women. We have an amazing nation when people say, "I want to volunteer to defend this country." I am constantly amazed, enthralled, and buoyed by the fact that I'm the Commander in Chief of honorable, decent, courageous men and women. And I thank you for coming to say hello.

I'm also proud to be here with our military families. I understand the sacrifices that you make on a daily basis for this country. So, as the President of the United States, I want to tell you plain and simple, the American people respect you, they appreciate you, and I'll do everything in my power to make sure the families and those who wear the uniform have all the support necessary to win this war on terror.

I'm impressed by the record of the folks here at Charleston Air Force Base. I'm impressed by your accomplishments and what you've done on behalf of this grateful Nation. Since September the 11th, 2001, the folks who fly the airplanes, maintain the airplanes, and load the airplanes—and fill up the tires—[*laughter*]—have launched more than 14,000 C–17 missions from here. You have airlifted more cargo to Operation Iraqi Freedom than any other unit in the United States. You are the only unit in the world tasked with providing strategic airlift to our Special Operation forces.

The men and women here in Charleston have also done more than just provided supply to the war zones. You have provided humanitarian aid that has saved countless lives. The folks here have airdropped 2.4 million rations of humanitarian aid to the people of Afghanistan at the start of Operation Enduring Freedom. You delivered 53,000 pounds of relief supplies to the tsunami victims in Indonesia. And after Hurricane Katrina, you delivered 2.5 million pounds of relief supplies and evacuated 2,400 citizens from New Orleans. You have

shown the great compassion of the American people, and I thank you for your service.

We are engaged in a global war on terror. After September the 11th, 2001, I vowed to the American people that I would use everything at our disposal to do the number-one job of government, and that is to protect you from further attack. And I have been aided in protecting the American people by the fine United States military.

We face an enemy that knows no bounds and no conscience. They're ideologues, but their ideology is the exact opposite of ours. They kill innocent people to achieve their evil objectives. But make no mistake about it, they have objectives. They have clearly stated that they want to drive the United States from the world so they can establish a caliphate, a governing organization, from Indonesia to Spain that would allow them to spread their ideology of hate, allow them to dominate a society in which people could not worship freely or speak freely, in which people who did not adhere to their point of view would be punished. They seek safe haven from which to launch further attacks to achieve their objective. And their attacks would aim right here at the United States of America.

I want you to think about a world in which rival forms of radicals competed for power in the Middle East to deny the hopes and aspirations of millions of people who simply want to live in peace. They would topple moderate governments. They would use oil as an economic weapon to bring the West to her knees. And to mix all that in with a country with a nuclear weapon, and 20 or 30 years from now, if that were to happen, people would look back and say, "What happened to them in 2006? How come they couldn't see the challenge? How come they couldn't see the threats to a generation of Americans?"

I'm proud to be with people who see the threats and know that the best way to protect the American people is to defeat the enemy overseas so we do not have to face them here at home.

One of the lessons of September the 11th is that when this country sees a threat, we must deal with that threat before it fully materializes. If we see a threat, we must take care of that threat. Otherwise, that threat could come to haunt us, to destroy innocent life. I saw a threat in Saddam Hussein. The world saw a threat in Saddam Hussein. Getting rid of Saddam Hussein was the right decision, and the world is better for it.

And now you're involved in this global war on terror, in the central front, which is Iraq. I know some in America don't believe Iraq is the central front in the war on terror, and that's fine. They can have that opinion. But Usama bin Laden knows it's a central front in the war on terror. He has called Iraq the third world war. He has said of Iraq that he will lead to victory or glory or humiliation. We have made our decision. Iraq will lead to victory and glory for the United States, for the Iraqis, and for the moderates around the world.

And it's tough fighting, because the enemy understands the stakes of a free Iraq. It's hard fighting, and we've got a lot of brave citizens of ours in the midst of the fight. But we have a plan for victory. We are in Iraq to help that young democracy fight off the radicals and the extremists. We're in the fight in Iraq to make sure there is not a safe haven from which to launch further attacks on the United States. Our plan for victory says that we want an Iraq that can defend itself and govern itself and sustain itself.

And we've got some great things going for us. We've got a military that is constantly adjusting to the enemy on the ground. We've got commanders who are wise and brave and are bringing justice to our enemies there in Iraq. And we've also got at our side brave Iraqis who have suffered unbelievable loss but yet still cling to the hope, as reflected in the voices and

votes of 12 million people who defied the car bombers and the terrorists. They want to live in freedom.

I believe in the universality of freedom. I believe in everybody's soul is the desire to be free. It is in this country's interests that we defeat the enemy in Iraq and help this young democracy survive. You see, this is a different kind of war. And make no mistake about it, if the United States of America were to leave before the job is done, the enemy will follow us here. And that is why we will support our military, and that is why we will fight in Iraq, and that is why we will win in Iraq.

And I thank you for being a part of this noble and just and important cause. You're fighting in a war that will set the course of a new century. The outcome will determine the destiny of millions across the world. The outcome of this fight will determine whether or not our children can grow up in the peace we want them to grow up in. Defeating the terrorists and the extremists is the challenge of our time and the calling of this generation. And like generations before us, we will do the hard work now, to make sure our children can grow up in freedom and peace.

The time of war is a time of sacrifice. I know the sacrifices you all make. But some have paid the ultimate price. Really good men and women have lost their lives in this struggle. We will pray for their families. And I make them this pledge: We will honor their sacrifice by completing the mission, by defeating the terrorists, and by laying the foundation of peace for generations to come.

I can't thank you enough for coming to say hello. May God bless you all, and may God continue to bless the United States.

NOTE: The President spoke at 4:48 p.m. In his remarks, he referred to Col. Glen G. Joerger, commander, USAF, 437th Airlift Wing; Col. Timothy J. Wrighton, USAF, commander, 315th Airlift Wing; former President Saddam Hussein of Iraq; and Usama bin Laden, leader of the Al Qaida terrorist organization.

Joint Statement by President George W. Bush and Prime Minister Nuri al-Maliki of Iraq
October 28, 2006

We were pleased to continue our consultations today. Via secure video, we discussed a range of issues of great importance to our common mission in Iraq, including the development of Iraqi security forces, efforts to promote reconciliation among all Iraqis, and the International Compact for Iraq and the economic reforms associated with it. As leaders of two great countries, we are committed to the security and prosperity of a democratic Iraq and the global fight against terrorism which affects all our citizens.

We have three common goals: accelerating the pace of training the Iraqi Security Force, Iraqi assumption of command and control over Iraqi forces, and transferring responsibility for security to the Government of Iraq. We have formed a high-level working group including the Iraqi National Security Advisor, Minister of Defense, Minister of Interior, General Casey, and Ambassador Khalilzad to make recommendations on how these goals can be best achieved. This working group will supplement existing mechanisms to better define our security partnership and enhance our coordination.

We are committed to the partnership our two countries and two governments have

formed and will work in every way possible for a stable, democratic Iraq and for victory in the war on terror.

NOTE: An original was not available for verification of the content of this joint statement.

Letter to Congressional Leaders on Continuation of the National Emergency Regarding the Proliferation of Weapons of Mass Destruction
October 27, 2006

Dear Mr. Speaker: (Dear Mr. President:)

Section 202(d) of the National Emergencies Act (50 U.S.C. 1622(d)) provides for the automatic termination of a national emergency unless, prior to the anniversary date of its declaration, the President publishes in the *Federal Register* and transmits to the Congress a notice stating that the emergency is to continue in effect beyond the anniversary date. In accordance with this provision, I have sent the enclosed notice to the *Federal Register* for publication, stating that the emergency posed by the proliferation of weapons of mass destruction and their means of delivery declared by Executive Order 12938 on November 14, 1994, as amended, is to continue in effect beyond November 14, 2006.

Because the proliferation of weapons of mass destruction and the means of delivering them continues to pose an unusual and extraordinary threat to the national security, foreign policy, and economy of the United States, I have determined the national emergency previously declared must continue in effect beyond November 14, 2006.

Sincerely,

GEORGE W. BUSH

NOTE: Identical letters were sent to J. Dennis Hastert, Speaker of the House of Representatives, and Richard B. Cheney, President of the Senate. This letter was released by the Office of the Press Secretary on October 30. The notice of October 27 is listed in Appendix D at the end of this volume.

Remarks at a Georgia Victory 2006 Rally in Statesboro, Georgia
October 30, 2006

The President. Thank you all very much. Thank you for the warm welcome. It is great to be back in the State of Georgia. It is even better to be here with the next Congressman from this district, Max Burns.

Max knows what it takes to be a United States Congressman because he's done it before. And when you turn out on November 7th, he's going to do it again.

He understands Georgia values because he was born and raised in this district, and he still lives on a family farm outside Syl-

vania. I've been in Washington long enough to know that it makes sense to have people who live on a family farm, in the Halls of the United States Congress.

I appreciate the fact that Max was a teacher. As a matter of fact, he taught right here at Georgia Southern. I hope he gave a few of the students A's. [*Laughter*] And for those of you who did get an A, you might as well vote for him. [*Laughter*] I appreciate the fact that when he was a Member of the United States Congress that

he passed key legislation that helped farmers, that helped seniors file their taxes, and helped our public schools recruit more math and science teachers. In other words, he has the record to run on. He's got something to say when he's out on the campaign stop, and he's also got a record to point to. There's no doubt in my mind that Max Burns is the right man to be the United States Congressman.

You know who else agrees with that is Laura. She knows Max and Lora. She likes the Burnses. She likes a man of integrity, like Max Burns. She says, like I'm saying, work hard; turn out the vote; and send this good man back to the United States Congress.

And by the way, when you're out there voting for Max, make sure you send a man who has done a fabulous job as your Governor back to the statehouse, and that's Sonny Perdue. Sonny has got him a pair of boots he can be proud of. By the way, it makes me feel comfortable to be a in a State where your Governor wears cowboy boots. And I know it makes you feel comfortable to live in a State where you got you a Governor who's accomplished and can get the job done.

I'm really pleased that Congressman Charlie Norwood has come over from his United States congressional district to help his friend Max Burns run. Welcome, Charlie Norwood.

And I want to thank the mayor. Mr. Mayor Bill Hatcher, thank you for welcoming us; thank you for being here. I appreciate Perry McGuire, who is the candidate for attorney general, joining us. I know you'll support Perry if you want good law enforcement in your State. And I want to thank Eric Johnson, who is the senate president pro tem. Mr. Senator, thanks for coming; good to see you again. I appreciate Jesse Tyler, president of Georgia Southern University College Republicans, for helping organize this event. I do want to thank the president of Georgia Southern for letting us come as well.

We are 8 days away from the election, and you can bet one thing: We're going to sprint to the finish line. And we need your help. I appreciate you coming out because I know you know what I know: This election is far from over, although there are some people in Washington who already think they know the outcome of the election. Some of them are already picking out their new offices at the Capitol.

Audience members. Boo!

The President. You might remember that around this time in 2004, some of them were picking out their new offices in the West Wing. [*Laughter*] The movers never got the call. [*Laughter*] And this November 7th, when our voters show up at the polls, we're going to elect people like Max Burns to the Congress, and we will keep control of the House and the Senate.

We will win this election because Republicans understand the values and priorities of the American people. We will win this election because our priorities and our values do not shift with the latest political opinion poll or focus group. We will win this election because we got a good record to run on.

For decades, our public school system failed too many American children, so we passed the No Child Left Behind Act and demanded that schools show results in return for Federal dollars. Test scores are rising. The achievement gap is beginning to close, and we are bringing America closer to the day when every single child gets a good education.

For decades, America has been growing more dependent on foreign oil, and so we took the lead. We passed a good energy bill that supports conservation and expands domestic production and expands new monies on technology. See, here's what we want—Max Burns wants this, Sonny wants this, and so do I—we want Georgia farmers growing the fuel that will energize our automobiles in the future. When you start running your car on Georgia corn, we'll

become less dependent on foreign sources of oil.

For decades, Medicare was an outdated program that wasn't serving our seniors as well as it could, so we passed landmark legislation that modernized the Medicare system. And today, more than 33 million seniors have more choices and access to affordable prescription drugs. And the days of our poor seniors having to choose between medicine and food are over.

For decades, we haven't had complete control over our southern border, and illegal immigration has been on the rise. So I acted. I sent the National Guard troops to help our Border Patrol. We're adding thousands of new Border Patrol agents. We are modernizing our border. We will reform our immigration system, and we will uphold the immigration laws of the United States.

For decades, activist judges have tried to redefine America by court order. Just this last week in New Jersey, another activist court issued a ruling that raises doubt about the institution of marriage. We believe that marriage is a union between a man and a woman and should be defended. And I believe I should continue to appoint judges who strictly interpret the law and not legislate from the bench. America is better off because John Roberts and Sam Alito are serving on the Supreme Court of the United States.

We've got a good record to run on. And with Max Burns back in the United States Congress, we will build on that record.

Now, there are big differences in Washington between Republicans and Democrats. Perhaps the biggest difference are on the two biggest issues that we face: Which party is going to keep your taxes low and keep this economy growing, and which party will take the necessary steps to protect you from terrorist attack?

Let me start with taxes. Max and I have a philosophy: We believe that you know how to spend your money far better than the Federal Government does. We believe

that when you have more of your own money in your pocket to save, spend, or invest, the economy benefits. Democrats believe they can spend your money better than you can. So over the past 5 years, we have acted on our philosophy and passed the largest tax relief since Ronald Reagan was in the White House.

In other words, we just didn't talk about philosophy—there's too many philosophers in Washington—we acted. We got the job done. We cut the taxes on everybody who pays income taxes. We doubled the child tax credit. We reduced the marriage penalty. We cut taxes on small businesses. We cut taxes on capital gains and dividends to promote investment and jobs. And to reward family businesses and farmers for a lifetime of hard work and savings, we put the death tax on the road to extinction.

We had a ferocious debate over taxes in Washington. The Democrats in Washington predicted tax cuts wouldn't create jobs, wouldn't increase wages, and would cause the Federal deficit to explode. Well, the facts are in. The truth is, the tax cuts have led to a growing economy that's added 6.6 million new jobs since August of 2003. The truth is, real wages rose 2.2 percent over the past 12 months, and we have cut the deficit in half 3 years ahead of schedule.

Now those Democrats in Washington are making another prediction. They're telling you they're going to win on election day. Well, if their electoral predictions are as reliable as their economic predictions, November 7th is going to be a good day for the Republican Party. [*Laughter*]

Now, during this campaign, the Washington Democrats really don't want you to know their plans. As a matter of fact, the top Democrat leader in the House made an interesting declaration. She said, "We love tax cuts." But given her record, she must be a secret admirer. [*Laughter*] She and her party voted against every single one of the tax cuts we passed. She voted against reducing the marriage penalty. She

voted against cutting taxes on small businesses. She and her party voted against lowering taxes for families with children. Time and time again, when she and the Democrat Party had an opportunity to show their love for tax cuts, they voted no. If that's the Democrats' idea of love, I sure wouldn't want to see what hate looks like. [*Laughter*]

See, here's the way it's working in Washington: If we do not make the tax cuts permanent or if the tax cuts are not extended, you're going to get a tax increase. Recently they asked a man who wants to be head of the House Ways and Means Committee, if the Democrats win, what he thinks about extending the tax cuts. He said he couldn't think of one of the tax cuts he would extend. This is what the Washington Democrats are saying about your taxes. He couldn't think of one of the tax cuts we passed that he would leave in place.

And so if you're a small-business person and pay taxes at the income—at the individual income tax rate, it means the Democrats will raise your taxes. If you're a small-business owner who wants to expand and invest in new equipment, the Democrats are going to raise your taxes. If you're a small-business owner who wants to pass your life's work to your children and grandchildren, the Democrats want to raise your taxes. If you're a small-business owner, my advice is, vote for Max Burns.

Now, if you happen to have children, I want to just talk to you about what it means to not extend the tax cut, just like the man who is going to be running the tax committee said he's going to do, not extend the tax. You see, if the child credit doesn't get extended, it means the tax credit gets cut in half from $1,000 per child to $500 per child. So this evening when you're sitting around the table eating dinner and you've got children around your table, just count the number of children you have and multiply it by 500, and that's what the tax increase is going to be. So if you've

got four children, four times 500 is 2,000. Your tax bill will go up if the Democrats take control of the House by $2,000. If you got three kids, it's $1,500. It's easy to calculate.

I guess the $2,000 doesn't seem like a lot of money to the people in Washington, DC, but I know it's a lot of money for your family. I know the child tax credit has meant a lot for people working for a living. And therefore, if you want to keep that money in your pocket instead of sending it to Washington, DC, you vote for Republicans on election day.

This election is taking place in an historic time for our country. Our children and grandchildren are going to look back on this period, one question will overwhelm all the rest: Did we do everything in our power to fight and win the war on terror? That's the question people will ask: Did this country do everything in our power to protect you?

We face an enemy that is brutal. They kill innocent people to achieve ideological objectives. They're totalitarian in nature. They hate freedom. We love freedom, and that is why they view us as their enemy. You cannot negotiate with these people. You can't try to talk sense into these people. The best way to protect you is to bring them to justice before they hurt America again.

I understand this is a different kind of war, and so do people in this congressional district need to know it's a different kind of war. I know we've got some vets here, and I want to thank you for serving. But in previous wars, particularly, say, World War II, it mattered how many airplanes you could shoot out of the sky or how much territory an army took. This is a different kind of war. This is a war where people plot and plan in secret and then launch lethal attacks, which means our professionals need to have all the tools necessary to protect you. You see, the challenge facing the United States is that we have to be right one time—I mean 100

percent of the time, and the enemy has to be right one time, in order to protect you.

And so when I found out there was laws preventing the intelligence community from talking to the enforcement community, I asked Congress to pass the PATRIOT Act to tear down those walls so our folks had the tools necessary to protect you. I believe that if Al Qaida or an Al Qaida associate is making a phone call from outside the United States to inside the United States, we need to know why in order to be able to protect you.

This is a different kind of war that requires us to get good intelligence in order to protect the American people. That's why I asked the CIA to develop a program that would question detainees that we picked up off the battlefield about what they know.

Now let me give you an example. We captured a fellow named Khalid Sheikh Mohammed. The intelligence community believes he was the man who mastermind the September the 11th attacks. I thought it made sense—if our most important job is to protect you, it made sense to find out what Khalid Sheikh Mohammed knew. In other words, we've been giving the professionals the tools necessary to defend America in this new kind of war.

And recently there were votes in the floor of the House of Representatives, in the floor of the United States Senate to provide these critical tools. In other words, Congress voted on these tools. And I want everybody in this district and in this State and around the country to understand those votes, because they were critical votes. And it shows the difference of attitude between the two parties and the leaders in the two parties about our responsibility to protect you.

When it came time to renew the PATRIOT Act, more than 75 percent—75 percent—of the House Democrats voted against it. When it came time to vote on whether or not the CIA continue its program to detain and question captured ter-

rorists, almost 80 percent of the House Democrats voted against it. They just have a different point of view. They don't see it the way I see it or the way you see it. Otherwise, why wouldn't they give the professionals the tools necessary to protect you? When it came time to vote on whether the National Security Agency should continue to monitor terrorist communications, almost 90 percent of the House Democrats voted against it. In all these vital measures for fighting the war on terror, the Democrats just follow a simple philosophy: Just say no.

When it comes to listening to the terrorists, what's the Democrats' answer? It's, just say no. When it comes to detaining terrorists, what is the Democrats' answer? Just say no. When it comes to questioning terrorists, what's the Democrats' answer?

Audience members. Just say no!

The President. When it comes to trying the terrorists, what's the Democrats' answer?

Audience members. Just say no!

The President. So when the Democrats ask for your vote, what's your answer?

Audience members. Just say no!

We're going to continue to make sure our professionals have the tools necessary to protect you, and you can count on Max Burns's vote.

One of the lessons of September the 11th, 2001, is that when this country sees a threat, we must take those threats seriously before they come home to hurt us. I saw a threat in Saddam Hussein. Members of both political parties in the United States Congress saw a threat in Saddam Hussein. The United Nations saw a threat in Saddam Hussein. Getting rid of Saddam Hussein was the right decision, and the world is better off.

And now Iraq is the central front in this global war against these ideologues who murder innocent people to achieve their objectives. You know, I think it's very important for the Commander in Chief, as well as our citizens, to listen to the words

of the enemy. You know, in Washington, you hear people say, "Well, Iraq is just a distraction from the war on terror." I believe it is a central part of the war on terror. And so does Usama bin Laden. Usama bin Laden calls this fight the third world war. He says victory for the terrorists in Iraq will mean America's defeat and disgrace forever.

They have made it clear they want to create as much carnage and death as possible to cause us to leave before the job is done. They have ambitions: They want to topple moderate governments; they want to control oil to blackmail the West; they want us to leave and dash the hopes and aspirations of millions of people who want to live in peace. And we have a different point of view.

I want you to hear the words of a senior Democrat in the House of Representatives. She said, "The President says fighting them there makes it less likely we will fight them here. The opposite is true," she said, "Because we are fighting them there, it may become more likely that we have to fight them there."

Here's what this person and the leaders of the Democrat Party in Washington seem to not understand: Iraq is not the reason the terrorists are at war against us. I would remind the House Democrats, our troops were not in Iraq when the terrorists first attacked the World Trade Center in 1993. We were not in Iraq when they bombed the USS *Cole* or the Embassies in Kenya and Tanzania. And we were not in Iraq when they killed nearly 3,000 people on September the 11th, 2001.

You do not create terrorists by fighting the terrorists. The best way to protect you, the best way to protect the American people is to stay on the offense and defeat them overseas so we do not have to face them here at home.

Our goal in Iraq is victory. Victory in Iraq will come when that young democracy can sustain itself and govern itself and defend itself and be a strong ally in the war

against the terrorists. The fighting in Iraq is tough, and I understand it's tough, and you know it's tough, and so does the enemy. They have no conscience. They kill innocent men, women, and children. They film the atrocities. They broadcast them for the world to see. They offer no hopeful vision. The only thing they know is death and destruction, but they hope these violent images will cause us to lose our nerve.

They make a big mistake. They do not understand the true strength of the United States of America. We don't run in the face of thugs and assassins. We will defend ourselves. We will defeat them. We will defeat them because our commanders on the ground have all the flexibility necessary to make sure that we constantly stay ahead of the enemy. We'll defeat them because we've got a fantastic United States military. And I know I can count on Max Burns. And I know you can count on Max Burns and I can count on Max Burns by making sure our troops have all that is necessary to do their job to defend the United States.

We will succeed in Iraq because the Iraqis want to live in a peaceful society. Nearly 12 million defied car bombers and assassins and terrorists and went to vote. They held up their purple ink-stained fingers, saying to the world, "We want to be free." And they got a unity Government that is working hard to repel the extremists who are preventing them. I believe strongly that with our help, they will be able to defend themselves. And I believe strongly that they'll become a government of the people and by the people and for the people. As a matter of fact, I believe the only way we cannot succeed is if we leave before the job is done.

And when you listen to this debate— and it's raging across the country, this debate on Iraq—if you listen carefully for a Democrat plan for success, they don't have one. Iraq is the central front in the war on terror, yet they don't have a plan for victory.

Last week, a Senator, Democrat Senator explained her party's position this way. She said, "We haven't coalesced around a single plan, but we're in general agreement on basic principles." She's right; the agreement—they are in agreement on one thing—they will leave before the job is done. That's what they're in agreement on. They've come up with a lot of creative ways to describe leaving Iraq before the job is done. Sometimes they say, immediate redeployment. Sometimes they say they wouldn't spend another dime on our troops. Sometimes they say, the idea that we're going to win this war is an idea that, unfortunately, is just plain wrong. However they put it, the Democrat approach in Iraq comes down to this: The terrorists win, and America loses.

That's what's at stake in this election. The Democrat goal is to get out of Iraq. The Republican goal is to win in Iraq.

I'm not saying these Democrats are unpatriotic; I'm just saying they're wrong. You cannot win a war unless you're willing to fight the war. Retreat from Iraq before the job is done would embolden the enemy and make us more vulnerable to attack. Retreat would allow the terrorists to gain a new safe haven from which to plot and plan, just like they had in Afghanistan. Retreat would enable the enemy to be more able to recruit. Retreat would say to people in the Middle East, you can't count on America. It would say to those folks desperate to live in freedom and peace, we no longer care or hear your cries. Defeat would dishonor the sacrifice of the men and women who wear the uniform of the United States of America. The consequences of retreat from Iraq will be felt for generations.

I want the folks all throughout America to envision a Middle East where extremism are battling for power, moderate governments are toppled, oil is controlled to use for blackmail, and a country has a nuclear weapon. If that were to happen, people would look back at the year 2006 and ask, "What happened to them? How come those folks couldn't see the threat? How come they couldn't see the danger for a generation of Americans who were growing up?" I want you to know, I see the threat. I see the danger. That is why we will support our troops. We will fight, and we will win in Iraq.

I want to share with you right quick a history lesson; at least, I see it as history; after all, we're on a college campus. [*Laughter*] It's the power of freedom. You know, recently I went to—with the former Prime Minister of Japan—he was sitting Prime Minister of Japan then—down to Elvis's place. Memphis, Tennessee—I don't know if you've ever been there or not, but—[*applause*]—yes, you have? Well, I liked going there. It was interesting. And he really wanted to go there because he liked Elvis. [*Laughter*]

But I wanted to tell an interesting story. It's a story about a Navy fighter pilot who, at the age of 18, volunteered, and he said, "I want to serve my country because the Japanese have just attacked us." You've got relatives who did the same thing. You've got a grandfather or a father, like I got, who said, "I want to fight the Japanese." They were the sworn enemy. Thousands of people lost their lives. This country went to war against an enemy which attacked us.

You know what's interesting? On the way down from Washington to Memphis, Tennessee, right there on Air Force One, Prime Minister Koizumi—the Prime Minister of the former enemy of the United States of America—and I discussed the peace. We talked about the fact that this country had 1,000 troops in Iraq to defend the young democracy. He knows what I know: We're in an ideological struggle between people who hate and people who have hope. We've been through ideological struggles before. Freedom wins every time, if we don't lose our nerve.

And that's the lesson I learned from my friend Prime Minister Koizumi. It's amazing what has happened between when 18-year-old fighter pilot George H.W. Bush fought this—fought the enemy, and his son is talking about keeping the peace with the same country. And the lesson is, liberty has got the capacity to change enemies into allies. And my citizens, liberty has got the capacity to turn regions of hate to regions of hope. Liberty has got the capacity to yield the peace we want.

Someday an American President will be sitting down with duly elected leaders talking about the—duly elected leaders from the Middle East talking about the peace, and generation of Americans will be better off for it.

And so these are the stakes in this election. It's an important election year. And I know Max Burns joins me in saying, thanks for coming out. Thanks for giving me a chance to share what's on my heart and where I want to lead this country. And

I thank you for getting ready—for doing what you're fixing to do, which is to go out of this hall and find fellow Republicans and discerning Democrats and reasonable independents and remind them that if they want more money in their pocket, you vote Republican. And if you want this country to do everything we can to protect you from further attack and lay the foundations for peace, you vote Republican.

I'm proud you've come today. May God bless you, and may God continue to bless the United States of America.

NOTE: The President spoke at 11:07 a.m. at Georgia Southern University. In his remarks, he referred to Lora Burns, wife of Max Burns, candidate for Congress in Georgia's 12th Congressional District; Mayor William S. Hatcher II of Statesboro, GA; Bruce Grube, president, Georgia Southern University; former President Saddam Hussein of Iraq; and Usama bin Laden, leader of the Al Qaida terrorist organization.

Remarks at a Texas Victory 2006 Rally in Sugar Land, Texas
October 30, 2006

The President. Thank you all very much. Thank you. I always feel better when I'm in Texas. Thanks for coming out. I'm honored you are here. I appreciate you taking time out of your day.

I thank you for joining me and saying loud and clear to the people of the 22d Congressional District: Shelley Sekula Gibbs is the right person to serve you in the United States Congress. She served in public office before, you might remember, she was a member of the Houston City Council, where she helped pass tax cuts. She's a doctor. She's a doctor, where she's helped heal broken bodies. She is going—she's a mother who understands the importance of family values. She's the right person to send to Washington, DC.

If you'll give me a chance maybe to, kind of, serve as the secretary of state for Texas for a second—[*laughter*]—for those folks who haven't been paying attention to this election yet—want good government, you get to vote twice for Shelley. You get to check her name in the special election portion of the ballot, and then you get to write her name in. See, if you want to send Shelley to the United States Congress, you're going to have to take a pencil into the ballot box.

Now, you can bring a piece of paper with you that's got her name on it, so you can copy it down on the ballot. So remember, when you show up to vote on November the 7th, bring your pencil, bring your

paper, and write Shelley's name in for good government.

Laura sends her love. As President, I make a lot of decisions, but the best decision I have made as a person is asking Laura to marry me. Some of her friends are still wondering whether the best decision she ever made was to say yes. [*Laughter*] But I'm real proud of her. She's a fantastic wife, a great mom, and a great First Lady for the United States.

Speaking about great ladies, this State is fortunate to have Kay Bailey Hutchison as the United States Senator. She is effective; she is capable; she's all Texan. And it's important for this State to send her back to the United States Senate with a strong, strong vote. I appreciate Kevin Brady joining us. He's the Congressman from over there. [*Laughter*] I know him well. He's a good one.

And I want to thank my friend Commissioner Michael Williams, who's joined us today. I want to thank all the statehouse folks; they're sitting behind me. I remember serving with them when I was their Governor—a little different here in Texas than it is in Washington. [*Laughter*] These are good people, and I appreciate them joining us.

I want to thank the mayor, Mayor David Williams [Wallace], ° right here from Sugar Land, Texas, for joining us. I thank all the grassroots activists who've joined us. I want to thank you for the job you're going to do, and that is, turn out your neighbors on November the 7th with a pencil and a piece of paper, and tell them to write in Shelley Sekula Gibbs to be the next United States Congresswoman.

I don't know about you, but I'm looking forward to sprinting to the finish line. I'm looking forward to this campaign. I like campaigning. I like getting out and about the people. I like telling them what's on my mind. You know, what's interesting in Washington, some of the folks over there

—————
° White House correction.

are already picking out their new offices. [*Laughter*]

Audience members. Boo!

The President. That's not the first time it's happened since I've been in Washington. You might remember in 2004, some of them were measuring the drapes in the West Wing. [*Laughter*] They had their office suites all picked out. Except their problem was, the movers weren't needed. [*Laughter*] And the same thing is going to happen this year. We're going to elect Shelley, and we're going to control the House and the United States Senate.

We've got a record to run on. We've done some things that are positive for the United States of America. For decades, the public schools failed too many children. And so we passed the No Child Left Behind Act, which demanded results in return for Federal money. And now test scores are rising, the achievement gap is beginning to close, and we're bringing closer to the day when every single child in America gets their quality education.

For decades, we've been growing too dependent on foreign oil. So we passed a good energy bill that encourages conservation, additional production for oil and gas in the United States. We're doing something else that's smart too: We're spending money on technology so that our automobiles will be able to be running on crops grown right here in the State of Texas. We want to be less dependent on foreign sources of oil.

For decades, Medicare was outdated, so we did something about it. We passed landmark legislation that modernized the Medicare system. Today, 33 million seniors have more choices and more access to affordable drugs, and because of our action, poor seniors no longer have to choose between food and medicine.

For decades, we hadn't had complete control over our southern border. Illegal immigration has been on the rise. So we acted. I sent the National Guard down there to help the Border Patrol do their

job. We're adding thousands of new Border Patrol agents. We're modernizing this border. We will reform our immigration system, and this country of ours will enforce our immigration laws.

For decades, activist judges have tried to redefine America by court order. I don't know if you've been following what happened in New Jersey recently. Another activist court issued a ruling that raises doubts about the institution of marriage. We believe marriage is a union between a man and a woman and should be defended. And I believe I must continue to appoint judges who will strictly interpret the law and not legislate from the bench.

No, we got a strong record to run on. This country is better off because John Roberts and Sam Alito are serving on the Supreme Court of the United States. And I want to thank Senator Kay Bailey Hutchison for her strong support helping get those nominees on the floor of the Senate and getting them confirmed as Supreme Court Justices.

Now, there are big differences between the Democrats and the Republicans. Perhaps the two biggest differences can be seen in these two issues: One, which party is going to keep your taxes low to keep this economy growing? And which party is going to take the necessary steps to protect the United States of America?

Let me start with taxes. Shelley and I have a clear philosophy: We believe that you know how to spend your money far better than the Federal Government can. We believe that when you have more money in your pocket to save, invest, or spend, the economy benefits.

The Democrats want more of your money because they think they can spend it better than you can.

Audience members. Boo!

The President. Over the past 5 years, we've acted on our philosophy. In other words, we just didn't go to Washington to talk. We went to Washington to get a job done on your behalf. We passed the largest

tax relief since Ronald Reagan was the President of the United States.

When you're out there rounding up votes, remind them of this record: We cut taxes on everyone who pays income taxes; we doubled the child tax credit; we reduced the marriage penalty; we substantially cut taxes on small businesses; we cut taxes on capital gains and dividends to encourage investment and jobs; and to reward family businesses and farmers and ranchers for a lifetime of work, we put the death tax on the road to extinction.

I know Senator Hutchison and Congressman Brady remember the debate in Washington. They remember those Democrats predicting that the tax cuts would not create jobs, would not increase wages, and would increase the Federal deficit. Well, the facts are in. The truth is, the tax cuts have led to a growing economy that has added 6.6 million new jobs since August of 2003. Real wages are on the rise, and we cut the deficit in half 3 years ahead of schedule.

Around this country, a lot of people don't understand the Democrats' position on taxes. So part of my job is to clarify matters, is to make it clear their intentions. Part of the confusion comes about because the leading lady in the Congress proclaimed this—you're not going to believe what she said, but she actually said this on TV the other—she said, about the Democrats: "We love tax cuts." The problem is, given her record, she must be a secret admirer. [*Laughter*]

She and her party voted against reducing the marriage penalty, voted against cutting taxes on small businesses, voted against taxes—lowering taxes for families with children, voted against reducing taxes on capital gains and dividends, voted against eliminating the death tax. That's their record. Time and time again, when she had a chance to show her love for tax cuts, she voted no. My attitude is, if this is the Democrats' idea of love, I don't want to see what hate looks like. [*Laughter*]

Here's what happens: If we do not make the tax cuts we passed permanent or extend the tax cuts, you'll get a tax increase. That's just the way it is. You know, it's interesting; they asked the man who would be the chairman of the House Ways and Means Committee—the Democrat who will be the chairman of the Ways and Means Committee, if the Democrats were to take over the House—which they're not—[applause]. And here's what he said—it's important for Americans to know the facts. Here's what he said. He said, when asked about extending the tax cuts or making them permanent, he said he couldn't think of one of the tax cuts he would extend. In other words, what they're telling you is, they're going to raise your taxes.

I want you to think about this. I want you to think about this: If the child tax credit were to expire, your taxes will go up by $500 per child. See, in other words, we increased the child tax credit from $500 to $1,000 per child. For those of you with children, you know what I'm talking about. If that tax cut were to expire—just like the man who wants to be the head of the tax committee said—your taxes per child go up $500. So when you're eating dinner tonight and you're looking around the table, you can take the number of children around your table and multiply it by $500, and that's going to be part of the tax increase you have to pay.

Audience members. Boo!

The President. You take a family working hard to get ahead, and they got four children; they're looking at a $2,000 tax increase. That may not seem like a lot to Democrats in Washington, DC, but it seems like a lot to me. And I know it's a lot for you. And the best way to make sure it doesn't happen is to send Shelley to the United States Congress.

So when they're out there campaigning and somebody comes up and says, "Shel, tell me the difference between what the Republicans are going to do and the Democrats," it's real easy. We're going to keep your taxes low, and they're going to raise your taxes. And a tax increase would not only be bad for your wallet; a tax increase would be bad for the economy of the United States of America.

We're meeting in historic times. This election is happening during historic times. And when our children and grandchildren look back at this period, one question is going to overwhelm all the rest: Did we do everything in our power to fight and win the war on terror?

We face an enemy that is brutal. They have an ideology. It's the opposite of our ideology. We love freedom. They hate freedom. They will kill innocent people to achieve their objectives. You cannot negotiate with these radicals and extremists. You can't hope for the best with these radicals and extremists. The only way to protect America, which is our most important job, is to stay on the offense and bring them to justice before they can hurt us again.

Our most important job is to protect you. I wish I didn't have to report that there's an enemy still out there, but there is. And they want to attack again. We have to be right 100 percent of the time to protect the American people, and they have to be right one time in order to achieve their objectives. And that's why I put some tools in the hands of our professionals, so they could better do their job.

You know, when I—right after 9/11 when we analyzed part of the problem, there was a wall that existed between our intelligence gathering people and our law enforcement, and they couldn't share information. I know that's hard for you to believe, but that's the way it was. So I asked Congress to pass the PATRIOT Act, and thanks to Senators like Kay Bailey Hutchison and Congressmen like Kevin Brady, we passed the PATRIOT Act.

In this different kind of war, we must understand what the enemy is thinking, in order to be able to protect you. And so therefore, when we found Al Qaida or Al Qaida affiliates making phone calls into the

United States, I thought it was important to understand why, in order to protect you. We are picking up the enemy on the battlefield. And when we pick people who understand what the plans are about attacks, we need to know what they're thinking.

See, this is a different kind of war. It requires pinpoint intelligence, advanced knowledge in order for us to do our job. And so we picked up people off the battlefield, like Khalid Sheikh Mohammed. You might have heard of him. He was the mastermind of the 9/11 attacks; at least that's what our intelligence people think. In other words, he was the—they think he was the person that organized and ordered the attacks that killed nearly 3,000 people on one day. I thought it was important to have the CIA be in a position to question him to find out what he knew, in order to protect America.

If anybody has any doubts about the differences of opinion in Washington, DC, between Republicans and Democrats, I want them to analyze the recent votes that took place on these important programs. When it came time to renew the PATRIOT Act, more than 75 percent of the House Democrats voted against it.

Audience members. Boo!

The President. When it came time to vote on whether or not to allow the CIA to continue its program to detain and question captured terrorists, more than 80 percent of House Democrats voted against it.

Audience members. Boo!

The President. When it came time to vote on whether the National Security Agency should continue to monitor communications that we think would be—contain information that would protect you, more than 90 percent of the House Democrats voted against it.

Audience members. Boo!

The President. In all these vital measures for fighting a war on terror, the Democrats in Washington follow a simple philosophy: Just say no. [*Laughter*] When it comes to

listening in on the terrorists, what's the Democrats' answer?

Audience members. Just say no!

The President. Just say no. When it comes to detaining terrorists, what's the Democrats' answer?

Audience members. Just say no!

The President. When it comes to questioning terrorists, what's the Democrats' answer?

Audience members. Just say no!

The President. When it comes to trying terrorists, what's the Democrats' answer?

Audience members. Just say no!

The President. And so when the Democrats ask for your vote on November 7th, what's your answer?

Audience members. Noo!

The President. No doubt in my mind, I can count on Shelley Sekula Gibbs to make sure that our professionals have the tools necessary to protect you in this dangerous world. But the best way to protect you, the best way to make sure that an enemy is unable to do us harm, is to stay on the offense and keep the enemy on the run. It is hard to plot, plan, and attack when you're on the run. And that's precisely what we're doing.

I can't tell you how honored I am to be a Commander in Chief of a military full of decent and honorable Americans who have volunteered to protect this country. And one of the things that I make a pledge to the families of those who wear our uniform is that we'll continue to make sure our troops have all that is necessary to be able to do the job that I have asked them to do. And I know that Congresswoman Shelley Sekula Gibbs will be a strong and steady vote for the men and women of the United States military.

One of the lessons of September the 11th is that this Nation must take threats seriously before they come home to hurt us. We must take every threat we see overseas very seriously. Otherwise, if we don't, there's an enemy that lurks and intends to hit us again. I saw a threat in Saddam

Hussein. Members of both political parties saw a threat in Saddam Hussein. The United Nations saw a threat in Saddam Hussein. I made the right decision to get Saddam Hussein out of power.

We're in a global struggle against these killers. And the war is fought on many fronts, but right now, the central front in this war on terror is Iraq. Oh, I hear them in Washington say, "Iraq is a distraction from the war on terror." Well, they shouldn't take my word for it; they should take the word of Usama bin Laden, who has said that the fight in Iraq is the third world war. He said victory for the terrorists in Iraq will mean America's defeat and disgrace forever. That is what the enemy has said. It's important for all Americans to listen carefully to the words of the people who would do us harm.

Now I want you to listen to the words of a senior Democrat in the House of Representatives, one of the leaders. She said, "The President says that fighting them there"—she's talking about Iraq—"makes it less likely we will have to fight them here." This is exactly what I've said. She went on to say, "The opposite is true; because we're fighting them there, it may become more likely we will have to fight them here."

Here's what the person doesn't understand: Iraq is not the reason the terrorists are in the war against us. I would remind the House Democrat, our troops were not in Iraq when the terrorists first attacked the World Trade Center in 1993. We weren't in Iraq when they blew up our Embassies in Kenya or Tanzania, or blew up the USS *Cole*. And we were not in Iraq when they killed nearly 3,000 people on September the 11th, 2001. We do not create terrorists by fighting the terrorists. The best way to protect you is to stay on the offense and bring the terrorists to justice wherever we find them.

Our goal in Iraq is clear: It's victory. We want to help this young democracy grow so it can sustain itself and govern itself and defend itself and become an ally in the war on terror. And the fighting is tough. I know it's tough, and you know it's tough. It's tough because we fight an enemy that has no conscience. We fight an enemy that can't stand the thought of a free society. We fight an enemy whose ideology is the opposite of our ideology.

The enemy kills innocent men, women, and children. They film the atrocities, and they broadcast them for the world to see. Our enemies hope these violent images will cause us to lose our nerve and pull out before the job is done. They don't understand the United States of America. We will not run from thugs and assassins.

I'll make sure our commanders have what they need to complete this job. If they want more troops, they get more troops. If they want less troops, they get less troops. They are flexible. We're constantly adjusting our tactics to meet the tactics of the enemy.

We got another asset going for us beside our military, and these are brave Iraqis. They have suffered unspeakable violence, yet they're committed to a free society. They're committed to reject the extremists and radicals who try to overturn their will. They voted—nearly 12 million people—to say, "We want to be free." It's in the United States interest to help them succeed. It's in our interest to defeat the radicals. It's in our interest to defeat the extremists. The only way we won't succeed in Iraq is by leaving before the job is done.

You listen to the debate about Iraq, the Democrat plan for success, well, they don't have a plan for success. [*Laughter*] It's a serious political party in the midst of a war, and they have no plan for success. They don't even have a plan for victory. [*Laughter*] Last week, one Democrat Senator described her party's position: "We haven't coalesced around a single plan, but we're in general agreement on the basic principles." She's right; the only principle about which they can agree is, get out before the job is done.

You know, they put it different ways. Some say, immediate redeployment. Some say they wouldn't spend another dime on our troops in Iraq. Some say that the idea that we're going to win this war is an idea that, unfortunately, is just plain wrong. Well, however they put it, their approach comes down to this: The terrorists win, and America loses.

Audience members. Boo!

The President. The Democrat goal is to get out of Iraq. The Republican goal is to win in Iraq.

I'm not saying that these Democrats are unpatriotic, I'm just saying they're wrong. You can't win a war unless you're willing to fight the war. Retreat from Iraq before the job was done would embolden an enemy and make this country more vulnerable to attack, would allow the terrorists to gain a new safe haven, which is precisely what they said is part of their plan, in Iraq. And why do they want a safe haven? They want a safe haven like they had in Afghanistan so they can launch further attacks.

Retreat from Iraq would strengthen the hands of these radicals and extremists and enable them to recruit better. Retreat from Iraq before the job was done would dishonor the sacrifice of the men and women who have worn the uniform of the United States of America in Iraq to protect us. The consequences of failure in Iraq would be felt for generations.

You see, the enemy has clearly stated they want us to retreat. They want to topple moderate governments. They want their extremism to become the philosophy of a governing structure that stretches from Indonesia to Spain. It's called a caliphate. That's what they've said. Imagine a Middle East in which violent forms of extremists compete for power, moderate governments are overturned, oil-rich states are controlled by the radicals who will use the energy to create blackmail for the United States, and in the midst, a country with a nuclear weapon that can't stand us. Thirty years from now, if that were to happen, people will look back and they'll say, "What happened to that generation in 2006? How come they couldn't see the impending danger? How come they couldn't see the threat?"

I want you to know, I see the threat. That is why we will support our troops, we will fight, and we will win in Iraq.

We've got another powerful tool at our disposal, and it's called freedom. I would like to share a story with you about a recent experience I had. Well, it's when I went down to Elvis's place. [*Laughter*]

You might remember, my guest was the then-sitting Prime Minister of Japan. Laura said, "Why you going down there?" I said, because I never been. [*Laughter*] By the way, she decided to come too. Prime Minister Koizumi wanted to go because he loved Elvis.

But I wanted to tell a story to the American people about the power of liberty, and I want to share it with you right quick. You see, after the Japanese attacked America, where more people—by the way, more people died on September the 11th than the attack of Pearl Harbor. When they attacked, a lot of brave Americans, including one George H.W. Bush, volunteered to defend America.

I bet you a lot of folks out here had relatives who did the same thing. They said, "I volunteer to protect this country against a mortal enemy." I'm flying down on Air Force One with the Prime Minister of the sworn—the country that used to be our sworn enemy talking about keeping the peace. I was talking to him about the fact that Iraq had 1,000 troops—I mean, Japan had 1,000 troops in Iraq because he knows what I know: In this ideological struggle, when we find young democracies, which will serve as a major defeat for ideologues who hate, that we've got to support them. We talked about convincing the leader of North Korea to give up his nuclear weapon for the sake of peace.

In other words, we were talking about peace. Isn't it interesting? My dad fought

the Japanese as a sworn enemy; his son is sitting down with the leader of that country talking about peace. Let me tell you something: Liberty has got the capacity to change an enemy into an ally. And liberty has got the capacity to change a region of the world that is so desperate for freedom into a place of peace. Someday an American President will be sitting down with duly elected leaders from the Middle East talking about the peace, and a generation of Americans will be better off.

So these are the stakes in this election, and I thank you for giving me a chance to come out and urge you on, to urge you to go to the polls and to take your friends. Find Republicans, discerning Democrats, discerning independents, and remind them,

if you want more money in your pocket, vote Republican, and if you want a party who will take the steps necessary to protect you today and to protect a generation of Americans coming up, vote for Shelley and vote for Republicans.

God bless. God bless America.

NOTE: The President spoke at 5:04 p.m. at the Sugar Land Regional Airport. In his remarks, he referred to Michael L. Williams, commissioner, Texas Railroad Commission; former President Saddam Hussein of Iraq; Usama bin Laden, leader of the Al Qaida terrorist organization; former Prime Minister Junichiro Koizumi of Japan; and Chairman Kim Jong Il of North Korea.

Letter to Congressional Leaders Reporting on Blocking Property of Certain Persons Contributing to the Conflict in the Democratic Republic of the Congo
October 27, 2006

Dear Mr. Speaker: (*Dear Mr. President:*)

Consistent with subsection 204(b) of the International Emergency Economic Powers Act, 50 U.S.C. 1703(b)(IEEPA), and section 301 of the National Emergencies Act, 50 U.S.C. 1631 (NEA), I hereby report that I have issued an Executive Order (the "order") blocking the property of certain persons contributing to the conflict in the Democratic Republic of the Congo. In that order, I declared a national emergency to deal with the unusual and extraordinary threat to the foreign policy of the United States posed by that conflict, as described below.

The conflict in the Democratic Republic of the Congo has been the deadliest conflict since World War II, with an estimated four million dead since 1996, many from hunger and disease resulting from the fighting. The United Nations Security Council, in Resolution 1596 of April 18, 2005, Reso-

lution 1649 of December 21, 2005, Resolution 1698 of July 31, 2006, and numerous other resolutions, has expressed serious concern over the presence of armed groups and militias in the Democratic Republic of the Congo, which perpetuate both the conflict in the country and a climate of insecurity throughout the entire region.

The conflict has been marked by serious violations of human rights and international humanitarian law by these militias and armed groups, including the massacre of civilians, sexual violence against women and girls, and the recruitment and use of children in the hostilities. The perpetuation of the conflict undermines the progress and promise of the Global and All-Inclusive Agreement on the Transition in the Democratic Republic of the Congo, signed in 2002, which created a process that can lead to the long-term restoration of peace and

stability, national reconciliation, and establishment of the rule of law.

The order blocks the property and interests in property in the United States, or in the possession or control of United States persons, of the persons listed in the Annex to the order, as well as of any person determined by the Secretary of the Treasury, after consultation with the Secretary of State

- to be a political or military leader of a foreign armed group operating in the Democratic Republic of the Congo that impedes the disarmament, repatriation, or resettlement of combatants;
- to be a political or military leader of a Congolese armed group that impedes the disarmament, demobilization, or reintegration of combatants;
- to be a political or military leader recruiting or using children in armed conflict in the Democratic Republic of the Congo in violation of applicable international law;
- to have committed serious violations of international law involving the targeting of children in situations of armed conflict in the Democratic Republic of the Congo, including killing and maiming, sexual violence, abduction, and forced displacement; or
- to have directly or indirectly supplied, sold, or transferred to the Democratic Republic of the Congo, or been the recipient in the territory of the Democratic Republic of the Congo of, arms and related materiel, including military aircraft and equipment, or advice, training, or assistance, including financing and financial assistance, related to military activities.

The designation criteria will be applied consistent with applicable Federal law, including, where appropriate, the First Amendment to the United States Constitution.

The order also authorizes the Secretary of the Treasury, after consultation with the Secretary of State, to designate for blocking any person determined to have materially assisted, sponsored, or provided financial, material, or technological support for, or goods or services in support of, the activities listed above or any person listed in or designated pursuant to the order. I further authorized the Secretary of the Treasury, after consultation with the Secretary of State, to designate for blocking any person determined to be owned or controlled by, or acting or purporting to act for or on behalf of, directly or indirectly, any person listed in or designated pursuant to the order. The Secretary of the Treasury, after consultation with the Secretary of State, is also authorized to determine that circumstances no longer warrant the blocking of the property and interests in property of, or the prohibiting of transactions with, a person listed in the Annex to the order.

I delegated to the Secretary of the Treasury, after consultation with the Secretary of State, the authority to take such actions, including the promulgation of rules and regulations, and to employ all powers granted to the President by the IEEPA and the United Nations Participation Act, as may be necessary to carry out the purposes of the order. All executive agencies are directed to take all appropriate measures within their authority to carry out the provisions of the order.

The order, a copy of which is enclosed, became effective at 12:01 a.m. eastern standard time on October 30, 2006.

Sincerely,

GEORGE W. BUSH

NOTE: Identical letters were sent to J. Dennis Hastert, Speaker of the House of Representatives, and Richard B. Cheney, President of the Senate. This letter was released by the Office of the Press Secretary on October 31. The Executive order of October 27 is listed in Appendix D at the end of this volume.

Remarks Following a Meeting With Special Envoy to Sudan Andrew S. Natsios
October 31, 2006

I've just had a meeting with the Presidential Special Envoy to Sudan, Andrew Natsios. I asked Andrew to serve our country and really serve the cause of humanity by taking on this important assignment. He's working very closely with Secretary Rice. He brought—he was just there for 10 days, and he came back with a grim report about the human condition of a lot of people who suffer.

And, you know, Andrew—the good thing about Andrew is—one thing, he puts a report out there, but he also understands we've got to do something about it. And the United States is going to work with the international community to come up with a single plan on how to address this issue and save lives. And Andrew is going to work with other partners in peace, and they'll take that plan to the current Government of Sudan.

One element of the plan is something that I strongly supported all along, and that there needs to be a credible and effective international force to go into Darfur to save lives, to make it clear that the international community respects human life and the international community will work in concert to save human life.

Andrew, I want to thank you for taking on this assignment. The situation in Darfur is on our minds. The people who suffer there need to know that the United States will work with others to help solve the problem. And the Government of Sudan must understand that we're serious—when you deliver a message to them on behalf of our Government, that we're earnest and serious about their necessity to step up and work with the international community. So thank you, Andrew, for that.

Today, as well, we had news out of the Far East. There is an agreement to restart the six-party talks concerning North Korea. I'm pleased, and I want to thank the Chinese for encouraging the meeting that got the agreement to get the six-party talks restarted. I've always felt like it is important for the United States to be at the table with other partners when it comes time to addressing this important issue.

And so I thank not only the Chinese but the South Koreans, the Japanese, and the Russians for agreeing to come back to the table with North Korea. We'll be sending teams to the region to work with our partners to make sure that the current United Nations Security Council resolution is enforced, but also to make sure that the talks are effective, that we achieve the results we want, which is a North Korea that abandons their nuclear weapons programs and her nuclear weapons in a verifiable fashion, in return for a better way forward for her people.

And so I'm very pleased with the progress being made in the Far East. Obviously, we've still got a lot of work to do. But I want to thank the Secretary for her good work when she went out to the region, and assure the American people, we'll continue to work to resolve this in a peaceful way.

Thank you.

NOTE: The President spoke at 9:26 a.m. in the Oval Office at the White House. The Office of the Press Secretary also released a Spanish language transcript of these remarks.

Remarks at a Georgia Victory 2006 Rally in Perry, Georgia
October 31, 2006

The President. Thank you all very much. Thanks for coming. Thanks for the warm welcome. It's great to be back in the State of Georgia. Just seems like I was here yesterday. [*Laughter*] I must have Georgia on my mind. [*Laughter*]

I got something else on my mind, and that is to make sure Mac Collins becomes the next United States Congressman from this district. I appreciate you coming. He's a self-made guy. He's a no-nonsense fellow. He's got a lot of common sense, just the kind of person you want representing you in Washington, DC.

You know, he kind of reminds me of a lot of folks in my home State. See, they didn't start off as a Republican. He was a Butts County commissioner, and he ran as a Democrat—a Reagan Democrat. And then he saw the direction of where the Washington, DC, Democrats were taking his party, so he came home. He came home to a party—[*applause*]—he feels like I feel: We don't want Washington Democrats running the House of Representatives.

And I appreciate you coming to express your support for Mac. I'm honored you're here. With your hard work, Mac Collins will be elected, and we're going to keep control of the House and the Senate.

I'm proud to be here with Julie—that's Mac's wife. She, like my wife, is a very patient person. Mac married above himself—[*laughter*]—so did I. Laura sends her love. She sends her love to the Collinses, but she also sends her love to your Governor. You talk about a man who deserves to be reelected, and that's Sonny Perdue. He's done in office exactly what he said he's going to do, and the State of Georgia is better for it.

I'm proud to be here with two United States Senators who are making a huge difference in the Nation's Capital, folks who represent your State with a lot of class and

a lot of dignity, Senator Saxby Chambliss and Senator Johnny Isakson.

It's a good sign when you've got sitting Members of the United States Congress coming in to help one of their former colleagues, see. It means they know him; they respect him; they like him. So please join me and welcome Charlie Norwood, Phil Gingrey, and Tom Price.

I'm proud to be here with the next Lieutenant Governor of the State of Georgia, Senator Casey Cagle. I thank all the other candidates, and I thank all the grassroots activists. You're the people who put up the signs, make the phone calls, convince people to go to the polls. I want to thank you in advance for what you're going to do.

We're driving toward victory. Now I know up in Washington, they've already decided the outcome of the election.

Audience members. Boo!

The President. They're measuring the drapes in their new offices.

Audience members. Boo!

The President. The same thing happened in 2004, you might remember. In 2004, the movers never showed up, and they're not going to show up in 2006.

One reason we're going to win this election is because we've accomplished a lot. We've done what the people expect us to do. We went up and represented the people's interests. You know, for decades, the public school system failed too many children, so we passed the No Child Left Behind Act and demanded schools show results in return for money. Test scores are rising; an achievement gap is closing; and we're bringing America closer to the day when every single child gets a quality education.

For decades, we've been growing too dependent on foreign oil, so we decided to do something about it. We passed a good

piece of energy legislation that encourages conservation, encourages domestic production. But it does something else: It spends your money on new technologies so that we can use Georgia crops to fuel and power automobiles.

One thing you don't have to worry about Mac, he understands what I know: If the farm economy is strong, the American economy benefits. So for the sake of national security, we want our farmers growing the fuel of the 21st century.

Medicare was an outdated program. It's an important program. If you're a senior, you know how important Medicare is. But you might remember, Medicare was becoming old, and it needed to be modernized. As a result of legislation that I signed, 33 million seniors have more choices and access to prescription drugs, but more importantly, the days of poor seniors having to choose between food and medicine, they're over.

For decades, we haven't had complete control over our southern border. Illegal immigration has been on the rise, so we acted. I sent the National Guard down on the border to help our Border Patrol. We're in the process of modernizing that southern border. We're adding Border Patrol agents. We'll reform our immigration system, and we will uphold the immigration laws of the United States.

For decades, activist judges have tried to redefine America by court order. I don't know if you paid attention recently to that New Jersey case, another activist court issued a ruling that raises doubt about the institution of marriage. We believe that marriage is a union between a man and a woman and should be defended.

And I will continue to appoint judges who strictly interpret the law and not legislate from the bench. When you're out rounding up the votes, you remind people that America is better off with John Roberts and Sam Alito as members of the Supreme Court. And I want to thank these two United States Senators for helping these two fine men become confirmed.

We've got something to run on. We've got a record to run on. And with Mac Collins back in the Congress, we're going to build on that record. Obviously, there are big differences between how Republicans think and Washington Democrats think. Perhaps the two biggest areas of difference, though, come down to how much money you're going to have in your pocket—that's taxes—and which political party is going to take the necessary steps to defend you.

First, let me talk about taxes. Mac and I have a philosophy. It says, you can spend your money better than the Government can. As a matter of fact, we believe that when you have more money in your pocket for you to save or spend or invest, the economy benefits. The Democrats believe they need more of your money to spend because they can spend it better than you can.

Audience members. Boo!

The President. But, you know, sometimes philosophers don't act. We act. See, we say we're going to do something, and we do it. And we cut the taxes on everybody who pays income taxes; we doubled the child tax credit; we reduced the marriage penalty; we cut taxes on small businesses; we cut taxes on capital gains and dividends; and for the sake of our family businesses and farmers, we put the death tax on the road to extinction.

Oh, you might remember the debates; I certainly remember them. Democrats in Washington predicted the tax cuts would not create jobs, would not increase wages, and would cause the Federal deficit to explode. Well, the facts are in. The tax cuts have led to a strong economy that's added 6.6 million new jobs since August of 2003. Real wages are on the rise, and the deficit has been cut in half 3 years ahead of schedule.

Tax cuts work, and Mac Collins understands that, and the Democrats don't. I

want the folks out there who are trying to make up their mind about this election to understand that the Democrats don't want you to know what their tax plans are. They just don't want you to know.

Recently the top Democrat leader in the House made this observation. She said, "We love tax cuts." Given her record, she must be a secret admirer. [*Laughter*] She and her party voted against reducing the marriage penalty, reduced—voted against cutting taxes on small businesses, voted against lowering taxes for families with children, voted against every single tax cut. If this is her definition of love, I'd hate to see her definition of hate. [*Laughter*]

See, it's important for you to understand, when you're out there hustling for the vote, that if these tax cuts are not made permanent or not extended, your taxes are going up. See, that's what happens. If they don't extend the tax cuts or pass a law that says they'll be a permanent part of the law, you can count on your taxes going up. I think it is interesting to note that the person who wants to be the head of the Ways and Means Committee for the Democrats said that he can't think of one tax cut that he would extend. See, that's code word for "get ready." If the Democrats take the House, your taxes are going up.

Audience members. Boo!

The President. And it's a fundamental issue in this campaign. They may try to hide their intentions, but that's what's going to happen. And I want you to think about it: If the tax cuts aren't made permanent or not extended and you've got a child, your taxes will go up $500 a child. The tax credit is now $1,000 per child, thanks to people like Mac Collins.

The man who wants to be the head of the tax committee said they're not going to extend those tax cuts, which means the tax credit goes from $1,000 a child to $500 a child. So when you get to dinner tonight and you're sitting around the table with your children, you can just count heads— [*laughter*]—and multiply that by $500. So

if you're a family with four children, that's four times 500, is 2,000. That's a $2,000 tax increase. That may not sound like a lot to Washington Democrats, but it sounds like a lot to me and Mac Collins, and we're going to keep your taxes low.

This election is taking place in an historic time. When our children and grandchildren look back on this period, one question will overwhelm all the rest: Did we do everything in our power to fight and to win the war on terror? That's the fundamental question this generation faces.

We face an enemy that is brutal. There is no negotiation with these people. You can't try to talk reason into these totalitarians. They have an ideology. Make no mistake about it, they believe things. What they really believe is, they believe freedom is bad. They can't stand the thought of free societies. And that's why they hate what the United States of America stands for: the ability for people to worship freely. The ability for people to vote and to express their opinion freely is something we hold dear. It's the exact opposite of what these ideologues believe in and what they're trying to impose on other parts of the world.

The best way to protect the American people is to bring the enemies to justice before they hurt us again. And the best way to protect you is to make sure our professionals have all the tools necessary to do their job. When it comes time to protecting the homeland, the United States of America must be right 100 percent of the time, and the enemy, which desires to strike us again, only has to be right once.

And that's why I decided to work with the Congress and our professionals to change some things. I decided it didn't make any sense to have a wall between our intelligence and our law enforcement folks. It may be hard for you to believe, but right around September the 11th, 2001, the folks in charge of protecting you couldn't share intelligence. And so I asked Congress to pass the PATRIOT Act to tear

down that wall—[*applause*]—that enabled people to share information.

This is a different kind of war. I know there's probably some World War II vets out there. In those wars, you could measure progress by how many airplanes you were able to shoot down, or you were able to measure progress by how much landmass you took. This is a different kind of war. This is a war that requires good information in order for this Government to do its most important job, which is to protect you. And so therefore, I felt it was important, if Al Qaida or an Al Qaida affiliate was making a phone call into the United States, we better understand what they're calling about.

In this different kind of war, we pick up people off the battlefield. We captured people like Khalid Sheikh Mohammed, who our intelligence officers believe was the mastermind of the September the 11th attacks. I felt it was important for the Central Intelligence Agency to be in a position to question this person to determine if he knew information that would be necessary to protect you.

Now I want you to—when you're out rounding up the vote, and people say, "Well, there's no difference between them," or they're saying, "Well, maybe I feel comfortable with the Washington Democrats," I want you to remind them about these three votes we just recently had. There's a clear pattern. When it came time to renew the PATRIOT Act, more than 75 percent of the Members—Democrat Members in the House of Representatives voted no.

Audience members. Boo!

The President. When it came time to vote on whether to allow the CIA to continue its program to detain and question captured terrorists, almost 80 percent of the House Democrats voted against it.

Audience members. Boo!

The President. And when it came time to vote on whether the National Security Agency should continue to monitor terrorist communications, almost 90 percent of the House Democrats voted against it.

Audience members. Boo!

The President. On all these vital measures—measures necessary to protect you—the Democrats in Washington follow a simple philosophy: Just say no. When it comes to listening in on the terrorists, what's the Democrats' answer? Just say no. When it comes to detaining terrorists, what's the Democrats' answer?

Audience members. Just say no!

The President. When it comes to questioning terrorists, what's the Democrats' answer?

Audience members. Just say no!

The President. When it comes to trying the terrorists, what's the Democrats' answer?

Audience members. Just say no!

The President. So when the Democrats ask for your vote on November the 7th, what's your answer?

Audience members. Noo!

The President. One thing is, the people in this district don't have to worry about Mac Collins giving the professionals the tools necessary to protect you. Those tools are necessary, no question about it. But the best way to protect you is to stay on the offense, is to keep the pressure on the enemy. It's hard to plan and plot attacks against America if you're on the run, and that's exactly what our brave professionals are doing.

It's important that the United States not forget the lessons of September the 11th, 2001. I assure you I'm not going to forget them. And one of the important lessons is that when we see a threat overseas, we've got to take that threat seriously. When you see a threat, you just can't hope for the best in this day and age where terrorists are capable of inflicting damage on the homeland. I saw a threat in Saddam Hussein. Members of the United States Congress from both political parties saw that same threat. The United Nations saw the

threat. I made the right decision in getting Saddam Hussein out of power.

In this global war against extremists who use murder as a weapon, Iraq is now the central front. Oh, I've heard all of the voices in Washington, DC. They say—a lot of them say, "It's just a distraction in the war on terror," that it's not a part of the war on terror, people in Washington— Democrats say. Well, all I ask if you're undecided about this important issue is just listen to the words of Usama bin Laden or Mr. Zawahiri, the number-two of Al Qaida. Usama bin Laden calls this fight the third world war. He has said that victory for the terrorists in Iraq will mean America's defeat and disgrace forever. It's important to listen to the words of the enemy if you're in war.

Now I want you to listen to the words of a senior Democrat in the House of Representatives. The reason I bring this up is, I want you to understand there is a different mindset in Washington. She said, "The President says that fighting them there in Iraq means it's less likely we will have to fight them here." I did say that, and I strongly believe it. "The opposite is true," she went on to say, "Because we are fighting them there, it may become more likely we will have to fight them here."

I want to remind that person that Iraq is not the reason that the terrorists are in war against us. We were not in Iraq when the terrorists bombed the World Trade Center in 1993. We weren't in Iraq when they blew up the USS *Cole* or the Embassies in Kenya and Tanzania. And we were not in Iraq on September the 11th, 2001, when they killed nearly 3,000 citizens on U.S. soil. You do not create terrorists by fighting the terrorists. The best way to protect you is to find the terrorists where they exist and bring them to justice so they can't hurt you again.

Our goal in Iraq is victory. Our goal is for a young democracy to be able to sustain itself, govern itself, and defend itself and

serve as an ally in the war on terror. And the fighting is tough. No question about it, it's tough. It's tough because we face a brutal enemy without conscience. It's tough because the enemy kills innocent men, women, and children. It is tough because they film the atrocities, and they broadcast them for the world to see. You see, they believe that the United States does not have the will necessary to complete the mission. That's what they believe. They don't understand this country. We will never run in the face of thugs and assassins. We will defend ourselves.

Our goals haven't changed, but our tactics constantly adjust. Our commanders on the ground have what it takes to succeed. And if they don't, I'll make sure they do. The enemy changes; we change. We got a lot of good things going for us in Iraq, starting with one of the finest United States militaries ever.

In the midst of a heated campaign season, there are some things we should all be able to agree on. And one of the most important is that every one of our troops deserves our respect and our gratitude.

Yesterday my opponent in 2004 Presidential race, Senator Kerry, was speaking to a group of young people in California.

Audience members. Boo!

The President. I want you to listen to what he said. He said, "You know education, if you make the most of it, you study hard, you do your homework, and you make an effort to be smart, you can do well; if you don't, you get stuck in Iraq."

Audience members. Boo!

The President. The Senator's suggestion that the men and women of our military are somehow uneducated is insulting and it is shameful. The members of the United States military are plenty smart, and they are plenty brave, and the Senator from Massachusetts owes them an apology.

Whatever party you're in, in America, our troops deserve the full support of our Government. And I don't have any doubt that Mac Collins will stand strong for the

men and women who wear the uniform of the United States.

Something else is going for us when it comes to victory in Iraq, and that is the Iraqi citizens. They've endured unspeakable violence, but they are determined to repulse the extremists and the radicals. Nearly 12 million went to the polls and said, "We want to be free." You know, I was pleased with the turnout, but I wasn't surprised because I believe there is an Almighty. And I believe one of the great gifts of the Almighty to every man and woman on the face of the Earth is freedom.

We'll help the Iraqis build their economy. We'll help them make sure their political system unites the country, and we'll help them defend themselves. The only way we can lose in Iraq is if we leave before the job is done. This is a vital issue for the security of our children. And yet when you listen to the national Democrats in Washington for their plan, if you listen for a plan, you will find they don't have one. They do not have a plan for victory on this vital issue.

Iraq is a central front in the war on terror, but the only thing they want to do is leave before the job is done. I want you to hear some of the voices of leading Democrats. They say we should pull our troops off the battlefield right away. My opponent in 2004 said there should be a fixed date for withdrawal. Others suggest that we ought to move our troops some 5,000 miles away to an island. Nineteen House Democrats introduced legislation that would cut off all the funds for the troops in Iraq.

Audience members. Boo!

The President. I thought it was illustrative to listen to a United States Senator from the Democrat Party say last week, "We haven't coalesced around a single plan, but we're in a general agreement on basic principles." She's right; they are in agreement. They will leave before the job is done.

Audience members. Boo!

The President. However they put it, the Democrat approach comes down to this: The terrorists win, and America loses. And that's what's at stake in this election. The Democrats want to get us out of Iraq, and the Republican goal is to win in Iraq. I'm not saying these good folks are unpatriotic; I'm just saying they're wrong. You can't win a war if you're not willing to fight it.

I want you to go home and think about what retreat from Iraq would mean, before the job is done. It would embolden the enemy. It would enable them to ridicule countries like the United States to folks who are wondering where the balance of power will lay in the world. It will embolden the extremists and radicals. It will enable them to gain a new safe haven from which to launch further attacks on the United States. It would strengthen the hand of the extremists and deny hope to millions and millions of people who simply want to live a peaceful life. It would dishonor the sacrifice of the men and women who have worn our uniform.

I want you to understand, in this different kind of war, if we leave Iraq before the job is done, the enemy will follow us here. Envision a world in which moderate governments have been toppled by the extremists because we left; envision a world in which people use oil—extremists use oil as blackmail to the Western World; envision a world in which a country which can't stand America has a nuclear weapon. And people will look back and say, "What happened to them in the year 2006? How come they couldn't see the impending danger to a generation of young Americans? Why weren't they willing to defend our security at that moment?"

I see the impending danger. I will use all assets at my disposal to do the most important job of the Government, and that is defend you. We will fight in Iraq, and we will win in Iraq. Oh, I know there are Democrats and independents in a great State like Georgia who do not share the

views of the Democrat leadership in Washington. You may not agree with Republicans on every issue, but you should also realize what voting Democrat in this election would mean for the war on terror.

When you vote next Tuesday, your vote will determine more than who is your local Congressman. It will also determine which party's leadership will set the agenda on Capitol Hill. A vote to send a Democrat to Congress is a vote for the liberal Democrat leadership in Washington, DC. A vote to send a Democrat to Congress is a vote to make the Senate majority leader a man who bragged about killing the PATRIOT Act. A vote to send a Democrat to Congress is a vote to make the chairman of the Senate Intelligence Committee a man who said the world would be better off if Saddam Hussein were still in power.

Audience members. Noo!

The President. A vote to send a Democrat to Washington is a vote to make the chairman of the House Ways and Means Committee a man who has suggested cutting off funds for our troops on the battlefield.

Audience members. Noo!

The President. A vote to send a Democrat to Congress is a vote to make the Speaker of the House—the third person in line for the Presidency—a woman who said that capturing Usama bin Laden would not make America any safer.

Audience members. Noo!

The President. If you want leaders in the United States Congress who will do what it takes to defend America and keep our country safe, then vote for Mac Collins on November the 7th.

I can't thank you enough for coming. I hope you go forth from the hall and round up our fellow Republicans, discerning Democrats, discerning independents and remind them about the stakes in this election. If you want your taxes low, if you want more of your own money to spend the way you see fit, vote Republican and vote Mac Collins. If you want this country to stay on the offense, to do everything we can to protect you, to do everything we can to do our most fundamental duty—and that is to protect the United States of America—vote Republican and send Mac Collins to the United States Congress.

I'm sure glad to be back in Georgia. I thank you for coming. May God bless you, and may God continue to bless the United States of America.

NOTE: The President spoke at 5:09 p.m. at the Georgia National Fairgrounds and Agricenter. In his remarks, he referred to former President Saddam Hussein of Iraq; and Usama bin Laden, leader of the Al Qaida terrorist organization. The Office of the Press Secretary also released a Spanish language transcript of these remarks.

Letter to Congressional Leaders on Continuation of the National Emergency With Respect to Sudan
November 1, 2006

Dear Mr. Speaker: (Dear Mr. President:)

Section 202(d) of the National Emergencies Act (50 U.S.C. 1622(d)) provides for the automatic termination of a national emergency unless, prior to the anniversary date of its declaration, the President publishes in the *Federal Register* and transmits to the Congress a notice stating that the emergency is to continue in effect beyond the anniversary date. In accordance with this provision, I have sent the enclosed notice to the *Federal Register* for publication,

stating that the Sudan emergency is to continue in effect beyond November 3, 2006.

The crisis constituted by the actions and policies of the Government of Sudan that led to the declaration of a national emergency on November 3, 1997, and the expansion of that emergency on April 26, 2006, has not been resolved. These actions and policies are hostile to U.S. interests and pose a continuing unusual and extraordinary threat to the national security and foreign policy of the United States. There-fore, I have determined that it is necessary to continue the national emergency and to maintain sanctions against Sudan.

Sincerely,

GEORGE W. BUSH

NOTE: Identical letters were sent to J. Dennis Hastert, Speaker of the House of Representatives, and Richard B. Cheney, President of the Senate. The notice is listed in Appendix D at the end of this volume.

Remarks at a Montana Victory 2006 Rally in Billings, Montana
November 2, 2006

The President. Thank you for the warm welcome. It's good to be in a part of the world where the cowboy hats outnumber the ties. And I'm proud to be here in Big Sky country with a fine United States Senator in Conrad Burns.

You might call him a plain-spoken fellow. [*Laughter*] As a matter of fact, I've heard some of them say that he's a little rough on the English language. [*Laughter*] Where have I heard that before? [*Laughter*]

Conrad, I'm keeping good company. We don't need a lot of doublespeak in Washington. I think somebody who speaks plainly for the values of Montana is somebody you need to send back as your United States Senator.

Laura sends her love. See, Conrad and I married above ourselves. [*Laughter*] I'm really proud to be here with Phyllis Burns. Phyllis, thank you for coming. There's nothing better than having a First Lady that you can be proud of. And I'm really proud of my First Lady, and I know you are as well. She knows Phyllis and Conrad well, and she joins me in saying: For the good of this State and for the good of the United States, send Conrad Burns back to Washington.

I'm proud to be here with Denny Rehberg. He's one of the strong Members of the United States Congress. Given my age and Conrad's age, I guess you could say he's a young star. [*Laughter*] But I'm proud to be with Denny and Jan. I want to thank the secretary of state, Brad Johnson, who is with us. The former Governor, Judy Martz, is with us. I want to thank all the grassroots activists. Here's what a grassroots activist is: A grassroots activist is somebody who is putting up the signs and making the phone calls and turning out the vote. I want to thank you in advance for what you're going to do in these last days of the campaign: turn out the vote and send this man back to Washington.

And I know you'll join me in sprinting to the finish line. It's interesting what's happening in Washington, however. Some of them are already measuring the drapes for their new offices. [*Laughter*] See, they think this election is over. They don't understand that the people of Montana haven't voted yet.

Oh, we've been through this before. You might remember 2004. Some of them were picking out their new offices in the West Wing. [*Laughter*] The movers never got the

call. [*Laughter*] And the same thing is going to happen on November the 7th. We will win the Senate, and we will win the House.

And we're going to win these elections because we understand the values and priorities of the American people. We're going to win this election because our values and our priorities do not shift because of the latest public opinion poll. We're going to win because we've got an optimistic and hopeful agenda.

Let me tell you something about Conrad Burns. I've worked with him closely. He understands that when the ag economy is strong, the national economy benefits. He spends a lot of time talking to me about— saying, "Let's get those foreign markets open for Montana beef." We worked together on a good piece of farm legislation that's helped Montana's farmers and ranchers. If I were a farmer and rancher in this State, I'd want to make sure this man is sent back to the United States Senate.

We got a lot to do. We're going to continue to work to make sure this country is less dependent on foreign oil. So we worked together to pass good energy legislation that supports conservation, expands domestic production, and invests in cutting-edge technologies. You got a lot of coal in this State. It's very important for us to be able to use your coal in environmentally friendly ways. That's why Conrad Burns promotes clean coal technology. And we're also investing to bring alternative sources of fuel like ethanol and biodiesel to the markets quicker. Here's what I want: I want Montana farmers growing crops that fuel our automobiles so I can tell the American people, we're less dependent on oil from parts of the world where people don't like us.

And Senator Conrad Burns understands the importance of having good judges on the Federal bench. We believe that judges ought to strictly interpret the law and not legislate from the bench. Confirming Federal judges is one of the most important

responsibilities of the Senate, and it is one of the most important issues at stake in this election.

When the people of Montana cast the ballot on Tuesday, your vote will determine more than who represents you in the Montana—from Montana in the Senate. It will also determine what kind of judges sit on Federal courts all across the United States.

At this moment, there are 50 vacancies on the Federal bench, and it is vital to maintain a Republican Senate so we can confirm the men and women I have nominated to fill those positions. Our record on appointing judges is clear. With the support of Senators like Conrad Burns, we have confirmed good judges, solid thinkers to the district court, to the circuit courts, and to the Supreme Court.

America is better off because John Roberts and Sam Alito are now serving on the Supreme Court of the United States. The people of Montana have got to understand, a vote for a Democrat Senator would be a vote against highly qualified judges like these. All you have to do is look at the record. When the Democrats held the Senate, they denied a hearing to over one-third of my nominees for the Court of Appeals. When they lost the majority in 2002, the Democrats didn't change their tactics. They filibustered or opposed 19 of my nominees to the Court of Appeals.

They tried to use the same tactics when Sam Alito's Supreme Court nomination came before the Senate. More than half of the Senate Democrats voted to filibuster him. And when he finally did get a vote, 40 of the 44 Democrats voted no. If the Democrats had their way, this man would not be sitting on the Supreme Court.

John Roberts had to overcome strong Democrat opposition in the Senate to make it to the Federal bench. More than a decade ago, another President Bush nominated John Roberts to serve on the DC Court of Appeals. A Democrat-controlled Senate denied him even a hearing. When I took office, I renominated him to that seat, and

another Democrat chairman of the Senate Judiciary denied him a hearing. I think you're beginning to see the pattern. It was only after the Republicans took the Senate back in 2002 that John Roberts got his hearing and got his vote and was confirmed for the DC Circuit. And then I put him up for the Supreme Court, and we confirmed him as Chief Justice last year.

Now I want you to hear this loud and clear: If the Democrats controlled the Senate, John Roberts would not be the Chief Justice today. He'd still be waiting for the Democrats to give him a hearing for his seat on the Court of Appeals. If the people of Montana want good judges, judges who will not legislate from the bench, judges like John Roberts and Sam Alito, you vote for Conrad Burns for the United States Senate.

Now, there's a lot of big issues facing the voters around the country. The two biggest issues are these: Which party is going to keep your taxes low and keep this economy growing; and which party is going to take the necessary steps to protect you in this war on terror?

First, let me talk about taxes. See, we have a philosophy; Conrad and Denny and I have a philosophy: We believe that you know how to spend your money far better than the Federal Government does. That stands in stark contrast to the Democrats, who want to take more of your own money because they think they can spend it better than you can spend it.

Audience members. Boo!

The President. We believe that when you have more money in your pocket to save, invest, or spend, the economy benefits. The difference between some of them in Washington and those on the stage here is, we don't just talk philosophy; we act. And so we passed the largest tax cuts since Ronald Reagan was the President. We cut taxes for everybody who pays income taxes. We doubled the child tax credit. We reduced the marriage penalty. We cut taxes on small businesses. We cut taxes on capital gains

and dividends to encourage investment and jobs. And to reward family farmers and small-business owners for a lifetime of hard work, we put the death tax on the road to extinction.

We got a record to run on. You might remember the debate in Washington. The Democrats predicted the tax cuts would not create jobs; they predicted they would not increase wages; and they said the Federal deficit would explode. Well, the facts are in. The truth is, the tax cuts have led to a growing economy that has added 6.6 million new jobs since August of 2003. The unemployment rate in the great State of Montana is 3.6 percent. Real wages are on the rise, and we cut the deficit in half 3 years ahead of schedule. The tax cuts we passed are working.

The Democrats are going to raise your taxes. They got a record too; they just don't want you to know about it. Interestingly enough, the top Democrat leader in the House made this statement: She said, "We love tax cuts," speaking about the Democrats. Well, given her record, she must be a secret admirer. [*Laughter*]

She and her party voted against reducing the marriage penalty. They voted against cutting taxes on small businesses. They voted against lowering taxes for families with children. They voted against reducing capital gains and income—dividends, taxes on dividends and capital gains. They voted against getting rid of the death tax. They voted against every single tax cut. Time and time again, when the Democrats in Washington had a opportunity to show their love for tax cuts, they voted no. If that's their idea of love, I sure would hate to see what hate looks like.

Those House Democrats have got a lot of company in the Senate too. We cut taxes in 2003; 46 of 48 Democrats voted against it. During the debate over tax cuts, one senior Democrat in the Senate called our policies insulting. See, there's a mindset; when you get in that box, I want you to remember, there's a mindset amongst the

Democrats: It's insulting for you to have more of your own money. And others said the tax cuts were the wrong prescription for our economy.

When people in Montana get in that voting booth, you remember what those tax cuts have done for our economy. If they take control of the Senate and the Congress, they don't have to lift a finger to raise your taxes. See, these tax cuts are set to expire. And their leaders have said they're going to let it expire. And if those tax cuts expire, it means your taxes are going up.

Let me give you an example. If the child tax credit were to go from $1,000 to $500 per child—which is what would happen if these tax cuts were not extended or made permanent—those of you with children get to pay $500-a-child tax increases. So when you get home this evening, I want you to think about the Democrat plan for you. You can go around the table and count the number of children that are eating dinner, and you can multiple that by $500 a child. So if you've got four children and it's 500 a child—the Democrats win, you're paying $2,000 more in taxes. That may not seem like a lot to the Democrats in Washington, DC, but Conrad and I know it's a lot, and that's why we're going to keep your taxes low.

I want you to not fall prey to one other trick the Democrats like to say. They like to say, "Oh, we're just going to tax the rich; we'll only tax people who make a lot of money." That's not how it works in Washington. Their spending appetite exceeds their capacity to raise taxes. You might remember 1992; they went around the country saying, "Vote for us; we'll give the middle class a tax cut." Well, that middle class tax cut turned out to be one of the largest tax increases in the history of the United States. When it comes to taxes, the Democrats are going to tax whoever they can find, and we're not going to let them because we're going to put Conrad Burns back in the United States Senate.

This election is taking place in an historic time for this country. When our children and grandchildren look back on this period, one question will overwhelm all the rest: Did we do everything in our power to fight and win the war on terror? I wish I could report to you that there wasn't a war, but there is. There's still an enemy that like— would like to strike the United States. These people are brutal. They have no conscience. They do have an ideology. They believe exactly the opposite of what we believe. We believe in basic freedoms: freedom to worship; freedom to dissent; freedom to speak. They do not believe in those freedoms.

And yet they have a plan that says they're going to extend their vision as far as they can extend it. It's called a caliphate. You cannot negotiate with these people. You cannot hope for the best in dealing with these people. The best way to protect the American people is to find them and bring them to justice before they hurt us again.

So our strategy is twofold. We're on the offense overseas, and we're doing everything we can to protect you here at home. And it's a tough task because the enemy only has to be right one time, and we have got to be right 100 percent of the time to do our most important job, which is to protect the American people.

And so that is why, after the enemy hit us, I worked to figure out ways to give the professionals on the frontline of protecting you the tools necessary to do so. There was a wall that prevented our intelligence folks from sharing information with law enforcement. In this different kind of war, we need to have the best kind of intelligence so we can protect you. We need to know what the enemy is thinking so that we can do everything we can to stop attacks.

We designed a piece of legislation that protects our citizens and protects our civil liberties. It was called the PATRIOT Act. And this act—[*applause*]—and this vital law has helped break up terror cells across the

United States. It's an important piece of legislation. If you expect the President and the professionals in Washington to do our jobs and protect you, you must put people in the Congress who will make sure we have the tools to do so.

When it comes to this piece of legislation, the Senate Democrats wanted to have it both ways. In the 2000—2001, the Senate passed this bill 98 to 1. But when the bill came up for renewal in 2005, the Senate Democrats filibustered it. In fact, the Senate leader bragged, "We killed the PATRIOT Act." There's just a different mindset in Washington amongst these people.

The Democrat attempt to filibuster the PATRIOT Act follows an approach that might sound familiar. They voted for it, right before they voted against it. [*Laughter*] Well, thanks to Senators like Conrad Burns, we overcame their filibuster. And I signed this important piece of legislation.

I want to talk about two other measures, two other steps I've taken to make sure that this Government of ours can protect you. If Al Qaida is making a phone call into the United States, or an affiliate of Al Qaida is making a phone call into the United States, we want to know why. We want to know why they're making a call into our country. So when we created— I sent this bill up to the House, Denny supported it; 90 percent of the Democrats voted against it. It hasn't made it to the Senate floor yet, but rest assured, the folks there have a different attitude about what it takes to protect you. I felt it was important in this different kind of war to understand what the enemy is thinking.

And so when we captured people off the battlefield, I instructed the professionals at the Central Intelligence Agency to interrogate them. We picked up a man named Khalid Sheikh Mohammed—let me tell you about him. Our intelligence folks thinks he was the mastermind of the September the 11th attacks. He's the person that organized and ordered the attacks. When we picked

him up, I felt it was important, in order to protect you, that we found out what he knew. See, if he was the mastermind of one attack, he might be masterminding another attack, and therefore it made sense—if our most important job is to protect you—to find out what he knew.

This bill came on the Senate floor. Conrad Burns strongly supported. Seventy percent of the Senate Democrats voted against it.

Audience members. Boo!

The President. On all these vital measures—measures necessary to fight and win the war on terror—the Democrats in Washington have followed a simple philosophy: Just say no. When it comes to listening on to the terrorist—listening to the terrorists, what's the Democrats' answer? Just say no. When it comes to detaining terrorists, what's the Democrats' answer?

Audience members. Just say no!

The President. When it came time to renew the PATRIOT Act, what was the Democrats' answer?

Audience members. Just say no!

The President. When it comes time to questioning the terrorists, what's the Democrats' answer?

Audience members. Just say no!

The President. And so when the Democrats ask for your vote on November the 7th, what's your answer?

Audience members. Noo!

The President. We are on the offense against the enemy wherever we can find them. One of the important lessons of September the 11th, in this new kind of war, America must take threats seriously before they come to the homeland. It's important for the people of this State to understand that lesson. In other words, when we see a threat, we just can no longer hope that oceans will protect us. We can no longer hope for the best—that in order to protect you, we must be on the offense. I saw a threat in Saddam Hussein. Members of both political parties saw a threat in Saddam Hussein. The United Nations saw a

threat in Saddam Hussein. I made the right decision to take Saddam Hussein from power.

And now Iraq is the central front in the war on terror. See, this is a global war. It is being fought on a variety of fronts. And Iraq is now the central front in this war. Oh, I hear them in Washington all the time saying, Iraq is just a distraction from the war on terror. I don't believe it's a distraction. Our troops know it is not a distraction in the war on terror. And guess who else doesn't think it's a distraction? Usama bin Laden. He has called Iraq the third world war. He says that victory for the terrorists in Iraq will mean America's defeat and disgrace forever.

I want you to listen to the words of a Democrat leader in Washington about Iraq, just to give you a sense of the difference of opinion, a different mindset: "The President says that fighting them makes—fighting them there makes it less likely we'll have to fight them there." That's exactly what I said. I said it then; I'm going to keep saying it because it's true. "The opposite is true," this lady went on to say, "Because we're fighting them there, it may be more likely that we will have to fight them here." I want to remind the Democrats that you do not create terrorism by fighting terrorists.

Our troops were not in Iraq when the terrorists first hit the Trade Center in 1993. Our troops were not in Iraq when they attacked in Kenya and Tanzania and the USS *Cole*. And our troops were not in Iraq on September the 11th, 2001, when they killed nearly 3,000 people. The best way to protect you is when we find a terrorist, is to bring them to justice. And that's exactly what we're going to continue to do.

We have a plan for victory in Iraq. I'm not going to leave our troops there unless I can tell you we're going to win. And our plan for victory is an Iraq that can govern itself, sustain itself, and defend itself and serve as an ally in the war on terror. And no question about it, the fighting in

Iraq is tough. It's tough because we face a brutal enemy that is willing to kill innocent men, women, and children in order to achieve their objective. And their objective is to shake the will of the United States. Their objective is to get enough carnage on the TV screens so that we withdraw before the job is done. I've got a message to the terrorists: America does not flee in the face of thugs and assassins.

Our military is constantly adjusting to tactics necessary to stay ahead of the enemy. When the enemy makes a decision, we move. And our troops are performing brilliantly in combat. No matter what your opinion is about my decision to go into Iraq, America needs to support the men and women who wear our uniform. And I know the people of Montana can count on Conrad Burns to make sure our troops have all that is necessary to do the jobs I've asked them to do.

Our troops are brave, and so are the Iraqis. They've been suffering unspeakable violence, yet they are dedicated to having a government of and by and for the people. It's easy to forget, but nearly 12 million people went to the polls to defy car bombers and assassins and said, "We want to live in a free society." I was pleasantly pleased, but I wasn't surprised, because I believe freedom is universal. I believe there's an Almighty, and I believe in the heart of every soul is the desire to be free.

So we'll help this Government politically; we'll help them economically; and we'll help train their security forces so they can take the fight to the enemy. And we'll succeed. The only way we can fail is if we leave before the job is done. And that's exactly what the Democrats want to do.

You know, imagine this: We're in the middle of a war on terror, and one of the most fundamental fights is in Iraq, and yet the Democrats have no plan for victory. They have no idea how to win. Harsh criticism is not a plan for victory. [*Laughter*] Leading Democrats argue we ought to pull our troops off the battlefield right now.

Others suggest we ought to withdraw at a—on a specific date, even though the job may not have been finished. Others recommend moving our troops to an island some 5,000 miles away. These are serious leaders making these kinds of suggestions.

Nineteen House Democrats introduced legislation that would cut off funds for our troops in Iraq. Last week, one of Conrad's colleagues, a Democrat Senator, explained her party's positions this way: "We haven't coalesced around a single plan, but we're in general agreement on the basic principles." She's right; they're in agreement that we ought to leave Iraq before the job is done. I'm not saying these people are unpatriotic; I'm saying they're wrong. You can't win a war unless you're willing to fight the war.

Retreat from Iraq before the job is done would embolden the enemy. It would make this country more vulnerable to attacks. This is a different kind of war. In this war, if we leave early, if we leave before the job is done, the enemy will follow us here. If we leave Iraq before the job is done, it would enable these extremists and radicals to be able to recruit. If we leave before the job is done, it would embolden the extremists and it would dishonor the sacrifice of the men and women who have worn the uniform of the United States of America.

The consequences of retreat from Iraq would be felt for generations. The enemy has said that they want to drive us out of Iraq because they want to establish safe haven, because they believe they can topple moderate governments. I want you to envision a world in which extremists battle for power, in which moderate governments have been toppled, in which these radicals are then capable of using oil to extract blackmail from the West.

Couple all that with a country with a nuclear weapon that can't stand America, and a generation of Americans will say, "What happened in 2006? How come the leaders couldn't see the impending dan-

gers? Where were they when the warning signs were evident?" I want you to understand, I see the impending danger. That is why we will support our troops; that is why we will fight the enemy; and that's why we will win in Iraq.

Victory in Iraq will be a blow to the terrorists and the extremists and the radicals. Victory will say to those in the Middle East who long for peace, you've got a friend in America. Victory will make Iraq an ally in the war on terror. Victory will say to young democracies, we're willing to stand with you. You see, we not only got great assets in our military; we got a fantastic asset in the power of liberty.

I want to share a story with you before we—before I unleash you to go turn out the vote. [*Laughter*] It's a story of my recent trip to Elvis's place. You might have heard about that. I went down there with then-sitting Prime Minister Koizumi of Japan.

People said, "Well, why did you go to Elvis's place?" Well, one, I had never been down there. And Laura was kind of— [*laughter*]—pushing me. She said, it's about time we took a family vacation. [*Laughter*] Secondly, Prime Minister Koizumi wanted to go to Elvis's place. He's a big believer in—he loved Elvis, in other words.

But I also wanted to tell a story, and it's a story that many of you share here, too, because you had a relative, just like I did, that fought the Japanese. World War II came about; the Japanese attacked us at Pearl Harbor. In Pearl Harbor, we lost fewer people than we did at the World Trade Center and in Lancaster, Pennsylvania, and at the Pentagon. But it was an attack on the homeland. Thousands of young Americans volunteered, just like happening today, by the way.

One of those volunteers was George H.W. Bush, Navy fighter pilot. And he, like a lot of other youngsters, fought hard against the Japanese. Thousands and thousands died. It was a bloody war. I find it very interesting that on the plane down

to Elvis's place, I was talking about keeping the peace with the Prime Minister of the former enemy. Something happened between my dad's being in the Navy and your relatives being in the military fighting the Japanese, and in 2006, the President of the United States talking about the peace.

See, we're talking about the fact that Japan had 1,000 troops in Iraq. Prime Minister Koizumi understands what I know: In this ideological struggle of moderation versus extremism, when you find a young democracy, you support that democracy. We talked about working to end the scourge of HIV/AIDS on the continent of Africa, understanding, to whom much is given, much is required. We were talking about the North Korean and how we must work together to convince him to give up his nuclear weapons.

Something happened between World War II and talking about the peace: Japan adopted a Japanese-style democracy. The lesson of history is, liberty has got the capacity to convert an enemy into an ally. Liberty has got the capacity to turn regions of despair into regions of hope. Freedom is universal. People desire to be free, and the more people that become free, the more likely it is our children will live in peace.

Someday duly elected leaders from the Middle East will be talking about keeping the peace with an American President, and generations of Americans will be better off

for it. And that's why I say these are historic times. In the election—the differences of opinion in this election are clear. If you want your taxes to go up, just go ahead and vote Democrat. If you want your taxes to stay low so this economy continue to grow and create opportunity, elect Conrad Burns to the United States Senate. If you want this country to do everything in its power to protect the American people, to stay on the offense against an enemy, and at the same time, create the conditions for lasting peace, you vote for Conrad Burns for the United States Senate. And while you're in there, make sure Denny goes back to Washington too.

So my call for our fellow citizens is to leave the hall, find our fellow Republicans, and tell them we have a duty to vote; find discerning Democrats, and remind them about the stakes; find discerning independents, and tell them what's at stake in this election. Work hard between now and election day. Turn out the vote, and Conrad Burns will be reelected for the United States Senate.

God Bless.

NOTE: The President spoke at 11:27 a.m. at the MetraPark Arena. In his remarks, he referred to Janice Rehberg, wife of Rep. Rehberg; former President Saddam Hussein of Iraq; Usama bin Laden, leader of the Al Qaida terrorist organization; and Chairman Kim Jong Il of North Korea.

Remarks at a Nevada Victory 2006 Rally in Elko, Nevada
November 2, 2006

The President. Thanks for coming. I appreciate the warm welcome. It is nice to be in a part of the country where the cowboy hats outnumber the ties. I can't thank you enough for coming out to say hello.

And I'm proud to be here with three people who I know you're going to make

sure win elections, starting with a fine United States Senator in John Ensign. His family settled in Nevada 100 years ago, so it's safe to say he's got Nevada in his blood. I'm proud to be here with the next Congressman from this congressional district, Dean Heller. And finally, I'm pleased to

be up here with the current Governor, my friend Kenny Guinn, and the future Governor, Congressman Jim Gibbons.

Laura sends her best. I wish she were here in Elko with me. We were both raised in a part of the world that's kind of like this, except the land was flat. [*Laughter*] But the people were warm. Down-to-earth, commonsense people live right here. And that's the kind of people we need in Washington, DC. We've got plenty of highfliers over there; what we need is down-to-earth, commonsense people like John Ensign and Dean Heller.

I want to thank State Senator Bill Raggio for joining us today. I appreciate your mayor, Mayor Mike Franzoia. Thank you, Mac. Good to see you again. I go over to Reno to do an event, and I get off Air Force One, and guess who's at the foot of Air Force One, your mayor. He welcomed me in Reno, and he's welcomed me here to Elko. Mr. Mayor, thank you very much. I appreciate you and Anita being here today. I'm proud to be with you.

I want to thank the Elko High School Band. Let me ask you something. You're not skipping school, are you? [*Laughter*] You are? Well, I'm glad to provide a convenient excuse. [*Laughter*] If you're 18, just remember who got you out of school today—[*laughter*]—and vote for who I ask you to vote for. If not, get a substitute for you in the polls—[*laughter*]—like mom or dad, brother or neighbor. Because see, we're here talking about an election that is 5 days away.

By the way, in Washington, some of them are already measuring the drapes in their new offices. [*Laughter*]

Audience members. Boo!

The President. The pundits have already got it figured out what's going to happen on election day, even before the people of Nevada vote.

Audience members. Boo!

The President. Oh, I'm used to that kind of stuff. I know you are. You might remem-

ber 2004. They were already picking out their offices in the West Wing. [*Laughter*] Except things turned a little differently, and they didn't need the movers. And the same thing is going to happen this November 7th. When you turn out the vote, we're going to hold the House and hold the Senate, and America is going to be better off for it.

We're going to win these elections because Republicans understand the values and the priorities of the American people. The other thing about Republicans is, our values and our priorities do not shift because of the latest poll or focus group. We got a record to run on. See, we've done a lot to raise standards and accountability in public schools so no child is left behind. We're working to reduce this country's dependence on foreign oil. We're working to make sure Americans have quality health care and that our seniors have got affordable prescription drugs. We're providing compassionate care for America's veterans. You don't have to educate this political party about what it's like to be a rancher or a farmer or a hunter. With John Ensign in the Senate and Dean Heller in the House and Jim Gibbons in the Governor's office, the lives of your fellow citizens are going to improve.

And I want to thank you for coming out and giving me a chance to tell you what's on my mind. One of the biggest threats to the values we share is activist judges. John Ensign understands what I know, that a good judiciary is one in which we've got judges who strictly interpret the law and not legislate from the bench.

So when you cast your ballot on Tuesday, your vote will determine more than who represents Nevada in the United States Senate. It will also determine what kind of judges sit on Federal benches around the United States. At this moment, there are about 50 vacancies on the Federal bench, and so it's vital to maintain a Republican Senate so we can confirm the men and women I have nominated.

Our record on judges is clear. With the support of Senators like John Ensign, we have confirmed good judges to the district courts, the circuit courts, and the Supreme Court. And this country is better off with John Roberts and Sam Alito as members of the United States Supreme Court.

A vote for a Democrat Senator in this State or in any State in which there's a senatorial election is a vote against highly qualified judges like these. All you have to do is look at the records. When the Democrats held the Senate, they denied hearings to one-third of my nominees to the court of appeals. See, they've got a record. You can rest assured what's going to happen if the Democrats take over the Senate. When they lost the majority in 2002, they changed their tactics. Instead of not giving them hearings, they just simply filibustered them. They tried the same tactics when Sam Alito's Supreme Court nomination came before the Senate. More than half of Senate Democrats voted to filibuster him. When he finally got his vote, 44 Democrats voted no. Thankfully, we had a Senator like John Ensign representing Nevada, who understands a good judge when he sees one.

The same thing happened to John Roberts. When I nominated him for the DC Circuit, it took—he had been denied a hearing when another President Bush named him. So he finally got his name up, he got in, and then the Senate finally confirmed him. I will just tell you this: If the Senate were controlled by Democrats, John Roberts would still be waiting for a hearing. There's a fundamental difference in this campaign. If you want good, sound, conservative judges who will not legislate from the bench, you send Republicans back to the United States Senate.

I want to talk about two other issues that divide us, two issues that clearly show the difference between how we think and how the other bunch thinks. And the first issue I want to talk about are taxes, and the second issue I'm going to talk to you about is who best to protect you from an enemy that wants to hurt us again.

First let me talk about taxes. Here's what those of us on this stage think. We think you can spend your money far better than the Federal Government can. Make no mistake about it, the Democrats in Washington think they can spend your money better than you can. And that's why if they get control of the House and Senate, they're going to run up your taxes.

Audience members. Boo!

The President. Over the past 5 years, we have done more than just talk philosophy. People of Elko, Nevada, want more than philosophers in Washington, DC. You want doers. When I campaigned in this State in 2000, I said, if you give me a chance to be your President, I'd work with the Congress to cut your taxes, and that's exactly what we've done. We delivered the largest tax cut since Ronald Reagan was the President of the United States.

We cut taxes on everybody who pays income taxes. We doubled the child tax credit. We reduced the marriage penalty. We cut taxes on small businesses. We cut taxes on capital gains and dividends. And we put the death tax on the road to extinction.

All you remember the debate where Democrats in Washington predicted the tax cuts wouldn't create jobs, wouldn't increase wages, and would cause the deficit to explode. Well, the facts are in. The truth is, the tax cuts have led to a growing economy that has added 6.6 million new jobs since August of 2003. The people in this State are working, and real wages are on the rise, and we cut the deficit in half 3 years ahead of schedule.

Cutting taxes works. The amazing thing is, in spite of the record, the Democrats are going to raise your taxes. No, I know they don't want you to know it. As a matter of fact, the top Democrat in the House made an interesting declaration the other day. She said, "We love tax cuts." Well, given her record, she must be a secret admirer. [*Laughter*] She and her party voted

against reducing the marriage penalty, against cutting taxes on small businesses, against lowering taxes for families with children, against reducing the taxes on capital gains and dividends, and against getting rid of the death tax. Time and time again, when she and the Democrat party had a chance to show their love—[*laughter*]—they voted no. [*Laughter*] If that's their idea of love, I sure would hate—I'd hate to see what hate looks like. [*Laughter*]

And by the way, this attitude doesn't extend just to the House. John Ensign will tell you that the Senate—46 Members of the 48 Members of the Democrat Senate voted against the tax cuts we passed. Now, let me tell you how it's going to work. If we don't have people in the Congress like Dean and John Ensign, who are willing to extend the tax cuts or make them permanent, your taxes are going up.

Audience member. Make them permanent.

The President. I agree. [*Laughter*] That man knows what he's talking about over there. [*Laughter*] He said, make it permanent. There way be won't any doubt about it. But, see, they asked the man who wants to be the top tax man in the Congress, the Democrat, "Would you extend any of the tax cuts?" He said, "Not a one." That's what's at stake in this election.

See, when you have the top tax man, the head of the Ways and Means Committee to be, say they're not going to extend any tax cuts, that's code for, your taxes are going to go up. That's exactly what's going to happen. That's why we've got to put Dean Heller in the United States Congress.

Let me give you an example of what I'm talking about. You might remember, we raised the child tax credit from $500 a child to $1,000 a child. Those of you with children understand what I'm talking about, particularly when it came time to fill out your tax form. If those tax cuts are allowed to expire, just like the Democrats want, your taxes go up by $500 a child. So when you're sitting around the table this evening, count the number of children—[*laughter*]—and multiply by 500. So if you've got four children, your taxes are going to go up four times 500, which is 2,000. Now, that may not seem like a lot to Democrats in Washington, DC, but it seems like a lot to those of us on this stage. That's why you're going to get Dean Heller and John Ensign back to Washington, and we're going to keep your taxes low.

This election is taking place at an historic time for this country. When our children and grandchildren look back on this period, one question will overwhelm all the rest: Did we do everything in our power to fight and win the war on terror? That's the fundamental question facing this country right now.

We face an enemy that's brutal. I wish I could tell you we weren't at war, but we are. I think about this every day. I understand there's an enemy that wants to attack us, and the most important responsibility I have and the most important responsibility people elected to Government in Washington have is to protect you. It is the fundamental responsibility of the Federal Government, and we face an enemy that's brutal. They have no conscience; they kill to achieve ideological goals.

They have an ideology. It's an ideology based upon hate. They do not believe in freedom. They don't believe in freedom to worship. They don't believe in freedom to speak. They don't believe in freedom of dissent. They don't believe in freedom for women. We believe in the exact opposite, and that's why they consider us their enemy. And because we're not going to change, they will continue to try to inflict damage on the American people.

Let me tell you, my most important job is to protect you at home. We got to be right 100 percent of the time to do so, and the enemy only has to be right one time, and that's the challenge. And so after

9/11, I decided to review all the tools available for our professionals, and if they didn't have them, let them have them so they can protect you. See, this is a different kind of war. In old times, you could measure progress based upon territories seized or the number of airplanes shot down or the number of ships sunk. In this kind of war, in order to protect you, we got to know what the enemy is thinking. We've got to know what's on their mind, and we've got to make sure our professionals have got the capacity to be able to protect you.

And so I saw walls that prevented the intelligence folks from sharing information with the law enforcement people. I know that it's hard for you to believe. But that's what had happened over time. And so you had a professional say, "I know something that the enemy is thinking," but you couldn't give it to law enforcement. And that's why I asked the Congress to pass the PATRIOT Act, which tore down the wall and, at the same time, protected your civil liberties.

Right after 9/11, the Senate voted 98 to 1 to put the law in place. However, when it came up for renewal in 2005, they filibustered. As a matter of fact, your Senator—not this one, but the other one—[*laughter*]—bragged, "We killed the PATRIOT Act."

Audience members. Boo!

The President. That's what he said, "We killed the PATRIOT Act." Well fortunately, they didn't kill the PATRIOT Act. I was able to sign it into law. Most of the House Democrats voted against the bill. And so you had a Senate bragging, we tried to kill it—a leading Democrat. You can get a sense that there's a difference of opinion.

When I found out that we had the capacity to listen to phone calls on Al Qaida and affiliates that they're making inside the country, I said, "Let's do that." In this new kind of war, if Al Qaida is making that phone call in the country, we want to know why, in order to be able to protect you.

Ninety percent of the House Democrats voted against that bill.

Audience members. Boo!

The President. See, there's just a different mindset. The people in Elko, Nevada, have got to understand that the people—a lot of people in Washington, particularly the Democrats, don't share the same point of view we do when it comes time to protecting you.

We're picking a lot of these people up off the battlefield, and I think it's important for us to know what they know. See, we picked up a man named Khalid Sheikh Mohammed; the intelligence folks think he was the mastermind of the September the 11th attacks. And when we had him in our custody, I approved of a CIA program to question him. I tell you why I did it. If he had knowledge of the September the 11th attacks, we needed to know if he had knowledge of another attack.

Audience members. Yes!

The President. Our most important job is to protect you from attack. This capacity to detain these terrorists and question them came up in front of the House and the Senate. The vast majority of Democrats voted against giving us the tools necessary to protect you.

In all these vital measures for protecting you in this war on terror, the Democrats in Washington follow a simple philosophy: Just say no. [*Laughter*]

When it comes to listening on the terrorists, what's the Democrats' answer: Just say no.

When it comes to detaining terrorists, what's the Democrats' answer?

Audience members. Just say no!

The President. Yes, when it comes to questioning terrorists, what's the Democrats' answer?

Audience members. Just say no!

The President. When it comes to trying the terrorists, what the Democrats' answer?

Audience members. Just say no!

The President. When it comes to trying the terrorists, what's the Democrats' answer?

Audience members. Just say no!

The President. So when the Democrats ask you for their vote on November the 7th, what's your answer?

Audience members. Just say no!

The President. John Ensign and Dean Heller will make sure the professionals have the tools necessary to do their jobs to protect you. The best way to protect you, however, is to go on the offense and defeat the enemy overseas so we do not have to face them here at home.

One of the lessons of September the 11th is, when this Nation sees a threat, we must take it seriously, before it comes home to haunt us. When we see a threat, you just can't ignore it anymore. If you see something that's brewing out there, we're going to have to deal with it. I saw a threat in Saddam Hussein; members of both political parties saw the same threat in Saddam Hussein; the United Nations saw the threat in Saddam Hussein. Getting rid of Saddam Hussein was the right decision.

And now Iraq is the central front in this war on terror. See, we're in a global conflict. If the goal is to defeat the enemy overseas so we don't have to face them here, we confront the enemy where we find them. And the central front of this global war is Iraq. Oh, there's all kinds of opinions in Washington about this. The predominant opinion amongst the Democrats is, Iraq is a distraction from the war on terror. They just couldn't be more wrong.

But don't take my word for it. Take the word of Usama bin Laden. He calls this fight the third world war. Usama bin Laden has said that victory for the terrorists in Iraq will mean America's defeat and disgrace forever.

Or listen to the words of leading Democrats in Washington. Here is what one woman said. She said, "The President says that fighting them there makes it less likely we'll have to fight them here"—that's exactly what I say. She said, "The opposite is true. Because we're fighting them there, it may become more likely that we have to fight them here."

Audience members. Boo!

The President. You do not create terrorism by fighting the terrorists. Iraq is not the reason the terrorists are at war with us. I would remind that Democrat that we were not in Iraq when the terrorists struck the World Trade Center in 1993; we were not in Iraq when they blew up the Embassies in Kenya and Tanzania; we were not in Iraq when they blew up the USS *Cole*; and we were not in Iraq on September the 11th, 2001, when they killed nearly 3,000 of our citizens.

The best way to protect the American people is to stay on the offense and bring these terrorists to justice before they hurt us again. Our goal in Iraq is victory. If I didn't think we could win in Iraq, I wouldn't have our sons and daughters there.

The mothers and fathers of our troops have got to understand that the cause is noble and just, and the sacrifice is important. And if I didn't believe we could succeed the mission, I'd pull them out. But I know we can succeed, and success is a government that can defend itself and govern itself and sustain itself, a new democracy in Iraq, in the heart of the Middle East.

But this is a tough fight. This is a tough fight because the enemy understands the stakes. This is a tough fight because we face an enemy that kills innocent people in order to achieve their objective. This is a tough fight because the enemy knows when they get images of carnage on our television screens, it causes some Americans to wonder whether it's worth it. But they don't understand this administration, and the enemy doesn't understand our country. We will never run from thugs and assassins.

And we've got a plan to defeat them. Our commanders are constantly adjusting our tactics on the ground. We're staying ahead of the enemy. We're inflicting damage. And at the same time, we're helping this young Iraqi democracy succeed. We've got tremendous stuff going for us, starting with the finest United States military ever assembled.

And whether or not you agree with my decision to go into Iraq, all Americans owe a debt of gratitude for the men and women who wear the uniform of our military. And I know Dean and Ensign will join me in making sure they have all the equipment and all the support necessary to do the jobs that I have asked them to do.

We've got—also got something. We've got brave Iraqis who want to succeed. These people have suffered unspeakable violence. And yet they want a government of and by and for the people. Remember, it was 12 million people—nearly 12 million people defied the car bombers and assassins to make a declaration, they want to be free. I was pleased with the results, but I wasn't surprised. I'll tell you why. One, I believe in an Almighty. Two, I believe a great gift of the Almighty is freedom. Three, I believe freedom is universal.

So we'll help them on the political front. We'll help their economy grow, and we'll train Iraqi troops and Iraqi police so they can take the fight. And that's what's happening. Matter of fact, the only way we can lose is if we leave before the job is done.

Oh, I've heard the Democrats. I'm sure you have too. If you listen for their plan on Iraq, they don't have one. On this crucial issue facing the country, they don't have a plan for victory. And I want to remind our fellow citizens, harsh criticism and second-guessing is not a plan.

Oh, they've got some ideas. Some of their leaders say we ought to pull out right now. Others suggest we withdraw on a specific date, even though the job might not be done. One of the House leaders, Demo-

crat House leaders said, why don't we move the troops to an island 5,000 miles away. [*Laughter*] Nineteen House Democrats said they're going to cut off the funds for our troops in Iraq. One of John Ensign's fellow Senators, a Democrat lady, she said, "We haven't coalesced around a single plan, but we're in general agreement on the basic principles." She's right; they're in general agreement about this: Get out of Iraq before the job is done, is what their message is. I'm not saying these people are unpatriotic; I'm saying they're wrong.

You can't win a war if you're unwilling to fight the war. Retreat from Iraq before the job is done would embolden the enemy and make this country more vulnerable. Unlike other wars we have fought, this one is different. If we leave Iraq before the job is done, the enemy will follow us here. Leaving Iraq before the job is done would provide a tremendous propaganda boost for these killers, which would enable them to recruit more. Leaving before the job was done would dash the hopes of millions of people who simply want to live in peace, millions of people in the Middle East who hunger for something other than their extremist and radical agenda. And leaving before the job is done would dishonor the sacrifice of the men and women who wear our uniform. And that is why we'll win in Iraq.

I want to tell you something. If we leave before the job is done in Iraq, the consequences of that decision will be felt for generations. Our enemies have made it clear that they believe we don't have the stomach for the fight, and that it's just a matter of time before we abandon our commitments. And that's something they want us to do because they need to establish new safe haven from which to launch further attacks, a safe haven like that which they had in Afghanistan, where they trained thousands of killers and plot—and planned the attacks of September the 11th. They have made it clear they want to topple moderate governments in the Middle East.

They've made it clear that they would like to use oil as an economic weapon against countries which stand against them.

Now you can imagine all that with a nation that doesn't like America with a nuclear weapon. And 20 or 30 years from now, people will look back at this period of time, and they'll ask, "What happened to those folks in 2006? How come they couldn't see the impending danger for a generation of Americans? What in the world clouded their vision to the threats that the free world would face?"

I'm going to tell you something: I see the threat. I understand the consequences of retreat. I understand what will happen if America tries to isolate ourselves off from the problems of the world, and that is why we will support our troops. We will stand, and we will fight in Iraq, and we will win.

And a victory will be a blow to these extremists and radicals. A victory will say to rational, moderate people, we hear your cries for a peaceful life. A victory will mean we'll have allies in the war on terror. A victory will prevent them from spreading their radical view across the Middle East.

You know, we've got a lot going for us. We got great courage. We've got a fantastic country and a great military. We got something else going for us, and that is the power of liberty. I want to share a quick story with you. It's the story about Prime Minister Koizumi, who was sitting Prime Minister at the time, and my trip to Elvis's place. [*Laughter*] See, I went down to Memphis with the Prime Minister of Japan. People say, "Why did you go to Elvis's place?" Well, Laura and I hadn't been on a trip for a while—[*laughter*]—and Prime Minister Koizumi wanted to go to Elvis's place. He liked Elvis. Like probably some of you, he thought Elvis was cool. [*Laughter*]

But I also wanted to tell a story. I wanted to tell a story to generations of Americans who really haven't thought much about the consequences of World War II. See, like your relatives, my dad joined the

Navy after our country was attacked. That's what's happening today, by the way. Thousands of young Americans have joined the military; many have reenlisted; a lot are continuing to join, because they understand the Nation was under attack.

Same thing happened in the forties. And like your relatives and my dad, thousands fought—thousands died in a bloody conflict. I think it's—found it really interesting when I was flying on Air Force One to Memphis, talking to the Prime Minister of the former enemy about keeping the peace. See, we were talking about North Korea, how we can work together to make sure the Korean Peninsula is nuclear weapons-free. We were talking about the fact that Japan has 1,000 troops in Iraq. See, the Prime Minister knows what I know, that when you find a young democracy that's willing to reject extremists and radicals, it's in our interest, it's in our mutual interests as free societies to support societies based upon liberty. We talked about the scourge of HIV/AIDS on the continent of Africa, and why our nations ought to be involved with helping to eradicate that pandemic. To whom much is given, much is required. See, that's what we were talking about, the peace.

Isn't it interesting? My dad fought the Japanese, and his son is talking about keeping the peace. Something happened. What happened was, Japan adopted a Japanese-style democracy. The lesson is, liberty has got the capacity to transform enemies into allies. Liberty has got the capacity to transform a region of hopelessness and despair into a region of light and optimism. The best way to defeat this enemy in the long run is to deny them the recruiting tools and recruitments made possible by resentment and hatred. Liberty is a powerful force.

Someday elected officials in the United States will be sitting down with duly elected leaders in the Middle East talking about how to keep the peace, and a generation

of Americans is going to be better off for it.

The stakes are high in the election. And I thank you for giving me a chance to come and visit with you and talk about the stakes. And I ask you to go—go from here and find fellow Republicans and discerning Democrats and wise independents, and tell them we have an obligation to vote, and make sure they clearly understand the stakes. If you want your taxes low, if you want more money in your pocket so you can save, spend, or invest, vote for John Ensign and Dean Heller.

Remind them that we're at war. And if you want your Government to do everything in our power to protect you and to stay on the offense and to lay the founda-tion of peace for generations to come, you vote for Dean Heller and you vote for John Ensign.

I can't wait to tell Laura how much fun it was to come to Elko. You got beautiful country here, and you got great people. And it's my honor to be with you.

God bless you, and God bless the United States.

NOTE: The President spoke at 1:35 p.m. at the Elko Regional Airport. In his remarks, he referred to Mayor Michael J. Franzoia of Elko, NV, and his wife, Anita; former President Saddam Hussein of Iraq; Usama bin Laden, leader of the Al Qaida terrorist organization; and former Prime Minister Junichiro Koizumi of Japan.

Remarks at a Missouri Victory 2006 Rally in Springfield, Missouri
November 3, 2006

The President. Thank you all. Thanks for coming. Thank you for the warm welcome. It's good to be back here in southwest Missouri. This isn't my first time here. It's not going to be my last time here, either. The reason why is, I like the people from this part of the world. Good, down-to-earth, commonsense people live in southwest Missouri. And that's the kind of Senator you need in Washington, DC, from this State— good and decent, down-to-earth and talented.

I appreciate you coming, giving me a chance to share with you some of my thoughts about Jim Talent. I've gotten to know him. He's effective. He's a leader. He does not need to take a political opinion poll to tell him where to stand. I want to thank you for supporting him, and I urge you to turn out the vote for Jim Talent. Jim's election will be good for Missouri, and it will be good for the United States of America.

I not only feel that way in my family; so does Laura. She sends her love to our friends here in Missouri. She sends her support to the Talents, and she, like me, urges you to get out and vote on November the 7th.

I'm proud to be here with Brenda Talent and their daughter, Chrissy. I don't know if you know much about the Talent family, but this man puts his family first. He just doesn't talk family values; he lives family values. And that's the kind of Senator you need from the State of Missouri.

I'm proud to be here with the Governor, this boy's son—that boy's son. Where is the Governor? Blunt—how you doing, Blunt? Governor Matt Blunt. It looks like it's—[*applause*]. People from this part of the world know how to find and elect and nourish good public servants. You not only nourished one Blunt; you nourished another Blunt. I'm proud to be up here with the majority whip of the United States Congress, Congressman Roy Blunt.

I want to thank an effective Senator for joining us today. He's the senior Senator from Missouri. He doesn't like me to emphasize the senior part. He is—[*laughter*]—he likes—he, like Jim Talent, every time I'm around him, talk about one thing, what's good for Missouri—and that's Senator Kit Bond.

I want to thank the Lieutenant Governor, Peter Kinder, for joining us. I appreciate all the elected officials. I want to thank all the grassroots activists who are here. Grassroots activists are those who put up the signs, those who make the phone calls, those who turn out the vote. When Jim Talent wins, it's going to be because he's a man of character, because he's got good ideas, and because you're going to help turn out the vote to get him elected on November the 7th.

We're going to sprint to the finish line. We got 4 days to go. What's interesting, however, is in Washington, DC, the pundits have already decided who's going to win.

Audience members. Boo!

The President. They forgot the people of Missouri hadn't voted yet. Oh, that's not the first time they've been forecasting elections. You might remember, in 2004, some of the folks in Washington listened to the prognosticators, and they started picking out their offices in the West Wing. And then it turned out the people went to the polls, and the movers weren't needed.

With your hard work for the next 4 days, you'll elect Jim Talent to the United States Senate. We'll keep control of the House, and we'll keep control of the Senate. And the reason why I believe we're going to win around this country is because Republicans understand the values and the priorities of the American people. We're going to win this election because we got a record to run on. We've done some things that have made this country a better place.

Let me start off with Jim Talent's record. He and I have worked closely to achieve a great national objective, and that is to become less dependent on foreign oil. He

has delivered for Missouri farmers. Let me say, if the farm economy is good, the national economy is good. The farmers and ranchers in Missouri need to send this man back to the United States Senate. But we're working on new technologies so that the automobiles you drive will be powered by crops grown right here in Missouri. And Jim Talent is the leader in this effort. If you want to become less dependent on foreign oil, you need to send him back to the United States Senate.

Jim Talent is a friend of the small-business owner. You see, small businesses are important to our economic vitality. Small businesses are important to a hopeful America. And he understands that insurance costs are making it difficult for small-business owners. And so that's why he has proposed and passed, when he was in the House of Representatives, what's called association health plans. These plans enable small businesses to bind together so they can buy insurance at the same discount that big businesses get to buy insurance. If you're a small-business owner in the State of Missouri, Jim Talent is the right man to represent you in the Senate.

If you're somebody who is worried about methamphetamines in your State, Jim Talent is the right man to represent you. He's introduced and passed tough anti-meth legislation that gives law enforcement new tools to defeat this deadly drug and to shut down meth labs not only here in Missouri but around the country. He's a leader. He's getting the job done.

And I want to talk about one other vital issue, and that is the nature of our judiciary. See, my job is to pick judges who will strictly interpret the law and not legislate from the bench. And so when people go to the polls here in Missouri, you're not only voting for the United States Senator; you're voting to determine what kind of judges will sit on the bench. And here's why. If the Democrats were to control the Senate—which they're not—but they would prevent judges like Sam Alito and John

Roberts from ever making it to the Supreme Court of the United States.

I want to thank Jim Talent for being a strong voice for judicial restraint, a strong voice for talented judges, and a strong advocate for Judge Roberts and Judge Alito. This country is better off by having those two men on the Supreme Court.

There's a lot of issues where there are differences between how we think and how the Democrats think. But there's no two more clear issues than what's going to happen to your taxes and whether or not this country will do everything in our power to protect you.

First, let me start with taxes. We have a clear philosophy: We believe you can spend your money better than the Federal Government can. And the Democrats want to raise your taxes because they think they can spend your money better than you can.

Audience members. Boo!

The President. We believe that when you have more of your own money in your pocket to save, invest, or spend, the economy benefits. Over the past 5 years, we have done more than just philosophize. You don't want philosophers representing you; you want doers representing you. And so we passed the largest tax relief since Ronald Reagan was the President of the United States. We did more than just talk; we acted. We cut the taxes on every American who pays income taxes. We doubled the child tax credit. We reduced taxes on small businesses. We reduced the marriage—the tax on the marriage penalty. We cut taxes on capital gains and dividends. And to reward family businesses and farmers here in the State of Missouri, we put the death tax on the road to extinction.

Oh, you might remember the debate that took place in Washington. The Democrats predicted the tax cuts would not create jobs, they predicted the tax cuts would not increase wages, and they predicted that the tax cuts would cause the deficit to explode. Well, the facts are in. The tax cuts have led to a strong and growing economy, and this morning we got more proof of that. The national unemployment rate has dropped to 4.4 percent. That is the lowest rate in 5½ years. Our economy added 92,000 jobs in the month of October, and over the past 3 months, America has added 470,000 new jobs. Real wages rose 2.4 percent over the past year, which means an extra $1,327 for the typical family of four with two wage earners. And finally, thanks to our growing economy and fiscal restraint, we cut the deficit in half 3 years ahead of schedule.

All those forecasts by the Democrats turned out to be wrong. And now they're forecasting they're going to win the elections. Well, if their election forecasts are as good as their economic forecasts, we're going to have a great day on November the 7th.

The Democrats don't want you to know where they stand on taxes. You know, it's interesting, the top Democrat leader in the House made this declaration: She said, "We love tax cuts." Well, given her record, she must be a secret admirer. [*Laughter*] See, when you all round up the vote, I want you to remind undecided citizens in this State that she and her party voted against reducing the marriage penalty, voted against cutting taxes on small businesses, voted against lowering the taxes for family with children, voted against reducing taxes on capital gains and dividends, and voting against cutting the death tax. That's their record. Time and time again, when she and the Democrats had a chance to show their love for tax cuts, they voted no. If that's their definition of love, I'd sure hate to see what hate looks like.

You see, their plan is to let the tax cuts we passed expire. If we don't make the tax cuts permanent or extend the tax cuts, you get a tax increase. And they've asked leading Democrats, do they have any plans to keep the tax cuts in place? And they don't, because they want to raise your taxes. A big issue in this campaign is whether

or not we're going to have low taxes or higher taxes.

If those tax cuts expire—just like the man who aspires to be the head of the Ways and Means Committee in the House has said is going to happen—I want you to think about this: If you've got a child and those tax cuts expire, your taxes just went up by $500. The child tax credit is 1,000. If the tax cuts are not extended or made permanent, the child tax credit drops to $500 a child. So when you're at dinner this evening, you count the number of children you've got around the table. [*Laughter*] And then you multiply it by $500 per child. So if you're a family—have got four children, just go, one, two, three, four times 500—that's $2,000. That's a $2,000 tax increase if the Democrats take over. That may not seem like a lot to the Democrats in Washington, DC, but it seems like a lot to me, and it seems like a lot to Roy, and it seems like a lot to Senator Talent. Therefore, send him to the Senate, and we'll keep your taxes low.

This election is taking place in an historic time for our country. And when our children and grandchildren look back at this period, one question will overwhelm all the rest: Did we do everything in our power to fight and win the war on terror? That is the fundamental question facing this generation. I wish I could report to you that we were not at war, but we are. We face an enemy that is brutal, an enemy that is determined to inflict damage on America because of what we stand for.

See, they have an ideology. Their ideology is the opposite of our ideology. They don't believe in basic freedoms. They don't believe in the freedom to worship; we do. They don't believe in the freedom of dissent, the freedom of speech. They don't believe in the basic freedoms that have helped define the societies of those of us who embrace liberty. And they want to impose their view on the world. They believe that they should establish a caliphate, a governing body, a governing organization, based upon their ideology of hate that extends, initially, from Indonesia to Spain. That is their declared intentions.

The best way to protect you from these enemies is to stay on the offense and to bring them to justice before they can hurt you again. Part of our strategy is to do just that, and we're doing that. The other part of our strategy is to protect this homeland. The enemy has to be right one time in order to attack us; we've got to be right 100 percent of the time in order to protect you. And that is why I made sure, as did these two gentlemen, that our professionals on the frontline of protecting you have the tools necessary to do so.

For example, there were walls that prevented our intelligence services from sharing information with our law enforcement. Now, I understand that—you probably say, "Well, how did that happen?" Well, it just happened. You cannot fight and win this war and protect the American people unless our intelligence folks can share the information they have gotten with those who are responsible for protecting you. And that's why we designed the PATRIOT Act, to make sure our professionals have the tools, and at the same time, protect civil liberties.

When it came time to renew the PATRIOT Act, the Senate Democrats voted against it. As a matter of fact, the Senate minority leader, the Democrat leader in the Senate, bragged, "Well, we killed the PATRIOT Act." Fortunately, we had Senators like Jim Talent who understand our most important responsibility is to protect you in this new war.

This is a different kind of war that requires a strategy that says we're going to find out what the enemy is thinking in order to protect you. And that's why I authorized a program that said if Al Qaida or an Al Qaida affiliate is making a phone call into the United States of America, we want to know why. We want to understand their intentions. When this bill came for a vote in the House of Representatives,

the overwhelming number of House Democrats voted against giving our professionals the tools necessary to protect you.

See, there's a different mindset in Washington. There's an attitude that says, "It's okay to wait," and, "We'll respond after we're attacked." Our attitude is, we're going to prevent the attacks from happening in the first place.

When we pick an enemy up on the battlefield, we need to be able to question that person. So I authorized the Central Intelligence Agency to question people we have picked up on the battlefield. Let me explain why. We picked up Khalid Sheikh Mohammed; our intelligence folks thinks he was the person that masterminded the September the 11th attacks. So you can imagine why I wanted to know what he knew. If he knew one attack, he might know another attack. If my job is to protect you, we better give the professionals the tools necessary to do so. And yet, when this program came up on the floor of the United States Senate and the United States House of Representatives, the overwhelming number of Democrats voted against it.

Audience members. Boo!

The President. We need people in the Congress who understand the stakes of this war. We need people in the Senate and the Congress who understand our most important job is to protect you. We need to make sure our professionals have the tools necessary to do so. That's why you've got to send Jim Talent to the United States Senate.

We're on the offense. Every day, this country is on the offense against those who would do you harm. You cannot plot and plan if you're on the run. It is hard to organize a strike on America if you're hiding. So you just got to know, there's a lot of really brave people on the hunt.

One of the lessons of September the 11th is that when we see a threat, we have got to take that threat seriously before it materializes. It's an essential lesson in this new war. I saw a threat in Saddam Hus-

sein; Members of the United States Congress, both political parties, saw the same threat; the United Nations saw the threat. Removing Saddam Hussein was the right decision, and the world is better off for it.

We're in a global war against these terrorists, and we're fighting on a variety of fronts. The most important front is Iraq. I've heard all the language out of Washington—I'm sure you have as well—that said, Iraq is a distraction in the war on terror. That's what the Democrats say. I believe Iraq is central to the war on terror. But don't take my word for it. Don't take my word for it; listen to Usama bin Laden. He has called Iraq—the fight in Iraq the third world war. He understands the stakes. He says that victory for the terrorists in Iraq will mean America's defeat and disgrace forever. That's what the enemy says.

Now I want you to listen to the words of a leading senior Democrat in Washington, DC, about Iraq. She said, "The President says fighting them there makes it less likely we will have to fight them here." That's what I have said, and that's what I'm going to continue to say, because it's the truth. [*Applause*] Hold on for a minute. She went on to say, "The opposite is true: Because we are fighting them there, it may become more likely we'll have to fight them here."

Audience members. Noo!

The President. Iraq is not the reason why the terrorists are at war against us. When you're out rounding up the vote, you remind people that we were not in Iraq when they attacked the World Trade Center in 1993. We were not in Iraq when they blew up our Embassies in Kenya and Tanzania. We were not in Iraq when they blew up the USS *Cole*. And we were not in Iraq on September the 11th, 2001, when they killed nearly 3,000 of our citizens. You do not create terrorists by fighting the terrorists. The best way to protect you is to stay on the offense and defeat them overseas

so we do not have to face them here at home.

Our goal in Iraq is victory. Victory in Iraq will mean a country which can sustain itself, govern itself, and defend itself and serve as an ally in the war on terror. And there's no question, the fighting is tough, because the enemy understands the stakes of what a free society will mean to their ambitions to spread their dark vision throughout the Middle East and then the world. See, they understand the stakes, and we must understand the stakes. The enemy kills innocent people in order to shake the will of the Iraqis, in order to create concern amongst the American people. They have got a weapon, and that is their willingness to take innocent life. Americans value life. We appreciate life. But I want the enemy to understand this country. We will not run in the face of thugs and assassins.

We have a plan for victory that gives our commanders all the flexibility they need to stay ahead of the enemy. And we've got some unbelievably brave and courageous people wearing the uniform of the United States of America. Our troops understand the stakes in Iraq. They understand this is a central front in the war on terror. And that is why I am pleased to tell you that there's no doubt in my mind, when it comes time to making sure our troops have all that is necessary to do the jobs I have asked them to do, Senator Talent is strong for the military.

Something else we've got going for us to achieve our goal, and those are the Iraqis. They've suffered unspeakable violence. Yet, you might remember, nearly 12 million of them said, "We want to be free." I was pleased, but not surprised, that people said, "We want to be free." I believe a gift from the Almighty to every soul on the face of the Earth is the desire to be free. I believe in the universality of freedom, and I believe it is in our interest that we help people who desire to be free to be so.

And therefore, we'll help this young Government politically. We will help them economically, to realize their vast potential. We will continue to train their military so they get to take the fight, so they're the ones who win, so they're the ones who defeat the extremists. And I believe that one day, Iraq will be a government of and by and for the people, unless we leave before the job is done. The only way we can lose is if we leave before the job is done. And that's a central part of the debate in this campaign.

You listen to the debate, and try to listen carefully for the Democrat plan for success. Don't listen too long because they don't have one. They don't have a plan to win this important front in the war on terror. Oh, some of the leading Democrats in Washington argue we should pull out right now. Then you got other voices saying we should withdraw on a specific date, even though the job hasn't been completed. You actually had a Member of the House recommend moving troops to an island 5,000 miles away, as part of their plan. Nineteen House Democrats introduced legislation that would cut off funds for our troops in Iraq.

One of Jim Talent's colleagues, a Democrat Senator, explained her party's position this way: "We haven't coalesced around a single plan, but we're in general agreement on the basic principles." Well, she's right. They're in agreement about one thing: They will leave before the job is done. I'm not saying these people are unpatriotic; I'm just saying they're wrong.

On this vital issue, on the issue that will determine the security of this country, the Democrats have taken a calculated gamble. They believe that the only way they can win this election is to criticize us and offer no specific plan of their own. Here's how one Democrat senior describes their strategy: "The election is about them," this person said. So far, the Democrats have refused to tell us their plan on how they're going to secure the United States. There's

still 4 days left before the election, and there's still time for the Democrats to tell the American people their plan to prevail in this war on terror.

So if you happen to bump into a Democrat candidate, you might want to ask this simple question: What's your plan? If they say they want to protect the homeland but oppose the PATRIOT Act, ask them this question: What's your plan? [*Laughter*] If they say they want to uncover terrorist plots but oppose listening in on terrorist conversations, ask them this question: What's your plan? If they say they want to stop new attacks on our country but oppose letting the CIA detain and question the terrorists who might know what those plots are, ask them this question: What's your plan? If they say they want to win the war on terror but call for America to pull out from what Al Qaida says is the central front in this war, ask them this question: What's your plan?

Audience members. What's your plan?

The President. The truth is, the Democrats can't answer that question. Harsh criticism is not a plan for victory. Second-guessing is not a strategy. We have a plan for victory. We have a plan to secure this country, and part of our plan is to send Jim Talent back to the United States Senate.

Victory is vital for the future of this country. Retreat from Iraq before the job is done would embolden the enemy. It would make our country more vulnerable to attacks.

This is a different kind of war. I know I keep saying that, but it's important for you to understand how different it is. Unlike other wars, if we were to leave Iraq before the job is done, the enemy would follow us here. Victory—defeat in Iraq, leaving before the job is done, would give the enemy a new safe haven, just like they had in Afghanistan, from which to plan and plot further attacks. It would enable the enemy to recruit. It would strengthen the hand of the radicals and extremists. It

would dash the hopes of millions of people in the Middle East who want to live in peace. And it would dishonor the sacrifice of the men and women who have worn the uniform of the United States of America.

The consequences of retreat would be felt for generations. I see a lot of young folks here today. My job is to think not only how to protect you today but how to create the conditions for peace in the long run. Retreating from the Middle East because of the unspeakable violence that the enemy inflicts on others as well as their own troops would create a dangerous world for you to grow up in. You see, the enemy has made it clear that they expect us to lose our nerve. They have made it clear that they don't believe America has what it takes to defend ourselves. They want to topple moderate governments. They want to be able to use energy as a tool to blackmail the United States.

Imagine the radicals and extremists taking over a country, and they were able to pull millions of barrels of oil off the market, driving the price up to 3 or $400 a barrel, whatever it would be, and saying, "Okay, we'll reduce the price, all you've got to do is surrender. All you've got to do is abandon your alliance with Israel, and we'll lower the price. All you've got to do is retreat." And couple that with a country which doesn't like us, with a nuclear weapon, and a generation of Americans will say, "What happened to them in 2006? How come they couldn't see the impending danger? What was it that clouded their vision?"

Well, I want to assure you, I clearly see the threats facing a generation of Americans. I see the problems we face, and that is why we will stay in Iraq. And that is why we will fight in Iraq. And that is why we will win in Iraq. Victory will be a blow to the terrorists, a blow to the plans of the extremists and radicals. Victory will help moderates—moderate people, people who want to bring their children up in a peaceful world, to have the boldness to

help us marginalize those radicals. Victory will say to reformers and women who long for freedom, America will not abandon you. Victory will say to those who believe they can impose their tyrannical vision on others, liberty is powerful.

I want to share a story with you about the power of liberty. You might remember, recently Laura and I took Prime Minister Koizumi, who was then sitting as the Prime Minister of Japan, to Elvis's place. It was in Memphis, Tennessee. You been there probably. See, I had never been there. Laura said, "It's about time we took a family vacation; take me down to Elvis's place." [*Laughter*] We also went because Prime Minister Koizumi, the Prime Minister of Japan, loved Elvis. [*Laughter*] But I also wanted to tell a story, and I want you all to listen to this story, because it's a powerful story about liberty.

See, after Japan attacked America— where, by the way, we lost fewer people in Pearl Harbor than we did on September the 11th—a lot of young Americans volunteered to defend our Nation, one of whom was my dad, and I'm certain some of your relatives did the same thing. Thousands of Americans volunteered to fight the enemy in a bloody war in which thousands and thousands of citizens on both sides of this war lost their lives.

And here I am, on Air Force One, flying down to Elvis's place with the Prime Minister of the former enemy, talking about the peace, talking about working together to secure peace. Isn't that interesting? Something happened between World War II and 2006, when I'm on the airplane talking about how we can work together to send a clear message to the leader in North Korea, no nuclear weapons; or how we can work together to fight the scourge and the pandemic of HIV/AIDS on the continent of Africa; or how we can work together to feed the hungry.

I thanked him for the 1,000 Japanese troops in Iraq, because he understands what I know: In this ideological struggle,

when we find young democracies that are willing to stand strong against the extremists and radicals, those of us who live in liberty have a duty to help these young democracies succeed for the sake of peace. Isn't it interesting? My dad fought the Japanese, and his son is talking about keeping the peace. Something happened: Japan adopted a Japanese-style democracy.

The lesson for all to hear is that liberty has got the capacity to transform an enemy into an ally. Liberty has got the capacity to transform a region of frustration and resentment into a region of hope. Someday American leaders will be sitting down with duly elected leaders from the Middle East talking about keeping the peace, and a generation of Americans will be better off for it.

And so these are the stakes in this election. These are historic times, and you can make a significant difference in how our country responds. When you leave the hall, go find your fellow Republicans, discerning Democrats—[*laughter*]—and openminded independents, and remind them of the stark differences in this campaign. And the message is this: If you want low taxes and a correspondingly strong economy, vote Republican and send Jim Talent back to the United States Senate. If you want this country of ours to give the professionals they need—the tools they need to protect you and if you want the United States of America doing everything we can to defeat an enemy and lay the foundation for peace, vote Republican and send Jim Talent back to the United States Senate.

I am honored you're here. I'm grateful for your time. I appreciate your enthusiasm. God bless you, and God bless the United States.

NOTE: The President spoke at 9:16 a.m. at the Springfield Exposition Center. In his remarks, he referred to former President Saddam Hussein of Iraq; Usama bin Laden, leader of the Al Qaida terrorist organization; and Chairman Kim Jong Il of North Korea.

Remarks at a Missouri Victory 2006 Rally in Joplin, Missouri
November 3, 2006

The President. Thanks for the warm welcome. It's good to be here in Joplin.

Audience members. Welcome to Missouri, George W. Bush! Welcome to Missouri, George W. Bush!

The President. As I was saying—[laughter]—it's good to be back here in southwest Missouri. I like coming here. You've got pretty countryside, and you've got hardworking, commonsense people. And that's what you need in the United States Senate, someone with common sense, someone who brings good, sound Missouri values to the United States Senate, someone who has got the right priorities, starting with his family, in the United States Senate. And that someone is Jim Talent.

I appreciate you coming. I appreciate your interest in this campaign, and I urge you to do your duty as a citizen and vote. And when you vote, your vote is not only going to be good for Missouri; it's going to be good for the United States when you send Jim Talent back to the Senate.

There's unanimity in my family about who ought to be your Senator from Missouri; Laura believes that Jim Talent ought to be the Senator from Missouri as well. She's not with me today; she's campaigning elsewhere. Tomorrow evening, however, I'm going to celebrate with her her 60th birthday party. But don't tell anybody. [Laughter] I want it to be a surprise. [Laughter] She sends her love. She sends her thanks. She knows what I know: Jim Talent is about as fine a United States Senator as you'll ever have.

I'm proud to be with your Governor. I was a Governor one time, but I didn't look as young as he looks. [Laughter] But he's doing a fine job, and you did a smart thing by sending him to the statehouse. I'm proud to be with the Governor's father, Majority Whip Roy Blunt, and Majority Whip Roy Blunt's son Charlie, and today happens to be his second birthday. And from the looks of things, he's trying to figure it out. [Laughter]

I want to thank Lieutenant Governor Peter Kinder for joining us today. Your mayor, Jon Tupper, is joining us today. Mr. Mayor, thanks for coming. Party Chairman Doug Russell, all the grassroots activists, I thank you for coming. Grassroots activists are those who put up the signs, make the phone calls, put the envelopes in the mail. In other words, you're the ones who are going to join Jim Talent in working hard until election day and turn out the vote. Thank you for doing what you're doing.

I want to thank the Pierce Arrow Band. I'm sorry I wasn't here to hear them. [Laughter] But from all accounts, they did a fabulous job.

Election is four days away, and I'm sprinting to the finish line, and Talent is sprinting to the finish line, and we're asking you to join us as we sprint to the finish line.

You probably heard all the reports from the punditry—[laughter]—in Washington, DC. Some of them are already measuring for new drapes. That's not the first time, by the way, people have said the election's over before the people vote. You might remember 2004. Some of the crowd up there was picking out their offices in the West Wing. [Laughter] Then the people of Missouri and people from around the country voted, and the movers were not needed.

And the same thing is going to happen on November the 7th, 2006. With your help, we'll send Jim back to the United States Senate, and we're going to keep control of the House and the Senate. And there's a reason why: Because our party understands the values and the priorities of the American people. We don't need to take an opinion poll to tell us what to think, and we've delivered.

First, let me talk about some of the work that Jim Talent has done in Washington. See, I've seen him up close. I know he cares a lot about the people of Missouri, and he understands that this Nation is at risk if we remain dependent on foreign oil.

When you get oil from parts of the world where people don't like you, it's a national security problem. And that's why I have worked closely with Jim to advance new technologies that will enable us to use Missouri farm products to power our automobiles. We understand, by the way, that when the farmers and ranchers are doing well, the American economy does well. And if you're a Missouri farmer or a Missouri rancher, it makes economic sense to send Jim Talent back to the United States Senate.

Jim understands small businesses. If you're a small-business owner, he understands you. See, he understands small businesses are having trouble getting insurance, and so he's proposed a plan called associated health plans, which enable small businesses to join together to pool risk so they can buy health insurance at the same discounts big companies get to do. If you're a small-business owner in the State of Missouri, it's in your interest to send Jim Talent back to the United States Senate.

Jim understands that this Nation must have a focus on eliminating methamphetamines. He's done something about it. He passed good law that gives law enforcement new tools to defeat this deadly drug and to shut down meth labs in Missouri and around the United States. If you're concerned about what meth does to your fellow citizens, send Jim Talent back to the United States Senate.

I want to talk about another issue that's important, and that is the nature of the judiciary. A lot of people in Missouri understand what Jim and I know, that in order to have a good, sound judiciary, we need judges who strictly interpret the law and not legislate from the bench. The people of this State have got to understand, when you cast your vote on Tuesday, you're electing more than just a United States Senator. Your vote will determine what kind of judges we have.

You know, I named two really solid judges for the Supreme Court, smart and capable men who share our judicial philosophy. Thankfully, we had Senators like Senator Talent and Senator Bond from Missouri who worked hard to get these men confirmed. However, if the Democrats had control of the Senate, they wouldn't be sitting on the Supreme Court. You tell your friends and neighbors who are still undecided in this race that if you want a judiciary full of judges who will strictly interpret the law and not legislate, send Jim Talent back to the United States Senate.

There are big differences between what we think and what the other bunch thinks. Perhaps the two biggest issues can—two differences can be seen on two issues. One, what's going to happen to your taxes, and which party will take the necessary steps to defend you.

Let me start with taxes. We have a philosophy: We believe you can spend your money far better than the Federal Government can. Democrats want to raise your taxes because they believe they can spend your money better than you can.

Audience members. Boo!

The President. We believe that when you have more money to save, spend, or invest, the whole economy benefits.

We're not just people who philosophize. We're people who act. Thanks to Senators like Jim Talent and Congressmen like Roy Blunt, I signed the largest tax decreases since Ronald Reagan was the President of the United States. Remind people of our record: We cut the taxes on everybody who pays income taxes; we doubled the child tax credit; we reduced the marriage penalty; we cut taxes on small businesses; we cut taxes on capital gains and dividends; and we put the death tax on the road to extinction.

If you're a farmer here in Missouri, you need to remember which Senator—or which candidate strongly supports making sure that death tax stays dead. We don't think it's right you pay taxes while you're alive and then you pay taxes after you die.

You might remember the debate. All the Democrats in Washington predicted the tax cuts would not create jobs. They predicted they would not increase wages, and they predicted the tax cuts would cause the Federal deficit to explode. Well, the results are in. The tax cuts have led to a strong and growing economy.

Just this morning, we got additional good news. The unemployment rate around the United States has dropped to 4.4 percent. That's the lowest rate in 5½ years. Our economy added 92,000 jobs in the month of October, and over the past 3 months, America has added 470,000 new jobs. People are working in the United States. The tax cuts have worked. Real wages went up 2.4 percent over the past year, which means an extra $1,327 for the typical family of four with two wage earners.

And finally, you might remember all the forecasts, but we have cut the deficit in half 3 years ahead of schedule. If the Democrats' election predictions are as good as their economic predictions—[laughter]— we're going to have a good day on November the 7th.

Now in this campaign, whether it's here in Missouri or anywhere else across the country, the Democrats don't want you to know their tax plans. Listen to the words of the top Democrat leader in the House, when she said, "We love tax cuts." Well, given her record, she must be a secret admirer. [Laughter] She and her party voted against reducing the marriage penalty, against cutting taxes on small businesses, against lowering taxes for families with children, against reducing taxes on capital gains and dividends, and against cutting the death tax. I mean, time and time again, when they had their chance to show their love for tax cuts, they voted no. Now, if

this is their definition of love, I'd sure hate to see what hate looks like.

Now there's a difference of opinion in Washington, DC, about what to do with your money. If these tax cuts are not extended or made permanent, your taxes are going up. You see, if the tax cuts are not made permanent, you can bet the Federal Government is going to be in your wallet.

And that's precisely what the Democrats want to do. They asked the man who would be the chairman of the Ways and Means— that's the tax-writing committee in Washington—could he think of any tax cuts he would extend. And he said, "Not a one." Not a tax cut. Make no mistake about it, they may not be admitting it on the campaign trail, but they're going to raise your taxes.

If the tax cuts aren't extended, think about what that does to the child tax credit. Right now the tax credit is $1,000 per child. If those tax cuts are not extended, those tax credits go down to $500 a child, which means you've got yourself a $500 tax increase per child. So tonight, when you're sitting around the dinner table, just count the heads. [Laughter] If you've got two children, you can count on a $1,000 tax increase. If you got three little heads there, you can count on a $1,500 tax increase. I know some people here in Joplin may have four children. Yes, there you are— the man right there has got four children, so when you're having dinner this evening, just go, one, two, three, four times 500; that's a $2,000 tax increase, if the Democrats win.

That may not sound like a lot of money to Washington Democrats, but it's a lot of money to me, and it's a lot of money to Talent. It's a lot of money to you. So my strong advice is, if you're a small-business owner, if you've got children, if you pay income taxes, you're a farmer and you want to keep the money that you've worked hard to earn, vote for Jim Talent for the United States Senate.

This election is taking place in an historic time for our country. And when our children and grandchildren look back on this period, one question will overwhelm the rest: Did we do everything in our power to fight and win the war against the terrorists? That is the question which faces this generation.

I wish I could report to you here in Joplin that we were not at war, but we are. We face a determined enemy. They have no conscience. They kill the innocent in order to achieve objectives. These people are totalitarian, and they share an ideology that is the exact opposite of what we believe. We believe in the right of every person to worship freely; they don't. We believe in the freedom to dissent, freedom to speak. We believe every life is precious. We believe in human dignity.

Their totalitarian point of view is dark and dismal, and yet they have objectives, and they want to spread that point of view. And they want to create enough chaos and havoc to cause people to withdraw so they can spread their attitude. The best way to protect you is to stay on the offense and bring these people to justice before they hurt America again.

You can't negotiate with these people. You can't try to talk sense in these people.

Audience members. Noo!

The President. You must be firm and determined to protect you. At the same time, here at home, we've got to do enough to be able to say, we're doing our duty. See, my most important job and the important job of people elected to Washington is to protect the American people. That's the call of this generation.

The enemy has to be right one time when it comes time to attacking us again. We have to be right 100 percent of the time to protect you. And therefore, I made sure that our professionals had the tools necessary to protect you. There was a wall that separated the intelligence community from sharing information with the law enforcement folks.

It's hard to rationalize that that happened, but that is what happened prior to September the 11th. In other words, you had—somebody had some intelligence about somebody who might be coming our way, and he couldn't share that information with somebody whose job it was to stop them. I know it doesn't make sense, but it's the reality of what we faced.

So I asked the Congress to pass the PATRIOT Act, which brought down that wall. The Senate Democrats tried to filibuster that reauthorization of that important bill. As a matter of fact, the Senate minority leader, the head Democrat in the Senate, bragged, "We killed the PATRIOT Act." See, there's a different mindset. If our most important job is to protect you, we've got to make sure our professionals have the tools necessary to do so.

I guess, maybe if—I'm just trying to guess the mentality, but they must not think there's an enemy that wants to hit us again. It's the only justification I can give you for not making sure those professionals had the tools.

I decided to institute another program. If Al Qaida or an Al Qaida affiliate is making a phone call into the United States from outside the United States, it seems like it makes sense to know why. They hadn't voted on this bill in the Senate, but they did in the House, and by far, the overwhelming majority of House Democrats voted against the program.

Audience members. Boo!

The President. We have got to understand what the enemy is thinking, in order to be able to protect you. And that's why I authorized the program through the Central Intelligence Agency that would allow us to detain and question people we picked up off the battlefield.

And let me give you a reason why. See, we captured Khalid Sheikh Mohammed; our intelligence services think he's the person that ordered and masterminded the September the 11th attacks. And so when I heard we captured him, I thought it made

sense, common sense, to say to our professionals, "If he knew the first attack, he might have information on another attack, and why don't you see if you can find out if he does."

Seventy percent of the Senate Democrats voted against that bill.

Audience members. Boo!

The President. We're at war. It's a different kind of war, but is, in fact, a war. That war came home on September the 11th, 2001. You should expect people in Washington, DC, to give our professionals the tools necessary to protect you. It's a big difference in this campaign, between what Republicans think and what Democrats think. I'm going to tell you something: You can't wait to respond after we're attacked. We must take the necessary measures to make sure we're not attacked in the first place.

That's why I feel so strongly about a person like Jim Talent. He understands the stakes. He also understands what I know: When we see a threat overseas, we must take that threat seriously. That's one of the lessons of September the 11th. It's important never to forget lessons. That lesson is a clear lesson to me. I saw a threat in Saddam Hussein; members of both political parties in the Congress saw the same threat; the United Nations saw the threat in Saddam Hussein. The decision to get rid of Saddam Hussein was the right decision, and the world is better off for it.

We're in a global war that's being fought on a variety of fronts, and Iraq is the central front of that war. Now I understand you hear the voices out of Washington, they say, "Well, Iraq is a distraction in the war on terror." To me, that's a dangerous point of view, but nevertheless, that's what they say. Well, the doubters about Iraq ought to listen to Usama bin Laden before they make up their mind as to whether Iraq is the central front.

See, Usama bin Laden calls the fight we're in in Iraq the third world war. He says that victory for the terrorists in Iraq will mean America's defeat and disgrace forever. Now there's a difference of opinion. I want you to listen to the words of a senior Democrat in Washington who—she said this: "The President says that fighting them there makes it less likely we will fight them here." Yes, that's precisely what I said, and I strongly believe it's right. [*Applause*] She went on to say—hold on for a minute—she went on to say, "The opposite is true; because we are fighting them there, it may become more likely that we will have to fight them here."

Audience members. Boo!

The President. See, that's the kind of mentality that you're voting on on November the 7th. You do not create terrorists by fighting the terrorists.

Iraq is not the reason the terrorists are at war against us. We weren't in Iraq when the terrorists bombed the World Trade Center in 1993. We were not in Iraq when they bombed our Embassies in Kenya and Tanzania. We weren't in Iraq when they bombed the USS *Cole*, and we weren't in Iraq when they attacked us on September the 11th, 2001.

The best way to protect you is to bring the terrorists to justice wherever we find them. And they are fighting us in Iraq because they can't stand the thought of a democracy in their midst. And so they're fighting with brutality, the likes of which we haven't seen in a long time. See, they'll kill innocent people.

Our goal in Iraq is victory. Our goal in Iraq is an Iraq that can sustain itself, an Iraq that can govern itself, Iraq that can defend itself, an Iraq that will be an ally against these extremists and radicals. But this enemy, which understands the stakes, also understands that their violence, their unspeakable violence against innocent life gets on our television screens. And they are trying to shake our will because they think our will is shakable.

Audience members. Noo!

The President. They don't think we have the stomach necessary to defend ourselves

in the long run, but they don't understand this administration and many in our country. We will not run from thugs and assassins.

We are constantly adjusting our tactics to meet the enemy. The enemy adjusts; we adjust. I've given our commanders the flexibility necessary and whatever they need to win this war. And we've got a lot going for us. We got a strategy that helps us achieve victory, and we got a military that is the finest military any country has ever assembled.

And whether or not our citizens agree with my decision to fight the enemy in Iraq, all citizens owe a debt of gratitude to those who wear our uniform. And those of us in Washington owe it to our troops and their families to make sure they have the full support, all they need in order to do the jobs I've asked them to do.

Our troops have got no finer supporter than Senator Jim Talent, another reason to send him back to Washington. We've also got something else going for us, and that is brave Iraqis. Listen, these people have suffered unspeakable violence, and yet they still want to live under a free society. I was pleased at the outcome of the elections when the Iraqis voted, but I wasn't surprised. I believe freedom is universal. I believe there's an Almighty, and a great gift of the Almighty to each man and woman and child on the face of the Earth is the desire to be free.

I'm not surprised when 12 million people say, "I want to be free." It's in our interests we help this young democracy. It's in our interests we defeat the enemy where we find them. It's in interests we help people realize the blessings of liberty. And that's why our strategy is to help the politics of Iraq succeed, to help their economy grow, and to train Iraqi troops so they can take the fight. One day Iraq will be a government of, by, and for the people—unless we quit.

If I didn't think we'd win, I wouldn't have our troops there. If I didn't know

this mission is noble and important, I wouldn't have our troops there.

You know, the debate is interesting about this vital part of protecting the country. If you listen carefully to what the Democrats say about Iraq, you think about what they're saying about their plan for success, there isn't one. This is a major political party that has no plan for success in Iraq. As a matter of fact, their only plan is to leave before the job is done. Oh, you listen to some of them—they say we pull out the troops now. And then they got a bunch of them saying, "Let's have a fixed date," and we'll leave on that fixed date, regardless of whether the job is done. They've actually got a Member of the House of Representatives who has recommended moving our troops 5,000 miles away on another island—on an island. Nineteen House Democrats introduced legislation that would cut off funds for our troops in Iraq.

Here we are in the middle of a national campaign that will determine our future, and one of Jim Talent's Democrat colleagues put it this way—she said, "We haven't coalesced around a single plan, but we're in general agreement on the basic principles." She's right. The principle they agree on is, get out before the job is done.

Audience members. Boo!

The President. Look, I'm not saying these people are unpatriotic; I'm just saying they're wrong.

On this important issue of Iraq and the global war on terror, the Democrats have taken a calculated gamble. They believe that the only way they can win this election is to criticize and offer no plan of their own. Here's how one senior Democrat describes their strategy: "The election is about them," talking about me and us. So far, they've refused to tell how they plan to secure this country; but there's still 4 days left. [*Laughter*] There's still time. There's still time for them to tell us how they intend to prevail.

Listen, if you happen to bump into a Democrat candidate, you might want to ask

this simple question: What is your plan? [*Laughter*] If they say they want to protect the homeland but opposed the PATRIOT Act, ask them this question: What is your plan? If they say they want to uncover terrorist plots but oppose listening in on terrorist conversation, ask them the question: What's your plan? You know, if they say they want to stop new attacks on our country but opposed letting the CIA detain and question the terrorists who might know what the plots are, ask them the question: What's your plan?

Audience members. What's your plan?

The President. If they say they want to win the war on terror but called for America to pull out from what Al Qaida says is the central front in that war, ask them this question——

Audience members. What's your plan?

The President. They're not going to be able to answer that question. They have no plan. When you're rounding up the vote, remind people, harsh criticism is not a plan for victory. Second-guessing is not a strategy. You cannot win the war on terror if you don't have a plan to win the war.

The most important duty we have is to protect you. We have a plan, a strategy that we're implementing every single day, and part of our plan to make sure that America does everything we can to protect you is to send Jim Talent back to the United States Senate.

Retreat from Iraq before the job is done would embolden the enemy, make our country more vulnerable to attacks. This is a different kind of war. It's unlike any other war we have fought. If we retreat from Iraq before the job is done, the enemy will follow us here. Leaving before the job is done would enable these extremists and radicals to recruit better. Leaving before the job is done would dash the hopes of millions of people who reject the ideology of hate and who want to live a simple life that is a peaceful life. Retreating before the job is done would dishonor the sacrifice of the men and women who have

worn the uniform of the United States of America. Retreating before the job is done would be felt for generations to come.

The enemy has said they expect us to retreat, and they want us to retreat. This is their words, not mine. In a time of war, you must take the words of the enemy very seriously. They would like to have another safe haven from which to plot and plan attacks, similar to the safe haven they had in Afghanistan before we removed that safe haven. The enemy would like to be in a position to topple moderate governments. They would use any means necessary to do so. Can you imagine what the world would look like if they were able to get ahold of oil resources which they would then use to extract economic blackmail against those of us who want—need to protect ourselves, and, two, to help freedom expand.

See, imagine what would happen if they were able to control enough energy, if they pulled enough off the market to run the price of oil up, and then said, "Fine, we'll let the price back down unless you give up your alliance with Israel," or, "until you withdraw," so that they could establish their—what they've declared they want to do, which is a caliphate.

And in the midst, put a country that doesn't like us with a nuclear weapon. And what's going to happen 30 years from now is, people will say, "What happened to those folks in 2006? How come they couldn't see the impending danger? What clouded their vision?"

I want to tell you all, my vision is clear. I see the threat. I understand the consequences of the world in which we live. America must lead. We will support our troops in Iraq. We will fight in Iraq, and we will win in Iraq.

If you got a second, I'd like to share one other story about the power of liberty.

Audience member. [*Inaudible*]

The President. Thank you. [*Laughter*] Recently Laura and I took our friend, who was then the Prime Minister of Japan, to

Elvis's place. You might remember that. Oh, they said, "Why did you go to Elvis's place?" Well, I had never been there. [*Laughter*] Prime Minister Koizumi wanted to go there—he was an Elvis fan. I also wanted to tell a story. It's important for all people to understand this story, but particularly for people who are trying to figure out the world in which we live and the power of liberty.

See, after the Japanese attacked our country, a lot of young Americans signed up. You've got relatives who signed up to fight the sworn enemy, the Japanese. So did I: my dad. And then he, like thousands, went through a bloody battle. We lost a lot of Americans, and the Japanese lost a lot—it was a brutal war, brutal war. And yet it's amazing, isn't it, that years later his son is on the airplane with the Prime Minister of the former enemy flying to Elvis's place. And guess what we talked about? Keeping the peace. Isn't that interesting?

We talked about working together to convince the North Korean leader to give up his nuclear weapons. We talked about the fact that Japan has 1,000—had 1,000 troops in Iraq. The Prime Minister and I understand that when you find a young democracy in this ideological struggle against reason versus extremists, you got to help those young democracies. It's in our long-term interests that we help people realize the blessings of liberty. We talked about the need to help fight the pandemic of HIV/AIDS on the continent of Africa, which the United States is doing. We talked about feeding the hungry. We talked about keeping the peace.

My dad fought the Japanese; his son is talking about keeping the peace with the Japanese. Liberty—the lesson is this: Liberty has got the capacity to change an enemy into an ally, and liberty has got the capacity to change a region of despair and hopelessness into a region of light and hope. Liberty is the best way to defeat the enemies of freedom in the long run.

Someday an American President will be sitting down with duly elected leaders from the Middle East talking about keeping the peace, and a generation of Americans will be better off.

These are the stakes in this election, and I'm asking you to go from the hall and find fellow Republicans, discerning Democrats, and openminded independents, and remind them about the stakes in this election. If you want your taxes low so you can have more money to spend and this economy continues to be strong, vote for Jim Talent. If you want the United States to do everything that we can to protect you and to lay the foundation of peace for generations to come, vote for Jim Talent.

It's such an honor to be with you. I thank you for your time. May God bless you, and may God continue to bless the United States.

NOTE: The President spoke at 11:55 a.m. at Missouri Southern State University. In his remarks, he referred to Gov. Matt Blunt of Missouri; former President Saddam Hussein of Iraq; Usama bin Laden, leader of the Al Qaida terrorist organization; former Prime Minister Junichiro Koizumi of Japan; and Chairman Kim Jong Il of North Korea.

Remarks at an Iowa Victory 2006 Rally in Le Mars, Iowa
November 3, 2006

The President. Thanks you all very much. Thanks for coming. I've got something on my mind, but before I tell you, I want

to bring Congressman Steve King up here. He asked for a little air time. [*Laughter*]

Representative Steve King. And the President yielded the balance of his time to—no, he didn't. [*Laughter*] But I do want to make sure we give the warmest of Le Mars and Plymouth County welcome to the President. We can't do that without having the Bull Dogs up here to do that.

The President. I was hoping to get a Bull Dog shirt.

I'm glad to be back in Sioux land; I'm glad to be Le Mars, Iowa. And I can't thank you enough for coming. I like being in country like this. It's good to look at, but more importantly, this part of the world is full of decent, hard-working people with common sense. And that's what you need in the statehouse here in Iowa, and that's what we need in the Capitol in Washington, DC, good, old, plain common sense, with a strong dose of values.

I'm proud to be here with your next Governor, Jim Nussle. I've seen him in action. When he says he's going to do something, he'll do it. The thing about Jim Nussle is, he doesn't need to take a poll or have a focus group to tell him what to believe. When he says he's going to work to have a first-class education, he means it. When he says he's going to work to have affordable health care, Jim Nussle means it. When he says he's going to reduce your taxes, you can take it to the bank.

I appreciate you coming out to support Nussle, and I appreciate your support for Steve King. Let me tell you something about Steve King. He is a self-made businessman. Listen, we've got plenty of lawyers in Washington, DC. [*Laughter*] It makes sense to have somebody who understands what it means to make a payroll. And in Congressman King, you've got somebody who knows what it means to make a payroll. He understands what you're going through. Send him back to the United States Congress.

And finally, I'm glad to share the same stage with the chairman. That would be chairman of the Finance Committee; that would be one of the most important people in Washington, DC; that would be a good friend of mine, and that's a good friend of yours, Chuck Grassley. I have campaigned in your State with Chuck Grassley, and there's nothing like it. You're riding down the road, and he says, "That's where old Smith lives." [*Laughter*] And about two miles later, he says, "That's my friend Jones." I think he has shaken hands with every single person in this great State.

All three of these men love Iowa, and they love Iowans. You know how I know? They're always talking about you when I'm with them. And somebody else who loves Iowa in my family is my wife, Laura. She sends her best. She's been out on the campaign trail. She's working hard for our candidates, and she's working her way back to Crawford. See—don't tell her this—[*laughter*]—but tomorrow, I'm sliding back after one event because we're going to have a birthday party for her. I'm not going to tell you her age—[*laughter*]—but we were both born in the same year, and I turned 60 this year. I guarantee you she is just like the people you live next door to. She's raised in Midland, Texas. She is down-to-earth. She is a fabulous First Lady for this country, and I'm proud to call her wife.

I'm proud to be here, as well, with Jim's runningmate, Bob Vander Plaats, and his wife, Darla. Speaking about wives, we got the next first lady of Iowa with us, and that would be Karen Nussle. State Auditor Dave Vaudt is with us. I saw him the other day in Des Moines. I said, "How's your campaign going?" He said, "Pretty good. I don't have an opponent." [*Laughter*] What is that like? [*Laughter*]

My friend Mary Ann Hanusa is with us; she is running for the secretary of state. I say she's my friend—she used to work in the Oval Office. She'll be a fine secretary of state. Put her in there. Give her a chance.

Candidate for secretary of agriculture Bill Northey is with us today. I appreciate you coming, Mr. Secretary. Mayor Virgil Van Beek is with us. Mr. Mayor, thanks for coming. My only advice—you didn't ask for any—[*laughter*]—and I recognize I'm at the Federal level, but my only advice is, fill the potholes. [*Laughter*]

I want to thank Le Mars High School Marching Band for being here today. I want to thank the school for letting us come and use this fantastic facility. I want to thank the teachers who are here in this crowd. I want to thank you for working in a noble profession.

And I want to thank all the grassroots activists. One reason I have come is to remind you that all of us have a duty to vote, and on November the 7th, you have a duty to show up at the polls. I'd like you to encourage your neighbors to go as well.

You know, it's amazing what happens in Washington. Some of them have already begun to measure for new drapes. [*Laughter*] People are already deciding how this election is going to turn out, before the people of Iowa or anywhere else have shown up to vote. You know, I'm used to that. I remember 2004 campaign. The prognosticators said, "No way old George W. can carry Iowa." You proved them wrong. In 2004, a bunch of them in Washington were already picking out their offices in the West Wing. And then the people went to the polls, and the movers were not needed.

And the same thing is going to happen this year. The people are going to go to the polls, you're going to elect a Republican Governor, and we're going to have a Republican-controlled House and Senate, and the country will be better off for it.

We're going to win because we understand the values and the priorities of the American people. We understand—we understand you can't make decisions based upon political polls. You have to stand for something. You have to believe in something. We are working to raise——

Audience members. U.S.A.! U.S.A.! U.S.A.!

The President. We believe in raising standards for our public schools and measuring so we can make sure no child is left behind in America. We have worked hard to make sure our seniors have got affordable prescription drugs, and the days of poor seniors having to choose between drugs and food are over with.

We have got a record to run on. Jim Nussle has got a record to run on, and so does Steve King. We've got a record to run on when it comes to making sure we're less dependent on foreign oil. Oh, there's been a lot of talk about renewable fuels, but this administration and these public servants have delivered. We understand that when America's agricultural economy is strong, the whole economy is strong. And we are developing new technologies that will enable Iowa's farmers to produce the fuels necessary to run our automobiles.

When people around this country go in the polls to vote, particularly where there's a Senate race, they're voting for more than just a Senator. They're voting for what the judiciary will look like. When I campaigned here in Iowa, I said to the people here in this State, "If I'm fortunate enough to be your President, I will name people to the bench who will strictly interpret the law and not legislate from the bench." And that is exactly what I have done. And make no mistake about it, if the Democrats were to control the United States Senate, judges like Sam Alito and John Roberts would never have been confirmed to the Supreme Court. And I thank Senator Grassley for his stalwart support of the kind of judges you expect me to appoint.

There's a lot of issues in these campaigns. Jim Nussle talks about making sure this is a fine place to do business; he'll deliver. Jim Nussle talks about being fiscally wise with your money—he'll deliver.

There's a lot of issues—I want to talk about two issues that confront the good folks of Iowa and the folks around this country. The two big issues in this campaign are taxes and who best to defend the United States from attack.

Let me start with taxes. We believe you can spend your money better than the Federal Government can. The Democrats will raise your taxes, because they think they can spend your money better than you can.

Audience members. Noo!

The President. We believe that when you have more of your own money in your pocket to save, invest, or spend, the economy benefits. But you didn't send us to Washington just to be philosophers; you sent us to act. I was proud to sign the largest tax cuts since Ronald Reagan was the President of the United States. We cut taxes on everybody who pays income taxes. We doubled the child tax credit. We reduced the marriage penalty. We cut taxes on small businesses. We cut taxes on capital gains and dividends to encourage investment. And for the sake of our farmers and for the sake of our small-business owners, we put the death tax on the road to extinction.

And Grassley, Nussle, and King were strong supporters in making sure you had more money. You might remember the debate in Washington. Oh, the Democrats said the tax cuts would not create jobs, and the Democrats said the tax cuts would not increase wages, and the Democrats said that those tax cuts would cause the Federal deficit to explode. Well, the facts are in. Reality has now come to be. The tax cuts we passed have led to a strong and growing economy. And I want to share with you the news that came out this morning. The national unemployment rate is at 4.4 percent. We added 92,000 jobs in the month of October. Over the last 3 months, Americans added 470,000 jobs. People are working in this country, and the wages are going up. Real wages rose 2.4 percent over the past 12 months. That means an extra $1,300 for the typical family of four with two wage earners.

And let me talk about the deficit. Instead of exploding, we have cut the deficit in half, 3 years ahead of schedule. If the Democrats' economic predictions—let me say, if their election predictions are as good as their economic predictions, we're going to have a fine day on November the 7th.

The interesting thing about campaigns, if somebody is going to raise your taxes, they don't want you to know about it. Here are the words of the ranking Democrat in the House of Representatives. They asked her about tax cuts, and she said, "We love tax cuts." Given her record, she must be a secret admirer. [*Laughter*] The record they have to run on is that every single tax cut we passed was opposed by the Democrats. When we made it easier for families with children, they voted no. When we made it easier for small businesses, they voted no. When we said, "You shouldn't tax a fellow who owns a farm when he's living and then tax him after he dies," they voted no. Time and time again when they had the opportunity to show love for—their love for tax cuts, they said no. If that's their definition of love, I sure would hate to see what hate looks like.

Let me explain to you how it works: If we don't make the tax cuts we passed permanent or extend them, your taxes go up. And that's why people here in Iowa and around the country must take the words of those who want to run the Congress very seriously. The person who thinks he will be the head of the Ways and Means Committee, the head Democrat, said he couldn't think of one tax cut that he would extend. If that were to happen, the child tax credit would go from $1,000 a child to $500 a child.

Audience members. Boo!

The President. So when you get home and have dinner this evening, count the number of children you have at your table—[*laughter*]—and multiple by 500. See, if they take control of the House,

they're going to raise your taxes by not making the tax cuts we passed permanent. So if you've got three children, you can go one, two, three times 500, that's a $1,500 tax increase. If you happen to have four children—I bet somebody here has got four—[*laughter*]—there you go—you count them up, one, two, three—you got six? One, two, three, four, five, six. [*Laughter*] And you multiply those six children by $500 a head, you're paying $3,000 more in taxes. That may not seem like a lot to those folks in Washington, but it seems like a lot to us. And that's why it's important to send Steve King back to the United States Congress, to keep your taxes low.

This election is taking place in an historic time for our country. And when our children and grandchildren look back on this period, one question will overwhelm all the rest: Did we do everything in our power to fight and win the war on terror? I wish I could report to you all that there was no war, but there is. I see it every day. Our most important job in Washington is to protect you. It's by far the fundamental responsibility we have. And we face a brutal enemy that wants to kill Americans again. Let me share some thoughts with you about the enemy. You can't negotiate with them. You can't try to talk sense into them. The best way to protect you is to find them where they are and bring them to justice so they won't hurt Americans again.

I know some ask, "Well, why would they possibly want to hurt America?" We're full of decent and compassionate people, which we are. And the reason why is these folks are ideologues. They're totalitarians. They believe in something, and what they believe in is the opposite of what we believe in. We believe in the freedom of people to worship as they so choose; they don't. We believe in public dissent; they don't. We believe that you can criticize your government; they don't believe that. They are the opposite of what we stand for. And yet they have ambitions. They want to establish

a governing organization, a caliphate. They want to impose their will. And that's why I have called this struggle the ideological struggle of the 21st century.

And so we're on the offense, and that's part of our strategy. The other part of our strategy is do everything we can to protect you here at home, and it's a challenge. It's a challenge because we have to be right 100 percent of the time to protect Americans, and they only have to be right one time.

And that is why I have worked with Congress to provide our professionals with the tools they need to protect you. And let me share some of my thinking. You know that there was a wall that prevented our intelligence services from sharing information with law enforcement. That doesn't make any sense. I know it doesn't make any sense. It certainly had no common sense to it. But nevertheless, that's what happened. This is a different kind of war, and when we find intelligence, in order to protect you, it has to be shared with the people on the frontline of law enforcement. And yet we couldn't do it. That's why I went to the Congress and asked Congress to pass the PATRIOT Act. The PATRIOT Act protects civil liberties. On the other hand, it tears down the barrier that prevents people from sharing information. It was a vital piece of legislation.

When it came time to be renewed, the Senate Democrats filibustered the bill. They tried to kill it. As a matter of fact, the minority leader of the Senate said—bragged, "We killed that bill." See, there's a different mindset in Washington, and when people are thinking about going to the polls, they've got to understand the differences of opinion.

I felt like if an Al Qaida or an Al Qaida affiliate was making a phone call into the United States, we need to know why. If our job is to protect you, and this is a different kind of war that requires good, sound intelligence, we ought to know why. And yet when that bill came up in front

of the House of Representatives, by far the vast majority of Democrats voted against giving our professionals the tools. See, they must not think we're at war. Either that— they must think it's okay to respond after we're attacked. What we must do is to respond before we're attacked, to protect the American people.

We're picking up people on the battlefield. One day the—came in the Oval Office and said, "Mr. President, we have captured Khalid Sheikh Mohammed." Our intelligence folks believe he was the mastermind of the September the 11th attacks. I told the CIA that I think it's important for them, the professionals, to figure out what he knows. See, if he ordered the first attack, he might know something about another attack. And if our job is to protect you, we need to know what these radicals and extremists are thinking, what they're planning. And so I put the program in place. It came up for a vote; in both bodies, the vast majority of Democrats voted against giving the professionals the tools necessary to protect you.

Audience members. Boo!

The President. We need to put people in the Congress like Steve King. We need people all across the United States who are running for the Senate and the House of Representatives who understand we're at war and will give us the tools necessary to protect you from attack.

We've got a lot of great people who are on the hunt. It is hard to plan and plot when you're on the run. And that's exactly what we're doing. We're pressing on the offense. Anytime, anyplace we think there's an enemy who will do harm to the American people, we're moving. And you just need to know that.

One of the lessons of September the 11th is this—and it's a lesson no President can ever forget—that when we see a threat, we must take that threat seriously, before it comes home to hurt us. See, it used to be that if a threat were overseas, we could say, "It's overseas." September the

11th changed that. It changed it once and for all in this new kind of war. I saw a threat in Saddam Hussein; Members of the United States Congress in both political parties saw a threat in Saddam Hussein; the United Nations saw the threat in Saddam Hussein. I made the right decision to get rid of Saddam Hussein, and the world is better off for it.

We're in a global war against these terrorists. And we must fight them where we find them, and right now Iraq is a central front in that war. Oh, I've heard them in Washington; you know, they say Iraq is a distraction from the war on terror. Well, we just have a difference of opinion. I believe Iraq is central to the war on terror. Our troops believe Iraq is central to the war on terror. And so does Usama bin Laden. Usama bin Laden has said that the fight in Iraq is the third world war. He went on to say—and I want you to listen to the enemy's words—he said that victory for the terrorists in Iraq will mean America's defeat and disgrace forever. That's what he said.

But they think differently in Washington, particularly the Democrats. I want you to hear the words of one of the leading Democrats in Washington about this war on terror; she said, "The President says that fighting there makes it less likely we will have to fight them here." I agree; I did say that because I believe that. She went on to say, "The opposite is true. Because we are fighting them there, it may become more likely that we will have to fight them here."

Let me say something to you loud and clear: Iraq is not the reason why the terrorists are at war with us. We were not in Iraq when the terrorists attacked the World Trade Center in 1993. We were not in Iraq when they attacked the Embassies in Kenya and Tanzania. We were not in Iraq when they attacked the USS *Cole*. And we were not in Iraq on September the 11th, 2001, when they killed nearly 3,000 of our citizens. You do not create terrorists by

fighting the terrorists. The best way to protect you is to stay on the offense and bring these folks to justice, before they hurt the American people again.

Our goal in Iraq is victory. Our goal is to have a country which can govern itself, sustain itself, and defend itself and be an ally in the war on terror. And it's a tough fight. I know it's a tough fight, and you know it's a tough fight. It's a tough fight because we face an enemy that kills innocent people in order to achieve their objectives. And they're good at propaganda. They understand that the carnage they create will end up on our TV screens, and they believe that the American people do not have the will to protect ourselves in the long run. That's what they believe.

But they don't understand this administration, and they don't understand the American people. We're not going to run from thugs and assassins. My message to our commanders on the ground is, you will have what it needs to succeed. You can adjust your tactics the way you see fit, in order to be able to defeat the enemy. As the enemy changes, we change. As the enemy adjusts, we adjust.

We've got something going for us in Iraq—two things—that the American people must understand. We've got a strategy for victory that's being implemented by the finest United States military ever on the face of the Earth. And around this country—I understand people don't agree with my decision on Iraq, but let me say this: Whether you do or not, you owe the troops the full support.

When I went to the Congress to ask for the full support for our troops, I could count on Jim Nussle, and I could count on Steve King, and I could count on Chuck Grassley. You don't have to worry about these three people understanding that we owe it to our troops and their families to make sure they have everything they need to do the jobs I've asked them to do.

And there's something else that leads me to believe we'll win. I'm going to tell you something point-blank: If I didn't think we could win, I'd get our troops out. See, I can't look in the eyes of the loved ones who have got somebody in harm's way and not believe in my heart of hearts that the cause is noble and necessary and that we'll achieve victory.

The Iraqis want success. They're suffering unspeakable violence, yet they are firm in their resolve to be a country which can govern itself, sustain itself, and defend itself. You know, I was pleased when nearly 12 million people defied the car bombers and terrorists and voted, but I wasn't surprised. I'll tell you why I'm not surprised. I believe that one of the great gifts from an Almighty is a desire to be free in everybody's soul. I believe in the universality of freedom. It didn't surprise me that people, when given a chance, would say, "We want to live in a free society."

So our strategy is to help this young democracy defeat the extremists by encouraging a political system that unifies the country, by helping their economy grow, and by training Iraqis so they take the fight. And I believe we'll succeed in having a government of and by and for the people in Iraq, unless we leave before the job is done.

This is an important issue facing the American voters. If you listen carefully for the Democrats' plan for success in Iraq, you're not going to hear anything. They don't have a plan for success. Iraq is the central front in the war to protect you, and yet they don't have a plan for victory. You can hear all kinds of voices. You hear them say, "Pull out now." Then you hear other candidates say, "We're going to have a fixed date for withdrawal, regardless of whether or not we've succeeded." You've had a Member of the House of Representatives from the Democrat side saying his recommendation is to move our troops to an island 5,000 miles away. You've had 19 House Democrats say, "We're going to cut off the funds for our troops."

One of Chuck Grassley's colleagues, a Democrat Senator, explained her party's position this way: "We haven't coalesced around a single plan," she said, "but we're in general agreement on basic principles." She's right. The basic principle is, get out before the job is done. I'm not saying these people are unpatriotic, I'm saying they're wrong.

On this vital issue, the Democrats have taken a calculated gamble. They believe that the only way they can win this election is to criticize and not offer a plan. One Democrat said recently of the strategy, "This election is about them," talking about us. So far, they've refused to tell us how they intend to win in Iraq and how they intend to secure this country. But there are 4 days left in the election. There's still time. [*Laughter*]

If you happen to bump into a Democratic candidate, you might want to ask this simple question: What's your plan? If they say they want to protect the homeland but opposed the PATRIOT Act, ask them: What's your plan? If they say they want to uncover terrorist plots but opposed listening in on terrorist conversations, just ask them: What's your plan? If they say they want to stop new attacks on our country but oppose letting the CIA detain and question the terrorists who might know where those plots are, ask them: What is your plan? If they say they want to win in the war on terror but call for America to pull out from what Al Qaida says is the central front on the war on terror, ask them: What is your plan? See, they don't have a plan. They have no plan.

Harsh criticism is not a plan for victory. Second-guessing is not a strategy. If we were to leave Iraq before the job is done, the enemy would be emboldened. This is a different kind of war. Unlike other wars—you could leave the battlefield before the job was done, and nothing would happen here at home. In this war, if we were to leave before the job was done, the enemy will follow us here. If we were to leave

before the job is done, it would strengthen the hands of the radicals and extremists. If we were to leave before the job was done, it would dash the hopes of millions in the Middle East who want to simply live in peace. And if we were to leave before the job was done, it would dishonor the sacrifice of the men and women who have worn our uniform. The consequences of not fulfilling our strategy for victory would be felt for generations.

See, the enemy has made it clear that they believe they can drive us out of the Middle East so they can establish a safe haven from which to launch further attacks, just like the safe haven they had in Afghanistan. The enemy has made it clear that they would like to topple moderate governments to begin to impose their totalitarian ideology. The enemy has made it clear that they would like to use energy resources to be able to blackmail the West.

Imagine a Middle East where the radicals and extremists were able to use oil to say to America, "We're going to run your price of oil up unless you abandon your allies such as Israel," or, "We're going to run your price of oil up unless you just totally withdraw and let us be." And you couple all that with a country which doesn't like us having a nuclear weapon, and 30 years from now, people are going to look back and say, "What happened to them in 2006? How come they couldn't see the impending danger? What clouded their vision?"

My vision is clear. I see the danger. That is why we will support our troops. That is why we will fight in Iraq. And that is why we will win in Iraq.

I would like to share one story with you, and then we'll all go outside and get some oxygen. [*Laughter*] Pretty soon. Recently I went with the then-sitting Prime Minister of Japan to Elvis's place. [*Laughter*] I did so for a couple reasons: One, I had never been in Elvis's place, thought it would be fun to go. [*Laughter*] And Laura was kind of nudging me. [*Laughter*] Secondly, Prime

Minister Koizumi wanted to go to Elvis's place because he liked Elvis. Thirdly, I want to tell a story, and it's a story about the power of liberty.

The Japanese attacked us in the early forties. People like George H.W. Bush, people like your relatives said, "I want to join the military to defeat the sworn enemy," and a lot of people did—just like people are doing today, by the way. A lot of people—a lot of—[*applause*]. And it was a bloody conflict, and thousands and thousands of people lost their lives. And yet I'm on Air Force One, flying down to Memphis, Tennessee, talking to the Prime Minister of the former enemy about peace. I'm talking to him about how we can work together to convince the leader in North Korea to give up his nuclear weapons ambitions. I talked to him about the fact that Iraq has—I mean, Japan has 1,000 troops in Iraq. See, he understands what I know. In an ideological struggle against totalitarians, you can defeat them with liberty. And therefore, when we find young democracies, it's in our interest and the interest of our children to help those young democracies survive.

We talked about how to whom much is given, much is required, and that is why we will continue to help save lives on the continent of Africa by defeating the pandemic of HIV/AIDS. We talked about the need to feed the hungry. We talked about our responsibilities to do necessary work to keep peace.

Isn't that interesting, that my dad fought the Japanese, and yet his son was able to talk about keeping the peace. What happened was, was that Japan adopted a Japanese-style democracy. Liberty has got the capacity to change enemies into allies. And liberty has got the capacity to change regions of frustration and hopelessness to regions of hope. Someday an American President will be sitting down with elected leaders from the Middle East talking about keeping the peace, and a generation of Americans will be better off for it.

I'm honored you came out and let me share some thoughts with you. My thought to you is, go from here and find Republicans, discerning Democrats—[*laughter*]—openminded independents—[*laughter*]—and get them to the polls, and remind them about the stakes. You got a chance to have a fantastic Governor in Jim Nussle in the statehouse. The people in this State and around the country have an opportunity, in their votes, to decide how much money you have in your pocket. Make no mistake about it, one of the big issues in this campaign is whether or not your taxes are going to go up or whether they're going to go low. You know our choice. Our choice is, we're going to keep your taxes low.

And finally, the vote in 2006 will help determine whether or not this country will use everything in our power to protect the American people from attack and, at the same time, lay the foundation of peace for generations to come.

I'm honored you're here. May God bless you, and may God continue to bless the United States.

NOTE: The President spoke at 4:54 p.m. at Le Mars Community High School. In his remarks, he referred to former President Saddam Hussein of Iraq; Usama bin Laden, leader of the Al Qaida terrorist organization; and Chairman Kim Jong Il of North Korea.

The President's Radio Address
November 4, 2006

Good morning. I'm speaking to you today from the Mile High Coffee Shop in Englewood, Colorado. Mile High Coffee was founded by Brian Verbeck, who is the city's entrepreneur of the year. I'm here to have a cup of his famous coffee and have breakfast with a group of local entrepreneurs to discuss our strong and growing economy.

Yesterday we received more good news about our economy. The national unemployment rate has dropped to 4.4 percent. It's the lowest rate in more than 5 years. Over the past 3 months, America has added 470,000 new jobs, for a total of more than 6.8 million new jobs since August of 2003. Real wages rose 2.4 percent over the past year, which means an extra $1,327 for the typical family of four with two wage earners. Americans are finding jobs, and they're taking home more pay.

The main reason for our growing economy is that we cut taxes and left more money in the hands of families and workers and small-business owners. Entrepreneurs like the ones I'm having breakfast with this morning have put that money to good use. They expanded their businesses, and they're creating jobs in their communities.

One of the entrepreneurs with me today is Duke Hanson, the cofounder of a company called Crocs. Crocs produces a hugely popular line of lightweight shoes, and over the past 3 years, they've expanded dramatically. Three years ago, Crocs had just 11 employees. Today, Crocs provides jobs for hundreds of Americans, and his shoes are sold all over the world. Duke calls this "rocket-ship growth." Here's what he says: "We're bringing a lot of money in. We're employing people and providing a product that millions of people love."

Another entrepreneur with me today is Rich Lewis. Rich is the founder, president, and CEO of a technology company called RTL Networks. Rich's company sells and maintains computer network hardware and infrastructure. His business is growing as well. Over the past 4 years, RTL Networks has expanded from 1 to 19 employees. Rich says, "We've been growing. I feel more secure now as an entrepreneur and businessowner, and I see continued growth."

A third entrepreneur with me today is Luke Schmieder. He's the chairman and CEO and cofounder of Mesa Labs. His company sells kidney dialysis products, electronic measuring instruments, and biological indicators, which means they use technology to meet people's health care needs. His company got off to a rough start, until Luke mortgaged his house to turn things around. In the past 6 years, the company has grown 34 percent. Luke says, "Revenues are up; earnings are up. I say it's a good economy right now."

Our tax cuts have helped businesses like these create jobs and deliver prosperity across Colorado and across the Nation. Yet Democrats in Washington have consistently opposed cutting taxes. They predicted that the tax cuts would not create jobs, would [not] * increase wages, and would cause the Federal deficit to explode. American workers and entrepreneurs have proved all those predictions wrong.

But the Democrats are still determined to raise taxes. And if they gain control of the Congress, they can do so without lifting a finger. Under current law, many of the tax cuts we passed have to be renewed by Congress or they will expire. In other words, if Congress fails to act, your taxes will automatically go up. If Democrats take control of the House, the committee in charge of all the tax legislation would be chaired by a Democrat who recently said he can't think of one of our tax cuts he

---

* White House correction.

would extend. And if there's no legislation to renew and extend the tax cuts, every tax rate will go back up to its old, higher level.

Think what that would mean for the small-business owners like the ones with me today. If the Democrats have their way, small-business owners like Rich Lewis, who pay business taxes at individual rates, will see their taxes go up. Small-business owners who want to expand and invest in new equipment will face a tax hike as well. And small-business owners who hope to pass on their life's work to their children and grandchildren will have to worry about their families being hit by the return of the death tax.

The choice you make on Tuesday will have a direct impact on our economy, on the small businesses that are creating jobs, and on the workers who depend on them.

The last thing American families and small businesses need now is a higher tax bill, and that is what you'll get if the Democrats take control of the Congress.

America needs leaders in Washington who understand that you know how to save, spend, and invest your money better than the Federal Government. And we need leaders who will work to make the tax relief we delivered permanent. And now the decision is in your hands, and however you decide, I urge you to get out and vote on Tuesday.

I appreciate you listening.

NOTE: The address was recorded at 8:06 a.m. at Mile High Coffee in Englewood, CO, for immediate broadcast. The Office of the Press Secretary also released a Spanish language transcript of this address.

Remarks at a Colorado Victory 2006 Rally in Greeley, Colorado
November 4, 2006

The President. Thank you. Thank you all very much. I appreciate you coming. Thanks. It's great to be back in Greeley. Thanks for your hospitality. This isn't the first time I've been to Greeley. I like coming to places like Greeley, Colorado, because the people here are down-to-earth, hard-working; people here have a lot of common sense.

That's what we need in Washington, DC, common sense. And Marilyn Musgrave brings common sense to Washington, DC. I'm not surprised she is a native of this important State, and she was raised right here in this district. And you raised her well. She understands your values; she knows what you're thinking. Send her back to the United States Congress.

I appreciate you coming today. I'm sorry that Laura is not with me. Yes, well, I don't want her to know that I know it's

her birthday. [*Laughter*] Well, she knows I know. I'm just not telling you the gift I'm going to give her. It's a surprise. [*Laughter*] But she sends her very best to our friends here in Colorado. She understands what I know: Marilyn Musgrave is a fine United States Congresswoman and deserves your support.

I'm proud to be here with Senator Wayne Allard. He's doing a fine job for the people of this State. I know firsthand. I deal with him all the time; he's always got Colorado on his mind.

I'm proud to be here with a man who's done an excellent job as your Governor, Governor Bill Owens. And I'm also pleased that the next Governor of Colorado, Bob Beauprez, is with us. So when you're in that box voting for Marilyn, make sure you put your check by Beauprez's name as well.

You're going to get good, solid government with Bob Beauprez.

I appreciate very much that Mike Coffman is with us. I appreciate Bob Schaffer is with us. I want to thank the mayor, Tom Selders, who's with us. Mr. Mayor, thanks for coming. I want to thank all the candidates and local officials.

I particularly want to thank the grassroots activists who are here. You're the people putting up the signs and making the phone calls and turning out the vote. Rest assured, Marilyn is going to work hard, and she's counting on you to work hard with her.

This election is just 3 days away. Oh, you've probably heard them in Washington; all the pundits and prognosticators have already determined the outcome of the election. I want to remind them, the folks of Colorado haven't even voted yet. Oh, it's not the first time we've been through this. You might remember 2004. I suspect it was about the time I came to Greeley that some of them in Washington were already picking out their offices in the West Wing. [*Laughter*] And then you voted, and the movers weren't needed. They're not going to be needed on November the 7th. With your help, we will hold the House, Marilyn will win, and we will control the United States Senate.

And there's a reason. We've got a fantastic group of folks who will turn out the vote. But we also share the values with the majority of the American people. We share their priorities. We're going to win this election because our values and priorities don't change because of the latest poll or the latest focus group. We're going to win this election because we've got a good, strong record to run on.

See, I got to know the Congresswoman well. Last time I talked to her, she said, "Don't you ever forget those Colorado ranchers." By the way, it's good to be in country where the cowboy hats outnumber the ties. She said, "Don't forget, we've got farmers here." Let me tell you something: I know what she knows: If the ag economy is strong, the United States overall economy is strong.

I understand something about ranching and farming. You might remember, I was raised in west Texas. And I understand that we need to be opening up markets, and we are. I also understand we have a fantastic opportunity to use agricultural products grown right here in Colorado to make us less dependent on foreign oil. And Marilyn understands that as well. If you're a farmer or a rancher or count on the agricultural industry to make a living, it is in your interest to send Marilyn Musgrave back to the United States Congress.

One thing I don't have to worry about is her support for the United States military. I don't have to worry about her strong support for making sure our veterans get the benefits they deserve. She understands what I know: We will honor those who have worn the uniform and support those who wear it today.

Marilyn Musgrave understands the importance of defending traditional values. In Washington, she's worked to defend the Pledge Allegiance and to protect the flag from desecration. She has worked to prevent the institution of marriage from being redefined by activist judges. She understands your values, and that's another reason to send her back to the United States Congress.

Oh, there's big differences between how the Democrats think and how we think, and there's no clearer difference on two big issues: One issue is taxes, and the other issue is who best to defend the United States of America.

First, let me start with taxes. We have a clear philosophy. This philosophy says this: We believe you know how to spend your money better than the Federal Government does. I know that the Democrats want to raise your taxes because they think they can spend your money better than you can.

Audience members. Noo!

The President. We understand that when you have more of your own money in your pocket to save, invest, or spend, the whole economy benefits. But you didn't expect people to go off to Washington and just philosophize; you expected us to act. And that's what we have done. I have signed the largest tax cut since Ronald Reagan was the President of the United States, and Marilyn Musgrave is a strong supporter of lower taxes.

We cut the taxes for every American who pays income taxes. We doubled the child tax credit. We cut taxes on small businesses. We cut taxes on—we reduced the marriage penalty. We cut taxes on capital gains and dividends to encourage investment. And I want the farmers and ranchers to listen carefully—we put the death tax on the road to extinction. We don't think you need to be taxed when you're living and then when you die.

Oh, I'm sure you remember the debate in Washington, DC. Democrats in Washington predicted that the tax cuts would not create jobs, would not increase wages, and that the tax cuts would cause the Federal deficit to explode. Well, the facts are in. The truth is, the tax cuts have led to a strong and growing economy. And just yesterday we got additional good news. The national unemployment rate is down to 4.4 percent. Our economy added 92,000 months [jobs]° last month, and over the past 3 months, America has added 470,000 new jobs.

The ag economy is strong in the United States. Real wages rose 2.4 percent over the past year. And thanks to our growing economy and being wise with your money, we cut the deficit in half 3 years ahead of schedule. Our economic policies are working. And if the Democrats' election predictions are as good as their economic predictions—[*laughter*]—next Tuesday is going to be a great day for Republicans.

° White House correction.

It's important for people in this district and around the country to understand, the Democrats are going to raise your taxes, but they don't want you to know it. [*Laughter*] They asked the top Democrat leader in the House about tax cuts, and she made an interesting statement. She said, "We love tax cuts." But given her record, she must be a secret admirer. [*Laughter*] See, she and her party voted against reducing the marriage penalty, voted against cutting taxes on small businesses, voted against lowering taxes for families with children, voted against reducing taxes on capital gains and dividends, voted against putting the death tax on the road to extinction. Time and time again, when she had her opportunity to show love, she voted no. [*Laughter*] If that's their definition of love, I'd sure hate to see what hate looks like.

Let me explain to you how it works. Here's how it works: If these tax cuts we passed are not extended or not made permanent, your taxes are going to go up.

Audience members. Boo!

The President. In other words, if we don't have people in Congress who will join me in saying, "Let's make these tax cuts extend," or, "Make them permanent," you'll be paying more taxes.

And so they asked the person who wishes that he would be the head of the tax writing committee, the lead Democrat, whether any of the tax cuts we passed should be extended, and the person said, "Not a one." In other words, what they're advocating without coming out and saying it is, "We're going to raise your taxes."

And let me explain how it will work for you. If you have children, your child tax credit will go from 1,000 per child to $500 per child. So when you're sitting around the dinner table tonight, you count the number of heads you've got at the table with you, and then you multiply by $500 a child, the sum of which will be how much you're going to pay in increased taxes. So, just say you got three children, you go, one, two, three times 500; that's $1,500

additional taxes if the Democrats take over the House of Representatives. Somebody has got more than three children I bet in this crowd—[*applause*]. Yes, how many you got? Got four children. There you go. Well, then you're going to go, one, two, three, four, times 500; that's a $2,000 tax increase. That may not seem like a lot to people in Washington, DC, but it seems like a lot to me and Marilyn. And therefore, send her to the Congress, and we'll keep your taxes low.

And the American people must understand the facts. If you vote Democrat, you're voting for a tax increase. And if you're voting Republican, you're voting for low taxes and a strong economy.

The election is taking place in an historic time for our country. And when the children and grandchildren look back at this period, one question will overwhelm all the rest: Did we do everything in our power to fight and win the war against the terrorists? I wish I could come to Greeley and report this war is over. It is not. There's still an enemy which desires to inflict harm on America. I live it every day. I understand what I am talking about. Our most important job in Washington is to protect you from further attacks.

We face an enemy which has no conscience. They kill innocent people to achieve their objectives. They share an ideology, and it's an ideology that's foreign to the United States. It's an ideology that is the exact opposite of what we believe. We believe in basic freedoms. We believe in human dignity. We value human life. They use human life to achieve objectives. They don't believe in freedom. They are totalitarians, and they have a desire to spread their vision, their point of view throughout as much of the world as possible. And they recognize we stand in the way, and that's why they want to inflict damage on the United States of America. The best way to protect you is to find these enemies overseas so we do not have to face them here at home.

Part of our strategy is to stay on the offense, and the other part of the strategy is to give our professionals the tools necessary to protect you here at home. So after the attacks, I evaluated programs to determine what we could do better to do our most important job, and that is to protect you. One of the problems we had is that over time, there was a wall that built up that prevented the intelligence community from sharing information with law enforcement. That didn't make any sense. You see, in this new kind of war, we must understand what the enemy is thinking and what they're about to do, in order to protect you.

And so I asked the Congress to pass what we have called the PATRIOT Act, which makes it now possible for intelligence folks to give the information to law enforcement officials so they can do their jobs. Interestingly enough, by far, the vast majority of Democrats in the House of Representatives voted against the reauthorization of the PATRIOT Act. And the reason I'm telling you this, it's important, if you have not made up your mind in this election, to understand there is a different mindset between what Republicans and what you believe and what Democrats in Washington believe. See, they must not believe we're at war; otherwise, why wouldn't they have given them—our intelligence folks and law enforcement folks—the tools necessary to protect you?

I've always believed that if the enemy, Al Qaida or an Al Qaida affiliate, is making a phone call from outside the United States to inside the United States, we must understand why, if our job is to protect you. If we want to protect you and somebody that we know wants to harm a fellow citizen is calling in to somebody, it makes sense to understand why. Yet, when this program came up in front of the United States Congress, by far, the vast majority of Democrats voted against it. They must

think it's okay to respond after we're attacked. I believe we've got to do everything to prevent the attacks in the first place.

We capture the enemy on the battlefield. Recently—or not recently, a while ago, we picked up a fellow named Khalid Sheikh Mohammed. Our intelligence folks believe he's the man that masterminded the September the 11th attacks. And when they picked him up, I recognized it would be important to find out what he knew. See, if he ordered the first attack, he might know something about a further attack. And it makes sense, if our job is to protect you, to say to the CIA professionals, "Find out what he knows." It's a different kind of war. We must understand what the enemy is thinking in order to protect you. So I sent this bill up to the United States Congress. By far, the vast majority of Democrats in both bodies voted against giving our professionals the tools necessary to protect you. There's just a different mindset. If you want to be protected, you send Marilyn Musgrave back to the United States Congress.

We are on the offense overseas. It's hard to plot and plan if you're on the run. It's hard to plot and plan if you're hiding. There's some fantastic people who have volunteered to serve your country, who are keeping the pressure on this enemy.

One of the lessons of September the 11th, a vital lesson of September the 11th, a lesson any President must always remember is that when we see a threat overseas, we have got to take those threats seriously. You can't just hope for the best in a war against people who want to kill our citizens. And so when you see a threat, for the sake of our children, we must take those threats seriously. I saw a threat in Saddam Hussein; Members of the United States Congress from both political parties saw the same threat; the United Nations saw the threat. My decision to remove Saddam Hussein was the right decision, and the world is better off for it.

We are in a global struggle. By global struggle I mean, we will find and face the enemy wherever we can. And we're on a multiple of fronts, the most important of which is Iraq. It is the central front in the war on terror. I have heard Democrats in Washington say, Iraq is a distraction from the war on terror. What I'm describing to you over and over again, there is a different mindset, and voters have got to understand when they go into the polls, the difference of opinion. See, I know Iraq is the central front in the war on terror, and so do our troops. But I want people to listen to the words of Usama bin Laden. If you have doubt about whether Iraq is important to this war on terror, listen to the words of the enemy. Usama bin Laden calls this fight the third world war. He went on to say, victory for the terrorists in Iraq will mean America's defeat and disgrace forever. He understands the consequences.

But I want you to hear the words of a senior Democrat in the House of Representatives about her view. She said, "The President says fighting them there makes it less likely we will have to fight them here." I do say that, because I believe that. She went on to say, "The opposite is true. Because we are fighting them there, it may become more likely that we will have to fight them here." Iraq is not the reason why the terrorists are at war with us. You remind your citizens that we were not in Iraq when they attacked the World Trade Center in 1993. We were not in Iraq when they bombed our Embassies in Kenya—Tanzania and Kenya. We were not in Iraq when they attacked the USS *Cole*. And we were not in Iraq on September the 11th, 2001.

You do not create terrorists by fighting the terrorists. The best way to protect you is to stay on the offense and bring these people to justice before they can hurt us again.

Our goal in Iraq is victory. Victory means a country which can sustain itself, govern itself, and defend itself and will be an ally

in the war on terror. And this is tough fighting. I know it's tough fighting, and you know it's tough fighting. It's tough fighting because we face an enemy which is willing to kill innocent people in order to achieve an objective. See, they can't stand the thought of a young democracy succeeding in the midst of their plans to spread a totalitarian vision of darkness. And that's why you're seeing the struggle you're seeing.

And the enemy understands that if they put enough carnage on the TV screen that America will be shaken. At least that's what they believe. And that's what you're seeing. And that's why a lot of our fellow citizens are justifiably concerned about Iraq. But what the enemy doesn't understand about this administration and millions of Americans is we're not going to run in the face of thugs and assassins.

Our goals have not changed; our tactics constantly change. I have given our commanders all the authority they need to keep adjusting to the tactics of this enemy. And we are; we're constantly altering the tactics. As the enemy changes, we change. And we've got a lot going for us. We've got a good strategy that's going to work, and we've got a fantastic United States military that deserves the full support of the United States.

Whether or not the people of this country agree with my decision, one thing they need to do is to honor and respect the volunteers who wear the uniform. And you don't have to worry about Marilyn Musgrave making sure our troops have all they need to do the jobs I've asked them to do.

There's something else happening in Iraq. There are brave Iraqis who've endured unspeakable violence, and the reason they have is because they want to live in freedom. I was pleased at the outcome of their elections, but I wasn't surprised. I'll tell you why I wasn't surprised. I believe in the universality of freedom. I believe there's an Almighty, and one of the gifts

of the Almighty to each man and woman and child on the face of the Earth is a desire to be free.

So our strategy is to help this young democracy survive. And we'll help them politically. The 12 million people—nearly 12 million voted and said, "We want to be free." I believe there will be a government of, by, and for the people. They've got good resources, and we'll help them get their feet on the ground after years of tyranny. And we're going to help train—continue to train Iraqi troops so they take the fight, so they're capable of defending this country. There's no doubt, let me say to you, if you've got a relative in the military, I wouldn't have your loved one in the theater if I didn't think we'd win. I can't look at the mothers and fathers and husbands and wives of those who wear our uniform who may be in Iraq and say, "It's noble," but not think I can—we can win the—the only way we can win is if we leave before the job is—I mean, the only way we can lose is if we leave before the job is done. That's the only way.

You know, it's an amazing debate here coming down the stretch. Iraq is vital to our security. Iraq is the central front in this war on terror. But I've been listening for the Democrats' plan for success. [*Laughter*] There's national silence. [*Laughter*] They have no plan for victory. You know, some of the leading Democrats say we ought to pull out now. Others suggest we ought to pull out at a specific date, even though we may not have done the job. One leading Democrat suggested we move our troops 5,000 miles away to an island. [*Laughter*] Nineteen House Democrats introduced legislation that would cut off funds for our troops.

It was an interesting observation last week by a Democrat Senator who explained her party's position this way: "We haven't coalesced around a single plan, but we're

in general agreement on the basic principles." Well, she's right. They are in agreement on one thing: They will leave before the job is done.

Audience members. Boo!

The President. I'm not saying these people are unpatriotic; I'm just saying they're wrong. On this vital issue, the Democrats have taken a calculated gamble. They believe that the only way they can win this election is to criticize and not offer a plan of their own. One senior Democrat describes their strategy, "Well, the election is all about them"—that would be us. There's 3 days left in this election, and there's still time for them to explain to the American people what they intend to do. [*Laughter*]

If you happen to bump into a Democratic candidate, you might want to ask them this simple question: What's your plan? They say they want to protect the homeland but oppose the PATRIOT Act. Ask them this question: What is your plan? If they say they want to uncover terrorist plots but oppose listening in on terrorist conversations, ask them this question: What's your plan? If they say they want to stop new attacks on our country but oppose letting the CIA detain and question the terrorists who might know what those plots are, ask them this question: What's your plan?

Audience members. What's your plan?

The President. If they say they want to win the war on terror but call for America to pull out from what Al Qaida says is the central front on that war, ask them this question: What's your plan?

Audience members. What's your plan?

The President. Well, they don't have a plan. [*Laughter*] I want the people of this district and around the country to understand, harsh criticism is not a plan for victory. Second-guessing is not a strategy. You can't win a war if you don't think we're in a war. We have a plan for victory, and part of that plan is making sure we got

people in the Congress who understands the stakes. Vote for Marilyn Musgrave.

Retreat from Iraq would embolden the enemy and would make this country less secure. This is a different kind of war. I know I said it once; I'm going to keep saying it because it's important for people to adjust their thinking about the stakes. In this war, if we were to leave Iraq before the job is done, the enemy would follow us here. Leaving Iraq before the job is done would provide a tremendous victory for the extremists and radicals. It would enable them to further recruit. Leaving before the job is done would dash the hopes of the millions and millions of people in the Middle East who long for a peaceful life and who reject the extremists and the radicals. And leaving before the job is done would dishonor the sacrifice of the men and women who have worn the uniform of the United States of America.

The consequences of retreat from Iraq would be felt for generations. The enemy has made it clear that, one, they believe we'll leave because if the fighting stays tough, that we don't have the stomach for it. And they want us to leave because they want to, one, establish a safe haven, just like they had in Afghanistan. And the reason they want a safe haven is so they have a place from which to launch further attacks.

Secondly, they have an objective—by the way, this is all their words. I'm just telling you what they say. Secondly, they want to topple moderate governments. It's part of their desire to spread their caliphate, their governing regime across as much of the world as they can.

Thirdly, you can imagine a world in which these extremists and radicals got control of energy resources. And then you can imagine them saying, "We're going to pull a bunch of oil off the market to run your price of oil up, unless you do the following." And the following would be along the lines, "Well, retreat and let us continue to expand our dark vision," or it would

be, "Give up your alliance with Israel, because part of our objective is to destroy your ally" or——

Audience members. Noo!

The President. In other words, they would use energy as economic blackmail. And then you can compound that further by a nation which doesn't like us, at this point in history, with a nuclear weapon. And 30 years from now or so, people will look back and say, "What happened in 2006?" They'll look back at this period and say, "What went wrong with our leaders? How come their vision was clouded to the point where they could not see impending danger for young Americans growing up?"

Well, I want to assure you, I clearly see the danger. I understand the consequences of retreat. That's why we'll support our troops. That's why we'll fight in Iraq, and that's why we'll win in Iraq.

I have been sharing this story with our fellow citizens all around the country because I want people to pay attention to the power of liberty to help us defeat this ideology of hate. You might remember, Laura and I had the honor of taking then-sitting Prime Minister of Japan, Koizumi, to Elvis's place—[*laughter*]—Memphis, Tennessee. [*Laughter*] People said, "Why did you go down there?" Well, I'd never been. [*Laughter*] Secondly, the Prime Minister of Japan—he was the then-sitting Prime Minister; he's since been replaced—loved Elvis. So I thought it would be fun to take him down there. But I wanted to tell the story.

The Japanese attacked us at Pearl Harbor, and millions of Americans volunteered to fight against the enemy. By the way, the same thing is happening today. We got kids—men and women volunteering to fight the enemy. One of those people was my dad, and I'm certain some of your relatives did the same thing. They said, "We're under attack. We're now going to go do everything we can to defeat the sworn enemy." And it was a bloody war, and thousands of people lost their lives.

And here I am on Air Force One flying down to Memphis, Tennessee, with the Prime Minister of the former enemy talking about keeping the peace. We were talking about how we can work together to convince the leader in North Korea to give up his nuclear weapons. We were talking about the fact that Japan had 1,000 troops in Iraq. See, the Prime Minister and I know that when you find a young democracy that is willing to fight off extremists and radicals, we have a duty—those of us who are free have a duty—to support those young democracies. We're in an ideological struggle between extremists who cannot stand liberty and millions who want to live free.

We talked about the need for—to whom much is given, much is required. And we'll continue to save lives on places like the continent of Africa by battling HIV/AIDS. In other words, we talked about our obligations in the world to make it more peaceful.

I find it interesting that my dad fought the Japanese, and his son is working to keep the peace with the Japanese. Something happened after World War II: Japan adopted a Japanese-style democracy. And the lesson is, liberty has got the capacity to convert an enemy into an ally. Liberty is powerful. Liberty has got the capacity to change regions of hopelessness and despair, the type of thing that the extremists exploit to achieve their dark vision. It has the capacity to change regions to hope and optimism. Someday elected leaders from the Middle East will be sitting down with an American President talking about keeping the peace, and a generation of Americans will be better off for it.

And I thank you for giving me a chance to share with you the important issues facing our electorate. And these are fundamental issues, and they're important issues that will determine how you live and the world in which your children grow up.

See, if you think health care decisions should remain in the hands of bureaucrats

and insurance companies, then you ought to just vote for the Democrats. If you believe you and your doctor should control your health care decisions, vote Republican.

If you think trial lawyers should be allowed to continue driving out good doctors and honest job creators, vote Democrat. If you believe that we should rein in the trial lawyers and protect our physicians and small-business owners from junk lawsuits, support the Republicans.

If you think activist judges should be allowed to redefine our country and issue new laws from the bench, vote Democrat. If you believe that the role of the judge is to strictly interpret the Constitution and leave legislating to legislators, vote Republican.

If you think your family budget can afford more taxes, you vote Democrat. If you believe you pay more than enough in taxes and you would rather invest your money and save your money and spend your money the way you see fit, vote Republican.

And if you think the way to best protect America and win the war against these terrorists is to simply criticize and offer no plan, vote Democrat. But if you believe the way to win the war on terror and to protect the United States is to stay on the offense and to work hard to lay the foundation of peace for generations to come, you vote Marilyn Musgrave back to the United States Congress.

I'm proud to be with you. Go from this hall and turn out the vote. Find your friends and neighbors, and get them to the poll. And come election day, we'll have a great victory, and the country will be better off for it.

God bless. May God bless America.

NOTE: The President spoke at 10 a.m. at Island Grove Regional Park. In his remarks, he referred to Colorado State Treasurer Mike Coffman; former Rep. Robert W. Schaffer of Colorado; Mayor Tom Selders of Greeley, CO; former President Saddam Hussein of Iraq; Usama bin Laden, leader of the Al Qaida terrorist organization; and Chairman Kim Jong Il of North Korea.

Remarks on Former Iraqi President Saddam Hussein's Trial Verdict From Waco, Texas
November 5, 2006

Today Saddam Hussein was convicted and sentenced to death by the Iraqi High Tribunal for the massacres committed by his regime in the town of Dujayl. Saddam Hussein's trial is a milestone in the Iraqi people's efforts to replace the rule of a tyrant with the rule of law. It's a major achievement for Iraq's young democracy and its constitutional Government.

During Saddam Hussein's trial, the court received evidence from 130 witnesses. The man who once struck fear in the hearts of Iraqis had to listen to free Iraqis recount the acts of torture and murder that he ordered against their families and against them. Today the victims of this regime have received a measure of the justice which many thought would never come.

Saddam Hussein will have an automatic right to appeal his sentence. He will continue to receive the due process and the legal rights that he denied to the Iraqi people. Iraq has a lot of work ahead as it builds its society that delivers equal justice and protects all its citizens. Yet history will record today's judgment as an important achievement on the path to a free and just and unified society.

The United States is proud to stand with the Iraqi people. We will continue to support Iraq's unity Government as it works to bring peace to its great country. We appreciate the determination and bravery of the Iraqi security forces who are stepping forward to defend their free nation. And we give our thanks to the men and women of America's Armed Forces, who have sacrificed so much for the cause of freedom in Iraq. And they've sacrificed for the security of the United States. Without their courage and skill, today's verdict would not have happened. On behalf of the American people, I thank every American who wears the uniform, I thank their families, and I thank them for their service and their sacrifice.

Thank you very much.

NOTE: The President spoke at 1:17 p.m. at the Texas State Technical College Waco Airport. The Office of the Press Secretary also released a Spanish language transcript of these remarks.

Remarks at a Nebraska Victory 2006 Rally in Grand Island, Nebraska
November 5, 2006

The President. Thank you all very much. Thanks for coming. Thanks for inviting me. So Laura says, "What do you think we ought to do on our 29th wedding anniversary?" I said, "Why don't I go to Grand Island, Nebraska, because there are some people I want to thank in advance of what you're going to do on November 7th."

I want to thank you for working hard. I want to thank you for voting. I want to thank you for sending Adrian Smith and Pete Ricketts to Washington, DC. You'd be happy to hear she agrees. [*Laughter*] She said, "You go ahead on; you go tell them, I agree with you." So she sends her love, and on this, our 29th anniversary, I'm proud to say, I love her dearly.

Seems like to me, when you want somebody to represent you in the Congress, you need somebody who has lived here their whole life and who understands Nebraska values. Seems like to me, if you're from this part of the world, you'd better have you somebody who understands what it means to be a farmer and a rancher representing you in the United States Congress. And that person is Adrian Smith.

I also appreciate you coming out to support Pete Ricketts. He's a small-business man; he's a successful small-business man. Let me tell you, we've got too many lawyers in Washington. Send somebody to Washington who has met a payroll, and that person is Pete Ricketts for the United States Senate. I appreciate Susanne Ricketts for standing with Pete and working just as hard as he is.

I want to thank your Governor, Governor Dave Heineman, and his wife, Sally, for being with us today. One of these days, he and I are going to be members of the ex-Governors club. [*Laughter*] But I know you're proud of the job he's doing. He's setting high standards and working hard to accomplish that which he said he would do on the campaign trail.

I appreciate very much being here with a fine United States Senator, a man I call a friend and a person I know you call friend, Chuck Hagel. From the First Congressional District, Jeff Fortenberry and his wife, Celeste, is with us. And from the Second Congressional District, Lee Terry and his wife, Robyn, have joined us. It's a good sign when the Congressmen from neighboring districts are coming in. See, they smell a winner. They understand what's about to happen on election day.

Proud to be here with your Lieutenant Governor, Sheehy, your attorney general, Bruning, and your secretary of state, Gale. Thank you all for coming.

I had an opportunity to say hello to his honor, your mayor. Mr. Mayor, thank you for being here. I appreciate you coming. I'm honored you're here. My only advice is, pave the potholes. [*Laughter*] Although, Mr. Mayor, if you please, I didn't feel any on the way in.

I want to thank you all. I really do want to thank the grassroots activists, the people who worked hard to get these candidates to where they are. And I just urge you to keep working for the next 48 hours.

I know—I'm sure you've heard the same predictions I've heard. The prognosticators have already decided the outcome of this election before the good people of Nebraska have voted. But don't worry about it; the same thing happened in 2004. Some of them up in Washington had already picked out their new offices in the West Wing. [*Laughter*] They listened to the prognosticators. Then the people showed up to the polls, and the movers were not needed.

And the same thing is going to happen on November the 7th. You're going to elect Adrian Smith; you're going to elect Pete Ricketts. We're going to hold the House and hold the Senate.

And there's a reason: Because Republicans understand the values and the priorities of the American people. And by the way, we don't shift our values and we don't shift our priorities based upon the latest opinion poll. We're running on a record. We've raised standards for our public schools. No child is going to be left behind in America because of our reforms.

Adrian Smith and I understand, if the farm economy is doing well in Nebraska, the entire economy of the United States does well. Adrian, Pete, and I understand that we've got a problem because we're too dependent on foreign oil. And so we passed comprehensive energy legislation that encourages new technologies that will enable us to drive our cars as a result of crops grown right here in the great State of Nebraska.

We're taking the lead. I remember when I was campaigning with you, I said, "Vote for me; I will put judges on the bench who strictly interpret the law and not legislate from the bench." We've got a record to run on. I want to thank Senator Chuck Hagel for strongly supporting my nominees to the Federal bench, particularly Sam Alito and John Roberts. When you go in to vote for your United States Senator, just remember you're not only voting for an individual, you're voting for the style of judiciary we have.

And if the Democrats were to control the United States Senate, judges like Alito and Roberts would never have been seated on the Supreme Court.

No, we've got a record to run on, and we've got stands we take that are totally different from the Democrats. The two big issues in this campaign, as far as I'm concerned, is how many—how much tax are you going to pay, and whether or not this Government is going to do everything in our power to protect you.

Let me start with taxes. See, our philosophy is this: You can spend your money far better than the Federal Government can. I don't care what they're telling you in the races here, but the Democrats believe they can spend their money better than you can.

Audience members. Boo!

The President. Our philosophy says that if you've got more of your own money in your pocket to save, spend, or invest, the economy benefits.

We just didn't go to Washington to be philosophers. We went to Washington to act. I signed the largest tax cut since Ronald Reagan was the President of the United States. We cut the taxes for everybody who pays income taxes. We doubled the child

tax credit. We reduced the marriage penalty. We cut the taxes on the small businesses. We cut taxes on capital gains and dividends to encourage investment. And for the sake of our small-business owners and for the sake of our ranchers and for the sake of our farmers, we put the death tax on the road to extinction.

I don't know if you can remember that far back about the debate on taxes, but I can. Democrats in Washington predicted the tax cuts would not create jobs; they predicted the tax cuts would not increase wages; and they predicted that tax cuts would cause the Federal deficit to explode. That's what they predicted. Now the facts are in. The tax cuts we passed have led to a strong and growing economy. Last Friday, we had more good news about our economy. The national unemployment rate is down to 4.4 percent. Real wages rose 2.4 percent over the past year, and we cut the deficit in half 3 years ahead of schedule. The tax cuts we passed are working.

And the Democrats are going to raise your taxes.

Audience members. Boo!

The President. Oh, they're not going to tell you that. They won't admit it quite that bluntly. As a matter of fact, they really don't want you to know what they think. They asked the Democrat leader in the House recently about tax cuts and she said, speaking about the Democrats, "We love tax cuts." Well, given her record, she must be a secret admirer. [*Laughter*]

She and her party voted against reducing the marriage penalty, voted against cutting taxes on small businesses, voted against lowering taxes for families with children, voted against putting the death tax on the road to extinction. If this is their definition of love, I'd sure hate to see hate.

See, here's the way the tax cuts work: If they are not extended or made permanent, your taxes are going up. See, if the Congress doesn't act to say, we're going to extend the tax cuts, or we're just going to make the tax cuts permanent, then you

get to pay an increased tax. They asked the man who aspires to be the head of the Ways and Means Committee in the House of Representatives—that's the tax writing committee—they said, "Can you think of any of the tax cuts that were passed that you would extend?" He said, "I can't think of a one." In other words, that's the Democrats' view of extending your tax cuts. This election is important because it determines the size of your taxes.

I'm going to give you an example of what I'm talking about. Right now the child tax credit is up to $1,000. But if those tax cuts are not expired, it goes down to $500 a child. So when you're sitting around the dinner table tonight, count heads. [*Laughter*] Any of you got four children? Right here, here you go, okay. I'm going to use you all as an example. So you're at dinner, number one child, two children, three, four, multiply by 500; means that if the Democrats take control of the House of Representatives, you get yourself a $2,000 tax increase.

Audience members. Boo!

The President. Now, that may not sound like a lot to people in Washington, but it sounds like a lot to me. It sounds like a lot to Adrian Smith, and it sounds like a lot to Pete Ricketts. That's why we're going to keep your taxes low.

On these issues, the Democrat party has adopted a clear strategy of opposition and obstruction. Recently the House Democrat leader explained the advice she's been following since I was reelected in 2004. She said, "You must take him down." That him would be me. One newspaper described her approach as scorched-earth strategy, for refusing to negotiate with the GOP. Now I want you to think about that. Think about that kind of vision. It's a sad commentary on the Democrat party that its leaders have resorted to knee-jerk opposition as their guiding principle.

You know if you're wondering what— where the Democrats stand on a major

issue, there's an easy formula to figure it out: No matter what the issue, if the Republicans are for it, they're against it. [*Laughter*]

When we proposed tax relief for everybody who pays income taxes, the Democrats opposed it. When Republicans proposed an energy policy, an energy bill to make our Nation less dependent on foreign oil, the Democrats opposed it. When Republicans proposed association health plans to help small businesses get coverage, insurance coverage at the same discounts big companies get, Democrats opposed it. When Republicans proposed medical liability reform so our docs aren't run out of practice and your costs aren't run up, the Democrats opposed it.

And here's the way I see it: If the Democrats are so good about being the party of the opposition, let's just keep them in the opposition. And the best way is to send Adrian Smith to the United States Congress and Pete Ricketts to the Senate.

This election is taking place in an historic time for our country. And when our children and grandchildren look back on this period, one question will overwhelm all the rest: Did we do everything in our power to fight and win the war on terror? We face an enemy—[*applause*]. I wish I could report to you we weren't at war. Nobody wants to be at war. But the truth is, we face a brutal enemy that still desires to harm America. Many of our citizens say, "Why is that?"

Well, this enemy has an ideology. They believe the exact opposite of what we believe. We believe in basic, universal freedoms. We believe people ought to worship the way they see fit. We believe people ought to be able to express themselves. We believe in public dissent; they don't. They also have a vision to spread their ideology as far corners—to the far corners of the world, and we stand in their way. You can't negotiate with them. You can't hope for the best with them. Our most important job is to protect you, and the best way

to do so is to stay on the offense and bring them to justice before they hurt us again.

The strategy is to stay on the offense, and the strategy is to protect you here at home. We have to be right 100 percent of the time, and the enemy has to be right one time. And therefore, I reviewed all the procedures to make sure our professionals have what it takes to protect you. There is a wall—there was a wall that prevented our intelligence folks from sharing vital information with our law enforcement folks. I can't tell you why that happened; it just did; and it didn't make any sense in this new kind of war. If our job is to protect you, we better make sure the intelligence our people gathers is passed on to the people whose job it is to prevent the attacks here in the homeland.

And so I asked the Congress to pass the PATRIOT Act. The PATRIOT Act is a vital piece of legislation that has helped us break up terror cells around the United States. It's a piece of legislation that guarded your civil liberties. When that important piece of legislation came up for renewal, the vast majority of Senate Democrats and House Democrats voted against it. Now, they must have a different attitude about this war on terror.

See, my attitude is, you can't respond after we're attacked; you must respond before we're attacked. In this new kind of war, we'd better understand what the enemy is thinking. And so I talked to the—our phone boys, and I said, "If they're calling in, if Al Qaida is making a phone call from outside the United States to inside, or if somebody affiliated with the enemy is making a phone call from outside to inside, we better understand why." We need to know what they're thinking and what they're planning in order to protect you.

When the terrorist surveillance program came up for votes in the United States House of Representatives, by far the vast majority of Democrats voted against that legislation. They just see the world differently. When you're getting ready to go

into the ballot box, remember the attitudes of the folks in Washington, DC, about what it takes to protect you. We're picking up people off the battlefield, and we better know what they're thinking.

I'm going to give you a short story here. We found a man named Khalid Sheikh Mohammad. Our intelligence people think he was the mastermind of the September the 11th attacks. So I authorized the Central Intelligence Agency to find out what he knew. See, if he knew about one attack, he might know something about another attack. Our job is to protect you. When the authority for these CIA interrogators to continue their program came up in front of the House and the Senate, the vast majority of Democrats in both bodies voted against that legislation.

We need people like Adrian Smith and Pete Ricketts in the House and the Senate who understand our professionals need to be given the tools necessary to protect you. We are on the offense, and we're going to stay on the offense. It is hard to plot and plan against America when you're on the run. It is hard to plot and plan—America when you're hiding.

I want you to know—let me share a lesson about September the 11th that's important. When we see a threat overseas, we've got to take the threat seriously. It's important for our fellow citizens never to forget that lesson. The days are gone when you see a threat and just hope for the best. When we see threats, we must deal with them.

Saddam Hussein was a threat. I saw him as a threat; members of both political parties saw the threat; the United Nations saw the threat. My decision to remove Saddam Hussein was the right decision, and the world is better off for it.

And today we witnessed a landmark event in the history of Iraq. Saddam Hussein was convicted and sentenced to death by the Iraqi High Tribunal. Saddam Hussein trial is a milestone in the Iraqi people's efforts to replace the rule of a tyrant with the rule of law, and it's a major achievement for this young democracy. America congratulates the Iraqi people, and we give our thanks to the men and women of America's Armed Forces, who have— [*applause*]. Without their courage and skill, today's verdict never would have happened. And we are grateful for their sacrifice and service.

We are in a global war, and it's a war being fought on a variety of fronts. And the central front is Iraq. Oh, I've heard all the talk out of Washington. You probably have too. "Iraq is a distraction in the war on terror," they say. Well, I don't believe that. Our troops don't believe that. And Usama bin Laden doesn't believe that. Listen to his words: He calls Iraq the third world war. He says victory for the terrorists in Iraq will mean America's defeat and disgrace forever.

Now I want you to listen to the words of a senior Member of the House of Representatives from the Democrat Party. The reason I'm talking about this is the people of this district have got to understand, there is a different mentality in Washington than what you're used to. She said, "The President says that fighting them there makes it less likely we will have to fight them here." That's exactly what I say, and it's exactly what I believe. She went on to say, "The opposite is true. Because we are fighting them there, it may become more likely we will have to fight them here."

Iraq is not the reason why these extremists and terrorists are at war with us. We were not in Iraq when they bombed the World Trade Center in 1993. We were not in Iraq when they bombed the Embassies in Tanzania and in Kenya. We were not in Iraq when they attacked the USS *Cole*, and we were not in Iraq on September the 11th, 2001. You don't create terrorists by fighting the terrorists. The best way to protect you is to stay on the offense and defeat them overseas so we do not have to face them here at home.

And we got one goal in Iraq, and that is victory. There's a country that—we're working for a country that can sustain itself and govern itself and defend itself and be an ally in the war on terror, to be an ally in this struggle against extremists who want to defy the hopes of reasonable people around the Middle East, these extremists who want to come and attack America again. And it's a tough fight, no question about it. I understand how tough it is, and so do our troops, and so do the families of our troops.

It's tough because we face an enemy that is willing to kill innocent life to achieve their objectives. They have no conscience, and they understand that these violent acts will end up on our television screens. And they believe the United States does not have the stomach for the long fight. But what they don't understand about this administration and a huge number of Americans, we're not going to run from thugs and assassins.

Our goal is solid. Our tactics constantly change. I'm in touch with our commanders all the time. I tell them, "Whatever you need to win, you'll have." We give them the flexibility necessary to continue to adjust their tactics to meet the changes the enemy are doing on the ground. And we got a lot going for us. We got a strategy for victory that will work, and we got a fantastic group of young men and women who have volunteered to defend you in the United States military.

And whether my fellow citizens agree with my decisions or not, one thing they owe is they owe those who wear the uniform the utmost respect. And those of us at the Federal Government owe them all they need, all the support to make sure they can do the jobs that I've asked them to do.

And I thank Senator Hagel for his strong support. I thank the Members of Congress who are here for their strong support of the United States military, and there's no doubt in my mind Pete Ricketts and Adrian Smith will be strong supporters of the men and women in the United States military.

We have something else going for us, and those are brave Iraqis. Iraqi citizens have suffered unspeakable violence, yet they are committed to a government of and by and for the people. Our strategy is to help their politics move forward. Our strategy is to help their economy improve. And our strategy is to train Iraqis so they can take the fight to the few who want to dash the hopes of the many.

You know, when nearly 12 million Iraqis voted, I was pleased, but I was not surprised, and I'll tell you why I wasn't surprised. I believe there is an Almighty. I believe a great gift of the Almighty to every man, woman, and child on Earth is the desire to be free. And so when the Iraqis said, "We want to be free," it is part of my belief in the universality of freedom.

We have a strategy for victory, and the only way we won't achieve it is if we leave before the job is done. If you listen to this debate on Iraq, if you think about the Democrats' plans for success, there isn't one. This is a vital issue facing our country. This is a central front in the war on terror, and yet they have no plan for victory.

Oh, some of them are saying we ought to pull out now. Others are saying we ought to pull out at a fixed date, before the job is done. Actually, one of the Members of the House of Representatives, a distinguished Member, said the best way to handle the situation is to remove our troops to an island 5,000 miles away. I'm not kidding you. That's not a plan for victory. Nineteen House Members introduced legislation that would cut off the funds for our troops. One Democrat Senator, one of Chuck's colleagues, she said, "We haven't coalesced around a single plan, but we're in general agreement on basic principles." Think about that. Yes, they're in agreement on principles: Get out before the job is done.

They've taken a calculated risk. By the way, I'm not saying these folks are unpatriotic; I'm saying they're wrong. You can't win a war and protect the homeland if you're unwilling to fight the war. You know, the Democrats have taken a calculated gamble in this campaign. They think the only way they can win is to criticize and not offer a plan of their own. You know, let me say this to you: Anger is not a plan; criticism is not a plan; pessimism is not a plan. This country needs people who understand the stakes and are willing to support the fight to protect you.

Retreat from Iraq before the job is done would embolden the enemy and would make this country less secure. It's very important for our fellow citizens to understand this is a different kind of war, and if the United States were to leave before the job is done, the enemy would follow us here. Leaving before the job was done would make it easier for these extremists to recruit. Leaving before the job was done would dash the hopes of the millions upon millions of people who want to live a peaceful life in the Middle East. And leaving before the job is done would dishonor the sacrifice of the men and women who have worn the uniform of the United States.

And leaving before the job is done would be felt for generations to come. And let me explain to you why. The enemy has made it clear, they expect us to leave when the fighting stays tough because, one, they want a safe haven from which to launch further attacks on the United States, a safe haven similar to the safe haven they had in Afghanistan, where they trained thousands of people and where they planned and plotted to launch their attacks that killed nearly 3,000 of our citizens.

They have said that they want to establish a caliphate—a governing organization based upon their ideology—and it starts with toppling modern governments. They would like to get ahold of oil resources so they could then say to the West, "Abandon your alliance with Israel," or, "Withdraw from the Middle East; otherwise, you're going to be facing high priced oil, and we'll bring your economy down." And when you put all in the mix a country which doesn't like us with a nuclear weapon, 30 years from now, people are going to look back at this period in our history and say, "What happened to them in 2006? Could they not see the impending danger? Were they unable to see the threats to a generation of Americans?"

Well, let me assure you, I see the danger. I clearly see the stakes. That is why we will support our troops. That is why we will fight in Iraq, and that is why we'll win in Iraq.

I would like to share a story with you. I share this story all around the country, so if you've heard it, I apologize. It's a story about the power of liberty. It's a story about then-sitting Prime Minister of Japan, Koizumi, and me and Laura heading down to Elvis's place in Memphis, Tennessee. They said, "Why did you go down there?" Well, I hadn't been down there. I thought it would be fun to go.

Koizumi, Prime Minister Koizumi wanted to go because he loved Elvis. He was a fan of Elvis Presley. But also, I wanted to tell a story. It's the story about—I'm sure your relatives, just like my relative, my dad, volunteered to fight the Japanese after the attacks of Pearl Harbor. That's when the story begins. They attacked us. Thousands of our fellow citizens said, "I want to go, and I want to fight for our freedoms against an enemy which has attacked us." By the way, it's the same spirit today, around, where people have said, "I want to volunteer to defend America."

My dad went. Your relatives went. They fought like mad. Japan was the sworn enemy of the United States. I'm now on the airplane, Air Force One, flying down to Elvis's place, and I was talking about keeping the peace with the Prime Minister of Japan. We talked about how we got to work together to convince the North

Korean to give up his nuclear weapons ambitions. We talked about the fact that Iraq has 1,000 troops—I mean Japan had 1,000 troops in Iraq.

He understands what I know: In this ideological struggle of extremists versus rational, reasonable people who want to live in peace, when we find young democracies, we must support them for the sake of peace. We talked about how to whom much is given, much is required, and that we'll continue to take the lead in trying to eradicate the pandemic of HIV/AIDS in places like Africa. We talked about our responsibilities as friends and allies.

I find it amazing that my dad and your relatives fought the Japanese, and today—then his son was talking about keeping the peace. Something happened, and what happened was, Japan adopted a Japanese-style democracy. The lesson for all to hear is, liberty has got the capacity to transform an enemy into an ally. Liberty has got the capacity to transform a region of hate and resentment into a region of hope.

Someday American Presidents will be sitting down with duly elected leaders in the Middle East talking about keeping the peace, and a generation of Americans will be better off for it.

In 48 hours, you're going to be walking into the booth, and so will millions of citizens around our country, and people will be given a choice between two political parties with different philosophies. If you think your health care decisions should remain in the hands of bureaucrats, then you ought to vote for the Democrats. If you think that you and your doctors should control your healthcare decisions, vote Republican.

If you think that trial lawyers should be allowed to continue driving good doctors out of practice and running up your costs of medicine, you go ahead and vote Democrat. But if you believe that we should trade in the trial lawyers and protect our physicians from frivolous lawsuits, vote Republican.

If you think activist judges should be allowed to redefine our country and issue new laws from the bench, you need to go vote Democrat. If you believe the role of the judge is to strictly interpret our Constitution and laws and leave legislating to legislators, vote Republican.

If you think Medicare was serving our seniors just fine and didn't need to be reformed, vote Democrat. But if you believe we were right to expand choices for our seniors and provide better access for affordable prescription drugs, vote Republican.

If you think our farmers and ranchers ought to pay taxes while they're alive and then pay taxes after they're dead, you vote Democrat. But if you think that the death tax is punitive and we need to get rid of it, you vote Republican.

If you think you can afford more taxes, vote Democrat. But if you want our taxes low and if you want people who believe you can spend your money better than the Government can, you vote Republican.

And if you think the way to protect this country and win the war on terror is to criticize your opponents and offer no plan for victory, you vote for the Democrats. But if you believe the way to win this war is to stay on the offense and use every element of national power to protect you and lay the foundation of peace for a generation, vote Republican.

So I appreciate your coming. Thanks for giving me a chance to share something that's on my mind. I'm now asking you when you go forth to find fellow Republicans and say, you've got a responsibility to vote. But while you're doing it, don't overlook discerning Democrats and open-minded independents. Tell them to go to the polls. Tell them to vote for Adrian Smith and Pete Ricketts, and the United States will be better off for it.

God Bless, and God bless America.

NOTE: The President spoke at 3:58 p.m. at the Heartland Events Center. In his remarks, he referred to Lt. Gov. Rick Sheehy, attorney

general Jon Bruning, secretary of state John A. Gale of Nebraska; Mayor Jay Vavricek of Grand Island, NE; former President Saddam Hussein of Iraq; Usama bin Laden, leader of the Al Qaida terrorist organization; and Chairman Kim Jong Il of North Korea.

Remarks at a Kansas Victory 2006 Rally in Topeka, Kansas
November 5, 2006

The President. Thank you all very much. It's an honor to be here. Thanks for coming out tonight. So Jim Ryun says, "Do you want a race?" I said, "No, but I want you reelected to the United States Congress." I appreciate you coming. I'm proud to be here with Jim Ryun. He's a decent, honorable man who works hard on behalf of the people from Kansas. He deserves to be reelected Congressman.

He is a compassionate conservative. He has run his own business. By the way, we've got plenty of lawyers in Washington. [*Laughter*] Send somebody up there who has made a payroll. He started Sounds of Success, that helped children with hearing difficulties realize their full potential. He doesn't need a poll or a focus group to tell him what to believe.

I thank you for being here, and I'm asking you to send this good man back to the United States Congress. I'm not the only one in my family who feels this way; Laura feels this way. Some guy just yelled, "Happy anniversary." That's what I was supposed to say today. You know, no better way to spend your anniversary—your 29th anniversary—with somebody you love, than being here asking for the vote for Jim Ryun. She sends her very best to Jim and Anne.

I'm proud to be here, as well, with Senator Sam Brownback of the great State of Kansas. More importantly, his wife, Mary, is here. Proud to be here with Congressman Todd Tiahrt, who you just heard from, and his wife, Vicki; Jim Barnett, running for Governor, and he needs your vote;

Susan Wagle, running for Lieutenant Governor, she could use your vote as well.

I appreciate very much that Chuck Ahner is with us. He's running for the Third Congressional District here in the State of Kansas. We've got your attorney general for the great State of Kansas here, who's asking for the vote. Secretary of State Ron Thornburgh is with us today.

Most importantly, I want to say thanks to the grassroots activists who are here. You're the folks who put up the signs, make the phone calls, and get your fellow citizens to the polls. I want to thank you for what you have done, and I want to thank you for what you're going to do over the next 48 hours.

We're heading to the finish line, and we're asking for your help. Whatever you do, don't pay attention to the prognosticators, the pundits. See, a bunch of them have already decided that the verdict's in, but they forgot that the folks of Kansas hadn't got to the polls yet. But this isn't the first time this has happened. You might remember in 2004—some of the folks in Washington were listening to the prognosticators, and then they starting picking out their offices in the West Wing. [*Laughter*] And then the people actually voted; the movers weren't needed.

When you turn out the vote and vote yourself and put Jim Ryun back in the United States Congress, we're going to control the House, and we'll control the United States Senate as well. And there's a reason why we're going to win: One, we got you behind us, but also we're going

to win because we share the values and the priorities of the American people.

And we've got a record to run on. We've delivered results. One of the things that Jim and I talk about is the need to make sure our farm economy is strong. See, we believe if the ag sector is doing well, the entire U.S. economy does well.

We also understand that if you become dependent—if you stay dependent on foreign oil, it creates a national security risk. And so therefore, Jim Ryun has worked to make sure that we encourage renewable fuel standards. In other words, we're going to use Kansas products to power our automobiles so we become less dependent on oil. If you're somebody who makes a living because of agriculture, it is in your economic interest to send Jim Ryun back to the United States Congress.

Jim Ryun is a strong, strong supporter of programs to make sure our veterans' health care benefits work. See, he believes in supporting our veterans just like he believes in supporting those who wear the uniform today. If you're involved with defense here in this congressional district, I strongly urge you to support Jim Ryun.

I also want to talk about Jim's belief in family values. He lives them. He not only believes in family values, he practices family values. And he is working to prevent the institution of marriage being redefined by activist judges.

I want to talk about two issues that divide Republicans from Democrats. One of them is taxes, and the other one is the defense of this homeland. Let me start with taxes. We believe that you can spend your money better than the Federal Government can. I don't care what they're telling you here at home; Democrats believe they can spend your money better than you can.

Audience members. Boo!

The President. We also believe that if you have more money in your pocket, more of your own money in your pocket to save, spend, or invest, the economy benefits. That is our philosophy, but you don't ex-

pect us to be in Washington philosophizing. You expect us to be doing something about it. That is why I signed the largest tax cuts since Ronald Reagan was the President.

We cut the taxes on everybody who pays income taxes. We doubled the child tax credit. We reduced the marriage penalty. We cut taxes on small businesses. We cut taxes on capital gains and dividends to encourage investment. And for the sake of our family businesses and for the sake of our farmers and for the sake of our ranchers, we put the death tax on the road to extinction.

We had a spirited debate in Washington over these tax cuts. You might remember some of the Democrats' predictions. They said if we had tax cuts it wouldn't create jobs; if we had tax cuts, it would not increase wages; if we had tax cuts, it would cause the Federal deficit to explode. Well, the facts are in. The tax cuts have led to a strong and growing economy. Last Friday we got more good news about the economy. The national unemployment rate is down to 4.4 percent. In the last 3 months, we've added 470,000 new jobs. Real wages rose 2.4 percent over the past year, and we cut the deficit in half, 3 years ahead of schedule. If the Democrats' election predictions are as good as their economic predictions, we're going to have a good day on November the 7th.

If you live in this congressional district or in any other district around the country, you must understand that if you vote Democrat, you're voting for a tax increase.

Audience members. Boo!

The President. Now understand that in a campaign like this, that the Democrats don't want you to know their plans. Listen to the words of the leading Democrat in the House of Representatives, a woman who thinks she's going to be the Speaker, but she's not. She said—when they asked about tax cuts, she said, "We love tax cuts." Well, given her record, she must be a secret admirer. [*Laughter*] She and her party voted against every single one of the tax

cuts we passed. If this is their definition of love, I'd sure hate to see what hate looks like.

If the tax cuts we passed are allowed to expire, if the tax cuts we passed are not extended, if the tax cuts we passed are not made permanent, you get a tax increase. That's how it's going to work. And so they asked the person who thinks he's going to be chairman of the House Ways and Means Committee, "Can you think of any of the tax cuts we've passed that ought to be extended?" And see, the Ways and Means Committee is the tax-writing committee in the House. They said, "Can you think of one?" He said, "I can't think of one tax cut that should be extended." In other words, every one of the tax cuts we passed ought to lapse, which means your taxes go up.

I'll give you an example. If the tax cuts are not extended or made permanent, the child tax credit will go from $1,000 a child to $500 a child, see.

Audience members. Boo!

The President. So when you get home this evening and you're sitting around the table—anybody here got four kids? I'll use you as an example. There you are at the table; you got five, okay. Five, okay. She's got five kids. So when you get home: one, two, three, four, five times 500. That's $2,500. That's your tax increase if you vote Democrat. That's your tax increase if the Democrats take over the House of Representatives. That 2,500 may not seem like a lot to people in Washington, but it seems like a lot to me and Jim Ryun, and that's why we're going to keep your taxes low.

This election is taking place in an historic time for our country, and when our children and grandchildren look back on this period, one question will overwhelm all the rest: Did we do everything in our power to win the war on terror? I wish I could report to you that we were not at war, but we are. We face a brutal enemy that has no conscience, an enemy that does have an ideology.

People in our country wonder why an enemy would want to attack a compassionate people like those of us in the United States, and the answer is, because we thwart their ambitions to spread their dark vision around the world. They believe—we believe in freedom; they don't. We believe in liberty; they don't. They understand America won't change.

You cannot negotiate with these people. You can't hope for the best from these people. The best way to do our most important job—is to protect you—is to defeat them overseas so we do not have to face them here at home.

Part of our strategy is to stay on the offense. The other part of our strategy is to protect you on the homeland. Now, the problem we face is that the enemy has to be right one time, and we have to be right 100 percent of the time. So I went to Congress and said, here are some vital tools that are necessary to protect the American people.

Let me give you three examples. One, there was a wall that separated our intelligence folks from sharing information with our law enforcement people. Now, that's probably hard for you to understand, but that was the reality. In this new kind of war, we must have good intelligence, and the people who are responsible for protecting you must be able to act on it. So I asked the Congress to pass the PATRIOT Act, and the PATRIOT Act made sure that folks had the tools necessary to protect you. And when that bill came up for reauthorization, the vast majority of Democrats in the House and the Senate voted against it.

Audience members. Boo!

The President. It's important for people in this district and around the country to understand there is a different mindset. You cannot wait to respond to an attack. You got to act before the attack.

I felt like if Al Qaida was making a phone call into the United States from outside the United States, we better understand why. If our job is to protect you, we've got to have the tools necessary to do so. When this bill came up in front of the House of Representatives, the vast majority of Democrats voted against it. I felt like it was important that when we picked somebody up off the battlefield, we better understand what that person is thinking.

Let me give you an example. We captured Khalid Sheikh Mohammed. Our intelligence officers believe he was the mastermind of the September the 11th attacks. My attitude is, if he knew about one attack, he might know about another attack, and we better find out why and what he knows.

The vast majority of Democrats voted against giving our CIA professionals the tools necessary to question detainees. There is a different mindset in Washington. The best way to protect you is to make sure our professionals have the tools necessary to do so, and the best way to make sure they do is to send Jim Ryun back to the United States Congress.

We are in a global war against an enemy that wants to strike us. And this war is fought on a variety of fronts. One of the lessons of September the 11th is that when we see a threat overseas, we must take each threat seriously, before it comes to hurt us. It's a lesson that every President must understand in this new world we live in. I saw a threat in Saddam Hussein; Members of the Congress from both political parties saw the same threat; the United Nations saw the threat in Saddam Hussein. The decision I made to remove Saddam Hussein was the right decision, and the world is better off for it.

And today we witnessed a landmark event in the history of Iraq. Saddam Hussein was convicted and sentenced to death by the Iraqi High Tribunal. Saddam Hussein's trial is a milestone in the Iraqi people's efforts to replace the rule of a tyrant with the rule of law. It's a major achievement for this young democracy. We congratulate the Iraqi people, and as I do so, I congratulate the men and women who wear the uniform of the United States for their hard work. Without their courage and skill, this verdict never would have happened.

Iraq is the central front in this war on terror. Oh, I've heard all the lines, and I know you have as well. "No, it's a distraction in the war on terror," the Democrats say in Washington. Well, that's not what I think, and that's not what our troops think, and that's not what Usama bin Laden thinks. Usama bin Laden has called this fight the third world war. He has said that victory for the terrorists in Iraq will mean America's defeat and disgrace forever. They just think different in Washington. You just got to know that. When you go in the booth to vote, you all got to understand that people don't see this world the way I do. I understand that.

I want you to hear the words of the Democrat—leading Democrat in the House. She said, "The President says that fighting them there makes it less likely we will have to fight them here." I do say that because I believe that. She went on to say, "The opposite is true. Because we're fighting them there, it may become more likely we will have to fight them here."

Audience members. Boo!

The President. Iraq is not the reason the terrorists are at war with us. We were not in Iraq when they bombed the World Trade Center in 1993. We were not in Iraq when they blew up the Embassies in Kenya and Tanzania. We were not in Iraq when they bombed the USS *Cole.* And we were not in Iraq when they attacked us on September the 11th, 2001. You do not create terrorists by fighting the terrorists. The best way to protect you is to stay on the offense and bring them to justice before they can hurt us again.

Our goal is victory in Iraq. That is our goal, and we got a plan to achieve victory.

And victory means a government that can sustain itself, govern itself, defend itself, and serve as an ally in the war against these extremists and radicals and terrorists.

We got a plan to do just that, but the enemy has got a plan to prevent us. See, they kill innocent men, women, and children, knowing that those images will be on our TV screens. And they believe that the United States does not have the will or the capacity to stay in the fight for the long run. And they recognize that these images, which justifiably horrify many of our citizens, will cause us to leave before the job is done. But they don't understand this administration, nor do they understand millions of our citizens. We're not going to run from thugs and assassins.

Our goal remains the same. Our tactics constantly shift. I have given our commanders on the ground all the flexibility they need and all the tools necessary to achieve victory. And we got great assets for us. We have a plan for victory that will work, and we got a fantastic United States military.

Any time—first of all, no matter what your view about the decisions I have made to protect America, you owe, and everyone owes, a debt of gratitude for the men and women in the United States military. And those of us in Government owe the men and women in uniform all the support necessary, all the pay, all the training, so they can do the job we've asked them to, and Jim Ryun is a strong supporter for the United States military.

There's something else going for us in terms of victory in Iraq, and that's the Iraqis themselves. They have suffered unspeakable violence, yet they are committed to a government of, by, and for the people. You know, I was pleased when nearly 12 million people went to the polls saying, "We want to live in a free society," but I wasn't surprised. And the reason I wasn't surprised is I believe a gift from the Almighty to each man, woman, and child on the face of the Earth is the desire to be free, is liberty.

And I believe in the universality of freedom. And I believe it's in our interests to help this young democracy survive. It's in our interests to help them on the political track and on the economic track. And at the same time, we're training Iraqis so they can take the fight to the enemy. We'll succeed. Let me tell you this: If I didn't think we're succeed and if I didn't think the cause was noble and just, I'd pull our troops out.

I can't look at the eyes of a mother or wife or husband or dad of a troop in combat if I didn't believe it was essential to the security of this country. As a matter of fact, the only way we won't succeed is if we leave before the job is done. If people go to the polls, I want you to think about the Democrats' plan for victory: There isn't one.

Iraq is the central front on this war, and yet they have no plan for victory. Oh, some of them say we ought to pull out now. Others say we ought to pull out on a fixed date, even though the job hadn't been done. One of the leaders in the House of Representatives—one of the Democrat leaders said—well, they're going to move the troops 5,000 miles away to an island. Nineteen people in the House said, "We're going to cut off the funds right now." In other words, they're all over the lot, but they agree on one thing: Get out before the job is done.

Audience members. Boo!

The President. Listen, I'm not saying these people are unpatriotic; I'm just saying they're wrong. You can't win a war unless you're willing to fight the war. The Democrats have taken a calculated gamble in this election that—they think they can win by just criticizing. That's what they believe. You know, if you happen to run into a Democrat candidate, you might want to ask them the simple question: What's your plan?

See, if they say they want to protect the homeland but opposed the PATRIOT Act, ask them: What's your plan? If they say they want to uncover terrorist plots but opposed listening in on terrorists' conversations, just go ahead and ask them: What is your plan? If they say they want to stop new attacks on our country but oppose letting the CIA detain and question the terrorists who might know about what those plots are, ask them this question——

Audience members. What's your plan?

The President. If they say they want to win the war on terror but call for America to pull out of what Al Qaida says is the central front in the war on terror, ask them this question——

Audience members. What's your plan?

The President. They don't have a plan. Harsh criticism is not a plan for victory, and second-guessing is not a strategy. We have a plan, and part of our plan is to send Jim Ryun back to the United States Congress.

Retreat from Iraq before the job is done will make this country more vulnerable to attack. This is a different kind of war. If we were to leave before the job is done, the enemy would follow us here. Leaving before the job is done would embolden the extremists and the radicals and would dash the hopes of millions of people in the Middle East who want to live a peaceful life.

Leaving before the job is done would dishonor the sacrifice of the men and women who have worn the uniform of the United States. The consequences of leaving before the job is done will be felt for generations. The enemy has made it clear that they want to establish safe haven in order to launch further attacks, just like the safe haven they had in Afghanistan.

They have made it clear that they want to drive us out of the Middle East to topple moderate governments as a part of spreading their dark vision of the future throughout the Middle East. They have made it clear that they would like to control re-

sources like energy in order to extract economic blackmail from the West.

Imagine if these enemy were able to control countries and said, "We're going to pull a bunch of oil off the market to run up the price of your oil unless you abandon your alliances"—alliances with Israel, for example—or, "unless you withdraw from the Middle East." Coupled with all this is a country which doesn't like us trying to possess a nuclear weapon. Thirty years from now, people would look back, if this were to happen, and say, "What happened the folks in 2006? How come they couldn't see the impending danger? What clouded their vision—which caused them not to do their duty?"

I want to assure you, I see the impending danger. I see the threats to a future for our children. Therefore, we will fight in Iraq, and we will win in Iraq.

We got one other thing going for us, and that is the power of liberty. I don't know if you all remember, but recently Laura and I took then-sitting Prime Minister of Japan to Elvis's place in Memphis. [*Laughter*] I'd never been there. [*Laughter*] Koizumi wanted to go there. See, he loved Elvis.

But I also want to tell an interesting story about the power of liberty. After the Japanese attacked Pearl Harbor, my dad and many of your relatives said, "I want to go defend this country," and they signed up by the thousands. By the way, the same thing is happening now. And these Americans fought the Japanese as a sworn enemy in a bloody, bloody war.

And yet I'm on Air Force One, flying down to Memphis, talking about how to keep the peace. Isn't that interesting? My dad fought the Japanese, and his son is talking to the leader of the Japanese—the leader of the former enemy—talking about North Korea, what we can do to work together to prevent the North Korea peninsula from having nuclear weapons.

We were talking about the fact that Japan had 1,000 troops in Iraq. See, the

Prime Minister knows what I know. In this ideological struggle of the 21st century, when you find a young democracy—a form of government which defeats the radicals and extremists—you got to support it. We talked about, "To whom much is given, much is required," and therefore, we'll continue to lead the fight against HIV/AIDS on the continent of Africa.

My dad fought them, and I'm working to keep the peace with the leader of the very same country. Something happened. What happened was, Japan adopted a Japanese-style democracy. The message is, liberty has got the capacity to change an enemy into an ally, and liberty has got the capacity to change a region of the world that is resentful and hopeless to a region of the world that has got hope and optimism. Someday—someday American leaders will be sitting down with duly elected leaders from the Middle East talking about the peace, and a generation of Americans will be better off for it.

And these are the stakes in this election. And I thank you for coming out and giving me a chance to tell you what's on my mind. In 48 hours, our citizens around this country are headed into the box, and they've got clear choices to make. If you believe that your health care decisions ought to remain in the hands of bureaucrats, vote Democrat. If you believe that you and your doctors should control your health care decisions, vote Republican.

If you think trial lawyers should be allowed to continue driving good doctors and honest job creators out of business, vote Democrat.

Audience members. Boo!

The President. But if you believe that we should rein in the trial lawyers and protect our physicians and small-business owners from junk lawsuits, you vote Republican. You think activist judges should be allowed to redefine our country and issue new laws from the bench, vote Democrat.

Audience members. Boo!

The President. But if you believe that the role of the judge is to strictly interpret the Constitution and leave the legislating to the legislators, vote Republican.

If you think Medicare was serving our seniors just fine and did not need to be reformed, vote Democrat. But if you believe we were right to expand choices for our seniors and provide better access to affordable prescription drugs, you vote Republican.

You think your family budget can afford more taxes, vote Democrat.

Audience members. Boo!

The President. If you believe you pay more than enough in taxes as it is, and if you believe that you can spend your money better than the Federal Government can, vote Republican.

And finally, if you think the way to protect America and win the war on terror is to criticize your opponents and offer no plan of your own, vote Democrat.

Audience members. Boo!

The President. But if you believe that the way to win the war on terror is to stay on the offense, and if you believe it is necessary to lay the foundation of peace for generations to come, you vote Republican.

I thank you for coming. Go vote. Get your neighbors and friends to vote. And send Jim Ryun back to the United States Congress.

God bless. And God bless America.

NOTE: The President spoke at 6:10 p.m. at the Kansas Expocentre. In his remarks, he referred to Kansas State Attorney General Phillip D. Kline; former President Saddam Hussein of Iraq; Usama bin Laden, leader of the Al Qaida terrorist organization; and former Prime Minister Junichiro Koizumi of Japan.

Remarks at a Florida Victory 2006 Rally in Pensacola, Florida
November 6, 2006

The President. Thank you all very much. He just yelled, "Happy birthday," to Laura—and happy anniversary. Imagine, in a short period of time, a birthday and anniversary and Republican victory on Tuesday.

I appreciate you recognizing Laura. No doubt about it, she is the A Team in my family, and she's a great First Lady for the United States. And Jeb Bush has been a great Governor for Florida, and I want to thank you for standing with him during 8 years in which he worked hard to improve the lives of every single citizen in this State, regardless of their political party. Jeb is the kind of fellow who did in office what he said he was going to do, and he's going to go down as one of the great Governors in your State's history.

I'm proud to be here with Senator Mel Martinez, one of the fine United States Senators. Tomorrow you get to vote for a new Governor, and I strongly suggest you vote for Charlie Crist to be Governor of the State of Florida. He's experienced; he's compassionate; and he'll work hard on behalf of all the citizens of this important State. And while you're in there voting for Charlie, vote for Katherine Harris for the United States Senate and Bill McCollum to be the attorney general; Tom Lee to be the chief financial officer. And if you know anything about agriculture, you're going to want Charlie Bronson to be your secretary of agriculture.

I'm proud to be here in the district of a fine United States Congressman, Congressman Jeff Miller. I want to thank you and Vicki for being here. Miller always talks about the good folks in this district. Every time I see him he's saying, "Don't you forget the people in the panhandle." And I say, "Congressman, how could I forget them; I wouldn't be President without them."

We're 24 hours away from voting. Some of the folks in Washington already think they figured out the results.

Audience members. Boo!

The President. That's what happened in 2004. [*Laughter*] Some of them up there started listening to the prognosticators and started picking out their offices in the West Wing. [*Laughter*] Then the people in Florida voted, and the people around the country voted, and the movers weren't needed. The same thing is going to happen tomorrow. Republicans are going to turn out. It's going to be a great victory on November the 7th.

And I thank you all for coming out today. I thank you for your interest. I thank you for what you have done to help these candidates, and I thank you for what you're going to do for the next 24 hours. You're going to pick up the phone; you're going to make the phone calls; you're going to turn out your friends and neighbors; and we're going to win.

We're also going to win because over the past 5 years, we have accomplished great things. Together, we have taken an economy from recession to strong and lasting growth. Together, we have risen to the test of September the 11th and have taken the fight to the terrorists all across the world. Together, we found a calling for a generation of Americans, a freedom agenda to replace tyranny with liberty, oppression with democracy, and an ideology of hate with an ideology of hope.

History has called upon our generation to lead, and we have led. We're also going to win this election because Republicans understand the values and the priorities of the American people. We don't need an opinion poll to tell us what we believe. Our principles are rock solid. We're going to win because we have a hopeful, optimistic agenda.

I knew we were going to finish strong because I knew that when the American people paid attention to the two most important issues, they would understand we stand with them. And the two most important issues is, how much money are you going to have in you pocket—in other words, the size of the taxes—and which group of folks can best win the war on terror.

Let me start with taxes. See, our philosophy says, you can spend your money better than the Federal Government can. Our philosophy says when you have more money in your pocket to save, invest, or spend, the entire economy benefits. The Democrat philosophy is, they can spend your money better than you can, and that's why they want more of it.

Audience members. Boo!

The President. Oh, you might remember the debates that we had in Washington. They said the tax cuts—the Democrats said the tax cuts wouldn't increase job growth; it wouldn't increase wages; it would cause the deficit to explode. Well, the facts are in. Our economy is strong. Americans are working. The national unemployment rate is down to 4.4 percent. The unemployment rate in this great State is 3.2 percent. Real wages are going up, and we cut the deficit in half 3 years ahead of schedule.

People are beginning to pay attention to this election, and they understand that if the Democrats win, they're going to raise your taxes.

Audience members. Boo!

The President. Oh, I know they don't want you to know that. See, they're going to say everything they can to make sure you don't understand that reality. Matter of fact, I want you to listen to the words of the top Democrat leader in the House of Representatives. They asked her about tax cuts; she said, "We love tax cuts." Well, given her record, she must be a secret admirer. Every tax cut we passed—and by the way, they're the largest tax cuts since Ronald Reagan was the President. Every

tax cut we passed, whether it be increasing the child tax credit, or reducing the marriage penalty, or putting the death tax on the road to extinction, or cutting taxes on capital gains or dividends, or reducing all income taxes for people who pay taxes, she was against. And so were the Democrats in Washington. If that's their idea of love, I'd hate to see what hate looks like.

Now here's the way this works. See, if the tax cuts we passed are not made permanent or are not extended, your taxes are going up. And so they asked the man who thinks he is going to be the head of the tax writing committee—he's not, but he thinks he's going to be—they said, "Can you think of one of the tax cuts that you would extend?" He said he couldn't think of one. See, rather than saying, "I'm looking forward to raising the taxes on the American people," this Democrat shows a different way of saying he's going to raise taxes on—he just said, "I can't think of one of the tax cuts that I would extend." So, for example, the child tax credit will go from $1,000 a child to $500 a child.

Audience members. Boo!

The President. And if you've got four kids—right there. I'm going to use you as an example, if that's all right. So when you get to dinner tonight and you're sitting around the table, you go, one, two, three, four, and multiply that by $500 a child. That's $2,000. You'll be paying $2,000 more in taxes if people across this country vote Democrat. The best way for you to keep your taxes low is to vote Republican.

There are clear differences on this important issue. The Democrats want to raise taxes when you're born, when you're working, when you're retired, and when you die. [*Laughter*] In other words, the Democrats' philosophy is this: If it breathes, tax it. [*Laughter*] And if it stops breathing, find their children and tax them. [*Laughter*] Our philosophy is, we want you to have more of your own money because we know the tax cuts have worked to keep this economy strong.

These are historic times. When our children and grandchildren look back on this period, there will be one overriding question; one question will overwhelm all the rest: Did the United States do everything in our power to win the war on terror? I wish I could tell you we weren't at war, but we are. We face a brutal enemy that has an ideology, an ideology so backwards that many of our citizens can't possibly comprehend it. See, we believe in basic freedoms; they don't. We believe in the freedom to worship; they don't. We believe in freedom to dissent; they don't. We believe in freedom of a press; they don't.

And because we stand in the way of their ambitions, which is to spread their vision as far and wide as possible, they want to hurt us. And so my most important job—when it all boils down to Washington, DC, my most important job, and any of us in Washington's most important job, is to protect you. You can't negotiate with these people. You cannot hope for the best with these people. The best way to protect you is to find them and bring them to justice before they have a chance to hurt us.

And we've got to make sure we're doing everything at home to protect you. The enemy has got to be right one time, and we've got to be right 100 percent of the time to do our job to secure this country. And so that is why I worked with the Congress to tear down walls that prevented our intelligence services from talking to law enforcement. It probably didn't make any sense to you that's what happened, but that's the case. And so I asked Congress to pass the PATRIOT Act. And they did. But when it came time to be renewed, the overwhelming majority of the Democrats in the House and in the United States Senate voted no.

Audience members. Boo!

The President. And the reason I'm bringing this up to you is that there is a different mindset in Washington, DC, than what I believe. See, I believe our professionals have all the tools necessary to protect you;

Democrats don't. There's an attitude up there that says, "Well, we'll respond after we're attacked." My attitude is, we're going to respond before we're attacked.

I felt it was important if Al Qaida or an Al Qaida affiliate was making a phone call into the United States that we knew why. In this different kind of war, we must understand what the enemy is thinking, if our job is to prevent an attack. When that bill came up in front of the United States House of Representatives, the vast majority of Democrats voted against it.

I felt it was important that when we picked somebody up off the battlefield that we had an opportunity to question that person. See, we picked up Khalid Sheikh Mohammed, who our intelligence services think was the mastermind of September the 11th. Here's my way of thinking: If he knew about one attack, he might know about another attack. When this bill came up in front of the House and the Senate, the overwhelming majority of Democrats voted no. If the people of this country expect their Government to do its most important job, you better elect people who will give our professionals the tools necessary to protect you, and those people are Republicans.

We're involved in a global struggle, and we will face the enemy where we find them, no matter what the theater of war is. The most important theater, however, is Iraq. See, one of the lessons of September the 11th is that when we see a threat, we have got to take that threat seriously. I saw a threat in Saddam Hussein; Members of the United States Congress in both political parties saw the same threat; the United Nations saw the threat. My decision to get rid of Saddam Hussein was the right decision, and the world is better off for it.

Audience members. U.S.A.! U.S.A.! U.S.A.!

The President. On Sunday, we witnessed a landmark event in the history of Iraq.

Saddam Hussein was convicted and sentenced to death. We congratulate the Iraqi people. We appreciate the fact that they're converting their country from a rule of a tyrant to rule of law. And as we congratulate the Iraqi people, we've got to remember that there was a lot of brave men and women who wear our uniform that made sacrifices necessary so that Iraq got to that position in the first place.

In our efforts to protect you, Iraq is now the central front. Oh, you hear them all the time in Washington say, "Well, Iraq isn't the central front in the war on terror," or, "Iraq is a distraction from the war on terror." I don't think it is, our troops don't think it is, and neither does Usama bin Laden. He has said that the fight in Iraq is the third world war. He has said that victory for the terrorists in Iraq will mean America's defeat and disgrace forever. That's what he said.

Oh, you hear them in Washington say, the Democrats say, that because we're fighting them in Iraq, we're creating more enemies. Well, Iraq is not the reason that the terrorists are at war with us. We weren't in Iraq when they bombed the World Trade Center in 1993. We weren't in Iraq when they attacked our Embassies in Kenya and Tanzania. We weren't in Iraq when they attacked the USS *Cole*. And we were not in Iraq on September the 11th, 2001. You do not create terrorists by fighting the terrorists. The best way to protect you is to stay on the offense and defeat the enemy overseas so we do not have to face them again here at home.

Our goal in Iraq is victory, and victory means a country that can sustain itself and defend itself and govern itself and a country which will be an ally in the war on terror against these extremists and radicals. And we've got a lot going for us. First of all, we have a plan for victory. I have given our commanders on the ground all the flexibility and all the tools they need to be able to stay ahead of the enemy. And we got a fighting force equal to none.

We got the finest United States military ever.

I understand a lot of citizens don't agree that Iraq is important for your security, but our troops understand it. Morale is high. They understand what's going on in this combat zone. They understand the stakes. And therefore, those of us in government have the full responsibility to give them all the tools they need to do the jobs that I've asked them to do. And you don't have to worry about Martinez and Miller. They understand that when we've got a man or woman in harm's way, he or she deserves all the full support of the Federal Government.

We've got something else going for us, and those are brave Iraqis. These folks have suffered unspeakable violence, and yet they're still committed to a government of, by, and for the people. You know, when they went to the polls and defied the car bombers and assassins, I was pleased, but I wasn't surprised. And the reason I wasn't surprised is because I believe in an Almighty, and I believe a great gift of the Almighty in each man and woman's soul is the desire to be free. I believe in the universality of freedom. It shouldn't surprise you when people say, "I'd rather be free than live under the hand of a tyrant."

So we'll help the Iraqis. We'll help them politically; we'll help economically; and we will continue to train their security forces so they get to take the fight to the enemy. And I want you to know, if you've got a loved one in uniform, if you've got a loved one in Iraq, I would not have your loved one there if I didn't believe that the cause was noble and just and that victory was attainable. As a matter of fact, the only way we will not win is if we leave before the job is done.

This is an important part of this campaign. It's an important part for your future. And if you listen for the plan of the Democrats, there isn't one. Oh, they've got some ideas. Some of them say, "Get out right now." Some of them say, "Get out

at a fixed date," even though the job hasn't been done. One of them said, "Let's move our troops to an island some 5,000 miles away."

Audience members. Boo!

The President. They don't have a plan, but they've got a principle around which they're organized, which is: It's too tough; get out before the job is done. That's what they believe. I'm not saying they're unpatriotic; I'm saying they're wrong. They have taken a calculated gamble. They believe the only way they can win this election is to criticize and offer no plan. It's a huge election issue, and they don't have a plan. So if you happen to bump into a Democrat candidate, you might want to ask this question: What is your plan? If they say they want to protect the homeland but opposed the PATRIOT Act, ask them this question: What's your plan? If they say they want to uncover terrorist plots but opposed listening in on terrorist conversations, ask them this question: What's your plan?

Audience members. What's your plan?

The President. If they say they want to stop new attacks on our country but opposed letting the CIA detain and question the terrorists who might know what those plots are, ask them this question: What's your plan?

Audience members. What's your plan?

The President. If they say they want to win the war on terror but call for America to pull out from what Al Qaida says is the central front in the war on terror, ask them a simple question——

Audience members. What's your plan?

The President. They don't have one. [*Laughter*] I want you to remind your fellow citizens when you ask them to go vote, harsh criticism is not a plan for victory. Second-guessing is not a strategy. We have a plan for victory, and part of that plan is to make sure Republicans control the House and the Senate.

Retreat from Iraq before the job is done would embolden the enemy and would make this country less secure. In this war,

if we were to leave before the job is done, the enemy would follow us here to America. If we leave before the job is done, it would enable these radicals and extremists to be able to recruit. If we leave before the job is done, it would dash the hopes of millions upon millions of people in the Middle East who simply want to live a peaceful existence. It would condemn them to the violent ideology of these haters. And if we were to leave before the job was done, it would dishonor the sacrifice of the men and women who have worn our uniform.

The stakes in this fight in Iraq are important, not only for today's generation but for future generations. See, the enemy has made it abundantly clear that they believe we'll leave because we're soft. They believe if they can put enough unspeakable violence on the TV screens that America will lose its nerve. They don't understand; we don't run from thugs and assassins. They believe it's a matter of time for us to leave, and they want us to so they can have safe haven from which to launch further attacks. This is what they have said. They have said that they want us to leave so they can have room to topple moderate governments, to begin to expand their ideological vision.

Can you imagine a world in the Middle East in which they controlled oil resources? And then they would say to the West, "Abandon your alliance with Israel, abandon your alliance with moderate governments, withdraw; otherwise, we'll bring you to your knees, economically." And you couple that with a country with a nuclear weapon that doesn't like us, and people will look at this period of time and say, "What happened to them in 2006? How come they couldn't see the impending danger? What clouded their vision?" I want to assure you, I see the danger. That is why we will stay in Iraq, fight in Iraq, and win in Iraq.

One of my favorite stories that I like to share with our fellow citizens is the story about the time when Laura and I went

to Elvis's place with sitting Prime Minister Koizumi of Japan. People say, "What the heck did you go there for?" [*Laughter*] I said, "Well, I hadn't taken Laura on a vacation for a while." [*Laughter*] Koizumi himself wanted to go because he was an Elvis fan. [*Laughter*] But it also tells an interesting story about the power of liberty, about the capacity of liberty to change for the better.

See, the Japanese attacked us, and thousands of young Americans, like your relatives and our dad, said, "I volunteer. I volunteer to fight for the country." It's happening today, by the way. Thousands are doing the same thing. And he went, and thousands went, and thousands died in a bloody war. And yet his son is on Air Force One flying down to Memphis, Tennessee, talking about the peace, talking about peace on the Korean Peninsula, talking about the fact that Japan had 1,000 troops in Iraq. The Prime Minister and I understand we're in an ideological struggle between extremists and people who want a better life than what they offer. And the best way to defeat the ideology of hate is with an ideology of hope. We were talking about the admonition, to whom much is given, much is required, and that's why we'll continue to lead the fight against the pandemic of HIV/AIDS. We were talking about our global responsibilities to foster peace.

Isn't that interesting? Our dad fought the Japanese, and one of his sons is talking about keeping the peace. Something happened. Japan adopted a Japanese-style democracy. The lesson is that liberty has got the capacity to transform an enemy into an ally; liberty has got the capacity to transform a region of the world that is resentful and full of hate to a region of the world full of hope. Someday, an elected leader from the United States will be sitting down with elected leaders from the Middle East talking about the peace, and a generation of Americans will be better off for it.

And those are the stakes in this election. I urge our fellow citizens to go to the polls. I urge you to do your duty in this great democracy, and that is to exercise your right as an individual to determine the course of this Nation. And as you're going into those polls, remember, if you want your taxes low, vote Republican. And as you go to the polls, remember, we're at war. And if you want this country to do everything in its power to protect you and, at the same time, lay the foundation of peace for generations to come, vote Republican.

Laura and I are so pleased you're here. Thank you for coming out. Thank you for your interest. May God bless you, and may God continue to bless the United States.

NOTE: The President spoke at 1:24 p.m. at the Pensacola Civic Center. In his remarks, he referred to former President Saddam Hussein of Iraq; and Usama bin Laden, leader of the Al Qaida terrorist organization.

Remarks at an Arkansas Victory 2006 Rally in Bentonville, Arkansas
November 6, 2006

The President. Thank you all for coming. You know, Asa, I remember landing at this airport in 2000, on the next to last event of my quest for the Presidency. I was then here to ask for your vote for me. I'm coming back, asking for you to vote and work for Asa Hutchinson.

I want to thank you for the interest in his campaign. I appreciate those of you who are putting up the signs and making the phone calls and turning out the vote.

With your help, he'll become the next Governor of Arkansas. And by the way, when you get people going into the polls, make sure they send a great United States Congressman back to Washington, John Boozman.

Laura and I are pleased to be here to support the Hutchinsons. We got to know them in Washington. One thing you have to understand is he spent time in Washington, but he never lost his Arkansas values. I guess that's because he grew up on a farm near Gra-vette—Gra-vette. No one has ever accused me of being the best English speaker in America. [*Laughter*] But I try to talk plain so people know where I'm coming from. And here's where I'm coming from: Asa Hutchinson is the right man to be your Governor.

I liked the fact that he and Susan have been married for 33 years. As a matter of fact, Laura and I celebrated our 29th wedding anniversary. She was in Crawford, and I was campaigning. [*Laughter*] We've had quite a week there. She celebrated a birthday; we celebrated the 29th anniversary; and on November the 7th, we're going to celebrate a great victory.

I like the fact that when Asa was called by his Government to come and serve, he did. See, he understands that it's important to put service ahead of self. And I gave him some hard jobs. I didn't ask him to come to Washington just to push paper; I asked him to come to Washington to fight drugs, which he did a fine job of—and to help us organize the Homeland Security Department so we can better protect you.

I like the fact that Asa is running on a good platform. See, when I was running for Governor of Texas, I said, "Education is to a State what national defense is to the Federal Government." That's what Asa thinks. The top priority of your government is to make sure every single child gets a good education. He also understands, you need a Governor who is going to be strong about eradicating methamphetamines. You need a Governor who is going to help small

businesses flourish. You need a Governor that's going to keep your taxes low. And that Governor is Asa Hutchinson.

I'm sure glad to be here with John and Cathy. I appreciate them being up here on the stage. I appreciate your service. Boozman is well-respected in Washington. People like him up there because they understand he's consistent, and he tells everybody where he stands. And the most important thing he tells me is, "You make sure you remember northwest Arkansas, Mr. President."

I want to thank State Senator Jim Holt, who's the candidate for Lieutenant Governor, joining us today. Johnny Key is with us; he's the minority leader of the Arkansas House of Representatives. Johnny, thanks for being here. I want to thank—welcome Gunner DeLay, running for attorney general. Gunner, you're just going to win on your first name alone. [*Laughter*] I want to thank Jim Lagrone, who's running for the secretary of state. Chris Morris is running for treasurer.

I want to thank all the grassroots activists who are here. I want to thank you for what you're going to do here over the next 24 hours. I appreciate the members of the Shiloh Christian Saints Band that's been with us. I want to thank the Pine Bluff Drum Line that's with us. I don't know if you noticed, but I had quite a step coming in from Air Force One, thanks to you all. I want to thank everybody else who's performed here. But I want to really thank you all. Laura and I are so pleased you came out.

See, this election is coming soon, but you've probably been reading about the fact that some of the prognosticators have already decided the outcome of the election.

Audience members. Boo!

The President. That's not the first time that's ever happened. [*Laughter*] Oh, you might remember 2004. As a matter of fact, some of them had already started to pick out their offices in the West Wing in 2004. [*Laughter*] But then the people of Arkansas

voted, and people voted all around the country, and the movers were not needed. Same thing is going to happen this year. They can prognosticate all they want; then the people get to decide. And the people of Arkansas are going to send John back to Congress and Asa to the statehouse, and we're going to control the House and the Senate.

And there's a reason why. Over the past 5 years, we have accomplished great things together. We've taken the economy from recession to one that is strong and growing. We have risen to the test of September the 11th and have taken the fight to the terrorists all around the world. In other words, we've led. We've done what the people expected us to do. There's another reason we're going to win, is because we understand the values and the principles of the American people. We don't need polls and focus groups to tell us where we stand. Our principles are the principles of the majority of the people in this country. We're going to win this election because we're right on the big issues.

You know, I knew we were going to finish strong. I knew that we were going to come roaring into election day because we got the right position on taxes, and we got the right position on what it takes to protect you from attack.

Let me first start talking about taxes. It's a big issue in this campaign. We believe that you can spend your money better than the Federal Government can spend your money. We believe when you have more of your own money in your pocket to save, spend, or invest, the economy benefits. The Democrats believe they can spend your money better than you can, and that's why they want more of it.

Audience members. Boo!

The President. We have a philosophy, but you'll be happy to hear we did more than philosophize. [*Laughter*] We acted. I signed the largest tax cut since Ronald Reagan was President of the United States.

Oh, you might remember the debate in Washington when the Democrats said the tax cuts aren't going to cause any people to find jobs; the tax cuts aren't going to help wages; and the tax cuts will cause the deficit to explode. Well, when you're out rounding up the people to vote, remind them of the facts. Our economy is strong, and it's getting better. We found out last week that the national unemployment rate is 4.4 percent. These tax cuts are working. Real wages are on the rise, and we cut the deficit in half 3 years ahead of schedule.

Whether it's here in Arkansas or around the country, there's a difference in this campaign about taxes. And one of the interesting things about these national Democrats is they're not going to tell you that they're going to raise your taxes. Let me just give you one example of what I'm talking about. They asked the lady who thinks she's going to be the Speaker—but she's not—about tax cuts. And she said on TV, "We love tax cuts." Well, given her record, she must be a secret admirer, because when it came time to reduce the marriage penalty or cut taxes on small businesses, when it came time to lower taxes on families with children, when it came time to reducing taxes on capital gains and dividends, and when it came time to getting rid of the death tax, she and her party voted no.

Audience members. Boo!

The President. If that is their definition of love—[*laughter*]—I'd sure hate to see what hate looks like. [*Laughter*]

Now here's the problem we've got if the tax cuts we passed are allowed to expire or are not made permanent—you're paying more taxes, see. Now, they're going to go around the country, and they say, "Oh, we're just going to let the tax cuts expire." That means your taxes are going up. Don't take my word for it. Take the word of the person who thinks he is going to be the head of the Ways and Means Committee, which he's not. [*Laughter*] And so

they asked him, "Could you think of any of the tax cuts that you would extend," in other words, keep in place—he said, "I can't think of a one."

Well, let me give you an example of what that means for you. Anybody here got four kids, three kids? You got four? Four. Three, okay. [*Applause*] Shhh. All right, wait, wait. [*Laughter*] I don't know why I asked that? [*Laughter*] Oh, I know why I asked it. When you're at dinner tonight— and, say, you got four kids—if the tax cuts are not extended, the child tax credit goes from $1,000 per child to 500, see. And so then you can start counting heads to determine how much the Democrats are going to raise your taxes. If you've got four children, at dinner, you can just go, one child, two, three, four, times 500. That's a $2,000 tax increase. Now that may not seem like a lot to the Democrats in Washington, but it seems like a lot to me, to Asa, and to John. And that's why you need to vote Republican to keep your taxes low. And we're closing strong in this election because the American people have finally figured out our tax cuts work, and the Democrats are going to raise your taxes.

This election is taking place at a historic time for our country. And when our children look back at this period, they're going to have one question: Did we do everything in our power to protect America and win the war on terror? That's the fundamental question facing this country, and it's a fundamental question in this campaign. I wish I could report to you here in northwest Arkansas that we were not at war, but we are. And we're at war because of what we believe and what the enemy believes. And we're at war because we stand in the way of their ambitions to spread their ideology throughout the world.

Their ideology is the exact opposite of what we believe. We believe in the right for people to worship freely. We believe in the right for people to dissent. We believe in the right for people to participate in politics. We believe in government of,

by, and for the people. They don't. There is—these are coldblooded killers. You cannot negotiate with them. You cannot hope for the best. Therapy won't work. The best way to protect you is to defeat them overseas so we do not have to face them here at home.

And so that is part of our strategy. And the other part of our strategy is to protect this homeland. I've told you Asa was a part of an important reorganization to make sure that we can respond better. Right after September the 11th, I analyzed the laws to determine whether or not our professionals had what they need to protect you. And let me talk about three examples. First, there was a wall that prevented the intelligence folks from sharing information with law enforcement. It doesn't make any sense. I understand that, but nevertheless, that was reality. You can't protect you if our folks who know what the enemy may be doing can't tell the folks on the frontline of protecting you—with that information. And so I said to Congress, "Pass the PATRIOT Act, to make sure that we can share information across jurisdictions within government." And they passed the PATRIOT Act. But I want you to remember, when this important piece of legislation—legislation necessary to protect the American people—came up for reauthorization in the United States House and in the United States Senate, the vast majority of Democrats voted no.

Audience members. Boo!

The President. You see, there's a different mindset in Washington, DC. They must think it—one, we're not at war, or it's okay to respond after we're attacked. Our view is, let's make sure we're not attacked in the first place.

I believe if Al Qaida or an Al Qaida affiliate is making a phone call into the United States of America from outside our country, we better understand why. We better make sure that we understand the intentions of the enemy. When this piece of legislation came up on the floor of the

House of Representatives—the terrorist surveillance program, it's called—the vast majority of Democrats voted no.

Audience members. Boo!

The President. Your Congressman voted yes. We picked up Khalid Sheikh Mohammed—if you haven't heard that name, he's the person our intelligence officers believe masterminded the September the 11th attacks. And my attitude is, in order to protect you, we've got to be in a position to question him. And so I authorized the Central Intelligence Agency, the professionals in the Central Intelligence Agency, to question Khalid Sheikh Mohammed. I'll tell you why. If he knew about one attack, it's conceivable he might know about another attack.

And so when it came time to vote on this valuable program that has prevented attacks on the homeland, the vast majority of Democrats voted no. And so when people go to the polls, they have got to understand that we're at war, and if you want to make sure our professionals have the tools necessary to do our most important job, which is to protect the American people, you need to vote Republican.

This is a global war fought on a variety of fronts. Where we find the enemy, we will confront them. One of the lessons of September the 11th is that when this Nation sees a threat, it must take those threats seriously, before they come home to hurt us. I saw a threat in Saddam Hussein; the United States Congress—people in both parties—saw the same threat; the United Nations saw the threat. The decision I made to get rid of Saddam Hussein was the right decision, and the world is better off for it.

On Sunday, we witnessed a landmark event in the history of Iraq: Saddam Hussein was convicted of heinous crimes on his people. This is a country which is going from the rule of a tyrant to rule of law, and we congratulate the Iraqi people. And as we do, we remember that this never would have happened without the sacrifices of the United States military.

And Iraq is the central front in this war to protect you. Oh, I've heard them in Washington. I know you have as well. They say, "Well, Iraq is just a distraction; Iraq is not a part of the war." Well, I don't believe that, our troops don't believe that, and Usama bin Laden doesn't believe that. [*Laughter*] He has called the fight in Iraq the third world war. He has said that victory for the terrorists in Iraq will mean America's defeat and disgrace forever. We need to take his words seriously. It doesn't matter what party you're in, you need to listen to the enemy.

There's people in Washington who believe that when we fight for Iraqi democracy and when we fight to adhere to the policy, "defeat them there so we don't have to face them here," it creates terrorists. In other words, it makes the world more dangerous. But I want to remind you that the reason we're at war with the terrorists is not because of Iraq. See, we weren't in Iraq when they bombed the World Trade Center in 1993. We weren't in Iraq when they bombed our Embassies in Kenya and Tanzania. We weren't in Iraq when they bombed the USS *Cole*. And we were not in Iraq on September the 11th, 2001, when they killed nearly 3,000 of our citizens.

They just think different; the Democrats have a different view of the world. It's an important part of this election. I'm going to remind our citizens, you do not create terrorists by fighting the terrorists. The best way to protect this country is to stay on the offense and bring them to justice before they can hurt us again.

Our goal in Iraq is victory, and victory means a country which can govern itself, sustain itself, and defend itself and be an ally in the war on terror. And it's hard work. It is really hard work because the enemy understands the stakes of a democracy in the midst of a region that desires for liberty. They understand that success

in Iraq will be a major blow to their desires. They also are willing to use weapons that disturb the American people, and those weapons kill innocent men, women, and children. And the reason they do so is they have no conscience, and they are convinced it's just a matter of time before the United States loses its will.

What they don't understand is—they don't understand this administration; they don't understand the American people. We're not going to run from thugs and assassins. We've got a strategy for victory where the goal is the same but the tactics constantly change. I have told our commanders, whatever it takes to get the job done you can have from Washington, DC. Our tactics are flexible. We've got great assets at our disposal, starting with the finest United States military ever assembled.

And Boozman and I understand this fact: When you have anybody in harm's way representing the United States of America, our Government must give them everything they need in order to get the job done. And I'd like to share one other thought with you. Whether or not you agreed with my decision or not to remove Saddam Hussein, you owe it to support our troops.

We got something else going for us, and those are Iraqis that want to live in a free society. These folks are suffering unspeakable violence, yet they are determined to set up a government that will reflect the will of the nearly 12 million people who voted. Let me say something. I was pleased by the vote, but I wasn't surprised. I'll tell you why I wasn't surprised. I believe that an Almighty's gift to each man, woman, and child is the desire to be free. I believe in the universality of freedom. And so we'll help this Government unify the country, we'll help their economy grow, and we will train Iraqis so they can take the fight to defend their country.

I want you to know that if you have a loved one in harm's way, that I wouldn't have your son or daughter there if I didn't believe the cause was noble and just and if I didn't believe we could win. As a matter of fact, the only way we cannot win is if we leave before the job is done.

This is a serious issue, and yet if you listen to the debate, if you listen for the plan of the Democrats, they don't have one. It's the central front in the war on terror, and they have yet to describe to the American people what they intend to do. Oh, they're beginning to give us glimpses. Some of them have said, "Just get out now." Others have said, "Let's just set a date, and then get out before the job is done." One of the leaders in the House, one of the Democrat leaders, said, "Why don't we move our troops to an island 5,000 miles away?" Nineteen of them up there, of the Democrats, introduced legislation that would cut off the funds for their troops. They don't have a plan, but they have—they're united on principle, and that is, get out before the job is done.

No, I'm not saying these folks are unpatriotic; I'm just saying they're wrong. You can't win a war unless you're willing to fight the war. They've taken a calculated gamble. They believe the only way they can win this election is to criticize and not offer a plan. You know, there's 24 hours left; they still have an opportunity to step up and tell the American people what they intend to do to prevail in this war against these terrorists.

If you happen to run into a Democrat candidate, you might ask him these questions. If they say they want to protect the homeland but oppose the PATRIOT Act, just ask them this question: What's your plan? If they say they want to uncover terrorist plots but oppose listening in on the terrorist conversation, ask them this question: What's your plan? If they say they want to stop new attacks on our country but oppose letting the CIA detain and question the terrorists who might know about those plots, ask them this question: What's your plan?

Audience members. What's your plan?

The President. Yes. If they say they want to win the war on terror but call for America to pull out from what Al Qaida says is the central front in this war on terror, ask them a simple question——

Audience members. What's your plan?

The President. They can't answer it. Harsh criticism is not a plan for victory. Second-guessing is not a strategy. We have a plan for victory. We've got a strategy to win. And part of that is to elect Republicans to the Congress and to the Senate.

Retreat from Iraq before the job is done would embolden the enemy and make this country less secure. In this war, if we were to leave before the job is done, the enemy would follow us here. These radicals and extremists would be able to recruit better. Just imagine their propaganda, when they say, "We caused the mighty United States to retreat." It would dash the hopes of millions of people in the Middle East who want to live a peaceful life. If we were to leave before the job is done, it would dishonor the sacrifice of the men and women who have worn our uniform.

This issue on the war on terror, this issue about Iraq is a vital issue. And the victory there or retreat from Iraq would be felt for generations. And that's why we want to make sure that we understand that we're not only talking about this generation but generations of Americans coming up. And I'll tell you why. The enemy has made it abundantly clear that they want us to retreat so they can have, one, safe haven from which to launch further attacks, safe havens similar to that safe haven they had in Afghanistan. Secondly, they want us to retreat so they can topple moderate governments. They want to be able to spread their ideology as far and wide as possible, and they understand our presence prevents them from doing so. Thirdly, they would like to control energy resources.

Imagine a world in which these extremists and radicals, bound together by a hateful ideology, was able to say to the West, to the United States, for example, "If you do not abandon your alliances, if you do not withdraw, we will run the price of oil up to the point that it chokes your economy." You can imagine somebody saying, "Abandon Israel, or we will bring you to your knees," or, "Get out of our way, or we'll bring you to your knees." And couple that with a country which doesn't like us with a nuclear weapon, and people will look back at this period of time and say, "What happened to them in 2006? How come they couldn't see the danger? What clouded their vision?" Well, I want you to know I clearly see the danger. That is why we will fight in Iraq and win in Iraq.

I want to share a story with you about the power of liberty. Recently Laura and I had the honor of taking our friend the former Prime Minister—he was the sitting Prime Minister at the time—of Japan—to Elvis's place. They said, "Why did you go?" Well, we hadn't been on a vacation lately. [*Laughter*] We also went because Prime Minister Koizumi liked Elvis. But I also wanted to tell a story, a tale about history and the power of liberty.

Right after the Japanese attacked Pearl Harbor, thousands and thousands of our citizens—I'm sure your relatives—volunteered to fight the enemy. See, Japan was the sworn enemy of the United States, and we fought them in a bloody war, and thousands lost their lives. And here I am on Air Force One with the Prime Minister of the former enemy talking about the peace. See, we were talking about how do we make sure the Korean Peninsula doesn't have a nuclear weapon. We were talking about the fact that Japan had 1,000 troops in Iraq, helping this young democracy. The Prime Minister knows what I know: In this ideological struggle, with extremism on one hand and reasonable folks on the other, anytime you can help a young democracy survive, you're making the world more peaceful. You're marginalizing the extremists.

We talked about this concept, that whom much is given, much is required—that's

what I believe. And we talked about how we can work together, for example, to get rid of the pandemic of HIV/AIDS on the continent of Africa. In other words, we were talking about our duties as responsible citizens of the world to lay the foundation for peace. Isn't it interesting? My dad fought the Japanese, and his son is sitting down talking about the peace with the Prime Minister of the very same country. What happened was, Japan adopted a Japanese-style democracy.

The lesson is that liberty has got the capacity to change an enemy into an ally. And liberty has got the capacity to change a region of resentment, a region that needs hope, into a place where people can realize the benefits of a rational life, where people can realize the benefits of a free society. Someday American Presidents will be sitting down with elected leaders from the Middle East talking about keeping the peace, and a generation of Americans will be better off for it.

And these are the stakes in this election. And I thank you for your interest. I ask you to go forth and find fellow Repub-licans, discerning Democrats, and open-minded independents and convince them, if you want a good Governor, vote for Asa Hutchinson. Remind them that if they want more money in their pocket, remind them if they want government that trusts you to make the right decisions with your money, you vote Republican. And remind them that we're in a tough fight against an enemy that wants to do us harm. And if you want government that responds with all assets, a government that will do everything in our capability to protect you and, at the same time, lay the foundation for peace for generations to come, vote Republican.

Thanks for coming. God bless you, and God bless America.

NOTE: The President spoke at 4:23 p.m. at the Northwest Arkansas Regional Airport. In his remarks, he referred to Cathy Boozman, wife of Rep. John Boozman; Usama bin Laden, leader of the Al Qaida terrorist organization; and former Prime Minister Junichiro Koizumi of Japan.

Remarks at a Perry for Governor 2006 Rally in Dallas, Texas
November 6, 2006

The President. Thank you all very much. Rick, thanks for the kind introduction. Let me put it to you this way: Everything I learned, I learned right here in Texas. All I've tried to do in Washington is what you expected me to do when I was your Governor: Speak plainly, make decisions based upon principles, and stand strong with Texas values.

And that is exactly what Rick Perry has done. I'm proud to be here with him. You know, one of the great comforts that I had when I left the State to head up to Washington was knowing that Rick Perry was going to be the Governor. He's optimistic.

He's done in office what he said he would do, and he's got a record. He's got a strong record to run on: Taxes are low, budgets are down, surpluses aplenty, fix the school funding issue. People are working here in the State of Texas. He passed tort reform. Rick Perry has got a record and deserves to be reelected Governor of Texas.

Laura and I are honored to be with the Perrys. You know, we've had quite a week, well, quite a couple of days. First, we had Laura's birthday. I'm not going to tell you how old she is, but we were born the same year. [*Laughter*] And 60 ain't all that bad. [*Laughter*] Then we had our 29th wedding

anniversary. And Tuesday is going to be a great victory for Republicans here in Texas.

I appreciate Anita Perry, one of the fine first ladies in our State's history. I'm proud to be here with the Lieutenant Governor, David Dewhurst. He deserves to be reelected. He's working on safe schools; he worked with the Governor to do something about school funding. He's got a strong, solid record to run on, and when you get in there to vote for Rick, make sure you vote for Dewhurst as well.

I appreciate very much that the chairman of the Railroad Commission is with us, Elizabeth Ames Jones. A lot of people around the country think the Railroad Commission has a lot to do with railroads. [*Laughter*] The Railroad Commission has got a lot to do with whether or not this State has got wealth to invest in our schools. And I appreciate her leadership, and I appreciate the leadership of my friend Commissioner Michael Williams, who is with us. The speaker of the house, from Midland, Texas, Tommy Craddick—thanks for coming, Tommy.

Rick Perry knows what I know: That we need judges who strictly interpret the law and not try to write law from the bench. I named two fantastic judges for the Supreme Court, Sam Alito and John Roberts. Rick Perry understands that, and we've got three important Supreme Court nominees with us today, actually sitting on the bench: Justice Don Willett, Justice David Medina, and Justice Dale Wainwright.

I appreciate the Members of the United States Congress who are here: Michael Burgess, Jeb Hensarling, and Michael Conaway. Thanks for coming.

But most of all, thank you all for being here. It warms our heart to be with our fellow Texans. I must say, I miss it, living here in this State. But I want you to know, for the next 2¼ years, I'm going to sprint as hard as I can to make this country as great as it can be.

We're in the home stretch of this campaign, and you all will play an important part of making sure that our fellow citizens get to the polls. When you send them to the polls, don't overlook those discerning Democrats and wise independents, by the way, because we've got a philosophy that's best for this country and for this State.

Laura and I have been traveling quite a bit, and we're enthused by the enthusiasm we see. We're closing strong because we're right on the issues. I understand you got the largest phonebank in the country here in Texas. That's what I expect. I thank you for manning it. My encouragement to you is to go out and keep dialing and get people to the polls. Send Rick Perry back to the Governor's office, and the State will be better off for it.

Oh, there's a lot of issues we differ on with the Democrats. I want to talk about two of them today. First is taxes. And there are big differences. We have a clear philosophy. We think you can spend your money better than the Government can. We believe that when you have more money in your pocket to save, invest, or spend, the entire economy benefits. Democrats believe they can spend your money better than you can. That's why they want more of it.

Audience members. Boo!

The President. But you didn't elect us just to be philosophers. You elected us to get things done. Republicans have acted on that philosophy. We delivered the largest tax cut since Ronald Reagan was the President. You should have heard the debate. Democrats said the tax cuts wouldn't create jobs; it wouldn't increase wages; and it would cause the Federal deficit to explode. Well, the facts are in. The tax cuts have led to a strong and growing economy. The unemployment rate has dropped to 4.4 percent. People are working here in Texas, and they're working around the country. Over the last 3 months, we added 480,000 new jobs. Real wages are on the rise, and we cut the deficit in half 3 years ahead of schedule. The tax cuts worked.

Taxes are an issue in this campaign. See, I'm convinced that your taxes go up when Democrats win. Now I know they don't want you to know about it. Back in Washington, the Democrats will tell you, "We love tax cuts." But given their record, they must be secret admirers. They voted against reducing the marriage penalty, voted against cutting taxes on small businesses, voted against lowering taxes for families with children, voted against reducing taxes on capital gains and dividends, and voted against putting the death tax on the road to extinction. If that's their definition for love, I'd sure hate to see what hate looks like.

Here's how it's going to work. Unless these tax cuts are extended or made permanent, your taxes go up. And the Democrat leaders have laid out their position. They asked them about whether or not the tax cuts ought to be extended, and they said they can't think of one of them, see. So all they got to say is, "Well, we're just not going to extend the tax cuts." Really what they're saying is they're going to raise your taxes. And I want you to think about what that means. For example, if the child tax credit is not extended or made permanent, your taxes are going to go up if you have children.

So, for example, anybody got four kids, here? Nelson has got five. Senator Nelson has got five children. So when you're having dinner this evening, Senator, and you're sitting around the table, just count those heads—1 child, 2, 3, 4, 5—and multiply by 500; see, the tax credit goes from 1,000 to $500 a child if the tax cuts are not extended. So you can just multiply 500 by 5, that's $2,500. That may not sound like a lot of money to people in Washington. But Rick Perry knows it's a lot of money, and I know it's a lot of money, and that's why we're going to work to keep your taxes low.

This election is taking place in an historic time for our country. And when our children and grandchildren look back on this period, one question will overwhelm all the rest: Did we do everything in our power to fight and win the war on terror? I wish I could report to you that we're not at war, but we are. We face a brutal enemy. They're bound by an ideology that's the opposite of our ideology. We believe in basic freedoms, and they don't. They also have designs to spread their ideology to the far corners of the world if they're able, and they understand we stand in the way of that. And that's why they still want to inflict harm on us.

I want to tell you something about these folks. You cannot negotiate with them; you can't hope for the best with them. The best way to protect this country is to stay on the offense and bring them to justice so they don't hurt us.

That is part of our strategy. The other part of our strategy is to protect you here at home. See, that's our most important job. Those of us who are honored to serve you have got a vital job, and that is to protect you from further attack. And so when I—after September the 11th, I reviewed the tools to see whether or not our folks had the tools necessary to guard you. Let me talk about three items. It will give you a sense about how people are thinking in Washington, and thinking around the country, by the way.

First is, there was a wall that prevented our intelligence folks from sharing information with law enforcement. Now I know that doesn't make any sense to you, but that's what happened. See, in this new kind of war, we can't protect you unless the intelligence folks whose job it is to figure out the designs and thinking of the enemy can share the information they have with the people whose job it is to stop the attacks. It's called the PATRIOT Act. It's a vital piece of legislation. It's a vital piece of legislation, but when it came up for reauthorization, the vast majority of Democrats voted against it.

Audience members. Boo!

The President. There's just a different mindset. See, they must not think we're at war, or they must think it's okay to respond after we're attacked. Our view is, let's respond before we're attacked. Let's prevent the attack from happening in the first place. If the most important job of the Government is to protect you, I thought it was vital to listen to Al Qaida or Al Qaida affiliates making phone calls from outside the United States to inside the United States. The reason why we did that is because we've got to understand what the enemy is thinking in this new kind of war. When the terrorist surveillance program was brought to a vote on the floor of the House of Representatives, the vast majority of Democrats voted against it.

Audience members. Boo!

The President. When we pick somebody up on the battlefield, we've got to be in a position to detain and question those folks. And let me give you an example why. We picked up Khalid Sheikh Mohammed; in case you haven't heard of him, he's the person our intelligence officers think masterminded the September the 11th attacks. So my attitude was, if he knew about one attack, he might know about another attack. And therefore, we've got to question Khalid Sheikh Mohammed in order to protect you. This bill came up for a vote in the House and the Senate; the vast majority of Democrats voted against it.

Audience members. Boo!

The President. It is important that our professionals have the tools necessary to protect you, and I vow that so long as I'm the President, we'll give them those tools.

This is a global war we're fighting, and we're facing the enemy on a multiple of fronts. One of the lessons of September the 11th is, when we see a threat, the United States must take those threats seriously, before they come home to hurt us. And it's a lesson all Presidents must remember. I saw a threat in Saddam Hussein; Members of the United States Congress in both political parties saw the same threat; the United Nations saw the same threat. My decision to remove Saddam Hussein was the right decision.

And on Sunday, we witnessed a landmark event in the history of Iraq. Saddam Hussein was convicted. You're watching a country evolve from the rule of a tyrant to the rule of law. And we congratulate the Iraqi people. But I also want to remind our fellow citizens the reason this verdict was able to happen in the first place was because of the skill and the sacrifice of the United States military.

And now Iraq is a central front in this war on terror. You know it's—I hear all the talk out of Washington where the skeptics say, "Well, Iraq is a diversion from the war on terror," or, "Iraq isn't that vital to the war on terror." I don't think it's true; our troops do not think it's true; and Usama bin Laden doesn't think it's true. He has said the fight in Iraq is the third world war. He has said that victory for the terrorists in Iraq will mean America's defeat and disgrace forever.

Audience members. Boo!

The President. There's a different mindset that you just got to know about. See, people have claimed that fighting the terrorists in Iraq creates terrorists. I disagree. Fighting the terrorists in Iraq is not the reason why the terrorists are fighting us. We weren't in Iraq in 1993 when they bombed the World Trade Center. We weren't in Iraq when they bombed our Embassies in Kenya and Tanzania. We were not in Iraq when they bombed the USS *Cole.* And we were not in Iraq on September the 11th, 2001. You do not create terrorists by fighting the terrorists. The best way to protect this country is to find the enemy overseas and defeat them there so we don't have to face them here at home.

Our goal in Iraq is victory. And victory means a country which can govern itself, sustain itself, defend itself, and be an ally in the war against these extremists and killers. And we're on our way to victory, but

it's a tough fight, and I know it's a tough fight, and so do you. We face a brutal enemy that is willing to kill innocent men, women, and children in order to achieve their objective. And one of their objectives is to cause us to leave Iraq. They don't believe we have the stomach for the fight. They believe that these images of carnage on our TV screens will weaken our resolve. They don't understand this administration, nor do they understand millions of our fellow citizens. We're not going to run from thugs and assassins.

We have a plan to defeat them. I talk to our commanders on the ground all the time. We give them whatever they need to achieve our objective, and we make sure our tactics are constantly adjusting to those of the enemy. So not only do we have a good plan, we've also got unbelievable people carrying out that plan. We've got the greatest military ever. And Rick Perry, who has worn the uniform, knows what I know, that any time we have an American troop in harm's way, he or she deserves all the support, all the help necessary to do the jobs I've asked them to do.

And we've got something else going for us in this vital part of the war on terror, and that is the Iraqi citizens themselves. They've suffered unspeakable violence, yet they're still committed to a government of, by, and for the people. When the nearly 12 million Iraqis voted, I was pleased, but I was not surprised. And the reason I wasn't surprised is because I believe a gift from the Almighty to each man, woman, and child is the desire to be free. I believe in the universality of freedom. I don't believe freedom is America's gift to the world; I believe it is universal. And it doesn't surprise me when people demand to be free.

It's hard work for Iraq to have a government that can defend and govern itself, but we're on our way. We've got a political plan to help them. Their economy will get help to improve, and we'll continue to train the Iraqis so they can take the fight to the few who want to stop the dreams of the many. And we will succeed. I want you to know this: If I didn't believe the cause was noble and just and if I didn't believe we can achieve our objective, I wouldn't have our troops there.

We're going to succeed, unless we leave before the job is done. And this is an important issue for our citizens around the country to think about. We've got a plan for victory. But if you listen to the debate about Iraq from the Democrats, I don't hear their plan for victory. On this vital issue, they don't have a plan. Oh, they've got some ideas. Some of them say, "Get out now." Some of them say, "Have a fixed date and get out even though the job hasn't been done." One fellow up there said we ought to move our troops to an island 5,000 miles away. No, they don't have a plan, but they got a principle, and the principle is, get out before the job is done.

Audience members. Boo!

The President. I'm not saying these folks are unpatriotic; I'm saying they're wrong.

If you happen to bump into a Democrat, you might want to ask this simple question: What's your plan? If they say they want to protect the homeland but oppose the PATRIOT Act, ask them this question: What's your plan?

Audience members. What's your plan?

The President. If they say they want to uncover terrorist plots but oppose listening in on terrorists' conversations, ask them this question: What's your plan?

Audience members. What's your plan?

The President. If they say they want to stop new attacks on our country but oppose letting the CIA detain and question the terrorists who might know about the plots, ask them this question——

Audience members. What's your plan?

The President. Yes. If they say they want to win the war on terror but call for America to pull out from what Al Qaida says is the central front in the war on terror, ask them a simple question.

Audience members. What's your plan?

The President. I want to remind you they don't have a plan. Harsh criticism is not a plan for victory. Second-guessing is not a strategy. We have a plan. Stick with us, and the country will be better off.

Retreat from Iraq before the job is done would embolden the enemy and make this country less secure. In this new kind of war, if we leave before the job is done, the enemy will follow us here. Retreating from Iraq before the job is done will enable these extremists and radicals to better recruit. Imagine their propaganda when they tell young recruits, "We have conquered the great America; we have forced them to leave before the job is done." If we leave before the job is done, millions of people—who simply want to live a peaceful life in the Middle East—hopes will be dashed. And if we leave before the job is done, it would dishonor the sacrifice of the men and women who have worn the uniform of the United States.

The consequences of retreat from Iraq will be felt for generations, and that's important for our citizens to understand, because the enemy has made it clear what their ambitions are: One, they believe we will leave so they can establish safe haven from which to launch further attacks, safe haven like they had in Afghanistan, from which they trained—of which they launched the attacks after having trained thousands of killers.

Secondly, they believe—they want us to leave so they can topple moderate governments. They want to spread their totalitarian ideology as far and wide as possible, starting in the Middle East.

Thirdly, imagine a world in which they controlled energy resources. You can just imagine the demands of the radicals and extremists to the West and to the United States. They would say things like, "Abandon Israel; otherwise, we're going to run your price of oil up and crater your economy." Or they'll say, "Withdraw, so we can establish our caliphate." And you couple all that with—and a country that doesn't

like us with a nuclear weapon, and they will look back 30 years—they'll look back and say, "What happened to them in 2006?" See, if that's the world that we allow evolve, they'll look back and say, "What happened to those folks? Could they not see the impending danger? What clouded their vision? What made it impossible for them to see—to do their duty and see the threats?" Well, I want you to know I clearly see the threat. I understand the stakes. That's why we will stay in Iraq, fight in Iraq, and win in Iraq.

If you got a second, I'd like to share one story with you. It's a story about liberty. It happened recently when Laura and I took then Prime Minister of Japan Koizumi to Elvis's place. People say, "Why did you do that?" And I said, "Well, I had never been"—[*laughter*]—"and I thought it would be fun to go, and so did Laura." Secondly, the Prime Minister wanted to go because he's an Elvis fan. Thirdly, I wanted to tell a story about the power of liberty.

After Pearl Harbor was attacked, thousands of citizens signed up to defend the country, one of whom was my dad, and I'm sure some of your relatives did the same thing. And we fought a bloody war against a sworn enemy, and thousands of people lost their lives in this war. And yet I'm on Air Force One with the Prime Minister of the former enemy talking about keeping the peace. We talked about how to prevent the Korean Peninsula from having a nuclear weapon. We talked about the fact that Japan had 1,000 troops in Iraq. The Prime Minister knows what I know: That we're involved in a grand—in a great ideological struggle between extremists and reasonable people and that when we find young democracies, we have an obligation to help those democracies survive and thrive, for the sake of peace. We talked about the admonition, to whom much is given, much is required, and I assured him we'd continue to lead the fight against the

pandemic of HIV/AIDS on the continent of Africa.

I find it interesting that my dad fought the Japanese and I'm sitting down talking about keeping the peace with the Prime Minister of the very same country. Something happened: Japan adopted a Japanese-style democracy. The lesson for all to hear is that liberty has got the capacity to change an enemy into an ally, and liberty has got the capacity to change a region of the world that is full of hate and resentment, a region of the world from which people were recruited to launch attacks against us to a place of hope.

Someday an American President will be sitting down with duly elected leaders from the Middle East talking about keeping the peace, and a generation of Americans are going to be better off for it.

This is our last stop before voting, but it's been a tradition in our family that we always end up the last stop in Texas. And there's a reason why. And there's a reason why: Because Laura and I are inspired by our fellow Texans. We appreciate the prayers that uplift us on a daily basis. We thank you for your friendship. We encourage you to vote. Send Rick Perry back to the Governor's office, please.

God bless you, and may God bless Texas and the United States.

NOTE: The President spoke at 7:09 p.m. at Reunion Arena. In his remarks, he referred to Texas State Sen. Jane Nelson; former President Saddam Hussein of Iraq; and Usama bin Laden, leader of the Al Qaida terrorist organization.

Remarks on Election Day in Crawford, Texas
November 7, 2006

Laura and I know it's a privilege to be able to cast our vote, and I encourage all Americans to vote today.

We live in a free society, and our Government is only as good as the willingness of our people to participate in it. And therefore, no matter what your party affiliation or if you don't have a party affiliation, do your duty: Cast your ballot, and let your voice be heard. So we thank you for being

a good citizen. It's good to be here voting in Texas. We're going to be heading back up to Washington here pretty soon and watch the results.

Appreciate it. Thank you all.

NOTE: The President spoke at 7:10 a.m. at the Crawford Fire Station. The Office of the Press Secretary also released a Spanish language transcript of these remarks.

The President's News Conference
November 8, 2006

The President. Thank you. Say, why all the glum faces?

Yesterday the people went to the polls, and they cast their vote for a new direction in the House of Representatives. And while the ballots are still being counted in the

Senate, it is clear the Democrat Party had a good night last night, and I congratulate them on their victories.

This morning I spoke with Republican and Democrat leadership in the House and Senate. I spoke with Republican leaders,

Senator Frist and Senator McConnell and Speaker Hastert and John Boehner and Roy Blunt. I thanked them for their hard-fought contests. I appreciated the efforts they put in for our candidates.

I'm obviously disappointed with the outcome of the election, and as the head of the Republican Party, I share a large part of the responsibility. I told my party's leaders that it is now our duty to put the elections behind us and work together with the Democrats and independents on the great issues facing this country.

This morning I also spoke with the Democrats. I spoke with Senators Reid and Durbin. I congratulated them on running a strong campaign in the Senate, and I told them that, regardless of the final outcome, we can work together over the next 2 years. I also congratulated Congresswoman Pelosi and Congressman Hoyer. They ran a disciplined campaign. Their candidates were well-organized and did a superb job of turning out their vote.

I told Congresswoman Pelosi that I look forward to working with her and her colleagues to find common ground in the next 2 years. As the majority party in the House of Representatives, they recognize that in their new role, they now have greater responsibilities. And in my first act of bipartisan outreach since the election, I shared with her the names of some Republican interior decorators who can help her pick out the new drapes in her new offices.

I believe that the leaders of both political parties must try to work through our differences. And I believe we will be able to work through differences. I've reassured the House and Senate leaders that I intend to work with the new Congress in a bipartisan way to address issues confronting this country. I invited them to come to the White House in the coming days to discuss the important work remaining this year and to begin conversations about the agenda for next year.

The message yesterday was clear: The American people want their leaders in Washington to set aside partisan differences, conduct ourselves in an ethical manner, and work together to address the challenges facing our Nation.

We live in historic times. The challenges and opportunities are plain for all to see. Will this country continue to strengthen our economy today and over the long run? Will we provide a first-class education for our children? And will we be prepared for the global challenges of the 21st century? Will we build upon the recent progress we've made in addressing our energy dependence by aggressively pursuing new technologies to break our addiction to foreign sources of energy? And most importantly, will this generation of leaders meet our obligation to protect the American people?

I know there's a lot of speculation on what the election means for the battle we're waging in Iraq. I recognize that many Americans voted last night to register their displeasure with the lack of progress being made there. Yet I also believe most Americans and leaders here in Washington from both political parties understand we cannot accept defeat.

In the coming days and weeks, I and members of my national security team will meet with the members of both parties to brief them on latest developments and listen to their views about the way forward. We'll also provide briefings to the new Members of Congress so they can be fully informed as they prepare for their new responsibilities.

As we work with the new leaders in Congress, I'm also looking forward to hearing the views of the bipartisan Iraq Study Group, cochaired by Secretary James Baker and Congressman Lee Hamilton. This group is assessing the situation in Iraq and are expected to provide—and the group is expected to provide recommendations on a way forward. And I'm going to meet with them, I think, early next week.

The election has changed many things in Washington, but it has not changed my fundamental responsibility, and that is to

protect the American people from attack. As the Commander in Chief, I take these responsibilities seriously. And so does the man who served this nation honorably for almost 6 years as our Secretary of Defense, Donald Rumsfeld. Now, after a series of thoughtful conversations, Secretary Rumsfeld and I agreed that the timing is right for new leadership at the Pentagon.

Our military has experienced an enormous amount of change and reform during the last 5 years while fighting the war on terror, one of the most consequential wars in our Nation's history. Don Rumsfeld has been a superb leader during a time of change. Yet he also appreciates the value of bringing in a fresh perspective during a critical period in this war. Don Rumsfeld is a patriot who served our country with honor and distinction. He's a trusted adviser and a friend, and I'm deeply grateful to his service to our country.

I've asked Bob Gates to serve as the Secretary of Defense. Bob is a former Director of the CIA and current president of Texas A&M University. If confirmed by the Senate, Bob will bring more than 25 years of national security experience and a stellar reputation as an effective leader with sound judgment. He's served six Presidents from both political parties and rose from an entry-level employee in the CIA to become the Director of Central Intelligence. During his service at the CIA and at the National Security Council, Bob Gates gained firsthand knowledge that will help him meet the challenges and opportunities our country faces during the next 2 years. He is serving as a member of the Baker-Hamilton commission. He's a steady, solid leader who can help make the necessary adjustments in our approach to meet our current challenges.

I will have more to say about Secretary Rumsfeld and Bob Gates later today here at the White House.

Amid this time of change, I have a message for those on the frontlines. To our enemies: Do not be joyful; do not confuse the workings of our democracy with a lack of will. Our Nation is committed to bringing you to justice. Liberty and democracy are the source of America's strength, and liberty and democracy will lift up the hopes and desires of those you are trying to destroy.

To the people of Iraq: Do not be fearful. As you take the difficult steps toward democracy and peace, America is going to stand with you. We know you want a better way of life, and now is the time to seize it.

To our brave men and women in uniform: Don't be doubtful. America will always support you. Our Nation is blessed to have men and women who volunteer to serve and are willing to risk their own lives for the safety of our fellow citizens.

When I first came to Washington nearly 6 years ago, I was hopeful I could help change the tone here in the Capital. As Governor of Texas, I had successfully worked with both Democrats and Republicans to find commonsense solutions to the problems facing our State. While we made some progress on changing the tone, I'm disappointed we haven't made more. I'm confident that we can work together. I'm confident we can overcome the temptation to divide this country between red and blue. The issues before us are bigger than that, and we are bigger than that. By putting this election and partisanship behind us, we can launch a new era of cooperation and make these next 2 years productive ones for the American people.

I appreciate your interest. Now, I'll answer some questions. Terry [Terence Hunt, Associated Press].

U.S. Armed Forces in Iraq

Q. Thank you, Mr. President. Does the departure of Don Rumsfeld signal a new direction in Iraq? A solid majority of Americans said yesterday that they wanted some American troops, if not all, withdrawn from Iraq. Did you hear that call, and will you heed it?

The President. Terry, I'd like our troops to come home too, but I want them to come home with victory, and that is a country that can govern itself, sustain itself, and defend itself. And I can understand Americans saying, "Come home." But I don't know if they said, come home and leave behind an Iraq that could end up being a safe haven for Al Qaida. I don't believe they said that. And so I'm committed to victory. I'm committed to helping this country so that we can come home.

Now, the first part about——

Q. A new direction.

The President. Oh, a new direction. Well, there's certainly going to be new leadership at the Pentagon. And as I mentioned in my comments, that Secretary Rumsfeld and I agree that sometimes it's necessary to have a fresh perspective, and Bob Gates will bring a fresh perspective. He'll also bring great managerial experience.

And he is—I had a good talk with him on Sunday in Crawford. I hadn't—it took me a while to be able to sit down and visit with him, and I did, and I found him to be of like mind. He understands we're in a global war against these terrorists. He understands that defeat is not an option in Iraq. And I believe it's important that there be a fresh perspective, and so does Secretary Rumsfeld.

Steve [Steve Holland, Reuters].

Resignation of Secretary of Defense Rumsfeld

Q. Thank you, Mr. President. Last week, you told us that Secretary Rumsfeld will be staying on. Why is the timing right now for this, and how much does it have to do with the election results?

The President. Right. No, you and Hunt and Keil [Richard Keil, Bloomberg News] came in the Oval Office, and Hunt asked me the question one week before the campaign, and basically it was, "Are you going to do something about Rumsfeld and the Vice President?" And my answer was, they're going to stay on. And the reason

why is, I didn't want to inject a major decision about this war in the final days of a campaign. And so the only way to answer that question and to get you on to another question was to give you that answer.

The truth of the matter is, as well—I mean, that's one reason I gave the answer, but the other reason why is, I hadn't had a chance to visit with Bob Gates yet, and I hadn't had my final conversation with Don Rumsfeld yet at that point.

I had been talking with Don Rumsfeld over a period of time about fresh perspective. He likes to call it fresh eyes. He himself understands that Iraq is not working well enough, fast enough. And he and I are constantly assessing. And I'm assessing, as well, all the time, by myself about, do we have the right people in the right place, or do we got the right strategy? As you know, we're constantly changing tactics, and that requires constant assessment.

And so he and I both agreed in our meeting yesterday that it was appropriate that I accept his resignation. And so the decision was made. Actually, I thought we were going to do fine yesterday. Shows what I know. But I thought we were going to be fine in the election. My point to you is, is that, win or lose, Bob Gates was going to become the nominee.

Let's see here. Bret [Bret Baier, FOX News].

Bipartisanship in Congress

Q. Thank you, Mr. President. You said you're interested in changing the tone and committed to changing the tone in Washington. Just a few days before this election, in Texas, you said that Democrats, "No matter how they put it, their approach to Iraq comes down to terrorists win; America loses." What has changed today, number one? Number two, is this administration prepared to deal with the level of oversight and investigation that is possibly going to come from one chamber or two in Congress?

The President. What's changed today is the election is over, and the Democrats won. And now we're going to work together for 2 years to accomplish big objectives for the country. And secondly, the Democrats are going to have to make up their mind about how they're going to conduct their affairs. And I haven't had a chance to talk with the leadership yet about these issues, but we'll begin consultations with the Democrat leadership starting Thursday and Friday.

David [David Gregory, NBC News].

Implications of 2006 Midterm Elections/ War on Terror

Q. Mr. President, thank you. You acknowledged that this is a message election on the war in Iraq. And so the American public today, having voted, will want to know what you mean, in terms of "course correction on Iraq." And particularly in light of this fact, that last week the Vice President pointed out that you and he aren't running for anything anymore, and that it's full speed ahead on Iraq. So which is it? Are you listening to the voters, or are you listening to the Vice President? And what does that mean?

The President. David, I believe Iraq had a lot to do with the election, but I believe there was other factors as well. People want their Congressmen to be honest and ethical. So in some races, that was the primary factor. There were different factors that determined the outcome of different races, but no question, Iraq was on people's minds. And as you have just learned, I am making a change at the Secretary of Defense to bring a fresh perspective as to how to achieve something I think most Americans want, which is a victory.

We will work with Members of Congress; we will work with the Baker-Hamilton commission. My point is, is that while we have been adjusting, we will continue to adjust to achieve the objective. And I believe that's what the American people want.

Somehow it seeped in their conscious that my attitude was just simply, stay the course. "Stay the course" means, let's get the job done, but it doesn't mean staying stuck on a strategy or tactics that may not be working. So perhaps I need to do a better job of explaining that we're constantly adjusting. And so there's fresh perspective—so what the American people hear today is, we're constantly looking for fresh perspective.

But what's also important for the American people to understand is that if we were to leave before the job is done, the country becomes more at risk. That's what the Vice President was saying. He said, "If the job is not complete, Al Qaida will have safe haven from which to launch attacks." These radicals and extremists have made it clear they want to topple moderate governments to spread their ideology. They believe that it's just a matter of time before we leave so they can implement their strategies. We're just not going to let them do that. We're going to help this Government become a government that can defend, govern, and sustain itself and an ally in the war on terror.

Yes, sir.

Q. The message today is not full speed ahead? Is that right, that it's not——

The President. We've got another man with the mike, David, please.

Robert M. Gates

Q. Mr. President, thank you. Can I just start by asking you to clarify, sir, if, in your meeting with Steve and Terry and Dick, did you know at that point——

The President. I did not.

Q. ——you would be making a change on Secretary Rumsfeld?

The President. No, I did not. And the reason I didn't know is because I hadn't visited with his replacement—potential replacement.

Q. But you knew he would be leaving, just not who would replace him?

The President. No, I didn't know that at the time.

Q. Okay. May I ask you about Nancy Pelosi——

The President. The other thing I did know, as well, is that that kind of question, a wise question by a seasoned reporter, is the kind of thing that causes one to either inject major military decisions at the end of a campaign, or not. And I have made the decision that I wasn't going to be talking about hypothetical troop levels or changes in command structure coming down the stretch.

And I'll tell you why I made that decision. I made that decision because I think it sends a bad signal to our troops if they think the Commander in Chief is constantly adjusting tactics and decisions based upon politics. And I think it's important in a time of war that, to the extent possible, we leave politics out of the major decisions being made. And it was the right decision to make, by the way.

And secondly, I hadn't visited with Bob Gates. I told you I visited with him last Sunday in Crawford. You can't replace somebody until you know you got somebody to replace him with. And finally, I hadn't had my last conversation with Secretary Rumsfeld, which I had yesterday.

Representative Nancy Pelosi

Q. Mr. President, I'd like to ask you: Nancy Pelosi has been quite clear about her agenda for the first 100 hours. She mentions things like raising minimum wage, cutting interest rates on student loans, broadening stem cell research, and rolling back tax cuts. Which of those can you support, sir?

The President. I knew you'd probably try to get me to start negotiating with myself. I haven't even visited with Congresswoman Pelosi yet. She's coming to the Oval Office later this week. I'm going to sit down and talk with her. I believe on a lot of issues we can find common ground, and there's a significant difference between common

ground and abandoning principle. She's not going to abandon her principles, and I'm not going to abandon mine. But I do believe we have an opportunity to find some common ground to move forward on.

In that very same interview you quoted, one of these three characters asked me about minimum wage. I said, there's an area where I believe we can make some—find common ground. And as we do, I'll be, of course, making sure that our small businesses are—there's compensation for the small businesses in the bill.

Q. What about tax cuts?

The President. Keil.

Vice President Cheney

Q. Thank you, Mr. President. In our discussion with you last week, which you've referenced here several times——

The President. Are you bringing this up so everybody else gets kind of jealous? [*Laughter*]

Q. Certainly. Certainly.

The President. Like Gregory, for example—he wishes he were there. [*Laughter*]

Q. This is a very competitive environment. No, but we asked you about the fate of Secretary Rumsfeld and Vice President Cheney. Vice President Cheney, of course, has made—takes many of the same positions that Secretary Rumsfeld did on the war. Does he still have your complete confidence?

The President. Yes, he does.

Q. Do you expect him to stay——

The President. The campaign is over. Yes, he does.

Q. And he'll be here for the remainder of your term?

The President. Yes, he will. Thank you.

Suzanne [Suzanne Malveaux, Cable News Network].

Bipartisanship in Congress

Q. Thank you, Mr. President. With all due respect, Nancy Pelosi has called you incompetent, a liar, the emperor with no

clothes, and, as recently as yesterday, dangerous. How will you work with someone who has such little respect for your leadership and who is third in line to the Presidency?

The President. Suzanne, I've been around politics a long time. I understand when campaigns end, and I know when governing begins. And I am going to work with people of both parties.

Look, people say unfortunate things at times. But if you hold grudges in this line of work, you're never going to get anything done. And my intention is to get some things done. And as I said, I'm going to start visiting with her on Friday, with the idea of coming together.

Look, this was a close election. If you look at race by race, it was close. The cumulative effect, however, was not too close; it was a thumping. But nevertheless, the people expect us to work together. That's what they expect. And as I said in my opening comments, there comes responsibility with victory. And that's what Nancy Pelosi told me this morning. She said in the phone call she wants to work together. And so do I. And so that's how you deal with it.

This isn't my first rodeo. In other words, I haven't—this is not the first time I've been in a campaign where people have expressed themselves and in different kinds of ways. But I have learned that if you focus on the big picture, which, in this case, is our Nation and issues we need to work together on, you can get stuff done. For example, the No Child Left Behind Act is going to come up for reauthorization. There's an area where we must work together for the sake of our children and for the sake of a competitive America. And I believe we can get a lot done. And I know it's the spirit of the new leadership to try to get a lot done, and I look forward to talking to them about it.

Rutenberg [Jim Rutenberg, New York Times].

Implications of 2006 Midterm Elections

Q. Thank you, Mr. President. You just described the election results as a "thumping."

The President. I said the cumulative—make sure—who do you write for?

Q. The New York Times, Mr. President.

The President. Oh, yes, that's right. [*Laughter*] Let's make sure we get it—the facts. I said that the elections were close; the cumulative effect——

Q. Is a thumping.

The President. ——thumping. [*Laughter*]

Q. But the results——

The President. It's a polite way of saying—anyway, go ahead. [*Laughter*]

Q. But the results are being interpreted as a repudiation of your leadership style in some quarters. I wonder what your reaction is to that. And do you—should we expect a very different White House? Should we expect a very different leadership style from you in these last 2 years, given that you have a whole new set of partners?

The President. You know, I really haven't—I'm still going to try to speak plainly about what I think are the important priorities of the country, and winning this war on terror is, by far, the most important priority. And making sure this economy continues to grow is an important priority. And making sure our children have a good education is an important priority.

Obviously, there's a shift in the Congress, and therefore, in order to get legislation passed, we've got to work with the Democrats. They're the ones who will control the committees; they're the ones who will decide how the bills flow. And so you'll see a lot of meetings with Democrats and a lot of discussion with Democrats.

And in terms of the election, no question Iraq had something to do with it. And it's tough in a time of war when people see carnage on their television screens. The amazing thing about this election, and what surprised me somewhat—which goes to

show I should not try punditry—is that this economy is strong. And a lot of times, off years are decided by the economy. And yet obviously, there was a different feel out there for the electorate. The economy—the good news in the economy was overwhelmed by the toughness of this fight and toughness of the war.

And so, Jim, look, I understand people don't agree—didn't agree with some of my decisions. I'm going to continue making decisions based upon what I think is right for the country. I've never been one to try to fashion the principles I believe or the decisions I make based upon trying to—kind of short-term popularity. I do understand where the people—the heart of the people. I understand they're frustrated. I am too, as I said the other day. I wish this had gone faster. So does Secretary Rumsfeld. But the reality is, is that it's a tough fight, and we're going to win the fight. And I truly believe the only way we won't win is if we leave before the job is done.

Yes, Jim.

Bipartisanship in Congress

Q. May I follow that, sir?

The President. I know, terrible principle. I'm sorry.

Q. Thank you, sir.

Q. [*Inaudible*]

The President. You think I'm nuts? [*Laughter*] You think my sensibility has left me as a result of working hard on the campaign trail, Gregory? [*Laughter*]

Q. But to follow, we were speaking about the war, and during the campaign, two very different viewpoints of the war came out. You spoke a lot, as Bret mentioned, about what you saw as the Democratic approach to the war, which you were greatly concerned about. Are you worried that you won't be able to work with the Democrats, or do you feel like you have to prevail upon them your viewpoint?

The President. Well, I think we're going to have to work with them, but—just like

I think we're going to have to work with the Baker-Hamilton commission. It's very important that the people understand the consequences of failure. And I have vowed to the country that we're not going to fail. We're not going to leave before the job is done. And obviously, we've got a lot of work to do with some Members of Congress. I don't know how many Members of Congress said, "Get out right now"—I mean, the candidates running for Congress in the Senate. I haven't seen that chart. Some of the comments I read where they said, "Well, look, we just need a different approach to make sure we succeed"—well, you can find common ground there.

See, if the goal is success, then we can work together. If the goal is, get out now regardless, then that's going to be hard to work together. But I believe the Democrats want to work together to win this aspect of the war on terror.

I'm also looking forward to working with them to make sure that we institutionalize, to the extent possible, steps necessary to make sure future Presidents are capable of waging this war. Because Iraq is a part of the war on terror, and it's—I think back to Harry Truman and Dwight Eisenhower. I mean, Harry Truman began the cold war, and Eisenhower, obviously, from a different party, continued it. And I would hope that would be the spirit that we're able to work together. We may not agree with every tactic, but we should agree that this country needs to secure ourselves against an enemy that would like to strike us again. This enemy is not going away after my Presidency.

And I look forward to working with them. And I truly believe that Congresswoman Pelosi and Harry Reid care just about as much—they care about the security of this country, like I do. They see the—no leader in Washington is going to walk away from protecting the country. We have different views on how to do that,

but their spirit is such that they want to protect America. That's what I believe.

Just like I talked about the troops—I meant what I said. Look, the people that's—are going to be looking at this election—the enemy is going to say, "Well, it must mean America is going to leave." And the answer is, no, that doesn't—what it means. Our troops are wondering whether or not they're going to get the support they need after this election. Democrats are going to support our troops just like Republicans will. And the Iraqis have got to understand, this election—as I said, don't be fearful. In other words, don't look at the results of the elections and say, "Oh, no. America is going to leave us before the job is complete." That's not what's going to happen, Jim.

Yes, sir, Fletcher [Michael Fletcher, Washington Post].

District of Columbia Fair and Equal House Voting Rights Legislation

Q. Thank you, sir. There's a bill that could come before the lameduck session of Congress that would extend voting rights to the District of Columbia, in Congress, and also give an extra seat to Utah. You've been passionate about democracy in Iraq. Why not here in DC, and would you support this bill?

The President. Yes, I haven't—it's the first I've heard of it. I didn't know that's going to come up from the lameduck.

Q. ——Congressman Davis's bill.

The President. Yes, well, it may or may not come up. I'm trying to get the Indian deal done, the Vietnam deal done, and the budgets done. But I'll take a look at it. It's the first I've heard of it. Thanks.

Let's see here. Yes, sir.

Iraq/Vietnam Analogy

Q. Mr. President, you mentioned the prospect that your successor would be dealing with the war. You'll be making your first trip to Vietnam in roughly a week. Some people are still—are looking at the war as another Vietnam war. Are they wrong to do so? And if so, why?

The President. I think they are. I think they are. First of all, Iraq is—after the overthrow of the tyrant, voted on a Constitution that is intended to unite the whole country. And then they had elections under that Constitution, where nearly 12 million people voted for this unity Government. Secondly—which is different from Vietnam.

Secondly, in terms of our troops, this is a volunteer army. Vietnam wasn't a volunteer army, as you know. And in this Volunteer Army, the troops understand the consequences of Iraq and the global war on terror. That's why reenlistment rates are up, and that's why enlistment is high.

Thirdly, the support for our troops is strong here in the United States, and it wasn't during the Vietnam era. So I see differences; I really do. And you hear all the time, "Well, this may be a civil war." Well, I don't believe it is, and the Maliki Government doesn't believe it is. Zal, our Ambassador, doesn't believe it is. But we've got to make sure it isn't by implementing a strategy which helps—a politics strategy which helps unify the country and a security strategy that makes sure that the Iraqis are better capable of fighting off the extremists and the radicals that want to stop progress in Iraq.

So I don't think it is a parallel.

Mike [Michael Allen, Time].

President's Decisionmaking

Q. Thank you, sir. During this campaign season, some religious conservatives expressed support and appreciation for the work you've done. But some also expressed that they felt like they expended a lot of effort on your behalf without a lot of results. I wonder if you could tell us what parts of their agenda are still on your radar screen and if you think they're right to be frustrated?

And also, Mr. President, may I ask you if you have any metrics you'd be willing

to share about your reading contest with Mr. Rove.

The President. I'm losing. I obviously was working harder in the campaign than he was. [*Laughter*]

Audience members. Oooooh!

The President. He's a faster reader.

You know, Michael, I must confess, I cannot catalog for you in detail the different criticisms. In this line of work, you get criticized from all sides. And that's okay; it's just part of the job. And so I'm not exactly sure what you're talking about, but I can tell you that I believe the faith-based and community-based—the Faith and Community-Based Initiative is a vital part of helping solve intractable problems here in America. And I would hope that I could work with Congress to make sure this program, which has been invigorated, remains invigorated.

And the reason why I believe in it so much is that there are just some problems that require something other than government help, and it requires people who have heard a call to help somebody in need. And I believe we ought to open up grants to competitive bidding for these types of organizations, and we have done that. And it's very important that that program stay strong.

But, you know, Michael, you're probably following all these—the different lists of concerns people have with my Presidency, and I respect that. I just—frankly, I'm not sure exactly what you're talking about in this question. I'm sure there are some people who aren't perfectly content, but there are some people that aren't perfectly content from different parties and different philosophies. All I know to do is to make decisions based upon principles that I believe are important, and now work with Democrat leaders in the Congress because they control the committees and they control the flow of bills. And I'm going to do that for the good of the country.

Let's see here—yes, McKinnon [John McKinnon, Wall Street Journal].

Analysis of 2006 Midterm Elections

Q. Thank you, Mr. President. If you had any do-overs to do in this race——

The President. You don't get to do them. [*Laughter*] Sorry.

Q. Or if Mr. Rove had any do-overs to do in this race——

The President. You don't get do-overs. Anyway, go ahead.

Q. Well, what would they be? I mean, are there any tactical—[*laughter*].

The President. Look, yes, well, I, frankly, haven't analyzed the election nearly as much as some of you have. You know, again, I think when you really look close at the results—first of all, there's a lot of close elections. No question, Iraq had an impact. But it's hard to win an election when you're trying to win a write-off—a write-in campaign in our State of Texas. I mean, you could have the greatest positions in the world on issues and be the most articulate person on an issue, but to try to get—to win on a write-in is really hard to do.

We had the race in Florida, the Foley seat. That's a hard race to win in a Republican district because people couldn't vote directly for the Republican candidate. And all I'm telling you, John, is that there's a—when you dig into the races, there's a—look, I had to go down to Houston, in Sugar Land, and act as the secretary of state: Take your pencil into the box and then write it in. And my only—the reason I bring that up is, I'm not sure Iraq had much to do with the outcome of that election.

Now, it certainly did in other places. One of the interesting observations I had from last night was that if you take a look at New York State, Senator Clinton ran a very strong race, but she ran a race that appeared to me to be on—just a Senate race. She wanted to show people she had the capacity to help others win. And the same thing happened in Pennsylvania with Governor Rendell. He ran a very strong race,

as did Senator-elect Casey. And my only point to you is, is that I'm sure Iraq had something to do with the voters' mind, but so did a very strong turnout mechanism in those two important States.

So they're just going to have to analyze all the different results. As far as do-overs, look, talk to them.

Ann [Ann Compton, ABC News].

Bipartisanship in Congress

Q. Americans have heard it before, "There's going to be cooperation; we're going to get along." What can you do to show Americans that there—that you'll stop and avoid any gridlock? Because they've seen it come anyway.

The President. Well, we had some pretty good success early on in this administration. We got the No Child Left Behind Act passed, which was an important piece of bipartisan legislation. We got some tax cuts passed with Democrat votes.

Q. ——partisan——

The President. Let me—I know you're anxious, but—but so we've just now got to show people we're capable of doing it. I mean, you're right; there's—people are skeptical. And the way you defeat skepticism is perform. And I was very pleased with my conversation with Congresswoman Pelosi. It was a very gracious conversation and—albeit a little early in the morning, I must confess, but nevertheless, it was a good one. And my fault, since I was the person who initiated the call.

But I do believe we can get some things done. I think we can set an agenda—I hope so. I hope so. I didn't come to Washington just to occupy the office; I came to get some positive things done on behalf of the country. And there are some big issues we got to deal with. No Child Left Behind is one. Entitlements, that's going to be an interesting issue to try to deal with. And it's going to be very important in entitlements for people to feel comfortable about bringing ideas to the table and—people being Republicans and Democrats. If we

do not have Republicans and Democrats at the table for entitlements, nothing is going to happen.

And therefore, I've instructed Secretary Paulson to reach out to folks on the Hill to see if we can't at least get a dialog started that will enable us, hopefully, to move forward on a very important issue that will affect this country for a long time if we don't solve it, and that is the unfunded liabilities inherent in these entitlement programs.

We need to continue to talk about energy. Dependency upon foreign oil is a national security and economic security problem, and it's a problem that requires bipartisan cooperation. I know the Democrats are concerned about this issue, as am I.

So, in other words, there's areas where I believe we can get some important things done. And to answer your question, though, how do we convince Americans that we're able to do it? Do it. That's how you do it. You get something done. You actually sit down, work together, and I sign legislation that we all agree on. And my pledge today is, I'll work hard to try to see if we can't get that done.

Herman [Ken Herman, Austin American-Statesman].

Analysis of 2006 Midterm Elections

Q. I wanted to ask you about the thumpin' you took at yesterday's rodeo. You said you were disappointed; you were surprised——

The President. There you go. Rutenberg, you notice that? Taking one——

Q. And that was "thumpin' " without a "g," correct? I just want to make sure we have it right for the transcript. [*Laughter*] You said you were surprised; you didn't see it coming; you were disappointed in the outcome. Does that indicate that after 6 years in the Oval Office, you're out of touch with America, for something like this kind of wave to come and you not expect it?

And on a somewhat related note, does Nancy Pelosi look much like Bob Bullock to you?

The President. [*Laughter*] That's an inside joke; I'm not commenting on it.

Secondly, I'm an optimistic person, is what I am. And I knew we were going to lose seats; I just didn't know how many.

Q. How could you not know that and not be out of touch?

The President. You didn't know it, either.

Q. A lot of polls showed it.

The President. Well, there was a—I read those same polls, and I believe that—I thought when it was all said and done, the American people would understand the importance of taxes and the importance of security. But the people have spoken, and now it's time for us to move on.

Ken [Kenneth T. Walsh, U.S. News and World Report].

Social Security Reform

Q. Mr. President, you mentioned entitlements, and one of the big, hot-button issues for the Democratic Party is Social Security and the idea of partial privatization, which you have talked about. And I wonder if there's anything in your agenda in that way that you're willing to adjust, in the spirit of bipartisanship, or back off from, given how important that is to the core of the Democratic Party?

The President. I told—Ken, I told Hank Paulson to tell the Members that we'd sit down and we'd listen to everybody's ideas. I put out my ideas, as you recall, I think in the State of the Union last time. And we want to hear their ideas. And hopefully, out of this concept of folks sitting around a table sharing ways forward, that we will come up with commonality, that we are able to then say to the American people, "We've helped solve this problem."

But this is a tough issue. Look, I fully understand how hard it is. Social Security is—people are generally risk-adverse when it comes to Social Security. My problem with that is, is that the longer you wait, the more difficult the issue is going to become. And some will keep pushing it, and hopefully, we can get something done.

Richard [Richard Wolffe, Newsweek].

National Security

Q. A little earlier, you said that you truly believe that the Democratic leaders care about the security of this country as much as you do. Yet just about at every campaign stop, you expressed pretty much the opposite. You talked about them having a different mindset——

The President. I did.

Q. ——about having a different philosophy, about waiting—about being happy that America gets attacked before responding.

The President. What did you just say, "happy"?

Q. You said they will be satisfied to see America——

The President. No, I didn't say, "happy." Let's make sure.

Q. You left that impression, forgive me.

The President. With you. Go ahead.

Q. Well, I'm wondering, looking back at the campaign and previous campaigns, do you think that it's been harder to pull the country together after the election by making such partisan attacks about national security?

The President. Richard, I do believe they care about the security. I don't—I thought they were wrong not making sure our professionals had the tools, and I still believe that. I don't see how you can protect the country unless you give these professionals tools. They just have a different point of view. That doesn't mean they don't—want America to get attacked. That's why I said what I said.

Yes, Jackson [David Jackson, Dallas Morning News].

Immigration Reform

Q. Thank you, Mr. President. On immigration, many Democrats had more positive

things to say about your comprehensive proposal than many Republicans did. Do you think a Democratic Congress gives you a better shot at comprehensive immigration reform?

The President. You know, I should have brought this up. I do. I think we have a good chance. And thank you. It's an important issue, and I hope we can get something done on it. I meant to put that in my list of things that we need to get done.

I would hope Republicans have recognized that we've taken very strong security measures to address one aspect of comprehensive immigration reform. And I was talking to Secretary Chertoff today; he thinks that these measures we're taking are beginning to have measurable effects and that catch-and-release has virtually been ended over the last couple of months. And that's positive.

And that's what some Members were concerned about prior to advancing a comprehensive bill. In other words, they said, "Show me progress on the border, and then we'll be interested in talking about other aspects." Well, there's progress being made on the border, in terms of security, and I would hope we can get something done. It's a vital issue. It's an issue that—there's

an issue where I believe we can find some common ground with the Democrats.

Q. What are the odds for a guest-worker provision?

The President. Well, that's got to be an integral part of a comprehensive plan. When you're talking comprehensive immigration reform, one part of it is a guest-worker program, where people can come on a temporary basis to do jobs Americans are not doing. I've always felt like that would be an important aspect of securing the border. In other words, if somebody is not trying to sneak in in the first place, it makes—decreases the work load on our Border Patrol and lets the Border Patrol focus on drugs and guns and terrorists. But that's a—I appreciate you bringing that up. I should have remembered it.

Listen, thank you all very much for your time. I appreciate your interest.

NOTE: The President's news conference began at 1 p.m. in the East Room at the White House. In his remarks, he referred to former President Saddam Hussein and Prime Minister Nuri al-Maliki of Iraq; U.S. Ambassador to Iraq Zalmay Khalilzad; and Gov. Edward G. Rendell and Senator-elect Robert Casey, Jr., of Pennsylvania.

Remarks on the Resignation of Secretary of Defense Donald H. Rumsfeld and the Nomination of Robert M. Gates To Be Secretary of Defense
November 8, 2006

The President. Good afternoon, and welcome to the White House. Earlier today I announced my intent to nominate Robert Gates to be the next Secretary of the Defense, and now I'm pleased to introduce him to the American people. I also am looking forward to paying tribute to the man he will succeed.

America remains a nation at war. We face brutal enemies who despise our freedom and want to destroy our way of life.

These enemies attacked our country on September the 11th, 2001. They fight us in Afghanistan and Iraq, and they remain determined to attack our country again. Against such enemies, there's only one way to protect the American people: We must stay on the offense and bring our enemies to justice, before they hurt us again.

In this time of war, the President relies on the Secretary of Defense to provide military advice and direct our Nation's

Armed Forces as they engage our enemies across the world. The Secretary of Defense must be a man of vision who can see threats still over the horizon and prepare our Nation to meet them. Bob Gates is the right man to meet both of these critical challenges.

Bob is one of our Nation's most accomplished public servants. He joined the CIA in 1966 and has nearly 27 years of national security experience, serving six Presidents of both political parties. He spent nearly 9 years serving on the National Security Council staff. And at the CIA, he rose from an entry-level employee to become the Director of the Central Intelligence. And his experience has prepared him well for this new assignment.

Bob understands the challenges we face in Afghanistan. As President Reagan's Deputy Director of Central Intelligence, he helped lead America's efforts to drive Soviet forces from Afghanistan. Success in these efforts weakened the Soviet regime and helped hasten freedom's victory in the cold war.

Bob understands the challenges facing our Nation in Iraq. He served as Deputy National Security Adviser to the first President Bush during Operation Desert Storm, as American troops repelled Iraqi aggression and drove Saddam Hussein's forces from Kuwait. More recently, he served as a member of the Iraq Study Group, a distinguished independent panel of Republicans and Democrats led by former Secretary of State Jim Baker and former Congressman Lee Hamilton. As part of this commission, he has traveled to Iraq and met with the country's leaders and our military commanders on the ground. He'll provide the Department with a fresh perspective and new ideas on how America can achieve our goals in Iraq.

Bob understands how to lead large, complex institutions and transform them to meet new challenges. As Director of Central Intelligence following the collapse of the Soviet Union, he was responsible for leading all the foreign intelligence agencies of the United States. And he's brought that same leadership and abilities as his work as president of our Nation's sixth largest university, Texas A&M. When the A&M board of regents interviewed him for the job, he described himself as an agent of change. As president, he delivered on that promise, initiating wide-ranging reforms to almost every aspect of campus life. He'll bring that same transformational spirit to his work in the Department of Defense.

Bob Gates is a patriot whose love for country was nurtured in the Kansas community where he was raised. He's worn our Nation's uniform. He's a strategic thinker who was educated at three of America's finest universities, receiving his bachelor's degree from William & Mary, a master's degree in history from Indiana University, and a doctorate in Russian and Soviet history from Georgetown.

He's a leader in the business community who served on the boards of several major corporations. He's a man of integrity, candor, and sound judgment. He knows that the challenge of protecting our country is larger than any political party, and he has a record of working with leaders of both sides of the aisle to strengthen our national security. He has my confidence and my trust, and he will be an outstanding Secretary of Defense.

Bob follows in the footsteps of one of America's most skilled and capable national security leaders, Donald Rumsfeld. Don is the longest serving member of my Cabinet, and next month, he will reach another milestone when he becomes the longest serving Secretary of Defense in the history of our Nation. I appreciate his willingness to continue serving until his successor is in place, because in a time of war, our Nation cannot be without a strong and steady hand leading our Department of Defense.

Don has served in times of great consequence for our Nation. Few will forget the image of Don Rumsfeld as he helped

rescue workers carry the victims from the rubble of the Pentagon on September the 11th, 2001. In the weeks that followed, he directed the effort to plan our Nation's military response to an unprecedented attack on our soil. Under his leadership, U.S. and coalition forces launched one of the most innovative military campaigns in the history of modern warfare, driving the Taliban and its Al Qaida allies from power in a matter of weeks.

In 2003, on my orders, he led the planning and execution of another historic military campaign, Operation Iraqi Freedom, that drove Saddam Hussein from power and helped the Iraqi people establish a constitutional democracy in the heart of the Middle East. History will record that on Don Rumsfeld's watch, the men and women of our military overthrew two terrorist regimes, liberated some 50 million people, brought justice to the terrorist Zarqawi and scores of senior Al Qaida operatives, and helped stop new terrorist attacks on our people.

America is safer and the world is more secure because of the service and the leadership of Donald Rumsfeld. As he led the Pentagon in an unprecedented war, Don never took his eye off another vital responsibility: preparing America for the threats that await us as this new century unfolds. He developed a new defense strategy. He established a new Northern Command to protect the homeland, a new Joint Forces Command to focus on transformation, a new Strategic Command to defend against long-range attack, and transformed the U.S. Special Operations Command for the war on terror.

He led our efforts to create a new NATO Response Force that allows NATO to deploy rapidly anywhere in the world. He undertook the most sweeping transformation of America's global force posture since the end of World War II. He revitalized America's efforts to develop and deploy ballistic missile defenses and led a comprehensive review of America's nuclear forces that has

allowed us to undertake dramatic reductions in offensive nuclear weapons.

Don's work in these areas did not often make the headlines. But the reforms that he has set in motion are historic, and they will enhance the security of the American people for decades to come.

Over the past 6 years, I've relied on Don Rumsfeld's advice and counsel. I've come to know his character and his integrity. As the Secretary of Defense, he has been dedicated to his mission, loyal to his President, and devoted to the courageous men and women of our Armed Forces.

Don once famously said, "There are known knowns, there are known unknowns, and there are unknown unknowns." Well, Mr. Secretary, here is a known known: Your service has made America stronger and made America a safer nation. You will be missed, and I wish you and Joyce all the best in the years to come.

Don Rumsfeld is a tough act to follow. That's why I picked a man of Bob Gates's caliber to succeed him. When confirmed by the Senate, Bob will bring talent, energy, and innovation to the Department of Defense. He'll work every day to keep the American people safe and to make our Nation more secure. And he'll do a superb job as America's next Secretary of Defense.

Bob, I appreciate you agreeing to serve our Nation again, and congratulations.

[*At this point, Secretary-designate Gates and Secretary of Defense Rumsfeld made brief remarks.*]

NOTE: The President spoke at 3:30 p.m. in the Oval Office at the White House. In his remarks, he referred to former President Saddam Hussein of Iraq; and Joyce Rumsfeld, wife of Secretary of Defense Rumsfeld. The transcript released by the Office of the Press Secretary also included the remarks of Secretary-designate Gates and Secretary of Defense Rumsfeld. The Office of the Press Secretary also released a Spanish language transcript of these remarks.

Statement on Israeli Airstrike in Gaza
November 8, 2006

The United States is deeply saddened by the injuries and loss of life in Gaza today. We send our condolences to the families of all those affected. We have seen the Israeli Government's apology and understand an investigation has begun. We hope it will be completed quickly and that appropriate steps will be taken to avoid a repetition of this tragic incident. We call on all parties to act with care and restraint so as to avoid any harm to innocent civilians.

Remarks Following a Cabinet Meeting
November 9, 2006

The President. Earlier this week, the American people went to the polls, and they cast their ballots for a new Congress. The American people made their decision. I respect the results, and so does my Cabinet. I want to congratulate the Democrat leaders on the victory they achieved for their party.

In a few minutes, Congresswoman Pelosi and Congressman Hoyer will be here for lunch. I'm looking forward to that visit. I'm also looking forward to my visit with Senator Reid and Senator Durbin tomorrow. We'll discuss the way forward for our country, and I'm going to tell him what I just told our Cabinet: It is our responsibility to put the elections behind us and work together on the great issues facing America.

Some of these issues need to be addressed before the current Congress finishes its legislative session, and that means the next few weeks are going to be busy ones. First order of business is for Congress to complete the work on the Federal spending bills for this year, with strong fiscal discipline and without diminishing our capacity to fight the war on terror.

Another important priority in the war on terror is for the Congress to pass the Terrorist Surveillance Act. We also need to pass the bipartisan energy legislation that's now before Congress. And on the foreign policy front, we need to complete the work on legislation that will allow us to cooperate with India on civilian nuclear technology and pass trade legislation that will enable us to recognize Vietnam as a member of the WTO.

As the new Members of Congress and their leaders return to Washington, I've instructed my Cabinet to provide whatever briefings and information they need to be able to do their jobs. The American people expect us to rise above partisan differences, and my administration will do its part.

One of the most important challenges facing our country is the war on terror, and Iraq is the central front in this war. Our country now has more than 149,000 men and women serving bravely in that country. Whatever party we come from, we all have a responsibility to ensure that these troops have the resources and support they need to prevail. I'm open to any idea or suggestion that will help us achieve our goals of defeating the terrorists and ensuring that Iraq's democratic Government succeeds.

Yesterday I accepted the resignation of one of the original members of my Cabinet, Secretary Donald Rumsfeld. He could not be with us today because he's at Kansas State University to deliver the prestigious Landon Lecture and to help dedicate the

university's military science building as the General Richard B. Myers Hall.

Don has been an outstanding Secretary of Defense, a trusted adviser, and a loyal friend to me and his fellow Cabinet Secretaries. I've named a good man to succeed Don Rumsfeld, former CIA Director Bob Gates. Secretary Rumsfeld has agreed to stay until Bob is confirmed, and I'm deeply grateful to Don for his service to our country.

Thank you all very much.

NOTE: The President spoke at 11:28 a.m. in the Rose Garden at the White House. The Office of the Press Secretary also released a Spanish language transcript of these remarks.

Remarks Following a Lunch With Representatives Nancy Pelosi and Steny H. Hoyer
November 9, 2006

The President. We just had a really important lunch. First, I want to congratulate Congresswoman Pelosi for becoming the Speaker of the House, and the first woman Speaker of the House. This is historic for our country. And as a father of young women, it is—I think it's important, I really do. And I appreciate Congressman Hoyer coming as well. We've had a—I would call it a very constructive and very friendly conversation.

Both of us recognize—or all three of us recognize that when you win, you have a responsibility to do the best you can for the country. I was pleased with a wide-ranging discussion about important issues facing America. The elections are now behind us, and the Congresswoman's party won. But the challenges still remain.

And therefore, we're going to work together to address those challenges in a constructive way. We won't agree on every issue, but we do agree that we love America equally, that we're concerned about the future of this country, and that we will do our very best to address big problems.

And so I want to thank you for coming. This is the beginning of a series of meetings we'll have over the next couple of years, all aimed at solving problems and leading the country. So, welcome. Congratulations again.

[At this point, Rep. Pelosi made brief remarks.]

The President. Thank you. Steny.

[Rep. Hoyer made brief remarks.]

The President. Thank you, Steny. Thank you all.

NOTE: The President spoke at 1:04 p.m. in the Oval Office at the White House. The transcript released by the Office of the Press Secretary also included the remarks of Reps. Pelosi and Hoyer.

Remarks Following Discussions With President-Elect Felipe de Jesus Calderon Hinojosa of Mexico
November 9, 2006

President Bush. It is my pleasure to have welcomed the President-elect of Mexico here to the Oval Office. I have had a fascinating and important conversation. This is a man who won a very good election. I'm proud of the Mexican people for conducting an election that is—was open and honest. We've spent a lot of time talking about vital issues. I have made it very clear to the President-elect that Mexico is a priority of this administration.

I know a fair amount about Mexico; after all, I was the Governor of Texas. I assured him that we will work very closely together. We talked about trade. We talked about mutual interests, fighting drugs, and we talked, of course, about migration. And I assured the President-elect that the words I said in the very Oval Office that we sit, about a comprehensive immigration vision, are words I still believe strongly.

And so I want to welcome you here. I wish you all the best as you—on your inauguration, on your big day. And I'm looking forward to working very closely with you.

President-elect Calderon. Yes. Thank you, Mr. President.

[*At this point, President-elect Calderon spoke in Spanish, and no translation was provided.*]

President Bush. Si, senor. Gracias.
Did you understand that?
Q. No.

[*President-elect Calderon spoke in Spanish, and his remarks were translated by an interpreter as follows.*]

President-elect Calderon. President Bush and I had a very good conversation today. And we reaffirmed the purpose that we both had, which is to strengthen the bilateral relationship between Mexico and the United States even more.

I expressed to President Bush my concern regarding the issue of migration. President Bush was very open to all the arguments that I have presented to him. And we both stressed the need to have a comprehensive vision with which we can move forward. This is, of course, an extremely important issue. It is not the only issue in our bilateral relationship.

We want to foster our trade relationship, our economic relationship even more. We both understand that the only solution to many of the problems that we have is to create well-paid jobs in Mexico. And for that, we need even more investment. We will continue to show the importance of democracy, the importance of free trade, the importance of all of these issues that will make us an even stronger nation, which will also strengthen the bilateral relationship.

And we were able to have a conversation between two people—two people who have very much in common. And we both look forward to a very constructive relationship in the future.

President Bush. Gracias. Thank you.

NOTE: The President spoke at 2:31 p.m. in the Oval Office at the White House.

Statement on the Death of Ed Bradley
November 9, 2006

Laura and I are deeply saddened by the death of Ed Bradley. For over 40 years, the American people have turned to Ed as a trusted source of information about events that have shaped our Nation. From serving as a White House correspondent to his many years as a journalist for a television newsmagazine, he produced distinctive investigative reports that inspired action and cemented his reputation as one of the most accomplished journalists of our time.

Today our thoughts and prayers are with Mr. Bradley's family and colleagues.

Message to the Congress on Continuation of the National Emergency With Respect to Iran
November 9, 2006

To the Congress of the United States:

Section 202(d) of the National Emergencies Act (50 U.S.C 1622(d)) provides for the automatic termination of a national emergency unless, prior to the anniversary date of its declaration, the President publishes in the *Federal Register* and transmits to the Congress a notice stating that the emergency is to continue in effect beyond the anniversary date. In accordance with this provision, I have sent the enclosed notice to the *Federal Register* for publication, stating that the Iran emergency declared in Executive Order 12170 on November 14, 1979, is to continue in effect beyond November 14, 2006.

Our relations with Iran have not yet returned to normal, and the process of implementing the January 19, 1981, agreements with Iran is still underway. For these reasons, I have determined that it is necessary to continue for 1 year the national emergency declared on November 14, 1979, with respect to Iran.

GEORGE W. BUSH

The White House,
November 9, 2006.

NOTE: The notice is listed in Appendix D at the end of this volume.

Remarks Following a Meeting With Senators Harry Reid and Richard J. Durbin
November 10, 2006

The President. I want to thank Senator Reid and Senator Durbin. Dick and I have had a really good discussion with them. The elections are over; the problems haven't gone away. And I assured the Senators that we will cooperate as closely as we can to solve common problems. I, of course, said this after I congratulated them on great victories. I know they were proud of their team's efforts. And they ran good campaigns, and they talked about issues that the people care about, and they won.

My attitude about this is that there is a great opportunity for us to show the country that Republicans and Democrats are equally as patriotic and equally concerned about the future and that we can work together. Senator Reid and I are both from the West. I'm from west Texas; he's from Nevada. And we tend to speak the same language, pretty plain-spoken people, which should bode well for our relationship.

So I appreciate you all coming. I'm really looking forward to working with you.

[*At this point, Sen. Reid made brief remarks.*]

The President. Thank you, sir. Dick, do you want to say something?

[*Sen. Durbin made brief remarks.*]

The President. I was hoping you would notice that. Thank you all.

NOTE: The President spoke at 12:18 p.m. in the Oval Office at the White House. The transcript released by the Office of the Press Secretary also included the remarks of Sens. Reid and Durbin.

Remarks at the Dedication Ceremony for the National Museum of the Marine Corps in Quantico, Virginia
November 10, 2006

The President. Thank you all. Thank you for the warm welcome. General Hagee, thank you for your service to our country— Secretaries of the Army and Navy and Air Force. I'm proud to be here with the Chairman of the Joint Chiefs of Staff, General Pete Pace, the first United States marine to have ever held this position. Senator Warner and Congresswoman Davis; former Governor Warner and former Senator Glenn; honored guests; veterans; General Christmas and all those responsible for this fine museum; United States marines everywhere: Please join me in wishing a very happy Marine Corps birthday to every man and woman who has ever worn the eagle, the globe, and the anchor.

As Jim Lehrer reminded you, we celebrate the 231st birthday of one of the world's premier fighting forces. And we mark the opening of our Nation's most modern military museum. For too long, the only people to have direct experience of the Marine Corps have been the marines themselves and the enemy who's made the mistake of taking them on. The National Museum of the Marine Corps fixes this

problem. In this museum, you will experience life from a marine's perspective. In this museum, you'll feel what it's like to go through boot camp—no, thanks—[*laughter*]—make an amphibious landing under fire, or deploy from a helicopter in Vietnam.

The museum will not make you into a marine—only a drill instructor can do that—but by putting you in the boots of a marine, this museum will leave you with an appreciation of the rich history of the Corps and the pride that comes with earning the title United States marine.

The history of the Corps is as important to each marine as his rifle. Every marine knows the Corps traces its founding to a Philadelphia tavern in 1775. Every marine can name the famous battles, legends, and heroes that stretch from the halls of Montezuma to the deserts of Iraq. Every marine understands that the Corps' reputation for honor and courage is a sacred inheritance from marines past and a solemn trust to be passed on to marines to come. The marines believe that you cannot know what you stand for if you do not know where

you came from, and they teach their history because they are determined to repeat it.

The history of the Corps is now preserved within these walls. Many of you here today do not need a museum to tell you this history because you wrote it yourselves with your sweat and your sacrifice in places like Tarawa, Chosin, and Khe Sahn. These walls pay tribute to your contributions to American freedom. These walls remind all who visit here that honor, courage, and commitment are not just words. They are core values for a way of life that puts service above self. And these walls will keep the history of the Marine Corps alive for generations of Americans to come. This is an important place, and I thank you for supporting it.

The museum is shaped in the form of the famous photograph of the flag raising on Iwo Jima. Iwo Jima is one of the most important battles in American history. It is fitting that Iwo Jima is one of the most important exhibits in this museum. The Japanese who defended that island had learned from costly battles that they could not defeat American forces. Yet they believed that by inflicting maximum casualties on our forces, they would demoralize our Nation and make America tire of war.

In that battle, the Japanese succeeded in taking the lives of more than 6,000 men. They did not succeed in stopping the marines from achieving their mission. And that flag that was raised on Mount Suribachi would become an enduring symbol of American resolve and a lasting icon of a democracy at war.

The history of the Corps is now being written by a new generation of marines. Since the attacks of September the 11th, 2001, more than 190,000 men and women have stepped forward to wear the uniform of the Marine Corps. Like the marines who have come before them, this new generation is serving freedom's cause in distant lands. Like the marines who have come before them, this new generation faces determined enemies. And like the marines

who have come before them, this new generation is adding its own chapters to the stories of liberty and peace. And years from now, when America looks out on a democratic Middle East growing in freedom and prosperity, Americans will speak of the battles like Fallujah with the same awe and reverence that we now give to Guadalcanal and Iwo Jima.

Like the marines who have come before them, this new generation has also given some of its finest men in the line of duty. One of these fine men was Jason Dunham. Jason's birthday is November the 10th, so you might say that he was born to be a marine. And as far back as boot camp, his superiors spotted the quality that would mark this young American as an outstanding marine: his willingness to put the needs of others before his own.

Corporal Dunham showed that spirit in April 2004, while leading a patrol of his marines in an Iraqi town near the Syrian border. When a nearby Marine convoy was ambushed, Corporal Dunham led his squad to the site of the attack, where he and his men stopped a convoy of cars that were trying to make an escape. As he moved to search one of the vehicles, an insurgent jumped out and grabbed the corporal by the throat. The corporal engaged the enemy in hand-to-hand combat. At one point he shouted to his fellow marines, "No, no, no, watch his hand." Moments later, an enemy grenade rolled out. Corporal Dunham did not hesitate; he jumped on the grenade to protect his fellow marines; he used his helmet and his body to absorb the blast.

A friend who was there that terrible day put it this way: "Corporal Dunham had a gift from God. Everyone who came in contact with him wanted to be like him. He was the toughest marine but the nicest guy. He would do anything for you. Corporal Dunham was the kind of person everybody wants as their best friend." Despite surviving the initial blast and being given the

best of medical care, Corporal Dunham ultimately succumbed to his wounds. And by giving his own life, Corporal Dunham saved the lives of two of his men and showed the world what it means to be a marine.

Corporal Dunham's mom and dad are with us today on what would have been this brave young man's 25th birthday. We remember that the marine who so freely gave his life was your beloved son. We ask a loving God to comfort you for a loss that can never be replaced. And on this special birthday, in the company of his fellow marines, I'm proud to announce that our Nation will recognize Corporal Jason Dunham's action with America's highest decoration for valor, the Medal of Honor.

As long as we have marines like Corporal Dunham, America will never fear for her liberty. And as long as we have this fine museum, America will never forget their sacrifice.

May God bless you, may God bless the Marines, and may God bless the United States.

NOTE: The President spoke at 2:12 p.m. at the National Museum of the Marine Corps. In his remarks, he referred to former Gov. Mark R. Warner of Virginia; former Sen. John H. Glenn, Jr.; Lt. Gen. G.R. Christmas, USMC (Ret.), president, Marine Corps Heritage Foundation; Jim Lehrer, anchor of PBS's "NewsHour with Jim Lehrer"; and Dan and Deb Dunham, parents of Corp. Jason Dunham, USMC, who was killed near Husaybah, Iraq, on April 14, 2004.

The President's Radio Address
November 11, 2006

Good morning. This weekend, we commemorate Veterans Day, a day when America honors every man and woman who has worn the uniform of our military. In Veterans Day celebrations across our Nation, we remember those who have served in previous wars, those who are serving today, and those who did not live to become veterans. Especially in a time of war, we see in our veterans an example of people who stepped forward to serve a cause larger than themselves. This weekend, I ask you to take a moment to thank our veterans for their service and express your appreciation for the sacrifices they have made to preserve our freedom and way of life.

One freedom that defines our way of life is the freedom to choose our leaders at the ballot box. We saw that freedom earlier this week, when millions of Americans went to the polls to cast their votes for a new Congress. Whatever your opinion of the outcome, all Americans can take pride in the example our democracy sets for the world by holding elections even in a time of war. Our democratic institutions are a source of strength, and our trust in these institutions has made America the most powerful, prosperous, and stable nation in the world.

As a result of this week's elections, the Democrats now hold a majority in both Houses of Congress. After the elections, I called the Democratic leaders in the House and the Senate to congratulate them on the victory they achieved for their party. On Thursday, I had lunch with Congresswoman Pelosi and Congressman Hoyer, and on Friday, I met with Senators Reid and Durbin. We had good discussions. I told them what I have told the men and women in my administration: We must put these elections behind us and work together on the great issues facing America.

The elections will bring changes to Washington. But one thing has not

changed: America faces brutal enemies who have attacked us before and want to attack us again. I have a message for these enemies: Do not confuse the workings of American democracy with a lack of American will. Our Nation is committed to bringing you to justice, and we will prevail.

Iraq is the central front in this war on terror. I look forward to listening to ideas from the new leaders of Congress on the best way to support our troops on the frontlines and win the war on terror. I also look forward to hearing recommendations on the way forward in Iraq from a bipartisan panel led by former Secretary of State James Baker and former Congressman Lee Hamilton. In the meantime, I have made an important change to my national security team. On Wednesday, I accepted Don Rumsfeld's resignation as Secretary of Defense and announced my intent to nominate Bob Gates to replace him. Bob is a proven leader who has served six Presidents, four Republicans and two Democrats. As a former CIA Director and the current president of Texas A&M University, he has experience leading large and complex organizations, and he has shown that he is an agent of change. As Secretary of Defense, he will provide a fresh outlook on our strategy in Iraq and what we need to do to prevail.

Bob replaces the longest serving member of my Cabinet, Don Rumsfeld. History will record that on Secretary Rumsfeld's watch, the men and women of our military overthrew two terrorist regimes, brought justice to scores of senior Al Qaida operatives, and helped stop new terrorist attacks on our people. America is safer and the world is more secure because of the leadership of Don Rumsfeld, and I am deeply grateful for his service.

The message of this week's elections is clear: The American people want their leaders in Washington to set aside partisan differences, conduct ourselves in an ethical manner, and work together to address the challenges facing our Nation. This is important work that will demand the hard effort and good faith of leaders from both sides of the aisle, and I pledge to do my part.

Thank you for listening.

NOTE: The address was recorded at 12:15 p.m. on November 10 in the Cabinet Room at the White House for broadcast at 10:06 a.m. on November 11. The transcript was made available by the Office of the Press Secretary on November 10 but was embargoed for release until the broadcast. The Office of the Press Secretary also released a Spanish language transcript of this address.

Remarks at a Veterans Day Ceremony in Arlington, Virginia
November 11, 2006

Thank you. Thanks for coming. Secretary Nicholson, thank you for your kind words and for your leadership. Members of the Cabinet; Members of Congress; members of the United State military; all veterans; all volunteers who have sworn to uphold the security of the United States: I thank your families for being here, and I thank our veterans. I am proud to join you on this day of honor.

On this day, in this month, at this hour, our Nation remembers the moment when the guns of World War I went silent, and we recognize the service and the sacrifice of our Nation's veterans. From Valley Forge to Vietnam, from Kuwait to Kandahar, from Berlin to Baghdad, our veterans have borne the costs of America's wars, and they have stood watch over America's peace. The American people are

grateful to the veterans and all who have fought for our freedom.

Since the Presidency of Abraham Lincoln, the National Cemetery has reminded our citizens of the cost of liberty. The simple white markers testify to honor fulfilled and duty served. Most of these markers stand over graves of Americans who came home to enjoy the peace they earned. Too many stand over the graves of those who gave their lives to protect that peace. This day is dedicated to all who answered the call to service, whether they live in honor among us or sleep in valor beneath this sacred ground.

On this Veterans Day, we give thanks for the 24 million Americans who strengthen our Nation with their example of service and sacrifice. Our veterans are drawn from many generations and from many backgrounds. Some charged across great battlefields. Some fought on the high seas. Some patrolled the open skies. And all contributed to the character and to the greatness of America.

On this Veterans Day, we honor a new generation of men and women who are defending our freedom. Since September the 11th, 2001, our Armed Forces have engaged the enemy, the terrorists, on many fronts. At this moment, more than 1.4 million Americans are on active duty, serving in the cause of freedom and peace around the world. They are our Nation's finest citizens. They confront grave danger to defend the safety of the American people. They've brought down tyrants; they've liberated two nations; they have helped bring freedom to more than 50 million people. Through their sacrifice, they're making this Nation safer and more secure, and they are earning the proud title of veteran.

On this Veterans Day, we're humbled by the strong hearts of those who have served. Last week, Secretary Nicholson told me about a visit he made to New York City, where he met a group of veterans who lost limbs in this war. Secretary Nicholson asked them how they could keep their spirits up. One man answered,"Sir, it is because we feel the American people are so appreciative of our service." Many of our veterans bear the scars of their service to our country, and we are a nation that will keep its commitments to those who have risked their lives for our freedom. That young man was right; we do appreciate the service of those who wear our uniform.

To help Americans show our appreciation to those who have served, Secretary Nicholson has asked all our Nation's veterans to wear their medals today. I urge our citizens to go up to those men and women and shake a hand and give a hug and give a word of thanks. I ask you to consider volunteering at a veterans hospital or a nursing home. I encourage you to work with your local veterans group to help support our troops in the field and their families here at home.

As we raise our flag and as the bugle sounds "Taps," we remember that the men and women of America's Armed Forces serve a great cause. They follow in a great tradition, handed down to them by America's veterans. And in public ceremonies and in private prayer, we give thanks for the freedom we enjoy because of their willingness to serve.

I thank you for honoring those who serve today and for honoring those who have set such a sterling example, our Nation's veterans. May God bless our veterans, may God bless all who wear the uniform, and may God continue to bless the United State of America.

NOTE: The President spoke at 11:39 a.m. in the Amphitheater at Arlington National Cemetery.

Remarks at the Groundbreaking Ceremony for the Martin Luther King, Jr., National Memorial
November 13, 2006

Thank you all very much. I'm honored to join you today in today's ceremony. I'm proud to dedicate this piece of our Nation's Capital to the lasting memory of a great man.

We have gathered in tribute to Dr. Martin Luther King, to the ideals he held, and to the life he lived. Dr. King showed us that a life of conscience and purpose can lift up many souls. And on this ground, a monument will rise that preserves his legacy for the ages. Honoring Dr. King's legacy requires more than building a monument; it required the ongoing commitment of every American. So we will continue to work for the day when the dignity and humanity of every person is respected and the American promise is denied to no one.

This project has been over a decade in the making, and I thank those who have worked to bring about this day. I particularly want to thank my predecessor, the man who signed the legislation to create this memorial, President Bill Clinton. It sounds like to me they haven't forgotten you yet. [*Laughter*] He's become, as you know, my fourth brother. [*Laughter*]

I want to thank Harry Johnson. I appreciate the members of my Cabinet who are here. I welcome the Members of Congress. I thank my mayor, Tony Williams, who is here. I'm proud to be with the members of the King family. I thank the representatives of the community and civil rights groups who have joined us. I thank the Martin Luther King, Jr., National Memorial Project Foundation board members and executive cabinet. Most of all, thank you all for coming.

Our Declaration of Independence makes it clear that the human right to dignity and equality is not a grant of government. It is the gift from the Author of Life. And Martin Luther King considered the Dec-

laration one of America's great, as he called it, "charters of freedom." He called our Founders' words, "a promise that all men— yes, black men, as well as white men— would be guaranteed the unalienable right of liberty, life, and the pursuit of happiness."

Throughout Dr. King's life, he continued to trust in the power of those words, even when the practice of America did not live up to their promise. When Martin Luther King came to Washington, DC, in the summer of 1963, he came to hold this Nation to its own standards and to call its citizens to live up to the principles of our founding. He stood not far from here, on the steps of the Lincoln Memorial. With thousands gathered around him, Dr. King looked out over the American Capital and declared his famous words, "I have a dream."

His dream spread a message of hope that echoed from his hometown of Sweet Auburn, Georgia, to the pulpit of Dexter Avenue Baptist Church to the Edmund Pettus Bridge. An assassin's bullet could not shatter the dream. Dr. King's message of justice and brotherhood took hold in the hearts of men and women across the great land of ours. It continues to inspire millions across the world.

As we break ground, we give Martin Luther King his rightful place among the great Americans honored on our National Mall. The King Memorial will span a piece of ground between the Jefferson and Lincoln Memorials. And by its presence in this place, it will unite the men who declared the promise of America and defended the promise of America with the man who redeemed the promise of America.

The memorial will reflect the arc of Dr. King's life, his search for justice, and the enduring beauty of his words. The memorial will include a wall where visitors can

read passages from Dr. King's sermons and speeches through a stream of water. And on the banks of the Potomac, visitors will walk from the Mountain of Despair to the Stone of Hope, where Dr. King's image is rendered.

Today we see only these open acres, yet we know that when the work is done, the King Memorial will be a fitting tribute, powerful and hopeful and poetic, like the man it honors. As we break ground, we remember the great obstacles that Dr. King overcame and the courage that transformed American history. The years of Martin Luther King's life were tumultuous, difficult, and an heroic time in the life of our country. Across our Nation, African Americans faced daily cruelties and pervasive wrongs. In 1955, a woman, Rosa Parks, challenged these wrongs on a bus in Montgomery, Alabama, when she refused a driver's order to give her seat to a white man. Her act of defiance inspired a young Baptist minister and changed our Nation forever.

Within days of Rosa Parks's lonely protest, Dr. King helped organize a boycott that captured the attention of our country. When Dr. King's leadership—with Dr. King's leadership, the boycott forced America to confront the glaring contradiction between the sign on the bus and the words of our Declaration of Independence. And on this date, exactly 50 years ago, the Supreme Court ruled the segregation of public buses unconstitutional. And so today we celebrate the courage that won victories and helped spark one of the greatest movements for equality and freedom in American history.

Eventually, the civil rights movement would succeed in persuading Congress to pass sweeping legislation that represented a new founding for our Nation. On July 2, 1964, President Johnson signed the Civil Rights Act at the White House. As of that date, no longer could weary travelers be denied a room in a hotel or a table at a restaurant on account of their race. And no longer could any American be forced to drink from a separate water fountain or sit at the back of the bus just because of their race.

Dr. King liked to say that our Civil Rights Act was written in the streets by citizens who marched for the idea that all men are created equal. He was right. Yet there is no doubting that the law came as it did when it did because of the courage and leadership of Martin Luther King.

As we break ground, we recognize our duty to continue the unfinished work of American freedom. America has come a long way since Dr. King's day, yet our journey to justice is not complete. There are still people in our society who hurt; neighborhoods are too poor. There are still children who do not get the education they need to fulfill their God-given potential. There's still prejudice that holds citizens back. And there's still a need for all Americans to hear the words of Dr. King so we can hasten the day when his message of hope takes hold in every community across our country.

We go forward with the knowledge that the Creator who wrote the desire for liberty in our hearts also gives us the strength and wisdom to fulfill it. We go forward with trust that God, who has brought us thus far on the way, will give us the strength to finish the journey. And we go forward with the confidence that no matter how difficult the challenge, if we remain true to our founding principles, America will overcome.

Dr. King was on this Earth just 39 years, but the ideas that guided his work and his life are eternal. Here in this place, we will raise a lasting memorial to those eternal truths. So in the presence of his family, his coworkers in freedom's cause, and those who carry on his legacy today, I'm proud to dedicate this ground on behalf of the American people as the site of the Martin Luther King, Jr., Memorial.

May God bless you all.

Martin Luther King, Jr. National Memorial Project Foundation, Inc.; and Mayor Anthony A. Williams of Washington, DC.

Remarks Following Discussions With Prime Minister Ehud Olmert of Israel and an Exchange With Reporters
November 13, 2006

President Bush. Mr. Prime Minister, welcome back to Washington. The Prime Minister and I had a fascinating discussion the last time he was here. We were sitting on the Truman Balcony. We spent probably an hour-and-a-half strategizing about how we can work together to achieve peace. Our conversation today continued this—that important dialog.

I appreciate the Prime Minister's strategic thoughts. He cares deeply about his country, and he cares deeply about securing the peace. We talked about our commitment to a two-state solution. We talked about the need for a Palestinian Government to embrace the principles of the Quartet and the roadmap, which both our governments strongly support.

We spent a great deal of time on Iran and about how we can work together with other nations of the world to convince the Iranians to abandon their nuclear weapons ambitions. I recognize the threat to world peace that the Iranians propose, as does—that the Iranians pose, as does the Prime Minister. We talked about Iraq. We talked about a variety of issues.

But the whole central thrust of our discussions was based upon our understanding that we're involved in an ideological struggle between extremists and radicals versus people who just simply want to live in peace, and that as democracies we have an obligation obviously to listen to the will of our people, but at the same time, work together to help those who want to live

in a peaceful society achieve their ambitions.

Mr. Prime Minister, it has been a delight to be with you again, and welcome back.

Prime Minister Olmert. Thank you very much. President—there's nothing that I can add to the very accurate analysis that you made with regard to these big issues. We in the Middle East have followed the American policy in Iraq for a long time, and we are very much impressed and encouraged by the stability which the greatest operation of America in Iraq brought to the Middle East. And we pray and hope that this policy will be fully successful so that this stability which was created for all the moderate countries in the Middle East will continue.

We shared thoughts about the Iranian threat. There is no question that the Iranian threat is not just a threat for Israel but for the whole world. The fanaticism and the extremism of the Iranian Government, and the fact that the leader of a nation such as Iran can threaten the very existence of another nation, as he does towards the State of Israel, is not something that we can tolerate or will ever tolerate, and certainly not when we know that he is trying to possess nuclear weapons. And I'm very encouraged by our discussion and thoughts that we have exchanged about what needs to be done in the Middle East, Mr. President.

Finally, I say time and again, on different occasions, that we want to open a serious dialog with the Chairman of the Palestinian

Authority, and I will make every possible effort to help Abu Mazen to get into such a dialog with us. Indeed, we hope that the new Government will be established soon on the basis of the Quartet and the roadmap, and that will allow an immediate contact between him and me that I'm sure will lead into a serious negotiation process.

And again, Mr. President, it's always a great joy to be your guest. And I always thank you for your friendship—your personal friendship and, even more important, your friendship for the State of Israel.

President Bush. Thank you, sir. We'll answer two questions a side. Tom [Tom Raum, Associated Press].

Iraq Study Group

Q. Mr. President, the Senate—the incoming Senate Democratic leaders have called for a phased withdrawal of troops from Iraq. You met this morning with the Baker commission. Would you accept any solution that included a timetable, and what options did you discuss this morning with the Baker commission?

President Bush. Tom, I'm not going to prejudge the Baker commission's report. I was pleased to meet with them. I was impressed by the quality of the—of their membership. I was impressed by the questions they asked. They are—they want us to succeed in Iraq, just like I want to succeed.

And so we had a really good discussion. I'm not sure what the report is going to say. I'm looking forward to seeing it. I believe this: I believe that it's important for us to succeed in Iraq, not only for our security but for the security of the Middle East, and that I'm looking forward to interesting ideas. In the meantime, General Pete Pace is leading investigations within the Pentagon as to how to reach our goal, which is success, a government which can sustain, govern, and defend itself and will serve as an ally in this war on terror.

I believe it is very important, though, for people making suggestions to recognize

that the best military options depend upon the conditions on the ground.

And so it's an interesting period here in Washington, Mr. Prime Minister. You might realize the opposition party won, won the Senate and the House. And what's interesting is, is that they're beginning to understand that with victory comes responsibilities. And I'm looking forward to working with the Democrats to achieve common objectives.

Syria-Israel Relations

Q. Mr. President, do you see any change in the administration's position regarding Syria? Do you support the resumption of Israeli-Syrian negotiations? And the same question to the Prime Minister, if I may. In the past, you rejected the resumption of the Syrian and Israeli negotiations under—one of the reasons was the rejection of the American administration regarding the policies of Syria. Do you see now, after you discuss this matter with the President, any change in your position regarding Syria?

President Bush. My answer to your question is, Prime Minister Olmert knows how to run his own foreign policy. And he can figure out his policy towards them. My policy towards Syria is this: That we expect the Syrians to be, one, out of Lebanon so that the Lebanese democracy can exist; two, not harboring extremists that create— that empower these radicals to stop the advance of democracies; three, to help this young democracy in Iraq succeed. And the Syrian President knows my position. We have told that to him through my administration. We do have an Embassy there in Syria. But our position is very clear, and we would like to see some progress toward peace from the Syrians.

Prime Minister Olmert. I share the same opinion with President Bush. We are not against negotiations with Syria. We would love to be able to have negotiations with Syria, but that must be based on a certain reasonable, responsible policy, which is not

preformed by Syria for the time being. Everything that they are doing is to the other direction: in Lebanon, in Iraq, and the sponsorship of Hamas and Khaled Meshal as the main perpetrators of terror against the State of Israel. With some changes in the Russian—I'm sorry, in the Syrian attitude on these major issues, I hope that one day the conditions for contacts between them and us will be created. But to be honest, I don't think at the present time they manifest any such attitude. And that makes it impossible.

President Bush. Matt [Matt Spetalnick, Reuters].

Iran/Nuclear Weapons Development

Q. Yes. Mr. President, Tony Blair today is going to be calling for a reaching out to both Syria and Iran to help calm the situation in Iraq. What is your response to that?

President Bush. I haven't seen his comments, but you just heard my response on Syria. And my comments on Iran is this: If the Iranians want to have a dialog with us, we have shown them a way forward, and that is for them to verify—verifiably suspend their enrichment activities. We put that proposal on the table a while back. We said that if you want to have a dialog with us, we're willing to come to the table with the EU, as well as Russia and China, to discuss a way forward. But first, you must verifiably suspend your enrichment activities.

Our focus of this administration is to convince the Iranians to give up its nuclear weapons ambitions. And that focus is based upon our strong desire for there to be peace in the Middle East. And an Iran with a nuclear weapon would be a destabilizing influence. And so we have made it very clear, our position in regards Iran, and it hasn't changed.

Q. Mr. President, do you think that it's better to impose sanctions on Iran or to handle dialog with them?

[*At this point, a reporter asked a question in Hebrew, and no translation was provided.*]

President Bush. I think it's very important for the world to unite with one common voice to say to the Iranians that, "If you choose to continue forward, you'll be isolated." And one source of isolation would be economic isolation. In other words, there has to be a consequence for their intransigence. They have—we went to the United Nations; we made it very clear— "we" being a lot of the world—have made it clear that the Iranian nuclear weapons ambitions are not in the world's interest. And therefore, if they continue to move forward with a program, there has to be a consequence. And a good place to start is working together to isolate the country.

And my hope is, is that there are rational people inside the Government that recognize isolation is not in their country's interest. And I also, when I speak about Iran, speak about a government, not about the Iranian people. I believe the Iranian people want a better way forward. I don't think they want to confront the world. I believe they need—I believe they could benefit by more trade and more openness with the world. But their leaders have to make the decision, and the decision is abundantly clear to them. And I say this in the interest of world peace, that if Iran has a nuclear weapon, it will be incredibly destabilizing and obviously threatening to our strong ally.

And so my attitude is, let's work in concert to convince the Government that it's not just the Israeli voices speaking or the United States voices speaking, but there's a lot of other voices saying the exact same thing, and present them with a choice.

Assistant Press Secretary Joshua A. Deckard. Thank you all.

President Bush. Wait a minute. That seems a little unfair. He's got a strong answer coming—I can feel it. [*Laughter*]

Prime Minister Olmert. She said it in Hebrew, and you can't blame him; he

didn't understand the Hebrew part of the question. I'll answer in Hebrew for the Israeli voters.

President Bush. Sure.

[*Prime Minister Olmert spoke in Hebrew, and no translation was provided.*]

Prime Minister Olmert. And again, I want to thank you, President Bush, for being so gracious to me and to the State of Israel.

President Bush. Yes, sir. Proud to have you here.

Thank you all.

NOTE: The President spoke at 11:45 a.m. in the Oval Office at the White House. In his remarks, he referred to James A. Baker III, cochair, Iraq Study Group; and President Bashar al-Asad of Syria. Prime Minister Olmert referred to President Mahmud Ahmadi-nejad of Iran; President Mahmoud Abbas of the Palestinian Authority; and Khaled Meshal, leader of the Hamas terrorist organization. A reporter referred to Prime Minister Tony Blair of the United Kingdom.

Message to the Senate Transmitting the Geneva Act of the Hague Agreement Concerning the International Registration of Industrial Designs
November 13, 2006

To the Senate of the United States:

With a view to receiving the advice and consent of the Senate to ratification, I transmit herewith the Geneva Act of the Hague Agreement Concerning the International Registration of Industrial Designs (the "Agreement"), adopted in Geneva on July 2, 1999, and signed by the United States on July 6, 1999. I also transmit, for the information of the Senate, a report of the Department of State with respect to the Agreement.

This Agreement promotes the ability of U.S. design owners to protect their industrial designs by allowing them to obtain multinational design protection through a single deposit procedure. Under the Agreement, U.S. design owners would be able to file for design registration in any number of the Contracting Parties with a single standardized application in English at either the U.S. Patent and Trademark Office or at the International Bureau of the World Intellectual Property Organization (WIPO).

Similarly, renewal of a design registration in each Contracting Party may be made by filing a single request along with payment of the appropriate fees at the International Bureau of WIPO. This Agreement should make access to international protection of industrial designs more readily available to U.S. businesses.

In the event that the Senate provides its consent to ratify the Agreement, the United States would not deposit its instrument of ratification until the necessary implementing legal structure has been established domestically.

I recommend that the Senate give early and favorable consideration to this Agreement and give its advice and consent to its ratification, subject to the declarations described in the accompanying report of the Department of State.

GEORGE W. BUSH

The White House,
November 13, 2006.

Remarks Following a Meeting With Chief Executive Officers of United States Automobile Manufacturers
November 14, 2006

The Vice President and members of my Cabinet—Secretary of Treasury, Secretary of Transportation—members of my staff, and I have just had a constructive and meaningful dialog with CEOs of the U.S. automobile manufacturers.

First, these leaders have—are making difficult decisions, tough choices to make sure that their companies are competitive in a global economy. And I'm confident that they're making the right decisions, and that's good news for the American people because the automobile manufacturers play such a significant part of our economy and a vital part of our employment base.

We've had a fascinating discussion about a lot of major issues that we share in common. One, of course, is rising health care costs. And I assured these leaders that the Government is addressing rising health care costs through a variety of initiatives that I think, over time, are going to make a significant difference in not only their cost but the cost to the U.S. taxpayer as well.

We talked about our mutual desire to reduce our dependence on foreign oil. Obviously, as these automobile manufacturers begin to incorporate new technologies that will enable us to power our cars in different ways, it will make it easier for me to be able to tell the American people, we're using less foreign oil. And that's in our economic interests as well as in our national security interests.

And finally, they've—these gentlemen are well aware that I'm on my way overseas this evening. And one of the issues I'll be talking about with our partners in APEC is free trade, but fair trade. And my message to our trading partners is, just treat us the way we treat you. Our markets are open for your products, and we expect your markets to be open for ours, including our automobiles.

And so we've found a lot in common. We'll have a continuing dialog. It's in our interest that in Government we find out ways that we'll be able to work to make sure that this industry is as vibrant and solid as possible. And so this is the beginning of a series of discussions we'll have, not only with me but also with people in our Government. I really do want to thank you all for coming. I appreciate you coming.

Thank you very much.

NOTE: The President spoke at 2:03 p.m. in the Oval Office at the White House. Participating in the event were Alan Mulally, president and chief executive officer, Ford Motor Co.; Thomas W. LaSorda, chief executive officer and president, Chrysler Group; and G. Richard Wagoner, Jr., chairman and chief executive officer, General Motors Corp.

Remarks Following a Meeting With the New Leaders of the Republican National Committee
November 14, 2006

I have just been meeting with the new team that's going to run the Republican National Committee. I am so proud my friend Mel Martinez, Senator from Florida,

is going to be the honorary [general]° chairman. My friend Mike Duncan from Kentucky is going to be the chairman. And Jo Ann Davidson is going to be the cochairman.

I want to thank you all very much for agreeing to serve our party. I do want to say that Ken Mehlman did a whale of a job as the chairman of the Republican Party. It's been a joy working with you. I appreciate the fact that you went to neighborhoods where Republicans have never been to talk to people about our message of ownership and hope. And I wish you all the very best.

One of the things I like to tell my friends about the Republican Party is that we're a party that really believes in entrepreneurship and small businesses and good-quality education and accountability. And Mel Martinez represents what I believe our party stands for, and that is, his parents put him on a plane to come to the United States from Cuba because they love freedom. That was Mel's first taste for the beauty of liberty and freedom. And he worked hard, started with little, and ended up being here, the United States Senator from Florida and the honorary chairman

of our party. He's going to be an excellent spokesman for the Republican Party. He'll be a person who'll be able to carry our message as we go into an important year in 2008.

And Duncan has been involved with grassroots politics for a long period of time. He comes from a Democrat State that is now a Republican State because he understands that you win votes by organizing and turning out the vote. And of course, Jo Ann has been around our party for years. And she brings a lot of stability and a lot of common sense.

And so I do want to thank you three. I'm looking forward to working with you. I'm looking forward to reminding the people that we've got plans to keep the country secure and keep our prosperity strong. And once again, I want to thank you for your service.

NOTE: The President spoke at 3:17 p.m. in the Oval Office at the White House. The Office of the Press Secretary also released a Spanish language transcript of these remarks. A tape was not available for verification of the content of these remarks.

Message to the Senate Transmitting the Malaysia-United States Treaty on Mutual Legal Assistance in Criminal Matters
November 14, 2006

To the Senate of the United States:

With a view to receiving the advice and consent of the Senate to ratification, I transmit herewith the Treaty between the United States of America and Malaysia on Mutual Legal Assistance in Criminal Matters, signed on July 28, 2006, at Kuala Lumpur. I transmit also, for the information of the Senate, the report of the De-

partment of State with respect to the Treaty.

The Treaty is one of a series of modern mutual legal assistance treaties being negotiated by the United States in order to counter criminal activities more effectively. The Treaty should enhance our ability to investigate and prosecute a wide variety of crimes. The Treaty is self-executing.

° White House correction.

The Treaty provides for a broad range of cooperation in criminal matters. Under the Treaty, the Parties agree to assist each other by, among other things: providing evidence (such as testimony, documents, items, or things) obtained voluntarily or, where necessary, by compulsion; arranging for persons, including persons in custody, to travel to the other country to provide evidence; serving documents; executing searches and seizures; locating and identifying persons, items, or places; examining objects and sites; freezing and forfeiting assets or property; and identifying or tracing proceeds of crime.

I recommend that the Senate give early and favorable consideration to the Treaty, and give its advice and consent to ratification.

GEORGE W. BUSH

The White House,
November 14, 2006.

Statement on the Upcoming State Visit of Queen Elizabeth II of the United Kingdom and Prince Philip, Duke of Edinburgh
November 15, 2006

Laura and I welcome Her Majesty Queen Elizabeth II and His Royal Highness Prince Philip, the Duke of Edinburgh, for a state visit in May 2007 to celebrate the 400th anniversary of the Jamestown Settlement. The United States and the United Kingdom enjoy an extraordinary friendship that is sustained by deep historical and cultural ties and a commitment to defend freedom around the world. We look forward to Her Majesty's state visit as an occasion to celebrate these enduring bonds.

Letter to Congressional Leaders Certifying Exports to the People's Republic of China
November 15, 2006

Dear Mr. Speaker: (Dear Mr. President:)

In accordance with the provisions of section 1512 of the National Defense Authorization Act for Fiscal Year 1999 (Public Law 105–261), I hereby certify that the export to the People's Republic of China of the following items is not detrimental to the U.S. space launch industry and that the material and equipment, including any indirect technical benefit that could be derived from such exports, will not measurably improve the missile or space launch capabilities of the People's Republic of China:

• Twelve Honeywell model HG1138 inertial measurement units to be incorporated into oil pipeline inspection equipment by the United Kingdom firm PII Group.

Sincerely,

GEORGE W. BUSH

NOTE: Identical letters were sent to J. Dennis Hastert, Speaker of the House of Representatives, and Richard B. Cheney, President of the Senate. This letter was released by the Office of the Press Secretary on November 16.

Letter to Congressional Leaders Certifying Exports to the People's Republic of China
November 15, 2006

Dear Mr. Speaker: (*Dear Mr. President:*)

In accordance with the provisions of section 1512 of the National Defense Authorization Act for Fiscal Year 1999 (Public Law 105–261), I hereby certify that the export to the People's Republic of China of the following items are not detrimental to the U.S. space launch industry and that the material and equipment, including any indirect technical benefit that could be derived from such exports, will not measurably improve the missile or space launch capabilities of the People's Republic of China:

- 110,000 pounds of fine grain bulk graphite to be distributed to seven companies in the People's Republic of China for machining into industrial components; and
- A motorized mixer with a stainless steel vacuum mixing tank to Dow Corning (Shanghai) Company in the People's Republic of China.

Sincerely,

GEORGE W. BUSH

NOTE: Identical letters were sent to J. Dennis Hastert, Speaker of the House of Representatives, and Richard B. Cheney, President of the Senate. This letter was released by the Office of the Press Secretary on November 16.

Remarks Following Discussions With Prime Minister Lee Hsien Loong of Singapore in Singapore
November 16, 2006

Prime Minister Lee. Well, I have just a few words to say. I'm very happy to have President Bush here and visiting Singapore for the second time in 3 years. We've had a very good conversation on many issues. Our bilateral relationship is excellent. We've had a very good time talking about it. We discussed what was happening in the region, what's happening in the Middle East, what's happening all over Asia, our economic matters, as well as security issues, as well as terrorism.

And on many of these areas, we not only exchanged notes but found a significant degree of matching in our views. Maybe it's because we've exchanged views so many times and we know how each other think, but I think it's also because our interests are aligned. And Singapore is very happy that America has a stake in the region and is growing the stake in the region. And we would like to help this to happen and to ensure that this continues for a long time to come.

So welcome, sir.

President Bush. Mr. Prime Minister, thanks. Thank you for your hospitality, again. Laura and I feel very comfortable in your country, and we feel comfortable in your presence. You're right, we had a wide-ranging discussion. I always benefit when I get your advice and your counsel on the neighborhood. And I think America's presence in the Far East is very important for our own country. And therefore, when you share your thoughts with me, it makes it much easier for us to conduct wise foreign policy.

We've got a lot in common, particularly our desire to continue to promote free and

fair trade, because your country has shown that open markets are capable of lifting up an entire people. And I congratulate you on your leadership, congratulate the people of Singapore for really being a model for the neighborhood.

And I'm looking forward to the dinner tonight that you're giving.

Prime Minister Lee. Thank you very much.

NOTE: The President spoke at 2:29 p.m. at the Istana.

Remarks at the National Singapore University in Singapore
November 16, 2006

Thank you very much. Good evening. Laura and I are really pleased to be back in Singapore, and I appreciate the chance to come and speak to you at this fine university. I thank the Government, the people of Singapore for such gracious hospitality. I'm particularly pleased that my friend the Senior Minister Goh and his wife are with us today. Mr. Minister, thank you for joining us.

I also had a very fine meeting with Prime Minister Lee earlier. I've come to know him as a wise man. I appreciate his good counsel. He's a friend and a partner, and he's a strong voice for peace and prosperity in Asia.

Our roots, America's roots in Singapore are deep and enduring. I don't know if you know this or not, but our first counsel to Singapore arrived in the 1830s to promote American trade in this region. His wife was the daughter of one of America's most famous patriots, Paul Revere. She came to love the city, and she came to love its people. And to show that love, she donated a bell that was cast by the Revere Foundry to the old St. Andrew's Church. The Revere bell is now in the National Museum of Singapore, and it is a symbol of the long affection between the people of our two nations.

The story of Singapore is a story of people who overcame challenges and transformed a small port city into one of the most prosperous nations on Earth. Many of you have parents or grandparents who remember riding ox carts, and now fly across the oceans from one the world's most modern airports. Some learned four national anthems over their lifetime: Britain's, Japan's, Malaysia's, and finally, Singapore's. Others recall Singapore's early days and the pessimists who predicted that a small country with no natural resources was doomed to fail.

By your effort and enterprise, you have proven the pessimists wrong. And today, Singapore has one of the most vibrant economies in the entire world. In many ways, Singapore's transformation from a small trading outpost to a confident and prosperous leader is the story of Asia. Like Singapore, this region was mired in poverty after the Second World War. Like Singapore, the region had to overcome challenges that included war and occupation and colonialism. Like Singapore, the region faced threats from movements that sought to destabilize governments and impose their ideology on others. And like Singapore, the region has overcome these challenges, and the Asia we see today is the fastest growing and most dynamic region in the world.

The United States has long recognized that it is in our interests to help expand hope and opportunity throughout Asia. And our policies have reflected this commitment for more than six decades. By opening our doors to Asian goods, America has ensured

that Asian workers and businesses and entrepreneurs would have access to the world's largest economy. By maintaining a strong military presence in the region, America has helped provide stability. And with these actions, America has helped contribute to the modern and confident Asia we see today, a region where people's incomes and opportunities are rising, where businesses compete in the global economy, and where citizens know that a world growing in trade is a world expanding in opportunity.

In this new century, America will remain engaged in Asia because our interests depend on the expansion of freedom and opportunity in this region. In this new century, our trade across the Pacific is greater than our trade across the Atlantic, and American businesses see a bright future in your thriving economies and rising middle class.

In this new century, we see threats like terrorism and proliferation and disease that have the potential to undermine our prosperity and put our futures in doubt. Amid these challenges, we hear voices calling for us to retreat from the world and close our doors to its opportunities. These are the old temptations of isolationism and protectionism, and America must reject them. We must maintain our presence in the Pacific. We must seize on our common opportunities. We must be willing to confront our common threats. And we must help our partners build more hopeful societies throughout this vital part of the world.

Building more hopeful societies starts with opening up to the opportunities of a global trading system. By opening up to trade, countries attract foreign investment they need to provide jobs and opportunities for their people. By opening up to trade, countries help attract the know-how that will enable them to compete in a global marketplace. And by opening up to trade, countries build wealth and empower their citizens.

The United States has long been committed to a global trading system that is free and that is fair. And so is Singapore. Singapore was the host of the first meeting of the World Trade Organization in 1996, where we announced an important new agreement on information technology goods. A decade later, America and Singapore are again close partners working toward a common purpose: a breakthrough in the Doha negotiations. Only an ambitious Doha agreement with real market access can achieve the economic growth and development goals that this world has set, and we look to nations across the Asia-Pacific region to help put these vital talks back on track.

To help build momentum for more open global trade, we're also opening up markets with individual nations. On this side of the Pacific, America has negotiated free trade agreements with Singapore and Australia, and we're negotiating similar agreements with Malaysia and South Korea. On the other side of the Pacific, we have successful free trade agreements with Canada and Mexico and Chile, and we've concluded negotiations with Peru. America believes in free and fair trade, and we will continue to open up new avenues to commerce and investment across this region.

Tomorrow I'm going to travel to Vietnam for the annual summit of the Asia-Pacific Economic Cooperation Forum. APEC has a vital role to play in promoting more open trading. In 1994, in Bogor, Indonesia, APEC reached an historic agreement to liberalize trade and investment throughout the region by 2020, and the United States strongly supports this goal. Recently some APEC members have advanced the idea of a free trade agreement for the entire APEC region. I believe this idea deserves serious consideration. The United States believes that APEC is the premier economic forum in the region. We believe APEC has immense potential to expand free trade and opportunity across the Pacific, and we will do our part to help APEC

become a stronger organization that serves as an engine for economic growth and opportunity throughout the region.

The remarkable economic growth that this region has achieved points to a clear lesson: The expansion of trade is the most certain path to lasting prosperity. America will continue to pursue trade at every level with individual countries, across all regions, and through the WTO. We will work to remove barriers to trade and investment, and by doing so, we will help reduce poverty and promote stability. And we will give citizens on both sides of the Pacific a brighter future.

Building more hopeful societies means working together to confront the challenges that face the entire region. Open markets and the entrepreneurial spirit have set off historic economic booms in Asia. This economic growth creates new opportunities, and yet we've got to recognize it creates new challenges. We must find the energy to power our growing economies. We must counter the risk of pandemic disease. And we must bring more people into the circle of development and prosperity. Meeting these challenges will require the effort of every nation, and you can count on the commitment of the United States.

As the economies of the Asia-Pacific thrive and expand, one of our most pressing needs will be an affordable, reliable supply of energy. Four of the world's top five energy consumers are APEC members, and the region's need for energy is going to continue to rise. The answer to this challenge is familiar in Asia: Harness the power of technology. Together, we must unleash the same spirit of innovation and enterprise that sparked the Asian economic revolution to spark a new revolution in new energy technologies.

America knows the importance of developing new energy sources because we are too dependent on a single source, and that is oil. So we're investing aggressively in clean coal technology, renewable fuels like ethanol and biodiesel, and hydrogen fuel cells. Since 2001, we've spent nearly $10 billion on clean energy technologies, and we're going to invest even more in the years to come. Across this region, we're cooperating with friends and allies to share our discoveries. We are learning from your experiences, and we're going to work together to improve new energy technologies It's in our mutual interest to do so.

This cooperation includes several key initiatives that hold the promise of a cleaner and more energy-efficient world. Through the Asia-Pacific Partnership on Clean Development and Climate, the United States is working with Australia and China and India and Japan and South Korea to share best practices and deploy new energy technologies. Last month, our partnership announced nearly 100 new projects, ranging from clean coal to renewable energy to more efficient buildings. These new technologies are helping us to improve our energy security and, as importantly, are helping to improve air quality by cutting greenhouse gas emissions.

Through the Global Nuclear Energy Partnership, America is working with other leaders in nuclear energy, like Russia and France and Japan, to help developing nations use civilian nuclear energy, while guarding against weapons proliferation. And through the APEC Biofuels Task Force, we're working with nations across the region to search for new ways to replace oil with clean fuels made from palm oil and sugar cane and other natural products.

My hope is that the investments that we make today will enable you to drive different kind of automobiles and to heat your homes and air-condition your homes using different sources of energy. It's in the world's interest that we work together to end our addiction from oil.

Keeping our economies growing also requires protecting the health of our people. Four years ago, we saw the SARS virus inflict terrible damage on Asian-Pacific economies, a virus that claimed the lives of hundreds of people all across the world.

Now this region faces a new threat of avian flu, and we're working together to address that threat. Vietnam was recently among the nations hardest hit by avian flu. Then Vietnam's leaders started to share information with the international community and improve monitoring and public awareness and take the difficult step of culling birds that might be infected. Vietnam's decisive actions have paid off. When I arrive in Hanoi for the APEC summit tomorrow, the country will have gone more than a year without a human case of avian flu. Our strategy is beginning to work.

At our summit, leaders will reaffirm our mutual responsibilities to report new avian flu cases, to contain the spread of animal outbreaks, and to follow wise preparedness plans. We've taken the important steps to stop the spread of avian flu, but we must continue to increase cooperation to ensure that if the pandemic ever does break out, the world will be ready to deal with it.

America has committed over $15 billion to fight the spread of HIV/AIDS across the world. Today, Vietnam has an estimated 280,000 citizens who suffer from this deadly virus, and many more who are in danger of becoming infected. Through our Emergency Plan for AIDS Relief, we're working with Vietnam to do something about it. We've launched an ambitious 5-year program to help Vietnam meet three clear goals: to support treatment for 22,000 people, to support care for 110,000 people, and to support testing and prevention for 660,000 people.

Since 2004, we've provided more than $138 million for this plan. We've helped bring relief to thousands of Vietnamese. It is in our interest to help defeat the spread of HIV/AIDS. This is a global challenge that grows daily and must be confronted directly. And I look forward to working with our Asian partners to do our duty to defeat this disease.

Our partners also know they can count on the United States when a disaster strikes suddenly. After the tsunami struck in 2004,

we quickly dispatched military assistance and humanitarian relief to save lives and help devastated communities rebuild. By coming to the aid of people in dire need, America showed the good heart of our citizens and the depth of our friendship in this region.

Our commitments extend far beyond responding to disaster, and they must if we expect this world to be peaceful and prosperous. We're helping countries like the Philippines and Indonesia to provide their children an education that prepares them to succeed in the global economy. My administration started a new and bold foreign policy—foreign aid initiative called the Millennium Challenge Account. The United States will provide financial assistance to developing nations that govern justly—in other words, fight corruption—that invest in their people and enforce the rule of law. We've signed a Millennium Challenge threshold agreement with the Philippines. We will soon begin discussions with Peru. And tomorrow we will sign an agreement with Indonesia. By providing governments that are committed to reform vital aid, we will help bring this region closer to a day when the benefits of economic growth and prosperity reach every citizen.

America has a clear approach to the challenges of the Asia-Pacific region. We believe that alleviating poverty and fighting disease and harnessing the benefits of technology require partnership, not paternalism. And the United States makes this pledge: Every nation that works to advance prosperity, health, and opportunity for all its people will find a ready partner in the United States.

Building more hopeful societies depends on a foundation of security. At the start of this young century, the nations of the Asia-Pacific region face a profound challenge: The same technology and global openness that have transformed our lives also threaten our lives. The same innovations that make it easier to build cars and computers make it easier to build weapons

of mass destruction. The same advances in international transportation and finance that allow a manufacturer in Singapore to sell electronics to a store in San Francisco would also allow a proliferating regime in the Far East to sell dangerous technologies to a terrorist organization in the Middle East.

The danger is unmistakable. In an age of unprecedented technological advances, irresponsible behavior by a few can have catastrophic consequences for the entire world. The people of this region understand the threat that the world faces because they have been the targets of terrorist violence. The terrorists have attacked a nightclub in Bali, a hotel in Jakarta, a ferry packed with passengers in Manila Bay, a school full of children in Russia, Australia's Embassy in Indonesia, and other targets.

The killers who committed these acts of terror are more than criminals; they are followers of a clear and focused ideology that hates freedom and rejects tolerance and despises all dissent. Their stated goal is to establish a totalitarian Islamic empire stretching from Europe to Southeast Asia. The greatest danger in our world today is that these terrorists could get their hands on weapons of mass destruction and use them to blackmail free nations or to kill on an unimaginable scale. This threat poses a risk to our entire civilization, and all our nations must work together to defeat it.

In this region, the most immediate threat of proliferation comes from North Korea. America's position is clear: The transfer of nuclear weapons or materiel by North Korea to states or non-state entities would be considered a grave threat to the United States, and we would hold North Korea fully accountable for the consequences of such action. For the sake of peace, it is vital that the nations of this region send a message to North Korea that the proliferation of nuclear technology to hostile regimes or terrorist networks will not be tolerated.

After North Korea's recent nuclear test, the United Nations Security Council passed a unanimous resolution making it clear that the regime's pursuit of nuclear weapons is unacceptable. The resolution imposes sanctions on North Korea's regime, and America will work with our partners to enforce those sanctions. We'll also continue working with Japan and China and South Korea and Russia through the six-party talks. Our nations are speaking with one voice: The only way for North Korea to move forward, for the good of their people, is to abandon its nuclear weapons programs and rejoin the international community.

North Korea recently took an encouraging step when it agreed to come back to the table and restart the six-party talks. The United States wants these talks to be successful, and we will do our part. If North Korea chooses a peaceful path, America and our partners in the six-party talks are prepared to provide security assurances, economic assistance, and other benefits to the North Korean people.

Ultimately, the success of these talks depends on the regime in North Korea. Pyongyang must show it is serious by taking concrete steps to implement its agreement to give up its nuclear weapons and weapons programs.

As we work for a Korean Peninsula free of nuclear weapons, we're also strengthening defense cooperation in the Asia-Pacific region. Unlike Europe, where our security cooperation takes place through the NATO alliance, America's security cooperation in Asia takes place largely through bilateral defense relations.

America places the highest value on these partnerships. We're committed to strengthening our existing partnerships and to building new ones. With Japan, we continue to work closely to field a missile defense system to protect both our countries and others in the region from rogue regimes threatening blackmail and/or destruction. With South Korea, we have upgraded our deterrent capabilities, while reducing

our footprint and repositioning U.S. troops stationed in the country. With Australia, we're working to improve joint training of our forces and increase cooperation in areas such as intelligence and missile defense research. With the Philippines, we're working to improve the capabilities of the nation's armed forces to fight terrorism and other threats. With India, we signed an historic agreement to expand defense cooperation, increase joint exercises, and improve intelligence sharing. With Vietnam, our Navy has made four port calls over the past 3 years, the first visits by U.S. military ships since the Vietnam war. And with Singapore, we signed a new strategic framework agreement that provides for joint military exercises and cooperation in military research and development.

By building new defense relationships and strengthening existing alliances, we are ensuring that the forces of freedom and moderation in this region can defend themselves against the forces of terror and extremism.

In addition to these bilateral defense relationships, America welcomes the growing multilateral security cooperation in this region. Today, Singapore, Malaysia, Thailand, and Indonesia are coordinating patrols in the Strait of Malaka and working to combat terrorism, piracy, and human trafficking. Through the Proliferation Security Initiative, 80 countries are cooperating to stop the spread of weapons of mass destruction and related materiel through air, land, and sea. APEC members know that advancing trade and opportunity throughout the Pacific requires safe travel and transport, so we will continue to work together to improve the security of our ports and airports and transportation routes.

With all these efforts, the nations of this region are answering the threats of the 21st century. And in doing so, we are laying the foundation of security and peace for generations to come. In the long run, the surest path to security is the expansion of liberty and freedom. History shows that free societies are peaceful societies. Democracies do not attack each other. Governments accountable to voters focus on building roads and schools, not weapons of mass destruction. Young people who have a say in their future are less likely to search for meaning in extremism. And nations that commit to freedom for their people don't support terrorists and extremists but, in fact, will join together to defeat them.

America is committed to advancing freedom and democracy as the great alternatives to repression and radicalism. We will take the side of democratic leaders and reformers. We will support the voices of tolerance and moderation across the world. We will stand with the mothers and fathers in every culture who want to see their children grow up in a caring and peaceful society.

We recognize that every democracy will reflect the unique culture and history of its people. Yet we recognize that there are universal freedoms, that there are God-given rights for every man, woman, and child on the face of this Earth. The people of Asia have faith in the power of freedom because you've seen freedom transform nations across your continent.

At the beginning of World War II, this side of the Pacific had only two democracies: Australia and New Zealand. Today, millions of Asians live in freedom. Freedom has unleashed the creative talents of people throughout Asia. Freedom has helped prosperity sweep across the region.

In all that lies ahead, the people of this region will have a partner in the American Government and a friend in the American people. Together, the people of America and Asia have endured dark and uncertain hours. Together, we've seen modern nations rise from the rubble of war and launch dynamic economies that are the envy of the world. Together, we will confront the challenges of the new century and build a more hopeful and peaceful and prosperous future for our children and our grandchildren.

I appreciate your hospitality. Thank you for letting me come by and share some thoughts with you. May God bless the people of Singapore.

NOTE: The President spoke at 6:04 p.m. in the University Cultural Centre Theatre. In his remarks, he referred to Senior Minister Goh Chok Tong of Singapore, and his wife, Tan Choo Leng; and Prime Minister Lee Hsien Loong of Singapore.

Remarks at a Dinner Hosted by Prime Minister Lee Hsien Loong of Singapore in Singapore
November 16, 2006

President Bush. Thank you all. Mr. Prime Minister and Ms. Lee, thank you very much for your gracious hospitality. Laura and I are thrilled to be back here. I'm always amazed when I think about Singapore, a country that wasn't supposed to be; a part of the world where people basically said, "There's no chance for the good folks to survive and thrive." I'm amazed at your successes, and I appreciate the values on which your successes rest.

I congratulate the people of Singapore for being such a vivid example of enterprise and markets and hard work. I congratulate the Government for being visionary in its leadership. And I am thrilled that you allowed me to give a speech at one of your fine universities, talking about the importance of the Far East to the future of the United States.

I thank you very much for serving that meat. [*Laughter*] It was so good, it had to be from Texas. [*Laughter*]

The Prime Minister and I have had a lot of discussions about a variety of issues, and I shared with them one of my chief concerns, that our country would become—could possibly become isolationist and protectionist. In my speech today to the university, Mr. Prime Minister, I assured the listeners that it is in our interest to remain engaged in the world. It's in our economic interests and it's in our national interests that the United States work with strong friends and allies such as Singapore to spread prosperity and hope and to work to lay the foundations for peace.

Mr. Prime Minister, I appreciate your clear vision of the threats that we face. I appreciate the fact that you see the ideological struggle before us. I cannot think of a more steadfast leader in you and your willingness to make the hard steps necessary to deal with this challenge today so that our children won't have to deal with it in more severe terms tomorrow.

I'm proud to call you friend. Laura and I are proud to be in your presence. May God bless you and your important country.

Prime Minister Lee. Thank you very much.

NOTE: The President spoke at approximately 7:25 p.m. at the Istana. In his remarks, he referred to Ho Ching, wife of Prime Minister Lee. The transcript released by the Office of the Press Secretary also included the remarks of Prime Minister Lee. A tape was not available for verification of the content of these remarks.

Remarks Following Discussions With Prime Minister John Howard of Australia and an Exchange With Reporters in Hanoi, Vietnam
November 17, 2006

President Bush. I just had an enjoyable lunch with my friend John Howard. We talked about a variety of subjects. I talked to John about Iraq. I appreciate the Australian contributions to helping this young democracy succeed. There's a lot of questions, I know, in the press around the world about our troop posture and about the attitudes of our Government. I assured John that we will get the job done. We will continue to help this Maliki Government meet the aspirations of the Iraqi people.

And that—I'm sure there's some questions by the Australian press about what the elections mean. The elections mean that the American people want to know whether or not we have a plan for success, and that—and I assured John that any repositioning of troops, if that's what we choose to do, will be done in close consultation with John and his Government. But I also assured him that we're not leaving until this job is done, until Iraq can govern, sustain, and defend itself.

We talked about the climate. John has got some very strong ideas about the use of technologies to enable countries like our own and the rest of the world to be able to grow and, at the same time, protect the environment. And I appreciated his views. And I share those views. I assured him that we will continue to spend research dollars to develop technologies such as clean coal technologies, something that Australia is interested in, or the use of ethanol, for example, to power our automobiles, or money spent to develop hydrogen fuel cells, all aimed at changing our energy habits and, at the same time, protecting the environment.

We talked about the neighborhood that Australia is in. I always admire John's strategic vision of the world. I really appreciate the chance to have lunch with you.

Prime Minister Howard. Well, thank you very much, George. We did cover all of those subjects, and we spent a lot of time, naturally, talking about Iraq. Our views are very similar. It's not easy, but we hold to the view, and I've said it back in Australia, and I'd repeat it here today, that the idea of the coalition leaving in circumstances where the Iraqi people were not soon to be able to look after themselves and to enjoy the democracy they want would be a catastrophic defeat for our cause, not only in the Middle East, but it would embolden terrorists in that region. And it would embolden terrorism in countries like Indonesia.

Our discussions about climate change were very valuable. Our thinking is similar. We don't believe that Kyoto is the answer. Both our countries are committed to dealing with the growth of greenhouse gasses. We can have debate about the severity of the problem, but there's really no debate about the desirability of responding to it, provided we do it in a way that maintains economic growth in our societies and the world.

And we certainly have a similarity of commitment to doing things in the area of technology. And I indicated to the President that Australia is looking very seriously at the place of nuclear power in our own response. And the Australian media will be aware of the upcoming Switkowski report that is going to deal with the whole question of nuclear power in the overall equation.

President Bush. We'll answer a couple of questions. Jennifer [Jennifer Loven, Associated Press]. Hold on for a second, please. Jennifer.

Vietnam-U.S. Relations

Q. Thank you, sir. What does it mean to you personally and what do you think it means to other Americans who experienced some of the turbulence of the Vietnam war that you're here now, talking cooperation and peace with a former enemy?

President Bush. You know, Laura and I were talking about—we were talking about how amazing it is we're here in Vietnam. And one of the most poignant moments of the drive in was passing the lake where John McCain got pulled out of the lake. And he's a friend of ours. He suffered a lot as a result of his imprisonment, and yet we passed the place where he was, literally, saved, in one way, by the people pulling him out.

I guess my first reaction is, history has a long march to it and that societies change and relationships can constantly be altered to the good. And I'm looking forward to my meetings with the President and the Prime Minister here shortly. I found it really interesting, for example, that the Prime Minister's children were educated in the United States. The Prime Minister of Vietnam, who, as I understand it, was part of the Viet Cong, sends his children to our country to get educated, and one of his children ended up marrying a Vietnamese American. And it shows how hopeful the world can be and how people can reconcile and move beyond past difficulties for the common good.

Vietnam is an exciting place. It's a place with an enormous future, and they obviously have got to work through difficulties like religious freedom, for example, but nevertheless, there's certainly a new hopefulness to this country. And so I'm—thought a lot about what it was like, what my impressions of Vietnam were growing up, and here I am in this country today, and I guess my answer is, it's very hopeful.

Democracy Efforts in Iraq

Q. Are there lessons here for the debate over Iraq?

President Bush. I think one thing—yes, I mean, one lesson is, is that we tend to want there to be instant success in the world, and the task in Iraq is going to take a while. But I would make it beyond just Iraq. I think the great struggle we're going to have is between radicals and extremists versus people who want to live in peace, and that Iraq is a part of the struggle. And it's just going to take a long period of time to—for the ideology that is hopeful, and that is an ideology of freedom, to overcome an ideology of hate. Yet the world that we live in today is one where they want things to happen immediately.

And it's hard work in Iraq. That's why I'm so proud to have a partner like John Howard who understands it's difficult to get the job done. We'll succeed unless we quit. The Maliki Government is going to make it unless the coalition leaves before they have a chance to make it. And that's why I assured the Prime Minister we'll get the job done.

Do you want to ask somebody?

Australia-U.S. Cooperation on Iraq

Q. Mr. President, did the Prime Minister raise any new ideas on Iraq during your talks? Can you tell us what they are, and will you be taking them up?

President Bush. The Prime Minister's main concern was that we consult closely together. And I assured him that's going to be the case. That's the way it has been throughout this war on terror. We value Australia's commitments; I value John Howard's advice. And when our deliberations are complete—and as you may or may not know, we've got a lot of people looking at different tactical adjustments—once I make up my mind what those will be, I'll share it with him right off the bat.

Let's see here, yes, Steve [Steve Holland, Reuters].

U.S. Armed Forces in Iraq

Q. You mentioned troop postures in Iraq. There's a report that you may want to send

30,000 additional troops to Iraq. Is that something——

President Bush. Where was that report?

Q. In the Guardian newspaper.

President Bush. The Guardian newspaper? Well, I don't read that paper often. But I—look, I'm going to listen to our commanders, Steve. Ours is a condition-based strategy, and Pete Pace is conducting a thorough study—he's the Chairman of the Joint Chiefs. John Abizaid has got some ideas, and the Baker-Hamilton commission is looking. I want to hear from Democrats on Capitol Hill what their views may be. I want to hear from my fellow Republicans on Capitol Hill. And then I'll make up my mind. So I'm not aware of the Guardian article.

Q. Can I ask another question?

President Bush. Sure, since you fumbled that question. You might get—let Gregory [David Gregory, NBC News] substitute for you.

North Korea

Q. Are you getting sufficient cooperation from South Korea on North Korea? And will this be something you talk to them about tomorrow?

President Bush. Oh, absolutely. I'll remind——

Q. ——they're not following through on the sanctions as hard as they could have.

President Bush. I'll, of course, talk to the South Korean President about implementing the United Nations Security Council resolution. I'll talk to Vladimir Putin, Hu Jintao, and Prime Minister Abe as well. I'm meeting with all our partners in the six-party talks.

The APEC is an important summit; it's an important opportunity to talk about the importance of free trade. But it's also important to give us a chance to talk about other issues, and a key issue that John and I, by the way, talked about is going to be North Korea. We have a chance to solve this issue peacefully and diplomatically. It's important for the world to see that the Security Council resolutions which were passed are implemented. So part of my discussions will be how we fully implement those sanctions that the world has asked for, but also, it's a chance to set the conditions right so that the six-party talks will succeed. North Korea, as you know, has decided to come back to the table, and it gives us a chance to solve this problem peacefully.

Military Tribunals

Q. Mr. President, did you discuss the issue of David Hicks at all with the Prime Minister? And when do you think he might come to trial?

President Bush. Yes, we did. The Prime Minister brought it up. He was pleased that I was able to sign the military tribunal bill, in other words, a way forward for somebody like Hicks to be able to get a day in court. And he was asking me, do I have a timetable in mind as to when Hicks's trial will be coming forth? I told him I didn't, although we hope that Hicks is one of the early people that will have a day in court.

Interestingly enough, as I understand, Hicks has lawyers that may be trying to appeal certain aspects of the law we passed. If that's the case, he's having his day in court in an interesting way. But I believe Hicks deserves a trial and is going to get it.

Thank you all very much.

Prime Minister Howard. Thank you.

Q. One more, do you feel generous, one more?

President Bush. No, I'm not generous. It's also hot out here, Gregory. We're in the sun; you're not. [*Laughter*]

NOTE: The President spoke at 1:17 p.m. at the Sheraton Hanoi. In his remarks, he referred to Prime Minister Nuri al-Maliki of Iraq; President Nguyen Minh Triet and Prime Minister Nguyen Tan Dung of Vietnam; Gen. John P. Abizaid, USA, commander, U.S. Central Command; President

Roh Moo-hyun of South Korea; President Vladimir V. Putin of Russia; President Hu Jintao of China; Prime Minister Shinzo Abe of Japan; and Australian citizen David M. Hicks, a detainee at the U.S. Naval Station in Guantanamo Bay, Cuba.

Remarks Following Discussions With President Nguyen Minh Triet of Vietnam in Hanoi
November 17, 2006

Mr. President, thank you very much for your hospitality. Laura and I have been struck by the friendliness of the people of Vietnam. In our drive through this beautiful city, we were pleased to see thousands of your citizens with smiles on their faces. And we're so grateful.

I've been reading and studying about your country, and I have seen now first-hand the great vibrancy and the excitement that's taking place in Vietnam. You're like a young tiger, and I look forward to continuing to work to make sure our bilateral relations are close. And thank you for hosting APEC. And thank you for hosting a dinner for us tonight. We're really looking forward to it.

NOTE: The President spoke at 2:35 p.m. at the Presidential Palace. A portion of these remarks could not be verified because the tape was incomplete.

Joint Statement by the Socialist Republic of Vietnam and the United States of America
November 17, 2006

President Nguyen Minh Triet of the Socialist Republic of Vietnam was pleased to welcome United States President George W. Bush to Vietnam. Looking back on the June 2005 Joint Statement by President Bush and then Prime Minister Phan Van Khai, both leaders expressed satisfaction at the progress the bilateral relationship has made, resulting in a U.S.-Vietnam relationship today that is multi-faceted and forward looking. It encompasses significant and growing trade and economic ties, an emerging military-to-military relationship, successful cooperation on health and development issues, growing cultural and educational links, a commitment to resolving remaining issues stemming from the war, a shared interest in ensuring peace, stability, and prosperity in the Asia-Pacific region, and frank and candid discussion of differences. The two sides reaffirmed their efforts to ensure that bilateral relations are stable, constructive, broad-based, and conducted on the basis of sovereign equality and mutual benefit.

President Triet and President Bush applauded the historic milestone of Vietnam's accession to the World Trade Organization and President Bush reiterated his firm support for the earliest possible Congressional approval of Permanent Normal Trade Relations. President Triet confirmed that Vietnam would fully uphold the rules-based trading system embedded in the WTO and join other members in their efforts to create a level playing field based on fairness, openness, and transparency. He welcomed President Bush's assurances that the United

States would maintain open access to the U.S. market and support Vietnam's process of integration with the world economy. The two leaders anticipated an even greater amount of bilateral trade and investment, benefiting the people of both nations. President Bush also welcomed the Vietnamese leadership's determination to accelerate the course of doi moi reforms, build the rule of law, and combat corruption, and held that such efforts are important for Vietnam's economic vitality and favorable business and investment climate. The two Presidents also looked forward to the signing of a Maritime Transport Agreement at an early date to further accelerate growth in our vibrant economic relationship.

President Bush and President Triet discussed the growing cooperation between the United States and Vietnam to address regional and global concerns. President Bush welcomed Vietnam's active engagement in international affairs aimed at maintaining peace, cooperation and development in the Asia-Pacific region and the world, and noted his appreciation of Vietnam's support for a denuclearized Korean Peninsula and the consensus views of the UNSC as expressed in UNSCR 1718. President Triet welcomed the reconvening of the Six Party Talks and expressed the hope that a peaceful solution for the denuclearization of the Korean Peninsula would be reached.

The two leaders pledged to increase cooperation to halt the proliferation of weapons of mass destruction and related technology and materials in accordance with international and national laws and each country's capacities. They also pointed to the agreement on nuclear fuel replacement at the Dalat Research Reactor, and the signing of a Memorandum of Understanding between the U.S. Drug Enforcement Administration Vietnam's Ministry of Public Security, as examples of the diverse ways in which the two countries are working together to protect the safety and security of their peoples and others in the region.

The two leaders looked especially to cooperation on the health front as an example of the tangible benefits of the United States and Vietnam working closely together. President Bush praised Vietnam's timely, effective, and transparent response to avian influenza in the country, which has prevented any further human outbreaks in Vietnam since October 2005. He noted that Vietnam's efforts were a model for the region, and pledged continued U.S. support in responding to the threat of avian influenza. As Vietnam is one of the focus countries for President Bush's PEPFAR initiative on HIV/AIDS, the United States and Vietnam have also worked closely together to combat the scourge of this disease. The two leaders agreed to further strengthen the present positive cooperation. President Triet praised the work of the STAR initiative in Vietnam and the extension of this activity. President Triet also expressed appreciation for the U.S. Government's increasing development assistance to Vietnam and urged the U.S. side to increase humanitarian assistance including through cooperation on areas such as unexploded ordinance and continued assistance to Vietnamese with disabilities. The United States and Vietnam also agreed that further joint efforts to address the environmental contamination near former dioxin storage sites would make a valuable contribution to the continued development of their bilateral relationship.

President Bush explained the National Security Strategy of the United States, which stresses the importance to world peace and stability of the development in every country of full respect for human rights and fundamental freedoms. President Triet apprised President Bush of recently promulgated laws and regulations on religious freedom that are to be implemented in all localities of Vietnam. The two leaders also noted the importance of continuing to make progress in the bilateral human rights dialogue and reaffirmed that it should be

conducted in a comprehensive, constructive and results-oriented manner.

The two leaders expressed satisfaction with progress on resolving outstanding issues from the war and agreed that the two sides would continue cooperation in this respect. President Triet reaffirmed his Government's continued efforts to assist the United States to ensure the fullest possible accounting for Americans who remain missing in action, through both joint and enhanced unilateral actions. President Bush reaffirmed U.S. contributions to help obtain information on Vietnamese MIA cases.

Presidents Triet and Bush discussed cooperation in regional affairs, and President Bush praised Vietnam's hosting of APEC this year as a demonstration of Vietnam's active and important role in promoting trade and economic liberalization and strengthening security in the region. Presi-

dent Triet noted the robust engagement by the United States with ASEAN, and looked towards increasing that cooperation through the U.S.-ASEAN Enhanced Partnership. The two leaders pledged continued efforts to seek mutual understanding on issues of regional and global concern.

The two leaders noted the importance of high-level visits between the two countries to the development of Vietnam-U.S. relations in the future. President Bush invited President Triet to visit the United States in 2007 to continue these discussions; President Triet thanked President Bush and accepted the invitation with pleasure.

NOTE: An original was not available for verification of the content of this joint statement.

Statement on Senate Passage of United States-India Civil Nuclear Cooperation Legislation
November 17, 2006

The United States and India enjoy a strategic partnership based upon common values. Today the Senate has acted to further strengthen this relationship by passing legislation that will deliver energy, nonproliferation, and trade benefits to the citizens of two great democracies.

The U.S.-India civil nuclear cooperation agreement will bring India into the international nuclear nonproliferation mainstream and will increase the transparency of India's entire civilian nuclear program. As India's economy continues to grow, this partnership will help India meet its energy needs without increasing air pollution and

greenhouse gas emissions. It will also help reduce India's dependence upon imported fossil fuels. By increasing India's demand for civil nuclear technology, fuel, and support services, this historic agreement creates new business opportunities for American companies and enhances our trade relationship.

I appreciate the Senate's leadership on this important legislation and look forward to signing this bill into law soon.

NOTE: The statement referred to H.R. 5682, which was passed with amendments by the Senate on November 16.

Statement on the Death of Milton Friedman
November 17, 2006

America has lost one of its greatest citizens. Milton Friedman was a revolutionary thinker and extraordinary economist whose work helped advance human dignity and human freedom.

A champion of limited government and personal freedom, Friedman proposed bold ideas about school choice, tax reductions, and an all-volunteer army that serve as the foundation of many of America's most successful Government reforms. His work demonstrated that free markets are the great engines of economic development.

His writings laid the groundwork that transformed many of the world's central banks, helping deliver economic stability and improved living standards in countries around the world.

Milton Friedman, a recipient of the Nobel Prize, will be remembered as one of the most influential economists in history. The Nation is grateful for his profound contributions.

Our thoughts and prayers are with the Friedman family.

Remarks at a State Banquet Hosted by President Nguyen Minh Triet of Vietnam in Hanoi
November 17, 2006

Mr. President and Madam Chi, the reason I'm smiling is because I'm really happy to be here, and so is Laura. And we thank you for your warm hospitality. First, I want to congratulate you for your success on hosting APEC. I'm confident our fellow leaders will have the same sense of gratitude and respect that we feel from the Vietnamese people.

Vietnam is a remarkable country. For decades, you had been torn apart by war. Today, the Vietnamese people are at peace and seeing the benefits of reform. The Vietnamese own their own businesses, and today, the Vietnamese economy is the fastest growing in Southeast Asia. Vietnamese students have great opportunities here at home and abroad. The Vietnamese people are traveling around the world and sharing this ancient culture with peoples of the world. And the United States, as well as other APEC partners, look forward to strengthening our ties.

The American people welcome the progress of Vietnam. And we want to continue to work together to better our relations. We will work with you to help combat avian flu and HIV/AIDS. We have signed agreements to protect religious freedom. We strongly support Vietnam in the World Trade Organization.

Vietnam is a country that's taking its rightful place as a strong and vibrant nation. Mr. President, your leadership is helping your country succeed. I can see it as I drive on the streets; the people of your country have hope. And I hope they know, as a result of my visit, they have the friendship of the American people.

And so, Mr. President, I would like to propose a toast to you and Madam Chi and to the fine people of Vietnam.

NOTE: The President spoke at approximately 7:15 p.m. at the International Convention Center. In his remarks, he referred to Tran Thi Kim Chi, wife of President Triet.

Remarks Following a Meeting With President Roh Moo-hyun of South Korea in Hanoi, Vietnam
November 18, 2006

President Roh. Today President Bush and I had a very good discussion on the North Korean nuclear issue. We agreed on the principle that North Korea should dismantle its nuclear weapons and its nuclear program, that our two countries fully support the U.N. Security Council Resolution 1718, and our two countries will implement this resolution in a faithful manner.

Although the Republic of Korea is not taking part in the full scope of the PSI, we support the principles and goals of the PSI and will fully cooperate in preventing WMD materiel transfer in the Northeast Asia region. And we also agreed that we will actively seek to resolve the North Korean nuclear issue within the six-party talks framework and also by actively engaging in bilateral talks within this framework.

In conclusion, the President and I had very satisfactory discussions on this issue, and we had very useful and indepth discussions on resolving the North Korean nuclear issue.

President Bush. Mr. President, I agree. We had a discussion like you would expect allies to have a discussion. We are allies in peace. We are allies in working to improve the lives of our fellow citizens.

We did discuss 1718, Resolution 1718 and our mutual desire to effectively enforce the will of the world. I appreciate the cooperation we're receiving from South Korea on the Proliferation Security Initiative. Our desire is to solve the North Korean issue peacefully. And as I've made clear in a speech as recently as two days ago in Singapore, that we want the North Korean leader to hear that if he gives up his weapons and nuclear weapons ambitions, that we would be willing to enter into security arrangements with the North Koreans as well as move forward new economic incentives for the North Korean people.

I appreciate your commitment to peace, and I appreciate our mutual friendship, Mr. President. And I've enjoyed yet another meeting in our quest to achieve our common objectives.

Thank you very much.

NOTE: The President spoke at approximately 8:38 a.m. at the Sheraton Hanoi. In his remarks, he referred to Chairman Kim Jong Il of North Korea. President Roh spoke in Korean, and his remarks were translated by an interpreter.

Remarks Following a Lunch With Prime Minister Shinzo Abe of Japan in Hanoi
November 18, 2006

President Bush. Mr. Prime Minister, thank you very much for your time. We just had a very frank and full discussion. I admire the Prime Minister's intellect. I'm very comfortable with his style, and I'm very confident we'll be able to work together for the common good.

The relationship between Japan and the United States is strong, and we will keep it that way. And a strong relationship between our two countries is good for the security of the East. We talked a lot of issues. And we spent time talking about North Korea and our common commitment

to see that the six-party talks succeed. We spent a lot of time talking about bilateral issues. And one of the most interesting issues we discussed was our common desire to continue to cooperate on a ballistic missile defense.

I told the Prime Minister he needs to get over to the United States quickly. I'm looking forward to hosting you. And thank you for your time.

Prime Minister Abe. I was able to spend a very meaningful and wonderful time with the President today. So thank you very much, Mr. President.

Japan and U.S. share an alliance which is based on fundamental values, such as freedom, democracy, basic human rights, and the rule of law. And we agreed with each other that strengthening our alliance would be a good in maintaining peace and security of not just Japan and the region surrounding Japan but the entire world.

Also concerning North Korea, as the President mentioned, we agreed that we would take a coordinated approach to reach a final resolution of the issue and also to achieve some concrete results at an early stage. We also agreed to strengthen and accelerate our cooperation concerning ballistic missile defense, and we will instruct our foreign ministers and defense ministers to conduct consideration concerning this matter.

We are faced with many difficult issues, like North Korea, the fight against terror, and also Iraq. But we agreed that we will be utilizing the alliance we have between Japan and the United States for the good of the world and the region for a long time.

And I'm looking forward to visiting the United States sometime next year and seeing the President. Thank you.

NOTE: The President spoke at 12:47 p.m. at the Sheraton Hanoi. Prime Minister Abe spoke in Japanese, and his remarks were translated by an interpreter.

Remarks Prior to a Meeting With Prime Minister Shinzo Abe of Japan and President Roh Moo-hyun of South Korea in Hanoi
November 18, 2006

I want to thank the leaders of two of America's strongest allies, the President of South Korea and the Prime Minister of Japan, for joining in this trilateral discussion. It is an important dialog between three democracies, all of which are committed to peace and security. I look forward to discussing a wide range of issues with these two leaders. There is no doubt, when we work together, we can bring peace and stability and prosperity for our peoples.

And so I want to thank you all very much for joining. I appreciate your time, and I'm looking forward to our dialog. Thank you.

NOTE: The President spoke at 1:02 p.m. at the Sheraton Hanoi.

The President's Radio Address
November 18, 2006

Good morning. This week, I'm visiting Singapore, Indonesia, and Vietnam, where I'm attending the annual summit of the Asia-Pacific Economic Cooperation Forum. On this trip, I am carrying a message for the people of this region: America will remain engaged in Asia because our interests depend on the expansion of freedom and opportunity in this vital part of the world.

Asia is important to America because prosperity in our country depends on trade with Asia's growing economies. Today, America's trade across the Pacific is greater than our trade across the Atlantic, and we need to continue opening up markets in this part of the world to American goods and services.

My position is clear: As long as the playing field is level, America's farmers, small businesses, and workers can compete with anyone. So America will continue to pursue free and fair trade at every level with individual countries, across whole regions, and through the World Trade Organization. By opening new markets for American goods and services, we help create new customers for our products abroad and jobs and opportunities for our workers and small businesses at home.

Asia is also important to America because our nations face common challenges, like energy and disease, that transcend borders. Our growing economies are too dependent on oil, and we have a common interest in pursuing affordable, reliable energy alternatives. So we're working with our partners in this region to develop new energy technologies that will make us less dependent on oil, including clean coal and ethanol, biodiesel and hydrogen fuel cells.

We are also working with our partners in the region to address the threat of diseases like avian flu, which has the potential to claim many lives and inflict terrible damage on our societies if not detected and stopped quickly. So we're sharing information and putting wise preparedness plans in place to help ensure that we can contain the spread of avian flu and be ready if a pandemic ever occurs. By coming together to address these and other challenges, we're helping build more hopeful societies in Asia and stronger partners for America.

Finally, Asia is important to America because we face common threats to our security. The people of this region understand the terrorist threat because they have been targets of terrorist violence. Since September the 11th, the terrorists have attacked a nightclub in Bali, a hotel in Jakarta, a ferry packed with passengers in Manila Bay, a school full of children in Russia, Australia's Embassy in Indonesia, and many other targets. The killers who committed these acts of terror are followers of a clear and focused ideology that hates freedom, rejects tolerance, and their stated goal is a radical Islamic empire stretching from Europe to Southeast Asia.

The greatest danger in our world today is that these terrorists could get their hands on weapons of mass destruction and use them to blackmail free nations or kill on an unimaginable scale. This threat poses a risk to our entire civilization, and we're working with our partners in the Asia-Pacific to defeat it.

In my meetings with leaders in the region, we discussed the threat of proliferation from North Korea. After North Korea's recent nuclear test, the United Nations Security Council passed a unanimous resolution imposing sanctions on North Korea's regime, and America is working with our partners to enforce those sanctions. We will also continue working with Japan, China, South Korea, and Russia through the six-party talks. Our nations are speaking with one voice: North Korea must abandon its

nuclear weapons programs, and we will not tolerate North Korea's proliferation of nuclear technology to hostile regimes and terrorist networks.

In the long run, the surest path to security is the expansion of freedom. History shows that free societies are peaceful societies. So America is committed to advancing freedom and democracy as the great alternative to repression and radicalism. And by standing with our allies in the Asia-Pacific region, we will defend our free way of life, confront the challenges of a new century, and build a more hopeful, peaceful, and prosperous future for our children and grandchildren.

Thank you for listening.

NOTE: The address was recorded at 7:20 a.m., local time, on November 16 at the Shangri-La Hotel in Singapore, for broadcast at 10:06 a.m., e.s.t., on November 18. The transcript was made available by the Office of the Press Secretary on November 17 but was embargoed for release until the broadcast. Due to the 11-hour time difference, the radio address was broadcast after the President's remarks in Hanoi, Vietnam. The Office of the Press Secretary also released a Spanish language transcript of this address.

Statement on the Death of Glenn E. "Bo" Schembechler
November 18, 2006

Bo Schembechler was a true legend of college football. I was saddened to learn of his death. He inspired generations of players and fans by insisting that his teams play hard, play fair, and bring honor to themselves and their school by finishing their educations and contributing to society. He was an extraordinary leader and role model who will be missed. Laura and I join fans of the Big Blue in extending our sympathies to his wife, Cathy, and his family and friends.

Remarks Following a Church Service in Hanoi
November 19, 2006

Laura and I just had a moment to converse with God in a church here in Hanoi. We were touched by the simplicity and the beauty of the moment. We appreciate very much the congregation for allowing us to come and worship with them.

A whole society is a society which welcomes basic freedoms, and there's no more basic freedom than the basic—the freedom to worship as you see fit. And Laura and I were proud to worship with believers here in Hanoi. And we, again, thank the church for the opportunity to come by. My hope is that people all across the world will be able to express religion [religious] * freedom. And it's our way of expressing our personal faith and, at the same time, urging societies to feel comfortable with and confident in saying to their people, if you feel like praising God, you're allowed to do so in any way you see fit.

God bless, and thank you.

---

* White House correction.

NOTE: The President spoke at 8:14 a.m. at Cua Bac Cathedral.

Remarks Prior to a Meeting With President Hu Jintao of China in Hanoi
November 19, 2006

President Hu. It's a great pleasure to see you again, Mr. President. I remember, in the course of this year, we have already met each other three times, we had four telephone conversations, and we also maintained frequent exchange of letters. So it is fair to say that we are keeping very close touch, and this has vigorously promoted China-U.S. relations.

I'm pleased to see new progress in China-U.S. relations since our meeting in St. Petersburg in July this year. Our two countries have maintained a frequent exchange of visits at the top levels and at different levels. And actually, our trade has also been expanding very rapidly, and I do have a piece of good news to share with you. According to U.S. statistics, in first 7 months of this year, U.S. exports to China jumped 35 percent.

Nationally, our mechanism for having strategic economic dialog has also been launched, and the first inaugural dialog will be held in Beijing around the middle of next month. And Chinese naval ships have again paid a visit to the continental America for the first time in 6 years. And even as we speak, our naval ships of the two countries are conducting joint search and rescue maneuvers in Chinese waters.

So, all in all, we feel very happy about the healthy and stable extension of China-U.S. relations. I think we would not have achieved such a state of our bilateral relations had it not been for your outstanding leadership.

President Bush. Well, thank you.

President Hu. So, with this, I would like to turn it over to you.

President Bush. Thank you, Mr. President. You're right; you and I have had a lot of meetings. And the reason why is because we recognize that working together, we can accomplish a lot for the security of the world and for the prosperity of our people. China is a very important nation, and the United States believes strongly that by working together, we can help solve problems such as North Korea and Iran.

Our bilateral relations are very good, and we—you and I—are committed to keeping them that way. Obviously, with as much commerce between our countries as there is, there's going to be trade difficulties, but nevertheless, we both adopt a spirit of mutual respect and the desire to work through our problems for the common good of our peoples.

I strongly support your vision, Mr. President, of encouraging your country to become a nation of consumers and not savers, which will inure to the benefit of our manufacturers, both large and small, and our farmers as well.

I always enjoy our frank and friendly discussions, and I'm looking forward to this one as well. And I thank you for your hospitality.

Thank you, sir.

NOTE: The President spoke at approximately 8:34 a.m. at the Hanoi Daewoo Hotel. President Hu spoke in Chinese, and his remarks were translated by an interpreter.

Remarks Following a Meeting With President Vladimir V. Putin of Russia in Hanoi
November 19, 2006

President Bush. Today Vladimir and I are pleased to report that after a long set of negotiations, Representative Gref and Ambassador Schwab have signed agreements that will be good for the United States and good for Russia. And that is, we support Russia's accession into the WTO. I congratulate you all for your hard work, and thank you very much for the hard work.

I repeat: This is a good agreement for the United States. And equally important, it's a good agreement for Russia, and it's a good agreement for the international trading community. And I thank you very much, Vladimir, for working hard on this agreement.

As usual, we've had a very important dialog. And we talked about common interests and how we can work together to solve some of the world's problems, including North Korea and Iran. And I want to thank you for your time and friendship.

President Putin. On my part, I would like to add that we've been in the process of difficult and lengthy work, 5 years of intense effort which has been culminated today with the signing of a protocol on Russia's accession to the World Trade Organization, which has been a successful outcome of this effort.

And I would like to underscore that this would not have been possible to achieve without expert and professional involvement both on the side of the U.S. and Russia, and without good will expressed in this— should I say, in the right term would be to use here—very businesslike approach in their dealing.

On top of that, it would not have been possible without a political will, which has been here expressed by the President of the United States of America. And I agree with you, George, that this lays out very favorable conditions to us to jointly tackle the very pertinent and acute problems of international relations together.

It also lays out favorable conditions to further develop the scope and volume of commerce and economic interaction between the business partners—between our two countries involved with other countries.

NOTE: The President spoke at 4:16 p.m. at the Sheraton Hanoi. In his remarks, he referred to Minister of Economic Development and Trade German Oskarovich Gref of Russia; and Ambassador Susan C. Schwab, U.S. Trade Representative. President Putin spoke in Russian, and his remarks were translated by an interpreter.

Remarks Prior to a Meeting With Business Leaders in Ho Chi Minh City, Vietnam
November 20, 2006

Thank you all very much for—thank you very much for joining me and the Secretary of State. I find it really interesting that my first meeting in Ho Chi Minh City is at the stock exchange, and I'm meeting with entrepreneurs, people who have taken

a look at the markets in Vietnam and have decided that this is a good place to invest.

I want to thank you all for coming to share some of your stories with me. I'm very interested in hearing what the opportunities are like and the obstacles you face

and how, perhaps, the United States can help foster the market economy that is growing here.

I must tell you, I am, first of all, unbelievably grateful for the welcome that Laura and I have been received with here in Ho Chi Minh City; I've never seen as many people line the streets with such a friendly attitude. Secondly, when I read about the recent economic history of Vietnam, I am amazed at the size of the growth and the fact that are people are beginning to realize dreams. I recognize that some of you here at the table were born in Vietnam, came to the United States in the midseventies, and have decided to return. And I'm really interested in hearing what that has been like and the contrast in lifestyles and why you made the decisions you made.

And I do want to hear from you all.

NOTE: The President spoke at 9:15 a.m. at the Ho Chi Minh City Securities Trading Center.

Remarks Following a Tour of the Pasteur Institute in Ho Chi Minh City
November 20, 2006

Laura and I are honored to be here at the center of an effort to help Vietnam battle HIV/AIDS. And, doctor, thank you for this wonderful tour. We've got a comprehensive strategy involved through our PEPFAR program with the country. We've got a very strong mother-to-child transmission program to prevent the children from developing HIV/AIDS.

The doctor has been explaining to us their strategy on how to detect HIV/AIDS not only in the cities but in the Provinces. And part of our comprehensive strategy to help this country is to distribute antiretroviral drugs.

Laura and I have come by to thank the doctor and her staff for their compassionate work and to assure the Vietnamese people that we will still help them fight HIV/AIDS.

NOTE: The President spoke at 10:29 a.m. In his remarks, he referred to Nguyen Thi Kim Tien, director, Pasteur Institute.

Remarks in a Discussion With Civic Leaders in Bogor, Indonesia
November 20, 2006

Mr. President, thank you very much. Thank you all for joining. I'm really looking forward to this discussion. I admire Indonesia's pluralism and its diversity. I admire your President's commitment to reform and strengthening democracy. It's very important for the people of America to understand that this vast country has got not only tremendous potential, but it's got a prominent role to play in the world—showing how it's possible for people of good will to live together in peace and harmony. And that's the lesson I want to hear from you all as well. I'm looking forward to our discussion.

I cannot thank you enough for taking time out of your busy day to come up here and share thoughts with us. I'm very interested in learning how our Government can continue to work with your Government, as it so chooses, to help, particularly in areas like education and health.

And so with that, Mr. President, thank you very much for setting this up. I appreciate the opportunity to meet some of your fine citizens. Thank you.

NOTE: The President spoke at 5:35 p.m. at Bogor Palace. In his remarks, he referred to President Susilo Bambang Yudhoyono of Indonesia.

Remarks Following a Meeting With President Susilo Bambang Yudhoyono of Indonesia and an Exchange With Reporters in Bogor
November 20, 2006

President Yudhoyono. Your Excellency, President Bush, members of the press, allow me to speak in Bahasa Indonesia.

[At this point, President Yudhoyono continued his remarks in Bahasa Indonesia, and they were translated by an interpreter as follows.]

President Yudhoyono. Ladies and gentlemen, today we have received a visit of President Bush, who has come here to increase our cooperation and friendship between Indonesia and the United States. And we just discussed a number of agenda in order to improve—increase our relations.

In the bilateral meeting, I expressed my thanks for the cooperation and assistance given by the United States to Indonesia in the field of economics, investment, trade, education, health, technology, military, and so on. I also expressed thanks for the U.S. assistance, and also other countries, during the Aceh tsunami and also, more recently, during the earthquake in Yogyakarta and central Java, which shows solidarity and cooperation between the two countries.

After that, we discussed in detail a number of cooperation in our agenda. We discussed health cooperation, especially on how to fight avian flu and other infectious diseases, which are found in the tropical areas, especially in Indonesia.

On education, we already have a good cooperation, and we will continue this cooperation and hope this cooperation will be continued between Indonesia and the U.S. as part of our educational agenda.

We also discussed energy, and we spent time discussing bioenergy fuels. And I'm glad that President Bush has said that he would share technology in other matters relating to development of alternative energy.

Lastly, we discussed how to deal with natural disasters, especially on how to build an early warning system in Indonesia. I expressed my appreciation to the assistance given by the United States Government, and we also cooperate also with other countries on building this early warning system.

We also discussed a number of international issues, global issues, such as the situation in the Middle East, the situation in North Korea, Iraq, and also Palestine. And of course, we agree on the need to find a solution to these issues.

After the discussions, we had a meeting with civic leaders, and we discussed all the things that we discussed earlier in the bilateral meeting, especially on how to improve the quality of life and how to make Indonesia-U.S. partnership—contribute to improving this quality of life.

The discussions were open, frank, constructive, sometimes critical, and what is important is that we tried to discuss cooperation on how to make Indonesia-U.S. relations touch on the lives of our people.

President Bush. Mr. President, thank you very much. Thanks for the invitation to come back to your beautiful country. Laura and I are thrilled to be here, and we're looking forward to our dinner tonight with you and your wife and your delegation. You

lead a large and diverse nation with a very bright future.

During my visit here, we're going to continue to work to build a relationship between our two nations that will last beyond the immediate. It's a relationship that should last for decades to come. It's important to our nation that we have good, strong relations with Indonesia.

We've just come from the APEC summit in Vietnam, and the people of Indonesia should know that when their elected leader speaks, other leaders listen, as do I. Mr. President, you're well-respected in the international community, and I appreciate your perspective on global and international issues, and thank you for sharing them with me again today.

This afternoon we also discussed bilateral initiatives that will expand opportunity for the people of Indonesia and, at the same time, deepen our partnership. We support your country's reform efforts, Mr. President. I thank you for your leadership on that important issue. The Indonesian President understands that economic reform and fighting corruption and investing in people will help this important nation succeed.

We are committed to helping you on all these initiatives. Last week, we signed a $55 million Millennium Challenge Account threshold agreement. This agreement means that the American people will support Indonesia's efforts to reform its democratic institutions and strengthen governance. We would not have made this commitment, Mr. President, if you were, yourself, not committed to reform.

The agreement is going to help fund your strategy to immunize your children against deadly diseases. We support your attempts to modernize your education system. We have pledged and provided over $150 million to the Indonesian Government to help provide the tools that will give the next generation of Indonesians the chance to realize their enormous potential. One thousand schools spread across eight Provinces in Indonesia are now benefiting from our education partnership. And as I told you in our meeting, we will continue to help.

Our two nations continue to build strong trade and investment relationships. We're determined to grow our economies in a way that are sustainable. Last week, we signed an agreement to help Indonesia conserve its forests. Together our nations will fight illegal logging while promoting trade in forest products that does not threaten the region's environmental quality.

Our two nations recognize we must explore alternatives to fossil fuels. The President and I have spent quite a bit of time talking about this important issue. The people of Indonesia have got to know that, for national security purposes and for economic security purposes, America must spend research money to enable us to have alternative sources of energy from oil.

I told the President that I am committed to sharing technologies as they become developed to help us all become less dependent on oil. And I appreciate your commitment, sir, to biofuels as an alternative source of energy.

We talked about avian influenza. In this world of ours today, if there's an influenza outbreak in Vietnam, it could affect Indonesia or the people of America. And therefore, we need to work in a collaborative way to deal with this grave threat. We'll continue to fund our partnership on this issue, Mr. President, as well as our partnership to protect public health in Indonesia.

We support Indonesia's growing global role. Indonesia will soon take a seat on the United Nations Security Council. We discussed threats to global security and how together our two nations can help provide a peaceful way forward.

We discussed North Korea, and we discussed Iran. Both regimes have nuclear ambitions. Nuclear weapons in the hands of these regimes would make the people of the Middle East and Northeast Asia less secure. The President and I discussed how the International Atomic Energy Agency

and the six-party talks provide the best opportunity to seek peaceful, diplomatic solutions to our concerns about these weapons programs.

The United Nations requires reform to become a more effective institution, and I know that Indonesia will be a strong voice for positive change in the United Nations. And we look forward to having you on the Security Council.

The American people and the Indonesian people have both suffered from the acts of violent extremists. Our nations are determined to take effective action against terror networks that plot new attacks against innocent people. Indonesia is an example of how democracy and modernization can provide an alternative to extremism. And we appreciate your leadership, Mr. President. Your democracy is making Indonesia strong and better able to play a positive role in Southeast Asia and the world. Our talks today have been very constructive. I appreciate your hospitality. And I presume we'll take some questions.

President Yudhoyono. Thank you very much, Mr. President.

Democracy in Indonesia

Q. I would like to ask you—as you mentioned before, Indonesia now is growing toward democratization, and how do you think the process of democratization in Indonesia—the progress of democratization is going? And I have a second question.

President Bush. How many do you get to ask here in Indonesia?

Q. Excuse me?

President Bush. How many questions do you get to ask? [*Laughter*] Keep firing away. You're just setting a bad example for the American press corps. [*Laughter*]

Q. Well, lots of Indonesians think that you have a hidden agenda going here——

President Bush. Oh, yes?

Q. ——such as securing your Exxon deal in Natuna. And what is your comment on that?

President Bush. Well, we didn't discuss it.

Q. [*Inaudible*]

President Bush. No, we did not discuss it. You asked about Indonesian democracy—here's living proof right here. He ran a campaign; he said, "Vote for me; I will do the following things"; he's following through on his promises. The elections were open; the elections were clean; the elections were fair. And you elected a good President, who is working hard to—in a tough job. And I don't think the American people understand how big Indonesia is—17,000 islands, 6,000 of them inhabited, with a variety of demographics. The President kindly hosted a meeting today with civil society leaders, which points up to the diversity of this great nation—different religions, different backgrounds, different people, all united under a democratic—under a democracy.

And so I would say, your progress is very good. But we all have work to do in our respective democracies. Our transition to democracy wasn't all that smooth in America. If you study American history, we had some rough go for a while. And it's hard work to make sure the institutions are sound so that people can live in a free society that's based upon the rule of law. But the President is committed to it, and he's working hard to it, and I would say you're making good progress.

Terry Hunt [Terence Hunt, Associated Press]—go ahead and yell it.

U.S. Troops in Iraq

Q. Mr. President——

President Bush. Oops, don't yell it. [*Laughter*]

Q. Mr. President, you've talked about the dangers of leaving Iraq too soon, but you haven't talked about what risks might be involved in adding tens of thousands of troops to secure Baghdad, as Senator McCain has suggested. What are the downsides, if any, to that approach?

And I'd like to ask the President of Indonesia, what suggestions did you make to President Bush about his Iraq policy?

President Bush. Terry, we haven't made up—I haven't made any decisions about troop increases or troop decreases, and won't until I hear from a variety of sources, including our own United States military. As you know, General Pace, who is the Chairman of the Joint Chiefs of Staff, is in the process of evaluating a lot of suggestions from the field and from people involved with the Central Command as well as at the Pentagon. And they will be bringing forth the suggestions and recommendations to me here as quickly as possible.

But—so I haven't—there's no need to comment on something that may not happen. But if it were to happen, I will tell you the upsides and downside.

President Yudhoyono. My view on how could we work together at ending conflict in Iraq or in finding a proper and realistic solution for Iraq is that global community must be also responsible in solving the problems in Iraq. Talking about long-term state-building, nation-building in Iraq, I think it's not only the responsibility of the missions of the United States and other countries who are now involved in Iraq but, of course, is the roles and responsibility of other nations as well—other communities as well.

Indonesia believes very strongly, if we could work together, if we share and exchange of ideas, then there must be a proper and realistic solution in the long term in finding, again, a proper solution for Iraq that's good for Iraq, good for neighboring countries, good for the U.S., good for Indonesia, and good for all communities in the world.

Alternative Fuel Sources/Indonesia

Q. I would like to ask Mr. President Bush—President Bush—investment and trade relations between the United States and Indonesia is strong, and in energy sector, the United States is a longstanding partner of Indonesia. As you probably know, Indonesia is currently developing alternative energy, mainly biofuel. Are you willing to cooperate in this area? And can the United States share its technology with Indonesia and, for the example, trading biofuels. Thank you.

President Bush. Yes, thanks. I'm very supportive of biofuel initiatives, starting in our own country. It's important for us to develop alternative ways to power our vehicles if we want to become less dependent on oil. And so for example, we're now consuming about 5 billion gallons of ethanol, which is a fuel made, in our case, from corn. The President and I spent a fair amount of time talking about the ability to develop biofuels, particularly in Indonesia's case, from sugar cane as well as palm oil. And the technologies are available to convert sugar into ethanol. For example, the country of Brazil powers its automobiles with about 85 percent of all fuels from ethanol from sugar cane.

The other interesting fact for people to understand is that the technology to have a gasoline-driven automobile be powered by ethanol is very simple. It's what's called flex-fuel automobiles. And so there's—we're on the beginning stages of really a change in how we consume energy. And it's in the world's interest that we promote biofuels.

Where the United States needs to go though, is that we can't rely upon corn only to develop our ethanols. And so we're spending a lot of money on cellulosic research, and that is the ability to convert wood chips, for example, to ethanol. And as those technologies become feasible and economic, we will share them with other countries. It's in our interests, it's in the U.S. interest that others use biofuel, as well as our own.

And so I'm optimistic about the technologies that are developing. I'm also realistic to understand it's going to take a while to get them—to bring them to the—to make them economic. But we're spending

a lot of money on this type of research. And the President needs to know that as it becomes commercially capable, we'll share it.

Matt [Matt Spetalnick, Reuters].

U.S. Foreign Policy

Q. President Bush.

President Bush. Yes, Matt.

Q. Here in the world's most populous Muslim nation, thousands have demonstrated for days, saying that your policy in the Middle East and Iraq and elsewhere is anti-Islamic. How do you fight that impression? And doesn't it require more than just a reassertion of your existing foreign policy goals?

And for President Yudhoyono, did you, in your talks with President Bush, urge him to begin a withdrawal of U.S. forces from Iraq as soon as possible?

President Bush. I mean, I'll be glad to answer it for him: No, he didn't. But he can answer it for himself. [*Laughter*]

Look, I applaud a society where people are free to come and express their opinion. And it's to Indonesia's credit that it's a society where people are able to protest and say what they think. And it's not the first time, by the way, where people have showed up and expressed their opinion about my policies. But that's what happens when you make hard decisions.

My answer to people about whether or not—how do you comfort people of the Muslim faith that our policies are open, is that I believe freedom is universal and democracy is universal. I don't believe it's the sole right of the United States or the sole right of Methodists. I believe in the universality of freedom. And therefore— and I believe people desire to live in free societies, and I believe the vast majority of people want to live in moderation and not have extremists kill innocent people.

And so therefore, our policies are to promote that kind of form of government. It's not going to look like America; it's going to be different from America. And I also

would tell people that democracies yield peace. Democracies don't fight each other. One of the reasons why I am proud to call this President friend is because he understands the power of democracy, and he understands it's a universal right.

And so therefore, to say spreading democracy is antireligious—it's the opposite of that. Democracy means you can worship any way you choose, freely. And so, look, people protest; that's a good sign. It's a good sign of a healthy society.

President Yudhoyono. Well, to elaborate my first view on Iraq, I would like to say that probably we have to think about developing a triple-track solution. One is really important is having national reconciliation in Iraq, together with the empowerment of the existing national Government is very important, so Iraq can handle her own problem.

Second is, of course, we have to involve other parties. We have to probably deploy and employ new setup of security forces in parallel with some day, this on a proper timetable, the disengagement of U.S. military forces and other coalition forces from Iraq.

And of course, the third track is also not to be neglected, is how do the international community work together in conducting reconstruction and rehabilitation of Iraq after the conflict.

So I think we have to combine all those three solutions before, actually, the United States can determine what the possible policies to be developed in the future related to the withdrawal or disengagement of the U.S. forces from Iraq.

Q. So do you believe—[*inaudible*]—U.S. forces should remain in Iraq then?

President Yudhoyono. I think I have explained my view on those three tracks of solution. And the future disengagement of U.S. forces from Iraq must be connected to the other two that I have mentioned already.

Thank you.

NOTE: The President spoke at approximately 6:45 p.m. at Bogor Palace. In his remarks, he referred to Kristiani Herawati, wife of President Yudhoyono. President Yudhoyono spoke partly in Bahasa Indonesia, and those portions of his remarks were translated by an interpreter.

Joint Statement Between the United States of America and the Republic of Indonesia
November 20, 2006

President Susilo Bambang Yudhoyono and President George W. Bush today reaffirmed the strength and vitality of the bilateral relationship between Indonesia and the United States, and reviewed the highly positive development of U.S-Indonesia relations over the past two years. The two Presidents recognized the special and enduring bonds between the two countries and their people, demonstrated recently by the close cooperation following the devastating tsunami in Aceh and Hurricane Katrina. President Bush expressed his admiration for the resilience and determination of the Indonesian people and government in rebuilding areas affected by the earthquake in Yogyakarta and Central Java.

The two Presidents reaffirmed that Indonesia and the United States are bound by a broad-based democratic partnership based on equality, mutual respect, common interests and shared values of freedom, pluralism and tolerance. The Presidents committed themselves to broadening and deepening such partnership.

President Bush congratulated Indonesia on the successful signing and implementation of a Memorandum of Understanding that has brought peace to the province of Aceh, and renewed the United States' firm support for Indonesia's peace-building efforts in Aceh. President Bush also re-emphasized the United States' strong support for Indonesia's national unity and territorial integrity, and opposition to secessionist movements in any part of Indonesia. President Bush stressed the importance of a united, democratic, pluralistic and prosperous Indonesia to the region and beyond.

President Bush congratulated President Yudhoyono on signing an agreement with the Millennium Challenge Corporation for a $55 million Threshold program, noting that it represents a resounding endorsement of President Yudhoyono's anti-corruption program and "pro-growth, pro-job, and pro-poor" economic strategy. President Bush expressed confidence that the threshold program will have a transformative effect on Indonesia's development and international competitiveness.

Noting the strength and importance of educational and cultural links, the Presidents reviewed the excellent work being done through the US$157 million U.S-Indonesia Education Initiative on basic education, the cornerstone of U.S. assistance to Indonesia and a symbol of our forward-looking partnership. The Presidents highlighted the importance of education for democracy, tolerance and economic progress and reaffirmed their commitment to working together to revitalize their cooperation in education. The Presidents also expressed their desire to encourage more people-to-people contacts through travel, educational exchanges, and tourism between Indonesia and the United States.

President Yudhoyono and President Bush noted with satisfaction the continuing development of U.S-Indonesia economic and trade relations. They welcomed the strong

support by APEC Leaders for the conclusion of an ambitious Doha Round agreement and noted their joint commitment to do everything possible to realize the development goals of the Doha negotiations. President Yudhoyono briefed President Bush on his government's program to strengthen the investment climate by improving infrastructure, reducing red tape, enhancing the rule of law and respect for contracts. They welcomed a number of positive developments since their May 2005 meeting in Washington DC, including:

- The establishment of the ASEAN-U.S. Enhanced Partnership;
- Signing of a U.S.-ASEAN Trade and Investment Framework Arrangement (TIFA);
- The June 2006 extension of U.S. Export-Import Bank coverage to private Indonesian corporations for the first time since 1998;
- The upgrading of Indonesia from the Special 301 Priority Watch List in November 2006 based on steps to improve intellectual property rights enforcement; and
- The strengthening of our dialogue through our bilateral Trade and Investment Framework Agreement (TIFA) to further promote and facilitate trade and investment.

The Presidents praised two recently signed MOUs, one on Cooperation in Trade in Textile and Apparel Goods and another on Combating Illegal Logging and Associated Trade in the context of the TIFA between the two countries. They also applauded the resumption of cooperation and capacity building activities between the U.S. Forest Service and the Indonesian Ministry of Forestry.

The two Presidents discussed the grave threat posed by Avian Influenza (AI), and President Yudhoyono reiterated his Government's firm commitment to combating its spread. He briefed President Bush on Indonesia's completion of a unified national response plan, increase in the AI budget for 2007, and active participation in the International Partnership on Avian and Pandemic Influenza. President Bush announced the United States would increase its AI assistance to Indonesia to expand animal surveillance and response efforts and strengthen nation-wide public awareness. President Bush confirmed that the U.S. Centers for Disease Control and Prevention and Animal and Plant Health Inspection Service would assign permanent staff to Indonesia to build more effective partnerships with their counterparts in Indonesia. President Yudhoyono thanked President Bush for the United States' work in support of the Indonesian Ministry of Health's efforts to identify human AI cases and investigate AI outbreaks. The two Presidents stressed the imperative of continued and enhanced cooperation between Indonesian and American health workers and medical scientists to fight infectious diseases, including through the Naval Medical Research Unit (NAMRU–2), which has been in operation since 1968. They agreed that negotiations to extend the research work of NAMRU–2 should be expedited.

President Bush and President Yudhoyono reviewed the expanding partnership between the U.S. and Indonesia in the area of disaster management, emergency preparedness, and mitigation. The two Presidents noted the steady progress on constructing the west coast road in Aceh Province that will restore communication and economic links to communities that were devastated by the tsunami, and agreed on the importance of expediting land acquisition so that the road can be completed on schedule. President Bush applauded the significant progress made in reconstructing Aceh, paving the way for sustained peace and economic growth. President Bush and President Yudhoyono also welcomed the recent agreement between their two governments to cooperate on the development of a tsunami early warning system that will

safeguard Indonesia's tsunami-prone areas by 2009.

The two leaders noted the tremendous opportunities for cooperation between Indonesia and the United States in the areas of alternative fuels and environmental protection. President Yudhoyono briefed President Bush on his ambitious biofuel development initiative and the Presidents endorsed the U.S.-Indonesia Energy Policy Dialogue as a forum to discuss ways and means to acquire clean and safe alternative energy, including biofuels.

As the leaders of two nations which have both suffered terrorist attacks on their soil, the two leaders reaffirmed their solidarity in defeating the scourge of terrorism. Both Presidents expressed satisfaction at the successful arrest and conviction in Indonesia of suspects involved in the 2002 incident in Timika, and agreed to begin negotiations toward a Mutual Legal Assistance Treaty.

President Bush and President Yudhoyono discussed a broad range of regional and global security issues. President Bush and President Yudhoyono welcomed the successful restoration of bilateral military ties, and pledged to make such ties sustainable and mutually beneficial in the support of peace and stability. They agreed that such ties would be primarily targeted at increasing coordination on disaster relief, exchanges and training on the role of militaries in democratic societies, increasing mutual professional development and en-

hancing regional and maritime security. They agreed to explore the possibility of a Status of Forces Agreement.

President Bush congratulated Indonesia on its election as a non-permanent member of the United Nations Security Council. Both Presidents pledged to work closely together on issues before the Council in order to maintain international peace and security, especially the challenge posed by North Korea's nuclear weapons program. President Bush applauded Indonesia's participation in maintaining peace in southern Lebanon by volunteering forces to join UNIFIL. The two Presidents also discussed the Arab-Israeli conflict, and both Presidents stressed their support for the establishment of a viable, independent, democratic and sovereign Palestine state that would live side by side in peace with Israel.

The two Presidents stressed the importance of inter-civilizational and inter-faith dialogues. The two Presidents expressed their concern to see growing religious intolerance in some parts of the world and their common desire to work against it. President Bush expressed great admiration and respect for Indonesia's long history of religious tolerance and moderate Islamic thought.

NOTE: An original was not available for verification of the content of this joint statement.

Remarks to the Troops at Hickam Air Force Base in Honolulu, Hawaii
November 21, 2006

Thank you all. Admiral, thanks for the introduction. Thanks for the warm breakfast, and thanks for the good view. I appreciate the tight ship you run here. And I thank you all very much for serving our country.

Laura and I are honored to be with you. We're honored to say thanks on behalf of a grateful nation. And I'm pleased to tell you that the work you're doing will lead to peace for generations to come.

You serve at a time when we witness an ideological struggle between those who

love freedom and those who hate freedom. And the outcome of this struggle will determine how your children and grandchildren live. And I'm determined, like you are determined, that freedom prevails.

Today we saw again the vicious face of those who oppose freedom. We strongly condemn the assassination today in Lebanon of Pierre Gemayel, who was a minister in the Government of Prime Minister Siniora. We support the Siniora Government and its democracy, and we support the Lebanese people's desire to live in peace. And we support their efforts to defend their democracy against attempts by Syria, Iran, and allies to foment instability and violence in that important country.

I call for a full investigation of the murder to identify those people and those forces behind the killing. We call on the international community to support Prime Minister Siniora's Government. And one clear way to do so is for the United Nations Security Council to take all remaining steps needed to establish a special tribunal concerning the assassination of former Prime Minister Hariri and to assure that those behind that killing, and others that followed, are brought to justice. I strongly believe the United Nations Security Council ought to act today. For the sake of peace, the free world must reject those who undermine young democracies and murder in the name of their hateful ideology.

I want to thank our Secretary of State for joining us. You know, one of the jobs of the President is to surround himself with smart, capable, strong people, and I have done so in Condoleezza Rice.

I also did so at the altar. [*Laughter*] And I'm pleased Laura is here as well. We're on our way back home after a trip in Southeast Asia. I had meetings in Singapore and Indonesia, as well as a meeting at the Asia-Pacific Economic Cooperation in Vietnam. And they're important meetings. It gave me a chance to discuss with leaders from the Pacific region about our common threats: the common threat of terrorism;

the common threat of pandemic outbreaks; and the common threat of North Korea's nuclear weapons program.

I told them that the United States of America remains committed to Asia because we have key economic and national security interests in the region. It's in our national interests that we be involved in the Asia-Pacific region. And the Pacific Command bares the primary responsibility for defending our interests in that part of the world. You represent the oldest and largest unified command in the United States military. You cover an area that spans more than half of the surface area of the Earth. You've got a really important job, and I'm here to thank you for doing a good job.

You serve freedom's cause in a lot of ways. When you help deliver humanitarian relief to victims of natural disasters, you serve freedom's cause. When you fight terrorists wherever we find them, you serve freedom's cause. Every branch of our military is playing a vital role. The Army and Marine Corps have deployed thousands of soldiers and marines to Afghanistan and to Iraq. You've been joined by units from Hawaii's Army and Air National Guard.

Earlier this year, the Pacific fleet conducted one of the largest multinational maritime exercises in the world, involving 8 nations, 35 ships, 180 aircraft, and 19,000 personnel. You serve freedom's cause when you help others to be able to defend themselves. You serve freedom's cause when you help young democracies fight off the extremists who try to impose their hateful vision of the world. What happens in Asia-Pacific matters to America's security here at home.

The Air Force has brought humanitarian aid to victims in earthquakes and typhoons. You provided airlift support to places like East Timor. The Coast Guard works closely with China as part of an effort to improve enforcement of laws against maritime drug traffickers.

Some of the troops from this command who were deployed to combat operations in Iraq and Afghanistan didn't come home. We remember their courage. We pray for their families and loved ones left behind, and we resolve to honor their sacrifice by completing the missions for which they gave their lives.

The men and women who wear the uniform are the best that America has to offer. You belong to the finest Armed Forces the world has ever known. I appreciate the fact that you have volunteered to wear our uniform in these troubled times, that you have volunteered knowing the dangers into which you might be sent. It's an incredible country when people of character stand up and say, "I want to serve something greater than my self-interests."

I want to thank you for your sacrifice. I particularly thank your families for joining you in this noble cause. We'll succeed, and when we do, generations of Americans will look back on this period and say, "Thank God the United States had such men and women of character at the beginning of the 21st century."

God bless.

NOTE: The President spoke at 7:45 a.m. in the Officers Club. In his remarks, he referred to Adm. William J. Fallon, USN, commander, U.S. Pacific Command; and Prime Minister Fuad Siniora of Lebanon.

Statement on the Assassination of Minister of Industry Pierre Gemayel of Lebanon
November 21, 2006

Today's assassination of Lebanese Industry Minister Pierre Gemayel shows yet again the viciousness of those who are trying to destabilize that country.

The United States remains fully committed to supporting Lebanon's independence and democracy in the face of attempts by Syria, Iran, and their allies within Lebanon to foment instability and violence. Syria's refusal to cease and desist from its continuing efforts to destabilize Lebanon's democratically elected Government is a repeated violation of United Nations Security Council Resolutions 1559 and 1701. The United States will continue its efforts with allied nations and democratic forces in Lebanon to resist these efforts and protect Lebanon's sovereignty and democratic institutions.

We urge the U.N. Security Council and the Secretary-General today to take the remaining steps needed to establish the special tribunal for Lebanon that will try those accused of involvement in the assassination of former Prime Minister Hariri, and to ensure that that tribunal can also bring to justice those responsible for related assassinations, assassination attempts, and other terrorist attacks. We also demand that Syria treat Lebanon as a genuinely sovereign neighbor, establishing full diplomatic relations with Lebanon, and delineating its border with that country including, in particular, in the Shab'a Farms area, through a bilateral agreement.

Joint Statement by President George W. Bush and Prime Minister Nuri al-Maliki of Iraq
November 21, 2006

We are pleased to announce that we will meet in Amman, Jordan, on November 29–30 to continue our consultations on building security and stability in Iraq. We will focus our discussion on current developments in Iraq, progress made to date in the deliberations of the high-level Joint Committee on Transferring Security Responsibility, and the role of the region in supporting Iraq. We would like to express our gratitude to His Majesty King Abdullah II of the Hashemite Kingdom of Jordan, who has graciously offered to host our consultations. We look forward to meeting with His Majesty in Amman.

We reiterate our common commitment to building the foundations of a peaceful, democratic, secure, and unified Iraq, and to strengthening the partnership between our two nations.

NOTE: An original was not available for verification of the content of this joint statement.

Remarks at the Thanksgiving Turkey Presentation Ceremony
November 22, 2006

Good morning. Thanks for coming. Welcome to the Rose Garden. I appreciate being up here with Mike Briggs and Alice Johnson of the National Turkey Federation, and I thank you for bringing along our feathery guest. [*Laughter*] We're glad you're here. Mike, thanks for bringing your family as well.

The name of the National Thanksgiving Turkey has been chosen by online voting at the White House web site. By the decision of the voters, this turkey is going to be called Flyer. And there's always a backup bird, just in case the guest of honor can't perform his duties, and the backup bird's name is Fryer. [*Laughter*] Probably better to be called Flyer than Fryer.

These birds were hatched on a farm in Missouri and raised there by Matthew Nutt and his mom and dad, Carol [Donna] ° and Lynn, and we're glad you all are here. Thanks for coming. They did a fine job of raising these birds.

° White House correction.

I also welcome the Girl Scouts who've joined us. Thanks for coming—[*applause*]—yes, I'm glad you're here. These are troops from Virginia and Maryland and Washington, DC. And we thank you for being in scouting, and we thank your scout masters and your parents for setting such a good example for you.

We're here in the Rose Garden. This is a place where Barney likes to hang out. Barney is my dog. And he likes to chase a soccer ball here. He came out a little early, as did Flyer, and instead of chasing the soccer ball, he chased the bird. [*Laughter*] And it kind of made the turkey nervous. See, the turkey was already nervous to begin with. Nobody has told him yet about the pardon I'm about to give him. [*Laughter*]

Tomorrow is our day of thanksgiving. It's a national observance first proclaimed by George Washington. In our journey across the centuries from a few tiny settlements to a prosperous and powerful nation, Americans have always been a grateful people,

and we are this year as well. We're grateful for our beautiful land. We're grateful for a harvest big enough to feed us all, plus much of the world. We're grateful for our freedom. We're grateful for our families, and we're grateful for life itself.

So on Thanksgiving Day, we gather with loved ones and we lift our hearts toward heaven in humility and gratitude. As we count our blessings, Americans also share our blessings. We're a generous country. We're filled with caring citizens who reach out to others, people who've heard the universal call to love a neighbor as we want to be loved ourself. On Thanksgiving and every day of the year, Americans live out of a spirit of compassion and care, and I thank you for that. It's the spirit that moves men and women to be mentors to the young, to be scout leaders, to be helpers of the elderly, to be comforters of the lonely and those who are left out.

We love our country, and the greatest example of that devotion is the citizen who steps forward to defend our Nation from harm. The members of our military have set aside their own comfort and convenience and safety to protect the rest of us. Their courage keeps us free. Their sacrifice makes us grateful, and their character makes us proud. Especially during the holidays, our whole Nation keeps them and their families in our thoughts and prayers.

And now to the ceremonial task of the day. Why don't we have a look at Flyer? There you go. I think Flyer heard Barney barking over there. [*Laughter*] It's a fine looking bird, isn't it? Flyer is probably wondering where he's going to wind up tomorrow. He's probably thinking he's going to end up on somebody's table. Well, I'm happy to report that he and Fryer both have many tomorrows ahead of them. This morning I am grateful I am granting a full Presidential pardon so they can live out their lives as safe as can be.

In fact, it gets even better. Later today Flyer and Fryer will be on a plane to Disneyland—[*laughter*]—where they're going to achieve further celebrity as the honorary grand marshal of the Thanksgiving Day Parade.

Thank you all for coming. God bless, and happy Thanksgiving.

NOTE: The President spoke at 10:22 a.m. in the Rose Garden at the White House. In his remarks, he referred to Mike Briggs, chairman, and Alice L. Johnson, president, National Turkey Federation. The Thanksgiving Day proclamation of November 16 is listed in Appendix D at the end of this volume.

The President's Radio Address
November 25, 2006

Good morning. This week, Americans across our Nation gather with loved ones to give thanks for the many blessings we share. We're grateful for our friends and families, who fill our lives with meaning and purpose. We're grateful to live in a land of plenty and during a time of great prosperity. And we're grateful to Almighty God for the freedom to enjoy all these gifts.

Every Thanksgiving we remember the story of the Pilgrims who came to America in search of a better life and religious freedom. Much has changed in the four centuries since these humble settlers landed at Plymouth Rock. While they were only a shivering few, we are now a strong and growing nation of more than 300 million. And the desire for freedom that led the Pilgrims to the New World still guides our Nation today.

Americans believe that every person has the right to live, work, and worship in freedom. And we're thankful to the men and women of our Nation's Armed Forces who risk their lives to protect those rights. This Thanksgiving, we are mindful that many of our finest citizens are spending the holiday far from their homes and loved ones, and we know that their service makes it possible for us to live in freedom.

On Tuesday, I had the chance to visit our troops and their families at Hickam Air Force Base in Honolulu, Hawaii. Our servicemembers there have deployed around the world to fight the terrorists in Afghanistan and Iraq, conduct important maritime exercises in the Pacific, help deliver humanitarian aid to the victims of disaster, and fight drug trafficking. I told the men and women at the base that we're grateful for their bravery and service and that we will never forget those who have made the ultimate sacrifice.

One American who made the ultimate sacrifice was Marine Corporal Jason Dunham. Two-and-a-half years ago in Iraq, Corporal Dunham gave his life when he threw himself on top of an enemy grenade and absorbed the blast. His selfless act saved the lives of two of his fellow marines, and earlier this month, I announced that our Nation will recognize Corporal Dunham with our highest decoration for valor, the Medal of Honor.

Corporal Dunham's friends remember him as the kind of guy who would do anything for you, his superiors remember him as a model marine, and a grateful Nation will forever remember him as one of America's most valiant heroes. This Thanksgiving, our thoughts and prayers are with his family and with all military families, especially those mourning the loss of a loved one.

During this holiday season, we also think of those still working to recover from the devastating hurricanes that struck our Nation last year. We are grateful to the armies of compassion who rallied to bring food, water, and hope to those who had lost everything, and we renew our commitment to help those who are still suffering and to rebuild our Nation's gulf coast.

Thanksgiving reminds us that the true strength of our Nation is the compassion and decency of our people. And as we count our blessings, we remember that those blessings are meant to be shared. I encourage all Americans to look for a way to help those in need—from tutoring a child to working in a shelter to giving a hand to a neighbor. I thank all those Americans who volunteer this season, and Laura and I wish every American a safe and happy holiday.

Thank you for listening.

NOTE: The address was recorded at 11:20 a.m. on November 22 in the Cabinet Room at the White House for broadcast at 10:06 a.m. on November 25. The transcript was made available by the Office of the Press Secretary on November 24 but was embargoed for release until the broadcast. The Office of the Press Secretary also released a Spanish language transcript of this address.

Statement on the Deaths of Frank Madla, Mary Cruz, and Aleena Jimenez
November 26, 2006

Laura and I are deeply saddened by the deaths of Frank Madla, his mother-in-law, Mary Cruz, and his granddaughter, Aleena Jimenez. Frank was a dedicated public servant who devoted more than three decades of his life to serving his State and all its people in the Texas house and senate. Frank never hesitated to reach across

party lines to do what was best for his fellow Texans, and I was proud to work with him when I was Governor. Texas has lost a fine man. Laura and I pray for the full and speedy recovery of Frank's wife, Helen. We send our deepest sympathies to the entire family for their loss.

Statement on the Death of Police Officer Steve B. Favela
November 26, 2006

Laura and I are deeply saddened by the death of Officer Steve Favela of the Honolulu Police Department. Officer Favela died from injuries he suffered while protecting us during our visit to Hawaii. We send our condolences to his wife, Barbara, his entire family, and his fellow law enforcement officers. We pray that God will comfort them and that their friends and loved ones will sustain them in this difficult time.

Officer Favela risked his life every day to protect the people of his community. In this time of great sadness, we give thanks for his life of service.

Remarks Prior to Discussions With Prime Minister Andrus Ansip of Estonia in Tallinn, Estonia
November 28, 2006

[*The Prime Minister's remarks are joined in progress.*]

Prime Minister Ansip. ——once again, thank you very much for your support and for the support of your country.

President Bush. Thank you, Mr. Prime Minister.

Prime Minister Ansip. [*Inaudible*]

President Bush. Well, we're honored to be here. It's a great country. And I thank you for your leadership. I'm very proud of the economic accomplishments and your contributions to peace and liberty around the world. I've really been looking forward to coming here. I'm honored that you agreed to—[*inaudible*]. Thank you.

NOTE: The President spoke at approximately 9:37 a.m. at the Stenbock House.

Remarks Following a Meeting With Proponents of Democracy in Tallinn
November 28, 2006

It's an amazing country you have here. They've got an e-government system that should be the envy of a lot of nations. They've got a tax system that is transparent, open, and simple; people file their taxes over the Internet.

You're doing a fine job, Mr. Prime Minister. I'm proud of you.

NOTE: The President spoke at 10:31 a.m. at the Stenbock House. In his remarks, he referred to Prime Minister Andrus Ansip of Estonia.

The President's News Conference With President Toomas Ilves of Estonia in Tallinn
November 28, 2006

President Ilves. Again, I'm very happy to greet the President of the United States, George W. Bush, in our fall weather here in Tallinn. Unfortunately, the weather isn't better than it is, but that's how it happens. This visit and these very open meetings that we have had, President Bush has had with me as well as with the Prime Minister, Andrus Ansip, truly prove that Estonia and the United States are close allies.

One of the main messages today was the message of freedom to those states who, like us, have chosen the way to democracy and freedom and will not bow to pressure from any of their neighbors, and by these countries we mean Georgia, Ukraine, the Balkan States. We should not hesitate to support these states. And we should not falter when any of our allies are losing hope or faith, and we will help them in every way we can.

We will also not falter in making Afghanistan more secure, where Estonian soldiers are helping to protect the welfare of Afghan citizens, again, together, hand in hand with the United States. NATO's greatest foreign operation in the post-cold war period—it is the greatest challenge of the postwar period. It is a challenge not only for the neighbors of these countries but also for the whole world, as was proved by September the 11th.

We are hoping to strengthen the ties between European countries and the United States. Conflicts between us are minor or nonexistent, and any issues will be easy to resolve. President Bush's visit to Tallinn is taking place at a time immediately before the summit of NATO in Riga. This summit shows how far the Baltic States have developed and how strong the support of our allies is for us. We want to give a strong message at the summit, and that is that the doors to NATO are not closed and this is becoming a very mature, good organization.

And I want to tell Mr. Bush, welcome to Estonia.

President Bush. I'm proud to be the first sitting American President to visit Estonia. I'm really glad I came. Yours is a beautiful country and a strong friend and ally of the United States. I appreciate the warm welcome I've received. My only regret is that Laura is not with me. She's receiving the Christmas tree at the White House. She sends her very best, Mr. President.

We had a lot—we had a really good discussion. The President and I spent a lot of time talking about the issue of freedom and liberty and peace. I appreciate very much the leadership Estonia is providing inside NATO.

We talked about how our nations can cooperate to achieve common objectives and promote common values, values such as human dignity and human rights and the freedom to speak and worship the way one sees fit.

Estonia is a strong ally in this war on terror. I appreciate so very much the President's understanding of the need to resist tyranny. Of all the people in the world who understand what tyranny can do, it's the Estonian people. I appreciate very much the fact that Estonia is helping others resist tyranny and realize their dreams of living in a free society.

In Afghanistan, Estonians are serving as a part of NATO's International Security Assistance Force in a dangerous Province that the extremists, the Taliban, seeks to control. I appreciate the fact that your forces are serving bravely, Mr. President. The people of Estonia need to be proud of their military. It's a fine military. And the commitment of your people is important to helping secure the peace.

I appreciate the troops that you have sent to Iraq. I also understand Estonian soldiers have been wounded and two soldiers have given their lives. We hold their families in our hearts. We lift them up in prayer. And Americans are grateful to be serving alongside such brave allies.

Estonia is sharing its democratic experience with other nations. You have made a very successful transition to democracy, and you're helping other nations do the same, and that is a vital contribution to world peace. I appreciate the fact that you're training leaders from Georgia to Moldova to the Ukraine. I appreciate the assistance programs you're providing to the Afghan people. I also appreciate the fact that you work with your neighbors and through the European Union to promote freedom in this region and around the globe.

This morning the Prime Minister and I had a chance to meet as well, and he introduced me to some of your citizens who are helping to build democracies, and I thanked them for their work. We also discussed how Estonia has built a strong economy and raised the standard of living for the people. I appreciate the fact that you've got a flat tax; you got a tax system that's transparent and simple. I also am amazed by the e-governance you have here in your country. You really are on the leading edge of change, and you're setting a really strong example.

We talked about the fact that Estonians want to be able to travel to America visa-free. Both the President and the Prime Minister made this a important part of our discussions. They made it clear to me that if we're a ally in NATO, people ought to be able to come to our country in a much easier fashion. It is clear to me that this is an important issue for the Estonian people as well. I appreciate their leaders being straightforward and very frank. There's no question where they stand.

I am pleased to announce that I'm going to work with our Congress and our international partners to modify our Visa Waiver Program. It's a way to make sure that nations like Estonia qualify more quickly for the program and, at the same time, strengthen the program's security components.

The new security component of the Visa Waiver Program would use modern technology to improve the security regime for international travelers to and from the United States. In other words, we need to know who is coming and when they're leaving. And the more we can share information, the easier it will be for me to get Congress to make it easier for Estonians to travel to the United States.

We want people to come to our country. We understand a lot of Estonians have relatives in America. It's in our Nation's interest that people be able to come and visit, and it's important, at the same time, to make sure that those who want to continue to kill Americans aren't able to exploit the system.

I'm going to go to Riga right after our lunch. We have an ambitious agenda there. More than 50,000 NATO soldiers are providing security in six missions on three continents. These deployments have shown that our alliance remains as relevant today as it was during the height of the cold war.

Our alliance defends freedom and, so doing, helps make us all more secure. We will discuss NATO's largest deployment, and that is Afghanistan. We're partnering with Afghan security forces to defeat the

Taliban and strengthen that young democracy. To succeed in Afghanistan, NATO allies must provide the forces NATO military commanders require. And I appreciate Estonia's commitment. Like Estonia, member nations must accept difficult assignments if we expect to be successful.

In Riga, we'll discuss how our alliance must build on what we have learned in Afghanistan. We will continue to transform NATO forces and improve NATO capabilities so that our alliance can complete 21st century missions successfully. The threat has changed. Our capabilities must change with the threats if NATO is to remain relevant. The President understands that, and I appreciate our discussion along those lines today.

We're also going to discuss NATO's further enlargement. By inviting qualifying democracies to join our alliance at the next NATO summit in 2008, we'll continue to build a Europe that is whole, free, and at peace.

I want to thank you for your hospitality again. I know the people of this country are proud of their accomplishments. The American people would be amazed at what your country has done, and I'm proud for you. And I'm proud to call you friend. Thank you, Mr. President.

President Ilves. Thank you, Mr. President.

President Bush. Is there some questions?

U.S. Visa Policy

Q. I have a question for both Presidents. Mr. Bush, you said that you really appreciate everything that Estonia has done and that the U.S. is very interested in seeing Estonians visit your country. But you, as President, when will you be proposing to Congress this change in the visa laws to give us visa-free travel? And the second part of the question is, what should Estonia do in order to help you resolve this issue more quickly?

President Bush. ——to work on our 3-percent requirement, and at the same time,

assure Members of Congress that in loosening the visa waiver issue, or changing the visa waiver issue, that we'll still be able to protect our country from people who would exploit the Visa Waiver Program to come to our country to do harm. And that process is beginning shortly.

President Ilves. And I may add that Estonia is constantly—has been raising this question. I had a very long discussion, even back when I was a delegate in European Parliament. I would say that we have come quite a long way from the time we started these discussions 2 years ago with Nick Burns. And we are prepared—when the security requirements have been clarified, have been explained, then we will be able to implement them in our passports. And that is simply a technical problem, but it is resolvable.

President Bush. Are you going to call on anybody?

Russia-Georgia Relations

Q. First, my respect to both of you, Mr. Bush, Mr. Ilves. A question for Mr. Bush: You said that you discussed with Mr. Ilves the situation in Georgia. Estonia and the United States have helped in the development of this country of Georgia, and we are hoping to see some progress—in this country. But the conflict between Russia and Georgia is putting a stop to this. What do you think we should do to help resolve this conflict between Russia and Georgia?

President Bush. Precisely what we ought to do is help resolve the conflict and use our diplomats to convince people there is a better way forward than through violence. We haven't seen violence yet. The idea is to head it off in the first place. I spoke to Vladimir Putin about this very subject when I saw him in the Far East last week. I know that the President has spoken with President Saakashvili as well. The tenor of the conversation appears to be improving to me, that people understand that the best way to resolve their differences is to sit

down at the table and solve them diplomatically. And so we'll continue to work along those lines.

I don't know if you want to add anything to that.

President Ilves. Briefly, just that we sincerely hope that Russia will understand that a democratic state on its borders is not a danger to Russian security. And we hope Russia will understand that authoritarian states at its borders will not guarantee its own stability.

President Bush. That's Deb [Deb Riechmann, Associated Press], AP. Yes, Deb.

War on Terror/Democracy in the Middle East

Q. Mr. President, thank you, sir. What is the difference between what we're seeing now in Iraq and civil war? And do you worry that calling it a civil war would make it difficult to argue that we're fighting the central front of the war on terror there?

President Bush. You know, the plans of Mr. Zarqawi was to foment sectarian violence. That's what he said he wanted to do. The Samarra bombing that took place last winter was intended to create sectarian violence, and it has. The recent bombings were to perpetuate the sectarian violence. In other words, we've been in this phase for a while. And the fundamental objective is to work with the Iraqis to create conditions so that the vast majority of the people will be able to see that there's a peaceful way forward.

The bombings that took place recently was a part of a pattern that has been going on for about 9 months. I'm going to bring this subject up, of course, with Prime Minister Maliki when I visit with him in Jordan on Thursday. My questions to him will be: What do we need to do to succeed? What is your strategy in dealing with the sectarian violence? I will assure him that we will continue to pursue Al Qaida to make sure that they are unable to establish a safe haven in Iraq.

I will ask him, What is required and what is your strategy to be a country which can govern itself and sustain itself? And it's going to be an important meeting, and I'm looking forward to it.

Q. ——people who are saying that we're moving forward to a full war are wrong?

President Bush. Deb, there's all kinds of speculation about what may be or not happening. What you're seeing on TV has started last February. It was an attempt by people to foment sectarian violence, and no— no question, it's dangerous there and violent. And the Maliki Government is going to have to deal with that violence, and we want to help them do so. It's in our interest that we succeed. A democracy in the heart of the Middle East is an important part of defeating the radicals and totalitarians that can't stand the emergence of a democracy.

One of the interesting things that's taking place—and people have got to understand what's happening—is when you see a young democracy beginning to emerge in the Middle East, the extremists try to defeat its emergence.

That's why you see violence in Lebanon. There's a young democracy in Lebanon run by Prime Minister Siniora. And that Government is being undermined, in my opinion, by extremist forces encouraged out of Syria and Iran. Why? Because a democracy will be a major defeat for those who articulate extremist points of view.

We're trying to help get a democracy started in the Palestinian Territory. Prime Minister Olmert has reached out, at one point, to Prime Minister Abbas—or President Abbas. And you know what happens as soon as he does that? Extremists attack, because they can't stand the thought of a democracy. And the same thing is happening in Iraq. And it's in our mutual interest that we help this Government succeed.

And no question, it's tough, Deb; no question about it. There's a lot of sectarian violence taking place, fomented, in my opinion, because of these attacks by Al

Qaida, causing people to seek reprisal. And we will work with the Maliki Government to defeat these elements.

By far, the vast majority of the people want to live in peace. Twelve million people voted. They said, "We want to live under a Constitution which we approved." And our objective must be to help them realize their dreams. This is the—this is an important part of an ideological struggle that is taking place here in the beginning of the 21st century. And the interesting contribution that a country like Estonia is making is that people shouldn't have to live under tyranny—"We just did that; we don't like it." They understand that democracies yield peace. This President is a strong advocate for democracies because he understands what it means to live under subjugation, and he understands the hope that democracy brings to regions of the world. And I appreciate your steadfast leadership.

Toby [Tabassum Zakaria, Reuters]. Last question?

Q. Yes.

President Bush. I'll follow your instructions.

Iran-Iraq Relations

Q. Mr. President, would direct talks between the United States and Iran and Syria help stem the violence in Iraq? And would you agree to such a step?

President Bush. I think that, first of all, Iraq is a sovereign nation which is conducting its own foreign policy. They're having talks with their neighbors. And if that's what they think they ought to do, that's fine. I hope their talks yield results. One result that Iraq would like to see is for the Iranians to leave them alone. If Iran is going to be involved in their country, they ought to be involved in a constructive way, encouraging peace. That is the message that the Iranians—the Iraqis have delivered to the Iranians. That's the message that Prime Minister Maliki has made clear, that he expects the neighbors to encourage peaceful development of the country.

As far as the United States goes, Iran knows how to get to the table with us, and that is to do that which they said they would do, which is verifiably suspend their enrichment programs. One of the concerns that I have about the Iranian regime is their desire to develop a nuclear weapon, and you ought to be concerned about it too. The idea of this regime having a nuclear weapon by which they could blackmail the world is unacceptable to free nations. And that's why we're working through the United Nations to send a clear message that the EU–3 and the United States, Russia, and China do not accept their desires to have a nuclear weapon.

There is a better way forward for the Iranian people. And if they would like to be at the table discussing this issue with the United States, I have made it abundantly clear how they can do so, and that is, verifiably suspend the enrichment program. And then we'll be happy to have a dialog with them.

But as far as Iraq goes, the Iraqi Government is a sovereign government that is capable of handling its own foreign policies and is in the process of doing so. And they have made it abundantly clear, and I agree with them, that the Iranians and the Syrians should help, not destabilize this young democracy.

Thank you.

President Ilves. Thank you very much.

NOTE: The President's news conference began at 11 a.m. at the National Bank of Estonia. In his remarks, he referred to President Vladimir V. Putin of Russia; President Mikheil Saakashvili of Georgia; Prime Minister Nuri al-Maliki of Iraq; Prime Minister Fuad Siniora of Lebanon; Prime Minister Ehud Olmert of Israel; and President Mahmoud Abbas of the Palestinian Authority. President Ilves spoke in Estonian, and his remarks were translated by an interpreter.

Remarks at a Lunch Hosted by President Toomas Ilves of Estonia in Tallinn
November 28, 2006

Mr. President, thank you very much, and Mr. Prime Minister, thank you as well for your gracious hospitality. I'm really thrilled to be here in Estonia. I love being in a country that values liberty and freedom. I appreciate being in a country that understands there are duties and obligations beyond her border to help others realize the benefits of liberty and freedom. I'm very proud of your military, and I'm pleased to be in the presence of those who wear the uniform of Estonia. I know our military has great respect for the Estonian soldiers.

I am amazed to be in a country that has been able to effect a flat tax in such a positive way. I am impressed by the e-governance that you have here in Estonia.

All in all, this has been a very worthwhile and exciting visit for me, and I thank you for your warm hospitality. And I'd like to raise my glass to the leadership of this important country, to our friendship, and most importantly, to the people of Estonia.

NOTE: The President spoke at approximately 11:42 a.m. in the Estonian Theater. In his remarks, he referred to Prime Minister Andrus Ansip of Estonia. The transcript released by the Office of the Press Secretary also included the remarks of President Ilves.

Remarks Following Discussions With President Vaira Vike-Freiberga of Latvia in Riga, Latvia
November 28, 2006

President Vike-Freiberga. Well, ladies and gentlemen, it's been a great pleasure to have the President of the United States here in Riga for the second time in less than 2 years. And I expressed how delighted we are to be receiving him and his delegation here on the occasion of the Riga 2006 summit.

The United States has been our strong supporter all those years when Latvia was not free, has been our supporter after we regained our independence, and I'm most grateful to the United States for the understanding and support we got in our direction and our movement towards NATO. Now that we are fully members, Latvians certainly sleep better at night knowing that they are protected by an alliance that will spare them the sorts of experiences they had in earlier years.

But of course I'm delighted to be welcoming the President of the United States as the representative of what still remains as a shining example of the free world, of the sort of success one can achieve in a country that has been working at its democracy for a long time, that keeps perfecting it. I would hope that Latvia, as well, has the same opportunities; that we can go ahead, have our own choices, make our own mistakes, and do so with the help and understanding and support of fellow nations who share the same values as us.

. *President Bush.* Madam President, thanks for inviting me back to Riga. Our experience was so good the first time that we couldn't wait to get back. I want to congratulate you on hosting this very important NATO summit. You and your Government have done a spectacular job, and I want

to thank the people of Riga for accommodating all the world leaders who have come to this important meeting.

I appreciate very much your strong belief that liberty has got the capacity to transform the world for the good. I thank you and the Latvian people for supporting the young democracies in Afghanistan and in Iraq.

We spent time talking about our bilateral relations. Trade is good between the United States and Latvia, and that's very positive. The President brought up the Visa Waiver Program. She is deeply concerned that the people of Latvia aren't able to travel to the United States as freely as she would like. I fully understand your concerns, Madam President. And to this end,

I'll be sending to Congress a new proposal to make it easier for the citizens of Latvia to come to the United States and, at the same time, for us to share information to make sure that we're able to thwart any type of terrorist activities in our country. And I'm confident we can work this through.

And I want to thank you for working hard on this issue. Every time I've met with you, you brought it up, because you deeply care about the people of your country. I want to congratulate you on your strong leadership, and again, thank you for your very warm hospitality.

NOTE: The President spoke at approximately 3:40 p.m. at Riga Castle.

Remarks at Latvia University in Riga
November 28, 2006

Thank you all. *Labdien*. Madam President, thank you for your kind words. Thank you for your leadership, and thank you for your friendship. Mr. Speaker; Mr. Prime Minister; Senator Sessions from the great State of Alabama, who is with us; Marc Leland, my friend from a long period of time; I want to thank the rector of this important university. Distinguished guests, ladies and gentlemen, thank you for your warm welcome. I'm delighted to be back in Riga.

I appreciate the Latvian Transatlantic Organization, the Commission of Strategic Analysis, and the German Marshall Fund of the United States for organizing this important conference. This is my third visit to the Baltics as the President of the United States, and it's my second visit to this beautiful city. I just can't stay away. I'm thrilled and honored to be back here, and I bring the greetings and good wishes of the American people.

Not far from where we meet today stands Riga's Freedom Monument. It was erected in 1935, during this country's brief period of independence between the two World Wars. During the dark years of Soviet occupation, the simple act of laying flowers at the foot of this monument was considered a crime by Communist authorities. In 1989, the monument was the scene of one of the most remarkable protests in the history of freedom. Hundreds of thousands of people stood together and formed a human chain that stretched nearly 400 miles across the Baltics, from Tallinn in the north, through downtown Riga, and into the heart of Vilnius. By joining hands, the people of this region showed their unity and their determination to live in freedom, and it made clear to the Soviet authorities that the Baltic peoples would accept nothing less than complete independence.

It took more years of struggle, but today, the Baltic nations have taken their rightful place in the community of free nations, and

Latvia is a host for an important NATO summit, the first time our alliance has met in one of the "captive nations" annexed by the Soviet Union. This is a proud day for the people of Latvia and all the Baltic States. And on behalf of the American people, I thank you for your hospitality, your friendship, and the courage you are showing in the NATO alliance.

As members of NATO, you are a vital part of the most effective multilateral organization in the world and the most important military alliance in history. As NATO allies, you will never again stand alone in defense of your freedom, and you'll never be occupied by a foreign power.

Each of the Baltic countries is meeting its obligations to strengthen NATO by bringing new energy and vitality and clarity of purpose to the alliance. Your love of liberty has made NATO stronger. And with your help, our alliance is rising to meet the great challenges and responsibilities of this young century by making NATO the world's most effective united force for freedom.

One of the great responsibilities of this alliance is to strengthen and expand the circle of freedom here in Europe. In the nearly six decades since NATO's founding, Europe has experienced an unprecedented expansion of liberty. A continent that was once divided by an ugly wall is now united in freedom. Yet the work of uniting Europe is not fully complete. Many nations that threw off the shackles of tyranny are still working to build the free institutions that are the foundation of successful democracies. NATO is encouraging these nations on the path to reform, and as governments make hard decisions for their people, they will be welcomed into the institutions of the Euro-Atlantic community.

After I took office in 2001, I declared that the United States believes in NATO membership for all of Europe's democracies that seek it and are ready to share the responsibilities that NATO brings. The following year in Prague, we invited seven nations to join our alliance: Estonia, Latvia, Lithuania, Romania, Bulgaria, Slovakia, and Slovenia. Here in Riga, allies will make clear that the door to NATO membership remains open, and at our next summit in 2008, we hope to issue additional invitations to nations that are ready for membership.

Today, Croatia, Macedonia, and Albania are all participating in NATO's Membership Action Plan, and the United States supports their aspirations to join the Atlantic alliance. Georgia is seeking NATO membership as well, and as it continues on the path of reform, we will continue to support Georgia's desire to become a NATO ally. We are also supporting the leaders of Ukraine as they work to curb corruption, promote the rule of law, and serve the cause of peace. Our position is clear: As democracy takes hold in Ukraine and its leaders pursue vital reforms, NATO membership will be open to the Ukrainian people if they choose it.

We're also working with Russia through the NATO-Russia Council. We recognize that Russia is a vital and important country, and that it's in our interests to increase our cooperation with Russia in areas such as countering terrorism and preventing the spread of weapons of mass destruction. By building ties between Russia and this alliance, we will strengthen our common security, and we will advance the cause of peace.

As we help the new democracies of Europe join the institutions of Europe, we must not forget those who still languish in tyranny. Just across the border from here lies the nation of Belarus, a place where peaceful protesters are beaten and opposition leaders are "disappeared" by the agents of a cruel regime. The existence of such oppression in our midst offends the conscience of Europe, and it offends the conscience of America. We have a message for the people of Belarus: The vision of a Europe whole, free, and at peace includes

you, and we stand with you in your struggle for freedom.

Another great responsibility of this alliance is to transform for new challenges. When NATO was formed in 1949, its principal mission was to protect Europe from a Soviet tank invasion. Today, the Soviet threat is gone. And under the able leadership of the Secretary General, NATO is transforming from a static alliance focused on the defense of Europe, into an expedentiary [expeditionary] ° alliance ready to deploy outside of Europe in the defense of freedom. This is a vital mission.

Over the past 6 years, we've taken decisive action to transform our capabilities in the alliance. We created a new NATO transformation command to ensure that our alliance is always preparing for the threats of the future. We created a new NATO battalion to counter the threats of enemies armed with weapons of mass destruction. We created a new NATO Response Force, to ensure that our alliance can deploy rapidly and effectively.

Here in Riga, we're taking new steps to build on this progress. At this summit, we will launch a NATO Special Operations Forces Initiative that will strengthen the ability of special operations personnel from NATO nations to work together on the battlefield. We will announce a new Strategic Airlift Initiative that will ensure that participating NATO members have a dedicated fleet of C–17 aircraft at their disposal. We will launch the Riga Global Partnership Initiative that will allow NATO to conduct joint training and joint exercises and common defense planning with nations like Japan and Australia, countries that share NATO's values and want to work with our alliance in the cause of peace. We will launch a new NATO Training Cooperation Initiative that will allow military forces in the Middle East to receive NATO training in counterterrorism and counterproliferation and peace support operations. And as

---

° White House correction.

we take these steps, every NATO nation must take the defensive—must make the defensive investments necessary to give NATO the capabilities it needs, so that our alliance is ready for any challenge that may emerge in the decades to come.

The most basic responsibility of this alliance is to defend our people against the threats of a new century. We're in a long struggle against terrorists and extremists who follow a hateful ideology and seek to establish a totalitarian empire from Spain to Indonesia. We fight against the extremists who desire safe havens and are willing to kill innocents anywhere to achieve their objectives.

NATO has recognized this threat. And 3 years ago, NATO took an unprecedented step when it sent allied forces to defend a young democracy more than 3,000 miles from Europe. Since taking command of the International Security Assistance Force in Afghanistan, NATO has expanded it from a small force that was operating only in Kabul into a robust force that conducts security operations in all of Afghanistan. NATO is helping to train the Afghan National Army. The alliance is operating 25 Provincial Reconstruction Teams that are helping the central Government extend its reach into distant regions of that country. At this moment, all 26 NATO allies and 11 partner nations are contributing forces to NATO's mission in Afghanistan. They're serving with courage, and they are doing the vital work necessary to help this young democracy secure the peace.

We saw the effectiveness of NATO forces this summer, when NATO took charge of security operations in Southern Afghanistan from the United States. The Taliban radicals who are trying to pull down Afghanistan's democracy and regain power saw the transfer from American to NATO control as a window of opportunity to test the will of the alliance. So the Taliban massed a large fighting force near Kandahar to face the NATO troops head on. It was a mistake. Together with the

Afghan National Army, NATO forces from Canada and Denmark and the Netherlands and Britain and Australia and the United States engaged the enemy, with operational support from Romanian, Portuguese, and Estonian forces. According to NATO commanders, allied forces fought bravely and inflicted great damage on the Taliban.

General David Richards, the British commander of NATO troops in Afghanistan, puts it this way: "There were doubts about NATO and our ability to conduct demanding security operations. There are no questions about our ability now. We've killed many hundreds of Taliban, and it has removed any doubt in anybody's mind that NATO can do what we were sent here to do."

Taliban and Al Qaida fighters and drug traffickers and criminal elements and local warlords remain active and committed to destroying democracy in Afghanistan. Defeating them will require the full commitment of our alliance. For NATO to succeed, its commanders on the ground must have the resources and flexibility they need to do their jobs. The alliance was founded on a clear principle: An attack on one is an attack on all. That principle holds true whether the attack is on our home soil or on our forces deployed on a NATO mission abroad. Today, Afghanistan is NATO's most important military operation, and by standing together in Afghanistan, we'll protect our people, defend our freedom, and send a clear message to the extremists: The forces of freedom and decency will prevail.

Every ally can take pride in the transformation that NATO is making possible for the people of Afghanistan. Because of our efforts, Afghanistan has gone from a totalitarian nightmare to a free nation with an elected President, a democratic Constitution, and brave soldiers and police fighting for their country.

Over 4.6 million Afghan refugees have come home. It's one of the largest return movements in history. The Afghan economy has tripled in size over the past 5 years. About 2 million girls are now in school—compared to zero under the Taliban—and 85 women were elected or appointed to the Afghan National Assembly. A nation that was once a terrorist sanctuary has been transformed into an ally in the war on terror, led by a brave President, Hamid Karzai. Our work in Afghanistan is bringing freedom to the Afghan people; it is bringing security to the Euro-Atlantic community; and it's bringing pride to the NATO alliance.

NATO allies are also making vital contributions to the struggle for freedom in Iraq. At this moment, a dozen NATO allies, including every one of the Baltic nations, are contributing forces to the coalition in Iraq. And 18 NATO countries plus Ukraine are contributing forces to the NATO Training Mission that is helping develop the next generation of leaders for the Iraqi security forces. To date, NATO has trained nearly 3,000 Iraqi personnel, including nearly 2,000 officers and civilian defense officials trained inside Iraq, plus an additional 800 Iraqis trained outside the country. NATO has also helped Iraqis stand up a new military academy near Baghdad, so Iraqis can develop their own military leaders in the years to come. And NATO has contributed $128 million in military equipment to the Iraqi military, including 77 Hungarian T–72 battle tanks. By helping to equip the Iraqi security forces and training the next group of Iraqi military leaders, NATO is helping the Iraqi people in the difficult work of securing their country and their freedom.

Tomorrow I'm going to travel to Jordan where I will meet with the Prime Minister of Iraq. We will discuss the situation on the ground in his country, our ongoing efforts to transfer more responsibility to the Iraqi security forces, and the responsibility of other nations in the region to support the security and stability of Iraq. We'll continue to be flexible, and we'll make the changes necessary to succeed. But there's one thing I'm not going to do: I'm not

going to pull our troops off the battlefield before the mission is complete.

The battles in Iraq and Afghanistan are part of a struggle between moderation and extremism that is unfolding across the broader Middle East. Our enemy follows a hateful ideology that rejects fundamental freedoms like the freedom to speak, to assemble, or to worship God in the way you see fit. It opposes the rights for women. Their goal is to overthrow governments and to impose their totalitarian rule on millions. They have a strategy to achieve these aims. They seek to convince America and our allies that we cannot defeat them and that our only hope is to withdraw and abandon an entire region to their domination. The war on terror we fight today is more than a military conflict; it is the decisive ideological struggle of the 21st century. And in this struggle, we can accept nothing less than victory for our children and our grandchildren.

We see this struggle in Lebanon, where last week, gunmen assassinated that country's Industry Minister, Pierre Gemayel, a prominent leader of the movement that secured Lebanon's independence last year. His murder showed once again the viciousness of those who are trying to destabilize Lebanon's young democracy. We see this struggle in Syria, where the regime allows Iranian weapons to pass through its territory into Lebanon and provides weapons and political support to Hizballah. We see this struggle in Iran, where a reactionary regime subjugates its proud people, arrests free trade union leaders, and uses Iran's resources to fund the spread of terror and pursue nuclear weapons. We see this struggle in the Palestinian Territories, where extremists are working to stop moderate leaders from making progress toward the vision of two democratic states, Israel and Palestine, living side by side in peace and security.

In each of these places, extremists are using terror to stop the spread of freedom. Some are Shi'a extremists; other are Sunni

extremists; but they represent different faces of the same threat. And if they succeed in undermining fragile democracies and drive the forces of freedom out of the region, they will have an open field to pursue their goals. Each strain of violent Islamic radicalism would be emboldened in its efforts to gain control of states and establish new safe havens. The extremists would use oil resources to fuel their radical agenda and to punish industrialized nations and pursue weapons of mass destruction. Armed with nuclear weapons, they could blackmail the free world, spread their ideologies of hate, and raise a mortal threat to Europe, America, and the entire civilized world.

If we allow the extremists to do this, then 50 years from now, history will look back on our time with unforgiving clarity and demand to know why we did not act. Our alliance has a responsibility to act. We must lift up and support the moderates and reformers who are working for change across the broader Middle East. We must bring hope to millions by strengthening young democracies from Kabul to Baghdad to Beirut. And we must advance freedom as the great alternative to tyranny and terror.

I know some in my country and some here in Europe are pessimistic about the prospects of democracy and peace in the Middle East. Some doubt whether the people of that region are ready for freedom, or want it badly enough, or have the courage to overcome the forces of totalitarian extremism. I understand these doubts, but I do not share them. I believe in the universality of freedom. I believe that the people of the Middle East want their liberty. I'm impressed by the courage I see in the people across the region who are fighting for that liberty.

We see this courage in the 8 million Afghans who defied terrorist threats and went to the polls to choose their leaders.

We see this courage in the nearly 12 million Iraqis who refused to let the car bombers and assassins stop them from voting for the free future of their country. We see this courage in the more than 1 million Lebanese who voted for a free and sovereign government to rule their land. And we see this courage in citizens from Damascus to Tehran, who, like the citizens of Riga before them, keep the flame of liberty burning deep within their hearts, knowing that one day its light will shine throughout their nations.

There was a time, not so long ago, when many doubted that liberty could succeed in Europe. Here in the Baltics, many can still recall the early years of the cold war when freedom's victory was not so obvious or assured. In 1944, the Soviet Red Army reoccupied Latvia, Lithuania, and Estonia, plunging this region into nearly five decades of Communist rule. In 1947, Communist forces were threatening Greece and Turkey, the reconstruction of Germany was faltering, and mass starvation was setting in across Europe. In 1948, Czechoslovakia fell to communism, France and Italy were threatened by the same fate, and Berlin was blockaded on the orders of Josef Stalin. In 1949, the Soviet Union exploded a nuclear weapon. And weeks later, Communist forces took control in China. And in the summer of 1950, seven North Korean divisions poured across the border into South Korea, marking the start of the first direct military clash of the cold war. All of this took place in the 6 years following World War II.

Yet today, six decades later, the cold war is over, the Soviet Union is no more, and the NATO alliance is meeting in the capital of a free Latvia. Europe no longer produces armed ideologies that threaten other nations with aggression and conquest and occupation. And a continent that was for generations a source of instability and global war has become a source of stability and peace. Freedom in Europe has brought peace to Europe, and freedom has brought the power to bring peace to the broader Middle East.

Soon after I took office, I spoke to students at Warsaw University. I told them America had learned the lessons of history. I said, "No more Munichs and no more Yaltas." I was speaking at the time about Europe, but the lessons of Yalta apply equally across the world. The question facing our nations today is this: Will we turn the fate of millions over to totalitarian extremists and allow the enemy to impose their hateful ideology across the Middle East, or will we stand with the forces of freedom in that part of the world and defend the moderate majority who want a future of peace?

My country has made its choice, and so has the NATO alliance. We refuse to give in to the pessimism that consigns millions across the Middle East to endless oppression. We understand that, ultimately, the only path to lasting peace is through the rise of lasting free societies.

Here in the Baltic region, many understand that freedom is universal and worth the struggle. During the Second World War, a young girl here in Riga escaped with her family from the advancing Red Army. She fled westward, moving first to a refugee camp in Germany and then later to Morocco, where she and her family settled for 5½ years. Spending her teenage years in a Muslim nation, this Latvian girl came to understand a fundamental truth about humanity: Moms and dads in the Muslim world want the same things for their children as moms and dads here in Riga: a future of peace, a chance to live in freedom, and the opportunity to build a better life.

Today, that Latvian girl is the leader of a free country—the Iron Lady of the Baltics, the President of Latvia. And the lessons she learned growing up in Casablanca guide her as she leads her nation in this world. Here is how she put it earlier this year in an address to a joint meeting of the United States Congress: "We know the

value of freedom and feel compassion for those who are still deprived of it. Every nation on Earth is entitled to freedom," your President said. She said: "We must share the dream that someday there won't be a tyranny left anywhere in the world. We must work for this future, all of us, large and small, together."

Like your President, I believe this dream is within reach. And through the NATO alliance, nations large and small are working together to achieve it.

We thank the people of Latvia for your contributions to NATO and for the powerful example you set for liberty. I appreciate your hospitality at this summit. America is

proud to call you friends and allies in the cause of peace and freedom. May God bless you, and may God continue to bless America. Thank you very much.

NOTE: The President spoke at 4:30 p.m. in the Grand Hall. In his remarks, he referred to President Vaira Vike-Freiberga, Speaker of the Saeima Indulis Emsis, and Prime Minister Aigars Kalvitis of Latvia; Marc Leland, cochairman, German Marshall Fund; Ivars Lacis, rector, Latvia University; Secretary General Jakob Gijsbert "Jaap" de Hoop Scheffer of the North Atlantic Treaty Organization; and Prime Minister Nuri al-Maliki of Iraq.

The President's News Conference With Prime Minister Nuri al-Maliki of Iraq in Amman, Jordan
November 30, 2006

President Bush. Good morning. It's good to be in Amman. I first want to thank His Majesty King Abdullah for his gracious hospitality.

Prime Minister Maliki and I just had a very productive meeting. This is the third time we've met since he took office 6 months ago, and with each meeting, I'm coming to know him better. He's a strong leader who wants a free and democratic Iraq to succeed. The United States is determined to help him achieve that goal.

I told the Prime Minister we're ready to make changes to better support the unity Government of Iraq and that certain key principles behind our strategy remain firm, and they're fixed. First, we believe the success of Prime Minister Maliki's Government is critical to the success in Iraq. His Government was chosen by the Iraqi people through free elections in which nearly 12 million people defied terrorists to cast their ballots. I've told the Prime Minister that our goal in Iraq is to strengthen his Government and to support his efforts to

build a free Iraq that can govern itself, sustain itself, and defend itself and is an ally in the war against the terrorists.

Secondly, the success of the Iraqi Government depends on the success of the Iraqi security forces. During our meetings, the Prime Minister and I heard an update from an important group that our Government established last month: the Joint Committee on Accelerating the Transferring of Security Responsibility. We agreed on the importance of speeding up the training of Iraqi security forces. Our goal is to ensure that the Prime Minister has more capable forces under his control so his Government can fight the terrorists and the death squads and provide security and stability in his country.

Third, success in Iraq requires a united Iraq where democracy is preserved, the rule of law prevails, and minority rights are respected. The Prime Minister made clear that splitting his country into parts, as some have suggested, is not what the Iraqi people want, and that any partition of Iraq

would only lead to an increase in sectarian violence. I agree. In the long term, security in Iraq requires reconciliation among Iraq's different ethnic and religious communities, something the overwhelming majority of Iraqis want.

The Prime Minister and I also discussed the review of our strategy in Iraq that is now nearing completion. I assured the Prime Minister that our review is aimed at strengthening the capacity of the sovereign Government of Iraq to meet their objectives, which we share. As part of the review, I've asked our military leaders in the Pentagon and those on the ground in Iraq to provide their recommendations on the best way forward.

Others outside the Government are conducting their own review, and I look forward to hearing their recommendations. I want to hear all advice before I make my decisions about adjustments to our strategy and tactics in Iraq to help this Government succeed.

My consultations with the Prime Minister and the unity Government are a key part of the assessment process. And that's why I appreciate him coming over from Iraq so that we could have a face-to-face visit. The Prime Minister and I agree that the outcome in Iraq will affect the entire region. To stop the extremists from dominating the Middle East, we must stop the extremists from achieving their goal of dominating Iraq. If the extremists succeed in Iraq, they will be emboldened in their efforts to undermine other young democracies in the region, or to overthrow moderate governments, establish new safe havens, and impose their hateful ideology on millions. If the Iraqis succeed in establishing a free nation in the heart of the Middle East, the forces of freedom and moderation across the region will be emboldened, and the cause of peace will have new energy and new allies.

Mr. Prime Minister, I want to thank you again for your time. I appreciate your friendship, and I appreciate the courage you show during these difficult times as you lead your country.

Prime Minister Maliki. Thank you. In the name of God. Beginning, I would like to thank King Abdullah for hosting this meeting. And I would also like to thank the President of the United States for his response and for the role that he has shown in dealing most positively with all the files that we've discussed.

And I would like, during this occasion as we leave this transitional stage, we have won initially when we have accomplished democracy in Iraq and when we give Iraq the permanent Constitution and the Parliament and the unity Government. And all these are victories—that are victories with the principles that we believe in. And therefore, these victories were our decision not to let those who would like to tamper with the fates of the region, or those who oppose democracy, to win so that the despotic regime comes back. And Iraq will never be a safe haven for terrorists who are trying to spread darkness instead of light, the light that started in Mesopotamia.

We have many visions and many ideas about the transformation process, and we are determined to succeed in the face of all the challenges that we believe are probably—should exist in a situation such as the situation that Iraq is going through. These are not outrageous challenges. There are criminals, there are people who are breaking the law. But the steel strength of the national unity Government would help us face all those who are breaking the law, or those who are trying to take down democracy in Iraq, or those who are conspiring and trying to have coups or basically bring down the national unity Government.

We are active with anybody who are working within the framework of the Constitution. Because we established the Constitution, we'll abide by it, we'll protect it, and we'll be protected by it. We assure everybody that we are in alliance with international community in facing all the

challenges that the world is facing. And foremost in those challenges is terrorism. Terrorism is not a danger only to Iraq; it's a culture; it's an ideology. The whole civilized world must face it as one line, one unit. Some people might not understand the successes that we have as we daily face terrorism in Iraq and as the security forces in Iraq chase them down, arrest them. This is solid strength based on our vision, and our vision is that terrorism, terroristic ideology, extremism, sectarianism are all issues that will rob humans from happiness.

We are ready to cooperate with everybody who believe that they need to communicate with the national unity Government, especially our neighbors. Our doors are open, and our desire is strong that between us and our neighbors, we will have strong relationships based on mutual respect and staying away from everybody's internal business. Iraq is for Iraqis, and its borders will be sound, and we'll not allow anybody to violate these borders or interfere in our internal affairs.

So everybody who is trying to make Iraq—their own influences appear on the account of the Iraqi people needs to recalculate, because it will not happen. And all the political forces in Iraq have agreed on that. They want to form a very strong political base to support the national unity Government. We have visions in Iraq, and we are at the steps of transformation into a new stage where we'll have security plans that we will believe will be effective and will deliver what is required.

In Iraq, we don't only deal with terrorism. We're dealing with building a whole state in all its aspect—political, economic, security, militarily—and all these are signs of maturity that are now very obvious in Iraq. And we hope that they will be complemented and supported by the international community and by our neighbors, who I hope that will be supportive not only for the benefit of Iraq, for the benefit of those countries as well.

President Bush. We will take a couple of questions. Abramowitz [Michael Abramowitz, Washington Post].

Democracy Efforts in Iraq/Security Situation in Iraq

Q. Mr. President, the memo from your National Security Adviser has raised the possibility the United States should press Prime Minister Maliki to break with Muqtada Al Sadr. Is this, in fact, your strategy? And did you raise this issue with the Prime Minister this morning?

And to the Prime Minister, I'd like to ask, the President's Adviser has said that a central problem in Iraq is your close alliance with Mr. Al Sadr, and did you make any representations to the President that you would break with Al Sadr, and could your Government survive such a break?

President Bush. I will let the Prime Minister talk about his relations with Al Sadr. I will tell you that he and I spent a lot of time talking about the security situation inside of Iraq. I expressed my concern about the security situation; he expressed his concern about the security situation. After all, one of his most important jobs is to provide security for the Iraqi people. Part of the Prime Minister's frustration is, is that he doesn't have the tools necessary to take care of those who break the law.

I was reassured by his commitment to a pluralistic society that is politically united, and a society in which people are held to account if they break the law, whether those people be criminals, Al Qaida, militia, whoever.

He discussed with me his political situation, and I think it is best that he talk to you about the Sadr group or any other group he wants to talk about inside of Iraq.

Prime Minister Maliki. Matter of fact, my coalition is not with only one entity. The national unity Government is a government formed of all the entities that participated in it. Therefore, that coalition basically represent a national responsibility.

And Mr. Sadr and the Sadrists are just one component that participate in the Parliament or in the Government. And I think participating in the Government is a responsibility, and it's a mutual commitment, and those who participate in this Government need to bear responsibilities. And foremost upon those responsibilities is the protection of this Government, the protection of the Constitution, the protection of the law, not breaking the law.

Therefore, I do not talk about one side at the expense of the other. I'm talking about a state; I'm talking about law; I'm talking about commitments. And this should apply to all the partners in the Government who have chosen to participate in the political process.

As to the issues that would pertain to violating the law or breaking the law, we would deal with them the same way, because the most important principle is the sovereignty and the power and the establishment of the state that must be borne by the state, but only our partners should participate in that.

Insurgency and Terrorist Attacks in Iraq

Q. Hizballah has denied that his forces trained Muqtada Al Sadr forces, but do you have any information if Hizballah has actually trained the forces of Muqtada Al Sadr?

Prime Minister Maliki. I think—[*inaudible*]—expressed itself and expressed its responsibilities. And one—another time, I would like to say that Iraq and all the Iraqis in the political process—nobody has the right, outside of Iraq, to interfere in the political or the security situation inside of Iraq. We invite everybody to cooperate with us. But as far as this issue related to training, Hizballah denied, and they're responsible for their denial.

President Bush. Our objective is to help the Maliki Government succeed. And today we discussed how to further the success of this Government. This is a government that is dedicated to pluralism and rule of law. It's a government elected by the Iraqi

people under a Constitution approved by the Iraqi people, which, in itself, is an unusual event in the Middle East, by the way.

We talked today about accelerating authority to the Prime Minister so he can do what the Iraqi people expect him to do, and that is bring security to parts of his country that require firm action. It's going to—the presence of the United States will be in Iraq so long as the Government asks us to be in Iraq. This is a sovereign government. I believe that there is more training to be done. I think the Prime Minister agrees with me. I know that we're providing a useful addition to Iraq by chasing down Al Qaida and by securing—by helping this country protect itself from Al Qaida.

Al Qaida wants a safe haven in Iraq. Al Qaida made it clear earlier that suicide bombers would increase sectarian violence. That was part of their strategy. One of our goals is to deny safe haven for Al Qaida in Iraq, and the Maliki Government expects us and wants us to provide that vital part of security.

So we'll be in Iraq until the job is complete, at the request of a sovereign government elected by the people. I know there's a lot of speculation that these reports in Washington mean there's going to be some kind of graceful exit out of Iraq. We're going to stay in Iraq to get the job done, so long as the Government wants us there.

We want the people of Iraq to live in a free society. It's in our interests. In my judgment, if we were to leave before the job is done, it would only embolden terrorists. It would only embolden the extremists. It would dash the hopes of millions of people who want to live in a free society, just like the 12 million people who voted in the Iraqi election. They want to live in a free society. And we support this Government because the Government understands it was elected by the people. And Prime Minister Maliki is working hard to overcome the many obstacles in the way to a peaceful Iraq, and we want to help him.

Let's see, Martha [Martha Raddatz, ABC News].

Iraqi Military and Security Forces/Transfer of Security Responsibilities

Q. Mr. President, is there a time limit on meeting any of these goals for Prime Minister Maliki? And you keep mentioning that the U.S. goal is to fight Al Qaida. Does that mean you believe it's up to the Iraqis to stop the sectarian violence and quell the sectarian violence, and this is something you don't want U.S. troops involved in?

And, Prime Minister Maliki, can you tell us why you canceled the meeting last night?

President Bush. What was the first part of your three-part question? [*Laughter*]

Q. Time limit on meeting goals. Is there a time limit on meeting goals?

President Bush. A time limit, as soon as possible. But I'm realistic, because I understand how tough it is inside of Iraq. The Prime Minister is dealing with sectarian violence. The Prime Minister is having to deal with Al Qaida. The Prime Minister is having to deal with criminal elements. And we want to help him.

And, yes, I talked about making sure that Al Qaida doesn't take—doesn't provide—gets safe haven in Iraq. Sure, that's an important part of our strategy. But I also have said that the goal is a country that can defend, sustain, and govern itself. And therefore, to the extent that our troops are needed to help do that, we're willing to do that. That's part of the operation in Baghdad. Part of the plan in Baghdad was to prevent killers from taking innocent life.

Q. Including sectarian violence?

President Bush. Well that's—killers taking innocent life is, in some cases, sectarian. I happen to view it as criminal as well as sectarian. I think any time you murder somebody, you're a criminal. And I believe a just society and a society of—that holds people to account and believes in rule of law protects innocent people from

murderers, no matter what their political party is.

And I discussed this with the Prime Minister, and I don't want to put words in his mouth, but I received a satisfactory answer about the need to protect innocent life. And that's exactly what our troops have been doing, along with the Iraqis. My plan, and his plan, is to accelerate the Iraqis' responsibility. See, here's a man who has been elected by the people. The people expect him to respond, and he doesn't have the capacity to respond. And so we want to accelerate that capacity. We want him to be in the lead in taking the fight against the enemies of his own country.

And that's exactly what we discussed today. We had a Joint Committee on Accelerating the Transfer of Security Responsibility Report. And it was a report that General Casey, who is with us today, and our Ambassador, Zal Khalilzad, who is with us today, as well as the Prime Minister's team delivered to both of us about how to accelerate responsibility to the Iraqi Government so this person elected by the people can take the fight to those who want to destroy a young democracy.

You had a question——

Q. Sir, there are no time limits here?

President Bush. As quick as possible, Martha. As quick—I've been asked about timetables ever since we got into this. All timetables mean is that it is a timetable for withdrawal. You kept asking me those questions. All that does is——

Q. Mr. President——

President Bush. Hold on a second. All that does is set people up for unrealistic expectations. As soon as possible. And today we made a step toward as soon as possible by transferring a—accelerating the transfer of authorities, military authorities to the Prime Minister.

Q. Did you put any pressure——

President Bush. Hold on a second. Hold on, please, sir. Please. Thank you.

Prime Minister Maliki. I emphasize what the President has just said, that we have

agreed together, and we are very clear together, about the importance of accelerating the transfer of the security responsibility. And be assured that the Iraqi forces and the security forces have reached a good level of competency and efficiency to protect Iraq as a country and to protect its people.

As far as the other issue related to the meeting, I have met with King Abdullah, then have met again with his Prime Minister and a group of his ministers, and we've discussed bilateral relations that are of concern to both nations—Iraq and Jordan—and that relationship is based on mutual friendship and being a good host and a good neighbor. And there was not part of our agenda a trilateral meeting, so there is no problem.

Please.

Iraq-Iran Relations

Q. Did you discuss with the President the Iranian influence that is expanding in Iraq and how—and the almost complete Iranian control over Baghdad, as the press sources seems to indicate? In Iraq, did you build this big wall between Iraq and Iranian? So—and are you going to deal with——

President Bush. Did I—I didn't understand your first question.

Q. To deal with Iranian directly?

President Bush. Am I going to meet with the Iranians directly, is that the question?

Q. The question of Iraq, yes.

Prime Minister Maliki. As far as the first question that was mentioned by the reporter, I think these are wrong and exaggerated information, and they are being used as one of the propaganda mechanisms to give the impression of sectarian strife so that will reach a point of no return. Because we want to emphasize that we will not allow anybody to exert their control over any part of Iraq. If there is any talk about intervention in Iraq and all the discussion, all the talks about people or other nations exerting control over Iraq, this is

not true. This is a political process in Iraq. We want good relationships with our neighbors; we want complementary relationships with our neighbors to protect the region from tensions. But the main principle underlying all this is the respect of the Iraqi borders and the internal affairs of Iraq.

President Bush. I believe the Iranians fear democracy, and that's why they destabilized Lebanon; that's why they are worried about the establishment of a Palestinian state.

I appreciate the Prime Minister's views that the Iraqis are plenty capable of running their own business and they don't need foreign interference from neighbors that will be destabilizing the country. I am very worried, as should the world, about Iran's desires to have a nuclear weapon and, therefore, will continue to work with the world to send a clear message to the Iranians, the Iranian Government, that we will—they will become more isolated. And my message to the Iranian people is, we have no beef with the Iranian people. We respect their heritage; we respect their history; we respect their traditions. I just have a problem with a government that is isolating its people, denying its people benefits that could be had from engagement with the world.

I told the Prime Minister, we'll continue to work with the world community to insist that Iran abandon its nuclear weapons programs. And I have said that if they were to verifiably suspend their enrichment program, we would be a part of the EU–3 plus Russia plus China discussions. They know how to get us to the table. The choice is theirs to make. It's the choice of the Iranian Government as to whether or not they make the right decisions, for not only the sake of the diplomacy, but for the sake—more importantly, for the sake of their people.

We might as well keep going, Prime Minister.

Richard [Richard Wolffe, Newsweek]. Please, sir. Please. Thank you.

Prime Minister Maliki's Leadership

Q. When you were in Baghdad 6 months ago, you expressed the same kind of confidence in the Prime Minister and his Government that you've expressed today. Yet there have been repeated rounds of disappointments when it comes to the Prime Minister's Baghdad Security Plan, with his plans for reconciliation. I'm wondering, if anything, if you've had any doubts over the last 6 months about the strength of his Government, about the Prime Minister's own abilities. And what gives you such confidence today to think that he can achieve what he hasn't done over the last 6 months?

President Bush. Well, as you mentioned, he's been in power for 6 months, and I've been able to watch a leader emerge. The first thing that gives me confidence is that he wants responsibility. A sign of leadership is for somebody to say, "I want to be able to have the tools necessary to protect my people." One of his frustrations with me is that he believes we've been slow about giving him the tools necessary to protect the Iraqi people. And today we had a meeting that will accelerate the capacity for the Prime Minister to do the hard work necessary to help stop this violence. No question, it's a violent society right now. He knows that better than anybody. He was explaining to me that occasionally the house in which he lives gets shelled by terrorists who are trying to frighten him.

And so the second point I make to you is that I appreciate his courage. You can't lead unless you have courage. And he's got courage, and he's shown courage over the last 6 months.

Thirdly, he has expressed a deep desire to unify his country. You hear all kinds of rumors about the politics inside of Iraq. I'm talking to the man face to face, and he says that he understands that a unified government, a pluralistic society, is important for success. And he's making hard decisions to achieve that.

No question, it's been tough. It would have been a lot easier had people not tried to destabilize the young democracy. His job would have been more simple had there not been terrorists trying to create sectarian violence.

Now, I want everybody to remember that it was Mr. Zarqawi of Al Qaida who said, "Let us bomb Shi'a in order to create the conditions necessary for sectarian violence." The Samarra bombing started off this new phase of violence. The Prime Minister comes in about halfway through that phase in order to—he'd been selected, and now he's dealing with a serious situation on the ground. And what I appreciate is his attitude. As opposed to saying, "America, you go solve the problem," we have a Prime Minister who's saying, "Stop holding me back. I want to solve the problem."

And the meeting today was to accelerate his capacity to do so. It's not easy for a military to evolve from ground zero, and I appreciate our forces and I appreciate General Casey, who have worked very hard to train the Iraqis so they become a capable fighting force as well as a unifying element for Iraq. But it's one thing to put people in uniform and another thing to have clear command structure, or the capacity to move troops from point A to point B, or the capacity to make sure that the troop carrier from point A to point B has got the necessary air in its tires or oil in its engine. In other words, this is a sophisticated operation, to get a unifying army stood up.

And one of the reasons I appreciate the Prime Minister is that he, on the one hand, sees that it's a sophisticated operation to get a military up from zero, but on the other hand, is frustrated by the pace. And the reason why he's frustrated is because he wants to show the people who elected him that he is willing to take the hard tasks on necessary to provide security for the Iraqi people, such as hunting down those who are killing the innocent. And the reason I came today to be able to sit

down with him is to hear the joint plans developed between the Iraqi Government, the sovereign Government of Iraq, and our Government, to make sure that we accelerate the transfer of capacity to the Prime Minister. And I know he's looking forward to more capacity being transferred so he can do his job.

Anyway, he's the right guy for Iraq, and we're going to help him, and it's in our interest to help him, for the sake of peace.

Situation in the Middle East

Q. Mr. President—[*inaudible*]—what is your—[*inaudible*]—Prime Minister Olmert and President Abu Mazen to keep this cease-fire agreement? And what should be done—[*inaudible*].

President Bush. Well, first of all, there's no question that if we were able to settle the Palestinian-Israeli issue, it would help bring more peace to the Middle East. And therefore, our Government is focused on helping develop the two-state solution. As a matter of fact, I was the—our Government strongly believes in the two-state solution, and I believe it's in the Palestinian people's interest that they have their own state, and I believe it's in Israel's interest that there be a democracy on her border. And therefore, we're working to that end.

Look, there are extremists who want to stop the development of a Palestinian state, just like there are extremists who want to destabilize Lebanon—and we're strongly in support of the Siniora Government—just like there are extremists who want to destabilize this young democracy. Isn't it interesting that the radicals and extremists fear democracy so much that they're willing to kill innocent people? And the task at hand is to support moderate, reasonable people in their quest for free societies. And that means that Abu Mazen, who I believe wants there to be a Palestinian state living side by side with peace in Israel, deserves the support of the world. And he deserves support in peeling his Government away

from those who do not recognize Israel's right to exist.

And therefore, Condoleezza Rice will be going to talk to Abu Mazen tomorrow, as well as Prime Minister Olmert, working with both parties together to see how we can advance the vision that the Prime Minister himself talked about earlier this week.

Q. And your advice to both of them?

President Bush. My advice is, support reasonable people and reject extremists. Understand that most people want to live in peace and harmony and security. It's very important for the American people to understand that most Muslim mothers want their children to grow up in peace, and they're interested in peace. And it's in our interest to help liberty prevail in the Middle East, starting with Iraq.

And that's why this business about graceful exit just simply has no realism to it at all. We're going to help this Government. And I'm able to say that it is—that we have a government that wants our help and is becoming more capable about taking the lead in the fight to protect their own country. The only way that Iraq is going to be able to succeed is when the Iraqis, led by a capable person, says, "We're tired of it. We don't want violence; we want the peace that our 12 million people voted for." And it's in the world's interest that Iraq succeed.

Mr. Prime Minister, you want to answer some more questions? [*Laughter*] Go ahead. Hold on for a minute. Wait, wait, wait.

Prime Minister Maliki. We said six question; now this is the seventh—this is the eighth—eight questions. Mr. President?

President Bush. Yes, this guy?

Progress in Iraq

Q. In light of the war that the United States is fighting against terror in Iraq, what has been accomplished? What do you expect to be accomplished after 3-year confrontation?

Another question, other people are accusing the United States of bringing terrorism to Iraq, and the proof is that what's going on in Iraq and what's going on in Afghanistan. The proof is that. And the biggest loser is the Iraqi citizen.

President Bush. It's an interesting analysis: The biggest loser for a free society is the Iraqi citizen, when this society was just liberated from the grips of a brutal tyrant that killed thousands and thousands of the Iraqi citizens.

What has been accomplished is the liberation of a country from a tyrant who is now sitting in jail getting a trial that he was unwilling to give thousands of people he murdered himself or had murdered.

Secondly, this country has a Constitution, which is one of the most modern constitutions ever written in the Middle East. This is a government that had been elected by the people. No question, it's tough. But the reason why terrorists are trying to stop the advance of freedom in Iraq is the very reason why we need to help them: Because they can't stand democracies, and they want to impose a hateful vision on as much of the world as possible. They want safe haven from which to launch attacks again. A safe haven in Iraq, a country that has got a lot of resources, would be very dangerous for America.

It didn't take but 19 people who were trained in Afghanistan to get on airplanes and come and kill over 3,000 citizens in my country. Threats that gather overseas must be taken seriously if we want to protect ourselves. And the best way to protect ourselves is to hunt down the terrorists and to help young democracies survive. Freedom and liberty is the great alternative to the hateful vision of those who are willing to murder innocent lives to achieve their objective.

And so you bet it's worth it in Iraq, and necessary. And I was very proud and pleased to see 12 million Iraqis go to the polls, to be able to express their desires, their wishes, as they helped put a government in place that this man now leads.

Prime Minister Maliki. Thank you very much.

President Bush. Good to see you. Thank you.

Prime Minister Maliki. Thank you.

President Bush. Thank you all.

NOTE: The President's news conference began at 9:43 a.m. at the Four Seasons Hotel Amman. In his remarks, the President referred to King Abdullah II of Jordan; Iraqi Shiite cleric Muqtada Al Sadr; Gen. George W. Casey, Jr., USA, commanding general, Multi-National Force—Iraq; Prime Minister Fuad Siniora of Lebanon; President Mahmoud Abbas of the Palestinian Authority; Prime Minister Ehud Olmert of Israel; and former President Saddam Hussein of Iraq. Prime Minister Maliki referred to Prime Minister Marouf al-Bakhit of Jordan. Prime Minister Maliki and some reporters spoke in Arabic, and their remarks were translated by an interpreter.

Joint Statement by President George W. Bush and Prime Minister Nuri al-Maliki of Iraq
November 30, 2006

We were pleased to continue our consultations on building security and stability in Iraq. We are grateful to His Majesty King Abdullah II of Jordan for hosting these meetings here in Amman.

Our discussions reviewed developments in Iraq, focusing on the security situation

and our common concern about sectarian violence targeting innocent Iraqis. In this regard, the Prime Minister affirms the commitment of his government to advance efforts toward national reconciliation and the need for all Iraqis and political forces in Iraq to work against armed elements responsible for violence and intimidation. The Prime Minister also affirms his determination with help from the United States and the international community to improve the efficiency of government operations, particularly in confronting corruption and strengthening the rule of law.

We discussed the plague of terrorism in Iraq which is being fomented and fueled by Al Qaeda. The people of Iraq, like the people of the United States and the entire civilized world, must stand together to face this common threat. The Prime Minister affirmed that Iraq is a partner in the fight against Al Qaeda. We agreed that defeating Al Qaeda and the terrorists is vital to ensuring the success of Iraq's democracy. We discussed the means by which the United States will enhance Iraq's capabilities to further isolate extremists and bring all who choose violence and terror to full justice under Iraqi law.

We agreed in particular to take all necessary measures to track down and bring to justice those responsible for the cowardly attacks last week in Sadr City. The Prime Minister has also pledged to bring to justice those responsible for crimes committed in the wake of this attack.

We discussed accelerating the transfer of security responsibilities to the Government of Iraq; our hopes for strengthening the future relationship between our two nations; and joint efforts to achieve greater cooperation from governments in the region and to counter those elements that are fueling the conflict.

We received an interim report from the high-level Joint Committee on Accelerating the Transferring of Security Responsibility, and encouraged the Committee to continue its good work. We agreed that reform of the Iraqi security ministries and agencies and addressing the issue of militias should be accelerated. The ultimate solution to stabilizing Iraq and reducing violence is true national reconciliation and capable and loyal Iraqi forces dedicated to protecting all the Iraqi people.

We are committed to continuing to build the partnership between our two countries as we work together to strengthen a stable, democratic, and unified Iraq.

NOTE: The Office of the Press Secretary also released a Spanish language version of this joint statement. An original was not available for verification of the content of this joint statement.

Letter to Congressional Leaders Transmitting an Alternative Plan for Locality Pay Increases Payable to Civilian Federal Employees
November 30, 2006

Dear Mr. Speaker: *(Dear Mr. President:)*

I am transmitting an alternative plan for locality pay increases payable to civilian Federal employees covered by the General Schedule (GS) and certain other pay systems in January 2007.

Under title 5, United States Code, civilian Federal employees covered by the GS and certain other pay systems would receive a two-part pay increase in January 2007: (1) a 1.7 percent across-the-board adjustment in scheduled rates of basic pay derived from Employment Cost Index data on changes in the wages and salaries of

private industry workers, and (2) a 6.9 percent locality pay adjustment based on Bureau of Labor Statistics' salary surveys of non-Federal employers in each locality pay area. According to the statutory formula, for Federal employees covered by the locality pay system, the overall average pay increase would be about 8.6 percent. The total Federal employee pay increase would cost about $8.8 billion in fiscal year 2007 alone.

Title 5, United States Code, authorizes me to implement an alternative locality pay plan if I view the adjustment that would otherwise take effect as inappropriate due to "national emergency or serious economic conditions affecting the general welfare." For the reasons described below, I have determined that it would be appropriate to exercise my statutory alternative plan authority to set an alternative January 2007 locality pay increase.

A national emergency, within the meaning of chapter 53 of title 5, has existed since September 11, 2001, that includes Operation Enduring Freedom in Afghanistan and Operation Iraqi Freedom. The growth in Federal requirements is straining the Federal budget. Full statutory civilian pay increases costing $8.8 billion in 2007 alone would interfere with our Nation's ability to pursue the war on terrorism.

Such cost increases would threaten our efforts against terrorism or force deep cuts in discretionary spending or Federal employment to stay within budget. Neither outcome is acceptable. Therefore, I have determined that a locality pay increase of 0.5 percent would be appropriate for GS and certain other employees in January 2007. Our national situation precludes granting larger locality pay increases at this time.

Accordingly, I have determined that under the authority of section 5304a of title 5, United States Code, locality-based comparability payments for the locality pay areas in amounts set forth in the attached table shall become effective on the first day of the first applicable pay period beginning on or after January 1, 2007. When compared with the payments currently in effect, these comparability payments will increase the General Schedule payroll by 0.5 percent.

Finally, the law requires that I include in this report an assessment of the impact of my decision on the Government's ability to recruit and retain well-qualified employees. I do not believe this decision will materially affect our ability to continue to attract and retain a quality Federal workforce. To the contrary, since any pay raise above what I have proposed would likely be unfunded, agencies would have to absorb the additional cost and could have to freeze hiring in order to pay the higher rates. Moreover, GS "quit" rates continue to be very low (2.0 percent on an annual basis), well below the overall average "quit" rate in private enterprise. Should the need arise, the Government has many compensation tools, such as recruitment bonuses, retention allowances, and special salary rates, to maintain the high quality workforce that serves our Nation so very well.

Sincerely,

GEORGE W. BUSH

NOTE: Identical letters were sent to J. Dennis Hastert, Speaker of the House of Representatives, and Richard B. Cheney, President of the Senate.

Remarks on World AIDS Day
December 1, 2006

Laura and I welcome our guests. This is World AIDS Day. It's a day for the world to recognize the fact that there are 39 million people living with HIV/AIDS and a day to remember the fact that 25 million people have died of AIDS. It's a day, as well, for the United States to remember that we have a duty to do something about this epidemic, this pandemic.

And today Laura and I met with the Secretary of HHS, as well as Mark Dybul, our U.S. Coordinator for our AIDS effort, and people who are involved with helping to save lives, people from our country and people from around the world who have come to share with us the stories of compassion and courage.

This country is committed—we're committed in helping solve this problem by dedicating a lot of resources to the battle against HIV/AIDS. The American taxpayers have funded over $15 billion to help groups around this table save lives. Before the PEPFAR program—that's the name of the program that we—that's what we call the program that we dedicate money to, to help save lives—before it became into being, there was about 50,000 people receiving lifesaving drugs. Today, there are over 800,000 people receiving lifesaving drugs, and we thank those who are on the ground in the countries around the world who are using taxpayers' money to save lives. We believe that it's one thing to spend money; we also believe it's another thing to say that we expect there to be results. And the American people need to know, we're getting good results with your money, and we'll continue to spend it wisely.

We also—as we think about people affected with HIV/AIDS in countries around the world, we remember those who have got HIV/AIDS here at home. And it's very important for the American people to understand we're spending over $18 billion to help save lives here at home. And I call upon the Congress to reauthorize the Ryan White Act. The bill has passed the United States House of Representatives; the Senate has time to act before it goes on recess. It is an important piece of legislation that will enable us to continue our fight against HIV/AIDS domestically.

I can't thank you all enough for coming, and I thank you for being such decent, compassionate people. The pandemic of HIV/AIDS can be defeated, and the United States is willing to take the lead in that fight. But we can't do it alone. And so for our international partners, we appreciate what you do. For the faith-based community, we thank you for hearing the universal call to love a neighbor. And for the taxpayers, we appreciate your generosity in showing the world the good heart and compassion of the American people.

Thank you.

NOTE: The President spoke at 10:41 a.m. in the Roosevelt Room at the White House. The World AIDS Day proclamation of November 26 is listed in Appendix D at the end of this volume.

Statement on the Northern Ireland Agreement
December 1, 2006

The United States welcomes the recent progress made by the Northern Ireland parties and the British and Irish Governments to implement the agreement reached at St. Andrews, and I recognize the leadership shown by the political party leaders.

The United States fully supports the agreed way forward for Northern Ireland: a power-sharing government by the end of March next year, based on support for the rule of law and policing.

The President's Radio Address
December 2, 2006

Good morning. I returned home this week from a visit to the Middle East. On my trip, I met with Prime Minister Maliki of Iraq to discuss how we can improve the situation on the ground in his country and help the Iraqis build a lasting democracy.

My meeting with Prime Minister Maliki was our third since he took office 6 months ago. With each meeting, I'm coming to know him better, and I'm becoming more impressed by his desire to make the difficult choices that will put his country on a better path. During our meeting, I told the Prime Minister that America is ready to make changes to better support the unity Government of Iraq and that several key principles will guide our efforts.

First, the success of Prime Minister Maliki's Government is critical to success in Iraq. His unity Government was chosen through free elections in which nearly 12 million Iraqis cast their ballots in support of democracy. Our goal in Iraq is to strengthen his democratic Government and help Iraq's leaders build a free nation that can govern itself, sustain itself, and defend itself and is an ally in the war on terror.

Second, the success of the Iraqi Government depends on the success of the Iraqi security forces. The training of Iraqi security forces has been steady, yet we both agreed that we need to do more, and we

need to do it faster. The Prime Minister wants to show the people who elected him that he's willing to make the hard decisions necessary to provide security.

To do that, he needs larger and more capable Iraqi forces under his control, and he needs them quickly. By helping Iraq's elected leaders get the Iraqi forces they need, we will help Iraq's democratic Government become more effective in fighting the terrorists and other violent extremists, and in providing security and stability, particularly in Baghdad.

Third, success in Iraq requires strong institutions that will stand the test of time and hardship. Our goal in Iraq is to help Prime Minister Maliki build a country that is united, where the rule of law prevails and the rights of minorities are respected. The Prime Minister made clear that splitting his country into parts is not what the Iraqi people want and that any partition of Iraq would lead to an increase in sectarian violence.

Security in Iraq requires sustained action by the Iraqi security forces, yet in the long term, security in Iraq hinges on reconciliation among Iraq's different ethnic and religious communities. And the Prime Minister has committed his Government to achieving that goal.

The Prime Minister and I also discussed the review of America's strategy in Iraq that is now nearing completion. As part of this review, I've asked our military leaders in the Pentagon and those on the ground in Iraq to provide their recommendations on the best way forward.

A bipartisan panel, led by former Secretary of State James Baker and former Congressman Lee Hamilton, is also conducting a review. And I look forward to receiving their report next week. I want to hear all advice before I make any decisions about adjustments to our strategy in Iraq.

I recognize that the recent violence in Iraq has been unsettling. Many people in our country are wondering about the way forward. The work ahead will not be easy, yet by helping Prime Minister Maliki strengthen Iraq's democratic institutions and promote national reconciliation, our military leaders and diplomats can help put Iraq on a solid path to liberty and democracy. The decisions we make in Iraq will be felt across the broader Middle East.

Failure in Iraq would embolden the extremists who hate America and want nothing more than to see our demise. It would strengthen the hand of those who are seeking to undermine young democracies across the region and give the extremists an open field to overthrow moderate governments, take control of countries, impose their rule on millions, and threaten the American people. Our Nation must not allow this to happen.

Success in Iraq will require leaders in Washington—Republicans and Democrats alike—to come together and find greater consensus on the best path forward. So I will work with leaders in both parties to achieve this goal. Together we can help Iraqis build a free and democratic nation in the heart of the Middle East, strengthen moderates and reformers across the region who are working for peace, and leave our children and grandchildren a more secure and hopeful world.

Thank you for listening.

NOTE: The address was recorded at approximately 7:50 a.m. on December 1 in the Cabinet Room at the White House for broadcast at 10:06 a.m. on December 2. The transcript was made available by the Office of the Press Secretary on December 1 but was embargoed for release until the broadcast. The Office of the Press Secretary also released a Spanish language transcript of this address.

Remarks at the Children's Holiday Reception
December 4, 2006

Thanks for coming. Laura and I want to welcome you all to the White House. We're really happy you're here. I think you're going to really enjoy this special occasion. My job is to introduce my wife, Laura Bush. [*Laughter*] Before I do so, though, I want to say something about your moms and dads. I thank you very much for supporting your mom and dad as they're on a very important mission for our country. I want you to know that they love you dearly, and the American people love and respect those who wear our uniform a lot.

I know it's tough to have your mom or dad overseas, and we wish you all the best. But it's really important work. And so we wanted to welcome you here to the White House to, first of all, thank you for your strength, and so that you would do me a favor and e-mail your mom or dad who is overseas how much the Commander in Chief respects them, admires them, and supports them.

So welcome to the White House. We're glad you're here. And now I'm going to introduce my wife, Laura Bush.

NOTE: The President spoke at 10:40 a.m. in the East Room at the White House. The transcript released by the Office of the Press Secretary also included the remarks of the First Lady.

Remarks Following a Meeting With Chairman Abdul Aziz Al-Hakim of the Supreme Council for the Islamic Revolution in Iraq
December 4, 2006

President Bush. Your Eminence, welcome back to the Oval Office. This is the second opportunity I've had to meet with one of the distinguished leaders of a free Iraq. This is a man whose family suffered unbelievable violence at the hands of the dictator, Saddam Hussein. He lost nearly 60 family members, and yet rather than being bitter, he's involved with helping the new Government succeed.

We talked about a lot of important issues. I appreciate so very much His Eminence's commitment to a unity government. I assured him the United States supports his work and the work of the Prime Minister to unify the country. Part of unifying Iraq is for the elected leaders and society leaders to reject the extremists that are trying to stop the advance of this young democracy. I appreciated very much His Eminence's strong position against the murder of innocent life.

We talked about the need to give the Government of Iraq more capability as quickly as possible, so that the elected Government of Iraq can do that which the Iraqi people want, which is to secure their country from the extremists and murderers. I told His Eminence that I was proud of the courage of the Iraqi people. I told him that we're not satisfied with the pace of progress in Iraq, and that we want to continue to work with the sovereign Government of Iraq to accomplish our mutual objectives, which is a free country that can govern itself, sustain itself, and defend itself, a free country which will serve as an ally in the war against the extremists and radicals and terrorists.

So, Your Eminence, welcome back. Thank you for the very constructive conversation we had.

Chairman Hakim. In the name of God, the merciful, the passionate, and blessing upon Prophet Mohammed and his purified family and his loyal companions. My meeting with President Bush today emerges from our shared commitment towards continued dialog and consultation among us and also on the basis of our conviction that the Iraqi issue is a mutual interest. It's an issue that requires coordination between the two sides in a way that concerns both of us politically and from a security point of view and economic point of view as well.

Therefore, our conversation today focused on ways to advance the work of the Iraqi Government, the elected Government, as well as to advance the whole situation in Iraq and move it forward. Also, we have discussed ways in order to provide all the necessities that the Iraqi Armed Forces will need, in terms of armament, in terms of trainings, in order to be in a position to assume the security file.

The Iraqi situation is being subjected to a great deal of defamation, and the true picture is not being presented in order to show a dark side of what's happening in Iraq. We see the attempts to defame and distort the situation in Iraq, not taking into consideration the democratic steps that that

country has taken, writing the Constitution and establishing a state that depends heavily on the Constitution, that it is unified and that it is strong. There are attempts to show the sectarian strife in an attempt to weaken the position in Iraq.

The U.S. interests, the Iraqi interests, the regional interests, they are all linked. Therefore, it is very important when we deal with this issue, we look at the interests of the Iraqi people. If we don't, this whole issue could backfire and could harm the interests of the region, the United States, and Iraq as well.

Therefore, we believe that the Iraqi issue should be solved by the Iraqis with the help of friends everywhere. But we reject any attempts to have a regional or international role in solving the Iraqi issue. We cannot bypass the political process. Iraq should be in a position to solve Iraqi problems. We welcome any effort that could enhance the democratic reality in Iraq and protect the constitutional role of that state.

We have gone a long way to establish a democratic and pluralistic society in Iraq. We have given a great deal of sacrifice toward achieving that objective. We cherish all the sacrifices that took place for the liberation and the freedom of Iraq, sacrifices by the Iraqi people, as well as friendly nations, and on top of that list, sacrifices by the Americans. We have now an elected government in Iraq, a government that it is so determined to combat both violence and terror, a government that it is—strongly believes in the unity of that government and of that country and the society, a government that deals and will deal with all the sources of terrorism regardless where they come from.

We will work very hard and seek all forms of cooperation at the international level and the regional level in order to defeat terrorism, that it is trying to use Iraq as a base in order to sabotage the future of that nation.

Thank you very much, Mr. President, for allowing me this opportunity to meet with you. I would like to take this opportunity also to thank the American people and their sympathy toward Iraq, those who helped Iraq to get rid of a brutal dictatorship and to enjoy freedom and liberties.

President Bush. Thank you, sir. Thank you all.

NOTE: The President spoke at 2:26 p.m. in the Oval Office at the White House. In his remarks, the President referred to former President Saddam Hussein and Prime Minister Nuri al-Maliki of Iraq. Chairman Hakim spoke in Arabic, and his remarks were translated by an interpreter.

Remarks on the Resignation of John R. Bolton as United States Permanent Representative to the United Nations
December 4, 2006

The President. I received the resignation of Ambassador John Bolton. I accepted; I'm not happy about it. I think he deserved to be confirmed. And the reason why I think he deserved to be confirmed is because I know he did a fabulous job for the country.

And I want to thank you and Gretchen for serving in a very important position, and doing so in a way that a lot of Americans really appreciate, John. We're going to miss you in this administration. You've been a stalwart defender of freedom and peace. You've been strong in your advocacy for human rights and human dignity. You've done everything that can be expected for an Ambassador.

And I accept your letter, and I wish you and Gretchen all the very best.

Ambassador Bolton. Many thanks.

The President. Thank you. Thanks for serving.

NOTE: The President spoke at 3:49 p.m. in the Oval Office at the White House. In his remarks, he referred to Gretchen Bolton, wife of Ambassador Bolton. The Office of the Press Secretary also made available Ambassador Bolton's letter of resignation.

Statement on the Resignation of John R. Bolton as United States Permanent Representative to the United Nations
December 4, 2006

It is with deep regret that I accept John Bolton's decision to end his service in the administration as Permanent Representative of the United States to the United Nations when his commission expires.

Over a year ago, I appointed Ambassador Bolton because I knew he would represent America's values and effectively confront difficult problems at the United Nations. He served his country with extraordinary dedication and skill, assembling coalitions that addressed some of the most consequential issues facing the international community. During his tenure, he articulately advocated the positions and values of the United States and advanced the expansion of democracy and liberty.

Ambassador Bolton led the successful negotiations that resulted in unanimous Security Council resolutions regarding North Korea's military and nuclear activities. He built consensus among our allies on the need for Iran to suspend the enrichment and reprocessing of uranium. His efforts to promote the cause of peace in Darfur resulted in a peacekeeping commitment by the United Nations. He made the case for United Nations reform because he cares about the institution and wants it to become more credible and effective.

I am deeply disappointed that a handful of United States Senators prevented Ambassador Bolton from receiving the up-or-down vote he deserved in the Senate. They chose to obstruct his confirmation, even though he enjoys majority support in the Senate and even though their tactics will disrupt our diplomatic work at a sensitive and important time. This stubborn obstructionism ill serves our country and discourages men and women of talent from serving their Nation.

I thank John Bolton for the dedication and skill with which he performed his duties, and his wife, Gretchen, and daughter, Jennifer Sarah, for their support as Ambassador Bolton served his country. All Americans owe John Bolton their gratitude for a job well done.

NOTE: The Office of the Press Secretary also made available Ambassador Bolton's letter of resignation.

Remarks Following a Meeting With Secretary of Defense-Designate Robert M. Gates
December 5, 2006

The President. Good morning. I just had a breakfast with my nominee to be the Secretary of Defense, Bob Gates. Bob Gates will be a fine Secretary of Defense. I appreciate the fact that he's getting a hearing today in the United States Senate. I hope for a speedy confirmation so he can get sworn in and get to work.

Those who wear the uniform know they'll have a friend in Bob Gates in the Defense Department. He admires our military; he respects those who have volunteered to serve our country. He's going to do an excellent job for us.

Again, Bob, I thank you for agreeing to serve.

Secretary-designate Gates. Thank you, Mr. President. Thank you very much.

The President. Best of luck up there on Capitol Hill. Good luck to you.

Secretary-designate Gates. Thank you.

The President. Thank you all.

NOTE: The President spoke at 7:48 a.m. in the Diplomatic Reception Room at the White House.

Remarks Following a Meeting With the Iraq Study Group
December 6, 2006

I just received the Iraq Study Group report, prepared by a distinguished panel of our fellow citizens. I want to thank James Baker and Lee Hamilton and the panel members for spending a lot of time on this really difficult issue. And I thank you for coming into the White House today to give me a copy of this report.

I've told the members that this report, called "The Way Forward," will be taken very seriously by this administration. This report gives a very tough assessment of the situation in Iraq. It is a report that brings some really very interesting proposals, and we will take every proposal seriously, and we will act in a timely fashion.

The commission is headed up to Congress, and I urge the Members of Congress to take this report seriously. While they won't agree with every proposal—and we probably won't agree with every proposal—it, nevertheless, is an opportunity to come

together and to work together on this important issue.

The country, in my judgment, is tired of pure political bickering that happens in Washington, and they understand that on this important issue of war and peace, it is best for our country to work together. And I understand how difficult that is, but this report will give us all an opportunity to find common ground, for the good of the country, not for the good of the Republican Party or the Democrat Party, but for the good of the country.

We can achieve long-lasting peace for this country, and it requires tough work. It also requires a strategy that will be effective. And we've got men and women of both political parties around this table who spent a lot of time thinking about the way forward in Iraq and the way forward in the Middle East, and I can't thank them enough for your time. You could be doing a lot of other things. You could have had

a lot more simple life than to allow your Government to call you back into service, but you did allow us to call you back into service, and you've made a vital contribution to the country. Our fellow citizens have got to know that it is possible for people of good will to come together to help make recommendations on how to deal with a very serious situation.

And we applaud your work. I will take it very seriously, and we'll act on it in a timely fashion. Thank you very much.

NOTE: The President spoke at 7:58 a.m. in the Cabinet Room at the White House. In his remarks, he referred to James A. Baker III and Lee H. Hamilton, cochairs, Iraq Study Group. The Office of the Press Secretary also released a Spanish language transcript of these remarks.

Remarks Following Discussions With President Oscar Arias Sanchez of Costa Rica
December 6, 2006

President Bush. Mr. President, welcome. I'm glad to welcome you back to the White House. I appreciate the very important discussions we had. Our discussions started with the bilateral relationship between the United States and Costa Rica. It is an important relationship. It's an important relationship when it comes to trade; it's an important relationship when it comes to interchanges between our governments and our peoples.

Mr. President, you spent a lot of time talking about the importance of education, and I respect you for that, and I appreciate your emphasis on education. And we will investigate ways to determine whether or not the United States can help, if you so desire, on matters of education. And I congratulate you on being very successful in educating the younger children of your country. And I, again, admire your focus on extending the education through all grades in Costa Rica.

Secondly, we spent time on CAFTA. It's an important initiative for this administration. I appreciate your dedication to the issue of trade. The President understands full well that trade is the best way to help reduce poverty around the world, and so he made it clear to me his deep desire

for the United States to take the lead on the Doha round of the trade discussions, which I assured him we would.

I appreciated very much your advice, Mr. President, on the neighborhood in which we live. I thank you for your clear vision when it comes to forms of government. And I appreciate you sharing with me your insights as to the different countries and different leaders and how best that we can work together to achieve peace and stability.

It's an honor to have you here, sir. You represent a fine country that a lot of Americans have had firsthand knowledge with. And I'm proud to welcome you.

President Arias Sanchez. Well, thank you, Mr. President, for your time. This room is familiar to me. I visited the Oval Office in the past, during the Reagan years and when President Bush was President. I was telling President Bush that in the past, every time I came to the White House, it was not to talk about Costa Rica, but about Nicaragua, and I'm very happy that we had a chance to talk about Costa Rica this time.

And as he just mentioned, my country is a small country. We produce what we do not consume, and we consume what

we do not produce. This is why trade is so important to us. Costa Rica is a very open economy, is the second-largest open economy in this hemisphere, after Chile. And this is why CAFTA is important to us, and this is why we're so determined to approve CAFTA, ratify CAFTA in our congress as soon as possible. And we are in the process of initiating negotiations with the European Union about free trade agreement with the whole of Europe, the European Union.

Concerning education, this is my priority. Peace was my priority 20 years ago; now it's education. I was asking President Bush that his program, No Child Left Behind, could be applied in many Latin American countries. You are all aware that what explains our failures, among other things, is the fact that average schooling in Latin American countries is only 6½ years, and that explains the social inequality and the poverty of our people.

So at the beginning of the 21st century, we're going to spend more on education, which is my dream and my determination to spend as much as 8 percent of GDP on education. We are simply condemning our children to remain poor as their grandfathers, and this is something that certainly the people of Latin America don't deserve.

President Bush. Thank you, sir. Glad you're here. Good job.

NOTE: The President spoke at 11:41 a.m. in the Oval Office at the White House. The Office of the Press Secretary also released a Spanish language transcript of these remarks.

Remarks Following a Meeting With Members of Congress
December 6, 2006

I've just met with Members of Congress from both political parties. My message is this: I want to work with the Congress; I want to work with people in both parties, so that we can send a message to the American people that the struggle for freedom, the struggle for our security is not the purview of one party over the other. The American people want us to work together, and my intention is to do just that.

Today the Baker-Hamilton commission, the Iraq Study Group put out what I thought was a very interesting report. There's some very good ideas in there. Not all of us around the table agree with every idea, but we do agree that it shows that bipartisan consensus on important issues is possible; really important for the American people to know that there are people of good will here in town willing to set aside politics and focus on the security of this country and the peace of the world.

And I want to thank you all for taking time out of your schedules to come. It means a lot to me, and I think it means a lot to the American people, to recognize that there are people in this town who are concerned more about the security of this country than they are about the security of their own political positions. And I'm proud to be with you. And I want to thank you for your thoughts. I take your comments very seriously. I take your ideas very seriously. And it's important to me that we continue to hear from the Congress as we fashion a way—a new way forward in Iraq, a new look, to achieve our objective of a country which can sustain itself, govern itself, defend itself, and be an ally in this war against extremism and terrorism.

Thank you all very much.

NOTE: The President spoke at 3:27 p.m. in the Cabinet Room at the White House.

Statement on Senate Confirmation of Robert M. Gates as Secretary of Defense
December 6, 2006

I am pleased the Senate has overwhelmingly voted to confirm Dr. Robert Gates as the next Secretary of Defense. In his confirmation hearing, Dr. Gates demonstrated he is an experienced, qualified, and thoughtful man who is well respected by members of both parties and is committed to winning the war on terror. Throughout his career, Dr. Gates has transformed the organizations he has led and

empowered them to successfully address complex issues. I am confident that his leadership and capabilities will help our country meet its current military challenges and prepare for emerging threats of the 21st century.

I thank Chairman Warner and Ranking Member Levin for leading dignified and constructive hearings, and I thank the Senate for moving quickly on this nomination.

The President's News Conference With Prime Minister Tony Blair of the United Kingdom
December 7, 2006

President Bush. Thank you all. Please be seated. I just had a good visit with Prime Minister Tony Blair. I appreciate you coming back, Mr. Prime Minister. I always enjoy our discussions. And I appreciate your clear view that we are confronted with a struggle between moderation and extremism, and this is particularly evident in the broader Middle East.

I talked about my recent trip to Jordan, where I talked to Prime Minister Maliki. I briefed the Prime Minister on my visit with His Eminence, Mr. Hakim, one of the major political players in Iraq. We discussed the report I received yesterday from the Iraq Study Group, a report chaired by Secretary of State—former Secretary of State James Baker and former Congressman Lee Hamilton. I told the Prime Minister I thought this was a very constructive report. I appreciated the fact that they laid out a series of recommendations, and they're worthy of serious study. I also updated the Prime Minister on the reviews that are being conducted by the Pentagon and the State Department and our National

Security Council. I talked to him about the consultations I'm having with the United States Congress.

We agree that victory in Iraq is important. It's important for the Iraqi people; it's important for the security of the United States and Great Britain; and it's important for the civilized world. We agree that an Iraq that can govern itself, defend itself, and sustain itself as an ally on the war on terror is a noble goal. The Prime Minister and I seek a wide range of opinions about how to go forward in Iraq, and I appreciate your opinions and your advice.

The increase in sectarian attacks we're seeing in and around Baghdad are unsettling. It has led to much debate in both our countries about the nature of the war that is taking place in Iraq. And it is true that Sunni and Shi'a extremists are targeting each other's innocent civilians and engaging in brutal reprisals. It's also true that forces beyond Iraq's borders contribute to this violence. And the Prime Minister put it this way, he said, "The violence is

not an accident or a result of faulty planning. It is a deliberate strategy. It is the direct result of outside extremists teaming up with internal extremists—Al Qaida with the Sunni insurgents and Iran with the Shi'a militia—to foment hatred and to throttle, at birth, the possibility of a nonsectarian democracy." You were right, and I appreciate your comments.

The primary victims of the sectarian violence are the moderate majority of Iraqis—Sunni and Shi'a alike—who want a future of peace. The primary beneficiaries are Sunni and Shi'a extremists, inside and outside of Iraq, who want chaos in that country so they can take control and further their ambitions to dominate the region.

These Sunni and Shi'a extremists have important differences, yet they agree on one thing: The rise of free and democratic societies in the Middle East, where people can practice their faith, choose their leaders, and live together in peace would be a decisive blow to their cause.

And so they're supporting extremists across the region who are working to undermine young democracies. Just think about the Middle East. In Iraq, they support terrorists and death squads who are fomenting sectarian violence in an effort to bring down the elected Government of Prime Minister Maliki. In Lebanon, they're supporting Hizballah, which recently declared its intention to force the collapse of Prime Minister Siniora's democratically elected Parliament and Government. In Afghanistan, they're supporting remnants of the Taliban that are seeking to destabilize President Karzai's Government and regain power. In the Palestinian Territories, they are working to stop moderate leaders like President Abbas from making progress toward the vision of two democratic states, Israel and Palestine, living side by side in peace and security.

In each of these places, radicals and extremists are using terror to stop the spread of freedom. And they do so because they want to spread their ideologies, their ideologies of hate and impose their rule on this vital part of the world. And should they succeed, history will look back on our time with unforgiving clarity and demand to know, what happened? How come free nations did not act to preserve the peace?

Prime Minister Blair and I understand that we have a responsibility to lead and to support moderates and reformers who work for change across the broader Middle East. We also recognize that meeting this responsibility requires action. We will take concerted efforts to advance the cause of peace in the Middle East. Prime Minister Blair informed me that he will be heading to the Middle East soon to talk to both the Israelis and the Palestinians, and I support that mission. I support the mission because it's important for us to advance the cause of two states living side by side in peace, and helping both parties eliminate the obstacles that prevent an agreement from being reached. And your strong leadership on this issue matters a lot.

We'll support the democratic Government of Prime Minister Maliki as he makes difficult decisions and confronts the forces of terror and extremism that are working hard to tear his country apart.

Britain and America are old allies, and the Prime Minister and I are strong friends. But Britain and America aren't standing together in this war because of friendship. We're standing together because our two nations face an unprecedented threat to civilization. We're standing together to prevent terrorists and extremists from dominating the Middle East. We stand together to prevent extremists from regaining the safe haven they lost in Afghanistan, a safe haven from which they launched attacks that killed thousands of our citizens. We stand together because we understand the only way to secure a lasting peace for our children and grandchildren is to defeat the extremist ideologies and help the ideology of hope, democracy prevail. We know the only way to secure peace for ourselves is to help millions of moms and dads across

the Middle East build what our citizens already have: societies based on liberty that will allow their children to grow up in peace and opportunity.

It's a tough time, and it's a difficult moment for America and Great Britain. And the task before us is daunting. Yet our nations have stood together before in difficult moments. Sixty-five years ago this day, America was jolted out of our isolationism and plunged into a global war that Britain had been fighting for 2 years. In that war, our Nation stood firm. And there were difficult moments during that war, yet the leaders of our two nations never lost faith in the capacity to prevail.

We will stand firm again, in this first war of the 21st century. We will defeat the extremists and the radicals. We will help a young democracy prevail in Iraq. And in so doing, we will secure freedom and peace for millions, including our own citizens.

Mr. Prime Minister, welcome.

Prime Minister Blair. Thank you very much, Mr. President. And thank you, firstly, for stressing again the strength of the relationship between our two countries, which is important for us, but I think it's important for the wider global community as well. Thank you also for the clarity of your vision about the mission that we're engaged in at the moment, which is a struggle between freedom and democracy on the one hand and terrorism and sectarianism on the other. And it's a noble mission, and it's the right mission, and it's important for our world that it succeeds.

And so the question is, how do we make sure that it does, indeed, succeed? And in respect of Iraq, I, like you, welcome the Baker-Hamilton study group. It offers a strong way forward. I think it is important now we concentrate on the elements that are necessary to make sure that we succeed, because the consequences of failure are severe. And I believe this is a mission we have to succeed in and we can succeed in.

And I think there are three elements that we can take forward. The first is to make sure that we are supporting the Maliki Government in making sure that that Government's nonsectarian nature is reflected in the policies of that Government and the way that it conducts itself. I think in respect of governance and security and capability—particularly economic capability—there is much that we are doing, but can do even more in order to make sure that they are supported in the vital work that they do and in the work of reconciliation, in bringing the different parts of Iraq together in order to give effect to the will of the Iraqi people, expressed in their democratic election.

I think, secondly, it's important that all of us who are engaged in this, but particularly those in the region, live up to their responsibilities in supporting the Maliki Government, in ensuring that Iraq is able to proceed in a democratic and non-sectarian way.

And I think that, finally, as you rightly emphasize, it is important that we do everything we can in the wider Middle East to bring about peace between Israel and the Palestinians. This is something that I know you feel deeply and passionately about. You are the first President who committed yourself to the two-state solution, and I believe that by moving this forward, we send a very strong signal not just to the region but to the whole of the world that we are evenhanded and just in the application of our values, that we want to see an Israel confident of its security and a Palestinian people able to live in peace and justice and democracy.

And that brings me back, finally, to the point that I began with, because I think it is the central point. Yes, it is immensely tough at the moment and very challenging, and everybody knows that. But there are only two ways that the Middle East can go. Its people can either be presented with a choice between a secular or a religious dictatorship, which is not a choice that any

free people would ever choose, or alternatively, they can enjoy the same possibilities of democracy that we hold dear in our countries. And this is not a view that we hold—I hold because of idealism alone; it is because I also believe that the only realistic path to security is by ensuring the spread of liberty.

So, Mr. President, thank you again for welcoming me here. And we will work closely with you in the time to come in order to achieve the mission we have set ourselves.

President Bush. Thank you, sir.

Prime Minister Blair. Thank you.

President Bush. We'll answer a couple of questions.

Iraq Study Group Report/Situation in the Middle East

Q. Mr. President and Mr. Prime Minister, neither of you has shown much doubt about your Iraq policies. Do you acknowledge that your approach has failed, as Baker-Hamilton suggests? And are you willing to engage directly with Syria and Iran and pull out most combat forces by early 2008, unless there's unexpected circumstances?

President Bush. The thing I liked about the Baker-Hamilton report is it discussed the way forward in Iraq. And I believe we need a new approach. And that's why I've tasked the Pentagon to analyze the way forward. That's why Prime Minister Blair is here to talk about the way forward, so we can achieve the objective, which is an Iraq which can govern itself, sustain itself, and defend itself and be an ally in the war on terror.

And the Baker-Hamilton report did some very interesting things. First, it shows that Republicans and Democrats can work together to achieve an—to come up with a strategy to achieve an objective, something the American people don't think is possible to happen. In other words, they've seen elections, and they saw all the bitterness and finger-pointing and name-calling and

wonder whether or not we can work together on this important cause. And I believe we can, and the Baker-Hamilton commission showed it's possible for people of good will to sit down at the table and design a way forward.

And so that's why I'm sitting down with the Members of Congress, to say to both Republicans and Democrats, "This is an important cause. It's important for our security. It's important to help lay the foundations for peace, and I want to hear your ideas." And I thought the report did a good job of showing what is possible. The Congress isn't going to accept every recommendation in the report, and neither will the administration, but there's a lot of very important things in the report that we ought to seriously consider.

And as the Prime Minister talked about, there's three aspects to the report. One is, how do we empower the Maliki Government so that the Maliki Government—the elected Government of the Iraqis—can help with the economy, can help secure peace, can do hard work necessary to achieve stability and to achieve the objective?

It talked about the regional—the countries in the region and the responsibilities of the region to help this Iraqi Government. And the idea of having an international group is an interesting idea. We've already got the compact, and I think the Baker-Hamilton report suggests that we broaden the Compact beyond just economic measures.

But one thing is for certain: When people—if people come to the table to discuss Iraq, they need to come understanding their responsibilities to not fund terrorists, to help this young democracy survive, to help with the economics of the country. And if people are not committed, if Syria and Iran is not committed to that concept, then they shouldn't bother to show up.

Thirdly, the Palestinian-Israeli conflict is an—is important to have—is important to be solved. I'm committed to a two-state

solution. I believe it is in Israel's interest and the Palestinian people's interest to have two states living side by side for peace. And the Prime Minister shares that goal, and he is willing to take time to go over and help remove obstacles toward achieving that goal.

And there are two notable obstacles. One is the prisoner, and secondly, is for there to be a unity government that recognizes the principles of the Quartet, with which Israel can negotiate. And we want to help.

And so I view this as a very important way forward, with important concepts. And the American people expect us to come up with a new strategy to achieve the objective which I've been talking about and which is laid out in the Baker-Hamilton report.

Prime Minister Blair. Look, I think the analysis of the situation is not really in dispute. The question is, how do we find the right way forward? And what we've got at the moment is something that is at one level very simple to describe but at another level very profound and difficult to deal with, and that is that the outside extremists are linking up with internal extremists, basically to create the circumstances of sectarianism, where it's very, very difficult then for democracy and ordinary institutions to function.

And I think the Baker-Hamilton report allows us to—as the situation has evolved in Iraq—to evolve our strategy in order to meet it in the ways that I've just described. But I think we've got to be very, very clear about this: It will require everybody to face up to their responsibilities—us, of course, because we are principal actors in this, but also the Iraqi Government. They've got to be prepared to make the moves necessary—full governance, full capability, reconciliation, and full help and security—and we will be there to support them.

But then there's responsibilities, as the President was saying a moment or two ago, on the region and the neighbors. And let me come directly to the Iran and Syria point. The issue for me is not a question of being unwilling to sit down with people or not, but the basis upon which we discuss Iraq has got to be clear, and it's got to be a basis where we are all standing up for the right principles, which are now endorsed in the United Nations resolutions, in respect of Iraq. In other words, you support the democratic elected Government; you do not support sectarians; and you do not support, arm, or finance terrorists.

Now, the very reason we have problems in parts of Iraq—and we know this very well down in the south of Iraq—is that Iran, for example, has been doing that. It's been basically arming, financing, supporting terrorism. So we've got to be clear the basis upon which we take this forward. And as I say, it's got to be on the basis of people accepting their responsibilities.

And finally, in relation to what the President was just saying a moment or two ago on Israel and Palestine, I mean, I think that one thing that is very clear is that the old Middle East had within it the origins of all the problems we see. I mean, this terrorist problem that we faced in the last few years, it didn't originate, I'm afraid, a few years ago. It's been building up over decades. It's come out of a series of states of oppression, of warped ideology based on a perverted view of the faith of Islam. This has been building up for a long period of time, and it has basically come out of the Middle East.

Now my view in the end is that you go back to the origins of this and say, well, how do we resolve it? And the only way we resolve it is by having the right vision and then the practical measures to achieve it.

Now I think the vision is absolutely correct. What we've got to do now—and this is exactly why the President is talking about the way forward—is that we've got to get the right way forward—this is where Baker-Hamilton helped—in order that we have the practical policy that bolsters and gives effect to the vision, because the vision is

the right vision. You leave a Middle East in which the Israel-Palestine issue is not solved, in which there's no moves towards democracy, in which Iraq goes back in its old state, in which the Iranian people have no chance to express themselves, maybe not in the months or 1 year, 2 years, but you'll have the same problem. You know, the reason we are faced with this issue is because in the end, everything that happened in that region erupted, in fact, on the streets of New York. But it—the origins of this went way, way back before that.

And so it is—there's a tendency, I think, sometimes, to see this as a battle between the idealists on the one hand and the realists on the other. In my view, the only modern form of realism is one that has ideals at the center of it.

War on Terror

Q. Mr. President, the Iraq Study Group described the situation in Iraq as grave and deteriorating. You said that the increase in attacks is unsettling. That won't convince many people that you're still in denial about how bad things are in Iraq, and question your sincerity about changing course.

President Bush. It's bad in Iraq. Does that help? [*Laughter*]

Q. Why did it take others to say it before you've been willing to acknowledge it to the world?

President Bush. In all due respect, I've been saying it a lot. I understand how tough it is, and I've been telling the American people how tough it is, and they know how tough it is. And the fundamental question is, do we have a plan to achieve our objective? Are we willing to change as the enemy has changed? The—and what the Baker-Hamilton study has done is, it shows good ideas as to how to go forward. What our Pentagon is doing is figuring out ways to go forward, all aiming to achieve our objective.

Make no mistake about it, I understand how tough it is, sir. I talk to the families who die. I understand there's sectarian vio-

lence. I also understand that we're hunting down Al Qaida on a regular basis and we're bringing them to justice. I understand how hard our troops are working. I know how brave the men and women who wear the uniform are, and therefore, they'll have the full support of this Government. I understand what long deployments mean to wives and husbands, and mothers and fathers, particularly as we come into a holiday season. I understand. And I have made it abundantly clear how tough it is.

I also believe we're going to succeed. I believe we'll prevail. Not only do I know how important it is to prevail, I believe we will prevail. I understand how hard it is to prevail. But I also want the American people to understand that if we were to fail—and one way to assure failure is just to quit, is not to adjust, and say, it's just not worth it—if we were to fail, that failed policy will come to hurt generations of Americans in the future.

And as I said in my opening statement, I believe we're in an ideological struggle between forces that are reasonable and want to live in peace and radicals and extremists. And when you throw into the mix radical Shi'a and radical Sunni trying to gain power and topple moderate governments, with energy which they could use to blackmail Great Britain or America or anybody else who doesn't kowtow to them, and a nuclear weapon in the hands of a government that is—would be using that nuclear weapon to blackmail to achieve political objectives, historians will look back and say, how come Bush and Blair couldn't see the threat? That's what they'll be asking. And I want to tell you, I see the threat, and I believe it is up to our governments to help lead the forces of moderation to prevail. It's in our interests.

And one of the things that has changed for American foreign policy is a threat overseas can now come home to hurt us. And September the 11th should be a wake-up call for the American people to understand what happens if there is violence and safe

havens in a part of the world. And what happens is, people can die here at home.

And so no, I appreciate your question. I appreciate—as you can tell, I feel strongly about making sure you understand that I understand it's tough. But I want you to know, sir, that I believe we'll prevail. I know we have to adjust to prevail, but I wouldn't have our troops in harm's way if I didn't believe that, one, it was important, and two, we'll succeed. Thank you.

Diplomatic Efforts in the Middle East

Q. Prime Minister, if I may, briefly— isn't what the——

Prime Minister Blair. You're not going to do a followup, are you? [*Laughter*]

Q. No, no, forgive me. I just wanted to ask you about your Middle East mission, if I may. Given your trip to the Middle East, isn't the truth of what the Arab-Israeli solution—sorry, isn't the truth of what the Arab-Israeli problem requires is not, however hard you try, another visit by a British Prime Minister, but the genuine commitment—and not merely in words—of an American administration that's serious about doing something about it?

Prime Minister Blair. Well, I believe that we have that commitment. And I mean, you're right in this sense, there would be no point in me going unless it was part of a mission that was supported fully by our American allies. But it is—we agree— the vision—I mean, the one thing that I find very frustrating about the situation, Israel-Palestine, is that there is actually an agreement as to the solution we want to see, which is a two-state solution. And really, everybody is agreed to that. So the question is, how do you get there?

And there are critical obstacles that stand in the way of that that require detailed attention and management, and it's not merely myself who's going to be engaged in this, of course, but as you know, the Secretary of State has been very closely involved in this. She's been visiting the re-

gion recently, and I know is, again, fully committed to it.

I think what is interesting from what you have from this today is an acceptance and, indeed, a clear belief that you look at these issues together. There is a kind of whole vision about how we need to proceed that links what happens inside Iraq with what happens outside Iraq. And again, I think that the Baker-Hamilton report put this very simply and very clearly.

And you know, there is no way that you ever succeed in these things unless you just carry on trying, and that's what we will do. And one of the things I learned in all the long years that you followed me in relation to Northern Ireland is that you just—you don't accept that you ever give up. You just carry on doing it. And I am sure that it is possible to resolve this, and I also do believe that if we do, then it would send a signal of massive symbolic power across the world.

President Bush. Steve [Steve Holland, Reuters].

War on Terror Strategy

Q. Thank you, sir. You mentioned Iran and Syria as part of this regional effort. Are you willing to engage with them directly as the report recommends? And back to the issue of the troops, is it possible to get them out of Iraq by early 2008, as the report talks about? And when do you hope to have this report? Sorry to——

President Bush. How many questions you got, Steve?

Q. Sorry about that. [*Laughter*]

President Bush. You mean, when do I hope to announce the strategy, is that what you're talking about?

Q. Yes, sir.

President Bush. After I get the reports. And Baker-Hamilton is a really important part of our considerations. But we want to make sure the military gets their point of view in. After all, a lot of what we're doing is a military operation. I want to make sure the State Department is able

to help us analyze the strategy to make sure that we've got the right political emphasis, not only inside Iraq but outside Iraq.

I appreciated the Prime Minister's answer to this lad—we call them lads, in Great Britain—lad's question, is that—[*laughter*].

Prime Minister Blair. You've made a friend, I think, there. [*Laughter*] It's a long time since anyone's called him that, yes. [*Laughter*]

President Bush. You got to understand—well——

Q. He calls me a number of other things.

President Bush. Our Secretary of State is very much engaged in this issue. She works hard on the issue. And as much as we'd like to impose the settlement, it's important for you to understand, sir, that the Israelis and the Palestinians must accept responsibility and must sign off on an agreement. It's kind of easy to sit back and say, okay, we're going to impose this on them. We can help, and we will help.

So, Steve, that's—we're spending a lot—I know, I'm heading back. We're spending a lot of time considering the new course, because the decisions that we make affect lives. They affect the lives of our soldiers; they affect the lives of the Iraqi people. But one thing is central to this new course, and that is, the Iraqi Government must be given more responsibility so they can prove to their people and to their allies that they're capable of making hard decisions necessary for their young democracy to move forward.

Second part of your long question?

Iran/Syria

Q. Well, are you willing to engage direct talks with——

President Bush. Oh, Iran and Syria.

Q. ——just a regional effort——

President Bush. No, no, I understand. Steve, let me talk about engaging Iran. We have made it clear to the Iranians that there is a possible change in U.S. policy,

a policy that's been in place for 27 years, and that is that if they would like to engage the United States that they've got to verifiably suspend their enrichment program. We've made our choice. Iran now has an opportunity to make its choice. I would hope they would make the choice that most of the free world wants them to make, which is, there is no need to have a weapons program; there is no need to isolate your people; there's no need to continue this obstinance, when it comes to your stated desires to have a nuclear weapon. It's not in your interest to do so.

And should they agree to verifiably suspend their enrichment, the United States will be at the table with our partners.

It's really interesting to talk about conversations with countries, which is fine; I can understand why people speculate about it, but there should be no mistake in anybody's mind, these countries understand our position. They know what's expected of them.

There is—if we were to have a conversation, it would be this one, to Syria: Stop destabilizing the Siniora Government. We believe that the Siniora Government should be supported, not weakened. Stop allowing money and arms to cross your border into Iraq. Don't provide safe haven for terrorist groups. We've made that position very clear.

And the truth of the matter is, is that these countries have now got the choice to make. If they want to sit down at the table with the United States, it's easy—just make some decisions that will lead to peace, not to conflict.

Is that the third part of your question? You've got to stop these long questions, Steven. Steven.

U.S. Troop Levels in Iraq/War on Terror

Q. Combat troops out by early 2008, is that possible——

President Bush. One of the things the report did mention, and I think you've said it in your comment, that if conditions so

allow—and we want our combat troops out as quick as possible. We want the Iraqis taking the fight. But it's very important to be—as we design programs, to be flexible and realistic. And as the report said—I don't got the exact words, but it was along the lines that, you know, "depending upon conditions," I believe is what the qualifier was. And I thought that made a lot of sense. I've always said we'd like our troops out as fast as possible. I think that's an important goal.

On the other hand, our commanders will be making recommendations based upon whether or not we're achieving our stated objective. And the objective, I repeat, is a government which can sustain, govern, and defend itself—free Government of Iraq that can do that—and will be an ally in this movement—against this movement that is threatening peace and stability. And it's real.

I like to remind people, it's akin to the cold war in many ways. There's an ideological clash going on. And the question is, will we have the resolve and the confidence in liberty to prevail? That's really the fundamental question facing—it's not going to face this Government or this Government because we made up our mind. We've made that part clear. But it will face future governments. There will be future opportunities for people to say, "Well, it's not worth it; let's just retreat." I would strongly advise a government not to accept that position because of the dangers inherent with isolationism and retreat.

Situation in the Middle East

Q. I'll try to be succinct. Mr. President, 2 years ago, you said that you were ready to expend political capital on the Israel-Palestinian situation. With hindsight, do you think you've fulfilled that intention? How closely do you see a linkage between what happens in Israel-Palestine and a settlement in Iraq, achieving your goals?

And Prime Minister, given that you were so recently in the Middle East and the situation hasn't exactly improved since then, is there anything specific you're hoping to achieve next week when you go back?

President Bush. Want me to start? I'm getting older, so you're going to have to repeat the second part of your question. [*Laughter*] Let me answer the first part. What's important is for people to accept the goal of two states living side by side for peace. And what has changed in the Middle East is that Israel and Palestine—at least the current leadership of both countries, or both—one entity and one country—accept that goal. That's important.

To that end, the previous Prime Minister made a decision to unilaterally withdraw from Gaza, which I felt was a good decision, which would expedite the potential arrival of a state. And so to answer your question, yes, we're spending a lot of capital getting people headed in the same direction, which if you look at the history of the Middle East, is a change.

Secondly, one of the reasons why there hasn't been instant success is because radicals and extremists are trying to stop the advance of a Palestinian state. Why? Because democracy is a defeat for them. That's what I strongly believe. I find it interesting that when Prime Minister Olmert reaches out to Palestinians to discuss a way forward on the two-state solution, Hizballah attacks Israel. Why? Because radicals and extremists can't stand the thought of a democracy. And one of the great ironies is that people in the Middle East are working hard to prevent people in the Middle East from realizing the blessings of a free society in a democracy.

And so no question, progress has been spotty. But it's important for people to understand, one of the reasons why is, is because radicals are trying to prevent it, and they're willing to kill innocent people to prevent progress. Now, our goal is to help the Abbas Government strengthen its security forces, and we're doing that. Our goal is to help the Abbas Government form a government that adheres to the principles

of the Quartet. We can't abandon the principles of the Quartet just because it may sound easy. We can't do that. When nations lay out principles, you've got to adhere to those principles, just like when we laid out a vision, you adhere to that vision.

And so the Prime Minister's visit, like Condi's visit recently to the Middle East, are all aiming to help countries remove obstacles necessary to achieve the vision. And it's hard work, but it's necessary work. And so I do believe there is a—I know there's a change of attitude. And now the fundamental question is, can we help the moderates prevail? And make no mistake about it, radicals and extremists will kill in order to stop the progress. And that's what's difficult. But it should be a signal to those of us who have got the comfort of liberty to understand the consequences of this ideological struggle we're fighting. One of the consequences is the denial of a Palestinian state.

This is ironic, isn't it? I think it is, and it's sad.

Prime Minister Blair. I mean, I think, first of all, it's important to understand how much has begun—how much work there's been. I mean, I know I've had many, many meetings on this issue over the past few months. I know Secretary Rice has been immensely active on it over these past months as well. Now, some of that is visible and out there at press conferences and meetings, and a lot of it is behind the scenes.

But in essence, what we've got to do is to try to resolve two issues. First of all, we need to get the release of Corporal Shalit, which, as Prime Minister Olmert made clear the other day, would then allow the release of many Palestinian prisoners as well. And this is obviously a very important issue.

But then, secondly, and this is, I think, really—one of the core questions is, we are prepared to release the money to the Palestinian Authority. We are prepared to take the peace process forward and get into a process of negotiation. But we need a government on both sides that is committed to the basic principles of that negotiation. And at the present time, we are not able to achieve a national unity government on the Palestinian side. And the reason for that is that we are saying, not as a matter of dogma at all, but you can't have a government that everyone can deal with and you can then negotiate a peace between Israel and Palestine, unless it's on the basis that everyone accepts the other's right to exist. So that's the difficulty. It's not a kind of technical point; it's absolutely at the heart of it.

Now, what we have got to do is to find either a way of unlocking the problem of forming that national unity government, on the principles laid down by the United Nations as well as the rest of the Quartet, or alternatively, a different way forward, but whatever way forward will have to be on the basis you get an empowered Palestinian Government with whom everyone can negotiate and deal with.

Now, you know, again, it's a very, very obvious thing. It's not just for the Israelis and the Palestinians but also for the whole of the region. You know, you can't negotiate this unless everyone accepts the basic principles of the negotiation. But if people were to do that—and after all, we're only asking people to accept the position that the United Nations and, really, the whole of the international community—you could move this forward quickly. I mean, I don't think there's any doubt at all that if you could get an empowered Palestinian Government able to negotiate, Israel has made it clear it is prepared to negotiate.

I'm not saying there aren't very tricky issues. There are—things like Jerusalem, the right of return, which are very, very difficult. But actually, it's not beyond our wit to put it together. We could put it together. But you need to get these initial steps taken.

Now, what I'm wont to do when I go out there is just explore what is the way

that we get that ability to get the negotiation underway, trying to work round these obstacles. And it's something—we were talking about Iran and Syria moments ago; it's something all of those countries could help with if they wanted to help with it. So I kind of feel one thing that is important is that everyone understands that there's no shortage of willingness, energy, commitment on our side.

And believe me, I've talked about this with the President many, many times, and I don't believe there's any shortage of those qualities on his part at all. But we need to get this—we need to get the door unlocked because it's kind of barred at the moment. It needs to be opened. And that's the task, I think, for the next period.

President Bush. Thank you. L.A. Times man, Jim [Jim Gerstenzang].

Iraq Study Group Report

Q. Mr. President, you have said that you have the Baker-Hamilton report; you also have the—you're waiting to hear from the Pentagon; you're waiting to hear from the State Department. This report was prepared by a bipartisan group, the only one you'll get. Secretary Baker has a special relationship with the family. Should this report not get extra consideration? Does it not carry more weight than any of the others?

President Bush. That's an interesting question. It's certainly an important part of our deliberations, and it was certainly an important part of our discussions this morning. Some reports are issued and just gather dust. And truth of the matter is, a lot of reports in Washington are never read by anybody.

To show you how important this one is, I read it, and our guest read it. The Prime Minister read a report prepared by a commission. And this is important. And there are some—I don't think Jim Baker and Lee Hamilton expect us to accept every recommendation. I expect them—I think—I know they expect us to consider every rec-

ommendation, Jim, that we ought to pay close attention to what they advise. And I told them yesterday at our meeting that we would pay close attention and would seriously consider every recommendation. We've discussed some of their recommendations here at this press conference. And we are—we will spend a lot of time on it.

And I—and so you ask its relative importance. I'd call it a very important report and a very important part of our working to a new approach, a new way forward in Iraq.

And I can't—I really do thank those citizens for taking time out of busy lives to spend time helping us look at different options. These are distinguished souls. They got plenty to do. They're busy people, and yet they took 9 months out. And they talked to a lot of people; they went to Iraq; they thought about it a lot. And it was a very considerate, important report. And I will take their recommendations very seriously.

War on Terror Strategy

Q. Mr. President, the Iraq Study Group said that leaders must be candid and forthright with people. So let me test that. Are you capable of admitting your failures in the past, and perhaps much more importantly, are you capable of changing course, perhaps in the next few weeks?

President Bush. I think you're probably going to have to pay attention to my speech coming up here when I get all the recommendations in, and you can answer that question yourself. I do know that we have not succeeded as fast as we wanted to succeed. I do understand that progress is not as rapid as I had hoped. And therefore, it makes sense to analyze the situation and to devise a set of tactics and strategies to achieve the objective that I have stated.

And so if the present situation needs to be changed, it follows that we'll change it if we want to succeed. What's really interesting is, the battle has changed in Iraq

from the rejectionists and former Ba'athists and definitely foreign fighters who have entered the country that were trying to destabilize the new Government to one that Mr. Zarqawi stated clearly—he said, "Look, let's kill Shi'a in order to create enough chaos and confusion and doubt of the Government, and set off a sectarian battle." And he succeeded in that extent. He didn't succeed at avoiding us, but he did succeed at starting off sectarian strife. And now the fundamental question is, what strategy is necessary to deal with this type of violence?

We'll continue after Al Qaida. Al Qaida will not have safe haven in Iraq. And that's important for the American people to know. We've got special operators. We've got better intelligence. And there is—Al Qaida is effective at these spectacular bombings, and we'll chase them down, and we are, along with the Iraqis. The strategy now is how to make sure that we've got the security situation in place such that the Iraqi Government is capable of dealing with the sectarian violence, as well as the political and economic strategies as well.

So yes, I think you'll see something differently, because it's a practical answer to a situation on the ground that's not the way we'd like it. You wanted frankness; I thought we would succeed quicker than we did, and I am disappointed by the pace of success.

Prime Minister Blair. I mean, look, there isn't any—as I said a moment or two ago, there isn't any doubt about how tough this is. It's hugely challenging. But what the report did not say is that we should just get out and leave it. What it did say is that it's immensely important that we succeed.

Now, the question is, therefore, how do we do it? And in that regard, I think the report is practical, it's clear, and it offers also the way of bringing people together.

The other thing that we want to do, because this is part of succeeding in this mission, is actually to make people understand that this is something where you've got to try and bring people together around a set of common objectives and a practical set of methods to achieve those objectives.

And, you know, the issues that the report raises—I mean, these aren't issues that, obviously, no one has ever thought of; these aren't issues that haven't been part of the continual discussion and debate and iteration within the coalition and, indeed, between us and the Iraqi Government. But those essential elements—we want to make sure, in the light of the changing situation that there is there, that, one, we have the Iraqi Government able to operate effectively, but in a nonsectarian way, because that's what we began with. Secondly, that we make sure that everyone in the region is supporting that. And thirdly, that we set this within the context of a broader vision for the Middle East, not least in respect of Israel and Palestine.

Now, in respect of the elements of that strategy, this report gives us a basis on which we can move forward, but we've obviously then got to look at the practical measures that are necessary in order to give effect to those elements. And that's what we'll do. And I think that, you know, the one thing that no one who is dealing with this on a day-to-day basis has any doubt about is how tough it is. But the question is, how we make sure that we overcome those tough conditions and succeed, because the need to succeed is so huge.

British Armed Forces in Iraq and Afghanistan

Q. Prime Minister, just a brief supplementary—sorry, I didn't get to ask you the question. You promised some time—I'm sorry.

President Bush. Look, I agree; this is a total violation of—[*laughter*]. Our press corps is calling you down, man. I mean, there you are—no, go ahead. [*Laughter*]

Q. You're encouraging it.

President Bush. I'm not encouraging it. He's not a member of the American press—it's the Prime Minister. [*Laughter*]

Prime Minister Blair. He's my guy. [*Laughter*]

Q. Only because you cut me off, Mr. President——

President Bush. Okay. [*Laughter*]

Press. Ooh! [*Laughter*]

Q. Prime Minister, you promised the British military whatever it takes to fight in Iraq and Afghanistan, but the former head of the British Army says the British military is not being funded properly for the job it's being asked to do. Do you accept that?

Prime Minister Blair. We get from our military advice as to what they need, and we do our level best to meet it. I mean, we'll—I haven't actually read Mike Jackson's comments. I think it's Mike's speech you're talking about. And let me tell you, he's someone I have enormous amount of respect for and did a fantastic job when he was chief of our staff.

But in relation to this, we've worked closely with the military the whole time. It's important we carry on doing it. And I simply make the point that in the last few years, and not least yesterday in the pre-budget report of the chancellor, we gave another significant increase in funding. But it's important we do this. I mean this is a mission in which it is—because it's important that we succeed, it's important that we equip our armed forces properly. But I've got nothing—if you'll forgive me, I've not got anything to comment on in detail until I've actually read the speech that he made. Not that—I'm not saying you wouldn't give me a fair resume of it. [*Laughter*]

President Bush. Thank you, buddy.

Prime Minister Blair. Okay.

President Bush. Good job. Thank you.

NOTE: The President's news conference began at 11:05 a.m. in Room 450 of the Dwight D. Eisenhower Executive Office Building. In his remarks, the President referred to Prime Minister Nuri al-Maliki of Iraq; Abdul Aziz Al-Hakim, chairman, Supreme Council for the Islamic Revolution of Iraq; Prime Minister Fuad Siniora of Lebanon; President Hamid Karzai of Afghanistan; President Mahmoud Abbas of the Palestinian Authority; Cpl. Gilad Shalit, an Israeli soldier captured and held captive by militants in Gaza since June 25; and Prime Minister Ehud Olmert and former Prime Minister Ariel Sharon of Israel. Prime Minister Blair referred to former Chief of the General Staff Michael Jackson of the United Kingdom.

Remarks on Lighting the National Christmas Tree
December 7, 2006

Thank you all very much. Laura and I are pleased to welcome you to the Christmas Pageant of Peace. Christmas is a season of glad tidings and a time when our thoughts turn to the source of joy and hope born in a humble manger 2000 years ago. And tonight we gather to observe one of the great traditions of our Nation's Capital, the lighting of the National Christmas Tree.

I'm really glad Santa made it. [*Laughter*] I'm glad he could find a place to park. [*Laughter*] And I'm glad you all joined us tonight.

I want to thank Vin for his leadership of the National Park Foundation. I thank Deputy Secretary of the Interior Lynn Scarlett for joining us. I am pleased to be here with members of my Cabinet; Members of the Congress; Mary Bomar, who is the Director of the National Park Service; Joe Lawler, Regional Director of the National Capital Region, National Park

Service. I want to thank all the National Park Service employees for their hard work.

I appreciate Dr. Robert Schuller for leading the invocation. I want to thank our fabulous entertainers for entertaining us tonight.

We have gathered for this ceremony for more than 80 years. We come together to celebrate a simple and inspiring story. It's a story of a miraculous birth in a humble place. It is a story of a single life that changed the world and continues to change hearts. And for two millennia, this story has carried the message that God is with us and He offers His love to every man, woman, and child.

During the Christmas season, we seek to reflect that love in our lives. Millions of Americans will celebrate at home in fellowship with friends and family. Millions will reach out with a compassionate hand to help brothers and sisters in need. And all will give thanks to the bonds of love and affection that bring fulfillment to our lives and the hope of peace around the world.

At this time of year, we give thanks for the brave men and women in uniform who are serving our Nation. Many of those who have answered the call of duty will spend this Christmas season far from home and separated from family. We honor their sacrifice. We are proud of their service and that of their families. We will keep them close to our hearts and in our prayers.

And now, as an expression of our own hope for peace in this Christmas season, we will light the National Tree. We've asked three representatives from the National Park Service's Junior Ranger Program to help. The Junior Ranger Program teaches children and families about science, nature, and stewardship of our national parks.

And so Attiyah Jenkins, Stephen Scott, and Dana Bederson will help me light the National Christmas Tree. Come on up, guys.

I ask all of you to join us in the countdown: five, four, three, two, one.

NOTE: The President spoke at 5:55 p.m. on the Ellipse at the White House. In his remarks, he referred to Vin Cipolla, president and chief executive officer, National Park Foundation; and Robert H. Schuller, minister, Reformed Church in America.

Remarks Following a Meeting With Congressional Leaders
December 8, 2006

I want to thank the Members of Congress—both Houses, both political parties—for joining me and the Vice President and members of my team. We just had a very constructive conversation. We talked about Iraq. We talked about the need for a new way forward in Iraq, and we talked about the need to work together on this important subject. We also talked about other key issues.

I assured the leaders that the White House door will be open when the new Congress shows up. And I think we ought to meet on a regular basis; I believe there's consensus toward that. And the reason you meet on a regular basis is so that the American people can know that we're working hard to find common ground. That's what they expect us to do; they expect us to work on big problems and solve them.

I want to say something about my two friends here. Senator Frist, we appreciate your service to the United States of America. You brought a lot of dignity to the office. And I appreciate the Speaker being,

as well—Mr. Speaker, you've done a fine job as Speaker.

I look forward to working with Senator Reid and Congresswoman Pelosi for doing what's right for the country. And again, I want to thank you all for coming down. I appreciate your interest, appreciate your advice, appreciate the input that you've given.

Thank you.

NOTE: The President spoke at 9:16 a.m. in the Cabinet Room at the White House.

Remarks Following a Meeting With President Thabo Mvuyelwa Mbeki of South Africa
December 8, 2006

President Bush. It's been my honor to welcome a man for whom I have a great deal of respect, and that is the President of South Africa, President Mbeki, here back to the Oval Office. I so very much appreciate the time you've given and the great discussion we just had.

We talked about a wide range of subjects. We talked about Darfur and the need for South Africa and the United States and other nations to work with the Sudanese Government to enable a peacekeeping force into that country to facilitate aid and save lives. And I expressed my concerns about the situation with the President. He shares my concerns that the situation is dire. And now is the time for action. And I appreciate your thoughts, Mr. President.

We talked about, interestingly enough, the Darfur [Doha]° round. The President is concerned about whether or not the World Trade Organization round will go forward. He recognizes, like I recognize, that trade will lift more people out of poverty than any other mechanism. And I told the President, I am committed to the Darfur [Doha]° round. I believe in trade, and I believe in the necessity of trade. And so we'll work to see if we can't get that issue solved.

We talked about a lot of issues. We talked about Iran; we talked about the Mid-

dle East; we talked about our bilateral relations and his Government's commitment to fighting HIV/AIDS and our willingness to provide over $600 million to the folks in South Africa to help deal with this terrible pandemic.

I would call our relations strong and good and necessary. And Mr. President, welcome back, and the floor is yours.

President Mbeki. Thank you very much, President. Well, I was very glad, indeed, that we had this opportunity to meet with the President to discuss precisely these matters that he has indicated. Of course of immediate importance to us is the support we get from the President and the U.S. Government with regard to the resolution of these African conflicts.

And indeed, we are, all of us, keenly interested that we must increase the troops deployed in Darfur, to address these issues that the President mentioned, and hopefully, the Security Council will move quickly on that to do that larger deployment of troops. It's very urgent, very necessary, and we will absolutely do everything to make sure that, from the African side, we remove any obstacles that might be to such bigger deployment in Darfur. It's very necessary.

° White House correction.

Because also I mentioned, I discussed with the President the impact of the situation in Darfur on the neighboring countries, particularly Chad and the Central African Republic. But also the difficult situation in Somalia——

President Bush. Yes, sir.

President Mbeki. ——and the President, together, we are very keen that, indeed, something must move there. This was a failed state. It's necessary to support transitional government, to restoring a government, and to reunify the country and so on. It's an important thing because the problem—one of the big problems is that as it is, it provides a base for terrorists—find safe haven there and then can spread out to the rest of the continent. It's something that is of shared concern.

But again, of course, I was very, very reassured when the President said he is committed to the success of the WTO negotiations. It's a very important part, in terms of addressing the agenda of the poor of the world. They need these market-access issues addressed, and so on. I was very, very pleased, indeed, that President said indeed we must work to make sure that WTO negotiating process succeeds.

We—finally, President, I'd like to say I was very pleased that, indeed, you said we shall need to work even—together even more intensely than we have in the past, because with effect from the 1st of January, South Africa, of course, joins the Security Council as a nonpermanent member. As I'm saying, I was very glad that the President said that's going to mean we'll need better interaction so that we could work together, indeed, to help to find solutions to all these wide range of issues that are on the agenda of the Security Council.

But thank you very much, Mr. President.

President Bush. Proud you're back. Thank you, sir. Thank you.

NOTE: The President spoke at 2:12 p.m. in the Oval Office at the White House.

Statement on the Death of Jeane J. Kirkpatrick
December 8, 2006

Laura and I are deeply saddened by the death of Jeane Kirkpatrick. As a professor, author, ambassador, and adviser to Presidents, she influenced the thinking of generations of Americans on the importance of American leadership in advancing the cause of freedom and democracy around the globe. She defended the cause of freedom at a pivotal time in world history, and her courageous service as our United Nations Ambassador inspired her fellow Americans and lovers of liberty around the world. Jeane's powerful intellect helped America win the cold war. Her insights and teachings will continue to illuminate the path ahead for the United States in the world. We send our condolences to Jeane's family and friends, and on behalf of all Americans, we give thanks for her extraordinary life.

Statement on the National Economy
December 8, 2006

Today we received a new report that confirms the continued strength of the American economy. The November jobs report showed that 132,000 more Americans found work last month and that job creation in previous months was stronger than first estimated, adding 42,000 jobs to the numbers released last month. The unemployment rate remained low at 4.5 percent. This is good news for American workers, and they are also seeing good news in their paychecks. As we look forward, our goal is to maintain the progrowth policies that have strengthened our economy and will stimulate the creation of good jobs and higher wages.

The President's Radio Address
December 9, 2006

Good morning. This week, I held important meetings at the White House about the situation in Iraq.

On Monday, I met in the Oval Office with one of Iraq's most influential Shi'a leaders, His Eminence Abdul Aziz Al-Hakim. We discussed the desire of the Iraqi people to see their unity Government succeed and how the United States can help them achieve that goal.

On Thursday, I had breakfast with Prime Minister Tony Blair of Britain. We discussed the sectarian violence in Iraq and the need to confront extremists inside Iraq and throughout the region. The Prime Minister explains it this way: "The violence is not an accident or a result of faulty planning. It is a deliberate strategy. It is the direct result of outside extremists teaming up with internal extremists—Al Qaida with the Sunni insurgents and Iran with Shi'a militia—to foment hatred and thus throttle, at birth, the possibility of nonsectarian democracy."

The Prime Minister and I also discussed the report I received this week from the Iraq Study Group, chaired by former Secretary of State James Baker and former Congressman Lee Hamilton. Their report provides a straightforward picture of the grave situation we face in Iraq. The Iraq Study Group's report also explicitly endorses the strategic goal we've set in Iraq: an Iraq that can "govern itself, sustain itself, and defend itself."

The report went on to say, quote, "In our view, this definition entails an Iraq with a broadly representative government that maintains its territorial integrity, is at peace with its neighbors, denies terrorism a sanctuary, and doesn't brutalize its own people. Given the current situation in Iraq, achieving this goal will require much time and will depend primarily on the actions of the Iraqi people."

I agree with this assessment. I was also encouraged that the Iraq Study Group was clear about the consequences of a precipitous withdrawal from Iraq. The group declared that such a withdrawal would, quote, "almost certainly produce greater sectarian violence" and lead to "a significant power vacuum, greater human suffering, regional destabilization, and a threat to the global economy." The report went on to say, "If we leave and Iraq descends into chaos, the long-range consequences could eventually require the United States to return."

The Iraq Study Group understands the urgency of getting it right in Iraq. The

group also understands that while the work ahead will not be easy, success in Iraq is important, and success in Iraq is possible. The group proposed a number of thoughtful recommendations on a way forward for our country in Iraq. My administration is reviewing the report, and we will seriously consider every recommendation. At the same time, the Pentagon, the State Department, and the National Security Council are finishing work on their own reviews of our strategy in Iraq. I look forward to receiving their recommendations. I want to hear all advice as I make the decisions to chart a new course in Iraq.

I thank the members of the Iraq Study Group for their hard work and for the example of bipartisanship that they have set. The group showed that Americans of different political parties can agree on a common goal in Iraq and come together on ways to achieve it. Now it is the responsibility of all of us in Washington—Republicans and Democrats alike—to come together and find greater consensus on the best way forward.

As part of this effort, I met this week with House and Senate leaders from both parties, as well as senior members of the Armed Services, Foreign Relations, and Intelligence Committees. We had productive discussions about our shared duty to forge a bipartisan approach to succeed in Iraq. The future of a vital region of the world and the security of the American people depend on victory in Iraq. I'm confident that we can move beyond our political differences and come together to achieve that victory. I will do my part.

Thank you for listening.

NOTE: The address was recorded at 7:50 a.m. on December 8 in the Cabinet Room at the White House for broadcast at 10:06 a.m. on December 9. The transcript was made available by the Office of the Press Secretary on December 8 but was embargoed for release until the broadcast. In his address, the President referred to Abdul Aziz Al-Hakim, chairman, Supreme Council for the Islamic Revolution in Iraq. The Office of the Press Secretary also released a Spanish language transcript of this address.

Statement on Congressional Passage of Outer Continental Shelf Legislation
December 9, 2006

I commend Congress for passing the Outer Continental Shelf legislation, which will help to reduce our dependence on imported sources of energy by increasing access to domestic sources of oil and gas. Developing these reliable domestic resources in an environmentally sound manner will help address high energy prices, strengthen our energy security, and protect manufacturing jobs. The bill also provides the producing States of Texas, Louisiana, Mississippi, and Alabama a share in the royalty revenues from OCS leases. I appreciate the commitment by the State of Louisiana to use revenues from these leases to restore coastal wetlands.

NOTE: The statement referred to H.R. 6111.

Statement on Congressional Passage of Legislation To Reauthorize the Ryan White Comprehensive AIDS Resources Emergency Act
December 9, 2006

In 1990, Congress passed the Ryan White Comprehensive AIDS Resources Emergency (CARE) Act to advance our domestic battle against HIV/AIDS. This landmark legislation has provided Americans in need with better access to medical care, antiretroviral treatments, and counseling and has helped them live longer lives. The act also supports HIV testing to prevent the further spread of this devastating disease.

Laura and I thank the House and Senate for reauthorizing the Ryan White CARE Act. This legislation focuses on lifesaving and life-extending services and increased accountability and will provide more flexibility to the Secretary of Health and Human Services to direct funding to areas of greatest need. The Ryan White CARE Act demonstrates the compassionate and generous spirit of America, and I look forward to signing this important legislation into law.

NOTE: The statement referred to H.R. 6143.

Statement on Congressional Passage of Legislation To Authorize Permanent Trade Relations With Vietnam
December 9, 2006

I commend the Congress for its bipartisan support for my request to approve legislation authorizing the grant of permanent normal trade relations to Vietnam. PNTR marks a significant step forward in the process of normalizing relations with Vietnam and will benefit both our nations. This designation will advance our trade and investment relations with Vietnam and ensure that the United States shares in the economic benefits generated by Vietnam's imminent membership in the World Trade Organization. Vietnam is demonstrating its strong commitment to continuing economic reforms, which will support political reform and respect for human rights. The American people welcome the remarkable transformation and economic progress in Vietnam, and we will continue to work together to strengthen our ties.

NOTE: The statement referred to H.R. 6406.

Statement on Congressional Passage of Fisheries Management Legislation
December 9, 2006

I applaud Congress for working in a bipartisan manner to pass a stronger Magnuson-Stevens Act. Our Nation is committed to maintaining our thriving commercial and recreational fishing communities. This bill embraces my priorities of ending overfishing and rebuilding our Nation's fish stocks through more effective, market-

based management and tougher enforcement. This landmark legislation also provides stronger tools to achieve progress internationally to ensure healthy fish stocks, promote better management, and halt destructive fishing practices based on sound science.

Since my administration released the Ocean Action Plan in 2004, we have been making great strides in our efforts to make our oceans, coasts, and Great Lakes cleaner, healthier, and more productive. Enactment of this bill is one of the top priorities of the Ocean Action Plan and is another significant bipartisan environmental achievement.

NOTE: The statement referred to H.R. 5946.

Statement on Congressional Passage of United States-India Civil Nuclear Cooperation Legislation
December 9, 2006

Congress has agreed upon bipartisan legislation that will strengthen the strategic relationship between America and India and deliver valuable benefits to both nations. I am pleased that our two countries will soon have increased opportunities to work together to meet our energy needs in a manner that does not increase air pollution and greenhouse gas emissions, promotes clean development, supports nonproliferation, and advances our trade interests.

I appreciate Congress's support for the U.S.-India civil nuclear cooperation initiative and would like to thank Chairman Hyde, Ranking Member Lantos, Chairman Lugar, and Ranking Member Biden for their leadership on this extraordinary legislation. I look forward to signing this bill into law soon.

NOTE: The statement referred to H.R. 5682.

Statement on the Situation in Darfur, Sudan
December 10, 2006

I send my greetings to those participating in events around the world protesting the situation in Darfur. It is only fitting that we take the time today to remember the value of every human life and the right of every person in the world to live in peace with dignity and respect.

Our Nation is appalled by the genocide in Darfur, which has led to the spread of fighting and hostility in the Republic of Chad and the Central African Republic. We call on the Government of the Republic of Sudan and the rebel groups to cease fighting and pursue peace.

We continue to work on establishing a credible and effective peacekeeping force to stop the violence in Darfur. To this end, we are aggressively engaging all stakeholders to implement U.N. Resolution 1706 to transition the African Union Mission in Sudan to a strong international peacekeeping operation. We are urgently seeking to broaden support for the Darfur Peace Agreement and pressuring all sides to implement an immediate cease-fire. We will continue to work with the Congress, the United Nations, the African Union, and the international community to provide aid to

those who are suffering. The United States is committed to achieving stability, lasting peace, and the restoration of basic human rights for the people of Darfur.

Remarks Following a Meeting With Senior State Department Officials
December 11, 2006

Thank you all for coming. I just had a briefing with my senior policy advisers here at the State Department. I want to thank you for your hospitality, Madam Secretary.

We talked about a lot of things. We talked about what's taking place on the ground in Iraq, particularly from the perspective of the State Department. I must tell you, there are some fantastic, brave souls who are heading PRTs, Provincial Reconstruction Teams. These are our civilian components on the ground there in Iraq. And we got a briefing from Baghdad, with one of our PRT leaders here in Washington, about the challenges and the tasks to help this Iraqi Government get a country that can sustain and govern and defend itself.

No question in my mind, there are some very brave State Department officials who are engaged in this really important endeavor, and I want to thank them and their families. I appreciate the advice I got from those folks in the field. And that advice is an important part and an important component of putting together a new way forward in Iraq. Like most Americans, this administration wants to succeed in Iraq, because we understand success in Iraq will help protect the United States in the long run.

We also talked about the neighborhood, the countries that surround Iraq and the responsibilities that they have to help this young Iraqi democracy survive. We believe that most of the countries understand that a mainstream society, a society that is a functioning democracy, is in their interests. And it's up to us to help focus their attention and focus their efforts on helping the Iraqis succeed.

I appreciate so very much the Iraqi leadership taking the lead in its neighborhood. After all, one of the things we're trying to do is help this Government get on its feet so it can govern and it can conduct its own foreign policy. But the role of America is to help this young democracy survive.

I'm looking forward to continuing my deliberations with the military. There's no question, we've got to make sure that the State Department and the Defense Department are—the efforts and their recommendations are closely coordinated so that when I do speak to the American people, they will know that I've listened to all aspects of Government and that the way forward is the way forward to achieve our objective: to succeed in Iraq. And success is a country that governs, defends itself, that is a free society, that serves as an ally in this war on terror.

And the reason why that's vital is because Iraq is a central component of defeating the extremists who want to establish safe haven in the Middle East, extremists who would use their safe haven from which to attack the United States, extremists and radicals who have stated that they want to topple moderate governments in order to be able to achieve assets necessary to effect their dream of spreading their totalitarian ideology as far and wide as possible.

This is really the calling of our time, that is, to defeat these extremists and radicals. And Iraq is a component part, an important part of laying the foundation for peace.

And so, Madam Secretary, thank you for the briefing. I want to thank your team here in Washington for their good work, and I thank those out in the field who have shown such incredible bravery to do the hard work necessary to secure our country.

Thank you all.

NOTE: The President spoke at 11:55 a.m. at the State Department.

Remarks Following a Meeting With Vice President Tariq al-Hashimi of Iraq
December 12, 2006

President Bush. It's been my honor to meet with the Vice President of Iraq again. I had the pleasure of meeting the Vice President in Baghdad. It was there that I invited him to come to Washington, DC, and I did so because I understand his importance to the future of Iraq.

The Vice President has suffered unspeakable violence in his family. He's lost loved ones to violent action. And yet, in spite of his grief and in spite of pain in his heart, he was willing to work for a united Iraq and a peaceful Iraq, an Iraq that can govern itself and sustain itself and defend itself, a free Iraq that will be an ally in the war against extremists and radicals.

And, Mr. Vice President, I respect your courage, and I respect your advice.

I spent time with the Vice President today talking about the conditions in Iraq and what the United States can do to help this Iraqi Government succeed. He brought me up to date on the terrible violence that is taking place in some of the neighborhoods in Baghdad. He spoke eloquently about the suffering that innocent families have gone through. And my heart goes out to those, Mr. Vice President, who have suffered at the hands of extremists and killers.

Our objective is to help the Iraqi Government deal with the extremists and killers and support the vast majority of Iraqis who are reasonable people who want peace.

And so, Mr. Vice President, my message to you today, and to the Iraqi people is, we want to help you. We want to help your Government be effective. We want your help—your Government live up to its words and ideals. And I thank you for being a leader of one aspect of Iraqi society—you're the leader of many Sunnis, and you're committed to a government that is Shi'a, Sunni, Kurdish, and everybody else in your country, every other group in your country that will help us yield peace.

And I welcome you; I thank you; and I praise your courage.

Vice President Hashimi. I would like to express my sincere thanks to Mr. President for the invitation, first of all, and too when he expedites my visit to the States, which left a really positive message to the Iraqi people that the American administration, while they are revising their strategy, they are looking for a balance and fair analysis from diversified leaders in Iraq.

So this visit coming after the visit of Mr. Hakim, I would like also to express my appreciation to the unique and unforgettable commitment of the President when he said, and continued saying, that we are committed to the success in Iraq. And I share his views and aspirations that there is no way but success in Iraq.

We have no other option in Iraq but to achieve that success. And with the cooperation with our friends and Mr. President and the American administration, we will join forces to achieve that success in the foreseeable future.

There is a chance, and I can assure you there is a great and real chance to get out of this present dilemma. It is a hard time that the Iraqis face in time being, but there is a light in the corridor. There is a chance, but we need a good will and a strong determination, the same strong determination that the Mr. President has. There will be a chance for the country and for Iraq to succeed.

During my discussion and dialog with the Mr. President, I had really a frank and positive dialog and conversation. We tackled key issues. And hopefully, at the end of the day, I would like to see my comments and observations welcomed, because at the end of the day, what I say to Mr. President is achieving—or could be seen as a genuine and—[*inaudible*]—part in the way of achieving the success.

I thank Mr. President again for the time given to myself and to my colleagues. And I leave United States with a great hope that we do have friends in Washington; that they are very much interested, in fact, to help us in these very difficult times, and to achieve the unforgettable, the long-waited success. Whatever the sacrifices, my family and the country, at the end of the day, we have no other option but to maintain this momentum and to struggle until we meet that success, *inshallah*.

President Bush. Thank you, sir. Thank you very much. Thank you.

NOTE: The President spoke at 1:51 p.m. in the Oval Office at the White House. Vice President Hashimi referred to Abdul Aziz Al-Hakim, chairman, Supreme Council for the Islamic Revolution in Iraq.

Remarks Following a Meeting With Senior Department of Defense Officials and an Exchange With Reporters in Arlington, Virginia
December 13, 2006

The President. I've just concluded a very productive meeting with the Secretary of Defense Rumsfeld and Chairman of the Joint Chiefs Pete Pace, the Joint Chiefs of Staff, Vice President. I thank these men who wear our uniform for a very candid and fruitful discussion about the—about how to secure this country and how to win a war that we now find ourselves in.

We spent a lot of time talking about a new way forward in Iraq, to help the Iraqi Government confront and defeat the enemies of a free Iraq. We all agree it's in our Nation's interest that we help this Government succeed. We recognize that there are enemies that would like to topple this young democracy so they could have safe haven from which to plot and plan attacks against moderate nations in the Middle East, as well as attacks against the United

States. It's in our interest that we help this Government succeed.

There have been a lot of violence in Iraq, and the violence has been horrific. Scores of innocent men, women, and children are being brutally killed by ruthless murderers. Our troops are engaged in offensive operations, and we mourn the loss of life. We are saddened by the loss of every single life amongst our service men and women. Our folks are very active in Al Anbar and in Baghdad, which is where the enemy is concentrated.

Our commanders report that the enemy has also suffered. Offensive operations by Iraqi and coalition forces against terrorists and insurgents and death squad leaders have yielded positive results. In the months of October, November, and the first week of December, we have killed or captured nearly 5,900 of the enemy.

While the enemy is far from being defeated, there should be no doubt in anybody's mind that every day and night, the Iraqi Government and our brave men and women of the Armed Forces are taking the fight to the enemy; that in spite of the fact that I am conducting a strategic review of the best way forward in Iraq, there are a lot of operations taking place, day and night.

Yesterday the Secretary and the Vice President and General Pace and I were on the SVTS with General Casey, and he's talking about the hard work our troops and Iraqi troops are doing to defeat these enemies.

I do want to say something to those who wear our uniform. The men and women in uniform are always on my mind. I am proud of them. I appreciate their sacrifices. And I want them to know that I am focused on developing a strategy that will help them achieve their mission. Oh, I know there's a lot of debate here at home, and our troops pay attention to that debate. They hear that I am meeting with the Pentagon or the State Department or outside officials, that my national security team and I are working closely with Iraqi leaders, and they wonder what that means. Well, I'll tell you what it means: It means I am listening to a lot of advice to develop a strategy to help you succeed.

There's a lot of consultations taking place, and as I announced yesterday, I will be delivering my plans, after a long deliberation, after steady deliberation. I'm not going to be rushed into making a difficult decision, a necessary decision, to say to our troops, "We're going to give you the tools necessary to succeed and a strategy to help you succeed." I also want the new Secretary of Defense to have time to evaluate the situation, so he can provide serious and deliberate advice to me.

I do want our troops to understand this, though: That this Government and this group of military leaders are committed to a strategic goal of a free Iraq that is demo-cratic, that can govern itself, defend itself, and sustain itself and be a strong ally in this war against radicals and extremists who would do us harm; secondly, that our troops deserve the solid commitment of the Commander in Chief and our political leaders and the American people.

You have my unshakable commitment in this important fight to help secure the peace for the long term. I pledge to work with the new Congress to forge greater bipartisan consensus to help you achieve your mission. I will continue to speak about your bravery and your commitment and the sacrifices of your families to the American people. We're not going to give up. The stakes are too high and the consequences too grave to turn Iraq over to extremists who want to do the American people and the Iraqi people harm.

I thank you for your service. I'm proud to be your Commander in Chief. We'll honor the sacrifices you are making by making sure your children and grandchildren can grow up in a more peaceful world.

God bless.

I'll take a couple of questions. AP man [Ben Feller, Associated Press].

War on Terror Strategy

Q. Mr. President, thank you. You've been gathering advice, as you said, from leaders here and from leaders in Iraq. As you've gone through that extensive process, have you heard any new ideas at all, anything that would change your thinking?

The President. I've heard some ideas that would lead to defeat, and I reject those ideas—ideas such as leaving before the job is done; ideas such as not helping this Government take the necessary and hard steps to be able to do its job.

I've heard interesting ideas. I won't share them with you because I want to make sure I continue to collect those ideas and put them together in a strategy that our military and the commanders and our national security team understands will lead

to an Iraq that can govern and sustain and defend itself.

I put off my speech—actually, I was quite flexible about when I was going to give my speech to begin with but—and one of the main reasons why is I really do want the new Secretary of Defense to have time to get to know people and hear people and be a part of this deliberation. And he will not be sworn in until next Monday. I also—one of the interesting things about this experience is that there's a lot of ideas and a lot of opinions. And I want to make sure I hear from as many of those ideas and opinions as possible.

Today I heard from some opinions that matter a lot to me, and these are the opinions of those who wear the uniform. These generals have spent a lot of time thinking about this issue. There's nobody who cares more about our troops than they do, and nobody who wants us to achieve more—than to achieve our objectives than they do. And it was a fascinating discussion we had. These are smart people and capable people and people whose judgment I listen to. And at the appropriate time, I will stand up in front of the Nation and say, "Here's where we're headed."

But one thing people got to understand is we'll be headed toward achieving our objectives. And I repeat: If we lose our nerve, if we're not steadfast in our determination to help the Iraqi Government succeed, we will be handing Iraq over to an enemy that would do us harm, the consequences of which—of leaving Iraq before the job is done, for example, would be grave for the American citizens.

As we learned on September the 11th, the enemy has got the capacity to strike us. And there's no doubt in my mind, a failure in Iraq would make it more likely the enemy would strike us. It would certainly make it more likely that moderate people around the Middle East would wonder about the United States will. Moderate people—moderate governments in the Middle East would be making irrational decisions about their future. It would be a disaster for governments that have got energy resources to be in the hands of these extremists. They would use energy to extract blackmail from the United States. And when you couple all that with a regime that is—doesn't like the United States having a nuclear weapon, you can imagine a world of turmoil. And we're not going to let it happen.

Caren [Caren Bohan, Reuters].

Iraq Study Group Report

Q. Thank you, sir. You said you would reject plans that would lead to defeat. Would you put the Baker-Hamilton report in that category?

The President. No, my opinion of Baker-Hamilton hasn't changed. One, I appreciated their look. Secondly, I thought it was interesting that both Democrats and Republicans could actually work in concert to help achieve an objective. And the objective they stated, that was necessary in their report, was a government that could defend itself, govern itself, sustain itself and serve as an ally in the war on terror. I thought there were some good ideas in there. And I—as I told both Baker and Hamilton and the American people after I received the report, I take every one of their considerations seriously.

War on Terror Strategy

Q. As you give the new Defense Secretary time to get more in the mix, what is the strategy that you're looking to build? Is it a military strategy for success in Iraq or a political one?

The President. I think that our military cannot do this job alone. Our military needs a political strategy that is effective. And that includes things such as an oil law passed by the Iraqis that basically says to the people, "All of you, regardless of where you live or your religion, get to share in the bounty of our Nation." It requires a reconciliation effort, including a rational de-Ba'athification law.

Q. That's not something you can do with your new strategy, is it?

The President. Oh, absolutely. Absolutely, I can do that with my new strategy. I mean, it is—I can hold people to account. It's something the military recognizes that they're not—that's not their job; it's my job to convince the Maliki Government to make the hard decisions necessary to move his country forward.

But the good news is, he agrees. In my conversations with him, I have said, you know, "Are you going to promote a unity government, or will you be so divisive in your approach that you can't achieve the objectives that the Iraqi people expect you to achieve?" How do I know they expect to achieve? They voted; 12 million of them actually went to the polls and expressed their opinions.

And so there needs to be a political track, and we're working very hard with the Maliki Government to achieve that political track. That's what I've been doing the last couple of days. As a matter of fact, today on the telephone I spoke to the two Kurdish leaders. These men have been outspoken about the desire to have a moderate governing coalition, which we support. I met with the major Sunni leader yesterday, all talking about how we hope that there is political reconciliation and a commitment to a political process that says to the Iraqi people, "You count; you matter for the future of our country."

There needs to be an economic component. As you know, part of our successful strategies in parts of Iraq have been based upon a "clear, hold, and build." Well, "build" means getting projects up and running in key parts of the country, so that people see the benefits of either working with coalition forces and/or the benefits of supporting a government. And so this is much more than a military operation.

And finally, there's the foreign policy piece that's necessary. And we spend a lot of time in our Government talking to people like Saudi Arabia or Egypt or Jordan or Turkey and sending messages, clear messages, to countries like Syria and Iran. And I believe, for example, the Saudis are committed to a government that will bring peace and stability, and that's a unity government. It's in their interest they do so. And we're working hard with them to figure out a strategy to help the Maliki Government succeed.

I'm pleased when Iraqi leaders go to Saudi Arabia and talk to my friend the King of Saudi Arabia, and talk about how they can work together to achieve stability. It's in Saudi's interest; it's in Jordan's interest; it's in the gulf coast countries' interest that there be a stable Iran, an Iran that is capable of rejecting Iranian influence—I mean Iraq that is capable of rejecting Iranian influence. It's in our interests that we succeed in Iraq so that we can continue to send a clear message to those in Iran that are desirous of a free society that freedom is possible in your neighborhood.

And so the stakes are high in this fight. Nobody knows that better than the gentlemen standing behind me. They clearly understand the stakes that are confronted—that confront this Nation. And I am proud to have listened to their points of view. And I'm proud to be working with them, as they help lead the greatest military ever assembled, a military, by the way, in which we've got brave volunteers, people who understand the stakes of this fight, saying, "I want to be in. I want to serve my country."

It's a remarkable period in American history right now. And as I deliberate the way forward, I keep in mind that we've got brave souls that need—to need to know that we're in this fight with a strategy to help them achieve the objectives that we've got.

Listen, thank you all very much.

NOTE: The President spoke at 2:45 p.m. at the Pentagon. In his remarks, he referred to Gen. George W. Casey, Jr., USA, commanding general, Multi-National Force—Iraq; Secretary of Defense-designate Robert

M. Gates; James A. Baker III and Lee Hamilton, cochairs, Iraq Study Group; Prime Minister Nuri al-Maliki, President Jalal Talabani, and Vice President Tariq al-Hashimi of Iraq; Masoud Barzani, president, Kurdistan region in Iraq; and King Abdallah bin Abd al-Aziz Al Saud of Saudi Arabia.

Statement on the Government of Syria
December 13, 2006

The United States supports the Syrian people's desire for democracy, human rights, and freedom of expression. Syrians deserve a government whose legitimacy is grounded in the consent of the people, not brute force.

The Syrian regime should immediately free all political prisoners, including Aref Dalila, Michel Kilo, Anwar al-Bunni, Mahmoud Issa, and Kamal Labwani. I am deeply troubled by reports that some ailing political prisoners are denied health care while others are held in cells with violent criminals.

Syria should disclose the fate and whereabouts of the many missing Lebanese citizens who disappeared following their arrest in Lebanon during the decades of Syrian military occupation. The Syrian regime should also cease its efforts to undermine Lebanese sovereignty by denying the Lebanese people their right to participate in the democratic process free of foreign intimidation and interference.

The people of Syria hope for a prosperous future with greater opportunities for their children and for a government that fights corruption, respects the rule of law, guarantees the rights of all Syrians, and works toward achieving peace in the region.

Remarks Following a Meeting With President Thomas Yayi Boni of Benin
December 14, 2006

President Bush. It's been my honor to have a visit with the President of Benin. We had a very long discussion about a variety of subjects. My administration is committed to helping the democracies on the continent of Africa deal with very significant problems. The President and I are about to go to a summit where the United States of America will commit resources, time, and talent to help rid much of Africa of malaria.

And, Mr. President, I'm proud to announce today that you're one of the countries that we'll be concentrating our help upon. We cannot succeed, however, unless there's an administration that is willing and capable to do the hard work necessary to educate people, spread nets, insecticides necessary to deal with a disease that can be defeated.

We talked about the Millennium Challenge Account. It's one of the most innovative foreign policy initiatives ever proposed by an administration. It's having a positive effect around the world. And I want to thank you for working toward that end.

We talked about the need for us to work together to deal with problems such as Darfur. The President recognized the genocide taking place in Darfur, as does the administration. We want to work through the United Nations to have a very strong

and capable AU force, augmented by United Nations help, to save lives.

One thing I'm impressed with is the President's commitment to democracy, rule of law, decency, and education. And to the extent that we can help—continue to help your country, Mr. President, we will do so.

Welcome, I'm glad you're here.

President Yayi. I have come here to, first and foremost, thank Mr. President Bush for all the initiatives that have been taken so far to eradicate poverty on the continents. As you may know, among these initiatives, we have the *agua* initiative, empowerment of women, the fight against HIV/AIDS, and the initiative of MCA, that is, Millennium Challenge Account. It is very important for us in Africa because the MCA will help us eradicate poverty. And I would like to thank President Bush for that last initiative he took.

Africa is aware of her responsibility in the roles she has to play, globally speaking, because we have to reach prosperity, and that prosperity has some conditions. We need peace. We need stability. We need security. And Africa—America has a leading role to play in our combat to restore a peaceful continent.

Of course, we have to be together with America to build—succeed in all these challenges, to take up all these challenges. And multilaterally, it should be also a part of concern of the American people. We are aware of the fact that America can really play a very important role to continue building capacity among the institutions like

IMF and the World Bank, and the institution of—[*inaudible*]—which is very important for us also.

And the efforts should continue being made by the American Government within the G–8 group, because Africa needs a lot from this G–8, and international exchanges also have to be reinforced. The Doha negotiations need to find a solution now—try to make it easier because cotton is but one of our important products in Africa, and in my country, two people out of three live out of cotton. It's the same reality in countries like Burkina Faso, Mali, Senegal, where cotton is a very important product.

So some subsidies granted to some countries like America here cause a kind of dysfunctioning in our country and on the continent also. So America should help us smooth this mechanism. I'm very happy to hear that America is trying to set up a parallel mechanism that would really help promote the production of cotton. So by the time the WTO will also reach an agreement, I think that this problem of Doha will be definitely solved.

Let me end my speech by saying that I want to thank the American Government, thank President Bush, and the American people for all they are doing to really help us eradicate poverty on African Continent.

President Bush. Thank you, sir.

NOTE: The President spoke at 11:02 a.m. in the Oval Office at the White House. President Yayi spoke in French, and his remarks were translated by an interpreter.

Remarks at the White House Summit on Malaria
December 14, 2006

The President. Thank you. Please be seated. Thanks for inviting me to what sounded like a festive occasion. [*Laughter*] I'm honored to be here. I'm pleased to visit with

you all here at the National Geographic Society, and I want to thank you for inviting me to come to this important conference. I appreciate all of today's speakers,

including my personal favorite—[*laughter*]—Laura.

As you conclude this summit, we turn our thoughts to those who carry the burden of sickness during this holiday season. There are members of our own families here in America who are ill, and they live in villages halfway around the world. For many of their illnesses, there is a known relief; for many, there is no known relief. Yet for malaria, we know exactly what it takes to prevent and treat the disease. The only question is whether we have the will to act. All of you have heard the call to act, and you have responded, and I appreciate your compassion.

Because of your work, children who once wanted [sic] to die are now preparing to live, and whole regions are replacing suffering and fear with hope and health. We can take pride in the progress we have made, and today we will renew our commitment to a world without malaria.

I've just had a state visit, an important visit, with a remarkable leader from Benin. Mr. President and Mrs. Yayi, welcome to America, and thank you for being here.

The President is committed to a free society. He understands the need to confront illness so his people can live in peace. And, Mr. President, I thank you very much for your commitment and your willingness to work with those who want to help to eliminate malaria in your country.

I want to thank members of my Cabinet who are here, particularly Madam Secretary of Education, Margaret Spellings. Thanks for coming. I thank Randy Tobias. He's the Director of USAID. He, by the way, led the initiative to help put America squarely in the fight to eliminate HIV/AIDS on the continent of Africa. Randy, you will have a wonderful legacy in your service to our country, and I want to thank you.

I appreciate Admiral Tony [Timothy]° Ziemer. He is the U.S. Malaria Coordi-

nator. I see a lot of people who are working hard in my administration on these initiatives, and I thank you for your participation. I thank members of the diplomatic corps who have joined us. I want to thank Members of Congress—I think that's Senator Leahy, Senator Frist—[*laughter*]—thank you all for coming. Thank you for taking an interest in it—Congressman Smith. I'd better stop. [*Laughter*] I think I'm going to leave somebody out. But I want to thank you all for your interest in this initiative.

I appreciate John Fahey—he's the president and CEO of National Geographic Society—and Gil Grosvenor. I want to thank Ray Chambers, who is the chairman of the board of Malaria No More. I thank all the social entrepreneurs who are here. I think people will understand that there is a call to act when we see a crisis at hand, and I want to thank you for acting. I appreciate Isaiah Washington, who is the emcee of this event. I want to thank all the program participants. Thank you all for coming.

By bringing together such a wide variety of people, this summit is sending a clear message that we are determined to defeat malaria. We are also sending a broader message about America's purpose in the world. In this new century, there is a great divide between those who place no value on human life and rejoice in the suffering of others and those who believe that every life has matchless value and answer suffering with compassion and kindness.

The contrast is vivid, and the position of America is clear: We will lead the cause of freedom, justice, and hope, because both our values and our interests demand it. We believe in the timeless truth, to whom much is given, much is required. We also know that nations with free, healthy, prosperous people will be sources of stability, not breeding grounds for extremists and hate and terror. By making the world more hopeful, we make the world more peaceful. And by helping others, the American people must understand, we help ourselves.

° White House correction.

One area in which America has a tremendous potential to help is in the fight against malaria. At home, malaria was eliminated decades ago. It is possible to eliminate malaria. In Africa, malaria remains a persistent killer. I think our citizens will be amazed to hear that last year, about a million Africans died of malaria. The vast majority were children under five, their lives ended by nothing more than a mosquito bite. In some countries, more people die of malaria than HIV/AIDS, and last week, a new study showed that people who contract malaria become more likely to spread HIV. The burden of malaria costs sub-Saharan Africa an estimated $12 billion a year. And if the disease continues to spread, the cost in lives and lost productivity is going to grow exponentially worse. Now is the time to act.

Allowing Africa to continue on that path is just simply unacceptable. So we are acting, and we're leading. And with partners across the world, we are helping the people of Africa turn the tide against malaria. The goal of defeating malaria is a challenging goal, yet it can be done. It's not going to require a miracle; it just requires a smart, sustained, focused effort. And that's what we're here to talk about.

Experts have identified four key steps for combating malaria in Africa: distributing insecticide-treated bed nets, expanding indoor insecticide spraying, providing antimalaria medicine to pregnant women, and delivering cutting-edge drugs to people with the disease. These are four things that, if done, will save lives. They are not impossible things to do. I believe that our country must help and continue to take the lead. That's why last year, I announced an initiative to increase our commitment to fighting malaria in Africa. And I want to thank the Members of Congress for supporting this initiative.

We're spending $1.2 billion over 5 years to provide bed nets and indoor spraying and antimalaria medicine in 15 African countries. We are focusing our efforts to eradicate malaria on 15 countries. We are insisting on measuring. This project is measurable. We can determine whether or not nets are being distributed or medicine is being provided. But more importantly, we can measure whether or not we're saving lives. We look—work toward this historic goal to cut the number of malaria-related deaths in half. That's what we're headed for, as quickly as possible.

The malaria initiative is off to a strong start. We have launched the program in three countries: Uganda, Angola, and Tanzania. I want our fellow citizens to hear this startling statistic: In a short period of time, more than 6 million people have benefited. It's in our interests that the 6 million people we've helped—lives have been improved. In Uganda, groups funded by our malaria initiative distributed more than 300,000 nets and almost 300,000 doses of medicine to children and pregnant women. In Angola, the initiative supported a spraying campaign that protected the homes of more than a half a million people. And in Tanzania, the initiative paid for local health clinics to distribute more than 130,000 nets and spray homes for more than a million people. We're in action. Your taxpayers' money is working to save lives.

The statistics are impressive, and behind them are the stories of families with renewed hope in the future. Not long ago, the Zanzibar islands off the coast of Tanzania were a hotbed of malaria infection. Then, with the support of the malaria initiative, local groups launched a campaign called "Kataa Malaria," which is Swahili for "Reject Malaria." Workers went door-to-door to teach people how to use bed nets, they launched a campaign of TV and radio ads, and they spoke in mosques about malaria prevention and treatment. Now the people of Zanzibar are beginning to see results. One island reported that in the first 9 months of this year, the number of malaria cases dropped almost 90 percent compared to the same time last year. One man said this: "Personally, the initiative gives me

a leap of faith. The ultimate outcome is that we should have a malaria-free Zanzibar. There is no turning back."

He's right; there's no turning back. We're going to continue to expand the malaria initiative to reach other countries across Africa as quickly as possible. Earlier this year, Laura announced that four nations will join the initiative in '07: Senegal, Malawi, Rwanda, and Mozambique. Today I am going to announce eight more countries will join in '08: Ghana, Madagascar, Mali, Zambia, Kenya, Liberia, Ethiopia, and Benin. President, I can assure the people that you are determined to beat malaria. And it's that determination by the leadership of a country that is required for our initiative to be as successful as quickly as it possibly can. You can count on us as a steady, reliable partner.

Defeating malaria is going to require a lot more work than just the action of the U.S. Government. Defeating malaria requires cooperation between government and grassroots volunteers. I want to thank the leadership of Malaria No More, which is energizing the grassroots and raising money and mobilizing thousands of volunteers to fight malaria. There's a lot of people out of our country who, if called to serve and to love, will do so. Rick Warren has got a church called Saddleback Church. He believes like I believe: To whom much is given, much is required. They're going to send thousands of volunteers into African villages and clinics. These groups rely upon the skill of doctors and nurses. And for doctors and nurses who are serving in Africa to help achieve the goal of eliminating malaria, I thank you on behalf of a grateful nation.

I am pleased to announce that I am going to expand a Federal program called Volunteers for Prosperity, which allows organizations that recruit skilled volunteers to receive Federal grants more easily. I believe it's in our interests to use taxpayers' money to encourage these private-sector initiatives. Organizations involved with the malaria initiative will find it easier to receive Federal funds, I hope. The point is, we're going to try to eliminate as much bureaucracy as possible to get money into the hands of those who are recruiting and encouraging volunteers to be on the frontline of fighting malaria.

I want to thank all the grassroots volunteers who are here. I want to thank you for doing what you're doing. I hope that you can do more, and I hope that this summit, which Laura and her team put together, enables you to go out and recruit, because the quicker we eliminate malaria, the better off the world will be.

Defeating malaria requires cooperation between Government and the private sector. When I announced the malaria initiative, I called on foundations and corporations to participate. In other words, I said, "You've got to be with us; the Government alone can't solve the problem. We can address it, we can fund it, but we need your help." I want to thank the Gates Foundation. Melinda, thank you for being here. This foundation is a fantastic example of social entrepreneurship. It was caused to be because of fantastic business entrepreneurship. It is now using the business acumen and the rewards of being smart to fund unbelievable programs. And I'm proud of what you're doing.

I want to thank the Red Cross. And, Bonnie, thank you very much. You've trained thousands of health workers in sub-Saharan Africa, and you're going to train more. I want to thank the Global Business Coalition that thus far has brought more than 200 companies together to raise money for bed nets and other supplies. Two hundred is a little short, as far as I'm concerned. In other words, I view it as a good start, kind of a down payment. [*Laughter*]

I want to thank ExxonMobil and Marathon Oil, who funded—which have funded antimalaria projects in some of Africa's most heavily affected nations. I think it's in your corporate interests that the people

of Africa see that you're willing to invest in the future of their countries. America's businesses and foundations are showing a lot of wisdom and generosity. I appreciate your support.

Defeating malaria requires cooperation between our country and the international community. We have given nearly $2 billion to the Global Fund to Fight AIDS—and I want to thank the leader of the fund, who is here today by the way—Fight AIDS, Tuberculosis, and Malaria. And nearly a quarter of that money has been used for antimalaria projects. We support the efforts to fight malaria being led by the WHO and the new leader, as well as UNICEF and my friend Ann Veneman, and the World Bank, where Paul Wolfowitz has made antimalaria projects a high priority. Some of our allies in Europe have committed resources to these efforts, and frankly, they should commit more. This is a global effort to fight malaria. The United States is proud to take the lead. I encourage other countries—to whom much is given, much is required—to step up and give. I want to thank those who understand that malaria is a global problem, and we've got to work to solve it together.

Defeating malaria requires cooperation between America and African nations. The malaria initiative is based on partnership, Mr. President, not paternalism. Leaders like you know your people, you know their problems, and you are determined to solve them. Our job is to help you. I fully understand that many times people have got great ambitions and great intentions, but they have no money to do—to help. And that's why this Government is committed to providing money and technology to help the leaders accomplish the objectives that we've set forth.

African leaders also understand, in the long run, that defeating malaria requires more than nets and sprays and drugs. It requires changing the conditions that help malaria thrive: poverty and the lack of education and unresponsive governments and

corruption and the HIV/AIDS pandemic. To help African leaders overcome these challenges, this administration has doubled development aid to Africa during my Presidency, and I propose to double it again by the end of this decade.

We've created the Millennium Challenge Account to support nations that govern justly. It doesn't make any sense for us to send taxpayers' monies to countries that steal the money. We give to—and part of the Millennium Challenge Account, headed by Ambassador Danilovich, is to encourage countries to invest in their people and to encourage economic freedom. And so far, we have signed compacts with five African nations, and we're working on more.

We launched one of the most important initiatives in American history, as far as I'm concerned, and that is the Emergency Plan for AIDS Relief, which thus far has brought lifesaving drugs to more than 800,000 people on the continent of Africa in 5 short years.

Development aid is one thing, but so is the capacity for us to help nations through trade. I appreciate the work of my predecessor, President Clinton, and subsequent Congresses to pass and now extend the African Growth and Opportunity Act, which has enabled me to report to you that between Africa and America, trade has doubled since 2001.

In all these ways, we stand with the people of Africa in their time of need. And by doing so, we help lift a burden of unnecessary suffering, and we help reduce the appeal of radicalism, and we forge lasting friendships on a continent that is growing in strategic importance.

As we come to the end of this historic summit, every citizen can be proud of the work our Nation is doing to fight disease and despair. Our development agenda in Africa and beyond is the most ambitious commitment America has made since the Marshall plan. And once again, our efforts are showing the world what kind of country America is. We're a nation of optimistic

people and generous people and decent people who value human life. We're a nation that believes that we're fortunate and that through our fortune, we ought to help others. We're a compassionate people who care deeply about the future of the world. And it is my honor to lead such a people.

God bless you all.

NOTE: The President spoke at 11:55 a.m. at the National Geographic Society. In his remarks, he referred to President Thomas Yayi Boni of Benin and his wife, Chantal de Souza Yayi; Gilbert M. Grosvenor, chairman of the board, National Geographic Society; Richard D. "Rick" Warren, pastor, Saddleback Church, Lake Forest, CA; Melinda French Gates, cochair, Bill & Melinda Gates Foundation; Bonnie McElveen-Hunter, chairman, American Red Cross; Richard G.A. Feachem, executive director, Global Fund to Fight AIDS, Tuberculosis, and Malaria; Margaret Chan, director-general-elect, World Health Organization; and Ann M. Veneman, executive director, United Nations Children's Fund.

Remarks on Presenting the Presidential Medal of Freedom
December 15, 2006

The President. Please be seated. Thank you all for coming. Welcome. Mr. Vice President, members of my Cabinet, Laura and I are pleased you could join us on this special occasion. We're delighted to welcome our distinguished honorees as well as their families and friends to the White House. Thanks for coming.

The Presidential Medal of Freedom is our Nation's highest civil honor. The Medal recognizes high achievement in public service, science, the arts, education, athletics, and other fields. Today we honor 10 exceptional individuals who have gained great admiration and respect throughout our country.

Norman Y. Mineta personifies the terms "public servant" and "patriot." He served as an Army intelligence officer, the mayor of San Jose, California, 10-term U.S. Congressman, and a Cabinet member under Presidents of both parties. He was my Secretary of Transportation. No Secretary of Transportation ever served longer or confronted greater challenges than Norm Mineta.

On September the 11th, 2001, he led the effort to bring thousands of commercial and private aircraft swiftly and safely to the ground. Norm was calm, and he was decisive in a moment of emergency. He showed those same qualities in the months and years afterward, ably transforming his Department to face the dangers of a new era.

Norm Mineta's whole life has been an extraordinary journey. At the age of 10, he was sent with his mom and dad to an internment camp for Japanese Americans. Such wrongful treatment could have left a person bitter, but not Norm Mineta. Instead, he has given his country a lifetime of service, and he's given his fellow citizens an example of leadership, devotion to duty, and personal character. Mr. Secretary, you're a good friend and a great man, and our country honors you.

With us today is Warren O'Neil, who will accept the Medal of Freedom on behalf of his brother, John Jordan "Buck" O'Neil. Buck O'Neil passed away in October, after a baseball career spanning more than seven decades. He joined the Negro League in 1938, as a first baseman for the Kansas City Monarchs. Buck O'Neil won two batting titles and played on nine championship teams, and as a manager, guided the Monarchs to four league titles. After finishing his playing career, Buck O'Neil

joined the Chicago Cubs as a scout and later as the first African American coach in the major leagues. He never did slow down. For the rest of his life, he was active in baseball, not just from the stands or the dugout.

In July of this year, he took a turn at bat in a minor league all-star game in Kansas City. They wisely pitched around him— [*laughter*]—he drew a walk—at the age of 94 years old. [*Laughter*] Buck O'Neil is also remembered as one of the game's best historians and ambassadors. He was the driving force behind the Negro Leagues Baseball Museum; he was proud to be its chairman. But he once said: "It never should have been a Negro League. Shouldn't have been." Buck O'Neil lived long enough to see the game of baseball and America change for the better. He's one of the people we can thank for that. Buck O'Neil was a legend, and he was a beautiful human being. And we honor the memory of Buck O'Neil.

One day in 1961, Ruth Colvin of Syracuse, New York, read a disturbing statistic in the morning newspaper. She learned that more than 11,000 people in her hometown could not read. Ruth wondered, "Why isn't somebody doing something about it?" Ruth decided that she would do something. Working out of her basement, she formed a network of citizens willing to donate their time as reading tutors. Before long, that network reached beyond Syracuse and beyond New York, and it had a name: Literacy Volunteers of America. Over the years, the volunteers have helped hundreds of thousands of adults learn the reading and language skills they need to build a better life. Ruth rightly says, "The ability to read and write is critical to personal freedom and the maintenance of a democratic society."

Ruth's good influence has continued to grow. She travels the world promoting literacy with her husband and best friend, Bob. She started literacy campaigns on multiple continents. Ruth has also made many dear friends, including another great crusader for literacy, my mother. [*Laughter*] Ruth's children, Terry and Lindy, know what I know—that you better listen to your mother. [*Laughter*] Ruth has said, "I am and always have been a volunteer." More than that, Ruth Colvin is a person of intelligence and vision and heart, and she has earned the gratitude of many and the admiration of us all. Congratulations.

Like Ruth, Dr. Norman C. Francis has dedicated his life to education. He achieved early distinction as the first African American to graduate from the Loyola University College of Law. In 1968, he became president of his alma mater, Xavier University in New Orleans, and he is today the longest serving university president in the United States. Dr. Francis is known across Louisiana and throughout our country as a man of deep intellect and compassion and character. He's an Army veteran. He led the United Negro College Fund. He was chairman of the board of the Educational Testing Service, and he holds only 35 honorary degrees. [*Laughter*]

Last year, after Hurricane Katrina did great damage to the Xavier campus, Dr. Francis vowed the university would overcome and reopen its doors by January, and he kept that pledge. Dr. Francis continues to help the people of southeast Louisiana as the leader of the Louisiana Recovery Authority. As they continue to rebuild from the devastation of the hurricanes, the people of the Pelican State will benefit from the leadership of this good man. And all of us admire the good life and remarkable career of Dr. Norman C. Francis.

Joshua Lederberg has always seemed ahead of his time. He was researching genetics when the field was scarcely understood. He was studying the implications of space travel before there were astronauts. And even three decades ago, he was warning of the dangers of biological warfare. All of his life, people have seen something special in this rabbi's son from Montclair, New Jersey. Someone who knew him in

college said, "You could tell that Joshua was in the lab because you could hear the breaking glass." [*Laughter*] "He was so young, bursting with potential."

He earned his Ph.D. in his early twenties. At the age of 33, he won the Nobel Prize. Dr. Lederberg has remained at the top of the scientific field as a professor, researcher, and writer. As a columnist and adviser to many administrations, he brought clear, independent thinking and wisdom to matters of public policy, especially in national security and nonproliferation. For his brilliant career, his high ethical standards, and his many contributions to our country, the United States thanks Joshua Lederberg.

Americans first came to know Natan Sharansky as a voice for freedom inside an empire of tyranny. As a Jew applying to immigrate to Israel, he was refused and harassed by the Soviet regime. Natan Sharansky became a leading dissident and advocate for human rights. And after a show trial, he was sentenced to a gulag for 10 years. The authorities may have hoped the world would forget the name Sharansky. Instead, leaders like President Reagan and Ambassador Kirkpatrick spoke often of his persecution, and the case of Natan Sharansky became a symbol of the moral emptiness of imperial communism.

Today, the Soviet Union is history, but the world still knows the name Sharansky. As a free man, he's become a political leader in Israel, winning four elections to the Knesset and serving more than 8 years in the Cabinet. He remains, above all, an eloquent champion for liberty and democracy. Natan reminds us that every soul carries the desire to live in freedom and that freedom has a unique power to lift up nations, transform regions, and secure a future for peace. Natan Sharansky is a witness to that power, and his testimony brings hope to those who still live under oppression. We honor Natan Sharansky for his life of courage and conviction.

The struggle between freedom and tyranny has defined the past 100 years, and few have written of that struggle with greater skill than Paul Johnson. His book, "Modern Times: The World from the Twenties to the Eighties," is a masterful account of the grievous harm visited on millions by ideologies of power and coercion. In all his writings, Paul Johnson shows great breadth of knowledge and moral clarity and a deep understanding of the challenges of our time. He's written hundreds of articles and dozens of books, including "The History of the Jews," "The History of Christianity," "The Quest for God," and "The Birth of the Modern." Obviously, the man is not afraid to take on big subjects. [*Laughter*]

Eight years ago, he published "A History of the American People," which Dr. Henry Kissinger said was "as majestic in scope as the country it celebrates." In the preface, Paul Johnson called Americans "the most remarkable people the world has ever seen." He said, "I love them, and I salute them." That's a high tribute from a man of such learning and wisdom, and America returns the feeling. Our country honors Paul Johnson and proudly calls him a friend.

One of America's unique gifts to the world is a music called the blues. And in that music, two names are paramount: B.B. King and his guitar, Lucille. [*Laughter*] It has been said that when John Lennon was asked to name his great ambition, he said, "to play the guitar like B.B. King." Many musicians have had that same goal, but nobody has ever been able to match the skill or copy the sound of the "King of the Blues."

He came up the hard way in the Deep South, living alone when he was 9 years old, walking miles to school and picking cotton for 35 cents a day. Barely out of his teens, he made his first trip to Memphis, Tennessee, with his guitar and $2.50 in his pocket. He made his name on Beale Street, and his studio recordings made him

a national favorite. B.B. King has sold more than 40 million records. He won 14 Grammys. He has a place on the Hollywood Walk of Fame. He's influenced generations of musicians from blues to rock, and he's performed in venues from roadside nightclubs to Carnegie Hall. He's still touring, and he's still recording, and he's still singing, and he's still playing the blues better than anybody else. In other words, the thrill is not gone. [*Laughter*] America loves the music of B.B. King, and America loves the man himself. Congratulations.

William Safire joined the White House staff nearly 38 years ago as a speechwriter to the President. President Nixon once introduced Bill this way: "This is Safire, absolutely trustworthy, but watch what you say—he's a writer." [*Laughter*] Writing has been at the center of Bill Safire's eventful life, going back to his days in the U.S. Army and as a PR man in New York. As a young speechwriter drafting remarks for a New York City official, he used the word "indomitable." When they asked Bill to find a better speech-word, he suggested "indefatigable." [*Laughter*] They fired him. [*Laughter*] We're a little more lenient about speechwriting here. [*Laughter*]

From the White House, Bill moved to the New York Times, where he spent more than 30 years as a columnist who was often skeptical about our Government but never cynical about our country. He always was committed to the cause of human freedom. His wit and style and command of English earned him another spot, his own page in the Times magazine every Sunday. Bill has said that his "On Language" column attracts more mail than any of his other work. People write me about my language too. [*Laughter*] Bill Safire has also written novels and a respected political dictionary. He won the Pulitzer Prize for commentary. He's a voice of independence and principle, and American journalism is better for the contributions of William Safire. Congratulations.

David McCullough has won the Pulitzer Prize twice, for "Truman" and "John Adams," two of the most successful biographies ever published. In person and on the printed page, David McCullough shares the lessons of history with enthusiasm and insight. He has written definitive works on the Johnstown flood, the building of the Brooklyn Bridge, and the digging of the Panama Canal. His first book out came— came out nearly 40 years ago; all of his books are still in print. David McCullough is also, for millions of Americans, the voice of history, as the narrator of Ken Burns's "The Civil War" and other films.

For those who question the importance of history, David likes to quote Harry Truman, who said, "The only thing new in the world is the history you do not know." David McCullough reminds us that "the laws we live by, the freedoms we enjoy, the institutions that we take for granted are all the work of other people who went before us." He's a passionate man about our responsibility to know America's past and to share it with every new generation. He's fulfilled that duty in his own career with splendid results. This chronicler of other times is one of the eminent Americans of our own time. The Nation owes a debt of gratitude to a fine author and a fine man, David McCullough.

Now the military aide will read the citations for the Presidential Medal of Freedom.

[*At this point, Lt. Cmdr. Robert A. Roncska, USN, Navy Aide to the President, read the citations, and the President presented the medals.*]

The President. Thank you all for coming. Congratulations to our honorees. Laura and I would like to invite you to a reception here to pay tribute to some of the finest citizens the Almighty has ever produced.

God bless you all.

NOTE: The President spoke at 10:18 a.m. in the East Room at the White House.

Remarks at an Armed Forces Full Honor Review for Secretary of Defense Donald H. Rumsfeld in Arlington, Virginia
December 15, 2006

Thank you all. Thank you. Thank you very much, Mr. Secretary and Joyce. Mr. Vice President, thank you for your kind words. Lynne and Senator Warner, Deputy Secretary England, Secretary Harvey, Winter, Wynne, General Pace, members of the Joint Chiefs of Staff, distinguished guests, men and women of the Armed Forces: I'm pleased to join you as we pay tribute to one of America's most skilled, energetic, and dedicated public servants, the Secretary of Defense, Donald Rumsfeld.

Don Rumsfeld has been at my side from the moment I took office. We've been through war together. We have shared some of the most challenging moments in our Nation's history. Over the past 6 years, I have come to appreciate Don Rumsfeld's professionalism, his dedication, his strategic vision, his deep devotion to the men and women of our Nation who wear the uniform, and his love for the United States of America.

That devotion began at an early age, inspired by a man in uniform he called dad. His father, George, was 37 when America was attacked at Pearl Harbor. Too old to be drafted, he volunteered for service in the United States Navy. One of Don's earliest memories is of standing on the hangar deck of his dad's aircraft carrier, the USS *Hollandia*, at the age of 11. He was taking in the sights and sounds of the ship as it prepared to leave for the Pacific war.

His father's example stayed with him, and after graduating from Princeton, Don Rumsfeld joined the United States Navy, rising to become a pilot, a flight instructor, and a member of the Naval Reserve for nearly 20 years.

In the decades since he first put on the uniform, Don Rumsfeld has served with distinction in many important positions: Congressman, Counselor to the President,

Ambassador to NATO, White House Chief of Staff, Secretary of Defense. Yet, to this day, the title that has brought him his greatest pride is dad, and now granddad. And so today, as we honor a fine man, we also honor his family, Joyce Rumsfeld and his children.

Don is the only man—Don Rumsfeld is the only man to have served as Secretary of Defense for two Presidents in two different centuries. [*Laughter*] In 2001, I called him back to the same job he held under President Gerald Ford, and I gave him this urgent mission: Prepare our Nation's Armed Forces for the threats of a new century.

Don Rumsfeld brought vision and enthusiasm to this vital task. He understood that the peace of the post-cold-war years was really the calm before the next storm and that America needed to prepare for the day when new enemies would attack our Nation in unprecedented ways. That day came on a clear September morning, and in a moment of crisis, our Nation saw Donald Rumsfeld's character and courage.

When the Pentagon was hit, Secretary Rumsfeld's first instinct was to run toward danger. He raced down smoke-filled hallways to the crash site so he could help rescue workers pull the victims from the rubble. And in the weeks that followed, he directed the effort to plan our Nation's military response to the deadliest terrorist attack in our Nation's history.

Under Secretary Rumsfeld's leadership, U.S. and coalition forces launched one of the most innovative military campaigns in the history of modern warfare, sending Special Operations forces into Afghanistan to link up with anti-Taliban fighters, to ride with them on horseback, and to launch a stunning assault against the enemy. In Operation Enduring Freedom we combined

the most advanced laser-guided weapons with one of the oldest tools in the military arsenal, a man with a weapon on a horse.

History will record that the first major ground battle in the 21st century involving American forces began with a cavalry charge. I guess that's what you get when you bring together a President from Texas with a Secretary of Defense who actually remembers when America had a cavalry. [*Laughter*]

In 2003, on my orders, Secretary Rumsfeld led the planning and execution of another historic military campaign, Operation Iraqi Freedom. In this operation, coalition forces drove Saddam Hussein from power in 21 days. And in the years that followed, Don Rumsfeld helped see the Iraqi people through the resumption of sovereignty, two elections, a referendum to approve the most progressive Constitution in the Middle East, and the seating of a newly elected Government.

On his watch, the United States military helped the Iraqi people establish a constitutional democracy in the heart of the Middle East, a watershed event in the story of freedom.

As he met the challenges of fighting a new and unfamiliar war, Don Rumsfeld kept his eyes on the horizon and on the threats that still await us as this new century unfolds.

He developed a new defense strategy and a new command structure for our Nation's Armed Forces, with a new northern command to protect the homeland, a new joint forces command to focus on transformation, a new strategic command to defend against long-range attacks, and a transformed U.S. special operations command ready to take the lead in the global war on terror.

He launched the most significant transformation of the Army in a generation. He led my administration's efforts to transform the NATO Alliance, with a new NATO response force ready to deploy quickly anywhere in the world. On his watch, NATO sent its forces to defend a young democracy in Afghanistan, more than 3,000 miles from Europe. It was the first time NATO has deployed outside the North Atlantic area in the history of the Alliance.

He helped launch the Proliferation Security Initiative, an unprecedented coalition of more than 80 nations working together to stop shipments of weapons of mass destruction on land, at sea, and in the air.

He undertook the most sweeping transformation of America's global defense posture since the start of the cold war, repositioning our forces so they can surge quickly to deal with unexpected threats and setting the stage for our global military presence for the next 50 years.

He took ballistic missile defense from theory to reality. And because of his leadership, America now has an initial capability to track a ballistic missile headed for our country and destroy it before it harms our people.

Most importantly, he worked to establish a culture in the Pentagon that rewards innovation and intelligent risk taking and encourages our military and civilian leaders to challenge established ways of thinking.

The record of Don Rumsfeld's tenure is clear. There have been more profound change—there has been more profound change at the Department of Defense over the past 6 years than at any time since the Department's creation in the late 1940s.

And these changes were not easy, but because of Don Rumsfeld's determination and leadership, America has the best equipped, the best trained, and most experienced Armed Forces in the history of the world. All in all, not bad for a fellow who calls himself a "broken-down ex-Navy pilot." This man knows how to lead, and he did, and the country is better off for it.

In every decision Don Rumsfeld made over the past 6 years, he always put the troops first, and the troops in the field knew it. A few years ago, the editors at

Time magazine came to his Pentagon office, and Don correctly suspected they were thinking of naming him "Person of the Year." Without hesitation, Don Rumsfeld told them, "Don't give it to me. Give it to our men and women in uniform." And that's exactly what Time magazine did.

Don Rumsfeld's selfless leadership earned him the admiration of our soldiers and sailors and airmen and marines. And we saw how they feel about him this week when he paid a farewell visit to our troops in Iraq.

Don Rumsfeld's strong leadership has earned him my admiration and deep respect. We stood together in hours of decision that would affect the course of our history. We walked amid the rubble of the broken Pentagon the day after September the 11th, 2001. He was with me when we planned the liberation of Afghanistan. We were in the Oval Office together the day I gave the order to remove Saddam Hussein from power.

In these and countless other moments, I have seen Don Rumsfeld's character and his integrity. He was—always ensured I had the best possible advice, the opportunity to hear and weigh conflicting points of view. He spoke straight. It was easy to understand him. He has a sharp intellect, a steady demeanor, and boundless energy. He began every day at the Pentagon with a singular mission—to serve his country and the men and women who defend her.

Mr. Secretary, today your country thanks you for 6 outstanding years at the Department of Defense. And I thank you for your sacrifice and your service and your devotion to the men and women of our Armed Forces.

I want to thank Joyce for her poise and her grace and for the example she has set for our Nation's military families. Laura and I will miss you both, and we wish you all the best in the years to come.

And now, ladies and gentlemen, I bring to this podium America's 21st Secretary of Defense, Donald Rumsfeld.

NOTE: The President spoke at 1:50 p.m. at the Pentagon. In his remarks, he referred to Lynne Cheney, wife of Vice President Dick Cheney; Secretary of the Navy Donald C. Winter; and Secretary of the Air Force Michael W. Wynne. The transcript released by the Office of the Press Secretary also included the remarks of Secretary of Defense Rumsfeld.

Message on the Observance of Hanukkah 2006
December 15, 2006

I send greetings to all those celebrating Hanukkah, the festival of lights.

During Hanukkah, Jewish people everywhere honor the liberation of Jerusalem and the great miracle witnessed in the Holy Temple more than 2,000 years ago. After Jerusalem was conquered by an oppressive king and the Jews lost their right to worship in freedom, Judah Maccabee and his followers courageously set out to reclaim Jerusalem from foreign rule. Though their numbers were small, the Maccabees' dedication to their faith was strong, and they emerged victorious. When they returned to their Holy Temple for its rededication, the Maccabees discovered enough oil to burn for only one day. Yet the oil lit the Holy Temple for eight days, and the light of hope still shines bright in Jewish homes and synagogues throughout the world.

Each year, the glow of the menorah is a reminder of the blessings of a just and loving God and the sacrifices made over the centuries for faith and freedom. Laura

and I pray that this holiday season will be a time of happiness in every home and a time of peace throughout the world.

Happy Hanukkah.

NOTE: An original was not available for verification of the content of this message.

The President's Radio Address
December 16, 2006

Good morning. Christmas is fast approaching, and I know many of you are busy trying to finish up your holiday shopping. This week, we received good news about the economy that should brighten the season and keep us optimistic about the year ahead.

First, the Commerce Department released figures showing that sales for America's retailers were up in November and that the increase is much larger than expected. These figures are important because for many American businesses November and December are their highest sales months for the year. So the healthy increase in retail sales is a good sign for American employers and workers.

America's working families also received another bit of holiday cheer this week: We learned that real hourly wages rose by 2.3 percent over the past year. That may not sound like a lot, but for the typical family of four with both parents working, it means an extra $1,350 for this year. At the same time, our growing economy continues to create jobs and that has brought unemployment down to just 4.5 percent. These numbers give all Americans a reason to celebrate. More people are working than ever before, and paychecks are going further than they used to.

When you decide how to spend your paycheck, you have to set priorities and live within your means. Congress needs to do the same thing with the money you send to Washington. That was one of the clear messages American voters sent in the midterm elections. And one of the best ways we can impose more discipline on Federal spending is by addressing the problem of earmarks.

Earmarks are spending provisions that are often slipped into bills at the last minute, so they never get debated or discussed. It is not surprising that this often leads to unnecessary Federal spending, such as a swimming pool or a teapot museum tucked into a big spending bill. And over the last decade, the Congressional Research Service reports that the number of earmarks has exploded, increasing from about 3,000 in 1996 to 13,000 in 2006. I respect Congress's authority over the public purse, but the time has come to reform the earmark process and dramatically reduce the number of earmarks.

Reforming earmarks is the responsibility of both political parties. Over the past year, the Republican Congress succeeded in eliminating virtually all earmarks for three major Cabinet Departments. And I'm pleased that Democratic leaders in Congress recently committed themselves to support reforms that would restore transparency and accountability to earmarks. For this year's budget, they pledged to maintain current levels of spending and not include any earmarks, and they agreed to a temporary moratorium on earmarks. This is a good start, but Congress needs to do much more. My administration will soon lay out a series of reforms that will help make earmarks more transparent, that will hold the Members who propose earmarks more accountable, and that will help reduce the

number of earmarks inserted into large spending bills.

Republicans and Democrats alike have an opportunity to demonstrate our commitment to spending restraint and good government by making earmark reform a top priority for the next Congress. When it comes to spending your money, you expect us to rise above party labels. By working together to cut down on earmarks, we can show the American people that we can be fiscally responsible with their money and that we can come together in Washington to get results.

Thank you for listening.

NOTE: The address was recorded at 9:40 a.m. on December 15 in the Cabinet Room at the White House for broadcast at 10:06 a.m. on December 16. The transcript was made available by the Office of the Press Secretary on December 15 but was embargoed for release until the broadcast. The Office of the Press Secretary also released a Spanish language transcript of this address.

Message on the Observance of Kwanzaa 2006
December 8, 2006

I send greetings to those observing Kwanzaa.

During the seven days of Kwanzaa leading up to the New Year, friends and family come together in a spirit of love and joy to honor their rich African heritage, reflect on the Seven Principles, and give thanks for the blessings of freedom and opportunity. Forty years after the first Kwanzaa, this hopeful occasion remains an opportunity to build the bonds of family, community, and culture and move ever closer to the founding promise of liberty and justice for all.

Our Nation is a better place because of the contributions African Americans have made to our strength and character over the generations. As you gather to celebrate your ancestry this Kwanzaa, I encourage you to take pride in your many achievements and look to the future with confidence in your abilities and faith in a brighter tomorrow.

Laura and I send our best wishes for a joyous Kwanzaa and a blessed New Year.

GEORGE W. BUSH

NOTE: This message was released by the Office of the Press Secretary on December 18. An original was not available for verification of the content of this message.

Letter to Congressional Leaders Reporting on the Deployments of United States Combat-Equipped Armed Forces Around the World
December 15, 2006

Dear Mr. Speaker: (*Dear Mr. President:*)

I am providing this supplemental consolidated report, prepared by my Administration and consistent with the War Powers Resolution (Public Law 93–148), as part of my efforts to keep the Congress informed about deployments of U.S. combat-equipped armed forces around the world. This supplemental report covers operations in support of the war on terror, Kosovo, and Bosnia and Herzegovina.

THE WAR ON TERROR

Since September 24, 2001, I have reported, consistent with Public Law 107–40 and the War Powers Resolution, on the combat operations in Afghanistan against al-Qaida terrorists and their Taliban supporters, which began on October 7, 2001, and the deployment of various combat-equipped and combat-support forces to a number of locations in the Central, Pacific, and Southern Command areas of operation in support of those operations and of other operations in our war on terror.

I will direct additional measures as necessary in the exercise of the U.S. right to self-defense and to protect U.S. citizens and interests. Such measures may include short-notice deployments of special operations and other forces for sensitive operations in various locations throughout the world. It is not possible to know at this time either the precise scope or duration of the deployment of U.S. Armed Forces necessary to counter the terrorist threat to the United States.

United States Armed Forces, with the assistance of numerous coalition partners, continue to conduct the U.S. campaign to pursue al-Qaida terrorists and to eliminate support to al-Qaida. These operations have been successful in seriously degrading al-Qaida's training capabilities. United States Armed Forces, with the assistance of numerous coalition partners, ended the Taliban regime and are actively pursuing and engaging remnant al-Qaida and Taliban fighters in Afghanistan. Approximately 10,400 U.S. personnel also are assigned to the International Security Assistance Force (ISAF) in Afghanistan. This number is higher than that stated in the last report because in late October 2006 additional U.S. forces were reassigned to ISAF. The total number of U.S. forces in Afghanistan is approximately 21,000. The U.N. Security Council authorized the ISAF in U.N. Security Council Resolution 1386 of December 20, 2001, and has reaffirmed its authoriza-

tion since that time, most recently, for a 12-month period from October 13, 2006, in U.N. Security Council Resolution 1707 of September 12, 2006. The mission of the ISAF under NATO command is to assist the Government of Afghanistan in creating a safe and secure environment that allows reconstruction and the reestablishment of Afghan authorities. Currently, all 26 NATO nations contribute to the ISAF. Eleven non-NATO contributing countries also participate by providing military and other support personnel to the ISAF.

The United States continues to detain several hundred al-Qaida and Taliban fighters who are believed to pose a continuing threat to the United States and its interests. The combat-equipped and combat-support forces deployed to Naval Base, Guantanamo Bay, Cuba, in the U.S. Southern Command area of operations since January 2002 continue to conduct secure detention operations for the approximately 435 enemy combatants at Guantanamo Bay.

The U.N. Security Council authorized a Multinational Force (MNF) in Iraq under unified command in U.N. Security Council Resolution 1511 of October 16, 2003, and reaffirmed its authorization in U.N. Security Council Resolution 1546 of June 8, 2004. In U.N. Security Council Resolution 1637 of November 8, 2005, the Security Council, noting the Iraqi government's request to retain the presence of the MNF, extended the MNF mandate for a period ending on December 31, 2006. In U.N. Security Council Resolution 1723 of November 28, 2006, the Security Council extended the MNF mandate until December 31, 2007. Under Resolutions 1546, 1637, and 1723, the mission of the MNF is to contribute to security and stability in Iraq, as reconstruction continues. These contributions have included assisting in building the capability of the Iraqi security forces and institutions as the Iraqi people

drafted and approved a constitution and established a constitutionally elected government. The U.S. contribution to the MNF is approximately 134,000 military personnel.

In furtherance of our efforts against terrorists who pose a continuing and imminent threat to the United States, our friends and allies, and our forces abroad, the United States continues to work with friends and allies in areas around the globe. These efforts include the deployment of U.S. combat-equipped and combat-support forces to assist in enhancing the counterterrorism capabilities of our friends and allies. United States combat-equipped and combat-support forces continue to be located in the Horn of Africa region, and the U.S. forces headquarters element in Djibouti provides command and control support as necessary for military operations against al-Qaida and other international terrorists in the Horn of Africa region, including Yemen. In addition, the United States continues to conduct maritime interception operations on the high seas in the areas of responsibility of all of the geographic combatant commanders. These maritime operations have the responsibility to stop the movement, arming, or financing of international terrorists.

NATO-LED KOSOVO FORCE (KFOR)

As noted in previous reports regarding U.S. contributions in support of peacekeeping efforts in Kosovo, the U.N. Security Council authorized Member States to establish KFOR in U.N. Security Council Resolution 1244 of June 10, 1999. The mission of KFOR is to provide an international security presence in order to deter renewed hostilities; verify and, if necessary, enforce the terms of the Military Technical Agreement between NATO and the Federal Republic of Yugoslavia (which is now Serbia); enforce the terms of the Undertaking on Demilitarization and Transformation of the former Kosovo Liberation Army; provide day-to-day operational direction to the Kosovo Protection Corps; and maintain a safe and secure environment to facilitate the work of the U.N. Interim Administration Mission in Kosovo (UNMIK).

Currently, there are 24 NATO nations contributing to KFOR. Eleven non-NATO contributing countries also participate by providing military personnel and other support personnel to KFOR. The U.S. contribution to KFOR in Kosovo is about 1,700 U.S. military personnel, or approximately 11 percent of KFOR's total strength of approximately 16,000 personnel. The U.S. forces have been assigned to the eastern region of Kosovo. For U.S. KFOR forces, as for KFOR generally, maintaining a safe and secure environment remains the primary military task. The KFOR operates under NATO command and control and rules of engagement. The KFOR coordinates with and supports UNMIK at most levels; provides a security presence in towns, villages, and the countryside; and organizes checkpoints and patrols in key areas to provide security, protect minorities, resolve disputes, and help instill in the community a feeling of confidence.

In accordance with U.N. Security Council Resolution 1244, UNMIK continues to transfer additional competencies to the Kosovo Provisional Institutions of Self-Government, which includes the President, Prime Minister, multiple ministries, and the Kosovo Assembly. The UNMIK retains ultimate authority in some sensitive areas such as police, justice, and ethnic minority affairs.

NATO continues formally to review KFOR's mission at 6-month intervals. These reviews provide a basis for assessing current force levels, future requirements, force structure, force reductions, and the eventual withdrawal of KFOR. NATO has adopted the Joint Operations Area plan to regionalize and rationalize its force structure in the Balkans. The UNMIK international police and the Kosovo Police Service (KPS) have full responsibility for public safety and policing throughout Kosovo. The UNMIK international police and KPS also

have begun to assume responsibility for guarding patrimonial sites and established border-crossing checkpoints. The KFOR augments security in particularly sensitive areas or in response to particular threats as needed.

NATO HEADQUARTERS IN BOSNIA AND HERZEGOVINA

Pursuant to the June 2004 decision made by NATO Heads of State and Government, and in accordance with U.N. Security Council Resolution 1575 of November 22, 2004, NATO concluded its Stabilization Force operations in Bosnia and Herzegovina and established NATO Head-quarters-Sarajevo to continue to assist in implementing the Peace Agreement in conjunction with a newly established European Force. The NATO Headquarters-Sarajevo, to which approximately 100 U.S. personnel are assigned, is, with the European Force, the legal successor to SFOR. The principal tasks of NATO Headquarters-Sarajevo are

providing advice on defense reform and performing operational supporting tasks, such as counterterrorism and supporting the International Criminal Tribunal for the Former Yugoslavia.

I have directed the participation of U.S. Armed Forces in all of these operations pursuant to my constitutional authority to conduct U.S. foreign relations and as Commander in Chief and Chief Executive. Officials of my Administration and I communicate regularly with the leadership and other Members of Congress with regard to these deployments, and we will continue to do so.

Sincerely,

GEORGE W. BUSH

NOTE: Identical letters were sent to J. Dennis Hastert, Speaker of the House of Representatives, and Ted Stevens, President pro tempore of the Senate. This letter was released by the Office of the Press Secretary on December 18.

Remarks on Signing the Henry J. Hyde United States-India Peaceful Atomic Energy Cooperation Act of 2006
December 18, 2006

Thank you all. Welcome; please be seated. Thanks for coming. Welcome to the White House. Today I have the honor of signing a bill that will strengthen the partnership between the world's two largest democracies. The relationship between the United States and India has never been more vital, and this bill will help us meet the energy and security challenges of the 21st century. I want to thank the Congress for delivering this historic bill to my desk. I'm look forward to signing it.

The Henry Hyde United States-India Peaceful Atomic Energy Cooperation Act passed with strong bipartisan support. It is a fitting tribute to its sponsor and the man

whose name it carries. During his 32 years in Congress, Chairman Hyde earned the respect of his colleagues on both sides of the aisle. I appreciate his effective and principled leadership. I wish him all the very best in his retirement.

I'm proud to be joined here by Secretary of State Condi Rice. This bill would not have happened without her leadership. I thank very much the Members of the Senate and the House who have joined us up here, people from both parties who worked hard to get this bill passed: Senator Bill Frist and Senator Dick Lugar and Senator George Allen; Congressman Gary Ackerman; Frank Pallone; Joe Crowley; Thad

McCotter. Thank you all for joining us. Thanks for your good work.

I appreciate our Ambassador, David Mulford, and wife, Jeannie, for joining us. Thanks for your good work, Ambassador. I'm also proud to be joined by Ambassador Jassal. I want to thank you for coming, Ambassador.

I thank the Indian American community leaders who are here today. The Indian American community was vital to explaining this strategic bill to our fellow citizens. I appreciate so very much your carrying the message not only here at home but in India. And I want you to know that your voice was very effective, and I welcome it.

The United States and India are natural partners. The rivalries that once kept our nations apart are no more, and today, America and India are united by deeply held values. India is a democracy that protects rule of law and is accountable to its people. India is an open society that demands freedom of speech and freedom of religion. India is an important ally in the war against extremists and radicals. Like America, India has suffered from terrorist attacks on her own soil. And like America, India is committed to fighting the extremists, defeating their hateful ideology, and advancing the cause of human liberty around the world.

The United States and India are working together to expand economic opportunities in both our countries. India's economy has more than doubled in size since 1991, and it is one of the fastest growing markets for American exports. If you visit India today, you are going to see a lot of people using goods and services made by American companies, and that helps raise the standard of living not only in India but here at home. Trade is good for both countries, and we're going to continue to work with India to promote free and fair trade.

In our meetings in Washington and in New Delhi, Prime Minister Singh, for whom I have a lot of respect, we discussed the importance of working together to meet the energy needs of our growing economies. We recognize that energy, clean energy is going to be important to the advancement of our economies. And on my visit to India earlier this year, we concluded an historic agreement that will allow us to share civilian nuclear technology and bring India's civilian nuclear program under the safeguards of the IAEA. This cooperation will help the people of India produce more of their energy from clean, safe nuclear power, and that, in turn, will help their economy grow. And it's in our interest that the Indian economy continue to grow. It helps make America more secure.

As part of the agreement, the United States and India have committed to take a series of steps to make nuclear cooperation a reality, and we're going to fulfill these commitments. The bill I sign today is one of the most important steps, and it's going to help clear the way for us to move forward with this process. The bill is going to help us achieve four key goals.

First, the bill will help us strengthen cooperation between India and United States on one of the most important challenges in the 21st century, and that is energy. India is now the world's fifth largest consumer of energy, and its demand for electricity is expected to double by 2015. The United States has a clear interest in helping India meet this demand with nuclear energy. By helping India expand its use of safe nuclear energy, this bill lays the foundation for a new strategic partnership between our two nations that will help ease India's demands for fossil fuels and ease pressure on global markets.

Second, the bill will help promote economic growth. This bill helps open a new important market for American businesses by paving the way for investment in India's civilian nuclear industry for the first time ever. This new trade will help American companies gain new customers abroad and create new jobs here at home.

Third, the bill will help make it possible for India to reduce emissions and improve its environment. Today, India produces nearly 70 percent of its electricity from coal. Burning coal produces air pollution and greenhouse gases, and as India's economy has grown, emission levels have risen as well. We must break the cycle, and with nuclear power, we can. We can help India do so, and we can do so here at home by the use of nuclear power.

Nuclear power is the one source of energy that can generate massive amounts of electricity without producing any air pollution or greenhouse gases. And by sharing advanced civilian nuclear technology, we will help our friend India meet its growing demand for energy and lower emissions at the same time.

Finally, the bill will help keep America safe by paving the way for India to join the global effort to stop the spread of nuclear weapons. India has conducted its civilian nuclear energy program in a safe and responsible way for decades. Now, in return for access to American technology, India has agreed to open its civilian nuclear power program to international inspection. This is an important achievement for the whole world. After 30 years outside the system, India will now operate its civilian nuclear energy program under internationally accepted guidelines, and the world is going to be safer as a result.

The bill I'm about to sign is evidence of the growing bonds of trust between our two countries. Congress acted quickly and passed it with overwhelming bipartisan support. You know why? Because the American people have come to see India as a friend. And I view the Prime Minister as a trustworthy man and a friend. I appreciate Prime Minister Singh's leadership on this very important issue. I look forward to continuing to work with him to make civil nuclear cooperation a reality.

And now it is my honor to sign the Henry J. Hyde United States-India Peaceful Atomic Energy Cooperation Act of 2006.

NOTE: The President spoke at 10:46 a.m. in the East Room at the White House. In his remarks, he referred to Raminder Singh Jassal, Deputy Chief of Mission, Embassy of India; and Prime Minister Manmohan Singh of India. H.R. 5682, approved December 18, was assigned Public Law No. 109–401.

Statement on Signing the Henry J. Hyde United States-India Peaceful Atomic Energy Cooperation Act of 2006
December 18, 2006

Today I have signed into law H.R. 5682, an Act containing the "Henry J. Hyde United States-India Peaceful Atomic Energy Cooperation Act of 2006." The Act will strengthen the strategic relationship between the United States and India and deliver valuable benefits to both nations.

Section 103 of the Act purports to establish U.S. policy with respect to various international affairs matters. My approval of the Act does not constitute my adoption of the statements of policy as U.S. foreign policy. Given the Constitution's commitment to the presidency of the authority to conduct the Nation's foreign affairs, the executive branch shall construe such policy statements as advisory. Also, if section 104(d)(2) of the Act were construed to prohibit the executive branch from transferring or approving the transfer of an item to India contrary to Nuclear Suppliers Group transfer guidelines that may be in effect at the time of such future transfer, a serious question would exist as to whether the

provision unconstitutionally delegated legislative power to an international body. In order to avoid this constitutional question, the executive branch shall construe section 104(d)(2) as advisory. The executive branch will give sections 103 and 104(d)(2) the due weight that comity between the legislative and executive branches should require, to the extent consistent with U.S. foreign policy.

The executive branch shall construe provisions of the Act that mandate, regulate, or prohibit submission of information to the Congress, an international organization, or the public, such as sections 104, 109, 261, 271, 272, 273, 274, and 275, in a manner consistent with the President's constitutional authority to protect and control information that could impair foreign relations, national security, the deliberative processes of the Executive, or the performance of the Executive's constitutional duties.

GEORGE W. BUSH

The White House,
December 18, 2006.

NOTE: H.R. 5682, approved December 18, was assigned Public Law No. 109–401. An original was not available for verification of the content of this statement.

Remarks at a Swearing-In Ceremony for Robert M. Gates as Secretary of Defense in Arlington, Virginia
December 18, 2006

Thank you all. I'm pleased to join you here at the Pentagon. We're here to congratulate Bob Gates on becoming our Nation's 22d Secretary of the Defense.

Bob Gates entered public service 40 years ago. He is an experienced and thoughtful leader. He has got a track record of steering large organizations through change and transformation. I know Bob Gates will be an outstanding Secretary of the Defense.

I want to thank Bob's wife, Becky, and their family and their many friends who are with us here today. I appreciate the fact that the Vice President is here to administer the oath. I want to thank the members of my Cabinet who have joined us in welcoming a new member to the Cabinet. I appreciate so very much Senator John Warner and Senator Carl Levin for joining us. I thank the other Members of the United States Congress who are with us today, not the least of whom is my Congressman, Chet Edwards, from central Texas. [*Laughter*] I suspect he's here because of the Texas A&M connection. [*Laughter*]

I want to thank Deputy Secretary England for joining us. I thank Dr. Harvey and Dr. Winter and Michael Wynne, Secretaries of the Army, Navy, and Air Force, for joining us here today. I appreciate so very much General Pete Pace, Chairman of the Joint Chiefs, and his wife, Lynne, as well as the other members of the Joint Chiefs of Staff. I thank our distinguished guests.

Most importantly, I thank those who wear our uniform. This has got to be an exciting time for Bob Gates. I can't tell you what an honor it is to be the Commander in Chief of unbelievably fine people, and I suspect he will share that same sense of enthusiasm as the Secretary of the Defense.

The job of Secretary of Defense is one of the most important positions in our Government. The Secretary must understand the challenges of the present and see the threats of the future and find the best ways

to prepare our Armed Forces to meet them.

We are a nation at war. And I rely on our Secretary of Defense to provide me with the best possible advice and to help direct our Nation's Armed Forces as they engage the enemies of freedom around the world. Bob Gates is the right man to take on these challenges. He'll be an outstanding leader for our men and women in uniform, and he's going to make our Nation proud.

Bob is a man of vision, integrity, and extensive experience. In 1966, Bob began his rise from an entry-level position at the Central Intelligence Agency to become its director. During his years of public service, Bob Gates has worked under six Presidents from both parties. He spent nearly 9 years at the White House working on the National Security Council staff. He's amassed nearly 30 years of experience in national security matters. Bob Gates's lifetime of preparation will serve him well as the Secretary of Defense.

Bob follows a superb leader at the Department of Defense. For nearly 6 years, Don Rumsfeld has served with exceptional strength and energy at a time of challenge and change, and he produced impressive results. During his tenure, he developed a new defense strategy, established a new command structure of our Armed Forces, helped transform the NATO Alliance, took ballistic missile defense from theory to reality, and undertook the most sweeping transformation of America's global defense posture since the start of the cold war. He led our Armed Forces with determination and distinction. And on Friday at the Pentagon, the men and women he led showed their admiration and devotion to him. I want to thank Don Rumsfeld for his service, and I wish him and his family all the very best.

As Bob Gates raises his hand and takes the oath of office, he does so at a time of great consequence for our Nation. He knows the stakes in the war on terror. He recognizes this is a long struggle against an enemy unlike any our Nation has fought before. He understands that defeating the terrorists and the radicals and the extremists in Iraq and the Middle East is essential to leading toward peace.

As Secretary of Defense, he will help our country forge a new way forward in Iraq so that we can help the Iraqis achieve our shared goal of a unified democratic Iraq that can govern itself, sustain itself, and defend itself and be an ally in our struggle against extremists and radicals.

Bob Gates is a talented and innovative leader who brings a fresh perspective to the Department of Defense. I'm pleased that he's answered the call to serve our Nation again. He has my trust and my confidence, and he has the gratitude and the prayers of the American people.

And so I look forward to working with Bob Gates. I congratulate you, sir. I appreciate you taking on this job. And now I'm going to ask the Vice President to administer the oath of office for our Nation's 22d Secretary of Defense.

NOTE: The President spoke at 1:22 p.m. at the Pentagon. The transcript released by the Office of the Press Secretary also included the remarks of Secretary of Defense Gates. The Office of the Press Secretary also released a Spanish language transcript of these remarks.

Remarks on Lighting the Hanukkah Menorah
December 18, 2006

Thank you all very much. Welcome to the White House. I'm pleased you all could join us. I appreciate members of my Cabinet who have joined us: Secretary Michael Chertoff, Ambassador Susan Schwab, and Chief of Staff Joshua Bolten.

Tonight is the fourth night of Hanukkah, a holiday which commemorates a victory for freedom and the courage and faith that made it possible. Laura and I are honored to have this Hanukkah menorah here at the White House. It's a symbol that the White House is the people's house, and it belongs to Americans of all faiths.

The story of Hanukkah celebrates a great miracle. More than 2,000 years ago, the land of ancient Israel was conquered, its most sacred temple was desecrated, and Jews were forbidden to practice their faith. A patriot named Judah Maccabee and his followers took a stand for freedom and rose up against their oppressors to take back Jerusalem.

When the Maccabees returned to reclaim their holy temple, the oil that should have lasted only one day burned for 8. That miraculous light brought hope. And today, by lighting the menorah, Jews around the world celebrate the victory of light over darkness and give thanks for the presence of a just and loving God.

We're honored to have a beautiful menorah here from Lisa and Alan Stern of Los Angeles. The ceramic plaques around the base feature biblical scenes of the Hanukkah story. And between the menorah branches are painted doves, which represent the eternal wish for peace.

I want to thank Ariel Cohen and her family for being here. Ariel, you did a wonderful job of saying the Hanukkah blessings and lighting the candles. I also thank the Indiana University's Hillel HooShir Choir for your wonderful performance. We're really glad you came. Thanks for coming.

On Hanukkah, we're especially mindful of the sacrifices that freedom requires. Our Nation is grateful to the men and women of every faith who serve our country in uniform and who are away from their families this holiday. We pray for them and their families, and we pray that those who still live in the darkness of tyranny will someday see the light of freedom.

The word "Hanukkah" means dedication, and the message of Hanukkah calls on us to dedicate ourselves to recognizing the miracles in our daily lives. This dedication has the power to lift our souls and to make us better people and to make the world a better place.

Laura and I wish all the people of the Jewish faith around the world a Happy Hanukkah, and thank you all for coming.

NOTE: The President spoke at 5:36 p.m. in the Bookseller's Area at the White House.

Message Sending Holiday Greetings to Members of the Armed Forces
December 18, 2006

To the Men and Women of the United States Armed Forces

On behalf of all Americans, Laura and I send our best holiday wishes to you and your families.

During this hopeful time of year, the hearts of Americans are filled with gratitude for the many blessings in our lives. We are especially thankful for the priceless gift of freedom that our Armed Forces help defend by serving the cause of peace and standing watch over our security. As courageous Soldiers, Sailors, Airmen, Marines, and Coast Guardsmen, you have set aside comfort and convenience to protect the rest of us, earning the respect of a grateful Nation and a proud Commander in Chief.

Many of you are confronting our adversaries abroad and observing the holidays in places far from home, but you are close to our hearts. You are serving at a time when our Nation needs you, and your fellow citizens appreciate the many sacrifices that you and your families are making every day. Over the holidays and throughout the New Year, we will continue to ask the Almighty to bestow His care on you and your loved ones.

Laura and I wish each of you a safe and joyous holiday season. May God bless and watch over you, and may God bless America.

GEORGE W. BUSH

NOTE: An original was not available for verification of the content of this message.

Message on the Observance of Christmas 2006
December 18, 2006

"For unto us a child is born . . . and His name will be called Wonderful, Counselor, Mighty God, Everlasting Father, Prince of Peace."

ISAIAH 9:6

For centuries, patient men and women listened to the words of prophets and lived in joyful expectation of the coming Messiah. Their patience was rewarded when a young virgin named Mary welcomed God's plan with great faith, and a quiet birth in a little town brought hope to the world. For more than two millennia, Christians around the world have celebrated Christmas to mark the birth of Jesus and to thank the Almighty for His grace and blessings.

In this season of giving, we also remember the universal call to love our neighbors.

Millions of compassionate souls take time during the holidays to help people who are hurt, feed those who are hungry, and shelter those who need homes. Our Nation also thinks of the men and women of our military who are spending Christmas at posts and bases around the world and of the loved ones who pray for their safe return. America owes a debt of gratitude to our service members and their families.

The simple story of Christmas speaks to every generation and holds a sense of wonder and surprise. During this time of joy and peace, may we be surrounded by the love of family and friends and take time to reflect on the year ahead. Laura and I pray that this season will be a time of happiness in every home and a time of

peace throughout the world. Merry Christmas.

GEORGE W. BUSH

NOTE: An original was not available for verification of the content of this message.

Statement on Signing the Combating Autism Act of 2006
December 19, 2006

For the millions of Americans whose lives are affected by autism, today is a day of hope. The "Combating Autism Act of 2006" will increase public awareness about this disorder and provide enhanced Federal support for autism research and treatment. By creating a national education program for doctors and the public about autism, this legislation will help more people recognize the symptoms of autism. This will lead to early identification and intervention, which is critical for children with autism. I am proud to sign this bill into law and confident that it will serve as an important foundation for our Nation's efforts to find a cure for autism.

NOTE: S. 843, approved December 19, was assigned Public Law No. 109–416. An original was not available for verification of the content of this statement.

The President's News Conference
December 20, 2006

The President. Thank you all. Good morning. This week, I went to the Pentagon for the swearing-in of our Nation's new Secretary of Defense, Bob Gates. Secretary Gates is going to bring a fresh perspective to the Pentagon, and America is fortunate that he has agreed to serve our country once again. I'm looking forward to working with him.

Secretary Gates is going to be an important voice in the Iraq strategy review that's underway. As you know, I've been consulting closely with our commanders and the Joint Chiefs of Staff on the strategy in Iraq and on the broader war on terror. One of my top priorities during this war is to ensure that our men and women wearing the uniform have everything they need to do their job.

This war on terror is the calling of a new generation; it is the calling of our generation. Success is essential to securing a future of peace for our children and grandchildren, and securing this peace for the future is going to require a sustained commitment from the American people and our military.

We have an obligation to ensure our military is capable of sustaining this war over the long haul and performing the many tasks that we ask of them. I'm inclined to believe that we need to increase in the permanent size of both the United States Army and the United States Marines. I've asked Secretary Gates to determine how such an increase could take place and report back to me as quickly as possible.

I know many Members of Congress are interested in this issue, and I appreciate their input. As we develop the specifics of the proposals over the coming weeks, I will not only listen to their views, we will work

with them to see that this becomes a reality.

Two thousand and six was a difficult year for our troops and the Iraqi people. We began the year with optimism after watching nearly 12 million Iraqis go to the polls to vote for a unity government and a free future. The enemies of liberty responded fiercely to this advance of freedom. They carried out a deliberate strategy to foment sectarian violence between Sunnis and Shi'a. And over the course of the year, they had success. Their success hurt our efforts to help the Iraqis rebuild their country. It set back reconciliation; it kept Iraq's unity Government and our coalition from establishing security and stability throughout the country.

We enter this new year clear-eyed about the challenges in Iraq and equally clear about our purpose. Our goal remains a free and democratic Iraq that can govern itself, sustain itself, and defend itself and is an ally in this war on terror.

I'm not going to make predictions about what 2007 will look like in Iraq, except that it's going to require difficult choices and additional sacrifices, because the enemy is merciless and violent. I'm going to make you this promise: My administration will work with Republicans and Democrats to fashion a new way forward that can succeed in Iraq. We'll listen to ideas from every quarter. We'll change our strategy and tactics to meet the realities on the ground. We'll never lose sight that on the receiving end of the decisions I make is a private, a sergeant, a young lieutenant, or a diplomat who risks his or her life to help the Iraqis realize a dream of a stable country that can defend, govern, and sustain itself.

The advance of liberty has never been easy, and Iraq is proving how tough it can be. Yet the safety and security of our citizens requires that we do not let up. We can be smarter about how we deploy our manpower and resources. We can ask more of our Iraqi partners, and we will. One

thing we cannot do is give up on the hundreds of millions of ordinary moms and dads across the Middle East who want the hope and opportunity for their children that the terrorists and extremists seek to deny them, and that's a peaceful existence.

As we work with Congress in the coming year to chart a new course in Iraq and strengthen our military to meet the challenges of the 21st century, we must also work together to achieve important goals for the American people here at home. This work begins with keeping our economy growing. As we approach the end of 2006, the American economy continues to post strong gains. The most recent jobs report shows that our economy created 132,000 more jobs in November alone, and we've now added more than 7 million new jobs since August of 2003. The unemployment rate has remained low at 4.5 percent. A recent report on retail sales shows a strong beginning to the holiday shopping season across the country, and I encourage you all to go shopping more.

Next year marks a new start with a new Congress. In recent weeks, I've had good meetings with the incoming leaders of Congress, including Speaker-elect Nancy Pelosi and Senate Majority Leader-elect Harry Reid. We agreed that we've got important business to do on behalf of the American people and that we've got to work together to achieve results. The American people expect us to be good stewards of their tax dollars here in Washington. So we must work together to reduce the number of earmarks inserted into large spending bills and reform the earmark process to make it more transparent and more accountable.

The American people expect us to keep America competitive in the world. So we must work to ensure our citizens have the skills they need for the jobs of the future and encourage American businesses to invest in technology and innovation. The American people expect us to reduce our dependence on foreign oil and increase our use of alternative energy sources. So we

must step up our research and investment in hydrogen fuel cells, hybrid plug-in and battery-powered cars, renewable fuels like ethanol and cellulosic ethanol and biodiesel, clean coal technology, and clean sources of electricity like nuclear, solar, and wind power.

Another area where we can work together is the minimum wage. I support the proposed $2.10 increase in the minimum wage over a 2-year period. I believe we should do it in a way that does not punish the millions of small businesses that are creating most of the new jobs in our country. So I support pairing it with targeted tax and regulatory relief to help these small businesses stay competitive and to help keep our economy growing. I look forward to working with Republicans and Democrats to help both small-business owners and workers when Congress convenes in January.

To achieve these and other key goals we need to put aside our partisan differences and work constructively to address the vital issues confronting our Nation. As the new Congress takes office, I don't expect Democratic leaders to compromise on their principles, and they don't expect me to compromise on mine. But the American people do expect us to compromise on legislation that will benefit the country. The message of the fall election was clear: Americans want us to work together to make progress for our country. And that's what we're going to do in the coming year.

And now I'll be glad to answer some questions. Terry [Terence Hunt, Associated Press].

Progress in Iraq

Q. Mr. President, less than 2 months ago, at the end of one of the bloodiest months in the war, you said, "Absolutely we're winning." Yesterday you said, "We're not winning; we're not losing." Why did you drop your confident assertion about winning?

The President. My comments—the first comment was done in this spirit: I believe that we're going to win. I believe that—and by the way, if I didn't think that, I wouldn't have our troops there. That's what you got to know; we're going to succeed.

My comments yesterday reflected the fact that we're not succeeding nearly as fast as I wanted when I said it at the time and that conditions are tough in Iraq, particularly in Baghdad. And so we're conducting a review to make sure that our strategy helps us achieve that which I'm pretty confident we can do, and that is have a country which can govern itself, sustain itself, and defend itself.

You know, I—when I speak, like right now, for example—I'm speaking to the American people, of course, and I want them to know that I know how tough it is, but I also want them to know that I'm going to work with the military and the political leaders to develop a plan that will help us achieve the objective. I also want our troops to understand that we support them, that I believe that tough mission I've asked them to do is going to be accomplished, and that they're doing good work and necessary work.

I want the Iraqis to understand that we believe that if they stand up—step up and lead—and with our help, we can accomplish the objective. And I want the enemy to understand that this is a tough task, but they can't run us out of the Middle East, that they can't intimidate America. They think they can. They think it's just a matter of time before America grows weary and leaves, abandons the people of Iraq, for example. And that's not going to happen.

What is going to happen is we're going to develop a strategy that helps the Iraqis achieve the objective that the 12 million people want them to achieve, which is a government that can—a country that can sustain itself, govern itself, defend itself, a free country that will serve as an ally in this war against extremists and radicals.

Caren [Caren Bohan, Reuters].

U.S. Military Forces in Iraq

Q. Thank you, Mr. President. If you conclude that a surge in troop levels in Iraq is needed, would you overrule your military commanders if they felt it was not a good idea?

The President. That's a dangerous hypothetical question. I'm not condemning you; you're allowed to ask anything you want. Let me wait and gather all the recommendations from Bob Gates, from our military, from diplomats on the ground—I'm interested in the Iraqis' point of view—and then I'll report back to you as to whether or not I support a surge or not. Nice try.

Q. Would you overrule your commanders——

The President. The opinion of my commanders is very important. They are bright, capable, smart people whose opinion matters to me a lot.

Bret [Bret Baier, FOX News].

War on Terror Strategy/Iraqi Government

Q. Thank you, Mr. President. You have reached out to both Sunni and Shi'a political leaders in recent weeks, and now there's word that the Grand Ayatollah Ali al-Sistani is supporting a moderate coalition in Iraq. Has the U.S. reached out to him? How important is he in the equation moving forward? And what do you say to people who say more troops in Iraq would increase the sectarian split and not calm things down?

The President. Well, I haven't made up my mind yet about more troops. I'm listening to our commanders; I'm listening to the Joint Chiefs, of course; I'm listening to people in and out of Government; I'm listening to the folks on the Baker-Hamilton commission about coming up with a strategy that helps us achieve our objective. And so as I said to Caren—probably a little more harshly than she would have liked—hypothetical questions, I'm not going to answer them today. I'm not going to speculate out loud about what I'm going

to tell the Nation, when I'm prepared to do so, about the way forward.

I will tell you we're looking at all options. And one of those options, of course, is increasing more troops. But in order to do so, there must be a specific mission that can be accomplished with more troops. And that's precisely what our commanders have said, as well as people who know a lot about military operations. And I agree with them that there's got to be a specific mission that can be accomplished with the addition of more troops before I agree on that strategy.

Secondly, whatever we do is going to help the Iraqis step up. It's their responsibility to govern their country. It's their responsibility to do the hard work necessary to secure Baghdad. And we want to help them.

Thirdly, I appreciate the fact that the Prime Minister and members of the Government are forming what you have called a moderate coalition, because it's becoming very apparent to the people of Iraq that there are extremists and radicals who are anxious to stop the advance of a free society. And therefore, a moderate coalition signals to the vast majority of the people of Iraq that we have a unity government, that we're willing to reconcile our differences and work together and, in so doing, will marginalize those who use violence to achieve political objectives.

And so we support the formation of the unity Government and the moderate coalition. And it's important for the leader Sistani to understand that's our position. He is a—he lives a secluded life, but he knows that we're interested in defeating extremism, and we're interested in helping advance a unity government.

Kelly [Kelly O'Donnell, NBC News].

Situation in the Middle East/War on Terror

Q. Good morning, Mr. President. Your former Secretary of Defense, Donald Rumsfeld, advocated for a lighter, more

agile military force. Have you now concluded that that approach was wrong?

The President. No, I strongly support a lighter, agile Army that can move quickly to meet the threats of the 21st century. I also supported his force posture review and recommendations to move forces out of previous bases that—you know, they were there for the Soviet threat, for example, in Europe. So he's introduced some substantive changes to the Pentagon, and I support them strongly.

However, that doesn't necessarily preclude increasing end strength for the Army and the Marines. And the reason why I'm inclined to believe this is a good idea is because I understand that we're going to be in a long struggle against radicals and extremists, and we must make sure that our military has the capability to stay in the fight for a long period of time. I'm not predicting any particular theater, but I am predicting that it's going to take a while for the ideology of liberty to finally triumph over the ideology of hate.

I know you know I feel this strongly, but I see this—we're in the beginning of a conflict between competing ideologies, a conflict that will determine whether or not your children can live in peace. A failure in the Middle East, for example, or failure in Iraq or isolationism will condemn a generation of young Americans to permanent threat from overseas. And therefore, we will succeed in Iraq. And therefore, we will help young democracies when we find them—democracies like Lebanon, hopefully a Palestinian state living side by side in peace with Israel, the young democracy of Iraq.

It is in our interest that we combine security with a political process that frees people, that liberates people, that gives people a chance to determine their own futures. I believe most people in the Middle East want just that. They want to be in a position where they can chart their own futures, and it's in our interest that we help them do so.

Jim [Jim Axelrod, CBS News].

Public Opinion on Iraq

Q. Thank you, Mr. President. In the latest CBS News poll, 50 percent of Americans say they favor a beginning of an end to U.S. military involvement in Iraq; 43 percent said, "Keep fighting, but change tactics." By this and many other measures, there is no clear mandate to continue being in Iraq in a military form. I guess my question is, are you still willing to follow a path that seems to be in opposition to the will of the American people?

The President. I am willing to follow a path that leads to victory, and that's exactly why we're conducting the review we are. Victory in Iraq is achievable. It hasn't happened nearly as quickly as I hoped it would have. I know it's—the fact that there is still unspeakable sectarian violence in Iraq, I know that's troubling to the American people. But I also don't believe most Americans want us just to get out now. A lot of Americans understand the consequences of retreat. Retreat would embolden radicals. It would hurt the credibility of the United States. Retreat from Iraq would dash the hopes of millions who want to be free. Retreat from Iraq would enable the extremists and radicals to more likely be able to have safe haven from which to plot and plan further attacks.

And so it's been a tough period for the American people. They want to see success, and our objective is to put a plan in place that achieves that success. I'm often asked about public opinion. Of course, I want public opinion to support the efforts. I understand that. But, Jim, I also understand the consequences of failure. And therefore, I'm going to work with the Iraqis and our military and politicians from both political parties to achieve success.

I thought the election said they want to see more bipartisan cooperation; they want to see us working together to achieve common objectives. And I'm going to continue to reach out to Democrats to do just that.

Sheryl [Sheryl Gay Stolberg, New York Times].

The Presidency/U.S. Military Casualties in Iraq

Q. Thank you, Mr. President. Mr. President, Lyndon Johnson famously didn't sleep during the Vietnam war, questioning his own decisions. You have always seemed very confident of your decisions, but I can't help but wonder if this has been a time of painful realization for you, as you yourself have acknowledged that some of the policies you hoped would succeed have not. And I wonder if you can talk to us about that.

The President. Yes, thanks.

Q. Has it been a painful time?

The President. The most painful aspect of my Presidency has been knowing that good men and women have died in combat. I read about it every night. My heart breaks for a mother or father, or husband or wife, or son and daughter; it just does. And so when you ask about pain, that's pain. I reach out to a lot of the families. I spend time with them. I am always inspired by their spirit. Most people have asked me to do one thing, and that is to make sure that their child didn't die in vain—and I agree with that—that the sacrifice has been worth it.

We'll accomplish our objective; we've got to constantly adjust our tactics to do so. We've got to insist that the Iraqis take more responsibility more quickly in order to do so.

But I—look, my heart breaks for them; it just does, on a regular basis.

Q. But beyond that, sir, do you question your own decisions?

The President. No, I haven't questioned whether or not it was right to take Saddam Hussein out, nor have I questioned the necessity for the American people—I mean, I've questioned it; I've come to the conclusion it's the right decision. But I also know it's the right decision for America to stay engaged and to take the lead and to deal with these radicals and extremists and to help support young democracies. It's the calling of our time, Sheryl. And I firmly believe it is necessary.

And I believe the next President, whoever the person is, will have the same charge, the same obligations to deal with terrorists, so they don't hurt us, and to help young democracies survive the threats of radicalism and extremism. It's in our Nation's interest to do so. But the most painful aspect of the Presidency is the fact that I know my decisions have caused young men and women to lose their lives.

McKinnon [John McKinnon, Wall Street Journal].

National Economy/Legislative Agenda

Q. Thank you, Mr. President. You mentioned a need earlier to make sure that U.S. workers are skilled, that U.S. businesses keep investing in technology. You also mentioned that you want targeted tax and regulatory relief for small businesses in the coming year. Can you describe those ideas a little more? And also, can we really afford new tax breaks at this point, given the cost of the war on terrorism?

The President. John, the first question all of us here in Washington ask is, how do we make sure this economy continues to grow? A vibrant economy is going to be necessary to fund not only war but a lot of other aspects of our Government. We have shown over the past 6 years that low taxes have helped this economy recover from some pretty significant shocks. After all, the unemployment rate is 4.5 percent and 7 million more Americans have been— have found jobs since August of 2003. And we cut the deficit in half a couple of years in advance of what we thought would happen.

The question that Congress is going to have to face, and I'm going to have to continue to face is, how do we make sure we put policy in place to encourage economic growth in the short term, and how

do we keep America competitive in the long term?

Part of the competitive initiative, which I have been working with Congress on, recognizes that education of young—of the young is going to be crucial for remaining competitive. And that's why the reauthorization of No Child Left Behind is going to be an important part of the legislative agenda going forward in 2007.

I also spoke about energy in my opening remarks. In my judgment, we're going to have to get off oil as much as possible to remain a competitive economy, and I'm looking forward to working with Congress to do just that. I'm optimistic about some of the reports I've heard about new battery technologies that will be coming to the market that will enable people who—people to drive the first 20 miles, for example, on electricity—that will be the initial phase—and then up to 40 miles on battery technologies. That will be positive, particularly if you live in a big city. A lot of people don't drive more than 20 miles or 40 miles a day. And therefore, those urban dwellers who aren't driving that much won't be using any gasoline on a daily basis, and that will be helpful to the country.

I'm pleased with the fact that we've gone from about a billion gallons of ethanol to over 5 billion gallons of ethanol in a very quick period of time. It's mainly derived from corn here in the United States. But there's been great progress, and we need to continue to spend money on cellulosic ethanol. That means that new technologies that—will enable us to use wood chips, for example, or switchgrass as the fuel stocks for the development of new types of fuels that will enable American drivers to diversify away from gasoline.

I spent a lot of time talking about nuclear power, and I appreciate the Congress's support on the comprehensive energy bill that I signed. But nuclear power is going to be an essential source, in my judgment, of future electricity for the United States and places like China and

India. Nuclear power is renewable, and nuclear power does not emit one greenhouse gas. And it makes a lot of sense for us to share technologies that will enable people to feel confident that the nuclear powerplants that are being built are safe, as well as technologies that will eventually come to fore that will enable us to reduce the wastes, the toxicity of the waste, and the amount of the waste.

I'm going to continue to invest in clean coal technologies. We've got an abundance of coal here in America, and we need to be able to tell the American people we're going to be able to use that coal to generate electricity in environmentally friendly ways.

My only point to you is we've got a comprehensive plan to achieve the objective that most Americans support, which is less dependency upon oil.

I think it's going to be very important, John, to keep this economy growing—short term and long term—by promoting free trade. It's in our interest that nations treat our markets, our goods and services the way we treat theirs. And it's in our interest that administrations continue to promote more opening up markets. We've had a lot of discussions here in this administration on the Doha round of WTO negotiations. And I'm very strongly in favor of seeing if we can't reach an accord with our trading partners and other countries around the world to promote—to get this round completed so that free trade is universal in its application.

Free trade is going to be good for producers of U.S. product and services, but free trade is also going to be the most powerful engine for development around the world. It's going to help poor nations become wealthier nations. It's going to enable countries to be able to find markets for their goods and services so that they can better grow their economies and create prosperity for their people.

So we've got a robust agenda moving forward with the Congress, and I'm looking

forward to working with them. And there are a lot of places where we can find common ground on these important issues.

Elaine [Elaine Quijano, Cable News Network].

CIA Employee Identity Disclosure Investigation

Q. Thank you, Mr. President. This week, we learned that Scooter Libby——

The President. A little louder, please. Excuse me—getting old. [*Laughter*]

Q. I understand, Mr. President.

The President. No, you don't understand. [*Laughter*]

Q. You're right; I don't.

This week, sir, we learned that Scooter Libby's defense team plans to call Vice President Cheney to testify in the ongoing CIA leak case. I wonder, sir, what is your reaction to that? Is that something you'll resist?

The President. I read it in the newspaper today, and it's an interesting piece of news. And that's all I'm going to comment about an ongoing case. I thought it was interesting.

Ann [Ann Compton, ABC News].

Mary Cheney

Q. Thank you, sir. Mary is having a baby. And you have said that you think Mary Cheney will be a loving soul to a child. Are there any changes in the law that you would support that would give same-sex couples greater access to things such as legal rights, hospital visits, insurance, that would make a difference, even though you've said it's your preference—you believe that it's preferable to have one man-one woman——

The President. I've always said that we ought to review law to make sure that people are treated fairly.

On Mary Cheney, this is a personal matter for the Vice President and his family. I strongly support their privacy on the issue, although there's nothing private when you happen to be the President or the Vice

President; I recognize that. And I know Mary, and I like her. And I know she's going to be a fine, loving mother.

Baker [Peter Baker, Washington Post], I'm not going to call on you again. You, like, got too much coverage yesterday, you know? [*Laughter*] Created a sense of anxiety amongst—no, no, you handled yourself well, though.

Don [Don Gonyea, National Public Radio].

Iran/Syria

Q. Thank you, Mr. President. A question about the Iraq Study Group Report. One of the things that it recommends is greater dialog, direct talks with Syria and Iran. James Baker himself, Secretary of State under your father, says that it's a lot like it was during the cold war when we talked to the Soviet Union. He says it's important to talk to your adversaries. Is he wrong?

The President. Let me start with Iran. We made it perfectly clear to them what it takes to come to the table, and that is a suspension of their enrichment program. If they verifiably suspend—that they've stopped enrichment, we will come to the table with our EU–3 partners and Russia and discuss a way forward for them. Don, it should be evident to the Iranians, if this is what they want to do.

I heard the Foreign Minister—I read the Foreign Minister say the other day that, "Yes, we'll sit down with America, after they leave Iraq." If they want to sit down with us, for the good of the Iranian people, they ought to verifiably suspend their program. We've made that clear to them. It is obvious to them how to move forward.

The Iranian people can do better than becoming—than be an isolated nation. This is a proud nation with a fantastic history and tradition. And yet they've got a leader who constantly sends messages to the world that Iran is out of step with the majority of thinkers, that Iran is willing to become isolated, to the detriment of the people.

I mean, I was amazed that, once again, there was this conference about the Holocaust that heralded a really backward view of the history of the world. And all that said to me was, is that the leader in Iran is willing to say things that really hurts his country and further isolates the Iranian people.

We're working hard to get a Security Council resolution. I spoke to Secretary Rice about the Iranian Security Council resolution this morning. And the message will be that you—"you," Iran—are further isolated from the world.

My message to the Iranian people is: You can do better than to have somebody try to rewrite history. You can do better than somebody who hasn't strengthened your economy. And you can do better than having somebody who's trying to develop a nuclear weapon that the world believes you shouldn't have. There's a better way forward.

Syria, the message is the same. We have met with Syria since I have been the President of the United States. We have talked to them about what is necessary for them to have a better relationship with the United States, and they're not unreasonable requests. We've suggested to them that they no longer allow Saddamists to send money and arms across their border into Iraq to fuel the violence—some of the violence that we see. We've talked to them about—they've got to leave the democrat Lebanon alone.

I might say—let me step back for a second—I'm very proud of Prime Minister Siniora. He's shown a lot of tenacity and toughness in the face of enormous pressure from Syria as well as Hizballah, which is funded by Iran.

But we made it clear to them, Don, on how to move forward. We've had visits with the Syrians in the past. Congressmen and Senators visit Syria. What I would suggest, that if they're interested in better relations with the United States, that they take some concrete, positive steps that promote peace as opposed to instability.

Knoller [Mark Knoller, CBS Radio].

Leak Investigations

Q. Thank you, sir. Mr. President, did you or your Chief of Staff order an investigation of the leak of the Hadley memo before your meeting with Prime Minister al-Maliki? And if the leak wasn't authorized, do you suspect someone in your administration is trying to undermine your Iraq policy or sabotage your meeting with Prime Minister al-Maliki a few weeks back?

The President. I'm trying to think back if I ordered an investigation. I don't recall ordering an investigation. I do recall expressing some angst about ongoing leaks. You all work hard to find information and, of course, put it out for public consumption, and I understand that. But I don't appreciate those who leak classified documents. And it's an ongoing problem here, it really is, not just for this administration, but it will be for any administration that is trying to put policy in place that affects the future of the country.

And we've had a lot of leaks, Mark, as you know, some of them out of the—I don't know where they're from, and therefore, I'm not going to speculate. It turns out, you never can find the leaker. It's an advantage you have in doing your job. We can moan about it, but it's hard to find those inside the Government that are willing to give, in this case, Hadley's document to newspapers.

You know, there may be an ongoing investigation of this; I just don't know. If there is, if I knew about it, it's not fresh in my mind. But I do think that at some point in time, it would be helpful if we can find somebody inside our Government who is leaking materials, clearly against the law, that they be held to account. Perhaps the best way to make sure people don't leak classified documents is that there be a consequence for doing so.

Jim [Jim Gerstenzang, Los Angeles Times].

Iraq/War on Terror Strategy

Q. Mr. President, if we could return to the reflexive vein we were in a little while ago——

The President. The what? Excuse me.

Q. Reflexive—reflective.

The President. Reflective stage.

Q. Part of the process of looking at the way forward could reasonably include considering how we got to where we are. Has that been part of your process? And what lessons—after 5 years now of war, what lessons will you take into the final 2 years of your Presidency?

The President. Yes, look, absolutely, Jim, that it is important for us to be successful going forward is to analyze that which went wrong. And clearly, one aspect of this war that has not gone right is the sectarian violence inside Baghdad, a violent reaction by both Sunni and Shi'a to each other that has caused a lot of loss of life as well as some movements in neighborhoods inside of Baghdad. It is a troubling, very troubling, aspect of trying to help this Iraqi Government succeed. And therefore, a major consideration of our planners is how to deal with that and how to help—more importantly, how to help the Iraqis deal with sectarian violence.

There are a couple of theaters inside of Iraq, war theaters. One, of course, is Baghdad, itself, where the sectarian violence is brutal. And we've got to help them. We've got to help the Maliki Government stop it and crack it and prevent it from spreading, in order to be successful.

I fully understand—let me finish. Secondly, is the battle against the Sunnis, Sunni extremists—some of them Saddamists, some of them are Al Qaida—but all of them aiming to try to drive the United States out of Iraq before the job is done. And we're making good progress against them. It's hard fighting. It's been hard work, but our special ops teams, along with Iraqis, are on the hunt and bringing people to justice.

There's issues in the south of Iraq, mainly Shi'a-on-Shi'a tensions. But primarily, the toughest fight for this new Government is inside of Baghdad. Most of the deaths, most of the violence is within a 30-mile radius of Baghdad, as well as in Anbar Province. In other words, a lot of the country is moving along positively. But it's this part of the fight that is getting our attention. And frankly, we have—it has been that aspect of the battle, toward a government which can defend and govern itself and be an ally in the war on terror that—where we have not made as much progress as we'd have hoped to have made.

Listen, last year started off as an exciting year with the 12 million voters. And the attack on the Samarra mosque was Zarqawi's successful attempt to foment this sectarian violence. And it's mean. It is deadly, and we've got to help the Iraqis deal with it.

Success in Iraq will be success—there will be a combination of military success, political success, and reconstruction. And they've got to go hand in hand. That's why I think it's important that the moderate coalition is standing up. In other words, it's the beginning of a political process that I hope will marginalize the radicals and extremists who are trying to stop the advance of a free Iraq. That's why the oil law is going to be a very important piece of legislation.

In other words, when this Government begins to send messages that we will put law in place that help unify the country, it's going to make the security situation easier to deal with. On the other hand, without better, stronger security measures, it's going to be hard to get the political process to move forward. And so it's—we've got a parallel strategy. So when you hear me talking about the military—I know there's a lot of discussion about troops, and there should be—but we've got to keep in mind we've also got to make sure we

have a parallel political process and a reconstruction process going together concurrently with a new military strategy.

I thought it was an interesting statement that Prime Minister Maliki made the other day about generals, former generals in the Saddam army, that they could come back in or receive a pension. In other words, he's beginning to reach out in terms of a reconciliation plan that I think is going to be important.

I had interesting discussions the other day with Provincial Reconstruction Team members in Iraq. These are really brave souls who work for the State Department that are in these different Provinces helping these provincial governments rebuild and to see a political way forward. And one of the things that—most of these people were in the Sunni territory, that I had talked to, and most of them were very anxious for me to help them and help the Iraqi Government put reconciliation plans in place. There's a lot of people trying to make a choice as to whether or not they want to support a government or whether or not their interest may lay in extremism. And they understand that a political process that is positive, that sends a signal, "We want to be a unified country," will help these folks make a rational choice.

And so it's a multifaceted plan. And absolutely, we're looking at where things went wrong, where expectations were dashed, and where things hadn't gone the way we wanted them to have gone.

Let's see here, Julie [Julie Hirschfeld, Baltimore Sun].

Legislative Agenda/Immigration Reform

Q. Thank you, Mr. President. You said this week that your microphone has never been louder on some of the key domestic priorities you've talked about, particularly Social Security and immigration. Your use of the Presidential microphone hasn't yielded the results that you wanted. So I'm wondering—the Democratic Congress, at this point, Republicans no longer controlling

things on Capitol Hill—why you think your microphone is any louder, and how you plan to use it differently to get the results that you're looking for?

The President. Yes, microphone being loud means—is that I'm able to help focus people's attentions on important issues. That's what I was referring to. In other words, the President is in a position to speak about priorities. Whether or not we can get those priorities done is going to take bipartisan cooperation, which I believe was one of the lessons of the campaigns.

I will tell you, I felt like we had a pretty successful couple of years when it comes to legislation. After all, we reformed Medicare; we put tax policy in place that encouraged economic growth and vitality; we passed trade initiatives; passed a comprehensive energy bill. I'm signing an important piece of legislation today that continues a comprehensive approach to energy exploration, plus extenders on R&D, for example, tax credits. It's been a pretty substantial legislative record if you carefully scrutinize it.

However, that doesn't mean necessarily that we are able to achieve the same kind of results without a different kind of approach. After all, you're right; the Democrats now control the House and the Senate. And therefore, I will continue to work with their leadership—and our own leaders, our own Members—to see if we can't find common ground on key issues like Social Security or immigration.

I strongly believe that we can and must get a comprehensive immigration plan on my desk this year. It's important for us because, in order to enforce our border, in order for those Border Patrol agents who we've increased down there and given them more equipment and better border security, they've got to have help and a plan that says, "If you're coming into America to do a job, you can come legally for a temporary basis to do so."

I don't know if you've paid attention to the enforcement measures that were taken

recently where in some of these packing plants they found people working that had been here illegally, but all of them had documents that said they were here legally. They were using forged documents, which just reminded me that the system we have in place has caused people to rely upon smugglers and forgers in order to do work Americans aren't doing.

In other words, it is a system that is all aimed to bypass no matter what measures we take to protect this country. It is a system that, frankly, leads to inhumane treatment of people. And therefore, the best way to deal with an issue that Americans agree on—that is, that we ought to enforce our borders in a humane way— is we've got to have a comprehensive bill.

And I have made a proposal. I have spoken about this to the Nation from the Oval Office. I continue to believe that the microphone is necessary to call people to action. And I want to work with both Republicans and Democrats to get a comprehensive bill to my desk. It's in our interest that we do this.

In terms of energy, there's another area where I know we can work together. There is a consensus that we need to move forward with continued research on alternative forms of energy. I've just described them in my opening comments, and be glad to go over them again if you'd like, because they're positive. It's a positive development. We're making progress, and there's more to be done.

So I'm looking forward to working with them. There's a lot of attitude here that says, "Well, you lost the Congress; therefore, you're not going to get anything done." Quite the contrary; I have an interest to get things done. And the Democrat leaders have an interest to get something done to show that they're worthy of their leadership roles. And it is that common ground that I'm confident we can get— we can make positive progress, without either of us compromising principle.

And I know they don't—I know they're not going to change their principles, and I'm not going to change mine. But nevertheless, that doesn't mean we can't find common ground to get good legislation done. That's what the American people want. The truth of the matter is, the American people are sick of the partisanship and name-calling.

I will do my part to elevate the tone, and I'm looking forward to working with them. It's going to be an interesting new challenge. I'm used to it, as Herman [Ken Herman, Cox News] can testify. I was the Governor of Texas with Democrat leadership in the house and the senate, and we were able to get a lot of constructive things done for the State of Texas. And I believe it's going to be possible here—to do so here in the country.

Michael [Michael Allen, Time].

President's Legacy

Q. Thank you, Mr. President. Merry Christmas.

The President. Thank you. Yes.

Q. I've just two questions related to the amazing fact that a quarter of your Presidency lies ahead. First, I keep reading that you'll be remembered only for Iraq, and I wonder what other areas you believe you're building, a record of transformation you hope will last the ages. And second, a followup on Julie's question, what is your plan for either changing your role or keeping control of the agenda at a time when Democrats have both Houses on the Hill, and when the '08 candidates are doing their thing?

The President. Well, one is to set priorities. That's what I've just done, setting a priority. My message is: We can work together. And here are some key areas where we've got to work together, reauthorization of No Child Left Behind, minimum wage. I hope we're able to work together on free trade agreements. We can work together

on Social Security reform and Medicare reform, entitlement reform. We need to work together on energy, immigration, earmarks.

The leadership has expressed their disdain for earmarks; I support their disdain for earmarks. I don't like a process where it's not transparent, where people are able to slip this into a bill without any hearing or without any recognition of who put it in there and why they put it in there. It's just not good for the system, and it's not good for building confidence of the American people in our process or in the Congress.

The first part of the—oh, last 2 years. I'm going to work hard, Michael. I'm going to sprint to the finish, and we can get a lot done. And you're talking about legacy. Here—I know—look, everybody is trying to write the history of this administration even before it's over. I'm reading about George Washington still. My attitude is, if they're still analyzing number 1, 43 ought not to worry about it and just do what he thinks is right and make the tough choices necessary.

We're in the beginning stages of an ideological struggle, Michael. It's going to last a while. And I want to make sure this country is engaged in a positive and constructive way to secure the future for our children. And it's going to be a tough battle.

I also believe the Medicare reform—the first meaningful, significant health care reform that's been passed in a while—is making a huge difference for our seniors. No Child Left Behind has been a significant education accomplishment, and we've got to reauthorize it. We have proven that you can keep taxes low, achieve other objec-

tives, and cut the deficit. The entrepreneurial spirit is high in this country, and one way to keep it high is to keep—let people keep more of their own money.

So there's been a lot of accomplishment. But the true history of any administration is not going to be written until long after the person is gone. It's just impossible for short-term history to accurately reflect what has taken place. Most historians, you know, probably had a political preference, and so their view isn't exactly objective—most short-term historians. And it's going to take a while for people to analyze mine or any other of my predecessors until down the road when they're able to take—watch the long march of history and determine whether or not the decisions made during the 8 years I was President have affected history in a positive way.

I wish you all a happy holiday. Thank you for your attendance. Have fun. Enjoy yourself. For those lucky enough to go to Crawford, perhaps I'll see you down there.

Thank you.

NOTE: The President's news conference began at 10 a.m. in the Indian Treaty Room of the Dwight D. Eisenhower Executive Office Building. In his remarks, he referred to James A. Baker III and Lee H. Hamilton, cochairs, Iraq Study Group; Prime Minister Nuri al-Maliki and former President Saddam Hussein of Iraq; Grand Ayatollah Ali al-Sistani, Iraqi Shiite Leader; Minister of Foreign Affairs Manuchehr Motaki and President Mahmud Ahmadi-nejad of Iran; and Prime Minister Fuad Siniora of Lebanon. A reporter referred to I. Lewis Libby, former Chief of Staff to the Vice President.

Remarks on Signing the Tax Relief and Health Care Act of 2006
December 20, 2006

Thank you all. Please be seated. Thanks for coming. Welcome to the White House.

In a few moments I'm going to sign a bill that will extend tax relief to millions of

American families and small businesses and add momentum to a growing economy. The Tax Relief and Health Care Act of 2006 will maintain key tax reforms, expand our commitment to renewable energy resources, make it easier for Americans to afford health insurance, and open markets overseas for our farmers and small-business owners.

This is a good piece of progrowth legislation, and I'm looking forward to signing it into law. And I appreciate members of my Cabinet who have joined me in thanking the Congress for their good work here at the end of this session. I want to thank Secretary of the Treasury Hank Paulson, Secretary of the Interior Dirk Kempthorne, and Ambassador Sue Schwab for joining us today. Thanks for your service.

I appreciate the Speaker for being here. Mr. Speaker, good piece of work. I thank you for your hard work at the end of the session. You deserve a lot of credit for this fine piece of legislation, as does Senator Bill Frist, Senate majority leader.

I appreciate key Members of the Senate and the House, who got this piece of legislation passed, for joining us today. I want to thank Pete Domenici and Mike DeWine and Rick Santorum for the Senate—I'm going to save the Louisianans here for a minute—and I want to thank the chairman, Bill Thomas, for not only this bill but a lot of other good pieces of legislation we were able to work together on.

I want to say something about these Louisianans. I appreciate them coming. This is a really important piece of legislation for Louisiana for a lot of reasons, not the least of which is it will help provide money so that we can help restore the wetlands in Louisiana. It's an issue that has united the people of Louisiana. People are rightly concerned about the evaporation of wetlands, and this bill is going to help deal with that important issue. And I want to thank Mary and David Vitter for good work on this important bill. Congratulations. Texas people kind of like Louisianans.

[*Laughter*] A lot of us spent some of our youth in Louisiana. [*Laughter*]

As we approach the end of 2006, our economy is strong, it's productive, and it's prosperous. The most recent jobs report shows that our economy created 132,000 new jobs in November. That's good. We have added more than 7 million new jobs since August of 2003, more than Japan and the European Union combined.

The unemployment rate has remained low at 4.5 percent. More Americans are finding work, and more American workers are taking home bigger paychecks. The latest figures show that real hourly wages increased 2.3 percent in the last year. For the typical family of four with both parents working, that means an extra $1,350 for this year.

As we look forward, our goal is to maintain progrowth economic policies that strengthen our economy and help raise the standard of living for all our citizens. The bill I sign today will continue important progress in four key ways. First, the bill will extend key tax relief measures that are critical to expanding opportunity, continuing economic growth, and revitalizing our communities.

To keep America competitive in the world economy, we must make sure our people have the skills they need for the jobs of the 21st century. Many of those jobs are going to require college, so we're extending the deductibility of tuition and higher education expenses to help more Americans go to college so we can compete.

And to keep our Nation leading the world in technology and innovation, we're extending and modernizing the research and development tax credit. By allowing businesses to deduct part of their R&D investments from their taxes, this bill will continue to encourage American companies to pursue innovative products, medicines, and technologies.

The bill will also extend vital provisions of the Gulf Opportunity Zone Act that I

signed last year. The bill will keep in place key tax credits that we passed to help rebuild gulf coast communities that were devastated by the hurricanes that hit the region in 2005. It will allow us to maintain our commitment to provide a 50-percent bonus depreciation for GO Zone properties in the hardest hit areas. It will encourage businesses to build new structures and purchase new equipment in Mississippi and Louisiana.

There is a great spirit of entrepreneurship on the gulf coast, and the incentives in this bill will help our fellow citizens help revive those communities. It's in our Nation's interest that this piece of legislation pass, and it's in our interest that the people of the gulf coast recover as quickly as possible.

Secondly, this bill will help expand and diversify energy supplies. The bill will increase America's energy security by reducing dependence on foreign sources of energy. And that's a key goal of the Advanced Energy Initiative that my administration has laid out. To encourage the development of new sources of energy, the bill will extend tax credits for investment in renewable electricity resources, including wind, solar, biomass, and geothermal energy. It will encourage the development of clean coal technology and renewable fuels like ethanol. And it will help promote new energy efficient technologies that will allow us to do more with less. In other words, it encourages conservation.

Meeting the needs of our growing economy also requires expanding our domestic production of oil and natural gas. If we want to become less dependent on foreign sources of oil and gas, it is best we find some here at home. This bill will allow access to key portions of America's Outer Continental Shelf so we can reach more than 1 billion additional barrels of oil and nearly 6 trillion cubic feet of natural gas.

By developing these domestic resources in a way that protects our environment, we will help address high energy prices, we'll protect American jobs, and we'll reduce our dependence on foreign oil.

The bill will help open new markets for American goods and services around the world. I believe in free and fair trade. I believe free and fair trade is in the interests of the working people of this country. The bill authorizes permanent normal trade relations with Vietnam. And Mr. Ambassador, thanks for joining us.

Vietnam will join the World Trade Organization in January. Isn't that amazing? I think it is. You'd be amazed at what it's like to be in Vietnam; Laura and I just returned. You were there, Mr. Ambassador. You saw the outpouring of affection for the American people. There's amazing changes taking place in your country as your economy has opened up. Vietnam is demonstrating a strong commitment to economic reform, and I believe that's going to encourage political reform and greater respect for human rights and human dignity.

With this bill, America will broaden our trade relations with Vietnam. It's going to help the Vietnamese people build a strong economy that's going to raise their standards of living. It's in our interest to help those who struggle. It's in the interest of the United States to promote prosperity around the world, and the best way to do so is through opening up markets and free and fair trade.

The bill is going to extend a series of programs with other developing nations to give duty-free status to products they export to the United States. By encouraging exports, we're going to help nations in sub-Sahara Africa, the Caribbean, and Latin America develop their economies and ultimately create new markets for U.S. goods and services.

Trade is an engine of economic growth, and I'm looking forward to continuing to work with the new Congress to open up markets for U.S. farmers and manufacturers

and service providers, and provide new opportunities for people around the world, and help eliminate poverty.

Fourth, the bill will help make health care affordable and accessible for more Americans. This bill strengthens health savings accounts, which we created in 2003. These accounts allow people to save money for health care tax free and to take their health savings accounts with them if they move from job to job. So far, an estimated 3.6 million HSAs have been opened in America.

To encourage even more people to sign up for HSAs, the bill will raise contribution limits and make accounts more flexible. It will let people fund their HSAs with one-time transfers from their IRA accounts. It will allow them to contribute up to an annual limit of $2,850, regardless of the deductible for their insurance plan.

We'll give them the option to fully fund their HSAs regardless of what time of year they sign up for the plan. These changes will bring health savings accounts within the reach of more of our citizens and ensure that more Americans can get the quality care they deserve.

With all these steps, we're working to improve the health and prosperity of the American people and to keep our economy growing. We're going to continue to support wise policies that encourage and enhance the entrepreneurial spirit in America, so this country of ours can remain the economic leader in the world.

I want to thank the Members of Congress for joining us. I appreciate the members of my Cabinet. It's now my honor to sign the Tax Relief and Health Care Act of 2006.

NOTE: The President spoke at 11:43 a.m. in Room 450 of the Dwight D. Eisenhower Executive Office Building. In his remarks, he referred to Sen. Mary Landrieu of Louisiana; and Vietnam's Ambassador to the U.S. Nguyen Tam Chien. H.R. 6111, approved December 20, was assigned Public Law No. 109–432.

Statement on Signing the Tax Relief and Health Care Act of 2006
December 20, 2006

Today I have signed into law H.R. 6111, the "Tax Relief and Health Care Act of 2006." The Act prevents tax increases that would have taken effect in the absence of the Act, facilitates effective use of health savings accounts, makes available natural resources of the outer continental shelf, and strengthens American laws in support of free trade.

The executive branch shall construe provisions of the Act, including section 406(c)(2) in Division A and section 203(b) in Division B, that call for executive branch officials to submit legislative recommendations to the Congress, in a manner consistent with the constitutional authority of the President to supervise the unitary executive branch and to recommend for congressional consideration such measures as the President shall judge necessary and expedient.

The executive branch shall construe as advisory provisions of the Act that purport to require concurrence of State officials as a precondition to execution of the laws, including section 415(b) of the Surface Mining Control and Reclamation Act of 1977 as amended by section 207 in Division C and section 311(d) in Division C, as is consistent with the Constitution's vesting in the President of the executive power and the duty to take care that the laws be faithfully executed.

The executive branch shall construe provisions of the Act, including section 4005(b) in Division D and section 213A(f) of the Caribbean Basin Economic Recovery Act as amended by section 5002 in Division D, that purport to make consultation with committees of Congress a precondition to execution of the law, to call for but not mandate such consultation, as is consistent with the Constitution's provisions concerning the separate powers of the Congress to legislate and the President to execute the laws.

GEORGE W. BUSH

The White House,
December 20, 2006.

NOTE: H.R. 6111, approved December 20, was assigned Public Law No. 109–432.

Statement on Signing the Postal Accountability and Enhancement Act
December 20, 2006

Today I have signed into law H.R. 6407, the "Postal Accountability and Enhancement Act." The Act is designed to improve the quality of postal service for Americans and to strengthen the free market for delivery services.

The executive branch shall construe sections 3662 and 3663 of title 39, United States Code, as enacted by section 205 of the Act, not to authorize an officer or agency within the executive branch to institute proceedings in Federal court against the Postal Regulatory Commission, which is another part of the executive branch, as is consistent with the constitutional authority of the President to supervise the unitary executive branch and the constitutional limitation of Federal courts to deciding cases or controversies.

The executive branch shall construe subsection 409(h) of title 39, as enacted by section 404 of the Act, which relates to legal representation for an element of the executive branch, in a manner consistent with the constitutional authority of the President to supervise the unitary executive branch and to take care that the laws be faithfully executed.

The executive branch shall construe section 407 of title 39, as enacted by section 405 of the Act, in a manner consistent with the President's constitutional authority to conduct the Nation's foreign affairs, including the authority to determine which officers shall negotiate for the United States and toward what objectives, to make treaties by and with the advice and consent of the Senate, and to supervise the unitary executive branch.

The executive branch shall construe subsections 202(a) and 502(a) of title 39, as enacted by subsections 501(a) and 601(a) of the Act, which purport to limit the qualifications of the pool of persons from whom the President may select appointees in a manner that rules out a large portion of those persons best qualified by experience and knowledge to fill the positions, in a manner consistent with the Appointments Clause of the Constitution. The executive branch shall also construe as advisory the purported deadline in subsection 605(c) for the making of an appointment, as is consistent with the Appointments Clause.

The executive branch shall construe subsection 404(c) of title 39, as enacted by subsection 1010(e) of the Act, which provides for opening of an item of a class of mail otherwise sealed against inspection, in a manner consistent, to the maximum extent permissible, with the need to conduct searches in exigent circumstances, such as to protect human life and safety against hazardous materials, and the need

for physical searches specifically authorized by law for foreign intelligence collection.

The executive branch shall construe provisions of the Act that call for executive branch officials to submit legislative recommendations to the Congress in a manner consistent with the constitutional authority of the President to supervise the unitary executive branch and to recommend for congressional consideration such measures as the President shall judge necessary and expedient. Such provisions include sub-section 504(d) and section 2009 of title 39, as amended by section 603 of the Act, and sections 701(a)(2), 702(b), 703(b), 708(b), and 709(b)(2) of the Act.

GEORGE W. BUSH

The White House,
December 20, 2006.

NOTE: H.R. 6407, approved December 20, was assigned Public Law No. 109–435.

Statement on Signing the National Transportation Safety Board Reauthorization Act of 2006
December 21, 2006

Today I have signed into law H.R. 5076, the "National Transportation Safety Board Reauthorization Act of 2006." The Act authorizes funding for the Board and makes adjustments to its authority and duties.

Section 2(a)(2) of the Act requires the Board to develop an operating plan for the National Transportation Safety Board Academy, obtain and respond to comments from a legislative agent regarding that plan, submit the plan to congressional committees with a description of modifications made in response to comments from the legislative agent, and then implement the plan within 2 years. The executive branch shall construe the provision in a manner consistent with the Constitution's provisions concerning the separate powers of the Congress to legislate and the President to execute the laws.

The executive branch shall construe section 1113(c) of title 49, United States Code, as amended by section 9(f) of the Act, which relates to the Board's review and comment or approval of documents submitted to the President, Director of the Office of Management and Budget, or Congress, in a manner consistent with the constitutional authority of the President to supervise the unitary executive branch and to recommend for the consideration of the Congress such measures as the President shall judge necessary and expedient.

The executive branch shall construe section 11(c) of the Act, relating to executive branch reports to the Congress concerning investigations of alleged criminal and fraudulent activities in connection with a specified project, in a manner consistent with the constitutional authorities of the President to supervise the unitary executive branch and to withhold information the disclosure of which could impair the performance of the Executive's constitutional duties, including the conduct of investigations and prosecutions to take care that the laws be faithfully executed.

GEORGE W. BUSH

The White House,

December 21, 2006.

NOTE: H.R. 5076, approved December 21, was assigned Public Law No. 109–443. An original was not available for verification of the content of this statement.

Statement on Signing the Palestinian Anti-Terrorism Act of 2006
December 21, 2006

Today I have signed into law S. 2370, the "Palestinian Anti-Terrorism Act of 2006." The Act is designed to promote the development of democratic institutions in areas under the administrative control of the Palestinian Authority.

Section 2 of the Act purports to establish U.S. policy with respect to various international affairs matters. My approval of the Act does not constitute my adoption of the statements of policy as U.S. foreign policy. Given the Constitution's commitment to the presidency of the authority to conduct the Nation's foreign affairs, the executive branch shall construe such policy statements as advisory. The executive branch will give section 2 the due weight that comity between the legislative and executive branches should require, to the extent consistent with U.S. foreign policy.

The executive branch shall construe section 3(b) of the Act, which relates to access to certain information by a legislative agent, and section 11 of the Act, which relates to a report on certain assistance by foreign countries, international organizations, or multilateral development banks, in a manner consistent with the President's constitutional authority to withhold information that could impair foreign relations, national security, the deliberative processes of the Executive, or the performance of the Executive's constitutional duties.

Section 620K(e)(2)(A) and 620L(b)(4)(B)(i) of the Foreign Assistance Act of 1961, as enacted by sections 2(b)(2) and 3(a) of the Act, purport to require the President to consult with committees of the Congress prior to exercising certain authority granted to the President by sections 620K and 620L. Because the constitutional authority of the President to supervise the unitary executive branch and take care that the laws be faithfully executed cannot be made by law subject to a requirement to consult with congressional committees or to involve them in executive decision-making, the executive branch shall construe the references in the provisions to consulting to require only notification.

The executive branch shall construe section 7 of the Act, which relates to establishing or maintaining certain facilities or establishments within the jurisdiction of the United States, in a manner consistent with the President's constitutional authority to conduct the Nation's foreign affairs, including the authority to receive ambassadors and other public ministers.

The executive branch shall construe as advisory the provisions of the Act, including section 9, that purport to direct or burden the conduct of negotiations by the executive branch with entities abroad. Such provisions, if construed as mandatory rather than advisory, would impermissibly interfere with the President's constitutional authorities to conduct the Nation's foreign affairs, including protection of American citizens and American military and other Government personnel abroad, and to supervise the unitary executive branch.

GEORGE W. BUSH

The White House,
December 21, 2006.

NOTE: S. 2370, approved December 21, was assigned Public Law No. 109–446. An original was not available for verification of the content of this statement.

Remarks Following a Visit With Wounded Troops at Walter Reed Army Medical Center
December 22, 2006

Laura and I are honored to be here to thank the folks working here at this service project. What you're seeing is some young kids wrapping gifts for children whose families are here in Washington, DC, as a result of an injury that they've received—that their parent received in combat.

We've also just come from Walter Reed. I got to tell you, it's a remarkable experience to go through the hospital. It's remarkable because of the unbelievable compassion and care of the people who work at Walter Reed. And it's also remarkable to me, these men and women who have volunteered to serve our country, who've received terrible wounds, but whose spirits are strong; their resolve is strong; and their dedication to our country remains strong.

I want all our fellow citizens to understand that we're lucky to have men and women who have volunteered to serve our country like those who wear our uniform. We're lucky to have their families support them so strongly. We owe them all we can give them, not only for when they're in harm's way, but when they come home, to help them adjust if they have wounds or help them adjust after their time in service. We owe a huge debt of gratitude for incredible men and women. And I—every time I come to Walter Reed, I am moved by the courage and bravery of the people I meet.

And so on behalf of a grateful nation, I want to thank our military families, thank the folks here who are wrapping gifts for the military families, and ask for God's blessings on our citizens.

Thank you.

NOTE: The President spoke at 12:01 p.m.

The President's Radio Address
December 23, 2006

Good morning. As families across our Nation gather to celebrate Christmas, Laura and I send our best wishes for the holidays. We hope that your Christmas will be blessed with family and fellowship.

At this special time of year, we give thanks for Christ's message of love and hope. Christmas reminds us that we have a duty to others, and we see that sense of duty fulfilled in the men and women who wear our Nation's uniform. America is blessed to have fine citizens who volunteer to defend us in distant lands. For many of them, this Christmas will be spent far from home, and on Christmas our Nation honors their sacrifice and thanks them for all they do to defend our freedom.

At Christmas, we also recognize the sacrifice of our Nation's military families. Staying behind when a family member goes to war is a heavy burden, and it is particularly hard during the holidays. To all our military families listening today, Laura and I thank you, and we ask the Almighty to bestow His protection and care on your loved ones as they protect our Nation.

This Christmas season comes at a time of change here in our Nation's Capital, with a new Congress set to arrive, a review of our Iraq strategy underway, and a new Secretary of Defense taking office. If you're

serving on the frontlines halfway across the world, it is natural to wonder what all this means for you. I want our troops to know that while the coming year will bring change, one thing will not change, and that is our Nation's support for you and the vital work you do to achieve a victory in Iraq. The American people are keeping you in our thoughts and prayers, and we will make sure you have the resources you need to accomplish your mission.

This Christmas, millions of Americans are coming together to show our deployed forces and wounded warriors love and support. Patriotic groups and charities all across America are sending gifts and care packages to our service men and women, visiting our troops recovering at military hospitals, reaching out to children whose moms and dads are serving abroad, and going to airports to welcome our troops home and to let them know they are appreciated by a grateful nation.

One man who's making a difference this holiday season is Jim Wareing. Jim is the founder of New England Caring for Our Military. This year Jim helped organize a gift drive by thousands of students from Massachusetts and New Hampshire. Students from kindergarten to high school collected more than 20,000 gifts for our troops abroad. The gifts are being sent to troops stationed in Iraq, Afghanistan, Kosovo, Korea, Japan, and Africa. The care packages include books and puzzles, board games, phone cards, fresh socks, and T-shirts, and about 7,000 handmade holiday greeting cards and posters. Jim says, quote, "It's probably always hard for troops to be far away from home, but especially hard on the holidays. I use this as an opportunity to try to pay them back for my freedom."

Citizens like Jim Wareing represent the true strength of our country, and they make America proud. I urge every American to find some way to thank our military this Christmas season. If you see a soldier, sailor, airman, marine, or a member of the Coast Guard, take a moment to stop and say, "Thanks for your service." And if you want to reach out to our troops or help out the military family down the street, the Department of Defense has set up a web site to help. It is americasupportsyou.mil. This web site lists more than 150 compassionate organizations that can use your help. In this season of giving, let us stand with the men and women who stand up for America.

At this special time of year, we reflect on the miraculous life that began in a humble manger 2,000 years ago. That single life changed the world and continues to change hearts today. To everyone celebrating Christmas, Laura and I wish you a day of glad tidings.

Thank you for listening, and Merry Christmas.

NOTE: The address was recorded at 7:35 a.m. on December 22 in the Cabinet Room at the White House for broadcast at 10:06 a.m. on December 23. The transcript was made available by the Office of the Press Secretary on December 22 but was embargoed for release until the broadcast. In his address, the President referred to Secretary of Defense Robert M. Gates. The Office of the Press Secretary also released a Spanish language transcript of this address.

Statement on the Death of James Brown
December 25, 2006

Laura and I are saddened by the death of James Brown. For half a century, the innovative talent of the "Godfather of Soul"

enriched our culture and influenced generations of musicians. An American original, his fans came from all walks of life and backgrounds. James Brown's family and friends are in our thoughts and prayers this Christmas.

Statement on the Death of Former President Gerald R. Ford
December 26, 2006

Laura and I are greatly saddened by the passing of former President Gerald R. Ford.

President Ford was a great American who gave many years of dedicated service to our country. On August 9, 1974, after a long career in the House of Representatives and service as Vice President, he assumed the Presidency in an hour of national turmoil and division. With his quiet integrity, common sense, and kind instincts, President Ford helped heal our land and restore public confidence in the Presidency.

The American people will always admire Gerald Ford's devotion to duty, his personal character, and the honorable conduct of his administration. We mourn the loss of such a leader, and our 38th President will always have a special place in our Nation's memory.

On behalf of all Americans, Laura and I offer our deepest sympathies to Betty Ford and all of President Ford's family. Our thoughts and prayers will be with them in the hours and days ahead.

NOTE: The Office of the Press Secretary also released a Spanish language version of this statement.

Remarks on the Death of Former President Gerald R. Ford in Crawford, Texas
December 27, 2006

My fellow Americans, all of us are saddened by the news that former President Gerald R. Ford passed away last night. I spoke with Betty Ford. On behalf of all Americans, Laura and I extend to Mrs. Ford and all President Ford's family our prayers and our condolences.

President Ford was a great man who devoted the best years of his life in serving the United States. He was a true gentleman who reflected the best in America's character. Before the world knew his name, he served with distinction in the United States Navy and in the United States Congress.

As a Congressman from Michigan and then as Vice President, he commanded the respect and earned the good will of all who had the privilege of knowing him. On August 9th, 1974, he stepped into the Presidency without ever having sought the office. He assumed power in a period of great division and turmoil. For a nation that needed healing and for an office that needed a calm and steady hand, Gerald Ford came along when we needed him most.

During his time in office, the American people came to know President Ford as a man of complete integrity who led our

country with common sense and kind instincts.

Americans will always admire Gerald Ford's unflinching performance of duty and the honorable conduct of his administration and the great rectitude of the man himself. We mourn the loss of such a leader, and our 38th President will always have a special place in our Nation's memory.

President Ford lived 93 years, and his life was a blessing to America. And now this fine man will be taken to his rest by a family that will love him always and by a nation that will be grateful to him forever.

May God bless Gerald Ford.

NOTE: The President spoke at 6:56 a.m. at the Bush Ranch. The Office of the Press Secretary also released a Spanish language transcript of these remarks. The related proclamation of December 27 announcing the death of Gerald R. Ford, the proclamation of December 28 on the national day of mourning for Gerald R. Ford, and the Executive order of December 28 providing for the closing of Government Departments and Agencies on January 2, 2007, are listed in Appendix D at the end of this volume.

Remarks Following a Meeting With the National Security Council in Crawford
December 28, 2006

I just had a meeting with my national security team, and this is the first time we've had a chance to sit down with Secretary Gates since he came back from Iraq. General Pace went with the Secretary. They reported firsthand what they saw, what they found. It's an important part of coming to closure on a way forward in Iraq that will help us achieve our objective, which is a country that can govern itself, sustain itself, and defend itself. And, Mr. Secretary, thank you for your timely trip, and thank you for this important briefing.

I've got more consultation to do until I talk to the country about the plan. Obviously, we'll continue to work with the Iraqi Government. The key to success in Iraq is to have a government that's willing to deal with the elements there that are trying to prevent this young democracy from succeeding.

We want to help them succeed. And so we'll continue to consult with the Iraqis. I'm going to talk to Congress; not only will I continue to reach out to Congress, but members of my team will do so as well.

I fully understand it's important to have both Republicans and Democrats understanding the importance of this mission. It's important for the American people to understand success in Iraq is vital for our own security. If we were to not succeed in Iraq, the enemy—the extremists, the radicals—would have safe haven from which to launch further attacks, they would be emboldened, they would be in a position to threaten the United States of America. This is an important part of the war on terror.

I'm making good progress toward coming up with a plan that we think will help us achieve our objective. As I think about this plan, I'm always—have our troops in mind. There's nobody more important in this global war on terror than the men and women who wear the uniform and their families. And as we head into a new year, my thoughts are with them. My thoughts are with the families who have just gone through a holiday season with their loved one overseas. My thoughts are with the troops as we head into 2007.

People always ask me about a New Year's resolution; my resolution is, is that they'll be safe and that we'll come closer to our objective, that we'll be able to help this young democracy survive and thrive, and therefore, we'll be writing a chapter of peace. I can't thank our families enough for supporting their loved one who wears the uniform, and I can't thank those who—

soldiers and sailors and airmen and Coast Guard men and women, folks in the Air Force—who represent the United States of America. May God continue to bless them.

Thank you all very much.

NOTE: The President spoke at 11:59 a.m. at the Bush Ranch. In his remarks, he referred to Secretary of Defense Robert M. Gates.

Statement on the Death of Former President Saddam Hussein of Iraq
December 29, 2006

Today Saddam Hussein was executed after receiving a fair trial, the kind of justice he denied the victims of his brutal regime.

Fair trials were unimaginable under Saddam Hussein's tyrannical rule. It is a testament to the Iraqi people's resolve to move forward after decades of oppression that, despite his terrible crimes against his own people, Saddam Hussein received a fair trial. This would not have been possible without the Iraqi people's determination to create a society governed by the rule of law.

Saddam Hussein's execution comes at the end of a difficult year for the Iraqi people and for our troops. Bringing Saddam Hus-

sein to justice will not end the violence in Iraq, but it is an important milestone on Iraq's course to becoming a democracy that can govern, sustain, and defend itself and be an ally in the war on terror.

We are reminded today of how far the Iraqi people have come since the end of Saddam Hussein's rule and that the progress they have made would not have been possible without the continued service and sacrifice of our men and women in uniform.

Many difficult choices and further sacrifices lie ahead. Yet the safety and security of the American people require that we not relent in ensuring that Iraq's young democracy continues to progress.

Statement on Signing the Office of National Drug Control Policy Reauthorization Act of 2006
December 29, 2006

Today I have signed into law H.R. 6344, the "Office of National Drug Control Policy Reauthorization Act of 2006" (the "Act"). The Act amends the Office of National Drug Control Policy Reauthorization Act of 1998 (Title VII in Division C of Public Law 105–277) (the "1998 Act") and adjusts the authorities and duties of the Director

of the Office of National Drug Control Policy.

The executive branch shall construe section 704(f)(5) of the 1998 Act, as amended by section 103(e) of the Act, which prohibits taking certain action if it is contrary to the expressed intent of the Congress, as referring to action contrary to a law.

The executive branch shall also construe provisions of the Act that refer to submission of requests to the Congress for reprogramming or transfer of funds, or to obtaining congressional committee approval, such as sections 708(c)(6) and 709(b)(2) of the 1998 Act, as enacted by sections 401 and 501 of the Act, as requiring only notification. Any other construction of these provisions would be inconsistent with the constitutional principles enunciated by the Supreme Court of the United States in *INS v. Chadha*.

The executive branch shall construe provisions of the Act that purport to authorize or require executive branch officials to submit legislative recommendations to the Congress in a manner consistent with the constitutional authority of the President to supervise the unitary executive branch and to recommend for congressional consideration such measures as the President shall judge necessary and expedient. Such provisions include section 711(a)(4) of the 1998 Act as enacted by section 103(f) of the Act and sections 1103(2)(D) and 1110(c) of the Act.

The executive branch shall construe provisions of the Act that concern the making of reports or the submission of classified national security information to the Congress in a manner consistent with the constitutional authority of the President to supervise the unitary executive branch and

to withhold information the disclosure of which could impair foreign relations, the national security, the deliberative processes of the Executive, or the performance of the Executive's constitutional duties. Such provisions include sections 704(c)(2)(A), 706, 711(a)(4), and 711(b)(4) of the 1998 Act, as enacted by sections 103(f), 105(b), and 201 of the Act, and sections 1104, 1109, and 1110 of the Act.

The executive branch shall construe provisions of the Act, including sections 704(c)(1)(C) and 704(c)(3)(C) of the 1998 Act, as enacted by section 105 of the Act, that purport to regulate the content of executive agency budget submissions to an officer within the executive branch in the development of the President's annual budget submission, in a manner consistent with the constitutional authority of the President to require the written opinions of the principal officers of the executive departments and to supervise the unitary executive branch.

GEORGE W. BUSH

The White House,
December 29, 2006.

NOTE: H.R. 6344, approved December 29, was assigned Public Law No. 109–469. An original was not available for verification of the content of this statement.

Message on the Observance of Eid al-Adha
December 29, 2006

I send holiday greetings to all Muslims gathered to celebrate Eid al-Adha.

For Muslims in America and around the world, Eid al-Adha is an important occasion to give thanks for their blessings and to remember Abraham's trust in a loving God. During the four days of this special observance, Muslims honor Abraham's example of

sacrifice and devotion to God by celebrating with friends and family, exchanging gifts and greetings, and engaging in worship through sacrifice and charity.

America is a more hopeful Nation because of the talents, generosity, and compassion of our Muslim citizens. This holiday reminds us of the values that so many of

our citizens hold in common, including love of family, gratitude to God, the importance of community, and a commitment to respect, diversity, tolerance, and religious freedom.

Laura and I offer our best wishes for a memorable holiday.

GEORGE W. BUSH

NOTE: An original was not available for verification of the content of this message.

The President's Radio Address
December 30, 2006

Good morning. This week, as Americans prepare to welcome a new year, we do so with heavy hearts and fond memories of our 38th President, Gerald R. Ford. We mourn the passing of a courageous leader, a true gentleman, and a loving father and husband. On behalf of all Americans, Laura and I send our prayers and condolences to Mrs. Ford and the entire Ford family.

Gerald Ford was a great man who devoted the best years of his long life to public service. He fought for his country during World War II. After returning home, he won the first of 13 elections to the United States Congress. The people of Michigan admired his dedication and decency, and so did his fellow Members of Congress. Gerald Ford rose to become a leader of his party, and he earned the respect and good will of all who had the privilege of knowing him.

Gerald Ford always believed in the importance of answering the call to duty, and he was there for the Nation when we needed him most. In December 1973, he accepted the responsibilities of the Vice Presidency. And the following August, he became President of the United States without ever seeking the office. Providence gave us Gerald Ford's steady hand and calm leadership during a time of great division and turmoil. He guided America through a crisis of confidence and helped our Nation mend its wounds by restoring faith in our system of government.

In his 2½ years as President, Gerald Ford distinguished himself as a man of integrity and selfless dedication. He always put the needs of his country before his own and did what he thought was right, even when those decisions were unpopular. Only years later would Americans come to fully appreciate the foresight and wisdom of this good man.

In recent years, Americans have honored Gerald Ford with the Presidential Medal of Freedom, the Congressional Gold Medal, and the John F. Kennedy Profile in Courage Award.

Through it all, Gerald Ford stayed true to the values that first led him to a life of public service, and he helped share that spirit with a future generation of leaders. He served as a mentor for Vice President Dick Cheney, former Secretary of Defense Don Rumsfeld, former Chairman of the Federal Reserve Alan Greenspan, and many others. He brought out the best in those around him and in our whole Nation.

To the end, Gerald Ford never lost the spirit that Americans grew to admire so much. This spring, I visited President and Mrs. Ford at their home in Rancho Mirage, California. At age 92 and battling health problems, he was still telling jokes and displaying the optimism that helped guide our Nation through some of its darkest hours.

Now America will stand with the members of the Ford family in the difficult hours and days ahead. Across the country, there has been an outpouring of grief and

affection for President Ford. I've ordered flags to fly at halfstaff for 30 days in his honor. This weekend, his body will lie in state at the United States Capitol. And on Tuesday, Laura and I will join former Presidents Clinton, Bush, and Carter at a funeral service at the National Cathedral as part of a National Day of Mourning.

Gerald Ford's life spanned nine decades and took him from the football fields of his boyhood in Michigan to the halls of power in Washington, DC. At every stage of his journey, he displayed a decency, patriotism, and courage that Americans will always admire. As we say goodbye to the year 2006, we bid farewell to one of the finest public servants America has ever

known. We give thanks for the gift of his remarkable life, for the caring man who touched so many lives, and the wise President who helped heal our Nation.

May God bless Gerald R. Ford. Thank you for listening.

NOTE: The address was recorded at 8:20 a.m. on December 29 at the Bush Ranch in Crawford, TX, for broadcast at 10:06 a.m. on December 30. The transcript was made available by the Office of the Press Secretary on December 29 but was embargoed for release until the broadcast. The Office of the Press Secretary also released a Spanish language transcript of this address.

Message on the Observance of New Year's Day 2007
December 31, 2006

Over the past year, we have reached important goals and confronted new challenges. At the start of this New Year, we move forward with trust in the power of the American spirit, confidence in our purpose, and faith in a loving God who created us to be free.

In 2006, the number of jobs steadily increased, wages grew, the unemployment rate dropped, and we achieved our goal of cutting the deficit in half three years ahead of schedule. Thanks to the hard work and innovation of the American people, our economy has been growing faster than any other major developed nation. Significant tax relief has helped our citizens keep more of what they earn and fuel an economy that is vigorous and healthy. My Administration will continue to work to help create more jobs, reduce the deficit, and spread prosperity to all our citizens.

Last year, America continued its mission to fight and win the war on terror and promote liberty as an alternative to tyranny and despair. In the New Year, we will re-

main on the offensive against the enemies of freedom, advance the security of our country, and work toward a free and unified Iraq. Defeating terrorists and extremists is the challenge of our time, and we will answer history's call with confidence and fight for liberty without wavering.

Our Nation depends on the fine men and women in uniform who serve our country with valor and distinction, and we remain mindful of their dedication and sacrifice. America's troops and their families exemplify the great character of our country, and they have earned the respect and admiration of a grateful Nation.

As we celebrate the New Year, we look with hope to the year ahead and the opportunities it will bring.

Laura and I send our best wishes for a happy New Year. May God bless you, may God bless our troops and their families, and may God bless America.

GEORGE W. BUSH

NOTE: An original was not available for verification of the content of this message.

Appendix A—Digest of Other White House Announcements

The following list includes the President's public schedule and other items of general interest announced by the Office of the Press Secretary and not included elsewhere in this book.

July 1

In the morning, at Camp David, MD, the President had an intelligence briefing.

The President declared a major disaster in New York and ordered Federal aid to supplement State and local recovery efforts in the area struck by severe storms and flooding beginning June 26 and continuing.

July 2

In the afternoon, the President and Mrs. Bush returned to Washington, DC.

The President declared a major disaster in Maryland and ordered Federal aid to supplement State and local recovery efforts in the area struck by severe storms, flooding, and tornadoes beginning on June 22 and continuing.

The President declared a major disaster in Ohio and ordered Federal aid to supplement State and local recovery efforts in the area struck by severe storms, tornadoes, straight line winds, and flooding from June 21–23.

July 3

In the morning, the President had an intelligence briefing. Later, he met with Secretary of State Condoleezza Rice. Then, in the Roosevelt Room, he participated in a bill signing ceremony for H.R. 5403, the Safe and Timely Interstate Placement of Foster Children Act of 2006.

The President announced his intention to appoint Kirk Van Tine as a member of the Presidential Emergency Board No. 239 and, upon appointment, to designate him as Chair.

The President announced his intention to appoint Roger P. Nober and Robert E. Peterson as members of the Presidential Emergency Board No. 239.

July 4

In the morning, the President had an intelligence briefing. Later, he traveled to Fort Bragg, NC, where, upon arrival, he met with USA Freedom Corps volunteer Benny Smith, Jr. He then toured U.S. Army Special Operations Command.

Later in the morning, at the 3d Brigade, 82d Airborne Division Dining Facility, the President had lunch with military personnel and their families.

In the afternoon, the President returned to Washington, DC. While en route aboard Air Force One, he participated in an interview with Stars and Stripes newspaper.

During the day, the President met with Secretary of Defense Donald H. Rumsfeld and Secretary of State Condoleezza Rice to discuss the situation in North Korea.

In the evening, in the Residence, the President attended a dinner party to celebrate the Fourth of July and his birthday.

July 5

In the morning, the President had an intelligence briefing and met with the National Security Council. Later, he met with members of the Commission for Assistance to a Free Cuba, who presented him with their official report. He then traveled to Alexandria, VA.

Later in the morning, the President returned to Washington, DC.

In the afternoon, the President had lunch with Vice President Dick Cheney.

The President announced that he has appointed Helgi C. Walker as a member of the District of Columbia Judicial Nomination Commission.

The President declared a major disaster in Delaware and ordered Federal aid to supplement State and local recovery efforts in the area struck by severe storms and flooding beginning on June 23 and continuing.

July 6

In the morning, the President had a telephone conversation with President Vladimir V. Putin of Russia. Later, he had an intelligence briefing. Then, in the Oval Office, he participated in a

photo opportunity with Alexa Ostolaza, the 2006 March of Dimes national ambassador.

In the afternoon, the President had a working lunch with Prime Minister Stephen Harper of Canada. Then, in the Blue Room, he and Mrs. Bush participated in an interview with Larry King of Cable News Network. Later, he traveled to Chicago, IL, where, upon arrival, he met with USA Freedom Corps volunteer Dave Kruger.

The White House announced that the President will host President Traian Basescu of Romania at the White House on July 27.

July 7

In the morning, the President had an intelligence briefing. Later, at Lou Mitchell's Restaurant, he had breakfast with local business leaders.

In the afternoon, the President traveled to Aurora, IL, where he toured Cabot Microelectronics Corp. Later, he returned to Washington, DC.

The President declared a major disaster in New Jersey and ordered Federal aid to supplement State and local recovery efforts in the area struck by severe storms and flooding beginning on June 23 and continuing.

July 8

In the morning, the President had an intelligence briefing.

July 10

In the morning, the President had an intelligence briefing.

In the evening, in the State Dining Room and the East Room, the President and Mrs. Bush hosted a social dinner and entertainment in honor of the Special Olympics.

The President announced his designation of the following individuals as members of a Presidential delegation to Abuja, Nigeria, to attend the Leon H. Sullivan Summit on July 19:

Alphonso R. Jackson (head of delegation);
John Campbell;
John A. Simon;
Herbert H. Lusk II; and
Anita Smith.

The President announced his designation of the following individuals as members of a Presidential delegation to Ulaanbaatar, Mongolia, to attend the 800th anniversary of the Great Mongolian State on July 12 and 13: Mike Johanns (head of delegation); and Robert M. Peck.

The President announced his designation of the following individuals as members of a Presidential delegation to Turkey to attend the opening of the Baku-Tbilisi-Ceyhan Pipeline on July 13: Jeffrey Clay Sell (head of delegation); and Ross Wilson.

July 11

In the morning, the President had breakfast with Republican congressional leaders. Later, he had an intelligence briefing. Then, in the Oval Office, he and Mrs. Bush met with President Alejandro Toledo of Peru and his wife, Eliane Karp de Toledo.

Later in the morning, in the Oval Office, the President had a telephone conversation with crewmembers of the Space Shuttle *Discovery*. He then participated in a photo opportunity with members of the National Council on the Arts.

In the afternoon, the President traveled to Port Washington, WI. Later, he traveled to Milwaukee, WI.

In the evening, the President returned to Washington, DC.

The President announced his intention to nominate Cindy Lou Courville to be U.S. Representative to the African Union with the rank of Ambassador.

The President announced his intention to nominate Philip S. Goldberg to be Ambassador to Bolivia.

The President announced his intention to nominate Henry M. Paulson, Jr., to be U.S. Governor of the following organizations: the International Monetary Fund; the International Bank for Reconstruction and Development; the Inter-American Development Bank; the African Development Fund; the Asian Development Fund; and the European Bank for Reconstruction and Development.

The President announced his intention to nominate John C. Rood to be Assistant Secretary of State for International Security and Non-Proliferation.

The President announced his intention to designate C.W. Bill Young as the President's Personal Representative at the Farnborough International Aerospace and Defense Exhibition and Air Show from July 17–23.

The President announced that he has appointed Peter W. Tredick as a member of the Presidential Emergency Board No. 239.

The President announced that he has appointed Kevin Sullivan as Assistant to the President for Communications.

July 12

In the morning, the President had an intelligence briefing. Later, he and Mrs. Bush traveled to Heiligendamm, Germany, arriving in the evening.

July 13

In the morning, the President had an intelligence briefing. He and Mrs. Bush then traveled to Stralsund, Germany. Later, in the Kollegien Room at the Town Hall, they participated in a guestbook signing ceremony and a greeting with local community representatives.

In the afternoon, in the Achtmannskammer Room of the Town Hall, the President had a working lunch with Chancellor Angela Merkel of Germany. Later, he and Mrs. Bush toured St. Nikolai Church.

In the evening, the President and Mrs. Bush traveled to Trinwillershagen, Germany, where, at the Zu den Linden restaurant, they attended a social dinner and entertainment hosted by Chancellor Merkel. They then returned to Heiligendamm, Germany.

The White House announced that the President will host Prime Minister Nuri al-Maliki of Iraq at the White House on July 25.

The President announced his intention to nominate Richard W. Graber to be Ambassador to the Czech Republic.

The President announced his intention to nominate Christopher A. Padilla to be Assistant Secretary of Commerce (Export Administration).

The President announced his intention to nominate Calvin L. Scovel to be Inspector General at the Department of Transportation.

The President declared a major disaster in Virginia and ordered Federal aid to supplement Commonwealth and local recovery efforts in the area struck by severe storms, tornadoes, and flooding from June 23 to July 6.

July 14

In the morning, the President had an intelligence briefing. Later, he and Mrs. Bush traveled to St. Petersburg, Russia. While en route aboard Air Force One, he had separate telephone conversations with King Abdullah II of Jordan, President Mohamed Hosni Mubarak of Egypt, and Prime Minister Fuad Siniora of Lebanon to discuss the situation in the Middle East.

Later in the morning, upon arrival in St. Petersburg, the President and Mrs. Bush participated in a wreath-laying ceremony at the Monument to the Heroic Defenders of Leningrad.

In the afternoon, the President and Mrs. Bush traveled to Strelna, Russia.

In the evening, in the Italian Guest Room at Konstantinovsky Palace, the President and Mrs. Bush attended a social dinner hosted by President Vladimir V. Putin of Russia and his wife, Lyudmila.

July 15

In the morning, the President had an intelligence briefing.

In the afternoon, at the Konstantinovsky Palace Complex, the President had a working lunch with President Vladimir V. Putin of Russia.

In the evening, the President traveled to Petrodvorets, Russia, where, at the Peterhof, he attended a G–8 summit social dinner and entertainment. Later, he returned to Strelna, Russia.

July 16

In the morning, at the Konstantinovsky Palace Complex, the President participated in G–8 summit meetings. He then met with Junior 8 student leaders.

In the afternoon, the President had a working lunch with G–8 leaders. Later, he participated in G–8 summit meetings.

In the evening, the President had a working dinner with G–8 leaders.

July 17

In the morning, the President had an intelligence briefing. Later, at the Konstantinovsky Palace Complex, he participated in G–8 summit meetings.

In the afternoon, the President had a working lunch with G–8 leaders. Later, he participated in a photo opportunity with G–8 leaders and leaders of international organizations. Later, he and Mrs. Bush returned to Washington, DC.

The President announced his designation of the following individuals as members of a Presidential delegation to Lima, Peru, to attend the inauguration of President Alan Garcia Perez of Peru on July 28: Carlos M. Gutierrez (head of delegation); and James Curtis Struble.

The President announced his intention to nominate Clyde Bishop to be Ambassador to the Marshall Islands.

The President announced his intention to nominate Mark R. Dybul to be Coordinator of the U.S. Government Activities to Combat HIV/AIDS Globally with the rank of Ambassador.

The President announced his intention to nominate Peter W. Tredick to be a member of the National Mediation Board.

The President announced his intention to nominate Stephen M. Prescott and Anne Jeannette Udall to be members of the Board of Trustees of the Morris K. Udall Scholarship and Excellence in National Environmental Policy Foundation.

The President announced his intention to appoint Louis Mead Treadwell II, Vera K. Metcalf, and Charles J. Vorosmarty as members of the National Arctic Research Commission.

The President announced his intention to appoint Tim Pawlenty as a member of the National Infrastructure Advisory Council.

The President announced his intention to appoint Sidney R. Unobskey as an alternate member of the Roosevelt Campobello International Park Commission.

July 18

In the morning, the President had an intelligence briefing. Later, in the Oval Office, he participated in a photo opportunity with members of the National Capital Area Council of the Boy Scouts of America. Then, in Room 350 of the Dwight D. Eisenhower Executive Office Building, he participated in a photo opportunity with 2006 Indianapolis 500 winner Sam Hornish, Jr., and his wife, Crystal.

In the evening, the President and Mrs. Bush hosted a dinner for former Archbishop of Washington Theodore E. Cardinal McCarrick, incoming Archbishop of Washington Donald W. Wuerl, and Papal Nuncio Archbishop Pietro Sambi.

July 19

In the morning, the President had an intelligence briefing. Later, in the Oval Office, he met with Secretary of Defense Donald H. Rumsfeld.

In the afternoon, in the Oval Office, the President met with Secretary of State Condoleezza Rice.

The White House announced that the President will welcome Salva Kiir Mayardit, First Vice President of Sudan and President of Southern Sudan, to the White House on July 20.

July 20

In the morning, the President had an intelligence briefing. Later, he had a telephone conversation with Prime Minister Recep Tayyip Erdogan of Turkey to discuss the situation in Lebanon and recent terrorist attacks in Turkey.

Also in the morning, the President dropped by a meeting between Vice Chairman of the Central Military Commission Gen. Guo Boxiong of China and National Security Adviser Stephen J. Hadley.

In the afternoon, the President had lunch with Vice President Dick Cheney.

The President announced his intention to nominate Sharon Lynn Hays to be Associate Director of the Office of Science and Technology Policy.

The President announced his intention to nominate Robert W. Johnson to be Commissioner of Reclamation at the Department of the Interior.

The President announced his intention to nominate James R. Kunder to be Deputy Administrator of the U.S. Agency for International Development.

The President announced his intention to nominate Mary Martin Ourisman to be Ambassador to Barbados, Ambassador to Saint Kitts and Nevis, Ambassador to Saint Lucia, Ambassador to Antigua and Barbuda, Ambassador to Dominica, Ambassador to Grenada, and Ambassador to Saint Vincent and the Grenadines.

The President announced his intention to nominate Bijan Rafiekian to be a member of the Board of Directors of the Export-Import Bank of the U.S.

The President announced his intention to nominate Karen B. Stewart to be Ambassador to Belarus.

The President announced his intention to nominate Todd I. Stewart to be a member of the National Security Education Board.

The President announced his intention to nominate Jane Marie Doggett to be a member of the National Council on the Humanities.

July 21

In the morning, the President had an intelligence briefing. Later, he traveled to Aurora, CO.

In the afternoon, the President traveled to Englewood, CO. Later, at a private residence, he made remarks at a reception for congressional candidate Rick O'Donnell. He then traveled to the Bush Ranch in Crawford, TX.

The White House announced that the President will welcome Prime Minister Tony Blair of the United Kingdom to the White House on July 28.

The President declared an emergency in Missouri and ordered Federal aid to supplement State and local response efforts in the area struck by severe storms beginning on July 19 and continuing.

July 22

In the morning, the President had an intelligence briefing.

July 23

In the morning, the President returned to Washington, DC.

In the afternoon, in the Oval Office, the President met with Minister of Foreign Affairs Saud al-Faysal bin Abd al-Aziz Al Saud of Saudi Arabia.

During the day, the President had a telephone conversation with 2006 Tour de France winner Floyd Landis to congratulate him on his victory.

July 24

In the morning, the President had an intelligence briefing. Later, at Walter Reed Army Medical Center, he met with U.S. military personnel injured in Iraq and presented Purple Hearts to four soldiers.

In the afternoon, in the Oval Office, the President participated in a bill signing ceremony for H.R. 42, the Freedom to Display the American Flag Act of 2005.

In the evening, at the historic Evermay house, the President attended a Republican National Committee reception.

The White House announced that the President will meet with Sudan Liberation Movement Army leader Minni Minawi at the White House on July 25.

July 25

In the morning, the President had an intelligence briefing.

In the afternoon, in the Old Family Dining Room, the President had a working lunch with Prime Minister Nuri al-Maliki of Iraq. Later, in the Oval Office, he met with Sudan Liberation Movement Army leader Minni Minawi. He then met with Republican congressional leaders to discuss legislative priorities.

The President announced his intention to nominate Margrethe Lundsager to be U.S. Executive Director of the International Monetary Fund.

The President announced his intention to nominate Ronald A. Tschetter to be Director of the Peace Corps.

The President announced his intention to nominate Dianne I. Moss to be a member of the Board of Directors of the Overseas Private Investment Corporation.

The President announced his intention to appoint W. Craig Vanderwagen as Assistant Secretary for Public Health Emergency Preparedness at the Department of Health and Human Services.

The President announced his intention to designate Stephen R. Larson as Acting General Counsel for the Department of the Treasury.

The President announced his intention to designate Arthur T. Hopkins as Acting Assistant to the Secretary of Defense for Nuclear and Chemical and Biological Defense Programs.

The President announced his designation of Ronald J. James as Acting Chief Human Capital Officer at the Department of Homeland Security.

July 26

In the morning, the President had an intelligence briefing. Later, in the Oval Office, he met with Secretary of Defense Donald H. Rumsfeld. Then, in the Indian Treaty Room of the Dwight D. Eisenhower Executive Office Building, he participated in a photo opportunity with recipients of the 2005 Presidential Early Career Awards for Scientists and Engineers.

In the afternoon, the President and Prime Minister Nuri al-Maliki of Iraq traveled to Fort Belvoir, VA. Later, he traveled to Charleston, WV, where, upon arrival, he met with USA Freedom Corps volunteer Joe Dailey. Then, at a private residence, he attended a Shelley Moore Capito for Congress reception.

In the evening, the President returned to Washington, DC.

July 27

In the morning, the President had a telephone conversation with Chancellor Angela Merkel of Germany to discuss the situation in the Middle East. Later, he had an intelligence briefing.

In the afternoon, the President had a working lunch with President Traian Basescu of Romania. Later, in the State Dining Room, he participated in a photo opportunity with members of the National Future Farmers of America Organization State Presidents' Conference.

The President announced his intention to appoint Donald G. Christensen, Jeffrey W. Gault, and Samuel Metters as members of the National Veterans Business Development Corporation.

The President announced his intention to appoint the following individuals as members of the National Cancer Advisory Board:

Anthony Atala (Science/Environmental Carcinogens);
Bruce Allan Chabner (Science);
Donald S. Coffey (Science);
Lloyd K. Everson (Public);
Judah Folkman (Science);
Robert A. Ingram (Public); and
Karen Dow Meneses (Science).

The President announced his intention to designate Carolyn D. Runowicz as Chairman of the National Cancer Advisory Board.

July 28

In the morning, the President had an intelligence briefing. Later, in the Oval Office, he participated in a photo opportunity with the Big Brother of the Year, Sylvester Fulton, and the Big Sister of the Year, Betsy Gorman-Bernardi.

In the afternoon, the President had lunch with Prime Minister Tony Blair of the United Kingdom. Later, in the Oval Office, he participated in a photo opportunity with the top 10 "American Idol" finalists. Then, in the East Room, he participated in a photo opportunity with the 2006 Boys and Girls Nation delegates.

July 29

In the morning, the President had an intelligence briefing.

July 30

In the afternoon, the President traveled to Miami, FL. While en route aboard Air Force One, he had a telephone conversation with Secretary of State Condoleezza Rice to discuss her ongoing visit to the Middle East. Upon arrival in Miami, he met with USA Freedom Corps volunteer Dorcas Piegari.

During the day, the President had several separate telephone conversations with Secretary of State Condoleezza Rice, Prime Minister Tony Blair of the United Kingdom, and National Security Adviser Stephen J. Hadley to discuss the situation in the Middle East.

In the evening, the President traveled to Miami Beach, FL, where he attended a dinner with community leaders. He then returned to Miami.

July 31

In the morning, the President had an intelligence briefing. Later, at the Versailles Restaurant and Bakery, he participated in an interview with Radio Mambi. He then visited the National Hurricane Center.

Later in the morning, at the U.S. Coast Guard Integrated Support Command, the President participated in an interview with Michael Putney of WPLG–TV Miami.

In the afternoon, at the U.S. Coast Guard Integrated Support Command, the President participated in separate interviews with Pedro Sevcec of Telemundo and Neil Cavuto of FOX News. Later, he traveled to Coral Gables, FL, where, at a private residence, he attended a Republican National Committee luncheon. He then returned to Washington, DC.

In the evening, the President met with Secretary of State Condoleezza Rice to discuss her recent visit to the Middle East.

The President announced his intention to nominate Randolph James Clerihue to be Assistant Secretary of Labor for Public Affairs.

The President announced his intention to nominate Susan E. Dudley to be Administrator of the Office of Information and Regulatory Affairs at the Office of Management and Budget.

The President announced his intention to nominate Michael F. Duffy to be a member of the Federal Mine Safety and Health Review Commission and, upon confirmation, to designate him as Chairman.

The President announced his intention to nominate Roger Romulus Martella, Jr., to be

Assistant Administrator of the Environmental Protection Agency (General Counsel).

The President announced his intention to nominate Arthur K. Reilly to be a member of the National Science Board (National Science Foundation).

The President announced that he has appointed Bryan Corbett as Special Assistant to the President for Economic Policy.

The President announced that he has appointed Kenneth Kiyul Lee as Associate Counsel to the President.

The President announced that he has appointed Andrea Becker Looney as Special Assistant to the President for Legislative Affairs.

The President announced that he has appointed Michael Magan as Special Assistant to the President and Senior Director for Relief, Stabilization, and Development of the National Security Council.

The President announced that he has appointed Scott Walter as Special Assistant to the President for Domestic Policy.

August 1

In the morning, the President had an intelligence briefing. Later, he traveled to Bethesda, MD, where, at the National Naval Medical Center, he had his annual physical examination and visited wounded U.S. military personnel and presented Purple Hearts to seven of them.

In the afternoon, the President returned to Washington, DC. Later, in the Solarium, he met with Republican Senators.

The President announced his intention to nominate C. Stephen Allred to be Assistant Secretary of the Interior for Land and Mineral Management.

The President announced his intention to nominate Carl Joseph Artman to be Assistant Secretary of the Interior for Indian Affairs and to appoint him as a member of the Board of Trustees of the American Folklife Center.

The President announced his intention to nominate Alex A. Beehler to be Inspector General of the Environmental Protection Agency.

The President announced his intention to nominate Wilma B. Liebman to be a member of the National Labor Relations Board.

The President announced his intention to nominate Leland A. Strom to be a member of the Farm Credit Administration Board.

The President announced his intention to nominate James H. Bilbray to be a Governor of the Board of Governors of the U.S. Postal Service.

The President announced his intention to nominate Charles R. Christopherson, Jr., to be a member of the Board of Directors of the Commodity Credit Corporation.

The President declared a major disaster in Ohio and ordered Federal aid to supplement State and local recovery efforts in the area struck by severe storms, straight line winds, and flooding on July 27 and continuing.

August 2

In the morning, the President had an intelligence briefing. Later, he met with Secretary of Defense Donald H. Rumsfeld. He then met with Republican Senators.

In the afternoon, the President met with Secretary of the Treasury Henry M. Paulson, Jr. Later, he participated in a photo opportunity with Make-a-Wish Foundation children. He then traveled to Mentor, OH.

Later in the afternoon, the President traveled to Kirtland Hills, OH, where, at a private residence, he attended a reception for Ohio gubernatorial candidate J. Kenneth Blackwell. He then returned to Washington, DC.

August 3

In the morning, the President had an intelligence briefing.

In the afternoon, the President traveled to McAllen, TX. While en route aboard Air Force One, he had a telephone conversation with Chancellor Angela Merkel of Germany to discuss the situation in the Middle East. Upon arrival in McAllen, he participated in a tour of Border Patrol and National Guard assets.

Later in the afternoon, the President traveled to Mission, TX, where he viewed a demonstration of the Border Patrol-National Guard Skybox. Later, he traveled to the Bush Ranch in Crawford, TX.

The President announced his intention to nominate Nelson M. Ford to be Assistant Secretary of the Army (Financial Management).

The President announced his intention to nominate Cynthia A. Glassman to be Undersecretary of Commerce for Economic Affairs.

The President announced his intention to nominate John K. Veroneau to be Deputy U.S. Trade Representative with the rank of Ambassador.

The President announced his intention to nominate Gerald Walpin to be Inspector General of the Corporation for National and Community Service.

The President announced his intention to nominate William H. Graves to be a member of the Board of Directors of the Tennessee Valley Authority.

The President announced his intention to nominate the following individuals to be Commissioners of the Mississippi River Commission:

Bruce Arlan Berwick;
Robert Crear and, upon confirmation, to designate him President;
Samuel P. De Bow, Jr.; and
Gregg F. Martin.

The President announced that he has appointed Jay Hein as Deputy Assistant to the President and Director of the Office of Faith-Based and Community Initiatives.

August 4

In the morning, the President had an intelligence briefing.

The President announced his designation of the following individuals as members of a Presidential delegation to attend the funeral of former Prime Minister Ryutaro Hashimoto of Japan on August 8: Norman Y. Mineta (head of delegation); and John Thomas Schieffer.

The President announced his designation of the following individuals as members of a Presidential delegation to attend the inauguration of President Alvaro Uribe Velez of Colombia on August 7: Henry M. Paulson, Jr. (head of delegation); Carlos M. Gutierrez; and William B. Wood.

The President declared a major disaster in Alaska and ordered Federal aid to supplement State and local recovery efforts in the area struck by snow melt and ice jam flooding from May 13–30.

August 5

In the morning, the President had an intelligence briefing.

During the day, the President met with Secretary of State Condoleezza Rice and National Security Adviser Stephen J. Hadley to discuss the situation in the Middle East.

August 6

In the morning, the President and National Security Adviser Stephen J. Hadley participated in a video teleconference with Prime Minister Tony Blair of the United Kingdom.

August 7

In the morning, the President had an intelligence briefing.

August 8

In the morning, the President had an intelligence briefing followed by briefings by National Security Adviser Stephen J. Hadley and Homeland Security Adviser Frances Fragos Townsend.

August 9

In the morning, the President had an intelligence briefing.

In the afternoon, the President had a telephone conversation with Prime Minister Tony Blair of the United Kingdom.

During the day, the President had separate telephone conversations with Secretary of State Condoleezza Rice and National Security Adviser Stephen J. Hadley.

The President announced that he has named Deb Fiddelke as Deputy Assistant to the President for Legislative Affairs.

The President announced that he has named Neal Burnham as Special Assistant to the President for White House Management.

The President announced that he has named Darren Hipp as Special Assistant to the President and Director of Presidential Correspondence.

The President announced that he has named Gregory Jacob as Special Assistant to the President for Domestic Policy.

The President announced that he has named Brent J. McIntosh as Associate Counsel to the President.

August 10

In the morning, the President had an intelligence briefing and a briefing on the arrests of suspected terrorists in Birmingham and London, England. Later, he traveled to Green Bay, WI, where, upon arrival, he met with USA Freedom Corps volunteer Karl Durant. He then participated in a tour of Fox Valley Metal-Tech, Inc.

In the afternoon, the President traveled to Oneida, WI, where, at a private residence, he attended a reception for congressional candidate John G. Gard. Later, at Oneida Police Department, he met family members of military personnel killed in Iraq. He then returned to the Bush Ranch in Crawford, TX.

August 11

In the morning, the President had an intelligence briefing.

In the afternoon, the President traveled to the Broken Spoke Ranch, where he attended a Republican National Committee reception. He then returned to the Bush Ranch.

Later in the afternoon, the President had a telephone conversation with Prime Minister Ehud Olmert of Israel to discuss the United Nations draft resolution to end fighting in Lebanon.

August 12

In the morning, the President had a telephone conversation with Prime Minister Fuad Siniora of Lebanon to discuss U.N. Security Council Resolution 1701 to establish a cease-fire in Lebanon. Later, he had an intelligence briefing.

August 13

In the afternoon, the President returned to Washington, DC.

August 14

In the morning, the President had an intelligence briefing. Later, he had a telephone conversation with Prime Minister Romano Prodi of Italy to discuss the situation in Lebanon. He then traveled to Arlington, VA.

In the afternoon, at the Pentagon, the President had a working lunch with experts on Iraq. Later, he returned to Washington, DC. Then, in the Oval Office, he participated in a bill signing ceremony for H.R. 5683, providing for the Federal acquisition of the Mt. Soledad Veterans Memorial in San Diego, CA.

August 15

In the morning, the President had an intelligence briefing. Later, he traveled to McLean, VA, where, at the National Counterterrorism Center, he participated in National Security Council and Homeland Security Council briefings.

In the afternoon, the President had a working lunch with counterterrorism and homeland security experts. Later, he met with his homeland security team. He then returned to Washington, DC.

The President announced his intention to appoint John Edward Niederhuber as Director of the National Cancer Institute at the Department of Health and Human Services.

The President announced his intention to appoint Marta Brito Perez as Chief Human Capital Officer at the Department of Homeland Security.

The President announced his intention to appoint the following individuals as members of the Congressional Executive Commission on the People's Republic of China: Christopher R. Hill (At Large Representative); Franklin L. Lavin (Department of Commerce Representative); and Barry F. Lowenkron (State Department Representative).

The President announced his intention to appoint Nancy Davenport as a member of the National Historical Publications and Records Commission.

The President declared a major disaster in Texas and ordered Federal aid to supplement State and local recovery efforts in the area struck by flooding beginning July 31 and continuing.

August 16

In the morning, the President had an intelligence briefing. Later, he granted pardons to 17 individuals.

In the afternoon, the President traveled to York, PA, where he toured Harley-Davidson Vehicle Operations. Later, he participated in a roundtable discussion on the economy with Harley-Davidson managers and workers. He then participated in an interview with USA Today.

Later in the afternoon, the President traveled to Lancaster, PA.

In the evening, the President returned to Washington, DC.

The White House announced that the President will welcome President Roh Moo-hyun of South Korea to the White House on September 14.

The President announced that he has named David McCormick as Deputy Assistant to the President and Deputy National Security Adviser for International Economic Affairs.

The President announced that he has named Jennifer Christie as Special Assistant to the President for Presidential Personnel.

August 17

In the morning, the President had an intelligence briefing. Later, he met with Secretary of Defense Donald H. Rumsfeld, military commanders, and senior military advisers to discuss the war on terror.

In the afternoon, the President traveled to Camp David, MD.

In the evening, the President met with his economic team.

August 18

In the morning, the President had an intelligence briefing.

The White House announced that the President will welcome President Alan Garcia Perez of Peru to the White House on October 10.

August 19

In the morning, the President had an intelligence briefing.

August 20

In the afternoon, the President and Mrs. Bush returned to Washington, DC.

August 21

In the morning, the President had an intelligence briefing.

August 22

In the morning, the President had an intelligence briefing. Later, he met with the Homeland Security Council to discuss avian influenza.

Also in the morning, the President had a telephone conversation with President Hamid Karzai of Afghanistan.

In the afternoon, the President traveled to Minnetonka, MN, where, upon arrival, he met with USA Freedom Corps volunteer David Jewison. Later, he traveled to Wayzata, MN, where he visited Glaciers Custard and Coffee Cafe. Then, at a private residence, he attended a reception for congressional candidate Michele Bachmann.

In the evening, the President returned to Washington, DC.

The President announced his intention to nominate Charles L. Glazer to be Ambassador to El Salvador.

The President announced his intention to appoint Dennis Prager as a member of the U.S. Holocaust Memorial Council.

The President announced his intention to appoint the following individuals as members of the Board of Trustees of the John F. Kennedy Center for the Performing Arts:

Edward William Easton;
James A. Haslam II;
Helen Lee Henderson;
Nancy G. Kinder;
Michael Frederic Neidorff; and
Dean A. Spanos.

August 23

In the morning, the President had an intelligence briefing. He then had a telephone conversation with President Pervez Musharraf of Pakistan to discuss U.S.-Pakistan relations and regional issues. Later, in the Oval Office, he met with Secretary of State Condoleezza Rice.

Also in the morning, in the Map Room, the President participated in separate interviews with WWL–TV, WVUE–TV, and WGNO–TV of New Orleans, LA, and WLOX–TV of Biloxi, MS. He also had a telephone conversation with United Nations Secretary-General Kofi Annan to discuss U.N. peacekeeping efforts in Lebanon and the situations in Iran and Darfur, Sudan.

In the afternoon, the President traveled to Alexandria, VA, where, at a private residence, he attended a reception for senatorial candidate George Allen.

In the evening, the President returned to Washington, DC.

August 24

In the morning, the President had an intelligence briefing. Later, he had separate telephone conversations with Prime Minister Romano Prodi of Italy and Chancellor Angela Merkel of Germany to discuss the situations in Lebanon and Iran.

Later in the morning, the President traveled to Kennebunk, ME, where, at Sea Road School, he met with family members of military personnel killed in Iraq, Afghanistan, and during the September 11, 2001, terrorist attacks.

In the afternoon, the President traveled to the Bush family home in Kennebunkport, ME.

August 25

In the morning, the President had an intelligence briefing.

The White House announced that the President and Mrs. Bush will host a White House Summit on Malaria in December.

August 26

In the morning, the President had an intelligence briefing.

August 27

In the afternoon, the President and Mrs. Bush returned to Washington, DC.

August 28

In the morning, the President had an intelligence briefing followed by a briefing on Hurricane Ernesto. He and Mrs. Bush then traveled to Biloxi, MS. While en route aboard Air Force One, they participated in an interview with April Ryan of American Urban Radio Network.

Later in the morning, upon arrival at Kessler Air Force Base in Biloxi, the President met with U.S. military personnel. Later, he and Mrs. Bush participated in a walking tour of a neighborhood damaged by Hurricane Katrina in 2005.

In the afternoon, the President and Mrs. Bush traveled to Gulfport, MS, where, upon arrival, he met with USA Freedom Corps volunteer Ken Wetzel. Later, they traveled to New Orleans, LA, where they had dinner with State and local officials.

August 29

In the morning, the President had an intelligence briefing. Later, at Betsy's Pancake House, he had breakfast with Mayor C. Ray Nagin of New Orleans, LA. Then, at the Windsor Court Hotel, he and Mrs. Bush participated in an interview with Garland Robinette of WWL Radio of New Orleans.

Later in the morning, at the St. Louis Cathedral, the President and Mrs. Bush attended a service commemorating the first anniversary of Hurricane Katrina.

In the afternoon, the President and Mrs. Bush toured the Musicians' Village housing development and hosted a lunch for Habitat for Humanity volunteers. He also presented a National Medal of the Arts to entertainer Antoine "Fats" Domino as a replacement for the original medal, which was lost during Hurricane Katrina.

Later in the afternoon, the President and Mrs. Bush participated in an interview with Brian Williams of NBC News. Later, at the Louis Armstrong New Orleans International Airport,

he and Mrs. Bush participated in a photo opportunity with the National Football League's New Orleans Saints. He then traveled to the Bush Ranch in Crawford, TX.

The President announced his intention to nominate Robert T. Howard to be Assistant Secretary of Veterans Affairs (Information and Technology).

The President announced his intention to nominate Collister Johnson, Jr., to be Administrator of the Saint Lawrence Seaway Development Corporation.

The President announced his intention to nominate Sara Martinez Tucker to be Under Secretary of Education.

The President announced his intention to nominate Peter E. Cianchette to be a member of the Internal Revenue Service Oversight Board.

The President announced his intention to designate Naomi Churchill Earp as Chairman of the Equal Employment Opportunity Commission.

The President announced his intention to designate James R. Kunder as Acting Deputy Administrator of the U.S. Agency for International Development.

August 30

In the morning, the President had an intelligence briefing. Later, he traveled to Little Rock, AR, where, upon arrival, he met with USA Freedom Corps volunteer Joy Cameron.

In the afternoon, at a private residence, the President attended a luncheon for gubernatorial candidate Asa Hutchinson. Later, he traveled to Nashville, TN, where, upon arrival, he met with USA Freedom Corps volunteer Patricia Gray.

In the evening, the President traveled to Salt Lake City, UT, where, upon arrival, he met with USA Freedom Corps volunteer Sam Delis.

The White House announced that the President will welcome Amir Sabah al-Ahmad al-Jabir al-Sabah of Kuwait to the White House on September 5.

The President announced his intention to nominate Terrence W. Boyle and William James Haynes II to be U.S. Circuit judges for the Fourth Circuit.

The President announced his intention to nominate William Gerry Myers III and Norman Randy Smith to be U.S. Circuit judges for the Ninth Circuit.

The President announced his intention to nominate Michael Brunson Wallace to be a U.S. Circuit judge for the Fifth Circuit.

The President declared a major disaster in New Mexico and ordered Federal aid to supplement State and local recovery efforts in the area struck by severe storms and flooding on July 26 and continuing.

August 31

In the morning, the President had an intelligence briefing. Later, he met with leaders of the Church of Jesus Christ of Latter-Day Saints (LDS) at their administration building.

In the afternoon, the President traveled to Camp David, MD.

The President announced his intention to recess appoint Paul DeCamp as Administrator of the Wage and Hour Division at the Department of Labor.

The President announced his intention to recess appoint Michael F. Duffy as a member of the Federal Mine Safety and Health Review Commission.

The President announced his intention to recess appoint Daniel Meron as General Counsel of the Department of Health and Human Services.

The President announced his intention to designate Michael J. Sullivan as Acting Director of the Bureau of Alcohol, Tobacco, Firearms, and Explosives.

September 1

In the morning, the President had an intelligence briefing.

The President announced that he has named Marc Thiessen as Deputy Assistant to the President and Deputy Director of Speechwriting.

The President announced that he has named Martha Miller as Special Assistant to the President for Presidential Personnel.

The President announced that he has named David Trulio as Special Assistant to the President and Executive Secretary of the Homeland Security Council.

The President announced that he has named Dennis C. Wilder as Special Assistant to the President and Senior Director for East Asian Affairs of the National Security Council.

September 2

In the morning, the President had an intelligence briefing.

September 3

In the afternoon, the President and Mrs. Bush returned to Washington, DC.

September 4

In the morning, the President had an intelligence briefing. Later, he traveled to Piney Point, MD.

In the afternoon, the President returned to Washington, DC.

September 5

In the morning, the President had an intelligence briefing. Later, he met with Secretary of the Treasury Henry M. Paulson, Jr.

In the afternoon, the President had a working lunch with Amir Sabah al-Ahmad al-Jabir al-Sabah of Kuwait.

The President announced his intention to nominate Mary E. Peters to be Secretary of Transportation.

The President announced his intention to nominate Robert K. Steel to be Under Secretary of the Treasury (Domestic Finance).

The President announced his intention to nominate Mary Amelia Bomar to be Director of the National Park Service and to appoint her as a member of the Board of Trustees of the American Folklife Center.

The President announced his intention to nominate Larry W. Brown, John E. Mansfield, and Peter S. Winokur to be members of the Defense Nuclear Facilities Safety Board.

The President announced his intention to nominate William W. Mercer to be Associate Attorney General and to designate him as Acting Associate Attorney General of the Department of Justice.

The President announced his intention to nominate Charles F. Conner to be a member of the Board of Directors of the Commodity Credit Corporation.

The President announced his intention to appoint Denis Bovin and Martin S. Feldstein as members of the President's Foreign Intelligence Advisory Board.

The President announced his intention to appoint Dallas Rob Sweezy as a member of the President's Committee for People With Intellectual Disabilities and, upon appointment, to designate him as Chair.

The President announced his intention to appoint the following individuals as members of

the President's Committee for People With Intellectual Disabilities:

Clayton Aiken;
Stephen Bird;
Valerie Billmire;
James Boles;
Stephanie Brown;
William J. Edwards;
Brian J. Kelly;
Mary Margaret Pucci;
Linda Hampton Starnes;
Stephen Henry Suroviec; and
William E. Tienken.

September 6

In the morning, the President had an intelligence briefing. Later, he participated in an interview with Katie Couric of the CBS Evening News.

The President announced that he has promoted Anita B. McBride to be Assistant to the President and Chief of Staff to the First Lady.

September 7

In the morning, the President had an intelligence briefing. Later, he traveled to Atlanta, GA. While en route aboard Air Force One, he participated in an interview with Charles Gibson of ABC News.

Later in the morning, the President traveled to Marietta, GA, where, upon arrival, he met with USA Freedom Corps volunteer Margaret Rose Halbert.

In the afternoon, the President traveled to Savannah, GA, where, upon arrival, he met with USA Freedom Corps volunteer Mary Nelson Adams. He then traveled to Pooler, GA. Later, he returned to Washington, DC. While en route aboard Air Force One, he participated in an interview with Paul Gigot of the Wall Street Journal.

The White House announced that the President will visit Tallinn, Estonia, on November 28 and Riga, Latvia, where he will participate in the North Atlantic Treaty Organization summit on November 28 and 29.

The President announced his intention to nominate Lauren M. Maddox to be Assistant Secretary of Education (Communications and Outreach).

The President announced his intention to nominate Jovita Carranza to be Deputy Administrator of the Small Business Administration.

The President announced his intention to nominate Donald Y. Yamamoto to be Ambassador to Ethiopia.

The President announced his intention to nominate Dean A. Pinkert and Irving A. Williamson to be Commissioners of the U.S. International Trade Commission.

The President announced his intention to designate Leslie Silverman as Vice Chairman of the Equal Employment Opportunity Commission.

The President declared a major disaster in Arizona and ordered Federal aid to supplement State and local recovery efforts in the area struck by severe storms and flooding from July 25 to August 4.

September 8

In the morning, the President had an intelligence briefing. Later, he participated in an interview with Matt Lauer of NBC News. He then traveled to Flint, MI, where, upon arrival, he met with USA Freedom Corps volunteer Greg Ybarra.

In the afternoon, the President traveled to Clarkston, MI, where, at a private residence, he attended a reception for senatorial candidate Michael J. Bouchard. Later, he traveled to Kansas City, MO, where, upon arrival, he met with USA Freedom Corps volunteers Bradley Fisher and Taylor Mayes. Later, at a private residence, he attended a reception for senatorial candidate James M. Talent.

In the evening, the President returned to Washington, DC.

September 9

In the morning, the President had an intelligence briefing.

September 10

In the afternoon, the President and Mrs. Bush traveled to New York City, where, at the site of the September 11, 2001, terrorist attacks, they participated in a wreath-laying ceremony commemorating the fifth anniversary of the attacks. Later, at the St. Paul's Chapel, they participated in a service of prayer and remembrance. Also in the afternoon, he toured the Tribute WTC Visitor Center commemorating the September 11, 2001, terrorist attacks.

September 11

In the morning, the President had an intelligence briefing. Later, at the Fort Pitt Firehouse, the President and Mrs. Bush had breakfast with New York City first-responders. Then, at 8:46 a.m., they participated in a moment of silence followed by a ceremony to commemorate the anniversary of the September 11, 2001, terrorist attacks.

Later in the morning, the President and Mrs. Bush traveled to Shanksville, PA, where, at the site of the crash of United Flight 93, they participated in a wreath-laying ceremony for victims of the September 11, 2001, plane crash.

In the afternoon, the President and Mrs. Bush traveled to Arlington, VA, where, at the Pentagon, they participated in a wreath-laying ceremony to commemorate the anniversary of the September 11, 2001, terrorist attacks. They then returned to Washington, DC.

September 12

In the morning, the President had an intelligence briefing. Later, he met with Secretary of Education Margaret Spellings. He then met with Secretary of Defense Donald H. Rumsfeld.

Later in the morning, the President participated in an interview with print journalists.

During the day, the President dropped by a meeting between National Security Adviser Stephen J. Hadley and Minister of the Interior and Regional Development Nicolas Sarkozy of France.

The White House announced that the President will welcome President Nursultan Nazarbayev of Kazakhstan to the White House on September 29.

The White House announced that the President will welcome Prime Minister Recep Tayyip Erdogan of Turkey to the White House on October 2.

The President announced his intention to nominate Frank Baxter to be Ambassador to Uruguay.

The President announced his intention to appoint Joseph B. Gildenhorn and Susan Hutchison as members of the Board of Trustees of the Woodrow Wilson International Center for Scholars.

September 13

In the morning, the President had breakfast with Secretary of State Condoleezza Rice. Later, he had an intelligence briefing.

In the afternoon, at the historic Evermay house, the President attended a Republican National Committee reception.

During the day, the President dropped by a meeting between Vice President Dick Cheney and Prime Minister Jaroslaw Kaczynski of Poland and a meeting between National Security Adviser Stephen J. Hadley and Minister of Foreign Affairs Tzipora "Tzipi" Livni of Israel.

September 14

In the morning, the President had an intelligence briefing. Later, at the U.S. Capitol, he made remarks to the House Republican Conference.

In the afternoon, the President had a working lunch with President Roh Moo-hyun of South Korea. Later, he met with the Smithsonian Institution Board of Regents.

In the evening, in the State Dining Room, the President and Mrs. Bush hosted a social dinner in honor of the Thelonious Monk Institute of Jazz followed by entertainment in the East Room.

The White House announced that the President will travel to New York City, to participate in the 61st United Nations General Assembly on September 18–20.

The White House announced that the President will welcome President Pervez Musharraf of Pakistan to the White House on September 22.

The White House announced that the President will welcome President Hamid Karzai of Afghanistan to the White House on September 26.

The President announced his intention to nominate Michele Davis to be Assistant Secretary of the Treasury (Public Affairs).

The President announced his intention to nominate Caroline C. Hunter to be a Commissioner of the Election Assistance Commission.

The President announced his intention to nominate David Palmer to be a Commissioner of the Equal Employment Opportunity Commission.

The President announced his intention to nominate Michael J. Astrue to be Commissioner of Social Security.

The President announced his intention to nominate Ned L. Siegel, Norman B. Coleman, and Barbara Boxer to be U.S. Representatives to the 61st Session of the United Nations General Assembly.

The President announced his intention to nominate Barbara McConnell Barrett and Cecil E. Floyd to be Alternate U.S. Representatives to the 61st Session of the United Nations General Assembly.

The President announced his intention to appoint Frank D. Stella as a member of the Board of Governors of the United Service Organizations, Inc.

The President announced his intention to appoint Duane R. Roberts, Jean Kennedy Smith, and Wilma E. Bernstein as members of the Board of Trustees of the John F. Kennedy Center for the Performing Arts.

The President announced that he has named Jeremy Katz and Myriah Jordan as Special Assistants to the President for Policy.

September 15

In the morning, the President had an intelligence briefing.

September 16

In the morning, the President had an intelligence briefing.

September 18

In the morning, the President had an intelligence briefing. Later, he and Mrs. Bush traveled to New York City, where, upon arrival, he met with USA Freedom Corps volunteer Patrick Gilligan. They then traveled to the Waldorf-Astoria Hotel.

In the afternoon, the President had separate meetings with President Elias Antonio Saca Gonzalez of El Salvador, President Manuel Zelaya Rosales of Honduras, and President Jakaya Mrisho Kikwete of Tanzania.

In the evening, at a private residence, the President attended a Republican National Committee reception. Later, he returned to the Waldorf-Astoria.

The President announced his designation of the following individuals as members of a Presidential delegation to Ukraine to attend the commemoration of the 65th anniversary of the tragedy in Babyn Yar on September 27:

Margaret Spellings (head of delegation);
William B. Taylor, Jr.;
Gregg Rickman;
Fred S. Zeidman; and
Vincent Obsitnik.

September 19

In the morning, the President had an intelligence briefing. Later, he traveled to United Nations Headquarters, where he met with United Nations Secretary-General Kofi Annan. He then met with Sheikha Haya Rashed Al Khalifa of Bahrain, President of the 61st Session of the United Nations General Assembly.

In the afternoon, the President participated in a roundtable discussion on democracy with other heads of state and leaders of nongovernmental organizations. Later, he returned to the Waldorf-Astoria.

The White House announced that the President will welcome President Pervez Musharraf of Pakistan and President Hamid Karzai of Afghanistan to the White House on September 27.

The President announced his intention to nominate Mark J. Warshawsky and Dana K. Bilyeu to be members of the Social Security Advisory Board.

The President announced his intention to nominate the following individuals to be members of the Board of Directors of the Inter-American Foundation:

Kay Kelley Arnold (Public Representative);
Gary C. Bryner (Public Representative);
Thomas Joseph Dodd (Public Representative);
Hector E. Morales (Government Representative);
John P. Salazar (Public Representative);
Thomas A. Shannon, Jr., (Government Representative); and
Jack C. Vaughn (Public Representative).

The President announced his intention to designate Sylvester J. Schieber as Chairman of the Social Security Advisory Board.

The President announced his intention to designate Jack C. Vaughn as Vice Chairman of the Board of Directors of the Inter-American Foundation.

September 20

In the morning, the President had an intelligence briefing. Later, he met with members of the U.S. mission to the United Nations. He then participated in an interview with Wolf Blitzer of Cable News Network.

In the afternoon, the President and Mrs. Bush returned to Washington, DC.

September 21

In the morning, the President had an intelligence briefing. Later, he met with Secretary of Defense Donald H. Rumsfeld. He then traveled to Tampa, FL, where, upon arrival, he met with USA Freedom Corps volunteer Zach Bonner.

Later in the morning, the President visited the National Football League's Tampa Bay Buccaneers training facility.

In the afternoon, the President traveled to Orlando, FL, where, upon arrival, he met with USA Freedom Corps volunteer Linda Feld.

In the evening, the President returned to Washington, DC.

The President announced his intention to nominate Curtis S. Chin to be U.S. Director of the Asian Development Bank with the rank of Ambassador.

The President announced his intention to nominate Steven R. Chealander to be a member of the National Transportation Safety Board.

The President announced his intention to nominate Ronald P. Spogli to be Ambassador to San Marino.

The President announced his intention to nominate Craig Stapleton to be Ambassador to Monaco.

The President announced his intention to designate Paul J. Hutter as Acting General Counsel of the Department of Veterans Affairs.

September 22

In the morning, the President had an intelligence briefing. Later, in the Oval Office, he participated in separate photo opportunities with 2006 National Spelling Bee champion Katharine "Kerry" Close and the 2006 Boys and Girls Club Youth of the Year Stacey Walker and regional finalists Kelly Barefield, Alyse Eady, Montorie Lee, and David Shelly.

In the afternoon, in the Oval Office, the President participated in a photo opportunity with recipients of the Secretary of Defense Employer Support Freedom Award.

In the evening, at the John F. Kennedy Center for the Performing Arts, the President and Mrs. Bush attended the musical drama "Asleep at the Wheel: A Ride With Bob."

The President declared a major disaster in Virginia and ordered Federal aid to supplement Commonwealth and local recovery efforts in the area struck by severe storms and flooding, including severe storms and flooding associated with Tropical Depression Ernesto, from August 29 to September 7.

September 23

In the morning, the President had an intelligence briefing.

The President announced his designation of the following individuals as members of a delegation to Beirut, Lebanon, to visit areas affected by recent conflict and to meet with Prime Minister Fuad Siniora of Lebanon and business leaders to discuss rebuilding priorities:

Dina Powell (head of delegation);
Jeffrey Feltman;
John T. Chambers;
Yousif Ghafari; and
Ray Irani.

September 25

In the morning, the President had an intelligence briefing. Later, he traveled to New York City, where, upon arrival, he met with USA Freedom Corps volunteer Katie Hustead. He then traveled to Riverside, CT.

In the afternoon, at a private residence, the President attended a Connecticut Republican Party luncheon. Later, he traveled to Cincinnati, OH, where, upon arrival, he met with USA Freedom Corps volunteer Robert "Kent" Wellington II. Later, he toured Meyer Tool, Inc.

In the evening, at a private residence, the President attended a reception for senatorial candidate Michael DeWine. Later, he returned to Washington, DC.

The President announced his designation of the following individuals as members of a Presidential delegation to Budapest, Hungary, to attend the 50th anniversary of the Hungarian Revolution on October 23:

George E. Pataki (head of delegation);
April H. Foley;
Peter K. Gogolak; and
Steven Udvar-Hazy.

September 26

In the morning, the President had a telephone conversation with President Ali Abdallah Salih of Yemen. Later, he had an intelligence briefing.

In the afternoon, in Room 350 of the Dwight D. Eisenhower Executive Office Building, the President participated in a bill signing ceremony for H.R. 5684, the United States-Oman Free Trade Agreement Implementation Act. Later, he

met with Republican congressional leaders to discuss legislative priorities.

In the evening, at a private residence, the President attended a reception for Iowa, Arkansas, and Wisconsin congressional candidates.

The President announced his intention to nominate Kevin M. Kolevar to be Assistant Secretary of Energy (Electricity Delivery and Energy Reliability).

The President announced his intention to nominate Jane C. Luxton to be Assistant Secretary of Commerce for Oceans and Atmosphere.

The President announced his intention to nominate Phillip L. Swagel to be Assistant Secretary of the Treasury (Economic Policy).

The President announced his intention to nominate Thurgood Marshall, Jr., to be a Governor of the Board of Governors of the U.S. Postal Service.

The President announced that he has named Tony Fratto as Deputy Assistant to the President and Deputy Press Secretary.

September 27

In the morning, the President had a telephone conversation with Prime Minister Shinzo Abe of Japan to discuss Japan-U.S. relations and to congratulate him on his September 26 election victory. Later, he had an intelligence briefing. He then met with Secretary of State Condoleezza Rice.

Later in the morning, the President traveled to Memphis, TN, where, upon arrival, he met with USA Freedom Corps volunteer Linda Smith.

In the afternoon, at a private residence, the President attended a luncheon for senatorial candidate Robert Corker. Later, he returned to Washington, DC.

In the evening, in the Old Family Dining Room, the President had a working dinner with Vice President Dick Cheney, Secretary of State Condoleezza Rice, National Security Adviser Stephen J. Hadley, President Hamid Karzai of Afghanistan, and President Pervez Musharraf of Pakistan.

September 28

In the morning, the President had an intelligence briefing. Later, he traveled to Hoover, AL, where, at the Hoover Public Safety Center, he participated in a briefing on energy. He then

participated in an interview with the Wall Street Journal.

In the afternoon, the President traveled to Birmingham, AL, where, upon arrival, he met with USA Freedom Corps volunteer Heather Shufelt. Later, he traveled to Columbus, OH, where, upon arrival, he met with USA Freedom Corps volunteer Eva Bradshaw. He then traveled to New Albany, OH.

In the evening, at a private residence, the President attended a reception for congressional candidate Deborah D. Pryce. He then returned to Washington, DC.

The White House announced that the President will welcome Prime Minister Ivo Sanader of Croatia to the White House on October 17.

The President announced his intention to nominate Dana Gioia to be Chairperson of the National Endowment for the Arts.

The President announced his intention to nominate Eric D. Eberhard to be a member of the Board of Trustees of the Morris K. Udall Scholarship and Excellence in National Environmental Policy Foundation.

The President announced his intention to appoint the following individuals as members of the Advisory Commission on Drug-Free Communities:

Catherine Thatcher Brunson (Public);
Dennis Griffith (National Substance Abuse Reduction Organization);
Steve Moak (National Substance Abuse Reduction Organization); and
Janet R. Wood (State Substance Abuse Reduction Organization).

September 29

In the morning, the President had an intelligence briefing.

In the afternoon, in the Oval Office, the President participated in separate bill signing ceremonies for S. 418, the Military Personnel Financial Service Protection Act, and S. 3850, the Credit Rating Agency Reform Act of 2006.

In the evening, at the Library of Congress, the President and Mrs. Bush attended the National Book Festival gala performance and dinner. Later, he traveled to Camp David, MD.

The President announced his intention to nominate Robert F. Hoyt to be General Counsel for the Department of the Treasury.

September 30

In the morning, the President had an intelligence briefing.

October 1

In the afternoon, the President returned to Washington, DC.

October 2

In the morning, the President had a telephone conversation with President Vladimir V. Putin of Russia. Later, he had an intelligence briefing followed by a briefing on the wildfires in California. He and Mrs. Bush then participated in planting an elm tree on the north grounds of the White House.

In the afternoon, the President traveled to Reno, NV, where, upon arrival, he met with USA Freedom Corps volunteer Elaine Nickovich.

In the evening, the President traveled to Stockton, CA, where, upon arrival, he met with USA Freedom Corps volunteer Masanobu "Mas" Kamigaki.

The President announced his intention to appoint Mary E. Peters as a member of the Amtrak Reform Board.

October 3

In the morning, the President had an intelligence briefing. Later, at the Radisson Hotel, he participated in a bill signing ceremony for S. 260, the Partners for Fish and Wildlife Act. He then traveled to the George W. Bush Elementary School, where he toured the school and met with students and faculty.

In the afternoon, the President traveled to El Dorado Hills, CA. Later, he traveled to Los Angeles, CA. While en route aboard Air Force One, he had a briefing on the wildfires in California.

Later in the afternoon, upon arrival in Los Angeles, the President met with USA Freedom Corps volunteer Matthew Cook.

In the evening, at a private residence, the President attended a Republican National Committee reception. Later, he traveled to Phoenix, AZ, where, upon arrival, he met with USA Freedom Corps volunteer Barbara MacLean. He then traveled to Scottsdale, AZ.

October 4

In the morning, the President had an intelligence briefing. Later, he traveled to Denver,

CO, where, upon arrival, he met with USA Freedom Corps volunteer Mary Lester. He then traveled to Englewood, CO.

In the afternoon, the President returned to Washington, DC.

October 5

In the morning, the President had an intelligence briefing. Later, he toured the Woodridge Elementary and Middle School Campus.

In the afternoon, in the Oval Office, the President met with Paul A. Morin, national commander, American Legion.

The President announced his intention to nominate Charles E. Dorkey III to be a member of the Advisory Board of the Saint Lawrence Seaway Development Corporation.

The President announced his intention to designate Stanley E. Taylor as Chairman of the Commission on Presidential Scholars.

The President announced his intention to appoint Mark B. Murphy as a member of the Advisory Board of the National Air and Space Museum.

The President announced his intention to appoint Debra Lynn Crisp as a member of the Klamath River Compact Commission (Federal Representative) and, upon appointment, to designate her as Chairman.

The President announced his intention to appoint Steven M. Colloton as a member of the Board of Trustees of the James Madison Memorial Fellowship Foundation (Federal Judiciary).

October 6

In the morning, the President had an intelligence briefing. Later, he had separate telephone conversations with President Abdoulaye Wade of Senegal to discuss the situation in Darfur, Sudan, and Prime Minister Stephen Harper of Canada to discuss international issues.

Later in the morning, the President toured the FedEx Express DCA Facility. Later, at the facility, he participated in a roundtable discussion on the national economy.

In the afternoon, in the Oval Office, the President participated in a photo opportunity with members of the Supreme Headquarters Allied Expeditionary Force/Headquarters European Theater of Operations U.S. Army Veterans Association.

The President declared a major disaster in Indiana and ordered Federal aid to supplement State and local recovery efforts in the area

struck by severe storms and flooding from September 12–14.

October 7

In the morning, the President had an intelligence briefing. Later, he and Mrs. Bush traveled to Langely Air Force Base, VA, where, upon arrival, he met with USA Freedom Corps volunteer Leah Hunkins. They then traveled to Newport News, VA.

In the afternoon, the President and Mrs. Bush returned to Washington, DC.

October 9

In the morning, the President had separate telephone conversations with President Hu Jintao of China, Prime Minister Shinzo Abe of Japan, President Vladimir V. Putin of Russia, and President Roh Moo-hyun of South Korea to discuss the situation in North Korea. Later, he had an intelligence briefing.

October 10

In the morning, the President had an intelligence briefing.

In the afternoon, the President traveled to Chevy Chase, MD. Later, he traveled to Robins Air Force Base, GA, where, upon arrival, he met with USA Freedom Corps volunteer Melissa Rosa. He then traveled to Macon, GA.

In the evening, the President returned to Washington, DC.

October 11

In the morning, the President had an intelligence briefing.

In the afternoon, in the Oval Office, the President met with Morris H. Chapman, president and chief executive officer, Southern Baptist Convention (SBC), and Frank Page, SBC Executive Committee president, and his wife, Dayle. Later, he met with Deputy Secretary of Veterans Affairs Gordon H. Mansfield, Gary Kurpius, commander-in-chief, Veterans of Foreign Wars, and Robert E. Wallace, executive director, Veterans of Foreign Wars Washington office.

The White House announced that the President will welcome President Leonel Fernandez Reyna of the Dominican Republic to the White House on October 25.

October 12

In the morning, the President had a telephone conversation with Prime Minister John Howard of Australia. He then had an intelligence briefing. Later, in the Oval Office, he met with State Councilor Tang Jiaxuan of China.

Later in the morning, the President traveled to St. Louis, MO, where, upon arrival in the afternoon, he met with USA Freedom Corps volunteer Tom Bailey, Jr.

Later in the afternoon, the President traveled to Chicago, IL.

In the evening, the President returned to Washington, DC.

The President announced that he has named David Broome as Special Assistant to the President for Legislative Affairs.

The President announced that he has named Gordon Johndroe as Special Assistant to the President and National Security Council Press Secretary.

The President announced that he has named Richard Klingler as Senior Associate Counsel to the President and National Security Council Legal Advisor and General Counsel.

The President announced that he has named Bobby Pittman, Jr., as Special Assistant to the President for African Affairs of the National Security Council.

October 13

In the morning, the President had an intelligence briefing. Later, on the South Portico, he participated in a photo opportunity with World War II veterans of the U.S. Air Force's 57th Bomb Wing.

In the afternoon, at the historic Evermay house, the President attended a Republican National Committee luncheon. Later, in the Oval Office, he participated in a photo opportunity with members of the U.S. Air Force Thunderbirds. He then traveled to Camp David, MD.

The White House announced that the President and Mrs. Bush will welcome King Carl XVI Gustaf and Queen Silvia of Sweden to the White House on October 23.

October 14

In the morning, the President had an intelligence briefing.

In the afternoon, the President and Mrs. Bush returned to Washington, DC. He and Mrs. Bush then traveled to Arlington, VA. Later, they returned to Camp David, MD.

October 15

In the afternoon, the President and Mrs. Bush returned to Washington, DC.

The President declared an emergency in New York and ordered Federal aid to supplement State and local response efforts in the area struck by a lake-effect snowstorm on October 12 and continuing.

October 16

In the morning, the President had separate telephone conversations with Prime Minister Manmohan Singh of India and Prime Minister Nuri al-Maliki of Iraq. Later, he had an intelligence briefing. Then, in the Oval Office, he met with Minister Mentor Lee Kuan Yew of Singapore.

Later in the morning, the President participated in an interview with Bill O'Reilly of FOX News, for later broadcast.

During the day, the President had a briefing on the October 15 earthquake and aftershocks in Hawaii.

The President declared a major disaster in Alaska and ordered Federal aid to supplement State and local recovery efforts in the area struck by severe storms, flooding, landslides, and mudslides on August 15–25.

October 17

In the morning, the President had an intelligence briefing. Later, in the Oval Office, he participated in a bill signing ceremony for H.R. 5122, the John Warner National Defense Authorization Act for Fiscal Year 2007. He then met with United Nations Secretary-General-designate Ban Ki-moon.

The President declared a major disaster in Hawaii and ordered Federal aid to supplement State and local recovery efforts in the area struck by an earthquake on October 15 and related aftershocks.

October 18

In the morning, the President had a telephone conversation with President Mohamed Hosni Mubarak of Egypt. Later, he had an intelligence briefing. He then traveled to Greensboro, NC, where, upon arrival, he met with USA Freedom Corps volunteer Michelle Gilmore.

In the afternoon, at Stamey's restaurant, the President had lunch with community leaders. Later, he toured Waldo C. Falkener Elementary School. He then traveled to Randleman, NC.

Later in the afternoon, the President participated in an interview with George Stephanopoulos of ABC News, for later broadcast. He then traveled to Greensboro, NC, where, at a private residence, he attended a Republican National Committee dinner.

In the evening, the President returned to Washington, DC.

October 19

In the morning, the President had an intelligence briefing. Later, he traveled to Avoca, PA, where, at the Wilkes-Barre/Scranton International Airport, he met with USA Freedom Corps volunteer Naomi Alamar. He then traveled to La Plume, PA.

In the afternoon, the President traveled to Clarks Summit, PA, where he visited patrons at Manning's Ice Cream and Milk. Later he traveled to Richmond, VA, where, upon arrival, he met with USA Freedom Corps volunteer W. Robert Floyd, Sr. He then stopped by the Pumpkin Patch and visited with owner William F. Gallmeyer.

In the evening, the President returned to Washington, DC.

The White House announced that the President will welcome President-elect Felipe de Jesus Calderon Hinojosa of Mexico to the White House on November 9.

The President announced his intention to nominate Katherine Almquist to be Assistant Administrator of the U.S. Agency for International Development (Bureau of Africa).

The President announced that he has recess appointed Richard E. Stickler as Assistant Secretary of Mine Safety at the Department of Labor.

The President announced that he has recess appointed Jeffrey R. Brown as a member of the Social Security Advisory Board.

October 20

In the morning, the President had an intelligence briefing. Later, at the Department of Health and Human Services, he participated in a roundtable discussion on Medicare. He then participated in an interview with Kevin Freking of the Associated Press.

The White House announced that the President will host Secretary General Jakob Gijsbert "Jaap" de Hoop Scheffer of the North Atlantic Treaty Organization at the White House on October 27.

October 21

In the morning, the President had an intelligence briefing. Later, in the Roosevelt Room, he met with National Security Adviser Stephen J. Hadley, Deputy National Security Adviser Jack D. Crouch II, State and Defense Department officials, military commanders, and Vice President Dick Cheney, who participated via video teleconference.

October 23

In the morning, the President had an intelligence briefing. Later, he met with Secretary of State Condoleezza Rice. He then met with Secretary of Defense Donald H. Rumsfeld.

Later in the morning, in the East Room, the President participated in a photo opportunity with crew members of the Space Shuttle *Discovery*, Space Shuttle *Atlantis*, and Space Station Expeditions 11, 12, and 13. Then, on the South Portico, he and Mrs. Bush participated in a photo opportunity with King Carl XVI Gustaf and Queen Silvia of Sweden.

In the afternoon, the President and Mrs. Bush had lunch with the King and Queen of Sweden. Then, at the Urban Trust Bank, he participated in a discussion on the economy with small-business owners and community bankers. Later, in the Old Family Dining Room, he participated in an interview with Maria Bartiromo of CNBC, for later broadcast.

The White House announced that the President will travel to Hanoi, Vietnam, to attend the Asia-Pacific Economic Cooperation Leaders' Meeting on November 18–19, to meet with President Nguyen Minh Triet and Prime Minister Nguyen Tan Dung of Vietnam on November 17, and that he will travel to Singapore and Indonesia.

October 24

In the morning, the President had an intelligence briefing. Later, he traveled to Sarasota, FL, where, upon arrival in the afternoon, he met with USA Freedom Corps volunteer Tom Cooney.

Later in the afternoon, the President traveled to Fort Lauderdale, FL, where, upon arrival, he met with USA Freedom Corps volunteer David Greenberger. He then traveled to Boca Raton, FL, where, at a private residence, he attended a Republican National Committee dinner.

In the evening, the President returned to Washington, DC.

The President declared a major disaster in New York and ordered Federal aid to supplement State and local recovery efforts in the area struck by severe storms and flooding on October 12–13 and continuing.

October 25

In the morning, the President had an intelligence briefing.

In the afternoon, in the Oval Office, the President participated in an interview with print journalists.

October 26

In the morning, the President had an intelligence briefing. Later, he traveled to Des Moines, IA, where, upon arrival in the afternoon, he met with USA Freedom Corps volunteer Sally Bates.

Later in the afternoon, the President traveled to Clinton Township, MI, where, upon arrival, he met with USA Freedom Corps volunteer George Kolf. He then traveled to Warren, MI.

In the evening, the President returned to Washington, DC.

October 27

In the morning, the President had an intelligence briefing. Later, in the Map Room, he participated in separate interviews with Laurie Kinney of Hearst-Argyle Television, Grant Rampy of Tribune Broadcasting, and Jim Fry of Belo Broadcasting.

In the afternoon, the President had a telephone conversation with Deputy Regional Forester Thomas Tidwell of the U.S. Forest Service to express his condolences for the deaths of four Forest Service firefighters in the wildfire near Palm Springs, CA.

The President declared a major disaster in Alaska and ordered Federal aid to supplement State and local recovery efforts in the area struck by a fire from August 3–4.

October 28

In the morning, the President had a telephone conversation with Prime Minister Nuri al-Maliki of Iraq. He then had an intelligence briefing.

Later in the morning, the President traveled to Sellersburg, IN, where, upon arrival in the afternoon, he met with USA Freedom Corps volunteer Judy Seelye.

Later in the afternoon, the President had a telephone conversation with Republican National Committee Chairman Kenneth B. Mehlman, which was broadcast to grassroots campaign supporters throughout the country. Later, he traveled to Charleston Air Force Base, SC.

During the day, the President had a telephone conversation with William O. DeWitt, owner, St. Louis Cardinals, to congratulate the team on winning the Major League Baseball World Series.

In the evening, the President traveled to Kiawah Island, SC, where, at a private residence, he attended a Republican National Committee dinner. Later, he returned to Washington, DC.

October 29

In the afternoon, in the Family Theater, the President and Mrs. Bush hosted a screening of the film "Children of Glory."

In the evening, in the Diplomatic Reception Room, the President and Mrs. Bush hosted a dinner for "Children of Glory" screening guests.

October 30

In the morning, the President had an intelligence briefing. Later, he traveled to Hunter Army Airfield, GA, where, upon arrival, he met with USA Freedom Corps volunteer Rebekah Rotton. He then traveled to Statesboro, GA.

In the afternoon, the President participated in an interview with Sean Hannity of FOX News, for later broadcast.

Later in the afternoon, the President traveled to Houston, TX, where, upon arrival, he met with USA Freedom Corps volunteer Pat McWaters. He then traveled to Sugar Land, TX.

In the evening, the President returned to Washington, DC.

The President announced his intention to appoint the following individuals as members of the Board of Trustees of the John F. Kennedy Center for the Performing Arts:

Elliott Bryan Broidy;
Emilio Estefan, Jr.;
Sheldon B. Kamins;
James V. Kimsey;
Norman Y. Mineta; and
Stephen A. Wynn.

October 31

In the morning, the President had a telephone conversation with President Luiz Inacio Lula da Silva of Brazil. He then had an intelligence briefing.

Later in the morning, in the Map Room, the President participated in separate interviews with Alison Burns of Cox Broadcasting, Morris Jones of Sinclair Broadcast Group, and Melissa Charbonneau of Christian Broadcasting Network.

In the afternoon, the President traveled to Robins Air Force Base, GA, where, upon arrival, he met with USA Freedom Corps volunteer Eloise Hadaway. He then traveled to Perry, GA.

In the evening, the President returned to Robins Air Force Base, where he met with military families and passed out Halloween candy. Later, he returned to Washington, DC.

November 1

In the morning, the President had an intelligence briefing. Later, in the Oval Office, he met with Secretary of State Condoleezza Rice.

Later in the morning, the President participated in a telephone interview with Rush Limbaugh of The Rush Limbaugh Show. He then met with Secretary of Defense Donald H. Rumsfeld.

In the afternoon, in the Oval Office, the President participated in an interview with Terence Hunt of the Associated Press, Steve Holland of Reuters, and Richard Keil of Bloomberg News.

November 2

In the morning, the President had an intelligence briefing. Later, he traveled to Billings, MT, where, upon arrival, he met with USA Freedom Corps volunteer Mark Polakoff.

In the afternoon, the President traveled to Elko, NV, where, upon arrival, he met with USA Freedom Corps volunteer Cathy McAdoo.

Later in the afternoon, the President traveled to Springfield, MO, where, upon arrival, he met with USA Freedom Corps volunteer Dennis Jones.

The President announced his designation of the following individuals as members of the Presidential delegation to observe the Presidential and legislative elections in Managua, Nicaragua, on November 5: Paul Trivelli; J. Bennett Johnston; and Bill Paxon.

The President announced his intention to nominate Dan Gregory Blair to be a member of the Postal Rate Commission and, upon confirmation, to designate him as Chairman.

The President announced his intention to nominate Scott A. Keller to be Assistant Secretary of Housing and Urban Development (Congressional and Intergovernmental Relations).

The President announced his intention to nominate Paul A. Schneider to be Under Secretary for Management at the Department of Homeland Security.

The President announced his intention to nominate the following individuals to be members of the National Council on the Arts:

Benjamin Donenberg;
Foreststorn Hamilton;
Joan Israelite;
Charlotte P. Kessler;
Robert Bretley Lott; and
William Francis Price, Jr.

The President announced his intention to appoint Juan Carlos Iturregui and Leonard Sands as members of the President's Export Council.

The President declared a major disaster in Missouri and ordered Federal aid to supplement State and local recovery efforts in the area struck by severe storms on July 19–21.

The President declared a major disaster in Louisiana and ordered Federal aid to supplement State and local recovery efforts in the area struck by severe storms and flooding on October 16 and continuing.

November 3

In the morning, the President had an intelligence briefing. Later, he traveled to Joplin, MO.

In the afternoon, the President traveled to Sioux City, IA, where, upon arrival, he met with USA Freedom Corps volunteer Earl Belt. He then traveled to Le Mars, IA.

In the evening, the President traveled to Englewood, CO.

The President announced that he has named Craig M. Albright as Special Assistant to the President for Legislative Affairs.

The President announced that he has named Ross Kyle as Special Assistant to the President for Cabinet Liaison.

November 4

In the morning, in Englewood, CO, the President had an intelligence briefing. Later, at Mile High Coffee, he had breakfast with small-business owners. He then traveled to Greeley, CO.

Later in the morning, he traveled to Aurora, CO, where, at Buckley Air Force Base, he met with family members of a Navy serviceman who was killed in Afghanistan.

In the afternoon, the President traveled to the Bush Ranch in Crawford, TX.

During the day, the President met with Robert M. Gates, president, Texas A&M University.

November 5

In the afternoon, the President traveled to Grand Island, NE, where, upon arrival, he met with USA Freedom Corps volunteer Holly Theis. Later, he traveled to Topeka, KS, where, upon arrival, he met with USA Freedom Corps volunteer Sharon Meissner.

In the evening, the President returned to the Bush Ranch in Crawford, TX.

November 6

In the morning, the President had an intelligence briefing. Later, he and Mrs. Bush traveled to Pensacola, FL, where, upon arrival in the afternoon, he met with USA Freedom Corps volunteer Honor Bell.

Later in the afternoon, the President and Mrs. Bush traveled to Bentonville, AR. Later, they traveled to Dallas, TX, where, upon arrival, he met with USA Freedom Corps volunteer Lori Whitlow.

In the evening, the President and Mrs. Bush returned to the Bush Ranch in Crawford, TX.

The White House announced that the President will welcome Prime Minister Ehud Olmert of Israel to the White House on November 13.

The President announced his intention to nominate Anthony W. Ryan to be Assistant Secretary of the Treasury (Financial Markets).

The President announced his intention to nominate Leon R. Sequeira to be Assistant Secretary of Labor (Policy).

November 7

In the morning, the President had an intelligence briefing. Later, at the Crawford Fire Station, he and Mrs. Bush voted.

Later in the morning, the President and Mrs. Bush returned to Washington, DC.

During the day, in the Oval Office, the President met with Secretary of Defense Donald H. Rumsfeld.

November 8

In the morning, the President had an intelligence briefing.

November 9

In the morning, in the Private Dining Room, the President had a breakfast meeting with Republican congressional leaders. Later, he had an intelligence briefing. Then, in the Oval Office, he and Mrs. Bush presented the 2006 National Medals of Arts and National Humanitarian Medals.

The President announced his designation of the following individuals as members of a Presidential delegation to Ankara, Turkey, to attend the funeral of former Prime Minister Mustafa Bulent Ecevit of Turkey on November 11: Jeffrey Clay Sell (head of delegation); Ross Wilson; and W. Robert Pearson.

The President announced his intention to nominate Andrew G. Biggs to be Deputy Commissioner of Social Security.

The President announced his intention to nominate Terry L. Cline to be Administrator of the Substance Abuse and Mental Health Services Administration of the Department of Health and Human Services.

The President announced his intention to nominate Richard Allan Hill to be a member of the Board of Directors of the Corporation for National and Community Service.

The President announced his intention to nominate Diane Humetewa to be a member of the Board of Trustees of the Morris K. Udall Scholarship and Excellence in National Environmental Policy Foundation.

November 10

In the morning, the President had a telephone conversation with President Alvaro Uribe Velez of Colombia. He then had an intelligence briefing.

In the afternoon, the President traveled to Quantico, VA. Later, he met with Dan and Deb Dunham, whose son, Corp. Jason Dunham, USMC, was killed in Iraq and posthumously awarded the Medal of Honor. He then returned to Washington, DC.

November 11

In the morning, the President had an intelligence briefing. Later, he and Mrs. Bush traveled to Arlington, VA, where they participated in a Veterans Day wreath-laying ceremony at the Tomb of the Unknowns in Arlington National Cemetery.

In the afternoon, the President and Mrs. Bush returned to Washington, DC.

During the day, the President and Mrs. Bush hosted a reception for members of the 555th Antiaircraft Artillery Battalion who served during World War II.

November 13

In the morning, the President had a telephone conversation with President Pervez Musharraf of Pakistan. He then had an intelligence briefing. Later, in the Roosevelt Room, he met with members of the Iraq Study Group.

In the afternoon, the President had a working lunch with Prime Minister Ehud Olmert of Israel. Later, he hosted a reception for newly elected Members of Congress.

The President announced his intention to nominate Mark Everett Keenum to be Under Secretary of Agriculture for Farm and Foreign Agricultural Services and to be a member of the Board of Directors of the Commodity Credit Corporation.

The President announced his intention to nominate Ellen C. Williams to be a Governor of the Board of Governors of the U.S. Postal Service.

November 14

In the morning, the President had an intelligence briefing.

In the evening, the President and Mrs. Bush traveled to Moscow, Russia, arriving the following afternoon.

November 15

In the morning, aboard Air Force One, the President had an intelligence briefing.

In the afternoon, upon arrival at Vnukovo II International Airport in Moscow, the President and Mrs. Bush met with President Vladimir V. Putin of Russia and his wife, Lyudmila.

Later in the afternoon, the President and Mrs. Bush traveled to Singapore, arriving the following morning.

November 16

In the morning, upon arrival in Singapore, the President and Mrs. Bush went to the Shangri-La Hotel. Later, he had an intelligence briefing.

Later in the morning, the President and Mrs. Bush visited the Asian Civilisations Museum. They then returned to the Shangri-La Hotel, where they greeted U.S. Embassy personnel and their families.

In the afternoon, the President and Mrs. Bush went to the Istana. He then met with Acting President J.Y. Pillay of Singapore. Later, he and Mrs. Bush returned to the Shangri-La Hotel.

In the evening, the President and Mrs. Bush went to the Istana, where they had dinner with Prime Minister Lee Hsien Loong and his wife, Ho Ching. Later, they returned to the Shangri-La Hotel.

November 17

In the morning, the President had an intelligence briefing. He and Mrs. Bush then traveled to Hanoi, Vietnam, where, upon arrival, they went to the Sheraton Hanoi.

In the afternoon, the President had lunch with Prime Minister John Howard of Australia. Later, he and Mrs. Bush went to the Presidential Palace, where they participated in an arrival ceremony and official photograph with President Nguyen Minh Triet of Vietnam and his wife, Tran Thi Kim Chi.

Later in the afternoon, the President and Mrs. Bush paid a courtesy call on President Triet and Mrs. Chi. He then had separate meetings with President Triet and Prime Minister Nguyen Tan Dung of Vietnam. Then, at Communist Party Headquarters, he met with General Secretary Nong Duc Manh of the Communist Party of Vietnam.

Later in the afternoon, the President returned to the Sheraton Hanoi.

In the evening, the President and Mrs. Bush went to the International Convention Center, where they participated in a state banquet. They then returned to the Sheraton Hanoi.

November 18

In the morning, the President had an intelligence briefing. Later, he went to the International Convention Center, where he met with leaders of the Association of Southeast Asian Nations.

Later in the morning, the President visited the Joint POW/MIA Accounting Command. He then returned to the Sheraton Hanoi, where he greeted U.S. Embassy personnel and their families.

In the afternoon, the President went to the National Conference Center, where he participated in the Asia-Pacific Economic Cooperation (APEC) Leaders Retreat I. Later, he participated in the APEC Leaders Dialogue with the APEC Business Advisory Council. He then returned to the Sheraton Hanoi.

In the evening, the President and Mrs. Bush went to the National Convention Center, where they attended a gala dinner and cultural performance. Later, they returned to the Sheraton Hanoi.

The President announced his intention to nominate Michael W. Tankersley to be Inspector-General of the Export-Import Bank.

November 19

In the morning, the President went to the National Conference Center, where he participated in the Asia-Pacific Economic Cooperation (APEC) Leaders Retreat II.

In the afternoon, the President participated in the APEC leaders official lunch and the APEC leaders official photograph. Later, he participated in the APEC Leaders Declaration. He and Mrs. Bush then traveled to Ho Chi Minh City, Vietnam.

November 20

In the morning, the President had an intelligence briefing. Later, he greeted U.S. Embassy personnel and their families. He then toured the Ho Chi Minh City Securities Trading Center.

Later in the morning, the President and Mrs. Bush went to the Pasteur Institute, where they participated in a briefing on HIV/AIDS and avian influenza. They then visited the Ho Chi Minh City History Museum.

In the afternoon, the President and Mrs. Bush traveled to Jakarta, Indonesia, where, upon arrival at Halim Perdanakusuma International Airport, they greeted U.S. Embassy personnel and their families. Later, they traveled to Bogor, Indonesia. Then, at Bogor Palace, he participated in a discussion with civic leaders.

In the evening, the President and President Susilo Bambang Yudhoyono of Indonesia participated in an education event hosted by President

Yudhoyono's wife, Kristiani Herawati, and Mrs. Bush. Later, he and Mrs. Bush had dinner with President Yudhoyono and Mrs. Herawati.

Later in the evening, the President and Mrs. Bush traveled to Honolulu, HI, crossing the international dateline and arriving in the evening. Upon arrival, he met with USA Freedom Corps volunteer Eloise Monsarrat.

Later in the evening, the President and Mrs. Bush had dinner with Adm. William J. Fallon, USN, commander, U.S. Pacific Command, and his wife, Mary.

November 21

In the morning, the President had an intelligence briefing. Later, at the Officers Club at Hickam Air Force Base, he and Mrs. Bush had breakfast with military personnel. Later, at the Nimitz-MacArthur Conference Center, he participated in a briefing by Adm. William J. Fallon, USN, commander, U.S. Pacific Command.

Later in the morning, the President and Mrs. Bush returned to Washington, DC, arriving in the evening.

November 22

In the morning, the President had an intelligence briefing.

In the afternoon, the President and Mrs. Bush traveled to Camp David, MD.

The White House announced that the President will welcome President Oscar Arias Sanchez of Costa Rica to the White House on December 6.

November 23

In the morning, the President had an intelligence briefing. Later, he had several Thanksgiving holiday telephone conversations with members of the U.S. military.

November 24

In the morning, the President had an intelligence briefing.

November 25

In the morning, the President had an intelligence briefing.

In the afternoon, the President and Mrs. Bush returned to Washington, DC.

November 27

In the morning, the President had an intelligence briefing. Later, he traveled to Tallinn, Estonia. While en route, aboard Air Force One, he had separate telephone conversations with President Hu Jintao of China, President Mohamed Hosni Mubarak of Egypt, and President Jacques Chirac of France.

In the afternoon, aboard Air Force One, the President had a telephone conversation with former Prime Minister Silvio Berlusconi of Italy.

In the evening, upon arrival in Tallinn, the President went to the Radisson SAS.

November 28

In the morning, the President had an intelligence briefing. Later, he met with U.S. Embassy personnel and their families.

Later in the morning, the President went to Kadriorg Palace, where he participated in an arrival ceremony and official photograph with President Toomas Ilves of Estonia. Later, in the State Council Hall, he met with President Ilves.

In the afternoon, the President went to the Estonian National Opera House, where he had lunch with President Ilves.

Later in the afternoon, the President traveled to Riga, Latvia, where, upon arrival, he went to Riga Castle and met with President Vaira Vike-Freiberga of Latvia. Later, he went to the Radisson SAS Daugava.

In the evening, the President went to the Latvian National Opera, where he attended a cultural performance. He then had a working dinner with North Atlantic Treaty Organization members. Later, he returned to the Radisson SAS Daugava.

The President announced his designation of the following individuals as members of the Presidential delegation to attend the inauguration of Felipe de Jesus Calderon Hinojosa as President of Mexico on December 1:

Former President George H.W. Bush (head of delegation);
Antonio O. Garza;
Alberto R. Gonzales; and
Carlos M. Gutierrez.

November 29

In the morning, the President had an intelligence briefing. He then met with U.S. Embassy personnel and their families. Later, he went to the Olympic Sports Centre, where he participated in a working session for the North Atlantic Council.

In the afternoon, the President participated in a North Atlantic Treaty Organization leaders group photograph. He then had lunch with North Atlantic Treaty Organization leaders.

In the evening, the President traveled to Amman, Jordan, where, upon arrival, he went to the Raghadan Palace and met with King Abdullah II of Jordan. They then had dinner.

Later in the evening, the President went to the Four Seasons Hotel Amman.

The President announced his intention to appoint Laura L. Rogers as Director of the Office of Sex Offender Sentencing, Monitoring, Apprehending, Registering, and Tracking at the Department of Justice.

The President announced his intention to appoint Carlos Marin as Commissioner of the International Boundary and Water Commission (United States and Mexico).

The President announced his intention to appoint the following individuals as members of the President's Board of Advisers on Tribal Colleges and Universities:

Verna Fowler;
Joseph George Hiller;
Richard Dennis Stephens; and
Edward K. Thomas.

The President announced his intention to appoint the following individuals to be members of the President's Board of Advisers on Historically Black Colleges and Universities:

Belinda Childress Anderson;
Delbert W. Baker;
Brett Everett Fuller;
Ivory V. Nelson; and
Beverly Daniel Tatum.

The President announced his intention to designate Mary Beth Buchanan as Designate Acting Director of the Office of Violence Against Women at the Department of Justice.

The President announced that he has named Scott M. Stanzel as Deputy Assistant to the President and Deputy Press Secretary.

The President announced that he has named Alan Swendiman as Special Assistant to the President and Director of the Office of Administration.

The President announced that he has named Christopher G. Oprison as Associate Counsel to the President.

The President announced that he has named Cheryl Stanton as Associate Counsel to the President.

November 30

In the morning, the President had an intelligence briefing. Later, he had breakfast with Prime Minister Nuri al-Maliki of Iraq. They then had a meeting.

In the afternoon, the President returned to Washington, DC.

The White House announced that the President will welcome President Thabo Mvuyelwa Mbeki of South Africa to the White House on December 8.

The President announced his intention to appoint Daniel J. Carroll, Jr., and Howard L. Lance as members of the President's National Security Telecommunications Advisory Committee.

The President announced his intention to designate Gary D. Forsee as Chairman of the President's National Security Telecommunications Advisory Committee.

The President announced his intention to designate Randall L. Stephenson as Vice-Chairman of the President's National Security Telecommunications Advisory Committee.

December 1

In the morning, the President had an intelligence briefing.

December 2

In the morning, the President had an intelligence briefing.

December 3

In the afternoon, in the East Room, the President and Mrs. Bush hosted a reception for Kennedy Center honorees.

In the evening, the President and Mrs. Bush went to the John F. Kennedy Center for the Performing Arts, where they attended the Kennedy Center Honors ceremony. Later, they returned to the White House.

December 4

In the morning, the President had an intelligence briefing.

In the afternoon, in the Oval Office, the President participated in an interview with Brit Hume of FOX News.

The White House announced that the President will host Prime Minister Tony Blair of the

United Kingdom at the White House on December 7.

The President announced his designation of the following individuals as members of the Presidential delegation to attend the inauguration of Joseph Kabila as President of the Democratic Republic of the Congo on December 6:

Elaine L. Chao (head of delegation);
Roger Meece;
Thelma J. Askey;
Jendayi E. Frazer;
Edward Brehm;
Michael E. Hess; and
John Fenn.

The President announced his intention to nominate Gregory B. Cade to be Administrator of the U.S. Fire Administration at the Department of Homeland Security.

The President announced his intention to nominate Sam Fox to be Ambassador to Belgium.

The President announced his intention to nominate Stanley D. "Dave" Phillips to be Ambassador to Estonia.

The President announced his intention to nominate Jill E. Sommers to be Commissioner of the Commodity Futures Trading Commission.

The President announced his intention to appoint Maria Cino as a member of the National Surface Transportation Policy and Revenue Study Commission.

The President announced his intention to designate Robert M. Couch as Acting General Counsel of the Department of Housing and Urban Development.

December 5

In the morning, the President had breakfast with Secretary of Defense-designate Robert M. Gates. Later, he had an intelligence briefing.

In the afternoon, the President had lunch with James A. Baker III, cochair, Iraq Study Group.

In the evening, the President and Mrs. Bush hosted a dinner for Secretary-General Kofi Annan of the United Nations and his wife, Nane Maria.

December 6

In the morning, the President had an intelligence briefing.

The President announced his intention to nominate Michael J. Burns to be Assistant to

the Secretary of Defense for Nuclear and Chemical and Biological Defense Programs.

The President announced his intention to nominate Rosemary E. Rodriguez to be a member of the Election Assistance Commission.

December 7

In the morning, the President had an intelligence briefing.

The White House announced that the President will welcome President Thomas Yayi Boni of Benin to the White House on December 14.

The President announced his designation of the following individuals as members of the Presidential delegation to attend the 60th anniversary of King Bhumibol Adulyadej's accession to the throne, to be held in Bangkok, Thailand, December 11: George H.W. Bush (head of delegation); Barbara Bush; and Ralph Boyce.

December 8

In the morning, the President had separate telephone conversations with Prime Minister Recep Tayyip Erdogan of Turkey and President Joseph Kabila of the Democratic Republic of the Congo. He then had an intelligence briefing.

Later in the morning, in the Yellow Oval Room, the President and Mrs. Bush participated in an interview with People magazine. Then, in the Oval Office, he had a meeting with Democrat Members of the House of Representatives.

In the afternoon, in an Oval Office ceremony, the President received credentials from newly appointed Ambassadors to the United States.

In the evening, on the State Floor, the President and Mrs. Bush hosted a holiday reception.

The President declared a major disaster in Alaska and ordered Federal aid to supplement State and local recovery efforts in the area struck by severe storms, flooding, landslides, and mudslides on October 8–13.

December 9

In the morning, the President had an intelligence briefing.

December 10

In the afternoon, the President and Mrs. Bush went to the National Building Museum, where they participated in the taping of the annual "Christmas in Washington" concert for later television broadcast.

In the evening, the President and Mrs. Bush returned to the White House.

December 11

In the morning, the President had an intelligence briefing.

In the afternoon, in the Oval Office, the President participated in an interview with Stephen F. Hayes of the Weekly Standard. Later, also in the Oval Office, he met with outside experts on Iraq.

The President announced his intention to appoint Patricia Hanahan Engman, Robert E. Peterson, and Peter W. Tredick as members of the Presidential Emergency Board No. 240, and, upon appointment, to designate Peter W. Tredick as Chair.

December 12

In the morning, in the Private Dining Room, the President had breakfast with Secretary of Defense-designate Robert M. Gates. Later, he had an intelligence briefing.

Later in the morning, in the Roosevelt Room, the President participated in a video conference call with U.S. military commanders and U.S. Ambassador to Iraq Zalmay Khalilzad.

In the evening, on the State Floor, the President and Mrs. Bush hosted two holiday receptions.

The President declared a major disaster in Washington and ordered Federal aid to supplement State and local recovery efforts in the area struck by severe storms, flooding, landslides, and mudslides on November 2–11.

The President declared a major disaster in New York and ordered Federal aid to supplement State and local recovery efforts in the area struck by severe storms and flooding on November 16–17.

December 13

In the morning, the President had an intelligence briefing. Later, he had separate telephone conversations with President Jalal Talabani of Iraq and Masoud Barzani, president of the Kurdistan region of Iraq.

In the afternoon, the President traveled to Arlington, VA. Then, at the Pentagon, he and Vice President Dick Cheney met with U.S. military personnel. Later, he returned to Washington, DC.

In the evening, on the State Floor, the President and Mrs. Bush hosted a holiday reception.

The White House announced that the President will welcome President Jose Manuel Durao Barroso of the European Commission to the White House on January 8, 2007.

The President announced the recess appointment of Dabney Langhorne Friedrich and Beryl A. Howell as members of the U.S. Sentencing Commission.

The President announced the recess appointment of John R. Steer as a member of the U.S. Sentencing Commission and designated him Vice Chair.

December 14

In the morning, the President had an intelligence briefing.

In the evening, on the State Floor, the President and Mrs. Bush hosted a holiday reception.

December 15

In the morning, the President had a telephone conversation with Prime Minister Abdullah bin Ahmad Badawi of Malaysia. He then had an intelligence briefing.

In the afternoon, the President traveled to Arlington, VA. Later, he returned to Washington, DC.

Later in the afternoon, the President and Mrs. Bush went to the State Department, where they participated in a holiday reception for members of the diplomatic corps. Later, they returned to the White House.

In the evening, on the State Floor, the President and Mrs. Bush hosted a holiday reception.

December 16

In the morning, the President had an intelligence briefing.

December 18

In the morning, the President had breakfast with Secretary of State Condoleezza Rice. Later, he had an intelligence briefing and met with the National Security Council. Then, in the Oval Office, he met with Secretary of Defense Robert M. Gates.

Later in the morning, in the Roosevelt Room, the President met with Jewish higher education leaders.

In the afternoon, the President traveled to Arlington, VA. Later, he returned to Washington, DC.

December 19

In the morning, the President had an intelligence briefing. Later, in the Oval Office, he signed H.R. 6143, the Ryan White HIV/AIDS Treatment Modernization Act of 2006, and S. 3678, the Pandemic and All-Hazards Preparedness Act.

Later in the morning, in the Oval Office, the President participated in an interview with the Washington Post.

In the afternoon, the President participated in a photo opportunity with U.S. Ambassadors. Later, in the Roosevelt Room, he met with White House Fellows.

In the evening, on the State Floor, the President and Mrs. Bush hosted a holiday reception.

December 20

In the morning, the President had an intelligence briefing.

The President announced his intention to appoint John V. Cogbill III as a member of the National Capital Planning Commission and, upon appointment, designate him as Chairman.

The President announced his intention to appoint Stephen J. Cassidy as a member of the Medal of Valor Review Board (Firefighting).

The President announced his intention to appoint M. Josephine Beach and Phillip M. Schofield as members of the Advisory Board on Radiation and Worker Health.

The President announced the recess appointment of Warren Bell as a member of the Corporation for Public Broadcasting.

The President announced the recess appointment of Wayne Cartwright Beyer as a member of the Federal Labor Relations Authority.

The President announced the recess appointment of Mark McKinnon as a member of the Broadcasting Board of Governors.

December 21

In the morning, the President had an intelligence briefing.

December 22

In the morning, the President had an intelligence briefing. Later, he and Mrs. Bush went to Walter Reed Army Medical Center, where he presented Purple Heart medals to 14 soldiers. They then volunteered to wrap gifts for family members of wounded soldiers.

In the afternoon, the President and Mrs. Bush traveled to Camp David, MD.

December 23

In the morning, the President had an intelligence briefing.

During the day, the President met with Secretary of Defense Robert M. Gates and Gen. Peter Pace, USMC, Chairman, Joint Chiefs of Staff, to discuss Iraq policy.

December 24

During the day, the President had several Christmas Eve telephone conversations with members of the U.S. military.

December 25

In the morning, the President had an intelligence briefing.

December 26

In the morning, the President had an intelligence briefing. Later, he had a telephone conversation with President Yoweri Kaguta Museveni of Uganda.

Later in the morning, the President and Mrs. Bush traveled to the Bush Ranch in Crawford, TX, arriving in the afternoon.

In the evening, the President had a telephone conversation with former First Lady Betty Ford.

December 27

In the morning, the President had an intelligence briefing.

December 28

In the morning, the President had an intelligence briefing.

The President announced that he has named Maggie Grant as Deputy Assistant to the President and Director of Intergovernmental Affairs.

The President announced that he has named Paul R. Eckert as Associate Counsel to the President.

December 29

In the morning, the President had an intelligence briefing.

The White House announced that the President will welcome Chancellor Angela Merkel of Germany to the White House on January 4, 2007.

The President declared a major disaster in Oregon and ordered Federal aid to supplement State and local recovery efforts in the area struck by severe storms, flooding, landslides, and mudslides on November 5–8.

The President declared an emergency in Illinois and ordered Federal aid to supplement State and local response efforts in the area struck by record snow from November 30 to December 1.

The President declared a major disaster in Missouri and ordered Federal aid to supplement State and local recovery efforts in the area struck by severe winter storms from November 30 to December 2.

December 30

In the morning, the President had an intelligence briefing.

Appendix B—Nominations Submitted to the Senate

The following list does not include promotions of members of the Uniformed Services, nominations to the Service Academies, or nominations of Foreign Service officers.

Submitted July 12

Philip S. Goldberg,
of Massachusetts, a career member of the Senior Foreign Service, class of Counselor, to be Ambassador Extraordinary and Plenipotentiary of the United States of America to the Republic of Bolivia.

Henry M. Paulson, Jr.,
of New York, to be U.S. Governor of the International Monetary Fund for a term of 5 years; U.S. Governor of the International Bank for Reconstruction and Development for a term of 5 years; U.S. Governor of the Inter-American Development Bank for a term of 5 years; U.S. Governor of the African Development Bank for a term of 5 years; U.S. Governor of the Asian Development Bank; U.S. Governor of the African Development Fund; U.S. Governor of the European Bank for Reconstruction and Development, vice John W. Snow, resigned.

John C. Rood,
of Arizona, to be an Assistant Secretary of State (International Security and Non-Proliferation), vice Stephen Geoffrey Rademaker, resigned.

Submitted July 13

Cindy Lou Courville,
of Virginia, to be Representative of the United States of America to the African Union, with the rank and status of Ambassador Extraordinary and Plenipotentiary.

Nora Barry Fischer,
of Pennsylvania, to be U.S. District Judge for the Western District of Pennsylvania, vice Robert J. Cindrich, resigned.

Richard W. Graber,
of Wisconsin, to be Ambassador Extraordinary and Plenipotentiary of the United States of America to the Czech Republic.

Sara Elizabeth Lioi,
of Ohio, to be U.S. District Judge for the Northern District of Ohio, vice Lesley Brooks Wells, retired.

Christopher A. Padilla,
of the District of Columbia, to be an Assistant Secretary of Commerce, vice Peter Lichtenbaum.

Calvin L. Scovel,
of Virginia, to be Inspector General, Department of Transportation, vice Kenneth M. Mead, resigned.

Submitted July 18

Clyde Bishop,
of Delaware, a career member of the Senior Foreign Service, class of Counselor, to be Ambassador Extraordinary and Plenipotentiary of the United States of America to the Republic of the Marshall Islands.

Mark R. Dybul,
of Florida, to be Coordinator of United States Government Activities to Combat HIV/AIDS Globally, with the rank of Ambassador, vice Randall L. Tobias, resigned.

Stephen M. Prescott,
of Oklahoma, to be a member of the Board of Trustees of the Morris K. Udall Scholarship and Excellence in National Environmental Policy Foundation for a term expiring April 15, 2011, vice Herbert Guenther, term expired.

Peter W. Tredick,
of California, to be a member of the National Mediation Board for a term expiring July 1, 2010 (reappointment).

Anne Jeannette Udall,
of North Carolina, to be a member of the Board of Trustees of the Morris K. Udall Scholarship

and Excellence in National Environmental Policy Foundation for a term expiring October 6, 2010 (reappointment).

Submitted July 21

Jane M. Doggett,
of Montana, to be a member of the National Council on the Humanities for a term expiring January 26, 2012, vice Stephen McKnight, term expired.

Sharon Lynn Hays,
of Virginia, to be an Associate Director of the Office of Science and Technology Policy, vice Kathie L. Olsen.

Ronald J. James,
of Ohio, to be an Assistant Secretary of the Army, vice Reginald Jude Brown.

Robert W. Johnson,
of Nevada, to be Commissioner of Reclamation, vice John W. Keys III, resigned.

James R. Kunder,
of Virginia, to be Deputy Administrator of the U.S. Agency for International Development, vice Frederick W. Schieck.

Mary Martin Ourisman,
of Florida, to be Ambassador Extraordinary and Plenipotentiary of the United States of America to Barbados, and to serve concurrently and without additional compensation as Ambassador Extraordinary and Plenipotentiary of the United States of America to St. Kitts and Nevis, Saint Lucia, Antigua and Barbuda, the Commonwealth of Dominica, Grenada, and Saint Vincent and the Grenadines.

Bijan Rafiekian,
of California, to be a member of the Board of Directors of the Export-Import Bank of the United States for the remainder of the term expiring January 20, 2007, vice Linda Mysliwy Conlin.

Karen B. Stewart,
of Florida, a career member of the Senior Foreign Service, class of Counselor, to be Ambassador Extraordinary and Plenipotentiary of the United States of America to the Republic of Belarus.

Maj. Gen. Todd I. Stewart, USAF (Ret.),
of Ohio, to be a member of the National Security Education Board for a term of 4 years, vice Arthur James Collingsworth, term expiring.

Submitted July 25

Margrethe Lundsager,
of Virginia, to be U.S. Executive Director of the International Monetary Fund for a term of 2 years, vice Nancy P. Jacklin, term expired.

Dianne I. Moss,
of Colorado, to be a member of the Board of Directors of the Overseas Private Investment Corporation for a term expiring December 17, 2007, vice John L. Morrison, term expired.

Ronald A. Tschetter,
of Minnesota, to be Director of the Peace Corps, vice Gaddi H. Vasquez, resigned.

Submitted July 27

Rodger A. Heaton,
of Illinois, to be U.S. Attorney for the Central District of Illinois for the term of 4 years, vice Jan Paul Miller, resigned.

Deborah Jean Johnson Rhodes,
of Alabama, to be U.S. Attorney for the Southern District of Alabama for the term of 4 years, vice David Preston York, resigned 2006.

Submitted August 1

C. Stephen Allred,
of Idaho, to be an Assistant Secretary of the Interior, vice Rebecca W. Watson, resigned.

Carl Joseph Artman,
of Colorado, to be an Assistant Secretary of the Interior, vice David Wayne Anderson.

Alex A. Beehler,
of Maryland, to be Inspector General, Environmental Protection Agency, vice Nikki Rush Tinsley, resigned.

James H. Bilbray,
of Nevada, to be a Governor of the U.S. Postal Service for the remainder of the term expiring December 8, 2006, vice John F. Walsh, resigned.

James H. Bilbray,
of Nevada, to be a Governor of the U.S. Postal Service for a term expiring December 8, 2015 (reappointment).

Charles R. Christopherson, Jr.,
of Texas, to be a member of the Board of Directors of the Commodity Credit Corporation, vice Joseph J. Jen.

Randolph James Clerihue,
of Virginia, to be an Assistant Secretary of Labor, vice Lisa Kruska.

Susan E. Dudley,
of Virginia, to be Administrator of the Office of Information and Regulatory Affairs, Office of Management and Budget, vice John D. Graham, resigned.

Michael F. Duffy,
of the District of Columbia, to be a member of the Federal Mine Safety and Health Review Commission for a term expiring August 30, 2012 (reappointment).

Wilma B. Liebman,
of the District of Columbia, to be a member of the National Labor Relations Board for the term of 5 years expiring August 27, 2011 (reappointment).

Roger Romulus Martella, Jr.,
of Virginia, to be an Assistant Administrator of the Environmental Protection Agency, vice Ann R. Klee, resigned.

Arthur K. Reilly,
of New Jersey, to be a member of the National Science Board, National Science Foundation, for a term expiring May 10, 2012, vice Michael G. Rossmann, term expired.

Leland A. Strom,
of Illinois, to be a member of the Farm Credit Administration Board, Farm Credit Administration, for a term expiring October 13, 2012, vice Douglas L. Flory, term expiring.

Submitted August 2

Dabney Langhorne Friedrich,
of Virginia, to be a member of the U.S. Sentencing Commission for the remainder of the term expiring October 31, 2009, vice Michael O'Neill.

Roslynn Renee Mauskopf,
of New York, to be U.S. District Judge for the Eastern District of New York, vice David G. Trager, retired.

Liam O'Grady,
of Virginia, to be U.S. District Judge for the Eastern District of Virginia, vice Claude M. Hilton, retired.

Lawrence Joseph O'Neill,
of California, to be U.S. District Judge for the Eastern District of California, vice Oliver W. Wanger, retired.

Submitted August 3

Brig. Gen. Bruce Arlan Berwick, USA,
to be a member of the Mississippi River Commission.

Brig. Gen. Robert Crear, USA,
to be a member and President of the Mississippi River Commission.

Rear Adm. Samuel P. De Bow, Jr., NOAA,
to be a member of the Mississippi River Commission.

Nelson M. Ford,
of Virginia, to be an Assistant Secretary of the Army, vice Valerie Lynn Baldwin.

Cynthia A. Glassman,
of Virginia, to be Under Secretary of Commerce for Economic Affairs, vice Kathleen B. Cooper, resigned.

William H. Graves,
of Tennessee, to be a member of the Board of Directors of the Tennessee Valley Authority for a term expiring May 18, 2007 (new position).

Col. Gregg F. Martin, USA,
to be a member of the Mississippi River Commission.

Rachel K. Paulose,
of Minnesota, to be U.S. Attorney for the District of Minnesota for the term of 4 years, vice Thomas B. Heffelfinger, resigned.

John K. Veroneau,
of Virginia, to be a Deputy U.S. Trade Representative, with the rank of Ambassador, vice Susan C. Schwab, resigned.

Gerald Walpin,
of New York, to be Inspector General, Corporation for National and Community Service, vice J. Russell George.

Submitted September 5

David Longly Bernhardt,
of Colorado, to be Solicitor of the Department of the Interior, vice Sue Ellen Wooldridge.

Mary Amelia Bomar,
of Pennsylvania, to be Director of the National Park Service, vice Frances P. Mainella, resigned.

Terrence W. Boyle,
of North Carolina, to be U.S. Circuit Judge for the Fourth Circuit, vice J. Dickson Phillips, Jr., retired.

Larry W. Brown,
of Virginia, to be a member of the Defense Nuclear Facilities Safety Board for a term expiring October 18, 2010, vice R. Bruce Matthews, resigned.

Peter E. Cianchette,
of Maine, to be a member of the Internal Revenue Service Oversight Board for a term expiring September 14, 2010, vice Nancy Killefer, term expired.

Charles F. Conner,
of Indiana, to be a member of the Board of Directors of the Commodity Credit Corporation, vice James R. Moseley.

John Ray Correll,
of Indiana, to be Director of the Office of Surface Mining Reclamation and Enforcement, vice Jeffrey D. Jarrett.

Charles L. Glazer,
of Connecticut, to be Ambassador Extraordinary and Plenipotentiary of the United States of America to the Republic of El Salvador.

William James Haynes II,
of Virginia, to be U.S. Circuit Judge for the Fourth Circuit, vice H. Emory Widener, Jr., retiring.

Tracy A. Henke,
of Missouri, to be Executive Director of the Office of State and Local Government Coordination and Preparedness, Department of Homeland Security, vice C. Suzanne Mencer, resigned.

Robert T. Howard,
of Virginia, to be an Assistant Secretary of Veterans Affairs (Information and Technology), vice Robert N. McFarland.

Collister Johnson, Jr.,
of Virginia, to be Administrator of the Saint Lawrence Seaway Development Corporation for a term of 7 years, vice Albert S. Jacquez, term expired.

John Edward Mansfield,
of Virginia, to be a member of the Defense Nuclear Facilities Safety Board for a term expiring October 18, 2011 (reappointment).

William W. Mercer,
of Montana, to be Associate Attorney General, vice Robert D. McCallum, Jr.

Mark Myers,
of Alaska, to be Director of the U.S. Geological Survey, vice Charles G. Groat, resigned.

William Gerry Myers III,
of Idaho, to be U.S. Circuit Judge for the Ninth Circuit, vice Thomas G. Nelson, retired.

James F.X. O'Gara,
of Pennsylvania, to be Deputy Director for Supply Reduction, Office of National Drug Control Policy, vice Barry D. Crane.

Halil Suleyman Ozerden,
of Mississippi, to be U.S. District Judge for the Southern District of Mississippi, vice David C. Bramlette, retired.

Norman Randy Smith,
of Idaho, to be U.S. Circuit Judge for the Ninth Circuit, vice Stephen S. Trott, retired.

Richard Stickler,
of West Virginia, to be Assistant Secretary of Labor for Mine Safety and Health, vice David D. Lauriski, resigned.

Sara Alicia Tucker,
of California, to be Under Secretary of Education, vice Edward R. McPherson, resigned.

Michael Brunson Wallace,
of Mississippi, to be U.S. Circuit Judge for the
Fifth Circuit, vice Charles W. Pickering, Sr.,
retired.

William Ludwig Wehrum, Jr.,
of Tennessee, to be an Assistant Administrator
of the Environmental Protection Agency, vice
Jeffrey R. Holmstead, resigned.

Peter Stanley Winokur,
of Maryland, to be a member of the Defense
Nuclear Facilities Safety Board for a term expiring October 18, 2009, vice John T. Conway,
term expired.

Otis D. Wright II,
of California, to be U.S. District Judge for the
Central District of California, vice Gary L. Taylor, retired.

George H. Wu,
of California, to be U.S. District Judge for the
Central District of California, vice Ronald S.W.
Lew, retiring.

Submitted September 6

Robert K. Steel,
of Connecticut, to be an Under Secretary of
the Treasury, vice Randal Quarles.

Submitted September 7

Jovita Carranza,
of Illinois, to be Deputy Administrator of the
Small Business Administration, vice Melanie
Sabelhaus, resigned.

Paul DeCamp,
of Virginia, to be Administrator of the Wage
and Hour Division, Department of Labor, vice
Tammy Dee McCutchen, resigned, to which position he was appointed during the last recess
of the Senate.

Michael F. Duffy,
of the District of Columbia, to be a member
of the Federal Mine Safety and Health Review
Commission for a term of 6 years expiring August 30, 2012 (reappointment), to which position
he was appointed during the last recess of the
Senate.

Lauren M. Maddox,
of Virginia, to be Assistant Secretary for Communications and Outreach, Department of Education, vice Kevin F. Sullivan, resigned.

Daniel Meron,
of Maryland, to be General Counsel of the Department of Health and Human Services, vice
Alex Azar II, to which position he was appointed
during the last recess of the Senate.

Mary E. Peters,
of Arizona, to be Secretary of Transportation,
vice Norman Y. Mineta, resigned.

Dean A. Pinkert,
of Virginia, to be a member of the U.S. International Trade Commission for the term expiring December 16, 2015, vice Jennifer Anne
Hillman, term expiring.

Irving A. Williamson,
of New York, to be a member of the U.S. International Trade Commission for the term expiring June 16, 2014, vice Stephen Koplan, term
expired.

Donald Y. Yamamoto,
of New York, a career member of the Senior
Foreign Service, class of Minister-Counselor, to
be Ambassador Extraordinary and Plenipotentiary of the United States of America to
the Federal Democratic Republic of Ethiopia.

Submitted September 13

Frank Baxter,
of California, to be Ambassador Extraordinary
and Plenipotentiary of the United States of
America to the Oriental Republic of Uruguay.

Thomas M. Hardiman,
of Pennsylvania, to be U.S. Circuit Judge for
the Third Circuit, vice Richard L. Nygaard, retired.

Submitted September 15

Michael J. Astrue,
of Massachusetts, to be Commissioner of Social
Security for a term expiring January 19, 2013,
vice Jo Anne Barnhart.

Caroline C. Hunter,
of Florida, to be a member of the Election Assistance Commission for a term expiring December 12, 2009, vice Paul S. DeGregorio, term expired.

David Palmer,
of Maryland, to be a member of the Equal Employment Opportunity Commission for a term expiring July 1, 2011, vice Cari M. Dominguez, term expired.

Submitted September 20

Kay Kelley Arnold,
of Arkansas, to be a member of the Board of Directors of the Inter-American Foundation for a term expiring October 6, 2010 (reappointment).

Dana K. Bilyeu,
of Nevada, to be a member of the Social Security Advisory Board for a term expiring September 30, 2010, vice Gerald M. Shea, term expired.

Barbara Boxer,
of California, to be a Representative of the United States of America to the Sixty-first Session of the General Assembly of the United Nations.

Gary C. Bryner,
of Utah, to be a member of the Board of Directors of the Inter-American Foundation for a term expiring June 26, 2008, vice Nancy Dorn, term expired.

Norman B. Coleman,
of Minnesota, to be a Representative of the United States of America to the Sixty-first Session of the General Assembly of the United Nations.

Thomas Joseph Dodd,
of the District of Columbia, to be a member of the Board of Directors of the Inter-American Foundation for a term expiring June 26, 2008, vice Nadine Hogan.

Cecil E. Floyd,
of South Carolina, to be an Alternate Representative of the United States of America to the Sixty-first Session of the General Assembly of the United Nations.

Hector E. Morales,
of Texas, to be a member of the Board of Directors of the Inter-American Foundation for a term expiring September 20, 2010, vice Jose A. Fourquet, resigned.

John P. Salazar,
of New Mexico, to be a member of the Board of Directors of the Inter-American Foundation for a term expiring September 20, 2012, vice Anita Perez Ferguson.

Thomas A. Shannon, Jr.,
of Virginia, a career member of the Senior Foreign Service, class of Minister-Counselor, to be a member of the Board of Directors of the Inter-American Foundation for a term expiring September 20, 2012, vice Roger Francisco Noriega.

Jack C. Vaughn,
of Texas, to be a member of the Board of Directors of the Inter-American Foundation for a term expiring September 20, 2012 (reappointment).

Mark J. Warshawsky,
of Maryland, to be a member of the Social Security Advisory Board for a term expiring September 30, 2012, vice Harold Daub, term expired.

Withdrawn September 20

Nadine Hogan,
of Florida, to be a member of the Board of Directors of the Inter-American Foundation for a term expiring June 26, 2008, vice Frank D. Yturria, resigned, which was sent to the Senate on January 24, 2005.

Nadine Hogan,
of Florida, to be a member of the Board of Directors of the Inter-American Foundation for a term expiring June 26, 2008 (reappointment), to which position she was appointed during the recess of the Senate from January 3, 2006, to January 18, 2006, which was sent to the Senate on February 10, 2006.

John E. Maupin, Jr.,
of Tennessee, to be a member of the Social Security Advisory Board for a term expiring September 30, 2010, vice Gerald M. Shea, term expired, which was sent to the Senate on September 6, 2005.

Submitted September 21

Steven R. Chealander,
of Texas, to be a member of the National Transportation Safety Board for the remainder of the term expiring December 31, 2007, vice Ellen G. Engleman, resigned.

Curtis S. Chin,
of New York, to be U.S. Director of the Asian Development Bank, with the rank of Ambassador, vice Paul William Speltz.

Ronald P. Spogli,
of California, to serve concurrently and without additional compensation as Ambassador Extraordinary and Plenipotentiary of the United States of America to the Republic of San Marino.

Craig Roberts Stapleton,
of Connecticut, to serve concurrently and without additional compensation as Ambassador Extraordinary and Plenipotentiary of the United States of America to Monaco.

Submitted September 26

Kevin M. Kolevar,
of Michigan, to be an Assistant Secretary of Energy (Electricity Delivery and Energy Reliability), vice John S. Shaw, resigned.

Jane C. Luxton,
of Virginia, to be Assistant Secretary of Commerce for Oceans and Atmosphere, vice James R. Mahoney.

Thurgood Marshall, Jr.,
of Virginia, to be a Governor of the U.S. Postal Service for a term expiring December 8, 2011, vice Ned R. McWherter, term expired.

Phillip L. Swagel,
of Maryland, to be an Assistant Secretary of the Treasury, vice Mark J. Warshawsky, resigned.

Submitted September 28

Michele A. Davis,
of Virginia, to be an Assistant Secretary of the Treasury, vice Antonio Fratto.

Eric D. Eberhard,
of Washington, to be a member of the Board of Trustees of the Morris K. Udall Scholarship and Excellence in National Environmental Policy Foundation for a term expiring October 6, 2012, vice Malcolm B. Bowekaty, term expiring.

Dana Gioia,
of California, to be Chairperson of the National Endowment for the Arts for a term of 4 years (reappointment).

Submitted September 29

John Roberts Hackman,
of Virginia, to be U.S. Marshal for the Eastern District of Virginia for the term of 4 years, vice John Francis Clark.

Robert F. Hoyt
of Maryland, to be General Counsel for the Department of the Treasury, vice Arnold I. Havens, resigned.

William Lindsay Osteen, Jr.
of North Carolina, to be U.S. District Judge for the Middle District of North Carolina, vice William L. Osteen, Sr., retired.

Martin Karl Reidinger,
of North Carolina, to be U.S. District Judge for the Western District of North Carolina, vice Graham C. Mullen, retired.

Thomas D. Schroeder,
of North Carolina, to be U.S. District Judge for the Middle District of North Carolina, vice Frank W. Bullock, Jr., retired.

Submitted November 9

John Robert Bolton,
of Maryland, to be the Representative of the United States of America to the United Nations, with the rank and status of Ambassador Extraordinary and Plenipotentiary, and the Representative of the United States of America in the Security Council of the United Nations.

John Robert Bolton,
of Maryland, to be Representative of the United States of America to the Sessions of the General Assembly of the United Nations during his tenure of service as Representative of the United States of America to the United Nations.

Submitted November 13

Katherine Almquist,
of Virginia, to be an Assistant Administrator of
the U.S. Agency for International Development,
vice Lloyd O. Pierson, resigned.

Andrew G. Biggs,
of New York, to be Deputy Commissioner of
Social Security for the remainder of the term
expiring January 19, 2007, vice James B.
Lockhart III.

Andrew G. Biggs,
of New York, to be Deputy Commissioner of
Social Security for a term expiring January 19,
2013 (reappointment).

Dan Gregory Blair,
of the District of Columbia, to be a Commissioner of the Postal Rate Commission for a term
expiring October 14, 2012, vice George A.
Omas, term expired.

Terry L. Cline,
of Oklahoma, to be Administrator of the Substance Abuse and Mental Health Services Administration, Department of Health and Human
Services, vice Charles Curie, resigned.

Benjamin Donenberg,
of California, to be a member of the National
Council on the Arts for a term expiring September 3, 2012, vice Maribeth McGinley, term
expired.

Charles E. Dorkey III,
of New York, to be a member of the Advisory
Board of the Saint Lawrence Seaway Development Corporation, vice James S. Simpson.

Foreststorn Hamilton,
of New York, to be a member of the National
Council on the Arts for a term expiring September 3, 2012, vice Mary Costa, term expired.

Richard Allan Hill,
of Montana, to be a member of the Board of
Directors of the Corporation for National and
Community Service for a term expiring June
10, 2009, vice Juanita Sims Doty, term expired.

Diane Humetewa,
of Arizona, to be a member of the Board of
Trustees of the Morris K. Udall Scholarship and
Excellence in National Environmental Policy

Foundation for a term expiring August 25, 2012,
vice Richard Narcia, term expired.

Joan Israelite,
of Missouri, to be a member of the National
Council on the Arts for a term expiring September 3, 2012, vice Don V. Cogman, term
expired.

Mark Everett Keenum,
of Mississippi, to be Under Secretary of Agriculture for Farm and Foreign Agricultural Services, vice J.B. Penn.

Mark Everett Keenum,
of Mississippi, to be a member of the Board
of Directors of the Commodity Credit Corporation, vice J.B. Penn.

Scott A. Keller,
of Florida, to be an Assistant Secretary of Housing and Urban Development, vice Steven B.
Nesmith, resigned.

Charlotte P. Kessler,
of Ohio, to be a member of the National Council on the Arts for a term expiring September
3, 2012, vice Katharine DeWitt, term expired.

Robert Bretley Lott,
of Louisiana, to be a member of the National
Council on the Arts for a term expiring September 3, 2012, vice Teresa Lozano Long, term
expired.

William Francis Price, Jr.,
of California, to be a member of the National
Council on the Arts for a term expiring September 3, 2012, vice Evelyn Dee Potter Rose,
term expired.

Anthony W. Ryan,
of Massachusetts, to be an Assistant Secretary
of the Treasury, vice Timothy S. Bitsberger.

Paul A. Schneider,
of Maryland, to be Under Secretary for Management, Department of Homeland Security, vice
Janet Hale, resigned.

Leon R. Sequeira,
of Virginia, to be an Assistant Secretary of
Labor, vice Veronica Vargas Stidvent.

Ellen C. Williams,
of Kentucky, to be a Governor of the U.S. Postal Service for a term expiring December 8, 2016 (reappointment).

Submitted November 14

Steven G. Bradbury,
of Maryland, to be an Assistant Attorney General, vice Jack Landman Goldsmith III, resigned.

Paul DeCamp,
of Virginia, to be Administrator of the Wage and Hour Division, Department of Labor, vice Tammy Dee McCutchen, resigned.

Elizabeth Dougherty,
of the District of Columbia, to be a member of the National Mediation Board for a term expiring July 1, 2007, vice Edward J. Fitzmaurice, Jr., term expired.

Elizabeth Dougherty,
of the District of Columbia, to be a member of the National Mediation Board for a term expiring July 1, 2010 (reappointment).

Arlene Holen,
of the District of Columbia, to be a member of the Federal Mine Safety and Health Review Commission for a term of 6 years expiring August 30, 2010, vice Robert H. Beatty, Jr., term expired.

Richard Stickler,
of West Virginia, to be Assistant Secretary of Labor for Mine Safety and Health, vice David D. Lauriski, resigned to which position he was appointed during the last recess of the Senate.

Kenneth Y. Tomlinson,
of Virginia, to be a member of the Broadcasting Board of Governors for a term expiring August 13, 2007 (reappointment).

Kenneth Y. Tomlinson,
of Virginia, to be Chairman of the Broadcasting Board of Governors (reappointment).

Peter W. Tredick,
of California, to be a member of the National Mediation Board for a term expiring July 1, 2009, vice Read Van de Water, term expired.

Withdrawn November 14

Elizabeth Dougherty,
of the District of Columbia, to be a member of the National Mediation Board for a term expiring July 1, 2009, vice Read Van de Water, term expiring, which was sent to the Senate on May 25, 2006.

Peter W. Tredick,
of California, to be a member of the National Mediation Board for a term expiring July 1, 2007, vice Edward J. Fitzmaurice, Jr., term expired, which was sent to the Senate on March 27, 2006.

Peter W. Tredick,
of California, to be a member of the National Mediation Board for a term expiring July 1, 2010 (reappointment), which was sent to the Senate on July 18, 2006.

Submitted November 16

Terrence W. Boyle,
of North Carolina, to be U.S. Circuit Judge for the Fourth Circuit, vice J. Dickson Phillips, Jr., retired.

William James Haynes II,
of Virginia, to be U.S. Circuit Judge for the Fourth Circuit, vice H. Emory Widener, Jr., retiring.

Peter D. Keisler,
of Maryland, to be U.S. Circuit Judge for the District of Columbia Circuit, vice John G. Roberts, Jr., elevated.

William Gerry Myers III,
of Idaho, to be U.S. Circuit Judge for the Ninth Circuit, vice Thomas G. Nelson, retired.

James Edward Rogan,
of California, to be U.S. District Judge for the Central District of California, vice Nora M. Manella, resigned.

Margaret A. Ryan,
of Virginia, to be a Judge of the U.S. Court of Appeals for the Armed Forces for the term of 15 years to expire on the date prescribed by law, vice Herman F. Gierke, term expired.

Benjamin Hale Settle,
of Washington, to be U.S. District Judge for the Western District of Washington, vice Franklin D. Burgess, retired.

Norman Randy Smith,
of Idaho, to be U.S. Circuit Judge for the Ninth Circuit, vice Stephen S. Trott, retired.

Scott Wallace Stucky,
of Maryland, to be a Judge of the U.S. Court of Appeals for the Armed Forces for the term of 15 years to expire on the date prescribed by law, vice Susan J. Crawford, term expired.

Michael Brunson Wallace,
of Mississippi, to be U.S. Circuit Judge for the Fifth Circuit, vice Charles W. Pickering, Sr., retired.

Submitted December 4

Robert M. Gates,
of Texas, to be Secretary of Defense, vice Donald Henry Rumsfeld, resigned.

Submitted December 5

Jeffrey Robert Brown,
of Illinois, to be a member of the Social Security Advisory Board for a term expiring September 30, 2008, vice Bradley D. Belt, resigned, to which position he was appointed during the last recess of the Senate.

Gregory B. Cade,
of Virginia, to be Administrator of the U.S. Fire Administration, Department of Homeland Security, vice R. David Paulison, resigned.

Sam Fox,
of Missouri, to be Ambassador Extraordinary and Plenipotentiary of the United States of America to Belgium.

Frederick J. Kapala,
of Illinois, to be U.S. District Judge for the Northern District of Illinois, vice Philip G. Reinhard, retiring.

Heidi M. Pasichow,
of the District of Columbia, to be an Associate Judge of the Superior Court of the District of Columbia for the term of 15 years, vice Anna Blackburne-Rigsby, elevated.

Stanley Davis Phillips,
of North Carolina, to be Ambassador Extraordinary and Plenipotentiary of the United States of America to the Republic of Estonia.

Jill E. Sommers,
of Kansas, to be a Commissioner of the Commodity Futures Trading Commission for the remainder of the term expiring April 13, 2009, vice Sharon Brown-Hruska, resigned.

Michael W. Tankersley,
of Texas, to be Inspector General, Export-Import Bank (new position).

Submitted December 6

Michael J. Burns,
of New Mexico, to be Assistant to the Secretary of Defense for Nuclear and Chemical and Biological Defense Programs, vice Dale Klein, resigned.

Beryl A. Howell,
of the District of Columbia, to be a member of the U.S. Sentencing Commission for a term expiring October 31, 2011 (reappointment).

Rosemary E. Rodriguez,
of Colorado, to be a member of the Election Assistance Commission for the remainder of the term expiring December 12, 2007, vice Raymundo Martinez III, resigned.

John R. Steer,
of Virginia, to be a member of the U.S. Sentencing Commission for a term expiring October 31, 2011 (reappointment).

Withdrawn December 6

Tracy A. Henke,
of Missouri, to be Executive Director of the Office of State and Local Government Coordination and Preparedness, Department of Homeland Security, vice C. Suzanne Mencer, resigned, which was sent to the Senate on September 5, 2006.

David H. Laufman,
of Texas, to be Inspector General, Department of Defense, vice Joseph E. Schmitz, resigned, which was sent to the Senate on June 5, 2006.

Submitted December 7

Thomas Alvin Farr,
of North Carolina, to be U.S. District Judge
for the Eastern District of North Carolina, vice
Malcolm J. Howard, retired.

Appendix C—Checklist of White House Press Releases

The following list contains releases of the Office of the Press Secretary which are not included in this book.

Released July 1

Statement by the Press Secretary on U.S.-Canada agreement on softwood lumber trade

Statement by the Press Secretary on disaster assistance to New York

Released July 2

Statement by the Press Secretary on disaster assistance to Maryland

Statement by the Press Secretary on disaster assistance to Ohio

Released July 3

Transcript of a press gaggle by Press Secretary Tony Snow

Statement by the Press Secretary announcing that the President signed H.R. 5403

Released July 4

Transcript of a press briefing by Press Secretary Tony Snow and National Security Adviser Stephen J. Hadley on the North Korea missile launches

Statement by the Press Secretary on North Korea missile launches

Released July 5

Transcript of a press briefing by Press Secretary Tony Snow

Statement by the Press Secretary on disaster assistance to Delaware

Fact sheet: Basic Pilot: A Clear and Reliable Way To Verify Employment Eligibility

Released July 6

Transcript of a press briefing by Press Secretary Tony Snow

Transcript of a press gaggle by Press Secretary Tony Snow

Transcript of a briefing on the President's visit to the G–8 summit in St. Petersburg, Russia

Statement by the Press Secretary: President Bush To Welcome President of Romania to the White House

Released July 7

Statement by the Press Secretary on disaster assistance to New Jersey

Fact sheet: A Day in Chicago: President Bush Highlights Economic Growth and Innovation

Fact sheet: Job Creation Continues—5.4 Million Jobs Created Since August 2003

Released July 10

Transcript of a press briefing by Press Secretary Tony Snow

Transcript of a press briefing by National Security Adviser Stephen J. Hadley on the President's upcoming visit to Russia and Germany

Statement by the Press Secretary announcing that the President signed H.R. 4912

Fact sheet: Commission for Assistance to a Free Cuba Report to the President

Released July 11

Transcript of a press gaggle by Press Secretary Tony Snow

Fact sheet: Strong Economic Growth and Fiscal Discipline Help Reduce Budget Deficit

Released July 12

Transcript of a press gaggle by Press Secretary Tony Snow

Statement by the Press Secretary: Condemnation of Hizballah Kidnaping of Two Israeli Soldiers

Released July 13

Transcript of a press briefing by Secretary of State Condoleezza Rice and National Security Adviser Stephen J. Hadley

Statement by the Press Secretary: President Bush To Welcome Prime Minister of Iraq to the White House

Released July 14

Transcript of a press gaggle by Press Secretary Tony Snow

Statement by the Press Secretary on disaster assistance to Virginia

Released July 15

Transcript of a press briefing by National Security Adviser Stephen J. Hadley, U.S. Trade Representative Susan C. Schwab, and Press Secretary Tony Snow

Statement by the Press Secretary on the U.S.-Russia Foundation for Economic Advancement and Rule of Law

Fact sheet: The Global Initiative To Combat Nuclear Terrorism

Released July 16

Transcript of a press briefing by Under Secretary for Political Affairs R. Nicholas Burns and Press Secretary Tony Snow on the G–8 leaders' joint statement on the situation in the Middle East

Transcript of a press briefing by Secretary of State Condoleezza Rice

Released July 17

Transcript of a press gaggle by Press Secretary Tony Snow

Fact sheet: The President's Accomplishments at the G–8 Summit

Released July 18

Transcript of a press briefing by Press Secretary Tony Snow

Released July 19

Transcript of a press briefing by Press Secretary Tony Snow

Statement by the Press Secretary: Visit by Salva Kiir, First Vice President of the Government of National Unity of Sudan and President of the Government of Southern Sudan

Statement by the Press Secretary announcing that the President signed S. 3504

Fact sheet: President Bush's Stem Cell Research Policy

Released July 20

Transcript of a press briefing by Press Secretary Tony Snow

Released July 21

Transcript of a press gaggle by Deputy Press Secretary Dana Perino

Transcript of a briefing by a senior administration official on the visit by Prime Minister Nuri al-Maliki of Iraq

Statement by the Press Secretary: Visit of British Prime Minister Tony Blair

Statement by the Press Secretary on disaster assistance to Missouri

Released July 24

Transcript of a press briefing by Press Secretary Tony Snow

Statement by the Press Secretary: Visit by Minni Minawi, Sudan Liberation Movement/Army Leader

Statement by the Press Secretary announcing that the President signed H.R. 42

Fact sheet: Honoring Immigrant Members of America's Armed Services

Released July 25

Transcript of a press briefing by National Security Adviser Stephen J. Hadley

Statement by the Press Secretary announcing that the President signed S.J. Res. 40

Fact sheet: Prime Minister Maliki's Meeting With President Bush

Released July 26

Transcript of a press briefing by Press Secretary Tony Snow

Statement by the Press Secretary announcing that the President signed S. 655

Released July 27

Transcript of a press briefing by Press Secretary Tony Snow

Statement by the Press Secretary: House Passage of India Civil Nuclear Cooperation Legislation

Statement by the Press Secretary announcing that the President signed H.R. 9, H.R. 2872, and H.R. 5117

Statement by the Press Secretary announcing that the President signed H.R. 5865

Fact sheet: Voting Rights Act Reauthorization and Amendments Act of 2006

Fact sheet: The Adam Walsh Child Protection and Safety Act of 2006

Released July 28

Statement by the Press Secretary: U.S. Support for Congolese Elections

Released July 30

Transcript of a press gaggle by Press Secretary Tony Snow

Released July 31

Transcript of a press briefing by Federal Emergency Management Agency Director R. David Paulison

Fact sheet: A Day in Miami: President Bush Highlights Economic Growth and Hurricane Preparedness Efforts

Released August 1

Transcript of a press briefing by Press Secretary Tony Snow

Statement by the Press Secretary: Renewal of the Burmese Freedom and Democracy Act of 2003

Statement by the Press Secretary announcing that the President signed H.J. Res. 86

Statement by the Press Secretary announcing that the President signed H.R. 2977, H.R. 3440, H.R. 3549, H.R. 3934, H.R. 4101, and H.R. 4108

Statement by the Press Secretary on disaster assistance to Ohio

Released August 2

Transcript of a press briefing by Press Secretary Tony Snow

Statement by the Press Secretary announcing that the President signed H.R. 4456, H.R. 4561, H.R. 4688, H.R. 4786, H.R. 4995, and H.R. 5245

Released August 3

Transcript of a press gaggle by Press Secretary Tony Snow

Statement by the Press Secretary announcing that the President signed H.R. 4019, S. 310, and S. 1496

Fact sheet: Operation Jump Start: Acting Now To Secure the Border

Released August 4

Transcript of a press gaggle by Press Secretary Tony Snow

Statement by the Press Secretary announcing that the President signed H.R. 5877 and S. 3741

Statement by the Press Secretary on disaster assistance to Alaska

Fact sheet: Job Creation Continues—More Than 5.5 Million Jobs Created Since August 2003

Released August 6

Transcript of a press briefing by Secretary of State Condoleezza Rice

Transcript of a press briefing by National Security Adviser Stephen J. Hadley

Released August 8

Transcript of a press gaggle by Press Secretary Tony Snow

Released August 9

Transcript of a press briefing by Press Secretary Tony Snow

Released August 10

Transcript of a press gaggle by Press Secretary Tony Snow

Fact sheet: National Strategy To Internationalize Efforts Against Kleptocracy

Released August 11

Transcript of a press gaggle by Press Secretary Tony Snow

Released August 14

Transcript of a press briefing by Press Secretary Tony Snow

Statement by the Press Secretary announcing that on August 12 the President signed S. 250,

H.R. 3682, and S. 3693 and on August 14 the President signed H.R. 5683

Released August 15

Transcript of a press briefing by Press Secretary Tony Snow

Statement by the Press Secretary on disaster assistance to Texas

Released August 16

Transcript of a press briefing by Press Secretary Tony Snow

Statement by the Press Secretary: Visit of President Roh Moo-hyun of the Republic of Korea

Released August 17

Transcript of a press briefing by Press Secretary Tony Snow

Statement by the Press Secretary on a Federal judge's ruling on the terrorist surveillance program

Statement by the Press Secretary on U.S. assistance to the Government of Colombia Airbridge Denial Program

Statement by the Press Secretary announcing that the President signed H.R. 4646, H.R. 4811, H.R. 4962, H.R. 5104, H.R. 5107, H.R. 5169, and H.R. 5540

Fact sheet: The Pension Protection Act of 2006: Ensuring Greater Retirement Security for American Workers

Released August 18

Transcript of a press briefing by Secretary of the Treasury Henry M. Paulson, Jr., Director of the Office of Management and Budget Robert J. Portman, and Council of Economic Advisers Chairman Edward P. Lazear on the President's meeting with economic advisers

Statement by the Press Secretary: Visit by President Alan Garcia of Peru

Released August 21

Fact sheet: United States Humanitarian, Reconstruction, and Security Assistance to Lebanon

Released August 22

Transcript of a press briefing by Gulf Coast Region Recovery and Rebuilding Coordinator Donald E. Powell, Federal Emergency Management Agency Director R. David Paulison, and Army Corps of Engineers Commanding General and Chief of Engineers Lt. Gen. Carl A. Strock

Transcript of a press gaggle by Deputy Press Secretary Dana Perino and Secretary of Health and Human Services Michael O. Leavitt

Fact sheet: Health Care Transparency: Empowering Consumers To Save on Quality Care

Released August 23

Transcript of a press briefing by Deputy Press Secretary Dana Perino

Released August 24

Transcript of a press gaggle by Deputy Press Secretary Dana Perino

Fact sheet: The One-Year Anniversary of Hurricane Katrina

Released August 25

Statement by the Press Secretary announcing that the President and Mrs. Bush will host a White House Summit on Malaria in December

Released August 28

Transcript of a press gaggle by Deputy Press Secretary Dana Perino

Fact sheet: President Bush's Visit to Biloxi and New Orleans

Fact sheet: A New Mississippi: Rebuilding in the Wake of Hurricane Katrina

Released August 29

Transcript of a press gaggle by Deputy Press Secretary Dana Perino

Transcript of a press briefing by Gulf Coast Region Recovery and Rebuilding Coordinator Donald E. Powell and U.S. Coast Guard Commandant Adm. Thad W. Allen

Fact sheet: Keeping the Promise of Jackson Square: A More Hopeful Louisiana

Released August 30

Transcript of a press gaggle by Deputy Press Secretary Dana Perino

Statement by the Deputy Press Secretary on the death of Egypt's Nobel Prize Laureate in Literature Naguib Mahfouz

Statement by the Press Secretary: The President and Mrs. Bush To Welcome the King and Queen of Sweden to the White House

Statement by the Press Secretary: Appointment of the New Secretary-General of the United Nations, Foreign Minister Ban Ki-moon

Statement by the Press Secretary announcing that the President signed H.R. 315, H.R. 562, H.R. 1463, H.R. 1556, H.R. 2322, H.R. 4768, H.R. 4805, H.R. 5026, H.R. 5428, H.R. 5434, S. 2856, S. 3661, and S. 3728

Statement by the Press Secretary announcing that the President signed H.R. 3127

Fact sheet: The President's Management Agenda: Making Government More Effective

Released October 15

Statement by the Press Secretary on disaster assistance to New York

Released October 16

Transcript of a press briefing by Press Secretary Tony Snow

Statement by the Press Secretary announcing that the President signed H.R. 138, H.R. 479, H.R. 3508, H.R. 4902, H.R. 5094, H.R. 5160, H.R. 5381, and S. 2562

Statement by the Press Secretary on disaster assistance to Alaska

Released October 17

Transcript of a press briefing by Press Secretary Tony Snow

Statement by the Press Secretary announcing that the President signed H.R. 4957 and H.R. 6197

Statement by the Press Secretary on disaster assistance to Hawaii

Fact sheet: The Military Commissions Act of 2006

Released October 18

Transcript of a press gaggle by Press Secretary Tony Snow

Fact sheet: A Day in North Carolina: President Bush Highlights the Success of No Child Left Behind

Released October 19

Transcript of a press briefing by Press Secretary Tony Snow

Statement by the Press Secretary: Visit by President-elect Felipe Calderon of Mexico

Released October 20

Transcript of a press briefing by Press Secretary Tony Snow

Statement by the Press Secretary: Visit of NATO Secretary General "Jaap" de Hoop Scheffer

Released October 23

Transcript of a press briefing by Press Secretary Tony Snow

Statement by the Press Secretary: President Bush To Attend the Asia-Pacific Economic Cooperation (APEC) Leaders' Meeting in Vietnam and Travel to Singapore and Indonesia

Released October 24

Transcript of a press gaggle by Deputy Press Secretary Tony Fratto

Statement by the Press Secretary on disaster assistance to New York

Released October 26

Transcript of a press gaggle by Deputy Press Secretary Dana Perino

Fact sheet: The Secure Fence Act of 2006

Released October 27

Transcript of a press briefing by Press Secretary Tony Snow

Statement by the Press Secretary on disaster assistance to Alaska

Released October 30

Transcript of a press gaggle by Deputy Press Secretary Dana Perino

Statement by the Press Secretary: Congolese Elections

Released October 31

Transcript of a press briefing by Press Secretary Tony Snow

Statement by the Press Secretary: U.S.-EU Economic Ministerial

Released November 18

Transcript of a press briefing by Press Secretary Tony Snow

Transcript of a press briefing by National Security Adviser Stephen J. Hadley

Statement by the Press Secretary on the President's acceptance of the recommendation of the Committee on Foreign Investment in the United States on the proposed merger of Lucent Technologies, Inc., and Alcatel

Statement by the Press Secretary announcing that on November 17 the President signed H.R. 6326 and H.J. Res. 100

Released November 19

Transcript of a press gaggle by Press Secretary Tony Snow

Transcript of a press briefing by Deputy National Security Adviser for International Economic Affairs David H. McCormick

Fact sheet: Asia-Pacific Economic Cooperation (APEC) 2006

Released November 21

Transcript of a press gaggle by Press Secretary Tony Snow and National Security Adviser Stephen J. Hadley

Transcript of a teleconference press briefing by National Security Council Senior Director for European Affairs Judith A. Ansley on the President's visit to Estonia and Latvia and the NATO summit

Transcript of a teleconference press briefing by Council of Economic Advisers Chairman Edward P. Lazear on the administration's updated economic forecast

Released November 22

Statement by the Press Secretary: Visit by President Oscar Arias Sanchez of Costa Rica

Released November 27

Transcript of a press gaggle by Press Secretary Tony Snow and National Security Adviser Stephen J. Hadley

Statement by the Press Secretary announcing that the President signed S. 435, S. 819, S. 1131, S. 2464, and S. 3880

Released November 28

Transcript of a press briefing by National Security Adviser Stephen J. Hadley

Fact sheet: NATO Summit 2006

Released November 29

Transcript of a press briefing by senior administration officials on the NATO summit

Transcript of a press briefing by a senior administration official on the President's dinner with King Abdullah II of Jordan

Transcript of a press briefing by senior administration officials

Transcript of a press gaggle by Counselor to the President Daniel J. Bartlett

Transcript of a press gaggle by Assistant Secretary of State for European and Eurasian Affairs Daniel Fried

Statement by the Press Secretary: Congolese Elections

Released November 30

Transcript of a press briefing by National Security Adviser Stephen J. Hadley on the President's meeting with Prime Minister Nuri al-Maliki of Iraq

Transcript of a press briefing by a senior administration official on the President's meeting with Prime Minister Nuri al-Maliki of Iraq

Statement by the Press Secretary on an economic grant agreement with El Salvador

Statement by the Press Secretary: President Bush To Welcome President Thabo Mbeki of the Republic of South Africa to the White House

Released December 1

Statement by the Press Secretary announcing that the President signed H.R. 409, H.R. 860, H.R. 1129, H.R. 3085, H.R. 5842, S. 101, S. 1140, and S. 4001

Fact sheet: World AIDS Day 2006

Released December 4

Transcript of a press briefing by Press Secretary Tony Snow

Statement by the Press Secretary: Visit of British Prime Minister Tony Blair

6316, S. 1346, S. 1998, S. 3938, S. 4044, and S. 4046

Fact sheet: Tax Relief and Health Care Act of 2006

Released December 21

Statement by the Press Secretary announcing that the President signed H.R. 1492, H.R. 3248, H.R. 6342, and H.R. 6429

Released December 22

Statement by the Press Secretary announcing that the President signed H.J. Res. 101, S. 214, S. 362, S. 707, S. 895, S. 1096, S. 1378, S. 1529, S. 1608, S. 2125, S. 2150, S. 2205, S. 2653, S. 2753, S. 3421, S. 3546, S. 3821, S. 4042, S. 4091, S. 4092, and S. 4093

Released December 26

Transcript of a press gaggle by Deputy Press Secretary Scott M. Stanzel

Released December 27

Transcript of a press gaggle by Deputy Press Secretary Scott M. Stanzel

Released December 29

Statement by the Deputy Press Secretary: President Bush To Welcome Chancellor Merkel

Statement by the Deputy Press Secretary: African Growth and Opportunity Act

Statement by the Deputy Press Secretary announcing that the President signed H.R. 5782

Statement by the Deputy Press Secretary on disaster assistance to Oregon

Statement by the Deputy Press Secretary on disaster assistance to Illinois

Statement by the Deputy Press Secretary on disaster assistance to Missouri

Appendix D—Presidential Documents Published in the Federal Register

This appendix lists Presidential documents released by the Office of the Press Secretary and published in the Federal Register. The texts of the documents are printed in the Federal Register (F.R.) at the citations listed below. The documents are also printed in title 3 of the Code of Federal Regulations and in the Weekly Compilation of Presidential Documents.

PROCLAMATIONS

PROCLAMATIONS—Continued

EXECUTIVE ORDERS

OTHER PRESIDENTIAL DOCUMENTS

OTHER PRESIDENTIAL DOCUMENTS—Continued

OTHER PRESIDENTIAL DOCUMENTS—Continued

Subject Index

Name Index

Abbas, Mahmoud—1388, 1397, 1407, 1412, 1435, 1465, 1473, 1496, 1498, 1500, 1508, 1671, 1675, 1695, 1696, 2124, 2140, 2154, 2161
Abdullah bin Ahmad Badawi—1665, 2259
Abe, Shinzo—1796, 1814, 2095, 2100, 2101, 2247, 2249
Abernathy, Juanita—1448
Abizaid, John P.—1533, 1540, 1576, 1587, 1592, 1660, 1908, 1913, 2095
Abraham, Jane—1928
Abraham, Spencer—1928
Ackerman, Gary L.—1737, 2196
Adams, Mary Nelson—2243
Aguila, Alex—1478, 1524
Aguilar, David V.—1486, 1919
Ahmadi-nejad, Mahmud—1338, 1344, 1371, 1398, 1605, 2210, 2211
Ahner, Chuck—2027
Aiken, Clayton—2243
Akin, Lulli—1834
Akin, W. Todd—1834
Alamar, Naomi—2250
Albright, Craig M.—2253
Alito, Samuel A., Jr.—1579, 1594, 1892, 1937, 1948, 1955, 1964, 1971, 1972, 1979, 1986, 1987, 1994, 2002, 2020, 2047
Allard, A. Wayne—1776, 2010
Allard, Joan—1776
Allen, George—1445, 1878, 2196, 2240
Allen, Susan—1878
Allen, Thad W.—1477, 1482, 1557, 1566, 1642
Allred, C. Stephen—2237, 2264
Almquist, Katherine J.—2250, 2270
Alvarez, Carlos—1477
al-Haili, Abu Zubair—1615
Ama Jan, Safia—1701
Anderson, Belinda Childress—2257
Annan, Kofi—1325, 1370, 1408, 1411, 1412, 1655, 1667, 1672, 2116, 2240, 2245, 2258
Annan, Nane Maria—1672, 2258
Ansip, Andrus—2120, 2122, 2126
Anuzis, Saulius—1928
Arias Sanchez, Oscar—2151, 2256
Armitage, Richard L.—1496, 1692
Armstrong, William L.—1777
Arnold, Kay K.—2245, 2268

Artman, Carl J.—2237, 2264
Asad, Bashar al- —1391, 2079
Asher, Robert B.—1516, 1872
Askey, Thelma J.—2258
Aspromonte, Ken—1892
Assayesh, Ali—1319, 1320
Astrue, Michael J.—2244, 2267
Atala, Anthony J.—2236
Aurakzai, Ali Muhammad Jan—1690
Austin, Al—1683
Ayad, Hamid—1586, 1596

Ba'Attash, Walid—1846
Bachmann, Michele—2240
Bailey, Tom, Jr.—2249
Baker, Delbert W.—2257
Baker, Howard H., Jr.—1574
Baker, James A., III—1818, 1822, 1905, 2053, 2054, 2056, 2059, 2065, 2074, 2079, 2095, 2146, 2150, 2152, 2153, 2156–2159, 2163, 2169, 2177, 2206, 2258
Ban Ki-moon—2250
Barbour, Haley R.—1557–1564
Barbour, Marsha D.—1557
Barefield, Kelly—2246
Barnett, Jim—2027
Barrett, Barbara McConnell—2245
Bartiromo, Maria—2251
Bartlett, Roscoe Gardner—1422
Barzani, Masoud—2178, 2259
Basayev, Shamil—1370
Basescu, Traian—1449, 2232, 2236
Basham, W. Ralph—1486, 1919
Bates, Sally—2251
Battle, Carlos—1787
Battle, Pamela—1787
Baxter, Frank E.—2244, 2267
Beach, M. Josephine—2260
Beauprez, Bob—1776, 2010
Beauprez, Claudia—1776
Bederson, Dana—2166
Beehler, Alex A.—2237, 2264
Bell, Honor, Sr.—2253
Bell, Warren—2260
Belt, Earl—2253
Bennett, Robert—1580, 1581, 1589, 1847
Benson, Bruce D.—1777
Berlusconi, Silvio—1367, 1368, 2256

Document Categories List

Communications to Congress—Continued
Industrial designs, international registration of, message transmitting the Geneva Act of the Hague agreement—2081
Iran, U.S. national emergency, message on continuation—2070
Latvia-U.S. Extradition Treaty, message transmitting—1740
Lebanon, letter on departure of American citizens—1420
Liberia, blocking property of certain persons and prohibiting the importation of certain goods, U.S. national emergency, message on continuation—1419
Malaysia-U.S. Mutual Legal Assistance in Criminal Matters Treaty, message transmitting—2083
Malta-U.S. Extradition Treaty, message transmitting—1741
Military commissions, message transmitting draft legislation—1620
Patent Law Treaty, message transmitting regulations—1611
Sudan
Blocking property of and prohibiting transactions with the Government, letter—1851
U.S. national emergency, letter on continuation—1969
Telecommunication Union Constitution and Convention, International, message transmitting amendments—1360
Terrorism, persons who commit, threaten to commit, or support, U.S. national emergency, message on continuation—1688
Terrorist attacks, U.S. national emergency, letter on continuation—1610
U.S. combat-equipped Armed Forces, deployment, letter reporting on—2193
U.S.-EU Extradition Agreement, message transmitting—1710
U.S.-EU Mutual Legal Assistance Agreement, message transmitting—1710
Weapons of mass destruction, U.S. national emergency, letter on continuation—1946

Communications to Federal Agencies

Combined Federal Campaign, memorandum—1642
Fisheries, promoting sustainable and ending destructive fishing practices, memorandum—1749
National parks, future of, memorandum—1554

Communications to Federal Agencies—Continued
Safety, Health, and Return-to-Employment (SHARE) Initiative, memorandum on extension—1734

Interviews With the News Media

Exchanges with reporters
Arlington, VA—2175
Aurora, CO—1433
Bogor, Indonesia—2107
Camp David, MD—1524
Gulfport, MS—1563
Hanoi, Vietnam—2093
Little Rock, AR—1573
New York City—1666
Strelna, Russia—1405
Washington, DC—1507
White House—1321, 1417, 1449, 1483, 1643, 1933, 2078
Interviews
ABC News—2243, 2250
American Urban Radio Network—2241
Associated Press—2250, 2252
Belo Broadcasting—2251
Bloomberg News—2252
Cable News Network—2232, 2245
CBS News—2243
Christian Broadcasting Network—2252
CNBC—2251
Cox Broadcasting—2252
Foreign journalists—1361
FOX News—1891, 2169, 2236, 2250, 2252
Hearst-Argyle Television—2251
NBC News—2241, 2243
People magazine—2258
Radio Mambi—2236
Reuters—2252
Rush Limbaugh Show, The—2252
Sinclair Broadcast Group—2252
Stars and Stripes newspaper—2231
Telemundo—2236
Tribune Broadcasting—2251
USA Today newspaper—2239
Various print journalists—2244, 2251
Wall Street Journal—2243, 2247
Washington Post—2260
Weekly Standard—2259
WGNO–TV New Orleans—2240
WLOX–TV Biloxi—2240
WPLG–TV Miami—2236
WVUE–TV New Orleans—2240
WWL Radio New Orleans—2241
WWL–TV New Orleans—2240

Above left: Walking with President Nursultan Nazarbayev of Kazakhstan on the Colonnade, September 29.

Left: Sitting with President Ellen Johnson Sirleaf, right, of Liberia during a discussion on democracy at the 61st United Nations General Assembly in New York City, September 19.

Above: Making remarks to reporters with President Pervez Musharraf of Pakistan, left, and President Hamid Karzai of Afghanistan, right, in the Rose Garden, September 27.

Right: Meeting USA Freedom Corps volunteer Zach Bonner in Tampa, FL, September 21.

Overleaf: Visiting the Ho Chi Minh City History Museum in Ho Chi Minh City, Vietnam, November 20.

PARTNERS IN DEMOCRACY

President Bush

Above left: Attending a speaking engagement in Clarkston, MI, September 8.

Left: Studying a press brief in the Oval
Office prior to a news conference in the
Rose Garden, September 15.

Above: Presenting the Presidential Medal
of Freedom to musician B.B. King in the
East Room, December 15.

Right: Walking with Prime Minister
Nuri al-Maliki of Iraq through the Cross
Hall to the East Room for a joint news
conference, July 25.